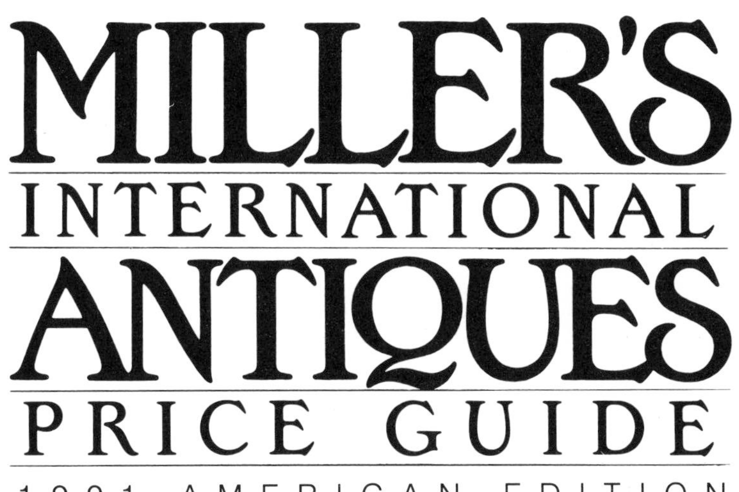

1991 AMERICAN EDITION

MILLER'S INTERNATIONAL ANTIQUES PRICE GUIDE

1991 AMERICAN EDITION

COMPILED AND EDITED BY
JUDITH AND MARTIN MILLER

HOW TO USE THE BOOK

Miller's uniquely practical *International Antiques Price Guide* has been compiled to make detailed information immediately available to the consumer.

The book is organized by category of antique: e.g. Pottery, Porcelain, Furniture, etc. (see Contents List on page 6); within each major category there are sub-categories of items in alphabetical order: e.g. basket, bowl, candlestick, etc., and these in turn are ordered by date. There are around 10,000 photographs of antiques and collectibles, each with a detailed description and price range. There is also a fully cross-referenced index at the back of the book.

This 1991 Edition contains 144 pages in full color — illustrating over 1,500 exceptional or attractive pieces.

In addition to individual entries there are special features throughout the book, giving pointers for the collector — likely condition, definitions of specialist terms, history, etc. — together with general articles, chapter introductions, glossaries, bibliographies where further reading is important, tables of marks, etc. As all the pictures and captions are new every year the selection of items included quickly builds into an enormously impressive and uniquely useful reference set.

PRICES

All the price ranges are based on actual prices of items bought and sold during the year prior to going to press. Thus the guide is fully up-to-date.

Prices are *not* estimates: because the value of an antique is what a willing buyer will pay to a willing seller, we have given not just one price per item but a range of prices to take into account regional differences and freak results.

This is the best way to give an idea of what an antique will *cost*, but should you wish to *sell* remember that the price you receive could be 25-30% less — antique dealers have to live too!!

Condition

All items were in good merchantable condition when last sold unless damage is noted.

ACKNOWLEDGEMENTS

Judith and Martin Miller wish to thank a large number of International auctioneers, dealers and museums who have helped in the production of this edition. The auctioneers can be found in our specialist directory towards the back of this edition.

Viking Penguin, a division of Penguin Books U.S.A. Inc., 40 West 23rd Street, New York, New York 10010, U.S.A.

Penguin Books Canada Ltd., 2801 John Street, Markham, Ontario, Canada L3R 1B4.

Designed and created by
Millers Publications
Sissinghurst Court
Sissinghurst
Cranbrook
Kent TN17 2JA, England

First published in 1990 by Viking Penguin, a division of Penguin Books U.S.A. Inc.
Published simultaneously in Canada
ISBN: 0-670-83540-4
ISSN: 0893-8857

Typeset in England by Ardek Photosetters, St. Leonards-on-Sea, East Sussex, England.
Color originated by Scantrans, Singapore.
Printed and bound in England by William Clowes Ltd, Beccles, England.

Editor's Introduction

by

Judith Miller

Martin and I started *Miller's Antiques Price Guide* in 1979. We produced a book which we believed was greatly needed by virtually everyone who had some interest in antiques, whether professional or as a collector.

We firmly believed that what was needed was a guide to the antiques market which was photographically illustrated, with detailed, concise descriptions and price ranges. The last 12 years have convinced me that this is what the buying public want. Initially, of course, we produced the kind of book that Martin and I wanted — and since we now sell well in excess of 100,000 copies of the British edition, it would seem we were not alone. The book in its various editions is now used all over the world as a major reference work to antiques and since we use in the region of 10,000 new photographs every year, the issues of the British Guide provide an unrivalled source to 100,000 different antiques.

Six years ago we decided, in conjunction with Viking Penguin, to produce a U.S. edition of the Guide. We were convinced that the U.S. market needed the clear, high quality photographs, detailed descriptions, and the price ranges which give a "ball-park" figure for the thousands of items featured in *Miller's International Antiques Price Guide*. These price ranges are researched from sold items and give readers an essential tool for buying and selling antiques and collectibles. We are constantly trying to improve our product and give the U.S. consumer information relevant to the antiques market in the States.

One interesting development I have noticed over the years is that the antiques market is becoming more international. Of course, each country has a special interest in items made by native craftsmen and it is the general trend that such pieces will sell better at a major saleroom in their country of origin. However, to balance this, when general prices achieved at auction in New York, London, Geneva and Hong Kong are compared, they show a striking similarity.

We try to include as many color photographs as is possible, and this year we have well over 1,500 items illustrated in color, all of which have been on the market in the year prior to compilation. All the pieces included, either in color or black and white, are antiques which have been available through dealers or auction houses; they are not museum pieces. The result is a strongly visual and encyclopedic reference guide to recognizing and buying antiques, to detecting trends and to planning one's future collecting. On my monthly trips to the U.S. I am in constant touch with dealers, antiques centers and auction houses to check and verify prices.

Finally our thanks are due to all those experts whose invaluable help and guidance has contributed so much toward this new edition.

CONTENTS

A dragonfly double overlaid and etched glass table lamp, by Emile Gallé, the domed shade overlaid in turquoise and brown etched to depict dragonflies, the base etched to depict irises and aquatic plants, cameo signatures on shade, 24in (61cm) high.
$90,000-130,000

POTTERY

During the past two years, since the heady days of 1987, the market for pottery has stabilised. Auction hype would have us believe that the boom is continuing, but the fact is that prices for more common mid-18thC wares have slipped back a little. Would-be sellers have recognised this trend and it seems that the major auction rooms have found it more difficult to tempt good things onto the market. When they do appear, however, they make predictably high prices especially when dealers and auctioneers use their undoubted expertise in accurate, painstaking and detailed cataloguing.

Some of the most interesting pieces to appear on the market are those which appear correctly catalogued for the first time having just been discovered or previously unidentified. One such piece appeared at Phillips on November 22nd, 1989. The unglazed back was inscribed Clifton Dish, thus identifying it as a product of Clifton Potteries, Cumbria, rather than a Staffordshire product as was assumed. A combination of family provenance, rarity, good condition and the all important involvement of at least two determined bidders carried the dish to £21,000, a substantial price for a mid-18thC piece.

However, two years ago the dish would probably have made an even higher price when the market was prone to spectacular results for such rarities. A glance at the London catalogues reveals one area where sellers are confident and there is a consequent strength in the range and quality of wares offered. This area is maiolica. This market began to pick up at about the same time as that for English pottery though it did not boom in the same way. Rather it progressed steadily forward and it seems set to continue in 1991.

Baskets

A Staffordshire creamware basket and stand, c1770, stand 11½in (29cm) wide.
$775-850

A stand for a chestnut basket, with scene after Claude Lorraine, by John and Richard Riley, early 19thC, 11in (28cm) wide.
$200-250

Bottles

A German stoneware bottle, c1720, 14½in (37cm).
$200-250

An earthenware bottle, probably Severn/Bristol Channel area, 14in (35.5cm).
$80-100

An earthenware bottle, 19thC, 9in (23cm).
$65-85

Bowls

A Jackfield teabowl, c1760.
$250-350

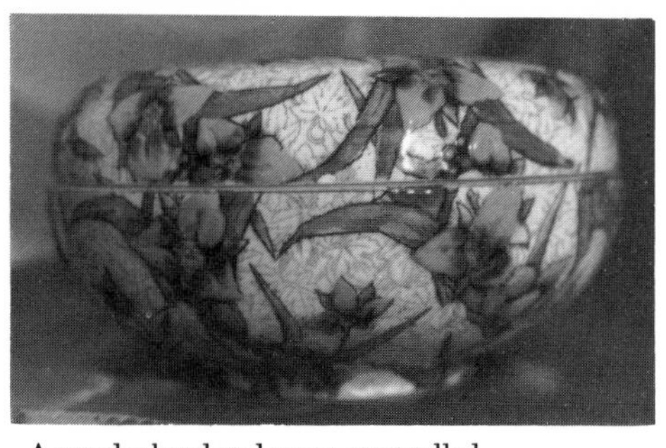

A powder bowl and cover, enamelled in relief in blue and green, Luneville-Keller & Guerin, mid-19thC, 6in (15cm) diam.
$125-150

A Quimper soup bowl, 5in (12.5cm).
$35-65

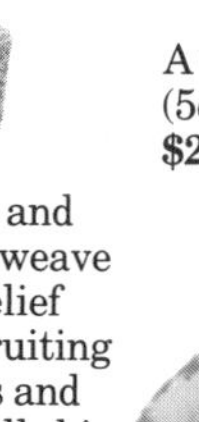

A Quimper blue and white bowl, 2in (5cm).
$25-40

A Minton majolica jardinière and stand, the pink glazed basketweave moulded sides decorated in relief with trailing flowering and fruiting strawberries, with ochre rims and pale blue glazed interior, small chip to footrim of jardinière, impressed marks, pattern No. 811 and date code for 1870, 8½in (21cm).
$2,000-3,000

A Quimper bowl, signed, c1920, 5½in (14cm) square.
$75-90

A Quimper bowl, 2in (5cm).
$25-40

A Quimper soup bowl, 7in (18cm) wide.
$40-75

A Wedgwood butter dish in glazed caneware, c1860, 7in (18cm) diam.
$350-400

A Quimper bowl, signed, c1900, 6in (15cm).
$40-50

A majolica dish with feet, c1880, 9½in (24cm) diam.
$100-120

A Staffordshire creamware bowl and cover, with flower finial and entwined rope twist handles, painted with scattered flowers, slight chips, c1780, 5in (12.5cm).
$250-350

A Wedgwood cream stoneware game pie dish, the cover with applied cabbage and carrot mounts, the sides with continuous fruiting vine decoration, 19thC, 8½in (22cm) diam.
$200-250

A Scottish porringer, with painted decoration, c1870, 3in (7.5cm) high.
$65-80

A faience pedestal bowl, painted in bright colours in blue, green and yellow, 12in (30.5cm).
$400-550

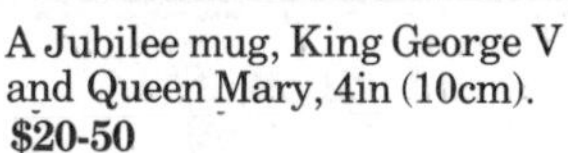

A Jubilee mug, King George V and Queen Mary, 4in (10cm).
$20-50

Commemorative

A mug, issued for Wesley centenary celebrations, 1839, 5in (12.5cm).
$230-250

A Coronation mug, King George VI and Queen Elizabeth, 1937, some damage, 3in (7.5cm).
$15-20

A child's plate, Lord Byron, 6in (15cm) diam.
$250-300

A Queen Victoria Jubilee tankard, some damage, 1887, 3in (7.5cm).
$55-65

Miller's is a price Guide not a price List

The price ranges given reflect the average price a purchaser should pay for similar items. Condition, rarity of design or pattern, size, colour, provenance, restoration and many other factors must be taken into account when assessing values. When buying or selling, it must always be remembered that prices can be greatly affected by the condition of any piece. Unless otherwise stated, all goods shown in Miller's are of good merchantable quality, and the valuations given reflect this fact. Pieces offered for sale in exceptionally fine condition or in poor condition may reasonably be expected to be priced considerably higher or lower respectively than the estimates given herein

Cottages

A Staffordshire cottage pastille burner, with removable roof, c1820, 3½in (9cm).
$850-950

A model of a windmill, flanked by a boy and a girl holding sheaves of wheat, c1855, 11½in (29cm).
$250-350

A Staffordshire lilac ground pastille burner and detachable base, modelled as Warwick Castle, applied with coloured flowers and white moss, enriched in gilding, castle restored, minor chipping to flowers, c1840, 6½in (16.5cm).
$900-1,000

A Staffordshire cottage pastille burner, outlined in lavender, 5in (12.5cm).
$150-250

A Staffordshire lilac ground pastille burner, applied with coloured flowers and enriched in gilding, the base with gilt rim, slight hair cracks and some chipping to flowers, finial restored, c1840, 8in (21cm).
$650-1,000

Cow Creamers

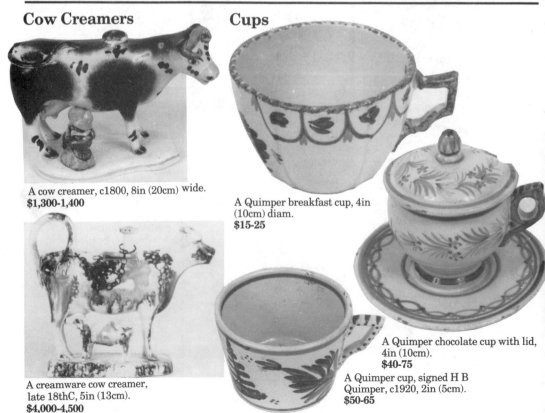

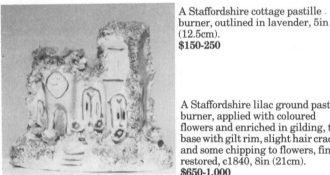

A cow creamer, c1800, 8in (20cm) wide.
$1,300-1,400

A creamware cow creamer, late 18thC, 5in (13cm).
$4,000-4,500

Cups

A Quimper breakfast cup, 4in (10cm) diam.
$15-25

A Quimper chocolate cup with lid, 4in (10cm).
$40-75

A Quimper cup, signed H B Quimper, c1920, 2in (5cm).
$50-65

A Quimper cup and saucer, signed, c1930, cup 2½in (6cm).
$100-130

A Jackfield loving cup, c1765, 4½in (11cm).
$210-240

A pearlware hound's head stirrup cup, with brown markings and green collar, cracked, 19thC, 5in (12.5cm) long.
$550-750

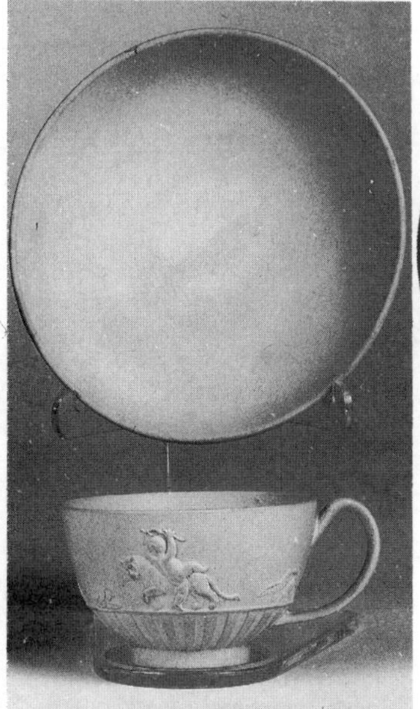

A pair of Wedgwood caneware teacups and saucers, the cups moulded in relief with putti at various pursuits above a fluted border, the undersides of the saucers similarly fluted, impressed marks, c1790.
$650-1,000

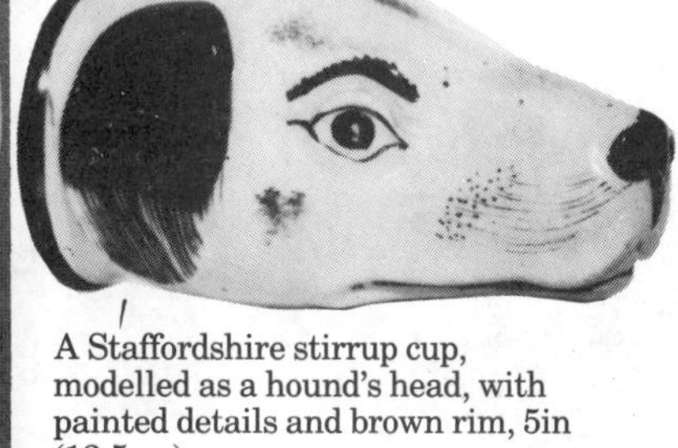

A Staffordshire stirrup cup, modelled as a hound's head, with painted details and brown rim, 5in (12.5cm).
$400-550

A pottery fox head stirrup cup, with red fur, yellow eyes and black collar, 5in (13cm).
$150-200

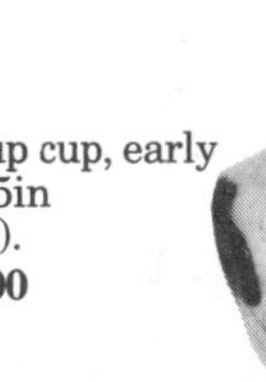

A stirrup cup, early 19thC, 5in (12.5cm).
$650-800

Figures – Animals

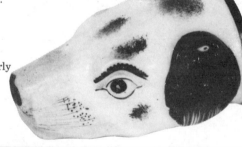

A Pratt ware hound, c1780, 4in (10cm) wide.
$1,200-1,400

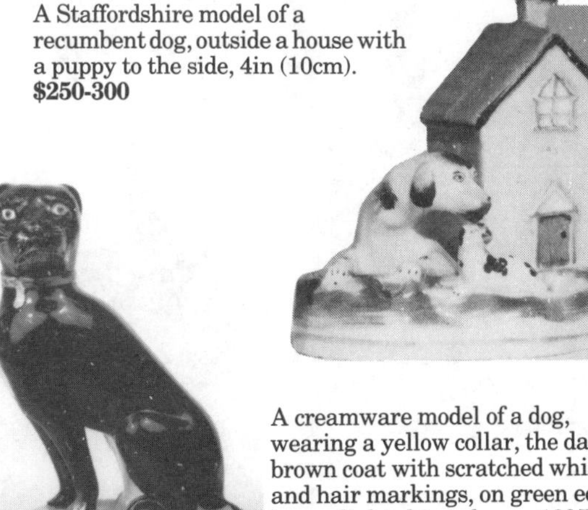

A Staffordshire model of a recumbent dog, outside a house with a puppy to the side, 4in (10cm).
$250-300

A creamware model of a dog, wearing a yellow collar, the dark brown coat with scratched whiskers and hair markings, on green edged base, slight chip to base, c1835, 8½in (22cm).
$1,300-2,000

A pair of figures of a herdsman and a milkmaid, on gilt lined bases, c1860, 9in (23cm).
$700-750

A Staffordshire pearlware model of a roaring lion with brown mane and muzzle, the base enriched in turquoise, minor restoration, c1790, 13in (33cm) long.
$3,500-4,000

A model of a seated whippet, with separate moulded front legs, and gilt collar, a dead hare at his feet, on waisted gilt lined base, c1840, 13in (33cm).
$500-600

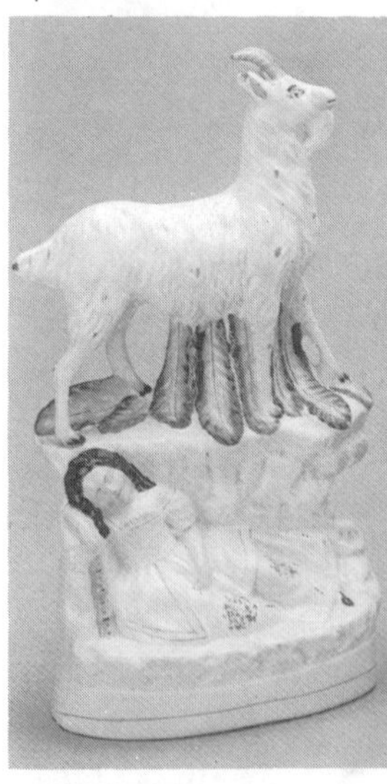

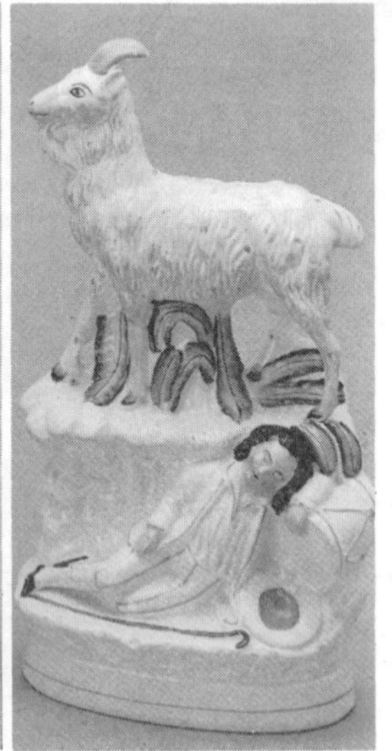

A pair of figures, depicting a girl and a boy sleeping with standing goats, on gilt lined bases, c1850, 12in (30.5cm).
$400-550

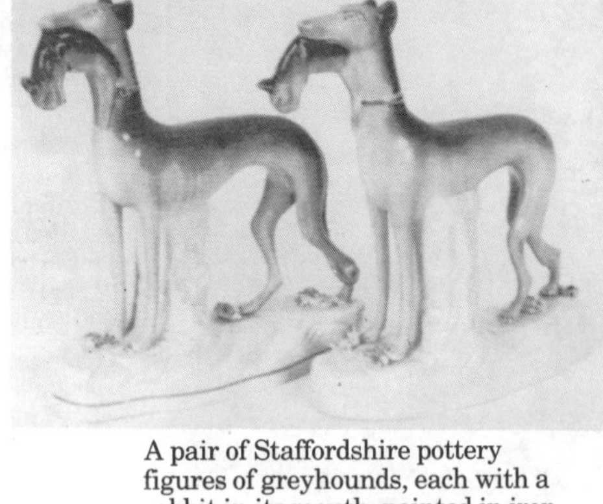

A pair of Staffordshire pottery figures of greyhounds, each with a rabbit in its mouth, painted in iron red, black, brown and gilt and raised on a rock moulded base applied with green painted tufts of grass, 19thC, 7½in (19cm).
$500-650

A pearlware cow, with a milkmaid and calf, decorated with sponged red, blue, black and ochre, Staffordshire or Yorkshire, restored, 5½in (14cm).
$1,200-1,400

A pair of spaniels, splashed with iron red, each with gilt collar and moulded fur, c1850, 10in (25.5cm).
$5,500-7,500

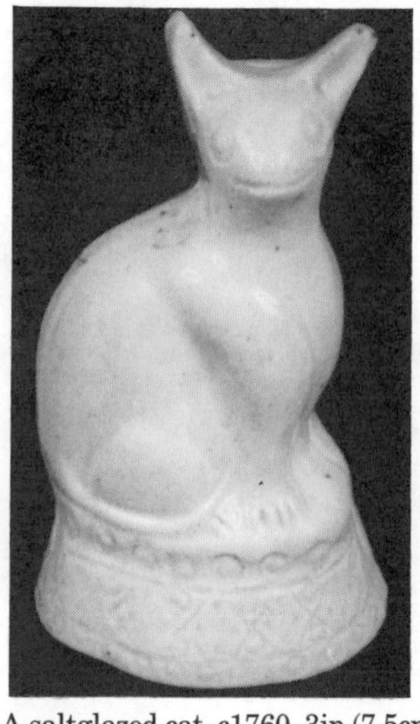

A saltglazed cat, c1760, 3in (7.5cm).
$1,500-2,000

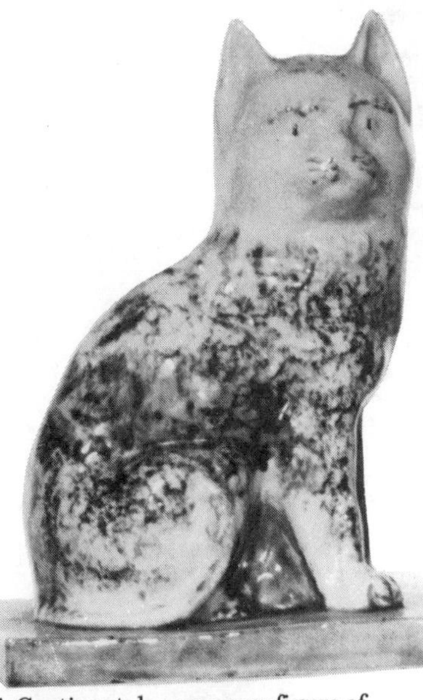

A Continental creamware figure of a cat, its fur sponged in black and yellow, on a green base, 5½in (14cm).
$350-400

A Staffordshire dog group, c1855, 7in (18cm).
$700-750

A Staffordshire bird whistle, early 19thC, 2in (5cm).
$650-800

A Staffordshire figure of an elephant, c1885, 9½in (24cm).
$700-800

A Staffordshire sheep, c1850, 5in (13cm).
$200-230

A Yorkshire buff pottery equestrian group, the rider wearing a brown hat, blue jacket and yellow breeches, damaged and chipped, c1790, 9in (23cm).
$5,000-5,500

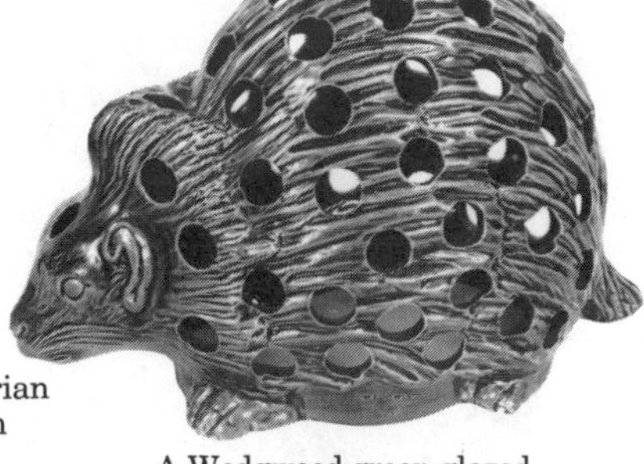

A Wedgwood green glazed hedgehog, 7in (18cm).
$1,000-1,200

Figures – People

A model of Auld Lang Syne, on gilt lined base, c1850, 8½in (22cm).
$400-550

A Staffordshire figure depicting Flora, emblematic of Spring, probably Enoch Wood, c1810, 13in (33cm).
$400-500

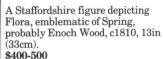

A Staffordshire figure, probably Sir Robert Peel, c1846, 8½in (22cm).
$400-500

An unidentified theatrical figure, on gilt lined base, c1850, 9½in (24cm).
$100-150

A Staffordshire group of the Princess Royal on a dog, c1850, 5in (13cm).
$275-300

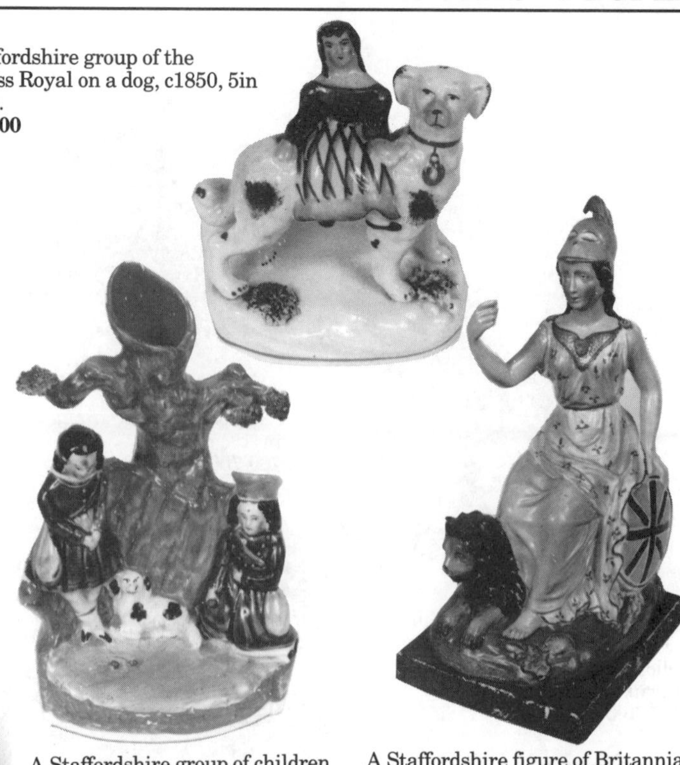

A Staffordshire group of children playing marbles, c1860, 8in (20cm).
$450-500

A Staffordshire figure of Britannia, by Thomas Pan, c1840, 14½in (36cm).
$800-900

A portrait of Anne Boleyn and King Henry VIII, on gilt lined base, c1850, 10in (25.5cm).
$1,000-1,200

A Staffordshire musician with dog, c1860, 9in (23cm).
$230-250

A Staffordshire group of Samson and the Lion, 11½in (29cm).
$400-500

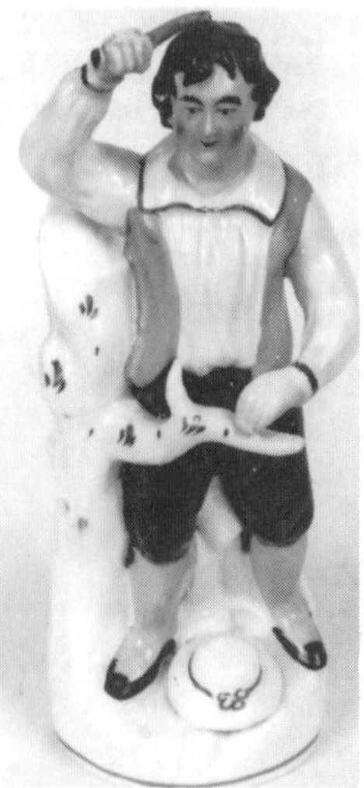

A Staffordshire woodcutter, c1840, 7½in (19cm).
$280-300

A Staffordshire boy with rats, c1840, 5½in (14cm).
$300-400

A Staffordshire figure of Vivandiere, c1850, 13in (32cm).
$600-650

A Staffordshire Welsh figure group, 10½in (26cm).
$700-800

A Staffordshire Whieldon type figure, c1765, 4½in (11cm).
$1,300-1,400

A Staffordshire flatback group, the lady balancing a bundle of sticks on her head, the man holding a pitcher, 12½in (32cm).
$100-150

A Staffordshire figure of Will Watch, c1860, 6½in (16cm).
$230-250

A Ralph Wood type figure, c1780, 9in (23cm).
$900-1,000

An Obadiah Sherratt tea-time group, modelled as a gallant and his companion before a yellow turreted building, with iron red table, some damage, c1830, 7½in (18.5cm) wide.
$5,000-6,500

Two Whieldon School figures of The Seasons, 7in (18cm).
$6,500-8,000

A Staffordshire figure, c1800, 5in (12.5cm).
$300-400

A Staffordshire pearlware group of The Parson and Clerk, wearing streaked brown clothes, supported by a green tree stump, on a green base, some restoration to hat, c1810, 10in (25cm).
$1,000-1,300

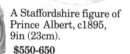

A Staffordshire creamware group of Venus and Cupid, of Ralph Wood type, the Goddess draped in a green robe with Cupid and a green dolphin at her side, the brown pedestal moulded with classical urns, restored, c1785, 10½in (27cm).
$650-800

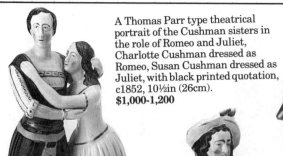

A Thomas Parr type theatrical portrait of the Cushman sisters in the role of Romeo and Juliet, Charlotte Cushman dressed as Romeo, Susan Cushman dressed as Juliet, with black printed quotation, c1852, 10½in (26cm).
$1,000-1,200

A figure of Falstaff, titled in raised gilt capitals on rococo moulded base, c1845, 16in (40cm).
$700-1,000

A Staffordshire figure of Prince Albert, c1895, 9in (23cm).
$550-650

In the Ceramics section if there is only one measurement it usually refers to the height of the piece

A Staffordshire pearlware figure of Neptune, of Ralph Wood type, scantily draped in green and holding a trident, repaired, c1785, 11½in (28.5cm).
$650-800

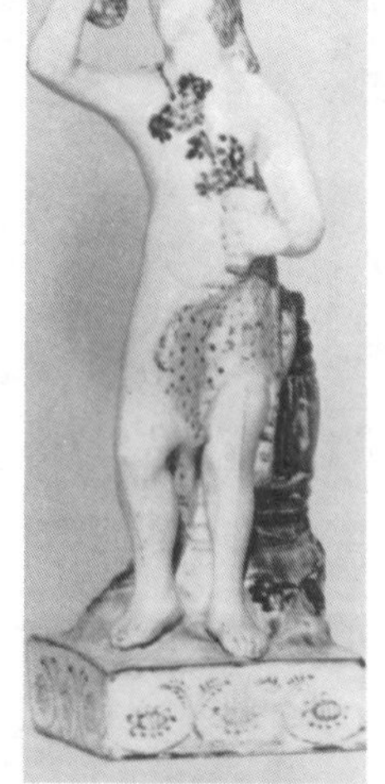

A pottery figure, emblematic of Autumn, scantily clad with fruiting vine beside a barrel on a square base, 7in (17.5cm).
$150-250

An Obadiah Sherratt group of Tam O'Shanter and Souter Johnny, the former in tartan jacket and blue striped breeches, the latter in brown coat and yellow smock, seated on a red and yellow couch, base restored, c1825, 8in (20cm).
$5,500-7,000

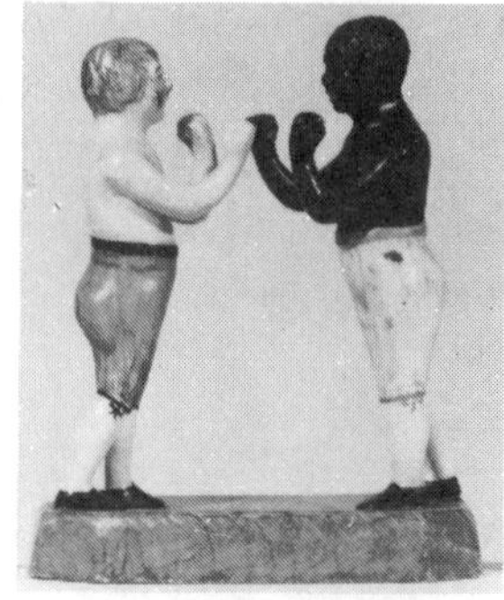

A group of Tom Cribb and Molyneaux, in grey and yellow breeches on a red base, repaired and chipped, c1811, 6in (15cm).
$5,000-5,500

A pair of Staffordshire figures of Royal children, c1845, 6in (15cm).
$650-800

Staffordshire Figures

A figure of Sir Robert Peel, in dark blue jacket and brown trousers, with scroll inscribed Repeal of the Corn Law, the base entitled in gilt Sir R. Peel, repairs to neck, c1846, 8in (20.5cm), (B1,2).
$650-800

A portrait of Dan O'Connell, wearing a black jacket enriched in gilt, green neckerchief and trousers, titled in gilt script on oval base, c1870, 17½in (44cm), (B,2).
$700-800

STAFFORDSHIRE FIGURES

The letters and figures in brackets refer to the book *Staffordshire Portrait Figures* by P. D. Gordon Pugh

A figure of Gladstone, named in raised capitals to the base, c1882, 13½in (34cm), (B16,54).
$300-400

A Staffordshire figure of the Duke of Wellington as a politician, c1850, 13in (33cm), (B,17).
$250-300

A pair of Staffordshire figures, previously suggested as portraying Lord Shaftesbury and Elizabeth Fry, but now believed to portray the Royal tutors with the Royal children, c1848, 7½in (19cm), (B,7/8).
$650-700

A figure of Franklin in dark blue coat and floral tunic holding a letter and hat in his hands, mis-titled Washington in raised gilt capitals to the base, c1855, 16in (40.5cm), (B24,71).
$900-1,200

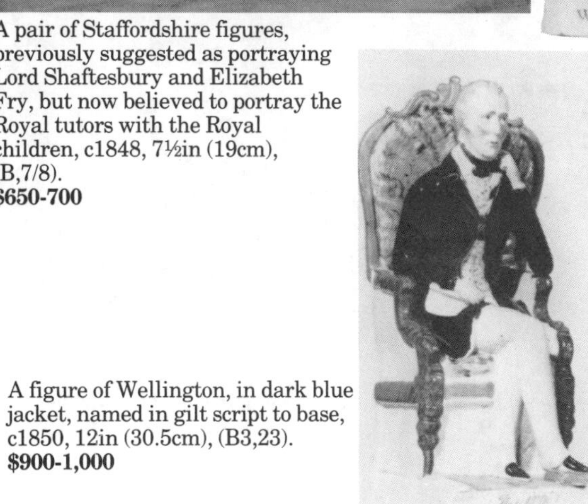

A figure of Wellington, in dark blue jacket, named in gilt script to base, c1850, 12in (30.5cm), (B3,23).
$900-1,000

A rare model of the Redan, a fortress near Sebastopol, painted mainly in grey and outlined with coloured flowers, flag restored, c1854, 8½in (21cm), (C70,189).
$2,500-3,000

A figure of Havelock, in dark blue military uniform and named in gilt script to the base, c1857, 9in (23cm), (C90,268).
$1,300-1,500

A Staffordshire figure of Omar Pasha, c1854, 13in (33cm), (C,130).
$550-650

A Staffordshire equestrian figure of Sultan Abd-ul-Medjid, c1854, 7½in (18cm), (C,167a).
$230-250

A pair of Staffordshire equestrian figures of General Brown and General Simpson, c1854, 13in (33cm), (C,149/150).
$1,300-1,500

A Staffordshire group depicting the Crimean War Victory, repairs to flags, c1856, 14in (36cm), (C,185).
$2,500-3,000

A Staffordshire figure of Maretta Alboni as Cinderella, wearing a blue dress, 9in (23cm), (E,20).
$550-650

A Staffordshire group depicting The Sailor's Return, c1855, 12½in (32cm), (C,197).
$650-700

A Staffordshire group of Napoleon III and Prince Albert, c1854, 14in (36cm), (C,225).
$400-500

A Staffordshire group depicting The Wounded Soldier, c1855, 10in (26cm), (C,194).
$300-400

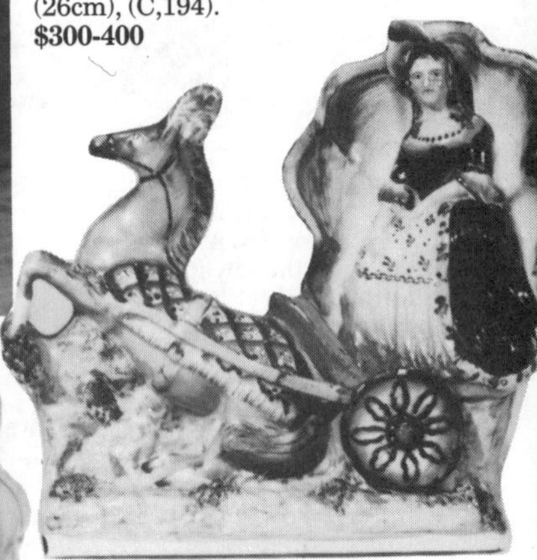

A figure of Mlle Alboni as Cinderella, in dark blue and floral dress, c1848, 9in (23cm), (E20,43).
$1,500-2,500

A figure of Luigi Lablanche as Dr. Dulcamara, in brown jacket and pink breeches, c1848, 8in (20cm), (E62,113).
$1,000-1,200

A group of Isaac Van Amburgh in Roman costume, with a leopard on his back and flanked by a lion, lioness and cub, named in script to the base, restored, c1839, 6in (15cm), (E100,200).
$1,200-1,300

A pair of figures of James Rush and Emily Sandford, the former in dark blue jacket and pink trousers, the latter in dark blue bodice and green dress, both named in gilt script, c1849, 10in (25.5cm), (G23,47/48).
$2,500-3,000

A group of Charles Kean, in mainly dark blue costume, c1856, 13in (33cm), (E78,152).
$300-400

A Staffordshire figure of Nellie Chapman, c1847, 12in (30.5cm), (E,150).
$1,200-1,400

A model of Stanfield Hall, with a blue roof, the building with white walls outlined with flowers and windows edged in puce, named in gilt script to the shaped base, c1849, 7in (17.5cm), (G25,52).
$900-1,000

A Staffordshire figure, possibly portraying Mr. Wood playing Atabarnes in Artaxerxes, maker Lloyd Shelton, c1840, 12in (30.5cm), (E,294).
$500-550

A Staffordshire group of Smith and Collier, 13in (33cm), (G,27).
$800-1,000

A group featuring Shakespeare flanked by figures representing Hamlet and Lady Macbeth, c1855, 10in (25.5cm), (H5,14).
$550-650

A Staffordshire figure of the Great Gate, Trinity College, Cambridge, c1860, 8in (20cm), (I,100).
$230-300

Flatware

A Bo'Ness plate, J. Marshall, c1865, 9½in (24cm).
$50-80

A pair of English tin glazed chargers, painted with flowers in green, blue, yellow and mauve, rim chips, 13½in (34cm).
$1,300-1,500

Use the Index!
Because certain items might fit easily into any of a number of categories, the quickest and surest method of locating any entry is by reference to the index at the back of the book. This has been fully cross-referenced for absolute simplicity

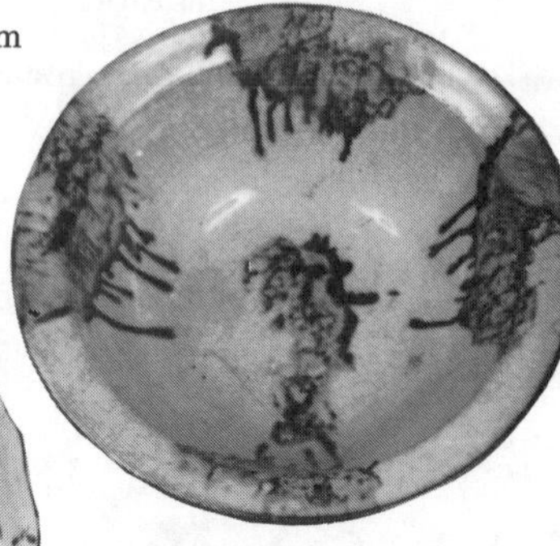

A set of 5 Welsh slipware bowls, 9½ to 15½in (24 to 39cm) diam.
$1,400-1,500

A Brameld tureen stand, Woodman pattern, c1820.
$200-250

Two Strasbourg faience plates, painted in colours with botanical specimens, with puce line rims, rim chips, H39 in blue for Joseph Hannong, c1750, 9½in (24cm).
$1,000-1,200

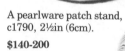

A Liverpool polychrome dish, c1765, 14in (35cm).
$900-1,000

A Nevers blue and white dish, the centre with figures beside a fence within a border of birds, flowers and buildings, the underside with trailing flowering branches, minute rim flaking, blue dagger and dot mark, c1680, 12in (30cm).
$900-1,000

A pearlware patch stand, c1790, 2½in (6cm).
$140-200

A Turin blue and white armorial dish, the centre painted within a border of foliage and flowerheads, restored, c1700, 19in (48cm) wide.
$550-700

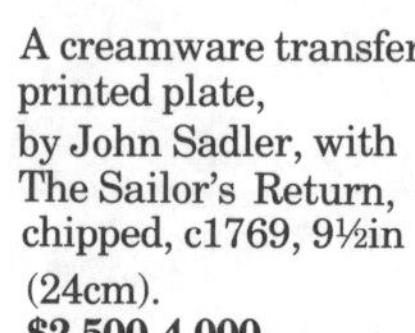

A creamware transfer printed plate, by John Sadler, with The Sailor's Return, chipped, c1769, 9½in (24cm).
$2,500-4,000

A pair of Quimper plates, signed H B Quimper, c1829, 5in (12.5cm).
$90-120

A Riley blue and white transfer printed plate, c1820.
$80-150

A Swansea rhyme plate, c1820, 5½in (14cm).
$150-200

A Swansea teapot stand, 7in (18cm) wide.
$200-250

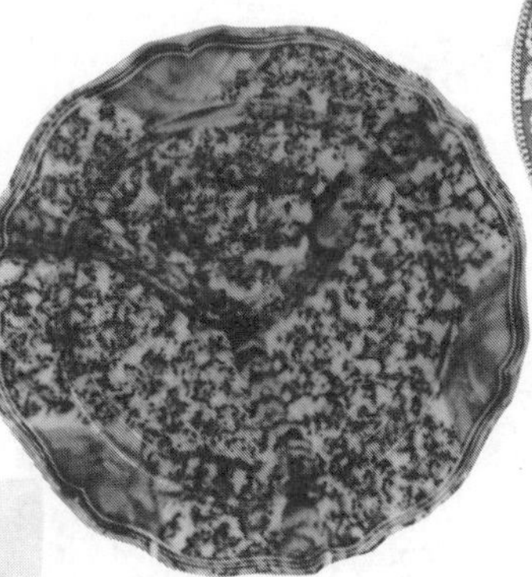

A Staffordshire Whieldon type plate, c1765, 10in (25.5cm).
$550-700

A Staffordshire plate, Clews & Co. Dr. Syntax series, Painting a Portrait, c1820, 10in (25cm).
$380-420

A pair of Quimper plates, 7½in (19cm).
$75-100 each

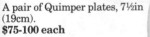

A Wedgwood earthenware fluted centre dish, with entwined double serpent handles, painted by Emile Lessore, the underside with a mottled tortoiseshell glaze, on short spreading foot, rim and handle restored, impressed mark, signed, c1865, 12½in (32cm) wide.
$1,300-1,500

Two Quimper plates, 5½ and 6½in (14 and 16cm).
$75-100 each

A Swansea, Dillwyn, plate, showing woman with baskets, marked, c1825, 10in (25cm).
$400-500

A Hispano-Moresque copper lustre dish, the central boss painted with a flowerhead, the outer border moulded with stylised palm leaves, damaged, mid-17thC, 15½in (39cm).
$1,200-1,500

A Montelupo fluted crespina, painted in colours within a yellow band, the borders with panels of exotic birds, flowers and foliate scrolls, yellow rim, minor rim chips, early 17thC, 10in (25cm).
$900-1,300

A Montelupo dish, painted in ochre and blue against a stylised landscape background with trees and blue mountains, small rim chips, c1640, 12½in (32cm).
$5,500-7,000

A pair of Italian pottery dishes, in the maiolica style, painted with classical figures among clouds within blue borders of mythical beasts and scrolling foliage, 24in (61cm).
$550-650

A Montelupo dish, painted with a pair of musketeers wearing green and orange striped doublet and trousers striding over hills, on a yellow and green ground, copper green rim, 3 brown concentric lines to the reverse, rim chip, c1650, 12½in (32cm).
$2,500-4,000

A Nevers Conrade dated blue and white dish, painted with a central galleon, surrounded by arches, trophies, castles and animals, one creature inscribed with the date 1644, the rim with trailing flowers, cracked and chipped, 16½in (42cm).
$5,000-6,000

Jars

A creamware wet drug jar, c1780, 7½in (19cm).
$300-350

A Sicilian albarello, painted on one side with a portrait bust and the other with a lion, in green, ochre, yellow and blue enamels, cracked, c1700, 12in (30cm).
$3,000-4,000

A pair of Catalan blue and white albarelli, painted with the name of the contents S.QUICX and S.CORIAND, neck rim chips, one with crack to body, glaze flakes, probably Talavera, 17th/18thC, 12in (30cm).
$2,500-3,000

A pill pot, probably London, c1760, 3in (7cm).
$650-800

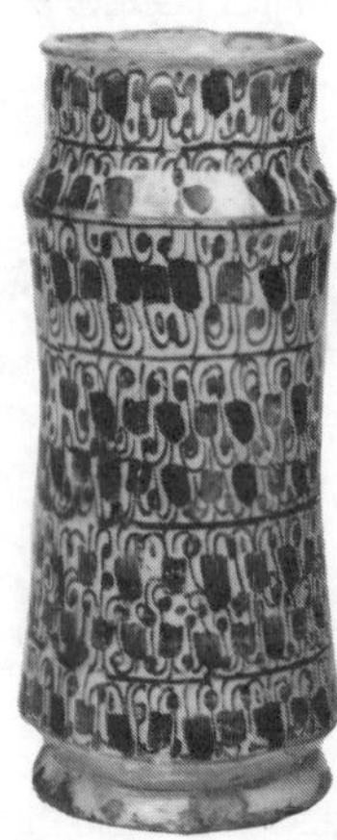

A Hispano-Moresque copper lustre and blue albarello, painted all over with concentric bands of stylised foliage between blue lines, rim chips, glaze flakes, blue retouched, late 15thC, 10½in (26.5cm).
$5,000-5,500

A Quimper pickle jar with lid, 6in (16cm).
$30-55

A Southern Italian dated albarello, painted in colours and inscribed S.P.Q.P. 1667 on a pale green ground, chips to neck, small crack, 9½in (23cm).
$1,400-2,000

A Catalan coloured albarello, painted in the workshop of Francisco Niculoso in the Deruta style, in blue and manganese on a yellow ground, broken and riveted, 17thC, 12in (31cm).
$4,500-5,500

A Southern Italian baluster pharmacy jar, painted in blue, green and yellow, the neck and waist with a band of green and yellow rope twist, minor chips to rims, restored, 17thC, 12in (31cm).
$2,500-3,000

An English wet drug jar, early 18thC, 7in (18cm).
$1,200-1,300

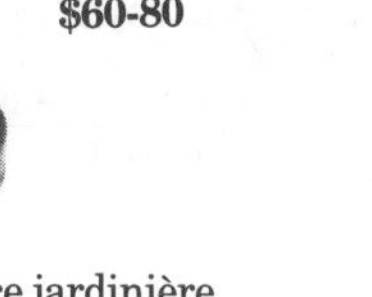

A Burmantofts faience jardinière and stand, cracked.
$300-500

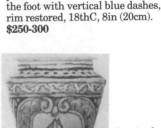

A banded slipware jar, Northern England, 11½in (29cm).
$60-80

A Venetian Berettino albarello, painted with an elaborate scroll inscribed with the name of the contents Mo Franda F, chip to base and rim, glaze flakes, 17thC, 13½in (34cm).
$5,000-6,500

An Italian maiolica albarello, painted in blue above a yellow band, the foot with vertical blue dashes, rim restored, 18thC, 8in (20cm).
$250-300

A pair of maiolica albarelli, painted in blue and yellow, damaged and restored, 10in (26cm).
$1,000-1,200

A Palermo maiolica albarello, painted with a yellow ground panel of a bishop saint, with patterns and stiff leaves painted in blue, yellow, brown and green between ribbon borders, glaze damaged, rim and foot chipped, 17thC, 11½in (29cm).
$2,000-2,500

A Ligurian blue and white waisted albarello, painted with a townscape and trees, with a crowned cartouche inscribed 'Charitas', the reverse with the date 1734, 9in (23cm).
$1,300-1,400

A Laterza squat waisted albarello, painted in blue with a seated figure among rockwork and trees, named in ochre, slight rim chip and crack, c1720, 8in (20cm).
$650-800

A pair of Caltagirone waisted albarelli, painted with portraits within yellow scroll cartouches, reserved on a blue ground with scrolling flowers and foliage in yellow and pale green, minor flaking, one cracked, 17thC, 9in (24cm).
$3,000-5,000

A waisted albarello, painted in blue and manganese, perhaps Savona, rim and footrim chips, c1700, 7½in (18cm).
$650-700

Jugs

A Derbyshire saltglazed stoneware jug, Brampton, possibly Oldfield, damage, c1840, 10in (26cm).
$130-150

A Liverpool pearlware cream jug, with S-scroll handle, painted in iron red with 2 swans, the trefoil lip and flared rim with a band of scrolls, rim cracked and chipped, Samuel Gilbody's factory, c1758.
$5,000-5,500

A North Devon jug with yellow slip, c1880, 5in (13cm).
$100-130

A Jackfield jug, with gilt decoration, rubbed, 4in (11cm).
$400-550

A Jackfield jug with moulded decoration, 5in (12.5cm).
$150-200

See page 104 in Miller's Collectables Price Guide 1990-91 for a further selection of Jackfield ware.

A Jackfield jug with moulded decoration, 4in (10cm).
$120-150

A Liverpool creamware jug, printed in black with Masonic motifs and verse, early 19thC, 5½in (14cm).
$250-300

A pair of Rye Pottery owl jugs, with dark green glaze on a terracotta body, c1870, 7in (17.5cm).
$130-150

A Pratt ware jug, c1800, 6in (15cm).
$500-550

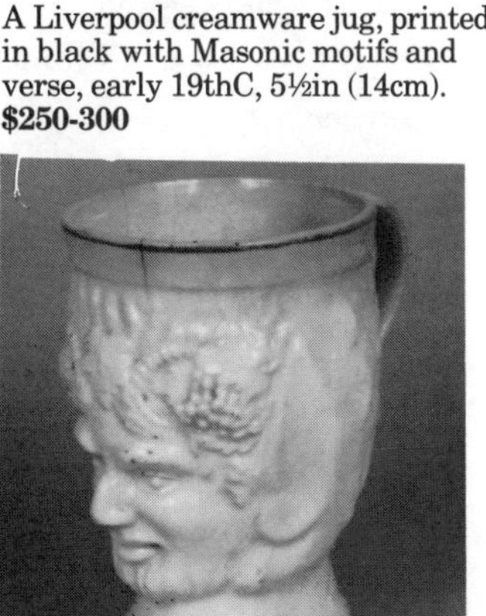

A Bacchus mask jug, 4½in (11cm).
£75-100 *SBA*

A gaudy lustre jug, with lion head spout, c1835, 5in (13cm).
$130-150

A Quimper jug, c1920, 7in (17cm).
$150-200

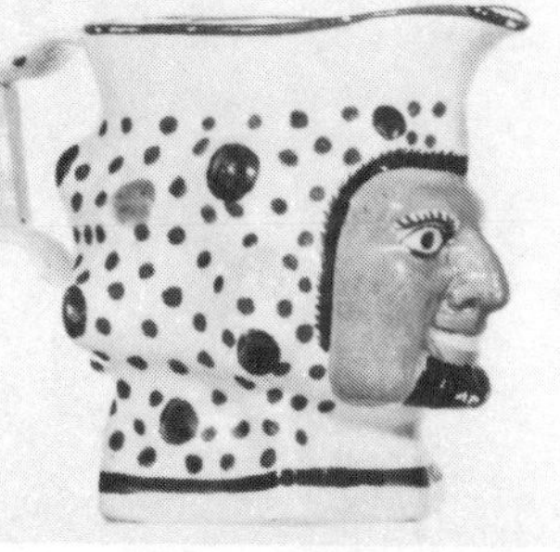

A Staffordshire pearlware Bacchus mask moulded jug, enriched in colours with puce, yellow and red dots, within brown lines, cracked and chipped, 5in (12.5cm).
£100-150 *CSK*

A Staffordshire enamelled saltglazed jug, c1765, 3½in (9cm).
$1,500-2,000

A silver lustre jug, c1814, 7½in (18cm).
$525-550

A pair of Spode jugs, printed and coloured in 'famille rose' style, printed marks, 12½in (32cm).
$2,000-2,500

A Quimper jug, marked H, c1890, 3½in (9cm).
$80-120

A Staffordshire blue and white jug, c1815, 11in (28cm).
$550-700

A Swansea gaudy lustre octagonal jug, c1835, 6½in (16cm).
$250-300

A saltglazed cream jug, c1755, 3in (8cm).
$1,200-1,300

A Staffordshire whiteware and pewter covered wine jug, c1870, 8½in (21cm).
$225-275

A jug with hand coloured enamel decoration, c1820, 6½in (16cm).
$300-350

A creamware baluster jug, the tortoiseshell ground applied with green swags of foliage, chips and cracks, interior staining, c1780, 6½in (16.5cm).
$650-800

A Staffordshire jug and bowl set, c1900, jug 7½in (19cm).
$250-300

A Swansea Cottage jug, with lion head spout, c1845, 5½in (14cm).
$250-300

A Leeds type creamware jug, handle restored, c1785, 4½in (11cm).
$300-400

A pottery jug, attributed to Swansea, early 19thC, 5½in (14cm).
$400-500

A creamware inscribed and dated jug, painted in colours, with inscriptions, perhaps Liverpool or Staffordshire, chipped, c1789, 10in (25cm).
$4,000-5,500

A cream jug, c1775, 2in (5cm).
$1,500-2,000

A jug with printed allegorical figure of Europe and verse, on a canary yellow ground, silver lustre decoration, 19thC.
$400-500

An English green glazed jug, 14th/15thC, 6in (16cm).
$400-500

A Quimper jug, 4½in (11cm).
$30-75

A blue and white jug, 8in (20cm).
$70-140

A Welsh jug made for the French market, c1840, 4½in (11cm).
$275-300

A French faience jug of fluted helmet shape, on spreading foot, painted in blue with a band of stylised scrolls, the handle with blue scrolling decoration, spout repaired, 8½in (21cm).
$150-250

Toby Jugs

A Staffordshire creamware Toby jug, with streaked brown jacket and shoes, white waistcoat and breeches, some restoration, c1760, 9½in (24cm).
$1,500-2,500

A Staffordshire creamware Toby jug of Ralph Wood type, in brown hat, pale brown jacket, green waistcoat, ochre breeches and dark brown shoes, a pipe between his feet, slight crack to base, c1775, 10in (25cm).
$1,400-2,000

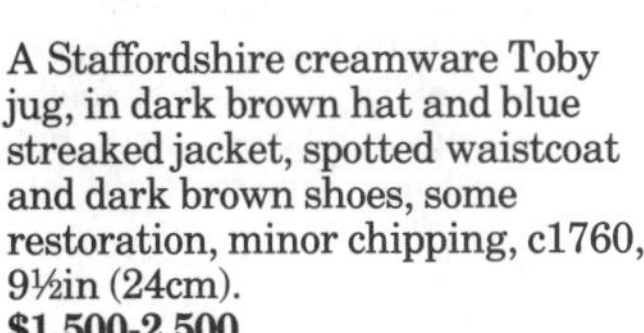

A Staffordshire creamware Toby jug, in dark brown hat and blue streaked jacket, spotted waistcoat and dark brown shoes, some restoration, minor chipping, c1760, 9½in (24cm).
$1,500-2,500

A Staffordshire creamware 'village idiot' Toby jug, in streaked brown hat, blue jacket and breeches, pale green waistcoat and brown shoes, his eyes outlined in blue, with pale pink face and hands, hat restored, c1775, 9½in (24cm).
$2,500-3,000

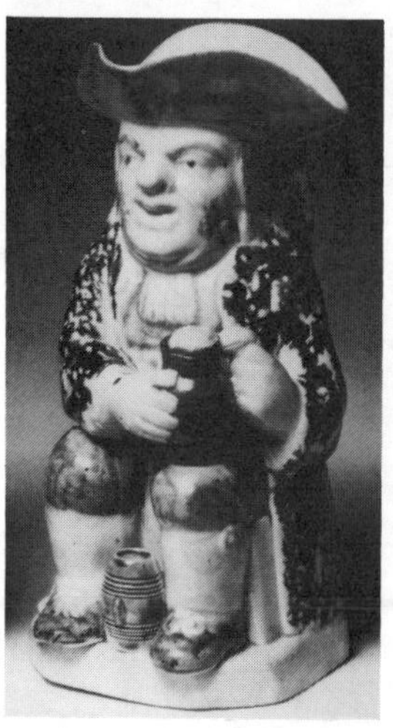

A Staffordshire pearlware sailor Toby jug, in opaque enamelled black hat, pink jacket, yellow waistcoat, white breeches and black shoes, hat restored, c1800, 11in (28cm).
$2,500-3,000

A pearlware Hearty Good Fellow jug, holding a pipe and striped jug of ale, in brown coat, patterned yellow, blue and ochre waistcoat, green breeches and white shoes with yellow buckles, traces of impressed mark, perhaps Yorkshire, c1800, 11½in (29cm).
$2,500-3,000

A Staffordshire pearlware Toby jug, holding a brown jug of ale, in grey hat, sponged blue jacket, yellow waistcoat, grey breeches and shoes, c1790, 10in (25cm).
$1,300-1,500

A pearlware 'convict' Toby jug, in brown hat, patterned blue and brown jacket, white waistcoat, ochre cuffs, yellow breeches and brown shoes, hat restored, perhaps Yorkshire, c1785, 9½in (24cm).
$2,000-2,500

A Staffordshire Pratt ware Toby jug, decorated in typical Pratt ware colours of yellow, blue and orange, hat repaired, c1790, 9½in (24cm).
$650-800

A Staffordshire Toby jug, in green coat and pink waistcoat, on a green circular base, c1800, 8in (19cm).
$300-400

A pearlware Toby jug, holding a jug of ale, with brown hair, patterned brown, ochre and blue jacket, green waistcoat, yellow breeches, striped blue stockings and brown shoes, hat restored, perhaps Yorkshire, c1800, 10in (25cm).
$1,300-1,500

A pearlware sailor Toby jug, in brown hat, yellow-edged blue jacket, white waistcoat, striped blue and ochre breeches and brown shoes, hat restored, perhaps Yorkshire, c1800, 11in (28cm).
$3,000-4,000

A pearlware Toby jug and cover, in black hat, ochre jacket, striped ochre, black and blue waistcoat, green breeches and black shoes, on a D-shaped base, hat restored, perhaps Scottish, c1800, 8in (20cm).
$1,000-1,400

A pearlware Toby jug, with ruddy hands and complexion, in yellow-edged brown hat, green jacket, white waistcoat, yellow breeches, striped stockings and brown shoes, on a sponged yellow and blue base, base restored, perhaps Yorkshire, c1800, 10in (25cm).
$1,200-1,500

A creamware Toby jug, in dark brown hat, blue jacket, grey waistcoat and breeches and black shoes, c1775, 13½in (34cm).
$2,500-3,000

A pearlware Toby jug of Pratt type, with brown hair, ochre-collared blue coat, chequered waistcoat, ochre breeches and black shoes, hat chipped, perhaps Yorkshire, c1800, 8in (20cm).
$800-1,000

A pearlware Toby jug, in green hat and jacket, brown breeches and grey shoes, restoration to hat and left shoe, c1800, 9½in (24cm).
$900-1,200

A squire Toby jug, of Ralph Wood type, decorated in coloured glazes, c1775, 11in (28cm).
$8,000-9,500

A Lord Howe Toby jug of the Ralph Wood school, c1775, 10in (25cm).
$5,000-5,500

Mugs

A Liverpool creamware dated and named mug, 3in (7.5cm).
$400-500

A creamware mug with lustre decoration and verse, 2½in (6cm).
$100-120

A Quimper mug, 5in (12cm).
$30-50

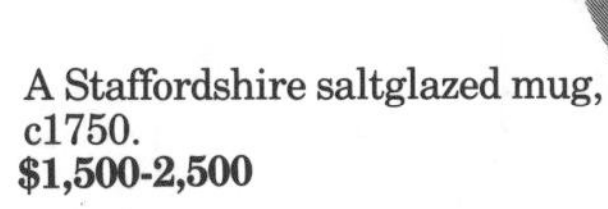

A Staffordshire saltglazed mug, c1750.
$1,500-2,500

A Staffordshire slipware mug, early 18thC, 3in (8cm).
$2,500-3,000

A Westerwald saltglazed tankard, 5½in (14cm).
$300-500

An agate bodied earthenware beaker, possibly Sussex, early 19thC, 3in (8cm).
$120-150

A Jackfield tankard, with original cold enamel decoration, c1780, 5in (12cm).
$450-500

A Staffordshire lead-glazed redware mug, c1750, 4½in (11cm).
$2,000-2,500

A copper lustre mug, with figure of a greyhound, c1840, 3in (7.5cm).
$200-250

A Jaco mug with blue transfer decoration, 4½in (11cm).
$400-450

A Shropshire Jackfield mug, c1750, 3½in (9cm).
$150-200

A creamware tavern pot or tankard, with inscription, late 18thC, 5½in (14cm).
$250-300

This form of tavern pot is often found in white and grey stoneware, delftware, heavier earthenware and ironstone, as well as in pearlware.

Make the Most of Miller's

CONDITION is absolutely vital when assessing the value of an antique. Damaged pieces on the whole appreciate much less than perfect examples. However a rare, desirable piece may command a high price even when damaged

A transfer printed pink lustre and enamelled mug, chipped, c1850, 4in (10cm).
$150-250

An agateware Royal armorial plaque, moulded in high relief with the Royal Arms and supporters, flanked by mantling and scrolls within a foliage moulded surround, covered in cream, brown and grey simulated agate glazes, perhaps Staffordshire, rim chips, c1750, 7in (17.5cm) high.
$2,500-4,000

A Mettlach plaque, decorated after Stahl in white relief on a blue grey ground, incised I.S. monogram, impressed castle mark 7040, 20½in (52cm).
$1,300-2,000

Pot Lids

Sandringham Cold Cream, green print, c1880.
$120-150

Pots

A Pratt ware pot, No. 402 'Uncle Tom', c1853, 4in (10cm).
$250-400

A saltglazed shop pot, London, mid-18thC, 9½in (24cm).
$80-100

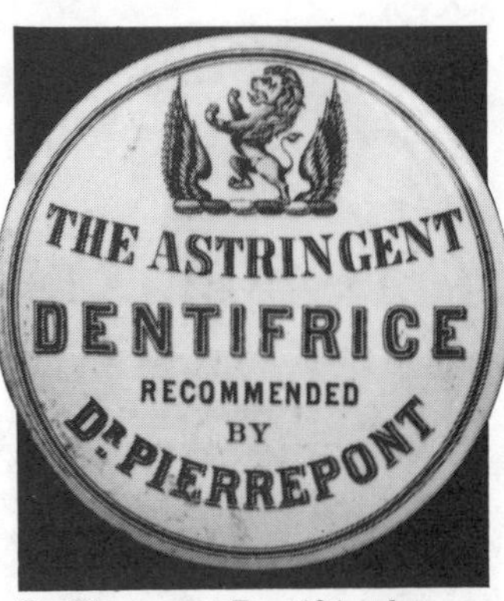

Dr. Pierrepont Dentifrice, late 19thC.
$80-120

Violette de Parme Toothpaste, purple print, c1880.
$120-150

A Quimper mustard pot, marked, c1925, 3in (7cm).
$55-75

A Quimper jam pot, 2½in (6cm).
$55-75

A Wedgwood basalt enamel ware sugar box, c1800, 4in (10cm).
$400-500

A Staffordshire blue chamber pot, gilded, 9in (23cm) diam.
$40-55

Pomade Sylphides, blue print, late 19thC.
$80-120

Almond Shaving Cream, sepia print, c1900.
$65-100

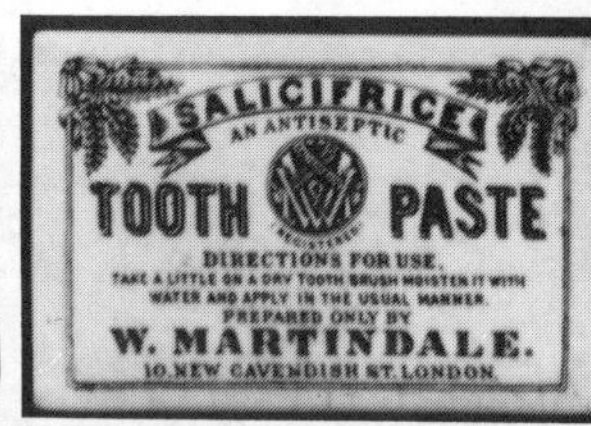

W. Martindale Tooth Paste, black print, 19thC.
$100-130

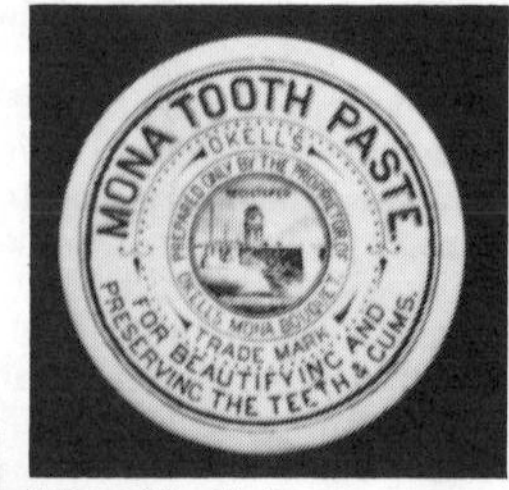

Mona Tooth Paste, black print, c1890.
$130-150

James Atkinson's Bears Grease, black print, c1890.
$80-120

Civil Service Rose Lip Salve, pink print, late 19thC.
$65-100

Thymol Tooth Paste, black print, c1880.
$30-50

Services

A Samuel Alcock tea service, decorated with leaves, scrolls and flowerheads on a pink ground, pattern No. 114, comprising 25 pieces, c1840.
$800-900

A Victorian Keeling & Co. dinner service, in the Stirling pattern, comprising: soup tureen with cover, ladle and stand, 2 vegetable tureens with covers, 2 sauce tureens with covers and ladles, 2 open tureens, 4 graduated meat plates, 12 soup bowls, 35 plates and one sauceboat.
$700-900

A Davenport stone china part dinner service, painted in pink, iron red and lavender blue, comprising: a meat dish, 2 serving dishes, 2 vegetable dishes and covers, 6 soup plates, 16 dinner plates, 16 dessert plates, some damage, printed Davenport Longport Staffordshire marks within a garter and pattern No. 79, c1845.
$5,000-6,500

A majolica tea set, c1875, teapot 5in (12.5cm).
$300-400

A pottery punchbowl, decorated with stylised flowerheads and gilt foliate painting, with gilt borders on circular flared foot, early 19thC, 11½in (29cm) diam.
$550-650

A Staffordshire creamware Whieldon type candlestick, cracked and chipped, c1750, 8in (21.5cm).
$20,000-25,000

A Faenza baluster famiglia gotica albarello, with bands of stylised leaves and flowerheads, footrim chip, c1480, 12in (30cm).
$65,000-73,000

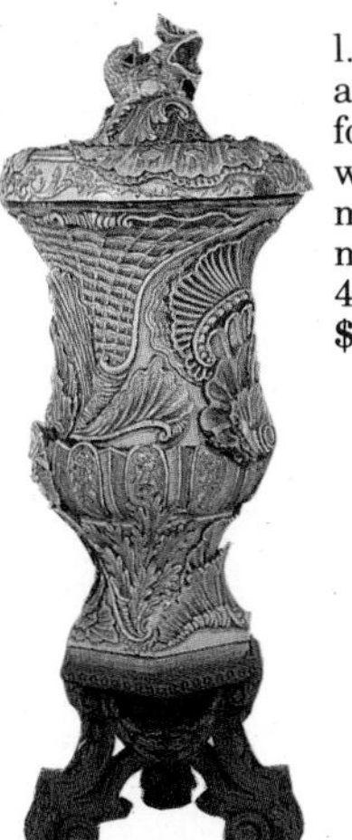

l. A rococo blue and white covered fountain, on later wooden stand, minor damage, mid-18thC, 49in (125cm).
$40,000-50,000

A Wemyss fruit bowl, 8½in (22cm) diam.
$150-250

An enamel decorated figure of Summer, probably North of England, c1820, 9in (23cm).
$250-300

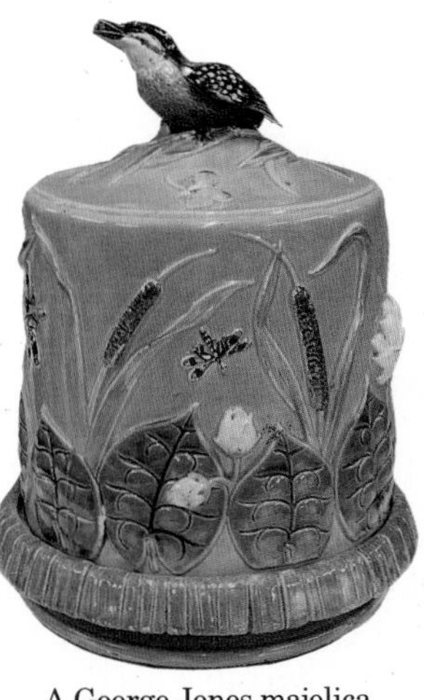

A George Jones majolica cheese bell and stand with kingfisher finial, repaired, late-19thC, 13½in (35cm) high.
$500-650

A French Mosanic hand painted pug, c1900.
$800-1,000

r. A Gallé cat with rare cream ground, signed Emile Gallé, c1900.
$7,000-8,000

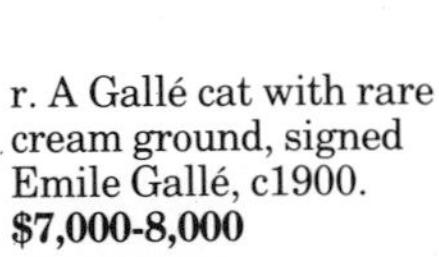

l. A creamware sauce-boat in the form of a duck, c1820, 8in (20cm) long.
$2,000-2,500

A Staffordshire pearlware group of Obadiah Sherratt type, extensively damaged, c1820, 13in (33.5cm) wide.
$16,000-20,000

A Deruta gold lustre tondino with portrait bust of a lady, slight chips, c1530, 9in (23cm).
$6,500-8,000

A Deruta Istoriato dish with Salome holding the head of John the Baptist before Herod and four attendants, c1580, 13½in (34cm).
$28,000-32,000

A Hispano-Moresque faience lustre dish, 16th/17thC, 17in (43cm).
$1,500-2,000

A Southwark delft polychrome La Fécondité dish, cracked and repaired, minor chips, c1650, 17in (43cm) wide.
$32,000-40,000

An Italian moulded dish with twin tailed mermaid, probably Angarano, late 17th/early 18thC, 18½in (47cm).
$5,500-7,000

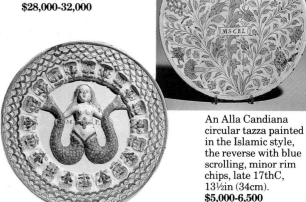

An Alla Candiana circular tazza painted in the Islamic style, the reverse with blue scrolling, minor rim chips, late 17thC, 13½in (34cm).
$5,000-6,500

A Bristol delft blue dash charger painted with a deer, c1710, 11½in (30cm).
$40,000-50,000

l. A London delft barber's bowl, c1716, 10in (26cm).
$40,000-50,000

A Dutch Delft plate, c1720, 8½in (21cm).
$150-250

l. A Castelli armorial plate painted by Aurelio Grue after a print from the 'Hunt Series' by Antonio Tempesta, c1725, 11½in (29cm).
$22,000-26,000

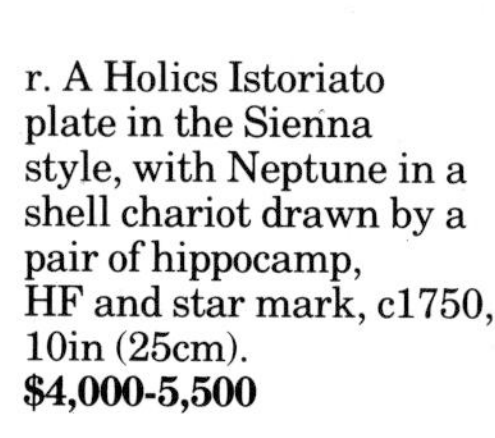

r. A Holics Istoriato plate in the Sienna style, with Neptune in a shell chariot drawn by a pair of hippocamp, HF and star mark, c1750, 10in (25cm).
$4,000-5,500

A French faience charger, Marseille factory of La Veuve Perrin, late 18thC, 14in (35.5cm) diam. **$650-800**

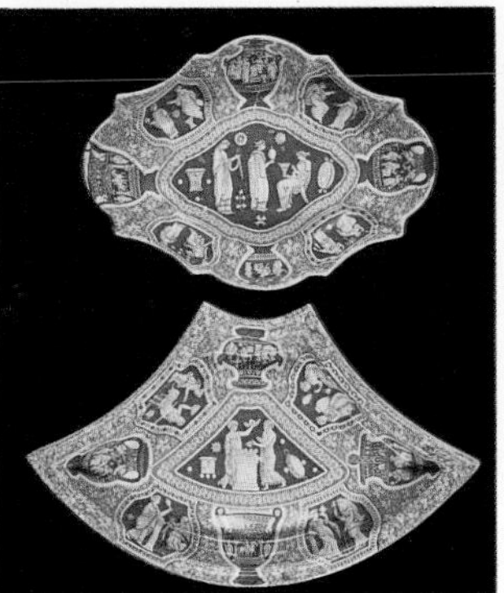

A Spode dessert dish and supper section, Greek patterns, c1805. **$150-250 each**

A Bathwell and Goodfellow soup plate, from the Rural Scenery series, Firewood pattern, c1820, 10in (25.5cm). **$120-200**

A dinner plate, with Fruit and Flowers pattern, c1815, 10in (25.5cm) diam. **$120-150**

A soup tureen stand, The Beemaster, maker unknown, c1820, 15in (38cm) wide. **$550-700**

A Bathwell and Goodfellow dinner plate, The Reaper pattern, c1820, 10in (25.5cm). **$120-200**

A Wemyss Gordon plate, with daisies and forget-me-nots, 8in (20cm) diam. **$300-400**

A Quimper teapot and cup and saucer set, teapot 5in (12.5cm) high. **$200-250**

A Staffordshire saltglazed soup tureen, cover and a stand, some damage, c1760. **$50,000-55,000**

A pair of Berlin baskets, underglaze and impressed marks, c1755, 9in (23cm). **$7,000-9,000**

A pair of delft vases and covers, Liverpool or London, some damage, c1760, 8½in (21cm). **$8,000-9,500**

A Staffordshire figure of Sir Robert Peel, c1850, 12in (30.5cm), (B,31). **$1,200-1,500**

A Wemyss pottery toilet set, with rose pattern and green border decoration, impressed and painted mark. **$6,500-8,000**

A Worcester armorial mug, with grooved loop handle, c1770, 5in (12cm) high. **$13,000-16,000**

A Meissen Kakiemon tankard and cover, chip to cover, blue caduceus mark, c1723, 4in (10.5cm) high. **$26,000-32,000**

A Worcester butter tub, painted with an Oriental, the interior with a flowering branch within a diaper and floral border, chip to footrim, c1754, 7½in (18.5cm) wide. **$30,000-32,000**

A Frankenthal snuff box and cover, c1770, with contemporary gilt metal mount, 4in (10cm) wide. **$16,000-20,000**

A Sèvres wine cooler, some damage, marked and letter H for 1760, 7½in (19.5cm) high. **$6,500-8,000**

A Chelsea leveret box and cover, red anchor and 110 marks, c1756, 4in (9.5cm) wide. **$22,000-26,000**

A Meissen tobacco box, painted in the manner of J. G. Horoldt, c1740 contemporary copper gilt mounts, 5½in (13cm). **$55,000-65,000**

A Worcester dish, rubbing and chips, blue square seal mark, c1770, 10½in (26cm) wide. **$9,500-12,000**

A Böttger figure, damaged, marked, c1717. **$16,000-20,000**

A Fürstenberg figure of Andromeda, restored, script and incised marks, c1774, later gilt chains, 11½in (28.5cm). **$2,500-4,000**

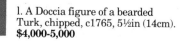

A Bow group of Harlequin and Columbine, some damage, c1765, 6½in (16cm) high. **$8,000-11,000**

l. A Doccia figure of a bearded Turk, chipped, c1765, 5½in (14cm). **$4,000-5,000**

A Höchst arbour group allegorical of Autumn, chips and repairs, wheel and incised mark, c1760.
$14,000-20,000

A pair of Höchst figures of street vendors, repairs, red and puce wheel marks, c1760, 7½in (19cm).
$20,000-25,000

A Mennecy group, two arms restored, incised d,v to base, 5½in (14cm).
$2,500-3,000

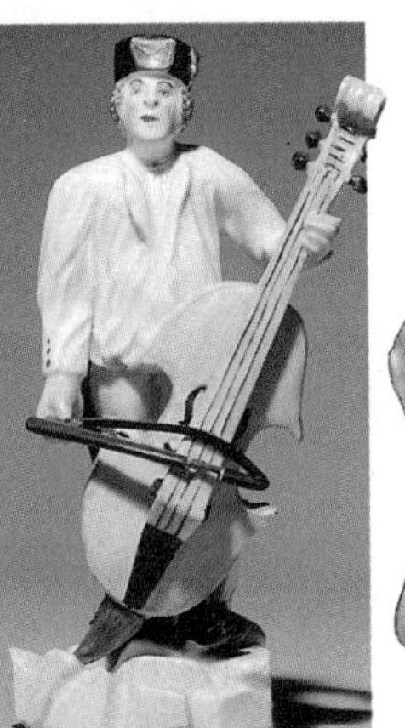

A Meissen miner musician, damaged and restored, blue crossed swords mark, c1730, 6in (15cm).
$16,000-20,000

A Meissen model by J. J. Kändler, extensively restored, faint blue mark to base, porcelain c1740, later decoration, 6½in (16cm).
$9,500-13,000

A Fulda Commedia dell'Arte figure of Harlequin, damaged, blue cross mark, c1770, 6½in (16cm).
$21,000-25,000

A Meissen salt by J. J. Kändler, repaired, marked, c1737, 7½in (19cm). **$13,000-16,000**

A French faience figure of an Oriental lady, repaired and damaged, c1730, 14½in (37cm).
$6,500-8,000

A Nymphenburg figure of Columbine from the Commedia dell'Arte, by Franz Anton Bustelli, repaired and chipped, impressed shield mark, c1762, 8in (20cm).
$20,000-25,000

A Sèvres biscuit figure of L'Abbé Fénélon after the sculpture by Lecomte, repaired and chipped, c1784, 19in (48cm).
$7,000-9,000

A Würzburg Commedia dell'Arte figure of Bagolin, possibly by Ferdinand Tietz, repaired, c1770, 5in (13cm). **$4,000-5,500**

A Chelsea group of 2 goats, restored and damaged, raised red anchor mark, c1751. **$9,500-13,000**

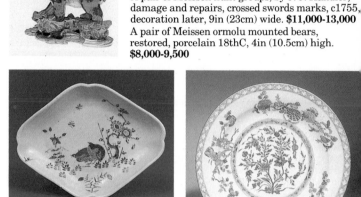

A pair of Meissen hunt groups, by J. J. Kändler, damage and repairs, crossed swords marks, c1755, decoration later, 9in (23cm) wide. **$11,000-13,000**

A pair of Meissen ormolu mounted bears, restored, porcelain 18thC, 4in (10.5cm) high. **$8,000-9,500**

A Meissen Hausmalerei plate, blue crossed swords mark, c1735, decoration later. **$40,000-50,000**

A Chelsea spoon tray, painted in the Kakiemon palette with the Quail pattern, glaze crack, raised anchor mark, c1750, 6in (15cm). **$8,000-9,500**

A Meissen plate, blue crossed swords mark, c1735, 15in (38cm). **$22,000-26,000**

A Meissen dish from The Red Dragon service, crossed swords and puce KHC mark, c1740, 11½in (29.5cm). **$4,000-5,500**

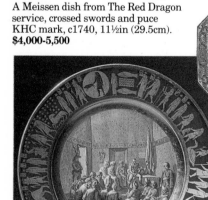

A Nymphenburg documentary tray, signed and dated 1813, impressed and incised marks, 15½in (39.5cm) wide. **$11,000-13,000**

A German dish, probably Ottweiler, border damaged, c1765, 12½in (31.5cm) diam. **$1,500-2,500**

l. A Dutch decorated Kakiemon dish, c1700, 7½in (18cm). **$8,000-9,000**

A Sèvres plate from The Egyptian service, various marks, 9½in (24cm). **$45,000-50,000**

A Vincennes 'bleu celeste' tray, with gilt dentil rim, interlaced L's enclosing date letter A for 1753, painter's mark, 11in (28cm) wide. **$8,000-9,500**

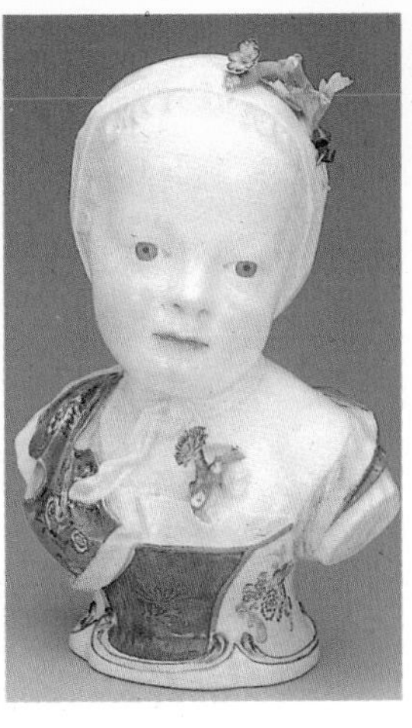

l. A Meissen portrait bust, by J. J. Kändler, some damage, crossed swords mark, c1755, 10in (25cm). **$14,000-20,000**

A Berlin K.P.M. Terrassenmalerei tête-à-tête, blue sceptre marks and gilder's dot mark to all pieces, various incised marks, c1790, the tray 13in (33cm) wide. **$11,000-13,000**

r. A Soviet porcelain propaganda plate, by the Imperial Porcelain Factory, 1921, 10in (25cm). **$8,000-9,500**

A Coalport Imari pattern part dinner service, comprising 86 pieces, some damage, c1805. **$16,000-20,000**

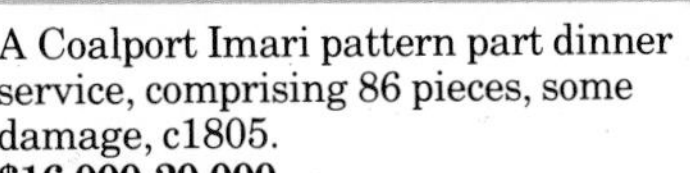

A Derby part dessert service, comprising 31 pieces, some damage, marked, c1800. **$65,000+**

l. A Bayreuth faience Hausmalerei 'famille rose' teapot and cover, cracked and repaired, c1740, 7½in (18.5cm) wide. **$13,500-16,000**

A Berlin K.P.M. part dinner service, comprising 43 pieces, sceptre marks and various gilder's marks, c1835. **$11,000-13,500**

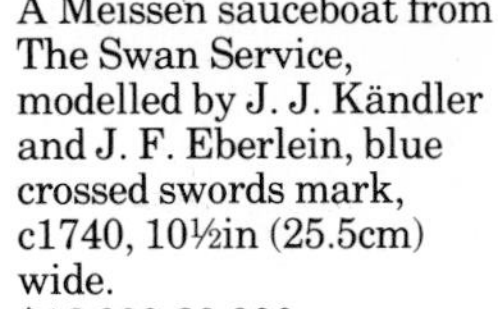

A Meissen sauceboat from The Swan Service, modelled by J. J. Kändler and J. F. Eberlein, blue crossed swords mark, c1740, 10½in (25.5cm) wide. **$16,000-20,000**

A set of 8 Meissen plates, blue crossed swords marks and Pressnummer 16, c1745. **$8,000-9,500**

A Naples cabaret, damage and repairs, blue crowned N marks, c1785, tray 12½in (32cm) wide. **$16,000-20,000**

r. A Bristol documentary sauceboat, Bristoll mark, incised mark, c1750, 8in (20cm). **$16,000-20,000**

A Chelsea moulded teapot and cover, with bamboo moulded handle, chipped and cracked, incised triangle mark, c1745, 4½in (12cm) high. **$40,000-50,000**

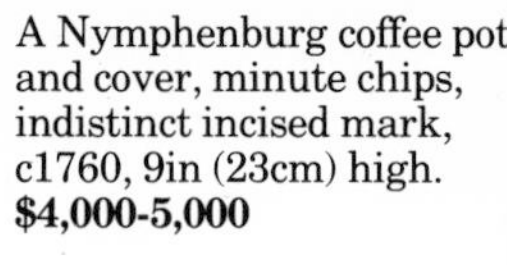

A Nymphenburg coffee pot and cover, minute chips, indistinct incised mark, c1760, 9in (23cm) high. **$4,000-5,000**

A Meissen teapot and cover, by J. J. Kändler, repairs, marked, c1735. **$7,000-9,000**

A Meissen underglaze blue teapot and cover, chipped and repaired, marked, c1724, 6½in (16.5cm) wide. **$20,000-25,000**

A Venice teapot and cover, repairs and chips, incised and iron red mark, c1725, 7in (17.5cm) wide. **$20,000-25,000**

Two Chelsea eel tureens, their tails forming the handles, one restuck and crack to cover, red anchor marks, c1755, 7½in (18.5cm) wide. **$35,000-40,000**

A Bow squat bowl and cover in a Kakiemon palette, incised R mark, c1750, 5½in (14.5cm) wide. **$32,000-40,000**

A Meissen two-handled écuelle and cover, painted by Bonaventura Gottlieb Hauer, crossed swords marks, c1745, 8in (20cm) wide. **$26,000-30,000**

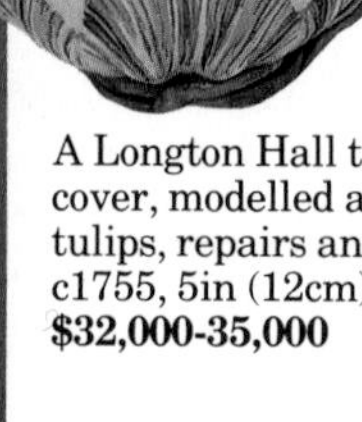

A Longton Hall tureen and cover, modelled as open tulips, repairs and chips, c1755, 5in (12cm) wide. **$32,000-35,000**

l. A Naples royal soup tureen and cover, from The Ercolanese Service, with inscription, repaired and gilding rubbed, c1781, on an almost contemporary gilt bronze mount, 14in (35.5cm) high. **$70,000-80,000**

A Böttger tea caddy and cover, slight damage, c1725, 4in (9.5cm) high. **$3,000-4,000**

A Chantilly pot pourri, the pierced cover with applied flowers, chips and repairs, c1750, 7½in (19cm) high.
$9,500-12,000

A pair of Chelsea vases and covers, minor damage, gold anchor marks, c1763.
$16,000-20,000

A pair of Chelsea vases, painted within gilt cartouches, chip to footrim, c1765, 7in (17.5cm) high.
$6,500-8,000

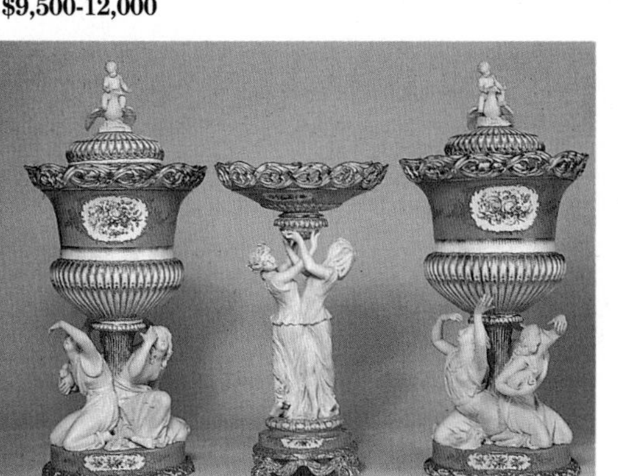

A Coalport garniture, comprising 2 ice pails, covers and liners and a fruit stand, some restoration, puce printed CBD marks incorporating retailer's marks for Daniell, c1855, ice pails 29½in (74cm) high. **$16,000-20,000**

A Sèvres caisse à fleurs, restored, marked, c1759, 7in (17.5cm) high.
$6,500-8,000

l. A Copenhagen vase, repaired, mark, c1810. **$40,000-50,000**

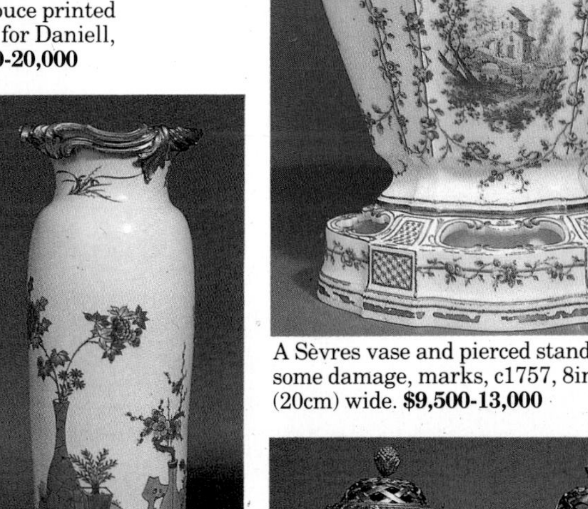

A Sèvres vase and pierced stand, some damage, marks, c1757, 8in (20cm) wide. **$9,500-13,000**

A porcelain vase, with ormolu mounts and brass liner, the ormolu c1830, 39in (99cm) high.
$3,000-6,500

A pair of Louis XV ormolu mounted Transitional blue and white vases, porcelain c1650, 19½in (49cm). **$40,000-50,000**

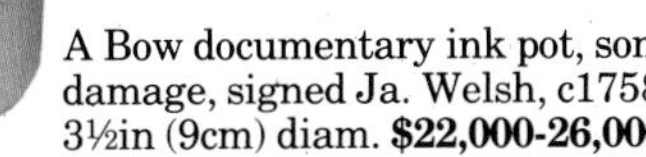

A Bow documentary ink pot, some damage, signed Ja. Welsh, c1758, 3½in (9cm) diam. **$22,000-26,000**

A pair of ormolu mounted jars and covers, the porcelain probably 18thC, the mounts later, 15in (38cm) high.
$11,000-16,000

A blue and white bottle vase, late Wanli, 7½in (18.5cm) high, wood box.
$16,000-20,000

A Kutani bottle, rim restored, c1670, 8in.
$11,000-16,000

An Arita blue and white bottle, c1680, 18½in (46cm) high.
$7,000-9,000

An Imperial 'famille verte' bowl, Yongzheng Yuzhi marks, 5½in (13.5cm) diam, box.
$80,000-95,000

A 'famille rose' mythological subject punchbowl, cracked, Qianlong, c1750, 15½in (39cm) diam.
$14,000-20,000

A water pot, decorated with copper red and iron red flowerheads, rim chips, Kangxi six-character mark.
$35,000-40,000

An Imari bowl, decorated with a continuous scene, restored, Genroku period, 15½in (39.5cm) diam.
$13,000-14,000

A ru-type bulb bowl, restored, underglaze blue Qianlong four-character seal mark and of the period, 9in (23cm). **$16,000-20,000**

l. A 'famille verte' enamelled biscuit bowl, Kangxi mark in underglaz blue within a double circle and of the period, 6½in (16.5cm).
$30,000-32,000

A Kakiemon blue and white bowl, kin mark, late 17thC, 8½in (22cm).
$9,000-9,500

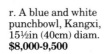

r. A blue and white punchbowl, Kangxi, 15½in (40cm) diam.
$8,000-9,500

A pair of yellow glazed bowls, one cracked, Qianlong seal marks and of the period, 4½in (12cm).
$20,000-22,000

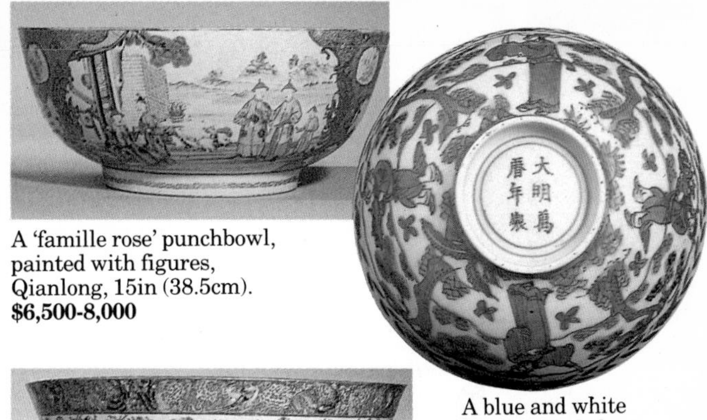

A 'famille rose' punchbowl, painted with figures, Qianlong, 15in (38.5cm).
$6,500-8,000

r. A Canton 'famille rose' punchbowl, early 19thC, 21in (52.5cm) diam.
$5,500-7,000

A blue and white bowl, encircled Wanli six-character mark and of the period, 6in (15cm).
$11,000-14,000

A Ming blue and white dragon bowl, star crack, Zhengde four-character mark in underglaze blue within a double circle and of the period, 6in (15cm) diam.
$40,000-50,000

A pair of blue and white bowls, painted with flying phoenix, some damage, encircled Jiajing six-character marks and of late in the period, 5in (12cm) diam, 2 boxes.
$2,000-2,500

A copper red glazed bowl, with finely pitted glaze, rim chip, Yongzheng mark within a double circle and of the period, 6in (15cm). **$1,500-2,500**

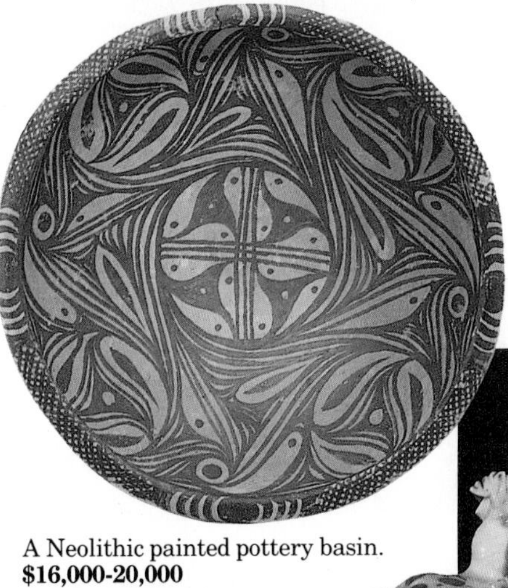

A Neolithic painted pottery basin.
$16,000-20,000

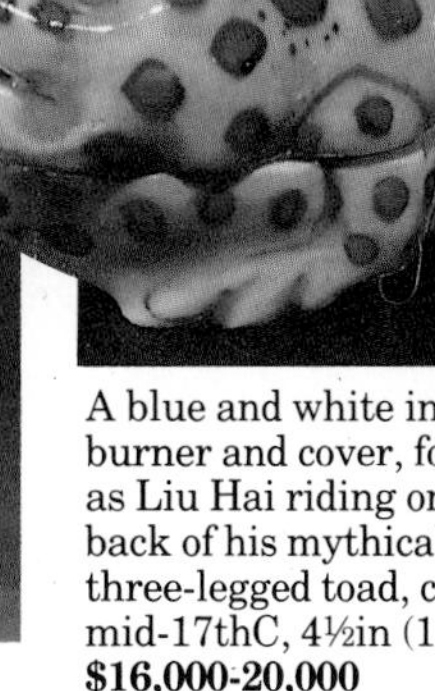

A blue and white incense burner and cover, formed as Liu Hai riding on the back of his mythical three-legged toad, chips, mid-17thC, 4½in (11cm).
$16,000-20,000

A pair of 'famille verte' dragon and phoenix bowls, Qianlong seal marks and of the period, 5½in (14.5cm), boxes. **$35,000-40,000**

Three blue and white eggshell month cups, painted with various flowers for December, September and January, cracks, Kangxi mark and of the period, 3in (8cm).
$2,500-3,000

A doucai cup, painted with chickens, Kangxi, 3½in (8cm), wood stand, box.
$40,000-50,000

A set of 5 blue and white sake cups, painted with spiral headed plum blossom and butterflies, one repaired in gold lacquer, one cracked, mid-17thC.
$5,000-6,500

A set of 5 blue and white cups, rims fritted, encircled Jiajing six-character marks, Chongzhen, 3in (7.5cm) diam.
$4,000-5,000

A blue and white stem cup, painted in underglaze blue with a continuous scene, the interior with a central medallion surrounded by a foliate diaper border at the rim, 16thC, 5½in (14cm) diam.
$13,000-16,000

A pair of yellow and blue glazed wine cups, Daoguang, 4½in (11cm) wide, fitted cloth box.
$1,500-2,500

A pair of Ming blue and white saucer dishes, rim chip, Jiajing mark and of the period, 6in (15cm) diam.
$25,000-30,000

A blue and white serving dish, Chinese or Japanese, firing cracks, possibly 17thC, 9in (23cm), wood box. **$20,000-22,000**

A set of 6 blue and white mukozuke, frits, one with underglaze blue Chenghua six-character mark, Chongzhen, 5½in (14cm), wood box.
$5,000-6,500

A set of 5 blue and white enamelled mukozuke, with scalloped borders and brown rims, rim frits, four-character seal marks, Chongzhen, 5½in (14cm), wood box. **$8,000-9,500**

l. A 'famille verte' dish, some damage, Kangxi, 12½in (31.5cm) diam.
$7,000-9,000

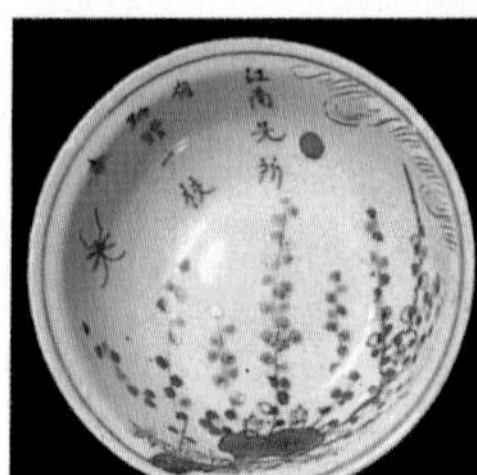

A set of 6 blue and white mukozuke, each painted with an underglaze blue Tang poem, rim frits, Tianqi, 5½in (14.5cm), wood box.
$7,000-9,000

A Kakiemon teabowl, decorated in enamels and gilt, the interior with a five-pointed floret, c1680, 3in (7cm). **$4,000-5,000**

Two Ming red lacquer carved boxes and covers, 16th/17thC. **$8,000-9,500 each**

A Ming stem cup, the iron red enamel laid over a yellow enamel ground, rim crack, Jiajing six-character mark and of the period, 6in (15cm) diam. **$4,000-5,000**

A blue and white display dish, rim chips, late Wanli, 13½in (34cm) diam, wood box. **$26,000-30,000**

A blue and white Shonzui style serving dish, fu seal mark, Chongzhen, 8in (20cm), wood box. **$16,000-20,000**

A blue and white Shonzui style serving dish, encircled Chenghua six-character mark, Chongzhen, 9in (23cm), wood box. **$11,000-15,000**

A blue and white Shonzui style serving dish, rim frits, Tianqi, 8in (20.5cm), wood box. **$6,500-8,000**

r. A 'famille verte' saucer dish, painted with the English coat-of-arms below a royal crown and inscription, some damage, Kangxi, 13½in (34cm). **$9,500-11,000**

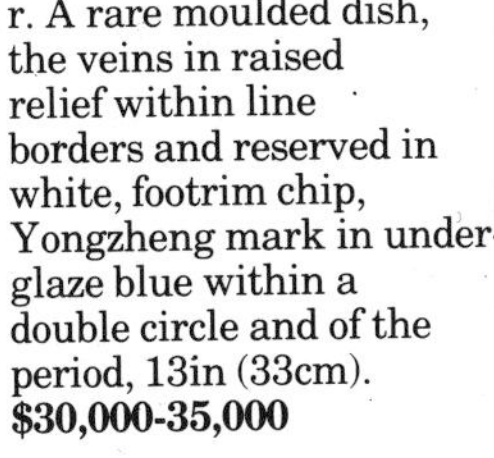

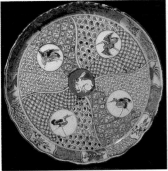

A blue and white enamel Shonzui style serving dish, fu mark within a double square, Chongzhen, 8in (19.5cm). **$25,000-30,000**

r. A rare moulded dish, the veins in raised relief within line borders and reserved in white, footrim chip, Yongzheng mark in underglaze blue within a double circle and of the period, 13in (33cm). **$30,000-35,000**

A pair of dishes, painted with a bust profile of Queen Anne, Qianlong, 14in (35.5cm).
$9,000-10,000

A pair of 'rose/verte' dishes, painted with court ladies and a young boy in a garden, rim frits, Yongzheng, 15in (38cm).
$18,000-20,000

Two 'famille rose' saucer dishes, Yongzheng mark and of the period.
$13,000-15,000

A pair of 'famille verte' dishes, the centre of each pencilled in under-glaze blue, rim crack, Kangxi, 13in (33cm).
$7,000-8,000

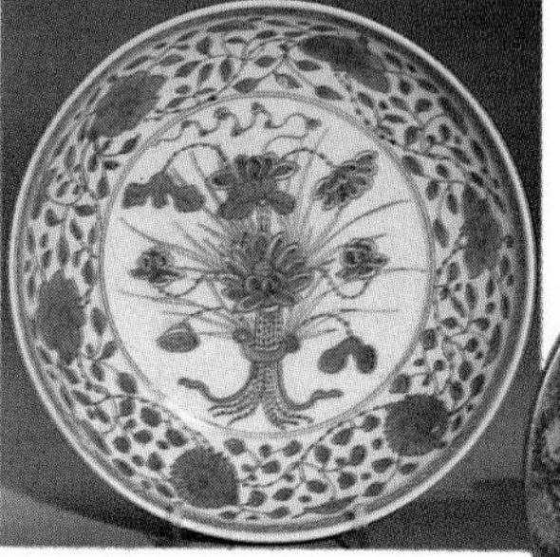

A Ming style saucer dish, Yongzheng mark and of the period, 8in (20cm).
$1,500-2,000

A pair of blue and white dishes, firing crack, Daoguang seal marks and of the period, 7in (18cm).
$3,000-5,000

l. A pair of Chinese 'famille rose' saucer dishes, mid-19thC.
$1,500-2,000

A pair of Arita blue and white dishes, small chip, late 17thC, 12½in (32cm) diam.
$5,500-8,000

A Kakiemon type dish, in coloured enamels on underglaze blue with a lakeside landscape, late 17thC, 10in (25cm).
$6,500-8,000

A pair of Kakiemon dishes, decorated in enamels with a bridge scene, footrim chip, late 17thC, 7½in (19cm).
$16,000-20,000

A pair of Arita blue and white saucer dishes, marks, early 18thC, 6½in (16cm).
$4,000-5,500

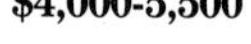

A pair of 'famille verte' dishes, painted with an aquatic scene, early 18thC, 14½in (38cm).
$11,000-14,000

An Imari dish, decorated in coloured enamels and gilt, Genroku period, 12½in (32.5cm).
$5,000-6,500

A Kakiemon dish, decorated with the Shiba Onko story, slight damage, c1680.
$13,000-16,000

A pair of Arita sake ewers modelled as minogame, in iron red enamel and gilt, late 17thC/early 18thC, 7in (18cm) long. **$11,000-16,000**

Two blue and white kendi for sake, l. late Wanli, 8in (20cm), r. rim frits, Chongzhen, 6in (15cm). **$6,500-9,500 each**

A ewer and fixed cover for serving sake, with tall hollow pierced bracket handle, rim frits, mid-17thC, 9½in (24.5cm) high. **$16,000-20,000**

l. A blanc de chine figure of Guanyin, cracks, incised and commendation marks, 18thC, 20in (51cm). **$25,000-30,000**
r. A pair of 'famille rose' export candle holders, one cracked, Jiaqing, 16in (41.5cm). **$21,000-25,000**

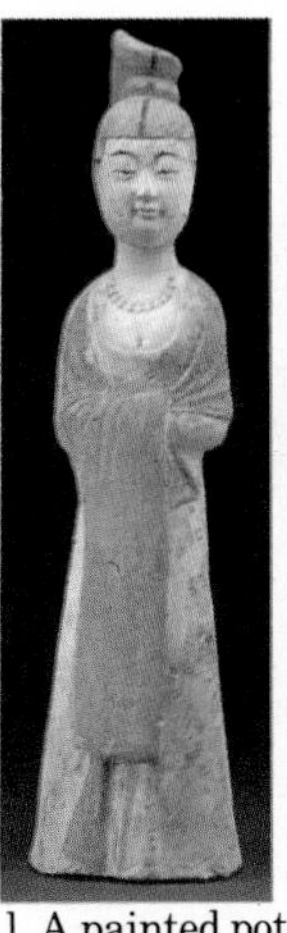

l. A painted pottery figure of a court lady, with traces of pigment and gilding, Tang Dynasty, 15½in (39.5cm). **$7,000-8,000**
above r. A pair of export figures of ladies, their robes embellished with gilt restored, heads later, Qianlong, 11½in (29cm). **$10,000-13,000**

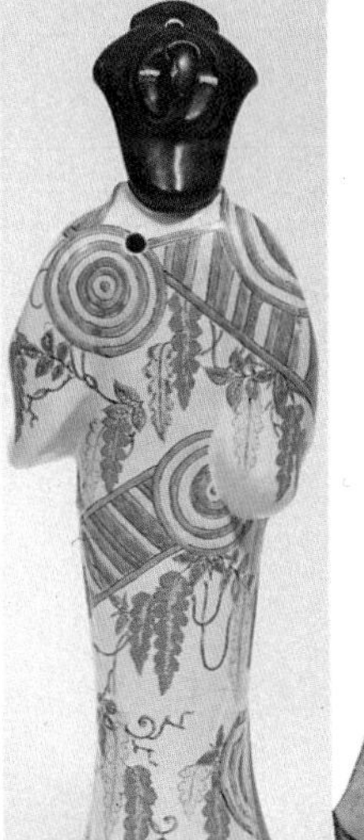

The rear view of a Kakiemon model of a bijin, restored, damaged, c1680, 15½in (39.5cm). **$50,000-80,000**
r. A figure of a matron, restored, Tang Dynasty, 18in (45cm). **$40,000-50,000**

A Sancai guardian figure, both hands and head unglazed, traces of black and red pigment, restored, Tang Dynasty, 18in (45cm). **$5,000-8,000**

l. A pair of painted pottery figures of soldiers, traces of pigment, restored, Northern Wei Dynasty, 14in (36cm). **$13,000-16,000**
c. A painted pottery figure of a kneeling lady, Han Dynasty, 18in (45.5cm). **$9,500-13,000**
r. A pair of painted grey pottery figures of dancers, traces of white slip and earth encrustation, restored, Northern Qi Dynasty. **$8,000-10,000**

A pair of Chinese warthogs, in green monochrome, restoration, c1820, 6½in (16cm) high.
$800-1,000

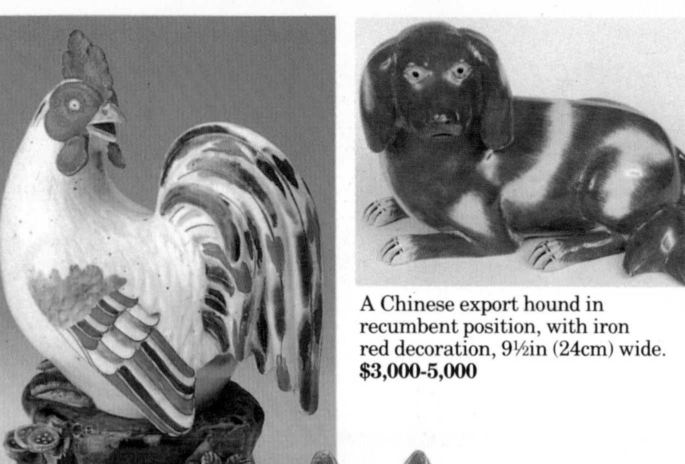

A Chinese export hound in recumbent position, with iron red decoration, 9½in (24cm) wide.
$3,000-5,000

r. An Imari model of a cockerel, painted in underglaze blue, iron red, black, green enamel and gilt, restored, Genroku, 10in (26cm).
$13,000-16,000

An amber glazed red pottery figure of a dog, restored, Han Dynasty, 12½in (31.5cm) long.
$8,000-11,000

A painted red pottery figure of a dog, Han Dynasty, 10½in (26.5cm) high. **$6,000-9,000**

l. A pair of grey pottery mythical beasts, Six Dynasties, 11in (28.5cm) wide. **$16,000-20,000**

A green glazed pottery dog, the glaze with shiny iridescent areas, some restoration, Han Dynasty, 13in (33cm) long. **$9,500-13,000**

l. A Chinese green glazed cockerel, c1820, 8½in (21cm) high.
$1,000-1,300

A pair of 'famille verte' enamelled Buddhistic lions, restored, Kangxi, 17in (43.5cm) high.
$20,000-25,000

r. An Arita model of a seated horse, after a Dutch Delft original, damaged, c1700, 7in (18cm) long.
$13,000-16,000

A moon flask, firing cracks, Qianlong six-character seal mark, 19½in (49.5cm).
$40,000-50,000

A moon flask, painted in iron red with peony blossom and other flowers and leaves, Kangxi, 9in (23cm). **$25,000-30,000**

A Sancai pottery flask, the flattened globular body moulded with a dense floral scroll beneath foliate loop handles, the glaze stopping irregularly at the spreading foot, enamel added to unglazed spots, Tang Dynasty, 6in (15.5cm). **$20,000-25,000**

A 'famille rose' jardinière, Yongzheng/early Qianlong, 14½in (37.5cm) wide. **$13,000-16,000**

l. A Ming cloisonné enamel moon flask, dents to enamels, 15th/16thC, 10½in (26cm). **$8,000-13,000**

A doucai jardinière, restored, Qianlong seal mark and of the period, 13in (33cm) diam. **$25,000-30,000**

A pair of 'verte' Imari cachepots, with lions' masks applied to the sides at the shoulder, fritting, mid-18thC, 8in (21cm) diam.
$14,000-18,000

A large green glazed pottery lian, restored, Han Dynasty, 12in (31cm) diam. **$10,000-15,000**

A blue and white jardinière, with gilt lacquered biscuit lions' masks, chips, Qianlong, 24½in (62cm) diam.
$20,000-25,000

A 'famille rose' jardinière, with gilt lacquered biscuit lions' masks, crack, fritting, Yongzheng/Qianlong, 25½in (64.5cm). **$20,000-25,000**

r. A blue and white jardinière, kiln adhesion polish to one side, 19thC, 24½in (62.5cm) diam. **$8,000-13,000**

A large Imari charger, painted with a fan shape panel, late 19thC, 24in (62cm). **$2,000-2,500**

A set of 5 blue and white serving plates, rim frits, Tianqi/Chongzhen, 6½in (16cm) diam, wood box.
$4,000-5,500

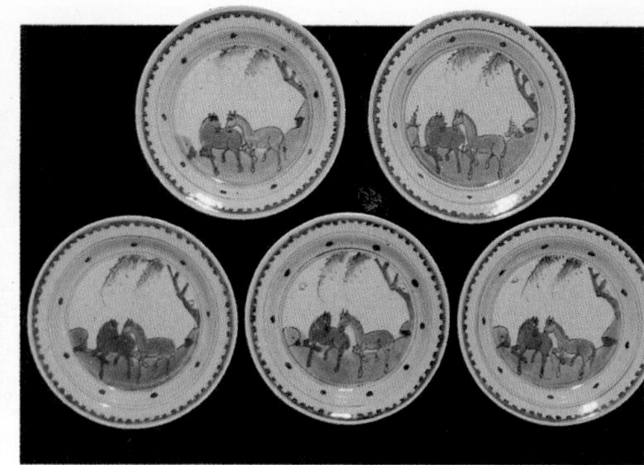

A set of 5 blue and white serving plates, chips and frits, Tianqi, 6in (15cm) diam, wood box.
$3,000-5,000

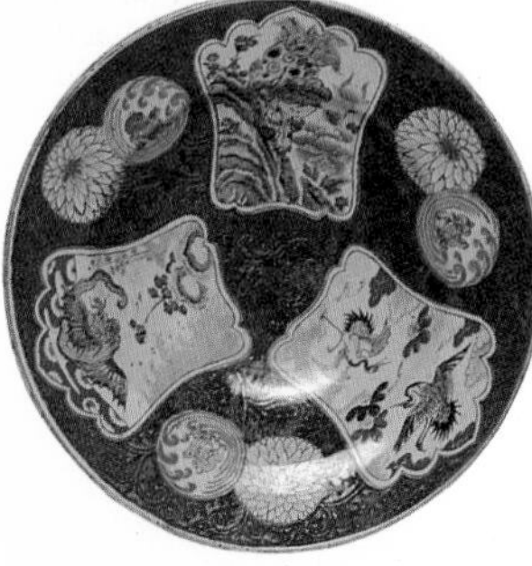

An Imari charger, Genroku period, 21½in (54.5cm).
$11,000-13,000

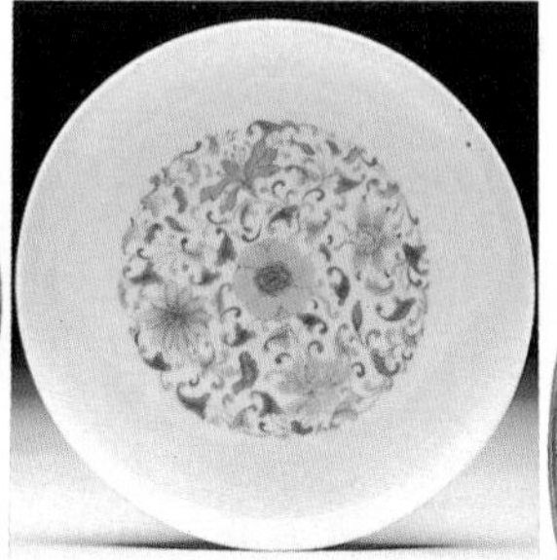

A pair of doucai dishes, enamels rubbed, 18thC, 6in (15cm), wood stands.
$20,000-25,000

A 'famille rose' eggshell deep plate, Yongzheng, 8½in (21cm) diam, box.
$25,000-28,000

A Ming blue and white cup stand, Wanli mark within a double circle and of the period, 6in (15cm) diam.
$5,500-7,000

A 'famille rose' five-piece garniture, decorated with Buddhist emblems, restoration and chips, iron red Qianlong six-character seal marks, 19thC, the beakers 11in (27cm). **$9,500-12,000**

A 'famille rose' plaque, mid-18thC, 16½in (42cm).
$3,000-4,000

r. A 'famille rose' dish, mid-18thC, 15in (38cm).
$4,000-5,000

An Imari garniture, decorated in enamels and gilt on underglaze blue, small cracks, Genroku period, the mounts later, vases 17in (43cm).
$16,000-20,000

An Imari oviform jar and cover, decorated in enamels and gilt on underglaze blue, cover damaged and restored, Genroku, 12in (31cm).
$6,500-8,000

A pair of Imari jars and covers, each decorated in iron red and black enamels and gilt, restored, late 17th/ early 18thC, 24in (62cm).
$40,000-50,000

A kettle and cover, after an archaic bronze prototype, rim and spout chips, body crack, Qianlong seal mark and of the period, 9½in (23.5cm) wide. **$10,000-12,000**

A pair of Ko-Imari teapots, decorated in enamels, repaired, late 17thC, 4½in (11.5cm) high.
$9,000-10,000

r. An Imari oviform vase, decorated in coloured enamels and gilt on underglaze blue, cracked base, c1700, 8½in (21cm). **$2,000-2,500**

A pair of 'famille rose' Mandarin pattern tureens, covers and stands, with animal head handles, covers with pomegranate finials, enamels rubbed, stands fritted, Qianlong, 15½in (39cm) wide.
$25,000-30,000

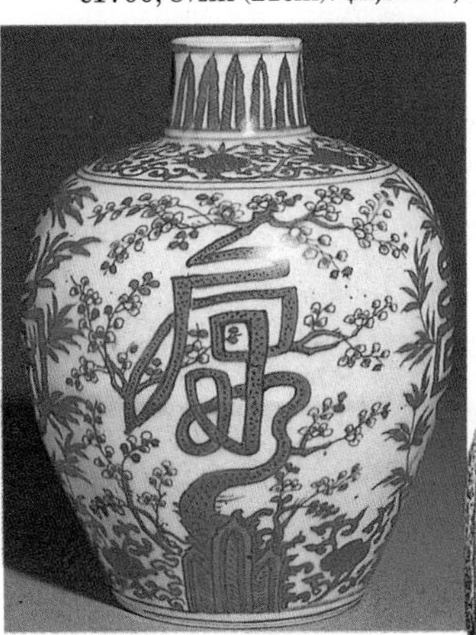

A late Ming vase, cracks and frits, Wanli mark and of the period, 8in (20cm).
$5,000-8,000

r. A pair of Canton vases, restored, 19thC, 51½in (130cm). **$16,000-20,000**

A pair of 'famille rose' tureens and stands, with dog finials, fritted, Qianlong, largest stand 16½in (42cm) wide.
$30,000-32,000

l. A Chinese export 'famille rose' baluster vase, mounted as a lamp, in the Ch'ien Lung style, 21½in (54.5cm) high.
$800-1,200

A 'famille rose' bottle vase, Qianlong seal mark and of the period, 20½in (52cm) high.
$32,000-40,000

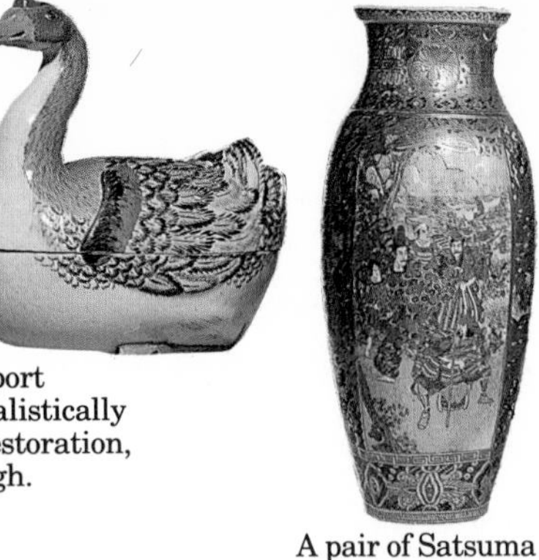

A pair of 'famille rose' export tureens and covers naturalistically painted, one with some restoration, Qianlong, 13in (33cm) high.
$95,000-110,000

A pair of Satsuma baluster vases, some damage, unsigned, late 19thC.
$11,000-12,000

A Yahu Meizan vase, gilt rubbed, Meiji period, 9in (22.5cm) high.
$12,000-13,000

A 'famille verte' rouleau vase, 19thC, 14in (36cm) high.
$1,000-1,200

An Imari vase, Genroku period, 21½in (54cm) high.
$21,000-25,000

An important oviform Kakiemon vase, decorated with coloured enamels in 3 panels, one crack, c1680, 15½in (39cm) high. **$400,000+**

Above r. A pair of Canton 'famille rose' barrel-shaped garden seats, 19thC, 18in (45.5cm) diam.
$8,000-9,500

l. A pair of Canton 'famille rose' vases, the necks with lion handles, one wood stand, 35½in (90cm) high.
$7,000-8,000

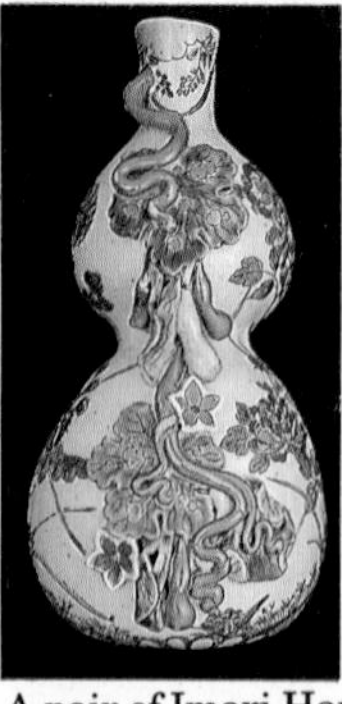

A pair of Imari Hanaike, some restoration, c1700, 8½in (21.5cm) high. **$9,500-11,000**

Above r. A gilt decorated 'famille rose' rotating triple vase, Qianlong seal mark and of the period, some damage, 9in (23cm) wide. **$40,000-58,000**

A glazed vase, 'lingzhi' mark, Kangxi, 9½in.
$3,000-5,000

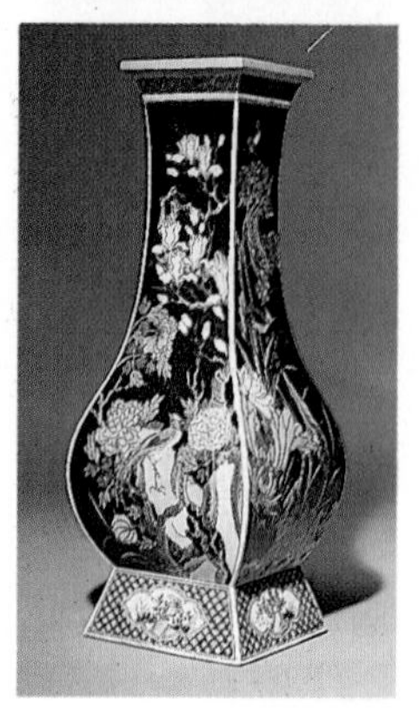

A 'famille noire' vase, base crack, porcelain Kangxi, 20½in (53cm).
$26,000-30,000

l. Two spirit decanters, c1780.
$300-350 each
c. A wine glass cooler, c1800.
$130-150
r. A spirit decanter for 'Shrub', c1800. **$300-500**

A set of 4 spirit decanters, with gilt simulated wine labels and gilt lozenge stoppers, c1800, 7½in (18.5cm). **$1,400-2,000**

An onion shaped carafe, c1830, 7½in (19cm).
$250-300

Three spirit flagons, with metal mounts and metal and cork stoppers, c1825, 8in (20cm).
$150-250 each

A mallet shaped decanter, engraved Rum and 'J.F' above, c1800, 8½in (21.5cm). **$550-650**

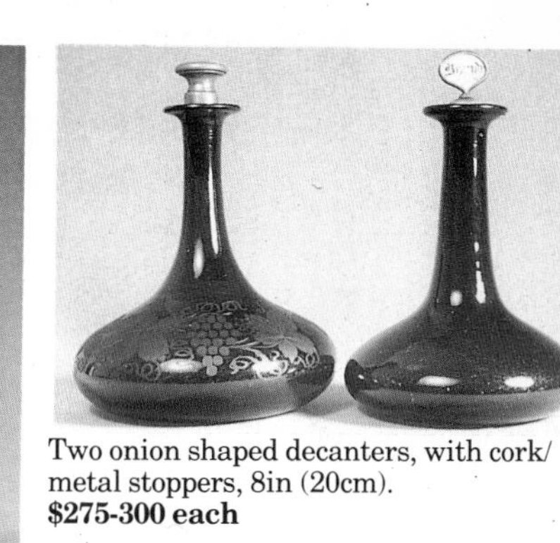

Two onion shaped decanters, with cork/ metal stoppers, 8in (20cm).
$275-300 each

A heavy engraved carafe, c1830, 8½in (21.5cm).
$300-400

A pair of broad flute decanters, with star cut bases and hollow cut mushroom stoppers, c1840, 9in (23cm).
$700-800

A pair of decanters, with star cut bases and hollow mushroom stoppers, c1840, 9in (23cm).
$550-650

l. An onion shaped amethyst carafe, c1840, 8½in (21cm). **$250-300**
r. A pair of engraved carafes, with cork/metal stoppers, c1840, 9in (23cm). **$550-650**

A pair of onion shaped blue opaline carafes, c1850, 8in (20.5cm).
$500-550

A cut glass chandelier, part 18thC, fitted for electricity, 44in (112cm).
$8,000-9,500

Purple amethyst bottles with l. plated cork mount, r. loop handled Britannia/cork mount, c1830, 8in (20cm).
$300-350 each

l. A pair of blue spirit bottles with annulated mouth rims, c1830, 11in (28cm). **$500-550**

A Central European enamelled glass-blower's flask, inscribed Johann Georich Hettne/anno 1767, 6½in (16cm) high.
$20,000-21,000

Two flute cut amber spirit bottles with cut pouring lips and cut spire stoppers, c1840, 9 and 12in (23 and 31cm) high.
$200-250 each

A pair of blue spirit bottles with turnover rims and cork/metal stoppers, c1830, 12in (30cm).
$550-650

Spirit bottles, amber wrythen with cork/metal stopper, plain amethyst with similar stopper, blue with plain lozenge stoppers, c1850, tallest 12in (30cm).
$250-400 each

A shell shaped satin glass dish, decorated with flowers, gilded branches and leaves in a silver plated figural stand, two reindeer pulling shell, 13½in (34cm) long.
$1,000-1,200

A set of 3 Bristol blue decanters, c1790, 8in (20cm). **$2,000-2,500**

A cylindrical bowl on solid glass round foot, engraved with design of fish, engraved signature Keith Murray S & W Brierley, 6in (15cm).
$4,000-5,000

r. A Monart footed bowl, with blue and purple stripes and bubbles, damaged. **$140-150** If perfect **$650-700**

A Webb cameo glass bride's bowl, on metal stand, marked, 10in (25cm). **$1,300-1,500**

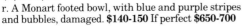

A blue bonnet glass, c1780, 3in (7cm). **$250-300**

l. A pair of green wines, with cup bowls, hollow knopped stems, c1850, 4½in (11.5cm). **$80-120** r. A set of 8 green wines, c1825, 5in (13cm). **$700-800**

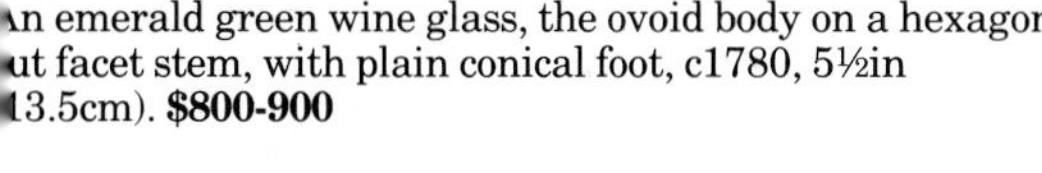

\n emerald green wine glass, the ovoid body on a hexagon ut facet stem, with plain conical foot, c1780, 5½in 13.5cm). **$800-900**

A wrythen moulded sugar basin and cream jug, c1800, bowl 3½in (8.5cm). **$200-250 each**

l. A set of 6 dimple moulded wine glasses, c1860, 5in (12cm). **$300-400**

A Nailsea bottle glass wine jug and carafe, with white marvered inclusions, c1810, jug 5½in (14cm). **$300-400** carafe **$250-300**

l. A black glass linen smoother, c1860. **$250-300**
r. A Nailsea cream jug, c1810, 4½in (11cm). **$400-500**

. & r. Clear glass scent bottles with silver/silver gilt nounts, c1850. **$250-300 each**
. A cut scent bottle, c1850, 4in (10cm). **$130-150**

Scent bottles, c1870, l. silver mount. **$130-150**
c. Silver gilt and gilt brass holder. **$1,300-1,500**
r. Diamond cutting. **$100-130**

'hree scent bottles, l. **$250-300**
. & r. With silver gilt mounts. **400-500 each**

Three scent bottles with gilt brass or silver gilt mounts, c1870. l. **$120-150**
c. & r. **$500-550 each**

A Louis XV gilt bronze, iron and rock crystal six-light chandelier, fitted for electricity, 38in (96.5cm) high.
$25,000-32,000

Three scent bottles, mid-19thC, l. with gilt metal mou
$200-250, c. with prism and star cut moulding **$400-50**
r. Bohemian with gold mount. **$400-500**

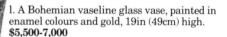

Three double-ended scent bottles, with hallmarke silver, silver gilt and gilt metal mounts, late 19th 5 to 6in (13 to 15cm). **$150-250 each**

l. A Bohemian vaseline glass vase, painted in enamel colours and gold, 19in (49cm) high.
$5,500-7,000

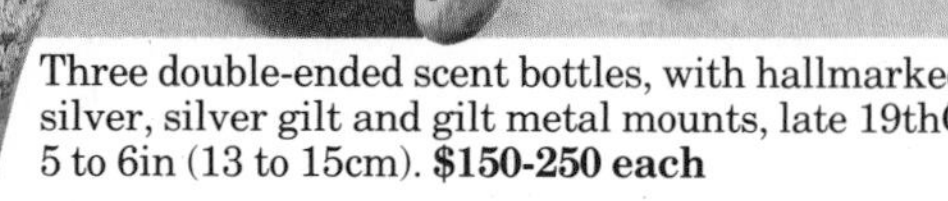

r. A blue glass pipe, c1860, 18½in (47cm).
$250-300

A cut glass scent bottle, with silver and enamel top, Birmingham 1930, 6in (15cm) high.
$300-400

A pair of ormolu mounted cut glass vases, on bronze plinths mounted with military trophies, inscribed Napoleon, 25½in (65cm) high.
$22,000-26,000

An enamelled Kurfursten Humpen, perhaps Bohemia, c1600, 11in (27.5cm).
$13,000-16,000

A set of 3 stained glass panels, entitled Sophocles, Aeschylus and Homer, some damage, 19thC, 79i (200cm) high. **$6,500-8,000**

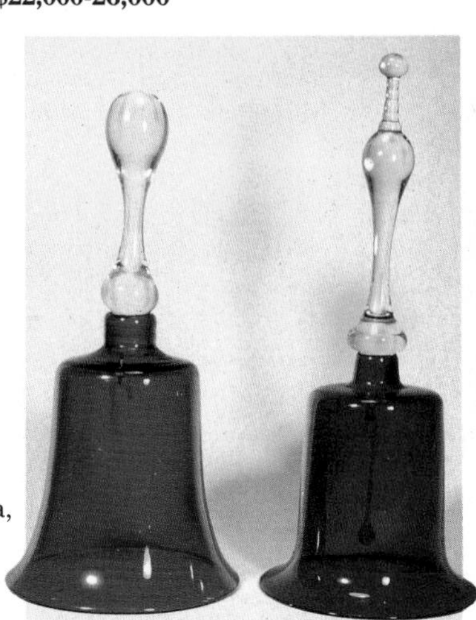

l. Two small bells with clear handles, c1860. **$200-250 each**

CHAPTER TWENTY FOUR

Deion and Mercedes sat next to Corrine's hospital bed. She'd been in a coma for a month and they were patiently waiting for her to wake up.

Mercedes was dressed in a pair of straight-leg blue jean pants, a hot-pink blouse, and a pair of hot-pink leather boots. Her wavy hair hung down her back and gold eye shadow accentuated her dark, flawless skin. Dressed in his usual jogging suit, Deion was asleep, snoring softly. Crossing her legs, Mercedes slowly folded her arms under her breasts and looked at Corrine. After going through many major surgeries for over a month, Mercedes and the rest of them were praying for her health to increase.

"Hey, girl!" Raynisha walked into the hospital room smiling, dressed in her police uniform and carrying a bouquet of flowers.

"Hey, Ray. You bought these for her? These are beautiful!" Mercedes smiled before giving her a welcoming hug.

"Yeah, girl. Wow, he's knocked clean out." Raynisha laughed, nodding at Deion.

Mercedes took the bouquet out of her hands before putting it on a nearby table where the rest of the "Get Well Soon" balloons and other flowers were located. Staring down at Corrine, Mercedes smiled. Turning back to face Raynisha, Mercedes took a seat next to her.

"I'm sorry I haven't really been home lately. I've been in the library studying to pass my GED classes and visiting her, so things have been a little hectic lately," Mercedes said.

"Girl, it's fine. Don't stress it. I'm glad that you're out of those streets, living with me, and back in school. Look at you, Mercedes. You're glowing! What did I tell you?"

"Let go and let God," they said in unison, bursting into a soft laughter.

"Raynisha. I can't believe it, either. I wish Tessa was here to see me now. But I know she's looking down at me and smiling right about now. And once Corrine gets out of here, I swear I'll do everything in my power to keep her off the streets and off of those drugs."

"Oh, yeah, I'll make sure she stays off those streets, too. Even if it takes all the strength in my body, this little girl will make it. I've already taken action and been appointed her legal guardian, so don't worry about her. You need to worry about yourself now, Mercedes. Have you thought about what you want to do with your life whenever you get your GED?"

"Yes, I want to go to school to be a sonogram technician."

"Good, and like I tell you all the time, anything is possible if you put your mind to it."

Mercedes nodded in agreement and turned when Corrine's doctor, Dr. Kennedy, walked into the room.

His bifocal glasses rested on the bridge of his nose as he tilted his head and looked at a chart that he held in his hands. He stared at Corrine, then back at the chart.

"Hello, is there a problem, doctor?" Raynisha asked, frowning.

"Yes, Ms. Williams, we have received the urine test back for Corrine Johnson, and it appears..."

"What? Appears what?"

"Ms. Johnson is four weeks' pregnant."

EPILOGUE

THREE MONTHS LATER...

Corrine weakly stepped out of the black BMW with a cane in her hand. She took baby steps, hesitantly walking toward the Pennsylvania Rehabilitation Center. Feeling hands on her, she stopped.

"Go ahead, baby girl. We're right by your side," Deion assured her with a warm smile.

He stood beside her, gently holding on to her frail arm and guiding her toward her future. Mercedes, who stood on the side of her, and Raynisha, who stood behind her, nodded their heads in agreement.

Corrine, who was dressed in a blue jean outfit that hung loosely on her body, flashed a fragile smile before taking a deep breath, clutched her small, pregnant stomach and continued to walk, but this time with much more confidence. When she finally reached the inside of the rehabilitation center and all three of them let go of her, she turned around, shielded her slanted eyes that now held hope in them, and waved goodbye to the only family she had left in this world.

Deion, now teary-eyed, ran and wrapped his strong, masculine arms around her petite frame, rocking her back and forth. She melted in his arms as he stroked her hair, telling her how much he loved her. Stepping back, he looked his little sister in the eyes. "I love you, baby girl. And I'm sorry for everything."

Remaining silent and giving him a reassuring smile, Corrine nodded before turning around and walking away.

Deion, Mercedes, and Raynisha waved her goodbye for the time being, hoping she'd walked into the center a girl and finally walk out a young woman.

✠ ✠ ✠

An hour later, Deion and Mercedes parted ways with Raynisha and they pulled up in front of an apartment in Northview. The sun was still shining and everyone in the neighborhood was out, enjoying the hot day. Dressed in an all-black cocktail dress and black stiletto pumps, Mercedes sat and stared at the house.

"So, this is where he stays at now?"

"Yeah, do you want me to handle this?"

Shaking her head, she reached into her leather pocketbook and pulled out her small .357. Turning around to face him, she said, "No, I want to do this by myself. I have to."

Getting out of the car, she walked toward the apartment with confidence, her head held high with each step.

Walking onto the porch, to her surprise, she found the front door unlocked. Turning the doorknob, she clutched her gun in her hand and looked around the living room with caution.

She shook her head in disgust and continued to stare around the usual smelly apartment. When she walked upstairs and found a man slumped over on a dirty mattress, she flipped him over.

Day'onne, who was in his usual drunken state of mind and looked like he was in good need of a wash, mumbled to himself and looked confused.

Mercedes turned her nose up and pointed her gun at him. "Big, bad-ass Day'onne, look at you now."

Day'onne, who was too much under the influence, continued to mumble under his breath and tried to stand, but quickly stumbled.

Cocking her gun and pointing it at his head, Mercedes took a deep breath, placing her hand on the trigger. Squinting her eyes, she said, "This is for Corrine."

Pulling the trigger, she watched as Day'onne's lifeless body limply fell to the dirty floor.

Exhaling, she walked out of the dirty room and house. Refusing to look back, she was finally happy to know she had closed that chapter of her life.

✠ ✠ ✠

Shay sat in her red Beemer, clutching her bulging stomach and looking through the windshield. She watched in envy as a beautiful, dark-skinned girl walked out of Day'onne's apartment, hopped into Deion's BMW and pulled off.

Getting out of the car, she walked on the porch and opened the door. A foul stench smacked her against her puffy cheeks, causing her to place her hand over her nose. She made her way up the stairs and into the first bedroom, not prepared for what she was about to see.

She held her swollen stomach as she made it out of the room as fast as she could. Walking into the living room, she doubled over and vomited. When she regained her composure, she walked back into the room and stared down at a lifeless Day'onne.

Turning, she walked out of the apartment and got back in her car. Always devious, she smiled mischievously, already plotting.

ABOUT THE AUTHOR

Paige Green is a high school senior from Pittsburgh, PA, where she grew up in the Northview Heights area. Since the age of 10, she has written plays, short stories, and eventually *Family Over Everything.* Motivated by her surroundings, she pushed herself to always strive for a more. Paige plans to attend college in one of the Southern states where she will major in Literature. Her main goal in life is to help young, at-risk females who are trying to find their way in life. Paige lives with her mother, two older brothers, and twin sister, Paris Green, in the Atlanta area.

If you enjoyed "Family Over Everything," please be sure to check out

Little White Lies

by Cole Riley

Coming Soon from Strebor Books

1 / HALLUCINATIONS

FALL 2006

The word around the neighborhood was that I was the good one, the levelheaded, ambitious boy who would make good one day. And never shame the family. I tried to be normal, the quiet nerd, the potential breadwinner. However, that was not to be the case.

My father said I reminded him of Doctor J, Elgin Baylor, Oscar Robertson, and even Michael Jordan when I found the proper stroke, the proper dribble, the proper pass. We used to shoot hoops in the backyard, and later on a tattered basketball court with tufts of grass peeking through the buckled asphalt. School was something I hated. I was never any good with numbers, grammar, or science. But put a basketball in my hands and I was an artist.

A rowdy crowd of supporters turned out to see us topple Cardozo by 12 points, allowing our team to capture a share of the division title. The Cardozo squad was playing without their top sophomore forward, Akim Lawrence, who was nursing a head cold. Still, the red-hot guards almost snatched the victory away in the third quarter with four three-pointers.

"Melvin, this win would mean a lot for our franchise and our school," Ron Faulk, our coach, said to me. "You've shown leadership throughout our entire season and you cannot let us down now. Not now. They're underestimating you and what you bring to our team. Kick some butt, son."

I thought back about how we beat Bishop Ford, Jefferson and even Nazareth. These dudes were a snap for us. I started rebounding and blocking shots, going out and putting my hand in the faces of the slick guards. Coach Faulk called our opposition Heckle and Jeckle, after the TV cartoon crows. Were they magpies?

Our 6-11 center, Houston Crown, stood in our huddle, grabbing me by the arm and speaking in his deep baritone voice. "They're talking a lot of smack out there. They say we're punks, we're chumps. Everybody thinks they can beat us. I take this personal and I know you guys do too."

"Shit, we cannot let them come to our house and talk a lot of shit," Emory Lewis, our point guard said. "We can't let them disrespect us and take the win. We've got to turn it up. We got to put them in their place. Smash-mouth ball, guys, smash-mouth ball."

The only game we lost all season was a blowout with Boys & Girl High in Brooklyn. They kicked our asses. I knew our team was better than that. I was real emotional 'bout that game. The reason I was not in the line-up was back spasms; it hurt to move, much less run up and down the court. Now, the guys were counting on me, looking at me and weighing whether I was up to the task.

Coach Faulk watched as one of the magpies shot the ball at the top of the key and it rimmed out. He called time out and we ran toward the sidelines in our snazzy red and black uniforms. All eyes were on me. The coach diagramed a play calling for me to shoot a jumper at the corner.

"We got to settle down," the coach said in a drained whisper. "Don't rush the shots. Play methodically. Focus. We got to put the ball in the hands of Melvin and he'll take care of business. Won't you, Melvin?"

I nodded. I shot the jumper but one of their players got a hard foul on me as I was going up with the ball. The ball went in on the foul shot, but the second one came out and bounced into the hands of the opposition.

The enemy called a time-out. We watched them and their coach, a loudmouth usually playing to the cameras. He gestured wildly and angrily, and slapped one of the boys on the back. They came back out and tried to do the play, which we stopped dead in its tracks. Emory picked off the pass and outran the speedy magpies to do a weak lay-up. Each team had another shot to end the game in regulation, until I put in a contested jumper as time expired.

They lifted me on their shoulders and carried me to the locker room. Spectators were pouring out of the stands, yelling and screaming my name. I felt damn good. As I was getting dressed, Coach Faulk smiled and said the sky was the limit for me. Emory walked past me and said we're going out to celebrate tonight.

I figured we had one game left to play, a brawl with St. Peter's Prep, and that would be a warm-up for the City Finals. Tonight, I'd act a total fool. I didn't want to think about how I got hurt during the game with Westinghouse just a year ago. One of the opposing players tangled my leg in his, maybe intentionally, as we went up for a rebound and I was writhing on the wood floor, unable to get up.

"Are you hurt, son?" my coach asked me. "Can you get up? Do you think you can get off the court unassisted?"

He was giving me a way out, to bravely get back up and trot off the court like a warrior. However, I felt like a punk, a sissy. Something had given away in my leg and my ankle when I fell. I felt it pull and later it burned like hell.

"Can you get up?" Coach Faulk wanted to do the right thing.

"Dammit, I don't think I can," I whined.

In no time, the coach waved over the trainers, who knelt beside me and manipulated my leg, then my ankle. All on the left side. I grimaced with pain and tried to hide my face with my shirt so the rest of the team wouldn't see how much I was suffering with this damn thing.

The coach whispered to the chief trainer in an urgent voice, gripping him on the arm. "Do you think he'll be able to play tonight?"

"Not in this game," the trainer replied. The arena was hushed while they waited to see if I would leave the court under my own power. I was lifted up, between two burly players and carried to the bench. Some of the team's admirers clapped and hooted while those in the know reserved their applause to see how badly I was hurt.

After the game, which we lost by eight points, I was told that I had a bad left mid-ankle sprain but there was nothing seriously wrong with my leg. When the doctor and the chief trainer told me the good news after I was X-rayed at the hospital, I was overjoyed. Coach Faulk said I would probably be out a week or two.

They wrapped my ankle tightly, gave me some painkillers, and sent me home.

"You gave a good acting job out there," my father hissed. He was always pushing me, pushing me. "You could have got up if you wanted to. You acted like a punk."

"Don't call me that," I protested. "The trainer said I hurt my ankle and that was that. The coach didn't want me to play."

"It's because of you that the team lost the game. You know that."

I shouted at him angrily. "That's not true!"

He smiled cruelly. "You punked out. You punked out when they needed you most. How does that feel, knowing that you didn't give your all?"

I turned from him and hobbled on my crutches to my room. My father was still yelling and ranting about how much of a coward I was, so I drowned him out with some jams from Biggie and Tupac. I knew how much he hated rap. Nigger baboon music, he called it.

"Turn that shit down," he screamed. "Turn that fuckin' shit down. Don't let me have to come in there. I'll knock the damn hell out of you."

I put on some headphones and listened to the music. There was something about him that reminded me about Drake Rice, whose father had high hopes for him as well. Drake's daddy was convinced he was going to play in the NBA and be a superstar. Just like Wilt or Bill Russell. My own father had those same damn dreams; one of many men living through their sons to reach goals that they could never attain.

About four years ago, Drake was leaving a party in East New York, a part of poorest Brooklyn, with a group of friends. Some dudes got out of a car and walked toward the high school basketball star. Two of them were waving guns when the cat with the hoodie yelled for the tall nigga not to move.

Everybody scattered and began running. Both of the thugs started firing wildly at the people. A girl later told the cops that you could hear the string of shots, pop-pop-pop-pop, the bullets whistling in the air past them. Drake stumbled and fell to the pavement and couldn't get up.

When they turned him over, he had two gunshots in the back. One of the parents carried him to his car and sped him to the hospital. Both of the bullets had hit his spinal cord, leaving him crippled from the waist down.

"Damn, they could've shot me in the head and my troubles would have been over," Drake told me when I visited him. "This is totally fucked up."

I completely agreed with him but I would never tell him to his face. God can be sometimes a trickster. Drake had everything in front of him. The good life. Everything. But now he was going to be trapped in that damn chair for life.

"Sure, we're pulling for you and living through you because if you can make the journey to the high life, then we will be a success too," my father said to me while going to the grocery store. "A lot of folks are counting on you. You've got a responsibility to not just yourself but to everybody. Remember that?"

Damn it, I thought. If people let me find my own way, everything would be cool. So much pressure, so much tension. I wanted to blow off steam but I didn't know how. I didn't do anything out of my character, nothing crazy, nothing to make my family ashamed of me.

2 / SHAME THE DEVIL

Joba Duane, a dude who used to play forward on our team, was running around with a crowd of roughnecks; most of them were former jailbirds. After one of the games, Joba offered me a joint but I refused it and man, he called me all kinds of names. So he and the crew were driving around the Bronx one night, and spotted somebody who owed Joba cash money.

"Hey spook, yo' owe me some cash, two large, and you been dodging me for three weeks," Joba shouted at the fleeing dude. "I told you I wants my money. You gon' gimme my money or I'll fuck you up."

The runner, panicked at the threat, fled between parked cars, zigzagging to prevent from getting shot. But the Beemer whipped around, squealed to a stop, and three of Joba's crew opened fire with heavy artillery. Some of the shots raked the front of an apartment building, sending sparks and shattered glass from the rooms with people living in them.

One apartment on the first floor contained a grandfather, an eighty-six-year-old, who was getting up to shut off his TV when the volley of shots came through the window, knocking him flat on the carpet. Later, his wife was on the news at eleven, saying he was reaching for the remote when the shots came through the window. He got it in the right jaw and the center of his chest.

"Henry kept saying I'm shot, I'm shot," his wife, tears in her eyes, said in a shaky voice to the reporters. "I didn't know what to do. So much blood. I went over to my neighbor's place and we called 9-1-1. Henry is lucky. He could be dead."

The news announcer gave a description of the vehicle, containing four black youths, armed and dangerous. She gave a number to the police tip line, saying all calls would be confidential.

Somebody tipped the cops off. Joba was singled out. The police staked him out for four days before they moved in, tailing him from the loading dock where he worked part-time, and surrounded him in his place. He lived there with his mother, his Dominican girlfriend and her baby. It wasn't his but he took care of it.

"They surrounded the house and moved in, trapping him like a rat," Luz said, clutching her baby. "They kicked down the door, slapped around his mother, and searched for him. He heard them when they came in and he went up the fire escape to the roof. They went up there after him."

"Did you see them shoot him?" the television reporter asked.

"No, they kept us inside," Joba's girlfriend sobbed. "They shot him in his belly, in his neck and in his hand. They said he was wrestling with them for the gun. He didn't have a gun. They shot him down like a dog."

"How is his mother taking it?" the reporter asked.

"What did you think?" Luz snapped. "She collapsed when they brought him out. She heard the sirens and the helicopters...and saw him when they carried him out in a body bag. She's crazy with grief, you know."

Oh man, my Pops, a used-to-be follower of Marcus Garvey and The Honorable Elijah Muhammad, went off about that Joba business. First, he started talking about the crumbling middle class, the recession, and how people were going nuts because the country cannot pay its debts. He babbled about reducing the deficit and how low-income families weren't ever going to move up the economic ladder.

"That's why these black boys robbin' and stealin' and killin' people, because they can't get any work," Pops added. "Joba didn't have a chance in this country. Most black boys don't have a chance. The cards are stacked against you guys."

I'd listen to him go off about the responsibility of young black men and the need to wake up to what's going on. The men and the boys are letting down the community, letting down the family, letting down the women, letting down the kids. But I couldn't see what he was doing to benefit anybody.

"Dad, somebody called you when you were out, said something about some money owed to a lawyer," I said. "I told him that you would call him back when you got in. He sounded like it was important."

"Everything's fuckin' important," my father growled.

"Are you going to be at the last game?" I asked him. "It's for the championship. The trainer and the coach say I should be ready so I'll play."

My father rubbed his chin and put his hand on my shoulder. "You've got to play your ass off. Coach Faulk said some pro and college scouts are going to be in the stands checking you out. You got to have your A game for that night."

"I will, I will." I grinned.

"Because it's all about the cash, the green stuff." My father lit a cigarette. "This is a capitalist society and everything is about money. You ain't shit until you got some money. Vultures and capitalism go hand in hand. One day I'll explain capitalism to you and how it works. As much money as this country generates, there should be no unemployment, no foreclosures, no lack, no poverty. The white man has this shit set up where poverty and capitalism go hand in hand. I'll explain it to you one day before you go out in the world."

"Explain what?"

"Explain how the real world operates, son." He took a deep drag of the smoke and let it out through his nostrils. The cigarette habit was something he had picked up recently. He always appeared stressed; jittery; worked up.

Our family had moved out of the projects into a fairly stable neighborhood bordering on a high crime area. For a time, we lived with our aunt in the Pink Houses in the East New York section of Brooklyn, but my father finally got some money coming in and we moved. Still, with all the money coming in the house, my parents were fussing and fighting. Pops accused her of spending money like it was growing on trees. Those were his words.

I plopped down on the couch. "Pops, what do you do? I have no idea what you do for a living. Somebody asked me and I didn't know what to tell them."

He pulled up a chair. It was crazy how much I looked like him. Mini-me. He lit another cigarette, frowned a little and stared out the window.

"What do you do, Pops?" I repeated.

"Hustle." He laughed roughly. "I'm a hustler. Every black man worth his salt is a hustler. If you want to be successful, then you will be a hustler."

I pulled up my feet and stared at him. "Then you're no better than Joba."

"Bullshit. No, Joba was a loser. He accomplished nothing with his life, except to spread misery and suffering. In fact, I'm glad he's dead. You know why I say that?"

"No." I wanted to hear this. Pops was in love with his voice. He loved to hear himself talk.

"Listen to me, son," my father said. "Martin Luther King was a hustler. Adam Clayton Powell was a hustler. Malcolm X was a hustler. Like I said, every black man wanting to do something is a hustler. These black men will do anything to have control in their lives. They want freedom. They want choices. And that is what I want for you. I want you to be a hustler."

At this point, my eyes were glazing over. Yak, yak, yak. I was thinking about going down to the Vicious Juice Bar on Atlantic Avenue, getting one of those frosty fruit smoothies or a Portobello mushroom wrap with sun-dried tomatoes and low-fat Mozzarella cheese. Joyce, my honey, hipped me to this place. She liked this health drink, a shake made with soy milk, protein powder and a little juice. She was on this health kick.

"Are you listening to me, son?" He stood up and got closer.

"Yes...yes." I was still thinking about Yvette. She was probably one of the most beautiful girls in the whole damn world. She was my cover girl and totally out of my league.

"See, that's what wrong with you," Pops said angrily. "And that's what wrong with most black boys and that's why they will not get anywhere in this world."

"That's not going to happen to me," I protested. "I've got potential. That's what everybody says. I'm not like most black boys."

"But hear me out. You must learn how to hustle."

In my mind's eye, I imagined how I would seduce Yvette when I finally got her alone. I almost had her alone on Valentine's Day but one of her lovelies came over to her place. Damn, she was a gorgeous female. Plus Joyce wasn't putting out. She wanted to remain a virgin until we got married. She was dull as shit.

Now, my old man was standing over me, shouting at me like I

was deaf. "If you're soft, you're gonna screw up. I think you're soft. I don't think you have what it takes."

I didn't like him looking down on me.

"Just because you're messed up in your life, Pops, that don't mean I'll do the same," I snapped back at him. "I'll be big one day and you'll see."

I hopped up from the couch and went to the fridge for a glass of Coke. Judging from his expression, I'd rattled his cage and put something on his mind to think about.

A Mason's Ironstone complete dinner service, c1835.
$11,000-13,000

A Sampson Hancock & Sons dinner service, in the Norman pattern, comprising: 4 tureens and covers, ladles and stands, a graduated set of 6 meat plates and 36 plates in 3 sizes, late 19thC.
$500-650

A Mason's Ironstone part dinner service, decorated in an Imari palette in blue, white, green and red, comprising: 13 soup bowls, 46 plates, 2 serving dishes, covers and stands, one soup tureen, cover and stand, 7 serving platters, 3 sauce tureens, covers and stands, and one separate stand, 19thC.
$5,500-7,000

A porcelain soup plate, from the design of Theodore R. Davis for President Rutherford B Hayes, with laurel leaf gilt edge, enclosing a polychrome okra plant and a hen, the exterior with a crested eagle, by Haviland and Co., Limoges, the underside marked Design patented August 10th 1880, No. 11933, in blue, 9in (23cm) diam.
$1,000-1,200

A porcelain Presidential dinner service soup plate, the leaf edge heightened by gilt, enclosing a view of a beach, various marks, including an intertwined TD monogram, and dated 1879, 9in (23cm) diam.
$5,000-6,000

The mark on this plate indicates it was part of 'first edition' china designed for the Rutherford B. Hayes administration in 1879 and delivered the following year. The patterns were used and re-ordered by Presidents Chester A. Arthur and Grover Cleveland.

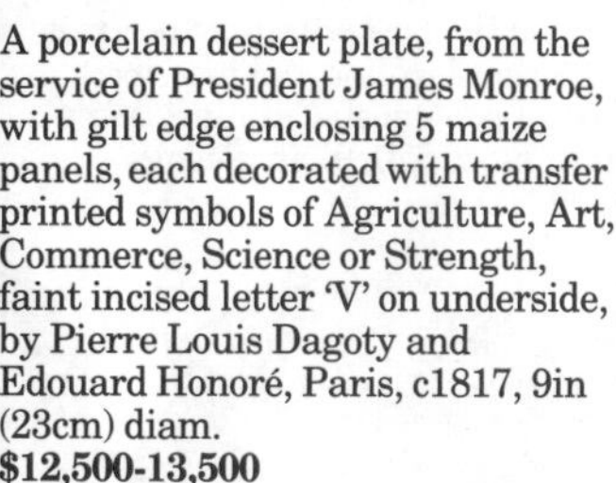

A porcelain dessert plate, from the service of President James Monroe, with gilt edge enclosing 5 maize panels, each decorated with transfer printed symbols of Agriculture, Art, Commerce, Science or Strength, faint incised letter 'V' on underside, by Pierre Louis Dagoty and Edouard Honoré, Paris, c1817, 9in (23cm) diam.
$12,500-13,500

James Monroe, the fifth President (1817-25) served as Minister to France during the administrations of Washington and Jefferson.

An Etruscan majolica tea set, in cauliflower form, with variations of maker's monogram on underside of each, by Smith and Hill, Phoenixville, Pennsylvania, c1890, together with a similar tea caddy, lacking lid, some damage.
$800-900

Tea Caddies

A Staffordshire tea canister, c1770, 4½in (11cm).
$900-1,000

A Staffordshire creamware cylindrical tea caddy, painted in colours, slight wear, 4in (10cm).
$80-150

An English tinglazed tea canister, c1780, 4in (10cm).
$1,000-1,200

Tea & Coffee Pots

A Brownfield earthenware novelty teapot in the form of a Chinaman, decorated in majolica type glazes, some damage, impressed registration mark.
$700-800

A chinoiserie pattern teapot, by William Greatbatch, c1755, 6in (15cm).
$1,400-2,000

A cauliflower teapot, by William Greatbatch, c1775, 6in (15cm).
$3,000-4,000

A Staffordshire teapot and cover, printed in black with bust portraits of Queen Caroline and inscribed 'Long Live Queen Caroline', some staining, c1820, 9½in (24cm).
$400-500

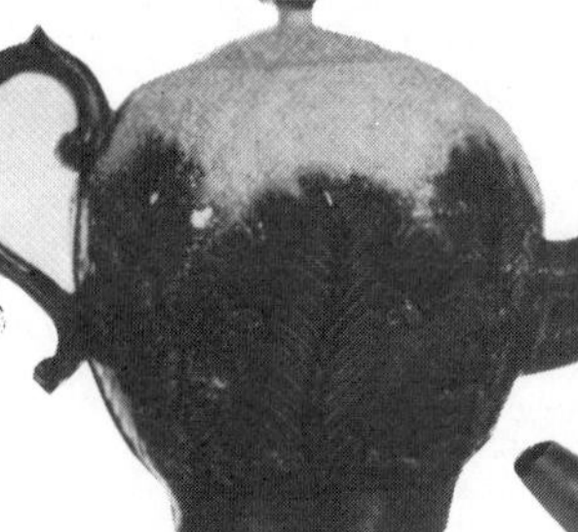

A Wedgwood type cauliflower moulded teapot and cover, the lower part covered in a bright green glaze, c1760, 11in (28cm) wide.
$2,000-2,500 *CSK*

A Jackfield teapot, c1770, 5½in (14cm).
$550-700

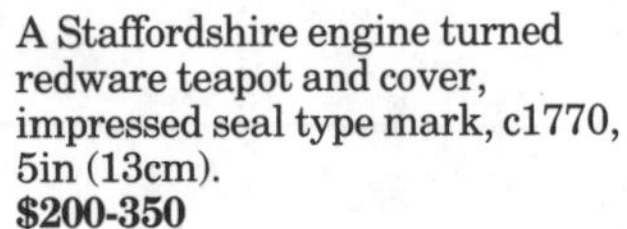

A Staffordshire engine turned redware teapot and cover, impressed seal type mark, c1770, 5in (13cm).
$200-350

A Whieldon teapot and cover, with crabstock handle and spout, in mottled green and yellow glaze, spout and cover restored, 3½in (8cm).
$300-400

A Staffordshire teapot, c1765, 5in (13cm).
$4,500-5,000

A Staffordshire saltglazed lobed teapot and cover, on 3 feet, some damage, late 18thC, 6in (15cm).
$3,000-4,000

A Whieldon type coffee pot, c1765, 7½in (19cm).
$5,000-5,500

A coffee pot and cover, decorated with a view of a Continental town enclosed by a mountainous landscape, cover cracked, minor restoration to spout, 10½in (26cm).
$150-250

A Quimper tea service, marked, c1930, teapot 7½in (19cm) high.
$400-500

A pearlware teapot, c1800, 7in (18cm).
$400-500

A Quimper coffee pot, 8in (20cm).
$100-140

An enamelled saltglazed coffee pot, c1765, 8½in (21cm).
$5,000-5,500

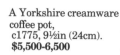

A Yorkshire creamware coffee pot, c1775, 9½in (24cm).
$5,500-6,500

A Staffordshire teapot and cover, splashed in manganese, green and yellow glazes, slight wear and chips, c1765, 7½in (18cm).
$800-1,200

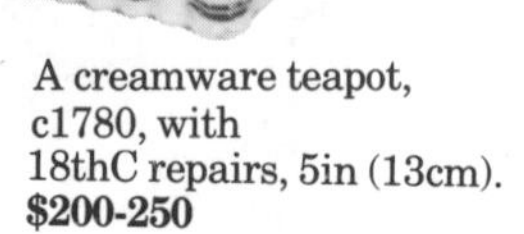

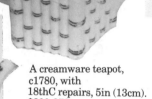

A creamware teapot, c1780, with 18thC repairs, 5in (13cm).
$200-250

A pearlware teapot and cover, small chips, c1800, 7½in (19cm).
$300-400

A coffee pot and cover, printed with a scene of Gothic style ruins in an extensive landscape, spout damaged, cover cracked, 9½in (24cm).
$150-250

Tiles

A Bristol tile, restored, c1760.
$140-150

In perfect condition – $300-350

A Liverpool tile, restored, c1750.
$80-100

A Liverpool biblical tile, c1750.
$65-80

A Bristol polychrome tile, c1765.
$400-500

A Liverpool wood block printed tile, c1757.
$500-550

A Liverpool tile, damaged, c1760.
$75-90

A London tile, c1775.
$65-100

A rare tile, possibly London.
$230-250

A London or Bristol tile.
$120-150

A Minton Shakespeare tile, 'Much Ado About Nothing', 6in (15cm) square.
$30-40

A set of 10 Poole pottery nursery tiles, designed by Dora Batty, comprising: 8 tiles depicting characters from nursery rhymes and 2 spacer tiles, painted in colours on a crackled cream ground, damaged, each 5in (12.5cm) square.
$550-650

A set of 6 Austrian terracotta hand painted and tin glazed blue and white tiles, Linz, c1800, 5in (12.5cm) square.
$800-1,000

A Low Countries fireplace tile, with stylised sun, 17thC, 6½ by 5in (16 by 12.5cm).
$550-650

A Dutch or German fireplace tile, a hound in relief, 16th/17thC, 5 by 3½in (12.5 by 8.5cm).
$350-400

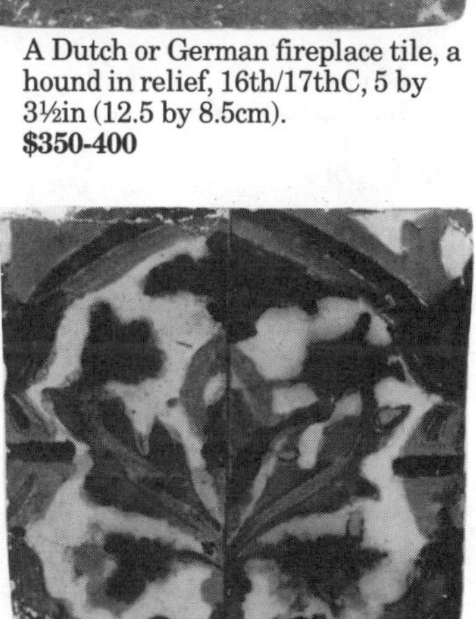

A Spanish floor tile, 16thC, 10in (25.5cm) square.
$50-65

A tin glazed flower tile, probably Flemish, 16thC.
$250-300

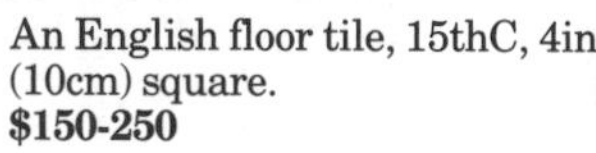

An English floor tile, 15thC, 4in (10cm) square.
$150-250

From a house in Chester.

A Low Countries relief fireplace tile, dated 1606, 6 by 4in (15 by 10cm).
$550-650

Tureens

A Leeds creamware sauce tureen and cover, in the form of an oval melon, with branch handle, c1785, 9in (23cm) wide.
$1,500-2,500

A tureen decorated with a dromedary pattern on a stippled ground, on rounded foot rim, 8½in (21cm).
$400-500

A Quimper tureen, 9½in (24cm).
$150-200

A Minton basket weave pattern game pie dish, the cover with dead game in relief, with rustic pattern handle, impressed Minton, 13in (33cm) wide.
$1,000-1,500

A Spode stone china tureen and cover, printed and painted with flowers in panels in Chinese style, 13½in (35cm) wide.
$300-400

A Continental faience quatrefoil tureen and cover, with pink and yellow scroll handles and naturalistic turkey's head finial, with an all over pattern of trellis with pink flowerheads and yellow fleur-de-lys, cracks restored, perhaps Buen Retiro, c1800, 17½in (44.5cm) wide.
$8,000-9,500

A Wedgwood soup tureen and ladle, with blue rose border and scene of the Tower of London, c1825.
$1,000-1,200

A Quimper tureen and cover with yellow background, 5½in (14cm).
$75-90

An English yellow ground tureen and cover, with black printed children's scenes, early 19thC, 8in (20cm) diam.
$400-550

A Milan (Clerici) maiolica partridge tureen and cover, the bird seated on a basket painted in colours, the plumage manganese, the wings black with yellow flashes, the breast iron red, cover repaired, 3 flanges missing, c1750, 6½in (17cm) wide.
$6,500-8,000

Vases

A Derbyshire stoneware vase, late 18thC, 9½in (24cm).
$550-650

A Wedgwood black basalt vase, with impressed marks, 10in (25cm).
$500-650

A Wedgwood baluster vase and cover, in white and gilt on a dark blue ground, cover cracked, gilding worn, impressed marks, 10½in (26cm).
$150-250

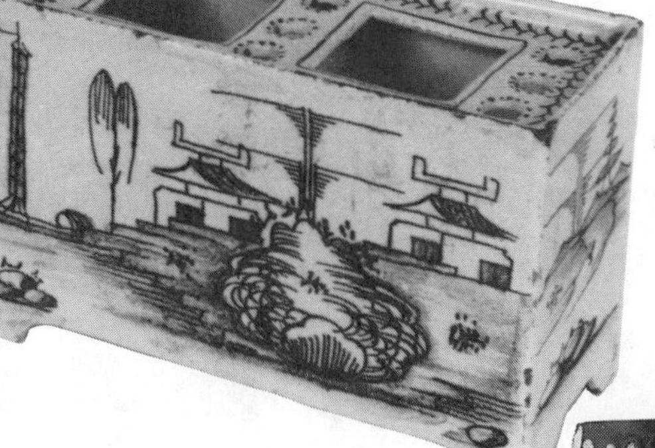

A Liverpool flower brick, decorated in manganese, c1760, 3½in (9cm).
$1,000-1,200

A Wedgwood & Bentley creamware two-handled vase and cover, applied with an oval medallion of the Three Graces, the handles moulded with leaves and female mask terminals, the foot with a circular laurel wreath, all with traces of gilding, plinth and cover chipped, c1770, 9in (23cm) high.
$1,400-2,000

A pair of Minton pot pourri vases, c1872, 15in (38cm).
$1,200-1,300

A Wedgwood black and white jasper vase, one rim ground, impressed mark Wedgwood, late 18thC, 10½in (26cm).
$800-1,000

A pair of late Wedgwood black basalt vases and covers, one cover repaired, impressed marks, 11½in (29cm).
$550-700

A garniture of 3 Mason's vases, c1815, 4 to 5in (10 to 12.5cm).
$450-500

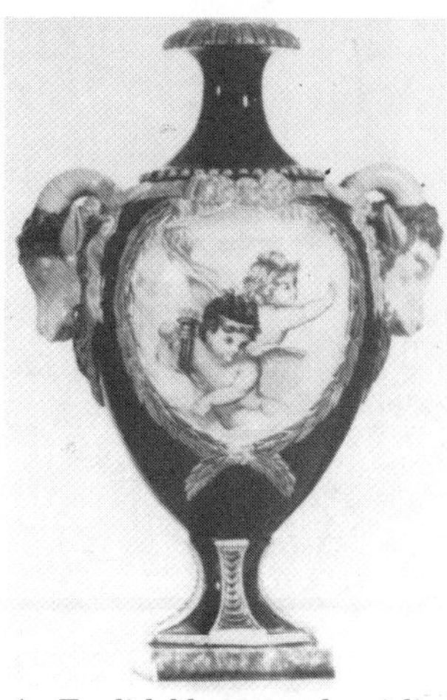

An English blue ground majolica vase, c1860, 13in (33cm).
$650-800

A Quimper vase, handle repaired, c1920, 11in (28cm).
$275-300

A Quimper tulip vase, c1930, 5½in (14cm).
$120-150

A South Wales type clock vase in copper lustre, c1825, 7½in (19cm).
$280-300

A Mason's vase and cover, with Peacock pattern, c1830, 18in (46cm).
$1,200-1,400

A Staffordshire castle spill vase, with 2 towers and outlined in coloured flowers, 5in (13cm).
$150-250

A sparsely coloured spill vase, c1860, 11in (28cm).
$300-400

A Staffordshire spill vase group, modelled as a boy seated and a girl standing, flanking a cauldron, 8in (20cm).
$80-150

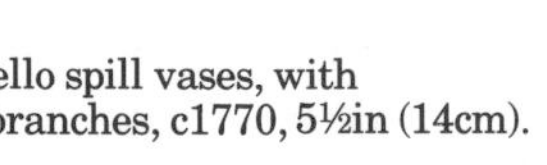

A pair of Portobello spill vases, with yellow birds on branches, c1770, 5½in (14cm).
$2,500-3,000

A Worcester polychrome spill vase, toes restored, c1870, 5½in (14cm).
$400-500

A Wemyss tankard decorated with black fowl on green base, with green band decoration and ribbed loop handle, impressed mark, 5½in (14cm).
$700-800

A Wemyss Gordon plate with Victoria plum design, 8in (20cm).
$150-250

Gordon plates all have indented rims and are often sold for use as dessert plates.

A Wemyss Gordon plate, with blackcurrants, 8in (20cm).
$250-300

A Wemyss pig with clover decoration, Scottish impressed mark, 7in (18cm) long.
$550-800

A Wemyss Gordon plate with buttercup design, 8in (20cm).
$400-500

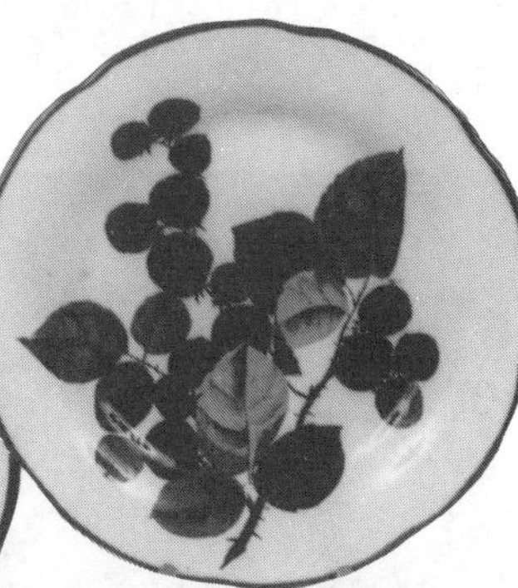

A Wemyss Gordon plate with bramble design, 8in (20cm).
$250-300

A pig with clover decoration, painted by Joseph Nekola, Bovey Tracey, 19in (48cm) long.
$3,000-5,000

A preserve pot decorated with strawberries, 5in (13cm).
$120-150

A Wemyss Gordon plate, with a honeysuckle design, 8in (20cm).
$400-550

A Wemyss marmalade cat, Bovey Tracey, c1935, 13in (33cm).
$3,000-5,000

A Wemyss early morning teaset.
$650-800

A jam pot with dish, impressed Wemyss, 7½in (18cm).
$500-800

A Dutch Delft basket and cover, with a dog of Fo finial, hairline cracks, marked with 5, late 17thC, 9in (22cm).
$9,500-11,000

A pair of Delft butter dishes and covers, painted in 'petit feu' colours in the Kakiemon style, the covers with dog of Fo finials, dashed in pink, minor chips, one cover marked 3 in overglaze red, the other marked 4, early 18thC, 5in (13cm) wide.
$4,000-5,500

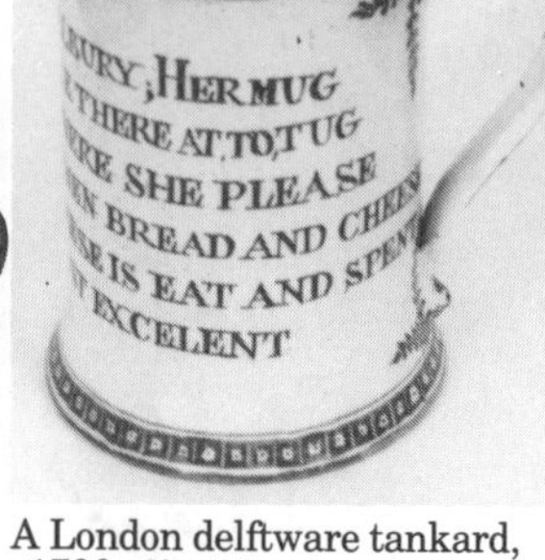

A London delftware tankard, c1790, 6in (15cm).
$4,000-5,000

A delft blue and white bottle, Liverpool or London, rim chip, c1760, 9in (23cm).
$700-1,000

A delft blue and white broth bowl and cover, painted with an all-over pattern of flower sprays, outlined in manganese, the loop handles with blue dash motifs, perhaps Bristol, slight crack to rim, c1730, 11½in (29cm) wide.
$2,500-3,000

A Bristol delft blue and white bowl, repaired and restored, c1740, 12in (31cm) diam.
$3,000-5,000

A Liverpool delft blue and white tea caddy, the sides painted with classical figures by a stream, in an extensive mountainous wooded landscape with goats and hounds, between hatch-pattern borders, slight rim chips, c1760, 6in (15cm).
$5,500-6,500

An English delft blue and white bowl, Bristol or London, rim and foot chipped, c1725, 14in (35cm).
$2,500-4,000

A Dutch Delft cabbage leaf bowl, naturalistically moulded in relief, the exterior as a yellow veined green cabbage with shaped overlapping leaves, the interior with a chinoiserie scene, hairline crack, c1770, 10½in (26.5cm).
$3,000-4,000

A Dutch Delft tea caddy and stopper, decorated in the Persian style, chips to edges, marked 3 above AL and 5 for De Grieksche A, late 17thC, 11in (28cm).
$9,500-11,000

A Dutch Delft figural fountain jug, hat restored and chipped, marked PVDB above 6 for Pieter van der Briel, 't Fortuyn, 1747, 14in (35cm).
$8,000-9,000

A Dutch Delft sweetmeat dish, minor chips, marked GVS for Geertruy Verstelle, c1760, 5½in (14cm).
$3,000-5,000

A Dutch Delft sweetmeat dish, naturalistically modelled in relief as a male figure in period costume after German porcelain examples, minor repair and chips, marked GVS for Geertruy Verstelle, c1760, 5in (13cm).
$3,000-5,000

A Dutch Delft figure of a young gentleman, possibly a pilgrim, painted in colours, carrying a child on his back, head of child repaired, c1780, 7½in (19cm).
$1,200-1,500

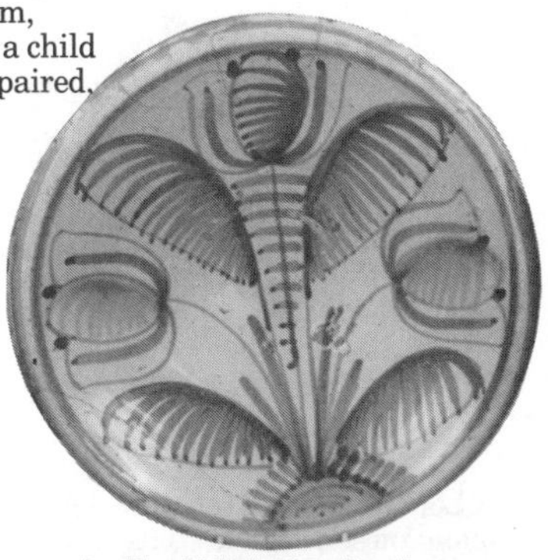

An English delft tulip charger, repaired, c1680, 13½in (34cm).
$1,300-1,500

A pair of Dutch Delft mixed technique figural butter dishes and covers, modelled in relief after Meissen porcelain examples, damaged, marked for de drie astonnekens, c1750, 5½in (14.5cm).
$13,000-14,000

A Dutch Delft figure of a young woman, possibly a pilgrim, painted in colours, c1780, 7in (18cm).
$1,200-1,500

An English delft blue dash Adam and Eve charger, outlined in manganese, a green boughed tree with striped yellow fruit, with blue dash rim, Brislington or Bristol, cracked and repaired, c1680, 13in (33cm).
$2,500-3,000

A Dutch Delft figure of a putto, emblematic of Summer, painted in blue, yellow and iron red, head re-stuck, chips to ears of corn, c1750, 16in (40cm). **$1,400-2,000**

A London delft pomegranate charger, the 3 fruits flanked by grey-green foliage edged in blue and divided by stylised blue flowerheads and foliage, within a green line rim, rim cracked, c1680, 13in (33cm).
$8,000-9,500

An English delft blue dash tulip charger, the centre painted with a blue and yellow tulip and 2 buds, within a border of yellow and green leaves, with blue dash rim, probably London, crack repaired, c1680, 14in (35cm).
$1,300-1,500

A Bristol delft blue dash pomegranate charger, boldly painted in blue, iron red, yellow and green, within a double yellow line and blue dash rim, crack riveted, rim chips, c1690, 14in (36cm).
$3,000-4,000

A Bristol delft polychrome dish, painted predominantly in iron red, yellow, green and blue, minor glaze flaking, the underside with circle and line under-rim markings, c1730, 13in (33cm).
$1,200-1,500

A Bristol delft blue dash oak leaf charger, painted with radiating green oak leaves and fruit, within a blue dash rim, cracked and repaired, c1720, 13½in (34.5cm).
$4,000-5,000

A London delft plate, painted in manganese and blue stylised vine within a border of pendant foliage, chips to rim, c1680, 8in (20cm).
$1,000-1,300

A Bristol delft polychrome plate, painted in blue and yellow flanked by sponged manganese trees and bushes, rim chips, c1740, 8in (20cm).
$1,000-1,200

A Bristol delft polychrome plate, painted with a bird in flight, flanked by manganese and iron red trees within a triple blue line rim, chips to rim, c1740, 9in (23cm).
$1,200-1,500

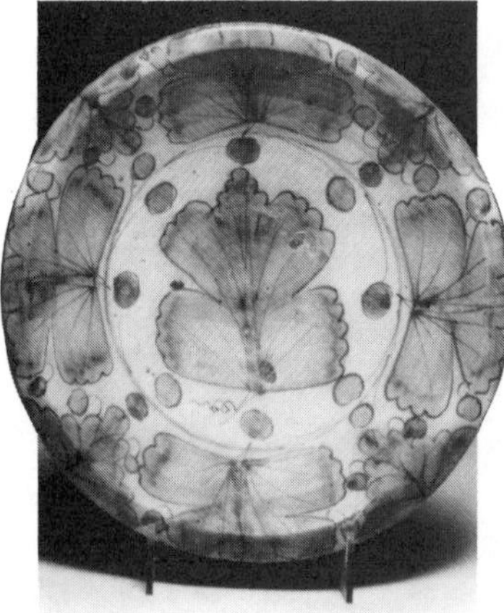

A London delft oak leaf charger, with a central pale green oak leaf edged in manganese, with blue and yellow fruit within a slightly sloping shallow rim, minute cracks to rim, c1690, 14in (35cm).
$3,000-4,000

A Bristol delft polychrome dish, painted in blue, green and iron red, with a narrow iron red diaper border reserved with panels of flowerheads edged in blue, the underside with star and line under-rim markings, minor glaze flaking, c1730, 13in (33cm).
$1,500-2,000

Two Bristol delft powdered manganese ground polychrome dishes, painted in blue, yellow and green, within a woolsack cartouche, the borders reserved with leaf shaped panels of flowers, chips to rim and foot rim, c1750, 13in (33cm).
$1,500-2,500

A Bristol delft blue and white dish, painted within a 'bianco-sopra-bianco' border of pinecones, flowers and foliage, slight glaze flaking to rim, c1760, 13½in (34cm).
$550-700

A Liverpool delft blue and white dated shipping plate, painted with a ship at full sail, the reverse inscribed P 1770, minute rim flaking, 1770, 9in (23cm).
$3,000-4,000

A Liverpool delft blue and white dated plate, painted with a ship flanked by harbour walls, the reverse inscribed P 1770, minute rim chips, 9in (23cm).
$2,500-4,000

Use the Index!

Because certain items might fit easily into any of a number of categories, the quickest and surest method of locating any entry is by reference to the index at the back of the book.
This has been fully cross-referenced for absolute simplicity

A Liverpool delft polychrome dish, painted in the Fazackerly palette, slight rim chips, c1760, 13½in (34cm).
$3,000-4,000

A London or Bristol delft plate, c1760, 7in (18cm).
$800-900

A delft blue and white serving dish, perhaps Dublin, restoration to flaked rim, c1760, 21½in (54cm) wide.
$1,300-2,500

A Lambeth delft polychrome dish, boldly painted with flowering plants issuing from pierced blue and yellow rockwork, within a border of sunflowers flanked by flowers and blue foliage, c1770, 13½in (34cm).
$650-1,000

A Liverpool delft polychrome dish, sketchily painted, cracked, rim chip and flaking, c1760, 13in (33cm).
$1,500-2,500

An English delft blue and white plate, probably London, c1770, 9in (23cm).
$400-550

A Liverpool delft blue and white dated shipping plate, painted with a sailing ship above an elaborate cartouche of flowers and foliage, inscribed J + S 1771, minute rim flaking, 9in (23cm).
$5,000-5,500

An early delft lobed dish, c1680, 13in (33cm).
$1,200-1,500

A Dutch Delft tripod herring-shaped dish, the concave border moulded with fins and tail, minor chips, marked for De Dissel, c1695, 11½in (29cm) wide.
$2,500-3,000

A Dutch Delft month dish, after an engraving by Jan van de Velde II, inscribed December, chipped, marked CK in underglaze blue for Cornelis Keyser, mid-17thC, 9in (24cm).
$800-900

This dish is one of the earliest examples from the month series.

A Delft charger, probably Dutch, crack and area of restoration, c1730, 14in (35.5cm).
$500-550

A London delft blue and white wet drug jar, named for S. Mororv, rim chips and glaze flaking, c1670, 7½in (19cm).
$2,500-3,000

A London delft blue and white posset pot and cover, with strap handles and curved spout, perhaps Vauxhall, spout restored, chips and cracks to cover, c1710, 8in (19.5cm).
$1,500-2,500

A London delft blue and white named drug jar, damaged and repaired, late 17thC, 4in (9.5cm).
$800-1,200

A London delft wet drug jar, with waisted cylindrical spout and flared base, inscribed S: Sambuci 1699, some damage, 7½in (18cm).
$1,400-2,000

A London delft blue and white baluster posset pot, with curved spout and S-scroll handles, painted with Orientals, edged in manganese, beneath a border of stylised lappets and manganese lines, spout and rim restored, slight crack, c1680, 4½in (11.5cm).
$700-1,000

A London delft blue and white named dry drug jar, top rim and foot restored, slight glaze flaking, c1680, 7½in (18.5cm).
$1,200-1,300

A Bristol delft dry drug jar, named in manganese for U;Basil;N within a cartouche, c1740, 8in (19.5cm).
$1,400-2,000

A pair of Dutch Delft blue and white named tobacco jars, chips to rims, marks of DE3 Klokken factory, c1750, 9½in (24cm).
$2,000-2,500

A Lambeth delft jug, c1760, 7½in (19cm).
$1,200-1,500

A Lambeth delft jug, with loop handle, restored and glaze flaking to rim, c1780, 8in (20cm).
$1,000-1,200

A London delft blue and white shield-shaped pill tile, painted in bright blue with the arms of The Worshipful Society of Apothecaries, with motto on a shaped cartouche, pierced for hanging, late 17thC, 12in (30cm).
$6,500-8,000

A Liverpool delft blue and white dated puzzle jug, with hollow loop handle connected to a cylindrical neck pierced with interlaced circles and with 3 short spouts, glaze flaking and re-touching to spout, dated 1766 on base, 9½in (24cm).
$7,000-9,000

A Liverpool delft blue and white inscribed and dated jug, with strap handle and mask spout, cracked body and repaired, crack to base of handle, 1773, 10in (25.5cm).
$3,000-4,000

A Liverpool delft blue and white puzzle jug, with hollow loop handle, the neck and rim with 3 short spouts, the neck pierced with hearts and ovals, with inscription, the interior with a cone-shaped strainer, spouts chipped, c1760, 8½in (21cm).
$2,500-3,000

A Lambeth delft tile, c1750, 5in (12.5cm) square.
$75-90

A medallion polychrome tilefield, comprising 28 tiles, 'spaartechniek' corners in blue, depicting various animals after engraving by Adriaen Collaert, restored, early 17thC.
$9,500-10,000

Miscellaneous

A bellarmine, possibly English, late 17th/early 18thC, 8in (20cm).
$1,000-1,200

A Bates, Brown-Westhead and Moore parian bust of Apollo, after a model by Delpech, Art Union stamp and dated 1861, 14in (35cm).
$650-700

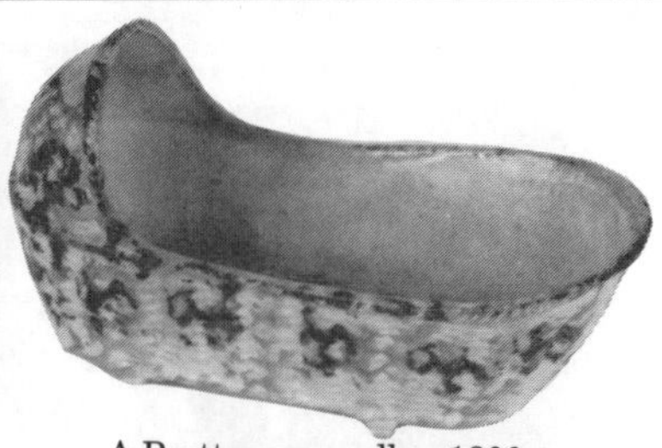

A Pratt ware cradle, c1800.
$400-500

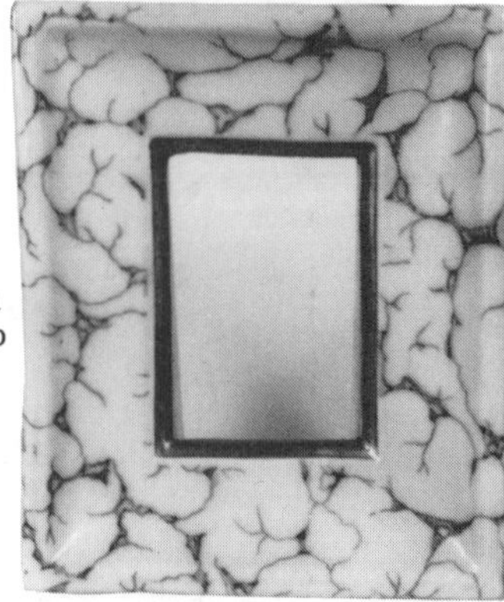

A Dillwyn & Co lazuli frame, c1850, 8 by 6in (20 by 15cm).
$400-550

A Pratt ware money box, c1830, 5in (12.5cm).
$800-1,000

A Mettlach saltglazed stoneware jardinière, impressed and incised marks, 9in (23cm) diam.
$550-700

A Wedgwood & Bentley blue and white jasper portrait medallion of Linnaeus, impressed lower case mark, contemporary stamped gilt metal frame, c1775, 3½in (8.5cm).
$2,000-2,500

A late Victorian cheese dish and cover, with floral decoration and gilded handle, 12in (30.5cm).
$80-130

An Italian maiolica ink stand, with large central aperture surrounded by 8 pen holders, the sides painted in blue, the upper surface inscribed, chipped, 18thC, 6½in (16cm) diam.
$400-550

A set of saltglazed furniture rests, depicting the Duke of Wellington, c1820.
$1,400-2,000

A Wedgwood black jasper-dip lamp base, 19thC, 9in (23cm).
$800-1,000

ENGLISH PORCELAIN

During the past year good Chelsea figures and some decorative Bow rarities have come onto the market. Price levels achieved for these pieces were uniformly high. This increase in price levels was reflected in the prices asked for fine Chelsea wares at Fairs and Exhibitions and some superb pieces were tempted onto the market.

However, this trend has not been reflected in prices generally. Price levels in most areas remained stable and it has been noticeable that single rarities, often poorly catalogued appearing at country auctions, have fetched more than comparable pieces in London.

As usual prices of Worcester, Lowestoft and Plymouth remain higher than for comparable wares away from 'home' and this is a natural reflection of local collecting interest.

Interest in wares previously ascribed to William Ball, Liverpool, has been stimulated by archaeological research at Vauxhall in London where it seems these wares may have been made. However, the relatively small number of collectors and their sensible approach to buying seems to have offset any tendency for new discoveries to overstimulate prices.

EUROPEAN PORCELAIN

Sales of European porcelain both here and in America have been strong. Estimates of good Meissen and other major European factories have very frequently been exceeded, often about double the anticipated figure has been the going rate.

Sales tend to be carefully timetabled to coincide with major fairs to take advantage of dealers and collectors in attendance.

Early Meissen has sold strongly as have du Paquier wares and Sèvres. More interest has been shown in decorative tureens, tea caddies, teapots and other domestic wares than in figures which have generally been more accurately estimated.

Baskets

A Belleek basket, with double entwined twig handles, the rim moulded and applied with lilies, slight damage, impressed ribbon mark, late 19thC, 11in (28cm) diam.
$550-650

A Lowestoft blue and white pierced basket of conventional type, transfer printed with The Pinecone and Foliage pattern, chip to one terminal, blue crescent mark, c1780, 9½in (24cm).
$900-1,000

A Spode basket and cover, c1820, 5½in (14cm).
$2,500-3,000

A Davenport basket and stand, slight damage, c1810, stand 10in (25.5cm) wide.
$800-1,000

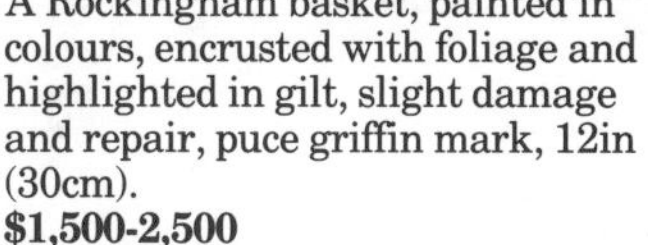

A Rockingham basket, painted in colours, encrusted with foliage and highlighted in gilt, slight damage and repair, puce griffin mark, 12in (30cm).
$1,500-2,500

A pair of Worcester baskets, both cracked, c1758, 8in (20cm) diam.
$3,000-4,000

A Worcester chestnut basket, in pea green, c1800, 6½in (16cm) high.
$2,000-2,500

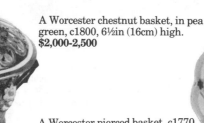

A Worcester pierced basket, c1770, 5in (12.5cm).
$650-800

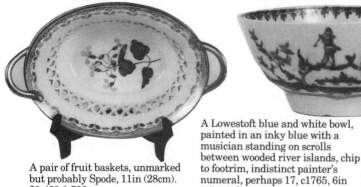

A pair of fruit baskets, unmarked but probably Spode, 11in (28cm).
$1,400-1,500

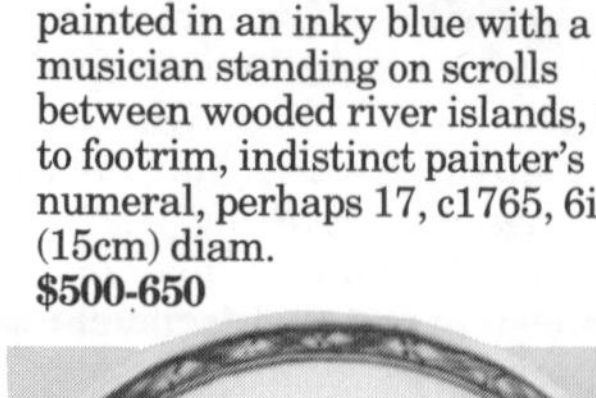

A Lowestoft blue and white bowl, painted in an inky blue with a musician standing on scrolls between wooded river islands, chip to footrim, indistinct painter's numeral, perhaps 17, c1765, 6in (15cm) diam.
$500-650

A Royal Crown Derby miniature cauldron shape bowl, in the Old Derby Witches pattern, c1917, 2½in (6cm) high.
$500-550

A Spode two-handled botanical centre dish, on spreading foot and with beaded rim, painted in bright colours with garlands of flowers, named on the underside, the branch handles with moulded and coloured fruit and leaf terminals, c1825, 11½in (29cm).
$1,500-2,500

A Caughley patty pan, with the Island pattern, c1785, 4in (10cm) diam.
$400-550

A Worcester sugar bowl and cover, painted with flowers, the cover with blue flower finial, restoration to finial, chips to footrim, c1758.
$800-1,500

A Worcester blue and white pierced quatrefoil chestnut basket and cover, with branch handles and finial, painted with flowers, restored, crescent marks, 8in (20cm).
$250-400

A Lowestoft blue and white flared patty pan, painted with trailing flowering branches, the centre with a butterfly, within a flowerhead rim, the exterior with trailing flowers, cracks to rim and base, c1765, 6in (15cm) diam.
$300-500

Bowls

A pair of Coalport bowls, covers and stands, decorated in the London studio of Thomas Baxter, within gilt cartouches, reserved on a gilt dot and red trellis pattern ground, between gilt foliage and hatch pattern borders, one stand with rim chip repair, c1805, the stands 6in (15cm) diam.
$3,000-4,000

A Minton bowl, painted with fishing boats off the Dutch coast, signed by J. E. (Teddy) Dean, impressed date codes, printed factory marks, c1915, 8½in (21cm) diam.
$1,000-1,200

A Lowestoft sugar bowl and flat cover, painted with scattered cornflowers and gilt foliage between gilt line rims, the cover with faceted conical finial, piece missing from rim of cover, some minor staining, c1795, 4½in (11.5cm) diam.
$2,000-2,500

A Caughley blue and white bowl, and painted with the Island pattern, c1780, 6in (15cm) diam.
$300-400

A pair of Victorian Grainger's Worcester bowls, painted with finches and gilt leaf sprays on a cream ground, 3in (7.5cm).
$300-400

A Wedgwood Fairyland lustre footed bowl, decorated after a design by Daisy Makeig-Jones, the exterior decorated on a shaded orange ground, some rubbing, printed Portland vase mark and pattern No. Z5360, c1920, 10½in (27cm) diam.
$3,000-5,000

A Worcester bowl, transfer printed in underglaze blue with uncommon European landscapes, c1780, 4½in (11cm) diam.
$300-400

A pair of ormolu mounted Vincennes bowls, painted with fruit, flowers and exotic birds with rich gilt and blue rims, on crisply cast scroll bases and foliage rims, cracked, 11in (28cm).
$1,400-2,000

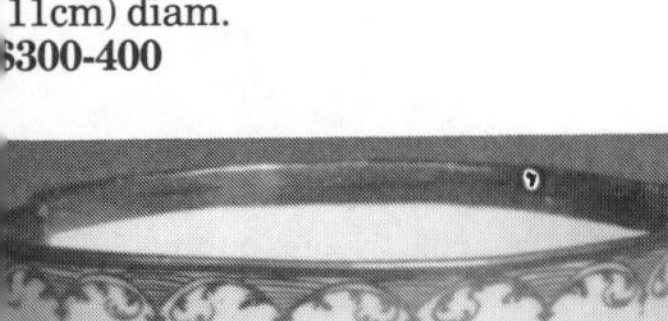

A Meissen sugar bowl, painted in the manner of Bonaventura Gottlieb Hauer, with a continuous scene beneath a border painted in gilt with 'Laub-und-Bandelwerk', blue crossed swords mark, c1740.
$1,500-2,500

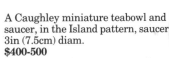

A Caughley miniature teabowl and saucer, in the Island pattern, saucer 3in (7.5cm) diam.
$400-500

A Meissen bowl, pierced with scrolls, with ram mask handles and 4 paw feet, some regilding, cancelled blue crossed swords, c1880, 15in (38cm) wide.
$1,300-1,500

Boxes

A Rockingham metal mounted box, griffin mark, c1830, 3in (7.5cm) diam.
$1,000-1,200

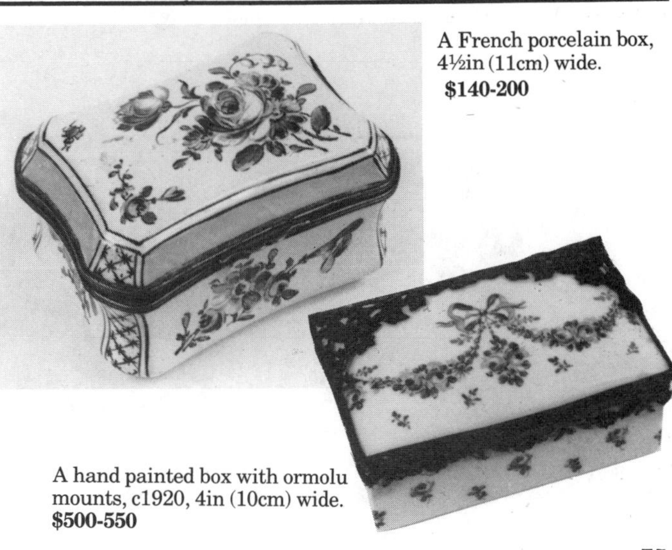

A French porcelain box, 4½in (11cm) wide.
$140-200

A hand painted box with ormolu mounts, c1920, 4in (10cm) wide.
$500-550

Centrepieces

A Coalport comport, c1840, 8½in (21cm).
$275-400

A Berlin centrepiece, modelled as 2 maidens supporting a pierced basket, one maiden wearing a pink robe with gilt flowerheads, the other wearing scanty yellow robe lined in pink, rim damaged, gilding worn, blue sceptre and circular medallion mark, c1850, 15in (38cm).
$700-900

A Meissen centrepiece and a pair of four-light candelabra, on shaped scroll moulded bases enriched with gilding, damaged, 19thC, centrepiece 11in (28cm).
$4,000-5,500

A Crown Staffordshire centrepiece, modelled as a vase of flowers, realistically coloured and modelled, some with bees, 20thC, 11in (28cm).
$400-500

A German pierced tazza, painted in colours and enriched with gilding, damage to extremities, impressed numeral, 16in (40.5cm).
$650-800

A Carl Thieme Potschappel centrepiece, decorated in coloured enamels and gilded, some damage, mark in underglaze blue, 21½in (55cm).
$1,500-2,000

A Worcester centrepiece, modelled as 4 deeply fluted shells surmounted by a bowl, one shell restored, restored rim chips, c1770, 14½in (36.5cm) wide.
$3,000-5,000

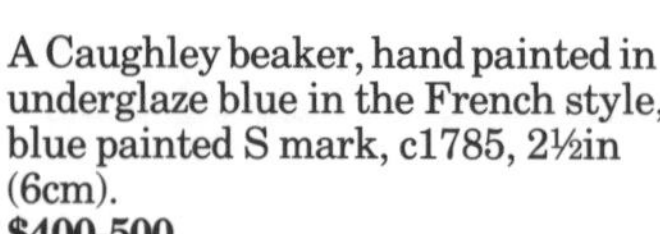

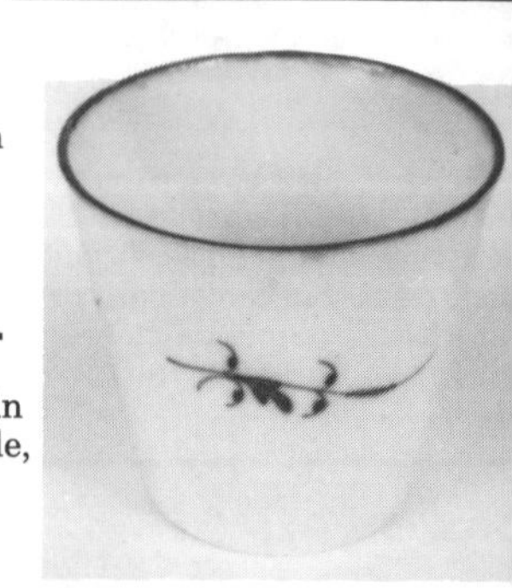

A Caughley beaker, hand painted in underglaze blue in the French style, blue painted S mark, c1785, 2½in (6cm).
$400-500

Cups

A Chamberlain trio, pattern No. 886, c1820, saucer 6in (15cm) diam.
$400-550

A Coalport cup and saucer, hand painted by Thomas Martin Randall, c1820.
$250-300

A Coalport teacup and saucer, decorated in the studio of Thomas Baxter, c1805.
$500-550

A Coalport coffee can and saucer, date code for 1929.
$110-150

A Davenport cup and saucer, c1825, 6in (15cm).
$400-550

A Coalport miniature cup and saucer in bamboo pattern, c1910, cup 1½in (3.5cm).
$250-300

A Derby trout's head stirrup cup, naturally modelled and coloured, the rim inscribed The Angler's Delight, between gilt lines, Robt. Bloor & Co., slight crack to one side, c1820, 5in (13cm).
$2,500-3,000

A Spode blue and white printed coffee can, c1805, 2in (5cm).
$80-150

A Coalport cup and saucer, in Green Dragon pattern, Empire shape, c1920, 3½in (9cm).
$50-80

A New Hall cup and saucer, bat printed with the Mother and Child pattern No. 1109, c1815, saucer 6in (15cm).
$250-300

A Coalport coffee cup and saucer, 1920.
$150-250

Five Lowestoft miniature teabowls and saucers, painted with a sailing boat between river islands with huts and trees, within loop and husk pattern borders, 2 teabowls with slight cracks, one chipped, traces of painter's numerals, c1765.
$2,000-2,500

A Lowestoft teabowl and saucer, painted with The Dragon pattern extending over the rim to the exterior, blue crescent mark, c1770.
$700-900

A Spode puzzle cup, containing an Oriental standing figure, with matching saucer, each piece painted with sprigs of flowers in enamel colours and gold on a deep blue ground within a gold line rim, pattern No. 3420, painted mark in red, early 19thC.
$550-700

A Worcester coffee cup, c1765, 2½in (6cm).
$550-650

Make the most of Miller's

Unless otherwise stated, any description which refers to 'a set' or 'a pair' includes a valuation for the entire set or the pair, even though the illustration may show only a single item

A Spode blue and sepia cup and saucer, c1810, saucer 5in (12.5cm).
$110-150

A Spode hand painted cup and saucer, c1825.
$110-150

A Worcester peach-shaped wine taster, with entwined brown branch handle, pink and yellow flower terminals on a basketweave pattern ground, the interior with a border of flowers, minute chip to handle, c1765, 4in (9.5cm) wide.
$6,500-7,000

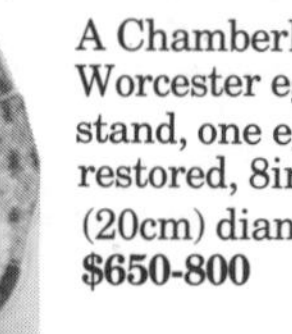

A Chamberlain's Worcester two-handled cup and saucer, pierced with gilt hexagons and iron red flowerheads between yellow borders, script marks, c1830.
$1,200-1,300

A Chamberlain's Worcester egg cup stand, one egg cup restored, 8in (20cm) diam.
$650-800

A Worcester First Period chocolate cup and saucer, with alternate panels of flowers, blue ground gilt trellis pattern and blue and white trellis pattern, scattered flowerhead motifs and prunus branches in the centre, the cup with branch handle, c1770. **$1,200-1,400**

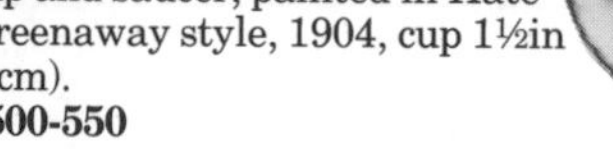

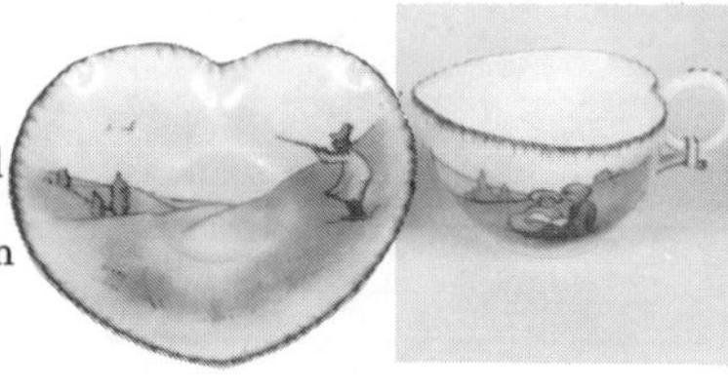

A Royal Worcester heart-shaped cup and saucer, painted in Kate Greenaway style, 1904, cup 1½in (4cm).
$500-550

A Worcester fluted coffee cup, painted in the Kakiemon palette, c1760.
$400-550

A Meissen Hausmalerei vine moulded coffee cup and saucer, painted in colours in the workshop of Mayor von Pressnitz, enriched with gilding, crossed swords marks, Pressnummer 17 to saucer, the porcelain c1740, the decoration a little later.
$3,000-4,000

A Sèvres cup and cover with flower finial, painted in pink monochrome, outlined in gilt and blue 'feuille de choux', with gilt dentil rims and gilt handle, rim chipped, blue interlaced L marks, date code indistinct but c1770, 4in (10cm).
$1,400-2,000

A Doccia armorial beaker, painted in colours in the manner associated with Klinger, chip to rim and 3 hair cracks, c1745, 3in (7.5cm).
$1,300-2,000

Ewers

A Royal Worcester ewer, painted by C. Baldwyn, on a matt pale blue ground, heightened in salmon pink and enriched with gilding, partially indistinct signature, green printed marks and date code for 1902, 14in (35cm).
$7,000-10,000

A Coalport hand painted ewer, c1850, 11in (28cm).
$550-650

A pair of Coalport royal blue ground ewers, c1840, 13in (33cm).
$1,500-2,000

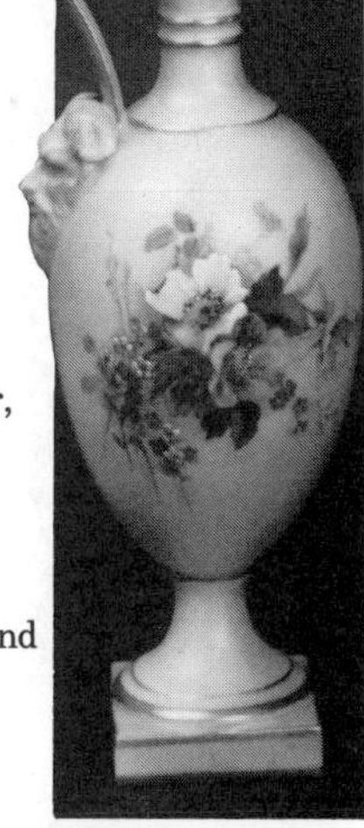

A Royal Worcester cream ground ewer, date code indistinct, 7in (17cm).
$300-400

Figures – Animal

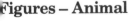

A Royal Worcester study of a group of young foxes, by Doris Lindner, shape No. 3131, introduced 1936, 12½in (32cm).
$500-650

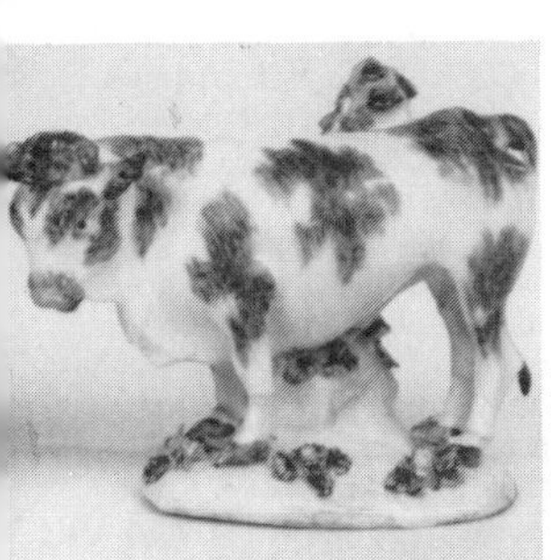

A Bow model of a bull, with brown markings, standing on an oval base by a flowering tree stump and rockwork, restored, chipping, brown 2 mark, c1758, 5½in (14cm) long.
$2,000-2,500

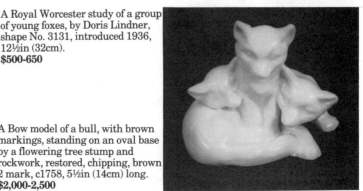

A Bow group of a goat and kid, naturally modelled with shaggy brown coats, minor restorations, c1758, 4½in (12cm), wood stand.
$2,000-2,500

A Minton model of a cat, sponged in green and yellow, seated on a gilt and yellow fringed and tasselled purple cushion, ears restored, c1830, 5in (12.5cm).
$650-800

A Royal Worcester model of Red Rum, by Doris Lindner, on wood stand, limited edition No. 88 of 250 with framed certificate, 9½in (24cm).
$500-550

A Samson group of a Queen perhaps Cybele, mounted on a white charger, 7½in (18.5cm).
$300-500

A pair of Samuel Alcock seated spaniels, their coats with grey patches, seated on pale yellow rockwork bases edged with a gilt line, glaze slightly worn, impressed number 121, c1835, 5½in (13cm).
$1,000-1,200

An English pug dog, with brown coat and black muzzle, and with a green collar tied by a red rosette, on a green base, perhaps Lowestoft or Derby, ear chipped, tail lacking, some rubbing, c1775, 3½in (9.5cm).
$1,500-2,000

A Worcester, Grainger, Lee & Co., recumbent dog, with brown markings, moulded with gilt foliage, ears restored, impressed mark, c1835, 4½in (11cm).
$300-500

A Royal Worcester model of HRH The Princess Anne on Doublet, by Doris Lindner, limited edition No. 288 of 750, with framed certificate, 11in (28cm).
$1,000-1,200

A Royal Worcester miniature tortoise, date code for 1910, 2in (5cm) wide.
$400-500

A Meissen figure of a recumbent lion, modelled by J. J. Kändler, painted with a brown coat, restoration, one tooth chipped, traces of crossed swords mark, Pressnummer 45, c1745, the decoration later, 9in (22cm) wide.
$2,500-3,000

A Bow figure of a dancer, modelled as a girl in plumed hat, blue bodice and flowered apron and skirt, enriched in puce, turquoise and gilding, restoration to one hand, waist and tree, some chipping, c1762, 7½in (18.5cm).
$800-1,000

A Bow figure of Mars, in plumed helmet, gilt and puce scale pattern cuirass and moulded and striped pink and iron red chiton, the scroll moulded base enriched in gilding, restoration, some chipping, anchor and dagger mark in iron red, c1768, 12½in (31.5cm).
$1,200-1,500

Two Bow arbour groups, each modelled as a sportsman and companion, in gilt flowered and patterned clothes standing before a pink, puce and iron red marbled wall fountain before flowering trees, the scroll moulded bases enriched in gilding, extensive restoration, anchor and dagger marks in iron red, c1770, 9in (23cm).
$3,000-4,000

Two Bow putti musicians, scantily draped in puce and turquoise, on pierced spreading marbled bases, one broken at base, both chipped and restored, c1762, 4½in (11cm).
$800-900

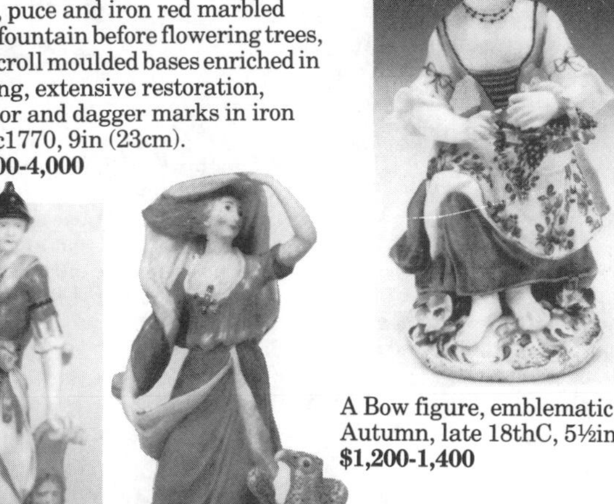

A Bow figure, emblematic of Autumn, late 18thC, 5½in (14cm).
$1,200-1,400

A Chelsea figure emblematic of Air, modelled as a nymph in yellow lined pink cloak and turquoise blouse and skirt, slight restoration, c1760, 8½in (22cm).
$1,200-1,300

A Bow figure of Minerva, in black helmet, yellow-lined flowered pink cloak and gilt scale pattern turquoise cuirass, the scroll moulded base enriched in puce, owl a restored replacement, other restoration, c1760, 13in (33cm).
$1,000-1,300

A Bow white figure of a toper, leaning against a tree stump on a shaped rockwork base, restoration, crack to barrel, chips, c1753, 6in (15cm).
$800-1,300

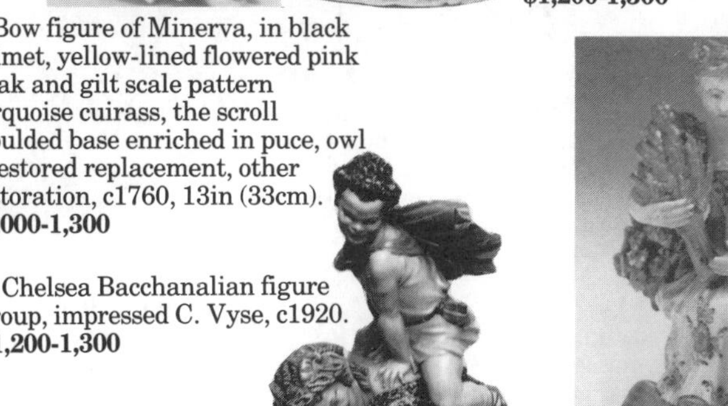

A Chelsea Bacchanalian figure group, impressed C. Vyse, c1920.
$1,200-1,300

A Derby group, minor damage, late 18thC, 5in (12.5cm).
$650-700

A pair of Derby figures, in yellow robes, on rococo mound bases, applied with flowers, incised Nos. 63 and 65, late 18thC.
$800-1,000

A pair of Derby figures, Stevenson and Hancock, damage to her fingers and flowers, puce printed marks, 7in (17.5cm).
$650-800

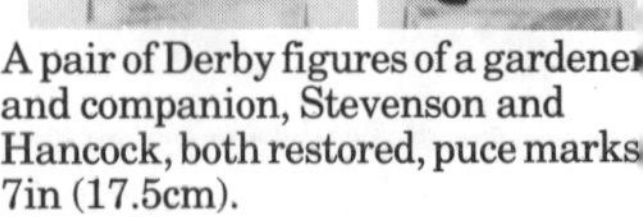

A pair of Derby figures of a gardener and companion, Stevenson and Hancock, both restored, puce marks, 7in (17.5cm).
$400-500

A Derby figure of Dr. Syntax, on a green base, Robert Bloor & Co., restorations, crown, crossed batons and D mark in red and incised No. 7, c1820, 4½in (11cm).
$250-300

A Longton Hall figure of a milkman, wearing a black tricorn hat, white shirt, yellow and puce spotted neckerchief, puce coat and brown breeches, the base enriched in purple, slight chipping, c1755, 10½in (27cm).
$5,000-5,500

A pair of Derby figures of the Welsh Tailor and companion, Stevenson and Hancock, restoration, puce marks, 5½in (14cm).
$550-700

A pair of figures of young women, the bases moulded with female masks and flowers, slight chipping, 24½in (62cm).
$2,500-3,000

A pair of Derby figures of a boy and girl, Stevenson and Hancock, on bases outlined in gilt, his left hand missing, damage to extremities, girl restored, puce marks, 7in (17.5cm).
$300-400

A Minton flat back model of The Dutch Pedlar, on gilt enriched base, restored, c1825, 5½in (14cm).
$550-650

A Derby figure of a young lady, in brightly painted 18thC costume, damage, some regilding, crossed swords marks, c1825, 10in (25.5cm).
$250-400

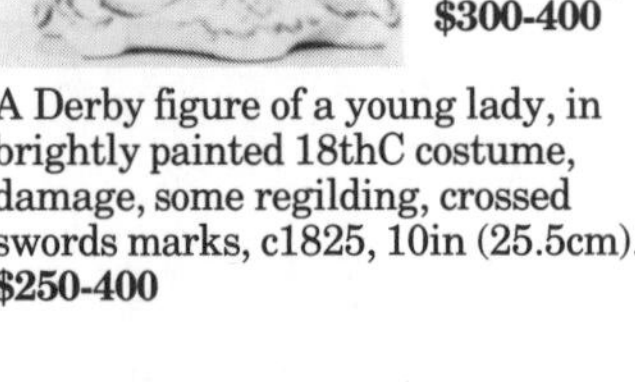

A Worcester crinoline figure, modelled as an unrecorded tea cosy top, colour scheme 2, shape No. 2620, c1916, 3in (7.5cm).
$700-800

The moulds were destroyed in 1920.

A pair of Royal Worcester figures of female musicians, each wearing gilt drapes and raised on moulded bases, printed mark in puce and date cipher for 1920, 10in (26cm).
$550-700

A Plymouth group, painted in enamel colours, some damage, c1770, 6in (15cm).
$1,000-1,200

A Royal Worcester equestrian group, entitled 'At the Meet', with wood plinth, 9in (23cm).
$650-700

A Royal Worcester equestrian group, entitled 'Huntsman and Hounds', on wood plinth, 9in (23cm).
$650-700

A Minton parian group entitled 'Naomi and her daughters-in-law', the base inscribed in indented capitals, minor damage, incised No. 183, 13½in (34cm).
$300-400

A Worcester majolica figure, c1862, 8½in (21cm).
$1,000-1,200

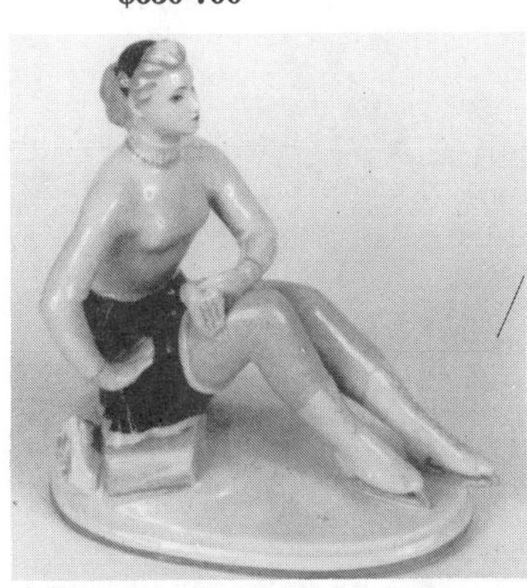

A European figure of a girl skater, c1930, 7in (17.5cm).
$100-150

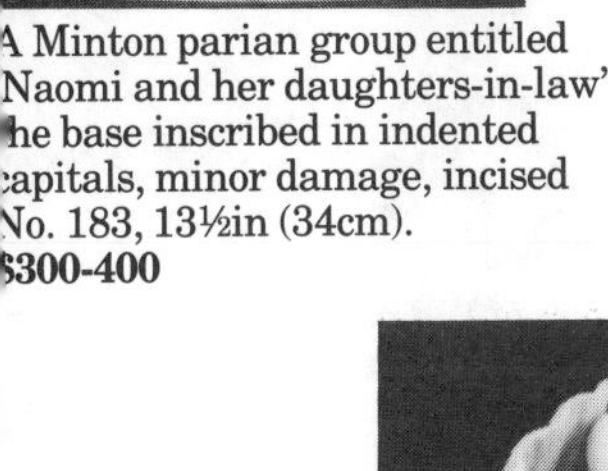

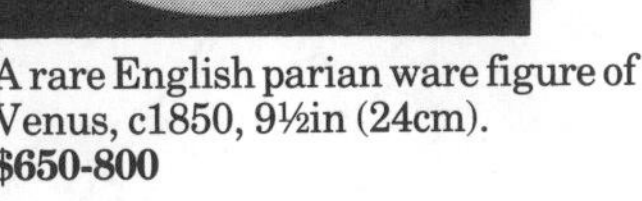

A rare English parian ware figure of Venus, c1850, 9½in (24cm).
$650-800

A pair of Continental figures of a seated lady and gentleman with dogs, on circular bases, blue printed mark, 19thC, 6in (15cm).
$1,400-2,000

A pair of Royal Worcester figures of Joy and Sorrow, modelled by James Hadley, Joy wearing pink robe, Sorrow wearing a green robe with dusted gilt highlights on coloured bases, puce printed factory mark and model number 2/57, date code for c1933, 9½in (24cm).
$800-1,000

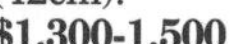

A Dresden group, painted in colours and enriched in gilding, the base heightened in pale pink and turquoise and enriched in gilding, minor chipping to flowers, blue crossed swords and dash marks, incised numeral marks, c1880, on a plush covered wood stand, 16½in (42cm).
$1,300-1,500

A Dresden group of a huntsman in 18thC costume and 2 leaping hounds, chips and restoration, 15in (38cm).
$1,000-1,200

A Meissen figure of St. Matthew, modelled by J. J. Kändler, with a long grey beard, wearing a long cloak with a purple and gilt scrolling border over a robe with scattered purple 'indianische Blumen' with gilt stems, an angel at his side, on a square chamfered base, crossed swords mark, c1740, 9½in (24cm).
$6,500-8,000

A Meissen group of The Hand Kiss, by J. J. Kändler, she wearing a puce crinoline with a flowered hem and yellow coat, he with a white coat enriched with gilding and purple revers, a black tricorn hat under his arm, damaged and repaired, c1740, 9in (23cm) wide.
$9,000-11,000

A Meissen figure of a bagpiper, modelled by J. J. Kändler, in black hat, green and yellow waistcoat and pink cloak with yellow stockings, on flower encrusted base, hair cracks to base, c1740, 9in (23cm).
$3,000-5,000

A Meissen rococo arbour group of lovers, modelled by J. J. Kändler and P. Reinicke, he in gilt trimmed jacket and waistcoat and black breeches, she in puce and gilt floral dress with black and blue bodice, the trellis modelled with trailing flowers, minor restoration, traces of crossed swords mark, c1745, 7½in (19cm).
$6,500-8,000

A Meissen figure of a Moor restraining a horse, modelled by J. J. Kändler, wearing a yellow striped turban, purple robe tied with a red striped sash and yellow boots, repair to the Moor, base and horse's fetlocks and ears, c1755, 9in (23cm).
$4,000-5,000

A late Meissen figure of Psyche seated on a tree stump, base cracked, some restoration, 21½in (54cm).
$2,000-2,500

A pair of Meissen figures of a Bulgar and Persian companion, from a series of Orientials modelled by J. J. Kändler and P. Reinicke, the man with fur-trimmed puce hat, buff lined pink cloak, cream coat reserved with sprays of flowers in puce and gold and with blue pantaloons, his companion dressed to match, his left arm, right sleeve and staff damaged, crossed swords mark at back, c1750, 9in (22cm).
$4,000-5,500

A Meissen equestrian figure, restored, 18thC, 8in (20cm).
$2,500-3,000

A Meissen figure of a monk carrying young lady wrapped in a sheaf into is monastery, modelled as a double cent bottle, 18thC, 4in (10cm).
2,500-3,000

A Meissen group, after Kändler, 19thC, 6in (15cm).
$1,200-1,500

A Meissen gardening group, painted in colours and enriched in gilding, minor chipping to flowers, blue crossed swords and incised numeral marks, late 19thC, 11½in (29cm).
$5,000-5,500

A Meissen figure of a moustached Saxon fusilier, wearing a black ricorn hat, buckled bandaliers, red rim to his waistcoat and jacket, black riding boots with spurs, the base enriched with puce, repairs, aint crossed swords mark to base, c1760, 9in (23cm).
$2,000-2,500

A Meissen group of children dressed as minstrels, 19thC, 8in (20cm).
$2,500-3,000

A set of 5 Meissen figures, emblematic of the Senses, each modelled as ladies in 18thC dress, painted in colours and enriched in gilding, the bases moulded with pink flutes enriched in gilding, minor chipping, blue crossed swords, incised and impressed numerals, late 19thC, 5 to 6in (12 to 15cm).
$7,000-9,000

A Meissen figure of Cupid, kneeling beside a target centred with a pink heart adorned with a flower garland, on a mound base and waisted plinth, slight damage, blue crossed swords and incised and impressed numerals, late 19thC, ½in (16cm).
700-800

A Meissen group of The Rape of the Sabine Woman, modelled as a scantily clad man carrying a woman over his shoulder, the base edged with gilt scrolls, lower arm restored and minute chipping to hand, crossed swords in underglaze blue and incised 1919, 19thC, 7in (17.5cm).
$300-400

A Meissen figure of a harlequin with pug dog, after J. J. Kändler, wearing a brightly enamelled diamond pattern jacket and octagonal sided hat, crossed swords in underglaze blue, impressed 3043, 20thC, 7½in (18.5cm).
$650-1,000

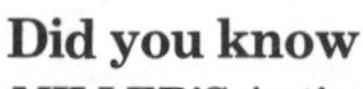

A Berlin figure of a putto, emblematic of Plenty, the base lined in gilt, slight chips to extremities, blue sceptre marks, 19thC, 7½in (19cm).
$300-400

A pair of Sitzendorf candle holder figures, modelled with a young man and woman, standing before stump supports on footed bases moulded with scrolls and applied and painted with flowers, slight chips, blue factory marks, 13in (33cm).
$650-700

A Würzburg figure, allegorical of Ceres, the scantily clad goddess holding a sheaf of corn and a scythe, her robe painted with scattered sprays of puce flowers, her hair and features naturalistically coloured, repaired, c1770, 6½in (16.5cm).
$3,000-5,000

Did you know
MILLER'S Antiques Price Guide builds up year by year to form the most comprehensive photo-reference system available

A Berlin figural group, modelled as a classical maiden wearing an orange robe lined in yellow, some damage, blue sceptre and iron red K.P.M. and globe mark, late 19thC, 16in (40.5cm).
$900-1,000

A pair of Sitzendorf figures of a young man and companion wearing 18thC style costume, the bases painted in predominantly pastel colours, damage to extremities, factory marks, 15½in (39cm).
$550-700

A Volkstedt figure of a female gardener, holding a watering can, in a black bonnet, yellow bodice and red dress, standing on a grassy mound base, restored, c1780, 7in (17cm).
$400-550

A pair of Doccia figures of Summer and Winter, she wearing a pink robe and blue cloak, Winter modelled as an old man draped in a fur lined cloak holding a cornucopia, both restored, c1780, 9in (23cm).
$1,400-2,000

A Vienna group, after a model by Anton Grassi, depicting a man and woman in 18thC costume, 11½in (29cm).
$1,500-2,500

Two Buen Retiro allegorical figures, Neptune standing with left arm raised, scantily clad and wearing a gilt crown, before a dolphin in blue and red, forearms missing, restored, and Laocoon loosely draped with a serpent entwined around his right arm, chipped, serpent's head missing and firing crack, c1770, 6in (15cm).
$2,000-2,500

A Coalport hand painted plate, with gilded decoration, c1845, 9in (23cm).
$200-275

A pair of Coalport plates, painted with landscapes, c1840.
$500-550

A pair of Coalport plates, painted with floral bouquets, c1840.
$300-400

A Coalport dish, painted with a rare view of Ludlow Castle, by Doe & Rogers, Worcester, c1820, 12½in (33cm) wide.
$950-1,100

A Chelsea silver shaped moulded dish, with red anchor mark, c1756, 8½in (21cm).
$500-650

A Coalport dish, c1825, 9in (23cm).
$550-700

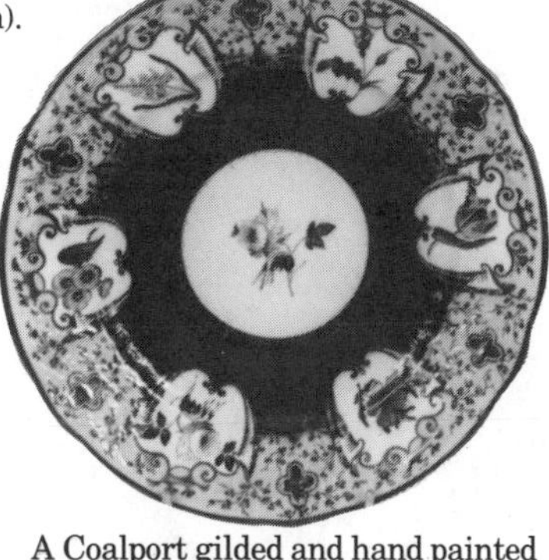

A Coalport gilded and hand painted plate, c1815, 9½in (23cm).
$300-400

A Chelsea blue ground plate, the well gilt with the egg-and-dart pattern within an underglaze blue border gilt with swags of vine, rim chip, gold anchor mark, c1765, 8½in (22cm).
$500-550

A Coalport plate, painted with birds perched on a nest among flowers, on a salmon pink ground and with pink border, enamels rubbed, 8½in (21cm).
$250-300

A Coalport soup dish, hand painted with the Tiger pattern, c1805, 9½in (24cm).
$120-150

A Coalport documentary crested plate, painted by John Duncombe Taylor, with The Exposure of Prince Bahman taken from Arabian nights, inscribed on the reverse, the gilt chequered pattern border reserved with an iron red crest, inscribed and dated July 1807, 8½in (21.5cm).
$650-1,300

A John Rose and Co. Coalport part dessert service, comprising: a comport, pedestal bowl and 8 plates, each piece finely painted with a flower within a pierced border, decorated in gold and turquoise, mid-19thC.
$5,500-6,500

A Coalport plate, with a painting of Lago Di Garda within a green border, c1855, 9½in (24cm).
$250-300

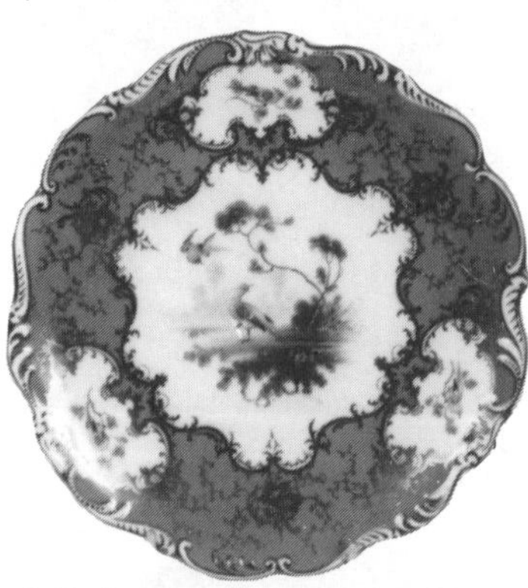

A Coalport plate, hand painted by Percy Simpson and signed, c1891, 8½in (21cm).
$450-550

A Coalport cabinet plate, entitled Clear Springs Valley, signed Arthur Perry, c1900, 9in (23cm).
$550-650

A Coalport plate, with a view of Windsor Castle within a pink border with gilt decoration, signed Arthur Perry, c1891.
$500-550

A Coalport soup plate, with heavy gilding, 10in (25cm).
$80-150

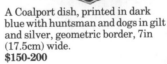

A Coalport dish, printed in dark blue with huntsman and dogs in gilt and silver, geometric border, 7in (17.5cm) wide.
$150-200

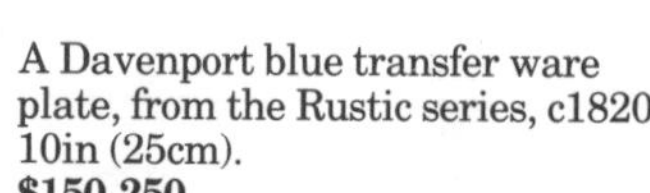

A Davenport blue transfer ware plate, from the Rustic series, c1820, 10in (25cm).
$150-250

A Coalport dish, with central painted landscape, c1900, 12½in (33cm).
$650-700

A finely painted Coalport plate, attributed to F. H. Chivers, c1910, 9in (23cm).
$350-450

A Derby dish, with the arms of Viscount Tamworth, Leicestershire c1820, 10in (25cm).
$1,300-1,400

A Derby armorial dish, the centre with the arms of Pigott impaling Cope, within an iron red and gilt chain border, 10½in (27cm).
$550-700

A Worcester blue ground lozenge shaped dish, the centre painted with exotic birds in a wooded landscape vignette, within a gilt scroll and diaper panelled cartouche, the border gilt with flowersprays, flakes to gilt rim, blue square seal mark, c1770, 10½in (27cm) wide.
$1,000-1,300

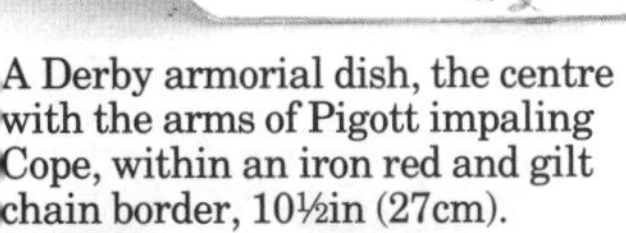

A Samson Imari deep dish, with everted rim, painted with a central river landscape, 18in (46cm).
$1,200-1,500

A Lowestoft blue and white fluted junket dish, painted in pale blue with flowers and insects, extended firing cracks, c1765, 9in (22cm).
$800-1,000

A Worcester leaf dish, the overlapping leaves with puce mid-ribs and raised veins, 2 small rim chips, c1760, 13in (35cm).
$1,400-2,000

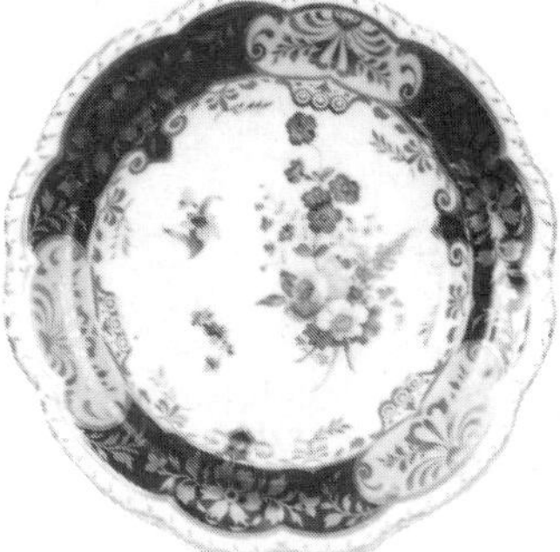

A set of 12 Ridgway dessert plates, with gadrooned gilt moulded border, with a blue and yellow alternate panel gilt decorated band, the centres with bouquet and sprigs of flowers, pattern No. 1385, double crest and ribbon motto in underglaze blue, 10in (25cm).
$2,000-2,500

A Nantgarw lobed dish, with finely painted flowers, impressed mark, c1818, 11½in (29cm).
$1,200-1,300

A Spode dish, Hunting Buffalo pattern, marked, c1820, 12½in (33cm) wide.
$900-1,000

Two Worcester blue ground plates, the centres painted with exotic birds in wooded landscapes within gilt gadroon cartouches and lobed gilt dentil rims, one rim chipped, blue square seal and blue W marks, c1770, 7½in (18.5cm).
$1,000-1,300

A pair of Ridgway plates, with 3 polychrome flower decorated reserve panels, on deep blue and buff coloured ground with gilt vine scroll and flower decoration, early 19thC, 9in (22cm).
$550-650

A pair of Samson 'famille rose' deep dishes, painted with peacocks among flowering shrubs and rockwork, within a floral border and iron red rim, 13in (33cm) diam.
$550-700

A pair of Chamberlain's Worcester armorial plates, red script mark, c1820, 10in (25cm).
$1,000-1,200

A set of 6 Worcester plates, decorated within egg shell blue border, with ornate pierced latticed rim, lined in pink, with gilt moulded lambrequins, impressed mark, c1865, 9in (23cm).
$300-400

An early Spode dish, painted with full blown roses, c1815, 10in (25cm).
$200-250

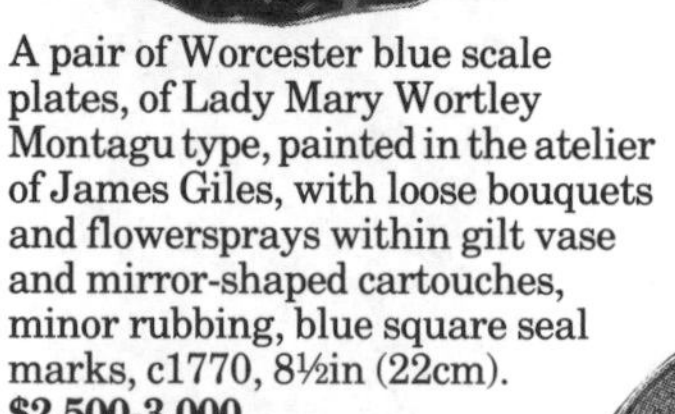

A pair of Worcester blue scale plates, of Lady Mary Wortley Montagu type, painted in the atelier of James Giles, with loose bouquets and flowersprays within gilt vase and mirror-shaped cartouches, minor rubbing, blue square seal marks, c1770, 8½in (22cm).
$2,500-3,000

A Royal Worcester dessert service, each piece painted in the centre with floral sprays, enclosed by a turquoise border, gilt with floral motif, comprising 2 tazzas and 6 plates, printed mark, c1882, 9in (23cm).
$400-500

A Swansea plate, painted by William Pollard within an elaborate gilt diaper and foliage well, reserved with gilt green berried foliage, within a gilt line rim, red stencil mark, c1820, 8in (20cm).
$1,500-2,500

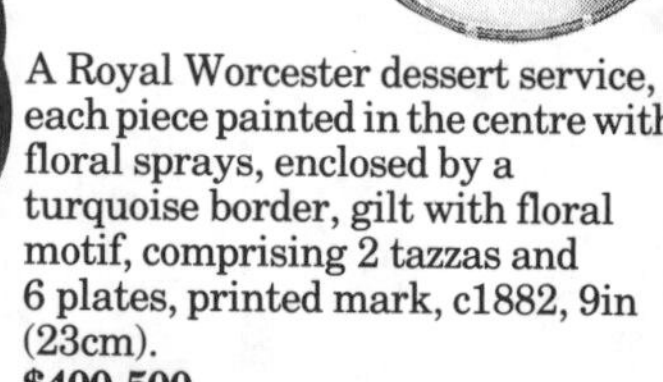

A Worcester green ground dish, c1775, 10in (25cm).
$1,400-1,500

A Barr, Flight & Barr, Worcester shaped armorial dish, with central arms and motto, flanked by gilt formal scrolling foliage, the border with a band of gilt anthemion, scrolls and foliage between gilt lines, slight wear, impressed and printed marks, c1816, 11in (28cm) wide.
$1,200-1,300

The Arms are those of Prendergast, 1st Viscount Gort.

A pair of Barr, Flight & Barr dessert plates, painted with figures in the centre, the white borders with meandering scroll and anthemion motifs in gilt, printed and impressed marks, 8½in (21cm).
$2,000-2,500

A pair of Chamberlain's Worcester dishes, the centres decorated with polychrome flowers, pink border surround with flower decorated panels, 10in (25cm).
$550-650

A Royal Worcester plate, signed by J. Freeman, c1950, 9in (23cm).
$120-150

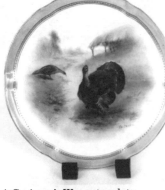

A pair of Royal Worcester dessert dishes, the hand painted central panel by J. Stinton, with deep blue and gilt decorated border surround with polychrome floral reserve panels, 9in (23cm).
$2,000-2,500

A Chamberlain's Worcester plate, from the Princess Charlotte service, c1816, 10in (25cm).
$1,300-1,500

A Grainger's Worcester plate, painted with birds in the centre, signed by James Stinton, c1899, 8½in (21cm).
$700-800

A pair of Worcester blue and white dishes, decorated with butterflies and floral and fruit sprays, 13in (34cm) wide.
$1,500-2,000

A pair of English porcelain 'jewelled' plates, c1880, 9in (23cm).
$550-650

A pair of Meissen plates, with a poppy, fritillary and insects, crossed swords marks, c1735, 9½in (24cm).
$2,500-3,000

Six Amstel plates, with dentilled gilt edge, marked Amstel in underglaze blue, c1790, 10in (25cm).
$4,000-5,000

An English dessert dish, with polychrome central reserve depicting Coniston Lake, in gilt scrolled border surround on pink ground, 11in (29cm) wide.
$650-700

A Quimper dish, signed, c1910, 9in (23cm) wide.
$90-120

A Royal Worcester comport raised on low foot, the dish painted by Po-Ling, within a gilt border, painted in coloured enamels in the Chinese 'famille rose' style, impressed marks, 9½in (24cm).
$500-650

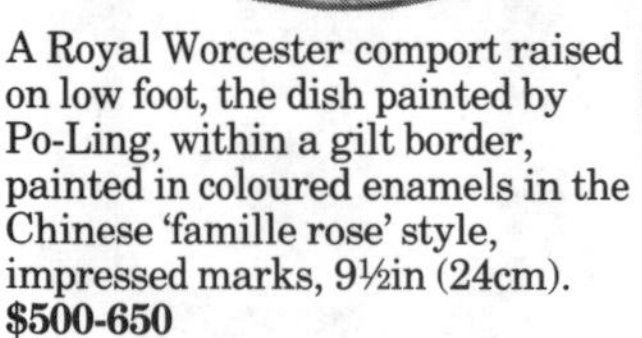

A Sèvres pattern turquoise ground tray, reserved and painted with a central portrait of Henri IV, surrounded by portraits of Court beauties, named on the reverse, within gilt band and foliage scroll cartouches, with gilt rim, some rubbing, imitation interlaced L marks, late 19thC, 19in (48cm) diam, on a carved stand enriched in gilding, damaged.
$3,000-4,000

A Vienna, Du Paquier, plate painted in the Oriental style, enriched with gilding, within an iron red diaper border, reserved with 4 panels of flowers, incised N c1735, 9in (23cm).
$1,500-2,500

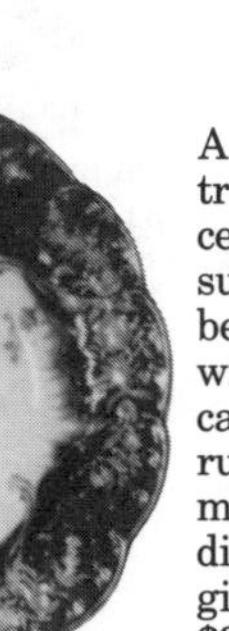

A Meissen plate, painted in colours and gilt within a surround of flowers and insects, the border painted in puce and gilt with gilt scrolling rim and turquoise feather painted edge, blue crossed swords and dot mark, gilding worn, c1770, 8½in (21cm).
$400-500

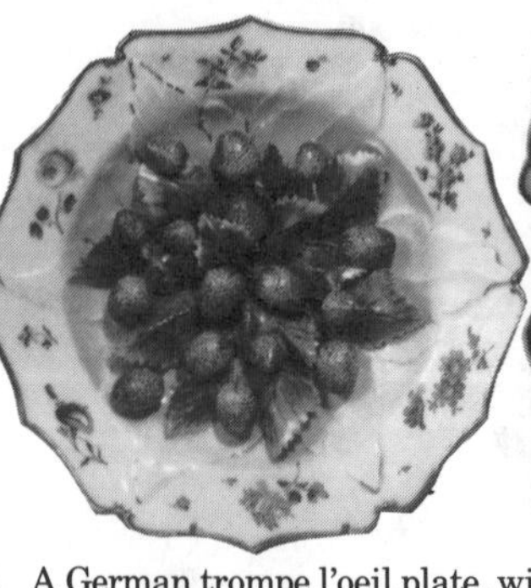

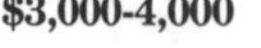

A German trompe l'oeil plate, with scattered flowers to the border, within a gilt rim, small chips to leaves, gilding rubbed, c1765, 9in (23cm).
$3,000-4,000

A pair of Ridgway dishes, c1820, 8½in (21cm).
$550-700

A pair of Meissen Schmetterling saucer dishes, painted in the Kakiemon style, with chocolate rims, crossed swords marks, c1740, 8in (20cm).
$2,000-2,500

A set of 5 Meissen pierced border plates, the borders with gilt latticework with alternating floral panels, 19thC, 8in (20cm).
$1,000-1,200

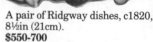

A Meissen Marcolini pierced plate, c1763, 9½in (23.5cm).
$650-700

ce Pails

pair of Coalport ice pails, covers nd liners painted within seeded lue borders edged with gilt foliage, ne liner and one stem repaired, rim hip, some staining, c1820, 10½in 26cm).
5,000-5,500

pair of Chamberlain's Worcester ucket shaped ice pails, covers and ners, with gilt shell and foliage andles and dolphin and cone nials, one body with crack to rim, ne handle restored, enamel aking, 3 small rim chips, script narks in puce, c1800, 10½in (27cm).
9,500-11,000

Jardinières

A Coalport flared flower pot and stand, decorated in the London studio of Thames Baxter, the stand with 3 gilt paw feet, gilding rubbed, c1805, 6½in (16.5cm) wide.
$1,000-1,200

A Sèvres bucket shaped jardinière, the blue and gold mosaic borders with 4 panels of flowers enclosed by gilt scrolls, gilt rim and footrim, gilding to footrim rubbed, blue interlaced L marks enclosing date letter H for 1760, painter's mark for Méreau jeune, incised 4, 9in (22cm) wide.
$3,000-5,000

Jugs

A Caughley jug with the Fisherman pattern, marked, c1780, 5½in (14cm).
$500-550

A Davenport jug, c1825, 5in (14cm).
$300-500

A Lowestoft blue and white moulded jug, painted between borders of moulded pendant leaves and flowers, painter's numeral 5, c1765, 10in (26cm).
$2,000-3,000

nkwells

Samuel Alcock inkstand in blue nd gilt, c1840, 15in (38cm) wide.
1,200-1,400

A Minton leaf-shaped inkwell, with branch handle, applied with flowers and leaves, chips and small cracks, one cover restuck, c1835, 8½in (21.5cm).
$2,500-3,000

wo Coalbrookdale inkwells of ushion shape, painted with flowers, lue factory marks, 5in (13cm).
300-400

Two Chamberlain's Worcester inkwells, modelled as groups of coloured shells on seaweed and rockwork moulds and square canted bases, in underglaze blue enriched with gilding, c1840, 3½in (8.5cm) wide.
$1,400-1,500

A Chamberlain's cream jug, decorated with the Japan pattern, c1820, 6in (15cm) wide.
$275-300

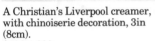

A Christian's Liverpool creamer, with chinoiserie decoration, 3in (8cm).
$800-1,000

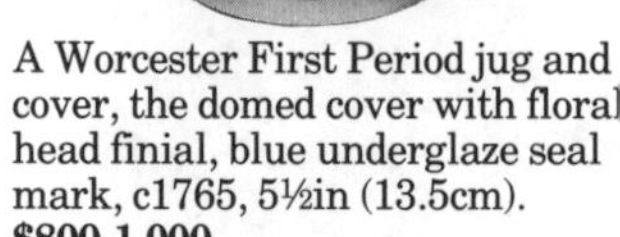

A Worcester First Period jug and cover, the domed cover with floral head finial, blue underglaze seal mark, c1765, 5½in (13.5cm).
$800-1,000

A Lowestoft cream jug, painted in a 'famille rose' palette, beneath a border of swags of flowers and an iron red line rim, minute crack to lip, c1790, 3in (8cm).
$300-400

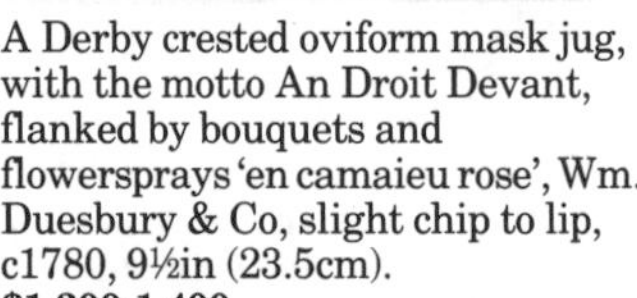

A Derby crested oviform mask jug, with the motto An Droit Devant, flanked by bouquets and flowersprays 'en camaieu rose', Wm. Duesbury & Co, slight chip to lip, c1780, 9½in (23.5cm).
$1,300-1,400

The crest is that of Molyneux.

A Grainger & Co., Worcester oviform jug, with scroll handle, painted with huntsmen wearing pink and a squire within a gilt cartouche, rim crack and restoration, script mark, c1805, 10in (25cm).
$1,500-2,500

A Staffordshire porcelain baluster jug, painted with a view of Worcester within a gilt panel and flanked by flowersprays on an apple green ground, the wide gilt neck inscribed in script 'J F S & L A M', 8in (20cm).
$300-400

A Lowestoft baluster cream jug, cracked body, rim chipped, c1785, 3in (7.5cm).
$300-400

A Royal Worcester miniature jug, dated 1909, 1½in (4cm).
$150-250

A Worcester jug, with chinoiserie decoration, c1760, 3½in (9cm).
$1,300-1,400

A Royal Worcester miniature jug, dated 1912, 2in (5cm).
$150-250

A baluster jug, with gilt angular handle, slight cracks to base, stencilled Pardoe Cardiff mark within a shaped rectangular cartouche, c1820, 6in (15cm).
$700-900

Use the Index!

Because certain items might fit easily into any of a number of categories, the quickest and surest method of locating any entry is by reference to the index at the back of the book.
This has been fully cross-referenced for absolute simplicity

Two miniature Spode jugs, c1820, 1½in (4cm). **$300-400**

Mugs

A Bow baluster mug, with grooved handle and heart-shaped terminal, painted in the 'famille rose' palette with flowers issuing from pierced rockwork, the rim with flowers reserved on a narrow diaper, minute chip to rim, crack to base of handle, painter's numeral 10, c1755, 5in (12.5cm).
$1,000-1,200

A Coalport mug, c1850, 3½in (8cm).
$80-110

A Coalport mug, transfer printed with a view in Shrewsbury, c1880, (3in) 8cm.
$70-100

A Coalport miniature mug, signed S. Schofield, 1½in (3.5cm).
$140-150

A Lowestoft blue and white mug, transfer printed with an Oriental crossing a bridge, the interior with a diaper pattern rim, c1780, 6in (14.5cm).
$700-1,000

A Coalport coffee can dated 1807, initialled J.V., 2½in (6cm).
$200-275

A Derby bell-shaped mug, with grooved handle, painted in colours on either side, slight damage, mid-18thC, 5in (13cm).
$1,200-1,400

A Hancock bell-shaped mug, The Masons Company of Edinburgh, small restoration, c1765, 5in (14cm).
$1,400-1,500

A bone china bat-printed mug, c1820, 3in (8cm).
$100-130

A Lowestoft blue and white baluster mug, with scroll handle, cracked, foot chipped, painter's numeral 4, c1765, 6in (15cm).
$500-550

A Pinxton mug, decorated with a yellow band, painted with stylised floral designs, letter P mark in gold, c1900, 4½in (11cm).
$700-900

A Worcester blue scale baluster mug, with grooved loop handle, reserved with mirror and vase shaped cartouches edged with gilt scrolls enclosing swags of garden flowers, the handle enriched in gilding, blue square seal mark, c1770, 6in (15cm).
$3,000-4,000

A First Period Worcester tankard, painted with the Walk in the Garden pattern, open crescent mark, c1760, 6in (15cm).
$2,000-2,500

Three miniature mugs, 1½in (4cm). **$50-100 each**

A Coalport mug, c1835, 3½in (8cm).
$70-100

A Copeland hand painted mug, c1850, 3in (8cm).
$130-150

A Worcester mug, painted in a typical 'famille rose' palette, with the Beckoning Chinaman pattern, crack to top of handle, painter's mark, c1758, 4in (11cm).
$1,200-2,000

A Worcester mug, painted with a bouquet and scattered flowers, minute crack to rim, c1760, 4½in (12cm).
$2,000-2,500

A Worcester blue and white baluster mug, printed with butterflies and flowersprays, handle cracked, crescent marks, c1770, 6in (15cm). **$250-300**

A mug, c1825, 2½in (7cm).
$100-110

A Worcester miniature mug, 1¼in (3cm).
$80-120

An English matt blue ground mug, with moulded scroll handle, painted with baskets of fruit and flowers within gilt cartouches, gilt monogram 'EMK' within oval reserves, c1820, 5½in (13cm).
$2,500-3,000

Plaques

A Worcester white glazed wall pocket, moulded as a young girl supporting a basket, within ivory border, 10in (25cm) high, mounted on a plush wall plaque.
$400-500

A pair of English plaques, painted with vases of flowers, one with hair cracks, both with restoration to decoration, mid-19thC, carved giltwood frames, 12½ by 9½in (32 by 24cm).
$5,000-6,500

A pair of small Fürstenberg rococo framed Imperial portrait plaques, painted in colours, of the Emperor Joseph II of Austria and the Empress Marie-Josephine of Austria, damaged and restored, marked to the glazed sloping sides with an underglaze blue F, late 1760s.
$25,000-30,000

A Berlin plaque, painted after the style of Guido Reni, with a portrait of the Virgin Mary wearing an ochre shawl and dark draped robes, impressed sceptre and KPM marks, c1880, 7½in (19cm) high, in carved giltwood frame.
$700-900

A Berlin plaque, impressed sceptre and KPM marks, late 19thC, 8½in (22cm) high, plush and giltwood frame. **$1,000-1,300**

A Vienna hand painted plaque, wit underglaze blue beehive mark to base.
$1,000-1,300

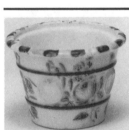

A Bow miniature flower pot with 4 yellow fixed ring handles, painted with flowe the body with raised brown ribs, the top rim with alternating puce and yellow gadroons, chip to foot, incised 26, c1760, 1½in (4cm).
$700-900

A Berlin plaque, painted in bright colours, inscribed on the reverse, impressed KPM and sceptre marks, imitation beehive mark, late 19thC, 10in (25cm) high, carved giltwood frame.
$7,000-8,000

A German plaque painted in colours, c1880, 3in (7cm), gilt frame.
$300-500

A Coalport D-shaped bough pot an pierced cover, the blue ground enriched in gilt with flowerheads, reserved with cartouches of garder flowers, cracked and chipped, feet re-stuck, c1805, 7½in (18cm).
$1,000-1,300

Pots

A Derby bough pot of demi-lune form, with twin lion mask terminals, painted and coloured with sprigs of roses, divided by gilt foliage within gilt bands, restored, gilding worn, puce factory marks, 5in (13cm).
$150-250

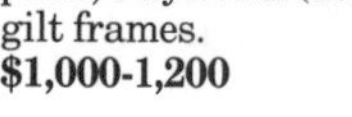

A pair of Continental plaques of putti, 7 by 5½in (17.5 by 14cm), in gilt frames.
$1,000-1,200

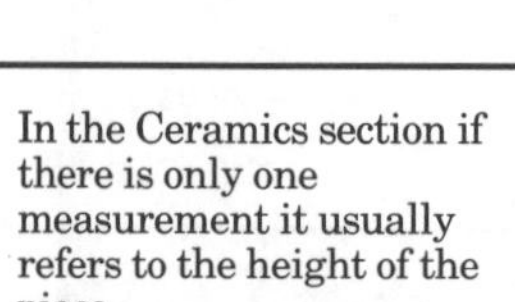

In the Ceramics section if there is only one measurement it usually refers to the height of the piece

Sauceboats

A Caughley blue and white sauce boat, c1780, 6½in (16cm) wide.
$400-500

Make the Most of Miller's

In Miller's we do NOT just reprint saleroom estimates. We work from realised prices either from an auction room or a dealer. Our consultants then work out a realistic price range for a similar piece. This is to try to avoid repeating freak results – either low or high

Scent Bottles

A Coalport scent bottle, encrusted with flowers, marked C.D., 3½in (9cm).
$300-350

An English navette-shaped scent bottle, bat printed and coloured with figures, within blue and gilt borders, c1810, 4in (10cm) long.
$150-250

Services

An armorial part dinner service, made as replacements to a Chinese service, comprising: 6 tureens, covers and stands, 7 oval meat dishes, 2 dishes, perhaps Coalport, soup tureen covers cracked, c1805.
$6,500-7,000

A Coalport part dessert service, painted with iron red bands with yellow scrolling foliage on a gilt and white diamond pattern ground, reserved with gilt navette shaped paterae between gilt line rims, comprising 22 pieces, gilding rubbed, some damage, c1810.
$4,000-5,500

A Coalport part tea and coffee service, comprising: 6 teacups and saucers, 6 coffee cups and saucers and 2 plates, c1860.
$800-1,000

A Coalport blue and white cabaret set, in Pine Cone pattern, including 6 cups and saucers, c1850.
$800-900

A Royal Crown Derby part coffee service, painted by W. E. J. Dean, comprising, a coffee pot and cover, a sugar bowl and cover, a box and cover, 2 trays and 6 cups and saucers, and a plate, yachts named on reverse, printed factory marks, 20thC.
$5,000-5,500

A Coalport blue ground part dessert service, painted with pink roses and vetch within pale yellow cartouches enriched with gilding, comprising 28 pieces, chips to stand, one dish repaired, c1820.
$8,000-9,500

A Derby Imari pattern composite part dinner, breakfast and coffee service, painted within gilt line rims, comprising 216 pieces, Robt. Bloor & Co., some staining, crown, crossed batons and D marks and printed crowned D marks in iron red, c1825.
$16,000-20,000

A Coalport composite gold ground part tea and coffee service, painted on a gold ground between bands of gilt scrolling foliage, diamond and loop pattern or anthemion, within gilt line rims, comprising 52 pieces, some minor rubbing to gilding, some pieces later replacements, c1810.
$9,000-10,000

A Royal Crown Derby fruit service, decorated in red on a white ground, bordered in deep blue and gilt, comprising: a pair of comports, 4 dishes and 12 plates.
$1,000-1,200

A Derby part dinner service, printed and painted in iron red and underglaze blue in the Imari pattern and enriched with gilding, comprising: meat dish, 2 vegetable tureens and covers, sauce tureen, cover, stand and ladle, a gravy boat and stand, 6 soup plates, and 21 plates, impressed and printed marks.
$1,500-2,500

A Copeland Imari pattern part dessert service, with flowers and foliage, enriched in gilding, comprising: 2 tazzas, 4 comports and 12 plates.
$1,500-2,500

A Derby armorial part tea service, painted in Smith's blue and gilt with a coat-of-arms and crest, within a shaped blue and gilt border, comprising: teapot, cover and stand, slop basin, 2 plates, sugar bowl cover, 12 teacups and 16 saucers, Wm. Duesbury & Co., some damage, crowned D marks in puce, c1785.
$3,000-4,000

The arms are possibly those of either the City or Bishopric of Durham.

A Derby part dessert service, the centres painted with urns and scattered bouquets within wide Smith's blue borders, gilt with scrolling anthemion between gilt and white dot pattern rims, comprising: a two-handled centrepiece, 3 dishes, 4 soup plates and 15 plates, some damage, Wm. Duesbury & Co., entwined anchor and D marks in gold, some pieces with crowned D mark in blue, c1775.
$2,500-3,000

A Royal Crown Derby part dessert service, decorated with central flower bouquets within a wide blue border with floral reserves, enriched with gilt floral sprays, comprising 18 pieces.
$2,500-3,000

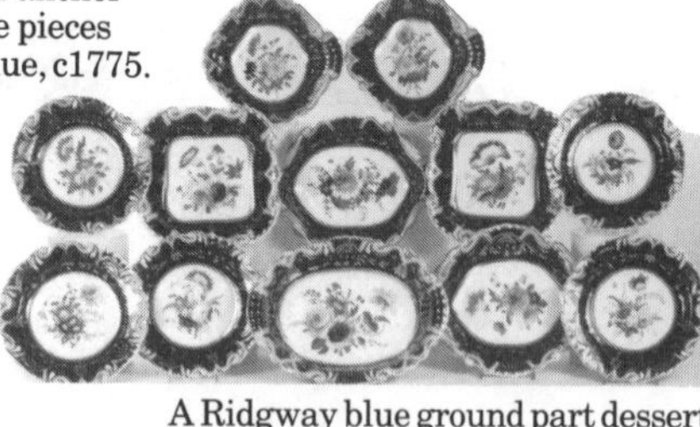

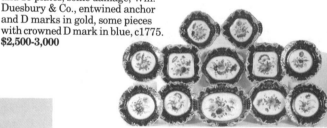

A Ridgway blue ground part dessert service, painted within a deep blue border gilt with foliage, within a moulded yellow scroll and gilt shell rim, comprising: 7 dishes, one riveted, some damage, and 12 plates, slight rubbing, pattern No. 733, c1830.
$3,000-5,000

A Derby part tea service, painted with the 'Imari' pattern in underglaze blue and iron red enriched in gilding, comprising: creamer, 9 teacups, 11 coffee cans and 11 saucers, the creamer and a coffee can cracked, gilding rubbed.
$1,000-1,300

A Staffordshire porcelain cabaret set, printed with panels of flowers in Imari colours comprising: teapot and cover, a sugar basin and cover, a milk jug, 4 teacups and saucers and a tray, some damage.
$650-1,000

A Worcester blue and white part tea service, painted with the Fence pattern and a Chinese pavilion on a rocky island and 2 flying wild ducks, the domed covers with flowerbud finials, comprising: teapot and cover, milk jug and cover, sugar pot and cover, cream pot and cover, broth bowl, basket with cover and stand, 12 cups and saucers and 2 cups, very minor chips, marked with an underglaze blue crescent, late 18thC.
$3,000-4,000

A pair of Niderviller porcelain dishes, painted in colours within gilt rims, blue crowned interlaced C's, Custine period, c1775, and a matching dish.
$2,000-2,500

A Meissen miniature tête-à-tête, each piece applied with coloured flowers beneath gilt rims, comprising: coffee pot and cover, milk jug, a sugar bowl and cover, 2 cups and saucers and a tray, some chipping to flowers, blue crossed swords marks, c1880, in fitted leather case, worn.
$5,000-6,500

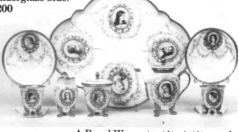

A Victorian Royal Worcester china dinner service, with Chinese vase and floral decoration, comprising 44 pieces.
$650-800

A Chamberlain's Worcester apricot ground part breakfast service, the centres with gilt paterae within a border of gilt radiating diamond pattern and a band of gilt scrolling foliage and paterae, comprising 18 pieces, pattern No. 305, some damage, c1800.
$5,000-6,500

A Jacob Petit porcelain neo-rococo tea service, comprising 32 pieces, some damage and repair, painted mark in underglaze blue.
$1,000-1,200

A Worcester, Flight and Barr, part tea service, painted in the Kakiemon palette with The Quail pattern, within gilt line rims, comprising: teapot, cover and stand, sugar bowl, milk jug, slop bowl, a saucer dish, 8 teacups and saucers, some damage, incised B marks, c1805.
$5,000-6,500

A Royal Worcester tête-à-tête, each piece painted within gilt band and beaded cartouche enclosed by pink roses and suspended from tied blue ribbon, on richly gilt claw feet, comprising 8 pieces, green and brown printed crown marks, c1865.
$3,000-4,000

A creamware crested part dessert service, each piece painted in iron red with a crest, comprising: 2 sauce tureens, covers and fixed stands, 2 plain ladles, 2 shallow dishes and 12 square plates, perhaps Wedgwood, some damage and staining, c1800.
$2,500-3,000

A Copenhagen celadon ground tête-à-tête, reserved and painted with views, comprising: teapot and cover, a sugar bowl and cover, 2 cups and saucers, and an oval tray, the centre with crowned LC monogram and inscribed, some repairs, blue waved line marks, c1860.
$3,000-5,000

A Meissen part dinner service, painted within 'Neubrandenstein' moulded borders and shaped gilt rims, comprising: a two-handled soup tureen, cover and stand, 2 vegetable dishes and covers, 2 serving dishes, and 23 dinner plates, some damage, blue crossed swords marks, c1900.
$6,500-7,000

A Sèvres pattern turquoise ground tea service, decorated in colours within gilt band cartouches, the rims gilt, comprising: a teapot and cover, milk jug, two-handled sugar bowl and cover, 12 teacups and saucers, and 14 plates, some damage, imitation interlaced L marks, late 19thC.
$3,000-5,000

An English porcelain part tea service, bat printed in grey with animals in their habitats, with chocolate rims, comprising: sugar bowl and cover, a miniature plate, one teacup, 6 coffee cans and 3 saucers, slight damage.
$800-900

A Rauenstein part tea service, moulded with wavy vertical ribs and painted in purple with landscape vignettes and scattered flowers, comprising: teapot and cover, tea caddy and cover, sugar box and cover, 3 teacups and saucers, puce crossed swords marks, c1780.
$1,500-2,500

Sucriers

A Wedgwood bone china sucrier and cover, painted in puce, marked, 5½in (14cm).
$300-400

A Samuel Alcock sucrier and cover, c1835, 6in (15cm).
$450-500

Tea & Coffee Pots

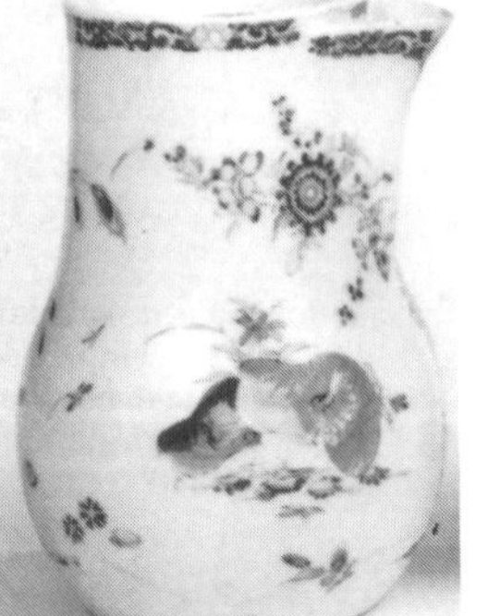

A Bow baluster chocolate pot and a Chinese cover, painted in a 'famille rose' palette with The Quail Pattern, the grooved loop handle with heart-shaped terminal, the cover with flowers, repaired and riveted, c1758, 6½in (16cm).
$500-650

A Minton teapot, cover and stand, c1825, 10in (25cm) wide.
$400-500

A Coalport teapot, with the Japan/Imari pattern, 7½in (18cm).
$250-300

A Coalport teapot and stand, with the Easter Lily pattern, John Rose & Co, c1805, 7½in (19cm).
$300-400

A Derby teapot and cover, with gilt ring handle and painted with cornflowers, finial restuck, crossed batons and D mark in puce, impressed initials BNP, c1795, 9in (23.5cm) wide.
$550-700

A Lowestoft blue and white transfer printed coffee pot and cover, slight crack to body, rim chip, c1780, 10½in (26.5cm).
$1,500-2,000

A Minton topographical part veilleuse, the teapot and cover with gilt borders of diaper pattern, trellis and dots, edged with gilt scrolls, the cover with gilt finial, base lacking, c1840, 7½in (19cm).
$550-700

A Lowestoft teapot and cover, painted in a 'famille rose' palette with Orientals, the cover with flowers and pink flower finial, the body extensively repaired, cover and finial chipped, c1772, 4½in (11.5cm).
$650-700

A coffee pot, possibly Grainger's Worcester, c1810, 10½in (26cm).
$300-400

A Worcester blue scale baluster coffee pot and cover, painted with flowers within cartouches, the cover with pink flower finial, chips to finial and footrim, blue square seal mark, c1768, 8½in (21.5cm).
$9,000-10,000

A Lowestoft teapot and cover, painted in pink 'camaieu', perhaps by the Tulip Painter, with borders of gilt scrolling foliage, cracked body, spout repaired, gilding rubbed, c1775, 5½in (14cm).
$2,000-2,500

A Meissen Hausmalerei white ground chinoiserie gilt teapot with cover and 6 teacups and saucers, in the style of F. J. Ferners, painted in underglaze blue, with flowers painted in colours, minor chips to spout, the cups and saucers marked with crossed swords, dotted hilts and central dot, c1755.
$5,000-5,500

A Worcester teapot, with different raised pattern each side, c1765, 4in (10cm).
$2,000-2,500

A Lowestoft teapot and cover, painted in a 'famille rose' palette, hair crack beneath the spout, c1785, 6½in (16cm).
$700-900

A Meissen Watteauszehen 'camaieu' purple coffee pot and domed cover, with artichoke finial, painted to each side with Italian Commedia dell'Arte figures and scattered 'Holzschnitt Blumen', all enriched with gilding, crossed swords mark, c1745, with silver gilt chased mount to the spout, 9in (23cm).
$2,500-3,000

A Worcester teapot, cover and hexafoil stand, enriched in dry blue, the centre of the stand with a dry blue flowerspray, within gilt dentil rims, spout restored, c1775, the stand 6in (15cm) wide.
$650-700

A Worcester teapot with chinoiserie pattern, crack to base, c1765, 6in (15cm).
$550-650

A Hochst teapot and a cover, painted in puce monochrome, with a pair of matching teacups and saucers, restored red wheel mark and impressed marks, c1750.
$150-250

Tureens & Butter Tubs

A Caughley polychrome tureen, c1780, 9in (23cm) wide.
$400-500

A Bow partridge tureen and a cover, naturally modelled in brown, yellow, blue and purple, the nest edged with yellow straw and green leaves, minor chipping to foliage, base crack, c1760, 5in (12.5cm) wide.
$1,400-2,000

A Derby two-handled sauce tureen and cover, the handles and paw feet terminating in lion heads, brightly painted on either side with sprays of flowers and gold scrolling foliage, painted mark in red, early 19thC, 7in (17.5cm).
$3,000-4,000

A pair of Rockingham sauce tureens, covers and stands, painted with flowers within gadroon, shell and foliage moulded rims, the gilt handles extending to 4 branch feet with leaf and acorn terminals, cracked and some staining, pattern No. 534, iron red griffin marks, c1830, 7in (17.5cm) wide.
$3,000-4,000

A Caughley blue and white butter dish and stand, c1785.
$500-550

A pair of Derby tureens and stands, c1820, 8in (20cm).
$1,500-2,000

A pair of First Period Worcester partridge-on-nest tureens and covers, each bird with naturalistic plumage, colour enamelled mainly in iron red, c1760, 4½in (11cm).
$4,000-5,500

A Chamberlain's Worcester armorial sauce tureen, ladle and stand, c1810, 7in (18cm).
$1,400-1,500

A Worcester Royal armorial sauce tureen and cover, from the service made to the order of the Duke of Clarence, the Arms with the Garter motto and with the Order of St. Andrew, the cover with entwined ribbons of the Orders of the Garter and Thistle, finial restored, crowned script Flight and crescent mark in blue, c1789, 7in (17cm) wide.
$1,300-1,500

Made in 1789 when Prince William was created Duke of Clarence and St. Andrew; this was the first Royal service made at Worcester.

A pair of Flight, Barr & Barr, Worcester pale blue ground sauce tureens and covers, with entwined gilt vinestock handles, painted with Malvern Abbey Church, and a church, the reverses with exotic birds in landscape vignettes, the bases edged in gilt and bronze, the covers with gilt cone finials, impressed marks, one with script marks and inscribed, c1815.
$6,500-8,000

A Worcester quatrefoil tureen and cover, with branch handles and finial, painted with bouquets and scattered flowers, 11in (28cm) wide.
$300-500

A Chelsea vase, painted in the Kakiemon palette beneath a border of scrolling blue foliage, the neck with iron red panels, extensively riveted, raised anchor mark, c1750, 9in (22.5cm).
$3,000-5,000

The price would be $2,000-3,000 without the raised anchor mark.

Vases

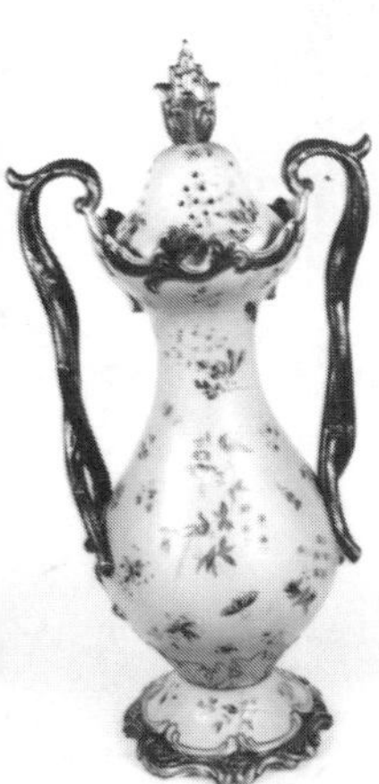

A pair of Samuel Alcock porcelain pot pourri vases, c1840, 25½in (65cm).
$2,000-2,500

A Bow flower vase, the top pierced with holes around a central aperture, the body applied with female masks surrounded by puce moulded scrolls and coloured flowers, some flowerheads and foliage lacking, indistinct painter's numeral in brown, c1762, 5in (12.5cm).
$1,300-1,400

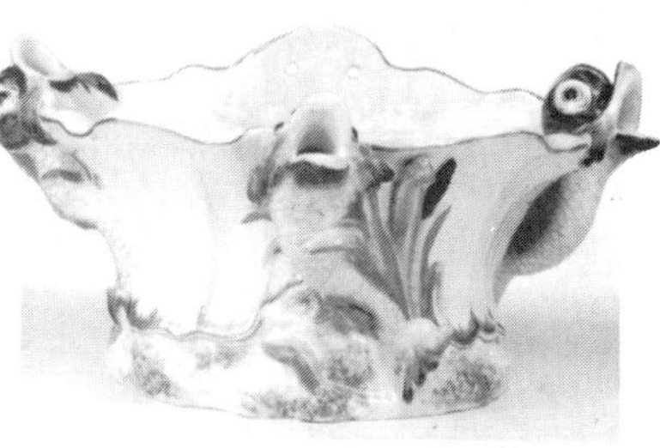

A Chelsea bough pot, the sides moulded and coloured with dolphins and bulrushes, the lower part with gilt 'feuille de choux' on a green rockwork base, restoration, red anchor mark, c1756, 13in (32cm) wide.
$3,000-4,000

A pair of Chelsea vases of scrolling form, with spreading pierced necks, pierced frill, minor damage and restoration, gold anchor marks, 8in (20cm).
$900-1,000

A Chelsea mottled claret ground vase and cover, with gilt loop handles, painted in the manner of Richard Askew, crack to rim, restoration, c1765, 12in (30cm).
$1,500-2,000

A Coalport two-handled campana vase, the gold ground reserved with brown ground panels and painted 'en grisaille', perhaps in the Studio of Thomas Baxter, with Hercules slaying the Lernaean Hydra, flanked by vertical bands of purple foliage, handles restored, some re-gilding, impressed number 25, c1805, 10in (25cm).
$550-700

A Coalport documentary vase, decorated in the London studio of Thomas Baxter, painted in sepia within a gilt oval cartouche, reserved on a gilt and white chequered ground between bands of gilt scrolling foliage, the neck and foot painted with bands of coloured flowers, slight rubbing to gilding, signed T. Baxter, 1802, 11½in (29cm).
$2,000-2,500

A Coalport pot pourri and cover, c1820, 5½in (14cm).
$800-1,000

A Coalport sponged pale blue ground vase and cover, with gilt rams mask handles, painted in the studio of Thomas Baxter, slight rubbing to gilding, c1805, 10½in (27cm).
$1,000-1,200

A Coalport pot pourri vase, painted and signed by E. O. Ball, c1891, 7in (18cm).
$1,000-1,200

A Coalport vase, with painted flowers attributed to Thomas Dixon, c1830.
$350-450

A pair of Coalport miniature vases, c1900, 4½in (11cm).
$650-800

A Coalport pot pourri vase and cover, painted on a royal blue ground, early 20thC, 7in (18cm). **$400-500**

A Derby vase and cover, decorated with classical figures and birds, slight restoration, c1760, 13in (33cm). **$1,300-1,400**

One from a garniture. If complete £3,000+

A pair of Derby vases and covers, with blue and gilt strapwork handles, painted in sepia with Minerva and Plenty and with Minerva and Juno, the covers with blue and gilt acorn finials, Wm. Duesbury & Co., cracks, chips and repairs, incised No. 101 G and with crown, crossed batons and D marks in gold, c1780, 10½in (26.5cm). **$13,000-14,000**

A Derby two-handled vase, with cracked ice ground, c1770, 6in (16cm). **$650-800**

A Derby inverted baluster vase of flowers, painted with a continuous fable scene, the neck applied with flowerheads, Wm. Duesbury & Co., flowers chipped, some glaze fritting, c1760, 5½in (14cm). **$2,500-3,000**

A Bloor Derby vase, painted by Richard Dobson, c1815, 10in (25cm). **$500-550**

A Royal Crown Derby miniature vase, in the Old Derby Witches pattern, c1916, 3in (8cm). **$400-500**

A Royal Crown Derby quatrefoil vase, in the Japan pattern, c1919, 3in (8cm). **$400-500**

A Royal Crown Derby miniature vase, in the Japan pattern, c1918, 3in (8cm). **$400-500**

A Royal Crown Derby miniature vase, in the Old Derby Witches pattern, dated 1820. **$500-550**

A Longton Hall vase, moulded with scrolls and shell bosses, the rim applied with a band of flowerheads, the body painted in colours with bouquets of flowers within puce cartouches, restored, 5in (12cm).
$400-500

A pair of Minton 'pâte-sur-pâte' two-handled vases and covers, with richly gilt entwined snake handles, c1894, 9½in (24.5cm).
$1,500-2,000

A vase, painted with a wide continuous panel of garden flowers within beaded and gilt borders, possibly Spode, minor cracks to foot, c1815, 6½in (16cm).
$600-700

A pair of Hicks & Meigh vases, c1835, 8in (20cm).
$1,300-1,500

A Samson giltmetal mounted pot pourri vase and cover, the rim applied with a giltmetal band pierced with scrolls and with caryatid handles, on a shaped square giltmetal base, late 19thC, 23in (58cm).
$4,000-5,000

A Spode vase, c1810, 4½in (11cm).
$1,000-1,200

A pair of Minton vases, richly painted with birds on flowering boughs, on 3 gilt peg feet, impressed marks, 7in (18cm).
$500-650

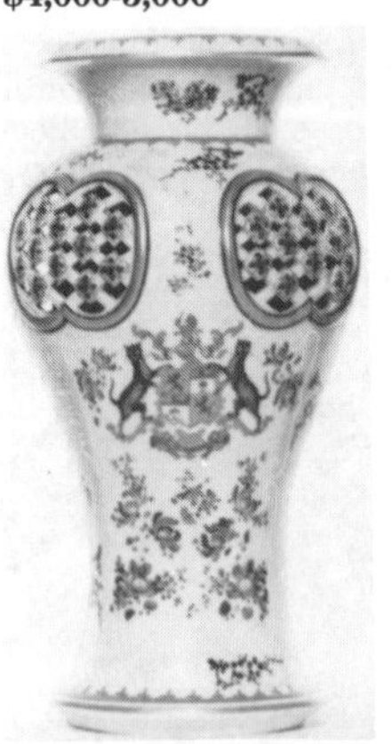

A pair of Samson armorial vases, painted in colours with scattered flowersprigs within bianco-sopra-bianco outlines, bases cracked, 12½in (32cm).
$700-900

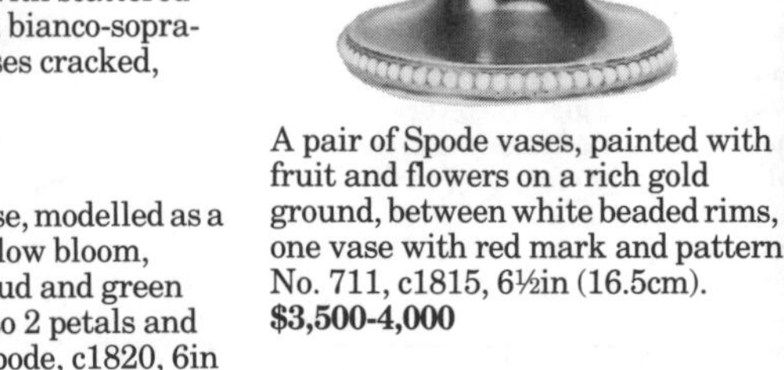

A pair of Spode vases, painted with fruit and flowers on a rich gold ground, between white beaded rims, one vase with red mark and pattern No. 711, c1815, 6½in (16.5cm).
$3,500-4,000

An English tulip vase, modelled as a red striped open yellow bloom, flanked by a tight bud and green leaves, restoration to 2 petals and 2 leaves, possibly Spode, c1820, 6in (15.5cm).
$3,000-4,000

Spode garniture of spill vases, 815, 5½in (14cm).
,200-1,300

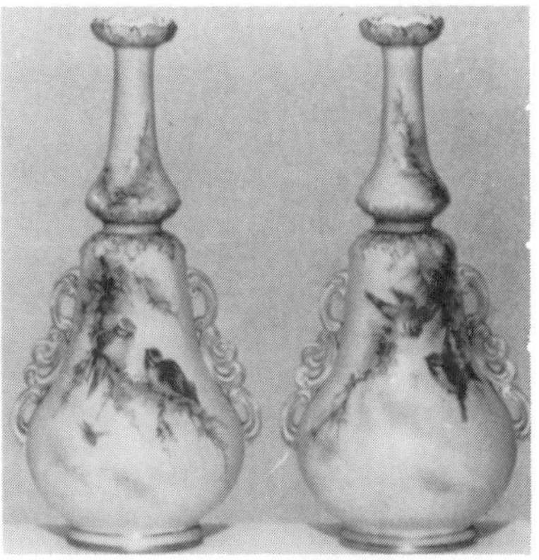
A pair of Grainger & Co., two-handled vases, painted in colours with birds, the pierced scrolling handles and leaf moulded rims enriched with gilding, 8in (20cm).
$650-800

pair of Chinese blue ground attened hexagonal vases, with gilt east handles, gilt in the London udio of Thomas Baxter, the key attern border between gilt line ms, one vase restored, c1802, 11in 8cm).
1,200-1,500

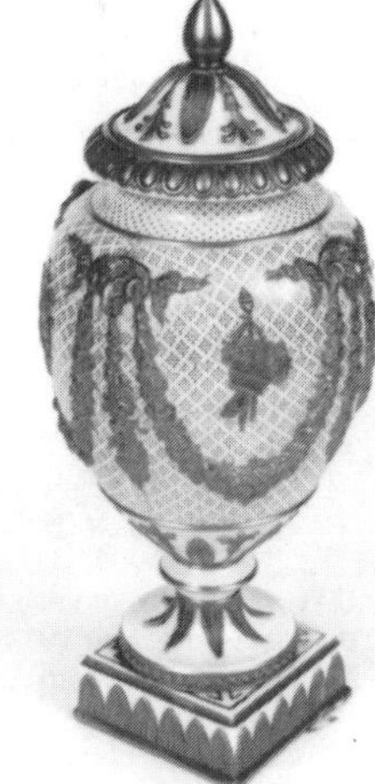
A Wedgwood lidded vase, finely gilded, c1895, 8½in (21cm).
$2,500-3,000

A pair of Royal Worcester vases, with gilt ring and scroll handles, the cream bodies printed in colours, puce printed marks and model number 1432, date code for c1892, 11½in (29cm).
$1,000-1,200

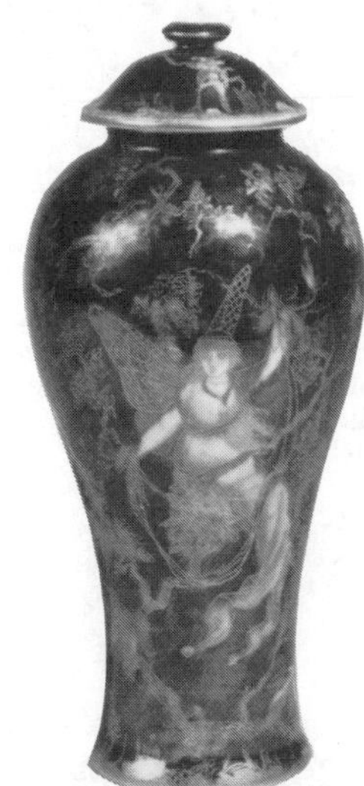
Wedgwood Fairyland Lustre vase nd cover, the iridescent black round printed in gold and coloured ith fairies, gilt Portland vase arks and numbers Z4968i to base nd cover, c1920, 8½in (21.5cm).
4,000-5,000

A Worcester, Flight, Barr & Barr, green ground vase, with entwined gilt serpent handles, painted with named views of Windsor Castle and the Straits of Menai, from Anglesey, one handle restored, script mark, c1820, 8in (20cm).
$3,000-4,000

A Grainger's Worcester cream ground vase, painted with a linnet, dated 1902, 3in (8cm).
$300-400

A Worcester, Flight, Barr & Barr vase, with a painted view, c1820, 3½in (9cm).
$1,200-1,400

A Royal Worcester green ground vase, painted by Jas. Stinton, the neck moulded and gilt beneath a gilt rim, the foot with a band of lappets, the base enriched in gilding, signed, puce printed mark and date code for 1897, shape No. 1794, 13in (33cm).
$3,000-4,000

A Grainger's Worcester pot pourri and cover, with a view of Malvern, 2½in (6cm).
$1,000-1,200

A Royal Worcester posy vase, with Union Jack flag mark of 1914-18, shape No. G161, 3in (7.5cm) diam.
$250-300

A Royal Worcester pierced vase, painted with a pheasant in a woodland setting, signed by Jame Stinton, dated 1908, 5in (14cm).
$650-700

A Worcester, Flight, Barr & Barr vase, painted flowers by Baxter, c1820, 3½in (9cm).
$1,200-1,400

A Royal Worcester vase, shape No. G957, 1916, 3in (7.5cm).
$250-300

A Barr, Flight & Barr, Worcester spill vase, painted with garden flowers, beneath a white beaded rim, the inner rim with a bronzed band of gilt 'caillouté', slight wear t gilding, c1810, 5½in (13.5cm).
$1,500-2,500

A garniture of 3 Staffordshire porcelain vases, c1830, 11in (28cm).
$2,400-2,800

A pair of Barr, Flight & Barr, Worcester pot pourri vases and pierced covers, with fixed gilt eagle's head and ring handles, the covers with gilt griffin finials, cracked, restored, wear to gilding, script marks, c1810, 7in (17.5cm).
$2,500-3,000

A pair of Royal Worcester posy vases, painted with a blue tit and a robin, c1913.
$550-650

Did you know

MILLER'S Antiques Price Guide builds up year by year to form the most comprehensive photo-reference system available

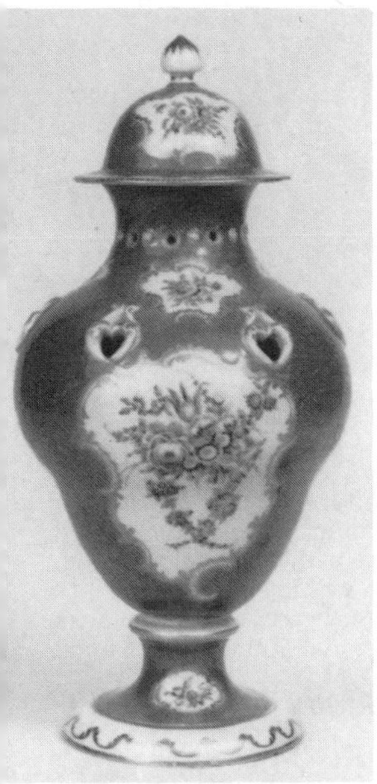

A Worcester pot pourri vase and cover, painted with flowers within C-scroll cartouches, the shoulder pierced with scroll moulded apertures, restoration, chip to cover, c1770, 13½in (34cm).
$1,000-1,200

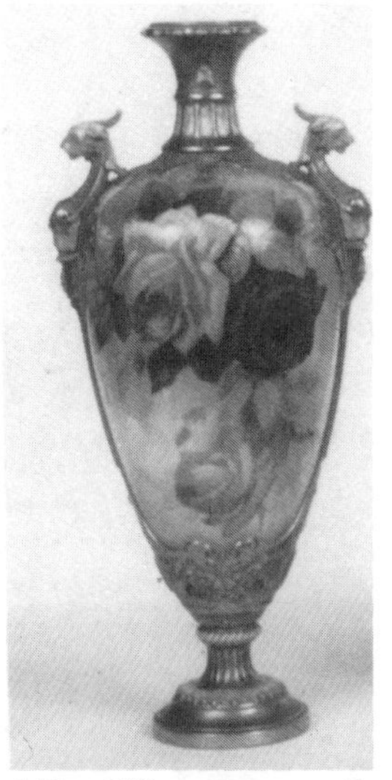

A Royal Worcester vase, the sides painted by Sedgley with red and pink roses pendant from the shoulder, the tinted ivory handles modelled as a griffin's head and enriched in gilding, signed, puce printed mark and date code for 1914, shape No. 1764, 14½in (36.5cm).
$1,200-1,400

A Royal Worcester pot pourri vase and cover, painted by J. Stinton, the handles covered in a rich bronzed and gilt patina, the foot and cover moulded with stiff leaves and enriched in similar patinas, signed, puce printed mark No. 1428 and date code for 1917, 12in (31cm).
$6,500-7,000

A Royal Worcester vase, with twin leaf moulded handles, painted by Jarman in colours on a shaded ivory ground, gilt highlights, puce printed marks and model No. 1459, date code for c1911, 12in (31cm) wide.
$800-1,000

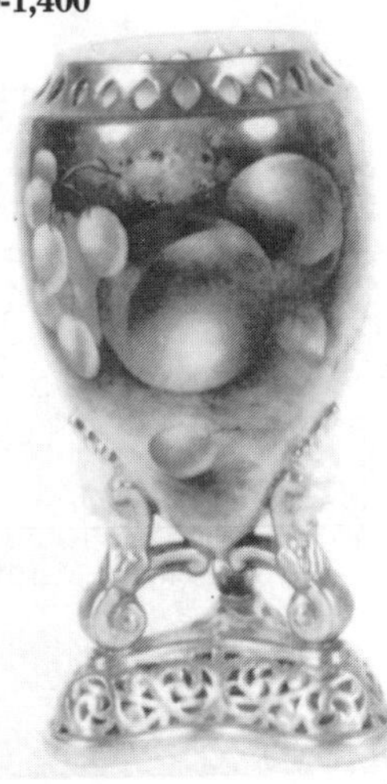

A Royal Worcester vase, painted in colours with peaches and grapes, the whole highlighted in gilt, signed by E. Townsend, printed mark in puce and date cipher for 1938, 6in (15cm).
$700-900

A Royal Worcester enamelled vase, decorated in colours and gilt with sprays of flowers on a yellow shading to pink ground, within pink and sky blue borders, printed mark in puce, 9in (23cm).
$400-550

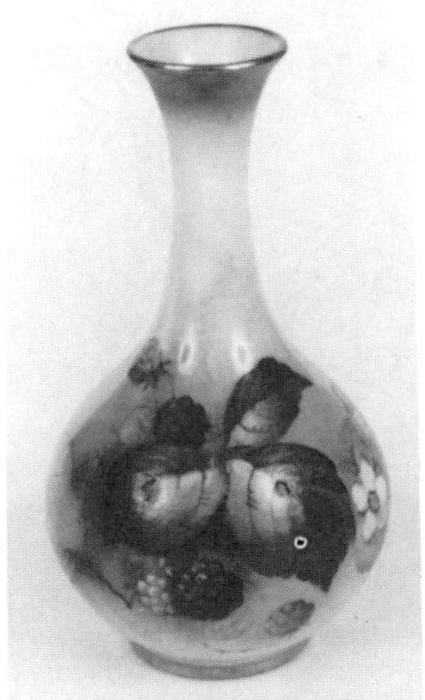

A Royal Worcester miniature vase, painted and signed by Kitty Blake, dated 1931, 4½in (11cm).
$400-500

An English bough pot and cover, painted with garden flowers, damaged, 8in (20cm).
$1,000-1,200

An English spill vase, painted on one side with exotic birds in a river landscape and on the other with an insect, reserved on a gold decorated semi-matt blue ground, early 18thC, 5½in (14cm).
$300-500

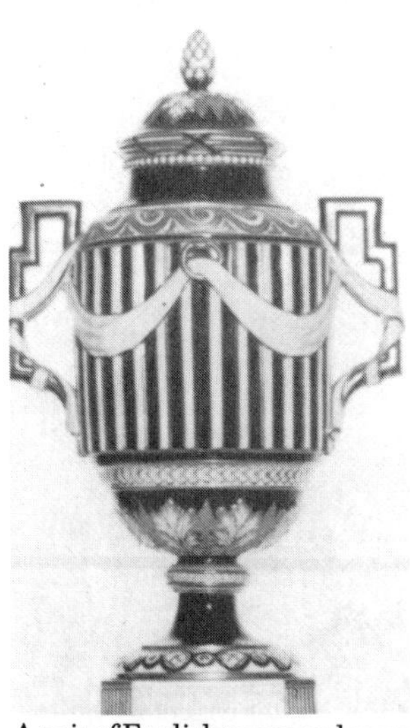

A pair of English vases and covers in Sèvres style, coloured in cobalt and white, with gilt highlights, pincecone finials, restoration and damage, 15in (39cm).
$1,300-1,500

A pair of English vases and covers, painted in colours, with all-over applied flower decoration, damaged, gilding rubbed, 17in (44cm).
$550-650

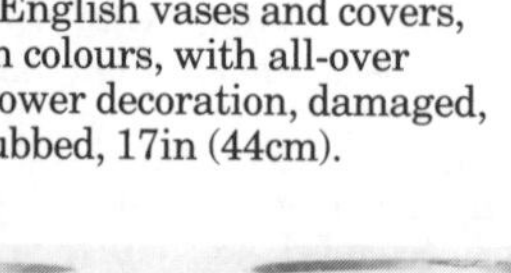

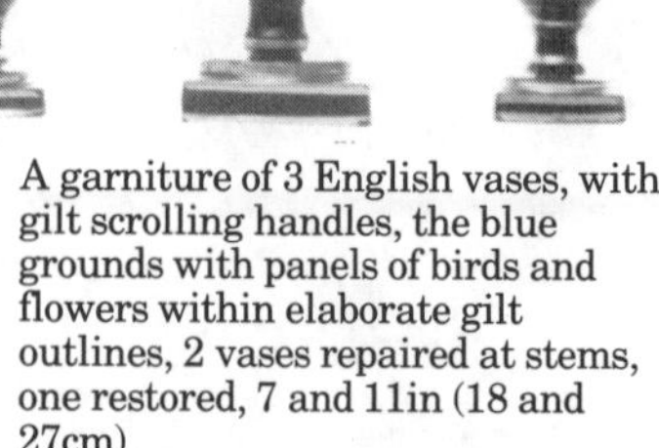

A garniture of 3 English vases, with gilt scrolling handles, the blue grounds with panels of birds and flowers within elaborate gilt outlines, 2 vases repaired at stems, one restored, 7 and 11in (18 and 27cm).
$1,000-1,200

An English vase, c1830, 8½in (21cm).
$700-800

A pair of Brussels gilt campana vases, manufactured by Frédéric Faber, painted in colours, possibly after J. B. Madou, the narrow pedestal foot on white square plinth, one rim restored, 1818-47, 12½in (32cm).
$4,000-5,000

A Copenhagen beige ground vase, the body painted within gilt cartouches, with crowned F and C monograms, the rim and foot richly gilt, blue waved line marks, c1865, 17in (43cm), fitted for electricity.
$2,500-3,000

Two English spill vases, the pink grounds reserved with panels of flowers within gilt borders, hairline cracks, some wear, 5in (14cm).
$250-350

A Copenhagen pale pink ground vase, reserved and painted within a gilt band and scroll cartouche, blue waved line mark, late 19thC, 10½in (26cm), fitted for electricity.
$900-1,000

A pair of Jacob Petit cornucopia vases, the bodies painted with flowers and moulded with leafy scrolls, with orange and gilt highlights, blue JP monogram, gilding worn, 19thC, 9in (23cm).
$700-900

. St. Clement bough pot, the bombé ides painted 'en camaieu' within uce cartouches, the scroll feet and ompartments enriched with puce ibbons and blue trailing flowers, hips to corners, one foot restuck, 1785, 10in (25cm) wide.
1,300-1,500

Jacob Petit figural vase, modelled s a lady seated, wearing a spotted ob-cap, green shawl and flower prigged gown, the pierced rococo crolling base decorated in colours nd gilt, damaged, underglaze blue ark, 11in (28cm).
550-700

pair of French gilt vases, probably imoges, painted in colours and pplied with flowers and scrolls in e Second Rococo Revival style, inor chips, marked with some npressed numbers and figures, arly 19thC, 20½in (52cm).
2,500-3,000

A pair of assembled Sèvres pattern gilt bronze mounted vases and a air of covers, the bodies decorated after Fragonard, with gilt bronze oliage moulded loose ring handles, he bodies signed Jeanne, late 9thC, 38in (98cm).
20,000-25,000

A pair of Sèvres pattern ormolu mounted vases and covers, the royal blue ground oviform bodies painted within gilt floral foliage cartouches, applied with ormolu caryatid handles, the domed covers reserved within gilt borders and with ormolu berried finials, c1865, 15in (38cm).
$4,000-5,000

A Sèvres pattern royal blue ground vase and cover, painted in colours and enriched with gilt, one handle and finial restored, imitation interlaced L marks, c1870, 20½in (52cm).
$2,500-3,000

A pair of Sèvres pattern jewelled pink ground gilt bronze mounted vases and covers, one cover restored, late 19thC, 14in (35cm).
$3,000-4,000

A pair of Sèvres pattern ormolu mounted turquoise ground vases and covers, decorated by Guillou, the waisted necks and domed covers enriched in gilding, the feet inscribed, signed, one rim repaired, late 19thC, 38in (98cm).
$14,000-20,000

A German vase modelled as an owl perched on a gnarled branch, naturalistically coloured plumage, leaves restored and chipped, blue factory marks, 12½in (32cm).
$500-550

A Sèvres pattern blue ground giltmetal mounted vase and cover, decorated by Poitevin within an oval gilt band cartouche, the reverse richly gilt on a blue ground, signed, c1900, 16in (40cm).
$5,000-6,500

A German pot pourri vase and pierced cover, painted in colours with gilt rims, finial chipped, impressed marks, 14½in (37cm).
$500-650

A pair of Meissen KPM vases, with pink and gilt pattern, one restored, 18thC, 12in (31cm).
$4,000-5,000

A pair of Dresden yellow ground vases and covers, reserved and painted within shaped cartouches, edged with black lines, the covers similarly decorated and with gilt spire finials, both vases restored, blue AR marks, c1900, 25in (64cm).
$5,500-6,500

A pair of Meissen Marcolini royal blue ground vases and covers, with gilt satyrs mask handles, the bodies enriched in gilding, the domed covers with a border of white and gilt stiff leaves in relief and with acorn finials, cover repaired, handles damaged, footrim chipped, blue crossed swords and star marks, c1800, 12½in (31.5cm).
$4,000-5,000

A pair of late Meissen vases, applied in relief with spiralling bands of forget-me-nots, blue crossed swords, incised and impressed numerals, 7½in (18cm).
$300-500

A Pottschappel vase and cover, the foot with encrusted floral garlands, small chip and crack to rim, blue crossed batons 'T' mark, 24in (61cm).
$1,000-1,200

A white glazed vase, decorated in bright colours of red, green, blue and yellow, with gilt Greek key pattern border, late 19thC, 10½in (26cm).
$400-500

Make the Most of Miller's

Every care has been taken to ensure the accuracy of descriptions and estimated valuations. Price ranges in this book reflect what one should expect to pay for a similar example. When selling one can obviously expect a figure below. This will fluctuate according to a dealer's stock, saleability at a particular time, etc. It is always advisable to approach a reputable specialist dealer or an auction house which has specialist sales

Miscellaneous

A Bow pierced stand, painted with insects and moths, the feet with moulded puce scrolls, the top with yellow, puce and blue marbling, c1762, 2½in (6cm).
$800-1,000

A Thuringian eye bath, modelled as the head of a man wearing a yellow hat, his buttoned waistcoast forms the bowl, restored, late 18thC, 3in (8cm) long.
$800-1,000

A Royal Worcester candle snuffer, date 1891, 3in (8cm).
$200-250

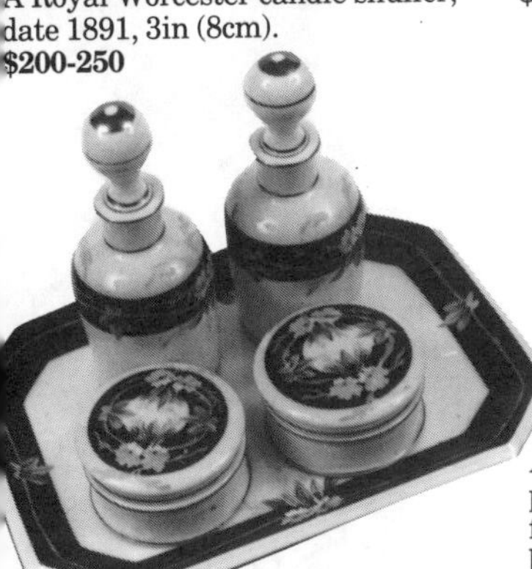

A Victorian toilet set, bottles 6in (15cm).
$130-150

A Coalport pin tray, c1885, 4in (10cm) wide.
$130-150

A Coalport horseshoe shaped pin tray, c1885, 5in (12.5cm) long.
$250-275

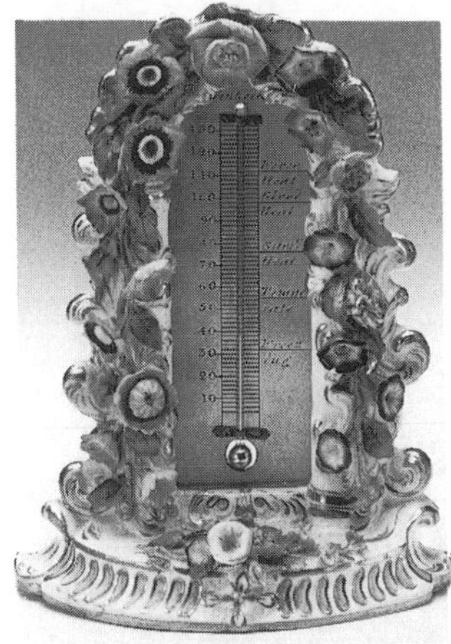

A thermometer in a Minton rococo frame, applied with flowers, on a semi-circular base, some damage, c1830, 7½in (18cm).
$275-400

A pair of Sèvres wine coolers, each painted with a colourful band of flowers and foliage, beneath a royal blue border of gilt tooled leafage and scrolls, incised numerals, printed mark and dated 1848, destination mark of Le Chateau des Tuileries, 5in (12.5cm).
$1,500-2,000

A pair of openwork wall pockets, probably Coalport, slight damage, mid-19thC, 8½in (21cm).
$550-700

A pair of Spode wine coolers, covers and liners, from the Lubbock Family Services, decorated with garlands of blue flowers, the rims and bases with white jewelled and gilt bands, the pierced covers with finials, on flower moulded gilt bases, minor damage, early 19thC, 16in (41cm).
$6,500-7,000

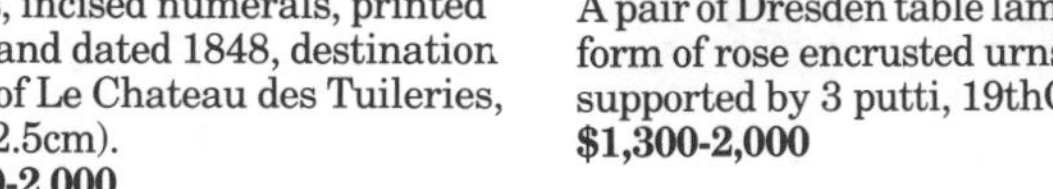

A pair of Dresden table lamps, in the form of rose encrusted urns supported by 3 putti, 19thC.
$1,300-2,000

ORIENTAL POTTERY & PORCELAIN

Bottles

A 'famille rose' bottle vase, painted with magpies among flowering peony and bush peony, Qianlong seal mark, 19thC, 21½in (54cm).
$9,500-11,000

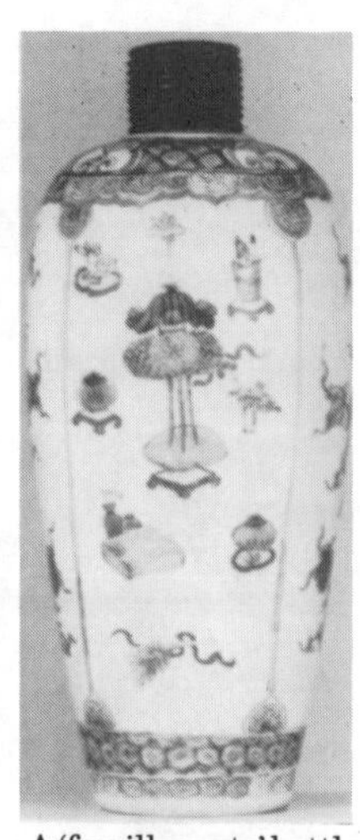

A 'famille verte' bottle, painted with alternate panels of vessels and emblems and flowering shrubs, above cell pattern at the foot and below lappets and trellis pattern at the shoulder, Kangxi, 9½in (24cm), wood cover.
$1,400-2,000

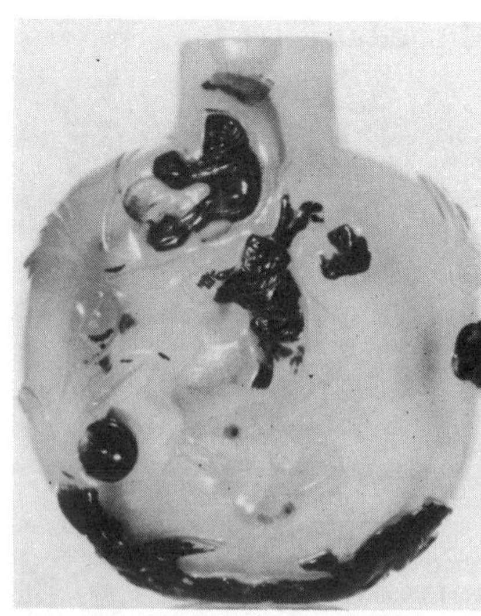

An agate flattened globular snuff bottle, carved in relief with 3 monkeys at play amongst pine and peach trees.
$500-650

A pair of Imari double gourd bottles, the upper sections with oval panels of ho-o, all on a ground of large stylised flowerheads and dense flowering shrubs, 17½in (44cm).
$5,000-6,500

A pair of Imari double gourd bottles, with spreading bulbous lower halves, painted with roundels of ho-o above flowers below flowering trees, all on grounds of scrolling chrysanthemum, rims restored, 9½in (24cm).
$1,000-1,200

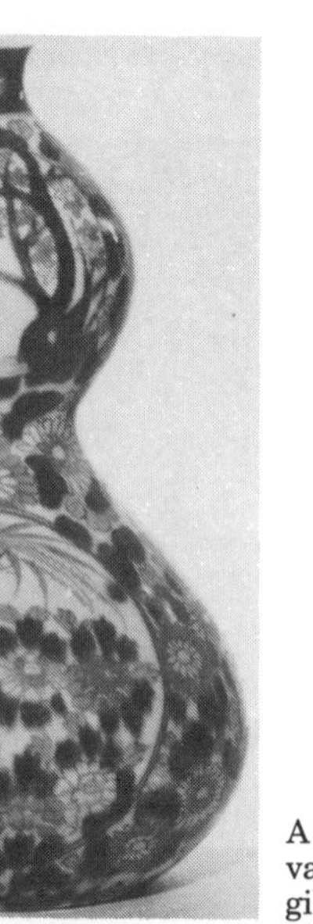

A Satsuma bottle vase, decorated in various coloured enamels and gilt, gilt rim, signed Tozan sei, 19thC, 4½in (10.5cm).
$1,400-1,500

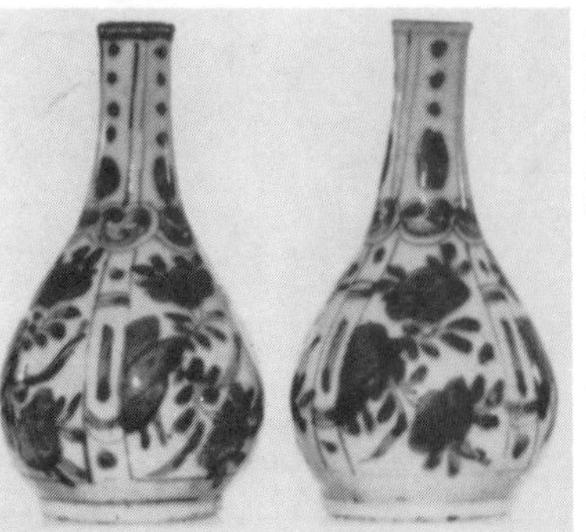

A pair of late Ming blue and white pear-shaped bottles, painted with panels of flowering shrubs below hanging tassels and lappets, Wanli, 5½in (14cm).
$1,500-2,000

A Satsuma bottle, painted with a gold ground roundel of numerous children on a ground of cranes wading in water below gilt clouds, 3½in (9cm).
$300-500

3owls

\ Sancai water pot, the glaze topping irregularly above the lattened base revealing the buff oloured body, Tang Dynasty, 2½in 6cm).
3,000-4,000

A Sultanabad deep bowl, painted in the interior with concentric blue, turquoise and black bands, 12th/13thC, 8in (20cm) diam.
$150-250

A Yuan blue and white bowl, the exterior with a band of lotus panels below a lingzhi scroll, the heavily potted sides resting on a thick solid foot, restored, c1340, 7½in (19cm) diam.
$1,500-2,500

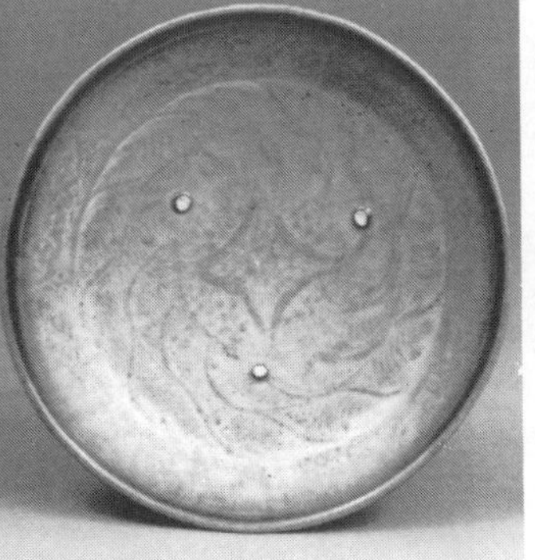

An amber glazed dish, moulded to the interior with scrolling foliage beneath a continuous floral garland in the well, all under a rich amber glaze deepening in tone at the rim and stopping unevenly above the buff pottery foot, the interior with 3 spur marks, Liao Dynasty, 5½in (13cm) diam.
$2,000-2,500

A Cantonese blue ground bowl for the Persian market, painted with panels of figures on terraces and gold ground panels of birds and flowers below a trellis pattern border, dated , 8in (20cm) diam.
$700-900

A blue and white foliate dish, painted in a pencilled style with an overall design of foaming and swirling waves, dotted with flowerheads and an unusual double headed eel-form fish to the centre, small rim chip and frits, Jiajing mark, 17thC, 6½in (16cm) diam.
$1,500-2,000

A large Swatow polychrome dish, painted to the centre below 6 ogival panels enclosing fruiting or flowering sprays on lozenge pattern grounds in the well, rim crack, 16thC, 16½in (42cm) diam.
$2,000-2,500

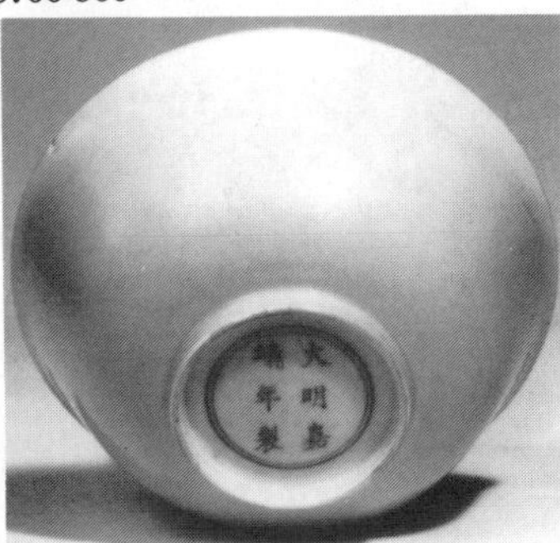

A Ming Imperial yellow glazed bowl, with slightly everted rim under a glaze of even tones thinning slightly at the rim, rim chip, glaze rubbed, encircled Jiajing six-character mark and early in the period, 8in (20cm) diam.
$8,000-11,000

A pair of 'famille rose' yellow ground bowls, painted with birds, 5in (14cm) diam.
$1,500-2,000

A Longquan celadon dish, carved to the centre, all under an even glaze of bright olive tones, 14th/15thC, 13in (33cm) diam.
$2,000-2,500

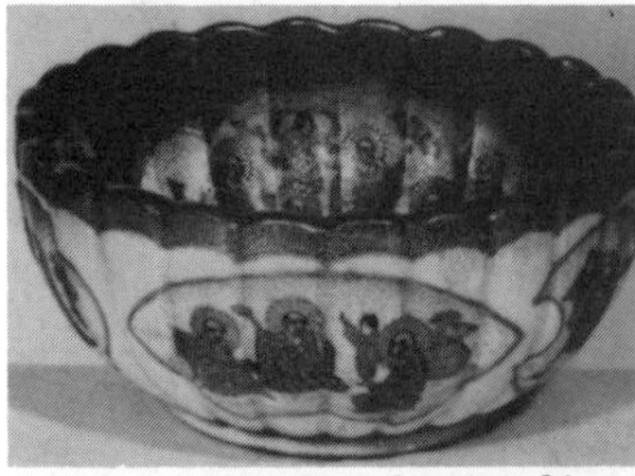

A Satsuma fluted bowl, painted in colours and richly gilt with numerous small shaped panels of seated Immortals and ladies, 5in (12cm).
$1,000-1,200

A Kakiemon deep bowl, painted with a flowering plum tree and iron red and turquoise birds in flight, the interior with a single flowerhead, late 17thC, 4in (10cm) diam.
$2,500-3,500

A pair of Arita bowls, late 17thC, 6½in (16cm) diam.
$800-1,000

A Longquan celadon bulb bowl, on 3 feet, the exterior decorated with an incised floral band, wide firing crack across base, late Ming, 11in (28cm) diam.
$550-700

An Imari saucer dish, with gilt metal stand, cracked, the porcelain late 17thC, 15½in (39cm) wide.
$1,400-1,500

A Chinese Imari barber's bowl, painted at the centre with peony and lotus, below cartouches reserved on a band of scrolling lotus at the border, the reverse with iron red flowersprays, fritted, early 18thC, 11in (28cm) diam.
$1,500-2,500

Two Imari tripod bowls, with everted foliate rims, on mask feet, the interiors with central flowersprays, c1700, 6in (15cm) diam.
$1,000-1,200

An Imari barber's bowl, painted in underglaze blue, yellow, green and iron red enamels and gilt, late 17th/early 18thC, 11in (28cm) diam
$4,000-5,000

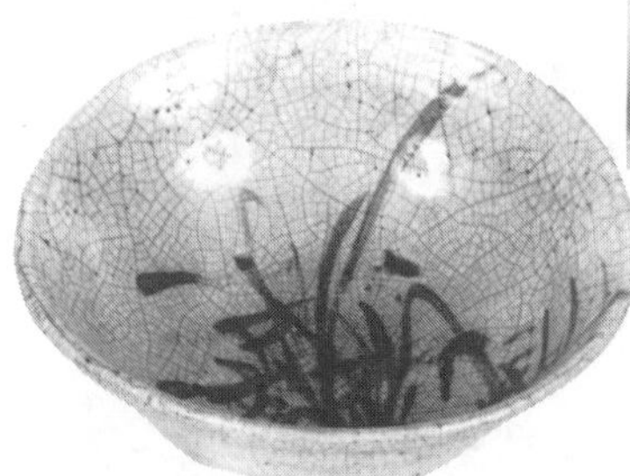

A Japanese Shino ware food bowl, 18thC, 9in (23cm) diam.
$2,500-3,000

A 'verte' Imari punchbowl, painted with sprays of chrysanthemum above a band of petals and whorl pattern at the foot, below a band of underglaze blue trellis pattern enriched with iron red and gilt, hairline crack, gilt slightly rubbed, foot rim chipped, base with square seal mark, early 18thC, 13½in (34.5cm) diam.
$2,500-3,000

A saucer dish, the exterior under a liver red glaze, the interior plain, encircled Yongzheng six-character mark and of the period, 6in (15cm) diam, with box.
$2,000-2,500

'wo late Ming blue and white ishes with everted rims, each ainted to the centre with a owerhead within panels of cell attern, swastika pattern and scale attern within rims of scrolling oliage, Tianqi, 8½in (21cm) diam.
1,000-1,200

A blue and white bowl, painted on the exterior with ruyi lappets, the interior with a central peony roundel beneath a band of trellis and swastika reserved with cartouches, rim frits, the base with square seal mark, Kangxi, 14in (35cm) diam.
$2,500-3,000

A blue and white bowl and cover, mounted with metal rings, Kangxi, 9in (23cm) diam.
$1,500-2,000

. pair of Imari bowls and covers, ainted and gilt with shishi lions, he interiors with flowersprays, the overs similarly decorated, minute hips, c1700, 6½in (16cm) diam.
1,200-1,300

A Chinese Imari dish, with pierced border, painted with peony and chrysanthemum on a cell pattern ground, hairline cracks, early 18thC, 8½in (21cm) diam.
$1,300-1,500

. Kyo-Satsuma deep bowl, painted colours and gilt, 6in (15cm) diam.
700-900

A 'famille rose' punchbowl, delicately painted with a continuous scene, restored, rim chipped, early Qianlong, 15½in (39cm) diam.
$5,000-6,500

A blue and white bowl, painted with flowers, fritted, chip restored, square seal mark to base, Kangxi, 13½in (34cm) diam.
$2,500-3,000

A Mandarin pattern 'famille rose' punchbowl, painted with figures reserved on a gilt scrolling ground above bands of cell pattern and iron red and gilt spear heads at the foot, cracked, Qianlong, 14in (35.5cm) diam.
$3,000-4,000

A Wucai bowl, painted with one ir red and one green enamelled five-clawed dragon, with Buddhis emblems at the rim, the interior with a five-clawed dragon, rim ch hairline cracks, Daoguang seal mark and of the period, 5in (15cm diam.
$1,500-2,500

A Chinese blue and white pierced flared oval basket and stand, early 19thC, stand 10in (25.5cm) diam.
$1,200-1,400

A 'famille rose' punchbowl, painted with scenes of Chinese figures, within underglaze blue floral surrounds, restoration to one side, Qianlong, 16in (40.5cm) diam.
$1,500-2,500

A 'famille rose' bowl, paint with European hunting scenes, cracks, Qianlong, 11in (28cm) diar
$1,000-1,300

A pair of Canton enamel bowls and covers, painted with continuous scenes of European figures reclining at leisure in wooded and rocky landscapes, between bands of scrolling foliage, Qianlong, 4½in (11cm) diam.
$250-300

A Chinese porcelain blue and white pouring bowl, Qianlong, c1750.
$1,400-1,500

These bowls with handles and spouts were possibly used to separate cream from milk. A rare item of salvage from the Nanking Cargo.

In the Ceramics section if there is only one measurement it usually refers to the height of the piece

Four blue and white square bowls with canted corners, variously decorated beneath broad bands at the rims, fritted, one base rim chipped, 2 cracked, late Qianlong, 10½in (25.5cm) wide.
$1,500-2,500

An Imari barber's bowl, painted with a large central vase of flowers on a table, the everted rim with buildings and flowers, restored, late 17thC, 11in (28cm).
$550-650

A 'famille rose' Rockefeller-type warming dish and cover, painted within a border of gilt tightly scrolling foliage reserved with smal panels of sepia landscapes and bird crack to base, chipped foot, one handle restored, Jiaqing, 14in (35.5cm) wide.
$2,500-3,000

. Cantonese punchbowl, painted ith panels of ladies divided by reen scroll gold ground bands, the aterior rim with a gold ground and, rim break restored, aoguang, 20in (50cm) diam.
6,500-8,000

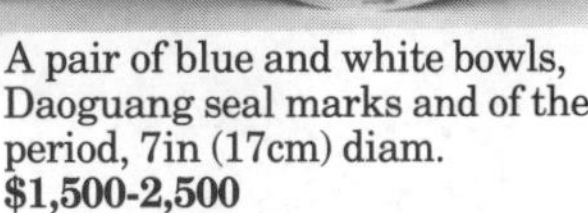

A pair of blue and white bowls, Daoguang seal marks and of the period, 7in (17cm) diam.
$1,500-2,500

A Satsuma bowl, decorated in various coloured enamels and gilt, with Yamato Takeru no Mikoto and his retainers, gilt rim, gilt rubbed and small chip, signed Choshuzan late 19thC, 9½in (24cm) diam.
$3,000-5,000

deep Imari bowl, decorated in arious coloured enamels and gilt a underglaze blue, bordered by a and of various Buddhistic nblems, the exterior with a similar and above sprays of peony, the base ith a pomegranate spray, late 9thC, 10in (25cm) diam.
2,500-4,000

A pair of 'famille rose' bowls and covers, one cover cracked, minor chips, blue enamel Xuantong six-character marks to cover and base and of the period, 8in (20cm) diam.
$2,000-2,500

A pair of 'famille rose' fish bowls, each painted with a continuous scene, the interiors with fish among aquatic plants, 18in (46cm) diam.
$2,500-3,500

Satsuma bowl, painted on the aterior with ducks beneath plum lossom and bamboo, the exterior ith flowersprays on a dark blue round, signed, 5in (12.5cm) diam.
500-800

A set of 20 small Arita blue and white bowls, enriched with gilding, 3½in (8cm) diam, two tier inscribed wood box. **$1,500-2,500**

A Cantonese flared punchbowl, painted with panels of figures on terraces and birds and butterflies among flowers on green scroll gold ground, rim chip restuck, 13in (33cm) diam.
$2,000-2,500

CHINESE PORCELAIN – VALUE POINTS

- ★ about 80% of the marks that appear on Chinese porcelain are retrospective
- ★ if a piece bears a correct, as opposed to a retrospective, reign mark then its value compared to an unmarked but comparable specimen would probably be of the magnitude of 3 to 4 times more
- ★ a piece of a known date but bearing the mark of an earlier reign would be adversely affected and could possible fetch less than an unmarked piece of the same vintage
- ★ as a rule condition will adversely affect a readily available type of ware more than a very rare or early type
- ★ original covers or lids can raise the price considerably – especially if the vessel appears more complete with it. Hence a baluster vase, for example, would be less affected than a wine ewer

A Satsuma fluted bowl, painted in blue enamel, iron red, colours and gilt on the exterior with 5 figures seated among furniture, the interior with chrysanthemum growing on a fence, rim crack, 7in (18cm) diam.
$800-1,200

A Japanese spittoon, Genroku period, late 18thC, 5in (12.5cm) diam.
$1,300-1,500

A Japanese teabowl, with bl decoration, Genroku period, (10cm) diam.
$1,000-1,300

A Satsuma pottery bowl, the interior decorated with a scene of a man and 3 ladies on a river bank, 10in (25.5cm) diam.
$250-400

Censers

An unglazed Shiwan pottery tripod censer and cover, on cabriole feet, the cover surmounted by a Buddhistic lion finial, the underside impressed with a hallmark Wunan Shitang, 19thC, 11in (27.5cm) high.
$2,500-3,500

A set of 3 'famille rose' bell-shaped mugs, each painted with a large panel of flowersprays flanked by four smaller quatrefoil floral panels, on underglaze blue cell-pattern grounds, late Qianlong, 4½ to 5½in (11 to 13cm).
$1,500-2,000

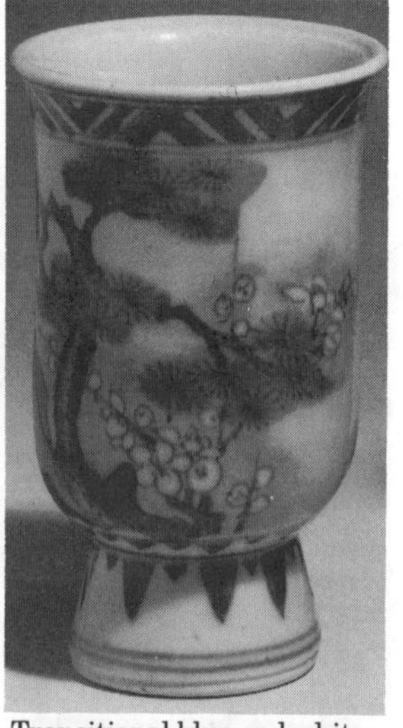

A Transitional blue and white cup, on tall spreading foot, painted with a bird in flight beside pine, prunus and bamboo, incised collector's mark, c1650, 6in (15cm).
$1,300-2,000

Cups

A Transitional blue and white stem cup, 17thC, 3½in (8.5cm).
$1,300-1,500

Two London decorated Chinese porcelain coffee cups, painted wit bouquets, flowersprays and a butterfly, showing 2 distinct style of painting, c1760.
$300-400

A Japanese cup, probably Noritak 2½in (6cm).
$15-50

Chinese Imari ormolu mounted ɪp, the porcelain early 18thC, the ıounts later, 6in (15cm).
3,000-4,000

A pair of 'famille rose' flared libation cups and stands, painted with panels of figures among furniture, on grounds of gilt scrolling foliage reserved with small pink panels, within borders of trailing flowers and bamboo, Qianlong, stands 6½in (16cm) wide.
$1,200-1,500

A pair of Doucai wine cups, painted on the exterior with phoenix among scrolling lotus, the interiors plain, Jiajing six-character marks, Kangxi/Yongzheng.
$3,000-4,000

:wers

Yingqing ewer with short spout, ɔbed handle and 2 looped handles ·low the flaring neck, the glaze at e body and mouth with iron spots, ·ng Dynasty, 4in (10cm).
,500-2,000

A late Ming blue and white kraak type kendi, painted with alternate panels of leaping horses and sprays of flowers, Wanli, 7½in (19cm).
$1,300-2,000

An Arita blue and white Kakiemon-type kendi, the neck and spout restored, c1700, 8in (20cm).
$800-1,300

A Shino ware ewer, 19thC, 4in (10cm).
$1,000-1,300

A set of 3 Imari pear-shaped jugs, covers and stand, painted with flowering shrubs, one handle repaired, one spout missing, late 17thC, 5in (12.5cm).
$2,500-3,000

TRANSITIONAL WARES

- ★ these wares are readily identifiable both by their form and by their style of decoration
- ★ forms: sleeve vases, oviform jars with domed lids, cylindrical brushpots and bottle vases are particularly common
- ★ the cobalt used is a brilliant purplish blue, rarely misfired
- ★ the ground colour is of a definite bluish tone, probably because the glaze is slightly thicker than that of the wares produced in the subsequent reigns of Kangxi and Yongzheng
- ★ the decoration is executed in a rather formal academic style, often with scholars and sages with attendants in idyllic cloud-lapped mountain landscapes
- ★ other characteristics include the horizontal 'contoured' clouds, banana plantain used to interrupt scenes, and the method of drawing grass by means of short 'V' shaped brush strokes
- ★ in addition, borders are decorated with narrow bands of scrolling foliage, so lightly incised as to be almost invisible or secret (anhua)
- ★ these pieces were rarely marked although they sometimes copied earlier Ming marks

A Hirado blue and white ewer and stopper, modelled in high relief with a dragon coiled around the neck and forming the handle and spout, the body painted with mountainous river landscapes, 10in (25.5cm).
$1,000-1,500

A late Ming blue and white kendi, painted with fish below a band of flowerheads and lappets at the shoulder, chipped and cracked, Wanli, 7in (18cm).
$3,000-4,000

A blue and white oviform wine ewer, applied at the shoulder with 4 mask loop handles above large ogival panels, painted with the 2 laughing twins, 'hehe erxian', on a scale ground, small spout chip and fritting to handles, Kangxi, 7½in (19cm), wood cover.
$1,500-2,500

Figures – Animal

A Chinese buff pottery standing figure of a camel, modelled with simulated tufted hair, some traces of pigment remaining on details, Tang Dynasty, 17in (43cm).
$5,000-5,500

A red pottery equestrian figure, traces of painted pigment, some restoration, Tang Dynasty, 12in (31cm).
$3,000-4,000

A painted buff pottery figure of a camel, some traces of pigment remaining, Tang Dynasty, 14½in (37cm).
$8,000-9,500

A rare Hirado 'Hanaike' modelled as a hawk, its feather details in underglaze blue and brown enamels, slight crazing, late 19thC 8½in (21cm).
$1,500-2,500

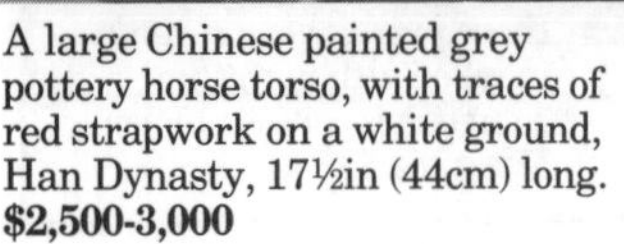

A large Chinese painted grey pottery horse torso, with traces of red strapwork on a white ground, Han Dynasty, 17½in (44cm) long.
$2,500-3,000

A Hirado blue and white candlestick, late 19thC, 7in (18cm) long.
$800-1,000

A pair of Arita goats, 19thC, 5½in (14cm) long.
$1,000-1,300

A late Kutani moulded model of a pug dog, decorated in iron red, green, blue, yellow and aubergine enamels and gilt, chips to front paws, slight crack to tail, mid-19thC, 10in (25cm) long.
$2,000-2,500

Two Cantonese candle holders, modelled as recumbent Buddhistic lions, with iron red and gilt fur markings and florally decorated saddle cloths, one candle holder missing, 4½ and 5in (11 and 12.5cm) long.
$1,500-2,000

Figures – People

A pair of late Ming blue and white figures of boys, wearing floral aprons, both on bases decorated with flowersprays, lotus leaf chipped, fritted, 17thC, 8½in (21cm).
$3,000-4,000

Two Chinese glazed ridge tiles, modelled with striding demon figures, in ochre, green and cream, Ming Dynasty, 14 and 15in (36 and 38cm).
$1,500-2,000

A pair of glazed buff pottery figures of warriors, their heads and clothes under an iridescent straw glaze with traces of red and green pigment remaining, Sui/early Tang Dynasty, 16in (41cm).
$4,000-5,500

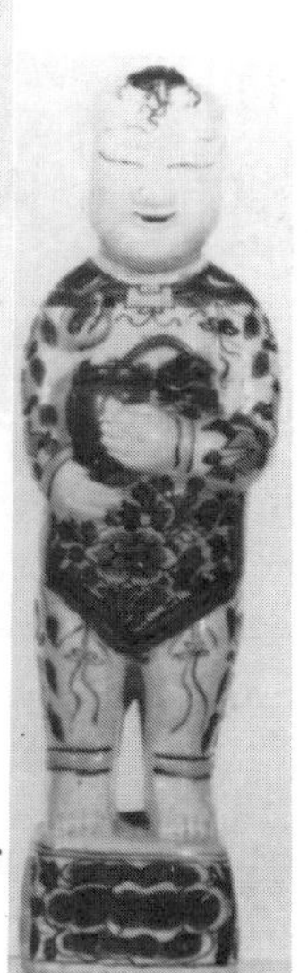

A pair of 'famille verte' figures of boys, painted with precious objects and with ruyi head collar, their hair tied in a bow at the front, minor damage, Kangxi, 11in (28cm).
$3,000-4,000

A pair of 'famille rose' moon flasks, applied on the shoulder with gilt 'kui' handles, the tall foot with a band of trellis pattern, 19thC, 11½in (29cm).
$2,000-2,500

Flatware

Three Ming blue and white dishes, with birds and foliage within panelled borders, repaired, 14 and 18in (35.5 and 46cm).
$1,200-1,300

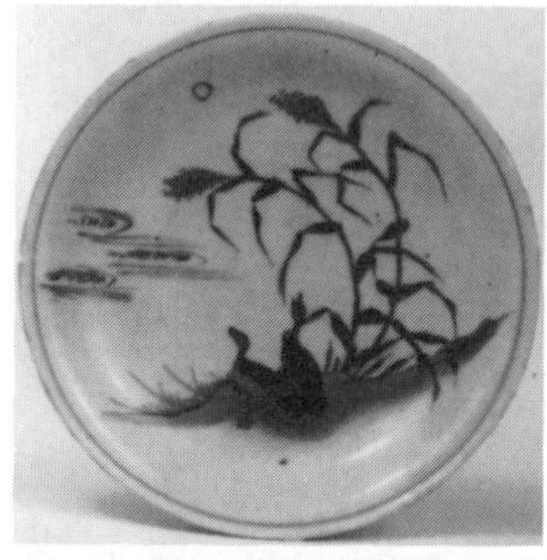

A pair of late Ming blue and white saucer dishes, each decorated with geese beneath grasses on a river bank, fritted, Chongzheng, 6in (15cm) diam.
$1,300-1,500

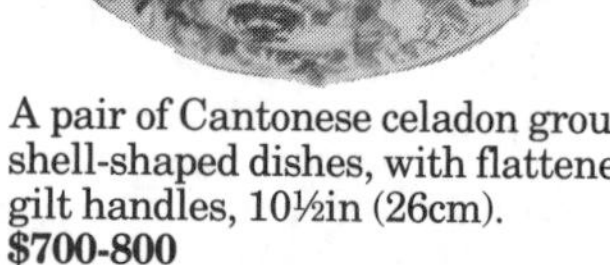

A pair of Cantonese celadon groun shell-shaped dishes, with flattened gilt handles, 10½in (26cm).
$700-800

A late Ming blue and white kraak deep dish, painted with birds below lotus on a river bank, the border with alternate panels of flowersprays and emblems, Wanli, 11½in (29cm).
$1,200-1,300

A late Ming blue and white dish, painted within a well of trailing foliage, the border with alternate panels of travellers in landscapes and stylised foliage, minor frits, c1630, 14in (35.5cm) diam.
$3,000-4,000

A late Ming blue and white saucer dish, painted with a central rounde of a vase, the border with butterflies in flight among flowering and fruiting branches, fritted, Xuande mark, Wanli, 11in (28cm).
$1,000-1,300

An Arita dish, modelled in the form of an 'uchiwa', decorated in various coloured enamels and gilt on underglaze blue, the reverse with scrolling foliage, Chenghua six-character mark, early 18thC, 7½in (19cm) wide.
$4,000-5,000

A late Ming blue and white 'kraak porselein' dish, painted in vivid blue tones at the centre, within a band of trellis and cell pattern divided by half flowerheads, the well decorated with quatrefoil lappets of flowers and fruit below the foliate rim, the exterior with similar lappets, fritted, Wanli, 18in (45cm) diam.
$6,500-7,000

late Ming blue and white 'kraak ›rselein' dish, fritted, Wanli, 14in ›5.5cm) diam.
2,000-2,500

A Transitional blue and white saucer dish, painted with a ferocious 'qilin' breathing flames beside plantain, the exterior plain, the base with four-character 'yutang jiaqi' mark, fine vessel for the jade hall, c1650, 14in (35cm) diam.
$1,400-2,000

A 'famille verte' dish, painted with chrysanthemum issuing from green rockwork within a cell pattern border reserved with panels of emblems, fritted, small cracks, Kangxi, 14½in (37cm) diam.
$1,500-2,000

ive late Ming blue and white raak' deep plates, each painted ariously to the centres, minor ıips, Wanli, 8½in (21cm) diam.
,000-1,300

A large Chinese blue and white saucer dish, with slightly flared rim painted, chipped, Kangxi, 15½in (40cm).
$800-1,000

A late Ming blue and white 'kraak porselein' dish, fritted and cracked, c1620, 18½in (47cm) diam.
$3,000-5,000

'famille verte' dish, with a pierced bbon border, painted within a rim trellis pattern, hairline crack, angxi, 12½in (32cm) diam.
,000-4,000

An Arita blue and white dish, in Kakiemon style, decorated in the centre with cranes bordered by branches of plum, pine and bamboo, the exterior with scrolling flowerheads and foliage, late 17thC, 8in (20cm) diam.
$1,500-2,000

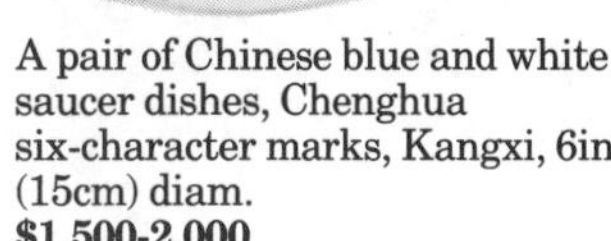

A pair of Chinese blue and white saucer dishes, Chenghua six-character marks, Kangxi, 6in (15cm) diam.
$1,500-2,000

A pair of 'famille verte' deep plates, minor frits, Kangxi, 8½in (21cm) diam.
$800-1,200

A blue and white dish, painted at the centre and reserved on a key pattern ground within a foliate rim, fritted, Kangxi six-character mark and of the period, 13½in (34.5cm) diam.
$3,500-4,000

A set of 4 Chinese blue and white deep dishes, with everted rims painted to the centres with sprays of finger citrus, within borders of further fruit sprays, Kangxi, 7½in (19cm).
$1,500-2,500

An Arita blue and white 'kraak' style charger, the central rounde containing branches of pomegranates surrounded by alternate panels of Buddhistic emblems and stylised flowerhead and foliage, linked by narrower panels of a single flowerhead, lat 17thC, 16½in (41cm) diam.
$2,500-3,000

A blue and white saucer dish, Kangxi, with a commendation mark, 9½in (24cm) diam.
$800-1,000

A 'famille verte' plate, Kangxi, 9in (23cm) diam.
$500-650

A 'famille verte' dish, painted in pencil underglaze blue to the cent with chrysanthemum sprays belo enamelled flower panels, on an ir red and gilt flowerhead band at th well and flowersprays at the borde Kangxi, 15in (38cm) diam.
$3,000-4,000

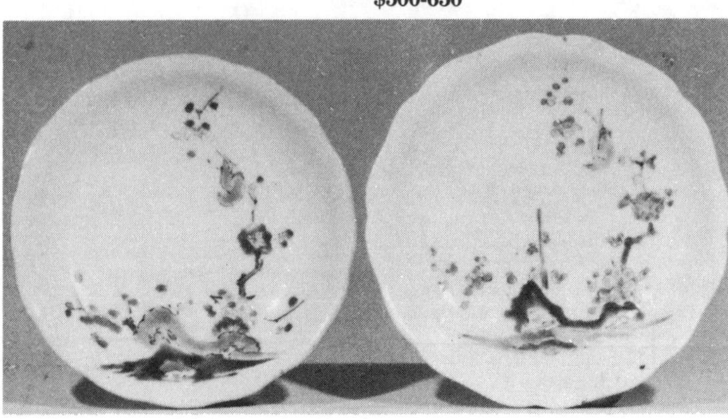

A set of 5 Kakiemon foliate dishes each painted in typical enamels with a bird perched in a plum tree above blue and green rockwork, damaged, late 17thC, 4½in (11cm) diam.
$2,500-3,000

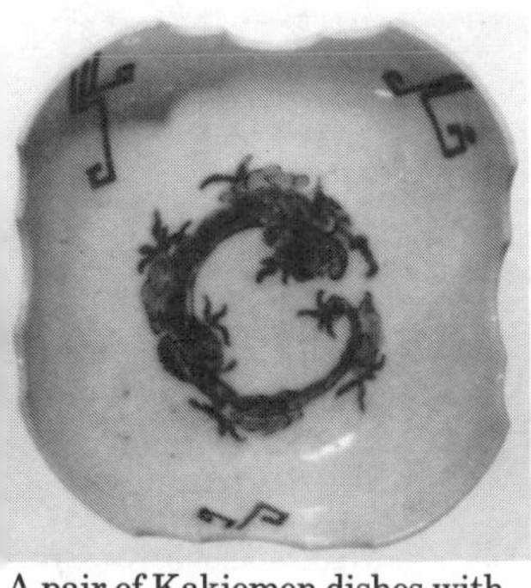

A pair of Kakiemon dishes with foliate rims, decorated in iron red, green, yellow, blue and black enamels with a dragon coiled beneath sheets of stylised lightning, ring feet, one with slight chip to rim, late 17thC, 3½in (8.5cm) wide.
$1,500-2,000

A pair of Arita blue and white saucer dishes, in the Kakiemon style, Fuku marks, late 17thC, 6in (15cm) diam.
$2,000-2,500

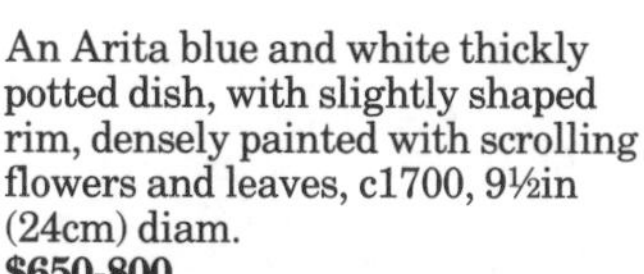

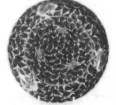

An Arita blue and white thickly potted dish, with slightly shaped rim, densely painted with scrolling flowers and leaves, c1700, 9½in (24cm) diam.
$650-800

A Chinese Imari charger, the broad rim with gold, iron red and blue chrysanthemum and peony decoration, 18thC, 14in (35.5cm) diam.
$550-700

A blue and white bowl, pencilled at the centre with scholars before pavilion on a terrace, rim slightly polished, seal mark on base, 18thC, 15½in (39cm) diam.
$2,500-3,000

A Chinese Imari shallow bowl, painted within a border of blue and gilt tightly scrolling foliage, early 18thC, 10½in (26cm) wide.
$2,000-2,500

Two 'famille rose' meat dishes, painted with bouquets of flowers within iron red and gilt spearhead wells and rims, the borders with flowersprays, Qianlong, 10 and 12in (25.5 and 30.5cm) wide.
$3,000-4,000

An Arita blue and white painted dish, small rim chip, Fuku mark, late 17thC, 8in (20cm) diam.
$650-1,000

A pair of Arita foliate rimmed blue and white dishes, minor chip, late 17thC, 11in (27cm) diam.
$3,000-4,000

A blue and white armorial dish, painted at the centre with a gilt coat-of-arms with a sepia squirrel beneath a coronet, Qianlong, c1745, 15in (38.5cm) wide.
$6,500-8,000

The arms are those of Sichterman, the family of the Dutch Governor of Bengal between 1734 and 1744. These arms with a squirrel have often been confused with the arms of the French family Foucquet whose name was close to the old French word 'fouquet' or squirrel.

A Chinese export meat dish, painted 'en grisaille' and gilt with a vase among flowers and emblems within 4 flowersprays and a gilt spearhead rim, Qianlong, 16in (41cm) wide.
$800-1,000

A set of 4 'famille rose' peacock pattern plates, each painted with peacocks perched among flowering chrysanthemum and rockwork, cracked and chipped, Qianlong, 9in (23cm).
$1,500-2,500

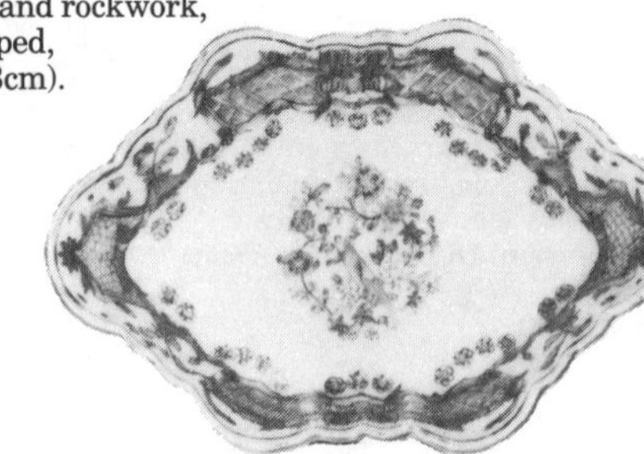

A 'famille rose' plate, painted with ducks swimming among water plants, the border with the 8 Immortals with attributes among breaking waves, Qianlong, 9in (23cm) diam.
$800-1,000

A pair of 'famille rose' fluted spoon trays, painted with central medallions of exotic birds and flowers within borders of feathers and flowersprays, one with star crack, Qianlong, 5in (12.5cm) wide.
$700-800

A 'famille rose' armorial dish, painted at the centre with a coat-of-arms surmounted by a crest within a band of underglaze blue cell pattern at the well and Fitzhugh-pattern at the shaped border, slightly fritted, Qianlong, c1790, 16½in (41.5cm) wide.
$2,500-3,000

The arms are those of Canning.

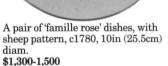

A pair of 'famille rose' dishes, with sheep pattern, c1780, 10in (25.5cm) diam.
$1,300-1,500

A 'famille rose' plate, painted with a central scene of the Czar's visit to Beijing, damaged, Qianlong, 15½in (39cm).
$500-650

A Chinese blue and white meat dish, painted within a cell pattern border reserved with panels of flowers, and later decorated iron red and gilt, small rim chips, one restored, Qianlong, 15in (38cm) wide.
$700-900

An Arita blue and white dish, boldly decorated with sprays of tree peony issuing from swirling waters beneath cumulus clouds, late 18thC, 9in (23cm) diam.
$2,500-3,500

A 'famille rose' dish, painted and gilt with a central scene within a gilt spearhead border and peony sprays to the rim, Qianlong, 15in (38cm) wide.
$1,200-1,300

A pair of 'famille rose' meat dishes, painted within underglaze blue butterfly, cell-pattern and floral borders and iron red and gilt rims, Qianlong, 13¼in (34cm) wide.
$3,000-4,000

A 'famille rose' European subject dish, painted with a lady wearing puce dress with green bodice and a yellow wrap, and a boy in an orange coat, blue breeches and white leggings, c1820, 15in (38cm) wide.
$2,500-3,000

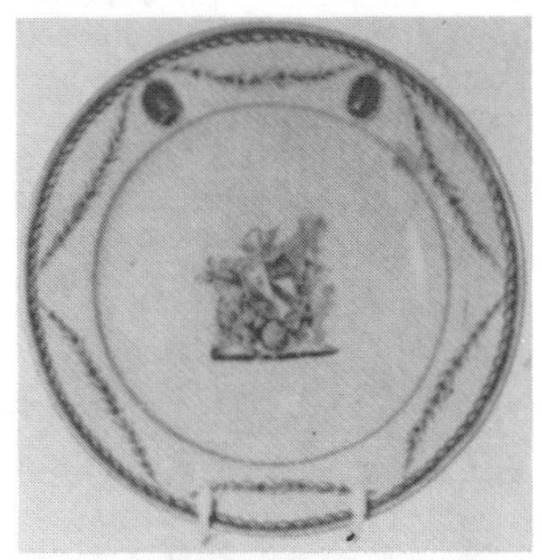

A set of 5 'famille rose' armorial plates, 2 cracked, Jiaqing, 7½in (19cm).
$1,500-2,500

A 'famille rose' Rockefeller-pattern dish, painted at the centre with a lady and a child peering out of the window watching a bearded gentleman leading a camel along a river bank, the camel with a banner, within a band of sepia trellis enriched with bird cartouches at the well, the curved border with further sepia cartouches on a rich gilt scrolling ground, rim repaired, c1800, 10in (25cm) diam.
$650-1,300

It appears from the large full beard and form of dress that the figure is a Middle Eastern, possibly Persian, quack advertising his medicinal services.

A pair of 'famille rose' soup plates, chipped, Daoguang, 10in (25cm).
$800-1,000

A large Imari dish, decorated in iron red enamel and gilt on underglaze blue, slight chip restored, late 19thC, 17in (43cm) wide.
$2,500-3,000

A Satsuma charger, decorated in various coloured enamels and gilt, with archers, warriors, standard bearers and horsemen in battle, a central roundel containing a 'kikugata' emblem bordered by a band of lappets, the border similarly decorated, late 19thC, 22½in (57cm).
$7,000-9,000

A Kinkozan dish, decorated in various coloured enamels and gilt on a deep blue ground, signed and impressed mark Kinkozan zo, painter's mark Hosui, late 19thC, 8½in (21cm) diam.
$1,500-2,500

A Satsuma dish, decorated in various coloured enamels and gilt, with a winding 'daimyo' procession, bearing a litter, standards and other trophies, within a key pattern border, signed Fuzan, late 19thC, 7½in (18cm) diam.
$1,300-1,500

A Chinese blue and white shallow basin, painted to the centre with a standing lady among flowers, Xuande six-character mark, 18thC, 11½in (29cm) diam. **$3,000-4,000**

An Imari charger, decorated in iron red and black enamels and gilt on underglaze blue, restored, Genroku period, 21½in (55cm) diam.
$3,000-4,000

A foliate rimmed Imari dish, decorated in typical coloured enamels and gilt on underglaze blue, the central panel with 'kirin' beneath branches of cherry blossom, each corner with a ho-o roundel, minor chip to rim, late 19thC, 12in (30.5cm) wide.
$800-1,000

A Cantonese meat dish, painted and gilt with alternating figures of warriors and ladies, 19in (48cm) wide. **$1,400-1,500**

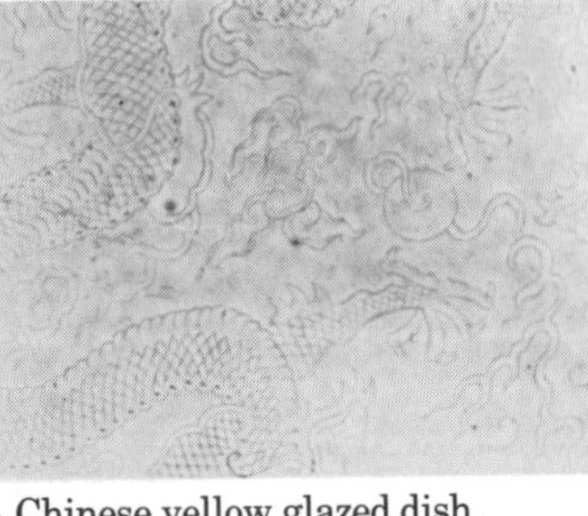

A Chinese yellow glazed dish, decorated to the centre with incised dragons chasing flaming pearls amongst cloud scrolls, Tongzhi six-character mark and of the period, 12½in (32cm) diam.
$6,500-7,000

An Imari charger, decorated in iron red enamel and gilt on underglaze blue, restored, Genroku period, 21½in (54cm) diam.
$2,500-3,000

A Cantonese meat dish, painted in the centre with figures, the border with iron red and gilt dragons chasing flaming pearls, 14½in (37cm) wide. **$800-1,000**

A Satsuma dish, painted and heavily gilt with a shaped panel bordered by a ho-o enclosing figures in a fenced garden, 12in (30.5cm) diam.
$1,300-1,500

A set of 5 Japanese Nabeshima-style saucer dishes, with combed foot rims, painted in underglaze blue, green and yellow enamels and iron red with sprays of daisies, 8in (20cm) diam.
$800-1,000

An Imari colander and tray, both decorated in typical coloured enamels and gilt on underglaze blue, tray restored, the tray with Ming six-character mark, Genroku period, colander 10in (25cm) diam.
$4,000-5,000

A set of 12 Kutani plates, painted and gilt with central scenes of ladies at leisure, within borders of floral, ho-o and geometric roundels among cloud scrolls, 3 damaged, 9½in (24cm) diam.
$1,300-1,500

A Chinese blue and white saucer dish, painted to the interior with scrolling lotus, small rim chips, Daoguang seal mark and of the period, 8in (20cm).
$500-650

An Arita Imari plate, late 17thC, 9in (23cm) diam.
$300-400

Jardinières

A 'rose/verte' jardinière, the interior painted with iron red fish among water plants, 19in (48cm) diam.
$1,000-1,200

A blue and white low jardinière, painted with a band of scrolling lotus between pendent dot lappets at the foot and key pattern at the rim, 18thC, 21in (53cm) diam.
$5,000-8,000

A 'famille verte' jardinière, painted with 4 panels of warriors and an audience scene, all reserved on a dense scrolling foliage ground enriched with flowerheads and butterflies above a band of iron red stiff lappets at the foot, beneath a 'ruyi' collar and a band of key pattern below the rim, 19thC, 21½in (54cm) diam, wood stand.
$5,000-6,500

A blue and white jardinière, base pierced, Kangxi, 9in (23cm) diam.
$1,400-2,000

A Satsuma pottery globular jardinière and stand, painted in colours and gilt, with moulded green leaves around the foot rim, 39½in (100cm) high.
$1,400-2,000

A pair of blue and white jardinières, painted on the exterior in mirror image with scholars and young boys, above a band of stiff lappets at the foot and below a 'ruyi' collar, the flat rim with a continuous band of scrolling foliage, fritted, one base restored, 19thC, 18½in (47cm) high, wood stands.
$5,000-6,500

Jars

A green glazed impressed jar, the top half covered with an olive green glaze stopping just above the mid-body, Zhou Dynasty, 15½in (39cm) wide.
$5,000-6,500

A Ming Fahua baluster jar, moulded in a cloisonné technique, painted predominantly in yellow and turquoise on a deep blue ground, the interior green glazed, neck restored, foot replacement, c1500, 13in (32.5cm) high, wood stand.
$5,000-5,500

A Wucai baluster jar and domed cover with knop finial, painted with a continuous scene of boys at play, repaired, Transitional, 17in (43cm).
$1,200-1,300

A late Ming blue and white jar, painted with a bird perched on rock between peony and chrysanthemum, above a band of whorl pattern, Wanli, 8½in (21.5cm).
$1,400-2,000

A Chinese blue and white baluster jar, painted with birds in flight, cracks, glaze chip to shoulder, early Kangxi, later replacement cover, 19½in (49cm).
$5,000-5,500

A Transitional blue and white oviform jar, rim interior with shallow chip, c1650, 9½in (24cm).
$5,000-6,500

A Chinese blue and white oviform jar and domed cover, Yuan/early Ming Dynasty, 5½in (14cm).
$650-1,000

A Ming blue and white baluster jar, painted with flowers below 'ruyi' heads and key-pattern at the shoulder and short neck, 16thC, 4¼in (11cm) high.
$800-1,000

A Transitional blue and white oviform jar, painted with two 'qilins' beside rockwork and plaintain on a terrace, rim crack, c1643, 10in (25cm) high, wood cover.
$3,000-4,000

A blue and white ginger jar and cover, with a cracked ice pattern ground enriched with prunus heads between bands of fret pattern at the foot and on the shoulder, the cover similarly decorated, Kangxi, 12in (30.5cm).
$1,500-2,500

A Japanese jar and cover, with lion mask ring handles, some pitting and finial missing, 8½in (21cm).
$500-650

A Chinese Imari jar and cover, painted with a pheasant among flowering shrubs and pierced rockwork in a fenced garden, Qianlong, 9in (23cm).
$2,500-3,000

A blue and white oviform jar, decorated in vivid blue tones, foot with glaze flake, Kangxi, 7½in (19cm), wood cover.
$2,500-3,000

A pair of Chinese blue and white oviform jars and domed covers, painted with figures standing in continuous rocky landscapes below bands of leaves at the shoulders, Yuan/early Ming Dynasty, 5in (13cm).
$1,000-1,200

A 'famille rose' jar, painted with phoenix among flowering shrubs issuing from pierced blue rockwork, Qianlong, 8in (20cm), with gilt metal tripod stand and pierced wood jade mounted cover.
$1,200-1,300

Two late Ming blue and white oviform jars, one painted with scrolling flowers and leaves below 'ruyi' heads at the shoulder, the other with flowering shrubs and grasses, Wanli, 5 and 5½in (13 and 14cm).
$800-1,000

An underglaze copper red and blue celadon ground jar of oviform shape, painted with peach sprays, the glaze pooling in places, some surface scratching, Kangxi, 6½in (16.5cm).
$1,500-2,500

A 'famille verte' tea caddy, painted on 2 sides with cockerels, the smaller sides with butterflies and flowers, Kangxi, 3in (7.5cm), white metal cover.
$800-1,000

A pair of Chinese blue and white jars and covers, decorated in inky cobalt, Kangxi, 12in (30.5cm).
$6,500-8,000

A Chinese blue and white square tea jar, painted with pagodas and boats in a rocky wooded river landscape, cracked, c1800, 12½in (32cm) high.
$2,000-2,500

A Chinese Imari oviform jar, painted with pheasants among flowering shrubs and rockwork in a fenced garden, Qianlong, 8½in (21cm).
$1,300-1,400

A 'famille rose' pale blue ground oviform jar and domed cover, painted with gilt shou characters below yellow lappets to the shoulder, star crack, cover chipped, iron red Daoguang seal mark and of the period, 9½in (24cm).
$1,300-1,400

A 'famille rose' jar and domed cover, 10½in (26cm).
$1,300-1,400

An Arita polychrome oviform jar and cover, with shishi and ball finial, painted with scenes above black and iron red ground panels of scrolling foliage at the foot and iron red key pattern on the neck and cover rim, body cracks, 37in (94cm).
$5,000-5,500

A Fukagawa cylindrical jar and flat cover, painted with figures below hanging leaves on a black ground, with bamboo finial, 6½in (16cm).
$2,500-3,000

A pair of Chinese blue and white jars and domed covers, painted with panels of figures at leisure, 12½in (32cm). **$2,500-3,000**

Chinese blue and white Fitzhugh ıttern soup tureen, domed cover ıd stand, with flowerhead and leaf nial and entwined strap handles, ıriched with gilding, inner cover ·stored, c1800, the stand 14in ·5.5cm) wide. **$2,500-3,000**

∖ pair of Cantonese celadon ground ·viform vases with gilt Buddhistic ·ion handles, painted in underglaze ›lue, iron red and gilt, and moulded n low relief, 24½in (62cm). **;3,000-4,000**

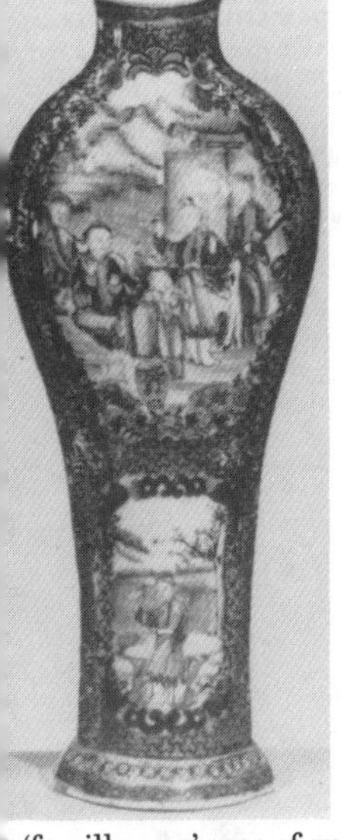

∖ 'famille rose' vase of quatrefoil ross section, painted with panels of igures in river landscapes within nderglaze blue floral surrounds, on ı ground of iron red, black and gilt 7-pattern, Qianlong, 11in (28cm). **;550-650**

Vases

A Chinese red pottery hu-shaped vase, with ring handles and bands of horizontal ribbing, under a thin pale greenish yellow degraded glaze, Han Dynasty, 13½in (34cm). **$1,000-1,300**

A Chinese blue and white beaker vase, cracked, Transitional 18in (45.5cm). **$2,500-3,000**

A green glazed red pottery baluster vase, with some iridescence, slight chips, Han Dynasty, 18½in (47.5cm). **$1,500-2,500**

A moulded Yingqing vase and integral stand, Yuan Dynasty, 1280-1367 AD. **$1,200-1,500**

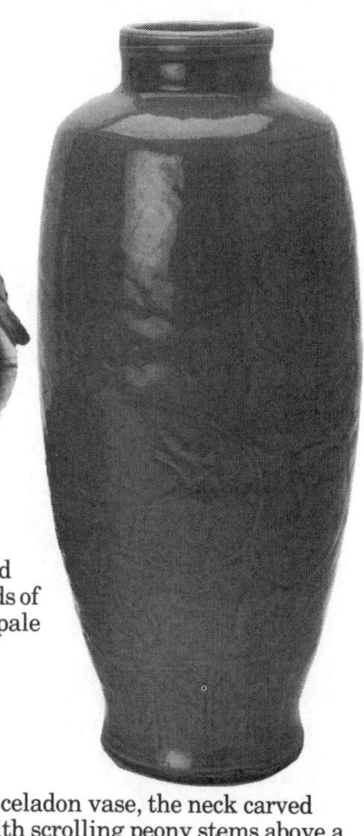

A celadon vase, the neck carved with scrolling peony stems above a band of stiff leaves, glaze cracks, firing crack in base, 15th/16thC, 10½in (26cm). **$1,200-1,500**

A Satsuma miniature conical two-handled tripod vase, painted in colours and gilt with figures in a continuous mountainous wooded landscape, 3½in (9cm). **$500-550**

Make the most of Miller's

Unless otherwise stated, any description which refers to 'a set' or 'a pair' includes a valuation for the entire set or the pair, even though the illustration may show only a single item

A late Ming blue and white 'kraak' bottle, painted with panels of leaping horses and flowering shrubs below a band of lappets, glaze fault, Wanli, 11in (28cm).
$1,500-2,000

A pair of Cantonese rouleau vases, painted in gilt with shaped panels of figures on terraces and birds and butterflies, on a green gold scroll ground, slight damage, 18in (45.5cm). **$2,500-3,000**

An Arita blue, white and biscuit vase, painted with flowers reserve on an iron oxide washed biscuit ground, Persian silver neck and cover with niello decoration, late 17thC, 10in (25cm).
$1,000-1,200

A Ming double gourd vase, painted in underglaze blue with sprays of camellia and peony, body cracks, 16thC, the red enamel probably later, 13½in (35cm).
$1,500-2,500

A Wucai vase, painted with a band of shaped panels of buildings in mountainous river landscapes, on an iron red wave pattern ground, Transitional, 13½in (34cm).
$800-1,000

A blue and white five-piece garniture, painted with audience scenes in river landcapes, the cove surmounted with Buddhistic lion finials, some restoration, four-character Kangxi marks, 19thC, baluster vases 15in (38cm).
$6,500-8,000

A Shoki Imari underglaze blue bottle vase, with everted rim, decorated with a hatched design below double lines, late 17thC, 7in (18cm).
$1,500-2,500

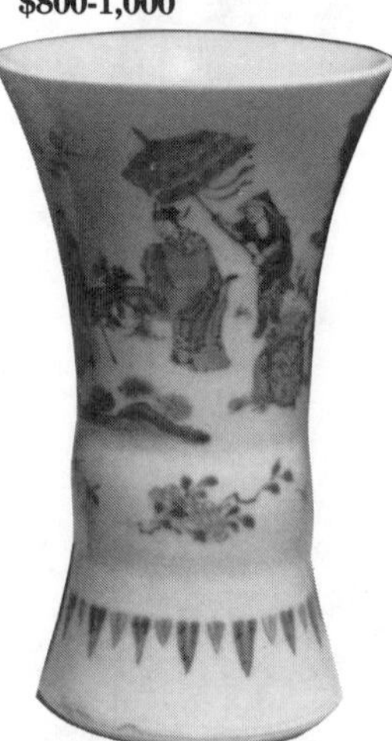

A Transitional blue and white beaker vase, rim polished, foot rim fritted, c1650, 8½in (22cm).
$1,300-2,000

A blue and white presentation vase damaged, Kangxi, 25½in (65cm).
$1,400-2,000

A 'famille verte' rouleau vase, painted with a continuous scene on a trellis pattern ground, gilt metal mounted, the cover with a recumbent elephant finial, body cracked, the porcelain Kangxi, the gilt metal mounts probably Qianlong, 17in (43cm).
$2,500-3,000

A Transitional blue and white vase, rim frit, c1650, 8in (20cm).
$2,000-2,500

An early Kangxi iron glazed monochrome vase, 7in (17.5cm).
$700-900

A powder blue glazed rouleau vase, gilt to one side, the other with a faint inscription below emblem cartouches at the shoulder and 'shou' characters dividing swastikas at the neck, Kangxi, 18in (45cm).
$2,500-3,000

A pair of blue and white moulded vases, painted with flowers on a diaper ground, between moulded lotus leaves at the shoulder, one cracked, some fritting, Kangxi, 10½in (26cm).
$2,000-2,500

A blue and white vase, Kangxi, 9½in (24cm).
$2,000-2,500

A Chinese powder blue slender vase, decorated and gilt with shaped panels, 18thC, 18in (45.5cm).
$1,500-2,500

A blue and white yanyan vase, base pierced, Kangxi, 18in (45cm).
$1,000-1,200

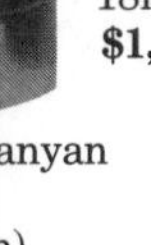

A Chinese black monochrome vase, 18thC, 9in (23cm).
$650-1,000

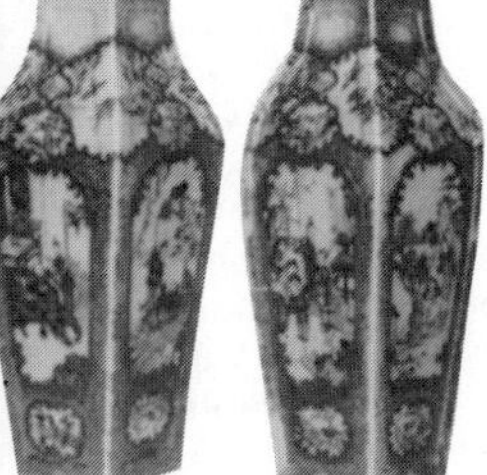

A pair of 'famille rose' square baluster vases, painted within iron red and gilt rococo borders on a gilt floral ground above and below smaller cartouches in iron red, sepia and 'grisaille' of birds and landscapes, chipped, gilt rubbed, Qianlong, 10½in (26cm).
$2,500-3,000

A blue and white baluster vase and cover, painted with flowers below blue ground lappets at the shoulder, heightened with gilding, Qianlong, 16½in (42cm).
$2,500-3,000

A 'famille verte' vase, fritted, Kangxi six-character mark, 20½in (51cm). **$2,500-3,000**

A pair of Chinese blue and white baluster vases, drawn with shaped panels of leafy branches above rockwork, the porcelain Kangxi, the silver Sheffield 1897, 9½in (24cm). **$2,500-3,500**

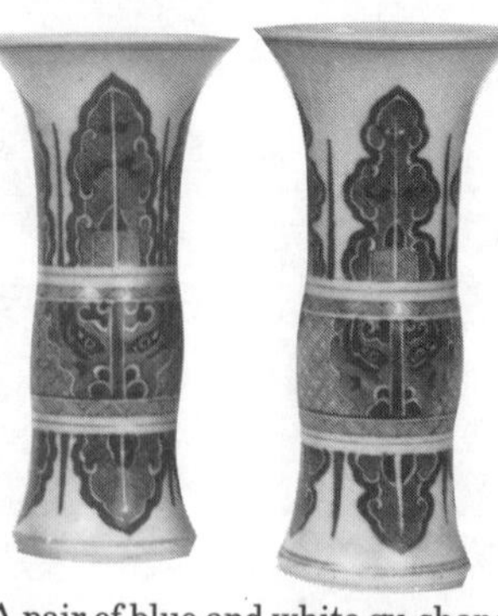

A pair of blue and white gu-shaped beaker vases, painted on the central section with 2 'taotie' masks on a trellis pattern ground, one rim with hairline crack, Kangxi, 10in (25.5cm). **$2,500-3,000**

A blue and white vase Kangxi, 6in (15cm). **$650-800**

A 'famille rose' beaker vase, decorated on a ground of gilt scrolling foliage, rim fritted, base chip, Qianlong, 16½in (42cm). **$2,500-3,000**

A blue glazed hexafoil baluster vase, applied at either side of the long neck with 'kui' handles, all under a deep blue glaze thinning at the extremities, 18th/19thC, 16in (41cm). **$1,300-1,500**

A 'famille rose' pear-shaped vase, painted with deer, applied at either side of the tapering neck with iron red and gilt scroll handles, Qianlong seal mark, 19thC, 18in (45.5cm). **$9,500-13,000**

A Canton 'famille rose' vase, the sides decorated in enamels and gilt, the shoulders applied with pairs of 'chilong', the neck with confronting shishi, 19thC, 32in (81cm). **$3,000-4,000**

A pair of Cantonese vases, the shoulders and necks moulded with shishi, the bodies decorated in brightly coloured enamels, the grounds with birds and flowers, one shishi fractured, 19thC, 18in (46cm). **$800-1,200**

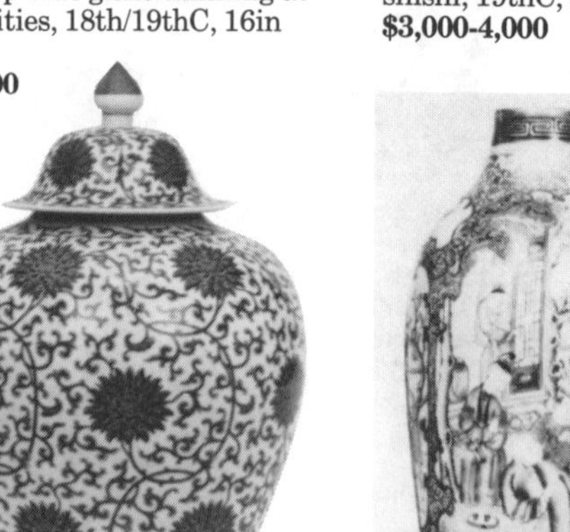

A pair of blue and white vases and covers, with knop finials, necks reduced, one with crack to rim, one cover cracked, Qianlong seal marks and of the period, 19in (48cm). **$8,000-9,500**

A pair of 'famille rose' semi-eggshell slender tapering oviform vases with narrow necks, painted with figures on grounds of gilt scrolling foliage, crack to rim, Qianlong, 8½in (21cm). **$1,200-1,400**

A pair of Chinese eggshell porcelain vases, early 20thC, 6in (15cm), in original box. **$300-500**

A pair of Chinese eggshell porcelain vases, early 20thC, 7½in (19cm). **$300-500**

A pair of Satsuma vases, with ring handles held in the claws of dragons, decorated in various coloured enamels and gilt with shaped panels, crack, other damage and signature rubbed, late 19thC, 37in (94cm). **$11,000-13,000**

An Imari oviform vase, decorated in various coloured enamels and gilt on underglaze blue, with a wide panel of ho-o birds amongst paulownia and peonies, the neck with iris sprays, restored, Genroku period, 16½in (42cm). **$3,500-4,000**

An Arita vase, decorated in various coloured enamels and gilt on underglaze blue with a continuous band of ho-o birds amongst peonies and rockwork, slight cracks, Genroku period, 12in (30cm). **$2,000-2,500**

A pair of 'famille verte' squat vases and covers, the cylindrical necks with cloud scrolls and the pierced domed covers with fruit and foliage beneath the iron red scroll finial, slightly chipped, 19thC, 19in (48cm). **$8,000-9,000**

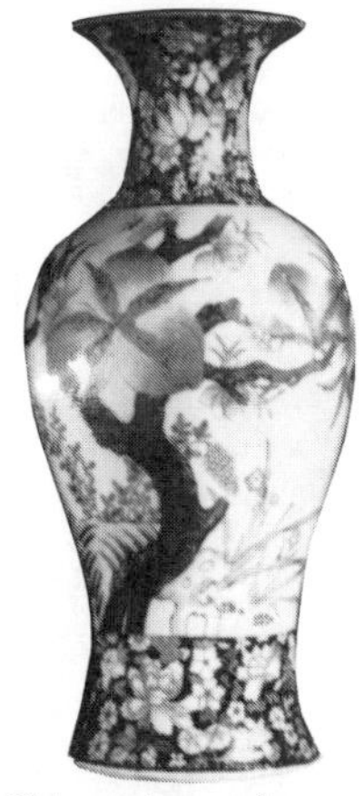

A Chinese tapered vase, painted with fruit and flowers on a black ground, 18in (45.5cm), on wood stand. **$400-500**

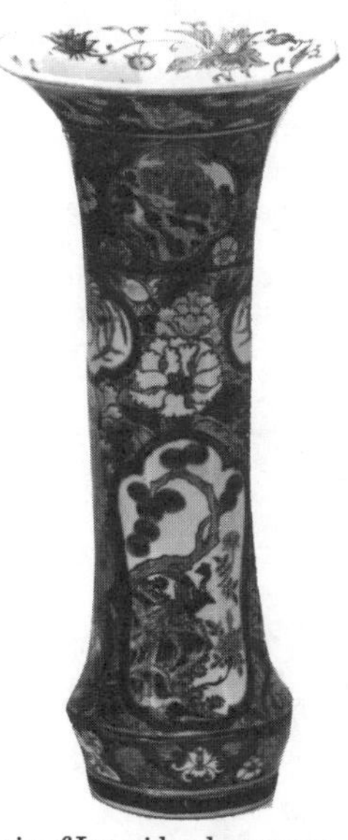

A pair of Imari beaker vases, painted in underglaze blue, iron red, green, aubergine enamels and gilt with panels of karashishi, ho-ho and other birds, on a dense 'kiku' and peony ground, both rims restored, Genroku period, 16½in (42cm). **$3,000-4,000**

An Imari vase and cover, decorated in iron red and black enamels and gilt on underglaze blue, the rim with chrysanthemum flowerheads, a scrollwork ormolu mount, the vase pierced for electricity, karashishi finial missing, Genroku period, the mount later, 23½in (59cm). **$9,000-10,000**

A pair of Cantonese vases, with gilt lion mask handles, 9in (23cm).
$1,300-1,500

A pair of Cantonese vases of quatrefoil cross-section, with gilt Buddhistic lion handles, painted on green scroll gold grounds, 1 cracked, 12in (31cm).
$1,300-2,000

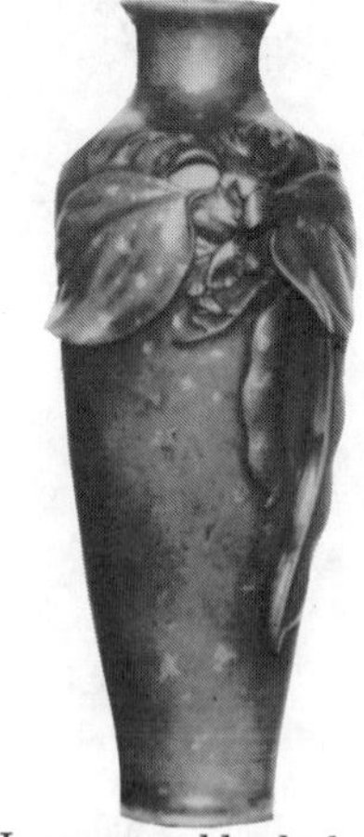

A Japanese gold splashed ovoid vase, decorated in relief with hanging bean pods, signed Yoshimasa, 10in (25.5cm).
$500-650

A pair of 'famille verte' vases, painted on each side with a warrior Immortal above yellow ground bands of scrolling foliage, 25in (63cm).
$2,500-3,000

A pair of Cantonese double gourd vases, painted with figures on green gold scroll grounds, 13in (33cm).
$1,200-1,300

A pair of Japanese cloisonné lacquered porcelain bottle vases, decorated in colours with birds amongst foliage on a brown ground, 8½in (22cm).
$500-650

A pair of Japanese Shibayama-style white metal mounted vases with flowerspray handles, the mounts with enamelled stylised flowerheads, signed on raised tablets, 4in (10cm).
$1,400-2,000

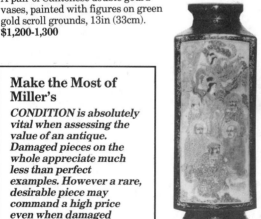

Make the Most of Miller's

CONDITION is absolutely vital when assessing the value of an antique. Damaged pieces on the whole appreciate much less than perfect examples. However a rare, desirable piece may command a high price even when damaged

A pair of Satsuma vases, painted in colours and gilt with panels of bijin and rakan on dark blue grounds enriched with gilding, 9½in (24cm).
$1,500-2,500

A pair of Kaga vases, painted in iron red, black and gilt with pheasants among flowers by a river, 15in (38cm).
$1,200-1,300

pair of Satsuma vases, painted in lours and gilt on one side with anels of ladies and children below amboo in gardens, cracked, signed hozan, 7½in (19cm).
2,000-2,500

A Satsuma vase, painted in colours and gilt on a ground of geometric designs, 4in (10cm).
$250-300

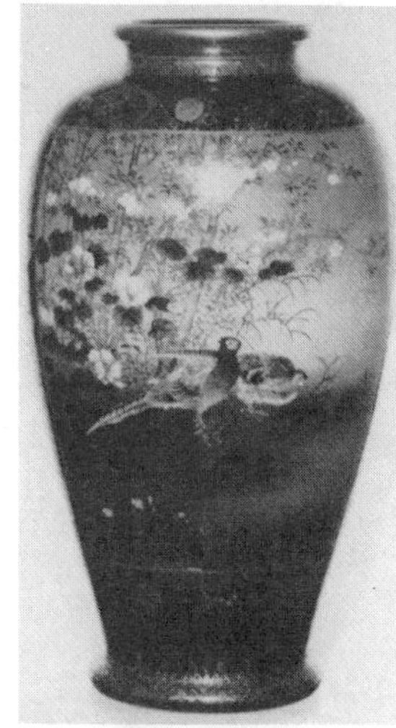

A Satsuma vase, painted on a dark blue gilt flowerhead ground and between bands of lappets, signed Kinkozan, 10½in (26cm).
$1,300-1,400

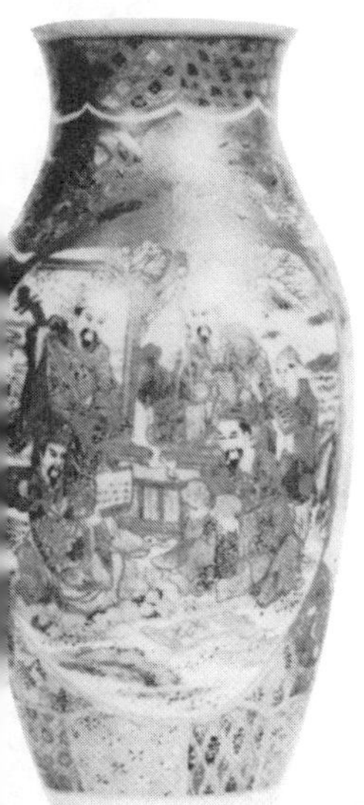

pair of Satsuma vases, inted in colours and richly lt, on dense floral and ometric grounds, 9½in 4cm).
,000-1,200

A pair of 'rose/verte' vases, with mask ring handles, 18in (45.5cm).
$1,400-1,500

A Satsuma pottery vase, with waisted neck heavily enamelled and gilt with panels of figures divided by geometric designs and flowers, 28in (71cm).
$650-700

A pair of Satsuma vases, moulded, painted and heavily gilt, signed, 9in (23cm).
$800-1,000

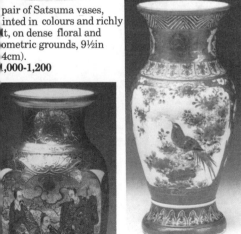

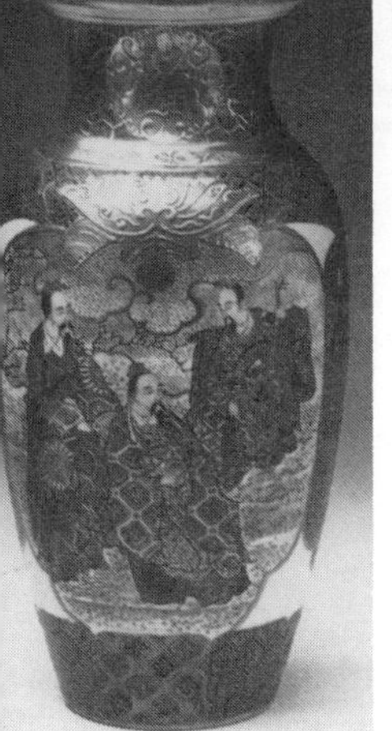

pair of Satsuma vases, painted ith figures on a brocade ground, in pical enamel colours and gold.
2,000-2,500

A pair of Kutani vases, painted with figures on one side and birds in a garden on the other, reserved on a gold decorated orange ground, 14in (35.5cm). **$1,000-1,200**

A Satsuma vase, painted with figures reserved within a narrow decorative band, the neck and foot painted with flowers and geometric designs, 4½in (12cm).
$650-800

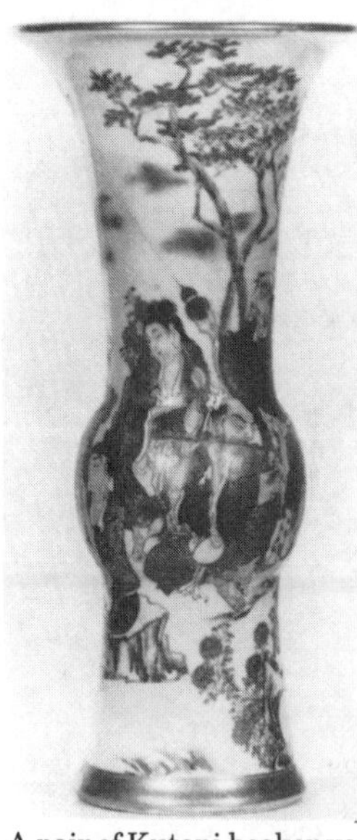

A pair of Kutani beaker vases, painted and heavily gilt with the 8 Buddhistic Immortals, one with a star cracked base, signed, 18in (45.5cm).
$2,500-3,000

A pair of Satsuma vases, with ring and tassel handles, each painted and gilt, the necks with panels of cell pattern, the rims with flowerhead bosses, both restored, 37½in (95cm), with marble inlaid wood stands. **$6,500-8,000**

A pair of Satsuma vases, 8in (20cm
$1,500-2,000

A pair of Satsuma vases, painted i colours and rich raised gilt with panels of warriors and Immortals, necks restored, 35½in (90cm).
$8,000-9,500

A pair of Cantonese vases, painted on a ground of flowerheads, fruit and butterflies between bands of lappets, all on a yellow ground, the interior with fruit sprays, some restoration, 24in (61cm).
$1,500-2,000

A pair of Satsuma vases, painted in colours and gilt on crackled cream grounds, 17in (43cm).
$4,000-5,000

A pair of 'famille rose' yellow groun beaker vases, 10½in (26cm).
$500-650

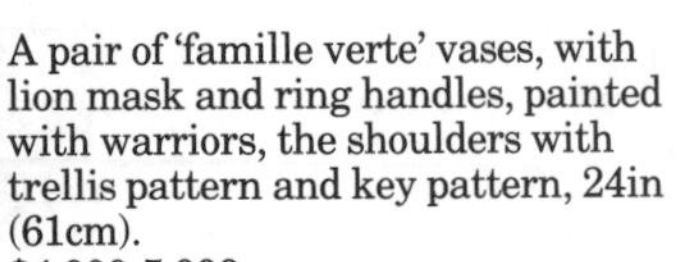

In the Ceramics section if there is only one measurement it usually refers to the height of the piece

A pair of 'famille verte' vases, with lion mask and ring handles, painted with warriors, the shoulders with trellis pattern and key pattern, 24in (61cm).
$4,000-5,000

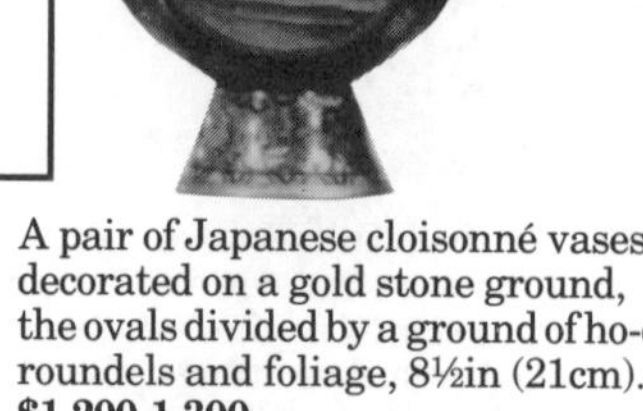

A pair of Japanese cloisonné vases, decorated on a gold stone ground, the ovals divided by a ground of ho-o roundels and foliage, 8½in (21cm).
$1,200-1,300

A pair of Cantonese vases, applied with Buddhistic lion and cub handles and gilt dragons, one riveted, 35in (89cm).
$6,500-7,000

Chinese dynasties and marks

Earlier Dynasties

Shang Yin, c.1532-1027 B.C.
Western Zhou (Chou) 1027-770 B.C.
Spring and Autumn Annals 770-480 B.C.
Warring States 484-221 B.C.
Qin (Ch'in) 221-206 B.C.
Western Han 206 BC-24 AD
Eastern Han 25-220
Three Kingdoms 221-265
Six Dynasties 265-589
Wei 386-557
Sui 589-617
Tang (T'ang) 618-906
Five Dynasties 907-960
Liao 907-1125
Sung 960-1280
Chin 1115-1260
Yüan 1280-1368

Ming Dynasty

洪武年製
Hongwu (Hung Wu)
1368-1398

永樂年製
Yongle (Yung Lo)
1403-1424

大明宣德年製
Xuande (Hsüan Té)
1426-1435

大明成化年製
Chenghua (Ch'éng Hua)
1465-1487

大明弘治年製
Hongzhi
(Hung Chih)
1488-1505)

大明正德年製
Zhengde
(Chéng Té)
1506-1521

大明嘉靖年製
Jiajing
(Chia Ching)
1522-1566

大明隆慶年製
Longqing
(Lung Ching)
1567-1572

大明萬暦年製
Wanli (Wan Li)
1573-1620

大明天啟年製
Tianqi
(Tien Chi)
1621-1627

崇禎年製
Chongzhen
(Ch'ung Chêng)
1628-1644

Qing (Ch'ing) Dynasty

大清順治年製
Shunzhi
(Shun Chih)
1644-1661

大清康熙年製
Kangxi (K'ang Hsi)
1662-1722

大清雍正年製
Yongzheng (Yung Chêng)
1723-1735

大清乾隆年製
Qianlong (Ch'ien Lung)
1736-1795'

嘉慶年製
Jiaqing (Chia Ch'ing)
1796-1820

大清道光年製
Daoguang (Tao Kuang)
1821-1850

大清咸豐年製
Xianfeng (Hsien Féng)
1851-1861

大清同治年製
Tongzhi (T'ung Chih)
1862-1874

大清光緒年製
Guangxu (Kuang Hsu)
1875-1908

大清宣統年製
Xuantong
(Hsuan T'ung)
1909-1911

洪憲年製
Hongxian
(Hung Hsien)
1916

GLASS – PRICE TRENDS

Over the past twelve months the marked increase in the price of all collectable glass has continued and, in some categories, accelerated and, whilst the present dearth of good glass coming onto the market continues, this situation is likely to remain. Having said that, this situation has brought a number of small collections of variable quality into the salerooms; quite insufficient, however, to satisfy demand.

One type of glass seldom seen on the market is Davenport. Better known for its pottery and porcelain in the 19thC, this firm made large quantities of run-of-the-mill table glass. Amongst this is a group of early 19thC glassware, mainly rummers with what appear to be acid etched decoration usually in the form of sporting activities and landscapes.

These pieces have a small etched rectangle marked 'Patent' under the base of the article, with no other mark. A small quantity appeared in the salerooms during the past year but did not go unnoticed: in one sale two goblets with very patchy decoration made £1,650. In another saleroom, where a small collection was on offer, two more goblets, or rummers, with, once again, patchy decoration made £968, whereas a ewer, a rare item, made £1,875.

Pressed glass, both clear and vitro porcelain (commonly called slag glass) continues to excite a lot of interest. Vitro porcelain has probably appreciated two- and three-fold over the past two years, however the type of decoration governs the price realised: pieces with inscriptions, nursery rhymes, etc., command high prices. In the Midlands last year, a very large private collection came onto the market. It was highly publicised, with a catalogue of its own, and some exceptional prices were realised.

Decanters are still appreciating strongly and any decanters with marked labels, Masonic decoration, etc., will easily make £500 or more at auction. Recently three fine decanters with cut spiral neck rings and engraved with the Beckford of Fonthill crest, made a hammer price of £6,000.

Early coloured glass is now very expensive and scarce as illustrated by a hammer price of £13,000 for a wine glass with blue bowl and foot and opaque twist stem. This is the only one recorded, but is probably from the same stable as similar glasses with green bowls and feet. As for colour twists, three garish wines, probably Victorian, made £1,000, £3,600 and £4,800.

As for clear glass, a reasonable cylinder knop wine glass made £3,800, and for the more ordinary examples, a good opaque twist wine glass c1760, that one could expect to get under the hammer for £70-100 two years ago, will now make about £140-200.

Continental glass hasn't appreciated as fast as English glass. A lovely Venetian gadrooned dish, c1500, with the usual enamelled dots and gilt scale decoration made £14,300. Also, a rare German 17thC amber coloured Rhine beaker, with conical bowl, three suspended rings and trailed decoration made £8,800.

R. G. Thomas

Beakers

A conical tumbler, engraved with a shepherd playing his pipe, his dog and sheep around, engraved on the reverse John and Anne Saxon, c1780, 4in (10cm).
$500-550

A North Bohemian Lithyalin beaker, attributed to Friedrich Egermann, the marbled iron red and dark blue sides cut with vertical flutes, Blottendorf, chipped, c1835, 4½in (11.5cm). **$3,000-5,000**

A North Bohemian Lithyalin beaker, from the workshop of Friedrich Egermann, in dark grey marbled glass, cut with wide flutes, Blottendorf, chips to rim, c1835, 4½in (11cm). **$1,300-1,500**

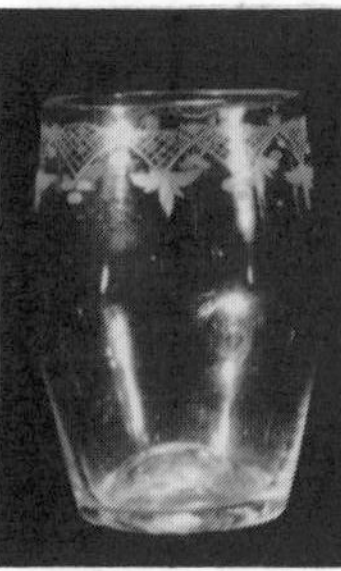

l. A barrel-shaped tumbler, with a band of hatched decoration, c1800, 4in (10cm).
$140-150

r. A tapered tumbler, with a band of hatched rose decoration and inscription 'George & Mary Owen 1835', 4in (10cm).
$140-150

A Bohemian transparent enamelled beaker, with raised panels painted in bright colours with chinoiserie figures, in the manner of C. von Scheidt, the underside of the foot flashed in pink, chipped footrim, c1840, 5in (12.5cm).
$3,000-4,000

A North Bohemian Lithyalin beaker, attributed to Friedrich Egermann, the marbled olive green exterior cut with wide flutes to reveal a translucent iron red ground with striated inclusions, each flute gilt with a letter spelling 'Erinnerung', gilt rim, Blottendorf, chipped and gilding rubbed, c1835, 4in (10.5cm).
$5,000-5,500

Bottles

An early sealed and dated dark green tint wine bottle, applied with a seal inscribed 'John Lovering Bidiford 1695', minor chipping to edge of seal and slight chip to rim, 5in (12.5cm).
$5,000-5,500

An armorial wine bottle, applied with a seal bearing a coat-of-arms, the neck with string ring and with kick-in base, damage and burial discolouration, c1680, 7in (17cm).
$1,400-2,000

The arms are those of Lowther.

A sealed green tint wine bottle, applied with an inscribed seal, the neck with modern silver replacement string ring and rim, c1660, 8½in (22cm).
$3,000-5,000

An early green tint wine bottle, the neck with string ring and with kick-in base, burial discolouration, c1660, 7in (17.5cm).
$3,000-5,000

Found in Stamford, Ct., U.S.A.

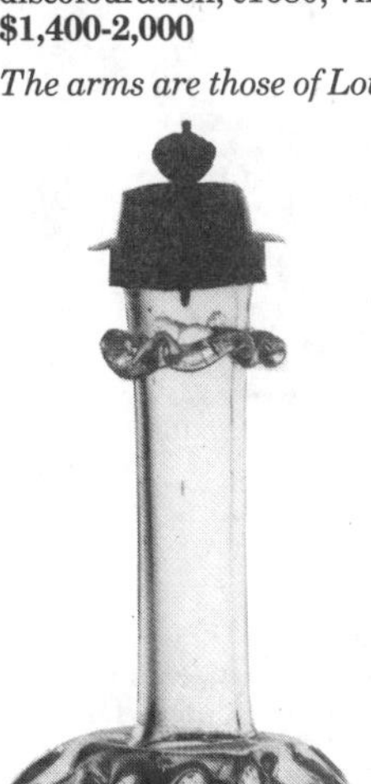

A Netherlands serving bottle with a silver gilt stopper, late 17th/18thC, the stopper mid-18thC, 6in (15cm).
$1,500-2,000

A sealed and dated green tint wine bottle, the shoulder applied with a seal inscribed 'Francis Young; de Rye 1700', the neck with a string ring and with a kick-in base, rim reduced and damage to string ring, 5½in (14cm).
$3,000-4,000

A sealed green tint wine bottle, with inscribed applied seal, the neck with string ring and with kick-in base, chipped, c1670, 8in (20cm).
$11,000-13,000

This bottle probably belonged to a member of the Loupe family.

A dark olive tint serving bottle, the slender neck with a pouring lip and applied loop handle with pincered thumbpiece, crack to base of handle, c1725, 6½in (17cm).
$1,500-2,000

A sealed olive green tint wine bottle, the shoulder applied with a seal marked 'VI', the neck with a string ring and with kick-in base, damage to string ring and some surface wear, c1690, 6in (15cm).
$800-1,200

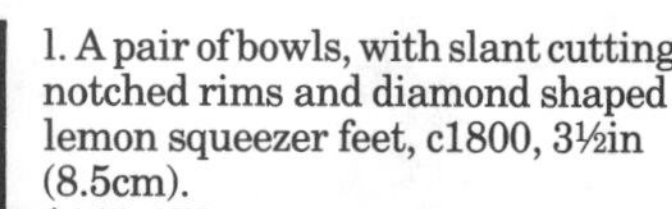

l. A pair of bowls, with slant cutting, notched rims and diamond shaped lemon squeezer feet, c1800, 3½in (8.5cm).
$110-150

r. A pair of cut bowls on lemon squeezer feet, c1810.
$110-150

A butter dish with fan cut handles, the body with diamond and flute cutting, star cut base, c1810, 8in (20cm).
$650-700

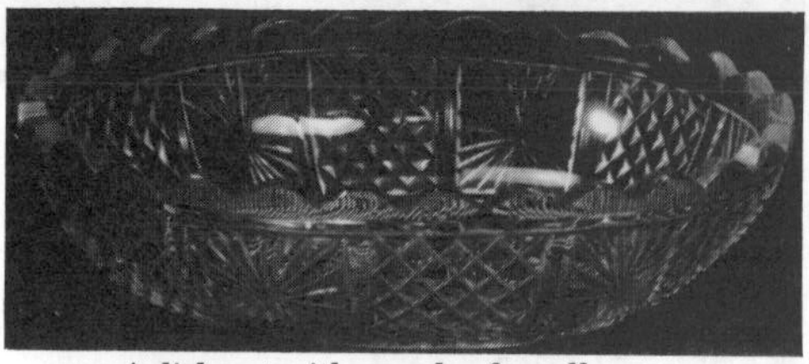

A dish cut with panels of small diamonds and stars, scalloped rim, star cut base, c1820, 8in (20cm) diam.
$140-200

A dish with diamond and flute cutting, star cut base, c1810, 10½in (27cm) diam.
$300-350

A tazza with rimmed platform, on a hollow conical foot with folded rim, c1720, 3in (7.5cm).
$500-550

A tazza, on hollow moulded Silesian stem, domed folded foot, c1780, 12in (30cm) diam.
$400-500

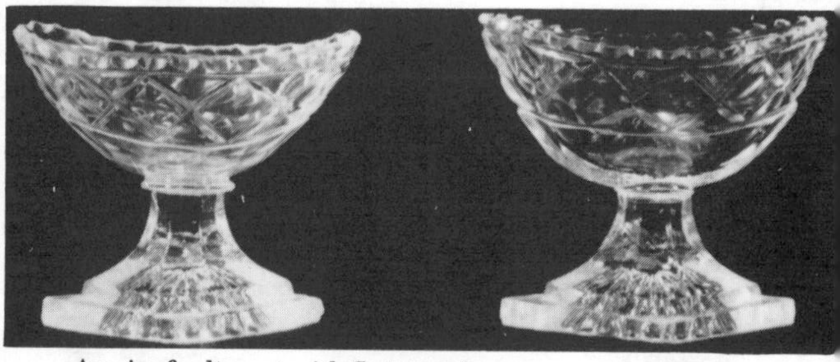

A pair of salts, cut with flutes and a band of diamonds, notched rims, c1810, 3in (8cm).
$200-250

An Irish fruit bowl, with turnover rim and geometric cutting, on a bobbin knopped stem and lemon squeezer foot, c1800, 8in (20cm).
$1,400-1,500

An Irish fruit bowl, with turnover rim, on a knopped stem, c1790, 8in (20cm).
$2,500-2,800

A Bohemian green tinted sweetmeat dish, with all-over gilt decoration, and alternate overlaid panels of portraits and gilt motifs, small chip, 19thC, 8in (20cm).
$700-900

A pair of comports and covers, cut with bands of diamonds, the bodies with French silver gilt hallmarked rims, on square pedestal lemon squeezer feet, c1830, 10½in (26cm) high overall.
$2,400-2,600

A Lynn green finger bowl, late 18thC, 4½in (11.5cm) diam.
$800-1,000

A bowl on detachable stand, the collared pedestal base cut underneath with hobnailing, early 19thC, 10½in (27cm) diam.
$500-650

A moulded and cut butter dish and cover, with looped band in relief, probably Irish, c1830, 6½in (17cm).
$750-850

l. An Irish sugar basin, with prism and flute cutting, everted notch cut rim, and plain foot, star cut, c1820, 4in (10cm).
$150-200

r. A comport and cover, the body cut with strawberry diamonds fluting and prisms, star cut foot, notched rim and domed cover similarly cut, with mushroom finial, c1825.
$350-400

A cut piggin and stand, the bowl with alternate panels of small diamonds and flutes, fan cut stave handle, the stand similarly cut and with lobed rim, c1810, stand 7½in (18.5cm) diam.
$1,000-1,200

An Irish cut bowl, with a band of shallow diamond-within-lozenge ornament beneath bevelled rim, the stem with swelling waist knop above an oval foot, moulded with flutes and with lemon squeezer base, minor rim chips, c1800, 15½in (39cm) wide.
$2,500-3,000

A cut bowl, with turnover rim, on a square stepped base, c1820, 7in (18cm).
$400-500

Candlesticks

A cut pedestal stemmed candlestick, the domed foot with facet and geometric ornament and with waved rim, mid-18thC, 10in (25cm).
$900-1,000

A pair of diamond cut candlesticks, with scalloped candle sockets and knopped stems, with domed diamond cut feet, c1830, 10in (25cm).
$1,400-1,500

A baluster candlestick, the cylindrical nozzle with everted rim, on a domed foot, c1750, 9½in (23.5cm).
$1,500-2,500

A baluster candlestick, the cylindrical nozzle with folded rim, supported on a cushion knop above an acorn knop, beaded ball knop and an annulated section, on a domed and terraced foot, repair, c1725, 7in (17.5cm).
$1,500-2,500

Chandeliers

A giltmetal 18-light chandelier, with foliate scrolled branches, each supporting 2 nozzles hung with faceted drops, fitted for electricity, 26in (66cm) wide.
$1,300-2,000

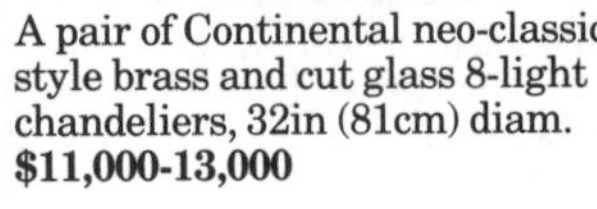

A pair of Continental neo-classic style brass and cut glass 8-light chandeliers, 32in (81cm) diam.
$11,000-13,000

Make the Most of Miller's

CONDITION is absolutely vital when assessing the value of an antique. Damaged pieces on the whole appreciate much less than perfect examples. However a rare, desirable piece may command a high price even when damaged

A pair of cut mallet shaped decanters and ball stoppers, the facet necks above strawberry diamonds and prisms, 10in (25cm).
$650-800

Three barrel shaped spirit decanters, with flute, prism and diamond cutting, cut mushroom stoppers, c1810, 6½in (16.5cm):
l. & r. **$150-250**
c. **$80-150**

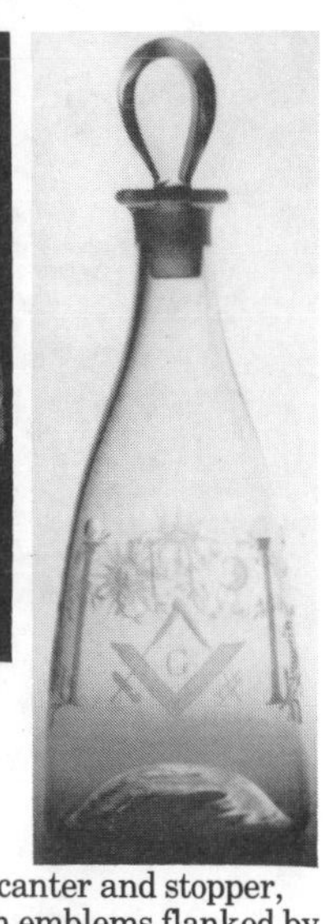

A Masonic decanter and stopper, engraved with emblems flanked by foliage, c1800, 12in (30cm).
$1,000-1,200

Two ovoid body spirit decanters, with base and neck fluting, 3 neck rings and cut lozenge stoppers, c1810, 7½in (19cm).
$150-250 each

Three spirit decanters with flute cutting, c1810:
l. With diamond cut neck rings, 7½in (19cm).
$150-200
c. With angular neck rings and lozenge stopper, 8½in (22cm).
$250-300
r. With sprig decoration and target stopper, 8in (20cm).
$150-200

A pair of heavy Irish cut decanters, with flute and diamond cutting, 3 annulated neck rings and cut mushroom stoppers, c1810, 8in (21cm).
$900-1,000

l. & r. A pair of ovoid flute cut spirit decanters, with cut neck rings and target stoppers, c1830, 7½in (18.5cm).
$500-550
c. A decanter with flute and diamond cutting, 2 diamond cut neck rings, and mushroom stopper, c1820, 8in (20cm).
$250-300

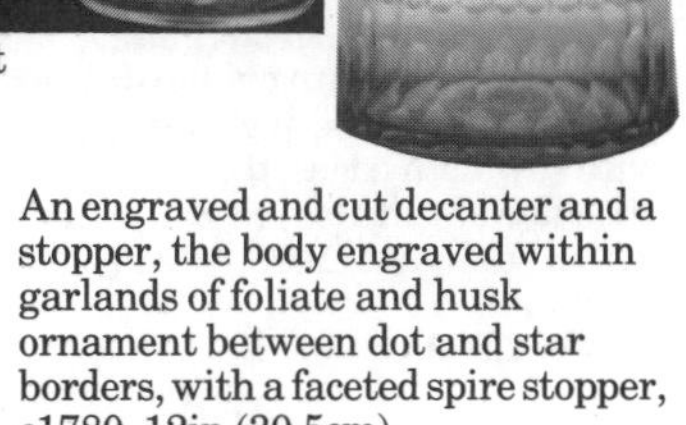

An engraved and cut decanter and a stopper, the body engraved within garlands of foliate and husk ornament between dot and star borders, with a faceted spire stopper, c1780, 12in (30.5cm).
$1,000-1,200

A Sunderland Bridge decanter and a stopper, engraved with a sailing ship passing beneath the Iron Bridge and inscribed 'Sunderland Bridge Span 236 feet Ht 100', early 19thC, 9in (23cm).
$1,500-2,500

l. A decanter with 3 annulated neck rings and target stopper, c1800, 8½in (22cm).
$300-400
c. A decanter with broad flute cut body, prism cut neck and target stopper, c1830, 7in (18cm).
$150-250
r. A decanter with bladed neck rings, c1800, 9in (22.5cm).
$300-400

An Irish decanter, with engraved ship and floral decoration, moulded mushroom stopper, c1810, 8½in (22cm).
$550-650

l. & r. A pair of decanters with blaze, printy, diamond and flute cutting, cut mushroom stoppers, c1815, 8in (20cm).
$1,000-1,200
c. A tapered decanter, with 3 bladed neck rings and cut lozenge stopper, c1780, 7½in (19cm).
$130-150

Three miniature green bottles and stoppers, named in gilt, enriched in gilding, with leather and metal stand, slightly damaged, early 19thC, the bottles 5½in (14cm).
$1,500-2,500

A pair of Anglo-Irish cut glass decanters, each with cylindrical neck and rings, the oval stoppers with sawtooth edges, the body cut with flowers and leaves, the bottom with a sunburst, c1825, 10½in (26cm).
$2,000-2,500

A mallet shaped decanter, with annulated neck ring and lip, c1730, 8in (21cm).
$500-550

rinking Glasses

baluster wine glass, the bell bowl ith a tear to the lower part, the em with a triple annulated oulder knop and basal knop and closing an elongated tear, on lded conical foot, c1720, 6in 5cm).
350-800

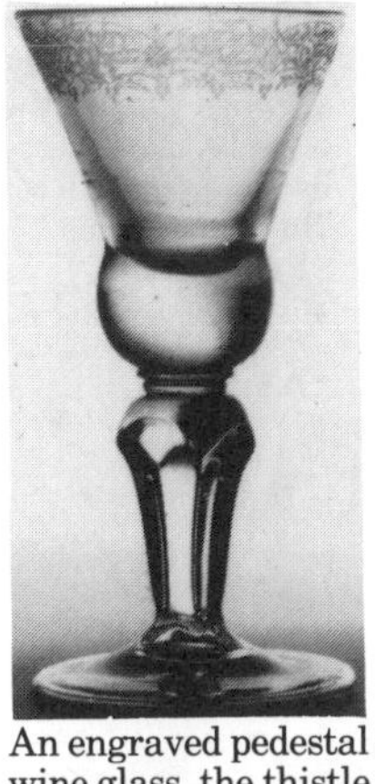

An engraved pedestal stemmed wine glass, the thistle shaped bowl engraved with a foliate border and with solid lower part, with folded conical foot, c1725, 6½in (16cm).
$1,000-1,200

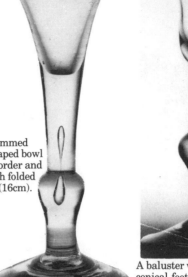

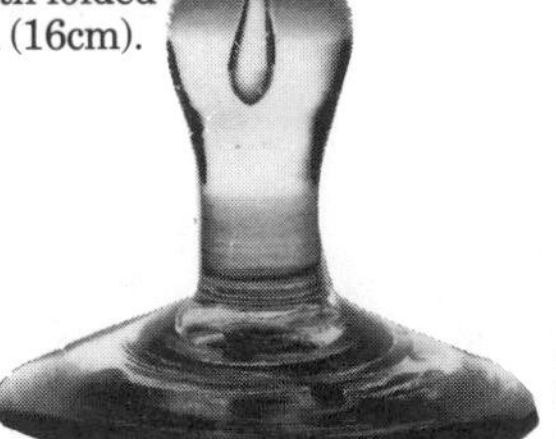

A balustroid wine glass of kit-kat type, on conical foot, c1720, 6½in (16.5cm).
$700-800

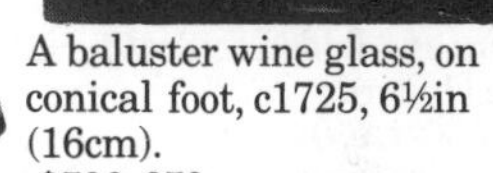

A baluster wine glass, on conical foot, c1725, 6½in (16cm).
$500-650

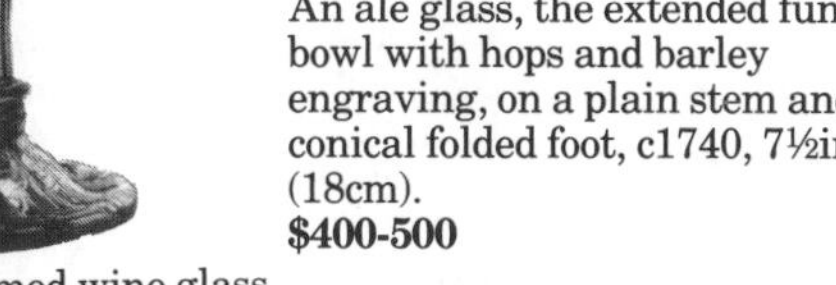

An ale glass, the extended funnel bowl with hops and barley engraving, on a plain stem and conical folded foot, c1740, 7½in (18cm).
$400-500

A pedestal stemmed wine glass, with vertically ribbed bowl supported on a beaded knop above an octagonal pedestal stem and radially ribbed domed and folded foot, c1750, 6in (15cm).
$800-1,000

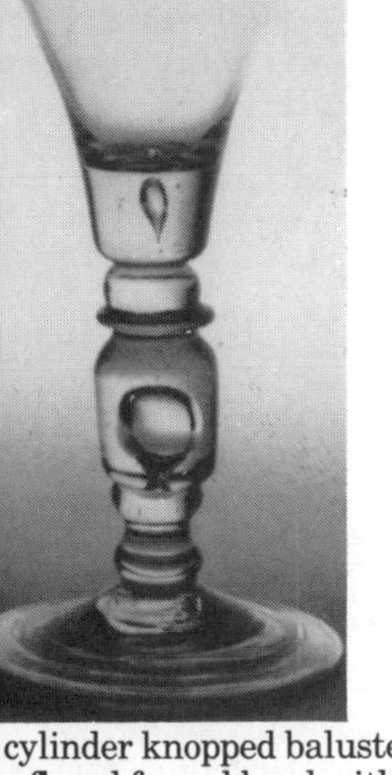

cylinder knopped baluster goblet, e flared funnel bowl with a solid wer part enclosing a tear, on a lded conical foot, c1715, 7in 7cm).
,500-7,000

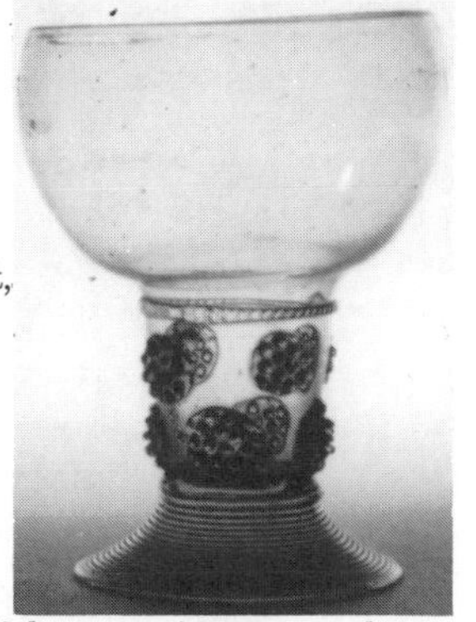

A light green tint roemer, the stem applied with raspberry prunts, The Netherlands or Rheinland, 17thC, 5in (12cm).
$1,500-2,000

A Bohemian goblet, the fluted funnel bowl with 4 medallions reserved on an elaborately engraved ground, the knopped and inverted baluster stem cut with facets and filled with spiral red and gilt threads, c1725, 11½in (28.5cm).
$11,000-13,000

A Nuremburg armorial goblet, the round funnel bowl engraved with 2 coats-of-arms within berried foliage cartouches, the conical foot with folded rim, foot detached and damaged, c1690, 11½in (29cm).
$1,500-2,500

A Dutch engraved armorial baluster goblet, the funnel bowl with crowned arms of Holland flanked by lion supporters above foliage scrolls, on a multi-knopped stem and domed foot, c1740, 8in (20cm).
$1,500-2,000

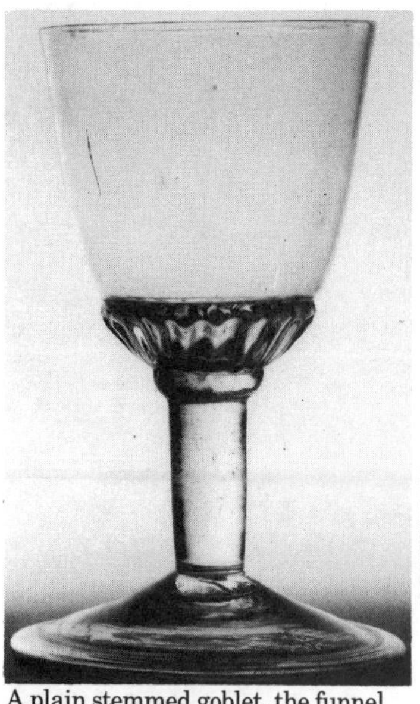

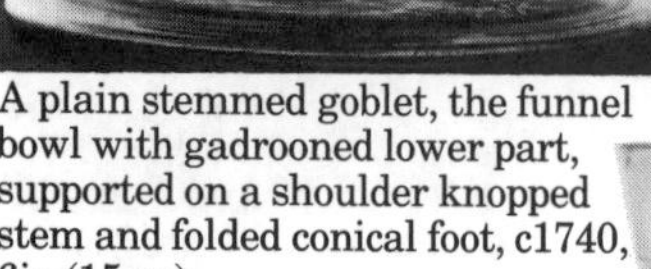

A plain stemmed goblet, the funnel bowl with gadrooned lower part, supported on a shoulder knopped stem and folded conical foot, c1740, 6in (15cm).
$1,300-1,400

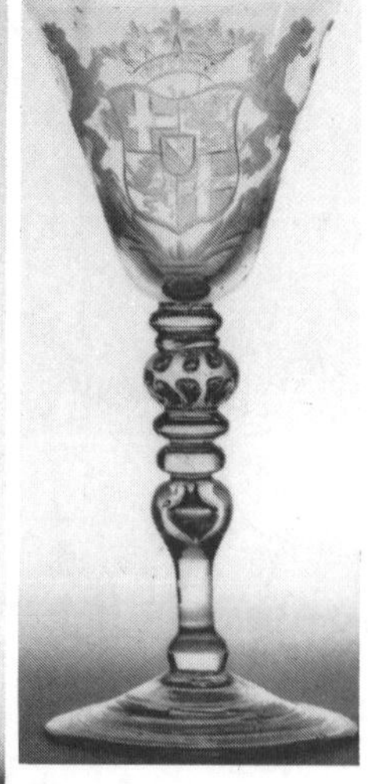

A Dutch engraved armorial baluster goblet, engraved with the crowned arms of the Province of Utrecht, the reverse with a stylised flowerspray, on a conical foot, c1750, 7in (17.5cm).
$1,400-2,000

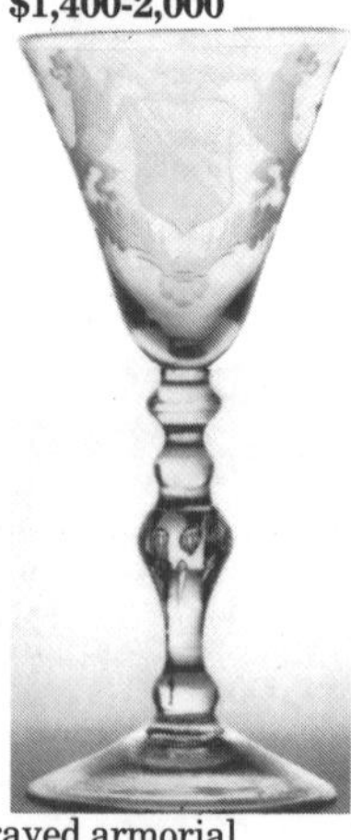

A Dutch engraved armorial baluster goblet, engraved with the arms of Utrecht, the multi-knopped stem including a beaded inverted baluster section, on a conical foot, mid-18thC, 7½in (19cm).
$1,500-2,500

A quadruple knopped air-twist wine glass, on conical foot, c1750, 7in (17.5cm).
$2,500-3,000

A mercury cordial glass, the bowl with honeycomb moulded lower part, the stem with a spiral air-core within a seven-ply spiral, on conical foot, c1750, 6½in (16.5cm).
$700-900

A Newcastle engraved baluster wine glass, the funnel bowl with a border of 'Laub-und-Bandelwerk', supported on a multi-knopped stem on a conical foot, c1750, 6in (15cm).
$800-1,000

An electioneering goblet, inscribed and dated, on plain stem and conical foot, 1761, 7in (17cm).
$1,200-1,500

A Newcastle baluster goblet, the funnel bowl supported on a multi-knopped stem enclosing tears, above a conical foot, c1750, 7½in (18cm).
$1,400-2,000

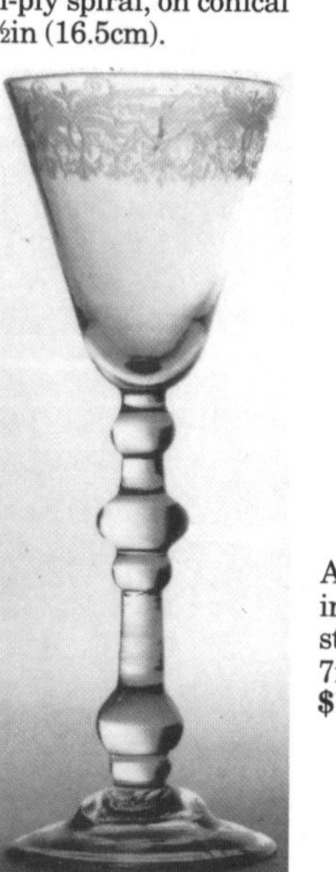

A Newcastle engraved baluster goblet, the funnel bowl supported on a multi-knopped stem including a beaded inverted baluster section with basal knop, above a conical foot, c1750, 7½in (18cm).
$1,500-2,500

A Newcastle baluster goblet, the funnel bowl supported on a knopped section above a beaded inverted baluster stem with basal knop, on a conical foot, c1750, 7in (17.5cm).
$1,000-1,200

An ale glass, engraved with hops and barley motif, on a stem with a double series air-twist, thick plain foot, c1750, 7½in (18.5cm).
$650-700

Three plain conical dwarf ales, with conical feet, c1810, 5in (12.5cm).
$65-100 each

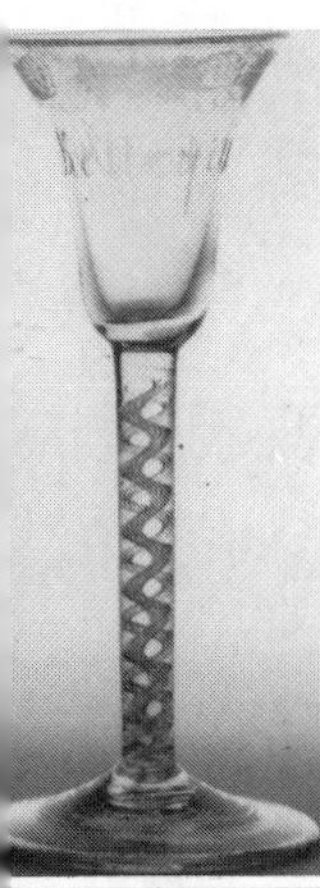

An engraved and dated air-twist wine glass, inscribed 'Jno. Keltey, 1754', beneath a border of engraved and polished fruiting vine, the stem with 2 entwined gauze spirals, on a conical foot, 6½in (16.5cm).
$1,000-1,200

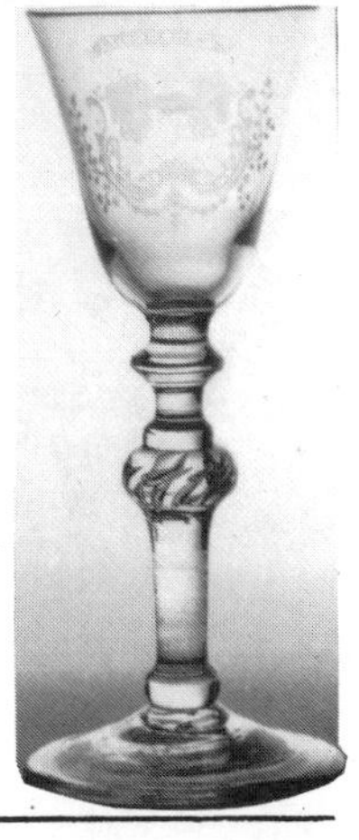

A Dutch baluster goblet, the funnel bowl engraved with 2 clasped hands, inscribed 'Ametitia', on a beaded multi-knopped stem terminating in a basal knop on a conical foot, c1750, 7in (17cm).
$1,500-2,000

GLASS APPENDIX

Drinking glasses

STEM FORMATIONS

ball knop

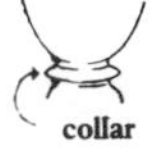
collar

annular knop

annulated knop

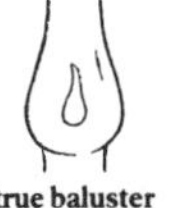
true baluster

swelling knop

flattened knop

cushioned knop

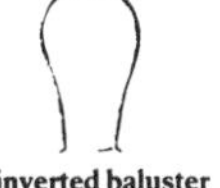
inverted baluster

the knop proper

cone knop

angular knop

acorn knop

drop knop

cylinder knop

wide angular knop

shoulder knop

mushroom knop

true baluster ridged

BOWL FORMS

pped bucket

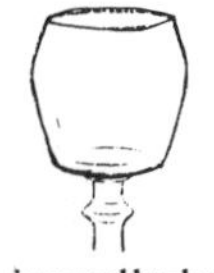
incurved bucket

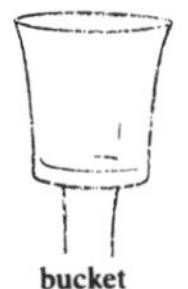
bucket

conical

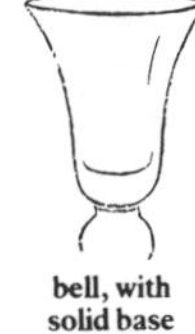
bell, with solid base

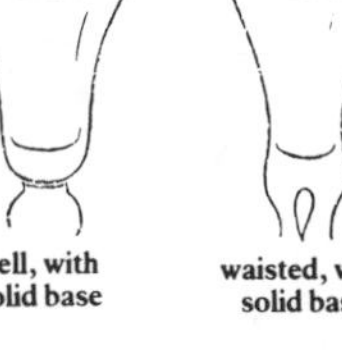
waisted, with solid base

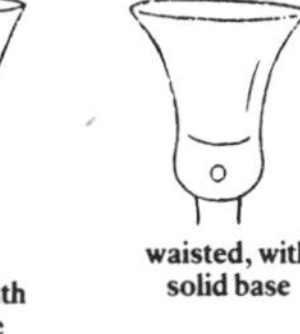
waisted, with solid base

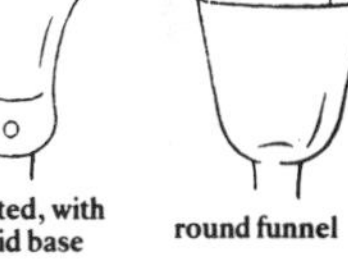
round funnel

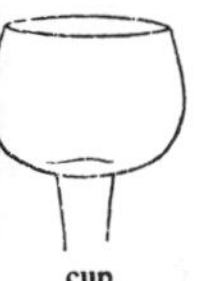
cup

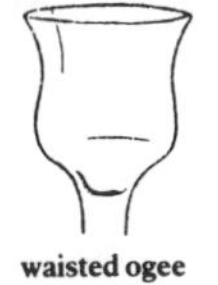
waisted ogee

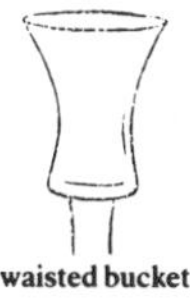
waisted bucket

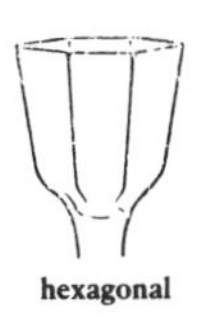
hexagonal

thistle

trumpet

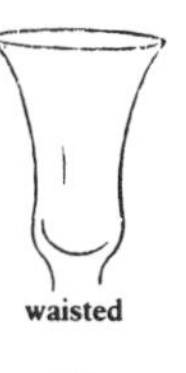
waisted

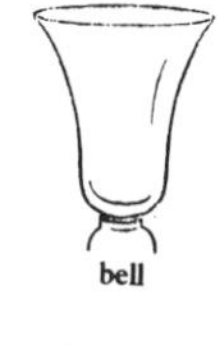
bell

lipped

pan-topped

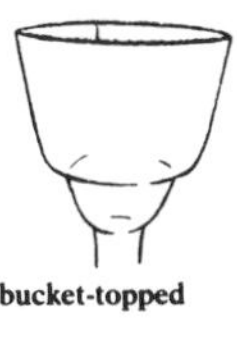
bucket-topped

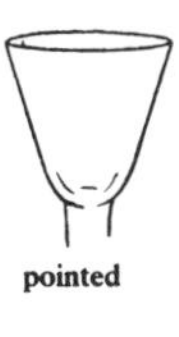
pointed

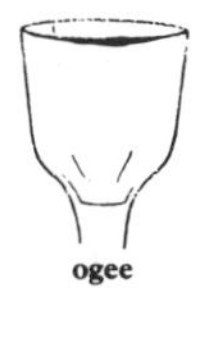
ogee

trumpet

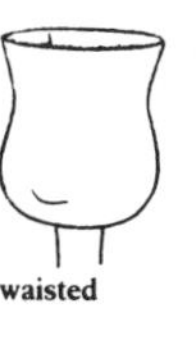
waisted

saucer-topped

FOOT FORMS

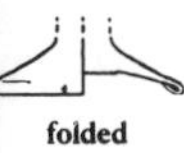
folded

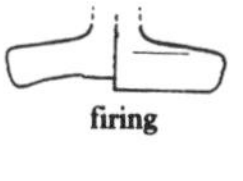
firing

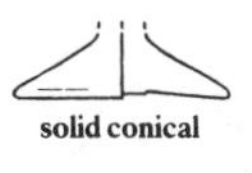
solid conical

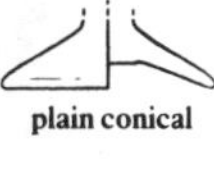
plain conical

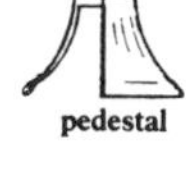
pedestal

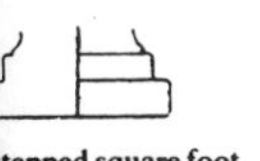
stepped square foot

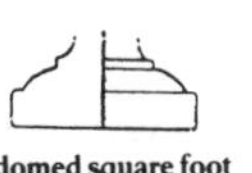
domed square foot

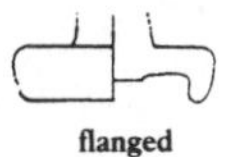
flanged

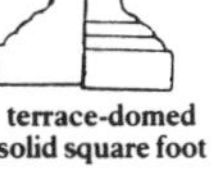
terrace-domed solid square foot

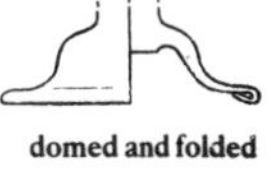
domed and folded

A pedestal stemmed goblet, c1740, 7in (17cm).
$550-700

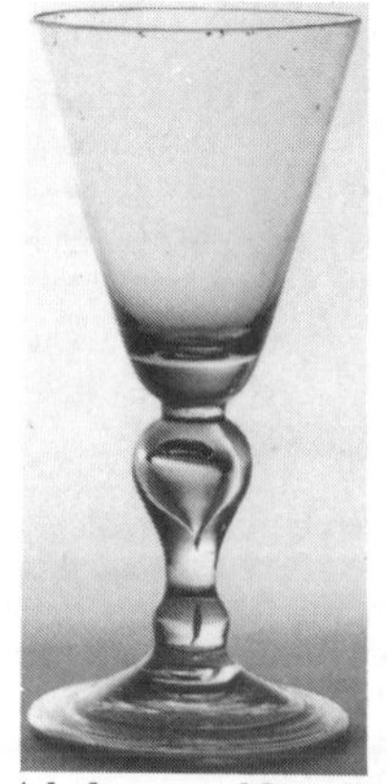

A baluster goblet, the inverted baluster stem enclosing a tear, and with a basal knop, above a folded conical foot, c1720, 6in (15cm).
$400-450

An armorial air-twist goblet, the funnel bowl engraved by a German hand, on a double knopped air-twist stem above a conical foot, the upper knop with inscription, c1750, 8in (20cm).
$4,000-5,000

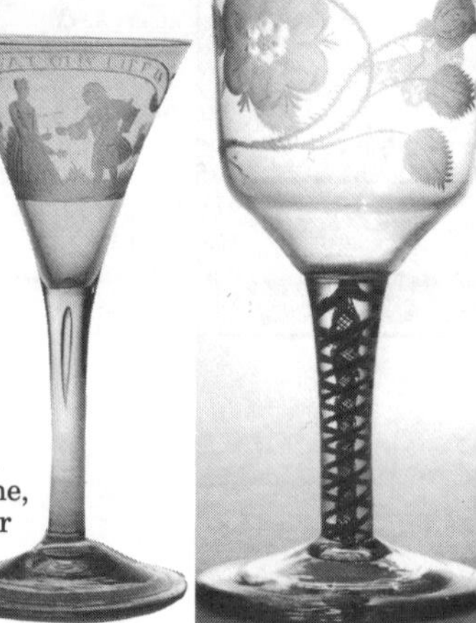

A Dutch engraved goblet, with inscription in a ribbon cartouche, the stem with an elongated tear above a folded conical foot, mid-18thC, 8in (20cm).
$1,200-1,300

A Jacobite opaque-twist goblet, the ogee bowl engraved with a rose and buds, the stem with 2 ribbon spirals on a conical foot, c1770, 8in (20cm).
$700-900

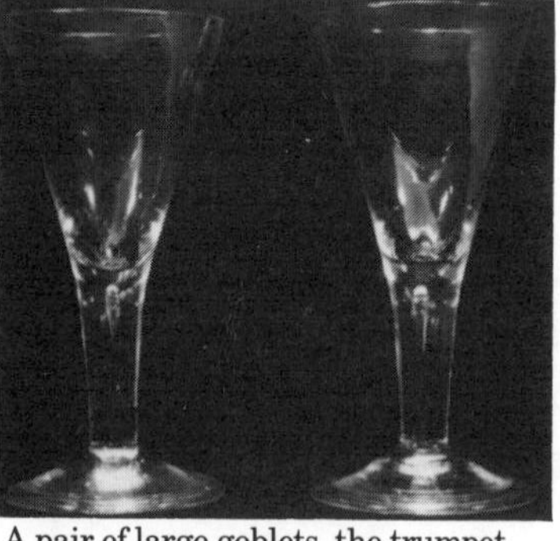

A pair of large goblets, the trumpet bowls on drawn stems with air tears, on folded conical feet, c1740.
$1,000-1,200

A Middle German engraved goblet, the flared ogee bowl on a teared multi-knopped stem divided by mereses, the conical foot with a band of foliage, perhaps Thuringia, c1735, 9½in (24cm).
$1,500-2,500

A Dutch engraved baluster goblet, with inscription beneath the rim, the slender inverted baluster stem on a conical foot, c1750, 7½in (18cm).
$2,000-2,500

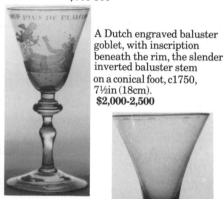

A baluster goblet, the waisted funnel bowl with a tear to the solid lower part, on a double drop knop stem, above a on a domed and folded foot, c1720, 8in (21cm).
$2,000-2,500

A Dutch engraved dated baluster goblet, with inscription and date 1765, the stem with an angular knop, beaded inverted baluster section and flattened basal knop, the foot with a foliate band, signed with initials 'I F' on the cartouche, c1765, 8in (20cm).
$6,500-7,000

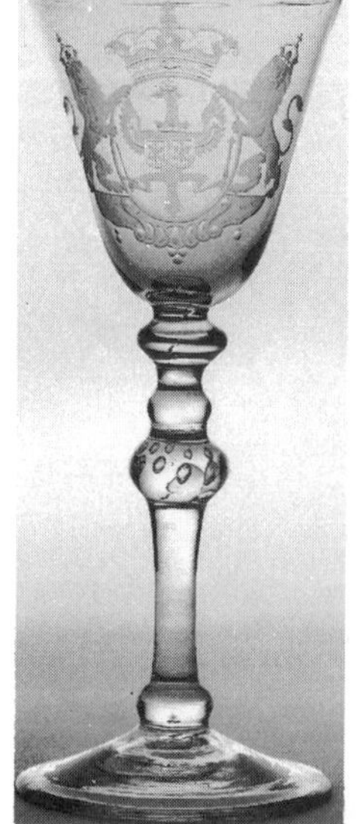

A Dutch engraved armorial baluster goblet, engraved with the arms of Princess Frederika Wilhelmina Sophia of Prussia, supported on a beaded multi-knopped stem above a conical foot, c1767, 7½in (18cm).
$4,000-5,000

Two rummers with ovoid bowls and square feet, c1810:
l. Bowl with engraved decoration and solid stepped foot, 5½in (13.5cm).
$110-140
r. Plain bowl, 4½in (12cm).
$100-130

Ovoid bowl rummers on capstan stems and square lemon squeezer feet, c1800:
l. 5½in (13.5cm).
$250-275 a pair
c. Engraved monogram 'JASC', 6in (15.5cm).
$120-150
r. Engraved TBF, 5½in (13.5cm).
$140-200

A Jacobite drawn trumpet wine glass, engraved with roses, the stem with a small tear, on a conical foot, mid-18thC, 6½in (16cm).
$1,000-1,300

A pair of heavy baluster wine glasses, the bowls with solid sections, on stems with inverted baluster air-teared knops and base knops, on domed folded foot, c1720, 7in (17.5cm).
$3,000-4,000

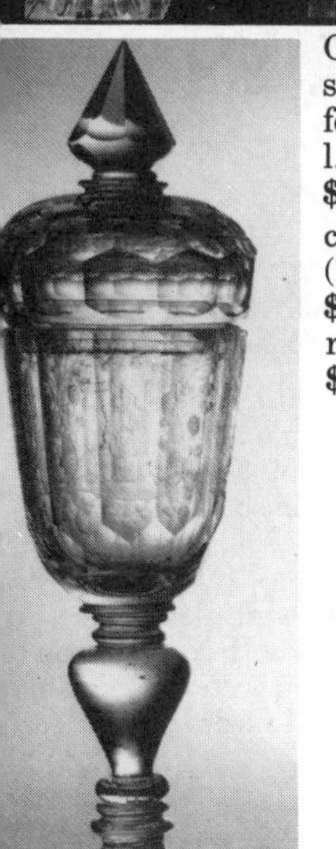

l. A bucket rummer with flute cut body, knopped stem and plain foot, c1825, 5in (13cm).
$100-130
r. A pair of similar rummers, c1830, 5in (13cm).
$200-250

Bohemian goblet and cover, ıgraved with a crowned mirror onogram, the reverse with a ırther crowned monogram, with ıted spire finial, c1730, 10½in 7cm).
2,500-3,000

Three rummers:
l. With capstan stem, c1810, 5in (12.5cm).
$65-100
c. With bowl engraved with hops and barley, c1810, 5in (12.5cm).
$140-200
r. Cup shaped bowl with cut printies, c1840, 5½in (14cm).
$65-100

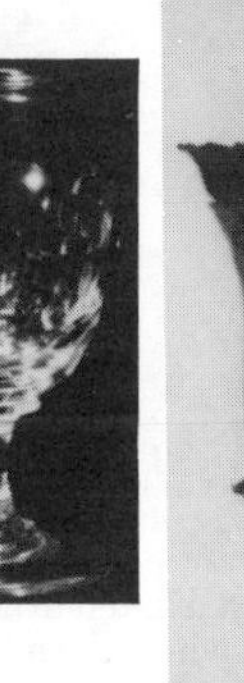

A large Bohemian ruby flash goblet and cover, engraved with a stag and numerous hind in a landscape, above an everted scalloped collar, on a knopped spreading octagonal stem with waved footrim, cover damaged, c1865, 21in (53cm).
$11,000-13,000

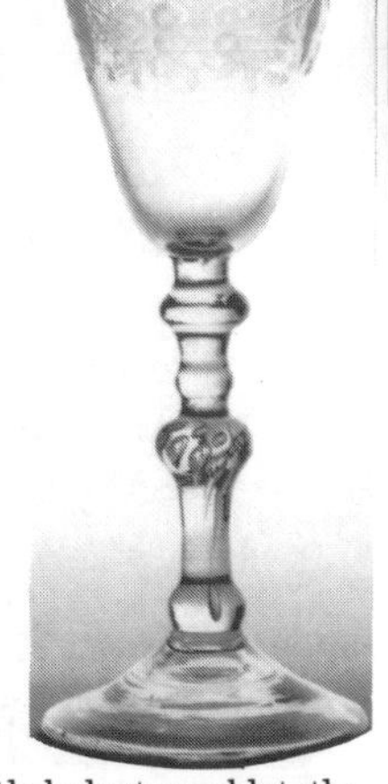

Newcastle baluster goblet, the ınnel bowl engraved with a border birds perched among 'Laub-und- ındelwerk', on a knopped section ove a baluster stem with basal ıop, on domed foot, c1750, 7in 7.5cm).
,200-1,500

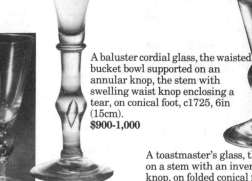

A baluster cordial glass, the waisted bucket bowl supported on an annular knop, the stem with swelling waist knop enclosing a tear, on conical foot, c1725, 6in (15cm).
$900-1,000

heavy baluster wine glass, the ınted round funnel bowl on a stem th an inverted baluster knop and tear, on folded conical foot, 710, 8in (20cm).
,400-1,500

A toastmaster's glass, the bowl set on a stem with an inverted baluster knop, on folded conical foot, c1710, 4½in (11cm).
$800-900

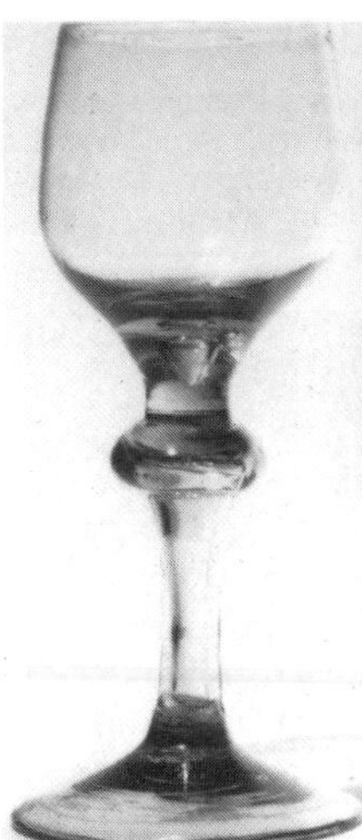

A green tinted wine glass, the cup-shaped bowl with a tear to the tapering lower part, set on a hollow shoulder knopped stem, on a conical foot, possibly English, possibly late 18thC, 6½in (16cm).
$500-650

A baluster wine glass, on a stem with air beaded knop and base knop, on plain domed foot, c1730, 6½in (16cm).
$1,200-1,300

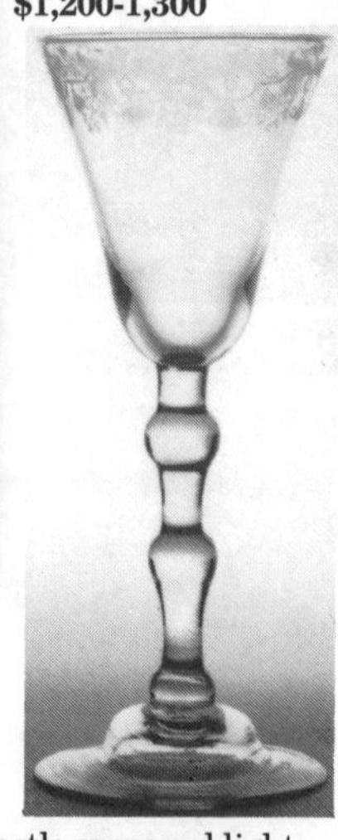

A Newcastle engraved light baluster goblet, the funnel bowl decorated with a border of birds perched among 'Laub-und-Bandelwerk', on a multi-knopped stem above a domed foot, c1750, 8in (20cm). **$1,300-1,500**

l. A wine glass, the bell bowl engraved with a band of fruiting wine, with shoulder, inverted baluster and base knops, folded conical foot, c1750, 6in (15cm).
$800-900
r. A baluster wine glass, the trumpet bowl with solid section ba knop and plain section conical foot c1750, 7½in (17.5cm).
$500-550

A Georgian glass with plain bowl and knopped stem, c1810, 4in (11cm).
$80-100

A Dutch engraved dated armorial baluster goblet, with inscription and date 1776, on a multi-knopped and beaded stem above a domed foot, 8in (20cm).
$5,000-5,500

An engraved baluster wine glass, on domed folded foot, c1730, 7in (17cm).
$1,300-1,500

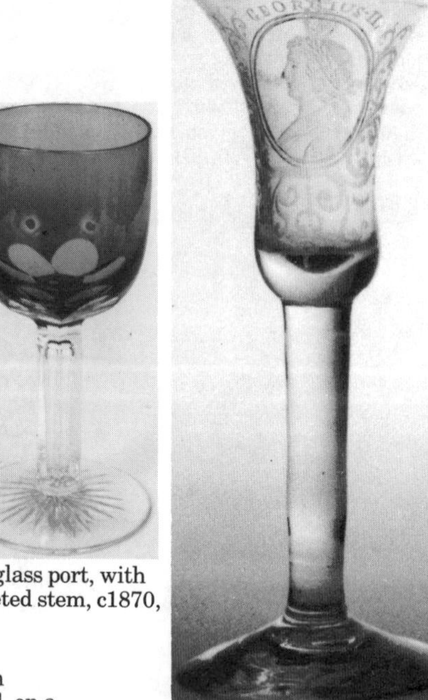

A Victorian ruby glass port, with long tear drop faceted stem, c1870, 5in (14cm).
$100-130

A Royal portrait glass, inscribed 'Georgius II', on a plain stem an conical foot, footrim slightly chipped, mid-18thC, 6½in (16cm
$1,000-1,300

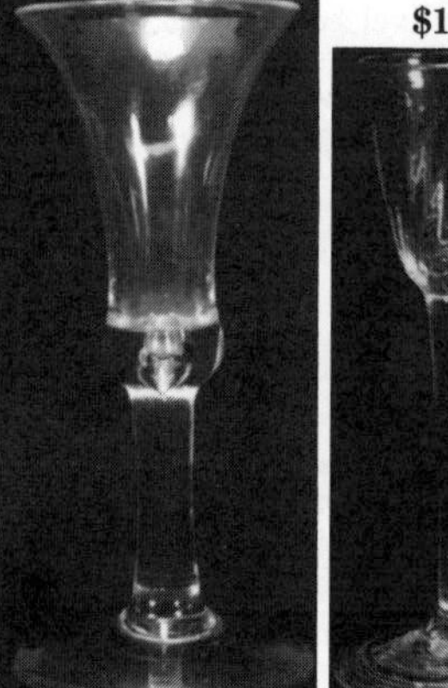

A wine glass with air tear in the base of the bowl, on plain stem and plain conical foot, c1750, 7in (17.5cm).
$200-250

A wine glass, with wrythen moulded round funnel bowl, on a plain stem, folded conical foot, c1750, 6in (15cm).
$230-260

A wine glass, with pan topped round funnel bowl, on air-twist stem, c1750, 6in (15cm).
$300-400

Did you know
MILLER'S Antiques Price Guide builds up year by year to form the most comprehensive photo-reference system available

A pair of facet stem wine glasses, on plain foot, c1780, 4½in (11cm).
$200-250

green tinted wine glass, the
uble ogee bowl on a plain stem
ove a domed and folded foot,
rhaps for export, c1765, 6in
5cm).
50-800

A green plain stemmed wine glass, the ovoid bowl with hammered flutes to the lower part, on a conical foot, c1765, 6½in (16.5cm).
$800-1,200

Newcastle wine glass, engraved
h the hands of friendship, the
m with bladed ball, air-beaded
erted baluster and base knops,
plain conical foot, c1750, 8in
cm).
000-3,500

A rare Williamite portrait glass, the trumpet bowl engraved with the monarch on horseback and inscribed 'The Glorious Memory of King William III', the plain stem enclosing a single tear and on circular foot with fold under rim, c1740, 6in (15cm).
$2,500-4,000

A Royal armorial baluster goblet, the funnel bowl engraved with the Royal Arms of England above scroll ornament, on a multi-knopped teared and beaded stem with basal knop, above a conical foot, c1750, 8in (20cm).
$4,000-5,000

A trumpet bowl wine glass, on plain drawn stem with air tear and folded conical foot, c1740, 6in (15cm).
$250-300

olour twist wine glass,
swelling waist knopped
m with a spiral of
lti-coloured threads
luding brick red, yellow,
e, white and pink, on a
in foot, late 18thC, 6in
cm).
,200-1,300

An engraved air-twist wine glass, perhaps Jacobite, inscribed 'Bien Venue', the double knopped stem filled with spiral threads above a conical foot, with a band of floral foliage, c1750, 6in (15cm).
$2,500-3,000

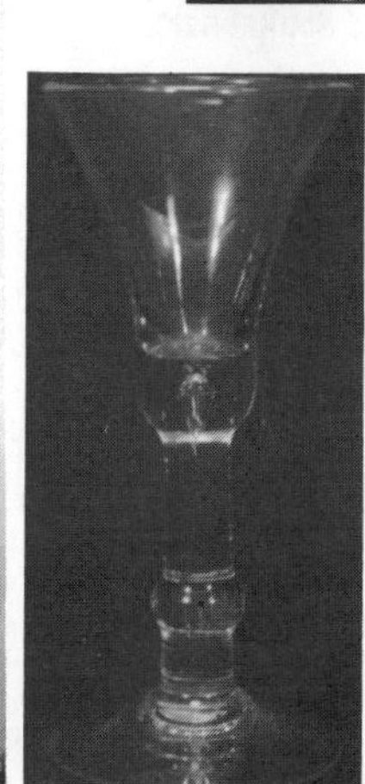

A baluster wine glass, with air tear in base, straight stem and cushion knop, on folded conical foot, c1750, 5½in (14.5cm).
$250-300

A baluster wine glass, engraved with a Jacobite rose, on a plain stem on folded conical foot, c1750, 6in (15cm).
$300-400

A wine glass with trumpet bowl on composite stem, plain inverted baluster over multi-series air-twist, c1750, 6in (16cm).
$500-550

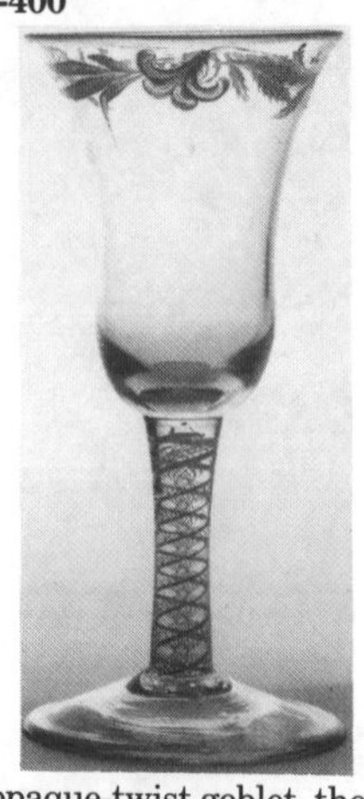

A Beilby opaque-twist goblet, the bowl enamelled in white, the rim with traces of gilding, on a double series stem and conical foot, footrim chipped, c1770, 8in (20cm).
$5,000-5,500

A wine glass with round funn bowl, on a stem with knopped multiple spiral air-twist, plai conical foot, c1750, 6in (16cm
$550-650

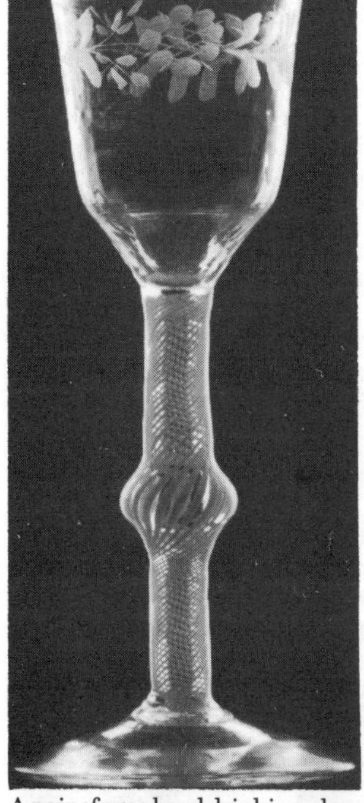

A pair of ogee bowl drinking glasses, with multiple spiral opaque twist stems on conical feet, 5½in (14cm).
$500-550

A rare Jacobite glass, engraved with a portrait of Prince Charles Edward, on a double air-twist and plain circular foot, c1750, 6in (15cm).
$5,000-5,500

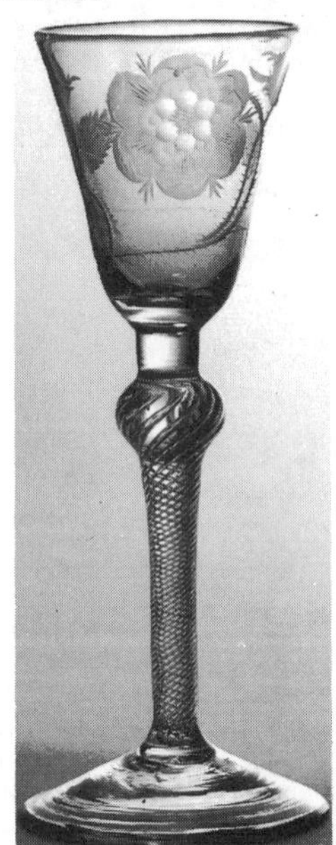

A Jacobite air-twist wine glass, supported on a shoulder knoppe stem filled with spirals above a conical foot, c1750, 6in (15cm).
$800-1,000

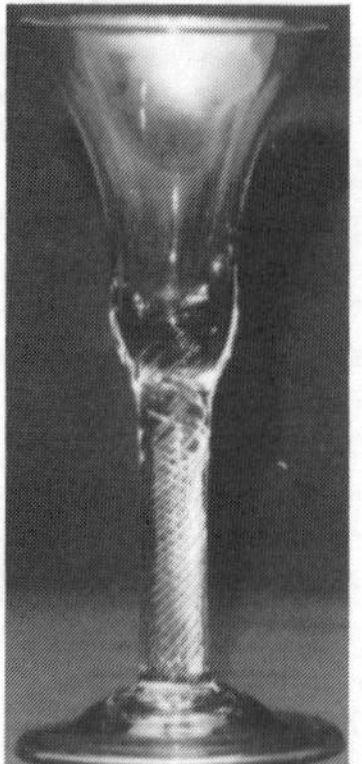

A wine glass with waisted bucket bowl, on multi-series air-twist stem with folded foot, c1745, 7½in (18.5cm).
$300-400

l. A baluster wine glass, the bowl with solid base and air tear stem with shoulder collar and baluster knop, folded conical foot, c1730, 6½in (17cm).
$1,000-1,200

r. A trumpet bowl glass, with shoulder knop and multiple spiral air-twist, plain conical foot, c1750, 7½in (18.5cm).
$500-600

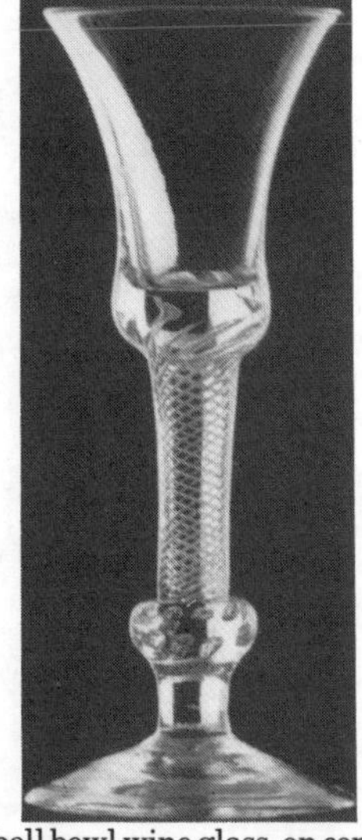

A bell bowl wine glass, on composite multiple air-twist stem over teared inverted baluster and conical foot, foot chipped, 6½in (16cm).
$250-300

l. A wine glass on a drawn stem, with multiple spiral air-twist, folded conical foot, c1745, 7in (18cm).
$300-400

r. A wine glass with bell bowl, on a plain stem domed foot, c1750, 8in (21cm).
$150-250

A wine glass, with round funnel bowl and wrythen base, on a double series opaque twist stem, c1760, 5½in (14cm).
$250-300

A Jacobite wine glass, on a drawn multiple spiral air-twist stem, folded conical foot, c1750, 6½in (16cm).
$1,300-1,400

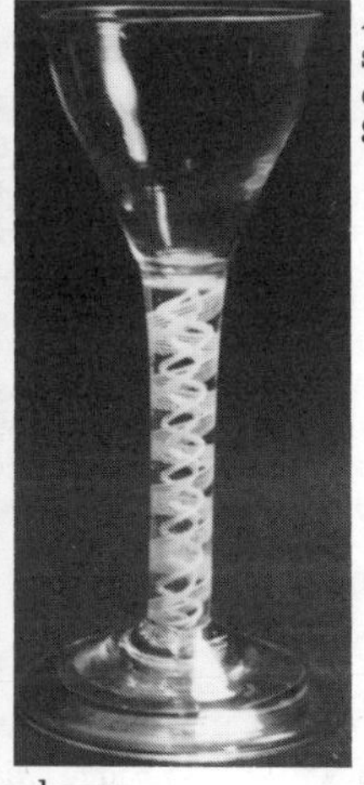

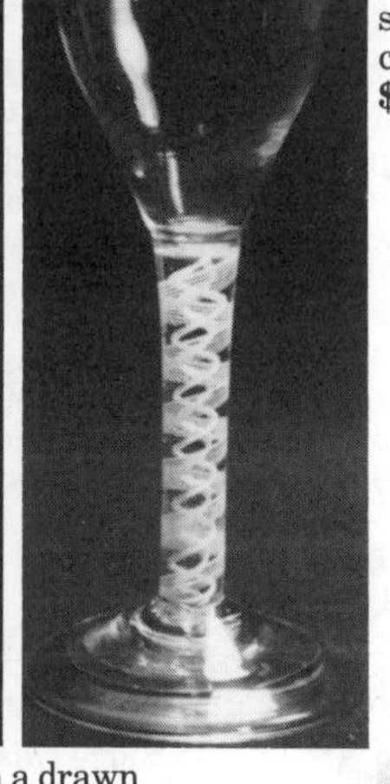

A wine glass, on a stem with double series opaque twist, on rare folded conical foot, c1760, 5½in (14cm).
$500-550

A colour twist wine glass, the stem with an opaque gauze core entwined by 2 blue/black ribbons, on a conical foot, c1765, 7in (17.5cm).
$4,000-5,000

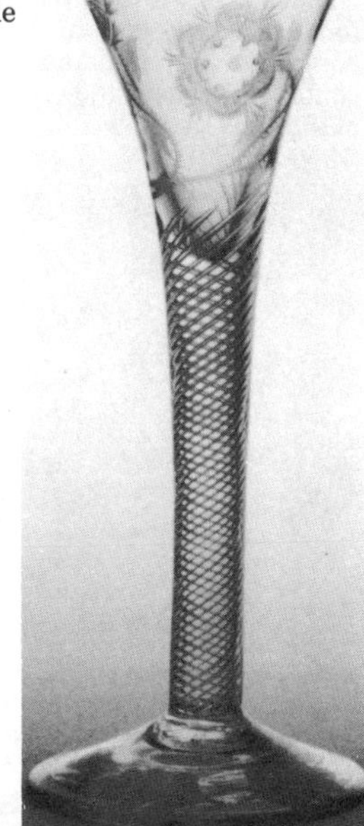

A Jacobite air-twist wine glass, inscribed with the motto 'Redi', the stem filled with spiral threads above a conical foot, c1750, 6in (15cm).
$1,200-1,400

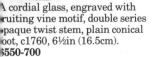

A cordial glass, engraved with fruiting vine motif, double series opaque twist stem, plain conical foot, c1760, 6½in (16.5cm).
$550-700

A wine glass, with pan topped round funnel bowl and floral engraving, on a mercury twist stem, c1750, 6in (15cm).
$550-650

l. A mixed twist wine glass, the bell bowl on a stem with a double series opaque twist and following air-twist thread, c1760, 6½in (16cm).
$500-550

r. A wine glass, the round funnel bowl on a stem with double series opaque twist, plain conical foot, c1760, 6in (15cm).
$250-300

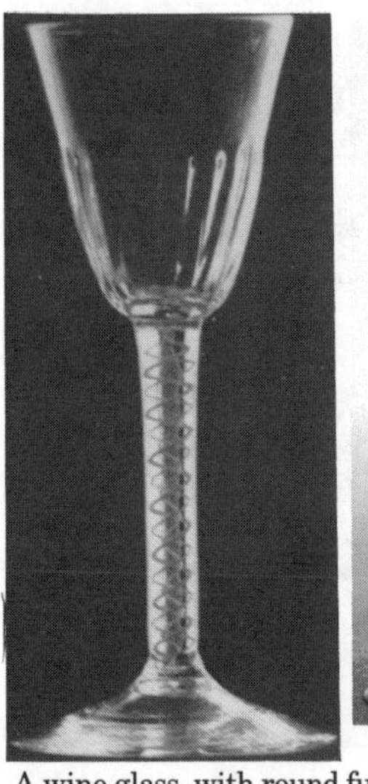

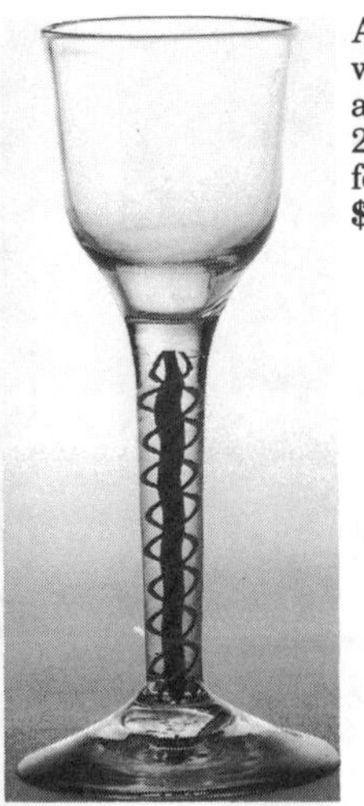

A colour twist wine glass, the stem with a solid white core incorporating a single yellow thread, within 2 white spiral threads, on a conical foot, c1765, 6in (15cm).
$2,000-2,500

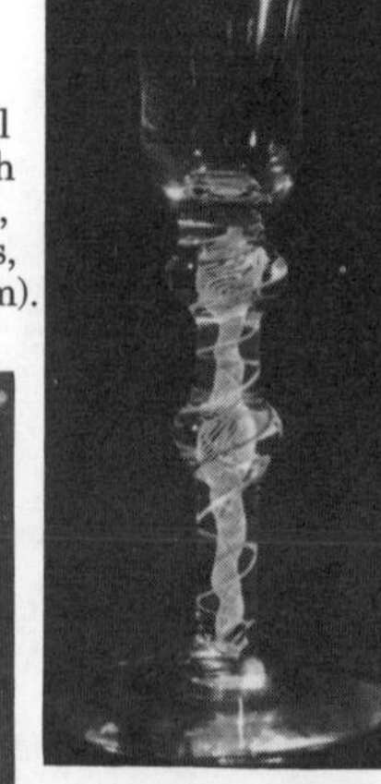

A colour twist wine glass, the bell bowl on a stem with 2 knops, with inner opaque white gauze spirals, and outer white and pink threads, plain conical foot, c1770, 6in (15cm).
$2,500-3,000

A wine glass, with round funnel bowl and basal flutes, on a double series opaque twist stem, 6½in (16cm).
$250-300

A Beilby opaque twist wine glass, enamelled in white with a pyramid flanked by trees and shrubbery, the rim with traces of gilding, on a double series stem and conical foot, c1765, 6in (15cm).
$4,500-5,000

A pair of St. Louis white overlay goblets, on red and blue twist stems and sunray cut feet, the bowls cut with tapering panels, 7in (18cm).
$1,000-1,200

A drinking glass, the ogee bowl with slight flaring rim, on double series opaque twist stem and conical foot, 6in (15cm).
$80-150

Two wine glasses, the ogee bowls on stems with double series opaque twists on plain conical feet, c1770, 5½in (14cm).
$1,000-1,200 each

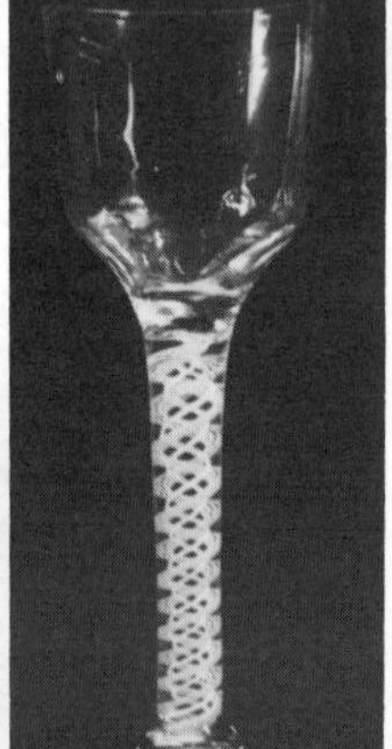

A wine glass, the stem with double series opaque twist, on plain conical foot, c1760, 5½in (14cm).
$250-275

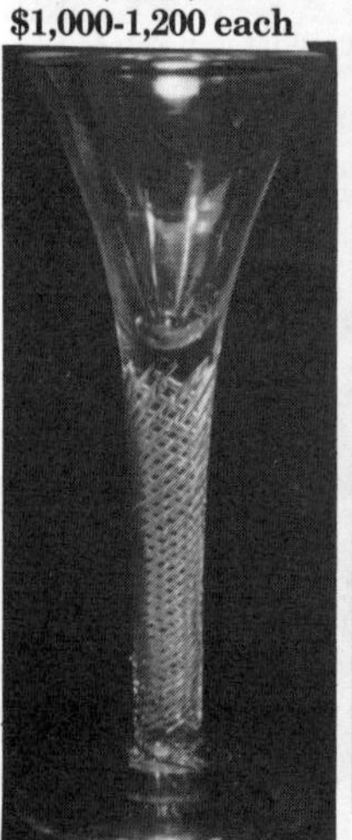

A wine glass on a drawn stem, with multiple spiral air-twist, plain conical foot, c1745, 6½in (16.5cm).
$250-300

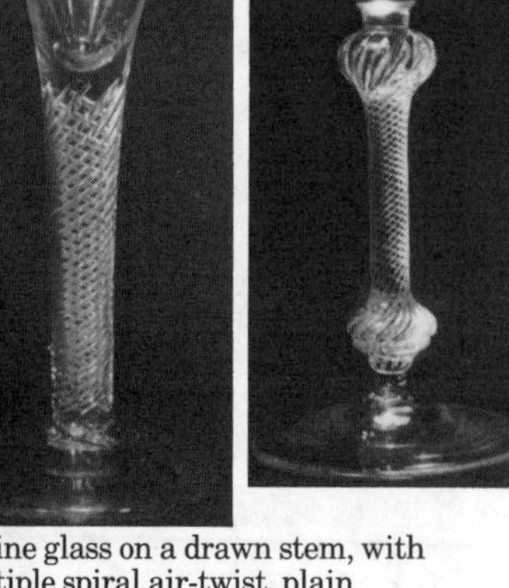

A wine glass on a multiple spiral air-twist, shoulder knop and annulated base knop, plain conical foot, c1750, 6½in (16.5cm).
$800-900

An air-twist wine glass, the bell bowl on a stem with single air-twist corkscrew, plain conical foot, c1745, 7½in (18.5cm).
$400-500

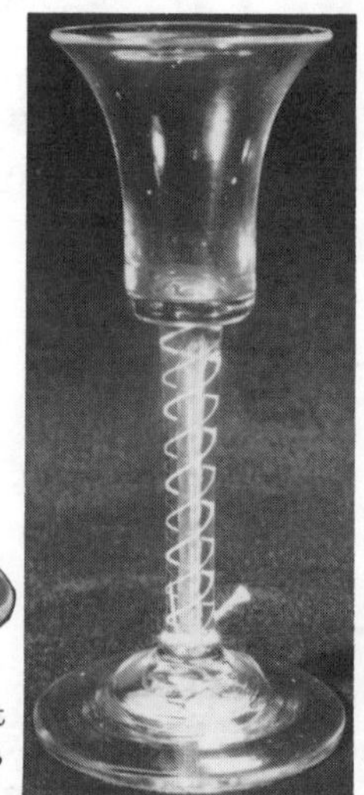

A mixed twist wine glass, on plain conical foot,c 1765, 6in (15cm).
$900-1,000

Jugs

A rock crystal jug, engraved with flowering prunus, Stourbridge, c1885, 7½in (19cm).
$1,300-1,500

The engraving was possibly executed by John Orchard at Stevens & Williams, Brierley Hill.

A two-handled posset pot, with 2 applied scroll handles, chip to spout, mid-18thC, 7½in (18.5cm).
$1,500-2,500

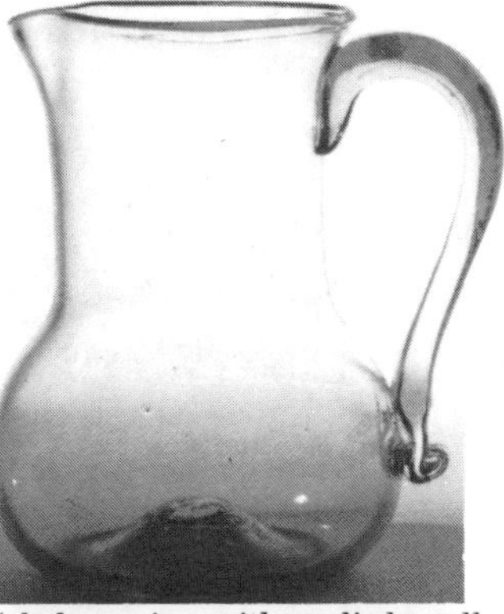
A baluster jug, with applied scroll handle, early 18thC, 5½in (14cm).
$650-700

A clear glass claret jug, with cut and etched fruiting vine and trellis decoration, with plated mount, high domed hinged cover and scrolling handle, 9½in (24cm).
$500-650

A magnum claret jug, with flute cut body, 2 neck rings and applied strap handle, star cut base, cut ball stopper, c1840, 10½in (27cm).
$1,500-2,500

Paperweights

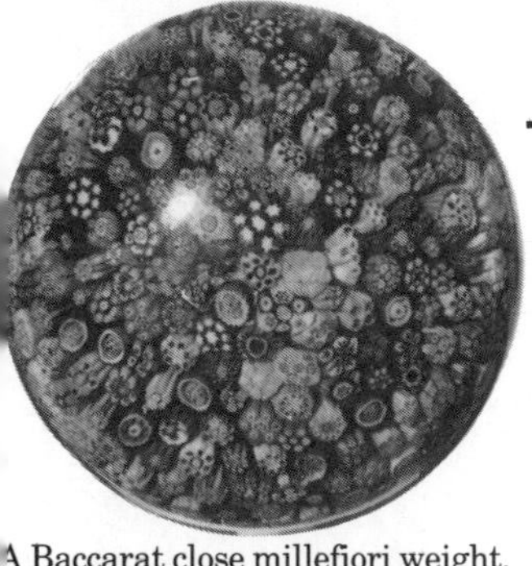
A Baccarat close millefiori weight, with closely packed brightly coloured canes including one inscribed 'B 1847', 3in (7.5cm) diam.
$800-1,200

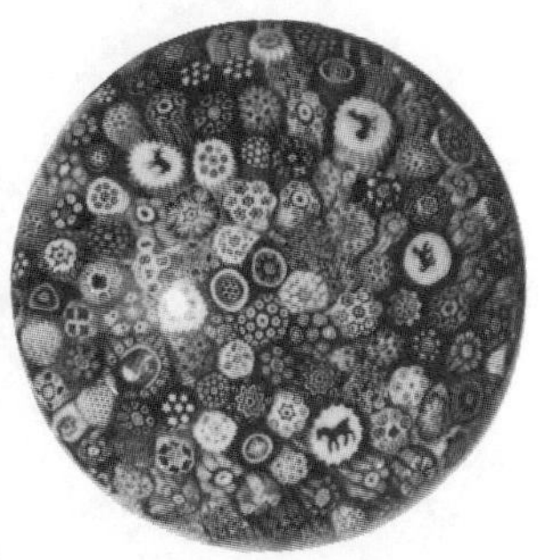
A Baccarat close millefiori weight, including 5 silhouette canes, revealing in places short lengths of latticinio ribbon, one cane inscribed 'B 1848', 3in (7.5cm) diam.
$1,000-1,300

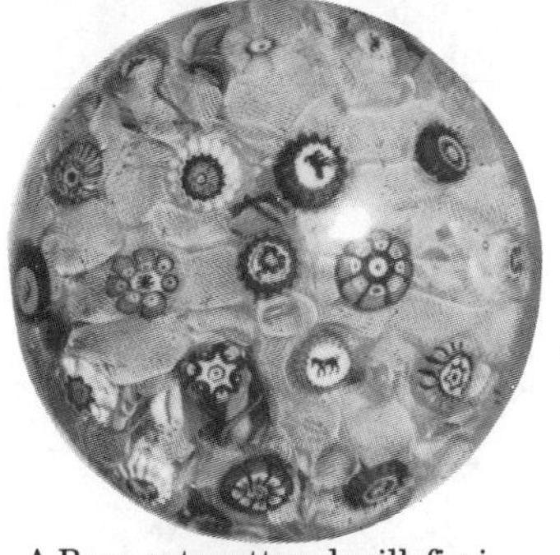
A Baccarat scattered millefiori weight, the brightly coloured canes set among short lengths of latticinio cable and coloured ribbon, one cane inscribed 'B 1848', scratched, 3in (7.5cm) diam.
$1,000-1,200

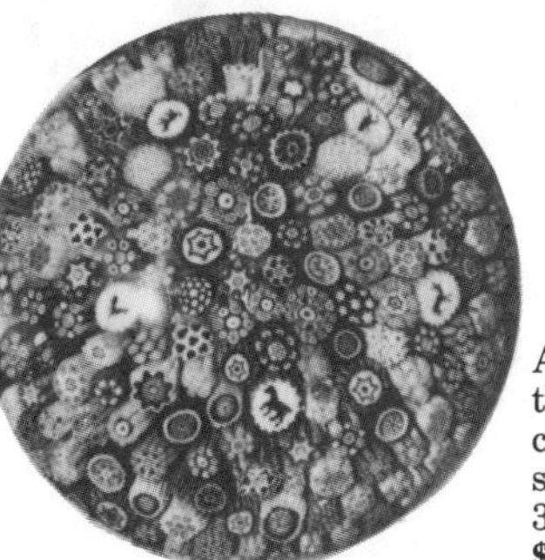

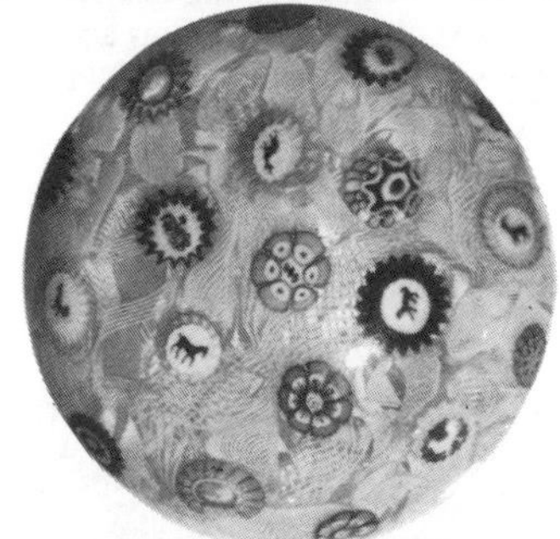
A Baccarat scattered millefiori weight, a cane inscribed 'B 1848', set among short lengths of latticinio cable and coloured ribbon, 3in (7.5cm) diam.
$1,000-1,200

A Baccarat close millefiori weight, the closely packed brightly coloured canes with numerous animal silhouettes, one inscribed 'B 1848', 3½in (8cm) diam.
$1,200-1,300

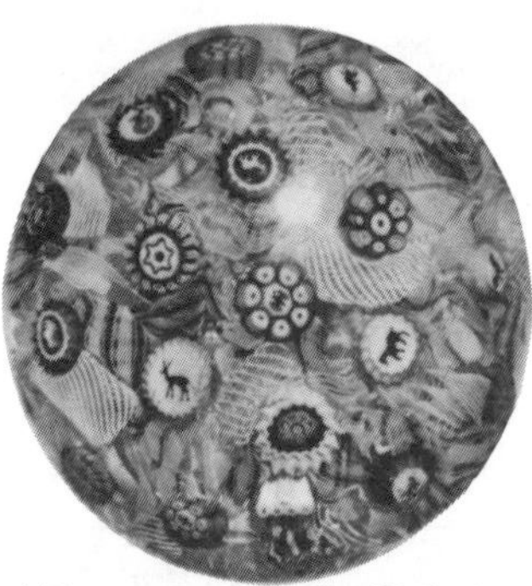

A Baccarat scattered millefiori weight, one cane inscribed 'B 1848', bruised, 3½in (8cm) diam.
$800-1,000

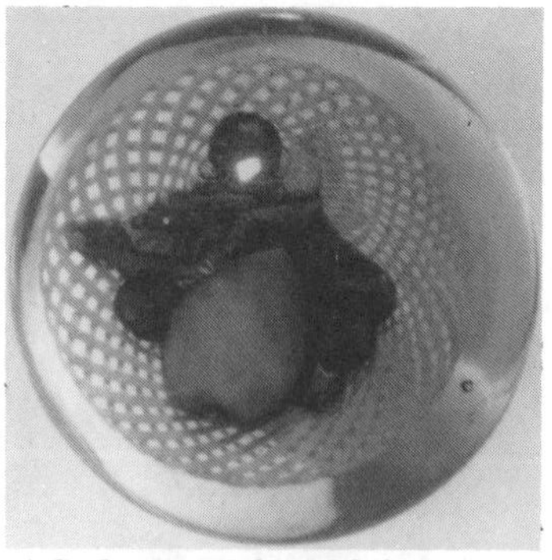

A St. Louis weight, with fruit on a cushion of opaque spiral latticinio thread, mid-19thC, 3in (7.5cm) diam.
$1,300-1,500

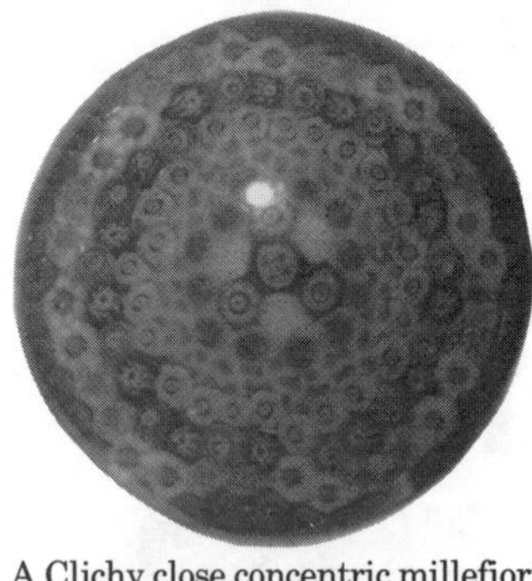

A Clichy close concentric millefiori weight, in pink, green, yellow, white and turquoise, mid-19thC, 3in (7cm) diam.
$650-800

A St. Louis faceted amber flash posy weight, in pink, yellow, white, blue and green, on an amber flash strawberry cut base, mid-19thC, 2½in (6.5cm) diam.
$1,500-2,000

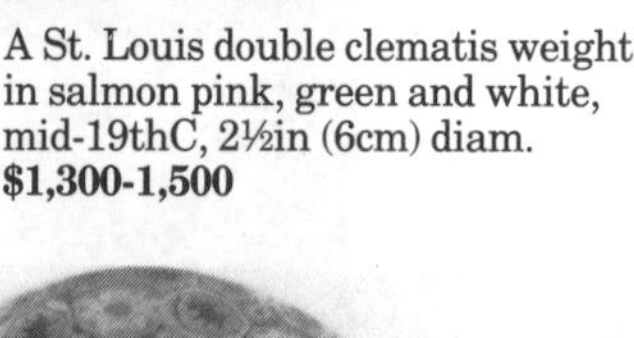

A St. Louis double clematis weight, in salmon pink, green and white, mid-19thC, 2½in (6cm) diam.
$1,300-1,500

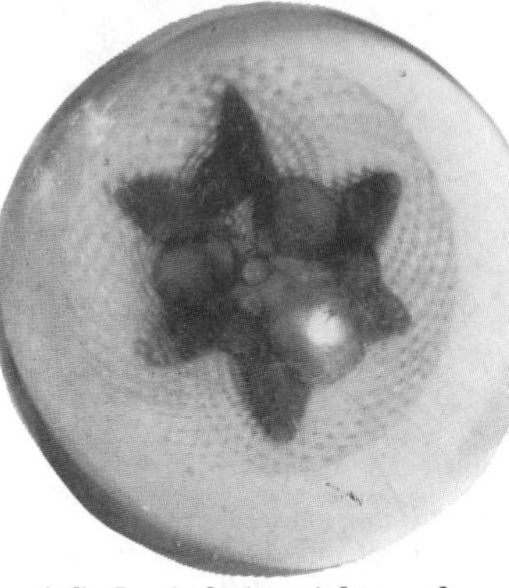

A St. Louis fruit weight, surface wear, mid-19thC, 3½in (8cm) diam.
$1,300-1,500

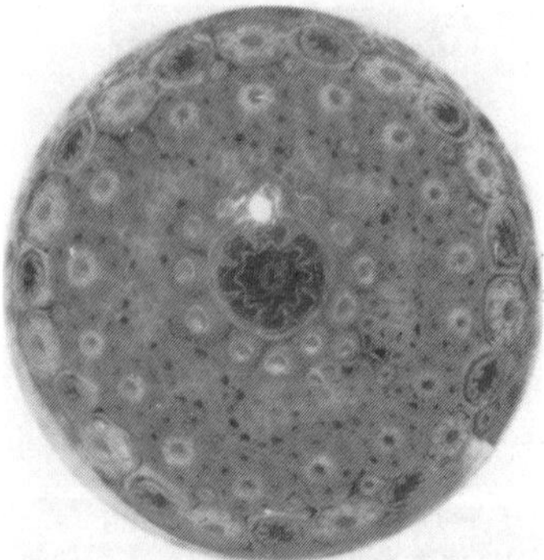

A Bacchus close concentric millefiori weight, in pink, mauve, blue, green, white and yellow about an iron red and white petal-shaped cane, mid-19thC, 3½in (8.5cm) diam.
$650-800

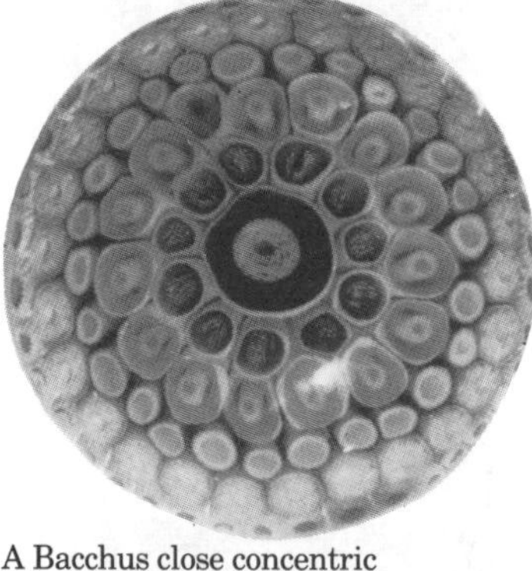

A Bacchus close concentric millefiori weight, in iron red, pale blue, cobalt blue, green and white, mid-19thC, 3½in (8.5cm) diam.
$1,300-1,500

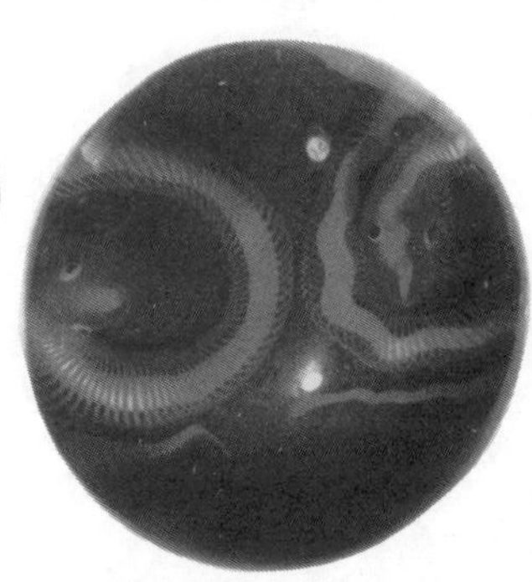

A Paul Ysart double snake pedestal weight, inscribed 'PY', on a black base, 20thC, 3in (7.5cm) diam.
$1,200-1,300

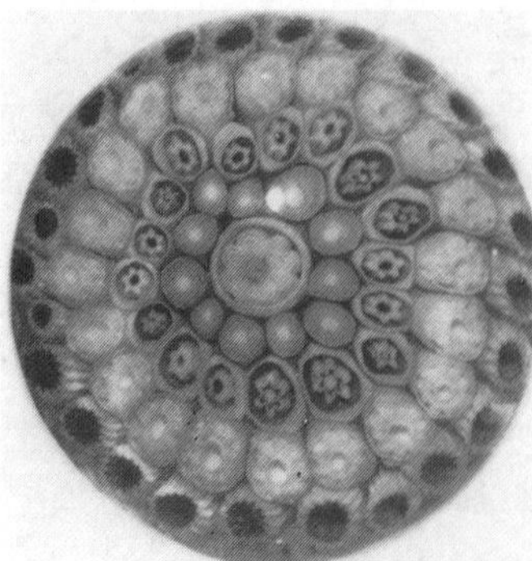

A Bacchus close concentric millefiori weight, in iron red, pale green, blue, pink and white, mid-19thC, 3½in (8.5cm) diam.
$500-650

A Baccarat garlanded pompom weight, with white flower, yellow stamen, green leaves and a green and white bud, on a star cut base, mid-19thC, 3in (7.5cm) diam.
$650-1,000

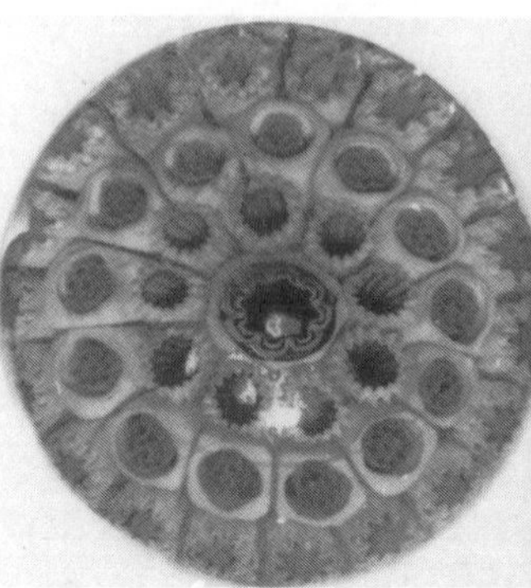

A Bacchus close concentric millefiori weight, in green, white, red, blue and mauve, mid-19thC, 3½in (8.5cm) diam.
$650-800

A Baccarat garlanded double clematis weight, the flower with ribbed pale mauve petals about a red and white star centre, set within a garland of alternate red and white canes, on a star cut base, mid-19thC, 2½in (6.5cm) diam.
$1,000-1,300

A Clichy swirl weight, the alternate dark green and white staves radiating from a central set-up of yellow rods and white star canes, mid-19thC, 3in (7cm) diam.
$650-1,200

A St. Louis faceted pink clematis weight, set on a cushion of white swirling latticinio thread, cut with a window and 6 printies, mid-19thC, 3in (7.5cm) diam.
$650-1,000

A Bacchus close millefiori weight, the tightly packed large canes in shades of turquoise, white, pale green, pink and brick red and including numerous portrait silhouette canes, mid-19thC, 3½in (8.5cm) diam.
$800-1,000

A Baccarat miniature primrose weight, inscribed on the base 18 4/72, mid-19thC, 2in (5cm) diam.
$1,300-1,500

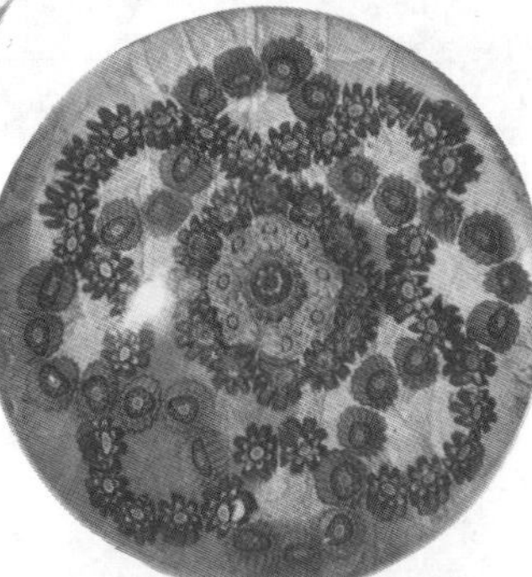

A Clichy patterned millefiori weight, in pale green, shades of dark blue and pink, on a muslin ground above a bed of horizontal cable, mid-19thC, 3½in (8cm) diam.
$650-1,200

A Baccarat garlanded butterfly weight, the insect with translucent purple body and marbled wings, set within a garland of alternate pink, green and white canes, on a star cut base, chipping to footrim, mid-19thC, 2½in (6.5cm) diam.
$1,300-1,500

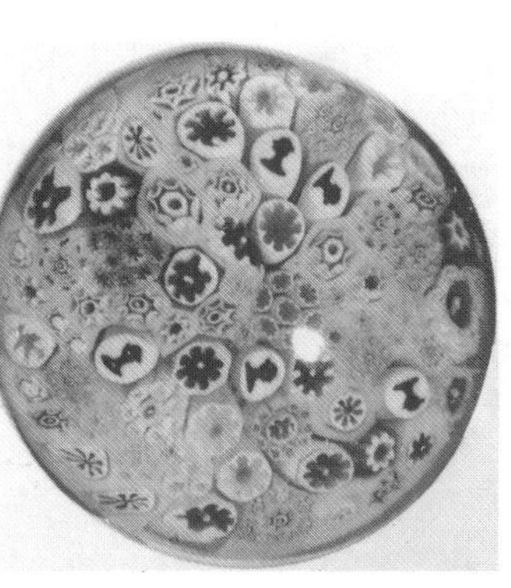

A Clichy patterned millefiori weight, with a tossed muslin ground above a bed of horizontal cable, mid-19thC, 3in (7cm) diam.
$1,200-1,400

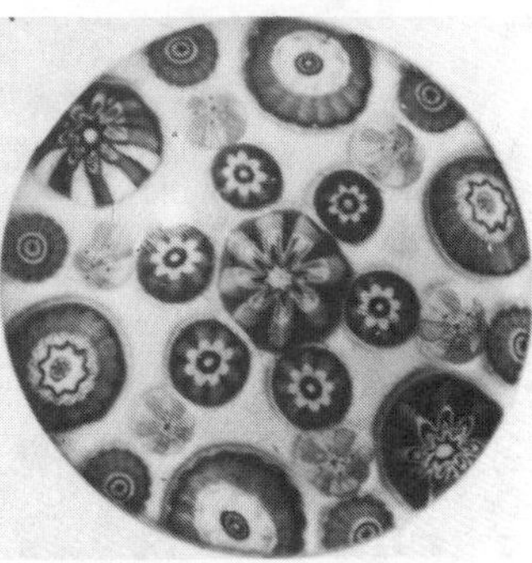

A Clichy 'sodden snow' ground patterned concentric millefiori weight, mid-19thC, 3½in (8.5cm) diam.
$500-650

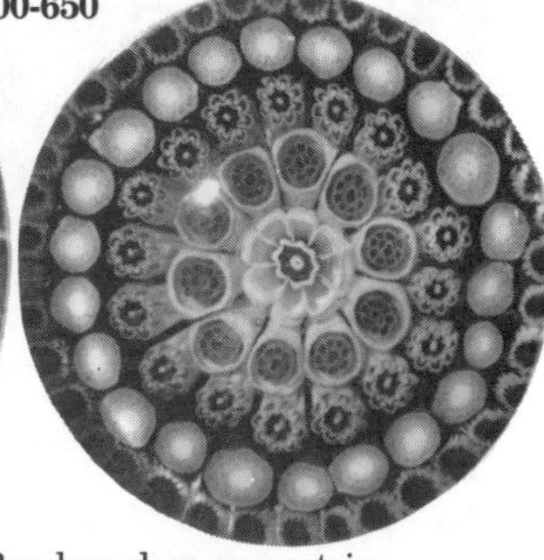

A Bacchus close concentric millefiori weight, in shades of pink, pale blue, dark blue, green and white within an outer circle of pale green lined white crimped tubes, mid-19thC, 3½in (8cm) diam.
$1,200-1,300

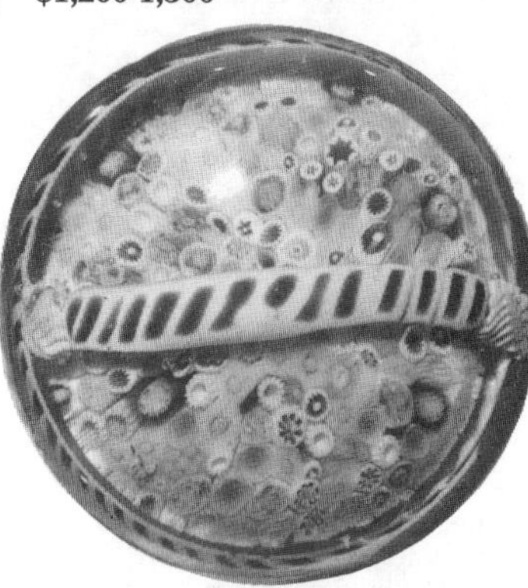

A Bacchus encased close millefiori basket weight, the tightly packed canes in predominant pale shades of white, red, turquoise and blue, mid-19thC, 4in (10cm) diam.
$2,500-3,000

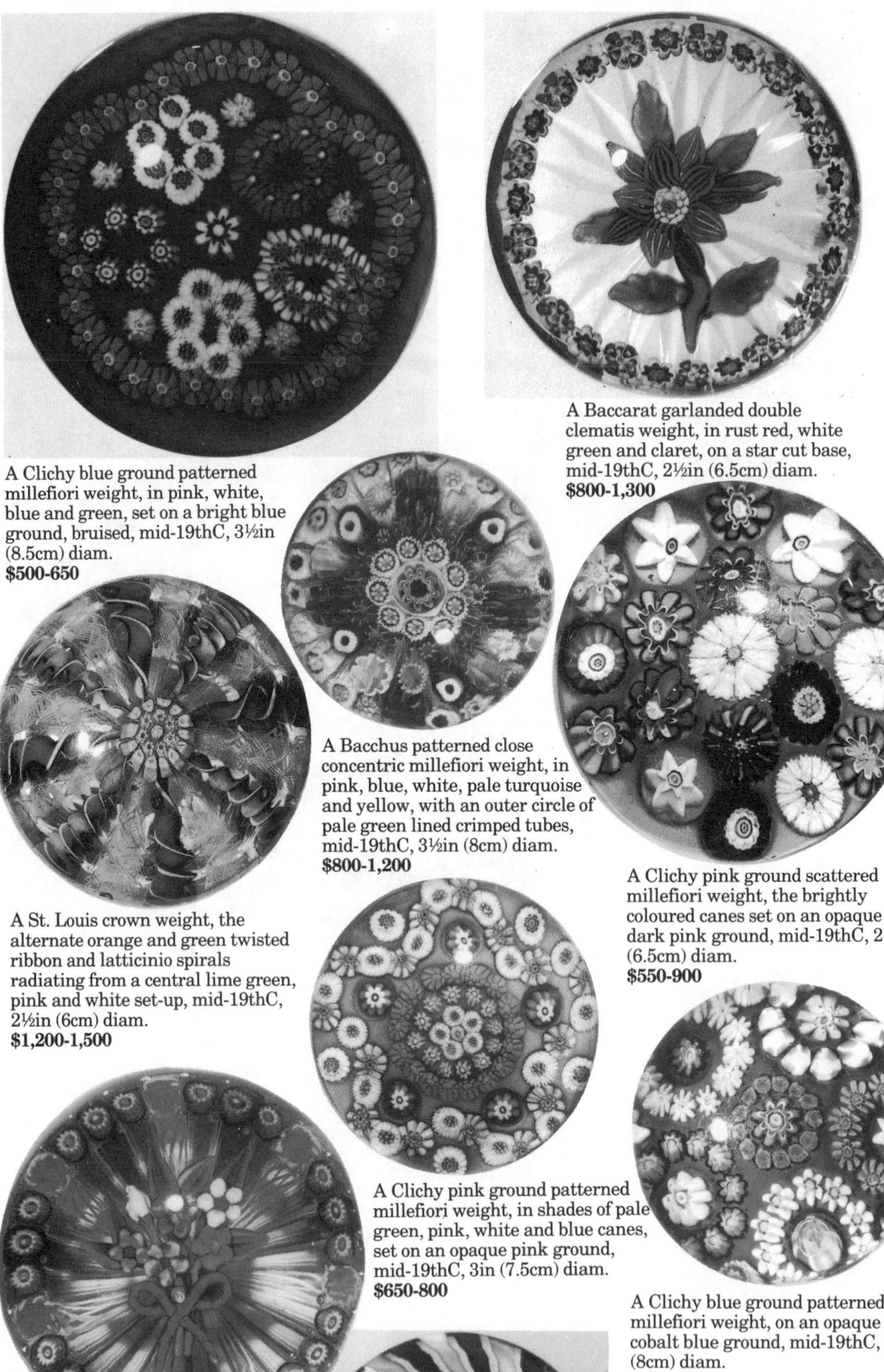

A Clichy blue ground patterned millefiori weight, in pink, white, blue and green, set on a bright blue ground, bruised, mid-19thC, 3½in (8.5cm) diam.
$500-650

A Baccarat garlanded double clematis weight, in rust red, white green and claret, on a star cut base, mid-19thC, 2½in (6.5cm) diam.
$800-1,300

A Bacchus patterned close concentric millefiori weight, in pink, blue, white, pale turquoise and yellow, with an outer circle of pale green lined crimped tubes, mid-19thC, 3½in (8cm) diam.
$800-1,200

A Clichy pink ground scattered millefiori weight, the brightly coloured canes set on an opaque dark pink ground, mid-19thC, 2½i (6.5cm) diam.
$550-900

A St. Louis crown weight, the alternate orange and green twisted ribbon and latticinio spirals radiating from a central lime green, pink and white set-up, mid-19thC, 2½in (6cm) diam.
$1,200-1,500

A Clichy pink ground patterned millefiori weight, in shades of pale green, pink, white and blue canes, set on an opaque pink ground, mid-19thC, 3in (7.5cm) diam.
$650-800

A Clichy blue ground patterned millefiori weight, on an opaque cobalt blue ground, mid-19thC, 3i (8cm) diam.
$1,000-1,200

A Paul Ysart bouquet weight, in blue, white, pink, purple, turquoise and lime green, inscribed 'PY', 20thC, 3in (7cm) diam.
$800-1,000

A Clichy swirl weight, the alternat cobalt blue and white staves radiating from a large central blue and white cane, mid-19thC, 3½in (8cm) diam.
$500-800

Scent Bottles

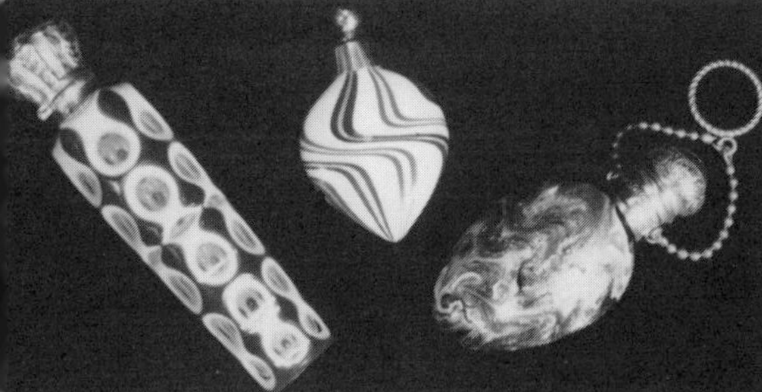

l. A clear scent bottle, with white and blue overlay, embossed white metal mount, c1860, 4in (10.5cm).
$500-550
c. A Nailsea type white opaque scent bottle, with red and blue swirls, gilt brass mounts, c1860, 2½in (6cm).
$110-150
r. A Venetian style scent bottle, with spangled inclusions, gilt brass mount and finger ring, c1820, 3in (7.5cm).
$100-150

A Victorian cut glass scent bottle, with gold cased mount.
$50-100

An Apsley Pellatt anti-slavery sulphide scent bottle and stopper, allover with hobnail within diamond cutting, slight bruising to rim and stopper, c1830, 6in (15cm).
$2,000-2,500

A Bohemian double overlay scent bottle, 3½in (9cm).
$200-250

l. A blue double-ended scent bottle, with gilt metal mounts, c1870, 4in (10cm).
$110-150
c. A red single-ended scent bottle, with embossed silver mount, hallmark 1876, 2½in (6.5cm).
$100-150
r. A red double-ended scent bottle, with embossed silver mounts, c1880, 4¼in (10.5cm).
$110-150

A scent bottle, Birmingham, c1904, 2½in (6.5cm).
$130-150

A Victorian green double overlay scent bottle, 7in (17.5cm).
$200-250

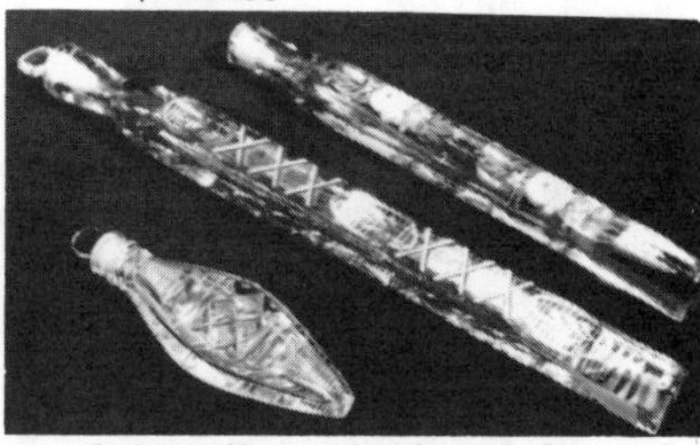

l. A small scent bottle with diamond and flute cutting, c1820, 3in (8cm).
$110-140
c. An Oxford lavender or throw-away scent bottle, with cut and gilt decoration, c1880, 8½in (21.5cm).
$80-110
r. A small scent bottle with enamelled floral decoration, c1880, 6in (15cm).
$80-110

A cut glass perfume bottle, with gilt top, 6½in (17cm).
$50-100

A French blue opaque glass scent bottle, decorated in gilt with berried foliage, gilt metal hinged cover and chain, 3in (7.5cm).
$100-130

A French glass and gold mounted perfume flask, the shoulders engraved with rococo scrolls and flowers, the gold jacket and domed hinged cover embossed and chased in rococo style and with engraved monogram, 4½in (11.5cm).
$550-700

Vases

A clear glass vase, designed by Clyne Farquharson, the body decorated in the Leaf pattern of cut leaves on engraved sinuous stems, engraved Clyne Farquharson NRD 39, 10in (25cm).
$400-550

A pair of Bohemian lustre vases, each with enamelled floral panels to the top, white overlaid bases and allover scrolling gilt decoration and hung with prism drops and lozenges, late 19thC, 13in (34cm).
$1,200-1,300

A pair of decalomania vases, decorated with coloured transfers, in shades of blue, yellow and green on buff grounds, some repainting to the interior, mid-19thC, 12in (30.5cm).
$5,500-7,000

A decalomania vase and cover, decorated with coloured transfers on a bright blue ground, one transfer lacking to cover and damage to decoration, mid-19thC, 9in (23cm).
$800-1,000

A pair of Victorian pink opaque glass lustre vases, with white enamelled decoration, bordered in gilt, 14in (36cm).
$900-1,000

An opaque white vase, with enamelled decoration of exotic birds in a chinoiserie scene, South Staffs. or London, c1760, 5in (13.5cm).
$1,500-3,000

A pair of Bohemian enamelled and gilt overlay vases, in dark cranberry glass overlaid in opaque white, the panels painted in colours, damaged 17in (43cm).
$900-1,000

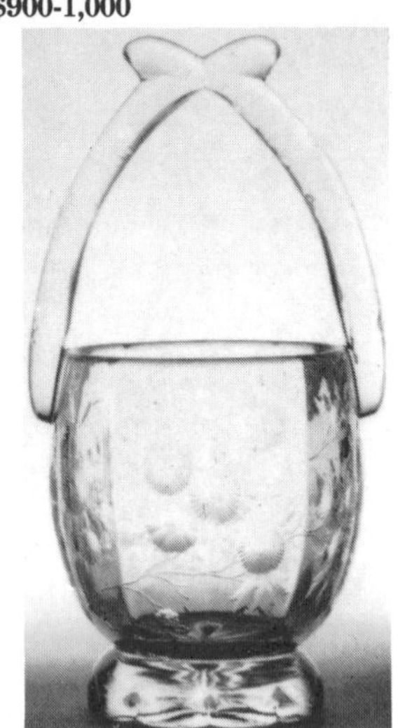

A rock crystal vase, in the form of a basket, Stourbridge, c1885, 9in (23cm).
$1,200-1,500

Miscellaneous

A Bohemian chinoiserie reverse painted and cut plate, the centre painted in colours with a youth standing holding an apple in one hand beside an exotic bird on a perch, possibly Buquoy Glasshouse South Bohemia, border crazed, rim damaged, c1835, 8½in (21cm) diam wood frame.
$650-1,000

A pair of Regency cut glass inkwells c1820, 2½in (6cm) high.
$140-150

OAK & COUNTRY FURNITURE

Beds

n oak cradle, with shaped hood nd sides, basically 17thC, 36½in 92cm) long.
1,000-1,300

n oak four-poster bed of panelled onstruction, the headboard with nlaid arched architectural panel, he tester carved with lozenges and oliage with foliate cornice, on ulbous turned posts, the footboard arved with lozenges, with box pring, 76in (193cm) long.
5,500-7,000

Bureaux

A George II oak bureau, with engraved brass plate handles and escutcheons, the interior fitted with stepped drawers, a centre cupboard and sunken well, on bracket feet, 36in (91.5cm).
$2,500-3,000

A George III oak bureau, with fitted interior, 2 short and 3 graduated long drawers, on bracket feet, adapted, 32in (81cm).
$2,000-2,500

A Queen Anne oak bureau, c1710.
$4,000-5,500

A small Queen Anne oak bureau bookcase, c1700.
$13,000-20,000

George III oak bureau bookcase, ith mahogany frieze, the hinged ope enclosing a fitted interior, on racket feet, 50½in (128cm).
1,500-2,500

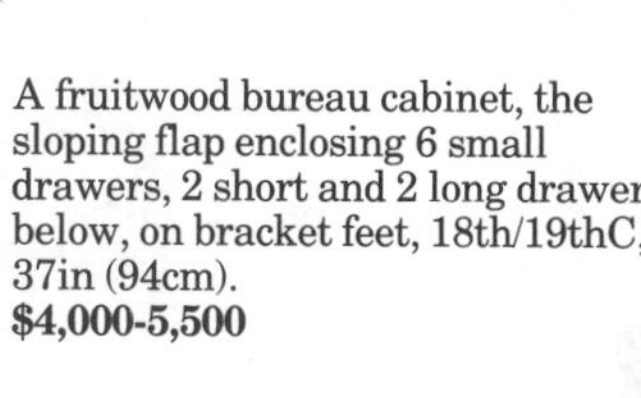

A George III oak bureau bookcase, c1760.
$9,500-14,000

A fruitwood bureau cabinet, the sloping flap enclosing 6 small drawers, 2 short and 2 long drawers below, on bracket feet, 18th/19thC, 37in (94cm).
$4,000-5,500

Cabinets

A Flemish cabinet-on-stand, heavily carved, the stand with deep frieze centred by a roundel of a trumpeting angel flanked by putti on bulbous turned sectional legs and ebonised feet, legs restored, early 17thC, 29½in (75cm).
$5,000-6,500

Chairs

An oak open armchair, the toprail with foliate scrolls, solid seat, on turned legs, with stretchers, 17thC.
$4,000-5,500

An oak open armchair, carved with a lozenge, with solid seat on turned legs with stretchers, lacking cresting, restored, 17thC.
$2,000-2,500

A Charles II carved oak wainsco chair, c1680.
$5,000-6,500

An oak wainscot chair, the square back with carved shaped arched cresting rail flanked by scroll ears, carved with the initials 'H.F.' flanking the date '1612', raised upon barrel turned and block supports and plain stretchers.
$400-550

A set of 6 Charles II style Derbyshire elm and oak dining chairs, the foliate waved rail backs above leather seats on baluster legs with stretchers.
$1,000-1,500

A Queen Anne oak armchair, the frieze initialled JL, dated in numerals 1710, the arms with S-scroll supports, with solid seat an shaped seat rail on S-scroll and squared legs, with stretchers, back legs replaced.
$1,400-2,000

A Charles II oak child's chair, the toprail with scrolled ends and the initials RT, the arms with turned supports, with solid seat on squared and turned legs with moulded stretchers.
$12,000-13,000

A pair of oak dining chairs, the canework seats on turned baluster and block supports, ending in tassled toes, joined by turned baluster stretchers, each chair initialled IP, late 17thC and later.
$2,500-3,000

A pair of oak hall chairs, with barley twist supports, upholstered seats, plain front legs with scrolling front stretchers, 18thC.
$550-700

A set of eight 17thC style oak dining chairs, including a pair of armchairs, with leaf and scroll carved pierced top rails, splat backs, panel seats on turned front supports.
$2,000-2,500

A pair of George I oak side chairs, c1725.
$1,300-2,000

A George III child's oak rocking chair, of plain plank construction with shaped sides.
$500-550

A comb back Windsor armchair, with scrolled arms above a shaped seat, on baluster turned splayed legs joined by a bulbous turned H-stretcher, Pennsylvania, loss to bottom of one arm, c1800.
$4,500-5,500

An oak side chair, c1700.
$1,000-1,200

A pair of bow back Windsor side chairs, each with bowed crest above bamboo turned spindles, over a shaped seat on bamboo turned legs joined by an H-stretcher, one branded Sanborn, Boston, Massachusetts, c1799, 37in (94cm).
$2,000-2,500

A set of 9 Restoration style carved oak chairs, with ornate leaf scroll and flower decorated high backs, overstuffed seats, raised understretchers and cabriole legs with paw feet, 19thC.
$3,000-5,000

A William and Mary painted maple side chair, on cylinder and ring turned front legs joined by a double arrow and ring turned stretcher, Essex County, Massachusetts, c1745.
$1,000-1,500

A cherrywood comb back Windsor armchair, c1760.
$2,500-4,000

A Welsh elm child's chair, with shaped top rail over spindle back, all raised on splay supports, mid-18thC, 14in (36cm) high.
$1,000-1,200

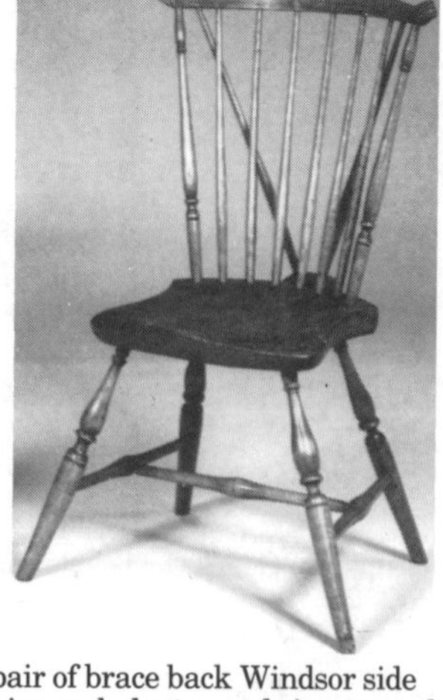

A pair of brace back Windsor side chairs, on baluster and ring turned legs joined by swelled stretchers, New England, late 18th/early 19thC.
$3,000-5,000

A slat back maple armchair, with ball and ring turned finials and flat arms, above a rush seat, on cylinder-and-ball turned legs joined by a double turned stretcher, New York or Connecticut, late 18thC.
$3,500-4,000

A George III elm armchair, c1780.
$1,200-2,000

A fan back Windsor armchair, with curved and scalloped crest rail over 7 spindles flanked by baluster turned stiles, above a shaped seat on splayed baluster turned legs, joined by a bulbous turned H-stretcher, Massachusetts, feet reduced, c1800.
$700-1,200

A set of 6 elm spindle back chairs, c1820.
$2,500-3,000

Did you know

MILLER'S Antiques Price Guide builds up year by year to form the most comprehensive photo-reference system available

A Windsor sack back armchair, on baluster and ring turned legs joined by turned stretchers, New England, 19thC.
$1,500-2,500

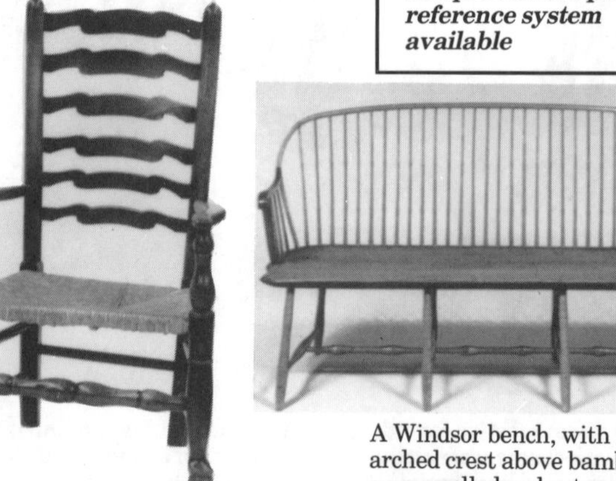

An 18thC style ladder back carver chair, with rush seat, on turned legs and stretcher.
$250-300

A Windsor bench, with incised arched crest above bamboo spindles over scrolled walnut arms, on bamboo turned legs joined by bamboo turned stretchers, Philadelphia, late 18th/early 19thC.
$12,000-13,500

. low bow armchair, with stick and ddle back, on turned legs.
500-650

A set of 6 ash matched ladderback chairs, c1810.
$5,000-5,500

A set of 6 elm Windsor wheelback chairs, c1830.
$2,500-3,000

ın Irish ash and elm famine chair, ı original colour, Kerry, c1840, 1in (54cm).
500-650

A large oak elbow hall chair and the matching set of 4 single chairs, carved in Jacobean style, supported on turned and carved feet with barley twist stretchers, each upholstered and covered to the back and seat with brown leather, 19thC.
$900-1,000

A pair of elm Windsor chairs, with crinoline stretchers, early 19thC.
$700-800

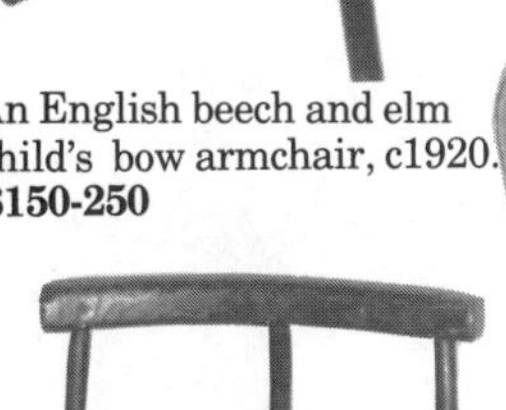
ın English beech and elm hild's bow armchair, c1920.
$150-250

A set of 6 Windsor wheelback kitchen chairs, 19thC.
$900-1,000

A Lincolnshire yew and elm Windsor chair, the high hoop back with pierced splat flanked by dowels, on baluster turned supports terminating in stylised hoof feet, tied by a crinoline stretcher.
$900-1,000

A primitive child's chair, with original red paint, 19thC, 18in 46cm).
$300-400

An elm chair, late 18thC.
$200-250

A set of 4 black-painted fan-back Windsor chairs, on splayed bamboo turned legs joined by a bulbous H-stretcher, New England, 19thC.
$2,500-3,000

A black painted Windsor child's armchair, with shaped fan-back above 7 spindles and flat-shaped set back arms over a saddle seat, on splayed baluster turned legs joined by a bulbous turned H-stretcher, 19thC.
$650-1,200

A yew wood bow arm high back Windsor chair, with pierced splat, solid seat, turned legs and stretcher.
$1,000-1,300

An English beech and elm carver chair, Sussex, c1870.
$350-450

An Irish stripped beech and elm smoker's chair, c1875.
$350-450

A set of 5 Irish beechwood penny seat and stick back chairs, c1890.
$650-800

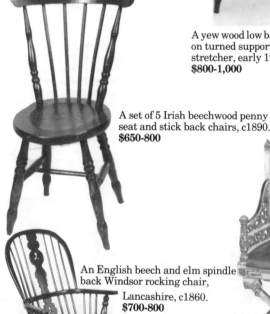

An English beech and elm spindle back Windsor rocking chair, Lancashire, c1860.
$700-800

A set of 4 beech and elm children's stick back chairs, c1880, 26in (66cm).
$650-800

A yew wood low back Windsor chair on turned supports with crinoline stretcher, early 19thC.
$800-1,000

A Continental parcel gilt oak throne, the upholstered back with crowned fleur-de-lys crest, the sides with foliate fretwork panels, on X-frame supports, 19thC.
$2,000-2,500

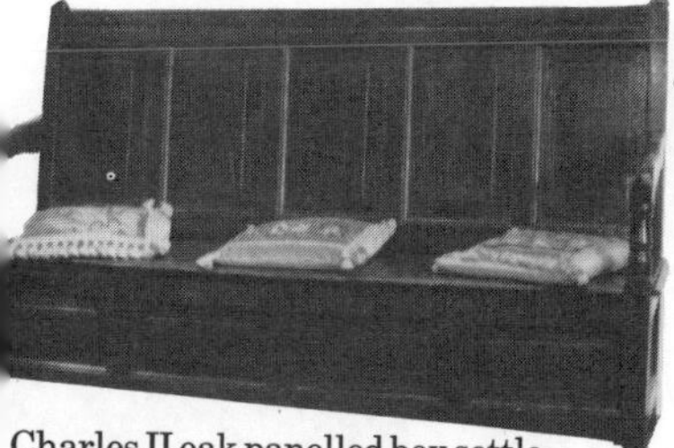

Charles II oak panelled box settle,
680.
,000-6,500

small oak panelled box settle,
760.
,000-5,500

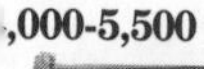

George I oak, ash and elm
nelled settle, c1720.
,500-3,000

An oak high wing back settle, of concave form, the seat with 2 drawers, 18thC, 50in (127cm).
$1,500-2,500

hests

n oak chest, with moulded hinged
, on square channelled legs, West
untry, early 17thC, 57in (145cm).
,000-4,000

An oak coffer with panelled top and front, shaped cornice and the legs formed from the reeded side stiles, 17th/18thC, 42in (106.5cm).
$1,000-1,200

A small Charles I oak arcaded and inlaid coffer, c1625.
$3,000-5,500

A Charles I oak coffer, Yorkshire, 49in (124cm).
$1,000-1,200

A carved oak arcaded coffer, c1660.
$4,000-5,500

A German metal bound oak coffer, with embossed bands, enclosed by a domed lid, with intricate lock mechanism and side carrying handles, on later turned feet, 18thC, 60in (152cm).
$1,200-2,000

An oak chest, the hinged top above an angled, panelled front with 2 short and one long drawer, on high bracket feet, early 18thC, 34in (86cm).
$2,000-3,000

An oak coffer with hinged panelled top, 17thC, 54in (137cm).
$3,000-4,000

An oak chest-on-stand, with two short and 3 graduated long drawers, the stand with 3 small drawers, on inverted cupped baluster legs and cross stretchers, basically 18thC, 40in (101.5cm).
$2,000-2,500

A George III oak chest, with 2 short and 3 long graduated drawers, on bracket feet, altered, 36in (91cm).
$800-1,000

A Charles II carved oak panelled coffer, c1680.
$2,500-4,000

A small oak chest of 4 drawers, with original brasses, c1745.
$1,500-4,000

A William and Mary burr oak chest of drawers, inlaid with fruitwood, c1695.
$5,500-8,000

Cupboards

A French Provincial chestnut armoire, the shaped apron carved with a heart, on cabriole feet, 18thC later moulded cornice, 62in (157cm
$2,500-3,000

A George III oak mule chest, with hinged moulded top, above a panelled front filled with ogee arches and fitted with 3 short drawers, distressed, 59½in (150cm).
$1,300-2,000

An oak chest, with moulded top above 3 geometrically panelled graduated long drawers, on bun feet, restorations, late 17thC.
$2,500-3,000

A French Provincial oak bas armoire, with frieze drawer, arched panel cupboard door, on square feet some restoration, late 18thC.
$1,000-1,200

A small Jacbobean oak chest, with moulded drawer fronts, on bunfeet, 33in (84cm).
$650-700

A French Provincial oak buffet, with planked and banded top, on tapering block feet, basically 18thC, 44½in (111.5cm).
$3,000-4,000

A carved oak blanket, on stump feet, 50½in (128cm).
$500-650

An oak coffer, some restoration required, 53in (134.5cm).
$1,400-1,500

An oak blanket box, the lid with a moulded edge above a 3 panelled front carved with the initials E.D., 48in (122cm).
$650-700

A French Provincial fruitwood buffet, with serpentine moulded top on squat cabriole legs, late 18thC, 52in (132cm).
$1,500-2,500

An oak court cupboard, South Wales, c1690.
$8,000-13,000

An oak court cupboard, ornately carved in flind fret style, with scrolling leaves and motifs, late 17th/early 18thC, 52in (132cm).
$1,300-1,500

An oak cupboard, with moulded cornice above 2 panelled doors, on moulded plinth and later bun feet, reduced in depth, mid-17thC, 58½in (148cm).
$6,500-8,000

A bowfront corner cupboard with double doors, 19thC.
$800-900

A Flemish oak cupboard, with moulded cornice, 2 pairs of ebony-set panelled doors divided by stop-fluted uprights and on later massive bun feet, 17thC, 52in (132cm).
$3,500-4,000

An oak court cupboard, with strapwork panels, the canopy top with 2 doors above 3 fielded cupboard doors, on block feet, c1668, 55½in (140cm).
$2,000-2,500

A Flemish oak cupboad, with a moulded cornice above a frieze applied with split bobbin turnings and roundels, the 2 geometrically panelled doors centred by roundels, a panelled front below, 17thC, 59in (149.5cm).
$1,300-1,500

An oak linen cupboard, the upper section with ogee moulded cornice, over hanging compartments, enclosed by a pair of arched double fielded panelled doors with brass hinges, knob handles and shaped escutcheons, over 3 drawers with later brass handles, flanked by quadrant stiles and raised upon ogee bracket feet, 18thC, 68in (172cm).
$3,000-4,000

A Georgian oak hanging corner cupboard, with stepped and dentil pediment, over 2 panel doors, enclosing 3 shelves, 34in (86cm).
$400-500

An oak press style cabinet, with 3 short and 4 long drawers, brass drop handles and escutcheons, bracket feet, 69in (175cm).
$2,500-3,000

A French oak armoire, with ornate brass escutcheons, full length base drawer with shaped sunk panel front with raised and fielded panel ends, 18thC, 65in (166cm). **$900-1,200**

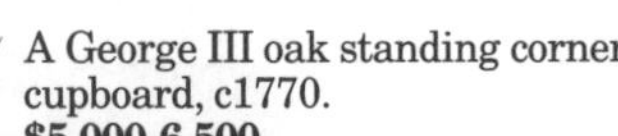

A George III oak standing corner cupboard, c1770. **$5,000-6,500**

A Georgian North Country oak corner cupboard. **$1,400-2,000**

An oak standing corner cupboard, profusely carved, on bracket feet, late 19thC, 46in (116.5cm). **$1,000-1,400**

An oak press cupboard, the top with moulded cornice and frieze dated '1733' and initialled 'P.E.K.', above a pair of fielded panelled doors, on a base of two similar short drawers, on block feet, 18thC, 53in (135cm). **$4,000-5,000**

A George III oak hanging corner cupboard, with original brasses and secret drawers to interior, c1770. **$4,000-5,500**

An oak court cupboard, carved with foliage and strapwork bands, initialled 'W.R.B.' and dated '1715', 47in (119cm). **$5,000-6,500**

A Georgian oak hanging corner cupboard, with mahogany crossbanding, dentil pediment over 2 panel doors enclosing 3 shaped shelves, 30in (76cm). **$400-500**

A George III mahogany standing corner cupboard, with a bolection moulded cornice, above a pair of fielded arched doors and a pair of panelled cupboard doors with canted angles on bracket feet, 48in (122cm). **$4,000-5,000**

Dressers

An oak dresser, inlaid with ivory and chequer bands, on turned bun feet, 55½in (140cm). **$2,500-3,000**

A late Georgian III oak dresser, the top section with a bolection cornice and open shelves above an arcaded base with 3 frieze drawers on baluster column supports and pot board with block feet, 73in (185cm). **$5,000-6,500**

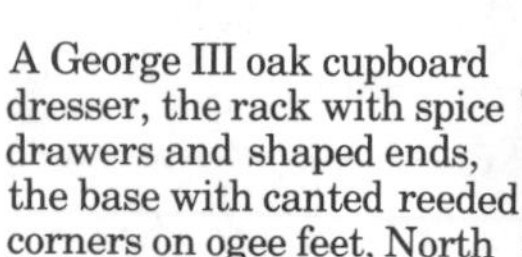

A George III oak cupboard dresser, the rack with spice drawers and shaped ends, the base with canted reeded corners on ogee feet, North Wales, c1785. **$13,000-20,000**

An oak dresser, the top section with a cavetto moulded cornice and open shelves, above 3 frieze drawers and twin false drawers, on baluster columns, 71½in (180cm).
$7,000-9,000

A George III oak, mahogany crossbanded and ebony lined dresser, the moulded top above 3 frieze drawers and 2 short drawers, flanked on either side by a pair of panelled cupboard doors, flanked by turned and fluted demi-column angles, on bracket feet, 72in (182.5cm).
$9,500-11,000

A Georgian oak dresser, the plate rack with moulded cornice and arcaded frieze, above 2 shelves fitted with iron books, the rounded top above 2 drawers and shaped apron, on square legs with rectangular undertier, 57in (145cm).
$5,500-7,000

Stools

An oak and elm joint stool, with moulded seat, ring turned legs and squared stretchers, 17thC, 18in (46cm). **$3,000-4,000**

An English beech and elm Windsor stool, c1860, 17in (43cm) high.
$90-110

An oak joint stool, with moulded seat, the seat rail carved with foliate lunettes, on ring turned legs with carved stretchers, 17thC with later top and restorations, 18in (46cm).
$1,200-1,300

Make the most of Miller's

Unless otherwise stated, any description which refers to 'a set' or 'a pair' includes a valuation for the entire set or the pair, even though the illustration may show only a single item

Tables

An oak side table, on bobbin turned legs joined by stretchers, late 17thC, 36in (91.5cm).
$1,500-2,500

An oak side table, with moulded top and frieze drawer, on baluster legs and conforming H-stretcher, one foot replaced, late 17thC, 34½in (88cm).
$1,300-2,000

A chestnut and polychrome-painted gateleg table, the top with single flap, on turned legs with turned and squared stretchers, restorations, 17thC.
$4,000-5,000

An oak lowboy, 18thC, 42in (106.5cm).
$1,200-1,500

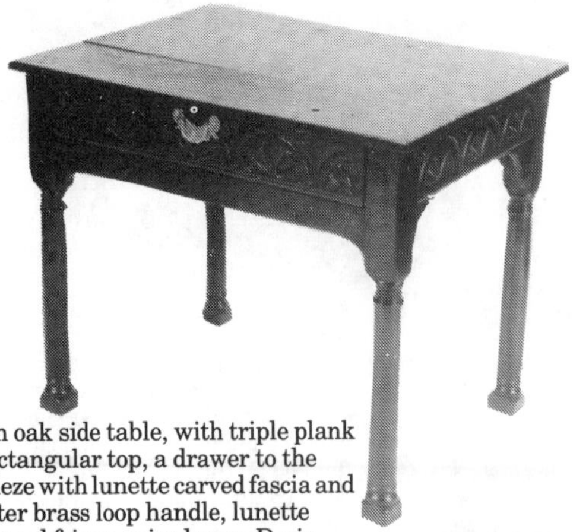

An oak side table, with triple plank rectangular top, a drawer to the frieze with lunette carved fascia and later brass loop handle, lunette carved frieze, raised upon Doric column supports, early 18thC, 34½in (87cm).
$700-900

A French Provincial chestnut table, on turned legs with moulded stretcher and later bun feet, 18thC, 57in (145cm).
$6,500-7,000

An oak gateleg table, the twin flap top and 2 frieze drawers, on baluster turned legs with stretchers, 78in (198cm).
$6,000-6,500

An Austrian elm work table with drawer, reduced in height, Tyrol, c1850, 33in (84cm).
$1,200-1,400

A Spanish oak and fruitwood serving table, the plank top above 3 frieze drawers on turned legs, tied by moulded stretchers, part 17thC, 73in (186cm).
$2,500-3,000

Miller's is a price Guide not a price List

The price ranges given reflect the average price a purchaser should pay for similar items. Condition, rarity of design or pattern, size, colour, provenance, restoration and many other factors must be taken into account when assessing values. When buying or selling, it must always be remembered that prices can be greatly affected by the condition of any piece. Unless otherwise stated, all goods shown in Miller's are of good merchantable quality, and the valuations given reflect this fact. Pieces offered for sale in exceptionally fine condition or in poor condition may reasonably be expected to be priced considerably higher or lower respectively than the estimates given herein

A Charles II style yew wood gateleg dining table, on a bobbin and reel baluster twin double gated underframe, joined with cross stretchers, 81in (205.5cm).
$4,000-5,000

An oak gateleg dining table, with plain plank top supported on barley twist legs and plain stretchers, 18thC, 47in (119cm).
$1,200-1,300

. tripod table, 18thC.
500-650

Victorian oak hall table, the ıarble top above 2 frieze drawers ırved with foliage, on bulbous ›liate carved square tapering legs, 6in (168cm).
3,000-4,000

. Charles II oak side table, the lank top above a frieze drawer and avy apron, on baluster turned legs, ›me restoration, 34in (86cm).
2,000-2,500

Make the Most of Miller's

CONDITION is absolutely vital when assessing the value of an antique. Damaged pieces on the whole appreciate much less than perfect examples. However a rare, desirable piece may command a high price even when damaged

An oak Jacobean style refectory table, with thick 2 plank top, on 6 square baluster supports, 139 (353cm) long.
$21,000-28,000

An 18thC style oak oval gateleg dining table, with single frieze drawer, supported on ring turned legs with plain stretchers, 40in (101.5cm).
$400-500

An oak carving, 17thC.
$400-500

Miscellaneous

An oak and fruitwood hanging shelf, the 3 shelves with turned supports, the central shelf with guilloche carved front and arcaded sides, 28in (71cm).
$3,000-4,000

A Queen Anne oak bookcase top, with moulded double arched cornice above 2 panelled doors, lacking lower section, 45in (114cm).
$800-1,300

An English iron bound oak wash tub on legs, Lincolnshire, c1890, 21in (53cm) diam.
$250-300

An Irish rustic pearwood turf or peat box, Connemara, c1840, 36in (92cm).
$900-1,000

FURNITURE

Beds

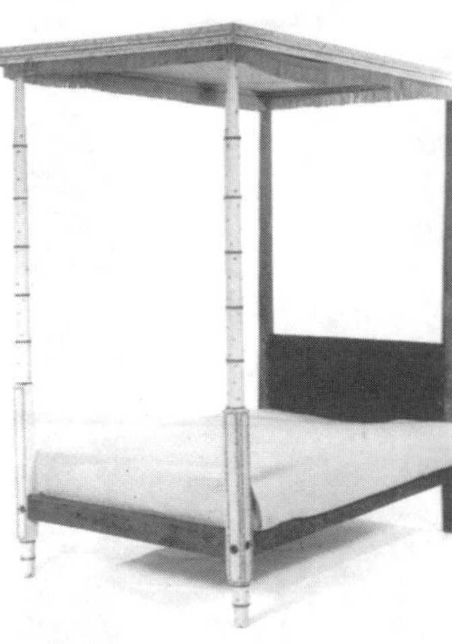

A Regency painted four-poster bed, with moulded cornice, supported on bamboo turned columns, 52in (132cm) wide.
$3,000-4,000

A Regency mahogany and cane panelled cradle, with ogee arched canopy and swing between acorned finialled turned uprights, joined by stretchers, 42in (106.5cm) long.
$1,400-2,000

A mahogany and pine four-poster bed, with carved canopy and fluted posts applied with acanthus scrolls on claw-and-ball feet, 18thC and later, 85in (216cm) long.
$3,000-5,000

A Louis XV walnut daybed, with conforming crisp carving on cabriole legs carved with flowerheads and foliage, possibly Liège, later blocks, restorations, one foot missing, 83in (21cm) long.
$2,500-3,000

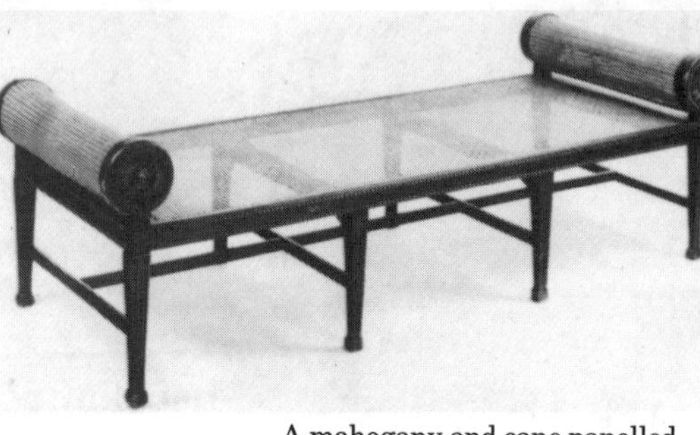

A mahogany and cane panelled daybed, the seat with bolster ends in a frame beaded and carved with paterae, on square tapered fluted legs joined by stretchers, with loose upholstered squab and 2 bolsters, late 18thC and later.
$2,500-3,000

A mahogany four-poster bed, the frieze with blind fret decoration supported on stop-fluted turned posts and shaped headboard, with pleated blue silk canopy and floral print chintz drapes, with box-spring and mattress, 86in (218cm) long.
$3,000-4,000

A late Federal carved mahogany high post bedstead, the footposts spiral turned with carved inverted balusters on inverted baluster and ring turned feet, Massachusetts, c1815, 58in (147cm).
$3,000-5,000

An Italian parcel-gilt, walnut and ebonised bed, with shaped foot rest and sides with turned finials and moulded columns headed by giltmetal capitals, on claw and block feet, distressed padded solid headboard, 70in (177.5cm).
$6,500-7,000

A French Provincial fruitwood daybed, with outscrolled ends and moulded rail, on bracket feet, 19thC, 78in (198cm).
$1,300-1,500

A Venetian rococo giltwood headboard, with cartouche-shaped padded back and pierced scrolling foliate crest issuing leafy scrolls, with vine leaves and grape clusters, upholstered in pale blue floral silk, 76in (193cm).
$6,500-8,000

Bonheur du jour

A Regency rosewood bonheur du jour, the mirrored shelf superstructure on S-scroll supports, with a subsidiary shelf on brass columns, the lower section with a frieze drawer, on turned and lobed legs headed by lotus carved capitals, 28in (71cm).
$8,000-9,500

An inlaid burr walnut bonheur du jour, with central mirror and drawer between two glazed cupboards, the fall enclosing fitted interior and well, with ormolu mounts, on cabriole legs, 19thC, 33in (84cm).
$2,000-2,500

A neo-classical style satinwood bonheur du jour, painted and decorated, the 3 frieze drawers and concave undertier on square splayed tapering legs, 24in (62cm).
$6,500-8,000

An Edwardian mahogany bonheur du jour, on tapered legs with brass casters, with satinwood banding and boxwood stringing, 31in (79cm).
$2,500-3,000

A Louis XVI style kingwood and aramanth breakfront bonheur du jour, the tambour shutter enclosing a fitted interior, with a brass galleried undertier, on cabriole legs with sabots and trophy mounted capitals, 26½in (68cm).
$3,000-4,000

Breakfront Bookcases

A William IV mahogany breakfront secretaire bookcase, the later moulded cornice applied with foliate motif above open shelves between moulded uprights, 112in (284.5cm).
$7,000-9,000

A George III style mahogany breakfront bookcase, with dentilled cornice, above glazed astragal doors and panelled doors on bracket feet, 80½in (204cm).
$7,000-9,000

A George III mahogany breakfront bookcase, with later moulded cornice, the base with a fitted interior, above a pair of panelled cupboards enclosing 3 graduated long drawers and with conforming cupboard doors, on later plinth, 90in (229cm).
$13,000-16,000

A George III mahogany breakfront secretaire bookcase, with central fitted writing drawer, above a pair of panelled doors flanked by 2 other doors, on platform base, 68in (172.5cm).
$10,000-12,000

An early Victorian mahogany breakfront library bookcase, with 5 glazed and 5 panelled doors, the whole raised upon a cushion moulded plinth, 139in (350cm).
$9,500-11,000

A Regency mahogany breakfront bookcase, the moulded cornice above 4 glazed doors, 4 drawers and 4 panelled doors on bracket feet, 102in (259cm).
$9,500-11,000

An Edwardian mahogany and satinwood banded breakfront bookcase, the lower section with 3 panel cupboard doors, on a plinth base, 72in (182.5cm).
$5,500-7,000

A Victorian mahogany breakfront bookcase, the cavetto moulded cornice above 4 glazed astragal doors and a pair of radial moulded panelled doors flanked by 8 side drawers, on plinth base, 98½in (250cm).
$8,000-9,500

A Victorian mahogany library bookcase, the panelled doors flanked by 10 drawers, on plinth base, 96in (244cm).
$3,000-5,000

A mahogany breakfront bookcase, with moulded cornice above 4 glazed doors and 4 radial panelled cupboard doors, on plinth base, 64in (162.5cm).
$2,500-3,000

A Georgian style mahogany and line inlaid breakfront library secretaire bookcase, 92in (233cm).
$35,000-40,000

A late Victorian oak breakfront library bookcase, on plinth base, labelled Sopwith & Co., Newcastle-on-Tyne, 98in (249cm).
$2,500-3,000

A mahogany breakfront bookcase, on plinth base, 142in (360cm).
$9,000-10,000

nahogany breakfront bookcase, :h Greek key cornice, above inlaid ted frieze and Gothic arch ragal glazed doors, the lower tion with a kingwood ssbanded drawer above oval neered cupboards, the sides with ther drawers above cupboards, n (249cm).
,500-13,000

A mahogany inverted breakfront bookcase, with additional later panelled mahogany and arched top, 180in (457cm).
$2,500-3,500

Bureau Bookcases

A mahogany bureau bookcase, with fitted interior, brass drop handles and escutcheons, fluted pilasters and ogee bracket feet, mid-18thC, 42½in (106.5cm).
$16,000-20,000

pair of Regency mahogany okcases, each with moulded rnice above a geometrically azed door and cupboard door iclosing shelves, on bracket feet, e side bowed and reeded, adapted, in (249cm) high.
,500-3,500

A George III mahogany bureau bookcase, with a fall flap revealing a fitted interior, the 4 long graduated drawers with brass and swan neck handles, on ogee bracket feet, 49in (124.5cm).
$4,500-5,000

A George II style walnut and featherbanded bureau bookcase, with a pair of candle slides, above a hinged sloping flap enclosing a fitted interior, on bracket feet, modern, 38in (96.5cm).
$3,000-4,000

Georgian mahogany secrétaire okcase, 42in (106.5cm).
,000-6,500

A George III mahogany bureau bookcase, the fall flap opening to reveal a fitted interior of pigeonholes, drawers and a cupboard, with 4 long graduated drawers under, on bracket feet, 44in (111.5cm).
$5,500-6,500

A George III mahogany bureau bookcase, the fall front enclosing small drawers and pigeonholes, with 4 graduated long drawers below, bracket feet, 47in (119cm).
$4,000-5,000

An Edwardian mahogany bureau bookcase, the shell inlaid flap opening to reveal plain interior, over 3 graduated drawers, raised on bracket feet, 24in (61cm). **$1,400-2,000**

An Edwardian mahogany and satinwood banded bureau bookcase, the fall front with an inlaid oval enclosing a fitted interior, above 4 long graduated drawers, on bracket feet. **$2,500-3,000**

An Edwardian inlaid mahogany bureau bookcase, with astragal glazed door, fall front and 3 drawers below with brass swan neck handles, on bracket feet, 93in (236cm) high. **$1,000-1,200**

An Edwardian mahogany and satinwood banded bureau bookcase, with a bolection moulded cornice, 37in (94cm). **$2,500-3,000**

A Sheraton mahogany revival period bureau bookcase, with satinwood crossbandings and swan neck cornice, 24in (61cm). **$2,000-2,500**

A walnut bureau bookcase, with arched top above 2 glazed doors, a featherbanded slope, 2 short and 2 long drawers, on bracket feet, 36in (91.5cm). **$3,000-4,000**

A Victorian walnut dwarf breakfront open bookcase, with fitted adjustable shelves, on a plinth base, 72in (183cm). **$2,000-2,500**

Dwarf Bookcases

A set of Regency mahogany open bookshelves, with swan neck pediment, on splay feet, 34in (86cm). **$700-900**

A Regency rosewood open dwarf bookcase, with 3 stepped shelves, baluster turned columns, turned legs and brass casters, 35in (89cm). **$2,500-3,000**

A rosewood open bookcase, with scrolled surmount, 5 graduated shelves with shaped sides and bead-and-reel moulding, 2 drawers below with turned knob handles, on 4 turned supports, early 19thC, 42in (106.5cm). **$1,500-2,500**

Regency mahogany bookshelf, the stepped shelves, with shaped sides ›ove a drawer on turned legs, 27in 9cm). **$3,000-4,000**

ɩ pair of walnut and parcel gilt warf open bookcases, each with a ıarble top, on turned feet, 19thC, 6in (66cm). **ı2,000-2,500**

ʟibrary Bookcases

ʌ George III style mahogany ›ookcase, with dentilled cornice ıbove a fluted frieze and a pair of ıstragal glazed doors, the base with luted frieze and enclosed by a pair ›f panelled doors, on bracket feet, 56in (142.5cm). **$3,000-4,000**

A mahogany dwarf open bookcase, the shelves with bobbin-turned fronts, clustered column supports, turned X-roundel side panels, with 2 drawers below, brass handles and turned feet, 18thC, 61in (155cm). **$4,000-5,000**

A pair of Victorian walnut open front dwarf bookcases, fitted with adjustable shelves, with parquetry Greek key pattern borders, on plinth bases, 33in (84cm). **$1,000-1,300**

A mid-Victorian mahogany bookcase, with pierced cartouche cresting above 4 glazed doors, the base with 4 convex strapwork drawers and 4 mirrored doors, on plinth base, 146in (370.5cm). **$8,000-9,500**

A pair of painted satinwood dwarf bookcases, on tapered feet, 19½in (49cm). **$1,500-2,000**

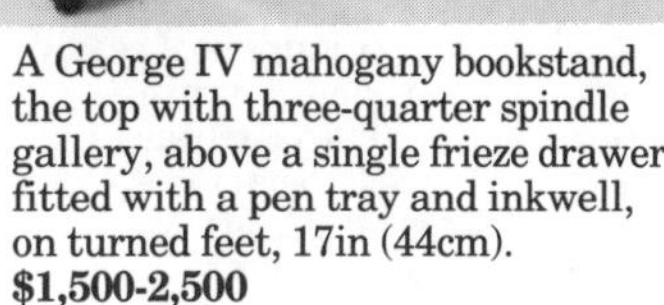

A George IV mahogany bookstand, the top with three-quarter spindle gallery, above a single frieze drawer fitted with a pen tray and inkwell, on turned feet, 17in (44cm). **$1,500-2,500**

A William IV rosewood bookcase, with moulded cornice, the lower section with 2 frieze drawers and 4 panelled doors, on plinth, stamped T. Willson, 68 Great Queen Street, London, 72in (182.5cm). **$7,000-9,000**

A George III mahogany secrétaire bookcase, the fascia hinged and falling to reveal pigeonholes and small drawers flanked by cupboards, enclosed by oval panelled doors, and with 3 long graduated drawers below, all with turned rosewood handles, flanked by cluster column stiles and raised upon shallow French bracket feet, 55in (138cm). **$6,500-7,000**

A George III mahogany secrétaire bookcase, the upper section with Greek key cornice, 44in (112cm). **$3,500-4,000**

A George III mahogany secrétaire bookcase, with moulded cornice, a pair of glazed cupboard doors above a fitted secrétaire drawer, 3 graduated long drawers, on splayed feet, 50in (127cm). **$5,000-6,500**

A Regency mahoga secrétaire bookcase on splayed bracket feet, 44½in (112cm). **$6,500-8,000**

A mahogany secrétaire bookcase, with rosewood banded writing drawer and panelled cupboard doors, on splayed bracket feet, adapted, early 19thC, 44½in (112cm). **$3,000-4,000**

A George III mahogany secrétaire bookcase, the base with fitted leather lined secrétaire drawer, above 2 short and 2 long drawers, on later blind fret carved bracket feet, 50in (127cm). **$5,000-8,000**

A late George III mahogany secrétaire bookcase, with a ball studded moulded cornice, a pair glazed astragal doors, a deep writing drawer, and pierced panelled doors on bracket feet, 48½in (123cm). **$2,500-4,000**

A Regency mahogany secrétaire bookcase, the top section with an inlaid frieze, 42in (106.5cm). **$2,500-3,000**

A late Georgian mahogany secrétaire bookcase, with shelved interior, the base with fully fitted secrétaire drawer and double cupboard below, on French bracket supports, 44in (111.5cm). **$4,000-5,000**

A Regency mahogany secrétaire bookcase, with beaded glass doors, fitted drawer and enclosed cupboar under, 44in (111.5cm). **$1,500-2,500**

brass bound bucket, with shaped andle, brass liner and shovel, 3½in (35cm) diam.
2,500-3,000

A Georgian staved mahogany plate bucket, with 2 wide brass bands and overhead swing handle, 14in (36cm) high. **$900-1,000**

Bureaux

A small William III walnut veneered bureau, with herringbone band inlay, oak lined drawers with engraved brass batswing plate handles and escutcheons, on replacement bun feet, 32½in (82cm).
$13,500-14,000

walnut bureau, inlaid with atherbands, the hinged slope nclosing a fitted interior, basically arly 18thC, 36in (91.5cm).
4,000-5,000

A walnut and pine bureau, with hinged sloping front enclosing a fitted interior, early 18thC, 36in (92cm).
$3,000-4,000

A Queen Anne walnut veneered bureau, with feather and cross banding, the fall front revealing a well, drawers and pigeonholes, with oak lined drawers double moulded outlined, on bracket feet, 34in (86cm).
$16,000-20,000

A walnut kneehole bureau, the fall front enclosing small drawers, pigeonholes, pillar drawers and a cabinet, the top, fall and drawer fronts all feather and crossbanded, bracket feet, early 18thC, 36in (91.5cm).
$5,000-6,500

walnut and featherbanded ureau, with hinged sloping front nclosing a fitted interior, on racket feet, basically early 18thC, 6in (92cm).
4,000-5,500

A mahogany bureau, with fitted interior, on bracket feet, distressed, early 19thC, 32in (81cm).
$2,500-3,000

A Dutch marquetry bombé bureau, the curved writing fall revealing a fitted interior, with ornate brass handles and escutcheon, profusely marquetry decorated within leafy scroll borders, early 19thC, 34in (87cm).
$3,500-5,000

A Provincial walnut bureau, with banded top and hinged sloping flap, enclosing a fitted interior, adapted, late 18thC, 45in (114cm).
$2,500-3,000

A walnut bureau, with stepped an fitted interior, 3 short and 3 long graduated drawers with brass handles and escutcheons, on brack feet, 18thC, 38in (96.5cm).
$13,500-14,500

A walnut marquetry bureau with shaped writing flap, stepped interior, single drawer under, on cabriole legs, 18thC, 34in (86cm).
$5,000-6,500

A burr walnut herringbone crossbanded bureau, with one simulated and 3 long drawers below, brass drop handles and bu feet, early 18thC, 38in (96.5cm).
$9,500-11,000

BUREAUX
- ★ Bureaux were not made in this country until after the reign of Charles II
- ★ this writing box on stand was initially produced in oak and then in walnut
- ★ these were originally on turned or straight legs but cabriole legs became popular in the last decade of the 17thC
- ★ note the quality and proportion of the cabriole legs – good carving is another plus factor
- ★ always more valuable if containing an *original* stepped interior and well
- ★ also the more complex the interior – the more expensive
- ★ from about 1680 most bureaux made from walnut, many with beautiful marquetry and inlay
- ★ from about 1740 mahogany became the most favoured wood, although walnut was still used
- ★ the 'key' size for a bureau is 38in (96.5cm), as the width diminishes so the price increases dramatically
- ★ original patination, colour and original brass handles are obviously important features for assessing any piece of furniture, but these are crucial when valuing bureaux and chests

A Dutch marquetry mahogany bureau of bombé form, on block feet, 18thC, 49½in (126cm).
$9,000-10,000

A mahogany bureau, the hinged sloping flap enclosing a fitted interior, on bracket feet, early 19thC, 47½in (120cm).
$1,500-2,500

A George I featherbanded walnut bureau, the hinged slope enclosing a fitted oak interior, on bracket feet, the drawers relined, 42in (106.5cm).
$8,000-9,500

A George I olivewood bureau, banded in walnut, restorations, 36i (91.5cm). **$4,000-5,500**

Antiques - Antiques - FOR SALE

20-foot and 40-foot Containerized
Hand Picked to Suit Your Requirements

THE GATEWAY TO A NEW WORLD OF ANTIQUES

OLD ENGLAND BROUGHT TO YOU IN FAMILY TRADITION
DELIVERED TO ANYWHERE IN THE WORLD. ESTABLISHED SINCE 1890

Swainbank
Antique Exporters
International Limited
- with compliments

"WORLD'S LARGEST SUPPLIER OF ANTIQUES"

Lord Hills' Estate
Coton Hall

COTON
WHITCHURCH
SHROPSHIRE
SY13 3LW

FAX: 094-872716
FAX: 051-277-2865

Telephone Direct:
011-4494-872-534

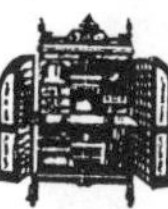

We offer a unique concept in buying antiques. You may select your merchandise from our special 100-page color brochure. Sent to you **free of charge.**

Why not invest your money wisely and turn over your capital into big profits from sales of antiques (off the floor sales) or (auction), whatever you prefer!

We guarantee excellent merchandise (30 days delivery). Just look at the prices of shipments for sale.

References available from many satisfied customers.

AMERICAN SHIPMENT PRICE LIST
CONTAINER GRADES AVAILABLE

The price of container required depends upon the Quality of Antiques you require for your clientele.

Price	Quality/Grade
$9,000	☐ ECONOMY (20ft. containers only)
$12,000	☐ BETTER ECONOMY
$15,000	☐ AUCTIONEERS WHOLESALE PACK
$20,000	☐ QUALITY WHOLESALE PACK
$25,000	☐ FINE ECONOMY (Extra)
$30,000	☐ SUPER QUALITY
$45,000	☐ DEPARTMENT STORE SPECIAL 18th & 19th Centry (bric-a-brac)
$50,000	☐ VIENNA HIGH GRADE ANTIQUES
$60,000	☐ MUSEUM QUALITY PACK (VIENNA)
$75,000	☐ CONTINENTAL ASSORTED PACK (EUROPE)
$100,000	☐ HISTORICAL/MUSEUM PACK (INC. ORIENTAL) Please check box required

Prices shown are for supply of 40 ft. Containers.
20 ft. Containers available to suit your requirements.

NOTE: PACKING BY EXPERTS *FREE OF CHARGE*

Calling Auctioneers
Antique Shop Owners
Antique Mall Owners
Collectors, Museums

We can supply you immediately

Please write today
or telephone
011-4494-872-534
Head Office (U.K.)

Vice president,
Mr. Mayhew
24 hours response
Telex or facsimile

"We're Ready" TO DEAL!!

"PERSONAL CALLERS TO ENGLAND ALWAYS WELCOME"

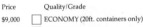

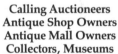

A George I walnut bureau, with herringbone banded and crossbanded fall, enclosing a fitted interior, c1720, 36in (92cm).
$6,500-7,000

A George III fruitwood bureau, the hinged slope enclosing pigeonholes and drawers, above 4 graduated drawers, on bracket feet, 36in (91.5cm).
$4,000-5,500

A George III mahogany bureau, with hinged slope and fitted interior, the 3 graduated long drawers on bracket feet, 44in (111.5cm).
$2,000-2,500

A George III mahogany writing bureau, with boxwood inlaid slope enclosing a secret drawer and leather inset, the drawers with original handles, raised on bracket feet, 46½in (117cm).
$2,000-2,500

A George I style burr walnut and featherbanded bureau, on bracket feet, 37in (94cm).
$1,400-2,000

A George III mahogany and marquetry inlaid bureau, with satinwood banded front enclosing a fitted interior, veneer distressed, 36in (91.5cm).
$2,500-3,000

A George III mahogany bureau, on ogee bracket feet, 44½in (112cm).
$1,400-2,000

A George II walnut bureau, feath and crossbanded, the drawers wit brass drop handles and butterfly backplates, on bracket feet, 39in (98cm).
$5,500-6,500

A George III inlaid mahogany bureau, 46½in (117cm).
$2,500-3,000

A George III mahogany bureau, t drawers with brass drop handles, flanked by reeded cylindrical columns, on bracket feet, 57in (114cm).
$2,000-2,500

A George II mahogany bureau, wi shaped, stepped and fretted interi original brass handles, c1750, 38i (96.5cm).
$6,500-8,000

George III inlaid mahogany ureau, fitted with 4 graduated rawers, and standing on bracket et, 36in (91.5cm).
2,000-2,500

A George III mahogany bureau, the fall above 4 graduated long drawers, on bracket feet, restorations, 39in (99cm).
$1,300-2,000

A Georgian mahogany bureau, fitted with 4 graduated drawers and standing on ogee bracket feet, 37in (94cm).
$1,200-2,000

A George III mahogany bureau, vith brass drop handles and utterfly back plates, on bracket eet, 36in (92cm).
3,000-4,000

A George III mahogany bureau, with elaborately fitted arcaded interior, on ogee bracket feet, 48in (122cm).
$3,000-4,000

A George III mahogany bureau, the hinged sloping flap enclosing a fitted interior and well, above 4 graduated long drawers, on bracket feet, 39in (99cm).
$1,000-1,400

A Georgian mahogany bureau, with 4 long graduated drawers, brass loop handles and pierced back plates, on bracket feet, 30in (76cm).
$4,000-5,000

A Georgian mahogany bureau, with fitted interior, over 4 long graduated drawers with knob handles, on splayed supports, 38in (96.5cm).
$1,400-2,000

A burr elm bureau, inlaid with chequered lines, the interior with arcaded drawers and pigeonholes flanking columns and a drawer, above 2 short and 3 long drawers on bracket feet, 28in (71cm).
$3,000-5,000

A late Victorian rosewood bureau, inlaid with ivory and marquetry panels, with fitted interior above 3 long drawers, on bracket feet, 31in (79cm).
$2,500-4,000

A Dutch walnut and marquetry bombé bureau, with fitted interior, on splayed feet, 42in (106.5cm).
$9,500-11,000

A lady's French rosewood and marquetry writing desk, the top with three-quarter cast gilt metal galleries, 32in (82cm).
$2,500-3,000

A French kingwood and rosewood banded bureau de dame with three-quarter pierced brass galler top, the gilt metal mounted conve fall with Vernis Martin panel, enclosing drawers and a well, on gi metal mounted cabriole supports and sabots, late 19thC, 26in (67cn
$1,500-2,500

A mahogany bureau, with satinwood inlay and banding, 3 drawers, 36in (91.5cm).
$800-1,500

A Chippendale carved cherrywood reverse serpentine desk, with thumb moulded slant lid enclosing a fitted interior, on short cabriole legs with claw-and-ball feet, repair to hinge portion of desk interior, Massachusetts, c1780, 44in (111.5cm).
$12,000-15,000

A Continental walnut and marquetry bureau, the fall front enclosing fitted interior, the fall an drawer fronts inlaid with floral an foliate swags and formal foliate spandrels, the sides with decorativ bandings, bracket feet, 36in (91.5cm).
$3,500-4,000

A neo-classical style satinwood and rosewood banded cylinder bureau, the top enclosing an adjustable leather lined writing plateau, the base with a knee-hole flanked by 3 drawers, on square tapering legs, 32½in (82cm).
$5,500-7,000

A Chippendale mahogany reverse serpentine slant front desk, with 4 blocked and cockbeaded moulded long drawers over a conforming base with central fan carved pendant, on ogee bracket feet, side carrying handles, Salem, Massachusetts, c1780, 45in (114cm).
$20,000-25,000

A Chippendale figured maple slant front desk, on shaped bracket feet, one interior short drawer restored, New England, c1770, 37in (94cm).
$12,000-15,000

Bureau Cabinets

A Dutch yew secrétaire à abattant with moulded frieze drawer, above fall front, 38½in (97cm).
$4,000-5,500

. South German walnut and ɔonised bureau cabinet, inlaid ith stars and geometric bands, the ncave elm and yew base with long drawers between canted ngles, on turned tapering bun feet, asically 19thC, 51in (129.5cm).
4,000-5,500

A German mahogany escritoire, with an applied carved cresting piece above on long drawer, the fall flap below enclosing a fitted interior of short drawers and a recess, 3 long graduated drawers under, flanked by reeded pilasters raised on turned feet, 19thC, 40in (101.5cm).
$2,500-3,000

A mahogany secrétaire cabinet, the top section with a dentilled moulded cornice, above a geometrically glazed mirrored door enclosing adjustable shelves, the base with secrétaire drawer lined in green baize, above 9 drawers, on square chamfered legs and block feet with scroll brackets, 33in (84cm).
$7,000-10,000

ʼisplay Cabinets

George III satinwood splay case, dapted, 18in (46cm).
1,200-1,500

A mahogany and satinwood banded side cabinet and associated bookcase top, early 19thC, 55in (139.5cm).
$1,400-2,000

An Edwardian Sheraton style mahogany display cabinet, 56in (142cm).
$3,000-4,000

ʌn early Victorian rosewood display abinet, on cabriole legs with law-and-ball feet, 64in (162.5cm).
5,000-6,500

An Edwardian mahogany china cabinet with marquetry inlaid back piece, single lead glazed front door, line inlays to pilasters and feet, 24in (62cm).
$650-800

A Victorian inlaid rosewood drawing room cabinet, 54in (137cm).
$3,000-4,000

An Edwardian mahogany serpentine front china cabinet, with hatch inlay, tapering legs with spade feet, 45in (114cm).
$1,300-1,500

An Edwardian inlaid mahogany shaped front corner display cabinet, with cupboard under enclosed by door, on square tapered legs, 30in (76cm).
$800-1,000

An Edwardian mahogany display cabinet, with velvet lined shelves with marquetry inlaid decoration urns, swags, flowerheads and scrolling leaves and outlined wit satinwood stringing, 48in (122cm
$1,500-2,500

An Edwardian mahogany china cabinet, the 2 pairs of doors about a fixed bowed centre section, the square section legs with Chinese fret brackets, 47in (119cm).
$1,000-1,200

An Edwardian mahogany display cabinet, with satinwood stringing decoration, supported on an Art Nouveau style base and feet, 57in (144.5cm).
$2,500-3,000

An Edwardian mahogany and inlaid display cabinet, with marquetry panels, shaped apro and raised on 4 splayed suppor 41in (104cm).
$1,300-1,500

An Edwardian rosewood display cabinet by Hindley & Sons, London.
$5,000-6,500

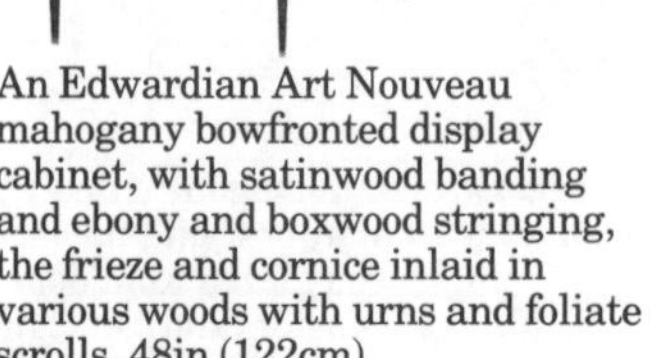

An Edwardian Art Nouveau mahogany bowfronted display cabinet, with satinwood banding and ebony and boxwood stringing, the frieze and cornice inlaid in various woods with urns and foliate scrolls, 48in (122cm).
$2,500-3,000

A Victorian walnut dwarf breakfront display cabinet, inlaid with symmetrical scrolling foliag and stringing, with velvet lined shelved interior, gilt metal beadir on a plinth base.
$2,500-3,000

Cabinets-on-Stands

A gilt metal mounted kingwood bombé vitrine, with a glazed door and side panels, on cabriole legs with sabots, 29in (74cm).
$1,400-2,000

A Queen Anne oyster walnut cabinet, with ogee frieze drawer, above 2 panel doors with geometric boxwood star and line inlays, enclosing a fitted interior, on later stand fitted with 3 drawers, on square cabriole supports and pad feet, 29½in (75cm).
$3,000-3,500

A black lacquer cabinet-on-stand, decorated in red and gilt, with 2 doors enclosing 11 drawers, the stand with waved apron on square legs, distressed, 18thC, 37in (94cm).
$2,500-3,000

late Victorian mahogany and ıtinwood banded pedestal display ıbinet, on square tapering legs ith spade feet, 42½in (106.5cm).
;50-1,000

A Regency lacquered collector's cabinet-on-stand, the stand with scroll frieze centered with lion's mask, on ring turned rear and cabriole front supports, containing the remains of the original collection of minerals, shells, seals and plaster casts, damaged, 42in (106.5cm).
$3,000-5,000

A Georgian mahogany toilet cabinet, with crossbanding, ebony and boxwood string inlays, single drawer, cupboard and X-stretcher.
$800-1,000

leather upholstered pedestal ıbinet, painted and decorated with ıimals and foliage, the platform ıse applied with gilt metal ıterae, on turned bun feet, lapted, basically early 19thC, 31in 9cm).
ı,200-1,500

Charles II style black lacquer and arcel gilt cabinet-on-stand, the chinoiserie decorated panelled ɔors with brass hinges and lock lates, on hipped spiral cabriole legs ith flowerheads and mask eadings, 42in (106.5cm).
ı,000-5,000

A black lacquer and chinoiserie cabinet-on-stand, the twin panelled doors with gilt metal hinges and lock plates, late 18thC on a later ebonised stand with cabriole legs and pad feet, 37in (94cm).
$3,000-4,000

Side Cabinets

A Dutch East Indies, Sri Lanka, brass mounted jackwood, kaliatur and ebony cabinet-on-stand, the scroll hinges engraved with fish, the stand with 2 frieze drawers, on bulbous baluster legs joined by stretchers, restorations, labelled Dutch Cabinet No. 1 His Excellency's Sitting Room, Queen's House, Colombo, 45in (115cm).
$3,000-5,000

A pair of rosewood console side tables, applied with gilt metal mounts, Carrara marble tops, with silk sunburst upholstered panelled interior, on plinth platform bases, parts early 19thC, 25in (64cm).
$2,000-2,500

An ormolu mounted boulle red tortoiseshell and ebonised side cabinet, the cupboard doors enclosing red velvet-lined shelve the sides with Bérainesque panel the top and side panels 18thC, 49½in (126cm).
$5,000-6,500

A rosewood and parcel gilt dwarf open bookcase, with verde antico marble top, basically early 19thC, 46in (117cm).
$2,500-3,000

A pair of breakfront amboyna wo and walnut side cabinets, each w heavy ormolu beading and moun Sèvres style plaques to the doors, with interior shelves and cupboar and marble tops, 19thC, 27in (69c
$13,000-16,000

A scarlet boulle ebonised and gilt metal mounted side cabinet, applied with acanthus clasps, with shaped plinth on block feet, distressed, mid-19thC, 76in (193cm).
$2,000-2,500

A George IV rosewood chiffonier, the frieze drawer flanked by roundels, the 2 panelled doors flanked by columns and on a plinth base, 39in (99cm).
$1,200-1,400

A burr ash side cabinet, with galleried back and panelled do applied with gilt metal crowne garter mounts, on gilt acanthu carved feet, early 19thC, 42in (107cm).
$4,000-5,000

A walnut and inlaid side cabinet, with gilt metal mounts and Sèvres style porcelain plaques, the centre cupboard flanked by a pair of bowed doors, on turned feet, mid-19thC, 66in (167.5cm). **$3,000-5,000**

Victorian mahogany serpentine
onted chiffonier, with a dummy
awer, 2 fielded panel doors,
rved decoration to the sides, on a
atform base, 46in (116.5cm).
,400-2,000

William IV mahogany chiffonier,
ith cushion fronted drawer and
cupboard doors, supported on lion
aw front feet, 42in (106.5cm).
00-1,200

pair of Regency style black and
old japanned side cabinets, with a
air of doors, painted with courtly
gures in a landscape and enclosing
elves, on turned tapering feet,
9in (124.5cm) wide.
16,000-18,000

A Regency ormolu-mounted rosewood chiffonier, the frieze with central plaque, the glazed doors backed with pleated green silk between turned columns on plinth base, 43in (109cm).
$6,500-8,000

A Regency mahogany and satinwood side cabinet, with crossbanded top, 2 frieze drawers above a pair of panelled cupboards, inlaid with ovals, with waved apron, and splayed feet, adapted, 36½in (93cm).
$1,500-2,500

A Regency mahogany side cabinet, with a pair of cupboard doors enclosing shelves, on bracket feet, early 19thC, 75in (190.5cm) high.
$2,500-3,500

A George IV Irish mahogany chiffonier, the top with raised superstructure of one shelf with scrolled cresting, panelled back and S-scroll supports, the frieze with a concave drawer, on Ionic column supports, the panelled back flanked by pilasters on a concave-fronted plinth base, 42in (106.5cm).
$3,000-4,000

A Victorian gilt metal mounted burr walnut and marquetry side cabinet, with a central painted porcelain plaque, 2 bowed glazed doors and Corinthian pilaster columns, on bun feet, 68in (172.5cm).
$6,500-7,000

A mahogany and marble top secrétaire à abattant, with a brass plaque inscribed, '. . . belonging to Jacob Lorillard 1774-1838, New York City', interior drawers possibly later, some damage, possibly New York, c1820, 39in (99cm).
$2,000-3,000

A William IV rosewood chiffonier, with mirrored back, 60in (152cm).
$1,200-1,400

A Victorian gilt metal walnut and ebonised credenza, with glazed door flanked by bowed doors divided by pilasters, on plinth, 66in (167.5cm).
$2,500-3,000

A Victorian inlaid walnut vitri
$2,500-3,000

A Victorian ormolu mounted walnut and marquetry display side cabinet, with shaped glazed door and clasp headed uprights on shaped plinth, 33in (84cm).
$1,300-1,500

A Victorian satinwood side cabinet, inlaid with paterae and foliate scrolls, 52in (132cm).
$5,000-6,500

A mid-Victorian walnut and marquetry inlaid dwarf serpentin side cabinet, applied with gilt met mounts, the yew wood crossbande top with a pierced three-quarter gallery, on turned tapering legs, 72in (182.5cm).
$6,500-8,000

A pair of Victorian ebonised and amboyna banded dwarf side cabinets, with gilt metal mounts, the eared tops with marquetry banded friezes, on turned tapering bun feet, labelled Frederick Gwilt, 36 High Oak, Pensnett, 32in (81cm).
$2,500-4,000

A Victorian walnut dwarf side cabinet, inlaid with marquetry and rosewood bands, applied with paterae, on plinth base, 36½in (92cm).
$2,000-2,500

A Victorian walnut and inlaid dwa side cabinet, with concave top abo 3 glazed doors, with gilt metal mounted pilasters, on plinth base, 55in (139.5cm).
$2,500-3,000

A Victorian walnut and boxwood strung breakfront side cabinet, the moulded top above scroll carved stiles flanking 3 glazed doors, on a plinth base, 74in (188cm).
$1,300-2,000

A Victorian ebonised and inlaid dwarf side cabinet, with gilt metal mounts, painted and decorated porcelain plaques, and on turned bun feet, 60in (152cm).
$1,400-2,000

A Victorian burr walnut and inlaid redenza, with moulded top, and eaded gilt metal stringing, on a linth base, 66in (168cm).
5,000-5,500

late Victorian walnut, foliate arquetry and gilt metal mounted reakfront side cabinet, with bonised panel centred by a ibbon-tied tulip motif, on a shaped linth with trade label Druce & Co. Jpholsterers and Cabinet Makers, Baker Street, Portman Square, 71½in (180cm).
3,000-4,000

Dutch mahogany side cabinet, vith broken pediment, on square apering block feet, basically late 18thC, 68in (172.5cm).
8,000-9,500

A green marblised and parcel gilt breakfront side cabinet, with four doors, each with a yellow silk pleated panel, 68in (172.5cm).
$1,300-2,000

A Victorian burr walnut dwarf pedestal side cabinet, the velvet lined shelved interior enclosed by a single panel door, inlaid with symmetrical leafy scrolls, gilt metal bordered and mounted pilasters, on a plinth base, 36in (92cm).
$2,000-2,500

An Adam design inlaid satinwood cabinet, with brass gallery, crossbanded in kingwood and inlaid with rosewood, on tapered legs, 42in (106.5cm).
$8,000-9,500

A Louis XV style walnut and marquetry inlaid meuble d'appui, applied with gilt metal mounts, on an undulating plinth base, 35in (89cm).
$3,000-5,000

An Edwardian music cabinet in rosewood, with satinwood inlay and mirror panel front, 22in (56cm).
$400-500

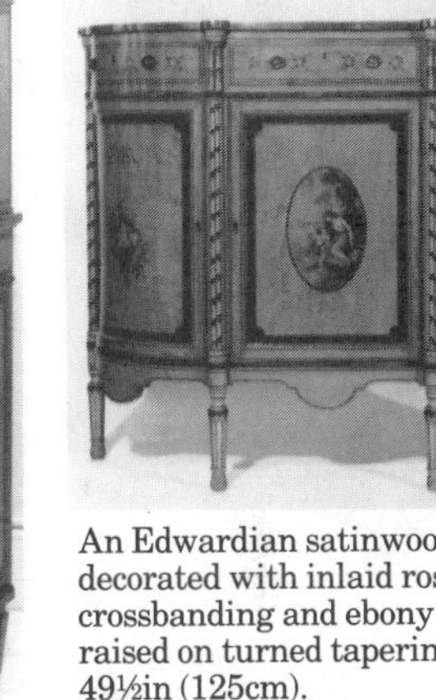

An Edwardian satinwood cabinet, decorated with inlaid rosewood crossbanding and ebony stringing, raised on turned tapering legs, 49½in (125cm).
$6,500-7,000

A Spanish painted pine cupboard, late 18thC, 46in (116.5cm) high.
$4,000-5,000

A French walnut credenza, of serpentine form with ormolu gadroon and beaded mounts, the frieze with marquetry inlaid panels, the doors and column stems with inlaid stringing and crossbanded decoration, mid-19thC, 63in (160cm).
$4,000-5,000

A French gilt metal mounted mahogany breakfront side cabinet, with eared Carrara marble top, 75in (190.5cm).
$3,000-5,000

A Louis Philippe cartonniere, in gil metal mounted quartered kingwooc with rosewood banding, the door with Sèvres floral medallion enclosing velvet interior with shelf, 28in (71cm).
$2,500-3,000

Canterburies

A George IV mahogany music canterbury, the front, back and two divisions, of butterfly shape and applied with draught-turned mouldings, on splayed legs with brass acanthus cast sockets with casters, drawer stamped 27006, c1825, 22½in (56cm).
$2,500-3,000

A Regency mahogany canterbury, the top with 4 dished dividers, on square supports above a divided drawer, on square tapering legs, 18in (46cm).
$4,000-5,000

A Victorian rosewood folio stand, with slatted, adjustable sides above aprons carved with fleur-de-lys, on moulded cabriole legs, with paw feet on casters, late 19thC, 21½in (54cm) wide. **$2,000-2,500**

A late Georgian mahogany canterbury, with plain railed divisions, single frieze drawer on turned supports, 19in (48cm).
$2,000-2,500

A George IV mahogany canterbury by L. W. Collmann, with an asymmetrical arrangement of 4 slatted divisions, turned corner supports with knob finials, on tapering turned feet with brass casters, 26in (66cm).
$1,300-2,000

A George IV mahogany canterbury of X-framed form, united by baluster turned spindles, on tapering turned legs with brass casters, 19in (48cm).
$1,500-2,500

A Victorian mahogany canterbury with single drawer, 4 squat legs and casters. **$900-1,000**

A Regency mahogany canterbury, on ring turned and fluted tapering supports, the base fitted with a drawer above a rosewood crossbanded apron, 19in (48cm).
$3.000-4.000

A mahogany music canterbury, with 4 divisions, drawer and turned ringed supports, fitted with casters, 19thC, 17½in (44cm).
$2,500-3,000

A Victorian rosewood grained canterbury, with spindle gallery and 2 compartments over a drawer, on turned legs, 19thC, 20½in (52cm) wide.
$1,000-1,500

A mid-Victorian walnut and crossbanded low music cabinet, the open shelves between canted angles, on turned feet, 20in (51cm).
$800-1,000

A mahogany canterbury, with one drawer, raised on turned supports with casters, early 19thC.
$2,500-3,000

A Victorian mahogany canterbury, the top centering 3 slatted compartments, flanked by shelves, on turned legs and casters, mid-19thC, 36in (91cm) wide.
$5,000-6,000

A mahogany canterbury with plain turned divisions and baluster side rails, above a shelf and brass casters, 19thC.
$500-650

A Sheraton period mahogany music canterbury, outlined with ebony stringing, the tapering square legs with brass sockets and casters, 17½in (44cm). **$9,000-10,000**

Open Armchairs

A walnut open armchair, upholstered in close-nailed gros and petit-point needlework, the outscrolled arms carved with foliage on scrolling supports, the front stretcher carved with a flowerhead and foliage, on scrolling legs with later paw feet and waved stretchers, part late 17thC.
$5,500-6,500

A George III mahogany carver chair, with reeded and carved decoration, on turned legs.
$400-500

A pair of walnut open armchairs, upholstered in 17thC tapestry, with foliate carved arm rests, on turned legs and stretchers.
$3,000-5,000

A George III mahogany open armchair, the channelled arms on downswept supports, above a padded seat covered in pink and cream trellis pattern material, on square tapering panelled legs and block feet headed by stiff leaves.
$1,000-1,200

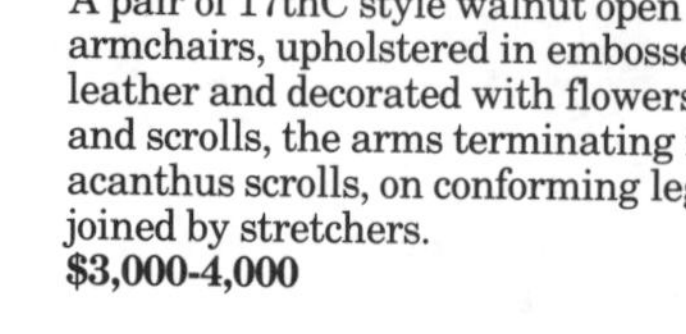

A pair of 17thC style walnut open armchairs, upholstered in embossed leather and decorated with flowers and scrolls, the arms terminating in acanthus scrolls, on conforming legs joined by stretchers.
$3,000-4,000

An early George III style mahogany open armchair, with shaped toprail and pierced interlaced splat, the arms carved with acanthus, the drop-in seat upholstered in green leather, on cabriole legs and hairy paw feet carved with C-scroll cabochons. **$1,000-1,400**

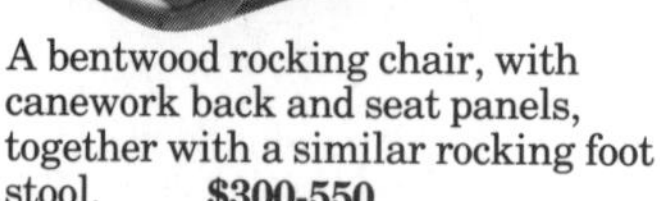

A bentwood rocking chair, with canework back and seat panels, together with a similar rocking foot stool. **$300-550**

CHAIRS
- ★ check seat rails are the same, with equal patination
- ★ top rail should never overhang sides
- ★ carving should not be flat
- ★ if stretchers low, chair could have been cut down
- ★ the height from floor to seat should be 18in (45.5cm)

A Venetian carved giltwood grotto chair, with shell seat and back, serpent arms, sea horse supports and serpent rockers, mid-19thC.
$4,000-5,000

A George III cream and pink painted open armchair, the padded back and seat with moulded frame and ribbon-tied cresting, the fluted seat rail on ribbed tapering legs with foliage bands.
$2,500-3,000

A George III style mahogany open armchair, with shaped toprail and pierced interlaced splat carved with foliage and scrolls, the shaped arms with scrolled ends, the padded seat upholstered in floral needlework, on square chamfered legs joined by stretchers.
$1,000-1,400

A George IV mahogany commode armchair, the solid hinged seat with brass recessed handle above 2 panelled doors, with buttoned green leather cushion, 25in (63.5cm).
$1,200-1,500

A pair of Regency mahogany open armchairs, each with scrolling curved toprail, pierced foliate horizontal splat, downswept reeded arms on baluster supports, with padded seats and turned legs, later blocks.
$2,500-3,000

A pair of George III beech framed open armchairs, with fluted oval frames to the padded backs, padded arms with acanthus terminals and upholstered bow front seats, on fluted leaf carved legs.
$3,000-4,000

A pair of Regency yew wood open armchairs, each with a spindle filled back, down curved arms and solid bowed seat, on square tapered legs.
$1,000-1,200

A set of 3 Regency ochre-painted beechwood open armchairs, the pierced back with crossed arrows joined by an oval medallion decorated with Prince of Wales feathers, with serpentine rush seat, on turned legs and conforming stretchers.
$2,000-2,500

Two George III mahogany library armchairs, with padded arms and seats upholstered in white floral damask, with downswept arm supports and square legs joined by stretchers, restorations and replacements. **$8,000-11,000**

A George IV mahogany framed open armchair, with overscrolled upholstered back and conforming padded arms, serpentine seat and on baluster legs. **$1,300-1,500**

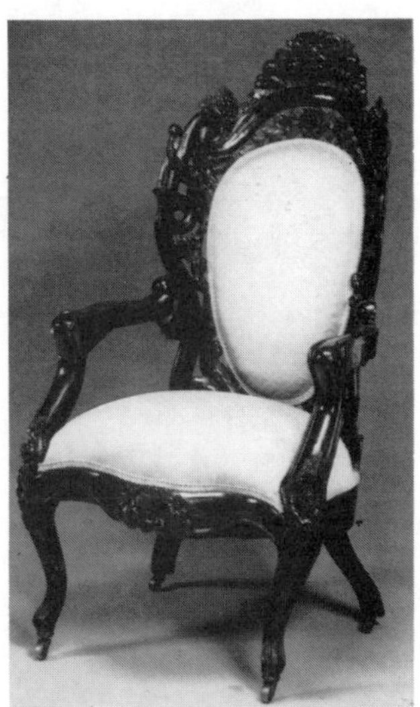

An American rococo revival laminated rosewood and grain painted mahogany open armchair, with arched pierced foliate scrolling back, with inset padded back, padded seat in moulded carved frame, on cabriole legs with brass casters.
$5,500-6,000

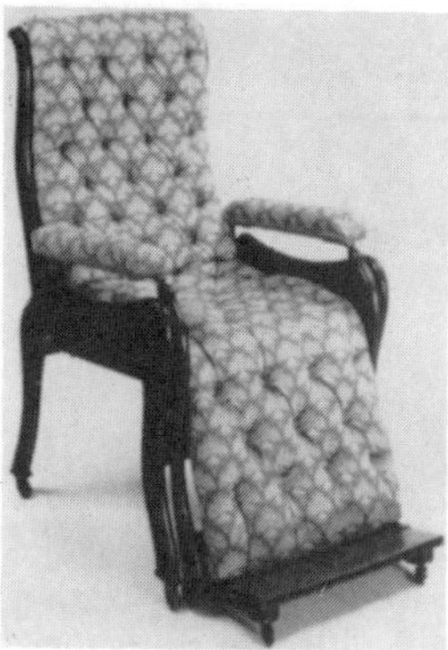

An early Victorian mahogany reclining chair, with buttoned panel back and adjustable seat upholstered in tapestry, on curved legs. **$1,300-1,500**

A Victorian walnut gentleman's armchair, the acanthus carved scrolling frame with buttoned back, circular seat and arms on cabriole legs; and the lady's chair en suite.
$2,500-3,000

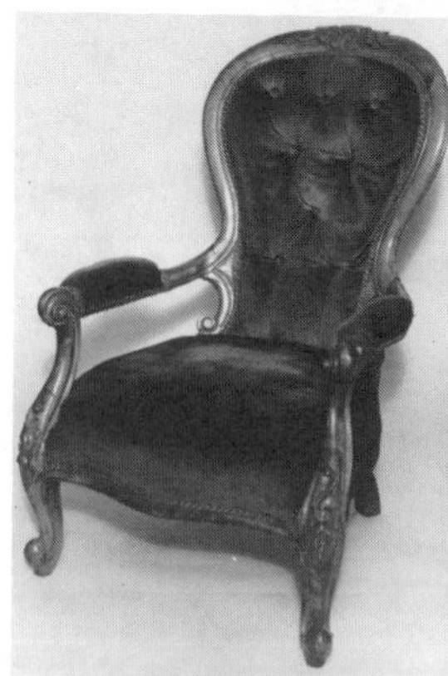

A Victorian walnut framed buttonback armchair, with carved decoration on cabriole legs.
$650-800

A Victorian carved walnut spoonback open armchair.
$2,500-3,000

A set of 6 Victorian carved oak dining chairs, with barleytwist supports, carved grape and vine leaf decoration and leather seats.
$1,500-2,500

A pair of Victorian lady's and gentleman's armchairs, with floral carved toprails, upholstered spoon shaped backs, scroll hand grips on floral carved cabriole supports and bowed seat rails, requiring restoration.
$5,000-5,500

A Victorian walnut gentleman's armchair, with C-scroll frame, upholstered seat, arms and spooned back with acanthus cresting, on cabriole legs; and a similar lady's chair.
$1,400-2,000

A late Victorian 5-piece rosewood drawing room suite, inlaid with marquetry and boxwood lines, on square tapering legs with spade feet.
$2,500-3,000

A late Victorian rosewood and foliate marquetry drawing room suite, with two tub chairs, each with an upholstered toprail and a pierced splat above a bowed seat, on turned legs, and a sofa with outscrolled end and pierced back, the arms carved with acanthus.
$2,000-2,500

A Victorian walnut open armchair, with waisted buttoned back, armpads and serpentine seat upholstered in green silk rep.
$2,500-3,000

\ Victorian walnut open armchair, ıpholstered in coral velvet, the ırms terminating in scrolls, on :abriole legs and scroll feet.
$800-1,000

A late Victorian walnut framed gentleman's chair, with carved tapering back, upholstered seat, on carved and turned front supports.
$650-800

An Edwardian inlaid mahogany parlour set of 8 chairs, and a 3 seater settee, all with boxwood string inlay.
$4,000-5,000

An Edwardian satinwood open armchair, of George III style, the seat upholstered in green damask, on square tapering legs.
$1,300-1,500

A mahogany framed armchair of Adam design, on square tapered and fluted front supports with carved paterae, and on block toes, upholstered in blue brocade.
$2,500-3,000

A pair of open armchairs, with padded serpentine seats, outscrolled arms and panelled tapering legs with spade feet, later blocks.
$2,000-3,000

A set of 14 mahogany open armchairs, with shield shaped backs and pierced splats above serpentine upholstered drop-in seats, on square tapered legs joined by stretchers, stamped F.S. and numbered.
$2,500-3,000

A pair of mahogany cockpen armchairs of Chinese Chippendale style, the padded seat upholstered with light blue cloth, on square chamfered legs carved with fret-work.
$2,000-2,500

A Chippendale mahogany elbow chair with leaf and floret carved cresting rail, scroll arms and moulded squared supports with carved angles, upholstered serpentine seat.
$4,000-5,000

A pair of George III style armchairs, with wheel back centered by a roundel over scrolling arms, the padded saddle seat upholstered in velvet, on moulded cabriole legs with toupie feet.
$4,500-5,000

A George III style mahogany ope armchair, with pierced crest rail centred by strapwork above a pierced vase shaped splat, the scrolling arms above a padded sea upholstered in brocade, on square legs edged with gadrooning.
$2,000-2,500

A pair of American Victorian rococo revival laminated rosewood open armchairs, with brass casters, by John Henry Belter, in the Rosalie pattern, mid-19thC.
$5,000-8,000

A Regency mahogany metamorphic library armchair, with bowed tablet crest rail and horizontal splat above scrolling reeded arms, the caned seat on reeded sabre legs, opening to reveal a set of 4 leather lined steps, early 19thC.
$4,000-6,000

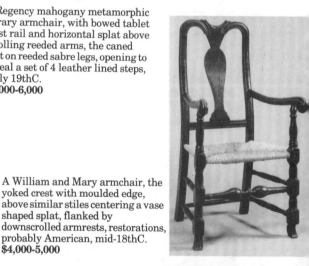

A William and Mary armchair, the yoked crest with moulded edge, above similar stiles centering a vase shaped splat, flanked by downscrolled armrests, restorations, probably American, mid-18thC.
$4,000-5,000

A William and Mary bannister back armchair, the double arched crestrail above 4 split bannisters flanked by turned stiles with double mushroom finials, flanked by scrolled arms, over a trapezoidal rush seat on cylindrical turned legs joined by a double box stretcher, feet restored, Connecticut, c1735.
$1,200-1,500

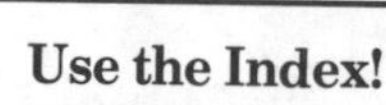

Use the Index!

Because certain items might fit easily into any of a number of categories, the quickest and surest method of locating any entry is by reference to the index at the back of the book.
This has been fully cross-referenced for absolute simplicity

ANTIQUE UPHOLSTERY

- ★ Condition is all-important. An early piece with sagging seat but with original or early needlework which is still largely intact will attract a higher value for its originality, but generally speaking an authentically re-upholstered item in good condition is clearly more valuable than an item requiring attention. Quality re-upholstery work is not cheap
- ★ Re-upholstery is acceptable provided it has been restored authentically with hand sewn hair borders, and hair padding, to the original contours of the design. Test the upholstery by prodding with one finger. Hair will crackle. Cotton flock and foam will not!
- ★ Pre-Regency furniture was not sprung, but was webbed on top of the seat rails and the upholstered pad invariably had a firm hair roll at the outer edge, and all hair stuffing. Later sprung upholstery is webbed beneath the seat rails to accommodate the springs
- ★ Originality of the cover fabric is immediately questionable if it is out of period. Textiles is a wide field but a study of fabric history and types, damasks, chintzes, crested, turkey-work, hand tapestry, brocades, etc, is well worthwhile to date an item
- ★ The use of dralon modern acrylic velvets will devalue an item in the same way as foam fillings, or similar low-grade upholstery work
- ★ The general quality of upholstery work is another pointer to value

A George IV mahogany framed wing armchair, the carved arm fronts over large lion's paw front supports and sabre rear supports.
$2,500-3,000

A George IV mahogany tub armchair, with shaped leather upholstered back, outscrolled arms and buttoned squab-seat with moulded arm supports and ring turned legs.
$3,000-4,000

A Regency brass inlaid simulated rosewood bergère, upholstered in peach cotton, the arms inlaid with foliage and paterae on reeded tapering legs, restorations.
$1,300-2,000

A Victorian walnut framed gentleman's button back armchair, with carved decoration and standing on cabriole legs.
$1,300-1,500

A George III armchair, upholstered in green hide, with serpentine seat, and on mahogany moulded square legs joined by stretchers.
$800-1,000

A Regency partially reeded mahogany frame tub shape library chair, upholstered in studded green hide, the arms with inverted tapering reeded supports, on turned tapering legs.
$3,000-4,000

A Regency mahogany bergère, with curved back, scrolled arms and padded seat upholstered in crimson velvet, on reeded tapering legs with lambrequin capitals.
$7,000-8,000

A pair of Louis XV white painted bergères, each with cartouche shaped back and bowed seat with a cushion upholstered in beige velvet, the moulded seat rails carved with flowerheads on cabriole legs, mid-18thC.
$5,500-6,500

A Chippendale mahogany easy chair, on square corner moulded legs joined by a moulded H-stretcher, upholstered in rose fabric with needlework floral and animal motifs, Salem, Massachusetts, c1780.
$8,500-9,500

A Federal mahogany easy chair, with arched crest flanked by shaped wings over horizontally scrolled arms, on square tapering legs joined by an H-stretcher, feet pieced, American, c1800.
$1,500-3,000

A Federal mahogany easy chair, on turned tapering legs with casters, Philadelphia, c1800.
$5,500-6,500

A George IV rosewood bergère, the curved back, arms and seat filled with cane, the seat cushion upholstered in floral cotton, on ribbed tapering legs.
$2,500-3,000

A Regency mahogany library armchair, with caned back, arms and seat, the padded arm rests, buttoned back and seat cushions upholstered in wine red hide, on ring turned legs.
$2,500-3,000

A Regency mahogany and caned bergère, the back with moulded frame and overscrolled arms, on sabre legs with brass casters.
$5,500-6,500

A Regency mahogany bergère, with caned back, arms and seat in a reeded frame, the scrolled arms on lion's paw supports, with padded seat cushion, on turned legs, back legs replaced.
$2,500-3,000

A Regency mahogany and caned bergère, the back with reeded frame and turned arm supports continuing to turned tapered legs.
$3,000-4,000

George III mahogany ning chair, with shield aped back and pierced lat carved with wheat rs, upholstered seat, square legs.
00-800

A pair of George III mahogany shield back dining chairs, with pierced Gothic pattern baluster splats, drop-in seats, and square legs.
$1,400-2,000

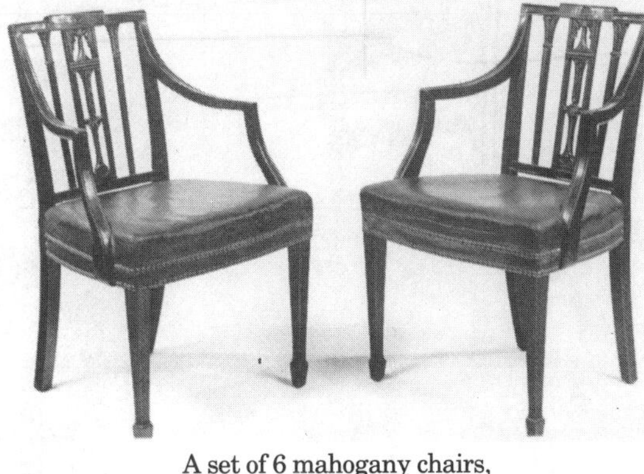

A set of 6 mahogany chairs, including a pair of armchairs, on square tapered legs with spade feet, 3 chairs, c1790, 3 later copies.
$3,000-4,000

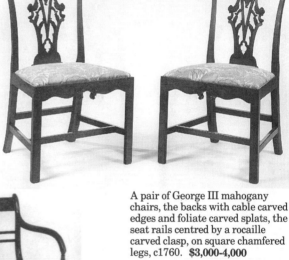

set of 8 mahogany dining chairs, cluding 2 armchairs, with holstered seats, on square pering legs, part George III.
,000-5,500

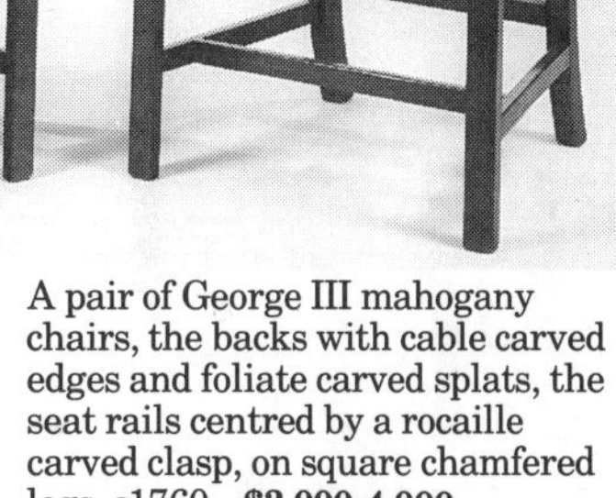

A pair of George III mahogany chairs, the backs with cable carved edges and foliate carved splats, the seat rails centred by a rocaille carved clasp, on square chamfered legs, c1760. **$3,000-4,000**

A set of 4 George III mahogany dining chairs, including one elbow chair, with stuff-over seats, on turned supports.
$1,200-1,400

set of 12 George III design ahogany dining chairs, including armchairs, on square tapering gs with Marlborough block feet ined by stretchers.
8,000-9,000

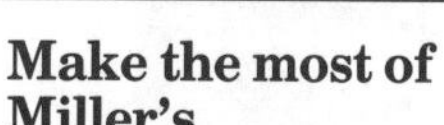

A set of 8 George III style mahogany dining chairs, including 2 armchairs, on square moulded legs joined by stretchers, 19thC.
$6,500-7,000

A set of 6 George III style mahogany dining chairs, with leather upholstered seats, on chamfered square moulded legs joined by cross stretchers.
$1,400-2,000

Make the most of Miller's

Unless otherwise stated, any description which refers to 'a set' or 'a pair' includes a valuation for the entire set or the pair, even though the illustration may show only a single item

A set of 8 George III mahogany dining chairs, the reeded bar and tablet backs above velvet seats, on ring turned tapering legs.
$7,000-8,000

A set of 6 Chippendale style dining chairs, comprising 2 armchairs and 4 side chairs, with pierced ladderback splats above needlework slip seats on straight square legs with moulded edges joined by box stretchers.
$1,500-2,500

A set of 6 George III mahogany dining chairs, the shaped toprails and pierced latticed splats above padded drop-in seats, on square tapering legs.
$2,500-4,000

A set of 8 mahogany dining chairs, including 2 armchairs, the pierced shield backs carved with the Prince of Wales' feathers, above leather seats, on square tapering legs with spade feet and bellflower headings, 19thC.
$5,000-6,500

A set of 6 mahogany dining chairs, with bowed bar toprails and cross bars pierced with roundels between reeded uprights, the padded drop-in seats on square moulded legs, late George III and later.
$4,000-5,500

A set of 4 late George III mahogany dining chairs, the bowed bar and latticed rail backs applied with roundels, above upholstered seats, on turned tapering legs.
$1,500-2,000

A set of 6 George III mahogany dining chairs, with serpentine toprails and pierced splats, above padded seats, on square chamfered legs joined by stretchers, restorations.
$4,000-5,500

A set of 6 late George III mahogany dining chairs, including 2 carvers, restorations.
$3,000-4,000

A set of 8 mahogany dining chairs, including a pair of open armchairs, the drop-in seats upholstered in aquamarine silk, on moulded sabre legs, early 19thC.
$8,000-9,500

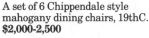

set of 8 mahogany dining chairs, ith foliate carved serpentine prails and formerly upholstered lats above padded seats, on square gs joined by stretchers.
,000-5,000

A pair of late George III mahogany dining chairs, each with a pierced lattice back and padded seat, on turned tapered reeded legs.
$1,500-2,500

A set of 6 Chippendale style mahogany dining chairs, 19thC.
$2,000-2,500

set of 8 mahogany dining chairs, ith bowed bar toprails centred by a blet, above pierced cross bars etween reeded uprights, the added drop-in seats on square pered legs joined by stretchers, 9thC.
7,000-9,000

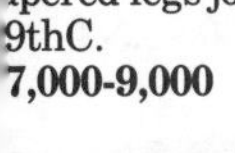

A set of 6 mahogany dining chairs, with bowed bar toprails and padded seats on square tapered legs joined by stretcher; and a similar armchair, 19thC.
$1,000-1,400

A set of 3 Regency dining chairs, with brass inlaid decoration cane seats and standing on sabre legs.
$400-500

set of 6 Regency mahogany dining hairs, with anthemion and scroll arved curved cresting rails, opetwist uprights pierced reeded ouble tie rails centred by foliate osettes, raised upon reeded sabre ont supports.
5,000-5,500

A set of 6 rosewood dining chairs with fluted legs, c1825.
$4,000-5,000

A set of 7 Regency beechwood dining chairs, the bowed toprails carved with rosettes, the reeded seat rails on sabre legs, the parcel gilt decoration distressed.
$1,400-2,000

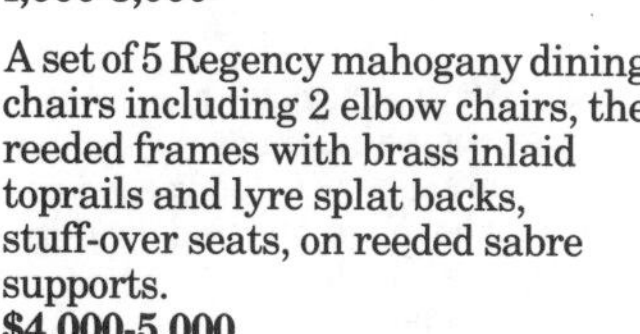

A set of 5 Regency mahogany dining chairs including 2 elbow chairs, the reeded frames with brass inlaid toprails and lyre splat backs, stuff-over seats, on reeded sabre supports.
$4,000-5,000

A set of 5 late Regency mahogany and brass strung dining chairs, with bowed toprails and bar splats, on ring turned tapered legs.
$1,400-2,000

A set of 6 Victorian mahogany spoon back dining chairs, upholstered in brown hide, standing on leaf capped cabriole supports.
$2,500-3,000

A set of 6 Regency period mahoga dining chairs, the backs with panelled fluted crests and hobna cut turned rails, with cane seats, sabre legs.
$5,000-5,500

A set of 3 Regency mahogany dining chairs, inlaid with brass rings and a shell scroll, the carved cross bar above a drop-in seat upholstered in green silk, on sabre legs; and 3 similar chairs, minor variations, partly early 19thC.
$3,000-5,000

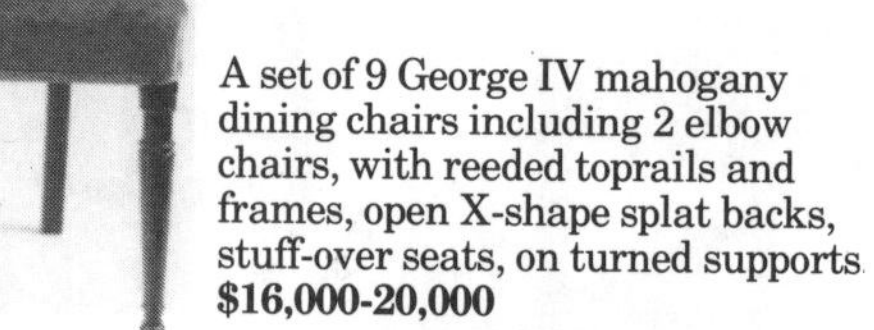

A set of 9 George IV mahogany dining chairs including 2 elbow chairs, with reeded toprails and frames, open X-shape splat backs, stuff-over seats, on turned supports.
$16,000-20,000

A set of 8 Regenc mahogany dinin chairs, upholste in wine rexhide and standing on turned taperi supports.
$5,500-6,500

A set of 10 mahogany and parcel gilt dining chairs, including 2 carvers, the seats upholstered in red needlecord, on turned tapered fluted legs, each with a stiff leaf collar, stamped Gillow, late 19thC.
$8,000-13,000

A set of 6 Regency beechwood dining chairs, including an armchair, with brass inlaid bowed and reeded rail backs, above upholstered drop-in seats, on sabre legs.
$3,000-5,000

A set of 6 Regency black painted a parcel gilt dining chairs, each wi curved eared toprail and X-shape splat, centred by a cane filled ova and rounded cane filled seat, on turned tapering legs all stamped GJ, 2 with additional K, and 3 wi JS.
$4,000-5,000

. set of 8 mahogany dining chairs, ncluding 2 armchairs, the canthus carved backs with padded eats and gadrooned aprons, on abriole legs with claw-and-ball eet, labelled S.S. & H. Jewell, 29-231 Little Queen Street, Holborn, WC.
6,500-8,000

A set of 6 rosewood dining chairs, upholstered in neo-classical manner in red velvet, the shell carved toprail with lion finials above a frame carved with acanthus, on square legs with lion's paw feet joined by a cross stretcher, stamped Maples.
$4,000-5,000

A set of 6 mahogany dining chairs, carved with foliage above a slightly bowed padded seat on square tapered legs and spade feet, with trade label Edwards & Roberts, Wardour Street.
$3,000-4,000

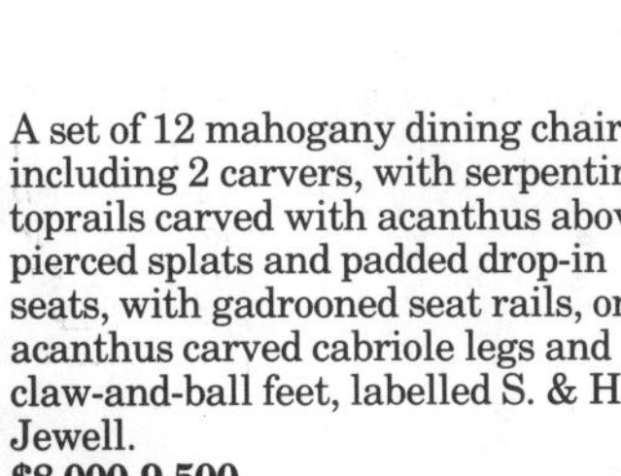

A set of 12 mahogany dining chairs, including 2 carvers, with serpentine toprails carved with acanthus above pierced splats and padded drop-in seats, with gadrooned seat rails, on acanthus carved cabriole legs and claw-and-ball feet, labelled S. & H. Jewell.
$8,000-9,500

A set of 10 mahogany dining chairs, including 2 carvers, with serpentine toprails and pierced splats above drop-in seats upholstered in leather, the gadrooned seat rails on cabriole legs and claw-and-ball feet.
$6,500-8,000

A set of 4 bamboo framed dining hairs, with cane seats and backs, on tretcher frames.
$400-500

A set of 15 mahogany dining chairs, including an armchair, with serpentine crestings and pierced splats above upholstered drop-in seats, on square chamfered legs joined by stretchers, labelled Maples.
$4,000-5,500

A set of 6 mahogany Chippendale style dining chairs, with pierced splats above upholstered drop-in seats, on claw-and-ball supports.
$1,500-2,000

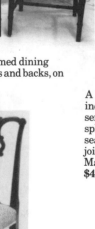

A set of 6 mahogany dining chairs, with pierced interlaced splats, padded seats and chamfered moulded square legs joined by stretchers.
$3,000-4,000

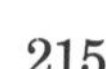

A set of 8 reproduction Chippendale style mahogany dining chairs including 2 elbow chairs, with pierced arched ladder backs, stuff-over floral wool tapestry seats, on moulded square chamfered supports united by stretchers.
$2,500-3,000

A set of 8 Hepplewhite style mahogany dining chairs, including 2 armchairs, with velvet upholstered seats, on square splayed tapering legs.
$5,000-5,500

A pair of Anglo-Indian Italian walnut dining chairs, the scrolled toprails over pierced carved splats incorporating foliage relief, over-stuffed seats raised on cabriole supports with carved knees and claw-and-ball feet.
$500-1,000

A pair of Portuguese fruitwood chairs, with shaped pierced toprails carved with foliage, the drop-in seats upholstered in floral material, on cabriole legs with claw-and-ball feet, back legs restored, mid-18thC.
$2,500-3,000

Three Federal carved mahogany side chairs, with arched and moulded crestrails, vertically pierced with splats over slip-in seats, on square legs with moulded corners, Salem, Massachusetts, c1800.
$4,000-5,000

Hall Chairs

A mahogany hall chair, with leaf carved back on turned supports, early 19thC. **$150-250**

A pair of Regency style mahogany hall chairs, each with a fluted oval back centering a painted crest and the motto 'Love, Serve' above a serpentine plank seat on square tapering legs and spade feet.
$2,500-3,000

A pair of mahogany hall chairs, late 18thC.
$8,000-9,500

A pair of early George III mahogany hall chairs, the cartouche shaped solid backs painted with the Royal Arms, within roundels, with moulded seats and shaped legs, the Arms possibly later.
$3,000-4,000

A Spanish oak armchair, early 17thC. **$3,000-4,000**

A set of 6 yew and elm Windsor armchairs, 19thC, Yorkshire. **$13,500-17,000**

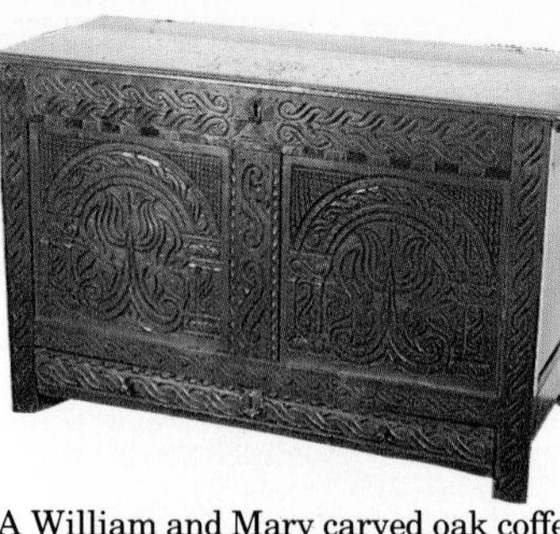

A William and Mary carved oak coffe 1691, English. **$1,500-3,000**

A harlequin set of 6 yew and elm Windsor chairs, c1810. **$8,000-11,000**

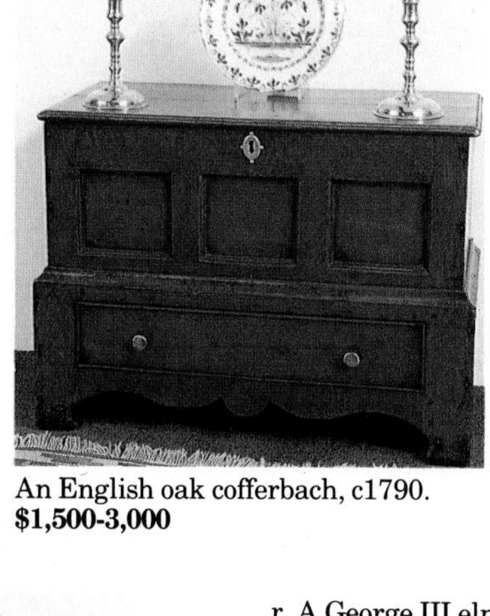

An English oak cofferbach, c1790. **$1,500-3,000**

A Welsh oak tridarn, mid-18thC. **$6,500-9,500**

A Charles II oak child's coffer, c1680. **$2,500-4,000**

r. A George III elm table, c1790. **$4,000-5,000**

An English oak box on cabriole legs, c1760. **$3,000-5,000**

l. An oak carved coffer, c1695. **$1,500-2,500**

r. An English oak plank coffer, c1580. **$5,000-6,500**

n oak four-poster bed, basically
7thC, with restorations and
lditions.
),500-13,000

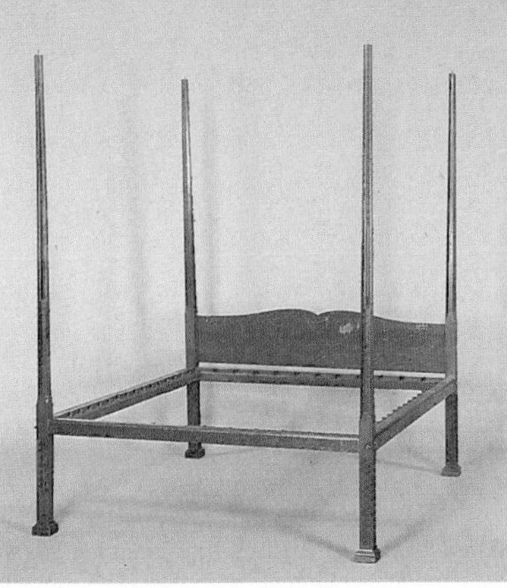

A Chippendale carved mahogany highpost bedstead, Newport, Rhode Island, c1770, 61in (155cm) wide.
$85,000-95,000

A George III painted parcel-gilt four-poster bed, 66in (168cm) wide.
$32,000-40,000

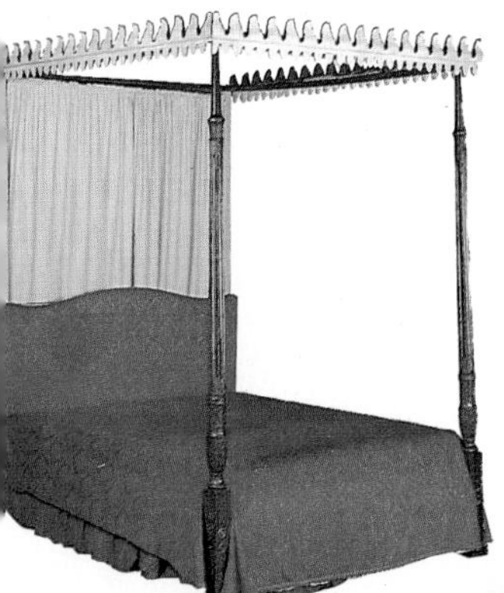

George III mahogany
ed, 70in (178cm) wide.
),000-10,000

An Empire mahogany ormolu mounted lit d'alcove.
$20,000-25,000

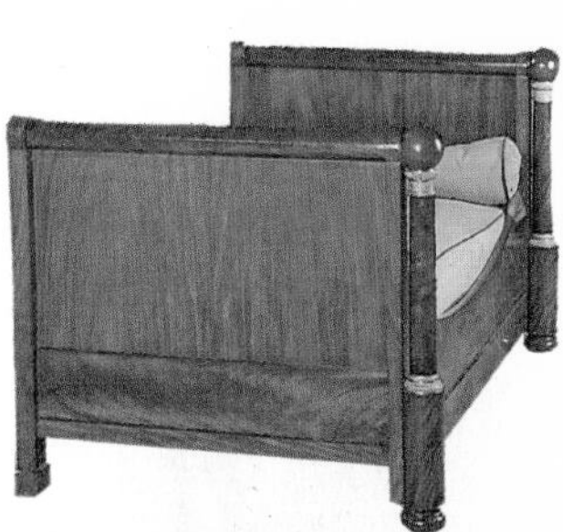

An Empire mahogany ormolu mounted lit en bateau.
$3,000-5,000

late Regency
ahogany
okcase, the
ors fitted with
ramah locks,
½in (151cm).
16,000-20,000

A Regency mahogany breakfront bookcase, with central oak lined slides, probably reduced, 96in (244cm). **$5,000-8,000**

A George III mahogany double breakfront bookcase, 145½in (369cm). **$32,000-40,000**

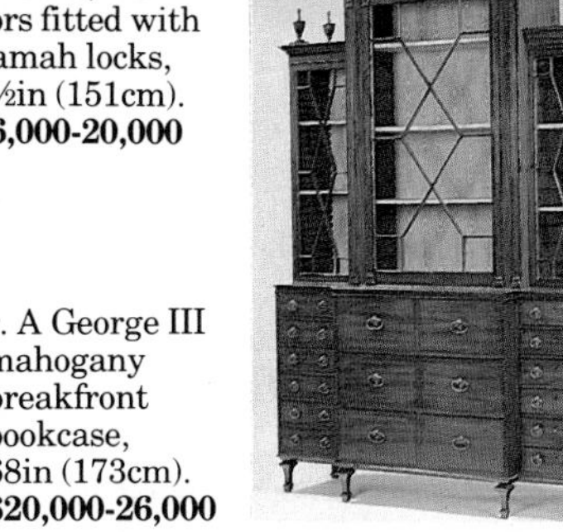

r. A George III mahogany breakfront bookcase, 68in (173cm).
$20,000-26,000

A Federal inlaid walnut breakfront bookcase, c1810, 76in (193cm). **$6,500-9,500**

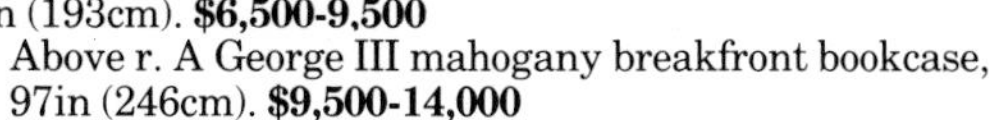

Above r. A George III mahogany breakfront bookcase, 97in (246cm). **$9,500-14,000**

A walnut bookcase, with moulded cornice above geometrically glazed doors and cupboard doors, on bracket feet, 38in (97cm).
$6,500-9,500

A George II mahogany bookcase, with moulded cornice above 2 glazed doors and 2 panelled doors, cornice cut, 104in (264cm) high.
$6,500-9,500

A George III mahogany bookcase, with pierced fretwork broken scroll pediment, the 2 panelled doors enclosing oak slides, inscribed George Shedden Esq., 60in (153cm).
$40,000-50,000

A George III mahogany bookcase, with pierced fretwork pediment, a pair of panelled doors enclosing 2 drawers and 2 slides, 49in (124cm).
$20,000-25,000

A George III mahogany bookcase, crossbanded with rosewood, 50½in (128cm). **$13,000-20,000**

A Regency mahogany breakfront bookcase, 103in (262cm).
$20,000-25,000

A Regency ormolu mounte rosewood breakfront bookcase, 81½in (207cm).
$22,000-26,000

A George III mahogany knee-hole secrétaire, 46in (117cm).
$16,000-20,000

A Federal inlaid mahogany secrétaire bookcase, in 2 parts, 40in (101.5cm).
$11,000-13,000

A Classical secrétaire bookcase, New York, c1830, 58in (147cm).
$40,000-50,000

A Regency rosewood, parcel gilt and bronze inlaid bookcase, 30½in (77.5cm).
$16,000-20,000

n Anglo-Indian padouk bureau
ıbinet, with fitted interior,
ıter bun feet, 41½in (105cm).
118,000+

A Dutch East Indies, Sri Lanka, kaliatur and calamander bureau cabinet, the hinged flap enclosing a fitted interior, above 6 drawers, on bun feet, 18thC, 57in (144.5cm).
$4,000-5,000

A George I walnut bureau cabinet, with fitted interior, later feet, 43in (109cm). **$50,000-58,000**

A William and Mary
valnut bureau cabinet,
n later feet, restored,
36½in (93cm).
$40,000-50,000

A George III mahogany bureau cabinet, fitted interior, on bracket feet, 30in (75.5cm).
$5,500-7,000

A North Italian walnut bureau cabinet, partly fitted interior, 44in (111.5cm).
$80,000-90,000

A red and gold japanned bureau cabinet, fitted interior, restorations, 40½in (103cm).
$70,000-80,000

l. A George III mahogany bureau cabinet, late 18th/early 19thC, 35in (89cm).
$18,000-21,000

r. An Anglo-Indian bureau cabinet, distressed, 18thC, 25in (63.5cm).
$14,000-16,000

A red lacquer bureau cabinet, with fitted interior, 40in (102cm).
$13,000-16,000

A Napoleon III ormolu mounted vitrine cabinet, 41in (104cm) wide.
$6,500-9,500

An inlaid Flemish cabinet-on-stand with later top and stand, 53½in (135cm) high.
$9,500-11,000

A William and Mary parquetry inlaid tulipwood 2-stage cabinet, the upper section with doors concealing 10 drawers, 69in (175cm) high.
$30,000-32,000

A Federal inlaid cherrywood linen press, c1800, 81½in (207cm) high.
$20,000-25,000

A Regency pollard elm clothes press, 83in (210cm) high.
$6,500-9,500

A Régence ormolu mounted kingwood armoire, c1720.
$50,000-55,000

A Federal inlaid mahogany sideboard and cabinet, possibly New Hampshire, possible old restoration, c1800, 70½in (178cm) high.
$10,000-15,000

A Federal grain painted step-back cupboard, some restoration, Vermont, early 19thC, 63½in (160cm).
$40,000-50,000

A pair of Louis XV kingwood and tulip wood parquetry encoignures, by RVLC, one with later marble top, 23½in (60cm) wide. **$20,000-25,000**

A pair of Louis XVI ormolu mounted tulipwood, mahogany, marquetry and parquetry corner cabinets, c1775, 30½in (78cm).
$22,000-26,000

A George III double corner cupboard, 93in (236cm) high.
$16,000-20,000

ı George III mahogany ecrétaire bookcase, he base with itted interior and nclosed slides, 42½in 108cm). **$11,000-14,000**

A George III style mahogany secrétaire cabinet, 31in (79cm). **$7,000-9,000**

A Classical mahogany and bird's-eye maple secrétaire a abattant, Philadelphia, c1825, 36½in (92cm). **$50,000-60,000**

A Classical rosewood and gilt-stencilled ladies secrétaire, in 2 sections, the glazed doors enclosing 2 shelves, the lower section with pull-out writing slide, New York, c1820, 37in (94cm). **$6,500-7,000**

ı Classical rosewood esk and bookcase, n two parts, robably Boston, c1830, 0in (127cm). **14,000-16,000**

A Louis XV ormolu mounted tulipwood and marquetry secrétaire a abattant, stamped C. C. Saunier JME twice, late 18thC, 29½in (75cm). **$18,000-21,000**

A green and black japanned and giltwood cabinet-on-stand, painted with chinoiserie scenes, the panelled cupboard doors enclosing 13 drawers around a cupboard door, 41½in (105cm). **$5,000-8,000**

ı Spanish parcel gilt and ebony reakfront cabinet-on-stand, the ides with carrying handles, 7in (195.5cm). **16,000-20,000**

A Louis XVI boulle cabinet en armoire, 42½in (108cm). **$14,000-20,000**

A William IV mahogany library cabinet, with leather lined articulated rounded rectangular top, the frieze with a brushing slide to either side, the sides with foliate bronze handles, on plinth base, 54in (137cm). **$30,000-32,000**

A Louis XVI Provincial mahogany bureau cabinet, with marble top and fitted interior, late 18thC, 44in (111.5cm) wide.
$10,000-15,000

A Louis XV tulipwood and marquetry secrétaire à abattant, restorations, 32in (81.5cm) wide.
$12,000-15,000

A Louis XVI ormolu mounted marquetry secrétaire à abattant, with Carrara marble top, fitted interior, stamped M. Ohneberg Jme, 38in (96.5cm) wide.
$25,000-32,000

A Regency secrétaire à abattant, 44in (111cm).
$5,000-8,000

A Flemish gilt metal mounted and kingwood strongbox-on-stand, the strongbox 17thC, 28in (71cm) wide.
$6,500-8,000

A Goanese inlaid cabinet-on-stand, 40in (101.5cm) wide.
$32,000-40,000

A walnut cabinet-on-chest, the top late 17thC, base 18thC. **$13,000-16,000**

A Charles II japanned cabinet-on-stand, regilded, 46in (117cm) wide. **$32,000-40,000**

Queen Anne burr walnut bureau,
e sloping flap enclosing a
ted interior of drawers and
cret drawers, on later bun feet,
½in (95cm).
3,000-32,000

A George I walnut bureau, the crossbanded fall enclosing a fitted interior, 31½in (80cm).
$12,000-14,000

A George I walnut bureau, the hinged flap lined with green baize, with fitted interior, on bracket feet, 26in (66cm).
$16,000-20,000

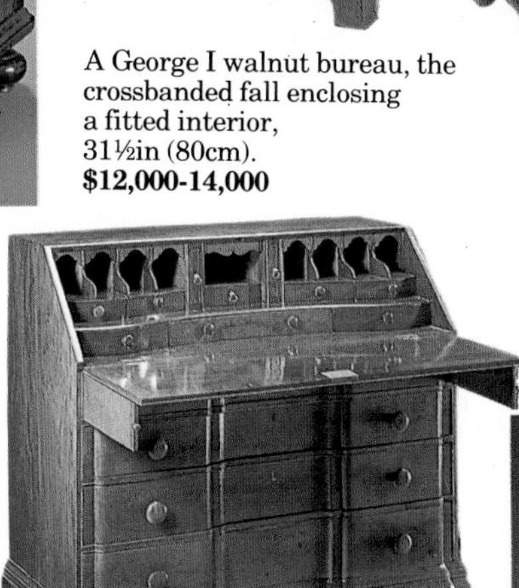

A Chippendale mahogany desk, with fitted interior, some damage, Connecticut, c1770, 47in (119cm).
$11,000-16,000

A cherrywood slant front desk, with fitted interior, labelled by Joseph Rawson, Providence, Rhode Island, feet damaged, c1790, 44in (111.5cm).
$20,000-25,000

Queen Anne cherrywood desk-on-
me, the upper part with fitted
erior, on cabriole legs with
l feet, sliding lid supports
laced, Connecticut, c1750,
n (89cm).
,000-60,000

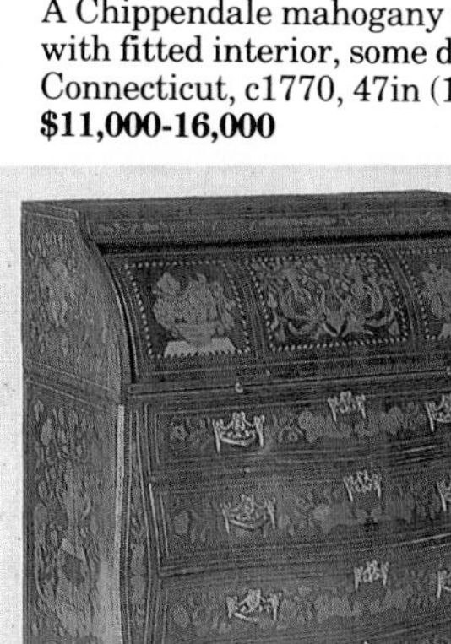

A Dutch marquetry and mahogany bombé cylinder bureau, with fitted interior, late 18thC, 45in (114cm).
$9,500-13,000

Chippendale carved mahogany
ck front desk, with
ed interior, on claw-and-
l feet, damage and
toration, c1780, 45in (114cm).
,000-32,000

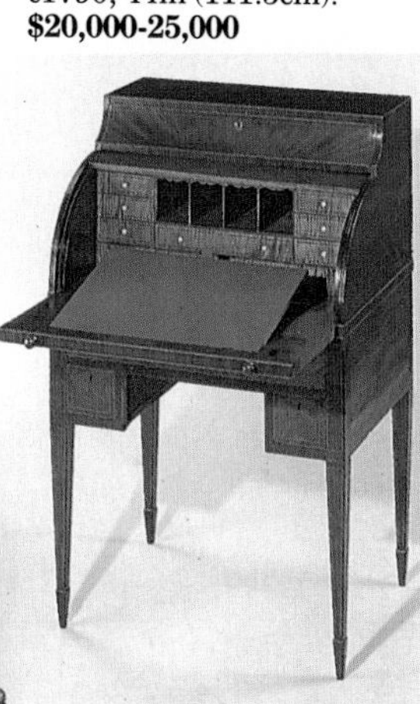

A George III mahogany cylinder bureau, inlaid with boxwood lines, with fitted interior, 48in (122cm).
$6,500-9,500

l. An ormolu mounted kingwood, amaranth and parquetry bureau, 46in (117cm) high.
$9,500-13,000

A mahogany dwarf cabinet, early 19thC, the superstructure possibly later, 30½in (77cm).
$8,000-9,500

A Flemish ebony, ivory and tortoiseshell table cabinet, the central door enclosing 5 drawers, the sides with carrying handles, late 17thC, 35½in (91cm).
$6,500-8,000

l. A George IV bird's-eye maple reading cabinet, 19in (48.5cm).
$22,000-26,000

A Regency mahogany, ebonised and parcel gilt dwarf breakfront side cabinet, with later marble top, restored, 74in (188cm). **$14,000-16,000**

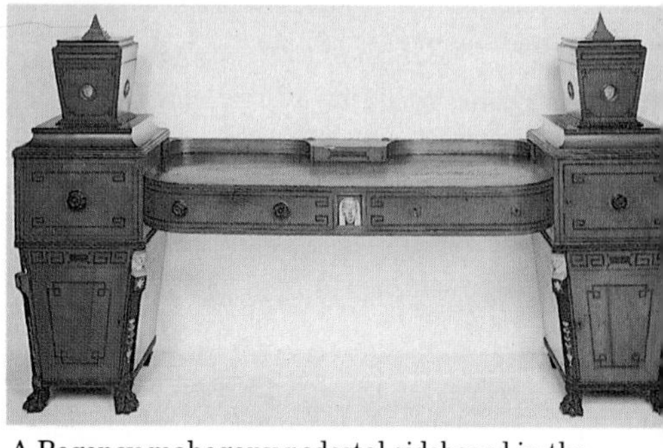

A Regency mahogany pedestal sideboard in the Egyptian style, formerly with a gallery, 109in (276.5cm). **$32,000-35,000**

A mid-Victorian ormolu mounted and marquetry side cabinet, with crossbanded breakfront top, 90in (229cm).
$6,500-9,500

A George III mahogany sideboard, with a central drawer above an arched kneehole, with 2 drawers to the left and deep drawer to the right, on block feet, 58in (147cm).
$11,000-14,000

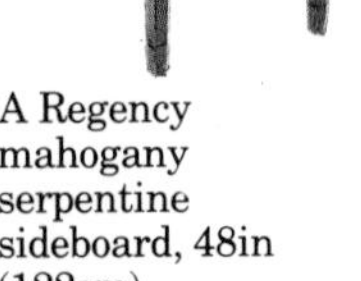

A Regency mahogany serpentine sideboard, 48in (122cm).
$9,500-13,000

A Federal inlaid cherrywood sideboard with serpentine top, repairs, c1800, 61in (155cm).
$25,000-28,000

A late George III mahogany bowfronted sideboard, 66in (168cm).
$22,000-26,000

r. A late George III mahogany sideboard, crossbanded and inlaid, 69in (175cm).
$9,500-14,000

A George III ormolu mounted and brass inlaid mahogany, rosewood and satinwood breakfront table cabinet, with fitted interior. **$32,000-50,000**

A Louis XVI mahogany console desserte, late 18thC, 56½in (143cm) wide. **$40,000-50,000**

A Regency penwork breakfront side cabinet, with later slate top and some redecoration, 48½in (123cm) wide. **$25,000-32,000**

An ormolu mounted ebo and boulle meuble d'appui. **$5,000-6,500**

A pair of American brass inlaid ebonised side cabinets, late 19thC, 95½in (242cm) wide. **$38,000-42,000**

A Victorian inlaid burr walnut credenza with serpentine doors and gilt mounts. **$5,500-6,500**

A pair of Victorian walnut display cabinets with glazed doors, 34½in (87cm). **$3,000-5,000**

r. A George III mahogany sideboard with bowfronted top, 73in (185cm) wide. **$16,000-20,000**

A George III mahogany sideboard edged with boxwood, 71in (180cm) wide. **$21,000-25,000**

r. A late George III mahogany sideboard, the ledge-back probably later, 72in (182.5cm). **$5,000-8,000**

A George I walnut wing armchair with early 18thC upholstery, the needlework restored, later blocks to feet.
$73,000-80,000

An early George II walnut wing armchair with shaped sides, carved cabriole front legs on claw-and-ball feet, swept back legs.
$9,500-13,000

A rare Chippendale carved mahogany easy chair on cabriole legs with ball-and-claw feet, rear legs spliced to chair frame, Boston, Massachusetts, c1775.
$50,000-60,000

A pair of Irish George III bergères in the French taste.
$13,000-16,000

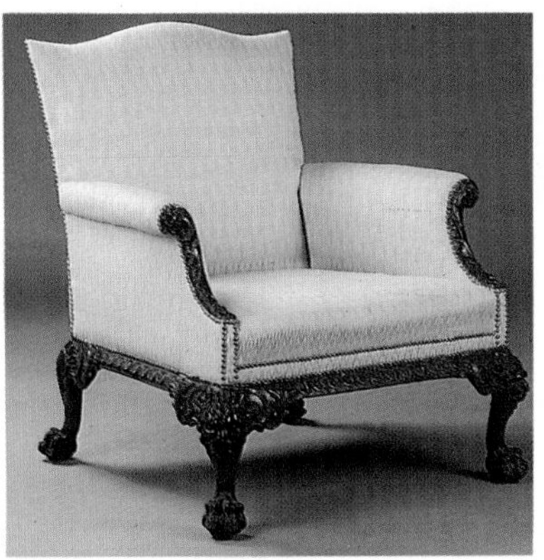

A mahogany armchair with serpentine top, the arms, seat rail and cabriole legs carved, restorations.
$14,000-20,000

A pair of Louis XVI walnut bergères with possibly matching tabouret, late 18thC.
$10,000-15,000

A pair of Louis XVI giltwood bergères by Georges Jacob and stamped, restored.
$40,000-50,000

A William IV mahogany tub armchair.
$16,000-25,000

A George I walnut open armchair with carved top-rail and drop-in seat, on cabriole legs with pointed pad feet, one later angle bracket and some restoration.
$20,000-25,000

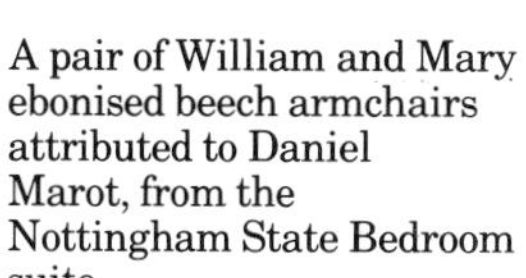

A pair of William and Mary ebonised beech armchairs attributed to Daniel Marot, from the Nottingham State Bedroom suite.

$80,000-88,000

A pair of George II mahogany library armchairs, with contemporary needlework upholstery.
$210,000+

A George III mahogany open armchair, covered in leather.
$9,500-13,000

A matched pair of George III mahogany library armchairs.
$22,000-26,000

A pair of George III mahogany armchairs, with buttoned backs and seats.
$13,000-20,000

A set of 4 George III painted armchairs, restored.
$5,000-8,000

A set of 8 George III mahogany open armchairs.
$55,000-65,000

A set of 4 George III giltwood open armchairs, some restoration.
$25,000-35,000

A suite of Louis XVI giltwood furniture, by Georges Jacob.
$25,000-35,000

A pair of Regency parcel gilt and painted armchairs.
$8,000-9,500

l. A set of 10 Regency mahogany dining chairs, with minor restorations.
$16,000-20,000

A Regency mahogany reading chair, with some restoration.
$13,000-16,000

A suite of Louis XVI style giltwood seat furniture.
$16,000-20,000

l. An Empire mahogany fauteuil-de-bureau with swivel seat, restored.
$2,500-3,000

l. A Russian brass mounted mahogany armchair, with silk upholstered seat, late 18thC.
$9,500-13,000

A George II walnut reclining wing armchair, with raked adjustable back.
$9,500-13,000

A pair of George III mahogany tub chairs, covered in green leather, one reduced.
$14,000-18,000

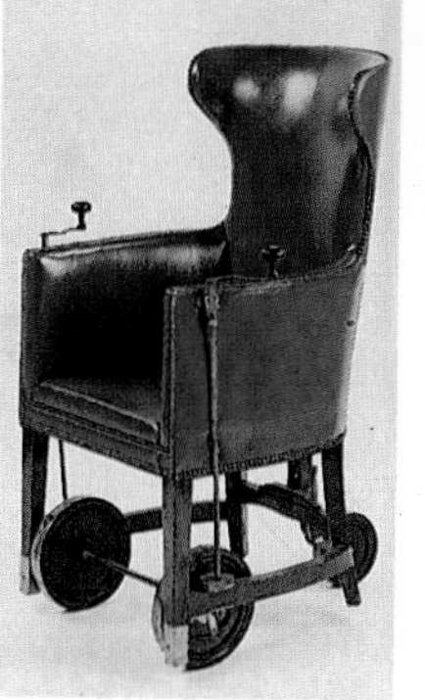

A George III mahogany invalid's chair, attributed to John Joseph Merlin.
$3,000-4,000

An Empire mahogany bergère.
$10,000-12,000

A pair of Louis XVI grey painted marquises, with reeded legs headed by paterae, late 18thC, 32½in (82cm).
$22,000-25,000

A pair of Louis XIII walnut fauteuils, with scrolled moulded arms.
$18,000-22,000

Two Transitional painted fauteuils, redecorated.
$5,000-6,500

A pair of giltwood fauteuils, stamped Bauve.
$53,000-58,000

l. A pair of George III grained rosewood open armchairs.
$6,500-9,500

A large George II mahogany open armchair, lacking some angle blocks, 32½in (82cm).
$5,000-6,500

A pair of George II mahogany library armchairs.
$200,000+

r. Two George II mahogany master's chairs, one with printed label 'Art Treasures Exhibition 1928', restorations.
$13,000-20,000

A pair of George III armchairs.
$5,000-8,000

l. A pair of Louis XV fauteuils, some restoration.
$25,000-32,000

A Regency mahogany reading chair, one arm with swing pen drawer, inscribed in ink A.S. twice, c1810. **$16,000-20,000**

A Regency mahogany reading chair, repairs to back legs, stamped IO. **$9,500-13,000**

A Regency simulated rosewood bergère, with cane seat and carved scroll legs. **$5,000-6,000**

A Federal fancy painted side chair, attributed to Samuel Gragg, Boston, U.S.A., some damage, c1820. **$5,000-6,500**

A pair of Regency rosewood tub bergères. **$6,500-9,500**

Below. A pair of Regency mahogany armchairs. **$13,000-16,000**

A Regency parcel gilt and ebonised armchair. **$13,000-20,000**

A pair of Empire mahogany fauteuils, c1810. **$14,000-16,000**

l. A pair of mahogany side chairs, c1760. **$95,000-110,000**

Below. A set of 8 Regency mahogany dining chairs, including 2 armchairs, some damage and repairs. **$22,000-26,000**

A Queen Anne painted carved side chair, attributed to John Gaines, c1730. **$32,000-40,000**

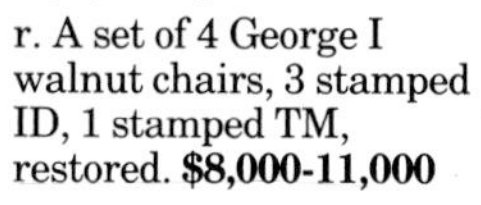

l. A pair of early Victorian mahogany armchairs. **$8,000-9,500**

r. A set of 4 George I walnut chairs, 3 stamped ID, 1 stamped TM, restored. **$8,000-11,000**

A set of 6 Federal carved mahogany side chairs, with X-pattern backs and over-upholstered seats, the feet possibly reduced slightly, probably Salem, Massachusetts, c1800, 34½in (87.5cm) high.
$10,000-15,000

l. A set of 6 George I walnut side chairs with caned panels and drop-in seats. **$16,000-20,000**

A set of 4 Regency oak side chairs in the Gothic style.
$6,500-8,000

Regency simulated
›sewood bergère with
›rched spoon-shaped back
›nd caned seat, on reeded
›bre legs.
;,500-8,000

An Empire giltwood chair with carved arched cresting.
$8,000-11,000

A set of 7 Regency brass inlaid mahogany dining chairs, including 2 open armchairs.
$32,000-35,000

A set of 6 William IV rosewood dining chairs with upholstered drop-in seats, curved toprail and scroll carved crossbar.
$2,500-3,000

A set of 8 George IV mahogany dining chairs with broad curved toprails and buttoned seats.
$9,500-16,000

A set of 8 William IV balloon-back dining chairs.
$4,000-5,000

A set of 12 mid-Victorian dining chairs, stamped 'Gillows Lancaster L23097'.
$28,000-32,000

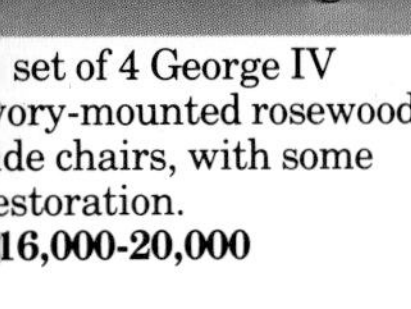

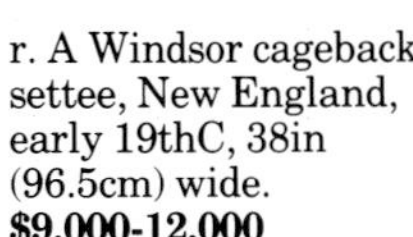

set of 4 George IV
›ory-mounted rosewood
›de chairs, with some
›storation.
16,000-20,000

r. A Windsor cageback settee, New England, early 19thC, 38in (96.5cm) wide.
$9,000-12,000

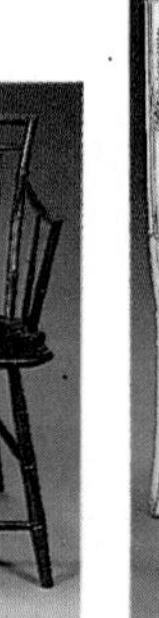

l. A suite of Empire white painted and parcel gilt furniture, some restoration to decoration, possibly Italian, early 19thC.
$130,000-140,000

A George III mahogany open armchair, with serpentine toprail and suede seat.
$3,000-5,000

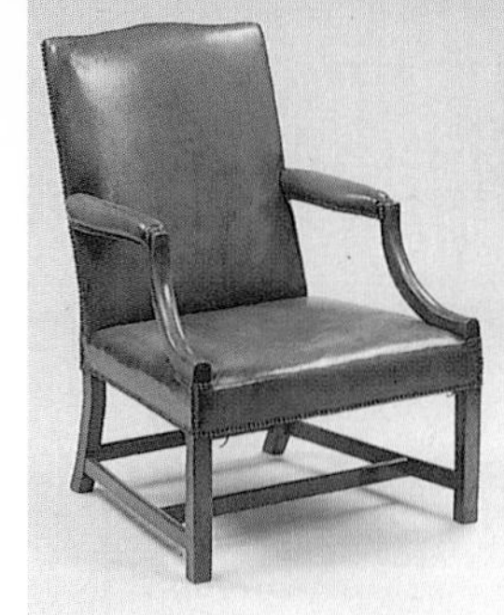
A George III fruitwood library armchair, with serpentine padded back, armrests and seat.
$5,000-6,500

A pair of mahogany open armchairs, with padded backs and bowed seats.
$8,000-9,500

A pair of Louis XVI fauteuils, c1780.
$16,000-20,000

A set of 10 late Regency mahogany dining chairs, including 2 armchairs.
$13,000-20,000

A pair of early Victorian rosewood open armchairs with shaped curved backs.
$9,500-11,000

A pair of Queen Anne red stained maple side chairs, some restoration.
$11,000-13,000

A Queen Anne carved maple side chair, possibly New Hampshire, c1735.
$9,500-13,000

A set of 6 Dutch walnut and marquetry chairs, c1730.
$32,000-40,000

A Queen Anne carved walnut side chair, attributed to John Goddard, Newport, Rhode Island, c1760.
$32,000-40,000

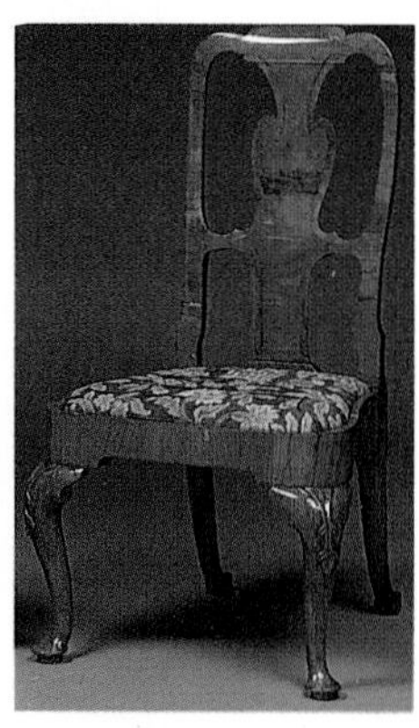
l. A set of 5 Queen Anne walnut dining chairs and 3 of later date, with drop-in seats on cabriole legs.
$38,000-40,000

A pair of Georg[e] II walnut side chairs, with padded backs a[nd] seats.
$18,000-20,000

l. A set of 8 George II walnut side chairs with padded backs and seats, on cabriole legs and pad feet, some restoration.
$32,000-35,000

l. A set of 10 German walnut side chairs, c1750.
$6,500-8,000

Chippendale carved
ıhogany side chair,
l repair to top of
ɛstrail.
2,000-40,000

A pair of early George III mahogany side chairs. **$80,000-88,000**

A set of 6 George III dining chairs. **$8,000-10,000**

A set of 4 George III mahogany dining chairs, restored. **$4,000-5,000**

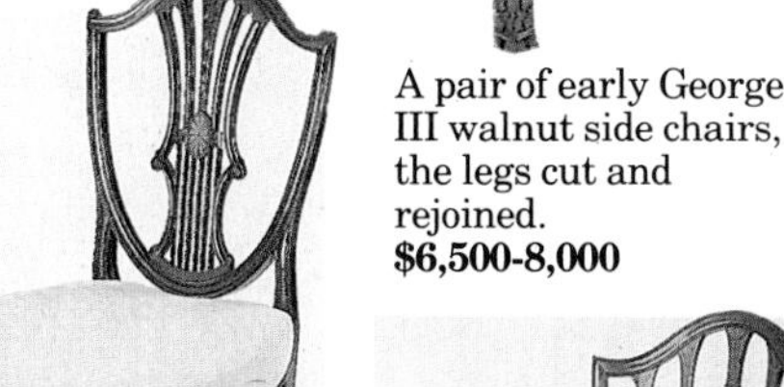

A pair of early George III walnut side chairs, the legs cut and rejoined. **$6,500-8,000**

ɔair of George III
ıhogany side chairs,
ɔairs, late 18thC.
,500-8,000

A pair of George III mahogany dining chairs, each with pierced shield back, and central fan medallion. **$2,500-3,000**

Eight George III mahogany chairs. **$20,000-25,000**

Six George III mahogany dining chairs, repairs. **$5,500-7,000**

ɛet of 4 George III
ıhogany dining chairs,
ɛ with slight
ɾiations.
,000-8,000

A pair of George III giltwood chairs. **$10,000-12,000**

A set of 4 mahogany chairs, 19thC. **$1,000-1,500**

l. A set of 6 George III mahogany dining chairs, including a pair of open armchairs, some restoration. **$6,500-9,500**

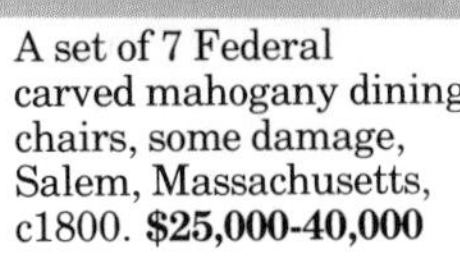

A set of 7 Federal carved mahogany dining chairs, some damage, Salem, Massachusetts, c1800. **$25,000-40,000**

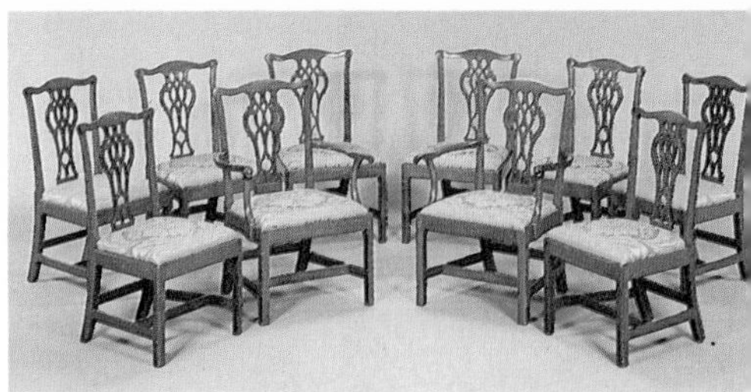

A set of 10 Chippendale mahogany dining chairs comprising 2 armchairs and 8 side chairs, Massachusetts, one repaired, c1770. **$60,000-65,000**

A set of 12 George III style mahogany dining chairs, including 4 armchairs, with waved crest rails and pierced splats. **$14,000-20,000**

A set of 6 George III mahogany dining chairs, including a pair of open armchairs, with later blocks. **$13,000-18,000**

A pair of Louis XV giltwood fauteuils, stamped Tilliard, mid-18thC. **$80,000-95,000**

A pair of Louis XVI giltwood fauteuils en cabriolet, stamped G. Jacob. **$25,000-40,000**

A set of 6 Federal carved mahogany side chairs and an armchair, each with carved and reeded bowed rectangular back with 4 square reeded vertical splats, each branded 'MB', various repairs to legs, Philadelphia, c1800. **$5,500-8,000**

A set of 8 Classical mahogany Klismos chairs, comprising 2 armchairs and 6 side chairs, each with a panelled tablet crest rail with a reeded and scrolled crest, the horizontal back rail with rope-twist and baluster turnings, the armchairs with open scrolled arms, Boston, c1820. **$30,000-40,000**

A Louis XVI giltwood fauteuil à la reine, the frame and downswept arm supports carved with flowers and acanthus, upholstery distressed, c1780. **$14,800-18,000**

A pair of Regency simulated bronze and parcel gilt bergères, after a design by George Smith, each with a scrolled back and deep toprail, centred by a Medusa mask, with double caned sides, redecorated. **$150,000-160,000**

An Empire giltwood fauteuil, the frame and seat rail carved with laurel leaves, re-gilded, stamped Jacob.D.R.Meslee, early 19thC. **$21,000-26,000**

walnut sofa, upholstered
early 18thC needlework,
7in (144.5cm).
28,000-32,000

A George I walnut double chairback settee, 50in (127cm).
$16,000-20,000

A Georgian walnut sofa.
$13,000-16,000

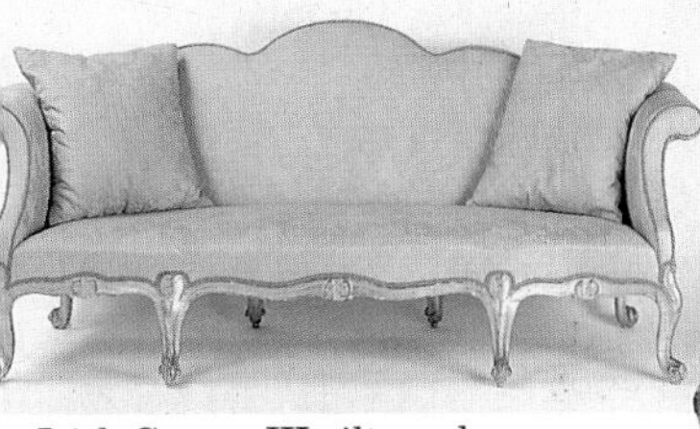

n Irish George III giltwood
ofa, with a carved moulded
eat rail, 83in (210.5cm).
8,000-11,000

A suite of Empire white painted and parcel gilt furniture, possibly Italian, early 19thC.
$130,000-150,000

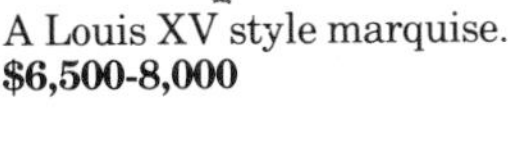

A Louis XV style marquise.
$6,500-8,000

Federal mahogany sofa, one front
ot pieced, c1800, 40in (101cm).
16,000-20,000

A pair of George IV oak window seats, some damage.
$28,000-32,000

r. A George III mahogany window seat, 37½in (70cm). **$5,000-6,500**

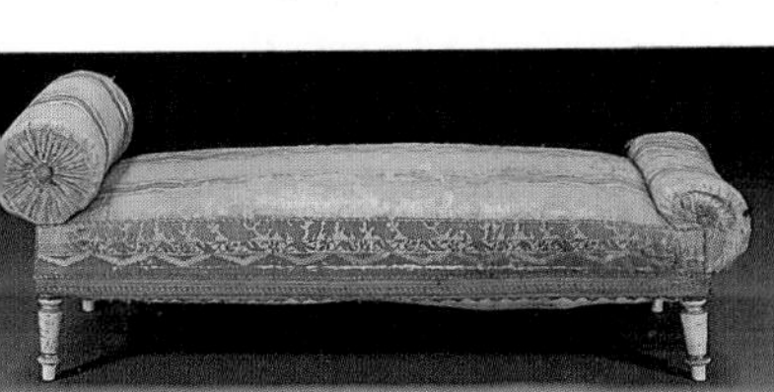

Neo-classic style white painted day
ed, 74in (188cm). **$1,500-3,000**

A pair of Regency window seats.
$36,000-40,000

r. A giltwood stool, with later blocks, 39in (99cm). **$11,000-13,000**

n early Victorian maple sofa,
7in (195.5cm). **$11,000-14,000**

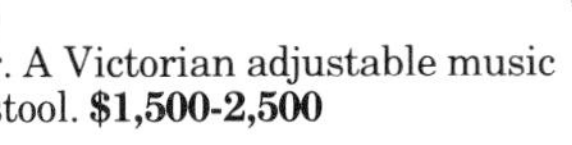

r. A Victorian adjustable music stool. **$1,500-2,500**

A pair of George IV mahogany window seats.
$14,000-16,000

A Directoire brass inlaid mahogany and amaranth gueridon, late 18thC, 29in (74cm) diam.
$8,000-9,500

A George III mahogany writing table, fitted with 2 drawers, the reverse with 2 slides, 48in (122cm).
$13,000-14,000

A George III ormolu mounted satinwood writing table, 34in (86cm).
$40,000-50,000

r. A Regency ormolu mounted amboyna writing table, restored, 45in (114cm).
$25,000-32,000

l. A Regency mahogany writing table, with 6 drawers, 74½in (189cm).
$32,000-40,000

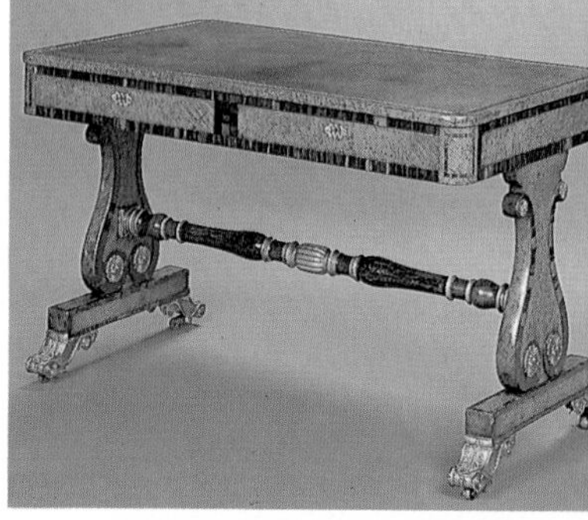

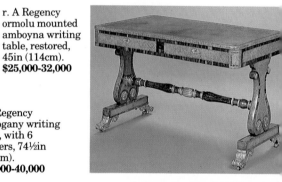

A Regency mahogany writing table, with moulded top and a drawer, on solid waisted end supports, labelled James Newton, 37in (94cm).
$8,000-9,500

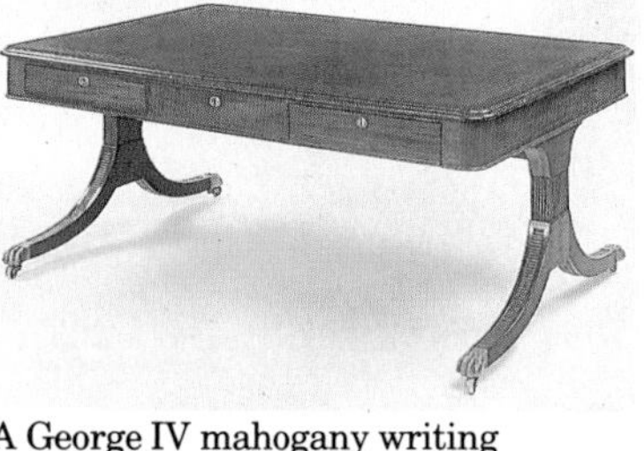
A George IV mahogany writing table, by Gillows of Lancaster, the frieze with 6 drawers on reeded end standards and downswept legs with paw caps, 72in (182.5cm). **$20,000-25,000**

A William IV plane writing table, with leather-lined rounded rectangular top, the frieze with 3 drawers, on turned legs, 54in (137cm). **$6,500-9,500**

l. A William IV brass inlaid rosewood library table.
$50,000-55,000

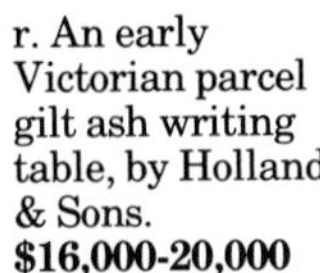

r. An early Victorian parcel gilt ash writing table, by Holland & Sons.
$16,000-20,000

l. A pair of William IV oak writing tables.
$14,000-16,000

r. An ormolu mounted tortoiseshell and boulle bureau plat, late 19thC.
$6,500-9,500

ueen Anne walnut bachelor's
st, with folding top,
torations, 29in (74cm).
,000-26,000

A George III mahogany chest, with original moulded handles and lock escutcheons, c1775, 36in (92cm). **$11,000-13,000**

eorge I walnut chest, the sides
h brass carrying handles,
torations to the feet,
n (81cm).
,000-30,000

A Federal figured maple chest of drawers, on modified French feet, c1810, 43in (109cm). **$5,500-7,000**

A George III mahogany secrétaire chest, with stepped fretwork superstructure, 31½in (80cm). **$20,000-25,000**

A George III satinwood serpentine chest of 4 long drawers, banded with tulipwood and inlaid with lines, on bracket feet, 37in (94cm). **$13,000-16,000**

eorge I walnut bachelor's
st, on later bracket feet,
torations, 27½in (70cm).
,000-16,000

A Régence ormolu mounted ebony and marquetry commode, the rectangular brass bordered top centred by a vase of flowers, above a mask flanked by scrolling foliage, restorations, 47in (119cm). **$65,000-80,000**

A North Italian walnut bombé commode, the sides with cupboards, on cabriole legs carved with flowerheads, with trefoil feet, 41in (104cm). **$8,000-11,000**

r. A Louis XV/XVI ormolu mounted tulipwood and marquetry commode, late 18thC, 44in (112cm). **$22,000-26,000**

A bronze mounted kingwood and parquetry bombé commode, 39in (99cm).
$11,000-14,000

A Restoration ormolu mounted mahogany commode with mottled grey marble top and decorated frieze drawer above 3 drawers, 50in (127cm).
$3,000-5,000

A German walnut and marquetry commode, top inlaid with geomet strapwork, on later bun feet, 18thC, 47½in (120.5cm).
$9,000-11,000

A Transitional ormolu mounted marquetry commode, the inlaid breakfront top possibly later, 57½in (146cm). **$110,000-130,000**

A George III mahogany serpentine commode, the doors enclosing slides above 2 short and 1 long drawer, on ogee bracket feet, 49in (124.5cm).
$14,000-20,000

A George III style mahogany and marquetry commode, 48in (122cm).
$12,000-13,500

A George III mahogany commode, with eared serpentine top, restorations, the stand possibly later, 48in (122cm).
$13,000-20,000

A Regency mahogany pedestal cupboard, with moulded square top above a cupboard door and drawer fitted with removable bin, on plinth base, early 19th(13in (38cm), together with a later brass-boun mahogany jardinière, 15in (38cm) diam.
$5,500-7,000

A Charles X bois satine commode with marble top, 52in (132cm).
$8,000-9,500

A late Victorian satinwood and marquetry commode, by Edwards & Roberts, with 3 panelled doors, on square tapering feet, 60in (152cm).
$18,000-21,000

n Italian rococo walnut commode, ı cabriole legs with toupie feet, id-18thC, 56½in (143cm) wide. **;0,000-65,000**

A Louis XV/XVI ormolu mounted kingwood, bois satiné and tulipwood parquetry commode, c1775. **$110,000-130,000**

. Louis XV/XVI ormolu mounted ılipwood and amaranth commode, ,amped N.Grevenich Jme, c1770,)in (127cm). **$65,000-80,000**

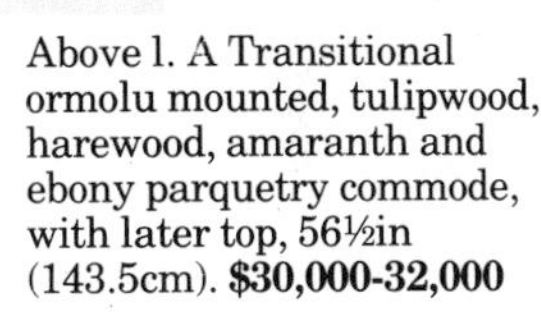

Above l. A Transitional ormolu mounted, tulipwood, harewood, amaranth and ebony parquetry commode, with later top, 56½in (143.5cm). **$30,000-32,000**

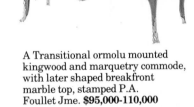

Louis XV/XVI ormolu mounted ılipwood and kingwood commode, 5½in (141cm). **$130,000-150,000**

A Swedish rococo ormolu mounted, tulipwood and walnut parquetry commode, the serpentine moulded crossbanded top inlaid with a lozenge panel, mid-18thC, 41in (104cm) wide. **$16,000-20,000**

A Transitional ormolu mounted kingwood and marquetry commode, with later shaped breakfront marble top, stamped P.A. Foullet Jme. **$95,000-110,000**

Transitional ormolu mounted marquetry commode, ınded in tulipwood and amaranth, with later top, amped P.A. Foullet Jme, 57in (145cm) wide. **:50,000-300,000**

A George III mahogany commode, with gilt tooled leather lined slide, the doors and drawers edged with ebony, 47in (119cm) wide. **$100,000-130,000**

A pair of ormolu mounted kingwood and amaranth petites commodes, with marble tops and frieze drawers above 2 drawers, 32½in (82cm) wide.
$14,000-16,000

A Louis XVI commode, late 18thC, 50in wide.
$15,000-20,000

A pair of South Italian walnut commodes, with composition marble tops above banded and inlaid drawers, 18thC, 23in (58.5cm) wide.
$11,000-16,000

A William and Mary oyster veneered chest, originally on bun feet, now on later stand, 37in (94cm) wide.
$13,000-16,000

An Empire ormolu mounted mahogany commode, with marble top above 2 panelled doors enclosing 3 drawers, later bun feet, adapted, 51in (129.5cm) wide. **$16,000-20,000**

A pair of George III mahogany dining pedestals, one fitted as a plate warmer, one with lead-lined compartments, 38in (96cm) high.
$11,000-16,000

r. A Queen Anne mahogany high chest of drawers in 2 sections, Boston area, Massachusetts, c1760, 86in (218.5cm) high.
$50,000-60,000

l. A Chippendale carved mahogany high chest of drawers in 2 sections, probably West Chester, Pennsylvania, c1775, 92½in (234cm) high.
$50,000-60,000

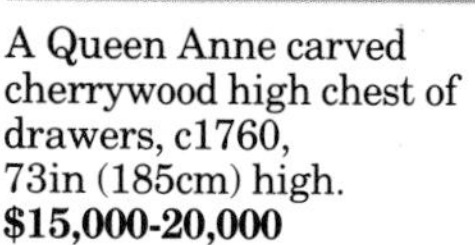

An early Georgian walnut tallboy on bracket feet, the drawers re-lined, restorations, 42in (106.5cm) wide.
$5,000-8,000

A Queen Anne carved cherrywood high chest of drawers, c1760, 73in (185cm) high.
$15,000-20,000

A Chippendale figured maple chest, adapted, c1785, 76in (193cm).
$25,000-30,000

A William and Mary walnut chest-on-stand, on later bun feet, c1690, 42½in (107cm) wide.
$6,500-8,000

A George I burr walnut tallboy, the base with a slide, 41in (104cm) wide.
$40,000-50,000

A George I burr walnut secrétaire tallboy, crossbanded and inlaid, 40in (101.5cm) wide.
$40,000-50,000

A Chippendale carved mahogany chest-on-chest, some damage, c1775, 45in.
$160,000+

A William & Mary wal veneer high chest of drawers, some restoration, c1725, 37in (94cm) wide.
$11,000-13,000

A Queen Anne maple high chest of drawers, Massachusetts, c1750.
$25,000-32,000

A Queen Anne carved cherrywood high chest of drawers, some restoration, c1750, 41in (104cm) wide.
$20,000-25,000

A carved maple high chest of drawers in 2 sections, c1750, 40in (101.5cm) wide.
$32,000-40,000

A Queen Anne burr walnut kneehole desk on later bun feet, 37in (94cm) wide.
$9,500-14,000

r. A Louis XIV ormolu mounted scarlet boulle bureau mazarin, with later turned feet, 38in (96.5cm) wide.
$25,000-32,000

A William & Mary walnut and marquetry chest-on-stand. **$28,000-32,000**

A George II mahogany kneehole desk with crossbanded top, 54½in (138cm) wide. **$32,000-40,000**

r. A Dutch kingwood and mahogany parquetry bonheur du jour, the interior fitted, late 18thC, 30½in (78cm) wide.
$6,500-8,000

A George III satinwood an rosewood inlaid desk.
$20,000-25,000

A mid-Georgian mahogany kneehole secrétaire desk. **$6,500-8,000**

A George III style mahogany writing desk, with a writing slide and recessed kneehole cupboard, 35½in (90cm). **$5,000-6,500**

Ȝeorge I walnut eehole desk, th one long awer, 6 short awers and a eehole drawer ound a recessed pboard door, on acket feet, in (76cm). **1,000-13,000**

A George III partners' desk, with leather lined top, 60in (152cm). **$30,000-32,000**

A George IV mahogany Carlton House desk, the impressed blue leather top fitted with a ratcheted slope, 64in (162.5cm). **$25,000-32,000**

l. A George III mahogany partners' desk, the drawer fronts restored, 55in (139.5cm). **$13,000-14,000**

l. A mahogany roll-top desk, possibly by Edwards and Roberts, c1900, 70½in (179cm). **$20,000-25,000**

A George III mahogany roll-top desk, restored, 44in (112cm). **$20,000-25,000**

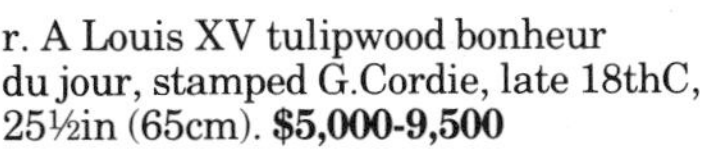

George II mahogany kneehole desk, ith later moulded top, 9in (125cm). **$16,000-25,000**

r. A Louis XV tulipwood bonheur du jour, stamped G.Cordie, late 18thC, 25½in (65cm). **$5,000-9,500**

A Regency satinwood secrétaire and dressing chiffonier, crossbanded with rosewood, 21in (53cm). **$65,000-70,000**

An Empire rosewood toilet mirror, the base inset with Paris porcelain plaques, 19½in (49.5cm) wide.
$5,000-6,500

An Italian carved and gilded tabernacle frame, with glass, 17thC, 41in (104cm) high.
$5,000-5,500

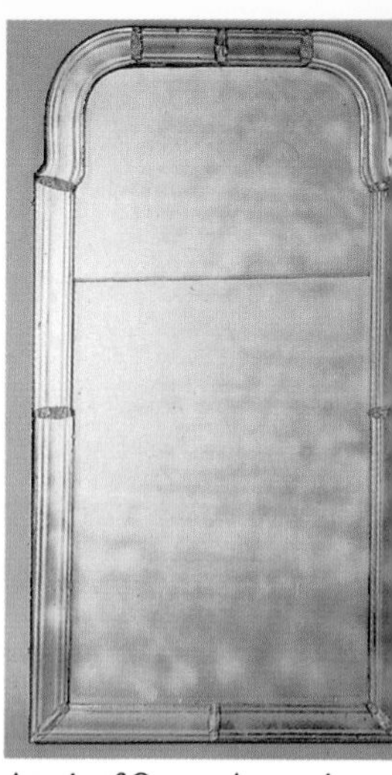

A pair of Queen Anne pier glasses, 58½in (148cm) high.
$80,000-95,000

A William and Mary overmantel mirror, with restorations and replacement glass, 60 by 74in (152 by 188cm).
$16,000-25,000

A Scandinavian lead-framed mirror, early 18thC, 60in (152cm).
$14,000-20,000

A George II giltwood mirror, 68in (173cm) high.
$25,000-30,000

An early George III giltwood overmantel, later plates and re-gilt, 36in (92cm) high. **$16,000-25,000**

A George III giltwood mirror, restored, 80in (203cm) high.
$16,000-25,000

A pair of George III giltwood girandoles restored, 51in (130c high. **$25,000-30,0**

A pair of Louis XV style giltwood mirrors, 39in (99cm) high.
$12,000-18,000

l. A George III style mirror. **$5,000-6,000**

walnut and parcel gilt
ilet mirror, with 3
awers, 31½ by 19in
0 by 48cm).
,500-2,500

A Queen Anne parcel gilt and lacquer toilet mirror, on later ogee bracket feet, 19in (48cm). **$5,000-6,500**

A Queen Anne japanned toilet mirror.
$4,000-5,000

A Charles II giltwood mirror, with a carved frame, re-gilded, 39½ by 29in (100 by 74cm).
$3,000-5,000

Charles II black,
lt and red japanned
irror, lacking cresting,
) by 40in (127 by 102cm).
,000-8,000

A Federal giltwood and eglomisé panel mirror, some damage, New York or Albany, c1800, 60 by 27½in (152 by 70cm).
$13,000-14,000

An Italian carved and gilded frame, 17thC, 41in (104cm) high.
$6,500-8,000

A Spanish carved, gilded and painted frame, 17thC, 59in (150cm) high.
$9,500-11,000

l. An Italian carved and gilded frame, 17thC.
$2,500-3,000

r. A Louis XIV carved and gilded frame, 47 by 39in (119 by 99cm).
$11,000-13,000

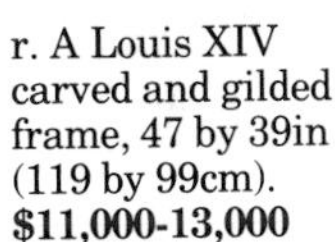

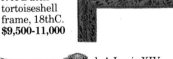

l. An English carved and gilded Chippendale frame, 18thC, 70 by 60in (176 by 151cm).
$5,000-6,500

n Italian blue and etched
lass giltwood mirror,
arly 18thC, 62 by 44in
57 by 112cm).
50,000-65,000

r. A Dutch tortoiseshell frame, 18thC.
$9,500-11,000

l. A Louis XIV style carved and gilded frame, 89in high.
$6,500-8,000

A George III giltwood mirror, 56 by 24in (142 by 61cm).
$5,000-6,500

An Italian carved and gilded frame, early 17thC.
$8,000-9,500

l. A Regency mahogany and rosewood breakfast table, 63in (160cm) wide.
$5,000-8,000

A William and Mary blac and gold japanned card table, some damage and repair, 31in (78cm) wide.
$15,000-20,000

A Queen Anne burr walnut card table, fitted interior, mid-18thC, 40in (101.5cm) wide.
$9,500-13,000

A William IV mahogany breakfast table, lacking bolts, 46in (116.5cm) wide.
$3,000-5,000

r. A George I burr walnut concertina-action card table, fitted interior, 33in (83.5cm) wide.
$65,000-80,000

A Chippendale carved walnut card table, repairs, c1770, 36in (92cm). **$20,000-25,000**

A George III mahogany card table, with inlaid D-shaped folding top, 42in (106.5cm) wide.
$8,000-9,000

A pair of George IV rosewood card tables, one with restorations, 36in (91.5cm) wide.
$6,500-8,000

A satinwood and painted card table, the D-shaped folding top and frieze inlaid, and with baize-lined interior, 36in (91.5cm) wide.
$8,000-9,500

A pair of early Victorian card tables, 36in wide. **$25,000-32,000**

r. A Dutch marquetry card table/dumb waiter, 19thC. **$5,000-6,000**

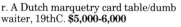

An early George III mahogany centre table, the top with moulded edge, 35in (89.5cm) wide.
$16,000-20,000

. George III mahogany drum table, ıe frieze inlaid with boxwood nes, with turned pedestal, ɔssibly reduced, 54in (137cm) ıam. **$11,000-16,000**

A Regency simulated calamander drum table, redecorated, 48in (122cm) diam.
$8,000-10,000

A Regency brass inlaid rosewood centre table, 48in (122cm) diam.
$30,000-32,000

. Regency rosewood and parcel gilt entre table, with inlaid marble anel, 47in (119cm) diam.
32,000-40,000

A Regency bird's-eye maple and rosewood centre table, top adapted, 29in (74cm) high. **$5,000-8,000**

A Regency rosewood centre table with inset marble top, on bun feet, 34in (86cm) diam.
$21,000-25,000

. Regency mahogany drum ıble, with leather-lined ɔp above 4 drawers, n turned shaft, 3in (84cm) diam.
6,500-9,500

A Dutch marquetry, ebony and bone inlaid centre table, late 19thC, 46½in (118cm).
$7,000-9,000

A Regency brass inlaid and ormolu mounted rosewood reading, writing and games table, with fitted drawers, 30in (76cm).
$16,000-20,000

n ormolu mounted kingwood and tulip-ood centre table, with oval leather-ned top and 4 drawers, 5in (139.5cm).
),500-13,000

A Regency mahogany twin-pedestal dining table with rounded rectangular end sections, each with a frieze drawer, on baluster shafts and splayed quadripartite bases, 67in (170cm) including one leaf.
$11,000-16,000

An early Georgian walnut rectangular chest of drawers, with brushing slide, 31in (79cm).
$10,000-11,000

A George II mahogany chest, with brushing slide above 4 graduated drawers on bracket feet, 31in (79cm).
$9,500-11,000

A George III mahogany serpentine chest of 4 long drawers, on splayed feet, 36½in (92cm).
$11,000-13,000

A Chippendale inlaid walnut blanket, chest, c1755.
$11,000-13,000

A Chippendale cherrywo chest of drawers, c1775.
$22,000-26,000

A Federal carved mahogany bowfront chest of drawers.
$14,000-18,000

A Chippendale cherrywood chest of drawers, c1790.
$21,000-22,000

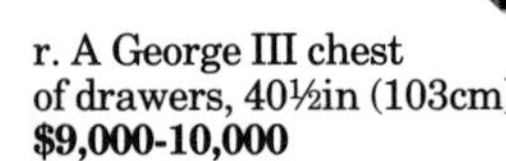

r. A George III chest of drawers, 40½in (103cm).
$9,000-10,000

A painted 2-drawer blanket chest, c1820, 51in (129.5cm). **$6,500-8,000**

l. A Chippendale cherrywood chest of drawers, c1790, 40in (101.5cm). **$6,500-8,000**

Regency mahogany serving table, with 4 frieze
awers centred by a lion's mask, 78½in (199.5cm).
1,000-25,000

r. A Regency parcel gilt rosewood and simulated rosewood side table, the specimen marble top inlaid with squares of various marbles and semi-precious stones, 43in (109cm). **$35,000-40,000**

George III satinwood and
sewood crossbanded sofa table,
laid with brass, the drawers
th turned ebonised handles,
in (147cm) wide.
8,000-22,000

r. A Regency mahogany sofa table, with crossbanded top, 60in (152cm).
$8,000-9,500

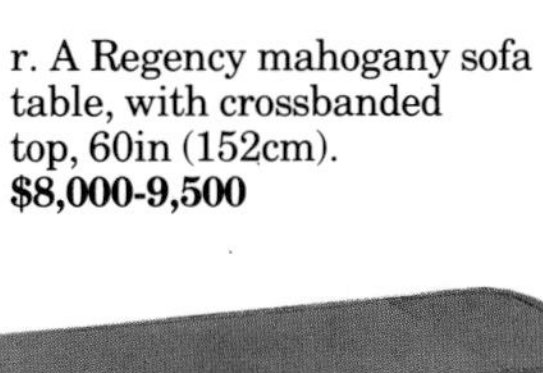

l. A Regency fiddleback mahogany sofa table, the frieze with 2 cedar-lined drawers, 48½in (123cm). **$8,000-11,000**

George IV mahogany sofa table,
laid with satinwood,
plied with roundels on spreading
aft, one leg replaced, 60in
52cm). **$5,000-8,000**

A George III mahogany library table, the top lined with gilt-tooled green leather, the frieze fitted with 6 drawers and 4 dummy drawers, 107in (272cm). **$50,000-60,000**

late George III mahogany writing
ble, the frieze fitted with 3
awers, 44in (111.5cm).
3,000-16,000

A Chippendale mahogany tilt-top tea table, attributed to John Goddard, Rhode Island, repaired, c1775.
$28,000-40,000

A George III padoukwood secrétaire table, with rectangular crossbanded twin-flap top, the deep frieze fitted with a fall flap simulated as 2 long drawers enclosing small drawers, 59½in (151cm) wide open.
$6,500-9,500

A pair of Louis XVI style ormolu mounted marble console tables, 19thC, 41½in (105cm) wide.
$30,000-40,000

A William IV mahogany serving table, 91in (231cm) wide.
$6,000-8,000

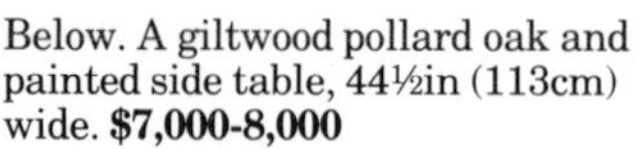

Below. A giltwood pollard oak and painted side table, 44½in (113cm) wide. **$7,000-8,000**

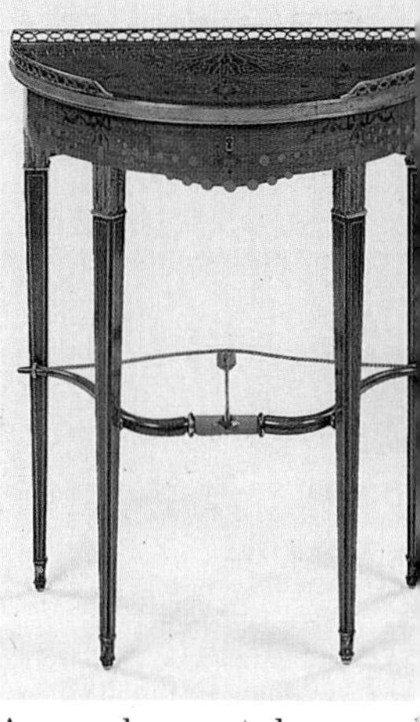

An ormolu mounted rosewood and marquetry side table, the frieze fitted with a drawer, 24in (61.5cm) wide.
$9,500-11,000

Above l. A Regency ormolu mounted rosewood side table with mirror-glazed top, formerly marble, possibly Continental, early 19thC, 53in (134.5cm). **$20,000-25,000**
r. A George II mahogany tripod table in the manner of John Channon, with brass and mother-of-pearl inlay, repaired, 25in (63cm) wide.
$16,000-25,000

A Regency rosewood sofa table in the manner of John Maclean, with cedar lined drawers, 65in (165cm) open.
$13,000-20,000

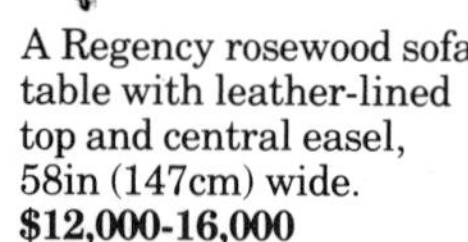

A Regency rosewood sofa table with leather-lined top and central easel, 58in (147cm) wide.
$12,000-16,000

A figured mahogany veneer sewing table, school of Thomas Seymour, Boston, c1812, 21½in (54cm) wide.
$11,000-14,000

A Regency brown oak writing-table attributed to George Bullock, the top with inlaid ebony band, 36in (91.5cm) wide.
$7,000-9,000

A Regency brass-inlaid rosewood writing table, 44½in (113cm).
$8,000-10,000

George II gilt gesso stand, with
ter grey and blue marble top,
e pierced frieze carved with
rolling foliage, 52in (132cm).
2,000-30,000

pair of George III style mahogany
rving tables, with crossbanded
ieze drawers, 50½in (128.5cm).
5,000-9,000

Louis XVI grey painted and
arcel gilt console table, with
ater Siena marble top, c1780,
7½in (146cm). **$16,000-20,000**

George III grained pier table,
vith semi-eliptical mahogany top,
arly 19thC, 76½in (194cm).
8,000-10,000

George III serving table,
he frieze centred by a tablet
nd fitted with a drawer, 72in
182.5cm). **$5,000-9,500**

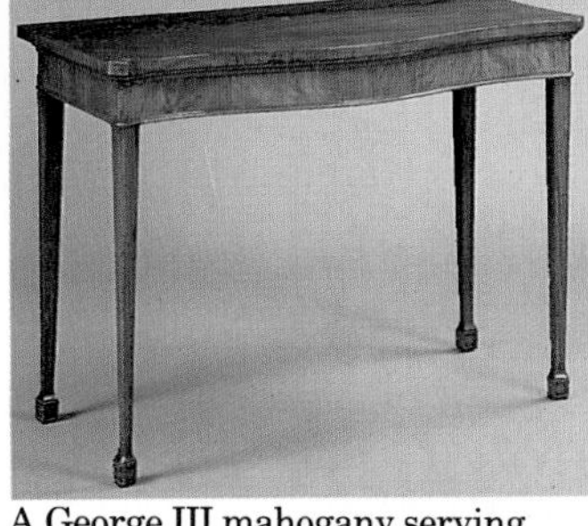

A George III mahogany serving table, with serpentine fronted top, 47½in (121cm). **$6,500-9,500**

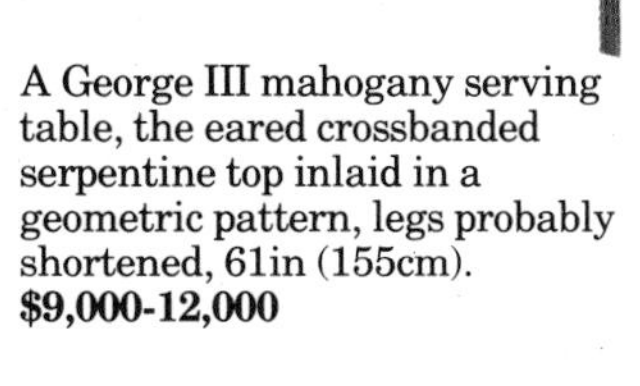

A George III mahogany serving table, the eared crossbanded serpentine top inlaid in a geometric pattern, legs probably shortened, 61in (155cm). **$9,000-12,000**

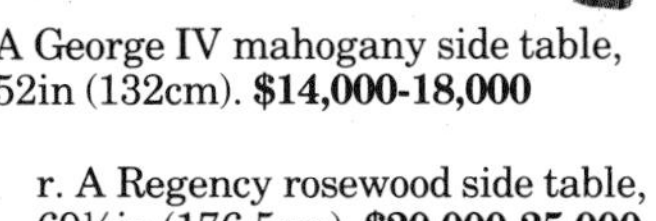

A George IV mahogany side table, 52in (132cm). **$14,000-18,000**

r. A Regency rosewood side table, 69½in (176.5cm). **$20,000-25,000**

A Louis XVI giltwood console table, with breakfront demi-lune black and white marble top and entrelac frieze, c1780, 34in (86.5cm). **$5,500-8,000**

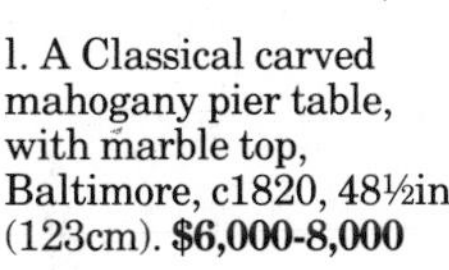

A Régence kingwood side table, with breccia marble top, the shaped frieze fitted with drawers mounted with ribbed handles and cartouche lockplates, 49½in (126cm). **$20,000-25,000**

l. A Classical carved mahogany pier table, with marble top, Baltimore, c1820, 48½in (123cm). **$6,000-8,000**

l. A Classical mahogany marble top pier table, with a mirrored backboard, New York, c1830, 42in (106.5cm). **$4,000-6,500**

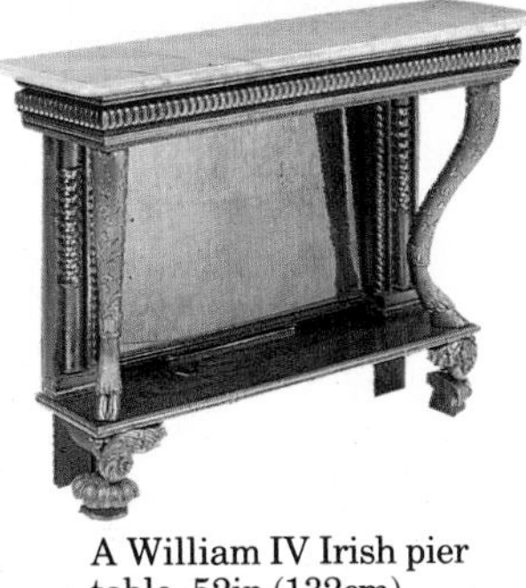

A William IV Irish pier table, 52in (132cm). **$16,000-25,000**

An Empire style ormolu and malachite centre table, after Jacob-Desmalter, 50in (127cm) wide.
$40,000-50,000

An early Victorian ormolu mounted satinwood, amboyna and marquetry centre table, 55in (139.5cm).
$43,000-50,000

A Regency grained oak centre table, on S-scroll legs applied with flower-head roundels, 54in (137cm) wide.
$7,000-9,000

A Victorian inlaid burr walnut loo table.
$6,500-8,000

A pair of early Victorian giltwood and rosewood centre tables, 36in (92cm) wide. **$14,000-16,000**

An early Victorian oak centre table, attributed to A. W. N. Pugin, 66in (167.5cm) wide.
$16,000-20,000

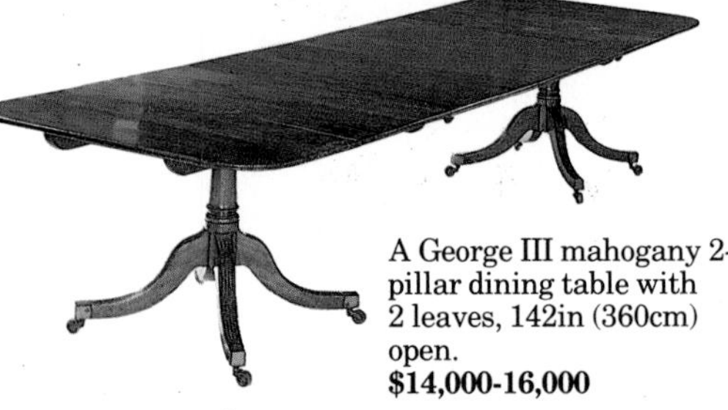
A George III mahogany 2-pillar dining table with 2 leaves, 142in (360cm) open.
$14,000-16,000

A Louis XVI mahogany dining table, 1 contemporary and 3 later leaves, 149in (377.5cm) long open.
$25,000-30,000

A specimen marble coffee table on mahogany stand.
$6,500-8,000

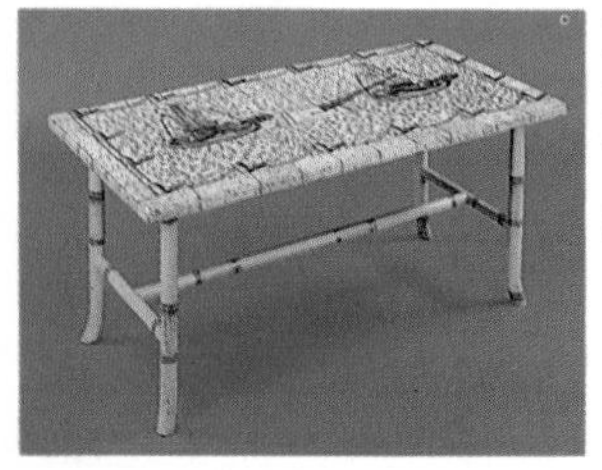
l. A decorated steel coffee table, by Piero Fornasetti, labelled, 17½in (45cm) high.
$3,000-5,000

A late Regency mahogany triple pillar dining table, with alterations, 184in (467cm) open. **$25,000-32,000**

A Victorian satinwood extending dining table.
$14,000-16,000

A mahogany twin pedestal dining table, Boston, c1825, 95in (241cm).
$28,000-32,000

A Queen Anne carved mahogany dressing table, Massachusetts, c1750.
$65,000-70,000

A Queen Anne figured maple dressing table, Delaware River Valley, c1760.
$40,000-50,000

A George III mahogany and marquetry dressing table with fitted interior.
$5,000-6,500

A George III ormolu mounted tulipwood and marquetry dressing table, with fitted interior, 32in (81cm).
$50,000-80,000

A Louis XV kingwood and marquetry table de toilette, with fitted interior, restorations, 34in (87cm).
$6,500-9,500

A George III mahogany dressing table, with divided interior, 26in (66cm).
$13,000-14,000

A Regency mahogany dressing table, with fitted interior, 48in (122cm).
$8,000-9,500

A George III mahogany Pembroke table. **$8,000-11,000**

A Federal inlaid mahogany Pembroke table, c1805.
$8,000-11,000

A Sicilian giltwood console table, c1700. **$32,000-40,000**

A pair of George I black and gold japanned side tables, 36in (92cm).
$32,000-50,000

George III white painted and parcel
lt mahogany console table, some
teration. **$5,000-6,500**

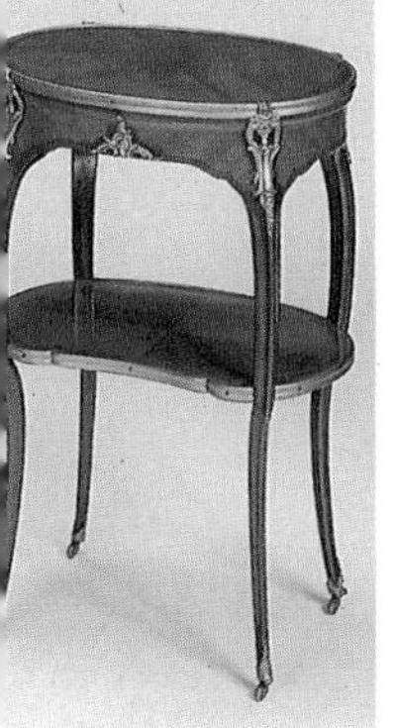

Louis Philippe gilt metal mounted,
ahogany and amaranth gueridon.
,000-4,000

Above r. A George III small table, 20½in (51.5cm). **$5,500-6,500**

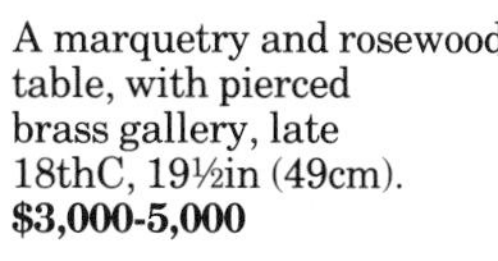

A marquetry and rosewood table, with pierced brass gallery, late 18thC, 19½in (49cm). **$3,000-5,000**

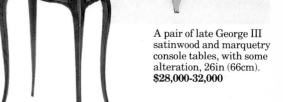

A pair of late George III satinwood and marquetry console tables, with some alteration, 26in (66cm). **$28,000-32,000**

A Regency rosewood work table, 20in (51cm). **$4,000-5,000**

George III
ahogany dumb-
aiter, 45½in
15cm) high.
,000-4,000

A mahogany vide poche, late 18thC. **$2,500-3,000**

A Transitional ormolu mounted tulipwood gueridon, 22½in. **$7,000-9,000**

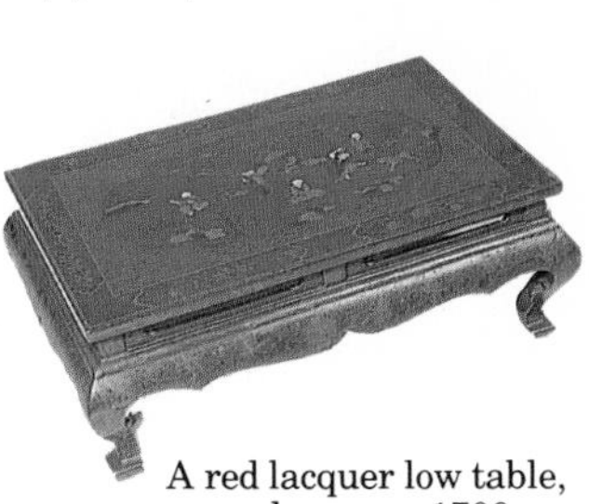

A red lacquer low table, some damage, c1700. **$8,000-9,500**

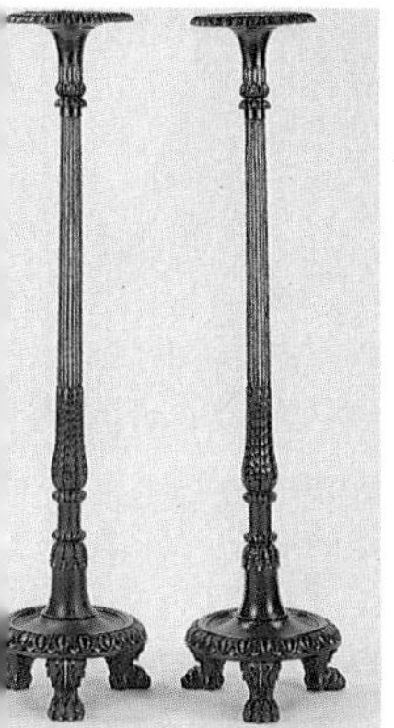

pair of torchères.
,500-13,000

A George III spinning wheel. **$2,500-3,000**

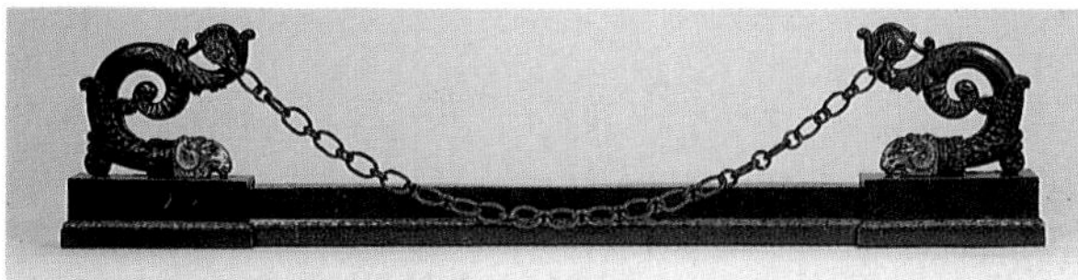

An Empire ormolu and bronze fender, 50in (127cm). **$2,500-3,000**

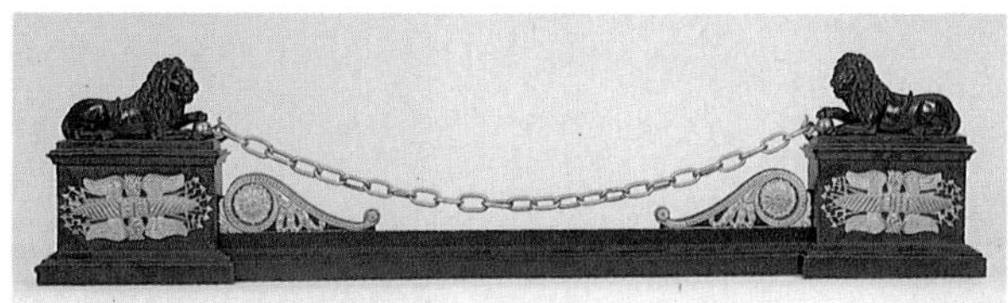

An Empire ormolu and bronzed adjustable fender, 59in (150cm). **$5,000-5,500**

A large Chinese mirror painting, decorated with a hilly river landscape, including figures, with a black and gold chinoiserie frame, 28½ by 46in (72 by 117cm). **$50,000-65,000**

A Dutch embossed leather four-leaf screen, 17thC. **$1,500-3,000**

A Dutch painte leather four-lea screen, the leather 18thC. **$7,000-9,000**

A George III mahogany breakfast table, with later bun feet and restoration to one leg, 64in (162.5cm) diam. **$20,000-22,000**

A Federal inlaid mahogany card table, Massachusetts, c1800. **$14,000-18,000**

A Regency faded mahogany breakfa table, 61in (155cm) wide. **$6,500-8,000**

An early George III mahogany concertina-action tea table, with moulded folding top, 36in (91.5cm). **$11,000-13,500**

A giltwood stand, with later marble top and bun feet, 17thC, restorations, 38½in. **$8,000-11,000**

A George III mahogany centre table, 48in (122cm) diam. **$13,000-16,000**

A Swedish mahogany centre table, the frieze fitted with 3 drawers, early 19thC, 55½in (141cm) diam. **$13,000-20,000**

A Chinese export scarlet and gilt lacquer centre table, the top inlaid in polychrome mother-of-pearl, 19thC, 44in (111.5cm) diam. **$37,000-40,000**

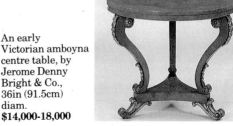

An early Victorian amboyna centre table, by Jerome Denny Bright & Co., 36in (91.5cm) diam. **$14,000-18,000**

An eight-leaf screen with Chinese decoration, each leaf 105in (266.5cm) high. **$6,500-9,500**

l. A painted leather chinoiserie five-leaf screen, 18thC, each leaf 86in (218cm) high. **$5,000-8,000**

. mahogany cheval fire-
creen with needlework
anel, 25½in (64cm) wide.
2,000-2,500

A pair of mahogany and parcel gilt pedestals, 45in (115.5cm) high. **$8,000-9,500**

A mahogany pedestal, after a Thomas Chippendale design, 44in (112cm) high. **$13,000-16,000**

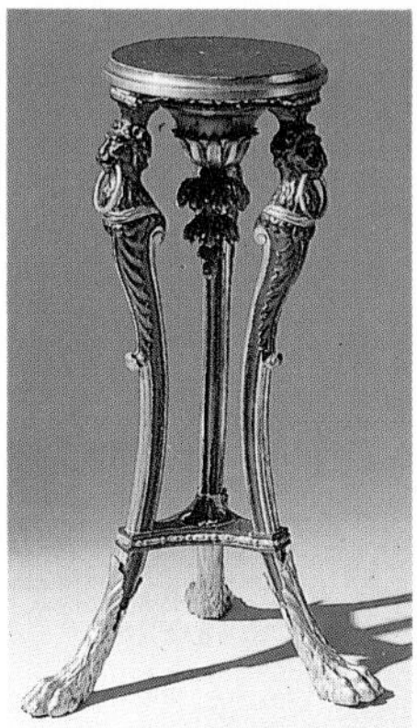

A pair of Regency ebonised and gilt torchères with circular tops, 30in (76cm) high. **$13,000-20,000**

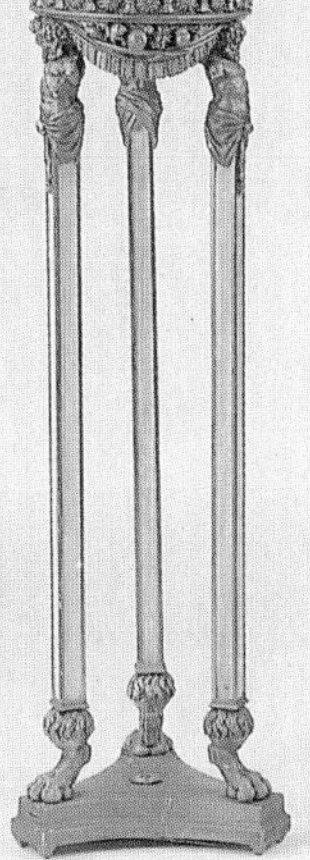

. pair of Regency
arcel gilt and
hite-painted
orchères,
9½in (125.5cm).
18,000-20,000

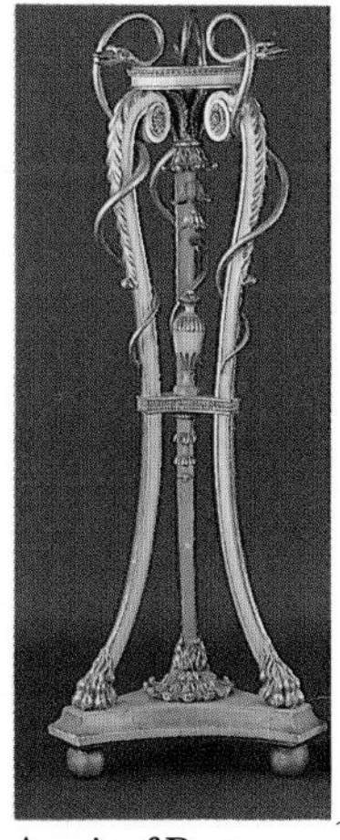

A pair of Regency parcel gilt and white painted torchères, 65½in (166.5cm). **$45,000-50,000**

An ormolu gueridon with blue-stained pink marble top, 32½in (82.5cm) high. **$32,000-40,000**

A Charles X ormolu, cut glass and scagliola gueridon, 23½in (59.5cm) diam. **$50,000-58,000**

l. A Louis XIV brass mounted boulle casket, 12½in (32cm). **$9,000-10,000**

r. A German ormolu mounted mahogany casket encrier, late 18thC, 10½in (26.5cm). **$5,000-8,000**

A Régence giltwood side table, with green and white veined marble top, carved frieze, apron, legs and X-stretcher, 63in (160cm).
$41,500-45,000

A Régence giltwood side table, with mottled red marble top, carved frieze, scrolled legs and stretchers, 64in (163cm). **$43,000-50,000**

A Louis XIV style side table, 19thC, 23½in (60cm wide. **$4,000-5,500**

l. A George III paperwork tea caddy, 6in (15cm) wide.
$2,500-3,000

A figured mahogany veneer cellaret, with fitted interior, attributed to Duncan Phyfe, New York, c1820, 25in (64cm) high.
$13,000-14,000

A George III ormolu mounted mahogany wine cooler, design attributed to Robert Adam, 34in (86cm) wide.
$80,000-95,000

A pair of late Victorian walnut miniature sentry boxes, with badge of Royal Lancaster Regiment, 22in (56cm) high.
$6,500-7,000

An ormolu mounted harewood, bois clair and mahogany marquetry overstrung grand piano by Steinway, c1882 recently reconditioned.
$113,000-118,000

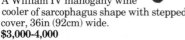

A William IV mahogany wine cooler of sarcophagus shape with stepped cover, 36in (92cm) wide.
$3,000-4,000

l. A pair of white marble urns on pedestals, ovoid shape, on turned bases, c1800, 82in (208cm) high.
$150,000-175,000

A pair of terracotta lions after the Antique, stamped Virebent Fres Toulouse, 44½in (113cm) wide.
$50,000-58,000

A Norwegian carved marriage box, with original metalwork and some original paint, mid-18thC.
$1,300-1,400

. Regency mahogany plate and
ıtlery stand on removable legs,
ne leg restored, 34in (86cm) wide.
11,000-16,000

An Italian Empire ormolu mounted and blue tôle jardinière, 24in (56cm).
$32,000-40,000

A Charles II oyster veneered olivewood, ebony and marquetry box on later feet, 11in (28cm) wide.
$2,600-3,000

. Napoleon III ormolu
ıounted corne verte, boulle
nd agate casket,
6in (41cm) wide.
4,000-5,000

An Embriachi style bone casket, slight damage to interior trays, in wooden travelling case, 27in (69cm) wide. **$9,500-11,000**

A pair of George III brass bound mahogany buckets, restored, 12½in (32cm) wide.
$4,000-5,500

Above l. A George III brass bound mahogany wine cooler, 13½in (35cm). **$10,000-12,000**

.bove r. A George III oval mahogany brass bound wine cooler,
2½in (32cm). **$6,500-8,000**

Below. A pair of George III mahogany dining room pedestals and lead lined urns, 68in (173cm) high.
$25,000-32,000

. Regency mahogany wine cooler with
ivided interior, 34in (86cm) wide.
;8,000-9,500

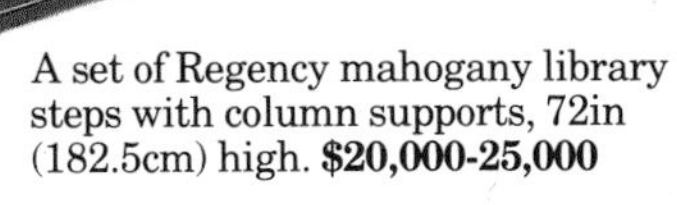

A set of Regency mahogany library steps with column supports, 72in (182.5cm) high. **$20,000-25,000**

A pair of elm kitchen chairs, c1880.
$150-250

A hand stripped oak dressing chest, c1910, 42in (106.5cm). **$500-550**

A hand stripped oak 4-drawer chest, c1895, 39in (99cm).
$300-400

An Austrian painted pine chest, c1854, 53in (134.5cm).
$1,000-1,500

A pine and walnut settle with shepherd's crook arms, c1800, 48in (122cm).
$1,000-1,200

A hand stripped ash dressing table, c1890, 42in (106.5cm).
$500-550

A Lancastrian pine chest with original decoration, c1850.
$1,200-1,300

A Danish pine chest of drawers, some restoration, c1820.
$1,100-1,200

A Spanish pine rocking crib, c1870, 39in (99cm) long. **$500-550**

An Irish pine farmhouse dresser, Galway, c1830.
$1,500-2,500

A French beech and lime vitrine in original condition. **$6,500-8,000**

An Irish astragal glaz corner cupboard, c182
$4,000-5,000

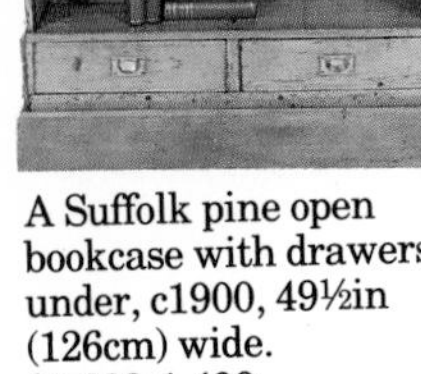

A Suffolk pine open bookcase with drawers under, c1900, 49½in (126cm) wide.
$1,200-1,400

r. An Irish pine open rack dresser typical of Co. Galway, feet replaced, c1840, 55in (139.5cm) wide.
$2,500-3,000

l. A pine corner cupboard, c1860. **$1,500-2,000**

A Lancashire pine washst c1860. **$800-1,000**

A finely carved Norwegian birch wood spice/tobacco jar, 19thC.
$400-500

A distinguished 'Folk Art' model of a pony and trap, in original condition.
$1,200-1,400

A Georgian yew wood veneered work box, in the form of a house, c1820.
$3,000-5,000

A Georgian child's money box, in the form of a bowfronted house, c1820.
$800-1,200

A Norwegian pudding box, carved and painted, c1800.
$1,300-2,500

A 'Folk Art' hand carved and painted model of a carthorse, c1860.
$550-800

Three Norwegian hand carved and polychrome painted ceremonial drinking vessels, 18th and 19thC.
$900-1,400 each

An English hand carved and painted wood pigeon decoy, 19thC.
$250-300

A rare English 'blackamoor' tobacco shop sign, with origin decoration, 18thC.
$1,500-2,500

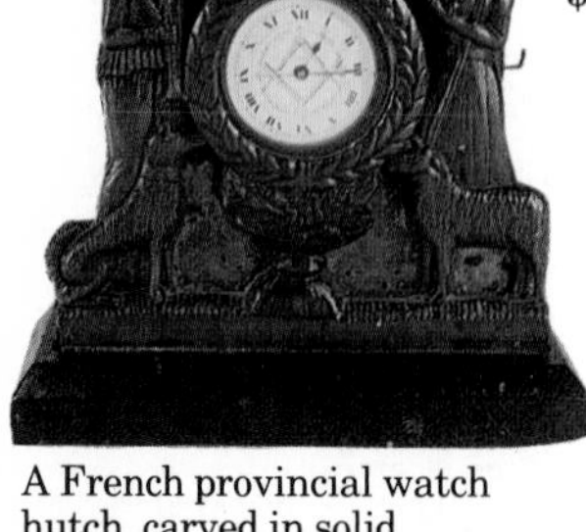

A French provincial watch hutch, carved in solid fruitwood, c1830.
$1,300-1,500

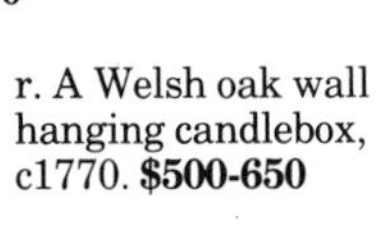

r. A Welsh oak wall hanging candlebox, c1770. **$500-650**

Two tea caddies, in pear and apple woods, c1800, 5in (12.5cm).
$3,000-4,000 each

THERE ARE MANY ANTIQUE

few, if any, who are as quality conscious Norman Lefton, Chairman and Manag- Director of British Antique Exporters l. of Burgess Hill, Nr. Brighton, Sussex. Nearly thirty years' experience of ship- g goods to all parts of the globe have nfirmed his original belief that the way build clients' confidence in his services to supply them only with goods which in first class saleable condition. To this d, he employs a cottage industry staff of er 40, from highly skilled antique storers, polishers and packers to presentative buyers and executives.

Through their knowledgeable hands sses each piece of furniture before it ves the B.A.E. warehouses, ensuring t the overseas buyer will only receive best and most saleable merchandise for ir particular market. This attention to tail is obvious on a visit to the Burgess ll showrooms where potential customers n view what must be the most varied sortment of Georgian, Victorian, lwardian and 1930s furniture in the UK. ne cannot fail to be impressed by, not ly the varied range of merchandise, but so the fact that each piece is in showroom ndition awaiting shipment.

The Company have a very good selec- on but cannot stock everything (neither n anyone else). If they have not got the tique you require in stock they do know nere to find it. This is one of their main rengths and for the 1990s they are also fering a new concept of buying on com- ission only. This enables the overseas aler to have a resident buying office in e U.K. for as little as 10% commission r goods purchased and provides the non- sident dealer with his exact requirements a precise specification.

As one would expect, packing is considered somewhat of an art at B.A.E. and the manager in charge of the works ensures that each piece will reach its final destination in the condition a customer would

SHIPPERS IN BRITAIN BUT...

wish. B.A.E. set a very high standard and, as a further means of improving each container load, their customer/container liaison dept, invites each customer to return detailed information on the saleability of each piece in the container, thereby ensuring successful future shipments.

This feedback of information is the all important factor which guarantees the profitability of future containers. ''By this method'' Mr. Lefton explains, ''we have established that an average $17,000 container will immediately it is unpacked at its final destination realise in the region of $25,500 to $34,000 for our clients selling the goods on a quick wholesale turnover basis.''

When visiting the warehouses various container loads can be seen in the course of completion. The intending buyer can then judge for himself which type of container load would be best suited to his market. In an average 20-foot container B.A.E. put approximately 75 to 100 pieces carefully selected to suit the particular destination. There are always at least 10 outstanding or unusual items in each shipment, but every piece included looks as though it has something special about it.

In the unlikely event of the merchandise not being suitable for any reason whatsoever the Company offers a full money back guarantee less one-way freight.

B.A.E. have opened several new showrooms based at its 15,000 square feet headquarters in Burgess Hill which is 15 minutes away from Gatwick Airport, 7 miles from Brighton and 39 miles from London on a direct rail link, (only 40 minutes journey), the Company is ideally situated to ship containers to all parts of the world. The showrooms, restoration and packing departments are open to overseas buyers and no visit to purchase antiques for re-sale in other countries is complete without a visit to their Burgess Hill premises where a welcome is always found

BRITISH ANTIQUE EXPORTERS LTD

SCHOOL CLOSE, QUEEN ELIZABETH AVENUE,
BURGESS HILL, WEST SUSSEX RH15 9RX, ENGLAND

Telephone BURGESS HILL (04 44) 245577.

Tel: from U.S. 011 44 4 44 245577 Fax: 011 44 4 44 232014

Members of L.A.P.A.D.A. and Guild of Master Craftsmen

A George III mahogany high chair, the shield shaped back with pierced splat set below with a medallion, the outswept arms on reeded supports and the drop-in seat on tapering square legs joined by stretchers.
$3,000-4,000

A set of 6 George IV mahogany Norfolk chairs, with horizontal curved splats, saddle seats and on turned legs.
$1,200-1,300

An early Victorian oak Glastonbury chair, the panelled back with shaped finials, the solid seat on X-legs inscribed below the seat Thomas Shepp...d(?) maker February 21, 1846 no.28.
$650-800

A George IV brass inlaid mahogany music chair, on slender splayed legs, c1830.
$3,000-4,000

A set of 5 Regency black painted and parcel gilt side chairs, with trellis-painted toprail, the back posts painted with acanthus, with caned seats, the seat rails centred by flowerheads, on ring turned tapering legs.
$3,000-4,000

.A Regency mahogany chair.
$1,500-2,500

A set of 6 French walnut salon chairs, the spoon backs with rococo scroll carved cresting and tie rails, over-stuffed seats upholstered in green velour, with serpentine seat rails carved with diapering and foliage, terminating in peg feet, labels to inside of seat rail, dated 1906.
$1,200-1,500

A set of 6 George IV rosewood side chairs, the seats covered in dralon, on front turned reeded tapering legs.
$3,000-4,000

A black painted ladderback side chair, with cylindrical legs, joined by a double box stretcher, formerly on rockers, paint worn, New England, late 18thC.
$300-500

A set of 4 Regency rosewood single chairs, each with a concave back and foliate carved rail, above a bergère cane seat and standing on sabre legs, with loose seat cushions
$1,500-2,500

pair of red painted Chippendale
le chairs, some wear, probably
airfield County, Connecticut, late
thC.
,000-2,500

A Gothic revival carved ladies' chair, with upholstered splat above a curved upholstered back rail over an upholstered seat, on raked trumpet turned front legs with hoof form feet, joined by a turned stretcher, acc. no. 71.1139, some damage, stamped Hunzinger, N.Y. Pat. March 30 1869.
$500-700

pair of Directoire walnut chairs,
ach with beaded crest rail above a
liate pierced splat and padded seat
pholstered in orange velvet, on
rned tapering legs and feet, early
thC.
,000-1,500

A Chippendale painted side chair, the serpentine crest with outcurved ears above an open work splat, flanked by square tapering stiles over a trapezoidal rush seat, repairs, New England, late 18thC.
$300-500

A set of 6 Federal mahogany 'Litchfield' chairs, on square tapering legs, joined by an H-stretcher, repairs, New York or Connecticut, c1790.
$3,500-4,000

An American rococo revival laminated rosewood slipper chair, with a curved pierced foliate scrolling back, crisply carved with a flower filled basket and inset with an oval pad, the serpentine padded seat over a conforming foliate carved seat rail on moulded cabriole legs with scroll feet and casters, upholstered in damask, restored, mid-19thC, possibly by John Henry Belter.
$2,000-2,500

A pair of George I style black and gold japanned side chairs, with eared crest rail above a vase shaped splat decorated with a pavilion in a landscape with courtly figures, over a caned seat, on cabriole legs with pad feet joined by stretchers.
$1,700-2,000

A Victorian rosewood framed chair with spiral twist side supports, top finials, tapestry seat and back, on cabriole front legs.
$400-550

A Victorian walnut spindle back captain's chair, with hide seat and back, c1870.
$650-1,000

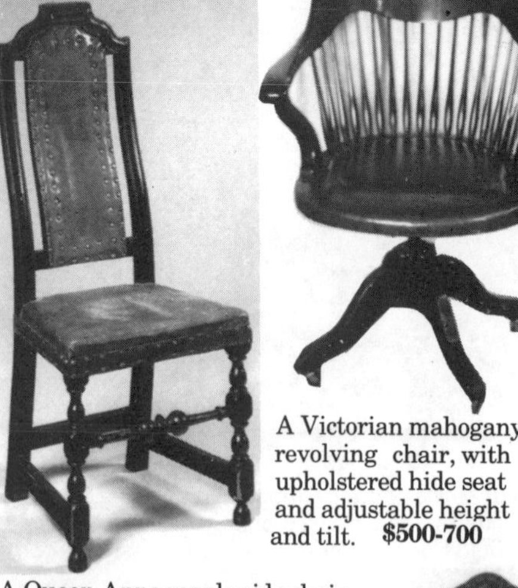

A Victorian mahogany revolving chair, with upholstered hide seat and adjustable height and tilt. **$500-700**

A Queen Anne maple side chair, with moulded shaped crest above a leather upholstered back and seat, on block and baluster turned legs with baluster feet, joined by a ring turned stretcher, Boston, c1740, feet pieced.
$2,000-2,500

A pair of Dutch walnut and marquetry inlaid side chairs, with bar shaped splat backs above upholstered tapestry drop-in seats, on etched cabriole legs with claw-and-ball feet.
$2,000-2,500

A pair of Louis XV caned beechwood chairs, with cartouche shaped caned back crested by a flowerhead, on cabriole legs headed by flowerheads and ending in scroll toes, mid-18thC.
$3,500-4,000

A set of 6 bamboo chairs, each with spindle back and paling toprail, the caned seats with grey cushions, the legs with brackets and stretchers.
$1,500-2,000

A Queen Anne red stained maple side chair, with carved yolk crest above a solid vase shaped splat flanked by moulded stiles, over a slip-seat with a shaped skirt, New England, c1740.
$1,500-2,500

A Queen Anne leather back mapl side chair, with moulded and shap crest above an upholstered leathe back flanked by moulded stiles above a slip-seat, on square cabric legs with incised decoration and paint brush feet joined by a ball a ring turned stretcher, Massachusetts, c1740.
$2,000-2,500

A Queen Anne black painted maple side chair, with carved yolk crest above a solid vase shaped splat flanked by moulded stiles over a slip-seat with a shaped skirt, New England, c1740.
$1,500-2,000

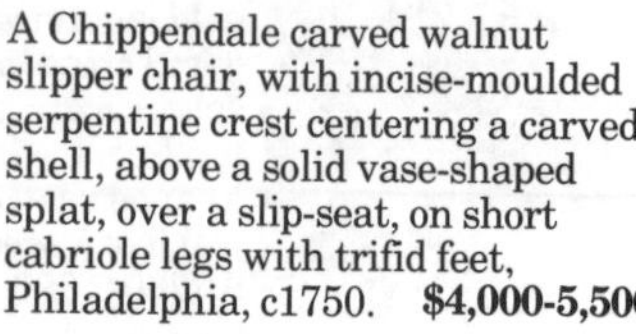

A Chippendale carved walnut slipper chair, with incise-moulded serpentine crest centering a carved shell, above a solid vase-shaped splat, over a slip-seat, on short cabriole legs with trifid feet, Philadelphia, c1750. **$4,000-5,500**

Small Chests

A William and Mary walnut and crossbanded chest, with marquetry inlaid brass pear drop handles and escutcheons, moulded apron and later bun feet, 40½in (104cm).
$11,000-13,000

A mahogany chest, on bracket feet, basically 18thC, 37½in (94cm).
$1,200-1,500

An early Georgian padouk bachelor's chest, the hinged moulded top lined in velvet above 2 short and 3 long pine-lined drawers, on ogee bracket feet, feet possibly replaced, restorations, 31½in (80cm).
$4,000-5,000

A Queen Anne walnut chest, on urned tapering bun feet, adapted, 37in (94cm).
5,000-6,500

A walnut straight front chest, with inlaid decoration, reeded edge to the top, 2 short and 3 long drawers, with brass drop handles on bracket feet, 18thC, 37in (94cm).
$1,200-1,500

An early Georgian walnut and oak chest, with moulded quarter veneered top, above 2 short and 3 long drawers, on bracket feet, 39in (99cm).
$3,000-5,000

walnut veneered chest of drawers, he top quarter veneered, feather nd crossbanded, bracket feet, early 8thC, 34½in (87cm).
4,000-5,000

A mahogany serpentine dressing chest, with 4 graduated drawers fitted bronze drop handles and escutcheons, on pointed ogee bracket feet, the top drawer missing fittings, mid-18thC, 37in (94cm).
$6,500-8,000

A walnut and yew dwarf chest, with featherbanded inlay, on bracket feet, basically 18thC, 28½in (72cm).
$5,000-6,500

Queen Anne burr walnut chest, e later quarter veneered top above short and 3 long herringbone nded drawers, on later bun feet, 715, 38in (97cm).
500-3,000

A walnut chest, with 3 small and 3 long drawers between fluted canted angles, on bracket feet, basically 18thC, 40½in (102cm).
$2,000-2,500

A walnut and mahogany chest, with crossbanded top and herringbone inlay, with brass handles, cushioned dividers between the drawers, bracket feet, 18thC, 39in (99cm).
$2,500-3,000

A George III mahogany bowfront chest, with 2 short and 3 graduated long drawers on splayed feet, 52in (132cm).
$1,500-2,500

A Federal mahogany and bird's-eye maple chest of drawers, the top with outset rounded corners and banded edge above 4 cockbeaded moulded and banded edge long drawers centering bird's-eye panels over a moulded arched apron flanked by reeded columns, on ring turned tapering feet, Salem, Massachusetts, c1800, 41in (104cm).
$4,000-4,500

A George III mahogany bow front chest, the frieze inlaid with a satinwood banding, on splayed bracket feet, 35in (89cm).
$2,000-2,500

A Georgian mahogany bowfront chest, with 2 short and 3 graduated drawers and standing on splay feet, 41in (104cm).
$800-1,200

A late George III mahogany bowfront chest, with 4 graduated long drawers, shaped apron and splayed bracket feet, 37½in (95cm
$1,400-2,000

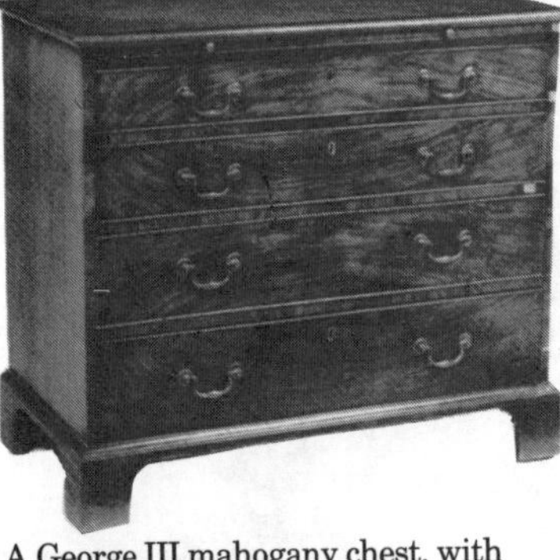

A George III mahogany chest, with figured crossbanded top above a brushing slide and 4 graduated long drawers, c1770, 37½in (95cm).
$3,000-4,000

A George III mahogany chest, the later top above a brushing slide and 4 graduated long drawers with brass swan-neck handles, on bracket feet, 31in (79cm).
$2,000-2,500

A George III mahogany dwarf che with a brushing slide, 2 short and 3 graduated long drawers on bracket feet, adapted, 35½in (90cr
$2,000-2,500

A George III mahogany bowfront chest, with 2 short and 3 long graduated drawers, waved apron and splayed feet, 38in (96.5cm).
$2,000-2,500

A George III mahogany chest, with moulded top above a slide and 4 graduated drawers, on splayed bracket feet, 35in (89cm).
$6,500-7,000

A George III mahogany Lancashi chest, with hinged top, above a fro fitted with 5 false drawers and 4 drawers between rounded flutec angles, on ogee bracket feet, 68½i (173cm).
$3,000-3,500

A Federal mahogany and bird's-eye maple chest of drawers, the top with reeded edge and outset rounded corners above 4 graduated and banded edge long drawers, each veneered with bird's-eye maple, over reeded arched apron, flanked by reeded columns, on fluted ring turned tapering feet, slight damage, Salem, Massachusetts, c1807, 42in (106.5cm) wide.
$4,000-5,000

A Dutch mahogany upright chest, inlaid with chequered bands, with 6 drawers, on square tapered legs, 19thC, 42in (106.5cm).
$1,500-2,500

Regency mahogany chest, with wed top above 2 short drawers r 3 graduated long drawers, on ted square legs, early 19thC, n (109cm) wide.
200-1,700

A North Italian walnut and fruitwood chest, the top and sides inlaid, on later square legs, late 18thC, 49in (124cm).
$2,500-3,000

A Victorian brass mounted walnut secrétaire military chest, with 5 drawers flanking a central fitted drawer, on turned tapering legs, 7 Duncannon Street, London, 39in (99cm).
$1,500-2,500

An oyster veneered walnut chest, on bracket feet, 31½in (80cm).
$2,000-2,500

A Victorian teak military chest, in 2 sections, with 2 short and 3 long graduated drawers with inset brass handles and corners, on turned bun feet, 41in (104cm).
$2,000-2,500

Regency mahogany bachelor's st, with hinged top and 4 long wers, on turned tapering feet, sides with carrying handles, n (84cm).
500-3,000

A William IV mahogany chest, with moulded top, above drawers flanked by fluted columns, on reeded bulbous supports, 48½in (123cm).
$3,000-4,000

A veneered walnut chest of drawers, with bracket feet, in need of restoration, 36in (91.5cm).
$5,500-6,500

A Victorian mahogany bowfront chest, with 2 short and 4 graduated long drawers on bracket feet, 45in (114cm).
$1,000-1,200

A Federal inlaid and mahogany veneer miniature chest, with banded and rope edged hinged top enclosing 3 compartments, on French feet, some damage, Connecticut or Rhode Island, c1800, 10½in (27cm).
$1,700-2,000

A Dutch walnut and crossbanded chest of drawers, with moulded edged top, broken serpentine shaped front, brass drop handles and escutcheons, moulded apron and bracket feet, early 18thC, 37½in (95cm).
$5,500-6,500

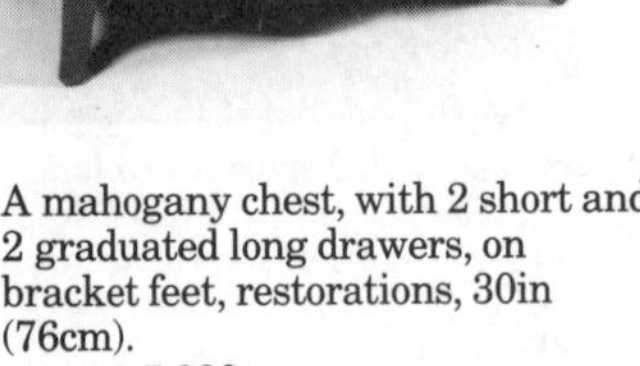

A Federal inlaid cherrywood bowfront chest of drawers, the top with bowed and banded front above 4 graduated long drawers, over a shaped apron, on flared French feet, New England, c1800, 40½in (102cm).
$3,000-5,000

A mahogany chest, with 2 short and 2 graduated long drawers, on bracket feet, restorations, 30in (76cm).
$4,000-5,000

A Chippendale walnut chest of drawers, with 2 short and 4 long drawers, repaired, mid-Atlantic states, late 18thC, 41in (104cm).
$4,000-4,500

A Federal inlaid mahogany bowfront chest of drawers, with line inlaid long drawers over a shaped skirt with lozenge pattern inlaid band, on French feet, Massachusetts, c1800, 42in (106.5cm).
$8,000-9,000

A Federal inlaid cherrywood bowfront chest of drawers, with ur inlaid escutcheons, shaped skirt, o French feet, New England, c1800, 41in (104cm) wide.
$3,500-4,500

A Federal carved mahogany chest o drawers, with 2 short and 4 cockbeaded moulded long drawer flanked by turned columns, each headed by a carved cornucopia on a star punched ground, on ball turne feet, Salem, Massachusetts, c1815, 44in (111.5cm).
$4,000-4,500

mahogany tallboy, with dentilled d cavetto moulded cornice above hort and 6 graduated long awers, between fluted canted gles, on bracket feet, late 18thC d later, 42in (107cm).
,500-3,000

walnut tallboy, with therbanded inlaid borders, on icket feet, early 18thC, 43in 9cm).
,000-6,500

George III mahogany chest-on-est, the upper section with dentil rnice above 2 short and 3 long awers, with canted angles, on a se of 3 long drawers and bracket t, 42in (107cm).
,000-4,000

A walnut and oak tallboy, with moulded cornice, brushing slide and on bracket feet, basically mid-Georgian, 41½in (104cm).
$7,000-9,000

An early George III mahogany chest-on-chest, with blind-fret carved frieze on later reduced bracket feet, 44½in (112cm).
$3,000-4,000

A George III mahogany chest-on-chest, with moulded Greek key pattern cornice, ornate brass drop handles and escutcheons, on bracket feet, 46in (117cm).
$2,000-2,500

A George III mahogany tallboy, with moulded cornice above 2 short and 6 graduated long drawers, on bracket feet, 43½in (109cm).
$1,400-2,000

A burr walnut tallboy, inlaid with stars and chequered boxwood lines, on bracket feet, 42in (106.5cm).
$3,000-4,000

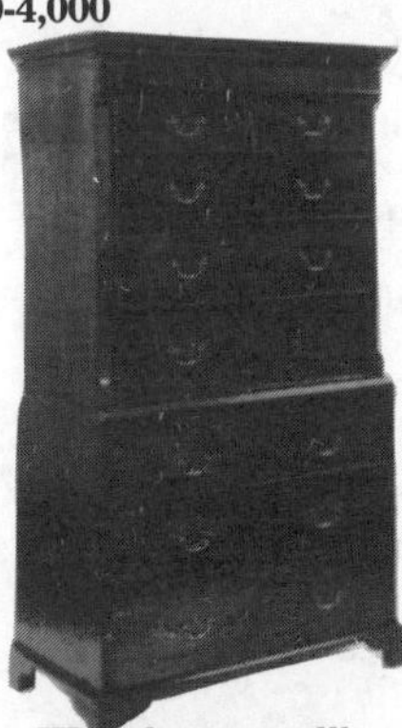

A George III mahogany tallboy, the top section with a dentilled cornice and canted angles, the lower section with a brushing slide and 3 drawers, on later bracket feet, 44½in (112cm).
$3,000-4,000

A George III mahogany tallboy, with moulded Greek key pattern cornice, above 2 short and 3 long drawers, the lower section with slide above 3 graduated long drawers on bracket feet, 44in (112cm).
$2,500-3,000

Chests-on-Stands

A William and Mary style burr walnut chest-on-stand, with floral marquetry panels, 19thC, 38in (96.5cm).
$4,000-5,000

A Queen Anne figured maple chest-on-stand, in 2 sections, on cabriole legs with padded disc feet, restoration to frame, New England, c1760, 40in (101.5cm).
$8,000-9,500

A Queen Anne walnut high chest of drawers, in 2 parts, on cabriole legs with pad feet, the rear legs of maple, patch to lower case, apron sides re-shaped, Massachusetts, c1750, 41½in (105cm).
$10,000-12,000

A Queen Anne carved cherrywood high chest of drawers, in 2 sections, the centre panel fan carved over an arcaded skirt centering 2 pendant acorn drops, on cabriole legs with pad and disc feet, brasses original, one drop restored, North Shore, Massachusetts, c1760, 38in (96.5cm).
$12,000-14,000

A Queen Anne walnut chest-on-stand, with later veneered moulded top above 2 short and 3 graduated long drawers, the reduced stand with 3 drawers, with shaped apron and later bun feet, the chest in 2 parts, 38in (96.5cm).
$3,000-4,000

A Dutch walnut and featherbanded chest-on-stand, with arcaded apron, on turned bun feet, parts 18thC, 38in (96.5cm).
$2,500-3,000

A walnut chest-on-stand, with fluted canted angles, the stand f with 3 short drawers, on cabriol legs and pad feet, 40in (101.5cn
$3,000-4,000

An early Georgian walnut chest-on-stand, on cabriole legs pad feet, 38½in (97cm).
$5,000-5,500

An early Georgian walnut chest-on-stand, on cabriole l pad feet, 38½in (97cm).
$5,000-5,500

ıate Federal mahogany veneer ırawer stand, on turned legs with ›ding, joined by a medial shelf, w on casters, mid-Atlantic states, ½in (57cm).
,700-2,000

A Federal inlaid figured maple tall chest of drawers, with cove moulded cornice above 3 short cockbeaded moulded and line inlaid drawers over 5 similar graduated long drawers, flanked by chamfered line inlaid corners above a shaped apron, on French feet, New England, c1800, 44½in (112cm).
$9,000-12,000

A Queen Anne maple high chest of drawers, in 2 parts, on cabriole legs with panelled feet, some repairs and restorations, Pennsylvania or New Jersey, c1735, 39½in (100cm).
$3,000-4,000

Queen Anne birch chest-on-chest, 3 parts, on cabriole legs with pad t, drawers in lower section ssibly not original, American, late thC, 37in (94cm).
000-5,000

A Philadelphia Chippendale style carved walnut dressing table, with moulded edge and notched corners above a long drawer over 3 short drawers, the centre drawer shell carved with applied tendrils, flanked by fluted quarter columns, above an elaborately shell carved skirt, on cabriole legs with similarly carved knees, on claw-and-ball feet, acc. no. 1973-158-1, 32½in (82cm).
$7,000-8,000

A Queen Anne walnut high chest of drawers, on cabriole legs with pad feet, some damage and repairs, Massachusetts, c1750, 41in (104cm).
$5,000-7,000

Queen Anne maple high chest of ıwers, in 2 parts, on cabriole legs h trifid-type feet on platforms, er brass, some repairs and cracks, bably Elijah Booth, Woodbury, nnecticut, c1760, 38in (96.5cm).
000-12,000

A George III mahogany tallboy, on bracket feet, adapted, 42½in (107cm).
$2,000-3,000

A Chippendale carved walnut high chest base, the top with applied moulding on 3 sides above a thumb moulded single long drawer over 3 thumb moulded short drawers, the centre drawer fan carved, above a scalloped apron, on cabriole legs with claw-and-ball feet, Salem, Massachusetts, c1775, 42in (106.5cm).
$6,000-7,000

A walnut and featherbanded chest-on-stand, on cabriole legs with pad feet, parts 18thC, 39in (99cm).
$1,500-2,500

A walnut chest-on-stand, with moulded top above 2 short and 2 graduated long drawers, the stand on spiral twist legs joined by an undulating flat stretcher, on bun feet, 38in (96.5cm).
$3,000-5,000

A Queen Anne design walnut and featherbanded chest, on a stand with cabriole legs and pad feet, 42in (106.5cm).
$1,000-1,200

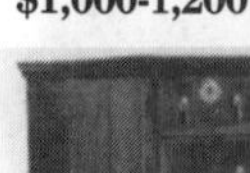

A walnut and banded chest-on-stand, on turned legs joined by a stretcher, 39in (99cm).
$2,000-2,500

A George I walnut chest-on-stand, the upper section with moulded edge, above 2 short and 3 long banded drawers, the stand with 3 small drawers above a shaped apron, on later turned club legs, c1730, 42½in (107cm).
$3,000-4,000

A George I walnut chest-on-stand, with featherbanded drawers with brass drop handles and engraved backplates, shaped apron, on later cabriole supports, 39in (98cm).
$1,500-2,500

Wellington Chests

A Victorian mahogany Wellington chest with 7 drawers, with turned knob handles, a locking bar to one side, raised on a plinth base, the top drawer stamped from S. & H. Jewells Furniture Warehouse, 29, 30 and 31 Little Queen Street, Holborn, 27in (69cm).
$2,500-3,000

A mahogany Wellington chest, wi pierced brass gallery, over 7 graduated drawers with turned wooden handles, 19thC, 27in (69cn
$1,000-2,000

A Victorian rosewood Wellington secrétaire chest, with fitted interi of small drawers and pigeonholes faced in maple wood, 22in (56cm).
$2,500-3,000

A Victorian Wellington chest, wit turned handles and scrolled capita to the front supports, 32in (81cm).
$1,300-1,500

Coffers

A Dutch East Indies camphor coffer, the top with brass studs, the angles with lotus-shaped straps, the sides with carrying handles, 18thC, 45in (114cm).
$650-1,000

A Louis XV style tulipwood and inlaid serpentine commode, with rouge royale marble top, above 3 long drawers between volutes mounted with cabochon clasps and sabots, early 19thC, 46in (116.5cm).
$5,500-7,000

A George III mahogany commode, inlaid with boxwood lines, with shaped apron, on bracket feet, adapted, 26½in (67cm).
$2,500-3,000

Commodes

A Louis XV style kingwood and marquetry bombé commode, applied with gilt brass mouldings and with mottled marble top, with inlaid drawers and frieze, on splayed feet, 26in (66cm).
$2,500-3,000

A South German walnut parquetry commode, with crossbanded overhung top inlaid with wide bands on an oysterwood ground, the drawer fronts and sides with walnut panels divided by ebonised lines, 18thC, 48in (122cm).
$21,000-25,000

A George III mahogany breakfront commode, the top enclosing fitted interior and concave sided fascia with one dummy and 3 drawers with turned wood handles and brass escutcheons, on 4 square tapered legs, 19½in (49cm).
$1,200-1,400

An ormolu mounted tulipwood and end-cut marquetry bombé commode, with eared serpentine 'breche violette' marble top above inlaid drawers, on tapering legs with sabots, stamped R. Roessle, 56in (142cm).
$2,500-4,000

A French kingwood and marquetry serpentine fronted 2 drawer commode, with marble top and ormolu mounts, on shaped legs, 19thC, 29in (74cm).
$1,500-2,500

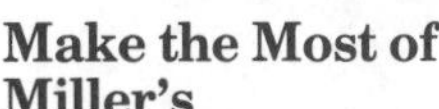

Make the Most of Miller's

CONDITION is absolutely vital when assessing the value of an antique. Damaged pieces on the whole appreciate much less than perfect examples. However a rare, desirable piece may command a high price even when damaged

A pair of George III mahogany night commodes, with pierced gallery tops above tambour shutter compartments, pull out pot holders with ebony stringing and brass swan neck handles, on square legs, 19in (48cm).
$13,000-14,000

A South German walnut commode, the crossbanded top inlaid with strapwork designs above two inlaid drawers highlighted with bone husk motifs, on later bun feet, c1740, with later back, 46in (117cm).
$5,000-6,500

A Louis XVI style commode, veneered in exotic woods, with metal mounts and marble galleried top.
$2,500-3,000

A George III mahogany crossbar and inlaid commode, with origir brass drop handles, on 4 square supports, 33in (84cm) high.
$1,200-1,400

A Continental marble top commode, with serpentine front, 3 drawers and cast metal handles and mounts.
$2,500-3,000

A North Italian walnut commode, the quarter-veneered top inlaid with a lobed medallion and broad barber's pole stringing, the serpentine front fitted with 3 long drawers, on short tapered legs, late 18thC, 55in (140cm).
$9,500-11,000

A Dutch oak bombé commode, with 4 graduated long drawers between canted volutes, on block feet, 19thC 33in (84cm).
$2,000-2,500

A South German kingwood and ormolu mounted commode, the bracket feet with sabots, lacking marble top, distressed, mid-18thC, 38½in (97cm).
$8,000-9,500

An Empire ormolu mounted mahogany commode, with black fossil marble top, on turned feet, 50in (127cm).
$2,500-3,000

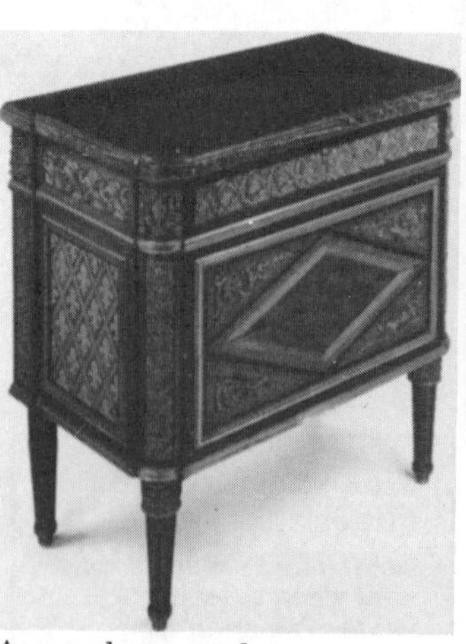

An ormolu mounted marquetry, mahogany and harewood commode, after Leleu, with drawers inlaid 'sans travers' with a lozenge, the sides inlaid with a trellis of fleur-de-lys, on turned tapering legs with acanthus capital, 34in (86cm).
$3,000-5,000

A pair of gilt metal mounted marquetry and parquetry commodes of transitional style, with green veined marble top, on cabriole legs with paw sabots, 46in (117cm).
$9,500-11,000

In the Furniture section if there is only one measurement it usually refers to the width of the piece

A North Italian fruitwood and banded serpentine commode, with 2 long drawers and a shaped apron, on bracket feet, late 18thC, 48in (122cm).
$3,000-4,000

An Italian blue painted and parcel gilt commode, decorated with a trailing flower-filled urn, and with 3 drawers, shaped apron on cabriole legs, 41in (104cm).
$1,200-1,400

An Empire ormolu mounted mahogany commode, with black marble top, above 3 graduated long drawers mounted with lion's mask pull handles, and flanked by pilasters headed by classical busts, on ebonised paw feet and later platforms, early 19thC, 50½in (128.5cm).
$6,000-8,000

A Louis XVI style gilt metal mounted mahogany commode, with mottled liver marble top, with false frieze drawer, on toupie feet with gadrooned collars, bearing label Charles Jenner & Co., Princes Street, Edinburgh, 52in (132cm).
$1,500-2,500

Bedside Cupboards

An early George III mahogany bedside cupboard, with pierced galleried top, open cupboard and chamfered square legs, 16in (40.5cm).
$1,500-2,500

A pair of late Georgian mahogany square pot cupboards with single door with satinwood stringing, on square tapered legs, 10in (25cm).
$1,400-2,000

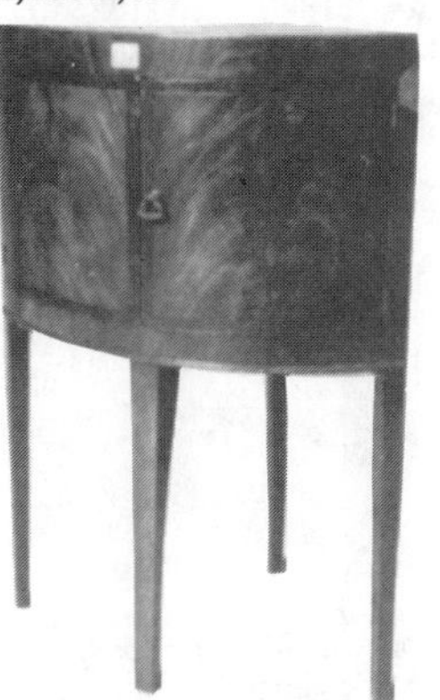
A William IV mahogany bowfront corner pot cupboard, with 2 doors, crossbanding and tapering legs, 20in (51cm).
$800-1,000

Corner Cupboards

A Georgian mahogany large bowfront hanging corner cupboard, inlaid stringing and crossbanding to the 2 doors, enclosing 3 shelves over one real and 2 dummy drawers, 35in (89cm).
$800-1,200

A Georgian oak and mahogany banded hanging corner cupboard, the cavetto cornice, above a moulded panel door, enclosing 3 shelves, 46in (116.5cm) high.
$300-650

A Federal mahogany corner cupboard, with moulded cornice above glazed double cupboard doors, over double cupboard doors, on base moulding with bracket feet, some damage, late 18th/early 19thC, 82in (208cm) high.
$4,000-5,000

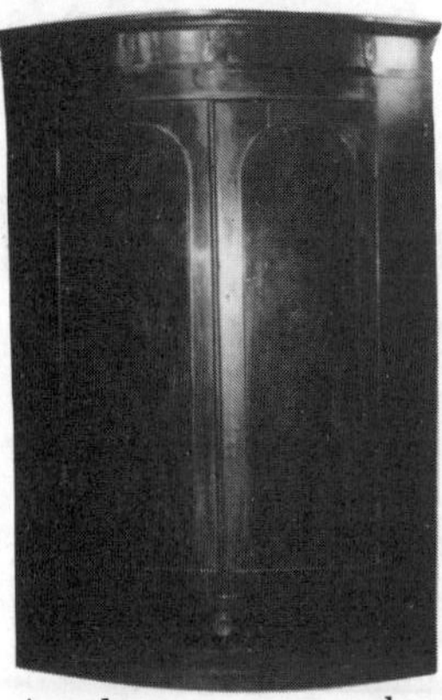
A mahogany corner cupboard, with double panel doors and small centre drawer, 19thC.
$400-650

A Georgian inlaid mahogany bowfront hanging corner cupboard, with a pair of doors enclosing 3 shelves and 3 spice drawers, 43in (109cm) high.
$1,500-2,500

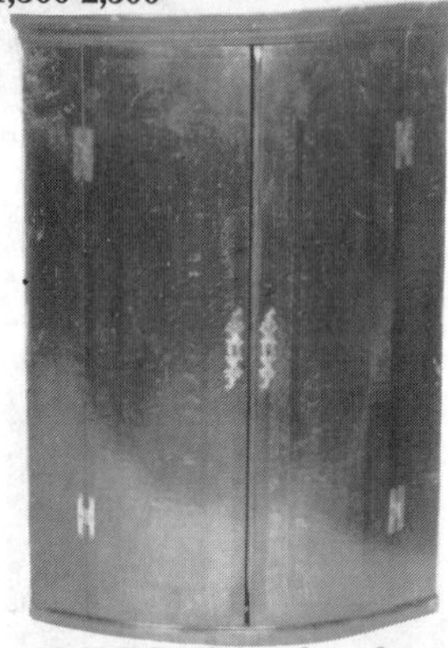
A mid-18thC oak bowfront hanging corner cupboard.
$1,000-1,400

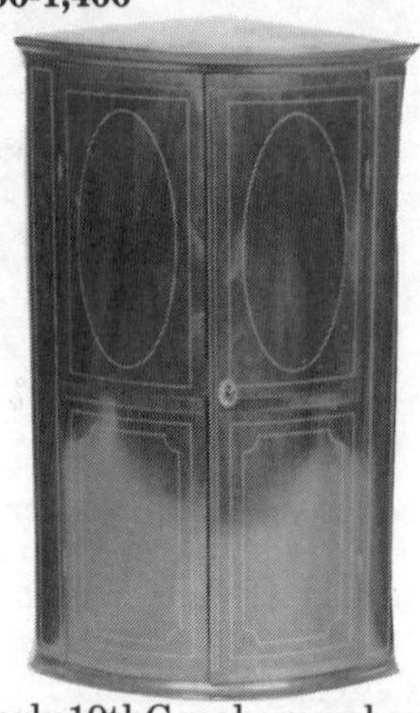
An early 19thC mahogany bowfront corner cupboard.
$900-1,300

A George III mahogany bowfronted corner cupboard with boxwood stringing and boxwood, ebony, satinwood and harewood inlay, with fitted interior, 30in (76cm).
$1,300-1,500

A Federal carved mahogany corner cupboard, with overhanging broken moulded cornice above 2 panelled cupboard doors, on bracket feet, some restoration, mid-Atlantic states, c1800, 52in (132cm).
$3,000-5,000

A Chippendale corner cupboard, the moulded pediment above a conforming case, on base moulding with bracket feet, some damage, late 18th/early 19thC, 86in (218.5cm) high.
$4,000-5,000

A Regency mahogany corner cupboard, with blind fret carved frieze, above 4 panelled doors flanked by reeded uprights, on plinth, 45½in (115cm).
$1,500-2,500

A Louis Philippe ormolu mounted kingwood and tulipwood corner cabinet of serpentine outline, with quarter-veneered doors, a shelf above and below, 37½in (95cm) high.
$1,000-1,300

A late Victorian mahogany corner standing display cabinet, inlaid with satinwood and boxwood lines, the dentilled cornice above a glazed lancet astragal door and a panel cupboard door between canted angles, on square tapering legs with spade feet, 27½in (70cm).
$1,200-1,400

A Regency mahogany linen press, with broken pediment applied with metal gilt paterae, the 2 oval panel doors above 4 graduated long drawers, on splayed bracket feet, 52in (132cm).
$3,000-4,000

A Regency mahogany bowfront linen chest, with moulded cornice, and 2 moulded panel doors, with 2 short and 2 graduated long drawers, on bracket feet, 56in (142cm).
$2,500-3,000

A Dutch mahogany linen press, with fret carved cresting, the lower section with 3 graduated long drawers between bellflower and acanthus carved canted angles, on square tapered fluted legs, early 19thC, 67in (170cm).
$6,500-7,000

A Victorian mahogany and inlaid linen press, with cavetto cornice above a pair of moulded panelled doors, 2 short and 2 graduated long drawers, on splayed bracket feet, 52in (132cm).
$2,500-3,000

A late Regency mahogany linen press, inlaid with geometric boxwood lines, with a dentilled moulded cornice, a pair of panelled doors with inset sliding trays above 2 short and 2 graduated long drawers on bracket feet, 54½in (138cm).
$1,500-2,500

A mahogany clothes press, with plain stepped pediment over 2 cupboard doors with Gothic panels, pillar sides, over a base with one long cushion fronted drawer and 3 further graduated drawers, on a platform base, 19thC, 58in (147cm).
$800-1,200

Cupboards – Wardrobes

A Sheraton style satinwood wardrobe, the pediment cornice with urn finials above a pair of fielded panel doors, the whole with tulipwood crossbanding, on bracket feet, c1880, 55in (140cm).
$5,000-5,500

Davenports

A George IV pollard oak davenport in the manner of Richard Bridgens, the top with undulating three-quarter gallery, 26in (66cm).
$3,000-4,000

An early Victorian rosewood davenport, the sliding top with brass balustrade and hinged leather-lined slope, 26in (66cm).
$2,000-2,500

A William IV mahogany davenport, with bobbin and reel beaded outlines, the hinged sloping flap below a galleried lidded compartment, on reeded baluster columns, flanking twin side panelled doors enclosing drawers on concave platform base, 30in (76cm).
$2,500-3,000

A Victorian walnut davenport, with fretwork gallery, the drawers with locking bars, on china casters, 20½in (52cm).
$2,500-3,000

A walnut veneer and mahogany davenport.
$1,300-1,500

A William IV rosewood davenport, 20in (51cm).
$4,000-5,500

A Victorian burr walnut davenport, with inset leather-lined hinged sloping front, below a galleried lidded stationery compartment, on foliate carved cabriole supports flanked by 4 side drawers on turned bun feet, 21in (53cm).
$2,500-3,000

A Victorian walnut davenport.
$1,500-2,000

A Victorian figured walnut davenport, with brass galleried lift-up stationery compartment, slant and 4 real and 4 dummy drawers, on china casters, 22in (56cm).
$2,500-3,000

A Victorian walnut davenport, the back with galleried hinged stationery compartment, above a leather-lined sloping front on turned feet, 22in (56cm).
$1,300-1,500

An early Victorian rosewood davenport, with sloping flap enclosing real and false drawers, o shaped plinth with casters, 28in (71cm).
$1,500-2,500

Use the Index!

Because certain items might fit easily into any of a number of categories, the quickest and surest method of locating any entry is by reference to the index at the back of the book.
This has been fully cross-referenced for absolute simplicity

\ Victorian walnut davenport, with
ainged stationery compartment,
en trays, and a lined slope,
nclosing a bird's eye maple
nterior, above 4 short drawers
pposed by false drawers, on a
linth, 21in (53cm).
$1,500-2,500

A Victorian walnut davenport, with inset brown hide panel enclosing fitted interior, 4 short and 4 dummy drawers to the side, on turned and carved knopped supports, plinth feet, 22in (56cm).
$1,500-2,500

A Victorian marquetry and inlaid rosewood davenport, on carved foliate cabriole front supports, flanking 4 small side drawers and pen drawers, on bar and turned bun feet, 22in (56cm).
$5,000-6,500

\ Victorian figured walnut and
narquetry inlaid davenport, the
ined surface enclosing a well, with
4 drawers, knob handles, and
arved scrolled brackets, 22in
56cm).
$3,000-4,000

A Victorian inlaid figured walnut davenport, with fitted stationery compartment, slant and 4 real and 4 dummy drawers, carved scroll front supports and bun feet, 21½in (54cm).
$2,500-3,000

A Victorian burr walnut veneered pop-up piano front harlequin davenport, with fitted interior, cabriole supports and gallery.
$5,500-6,500

\ Victorian walnut piano top
lavenport, with sprung stationery
ompartments, the interior fitted
vith a lined sliding writing surface
nd pen trough, with 4 short
lrawers to the right on bar feet and
asters, 22in (56cm).
$4,000-5,500

A Victorian walnut davenport, the serpentine front with fall flap inset with leather, with sandalwood fitted interior, the top with an ogee sided lidded stationery compartment with brass gallery, the sides with drawers and dummy drawers, knob handles, on leaf carved cabriole supports, bun feet and casters, 21in (53cm).
$2,500-3,000

A Victorian burr walnut veneered davenport, with boxwood and ebony string inlays and central inlaid panel.
$2,500-3,000

A walnut and mahogany veneer plantation desk, on ring and ball turned cylindrical legs with compressed ball feet, some damage, mid-Atlantic states, mid-19thC, 71in (180cm) high.
$3,000-4,000

An Edwardian mahogany lady's cylinder desk.
$1,400-2,000

A mahogany kneehole writing de[sk] with frieze drawer and 6 side drawers with brass drop handles, recessed cupboard with interior shelf, 18thC, 27½in (70cm).
$3,000-5,000

A Victorian mahogany partners' desk, with lined top and 6 frieze drawers, on pedestals each with 3 short drawers opposed by a cupboard door, on plinth, 72in (182.5cm).
$4,000-5,000

A Victorian mahogany partners' pedestal desk, with leather lined top, on plinth bases, 60in (152cm)
$3,000-4,000

A mahogany kneehole desk, the frieze with brushing slide and lon[g] drawer, on bracket feet, 31½in (80cm).
$1,500-2,500

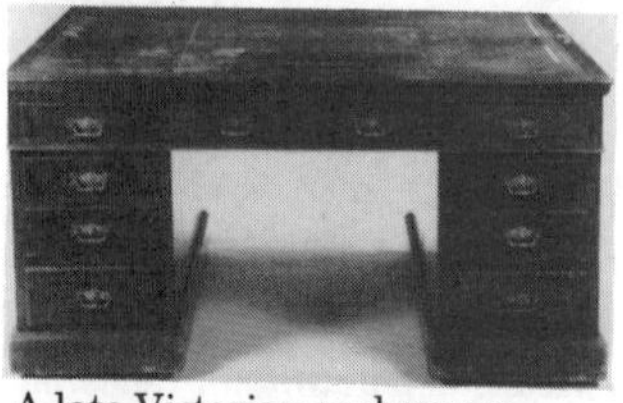

A late Victorian mahogany partners' kneehole pedestal desk, with inset leather lined top, on plinth bases, 60in (152cm).
$2,500-3,000

A walnut and featherbanded desk, the crossbanded rectangular top above 9 drawers, flanking a central kneehole panelled door, on bracket feet, 18thC, 33in (84cm).
$1,500-2,500

A mahogany roll-top desk, crossbanded and with string inlay, the fitted interior with satinwood faced small drawers, pigeonholes, ink pot and pen stands, fitted with 2 slides and 9 drawers surrounding the kneehole, bracket feet, veneered back, Maple & Co., metal label, 54in (137cm).
$5,500-6,500

An Irish mid-Victorian mahogany partners' desk, with 2 silver plaques, one in Irish, the other inscribed 'Presented to William T Cosgrave Esq Ltd President Executive Council Saorstat Eireann by Wm and P Thomson Ltt as an expression of their deep appreciation of the invaluable services rendered by him to the Saorstat during the critical period of its history', stamped J J Burne and Sons, Cabinet Makers and Upholsterers Henry Street Dublin, 75in (190.5cm).
$5,000-6,500

A child's mahogany desk, the adjustable 2 sided writing slope with baize lining and well under, brass drop handles, on stand with drawer and square tapered legs, la[te] 18thC, 19in (49cm).
$4,000-5,000

An early George III mahogany kneehole desk, with moulded edge, above a long drawer and columns of 3 drawers flanking a cupboard, with fielded panel door, 36in (91cm).
$2,500-3,000

A mid-Georgian mahogany kneehole desk, on ogee bracket feet, restorations, 34in (86cm).
$2,500-3,000

A mid-Victorian mahogany partners' desk, the top with 2 hinged writing slopes enclosing drawers, with 5 drawers and a door to each side, 66in (167.5cm).
$3,000-4,000

A Queen Anne maple miniature desk on frame, opening to an interior with 5 valanced pigeonholes above a long drawer flanked by 2 short drawers, the case with 2 long drawers, each thumb moulded, the frame with scalloped apron, on cabriole legs with pad feet, frame later, New England, c1750, 21½in (55cm).
$3,500-4,500

An elm and mahogany banded desk, the top above a long frieze drawer and 6 small drawers, flanking a central kneehole panelled cupboard door, on plinth base, part 18thC, 40½in (102cm).
$1,200-1,500

A mahogany partners' kneehole pedestal desk, with leather lined top above 6 drawers and a panelled door, the same to the reverse on plinth bases, 19thC and later, 62½in (158cm).
$5,000-5,500

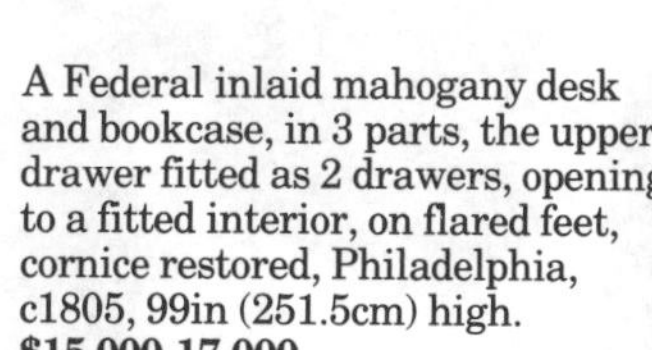

A Federal inlaid mahogany desk and bookcase, in 3 parts, the upper drawer fitted as 2 drawers, opening to a fitted interior, on flared feet, cornice restored, Philadelphia, c1805, 99in (251.5cm) high.
$15,000-17,000

A Victorian burr walnut pedestal desk, with lined kidney-shaped top, above 3 frieze drawers and 8 pedestal drawers, stamped W. Williamson & Sons, Guildford, 51in (129.5cm).
$13,000-14,000

A Chippendale mahogany slant front desk, the top above a thumb moulded slant front opening to a fitted interior, the dividers cockbeaded, on base moulding with claw-and-ball feet, 35in (90cm).
$3,000-4,000

A Chippendale walnut and grain painted slant front desk, with ogee bracket feet, some damage and restoration, Pennsylvania, late 18thC, 40in (101.5cm).
$12,000-13,000

A George III mahogany partners' desk, with brown leather lined top, the reverse with a panelled door on a plinth base, restorations, 59½in (152cm).
$9,500-11,000

A Victorian mahogany partners' desk, with leather lined top above 9 drawers, the reverse enclosed by a pair of panelled doors, on plinth bases, 48in (122cm).
$3,000-5,000

A Georgian clerk's desk, with 4 interior drawers and reading mould, c1820, on later stand, 48in (120cm) high.
$800-1,200

A Victorian walnut and elm kneehole pedestal desk, the inset leather lined top above 9 drawers between quadrant angles, on plinth bases, adapted, 54in (137cm).
$2,500-3,500

A Victorian larch and satinwood kneehole desk, the lined top above 9 drawers, on undulating plinth base, 54in (137cm).
$2,000-3,000

An oak partners' desk, c1860, 60in (152cm).
$3,500-4,000

A Flemish walnut and marquetry desk, the top with gadrooned edge depicting an episode from classical mythology, also carved back, 67½in (171cm).
$6,500-8,000

An Edwardian mahogany kidney-shaped pedestal desk, with green inset top, tooled leather, crossbanded with brass ring handles, the plinth bases on castors, 48in (122cm).
$2,500-3,000

A Victorian oak desk, 72in (182.5cm).
$1,500-2,000

A Victorian mahogany partners' desk, with leather lined top, on plinth bases, 60in (152cm).
$2,500-4,000

A mahogany pedestal desk, with leather lined top above 9 drawers, the reverse with simulated drawers, on plinth bases, 19thC and later, 49in (124.5cm).
$6,500-7,000

An ebony veneered and amboyna banded pedestal desk, fitted with 3 frieze drawers, each pedestal fitted with a further 3 drawers, stamped Edwards & Roberts, 48in (122cm).
$2,500-5,000

An Edwardian walnut kneehole pedestal desk, with inset leather lined top, below a galleried elevated cabinet back fitted with 4 small drawers, above 9 graduated drawers to the pedestals, on plinth bases, stamped Jas. Shoolbred & Co., 48in (122cm).
$1,400-2,000

Victorian gilt mirror, with bonised reeded slip in an acanthus arved and ball mounted cavetto rame with eagle cresting, 56 by 1in (142 by 79cm).
2,500-3,000

A George I walnut dressing glass, with later bevelled mirror plate, the stepped plateau with 3 short drawers over a long cushion drawer, on bracket feet, the whole with herringbone banding, 16½in (42cm).
$4,000-5,500

An early Georgian walnut mirror, the plate with re-entrant top corners and moulded frame, shaped arched cresting and conforming apron, 33½ by 19in (85 by 48cm).
$800-1,200

gilt girandole mirror, with two andlearms, damages and cracks, 1825, 38 by 22½in (97 by 57cm).
4,000-5,000

A Regency mahogany toilet mirror, inlaid with ebonised lines on ring turned supports, the serpentine base with 2 drawers, on turned legs, 22in (56cm).
$1,200-1,400

A George III style satinwood toilet mirror, with shield shaped bevelled plate on scrolled supports, with crossbanded serpentine base, on bracket feet, 18in (46cm).
$1,000-1,300

George III style giltwood mirror, with pierced frame carved with scrolls, acanthus flowers and fruit, he cresting with a foliate plume with flowers, 19thC, 26in (66cm) wide.
2,500-3,000

A Victorian mahogany cheval mirror, on turned reeded supports, the box top base with scroll legs and casters, 42in (106.5cm).
$3,000-4,000

A George II style pine wall mirror, with an eared frame carved with egg-and-dart, the frieze applied with shells and acanthus beneath a broken pediment, 72 by 37in (182.5 by 94cm).
$3,000-4,000

An Edwardian inlaid mahogany cheval mirror, with harebell inlay, on rectangular base with bracket feet, 69½in (176cm) high.
$650-800

A Federal giltwood églomisé mirror, flanked by coved pilasters with applied spiral twists, on a moulded base, some flaking to paint, probably Boston, c1815, 37in (94cm) high.
$1,200-1,500

A Chippendale mahogany and giltwood mirror, bearing the label 'James Musgrove carver, gilder', minor veneer damage, Philadelphia, c1780, 30in (76.5cm) high.
$3,500-6,000

A Régence style giltwood mirror, with arched central plate and mirrored slips carved with scrolling foliage, the eared frame with scrolling feet and a pierced rocaille cresting, 56½in (143cm) high.
$12,000-14,000

A Federal carved and inlaid mahogany and giltwood mirror, the broken scrolled crest with rosette terminals centering an urn above a rectangular frame enclosing a mirror plate, wear to gilt, damages, late 18th/early 19thC, 40in (101.5cm) high.
$3,000-3,500

An Empire giltwood pier glass mirror, with egg-and-dart decoration above a rectangular mirror plate flanked by Ionic pilasters on moulded bases, American, c1825, 89in (226cm) hig
$3,500-4,000

A pair of Portuguese mirror sconces with trefoil tops, with plain reeded borders, the bases each fitted with a scrolling tubular branch supporting a plain circular wax pan and spool shaped socket, Lisbon, c1880, maker's mark AFC, 15½in (39.5cm) high.
$12,000-13,000

Make the most of Miller's

Unless otherwise stated, any description which refers to 'a set' or 'a pair' includes a valuation for the entire set or the pair, even though the illustration may show only a single item

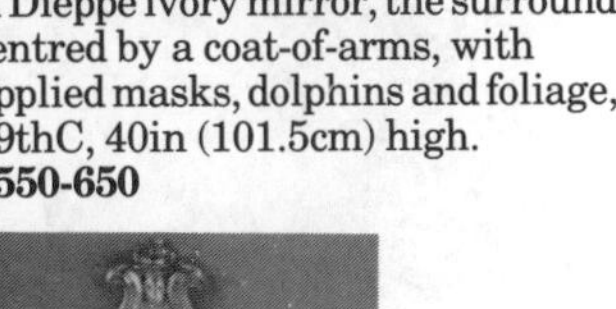

. Dieppe ivory mirror, the surround
entred by a coat-of-arms, with
pplied masks, dolphins and foliage,
9thC, 40in (101.5cm) high.
550-650

pair of William IV giltwood
irrors, each plate within a glazed
oulded frame carved with
rolling leaves and flowerheads
ith ribbon tied cresting and
rolled base, crestings damaged
nd one piece deficient, 56 by 24in
42 by 61cm).
11,000-13,000

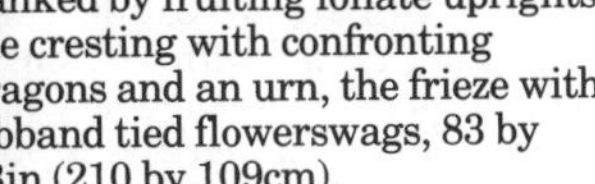

giltwood overmantel, the plate
anked by fruiting foliate uprights,
e cresting with confronting
agons and an urn, the frieze with
bband tied flowerswags, 83 by
3in (210 by 109cm).
,300-1,500

A pair of English carved and gilded landscape frames, with a shell cresting and opposed C-scroll corners, 18thC, 36½ by 49in (93 by 125cm).
$1,000-1,500

A gilt gesso rococo wall mirror, with bevelled plate, 45in (114cm).
$1,000-1,200

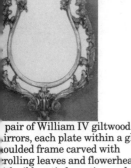

A carved giltwood frame wall mirror of asymmetric form, 18thC, 25½in (65cm).
$2,500-3,000

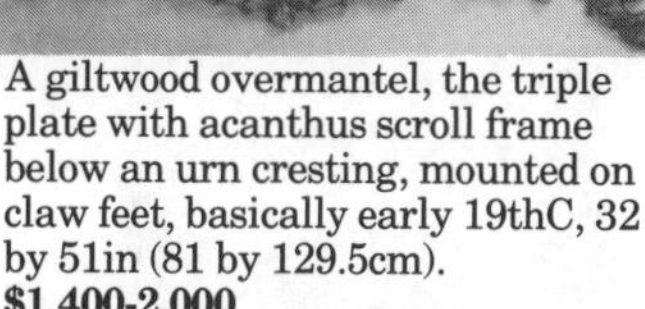

A giltwood overmantel, the triple plate with acanthus scroll frame below an urn cresting, mounted on claw feet, basically early 19thC, 32 by 51in (81 by 129.5cm).
$1,400-2,000

An English carved and gilded frame, foliate sight edge, 18thC, 35 by 30in (89 by 76cm).
$800-900

A Venetian engraved and moulded glass mirror, with arched bevelled plate, the shaped apron and cresting framed with C-scrolls and applied with flowers, mid-19thC, 72 by 37in (182.5 by 94cm).
$2,500-3,000

An English carved and gilded frame, the corners with rosettes flanked by pierced opposed C-scrolls and scrolling foliage and flowers, foliate sight edge, 18thC, 37 by 32in (94 by 81cm).
$1,400-2,000

A pair of Chippendale style giltwood mirrors, the plates surmounted by foliate and C-scroll crests with ho-ho birds, the sides with elongated C-scrolls, the aprons with C-scrolls and icicles, 50 by 26in (127 by 66cm).
$5,500-6,500

A Dutch carved ebonised frame, with various ripple and wave mouldings, 17thC.
$2,500-3,000

A pair of giltwood pier glasses, each with an arched bevelled plate in a gilt églomisé frame incorporating C-scrolls, distressed, 51 by 31in (130 by 79cm).
$4,000-5,000

A walnut and floral marquetry wall mirror, with rectangular plate, the broken pediment above an arched recessed frieze, 36 by 17½in (91.5 by 44cm).
$1,000-1,200

A giltwood mirror, with bevelled plate, the frame with flowerhead and ribbon entwined border within pierced acanthus scrolls, the cresting with flowerheads, part 18thC, 44 by 34½in (112 by 87cm).
$2,500-3,000

A walnut and parcel gilt mirror, with bevelled plate in a narrow moulded frame with shaped base and cresting, incised with foliage and with basket of flowers cresting, 33 by 19½in (84 by 49cm).
$2,000-2,500

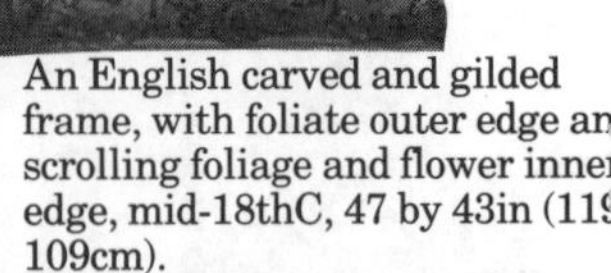

An English carved and gilded frame, with foliate outer edge an scrolling foliage and flower inne edge, mid-18thC, 47 by 43in (11 109cm).
$1,300-1,500

A giltwood mirror, the bevelled plate engraved with a chinoiserie scene, in a moulded frame applied a the corners with leaves, 33 by 26in (84 by 66cm).
$2,500-3,000

An English carved and gilded frame, 18thC, 38 by 30½in (96.5 b 77cm).
$800-1,000

A North Italian giltwood wall mirror, with waisted bevelled pl in a frame carved with C-scrolls foliage, pierced C-scroll and folia surmount and similar apron, 36 24in (92 by 61cm).
$1,300-1,500

A giltwood mirror, basically 18thC, 45 by 31½in (114 by 80cm).
$3,000-4,000

An Italian giltwood mirror, with arched inset plate in a fish scale gadrooned carved frame, decorated with masks and acanthus scrolls below a twin eagle and fruit festooned cresting, 19thC, 79 by 50in (200 by 127cm).
$4,000-5,000

A gilt pier mirror with acorn pendants over a frieze centering an applied scallop shell, above a double-plate mirror flanked by a pair of twist colonettes, over a moulded base, c1820, 45in (114cm) high.
$2,000-3,000

An Italian painted and giltwood wall mirror, of cartouche form, later mirror plate and repaired, 19thC, 57 by 35½in (144 by 90cm).
$3,000-4,000

An English carved and gilded Sunderland frame, with scrolling foliage and flowers centred by a cartouche, the base carved with a lion's mask, 17thC, 12½in (32cm) wide.
$1,200-1,300

A Dutch tortoiseshell and ebonised frame, with ripple moulding, 19thC, 24 by 20½in (61 by 52cm).
$4,000-5,000

An Italian carved and gilded frame, with foliate outer edge, ribband central panel and an overlapping leaf design running to the corners, 17thC, 29½ by 26in (75 by 66cm).
$1,200-1,500

A French Regency carved and gilded frame, foliate sight edge, 34 by 38½in (86 by 97cm).
$1,500-2,500

A French rococo carved and gilded frame, 31 by 19in (78 by 48cm).
$4,000-5,000

A Louis XIV style carved and gilded frame, 35in (90cm) wide.
$5,000-6,500

An Italian carved and gilded frame, with leaf corners and stylised foliate centres, 17thC, 40 by 53in (102 by 135cm).
$2,500-3,000

A George III style stripped pine overmantel, the frame pierced and carved with rocailles, scrolls and foliage and crested by a Chinaman in a pavilion flanked by ho-ho birds, the base with pierced scrolling foliage, 55 by 64in (139.5 by 162.5cm).
$12,000-14,000

An Italian carved and gilded frame, with pierced scrolling acanthus leaves, cherubs' heads, bunches of fruit and a bar-and-treble-bead inner edge, 27½ by 20½in (70 by 51.5cm).
$3,000-4,000

A Federal giltwood églomisé mirror, flanked by moulded pilasters with spiral twists, on a moulded base, Massachusetts, early 19thC, 41in (104cm) high.
$2,500-3,000

A George III gilt and composition pier glass, the frieze applied with flowerheads within beaded roundels.
$2,000-3,000

An Italian carved gilded and ebonised frame, with bar-and-double-bead outer edge and a foliate sight edge, 18thC, 14in (35cm) high.
$650-700

A Louis XIV carved and gilded laurel leaf corner frame, anthemia and flower corners and engraved reposes, 39 by 33in (99 by 84cm).
$2,500-3,000

An Italian carved and gilded frame, with anthemia corners and pierced scrolling acanthus leaves running to foliate clasp centres, 17thC, 32 by 29in (81 by 74cm).
$1,500-2,500

A gilt pier mirror, with acorn pendants over a foliate diaper-patterned frieze over a double-plate mirror, flanked by a pair of twist colonettes surmounted by Corinthian capitals, over a base moulding, probably American, c1820, 58in (147cm) high.
$2,500-3,500

ettees

A Victorian mahogany conversation seat, upholstered in apricot material, the seat rail hung with tassels, on turned legs, 32in (81cm) high.
$6,500-8,000

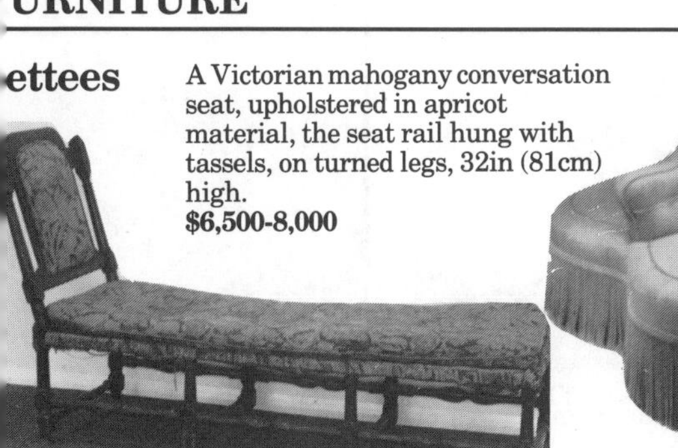

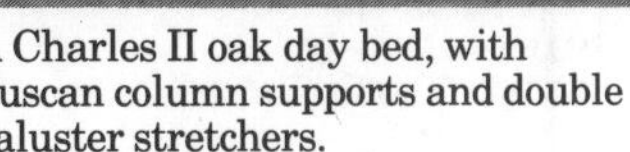

. Charles II oak day bed, with uscan column supports and double aluster stretchers.
1,200-2,000

A George III mahogany sofa, upholstered in striped floral damask, on square chanelled tapering legs headed by inlaid paterae, 53½in (136cm).
$6,500-7,000

William and Mary design walnut ›fa, tassled and upholstered in gros ›int tapestry, on scrolling legs ined by stretchers carved with liage and C-scrolls, 87in (221cm).
2,000-4,000

A Victorian metamorphic island sofa, upholstered in the original rose ground floral tapestry, the turned legs fitted with casters, late 19thC, 51in (129.5cm) diam.
$2,500-4,000

A Victorian walnut sofa, with buttoned upholstered arched back, bowed ends and seat, on fluted turned tapering legs with acanthus carved headings, 72in (182.5cm).
$1,200-1,500

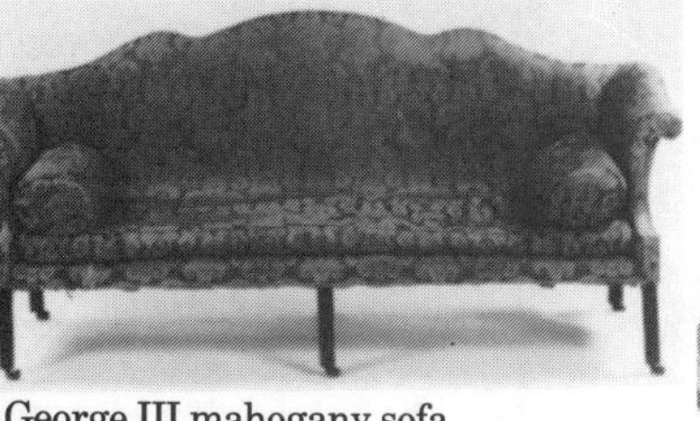

George III mahogany sofa, ›holstered in red damask, on ıamfered legs carved with blind etwork, later central back leg, .in (296cm).
,500-6,500

A Victorian walnut trefoil conversation seat, upholstered in red velvet, on turned tapered legs, restorations, 44in (112cm).
$1,300-1,500

A Regency olive green painted triple back settee, the toprail painted with ribbon tied swags of flowers and a central classical urn, with cane filled seat, green velvet squab on ring turned tapering legs, 59in (149.5cm).
$3,000-5,000

Victorian walnut framed ree-piece part lounge suite, the ch back rails with carved laurel ouldings, the arms and uprights eded, carved with acanthus leaves.
,500-2.500

sofa, with deep seat, low back, rolled arms and bolster cushions ›holstered in tartan with tasselled at rail, 132in (335cm).
,500-3,000

A Continental walnut framed canapé, upholstered in rose damask with fruiting vine needlework borders, the moulded outset arms continuing to moulded cabriole legs with scroll feet, basically mid-18thC, 59in (150cm).
$3,000-3,500

A Louis XVI style giltwood settee, with carved back and seat and elaborate foliate back panel and seat rail.
$2,500-3,000

A Regency beechwood open arm sofa, with simulated bamboo frame, on turned splayed tapering legs joined by abacus mounted cross stretchers, with loose upholstered seat squab, 74in (188cm).
$3,000-5,000

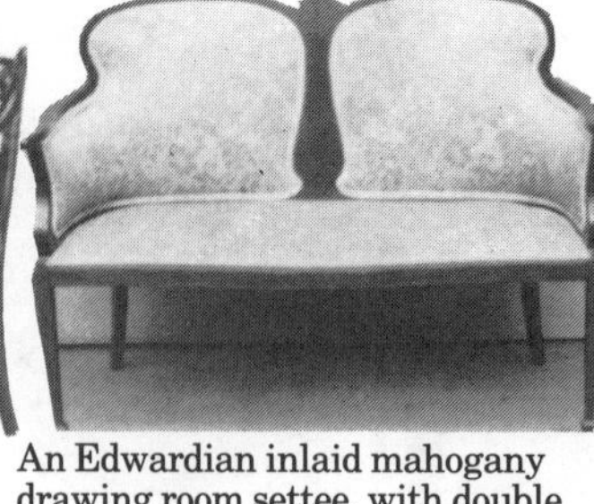

An Edwardian inlaid mahogany drawing room settee, with double arched back and bow fronted seat, upholstered in floral silk damask, and standing on square tapering supports with spade feet.
$1,000-1,200

A Victorian mahogany 3 seater sofa, with upholstered buttoned bowed back and seat, on cabriole legs with foliate knob feet, 82in (208cm).
$1,500-2,000

A three-piece mahogany bergère suite with upholstered backs, carved side panels with armrests ending in carved eagles heads, overstuffed seats, blind fret frieze, and carved cylindrical front legs with claw-and-ball feet, early 20thC.
$4,000-5,000

A Louis XVI giltwood salon suite, comprising a canapé, a pair of fauteuil and 4 single chairs with foliate carved serpentine seat rails, raised upon slender fluted cabriole front supports carved at the knees with flowerheads, and terminating in peg feet and casters.
$5,500-6,500

A mahogany Empire style two-seater settee, with cast brass plaques and carved Egyptian head, on cast brass claw feet.
$1,200-1,400

A Louis XVI style giltwood suite, comprising 4 fauteuils and a canapé, upholstered in 18thC tapestry, on turned fluted taperin legs, the upholstery with restorations, canapé 67in (170cm
$4,000-5,500

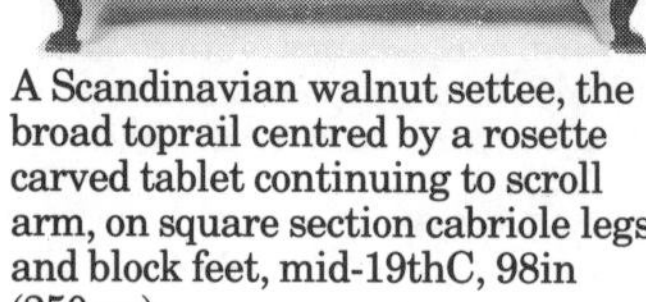

A Scandinavian walnut settee, the broad toprail centred by a rosette carved tablet continuing to scroll arm, on square section cabriole legs and block feet, mid-19thC, 98in (250cm).
$650-1,000

A pair of settees with double scr ends, finely carved frames with anthemion, acanthus scrolls anc paterae, 96in (243.5cm).
$25,000-32,000

A Classical carved mahogany chaise longue, with moulded curved half crest rail terminating in a leaf carved scroll, with gadrooned seat rail, on anthemion carved paw feet, attributed to Quervelle, Philadelphia, c1820, 72in (182.5cm) long.
$9,000-10,000

A Federal mahogany sofa, with moulded arched and curved back continuing to sloping arm supports above an over-upholstered seat, on square tapering moulded legs with spade feet, repairs, New York, c1810, 72in (182.5cm) long.
$8,000-10,000

Sheraton style satinwood and
oral painted settee, the toprail
ith 3 oval cane panels, on ring
ırned tapered legs, late 19thC,
9in (125cm).
1,500-2,500

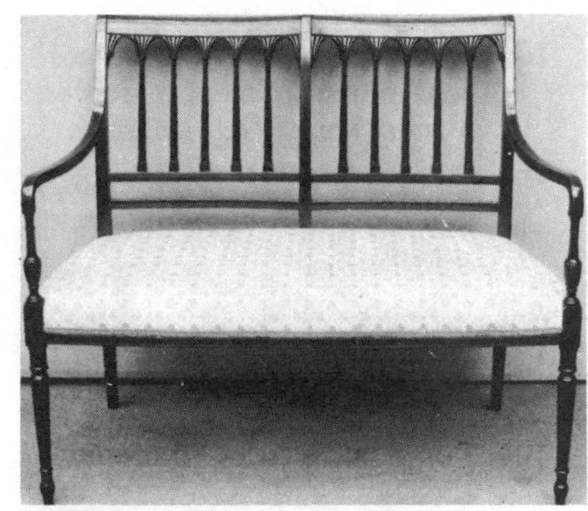

An Edwardian inlaid mahogany Hepplewhite style occasional settee, with double concave back above arched and reeded pilasters and floral upholstered seat, on slender turned supports, 42in (106.5cm).
$1,400-2,000

Sheraton design painted
atinwood settee, with radiating
ane work centred by painted panel,
3in (109cm).
4,000-5,000

An oak chaise longue, highly carved in the Jacobean manner, the backrail and stretchers embellished with earls coronets supported by dolphins.
$1,000-1,200

n 18thC style walnut chair-back
ttee, upholstered in brown floral
ocade and raised on 3 cabriole
ont supports carved at the knees
ith acanthus leaves, terminating
claw-and-ball feet and 3 outward
layed back supports, terminating
pad feet.
2,500-4,000

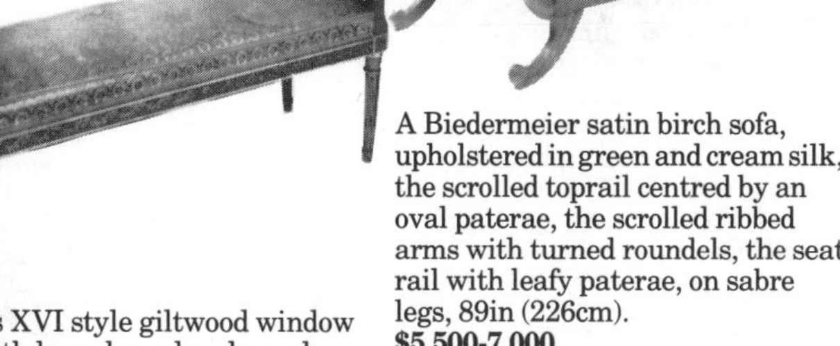

A Louis XVI style giltwood window seat, with lyre shaped ends, and carved bead and leaf mouldings, on fluted legs.
$1,200-1,400

A Biedermeier satin birch sofa, upholstered in green and cream silk, the scrolled toprail centred by an oval paterae, the scrolled ribbed arms with turned roundels, the seat rail with leafy paterae, on sabre legs, 89in (226cm).
$5,500-7,000

late George III cream painted and
t corner sofa, with triple panelled
airback, the toprail painted with
wers, the seat curved at one end,
turned tapering legs, 62½in
57.5cm).
,500-2,500

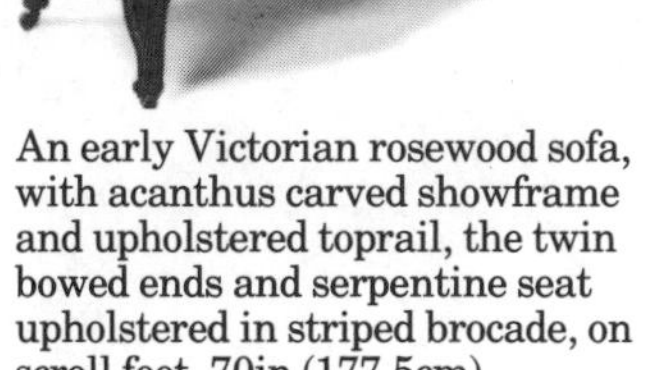

An early Victorian rosewood sofa, with acanthus carved showframe and upholstered toprail, the twin bowed ends and serpentine seat upholstered in striped brocade, on scroll feet, 70in (177.5cm).
$1,300-1,500

A Dutch East Indies, Sri Lanka, hardwood and ebony sofa, with shaped toprail, spindle back and scrolled arms, the caned seat on square bobbin turned legs joined by an H-stretcher, 17thC, 44in (112cm).
$1,300-2,000

A Directoire stained beechwood settee, the eared crest rail above foliate pierced splats and bowed arms on a padded seat and sabre legs, restorations, early 19thC, 61½in (156cm) wide.
$2,000-3,000

A Classical mahogany piano stool, the upholstered seat turning above a threaded support to adjustable height, on 4 turned tapering legs joined by a cross stretcher, top edge of rail and stretchers restored, New York, c1810, 14in (35.5cm) diam.
$800-1,000

A Classical carved and giltwood chaise longue, the scrolling half back carved with a lion's head terminal and acanthus leaves, wit leaf carved tapering baluster legs with casters, New York, c1830, 85 (216cm) wide.
$6,000-8,000

A Classical mahogany stool, the upholstered seat fastened to a rectangular box frame, on a scrolled curule base joined by a turned stretcher, Boston, c1825, 20in (50.5cm) wide.
$2,000-3,000

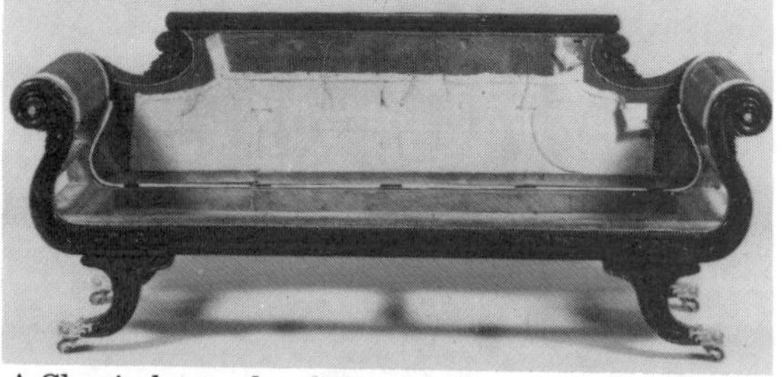

A Classical carved mahogany sofa, the arms with scrolled supports continuing to a bolection moulded seat rail, on carved sabre legs with leafy feet with casters, upholstery lacking, Boston, c1825, 85in (216cm) wide.
$8,000-9,000

An early Victorian mahogany lon bench, with turned scrolling arms above a padded seat upholstered i contemporary polychrome gros point needlework depicting leaves on turned legs with casters, 59½in (151cm) wide.
$5,000-6,000

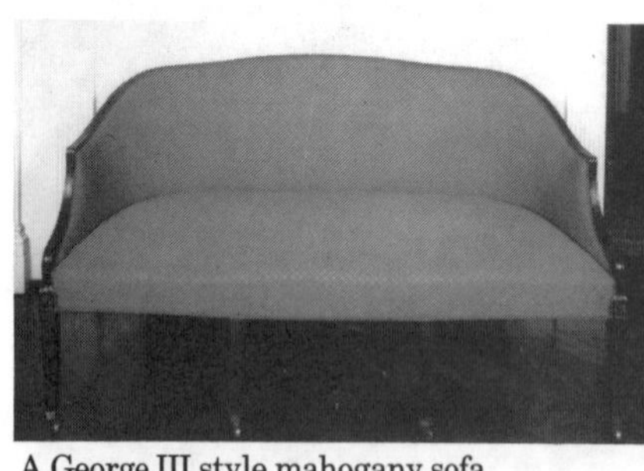

A George III style mahogany sofa, with downswept reeded crest rail and arms, the padded back and seat upholstered in cotton, on square tapering legs headed by rosettes on brass box feet and casters, 66in (167.5cm) wide.
$2,000-3,000

A Regency mahogany window bench, with padded seat with up-scrolling ends upholstered i velvet, the crossbanded X-fram mounted with gilt metal rosett and carved with fruit filled cornucopias, early 19thC, 51in (129.5cm) wide.
$2,000-3,000

ideboards

George III mahogany bowfront
deboard, on square tapering legs,
in (92cm).
,500-3,000

A mahogany and inlaid breakfront sideboard, with cellaret drawers, on square tapering legs, with spade feet, basically early 19thC, 48in (122cm).
$4,000-5,000

A George III mahogany sideboard, with D-shaped breakfront top, above a central drawer and arched kneehole drawer with 2 drawers below and cellaret drawer to the right, on square tapering legs and spade feet, 67in (179cm).
$2,000-3,000

. reproduction George III style
ahogany and inlaid sideboard,
ossbanded in rosewood, with brass
ng handles, raised on 6 square
pered legs, 54in (137cm).
,500-2,500

A George III mahogany demi-lune sideboard, the crossbanded top above a napery drawer flanked by cellaret drawers and further shallow crossbanded drawers, on square tapered legs inlaid with oval fan paterae and husk chains, c1780, 72in (183cm).
$7,000-9,000

A mahogany sideboard, with serpentine top inlaid with boxwood lines, on square tapering legs and spade feet, 47in (119cm).
$5,000-6,500

. mahogany and marquetry
owfront sideboard, with short
rawer and 2 panelled doors with
vag hung urns and stylised foliage,
n square tapered legs, 72in
.82.5cm).
1,300-2,000

A Regency mahogany and inlaid pedestal sideboard, on reeded turned tapering legs, 74in (188cm).
$1,500-2,500

A late George III mahogany sideboard, inlaid with boxwood lines, the crossbanded serpentine top above a drawer and central arch with recessed tambour shutter, 71in (181cm).
$6,500-8,000

. George III mahogany breakfront
ideboard, the apron drawer with
n spandrels, tapering square stop
uted supports with spade feet,
ome alterations, 49½in (125cm).
4,000-5,000

A serpentine front mahogany sideboard banded in boxwood and ebony, on square tapering supports, early 19thC, 56in (142cm).
$1,200-1,400

A Sheraton design serpentine fronted mahogany sideboard, the top banded in satinwood and with a brass rail, with inlaid satinwood bands, shell quadrants and oval panels, string inlaid, and angled square tapering legs, spade feet, 48½in (123cm).
$4,000-5,000

A Regency mahogany and marquetry bowfront sideboard, the top with 2 frieze drawers flanked by 2 cellaret drawers, on square tapering legs, adapted, 79in (200.5cm).
$4,000-5,000

A mahogany sideboard, t reverse breakfront top wi brass fan shaped loop handles and shaped back plates, raised on octagona tapering supports terminating in peg feet, early 19thC, 95in (241cm
$2,000-2,500

A mid-Victorian walnut sideboard, the back carved with boars heads above an open centre flanked by 2 panelled doors inset with carved game trophies, mirror-back missing, 150in (381cm).
$5,000-8,000

A mid-Victorian oak, sycamore ar alder sideboard, by Charles Bevar inlaid with dots, chevrons and stylised flowers, labelled Marsh a Jones, late Kendall & Co, 84½in (215cm).
$3,000-4,000

A late Victorian oak mirror-back sideboard, ornately carved with shells, scrolls, flowerheads and acanthus leaves, on ornate bracket feet, 84in (213cm).
$1,500-2,500

A William IV mahogany pedesta mirror-back sideboard, the crossbanded mahogany top over 4 frieze drawers with sunken half round fronts, the right hand pedestal with lead lined cellaret drawer, 89in (226cm).
$650-800

Stands

An early Victorian mahogany three-tier dumb waiter, with moulded edges and rounded corners, the graduated sides joined by a stretcher, and the upper and lower tiers adjustable, 36in (91.5cm).
$650-700

An early Victorian walnut folio stand, on shallow scroll legs and turned feet, some damage, c1840, 30in (76cm).
$3,000-4,000

A Victorian carved mahogany hallstand, with foliate cresting, shaped marble slab and glove drawer below, standing on cabriole supports, 50in (127cm).
$1,400-1,500

A Victorian free standing display stand, with moulded edge top, on turned fluted and reeded supports, the centre circular undershelf raised on 4 leaf carved supports, rectangular shelves on either side with shaped frieze, 65in (165cm). **$4,000-5,000**

A Georgian design lyre-shaped music stand, having brass rods and mounts, decorated with boxwood string inlay.
$650-700

An early Victorian rosewood duet stand, the lyre inset flaps raised on ratchets, supported on a turned column with leaf carved stem and tripod platform base.
$1,300-1,400

A Victorian oak shaving stand, on an arched tripod support ending in pad feet, 17in (44cm) diam.
$500-800

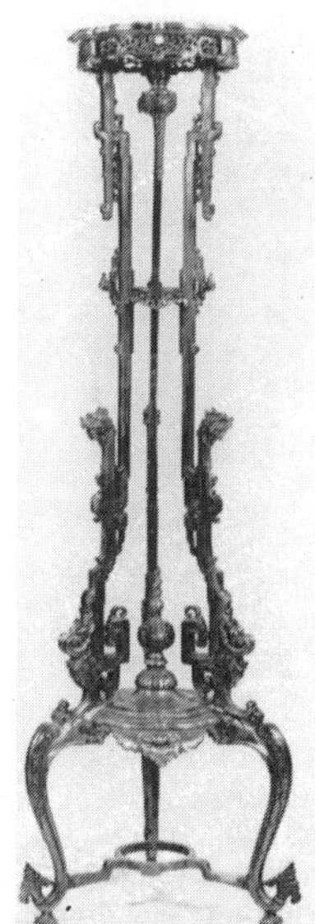

A pair of Victorian brass pedestals, in the Japanese style, c1880, 49in (125cm).
$4,000-5,000

A pair of mahogany bust stands, with partial fluted and wrythen turned columns to triple splay bases.
$800-1,000

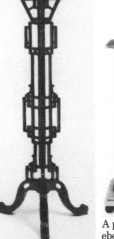

A pair of mahogany torchères, each with an hexagonal top with pierced gallery, on fretwork support and tripod base carved with foliate scrolls, 39in (99cm) high.
$1,300-2,000

A pair of fruitwood and ebonised fluted columns, with square capitals and plinths, 40in (101.5cm) high.
$1,400-2,000

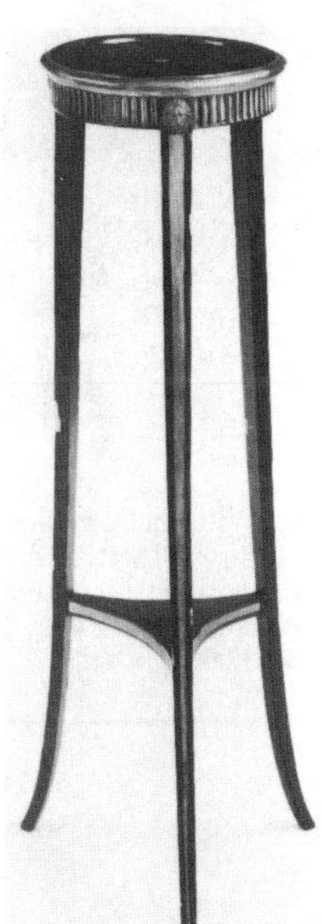

A pair of ebonised and gilded plant stands, with fluted friezes on square tapering splayed legs joined by triform stretcher, early 19thC, 34½in (87cm) high.
$1,300-2,000

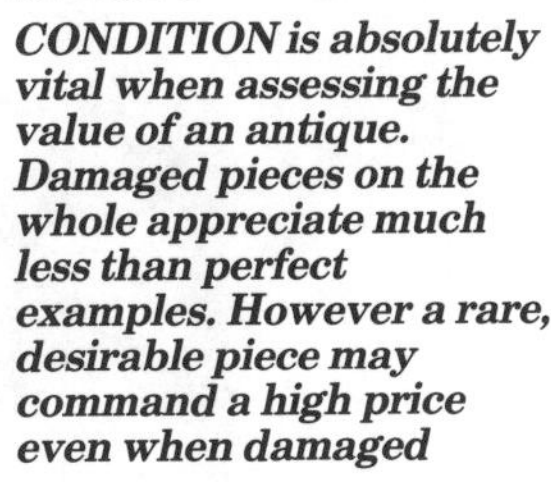

Make the Most of Miller's

CONDITION is absolutely vital when assessing the value of an antique. Damaged pieces on the whole appreciate much less than perfect examples. However a rare, desirable piece may command a high price even when damaged

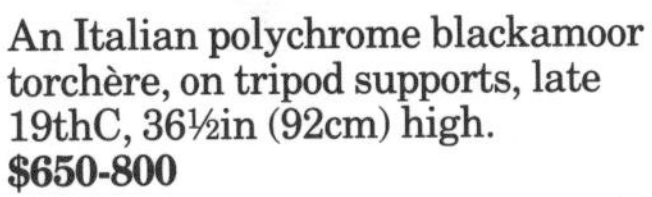

An Italian polychrome blackamoor torchère, on tripod supports, late 19thC, 36½in (92cm) high.
$650-800

A Victorian brass church lectern, the eagle crested rest mounted on an orbed baluster column decorated with cusps and cabochons, on a tiered platform base with claw feet, 67½in (171cm) high.
$3,000-4,000

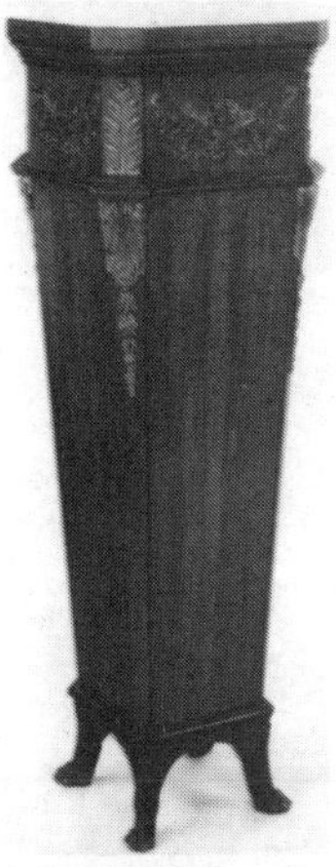

A Louis XVI style satinwood and ormolu mounted pedestal, inlaid with boxwood lines, on paw feet, 50½in (128cm) high.
$3,000-4,000

A French carved beechwood and caned hall stand, c1900, 46½in (117cm).
$1,200-1,300

A French Empire style mahogany jardinière stand, decorated with ormolu bands and 3 Sphinx motifs, with an urn below on tripod feet, 47in (119cm) high.
$700-800

A French rosewood veneered jardinière stand, with inlaid floral marquetry and gilt bronze mounts, the galleried top with a lidded interior revealing zinc liner, serpentine edge frieze on cabriole legs, 19thC, 26½in (67cm). **$2,000-2,500**

Steps

A set of William IV mahogany steps, lined in green leather, the top hinged, with pull-out middle, on turned legs, 16½in (42cm).
$2,500-3,000

Stools

An Irish mahogany stool, the seat upholstered in floral needlework, on cabriole legs and paw feet carved with foliage, restorations, 18thC, 28½in (72cm).
$2,500-3,000

A walnut stool, the needlework seat on shell carved cabriole legs with carved and pierced claw-and-ball feet, part early 18thC, 22in (56cm).
$1,200-1,300

A walnut stool, upholstered in emerald velvet, with turned baluster legs and stretchers, with restorations, late 17thC, 19in (48cm).
$2,000-2,500

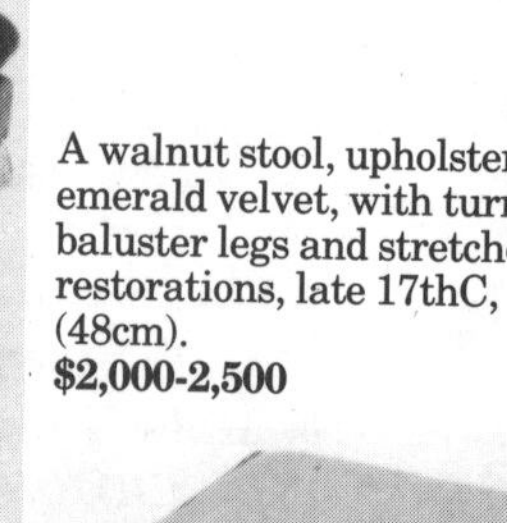

An early George III mahogany dressing stool, with slip in seat, 16½in (42cm).
$500-800

A George III mahogany stool, with drop-in seat on chamfered square legs and stretchers, 21in (53.5cm).
$700-1,200

. George III mahogany stool, with
oncave sided drop-in seat, on
quare legs and cross stretchers,
7in (43cm).
1,400-2,000

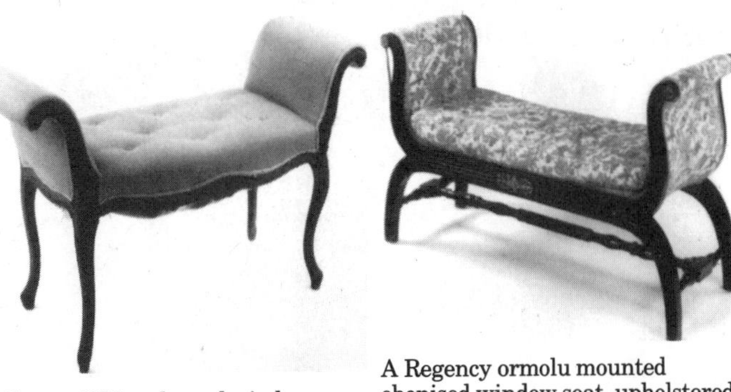

A George III beechwood window seat, with outscrolled arms, upholstered in peach rep, the waved frieze carved with a shell on cabriole legs, headed by foliage, restorations, 41in (105cm).
$1,400-2,000

A Regency ormolu mounted ebonised window seat, upholstered in floral cotton, the arms applied with flowerheads, the seat rail with anthemion and flowerhead plaques, on reeded legs with turned stretchers, stamped IM, 47in (119cm).
$2,500-3,000

A Regency ebonised window seat, with a concave reeded seat rail, on sabre legs.
$800-1,200

A mahogany stool, the top upholstered in close nailed dark brown leather, on 6 fluted and reeded legs, 35in (89cm).
$1,500-2,500

A mahogany fender stool, the padded seat upholstered in cream calico, on reeded legs, 49in (124cm).
$3,000-4,000

pair of Regency rosewood dressing
:ools, the drop-in seats upholstered
. green floral sculptured moquette,
aised on inverted X-frame supports
ed by a baluster turned stretcher.
2,500-3,000

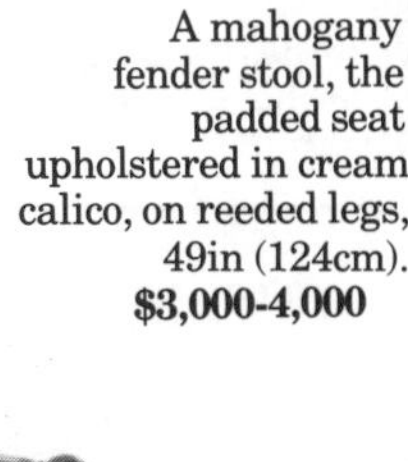

A Regency mahogany window seat, the padded seat covered in green damask, the scrolling X-frame applied with paterae and joined by spirally reeded arms and stretchers, the legs with restorations, 64½in (164cm).
$14,000-18,000

A William IV rosewood window seat, with padded seat on turned and ribbed tapering legs, 35½in (90cm).
$1,300-1,500

A Classical carved mahogany footstool, with scrolled ends joined by turned balusters, above a straight skirt, on reeded baluster feet, with a padded slip seat, English, c1820, 17½in (45cm).
$650-1,000

Architects Tables

An early George III mahogany architect's table, with crossbanded hinged and ratcheted top, above a frieze drawer with lined writing surface, on square chamfered legs, 34in (86cm).
$9,500-11,000

An early George III mahogany architect's table, the frieze with pull-out drawer, on chamfered legs with turned inner legs, adapted, top fixed down, 36in (91.5cm).
$1,500-2,500

A Georgian architect's mahogany table, with adjustable top and 2 slides, fitted with a drawer, on square chamfered legs, 34in (86cm)
$2,500-3,000

A George III mahogany architect's table, inlaid with satinwood fanned spandrels and geometric bands, the adjustable coffered top above a frieze drawer, on baluster column supports, adapted 39in (99cm).
$3,000-5,000

A George III mahogany secrétaire architect's table, with adjustable top with rests, above a writing drawer, on reeded turned tapering legs, with side carrying handles, 43in (109cm).
$8,000-9,000

A Georgian mahogany architect's desk.
$7,000-9,500

A George IV mahogany artist's table, the ratcheted top with a book rest on adjustable side supports, with double turned stretchers, the splay legs on brass sabots with casters, 27in (69cm).
$2,500-3,000

Billiards Tables

A mahogany slate bed bar billiar table, of plain design with heavy chamfered supports, together wit scoreboard, balls and cue, 73in (185cm) long.
$500-550

A mahogany slate bed bar billiards table, with heavy chamfered supports, together with scoreboards cues and balls, 78in (198cm).
$1,200-1,400

Breakfast Tables

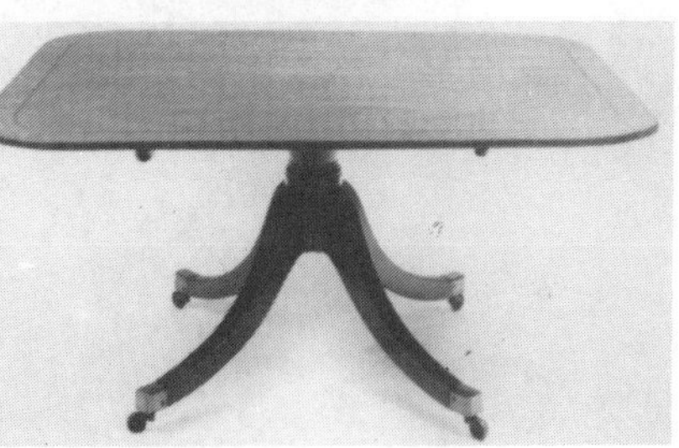

A George III mahogany breakfast table, on a quadripartite support with splayed reeded legs, 58½in (148cm).
$3,000-4,000

A Georgian mahogany breakfast table, with reeded edge to the tilt-top over a ring turned stem on 3 splayed part fluted legs, ending in brass cap casters, 51in (129.5cm).
$800-1,000

A George III mahogany breakfast table, on a quadripartite support with reeded legs, 52in (132cm).
$1,500-2,500

A George III mahogany pedestal breakfast table, with rosewood banded top and rounded ends, on a turned tapering shaft and quadripartite splayed legs with brass paw feet, 47in (119cm).
$1,400-2,000

A mahogany breakfast table, the tip-up top on a turned shaft with reeded splayed legs and lion's paw caps, Regency and later, 53in (134.5cm).
$2,000-2,500

A late Victorian walnut breakfast table, the moulded tip-up top on a turned quadripartite support with foliate carved splayed legs, restorations, 54in (137cm).
$1,200-1,500

A Regency figured mahogany breakfast table, the satinwood banded top on a ring turned column and quadripartite outswept legs, restorations to frame, 55½in (141cm).
$1,200-1,300

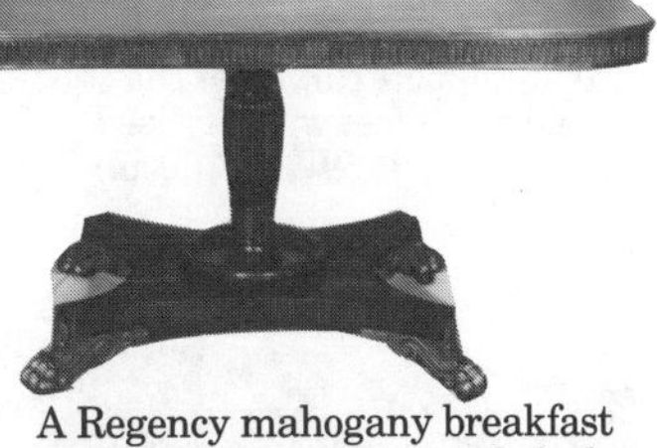

A Regency mahogany breakfast table with tip-up top, reeded edge and fluted frieze, the turned and reeded column on concave quadruple support and brass paw feet, 54in (137cm).
$2,500-3,000

A Regency mahogany tilt-top breakfast table, with wide zebrawood crossbanding, on turned shaped column and reeded quadruple splay support having brass terminals and casters, 52in (132cm).
$8,000-9,500

A George IV rosewood breakfast table, on a faceted column, concave platform and bun feet.
$8,000-9,500

A Regency mahogany tilt-top breakfast table, with egg-and-tongue-moulded edge, on a turned palm tree trunk column with ball decoration, terminating in brass acanthus leaf decorated caps and casters, 45½in (115cm).
$3,500-4,000

A mid-Victorian burr walnut breakfast table, the tip-up top inlaid with Tunbridgeware diamonds within boxwood line borders, on 4 column supports and foliate carved scrolling base with central finial, 56in (142cm).
$2,500-3,000

A William IV mahogany breakfast table, the D-end tilt-top on a pedestal carved with lotus leaves, the concave sided platform on turned feet, 61in (155cm).
$3,000-4,000

An early Victorian oak breakfast table, the tip-up top geometrically inlaid and centred by a sunburst design outlined in ebony, 49½in (125cm).
$1,400-2,000

A calamander breakfast table, with crossbanded top, on chamfered stepped triangular shaft with concave platform, scrolled legs and brass foliate caps, 48in (122cm).
$4,000-5,000

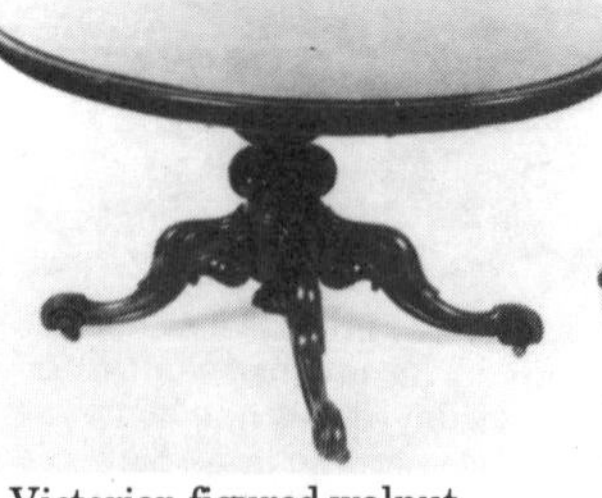

A Victorian figured walnut breakfast table, the snap-top quarter veneered, with thumb moulded edge, raised upon a boss and strapwork carved double baluster stem and cabriole quadruple support carved at the knees and scroll feet with stylised foliage, on casters, 59½in (150cm).
$2,000-2,500

A rosewood breakfast table, the moulded tip-up top on a turned shaft with 4 splayed legs carved with acanthus, on flattened bun feet, 19thC, 54½in (138cm).
$3,000-4,000

A rosewood and brass inlaid pedestal breakfast table, with crossbanded tip-up top, the splayed legs with brass paw feet, basically early 19thC, 50½in (128cm).
$3,000-5,000

A George III style mahogany spider gateleg table, with twin flap top above a frieze drawer on turned legs joined by stretchers on turned feet, late 19thC, 32in (81.5cm) long.
$1,500-2,000

A Classical carved mahogany breakfast table, the clover shaped top with 2 drop leaves above a long drawer, with an urn-turned pedestal, on reeded sabre legs with waterleaf carving and hairy paw casters, minor repair, small patch to legs, New York, c1820, 39in (99cm) long.
$5,000-8,000

A Federal inlaid mahogany breakfast table, the top with clover shaped drop leaves above a short drawer flanked by inlaid rectangular reserves, on tapering reeded ring turned legs with swelled feet and casters, feet slightly reduced, New York, c1815, 38in (96.5cm) long.
$3,000-4,000

A Regency style Cumberland-action breakfast table, with crossbanded twin flap top above columnar supports and quadripartite base with splayed reeded legs on brass box feet and casters, restorations, mid-19thC, 49in (124.5cm) wide extended. **$4,000-6,000**

'ard Tables

A George II Virginia walnut fold-over card table, with frieze drawer, brass drop handle, and cabriole legs with scroll carved knees and pad feet, 29in (74cm).
$3,000-4,000

A mahogany fold-over card table, with single frieze drawer supported on cabriole legs and pad feet, 18thC, 30½in (77cm).
$1,300-2,500

A George II mahogany card table, with eared folding top lined in green baize, the plain frieze on cabriole legs carved with foliage, and claw-and-ball feet, 31½in (80cm).
$2,500-3,000

A George III mahogany and inlaid demi-lune card table, with a fold-over top, crossbanded in tulipwood, raised on tapered supports, headed by oval burr walnut panels, 36in (91cm).
$3,500-4,000

A George II mahogany D-shaped card table, with fold-over top enclosing a well, on turned tapering legs and pad feet, 31in (79cm).
$2,500-3,000

A George III mahogany card table, the fold-over top with canted corners and kingwood crossbanding, the tapering square legs headed by oval fan medallions, some restoration, 36in (91.5cm).
$3,000-4,000

A mahogany card table, applied with urns, bellflower festoons and paterae carved in the Adam manner, on tapering legs with spade feet, 18thC and later, 34in (86cm).
$2,500-3,000

A Chippendale style mahogany fold-over card table.
$800-1,200

A George III mahogany veneered D-shape card table, with inlaid stringing, the flap top baize lined, with later brass knob handles, the square tapering legs on casters, c1800, 37in (94cm).
$1,200-2,000

A walnut card table, the eared top and single frieze drawer on shell headed club legs and pad feet, early Georgian and later, 32½in (82cm).
$2,000-3,000

A pair of Sheraton style satinwood card tables, each with a hinged top, decorated with inlaid rosewood crossbanding and stringing, raised on square tapering legs, 36in (91.5cm). **$5,000-5,500**

A George III satinwood card table, with mahogany crossbanded top, 36in (91cm). **$5,500-6,500**

A Regency brass inlaid mahogany card table, with D-shaped folding top inlaid with a band of quatrefoils, two legs repaired, 36in (91.5cm).
$4,000-5,000

A mahogany and inlaid pedestal card table, with rosewood crossbanded top, brass paw feet, early 19thC, 38in (96.5cm).
$650-700

An early Victorian mahogany card table, on leaf scroll feet, 36in (91.5cm). **$1,500-2,500**

A mahogany card table, with canted fold-over top banded in satinwood, with concave platform on splayed legs, early 19thC, 36in (91.5cm).
$3,000-4,000

A George IV rosewood card table, the rounded hexagonal stem with spreading base and on concave sided platform with lotus carved bun feet 36in (91.5cm).
$800-1,000

A Victorian walnut card table, the serpentine top on cabochon tapering shaft and scrolling quadruple supports, 36in (91.5cm).
$2,000-2,600

A Victorian walnut folding card table, with turned and reeded supports and carved scrolled splay feet. **$800-1,000**

A Victorian demi-lune fold-over card table.
$500-650

A Victorian walnut and marquetry inlaid serpentine card table, with quadruple splayed legs, adapted, 35in (89cm).
$1,200-1,400

A calamander and gilt metal card table, with a baize lined playing surface and counter wells above a bead moulded frieze, on turned tapered fluted legs each with a foliate collar, late 19thC, 36in (91.5cm).
$1,200-1,500

An Edwardian rosewood envelope card table decorated with inlaid floral scrolls and stringing, opening to reveal a green baize lining and counter wells, an undertier below raised on turned and square legs with splay feet, 23in (59cm).
$2,500-3,000

. Chippendale carved mahogany
ɪrd table, with hinged serpentine
ɪp above a conforming apron
ɪntering a single drawer above a
ɜad moulded skirt, on bracketed
ɪoulded square legs, repair to one
g, several brackets restored,
hode Island or Massachusetts,
1780, 32in (81.5cm) wide.
3,000-5,000

A Federal carved mahogany card table, the hinged top with cockbeaded moulded edge above a conforming apron with bead moulded skirt, on fluted, square tapering legs, Salem, Massachusetts, c1790, 32½in (82.5cm) diam.
$12,000-14,000

A late Federal carved mahogany card table, with hinged folding top above a conforming apron centering a rectangular reserve edged with crossbanding, flanked by crossbanded rectangular reserves, on ring turned reeded tapering legs with swelled feet and casters, New York, c1810, 36in (91.5cm) wide.
$5,000-7,000

ʌ Classical gilt stencilled
ɪahogany card table, with folding
ɔp above a conforming bolection
ɪpron with stencilled foliate
ɪecoration, on a hexagonal faceted
ɪedestal with a circular moulded
ɪase, on 4 acanthus carved legs with
ion's paw feet, New York, c1830,
36in (91.5cm) wide.
$2,000-3,000

An Italian burr yew card table, the banded top centred by an inlaid geometric motif on square tapered legs, 33in (84cm).
$2,500-3,000

A Dutch walnut card table, inlaid with urns, flowerheads and foliate marquetry, the concave arched rectangular fold-over top enclosing a chessboard, with 2 frieze drawers, on cabriole legs with pad feet, part late 17thC, 30½in (77cm).
$2,500-3,000

An ormolu mounted ebonised and scarlet boulle serpentine card table, the shaped frieze centred by a mask clasp, on cabriole legs and sabots, 19thC, 35in (89cm).
$1,500-2,500

A Federal inlaid mahogany card table, the hinged top with swept corners and line inlaid edge above a conforming apron with line inlaid panels over a pattern banded skirt, on square tapering legs, Massachusetts, c1800, 36in (91.5cm) wide.
$6,000-7,000

A burr walnut serpentine fold-over card table, veneered on mahogany with ormolu mounts, inlaid with boxwood and amboyna stringing and on cabriole legs, 19thC, 38in (96.5cm).
$4,000-5,000

Centre Tables

A Louis XVI ormolu mounted mahogany bouillotte table, with pierced galleried white marble top above a frieze fitted with 2 drawers, on circular tapering legs with casters, late 18thC, 26½in (67.5cm) diam.
$7,000-9,000

A George II design giltwood table with verde antico marble top, the pierced apron carved with scrollin foliage and fruit, on cabriole legs headed by shells, on hairy claw-and-ball feet, redecorated, restorations, 60in (152cm).
$30,000-33,000

An early Victorian black painted occasional table, the cartouche shaped top decorated with pavilions in a landscape, with a moulded frieze painted with foliage on scrolling supports and an incurved quadripartite base, mid-19thC, 26in (66cm) wide.
$3,000-4,000

A French rosewood and marquet centre table, with brass mounts t the serpentine sides, the top and frieze with floral and scroll marquetry, the whole supported cabriole legs ending in brass mounted feet, late 19thC, 40in (101.5cm).
$2,500-3,000

A Queen Anne design giltwood and black lacquer table, on cabochon headed cabriole legs joined by a stretcher, part 18thC, 36in (92cm).
$4,000-5,000

A Regency rosewood centre table, with inlaid brass stringing, 2 frieze drawers, stained beech column and sabre legs with brass paw casters, 48in (122cm). **$2,000-2,500**

A George III style mahogany centre table, with crossbanded and boxwood strung top inlaid to the corners, on square tapered legs and spade feet, 66in (168cm).
$1,500-2,500

A Victorian walnut salon table, with figured top, supported on 2 turned stems and splayed legs with turned stretcher, the legs carved with fruit and scrolls, 53in (134.5cm). **$4,000-5,000**

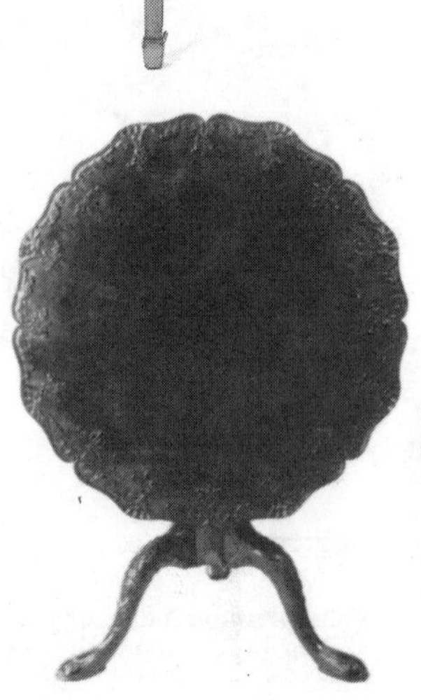

A mahogany centre table, with tip-up top on foliate carved splayed legs with dolphin head pad feet, part 18thC, 34in (86cm).
$2,500-3,000

A Victorian oak centre table in the Jacobean style, on 4 turned stems, splayed legs and reeded stretcher, the whole with carved flutings, masks and lines, 46in (116.5cm).
$700-900

. Regency rosewood centre table, vith brass inlaid wirework tringing gilded brass edging and ilt painted decoration, the plain upports with scroll mounts, upported on scrolling feet with urned stretcher, 45in (114cm).
5,000-5,500

A rosewood centre table, with pendant finials to the frieze, twist turned end supports joined by a stretcher and on downturned splayed feet with brass casters, mid-19thC, 52in (132cm).
$1,200-1,400

A Dutch walnut centre table, inlaid with marquetry with boxwood line borders, the coffered top with 2 frieze drawers, on spiralled baluster legs with latticed cross stretchers, labelled W. & J., Sloane Furniture, 5th Avenue, New York, 53in (134.5cm).
$3,000-4,000

A rosewood centre table, 36in (92cm).
$500-650

A Louis Philippe walnut centre table, with grey marble slab top, on a ribbed vase shaped shaft and 3 acanthus carved splayed legs with scroll feet, some moulding missing, 39½in (100cm) diam.
$2,500-3,000

A French kingwood, tulipwood and foliate marquetry centre table, on square supports joined by an undertier on cabriole legs with gilt metal sabots, 20in (51cm).
$1,300-2,000

A Victorian faded walnutwood centre table, the top with inset leather, raised on a well turned column with cabriole tripod carved with acanthus leaves, 30in (76cm).
$2,000-2,500

A Louis XVI design giltwood centre table, the top inset with a porcelain plaque surrounded by 12 plaques in egg-and-dart borders, above a foliate composition frieze on acanthus carved C-scrolling supports with cabochon headings and arched stretchers, labelled Comline di Roma, Scalo Termini, 26½in (68cm) diam.
$4,000-5,500

An ebonised parcel gilt and gilt metal mounted centre table, the top of serpentine outline centred by a porcelain plate within a border of portrait medallions, on foliate carved cabriole legs joined by a similarly mounted stretcher, late 19thC, 26in (67cm).
$3,000-4,000

A pair of rosewood snap-top centre tables, the supports carved with 3 entwined dolphins, the leaf carved concave sided triangular platform bases on 3 carved turtles, 19thC, 29in (73cm) diam.
$6,500-8,000

A Dutch walnut centre table, with quarter veneered tray top, above one convex frieze drawer, on cabriole legs and claw-and-ball feet, 35in (89cm).
$1,300-1,500

A French grey painted and parcel gilt centre table, the top lined in watered silk, 52in (132cm).
$1,500-2,500

A Flemish walnut ebony and ebonised centre table, the top inlaid with stars, the shaped frieze on bulbous baluster legs joined by a finialled stretcher, the top with trade label, 60in (152cm).
$2,500-3,000

An Italian walnut ebonised and bone inlaid centre table, decorated overall with stylised foliage, the top with bowed ends centred by a pewter tablet, on finialled pedestals, each with a square plinth joined by a flat stretcher on turned feet, 19thC, 49½in (125cm).
$1,500-2,500

Console Tables

A Régence oak console table, with serpentine brown marble top above a waved frieze centred by a pierced roundel, on scrolling cabriole legs joined by a pierced cartouche and block feet, early 18thC, 31½in (80cm) wide.
$9,000-10,000

A rosewood console table, applied with gilt flowerheaded paterae, with a platform base on turned bun feet, early 19thC, adapted, 23½in (60cm).
$1,200-1,500

A late Empire mahogany console table applied with ormolu mounts, with Carrara marble top and a mirror lined back and platformed base, stamped P. Lehaene, 35in (89cm).
$6,500-7,000

An early Victorian mahogany console table, with a frieze applied with foliate mouldings on 2 acanthus carved S-scroll supports backed by a mirror plate on a concave plinth, 54in (137cm).
$2,000-2,500

ining Tables

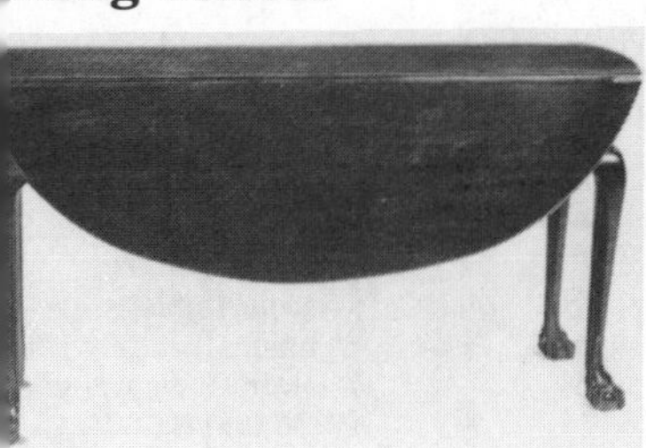

George II mahogany gateleg ining table, the top with a bevelled dge, on cabriole legs and law-and-ball feet, 58in (147cm).
5,000-5,500

An Irish mahogany drop-leaf dining table, with twin flap top on club legs with claw-and-ball feet, 18thC, 70in (177.5cm).
$4,000-6,500

A Georgian design mahogany 2 flap dining table, with carved scroll and leaf decoration to knees, cabriole legs and hoof feet.
$1,000-1,200

Georgian style mahogany D-end ning table, on twin turned shafts d splayed legs with brass caps, ith 2 leaves and rails, 106in 69cm).
,400-2,000

A George III mahogany extending dining table, on 4 baluster turned columns with a concave plinth and 4 foliate carved outswept legs, c1815, 2 later leaves, 86in (218cm) extended.
$10,000-12,000

A Regency mahogany two-part dining table, with crossbanded top over a frieze decorated with chevron banding, on square tapering legs with spade feet, with 2 leaves, early 19thC, 108in (274cm) extended.
$2,000-2,500

A Regency mahogany dining table, the folding top on ring turned tapering legs, including an extra leaf, 55in (139.5cm).
$1,500-2,500

late George III mahogany D-end ning table, on square tapered ted legs headed by a fanned oval, sociated, including an extra leaf, ½in (214cm).
,500-3,000

A mahogany twin pedestal dining table, with reeded edge, each pedestal with turned shaft and 3 moulded downswept legs, the pedestals early 19thC, 89in (226cm) extended.
$5,000-6,500

A Georgian style mahogany triple pedestal dining table, with plain top, reeded edge, supported on turned stems, splayed legs and brass cap casters, including 2 leaves, 144in (369.5cm) extended.
$3,000-5,000

A George III mahogany dining table, with ribbed tapering legs, later rails, the feet restored, including 2 leaves, 84in (213cm) extended.
$4,000-5,500

A mahogany and inlaid 3-part D-end dining table on 14 square tapering legs, basically early 19th 94in (238cm) exten
$5,000-6,500

A George III style mahogany D-end dining table, on triple ring turned tapering shafts and reeded down curving legs with brass paw feet, including 2 extra leaves, 140in (359.5cm) extended.
$5,000-6,500

A George III style mahogany D-end dining table, with satinwood banded top triple turned tapering columns and reeded splayed legs with bra paw feet, including 2 extra leaves, 144in (369.5cm) extended.
$4,000-5,000

A mahogany twin pedestal dining table, with rounded end sections on turned shafts and splayed legs, 104in (264cm).
$5,000-6,500

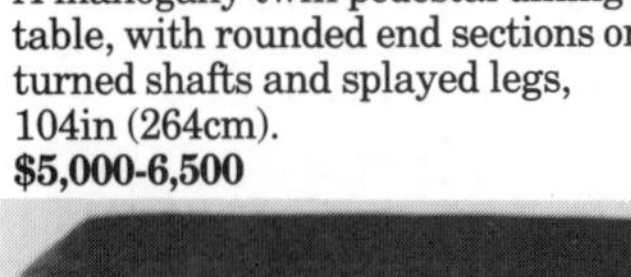

A George III mahogany D-end dining table, with plain veneered arched friezes and on square legs 114in (289.5cm).
$5,500-7,000

A Regency mahogany D-end dining table, with concertina action, on ring turned tapered legs, including 4 modern leaves, 132in (335cm).
$6,500-9,500

A Regency mahogany drop-lea dining table, with 2 detachable leaves on 6 turned tapered legs 66in (167.5cm).
$1,500-2,500

A mahogany D-end 3-pillar dining table, with moulded top on turned supports, basically 19thC, including 2 leaves, 118in (300cm) extended.
$3,000-4,000

Regency mahogany twin pillar ning table, on turned baluster afts and splayed quadripartite ipports, 102in (259cm).
28,000-32,000

A Regency mahogany extending dining table, with panelled frieze and ring turned legs, opening to include 3 further leaves, 94in (239cm) extended.
$6,500-9,000

. Regency mahogany extending ining table, on ring turned legs eaded by roundels, the action amped Wilkinson Patent Ioorfields and Patent 483, opening include 3 further leaves, ıcluding 3 leaves stamped 483, 6in (244cm).
8,000-9,500

Villiam and Thomas Wilkinson of and 10 Broker Row, Moorfields, ondon (1790-1811), specialised in xtending tables.

A mahogany pedestal dining table, the top on triple faceted tapering shafts with reeded collars above concave platform bases with scroll feet, adapted early 19thC, including 2 extra leaves, 12in (284.5cm) extended.
$9,000-10,000

. mahogany dining table, xpanding by means of a band of xtra leaves on 4 ring turned ipports joined by a circular retcher on splayed legs, including leaf cabinet, 84in (213cm) xtended.
1,400-2,000

A William IV mahogany extending dining table, on turned tapered legs, each with a lotus leaf carved collar on brass caps and spooned casters, including 3 extra leaves, 135in (244cm) extended.
$5,000-6,500

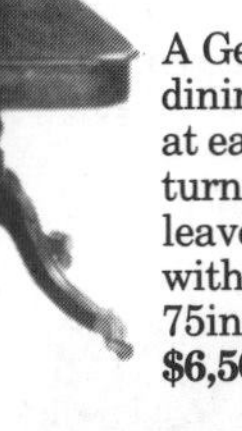

A George IV mahogany 2 pillar dining table, the frieze with tablets at each end, each pedestal with turned shaft lappeted with lotus leaves and 4 downswept legs carved with acanthus, including one leaf, 75in (191cm) extended.
$6,500-7,000

A mahogany D-end dining table, with fluted edge, deep frieze, raised upon reeded turned and tapering supports terminating in brass caps and casters, 19thC, 54in (134cm).
$1,400-2,000

A George IV mahogany 3 part dining table, the top with rounded ends and folding central section, on ring turned tapering legs, 81½in (206cm) extended.
$3,000-5,000

Display Tables

A mahogany bijouterie table, with a velvet lined fully glazed interior, supported on cabriole legs with undertier, early 20thC, 23in (59cm).
$550-650

A Louis XV style ormolu mounted tulipwood vitrine table, enclosed by a hinged lid, on cabriole legs with sabots, 32in (81cm).
$2,500-3,000

Drawleaf Tables

A mahogany drawleaf breakfast table, with boxwood stringing, one side inlaid to simulate 2 drawers, the other fitted with a single drawe flanked by simulated drawers, on square section tapering legs with brass casters, 45½in (115cm) extended.
$1,500-2,500

Dressing Tables

A Regency mahogany dressing table, inlaid with boxwood lines, with mahogany lined divided drawer, on turned tapering reeded legs with foliate carved feet, 32in (81.5cm).
$1,400-2,500

A parquetry and marquetry dressing table, part lined in maroon leather and enclosing 3 compartments, the shaped frieze fitted with 2 end drawers, on cabriole legs, 35in (89cm).
$2,500-3,000

A Victorian walnut dressing table, with swing mirror, on platform ba with 3 small drawers, 39in (99cm).
$1,200-1,400

A Classical gilt stencilled mahogany chest of drawers with dressing mirror, the mirror with a stencilled frame tilting between scrolled supports over a frieze of 3 short drawers, over a stencilled bolection drawer above 2 stencilled long drawers flanked by stencilled columns, on baluster-turned feet, New York, c1830, 37in (94cm) wide.
$3,000-4,000

A late Federal inlaid mahogany dressing table, with 6 drawers, on cylindrical legs with diamond carving and ball feet, 28in (71cm) wide. **$4,000-5,000**

A Queen Anne cherrywood dressin table, the top with moulded edge with one long drawer and 3 short drawers, above a shaped skirt on cabriole legs with pad feet, probabl Connecticut, 19thC, 33½in (85cm) wide.
$3,000-4,000

A George IV mahogany dressing table, the top above frieze drawers and a simulated panelled door flanking a kneehole on ring turned tapering legs, 45½in (115cm).
$1,400-2,000

Federal style mahogany and ırlwood dressing table, some ımage and repairs, 34in (86cm) ide.
1,500-2,500

A Queen Anne mahogany dressing table with thumb moulded rectangular top above one thumb moulded long drawer and 2 short drawers, on cabriole legs with pad feet, 27in (68.5cm) wide.
$10,000-12,000

A Queen Anne cherrywood drop leaf table, the top with 2 drop leaves with cusped corners above a shaped apron, on cabriole legs with pad feet, repair to apron, probably Connecticut, c1750, 44½in (113cm) long.
$2,000-3,000

ropleaf Tables

A Queen Anne cherrywood drop leaf table, with flat arched apron, on cabriole legs with pad feet, Massachusetts, c1750, 36in (91.5cm) wide.
$5,500-6,000

A Chippendale mahogany drop leaf table, with plain apron, on cabriole legs with claw-and-ball feet, Salem, Massachusetts, c1770, 41in (104cm) extended.
$6,000-8,000

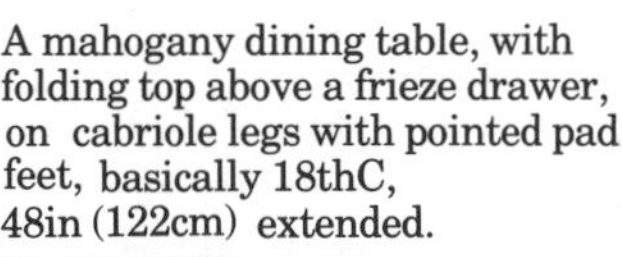

A mahogany dining table, with folding top above a frieze drawer, on cabriole legs with pointed pad feet, basically 18thC, 48in (122cm) extended.
$1,400-2,000

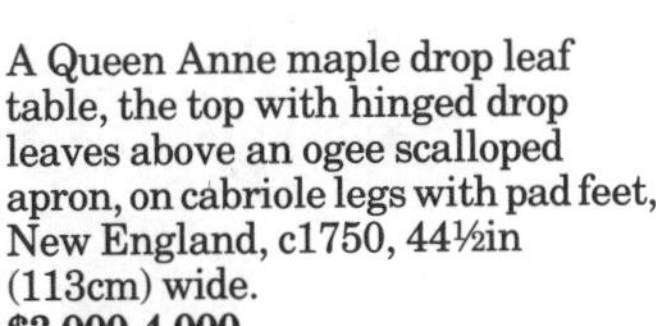

A Queen Anne maple drop leaf table, the top with hinged drop leaves above an ogee scalloped apron, on cabriole legs with pad feet, New England, c1750, 44½in (113cm) wide.
$3,000-4,000

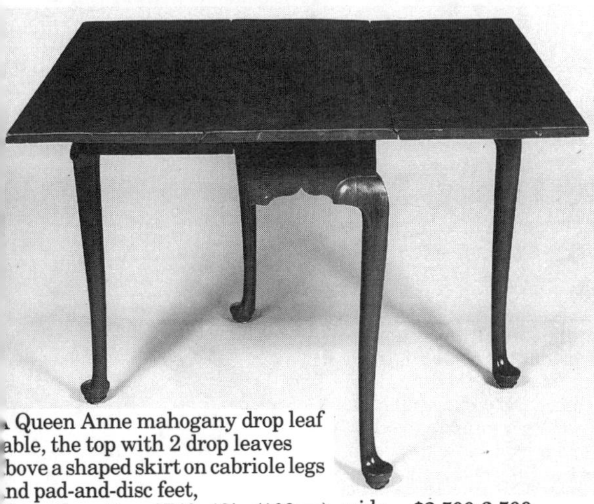

A Queen Anne mahogany drop leaf able, the top with 2 drop leaves bove a shaped skirt on cabriole legs nd pad-and-disc feet, Iassachusetts, c1740, 43in (109cm) wide. **$2,500-3,500**

A Queen Anne cherrywood drop leaf table, the oval top with hinged drop leaves above a plain apron, on turned legs with pad feet, repairs to gates, Massachusetts, c1750, 54in (137cm) extended.
$3,000-4,000

A mid-Georgian mahogany drop-leaf dining table, the twin-flap top on club legs and pad feet, 55in (139.5cm).
$1,500-2,500

A Federal mahogany pedestal bas drop leaf table, the top with D-shaped drop leaves above a concave and reeded apron over a ring turned pedestal, on 4 moulde sabre legs fitted with casters, Bosto or Salem, Massachusetts, c1810, 60½in (153cm) long.
$3,000-5,000

Drum Tables

A George IV mahogany drum library table, with gilt tooled red leatherette inset top, 4 fitted frieze drawers with brass ring handles, on a ring turned centre pillar and reeded quartet base, 48in (122cm).
$6,500-8,000

A Regency walnut drum table, with segmented top and carved border, on cluster column and triform platform support, with claw feet and casters, 29in (74cm).
$3,000-4,000

A Regency style yew wood drum table, the inset leather lined top above a simulated frieze fitted with 2 drawers, on a fluted tapering shaft and scrolling triform base joined with flat cross-stretchers, 24in (62cm).
$800-1,300

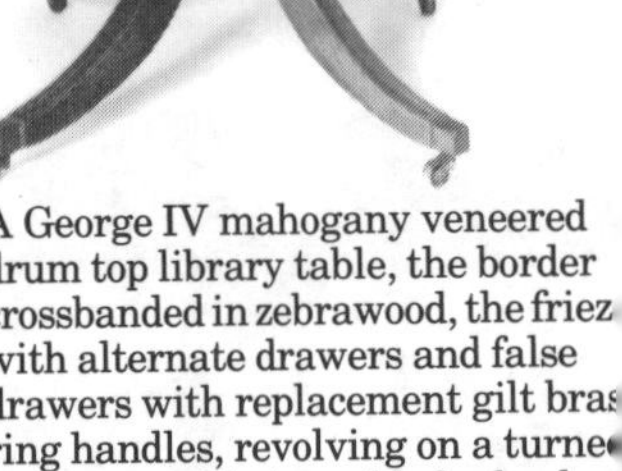

A George IV mahogany veneered drum top library table, the border crossbanded in zebrawood, the friez with alternate drawers and false drawers with replacement gilt bras ring handles, revolving on a turne vase stem with 4 moulded splay leg with brass sabots on casters, 49in (124.5cm).
$5,000-6,500

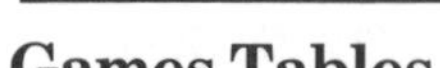

Games Tables

A William IV amboyna games/work table, with a writing easel and an upholstered bowed well, on trestle supports and turned feet, 30½in (80cm).
$2,500-3,000

A coromandel and ebony games table, with half balustrade, the reversible centre inlaid with a chequerboard and enclosing a backgammon board, on ring turn legs joined by stretchers with downcurved feet, 37½in (95cm).
$2,500-3,000

An Edwardian mahogany roulette table, the lift-off top revealing a fitted baize lined interior with roulette wheel and scoop, the shell and scroll carved aprons, on leaf carved slender cabriole supports, 38in (96cm).
$1,200-1,400

Make the Most of Miller's

In Miller's we do NOT just reprint saleroom estimates. We work from realised prices either from an auction room or a dealer. Our consultants then work out a realistic price range for a similar piece. This is to try to avoid repeating freak results – either low or high

ʌ Regency mahogany secrétaire ibrary table, the top with reeded dge, the deep secrétaire drawer vith partly hinged front enclosing a eather lined writing slide with alphabetically inlaid ompartments below, with panelled ngles on reeded tapering legs and rass socket casters, the casters tamped Rotary No. 7168, 43in .09cm).
6,500-8,000

A late Victorian mahogany and inlaid library table, with an inset top, 4 fitted drawers each side with brass handles, raised on 5 shaped square tapering
$2,100-2,500

A Victorian mahogany library writing table, with inset lined coffered top above 6 frieze drawers, on lotus leaf lappeted turned tapering bulbous legs, 72in (182.5cm).
$3,000-5,000

An early Victorian oak library table, with parquetry top, the frieze carved with lunettes and 16thC style portrait roundels and fitted with a drawer, the turned legs with foliate bases and capitals on plinth feet, 54½in (138cm).
$1,500-2,500

A Victorian oak library table, with leather lined top with 6 frieze drawers, on fluted turned tapering legs, 72in (182.5cm).
$1,300-2,000

A Victorian walnut library table, on heavily scrolled and carved supports with decorative stretcher, 54in (137cm).
$1,500-2,500

A Victorian library table, the inset leather lined top above 6 frieze drawers, on square tapering legs, 48in (122cm).
$6,500-7,000

..oo Tables

A Victorian rosewood loo table, the ilt-top with crossbanded decoration supported on a plain hexagonal stem, trefoil base and bun feet, 51in 129.5cm).
$1,200-1,300

A Victorian rosewood loo table, with plain tilt top on an octagonal baluster stem, trefoil base ending in lion paw feet, 50in (127cm).
$800-1,200

Nests of Tables

A nest of 3 mahogany tables, with crossbanded tops on ring turned legs and shaped feet, 19in (48cm).
$1,400-2,000

A nest of Regency burr walnut tables, with inlaid chevron borders, on slender bulbous supports, smallest 13in (33cm).
$3,000-4,000

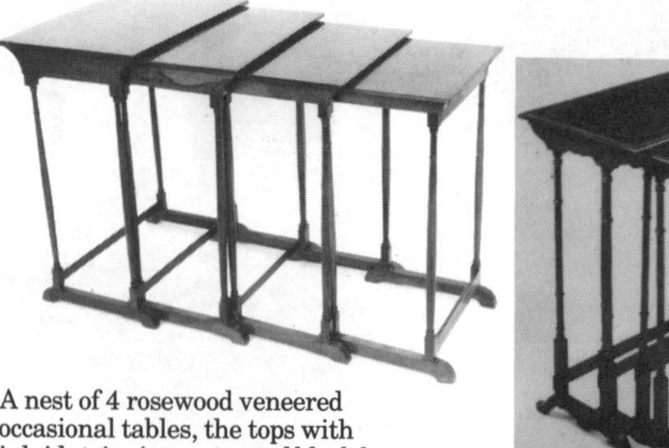

A nest of 4 rosewood veneered occasional tables, the tops with inlaid stringing on turned block legs with stretchered feet, restorations, early 19thC, smallest 15½in (39cm).
$1,400-2,000

A nest of 3 rosewood tables, with moulded top banded in satinwoo on ring turned supports and shap bar feet, 21½in (54cm).
$1,200-1,500

A nest of 4 rosewood tables, each top with a beaded rim, on turned supports and bar feet carved with acanthus scrolls, 19½in (49cm).
$3,000-4,000

A nest of 3 French walnut occasional tables, the tops etched with roundels and with shaped borders, on end standards with turned bun feet, 20in (51cm).
$650-800

A set of 3 rosewood tables, on twi turned tapering column end standards with down curving leg joined by bowed cross stretchers, 23in (59cm).
$2,000-2,500

A nest of 3 Edwardian bowfront mahogany and satinwood crossbanded tables.
$700-800

A nest of Edwardian mahogany occasional tables, decorated with inlaid satinwood crossbanding and boxwood stringing, raised on square tapering legs and understretchers, 25in (64cm).
$1,000-1,100

A nest of 4 mahogany tables.
$700-900

. William IV mahogany breakfast
ıble, the tip-up top with gadrooned
dge and bead moulded frieze, on
ibbed shaft with foliate carved
ocle, the concave sided platform on
ırned feet, associated, 48in
122cm).
3,000-5,000

A Victorian walnut salon table, the tilt-top with quarter-veneered decoration, on a carved bulbous stem and 4 carved scrolling supports, 59in (149.5cm).
$3,000-4,000

A Victorian mahogany pedestal table, with feathered and carved edge and carved triangular pedestal, 31in (79cm).
$2,500-3,000

A Victorian burr walnut pedestal dining table, the crossbanded moulded tilt-top inlaid with amaranth bands, on a carved tapering bulbous column and quadripartite base with scrolled feet, 53in (134.5cm).
$2,500-4,000

A Victorian walnut salon table, the tilt-top with figured quarter-veneer design, bordered with floral marquetry, stringing and crossbanded decoration, bears label for Constantine & Co's. Cabinet & Upholstery Warehouse, 40in (101.5cm).
$3,000-5,000

ʼembroke Tables

. George III mahogany Pembroke
able, the folding top above 2 frieze
rawers, on square tapering legs
oined by a platform cross stretcher,
dapted, 33in (84cm).
ı1,000-1,200

A George III mahogany butterfly Pembroke table, the twin flap top and frieze drawer on square moulded legs and spade feet, 38½in (97cm). **$2,500-3,000**

A Sheraton design satinwood Pembroke table, with rounded fall flaps, the top with broad rosewood band within ebony string lines, 36½in (93cm).
$3,000-4,000

A yew Pembroke table, the top inlaid with batswing stringing and a batswing medallion, with frieze drawers and false drawer, 18thC, 37in (94cm) extended.
$34,000-38,000

A Regency mahogany Pembroke table, with crossbanded twin flap top above a frieze drawer on moulded square tapering legs with brass box feet and casters, early 19thC, 37½in (95cm) wide extended.
$2,000-3,000

A satinwood and polychrome painted Pembroke table, with twin-flap top banded in trailing foliage and centred by an oval depicting 3 fishing putti, with a frieze drawer, on square tapered legs, 40½in (102cm).
$5,000-5,500

A late Federal figured maple and cherrywood Pembroke table, with 2 clover shaped drop leaves above a single drawer with an oval bird's-eye maple reserve over a straight apron, on spirally reeded tapering cylindrical legs and ring turned feet, signed by A. J. Baycock, Brookfield, Madison County, New York, c1820, 42½in (108cm) wide extended.
$4,000-5,000

A Georgian mahogany Pembroke table, with ebony stringing inlay and satinwood crossbanding, single drawer and cylindrical tapered legs.
$800-1,500

A Dutch oak and marquetry Pembroke table, with folding top above a frieze drawer, on cabriole legs with pointed pad feet, early 19thC, 27in (69cm).
$2,500-3,000

A mahogany crossbanded Pembroke table, with drawer, late 19thC.
$900-1,000

A Regency inlaid mahogany Pembroke table, with rosewood banded top, above a frieze drawer on square tapering legs with casters, 32in (81cm).
$4,000-5,000

A Federal inlaid mahogany Pembroke table, the top with 2 drop leaves and line inlay above a bowed line inlay apron flanked by oval inlay paterae, on square tapering legs with bellflower and line inlay with brass casters, Connecticut, c1800, 33in (83.5cm) long.
$6,000-8,000

A Georgian mahogany pedestal Pembroke table, with crossbanded top, single frieze and dummy drawers, on a turned baluster and fluted stem ending in 4 curving legs and brass cap casters, 36in (92cm).
$800-1,000

An Edwardian Sheraton inlaid mahogany Pembroke table, with single drawer , on tapered legs with spade feet, 27in (69cm).
$1,200-1,500

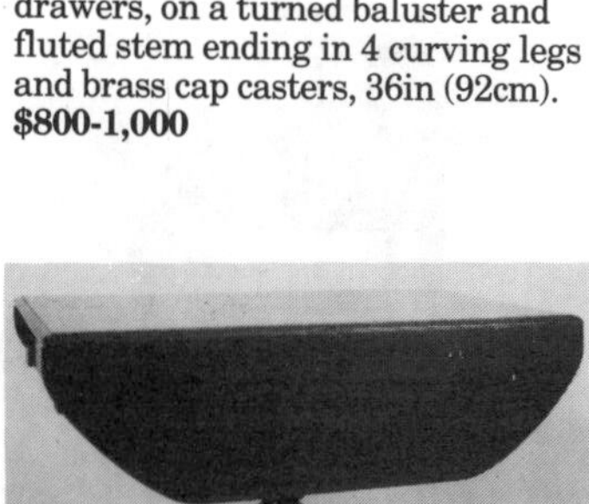

A Regency mahogany Pembroke table, with twin flap top on a ring and baluster turned pedestal, the quadripartite base with cabriole legs on brass paw feet and casters, early 19thC, 39½in (100cm) wide extended.
$2,000-3,000

PEMBROKE TABLES

★ became popular in the mid to late 18thC, possibly designed and ordered by Henry Herbert, the Earl of Pembroke (1693-1751)
★ on early examples the legs were square which are by far the most desirable
★ later tables had turned legs
★ the turned and reeded legs are much less popular
★ those with oval or serpentine tops more desirable
★ flaps should have three hinges
★ rounded flaps and marquetry again increase desirability
★ satinwood was greatly favoured, particularly with much crossbanding and inlay
★ many 18thC Pembroke tables have chamfering on the insides of the legs
★ the Edwardians made many fine Pembroke tables which have been known to appear wrongly catalogued at auction
★ Edwardian tables now in great demand

Classical rosewood marble top ier table, the white marble top bove a straight skirt with gold tencilled banding and applied with rmolu medallion and leafage, bove gilt scrolled supports and a lass plate joined by a medial shelf vith a gilt stencilled guilloche order, on gilt leaf carved feet, narble restored, Philadelphia, :1825, 42in (106.5cm) wide.
8,000-10,000

Classical rosewood marble top ier table, the white marble top bove a straight skirt with brass nlaid banding and applied with rmolu classical figures and lyres, n 2 white marble columns, each vith gilt base and columns and a lass plate flanked by 2 pilasters oined by a medial shelf with brass nlaid stringing, on gilt leaf carved nd lion's paw feet, marble restored, ome damage, New York, c1825, 2½in (108cm) wide.
10,000-12,000

A Victorian walnut Sutherland table on turned standards and legs 34in (86cm).
$700-1,000

A Portuguese walnut centre table with geometrically carved frieze fitted with 2 drawers, on baluster turned legs joined by an H-stretcher, early 18thC, 57in (144.5cm).
$4,000-5,000

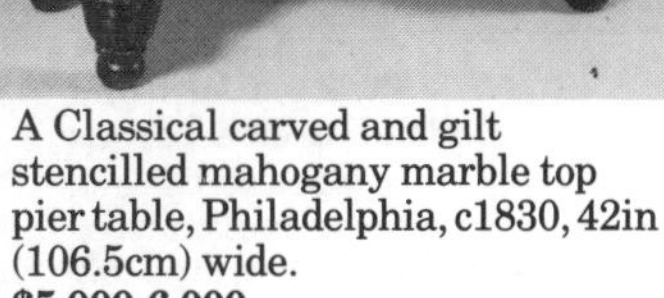

A Classical carved and gilt stencilled mahogany marble top pier table, Philadelphia, c1830, 42in (106.5cm) wide.
$5,000-6,000

A Chippendale mahogany pier table, the top with moulded edge above an apron with bead moulded skirt, on scroll bracketed Marlborough legs with blocked feet, restoration, top possibly not original, Philadelphia, c1770, 43in (109cm) wide.
$5,000-8,000

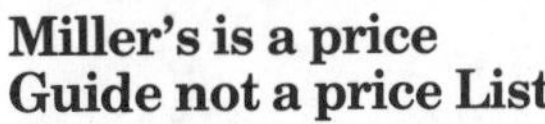

Miller's is a price Guide not a price List

The price ranges given reflect the average price a purchaser should pay for similar items. Condition, rarity of design or pattern, size, colour, provenance, restoration and many other factors must be taken into account when assessing values. When buying or selling, it must always be remembered that prices can be greatly affected by the condition of any piece. Unless otherwise stated, all goods shown in Miller's are of good merchantable quality, and the valuations given reflect this fact. Pieces offered for sale in exceptionally fine condition or in poor condition may reasonably be expected to be priced considerably higher or lower respectively than the estimates given herein

A George II mahogany silver table, the top on square tapering legs headed by later pierced brackets joined by chamfered H-stretchers on block feet, mid-18thC, 37in (94cm) wide.
$6,000-8,000

Reading Tables

A George IV mahogany reading table, with adjustable ratchet, on a baluster turned centre pillar and tripod base, 17½in (45cm).
$1,500-2,500

Serving Tables

A mahogany serving table, wit chamfered square legs headed pierced brackets, 54in (137cm). **$1,400-2,000**

A late Federal carved mahogany serving table, the reeded top with outset rounded corners above cockbeaded short drawers over a long drawer flanked by round reeded pilasters, with baluster supports centering a medial shelf on baluster-and-ring-turned legs, with button feet, New York, c1820, 36in (92cm) wide.
$3,500-4,500

An Irish mahogany serving table, with rope carved borders, on rope carved tapering legs with paw feet, parts early 19thC, 72in (182.5cm).
$5,500-6,500

A George III mahogany serpentine serving table, on square tapering legs, restored, 65in (165cm).
$3,000-4,000

A George III mahogany bowfront serving table, with boxwood stringing, on square tapering legs, inscribed in pen 'This sideboard belongs to Miss Florisida Norman Foyle Cottage, Vicarage Gardens, Clacton-on-Sea', 72in (182cm).
$5,500-6,500

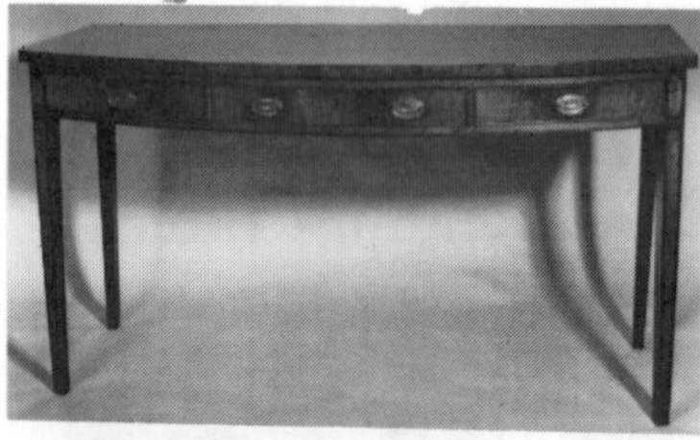

A mahogany serving table, with inlaid panels, late 18thC, 63in (160cm).
$2,500-3,000

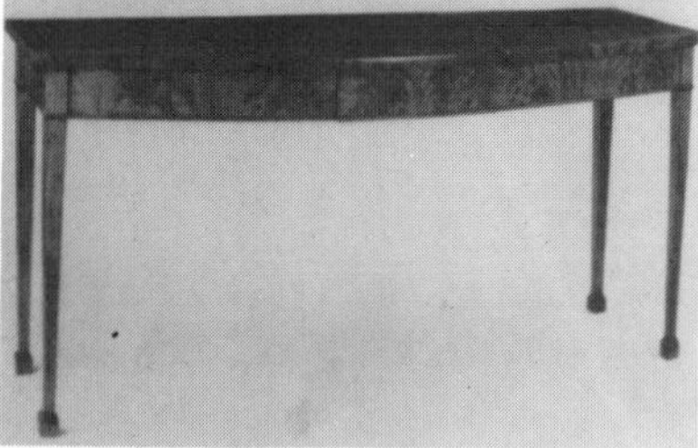

A George III mahogany bowfront serving table, with tablet centred frieze, on square tapering legs and block feet, the brass plaque on back inscribed Humphrey W. Cook Collection, 76½in (194cm).
$5,000-6,500

A Victorian carved mahogany serving table, decorated with a lion mask, supported on a pair of twin reeded legs joined by a platform and standing on acanthus capped scroll feet, by Fras & Jas Smith of Glasgow, 40½in (102cm).
$1,000-1,200

A William IV mahogany D-shaped serving table, with beaded border and frieze carved with vine leaves, on 8 ribbed baluster legs, 141in (358cm).
$8,000-9,000

. mahogany serving table, with lain top, 3 frieze drawers with lion ing brass handles, supported on arved turned and fluted front legs nding in lion paw feet, early 19thC, 5in (216cm).
3,000-4,000

A Victorian pollard oak serving side table, the serpentine top with an oak leaf carved border, above a shaped frieze carved with rockwork scrolls and centred by an armorial motif, on cabochon headed cabriole legs, 93in (236cm).
$2,500-3,000

ide Tables

. pair of neo-classical style atinwood pier tables, painted and ecorated with foliate scrolls and ellflower festoons, the elliptical noulded tops on square tapering egs, 45in (114cm).
2,000-2,500

A walnut side table, the crossbanded top above 2 short and a long frieze drawer, on later cabriole legs with pad feet, 38in (96.5cm).
$650-1,200

A Louis XVI grey painted side table, with eared white marble top above a beaded laurel leaf frieze on turned tapering fluted legs and turned feet, late 18thC, 48in (122cm) wide.
$6,000-8,000

A mahogany, sycamore and narquetry side table, the elliptical op on square tapering legs, asically late 18thC, 48in (122cm).
1,200-1,500

A Federal inlaid mahogany and figured maple sideboard, the top with banded inlay edge above 3 cockbead moulded and bird's-eye maple veneered short drawers over cockbead moulded cupboard doors flanked by similar doors flanked by figured maple panels, on turned tapering reeded legs, with turned feet, labelled in top right drawer, damaged and repaired, labelled by Joseph Rawson and Sons, Providence, Rhode Island, c1805, 58in (147cm) wide.
$10,000-12,000

An Adam style mahogany side table, with harewood inlaid and kingwood crossbanded top, carved fluted frieze, square tapered and fluted legs and moulded feet, 60in (152cm).
$5,000-5,500

An Adam pine side table, with an rched foliate and fleur-de-lys arved frieze on all sides with aterae corners, the fluted square apered legs carved with floral estoon, 42in (106.5cm).
650-800

A George III mahogany serpentine front side table, the top with moulded edge, 3 drawers to the frieze and raised upon square tapering supports, 31in (79cm).
$2,500-3,000

A late George III satinwood side table, inlaid with ebony lines, the D-shaped top crossbanded with tulipwood, with plain frieze on square tapering legs, 40in (102cm).
$5,000-6,500

A Regency mahogany secrétaire side table, the later top above a long writing drawer and 5 small drawers with inset brass handles, flanking a kneehole between quadrant angles on ring turned tapering legs, 39in (99cm). **$1,500-2,500**

A Regency mahogany side table, crossbanded in rosewood, with 2 drawers, on spirally reeded tapering legs, previously fitted with a work basket, 26in (66cm).
$1,500-2,500

A George IV mahogany side table, on plain end standards united by a turned centre stretcher, on reeded splayed supports, 31in (79cm).
$800-1,500

A Dutch walnut and foliate marquetry side table, decorated with birds and a flower-filled urn, with later mirror fitments, the frieze with 2 drawers with a shaped apron, on shell carved cabriole legs and claw-and-ball feet, 18thC, 27in (69cm).
$5,000-6,500

A Louis XVI mahogany and kingwood side table, with crossbanded top centred by a later floral marquetry oval, the panelle frieze fitted with a drawer, on square tapering legs, Franco Flemish, 25½in (64.5cm).
$3,000-5,000

A Victorian rosewood and walnut side table, with segmented veneered top decorated with mother-of-pearl and inlaid with harewood and satinwood marquetry, above an acanthus banded frieze, fitted with 2 small drawers, on guilloche and foliate carved tapering bulbous end standards with scrolling splayed legs, 53in (134.5cm).
$6,500-8,000

A gilt metal and rosewood side table, with acanthus banded supports, mirror back and plinth base, 45in (114cm).
$2,500-3,000

A white painted and brass mounted bowfront side table, with green speckled scagliola top and plain frieze, on 5 square conforming marbled legs and block feet, 63½in (162cm).
$1,500-2,500

Silver Tables

A mahogany silver table, with fret blind outlines, with galleried top, o chamfered square moulded legs with Marlborough block feet, 32½i (82cm).
$1,000-1,400

A George III flame mahogany Lancashire longcase clock, signed Henry Fisher, Preston, 101in (257cm) high.
$9,500-13,000

A George III mahogany longcase clock, signed Peter Fearnley, Wigan, 96in (244cm) high.
$12,000-15,000

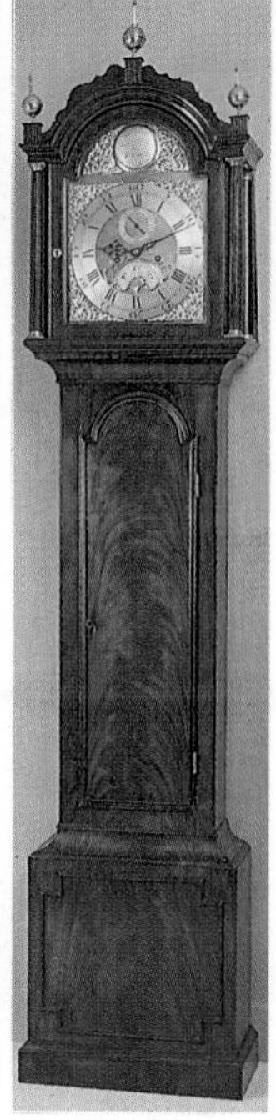

A mahogany 8-day longcase clock, by Wm. Hornsey, Exon, with a large date aperture, c1790.
$9,500-13,000

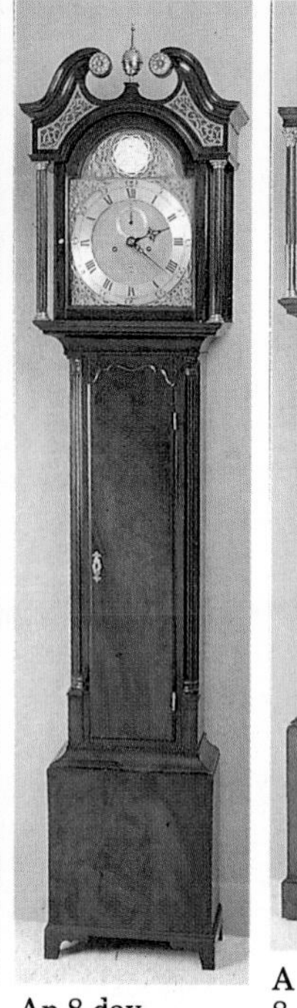

An 8-day longcase clock, east coast of Scotland, signed in the arch by John Memess Johnshaven, c1775, 87in (221cm) high.
$9,500-13,000

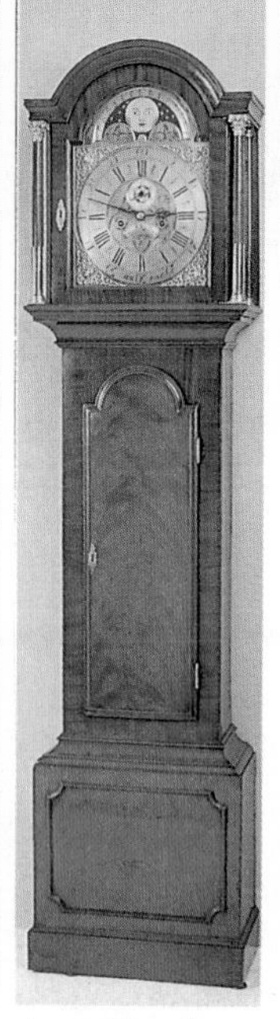

A small mahogany 8-day longcase clock, signed Dolly Rollisson of Halton, c1785, and numbered 479, 78in (198cm) high.
$9,500-13,000

An 8-day mahogany longcase clock signed by Samuel Shepl of Stockport, c1780, 82in (208cm) high.
$11,000-14,00

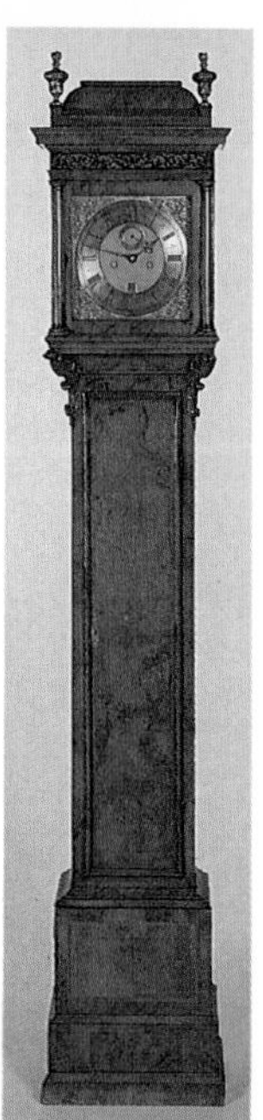

A burr walnut Queen Anne longcase clock, by Tho. Tompion, 92in (234cm) high.
$40,000-50,000

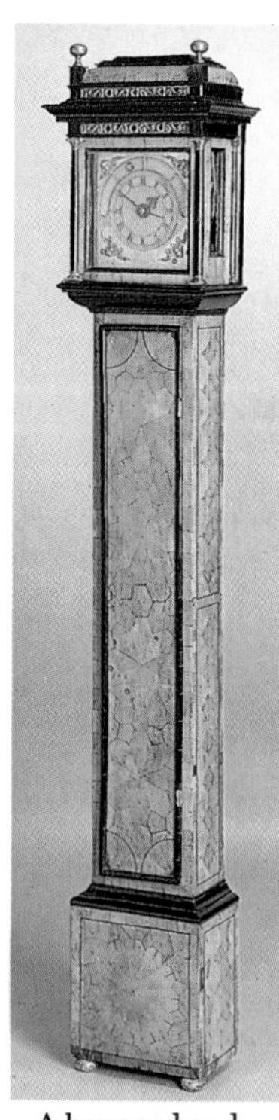

A boxwood and ebony parquetry, longcase clock, by Tho. Tompion, c1679, 73in high.
$1,200,000+

A Federal inlaid mahogany longcase clock, signed by Andrew Billings, New York, c1805, some repairs and minor in-painting to dial.
$14,000-18,000

A Federal inlaid cherrywood longcase clock, dial signed Caleb Davis, Virginia, with restored feet, dial chipped, c1804.
$8,000-12,000

A Chippendale mahogany longcase clock, by Thomas Harland, Connecticut, c1780, 92in (234cm) high.
$7,000-9,500

A Federal mahogany longcase clock signed by Joakim Hill, New Jersey, c1805, 101in (256cm) high.
$16,000-25,00

DIGBETH STREET, STOW-ON-THE-WOLD,
CHELTENHAM, GLOUCESTERSHIRE, GL54 1BN
Telephone: (0451) 30236

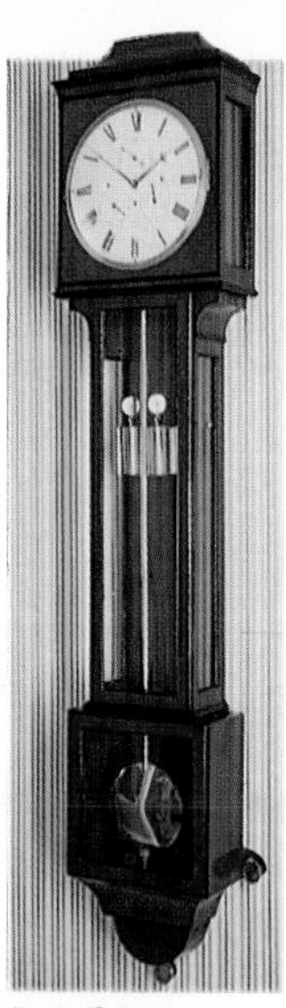

A striking Viennese regulator, by Brandl in Wien, c1811, 57in (144.5cm) high. **$50,000-65,000**

Three Viennese regulators, c1835, l. **$6,500-8,000,** c. **$4,000-5,500,** r. **$32,000-40,000**

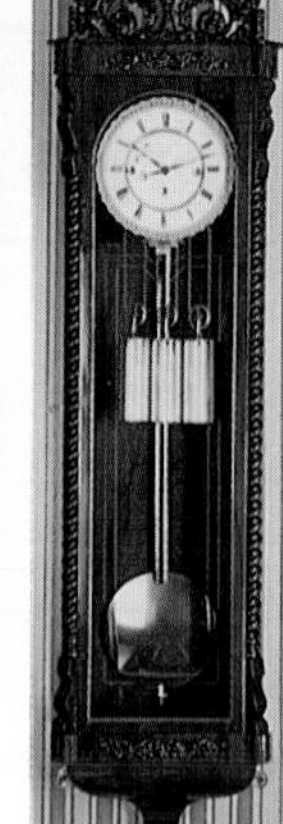

l. A Viennese grande sonnerie striking regulator, c1850, 50in high. **$9,000-10,000**

l. A George IV longcase regulator, by Brownbill, Liverpool. **$16,000-20,0**

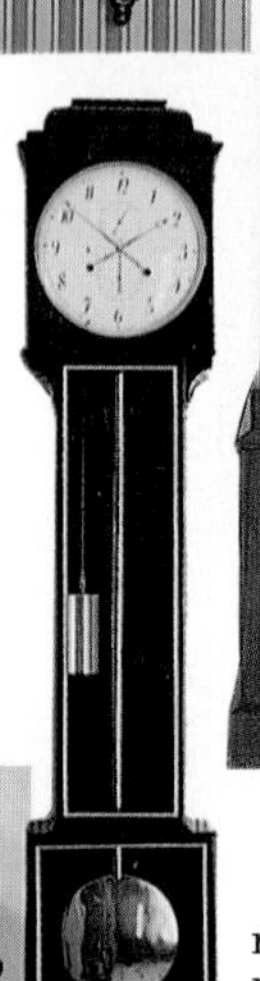

r. A Viennese regulator, by Brandl in Wien, c1811, 57in (144.5cm) long. **$40,000-50,000**

r. A Charles II month-going longcase clock, some alteration, 84in (213cm). **$20,000-25,000**

A walnut and panelled floral marquetry longcase clock, by Stephen Asselin, c1705, 85in (216cm) high. **$22,000-30,000**

A panelled marquetry longcase clock, with 8-day count wheel striking movement with latched pillars, by Wm. Garfoot, c1690. **$32,000-40,000**

An oak longcase clock by William Wall, Richmond, late 18thC. **$4,000-5,500**
Above r. A grandmother clock by John Carter of London, 1775, 69½in (176cm). **$15,000-17,000**
r. A longcase clock by Robert Dingley of London, late 17thC, 81in (205.5cm). **$9,500-11,000**

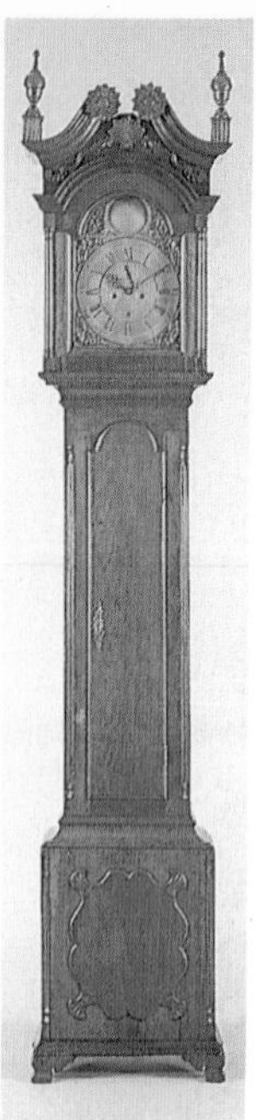

A Chippendale carved cherry-wood longcase clock, c1770, restorations.
$25,000-30,000

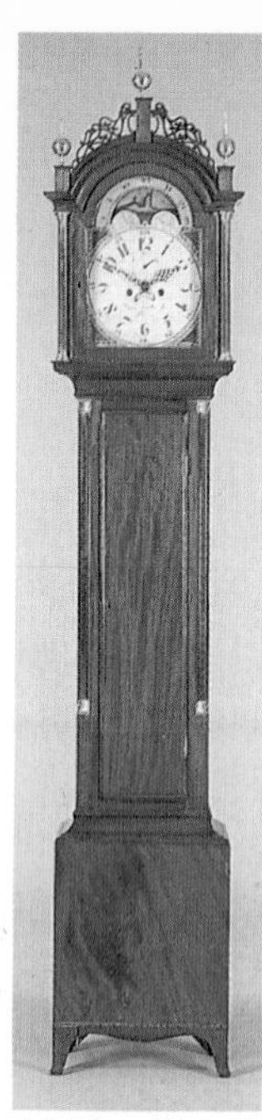

A Federal inlaid mahogany long-case clock, by Aaron Willard Jr., Boston, c1805, 100½in (255cm).
$25,000-30,000

A Federal inlaid mahogany long-case clock, by Aaron Willard Jr., Boston, slight damage, restored, c1805, 91in (231cm).
$45,000-50,000

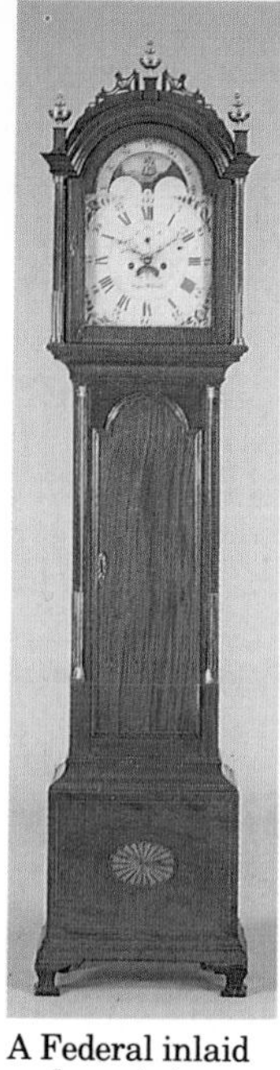

A Federal inlaid mahogany long-case clock by Simon Willard, Roxbury, Mass., c1810, 92in (233.5cm) high.
$55,000-60,000

A Dutch burr walnut longcase clock with planisphere, slight damage, mid-18thC, 116in (294.5cm).
$65,000-70,000

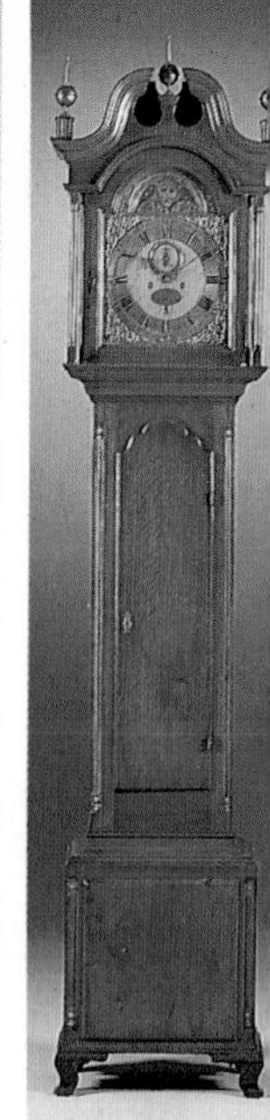

A Chippendale carved mahoga longcase clock by John Wood, Philadelphia, paint heightene on lunar dial, c1770, 96in (243.5cm) high.
$20,000-25,000

A Scandinavian longcase clock dated 1811.
$2,500-3,000

A Regency bronze and ormolu mounted clock, by George Bullock, 16in (40cm) high.
$22,000-26,000

Above. A Regency mantel clock by Vulliamy, in later case, inscribed Vulliamy, London 863, 16in (41cm) high.
$3,000-4,000

A Louis XV ormolu mantel clock, signed Charles Voisin à Paris, mid-18thC, 15½in (40cm) high.
$25,000-32,000

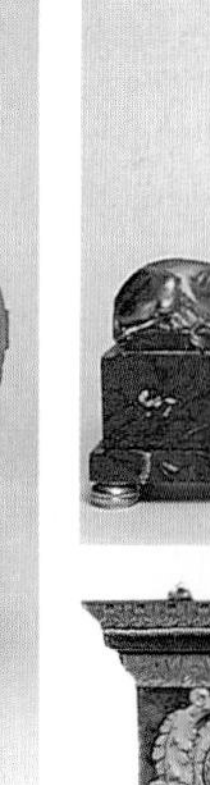

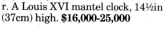

An Empire mantel clock, c1810. **$13,000-16,000**
l. An Empire mantel clock, signed Knab à Paris, 22in (56cm) wide.
$9,500-16,000
r. A Louis XVI mantel clock, 14½in (37cm) high. **$16,000-25,000**

ı George III musical
racket clock.
11,000-14,000

A late George III mahogany and ebony quarter chiming and Dutch hour striking calendar equation bracket clock.
$8,000-13,000

A Louis XIV cartel clock, 17½in (44cm) high.
$8,000-13,000

A French gilt metal mantel clock, late 19thC, 20in (51cm) high.
$500-650

ı Neuchatel musical calendar
racket clock.
20,000-22,000

A Dutch ebony veneered striking bracket clock, 15½in (39cm) high.
$9,500-13,000
r. A Louis XV bracket clock and bracket, signed Gudin À Paris.
$5,000-7,000

An early Louis XV bracket clock.
$6,500-9,500
Far l. A Charles II longcase clock.
$18,000-22,000
l. A panelled marquetry long-case clock.
$28,000-32,000

A Règence bracket clock, G. I. Champion.
$16,000-25,000
l. A Louis XV bracket clock.
$8,000-11,000

A George III ebonised striking bracket clock, signed, 17in (43cm) high.
$7,000-8,000

A fusee bracket clock, early 19thC.
$5,000-5,500

l. A Regency mahogany brack clock, the dial inscribed Wasbrough Hal and Co., Bristol.
$1,500-2,500

r. An Edwardian oak mantel clock, 3 train movement with Westminster chimes on 8 bells and gong, 25in (64cm) high.
$1,500-2,500

A George III mahogany striking bracket clock, 19½in (50cm) high.
$5,500-6,500

A George III scarlet japanned musical bracket clock, by Wm. Kipling, London, 25in (64cm) high.
$45,000-53,000

A Charles II ebony striking bracket clock, by Joseph Knibb, London, signed, restored, 15in (38.5cm) high. **$25,000-32,000**

A Charles II ebony bracket clock by Joseph Knibb, London, signed, escapement rebuilt, 11½in (29cm) high.
$30,000-32,000

r. A Charles II ebonised striking bracket clock, by Joseph Knibb, London, signed, restoration, 13in (33cm) high.
$32,000-40,000

A George III tortoiseshell musical bracket clock by Markwick Markhan London, 13in (33cm) high.
$25,000-32,000

A Regency mantel clock by Vulliamy, marked, 9½in (24cm). **$6,500-8,000**

A Napoleon III ormolu and bronze mantel clock, the movement within a blue enamelled globe, 23in (58.5cm). **$3,000-4,000**

A Louis Philippe portico mantel clock, signed Hry Marc À Paris, 17in (43cm) high. **$3,000-4,000**

A Louis XVI calendar clock, signed Bouchet à Paris. **$7,000-8,000**

An Empire ormolu mounted burr elm portico clock, dial and backplate signed, 18in (46cm). **$4,000-5,000**

A French 'swinging clock', the dial signed Breguet et Fils, 22½in (57cm) high. **$13,500-14,000**

l. A George II giltwood cartel clock, the dial signed, later movement, cover and eagle, 34½in (88cm) high. **$3,000-4,000**

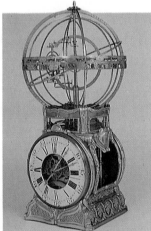

An orrery clock in glazed ormolu case above a bombé kingwood stand, c1770, 95in (241cm) high overall. **$960,000+**

l. An 'Around the World' clock. **$1,000-1,200**

An automaton magician in giltwood case below clock, 33in (84cm) high. **$7,000-9,000**

A Louis XVI ormolu and white marble clock, the dial signed, regilded. **$5,000-8,000**

r. A Louis XVI ormolu mounted porcelain mantel clock, the porcelain French, 19thC, 17½in (44.5cm) high. **$65,000-70,000**

A French spelter figural clock, 22½in (57cm). **$550-700**

A Charles X ormolu and bronze mantel clock, 1827, 26½in (68cm) high. **$3,000-5,000**

An ormolu mounted and Chinese porcelain mantel clock, 19thC, later movement. **$5,500-7,000**

An ormolu and marble mantel clock, with restorations, early 19thC, 18½in (47cm) high. **$2,000-2,500**

A neo-classical urn clock, 19thC, 23in (59cm) high. **$30,000-32,000**

r. A Napoleon III ormolu mantel clock, 21in (53cm). **$3,000-5,000**

A Louis XVI ormolu urn clock, the pedestal inset with marble, 16in (41cm) high. **$32,000-40,000**

An ormolu bronze table clock of Louis XVI design, 30in (76cm **$5,500-6,500**

l. A French ormolu and bronze matched clock garniture, mid-19thC, the clock 16in (41cm). **$9,000-10,000**

n enamelled gold keyless
ıronograph with perpetual
ılendar, signed J.W.
enson, London, No. 25069,
381, 5.5cm diam.
$5,000-70,000

A gold pair case
quarter repeating watch,
1773, later dial, 5cm.
$7,000-10,000
l. A minute repeating,
full calendar keyless
hunter pocket watch,
small chips to enamel.
$8,000-16,000

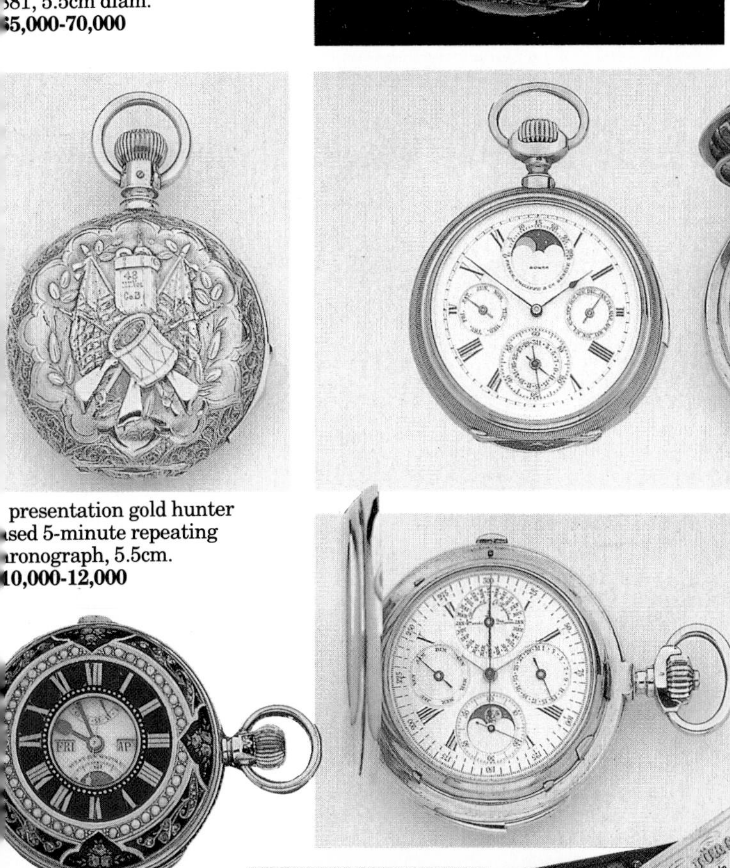

presentation gold hunter
ısed 5-minute repeating
ıronograph, 5.5cm.
10,000-12,000

A gold minute
repeating watch, signed
Patek Philippe, 1888.
$110,000-120,000
l. A Swiss gold hunter
chronograph, c1880.
$32,000-40,000

n enamelled half
unter gem set watch.
16,000-20,000
A pendant watch and
ıain by Patek Philippe.
4,000-5,000

l. An enamelled world
time watch, signed Patek
Philippe & Co.
$70,000-78,000
r. A presentation set of
chronograph and small
minute repeating watch.
$45,000-50,000

A rare early gold chronograph, by Patek Philippe, Genève, No. 860358, 18ct gold case, inscribed 1938. **$32,000-40,000**

Three circular wristwatches, one in 14ct gold case, the others gold filled, all signed Otto K. Kramer, Chicago. **$650-800**

An 18ct gold wrist chronograph with perpetual calendar, by Patek Philippe Genève, No. 863678 18ct strap, c1945. **$110,000-150,000**

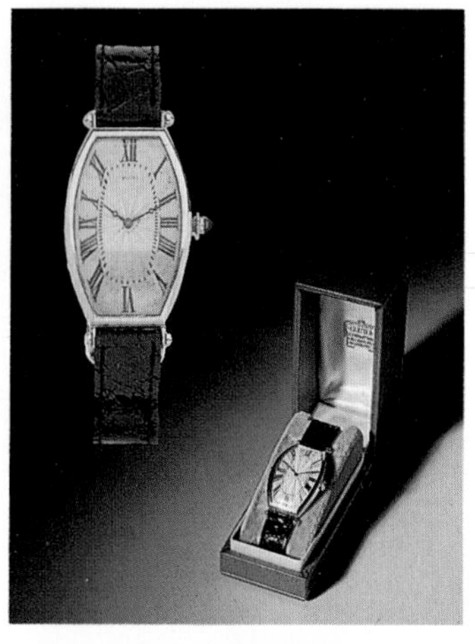

A gold jump hour time-zone wristwatch, signed Patek Philippe, Genève, No. 729422, 18ct case and buckle to leather strap, c1960. **$65-85,000**
r. A rare 18ct gold gentleman's curved wristwatch, with sapphire winding crown, signed Cartier, 24112/25881, c1933. **$24,000-26,000**

A George III mahogany baromete by George Adams with glazed door enclosing an engraved silver dial, inscribed, 37in (94.5cm). **$26,000-30,000**

A Louis XV kingwood barometer, with enamel dial, signed C. Bousson, the case and thermometer inscribed J. Bettally, restorations, c1771, 46in (117cm) high. **$30,000-32,000**

A French ormolu mounted mahogany barometer and clock, inscribed, 61in (155cm). **$20,000-22,000**
r. A Dutch brass theodolite signed J.M Kleman & Zoon Fecerunt, Amsterdam, c1800, 14½in (36.8cm). **$6,500-8,000**

A brass 4½in reflecting telescope, unsigned, mahogany case, 18thC, 27in (73cm). **$4,000-5,500**

A rare French lacquered brass 'Achromatique Universal' horizontal microscope of Charles Chevalier pattern but signed Lerebours et Secretan à Paris, with original accessories in fitted mahogany cabinet, 19thC, 17in (43.2cm) wid **$14,000-18,000**

Persian brass astrolabe, gned 'Made by Hājjī ılī', c1790, 3½in (8cm) ıam.
21,000-25,000

. French silver ıal, signed Butterfield, aris, 18thC, 3½in (8.5cm), ı fish skin case.
2,500-3,000

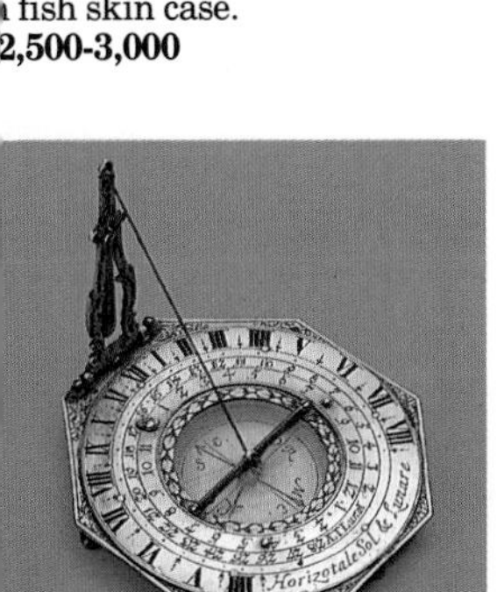

ı German silver and gilt rass horizontal dial, ıgned, 3in (8cm).
5,500-8,000

ı lecture galvanometer, 9thC, 10½in (26cm), ı fitted case.
1,000-1,500

l. A mariner's brass astrolabe, the scale divided into 4 quadrants, the alidade with 2 pin-hole sights, 17thC, 9in (23cm) diam. **$3,000-4,000**

A German painted fruitwood polyhedral dial, with 3 wire gnomons and 12 dials, 18thC, 8in (20cm) high.
$3,000-5,000

An Italian Copernican armillary sphere.
$5,500-7,000
Below. A large twin-plate machine.
$2,500-3,000

An English and gilded brass equinoctial ring dial, signed, late 18thC.
$40,000-50,000

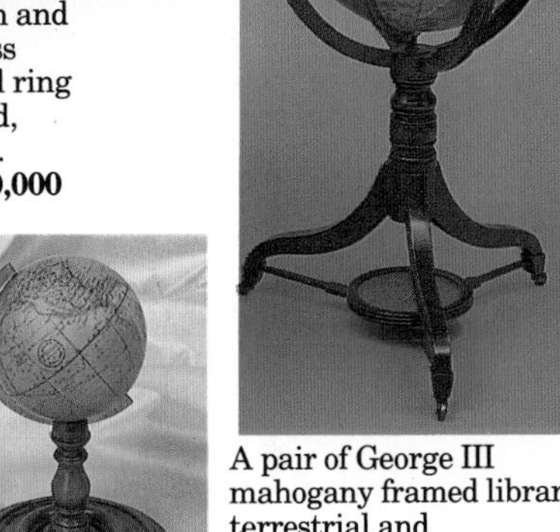

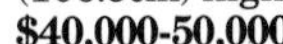

A pair of George III mahogany framed library terrestrial and celestial globes, with brass scales, 42in (106.5cm) high.
$40,000-50,000

A pair of table globes, early 19thC.
$5,500-6,500

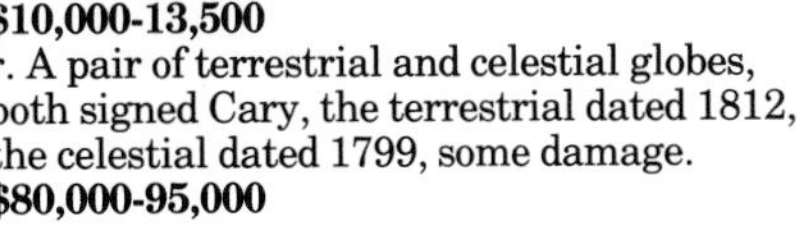

A pair of Regency table globes, by Cary, the terrestrial globe dated 1820, celestial globe 1815, 13½in (34cm) high.
$10,000-13,500
r. A pair of terrestrial and celestial globes, both signed Cary, the terrestrial dated 1812, the celestial dated 1799, some damage.
$80,000-95,000

A Victorian parcel gilt copy of The Howard ewer and basin, by Frederick Elkington, Birmingham, 1875, basin 18in (46cm) diam, 85oz.
$8,000-16,000

r. A German parcel gilt tankard, indistinct marks, c1600, 1,160kg.
$100,000-110,000

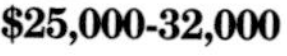

A George II bread basket, engraved with coat-of-arms, by Robert Brown, 1740, 11½in (29.5cm) diam, 50oz.
$25,000-32,000

A rare cake basket by van Voorhis & Schanck, New York, c1792, 13½in (35cm) wide, 34oz.
$60,000-73,000

A George II shaped oval bread basket, by Eliza Godfrey, 1744, 13½in (34cm) long, 53oz.
$21,000-25,000

A pair of William III candlesticks, by Philip Rollos, 1697, 5in (12cm), 14oz.
$20,000-25,000

A silver and glass punch bowl, Gorham, Providence, marked, 1893, 16in (41cm) diam, 352oz gross.
$25,000-30,000

A Queen Anne monteith by Robert Timbrell, 1705, repairs, 13in (33cm) diam, 92oz. **$32,000-40,000**

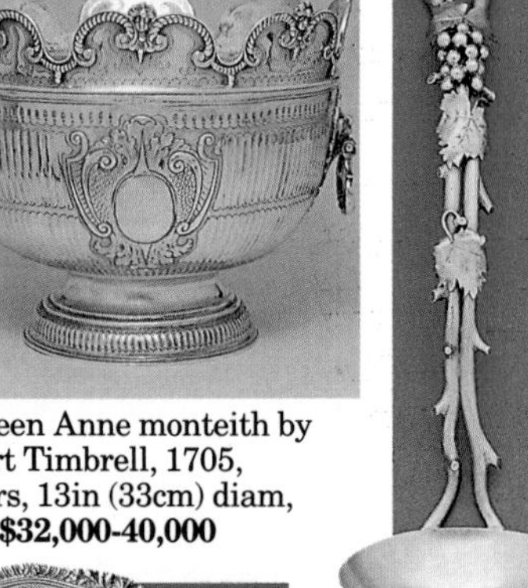

An American punch ladle, marked sterling, c1855, 11in (28cm), 7½oz.
$2,500-3,000

A pair of Georg II candlesticks, with detachabl nozzles, engraved twice with a crest, by Peter Taylor 1741, 8½in (21.5cm), 45oz.
$32,000-40,000

A George I monteith, with detachable rim, by John East, 1718, 10in (25cm) diam, 52oz.
$26,000-32,000

A set of 12 George IV dinner plates, by Paul Storr, 1820, 10in (26.5cm) diam, 284oz.
$40,000-50,000

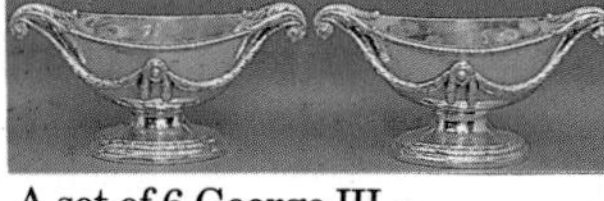

A set of 6 George III sauceboats, by Sir William Chambers, 1768, 169oz.
$32,000-40,000

A sauceboat by Joseph Lownes, c1785. **$16,000-20,000**
l. A William and Mary snuffer stand with a pair of matching candle snuffers. **$32,000-40,000**

A George III silver presentation wine cooler, 1806, 144oz. **$25,000-30,000**

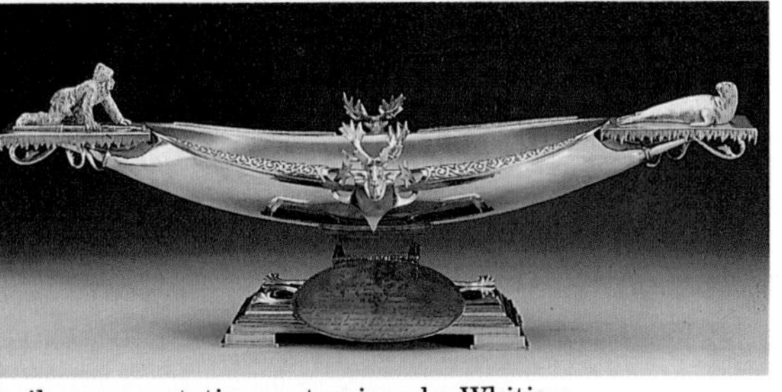

A silver presentation centrepiece, by Whiting Manufacturing Company, marked, c1873, 24½in (62cm) wide, 78oz. **$18,000-20,000**

A silver tureen and stand. **$26,000-30,000**

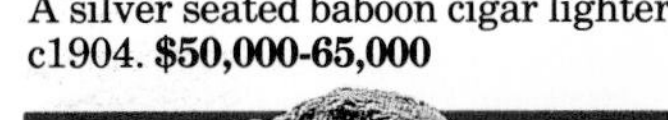

l. A George III silver tea urn, by Paul Storr, London, fully marked, c1809, 14in (35cm) high, 126oz. **$18,000-25,000**

A silver seated baboon cigar lighter, c1904. **$50,000-65,000**

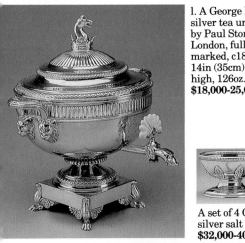

A set of 4 George II silver salt cellars. **$32,000-40,000**

A pair of George II silver two-handled soup tureens and covers, 1752, 13in (33cm) long, 196oz. **$40,000-50,000**

l. A pair of William IV silver wine coolers, with removable liners, c1830, Sheffield, marked, 14in (35cm) high, 176oz. **$40,000-50,000**

A set of 4 George III silver sauce tureens, 6in (15cm) high, 93oz. **$25,000-32,000**

l. A Continental shaving set, comprising: 6 razors, a mirror, comb, stone strop and pair of later scissors, c1740. **$6,500-9,500**

A George III Irish epergne, by Joseph Jackson, Dublin, 1791, fitted with 8 cut glass ewers, 4 casters with pierced covers, 1 broken, a central and 4 smaller baskets, 1 repaired, wood base on casters, fully marked, 23in (58cm) wide, 72oz. **$13,000-16,000**

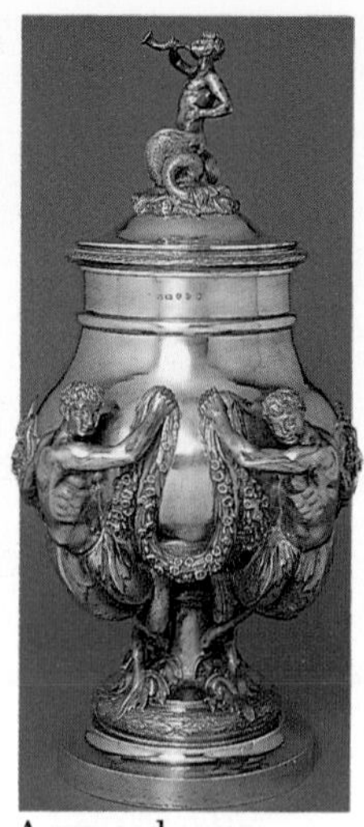

A cup and cover J. Garrard, 1882, 28in (72cm), 448oz. **$18,000-25,000**

A George III tea urn, by Paul Storr, 1816, engraved with coat-of-arms and crest, tap with fluted ivory knob, fitted with liner and cover, 15in (38cm) high, 200oz gross. **$21,000-25,000**

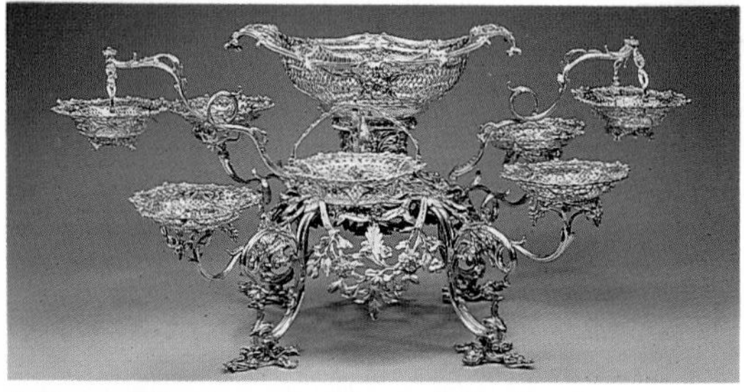

A George III epergne, by Thomas Pitts, London, 1765, 3 hanging baskets 1767 and one 1769, marked on frame, central dish, baskets and four branches, 31in (79cm) wide, 229oz. **$35,000-40,000**

A George II Irish four-branch epergne, by Robert Calderwood, Dublin, c1750, 14in (35.5cm) high, 155oz. **$32,000-40,000**

l. A George III epergne, by Thomas Pitts, 1781, 15in (38cm) high, 111oz. **$11,000-14,000**
r. A Danish soup tureen, cover and stand by Julius Diderichsen, Copenhagen, 1864, 18in (47cm), 190oz. **$12,000-15,000**

A rare teapot, the base engraved "EPL" probably initials of original owners Philip Lansing and Elsje Hun, married Albany 1757, and "IAH", unmarked, New York, c1750, 8in (21cm) high, 24.5oz gross. **$16,000-18,000**

A George II coffee pot, by John Swift, London, 1739, marked, 11½in (29cm), 54oz gross. **$60,000-65,000**

A George II kettle, stand and lamp, by Christian Hillan, 1740, 82oz gross. **$6,500-9,500**

An enamelled and stone set gold match safe, by Tiffany for the 1889 Paris Exposition, marked, 1.2oz.
$9,000-12,000
r. An 18ct gold statue of Henri IV of France, 19thC, 4in (10cm) long, gold, 394gr.
$9,000-9,500

A late Victorian 18ct gold cup and cover, by Sebastian Garrard, inscribed 'Won by Santoi, Ascot 1901', 25½in (65cm) high, 143oz.
$73,000-80,000

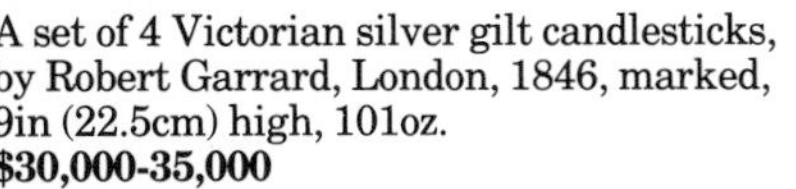

A set of 4 Victorian silver gilt candlesticks, by Robert Garrard, London, 1846, marked, 9in (22.5cm) high, 101oz.
$30,000-35,000

A George III inscribed goblet, mark 'R.B.' may be Robert Burton, c1780, 5½in (14cm), 7oz. 218gr.
$95,000-100,000

A Napoleon III silver gilt tea and coffee service, mark PQ, Paris 1860, 71oz gross.
$20,000-25,000

A pair of George III silver-gilt tureens by Paul Storr, 1805, 52oz.
$14,000-18,000

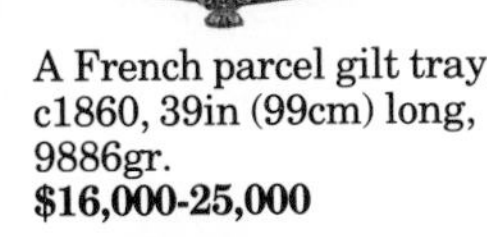

A French parcel gilt tray, c1860, 39in (99cm) long, 9886gr.
$16,000-25,000

A silver-gilt vase by Tiffany, small repair, marked, c1885, 8in (20cm) high, 10oz.
$6,500-9,500

A parcel gilt presentation punch bowl and ladle, inscribed, by Gorham, Providence, 1871, marked 'Sterling', 12in (30cm) high, 103oz.
$25,000-30,000

A set of 12 parcel gilt butter dishes, by Gorham, Providence, 1879, marked, each 3in (8cm) square, 13oz. **$10,000-12,000**

A pair of Louis XVI style ormolu chenets, mid-19thC, 26in (66.5cm) high.
$20,000-25,000

l. A pair of Louis XVI style ormolu and rose agate covered urns, 19thC, 17½in (44.5cm) high.
$7,000-8,000

A pair of Empire ormolu urns, attributed to Gérard-Jean Galle, c1820, 22½in high.
$45,000-50,000

An Empire ormolu surtout-de-table, stamped Thomire à Paris, 117in (297cm) long.
$40,000-50,000

A pair of Louis XVI style chenets, signed Henri Dasson 1885, 9in (22.5cm) high.
$10,000-15,000

An ormolu inkstand, mid-19thC, 17½in (44cm) wide.
$2,500-3,000

A pair of Louis XI V style pedestals, restorations, 53½in. **$28,000-32,000**

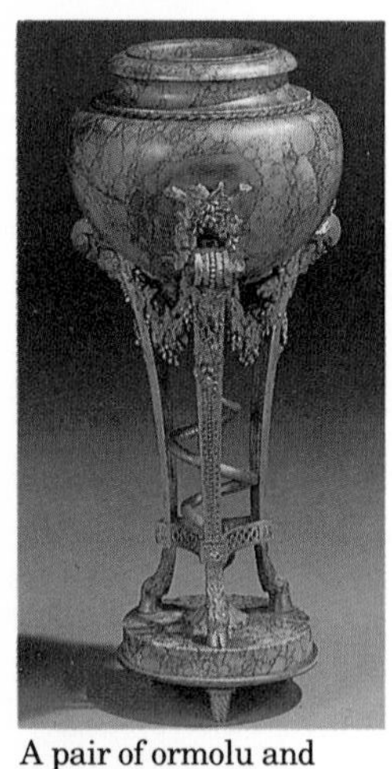

A pair of ormolu and marble brûle parfums, 20in (51cm) high.
$16,000-25,000

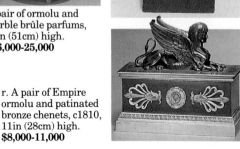

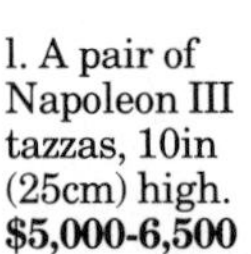

l. A pair of Napoleon III tazzas, 10in (25cm) high.
$5,000-6,500

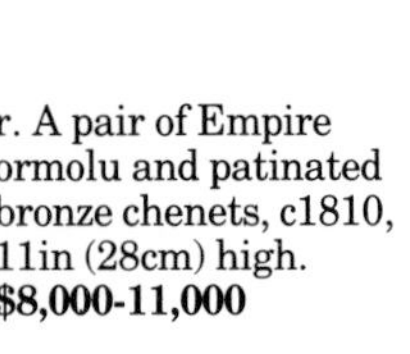

r. A pair of Empire ormolu and patinated bronze chenets, c1810, 11in (28cm) high.
$8,000-11,000

An Empire ormolu surtout-de-tabl
25in (63.5cm) diam.
$14,000-20,000

Paduan bronze Judith ith head of Holophernes, om the Workshop of evero da Ravenna, early 6thC, 7½in (19cm). **4,000-20,000**

A Venetian bronze figure of Bacchus, c1600, 12½in (32cm). **$30,000-40,000**

A Neapolitan bronze of Narcissus, with removable fig leaf, signed and inscribed, c1887, 24½in (63cm). **$40,000-50,000**

A Venetian bronze allegory of peace, base damaged, 16thC, 21in (54cm). **$21,000-25,000**

bronze cast of a nymph and satyr, fter Giambologna, heavily cast, ectangular marble pedestal, 17thC, by 12in (20 by 30cm). **16,000-20,000**

A French bronze, Rape of Proserpine, damaged, 18thC, 23in (59cm). **$14,000-18,000**

A pair of Empire candelabra, 45½in (116cm). **$200-210,000**

A pair of bronze urns, with twin swan's mask scrolling foliate handles, signed Heizler, 21in (53cm). **$8,000-9,500**

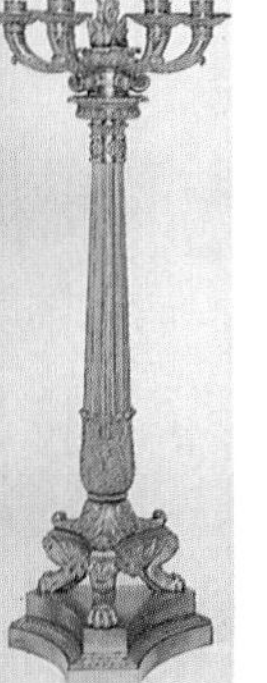

pair of Charles X ix-light ormolu andelabra, with flaming nials, 30½in (77.5cm). **6,500-9,500**

bove r. A pair of rmolu candlesticks, after .-D. Dugourc, 13in 33cm). **$16,000-20,000**

. A Venetian edarwood torchère, by Valentino Besarel, signed, ate 19thC, 69in (174cm). **28,000-32,000**

A Florentine ebony and pietra dura casket, mid-19thC, 20½in (52cm) wide. **$50,000-58,000**

A French bronze bust of an Egyptian harem girl, mid-19thC, 14½in (38cm) high. **$8,000-13,000**

Laurent, a Susse Frères 2-coloured bronze bust, signed, 23in (59cm). **$3,000-5,000**

A Florentine bronze group, early 18thC. **$20,000-25,000**

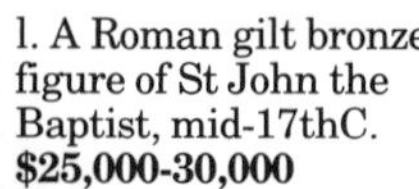

l. A Roman gilt bronze figure of St John the Baptist, mid-17thC. **$25,000-30,000**

A French bronze figure, by Christophe-Gabriel Allegrain, 18thC. **$65,000-80,000**

Gaudez, a bronze figure of a sword mender, 21in high. **$1,500-3,000**

Muller, a bronze figur
$2,500-4,000

Above l. Picault, a bronze figure. **$2,500-4,000**

A German life-size bronze statue, cast from a model by Arthur Lewin-Funcke, early 20thC. **$30,000-32,000**

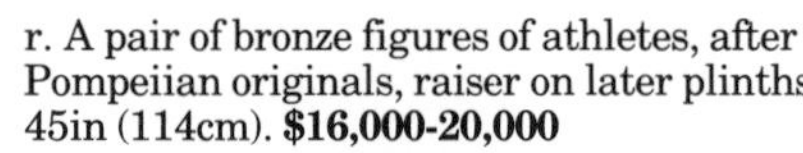

r. A pair of bronze figures of athletes, after Pompeiian originals, raiser on later plinths, 45in (114cm). **$16,000-20,000**

Boucharel, a bronze group of 2 seated bulldogs, signed, 19½in (49cm) high. **$3,000-5,000**

l. A French bronze model of the setter named 'Cora', cast from a model by Isidore Bonheur, 19thC, 12½in (32cm) high. **$6,500-9,500**

n Isnik tile panel, comprising 4 les of different sizes, some storation, c1725, 21 by 16in 4 by 42.5cm). **$7,000-9,500**

A Safavid dish and deep bowl in the Chinese kraak style, repaired, 17thC, dish 19½in (49.5cm) diam. **$2,500-4,000 each**

A rare fragmentary Abbasid red ground lustre bowl, restored, 9thC, 7½in (19.5cm). **$30,000-32,000**

Kashan moulded cobalt nd lustre inscription le, minor restoration, 3thC, 14 by 13¼in 5.5 by 33.5cm). **3,500-8,000**

A Kashan moulded cobalt and lustre inscription tile, minor chipping, 13thC, 18 by 5in (45.5 by 12.5cm). **$7,000-9,000**

r. An amber wheel cut glass bottle, very slight surface iridescence, Nishapur, 10thC, 5in (12.5cm) high. **$8,000-11,000**

An Ottoman rebab of turned wood with a skin covering, the neck inlaid with ivory, ebony and tortoiseshell, horsehair strung bow, minor restoration, 18thC, 37in (94cm). **$8,000-10,000**

An Ottoman gilt copper incense burner on tray, damaged, early 17thC, 9½in (24cm) high. **$5,000-8,000**

l. A Persian silver inlaid brass pen box, minor damage, signed and inscribed, c1200, 12in (30.7cm) long. **$22,000-26,000**

A French inlaid octagonal Islamic table, slight damage, late 19thC, 31½in (80cm) wide. **$2,500-3,000**

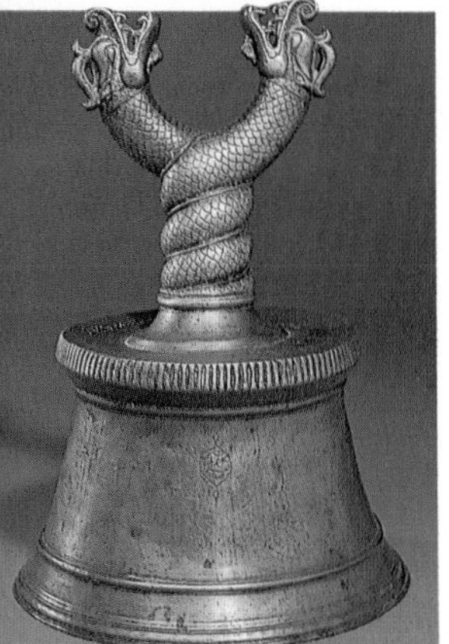

n early Safavid brass andlestick, inscribed, 6thC, 10½in (27cm). **45,000-50,000**

A Mesopotamian silver inlaid brass casket, 13thC, Jazira, 7½in (19cm). **$400,000+**

An Ottoman voided velvet and metal thread cushion cover, backed and stretched, slightly worn, one band of repair, 17thC, 43 by 25½in (110 by 65cm). **$6,500-9,500**

A carved oak and painted coat-of-arms of His Majesty King William III, late 17thC, 19in (49cm) high. **$3,000-4,000**

A German boxwood group, after Albrecht Durer, damaged, early 17thC, 5½in (14cm). **$16,000-20,000**

r. A Flemish oak relief, damaged, early 16thC, 48in (122cm). **$12,000-13,000**

A pine Angel Gabriel weathervane, American, 19thC, 41½in (105cm). **$2,500-3,000**

l. A set of 4 giltwood wall brackets, 21in (54cm) high. **$9,500-10,000**

A carved and painted soldier whirligig, some paint loss, one arm lacks axe, American, 19thC, 20in (51cm). **$30,000-32,000**

A parrot, 10in (25cm). **$7,500-8,000**

l. A set of 4 fruitwood candlesticks, c1800. **$10,000-11,000**

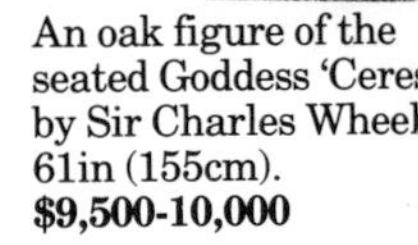

An oak figure of the seated Goddess 'Ceres by Sir Charles Wheel 61in (155cm). **$9,500-10,000**

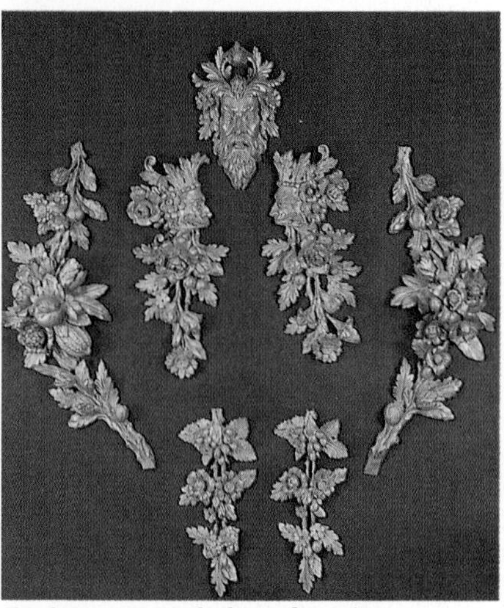

Twelve sections of giltwood carving, masks 24in (61cm). **$5,000-5,500**

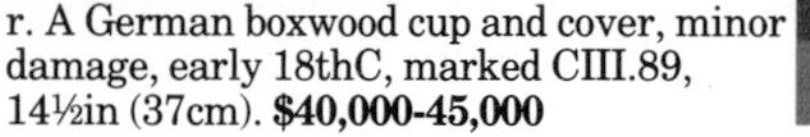

r. A German boxwood cup and cover, minor damage, early 18thC, marked CIII.89, 14½in (37cm). **$40,000-45,000**

A lignum wassail with 3 brass taps, 18thC, 20in (51cm). **$2,500-3,000**

et of 4 white marble garden
ıs, 19thC, 40in (101cm) high.
),000-25,000

A pair of Code stone urns, early 19thC, 40½in (102cm) high. **$7,000-9,000**

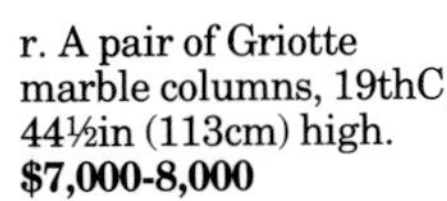

r. A pair of Griotte marble columns, 19thC, 44½in (113cm) high. **$7,000-8,000**

Above r. A pair of Napoleon III marble urns, 17in. **$2,000-3,000**
Above l. A set of 4 lead urns, early 19thC, 31½in (80cm). **$20,000-25,000**

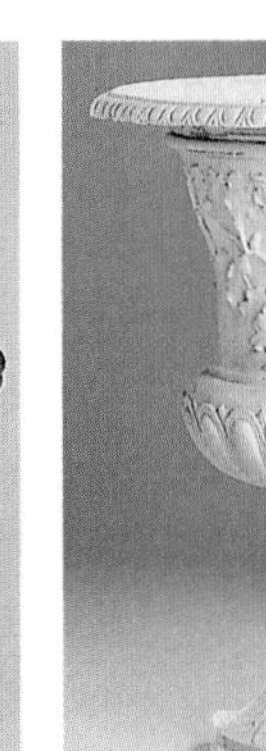

ıair of ormolu mounted
ıttled liver and grey-
ıen marble vases after
uthière, 15in (38cm).
1,000-16,000

A pair of French white marble urns, one with oak and laurel leaves, one with palm and olive leaves, some minor damage, c1700. **$80,000-88,000**

Above r. A red and brown marble column, early 19thC, 36in (91.5cm) high. **$3,000-5,000**

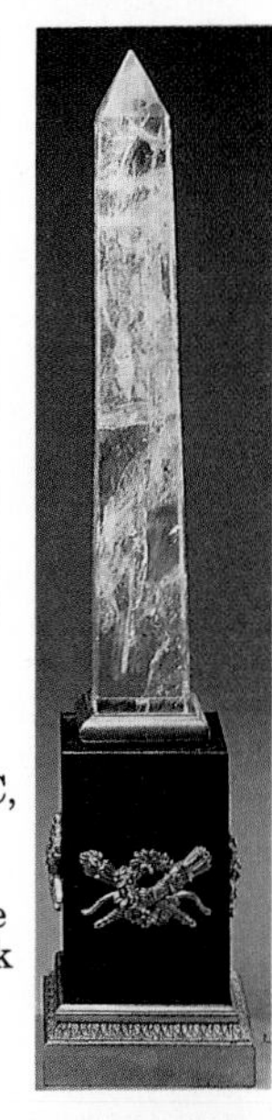

r. A pair of Empire style ormolu, marble and rock crystal obelisks, 18½in (47cm). **$9,000-10,000**

ı English marble bust of Venus by
seph Wilton, signed J. Wilton
ulp. 1782, late 18thC, 28½in
3cm).
'3,000-80,000

An alabaster bust of a young lady in pre-Raphaelite headdress, signed E. Fiaschi, 50in (127cm). **$1,500-2,500**

A carved marble lamp with matching shade, 25in (64cm). **$1,000-1,500**

l. An Italian marble statue of Pauline Borghese after Canova, some damage, mid-19thC, 35½in (90cm) high. **$9,500-11,000**

A Victorian 18ct gold almondine garnet brooch, 4in (10cm) wide.
$1,200-1,400
r. A Victorian gold and garnet bracelet, set with almondine garnets and one cabochon in the centre.
$1,500-2,000

A diamond set floral spray brooch.
$4,000-5,000

A French enamelled g locket, some restoration, c1650, 1in (2.5cm) high
$4,000-5,00

A pearl and diamond diadem, by Cartier, Paris, 1908, No. 1743, 5½in (14.2cm) wide. **$80,000-95,000**
l. An Edwardian diamond bow brooch, 5in (12.6cm) high.
$70,000-80,000

An important cushion shaped Fa Light Yellow 35.03 carat diamon single stone pendant, on a flattened curb link chain, 14½in (36.8cm) long.
$250,000-320,000

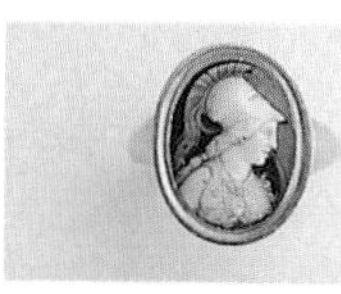

A sardonyx cameo with the head of Pallas Athene, inscribed 'LAV.R.MED.' in gold r setting, cameo 18thC, mount early 19thC.
$40,000-50,000

A necklace, comprising 19 gold mounted memori and love jewels with rock crystal covers, the central locket 2in (5cm) high. **$32,000-40,000**

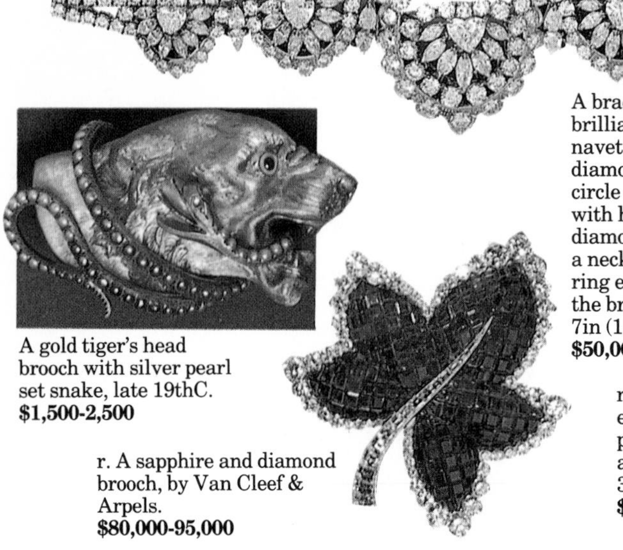

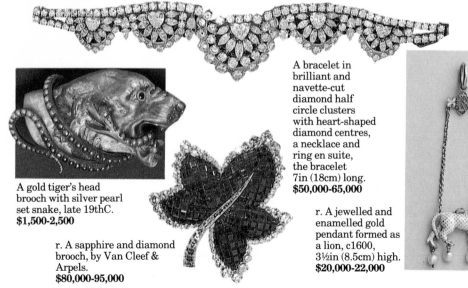

A bracelet in brilliant and navette-cut diamond half circle clusters with heart-shaped diamond centres, a necklace and ring en suite, the bracelet 7in (18cm) long.
$50,000-65,000

A gold tiger's head brooch with silver pearl set snake, late 19thC.
$1,500-2,500

r. A sapphire and diamond brooch, by Van Cleef & Arpels.
$80,000-95,000

r. A jewelled and enamelled gold pendant formed as a lion, c1600, 3½in (8.5cm) high.
$20,000-22,000

Dutch walnut and foliate arquetry silver table, the dished p decorated with spandrels and rds amongst foliage, the frieze ith a single drawer, on cabriole gs and pointed pad feet, 19thC, 6in (92cm).
4,000-5,000

Sofa Tables

A Queen Anne maple tavern table, with oval top above a shaped apron on tapering cylindrical legs with pad feet, some damage and repairs, 18thC, 36½in (92cm) long.
$2,000-4,000

A mahogany and rosewood crossbanded sofa table, with moulded apron drawers, on twin turned columns and moulded quadruple supports, brass toes and casters, late 18thC, 66in (167.5cm).
$6,500-7,000

A mahogany and inlaid sofa table, with folding top and 2 frieze drawers, on solid end standards and C-scrolling splayed legs with brass block terminals, part early 19thC, 57in (144.5cm) extended.
$3,000-4,000

rosewood sofa table, with inlaid ringing decoration, 2 real and dummy drawers, supported on a ng turned stem, ending in splayed legs and brass paw asters, early 19thC, 71in (182.5cm).
3,000-5,000

A rosewood sofa table, inlaid with brass, on quadruple baluster shaft with paw feet, early 19thC.
$8,000-9,500

A Regency mahogany sofa table, on later solid end standards with splayed feet, 70in (177.5cm).
$3,000-5,000

figured mahogany sofa table, with bony line inlay and wide rossbanding, 2 frieze drawers with urned brass handles, on 4 splay feet ith brass paw casters, 58in 147cm).
8,000-9,500

A red lacquer and gilt chinoiserie sofa table, with 2 frieze drawers, opposed by false drawers, on end standards joined by a turned stretcher on down curved legs, 46in (116.5cm).
$3,000-4,000

A Regency rosewood sofa table, with inlaid brass motifs and string lines, the brass feet with moulded florets scrolls and anthemia, casters, inlaid brass work defective in places, 60½in (153cm). **$5,000-6,500**

A Regency mahogany sofa table, with twin-flap top above 2 frieze drawers, on a square shaft with 4 splayed legs, distressed, 58in (147cm).
$2,500-3,000

A Regency rosewood games and sofa table, with wide burr walnut crossbanding, the underside with chequered games board, with brass handles and moulding, the lyre end standards gilt metal acanthus and roundel mounted, on swept supports terminating in brass claw casters, united by a later arched stretcher, 42in (107cm) extended.
$11,000-13,000

A Regency rosewood sofa table, with interlaced lozenge boxwood stringing, raised on ring turned double pillar end standards and outward splayed square tapering supports terminating in peg feet and brass casters, 62½in (159cm) extended.
$3,000-4,000

A Regency mahogany sofa table, with solid trestle ends and splaye legs, 66in (168cm) extended.
$3,000-5,000

A Regency satinwood sofa table, the crossbanded top with ebonised stringing above a pair of frieze drawers on trestle supports joined by an arching bracket on downswept legs with brass paw feet, early 19thC, 39in (99cm) wide.
$4,000-6,000

Sutherland Tables

A George III mahogany Sutherland table, with twin-flap top and turned gateleg supports on turned feet, restored, 32½in (85cm).
$1,500-2,500

A Victorian burr walnut and inlaid Sutherland tea table, with an inlaid scrolling foliate border and stringing, on turned and whorled end standards, united by a centre stretcher, on leaf carved scrolled supports, 35in (90cm).
$1,200-1,500

An early Georgian walnut tea table, with rectangular folding top and a drawer, on club legs and pad feet, 24in (61cm).
$2,500-3,000

A Victorian figured walnut pedest Sutherland table, the top quarter-veneered and with 2 shape flaps, the frieze with 2 drawers, on turned fluted shaft and 3 splayed legs, 30in (76cm).
$1,200-1,400

Tea Tables

A George II red walnut and mahogany serpentine tea table, the top enclosing a boxwood lined interior above a banded frieze, on chamfered square moulded legs with acanthus carved wings, adapted, 33in (84cm).
$2,500-3,000

A Victorian burr walnut Sutherland table, with shaped leaves and standing on a turned cheval base with quadruple carved spreading supports, 39½in (99cm).
$2,500-3,000

mahogany tea table, with ossbanded serpentine folding top chamfered legs with block feet, ½in (85cm).
,000-4,000

A late George III mahogany tea table, with D-shaped fold-over top above a frieze drawer with a gilt metal border, on turned tapering reeded legs, 40in (101.5cm).
$2,500-3,000

A mid-Georgian mahogany tea table, with folding top, fitted with a drawer concealed by the gateleg, on square chamfered legs, 28½in (72cm). **$1,200-1,500**

Regency rosewood fold-over top a table, with segmented ball feet, in (92cm).
1,200-1,500

A Regency mahogany fold-over tea table, on turned and fluted column, on quadruple base and casters, 36in (92cm) extended.
$1,200-1,400

A Chippendale mahogany birdcage tea table, the tilting top with moulded ring above a birdcage over a baluster and ring-turned pedestal on cabriole legs with claw-and-ball feet, one leg restored, Pennsylvania, c1770, 34in (86cm) diam.
$3,500-4,000

George IV figured mahogany ld-over top tea table, of D-form ith black line inlays, on 4 turned gs with ring detail and brass sters, 36in (92cm).
,400-2,000

A pair of William IV rosewood pedestal tea tables, with swivelling fold-over tops, on faceted tapering shafts and concave sided platform bases with turned bun feet, stamped Gillows Lancaster, 36in (92cm).
$5,000-6,500

A Chippendale mahogany tea table, with dished, tilting and revolving top above a birdcage support over a tapering columnar and compressed ball-turned pedestal, on tripod cabriole legs with claw-and-ball feet, Philadelphia, c1780, 28in (71cm) high, 32in (81cm) diam.
$7,000-8,000

satinwood tea table, inlaid with usical instruments and foliate arquetry arabesques, with square layed tapering legs joined by scrolling cross stretchers, 35in 9cm).
,500-2,500

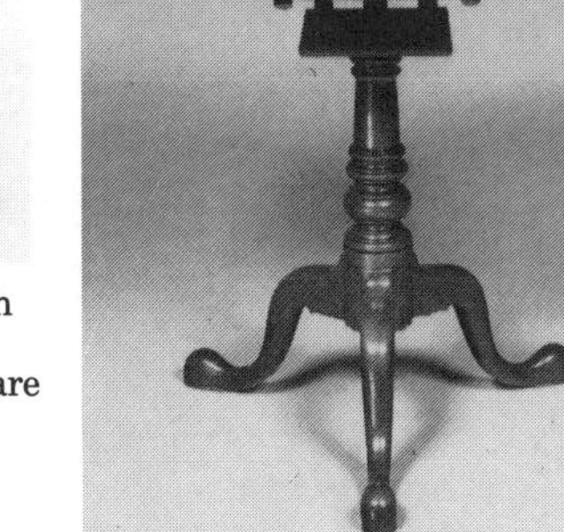

A Chippendale walnut tea table, the tilting top with moulded rim above a birdcage with ring-turned and compressed ball pedestal on cabriole legs with slipper feet, Pennsylvania, c1770, 33½in (85cm) wide.
$3,000-5,000

A Chippendale cherrywood tea table, the dish-top revolving and tilting above a birdcage support over a tapering columnar and compressed ball-turned pedestal, on tripod cabriole legs with claw-and-ball feet, Pennsylvania, c1785, 33½in (85cm) diam.
$8,000-9,000

Tray Tables

A William IV black japanned papi mâché tray, decorated in gilt and colours with a spray of flowers within a leafy border, the later stand with ring turned legs and X-stretcher, 30½in (77cm).
$1,000-1,400

Tripod Tables

A Chippendale mahogany tripod table, on later well carved blind fret and floral stem and supports, 20in (51cm).
$2,500-3,000

A George III mahogany tripod table, with snap-top, the ring turned baluster centre pillar, on a tripod base, 16½in (41cm).
$1,200-1,400

An Irish mahogany tripod table, each cabriole leg differently carve on shaped pad feet, mid-18thC, 36 (91cm). **$3,000-5,000**

A George III mahogany and inlaid tripod table, the snap-top with canted corners and kingwood crossbanding, the ring turned centre pillar on a tripod base, 20in (51cm).
$1,000-1,200

A mid-Georgian mahogany tilt-top table, on spiral fluted round tapering column to tripod cabriole supports, 31in (79cm).
$800-1,000

A mahogany tripod table, the top with spindled gallery, on turned shaft and arch splayed legs with paw feet carved with foliage, 28½in (72cm). **$1,300-1,500**

A George III mahogany table, wi dished snap-top, on a baluster turned centre pillar and tripod b 17½in (44cm).
$1,200-1,400

mahogany and padouk tripod ɔle, with pie crust top and luster shaft, the splayed base rved with foliage on claw-and-ball ɛt, 14in (36cm).
,000-2,500

A George III tilt-top table, the top above a bird cage base, with vase turned column and triple spreading supports, 31½in (80cm).
$1,400-2,000

An early George III mahogany tripod table, the top on a birdcage action and a baluster turned and spiral fluted column hipped outswept legs and pointed pad feet, 36in (91cm).
$1,400-2,000

mahogany pedestal table, the ɔ-up top with an undulating pie ust border, on a fluted tapering olumn and splayed legs with aw-and-ball feet and acanthus leaf eadings, 29in (74cm).
,000-1,200

An early George III mahogany occasional table, the tilt-top with a moulded edge, the fluted stem with ribbon paterae moulded edge, the fluted stem with ribbon paterae moulding on tied leaf spray carved cabriole legs, with claw-and-ball feet, 26in (66cm).
$9,000-9,500

A mahogany tripod table, the tip-up top with a waved border carved with shells and husks, on a turned foliate carved shaft and splayed legs, 31in (79cm).
$1,000-1,300

yew and mahogany ipod table, the top on a ırned shaft and splayed legs with ɔinted pad feet, ssociated, mid-18thC, 9in (48cm).
1,200-1,300

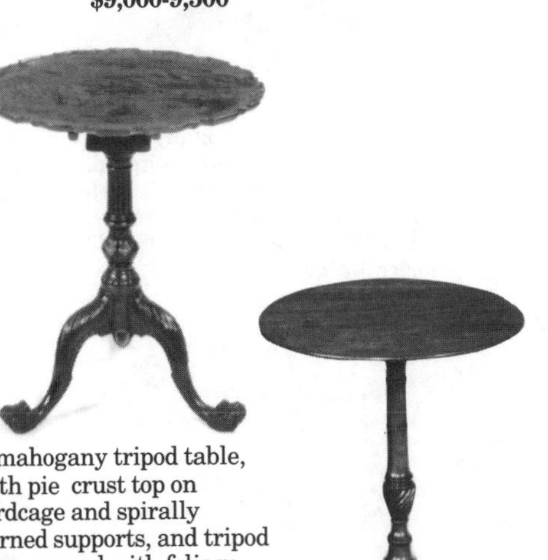

A mahogany tripod table, with pie crust top on birdcage and spirally turned supports, and tripod base carved with foliage, 26in (66.5cm).
$4,000-5,500

A mahogany tripod table, with plain fixed top, on turned and spiral reed stem, 19thC, 18in (46cm). **$500-650**

A Regency rosewood grained and parcel gilt tripod table, the top on spirally fluted column and scrolled legs, 18in (46cm).
$1,300-2,000

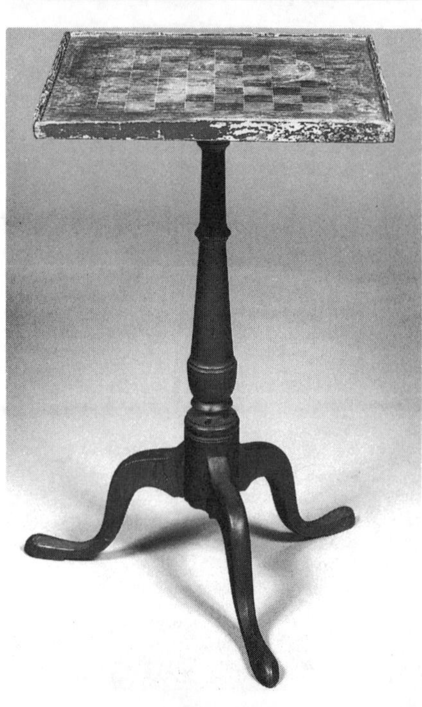

A Federal red painted candlestand with a gameboard top, Massachusetts, c1775, 17½in (44.5cm) square.
$1,000-1,500

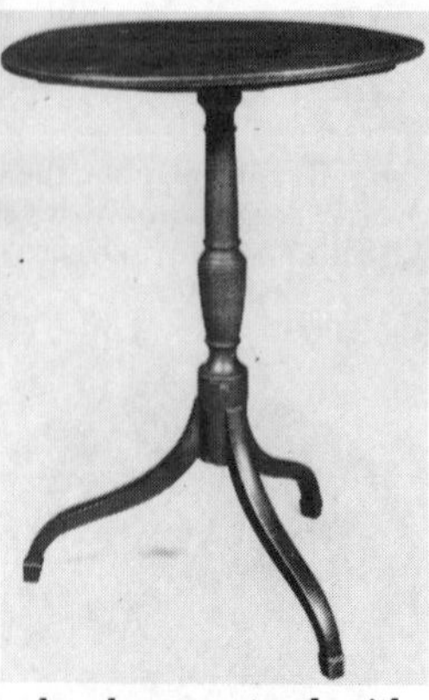

A Federal mahogany stand, with tilting top above a tapering urn-turned pedestal, on tripod arched legs with spade feet, one leg damaged, Salem, Massachusetts, c1800, 23in (58.5cm) wide.
$1,200-1,500

A Federal mahogany stand, the to above a tapering columnar and turned pedestal, on tripod cabriole legs with elongated pad feet, Salen Massachusetts, c1800, 15½in (39.5cm) diam.
$3,500-4,500

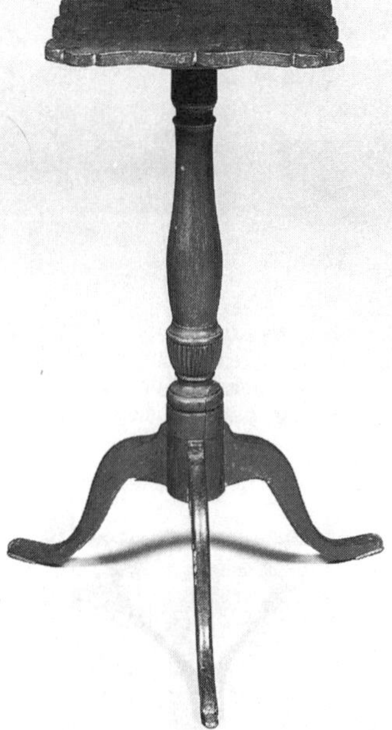

A late Federal grain painted maple candlestand, the top scalloped and joined by a cleat to a baluster support with a fluted urn, on 3 arched snake feet, the surface with grained paint, old repairs, New England, early 19thC, 12½in (31.5cm) square.
$7,000-9,000

A Federal mahogany tilt top stan the top with rounded corners and reeded edge tilting above a taperi columnar and squat baluster-turn pedestal, on tripod reeded sabre legs, fitted with brass ends and casters, Boston or Salem, Massachusetts, c1810, 28in (71.5cm).
$1,000-1,500

A Federal inlaid mahogany tilt top stand, the top with pattern inlaid edge tilting above a slender baluster turned pedestal, on tripod arch legs, Salem, Massachusetts, c1800, 22in (55.5cm) wide.
$3,000-5,000

A George III mahogany and oak tripod supper table, the moulded scalloped top carved with shells on a baluster stem and cabriole legs with pad feet, 33in (83.5cm) diam.
$4,000-5,000

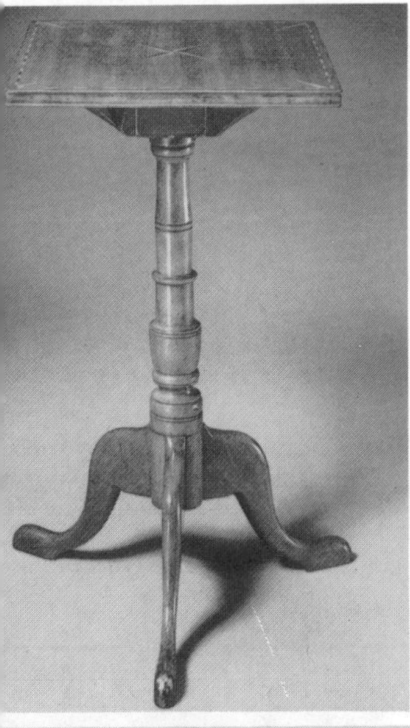

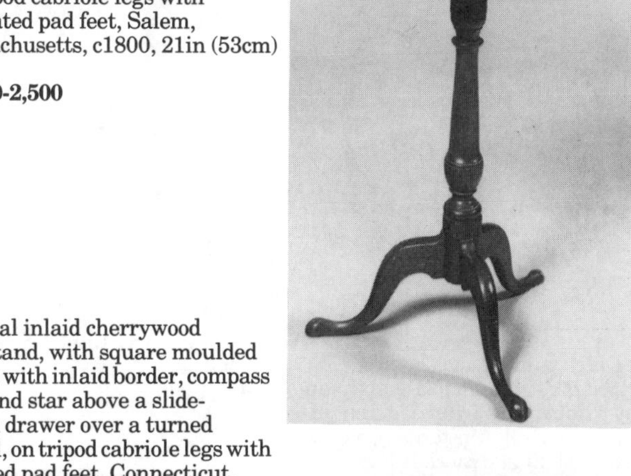

A Federal mahogany stand, with tilting top above a tapering columnar and urn-turned pedestal, on tripod cabriole legs with elongated pad feet, Salem, Massachusetts, c1800, 21in (53cm) wide.
$2,000-2,500

A Federal inlaid cherrywood candlestand, with square moulded edge top with inlaid border, compass points and star above a slide-through drawer over a turned pedestal, on tripod cabriole legs with elongated pad feet, Connecticut, c1800, 16½in (42cm) wide.
$4,000-6,000

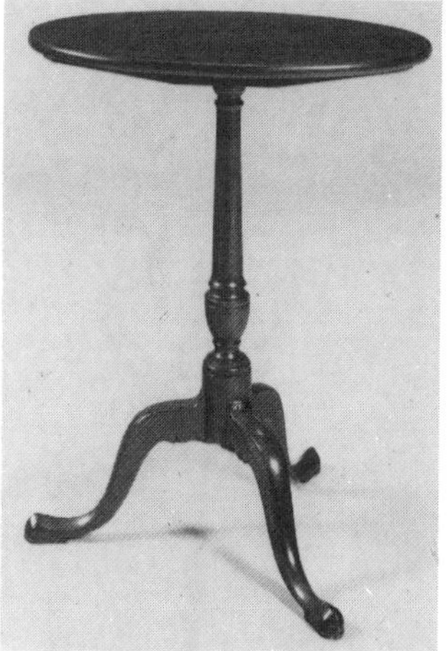

A Federal mahogany stand, with tilting top above a tapering columnar and urn turned pedestal, on tripod cabriole legs with pad feet, Salem, Massachusetts, c1800, 22in (55.5cm) wide.
$1,000-1,500

. George III mahogany tripod table, he piecrust top above a baluster edestal carved with stiff leaves on abriole legs headed by acanthus vith claw-and-ball feet, 29½in 75cm) diam.
4,000-4,500

A George III mahogany tripod table, the tilting top with guilloche pierced gallery and birdcage action on a reeded columnar pedestal, on cabriole legs headed by rosettes on claw-and-ball feet, 22in (55.5cm) wide.
$4,000-6,000

. George III mahogany tripod table, he later crossbanded top with eeded edge, the column and aluster turned stem on cabriole gs and pad feet, 29in (73.5cm) ide.
3,500-4,000

A George III rosewood tripod table, the tilt-top crossbanded and inlaid with narrow satinwood bands, on tapered reeded and fluted stem, the legs inlaid with satinwood bands, on peg supports, 20in (51cm).
$4,000-5,000

A mahogany tripod table, the moulded pie crust tip-top with birdcage action on a spirally fluted baluster shaft, the cabriole legs carved with cabochons, C-scrolls, acanthus and rockwork with claw-and-ball feet, 27in (69cm).
$3,000-5,000

A Dutch painted and ebonised tripod table, the shaped oval tip-up top painted with figures in front of the Town Hall, Amsterdam, on turned shaft and cabriole legs with pad feet, 18thC, 43in (109cm).
$5,000-6,500

A mahogany snap-top tea table, on ring turned column to a triple splay base, with cabriole legs and casters, early 19thC, 39in (99cm).
$1,000-1,200

A Regency mahogany tripod table, the rounded tip-up top and baluster shaft on moulded arched downswept legs with spade feet, 31in (79cm).
$800-1,300

An Austrian fruitwood, yew and specimen wood tripod table, the top inlaid with various woods in a radiating pattern, on 3 shaped supports and downswept legs applied with turned roundels, 27½in (70cm).
$2,500-4,000

Work Tables

Two Federal work tables, l. mahogany, with a short drawer, on square tapering legs, 28in (71cm) high, r. cherrywood, with tapering legs, 26in (66.5cm) high.
$2,500-3,000

Wine & Lamp Tables

A Regency mahogany lamp table, on a turned ribbed shaft with gadrooned socle and 4 scrolled feet, the top and bottom possibly associated, 22in (56cm).
$1,500-2,000

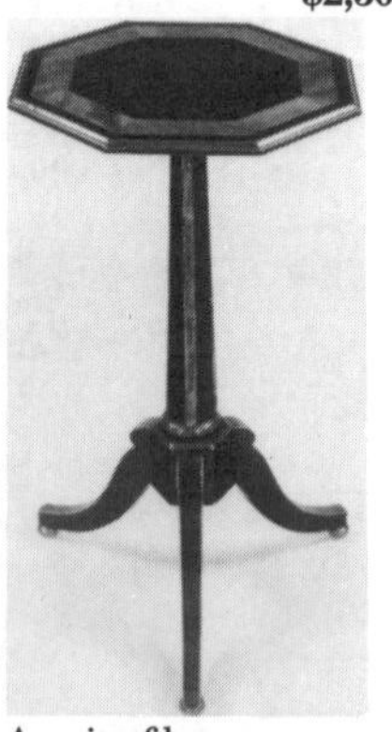

A pair of mahogany lamp tables, with ring turned shaft and 3 downswept legs with ball feet, 31in (79cm) high.
$3,000-5,000

A pair of brass mounted rosewood and satinwood lamp tables, each with octagonal top, square spreading shaft and tripod base with bun feet, 17in (43cm).
$3,000-4,000

A Regency rosewood sewing table, with crossbanded top and frieze drawer on open lyre supports and gilt metal claw feet, re-veneered, 19in (48cm).
$2,000-2,500

Georgian mahogany writing work ble, with 2 drawers, one fitted ith a writing slide, on refectory ıpports with splayed legs and sters, 21in (53cm). ,000-4,000

A Georgian mahogany work table, with an oval crossbanded panel and inlaid stringing, fitted with brass knob handles, a sliding wool box below, raised on turned tapering legs, 21in (53cm). **$2,500-3,000**

A Regency mahogany Pembroke work table, the twin flap top with rounded angles above 2 frieze drawers, on ring turned tapering supports, 33in (84cm) extended. **$1,500-2,500**

Regency satin birch work table, e top above a partially fitted frieze awer and work basket on -shaped support, the faceted shaft ith concave platform and scroll et, adapted, 18in (46cm). **,500-3,000**

A rosewood veneered sewing table, with segmented column, platform base and decorated with half bead moulding, early 19thC. **$2,300-2,500**

A George IV amboyna veneered work table, with a frieze drawer, sliding work compartment, tapering end standards joined by a pole stretcher and on trestle feet, 18½in (47cm). **$1,500-2,500**

A mahogany work table, with twin-flap top banded in kingwood, above 2 frieze drawers opposed by false drawers with a sliding well below, on lion's paw feet joined by a pierced stretcher, 32½in (82cm). **$2,000-2,500**

A Regency rosewood work table, the ridged top above a frieze fitted with a sewing basket, on lappeted tapering supports and turned feet, 16½in (42cm). **$2,000-2,500**

Victorian walnut sewing table, ith single drawer and sliding well ompartment, with shaped end ıpports joined by turned stretcher n brass casters, 21in (53cm). **700-800**

A Victorian kingwood pedestal work table, with crossbanded top, frieze drawer and work basket, supported on an octagonal tapering stem, ending in a quatrefoil base and scroll feet, 20in (51cm). **$800-1,000**

A Victorian burr walnut work table, the hinged top with marquetry inlaid and fret carved interior above an upholstered well, on scrolling end standards, 22in (56cm).
$1,500-2,500

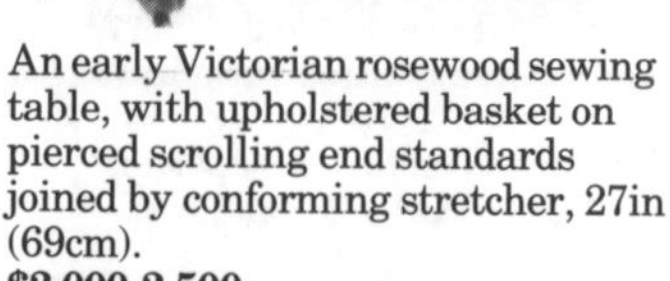

An early Victorian rosewood sewing table, with upholstered basket on pierced scrolling end standards joined by conforming stretcher, 27in (69cm).
$2,000-2,500

An Edwardian inlaid mahogany sewing table, with fitted interior, raised on slender square outswept supports, 16in (41cm).
$800-1,000

A Victorian rosewood opening to reveal fitted compartments and a central sewing well, on cabriole tripod carved at the knees with flowerheads terminating in scroll feet, 20½in (52cm).
$650-800

A Federal fancy painted work table, with square top above a short drawer embellished with stylised flowers, on ring-turned tapering cylindrical legs, the entire surface painted yellow, New England, early 19thC.
$2,500-3,000

A late Federal inlaid mahogany work table, with 2 short drawers above 2 long drawers, each with bird's-eye maple veneer and lion's mask pulls, on cylindrical legs with diamond carving, with ball feet, some drawer sides restored, probably Philadelphia area, early 19thC, 22in (55.5cm) wide.
$3,000-3,500

A Federal figured maple work table with a short drawer, on ball and ring-turned reeded tapering legs with ball-turned feet, 18in (45.5cm) wide.
$2,500-3,000

A Classical stencilled rosewood work table, the top with a side candleslide over 2 drawers, the upper one with a hinged velvet-covered work surface and 2 compartments, the lower one with dividers, above a sliding grain painted tambour velvet-lined compartment, on 4 scrolling legs joined to a circular base, on 4 gilt acanthus leaf carved lion's paw feet, the top and corners with gilt stencilling, New York, c1820, 29in (73.5cm) high.
$7,000-8,000

\ Federal inlaid mahogany work able, with 2 line inlay short lrawers, on square tapering line nlaid legs, small patches to drawer ronts and one leg slightly pieced, Jew England, early 19thC, 18in 45.5cm) wide.
2,000-2,500

Writing Tables

\ Regency mahogany writing table, n the manner of Gillows, the top ontaining an ink well with hinged lap, with 2 frieze drawers, on ring urned legs, 36in (92cm).
3,000-5,000

. William IV mahogany writing able, the top inset with later green eather, raised upon melon fluted urned and tapering supports erminating in brass caps and asters, one drawer stamped with aker's name, by T. Wilson of 8 Great Queen Street, London, 7in (94cm).
650-800

A William IV mahogany partners' writing table, with lined top, above 6 frieze drawers with false drawers to the sides, on solid end standards terminating in paterae on bar and lotus leaf feet, the locks labelled T Parsons patent, 63in (160cm).
$9,500-11,000

A Victorian satin birch writing/reading table, the top with a leather lined adjustable and sliding centre panel, above 2 frieze drawers and 2 pen drawers, on fluted turned tapering legs, stamped C. Hindley & Sons, 134 Oxford Street, London, No. 44435, 44in (111.5cm) extended.
$1,300-1,500

C. Hindley & Sons, 19thC furniture manufacturers becoming later Hindley & Wilkinson in 1899.

A William IV mahogany partners' writing table, the leather lined top above 6 frieze drawers, each fitted with a Bramah patent lock, on turned tapered ribbed legs, 60in (152cm).
$5,500-6,500

A William IV rosewood partners' writing table, with inset leather top, fitted with 2 drawers each side, on cheval frame with solid panelled ends applied with roundel motifs, joined by turned stretcher, on fluted bun feet, 57in (145cm).
$5,500-7,000

A William IV mahogany writing table, with crossbanded top and 2 concave frieze drawers, on trestle ends carved with bands of egg-and-dart with scrolling feet, 63½in (162cm).
$7,000-8,000

A Victorian mahogany writing table, fitted with 6 frieze drawers, on faceted turned tapering legs, stamped Webbs, 323 Grays Inn Road, 72in (182.5cm).
$2,500-3,000

A Victorian burr walnut and marquetry writing table, with tulipwood banded waved top with a frieze drawer, on cabriole legs mounted with sabots and gilt metal foliate headings, 44½in (112cm).
$3,000-4,000

An Edwardian mahogany and satinwood bowfront writing table, the elevated back with 4 small drawers above a leather lined plateau and 5 frieze drawers, on square tapering legs, 36½in (92cm).
$1,200-1,500

A mahogany writing table, maker's label in drawer, J. Batten, Rochester, Kent, late 18thC, 36in (92cm).
$2,500-3,000

A Victorian mahogany writing table, with inset leather lined top and 2 frieze drawers, the reverse with simulated drawers, on lyre end standards and lappeted scroll feet joined by stretchers, adapted, 41in (104cm).
$800-1,300

A mid-Victorian mahogany writing table, the lined moulded top above a frieze fitted with 8 drawers, on turned reeded legs and casters, 121in (307cm).
$4,000-5,000

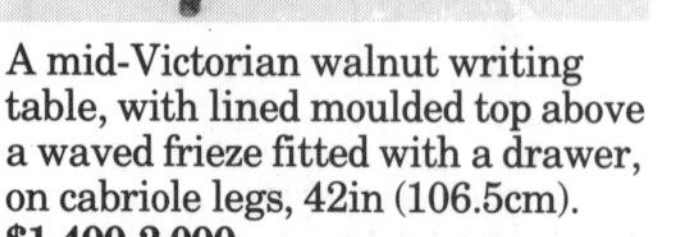

A mid-Victorian walnut writing table, with lined moulded top above a waved frieze fitted with a drawer, on cabriole legs, 42in (106.5cm).
$1,400-2,000

An Edwardian rosewood writing table, with floral inlay and satinwood stringing, 42in (106.5cm).
$1,400-1,500

A Louis XV style kingwood and marquetry inlaid bureau plat, applied with gilt metal mounts an borders, on cabriole legs and sabot 19thC, 45½in (115cm).
$5,500-6,500

A Louis XV style bureau plat, veneered in tulipwood with elaborate gilt metal mounts and leather top.
$6,600-8,000

A burr walnut wri table, with kingwo crossbanding and ormolu mounts, shaped galleried shelf, a drawer and on 4 cabriole legs, 19th(
$6,500-8,000

A mahogany table, with painted X-trestle ends and turned stretcher, early 19thC, 49in (124.5cm).
$2,000-2,600

A walnut and gilt metal mounted writing table, the lined top of serpentine outline, on clasp heade cabriole legs with sabots, restorations, late 19thC, 24½in (62cm).
$1,400-2,000

A Louis XVI design walnut and brass bureau plat, the top lined in gilt tooled green leather, on turned tapered fluted legs each with a brass capital and cap, 67½in (171cm).
$11,000-14,000

. mahogany burr elm and gilt ıetal mounted bureau plat, the ned top with a brass edge, above a haped frieze with 5 drawers, and pplied with acanthus and female ıask clasps, on cabriole legs with airy paw sabots, 71in (180cm).
6,500-8,000

Teapoys

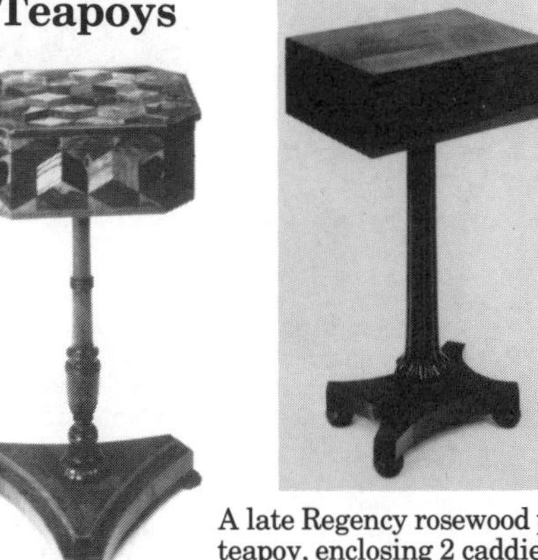

A Regency specimen wood parquetry pedestal teapoy, the octagonal top with a hinged lid enclosing 2 caddies and bowl apertures, the concave sided platform on gilt metal hairy paw feet.
$3,000-4,000

A late Regency rosewood pedestal teapoy, enclosing 2 caddies and mixing bowl apertures, on ribbed shaft and concave sided platform with bun feet, 18in (46cm).
$1,300-2,000

A William IV rosewood teapoy, with hinged slightly domed panelled top enclosing a fitted interior, 16in (41cm).
$3,000-4,000

\An Anglo Indian rosewood ;arcophagus teapoy, with fitted nterior, on stepped square shaft :arved with stylised foliage with :oncave sided platform base and scrolling foliate feet, mid-19thC, 18½in (47cm).
$1,200-1,500

An early Victorian mahogany teapoy, of sarcophagus form, on an octagonal tapered column with lotus collar on concave base with scroll feet, 20½in (52cm).
$650-800

A Regency mahogany tea chest, with hinged domed lid enclosing a fitted interior, above a pair of panelled doors, with side carrying handles, on bracket feet, 22½in (57cm).
$1,200-1,500

Vashstands

A Georgian mahogany washstand, with folding top, fitted interior, double doors, on square tapered legs.
$700-900

A Dutch mahogany washstand, with hinged top enclosing an interior fitted with 2 flaps, shelves and a bowl aperture, with 2 cupboard doors below, between canted angles, on square tapered legs, early 19thC, 48in (122cm).
$2,500-3,000

A pair of Regency mahogany washstands, in the manner of Gillows, each with three-quarter gallery, above a panelled frieze on turned tapering legs, 38½in (98cm).
$5,000-6,500

Whatnots

A Regency style mahogany washstand, the top with three-quarter gallery above a drawer, shelf and pair of cupboard doors on square legs with brass box feet and casters, 18in (45.5cm) wide.
$800-1,200

A Regency mahogany whatnot, with 4 shelves and a drawer on square legs with brass box feet and casters, 19thC, 18½in (47cm) wide.
$3,500-4,000

A Regency mahogany three-tier whatnot, each tier with a three-quarter gallery and rosewo[od] banded drawer with turned handles, the frieze with a gadroon[ed] moulding, spiral turned intermediate supports and graduated bead mouldings, on turned feet, 23in (59cm).
$4,000-5,000

A Regency mahogany whatnot, with three-quarter gallery on turned supports with iron cross-braces over 3 shelves, on turned feet, early 19thC, 33in (83.5cm) wide.
$5,000-5,500

A mid-Victorian oak tabernacle of architectural form, the fluted superstructure with pepperpot finials, 39in (99cm).
$2,500-3,000

Miscellaneous

An American stained beech candle rack, the central ring turned column support on a rectangular base with upright gallery and applied stepped mouldings, fitted with bronzed metal lion ring handles to the sides, 19thC, 17½in (44.5cm) wide.
$350-400

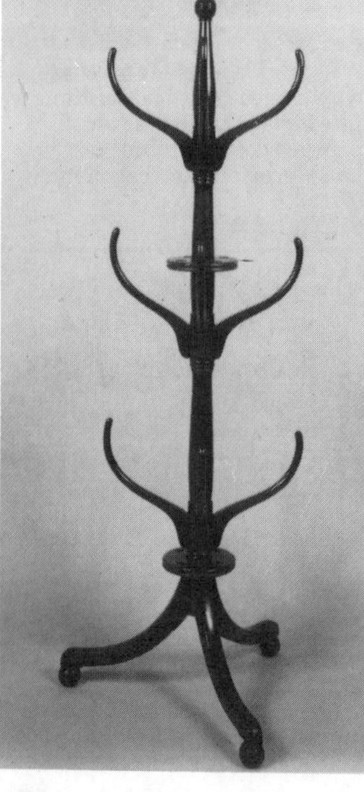

An early Victorian mahogany hat rack, in the manner of Gillows, the baluster and ring-turned shaft supporting 3 tiers of 4 scrolling arms on a tripartite base with downswept legs and ball feet, one arm pieced, 62in (157cm) high.
$2,000-3,000

A Directoire mahogany jardinière, with lead liner above a moulded frieze on columnar supports, flaring plinth and turned feet, early 19thC, 35in (89.5cm) high.
$2,000-2,500

ARCHITECTURAL ANTIQUES

Fire Irons

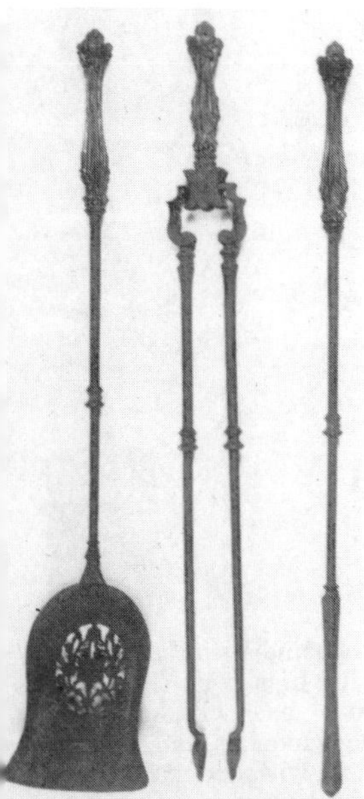

A set of 3 William IV ormolu mounted fire irons, comprising: a pierced shovel, tongs and a poker with foliate handles, restoration to tongs, 30in (76cm).
$1,200-1,400

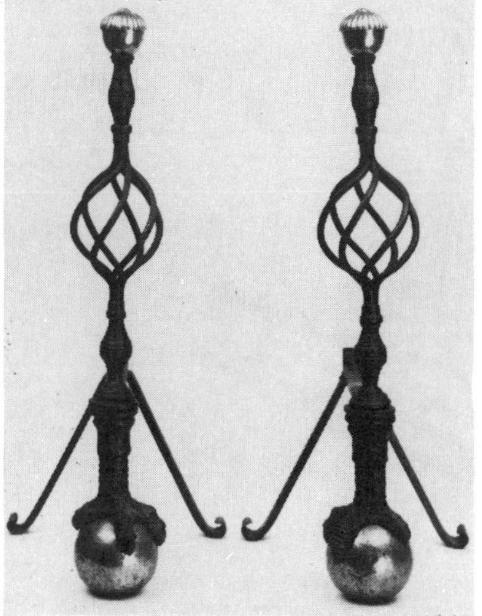

A pair of wrought iron and brass andirons, the ring turned uprights centred by spiral open twist knops, on claw-and-ball bases, late 18th/19thC, 25½in (65cm).
$1,000-1,300

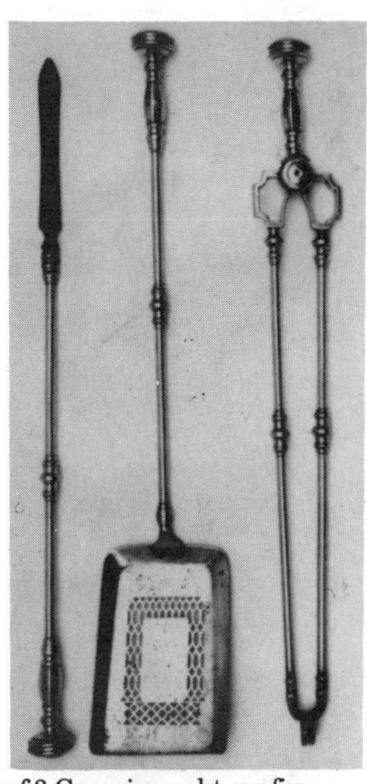

A set of 3 Georgian paktong fire irons, comprising: shovel, poker and tongs, the polygonal grips ring turned and with mushroom knops.
$4,000-5,500

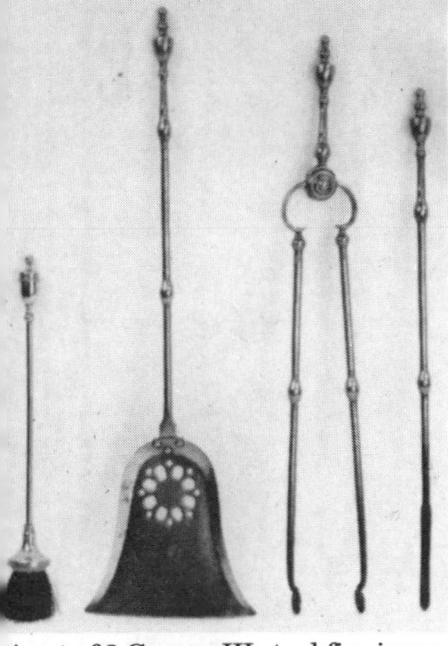

A set of 3 George III steel fire irons and associated brush, with pommel finials, 31in (79cm).
$1,000-1,300

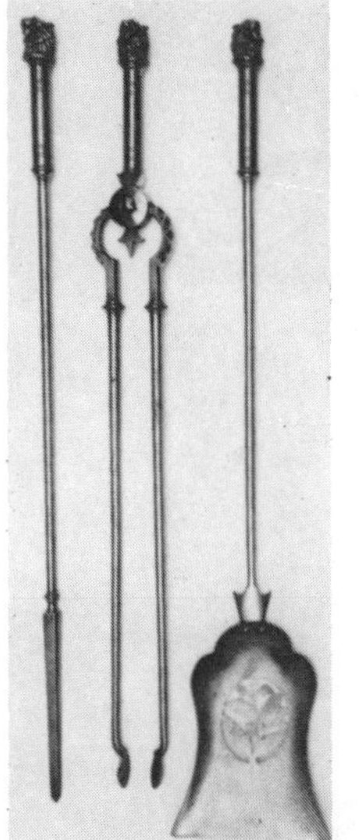

A set of 3 polished steel fire irons, the turned pommels with lion mask bosses comprising: a poker, a pair of tongs and a pierced shovel, the shovel 32in (81.5cm) long.
$1,400-2,000

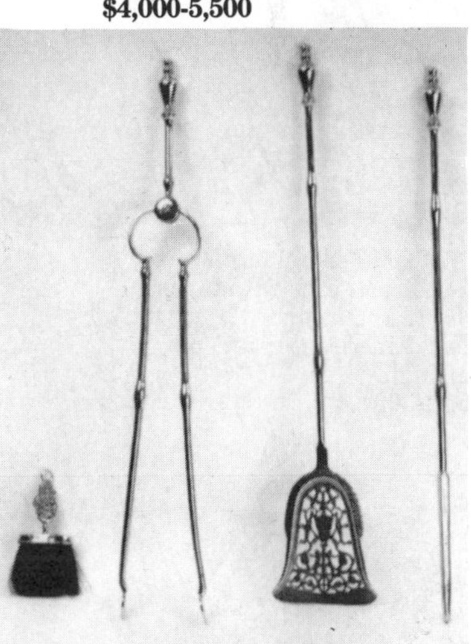

A set of 3 Georgian brass fire irons and a firebrush, with urn finials, the shovel 31in (79cm) long.
$1,300-1,500

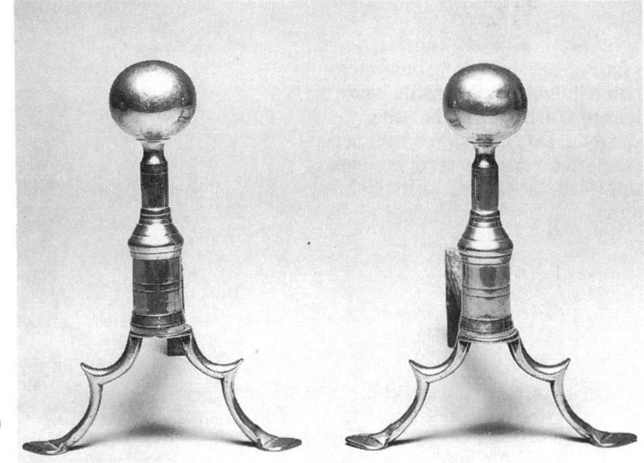

A pair of brass andirons, each with ball finial above a cylindrical standard, on spurred arched leg with spade feet and iron billet bar, American, late 18thC, 12in (30.5cm) high.
$1,200-1,500

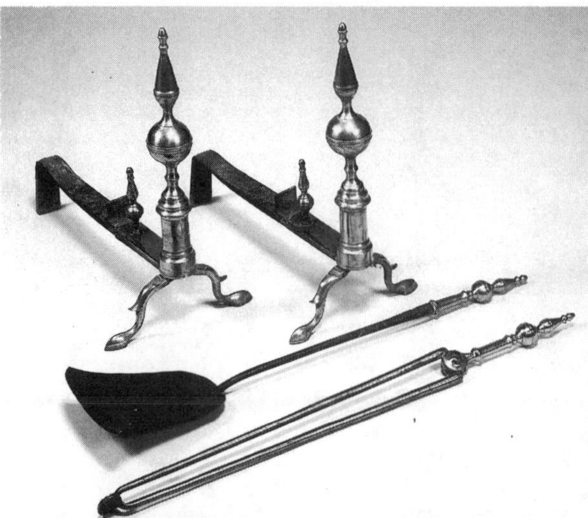

A pair of Federal brass andirons and 2 fire tools, New England, c1800, the andirons 21in (53.5cm) high.
$3,000-3,500

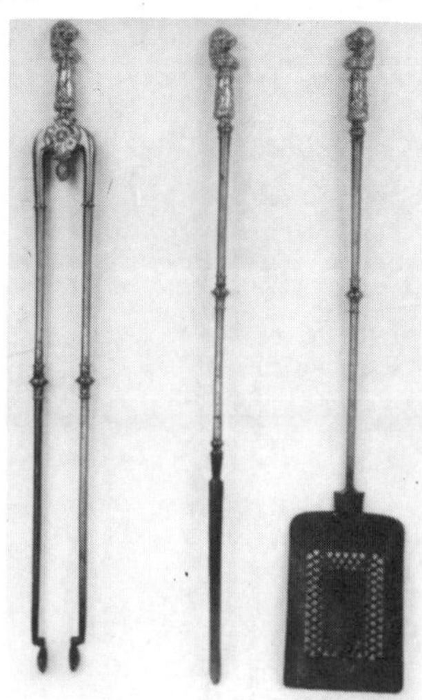

A set of 3 mid-Victorian steel and brass fire irons, with shovel, tongs and poker, each with lion and acanthus handles, and a pair of andirons, with lion mask finials, baluster stems and circular bases, 13½in (34cm) high.
$1,200-1,500

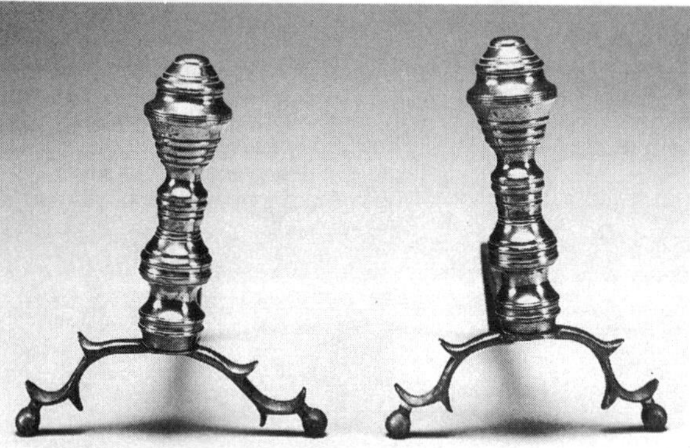

A pair of late Federal miniature brass andirons, each with turned standard on spur-arched legs with ball feet, American, 19thC, 6in (15cm) high.
$1,200-1,500

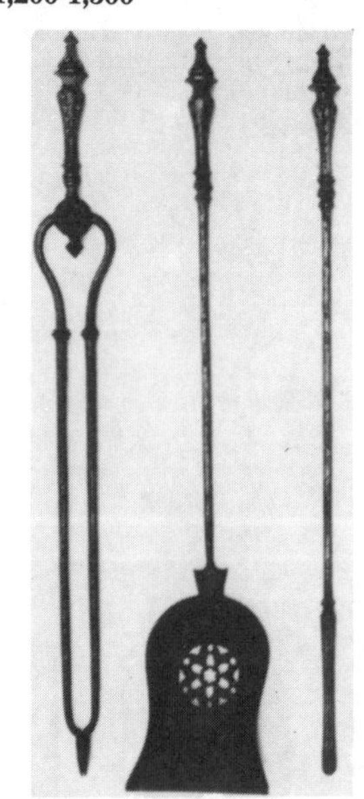

A set of 3 Georgian steel fire irons, the baluster brass grips chased with foliage. **$500-650**

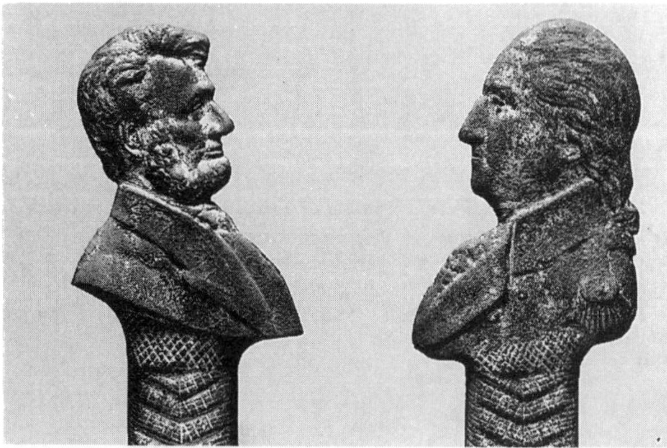

A pair of cast iron andirons, each with silhouette bust profile, one George Washington, the other Abraham Lincoln, above a diapered standard on slightly scrolled legs, American, late 19thC, 16in (40.5cm) high.
$2,000-2,500

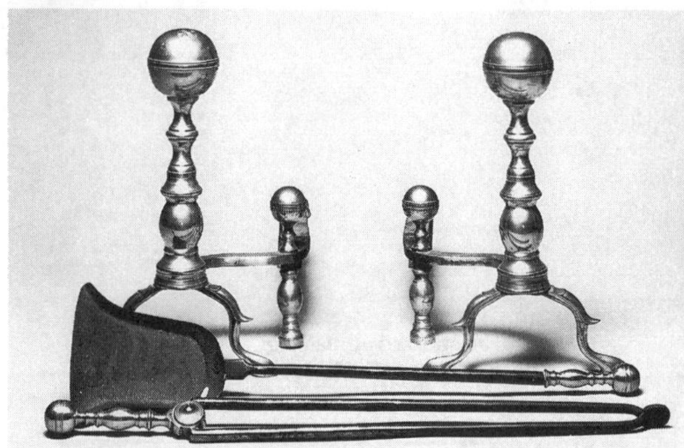

A pair of brass andirons with fire tools, Boston, late 18thC, 17in (43.5cm) high.
$800-1,200

Fenders

A French gilt bronze pierced fender, decorated with shell leaf sprays and hatched panels, 19thC, 67½in (171cm).
$1,400-2,000

A George III serpentine brass fender, the frieze pierced and engraved with linked lozenges and flowerheads, 44in (111.5cm).
$1,200-1,400

A George III serpentine brass fender, the frieze pierced and incised with foliate ornament, 48in (122cm).
$2,000-2,500

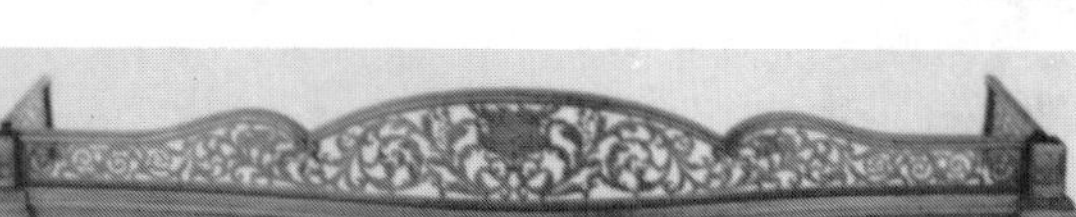

A serpentine brass fender, the frieze pierced and incised with an urn of flowers, dragons and scrolling foliage, flanked by applied coats-of-arms, late 19th/early 20thC, 90½in (229cm).
$2,000-2,600

A steel and brass fire kerb, with bead and Greek key border, with floral rectangular porcelain mounts and ropework twist rail over, 63in (160cm).
$1,000-1,200

A George III brass serpentine fender, pierced with urns, 49in (124.5cm) wide.
$800-1,200

A George III brass serpentine fender, pierced with flutes, paterae and entrelacs, 46in (117cm).
$650-1,000

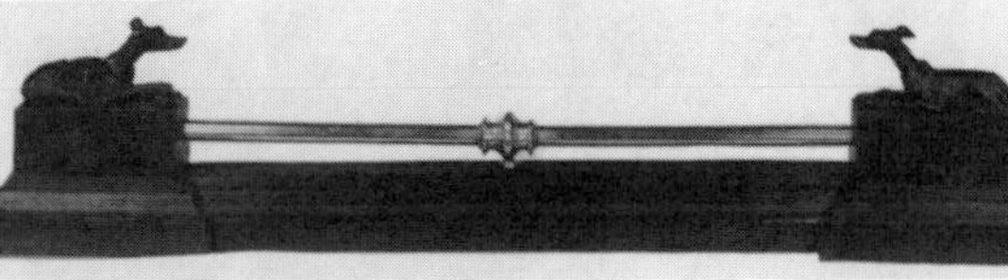

A bronze, steel and brass adjustable fender, with turned brass rail flanked by recumbent greyhounds with moulded plinth, 32in (91cm).
$650-1,000

An ormolu and bronze adjustable fender, of Louis XVI style, the pierced front and sides cast with scrolling foliage, with a cherub to each side warming his hands, stamped BFP 1681 twice, 71in (180cm) wide.
$1,500-2,500

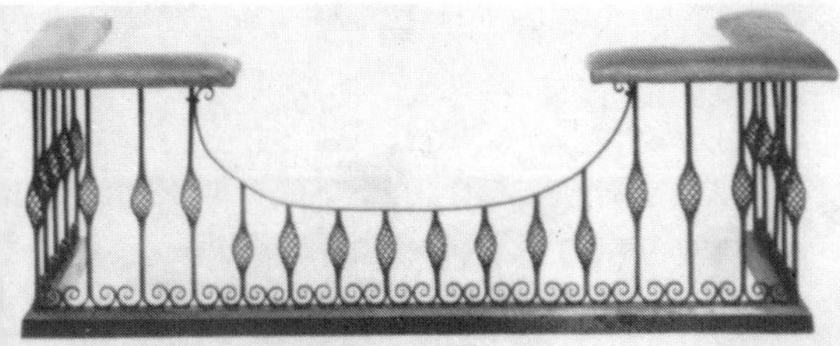

A black painted wrought iron club fender, the square uprights with central open spiral twist knops, terminating in scrolls, with green leather upholstered seats, 75½in (191cm).
$1,300-1,500

A George IV brass fender, the body pierced with anthemia, on claw feet, 35in (89cm).
$650-1,000

A William IV cast and polished steel and brass fender, with a frieze of stylised acanthus leaves and tulip motifs, on ball feet, 51in (129.5cm).
$500-650

A late Georgian steel fender, the lattice work frieze with applied lozenges, on ball feet, 48in (122cm).
$150-300

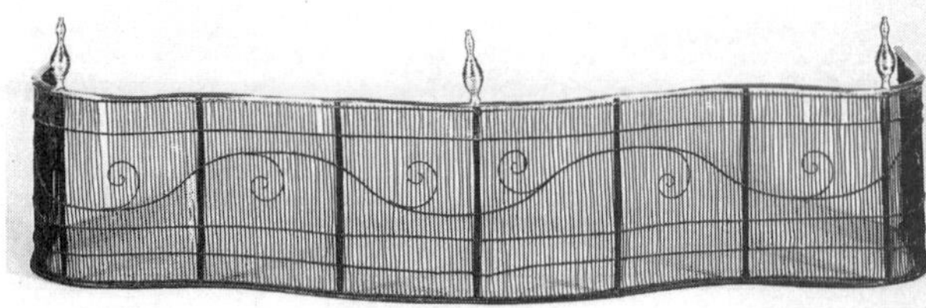

A serpentine brass and wire fire fender, with 3 beaded double lemon-turned finials, American, 19thC, 57in (144.5cm) wide.
$4,000-4,500

Fireplaces

An oak overmantel with carved decoration enclosing and surrounding needlework panels of the 4 elements, early 20thC, 65in (165cm) wide.
$1,000-1,200

An original fireplace, c178
$900-1,200

A Victorian white painted pine and gesso chimneypiece in the Adam taste, the inverted breakfront shelf with stiff leaf moulding above an egg-and-dart cornice, the centre tablet to the frieze depicting a classical hunting scene, flanked by swags and urns with conforming jambs, 70½in (178cm).
$1,500-2,000

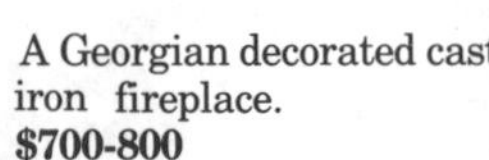

A Georgian decorated cast iron fireplace.
$700-800

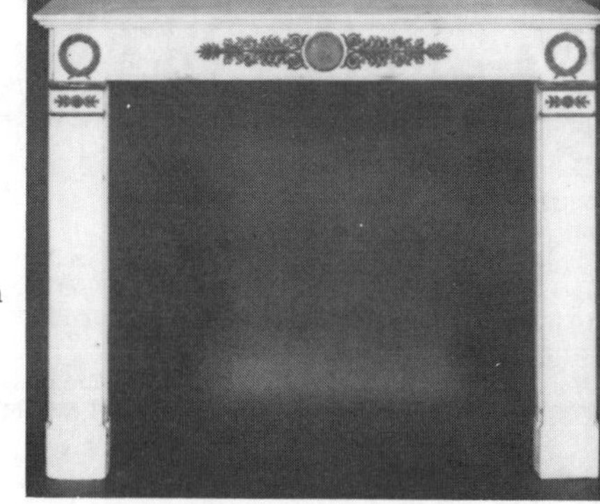

A Regency Carrara marble and bronze mounted chimneypiece, with moulded shelf above a plain frieze centred by an applied anthemion leaf motif flanked by wreaths, the conforming jambs with foliate capitals, 53in (134.5cm).
$2,500-3,500

A white painted pine chimneypiece, with eared top, the later frieze carved with a panel of Pegasus flanked by fluted panels, the jambs formed as fluted columns with composite capitals, 57in (145cm) wide.
$650-1,000

A mahogany fire surround, the inverted breakfront pediment with Greek key and blind fret carving over a plain panel within a beaded frame, all over a plain overmantel and outlined fire surround, the sides with carved double column mounts with fluted stems, 75in (190.5cm).
$550-700

A Regency giltwood overmantel mirror, with eared moulded ball encrusted cornice, the parcel ebonised frieze applied in relief, the bevelled plate flanked by cluster columns and appied lion masks, 57½in (146cm).
$5,500-6,500

Fire Grates

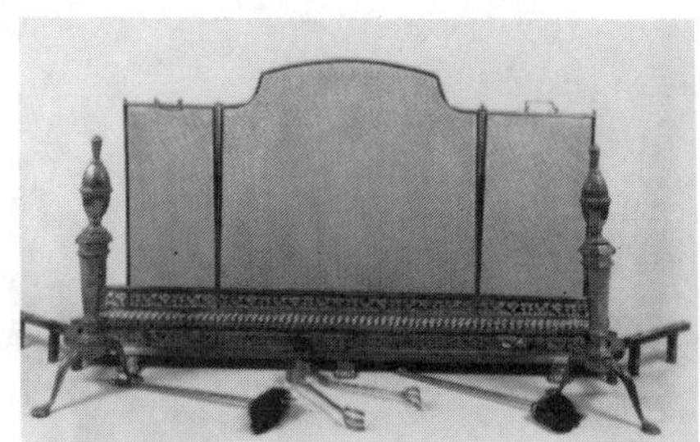

A set of George III style brass hearth equipment, comprising a pair of andirons, a gadrooned fire fender, a 3-panel brass and wire mesh fire screen, tongs, a shovel and a poker, the fender 59in (149.5cm) wide, together with a hearth brush with an ivory-mounted handle.
$3,000-4,000

Fire Grates

A cast iron and brass mounted fire grate, the serpentine railed front above a waved apron flanked by square section standards with spherical finials, the concave backplate in the form of a phoenix rising from the flames, 19thC, 36in (92cm).
$1,000-1,500

A late Georgian brass and cast iron fire grate in the Adam style.
$2,200-2,500

A Victorian cast iron and brass mounted fire grate, the railed front on paw feet with urn finials below an arched backplate, 21½in (55cm).
$1,200-1,400

A brass and iron serpentine fronted fire grate, incised with scrolling foliage and mythical beasts flanking an urn, the tapering standards with urn shaped finials, part 18thC, 31½in (80cm).
$700-1,000

A brass and steel serpentine basket grate, with pierced frame and scrolled supports, fitted for electricity, 21in (53cm).
$500-800

A polished steel and cast iron basket grate, with arched backplate flanked by scrolling serpents above drapery swags on square stepped base with pierced ash drawer, 22in (56cm).
$1,000-1,400

A Victorian cast iron and brass fire grate with serpentine railed front, the fret pierced with Vitruvian scrolls flanked by baluster column standards on fluted tapering supports, the arched backplate with raised swags, 24in (62cm).
$800-1,200

An iron and brass grate, the barred front above a pierced fret incised with dragons and foliage, the square section standards with urn shaped finials below an arched back plate, 28in (71cm).
$2,000-2,500

A Victorian iron and brass fire grate, with serpentine barred front above a pierced fret flanked by tapering standards with applied beaded mouldings, surmounted by urn finials, 27½in (70cm).
$1,400-2,000

An iron fire basket, 30in (77cm).
$650-700

A brass and iron grate, with finial and pierced fret frieze with pierced fret surmounted supports with cabriole legs, on paw feet, 18thC, 29in (74cm).
$1,300-2,000

Garden Statuary

A pair of lead jardinières, with rams' masks terminals and rope twist border above running frieze depicting Bacchanalian scenes, early 19thC, 32in (81cm) wide.
$6,500-8,000

A terracotta urn, c1880, 26in (66cm) diam.
$130-140

A painted garden figure, modelled as a full bodied stag, with applied antlers and moulded fur at the neck, American, late 19th/early 20thC, 61in (155cm) high.
$3,500-5,000

A pair of Sicilian marble urns, c1830, 34in (86cm) diam.
$23,000-25,000

A pair of black painted cast iron urns, of campana form, decorated with a Bacchanalian and a scene from the Iliad, 19thC, 21½in (55cm).
$4,000-5,000

A pair of cast iron garden urns, with egg-and-dart rims, on circular fluted socles and square bases, mid-19thC, 44½in (113cm) diam.
$5,000-6,500

A simulated granite urn, c1920, 33in (84cm) high.
$2,000-2,300

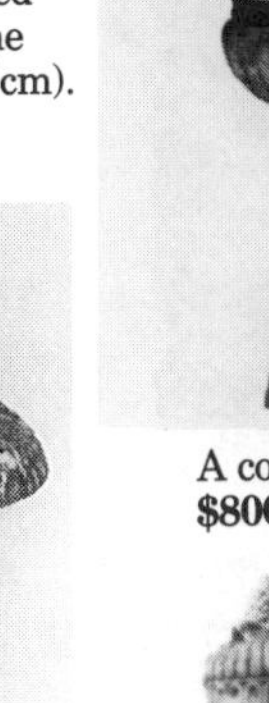

A composition urn, c1880.
$800-900

A pair of hardstone garden urns, of campana form, 32½in (82cm).
$2,000-2,500

A pair of sandstone urns and lids, with waisted leaf carved bodies, 31in (79cm) high.
$500-650

A pair of French garden urns, with fluted covers, repaired, 82in (208cm) high.
$5,500-6,500

A pair of stone urns, 21in (53cm) diam.
$550-700

A stone urn, the bulbous body with entwined double handles, on moulded socle with paw feet, 32in (81cm) diam.
$2,500-3,000

A pair of lead urns with covers, of Adam design, the lids with urn finials, mask side handles, 22in (56cm) high.
$5,500-6,500

A pair of Bath stone urns.
$7,000-9,000

A composition fountain, c1850, 62in (157cm) high.
$6,500-7,000

A bronze fountain modelled as a carp, with arched back, resting on its fins, 20thC, 59in (150cm) long.
$3,000-4,000

A stone carved fountain, 78in (198cm) high.
$7,000-8,000

An Italian stone fountain in the shape of a lion's mask, 20in (51cm) high.
$1,500-2,500

A cast iron fountain of a putto holding a fish, standing on 3 white painted shells on a shaft in the shape of 3 dolphins, on white painted hexagonal shaped base, 19thC, 49½in (126cm) high.
$4,000-5,000

A set of 10 sandstone garden gnomes, 18thC, 25in (64cm) high.
$6,500-7,000

A lead fountain figure, formed as a figure of Cupid, holding a fish, with spout, standing on domed octagonal base, 25½in (65cm) high.
$1,200-1,300

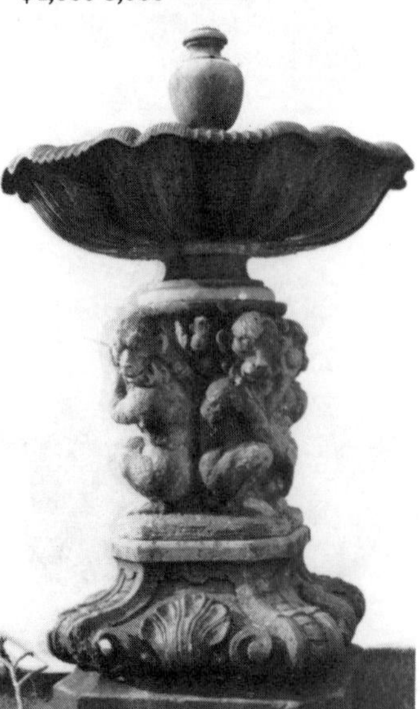

A Vicenza limestone fountain, possibly 20thC, 62in (157cm) high.
$9,000-9,500

A Regency stone sundial, 38in (96.5cm) high.
$5,000-5,500

A composition boar, c1850, 42in (106.5cm) high.
$8,000-8,500

A terracotta stoneware figure of Samuel Viscount Hood, 43in (109cm) high.
$1,000-1,100

A bronze fountain, the shaft with 3 addorsed musical putti, on gadrooned cylindrical spreading base, 20thC, 65½in (166.5cm) high.
$5,000-8,000

A terracotta group of 3 playing putti, on a cylindrical plinth decorated with a garland of foliage and flowerheads, 19thC, 85in (216cm) high.
$9,000-10,000

A lead figure of Mercury standing on a sphere, after Giambologna, 43½in (110cm) high.
$1,200-1,300

A Scottish limestone sundial, c1840, 68in (172.5cm) high.
$18,000-19,000

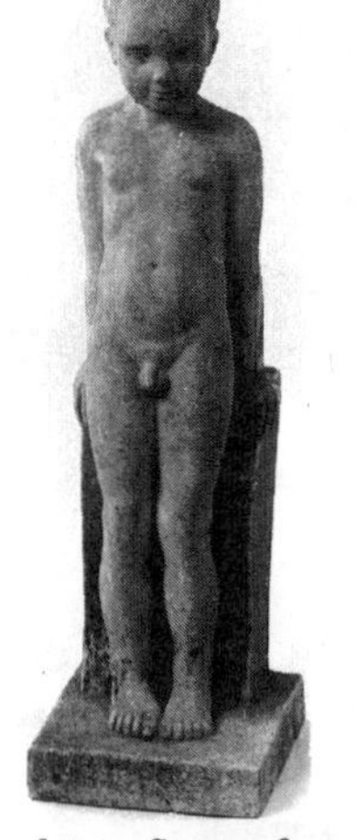

A sandstone figure of a nude boy, leaning against a ledge, the neck restored, 36in (92cm) high.
$900-1,000

A stone statue, 80in (203cm) high.
$3,000-4,000

A pair of sandstone figures of recumbent lions, on rock shaped bases, 19thC, 36½in (93cm) high.
$3,000-4,000

A lead figure of a boy gardener, in the style of John Cheere, on stepped base, late 18th/early 19thC, 53in (134.5cm) high.
$3,000-5,000

A lead figure of a heraldic lion, seated on its haunches, supporting a cabochon, on square base with cut corners, 17½in (44.5cm) high.
$300-400

A cast bronze fountain, in the form of a winged putti holding a dolphin with a water spout in its mouth, on marble plinth, 30in (76cm) high.
$1,000-1,200

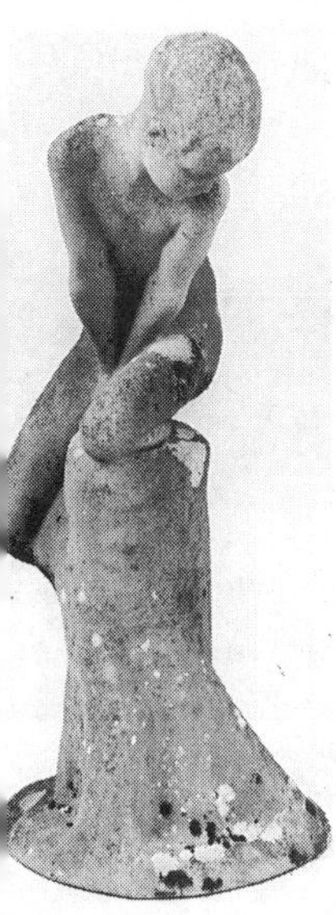

A lead cistern, moulded with rosettes and a tap on the bottom, early 19thC, 22in (56cm) wide.
$1,300-2,000

stone figure of a boy, 38in (96cm) igh.
800-1,000

A terracotta Herm statue of winter, damaged, 18th/19thC, 180in (457cm) high.
$2,500-3,000

A group of 3 composition putti, on limestone base, c1840, 88in (223.5cm) high.
$12,000-13,000

sandstone bird bath, the top with luted frieze, on a spiral fluted olumn carved with bumble bees, nd an oak leaf carved capital, with faceted square plinth, 23in (58cm) vide.
2,500-3,000

A sandstone figure of a female, the body partly shrouded in drapery, the right hand holding a cornucopia with corn, a smiling putto at her feet, 19thC, 67in (170cm) high.
$13,000-14,000

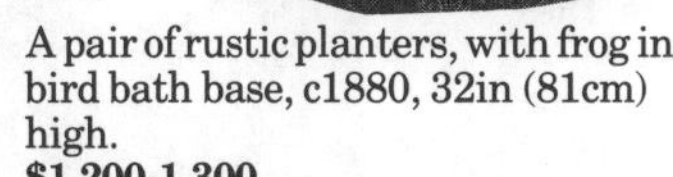

A pair of rustic planters, with frog in bird bath base, c1880, 32in (81cm) high.
$1,200-1,300

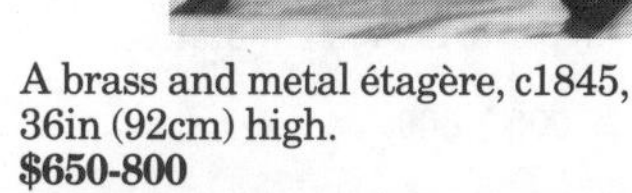

A brass and metal étagère, c1845, 36in (92cm) high.
$650-800

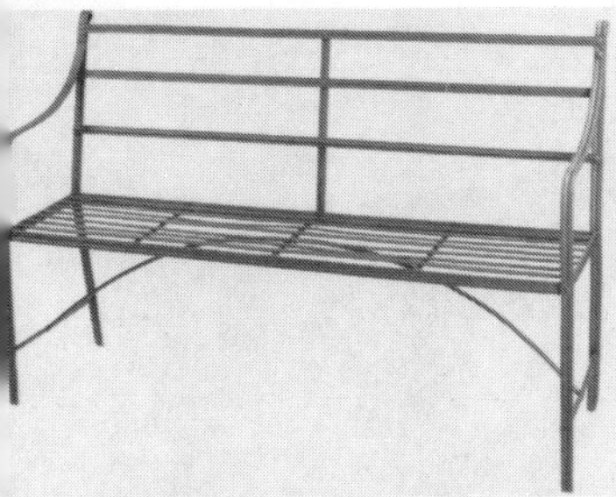

reeded wrought iron garden seat, vith down curved armrests and traight feet, the supports joined by curved stretcher, early 19thC, 0½in (133cm) wide.
1,000-1,500

A pair of wrought iron scrolled design armchairs, 37in (94cm) high.
$650-700

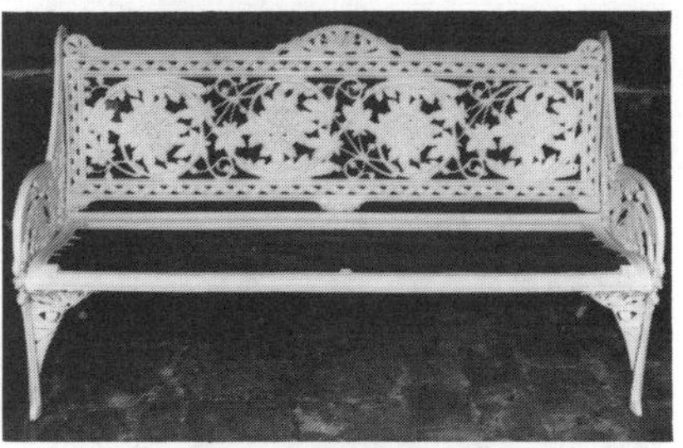

A cast iron Coalbrookdale garden bench, sweet chestnut design, c1865, 73½in (186cm) wide.
$4,000-4,500

A pair of sandstone planters, 24in (62cm) high.
$2,500-2,600

A German parcel gilt and white painted cast iron garden seat, in the manner of Schinkel, the pierced toprail with twin lyres and scrolling winged putti, with re-railed seat and ram's mask and iron supports on channelled X-frame legs and hoof feet, early 19thC, redecorated, 41in (104cm) wide.
$8,000-9,500

A cast iron garden table, with dolphin tripod, 28in (71cm) high.
$500-550

A white painted cast iron garden seat, the arched pierced back cast with foliate scrolls and rustic motifs, on down curved arm rests, wooden slatted seat and scroll feet, 49in (125cm).
$1,000-1,300

A pair of wrought iron gates, c1830, 62½in (158cm) high.
$1,000-1,100

A suite of rustic garden furnitu stamped J Hayward Phoenix Foundry Derby, c1850, bench 4 (124.5cm) wide.
Two chairs. **$3,800-4,500**
Two benches. **$3,500-4,000**

A white marble garden bench, the moulded top with scrolled frieze centred by grotesque mask, on addorsed lion mask monopodia end supports and rectangular bases, 55in (139.5cm) wide.
$6,500-7,000

A Regency reeded wrought iron garden seat, c1790, 70½in (178cm) wide.
$11,500-12,000

A pair of wrought-iron sprung garden seats, and a matching armchair, 32in (81cm) high.
Pair of chairs. **$300-400**
Armchair. **$300-400**

A garden table, with marble top an cast iron base, c1850, 27in (69cm) high.
$800-900

A brass letter box, 6½in (16cm).
$30-50

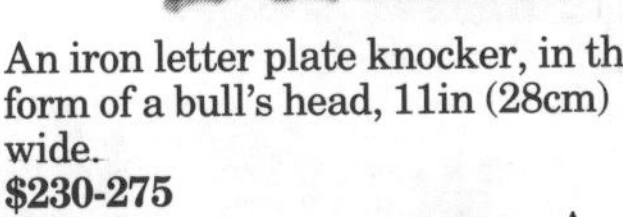
An iron letter plate knocker, in the form of a bull's head, 11in (28cm) wide.
$230-275

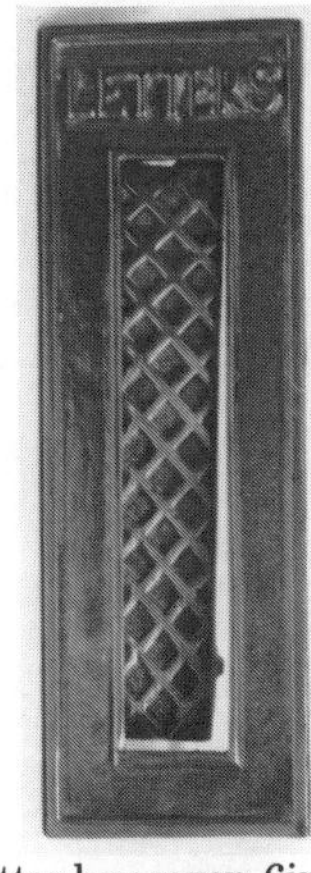

A small brass letter box cover, 6in (15cm).
$25-30

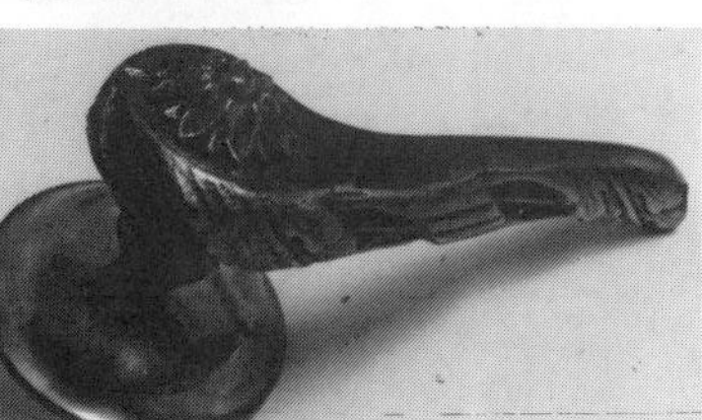
A brass door handle.
$75-90

A solid copper lion door knocker, 5in 13cm).
$130-150**

A china washbasin with brackets and brass taps.
$350-400

A brass lion's head bell pull, 4½in (11cm).
$140-200

A cast iron door handle.
$30-50

A brass door handle, 3in (8cm).
$30-65

A brass keyhole cover and door plate, 7½in (19cm).
$50-65

A pair of brass door pulls, 8in (20cm).
$100-130**

Four brass door hooks, 3 to 13in (8 to 33cm).
$15-30 each

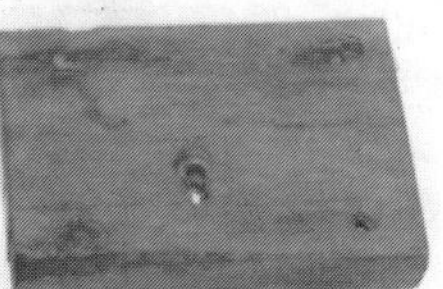
A pair of oak locks.
$15-30

A brass door latch, 11in (28cm).
$110-140

A pair of brass and turned wooden handles, 14in (36cm).
$110-130

A brass and copper door knocker letterbox, 10in (25cm).
$100-130

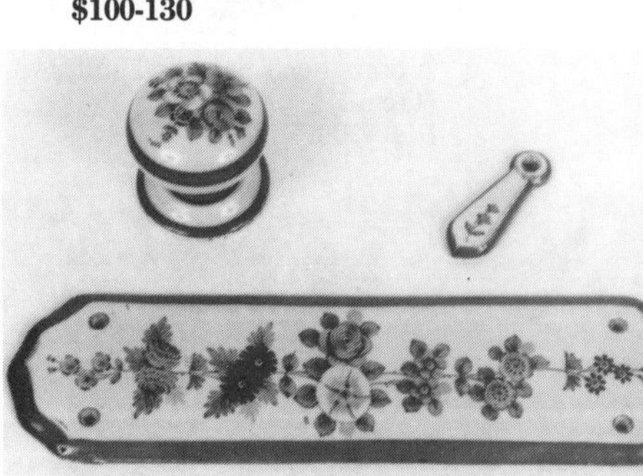

A set of Continental hand painted door furniture, c1900.
$80-110

A brass bell pull, 6in (15cm).
$120-140

A brass door bell pull on marble, 10in (25cm).
$140-200

A pair of copper door handles, 3in (8cm).
$30-55

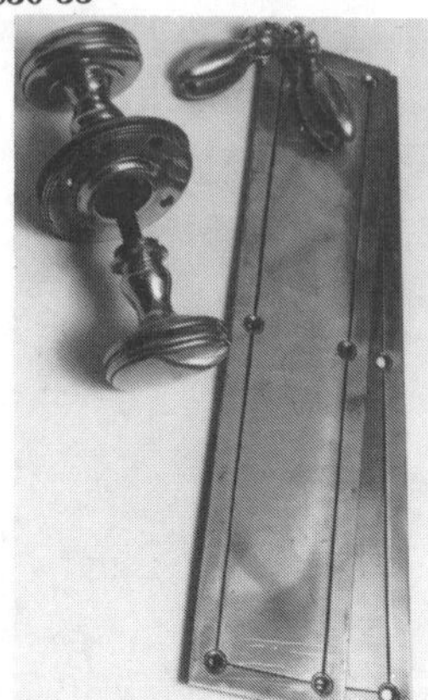

A set of brass door knobs, finger plates and escutcheons.
$55-65

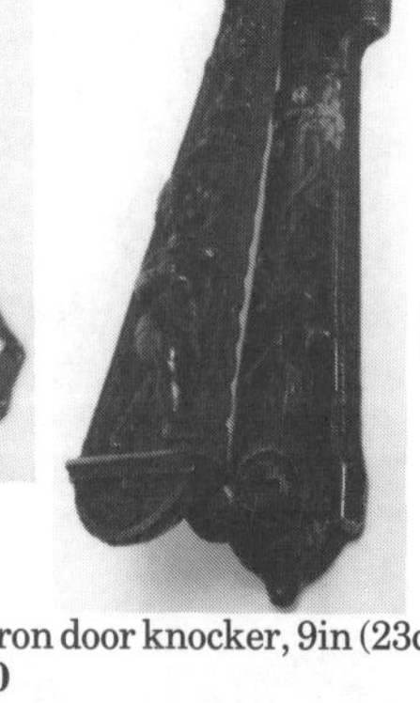

A cast iron door knocker, 9in (23cm).
$65-100

An elm country door, with original hinges and latch, 18thC.
$140-150

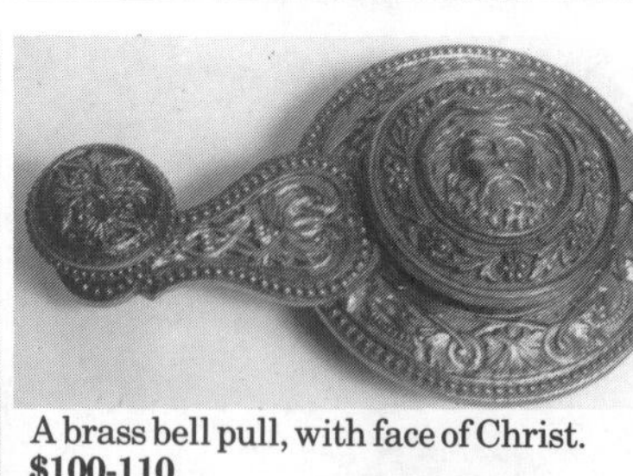

A brass bell pull, with face of Christ.
$100-110

A set of hand painted door furnitur
$15-25

A brass fox door knocker, 6in (15cm
$65-100

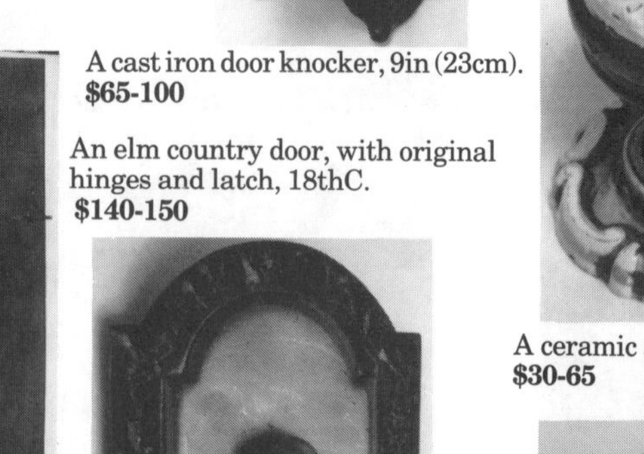

A ceramic and brass door handl
$30-65

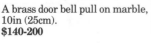

A pair of ceramic bell pushes, 3i (8cm).
$80-100

. cast iron door knocker, 9in (23cm).
110-150

A brass door knocker, 7in (18cm).
$140-200

A pair of large brass door knockers, 12in (31cm).
$150-230

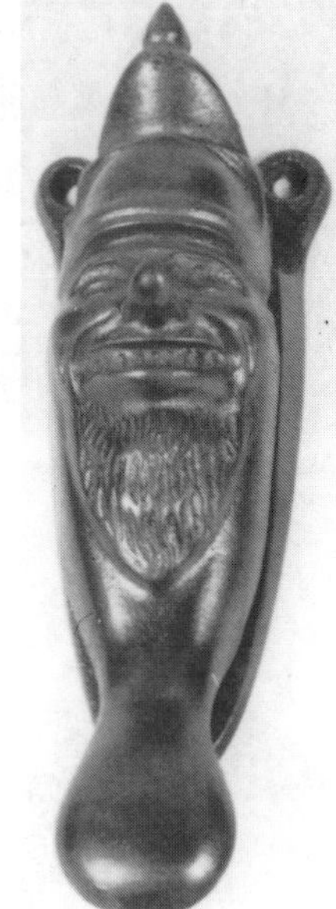

A metal door knocker, 6in (15cm).
$55-75

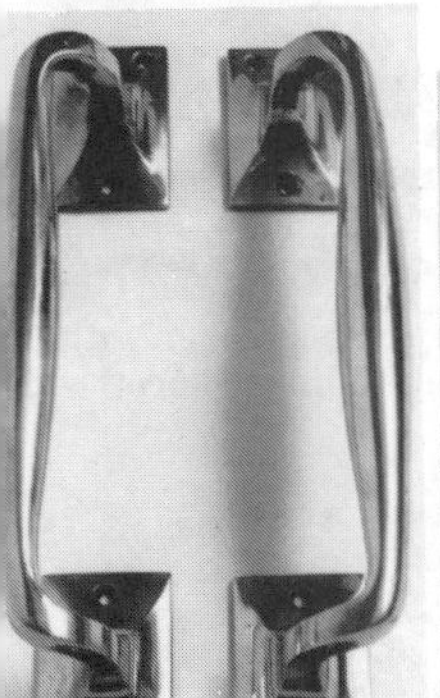

. pair of brass door pulls, in (23cm).
50-80

A pair of brass door plates, 8 and 12in (20 and 30.5cm).
$15-30 each

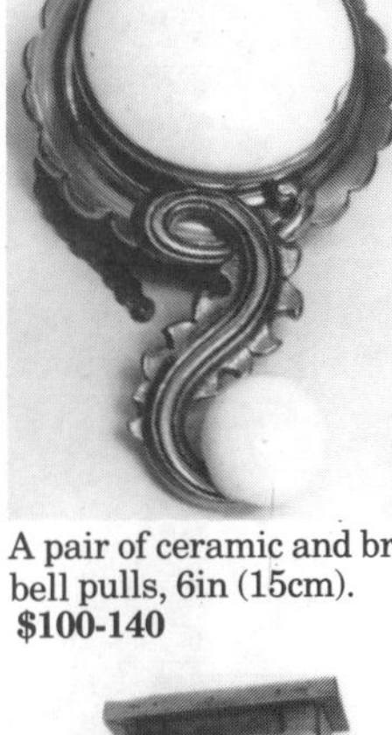

A pair of ceramic and brass bell pulls, 6in (15cm).
$100-140

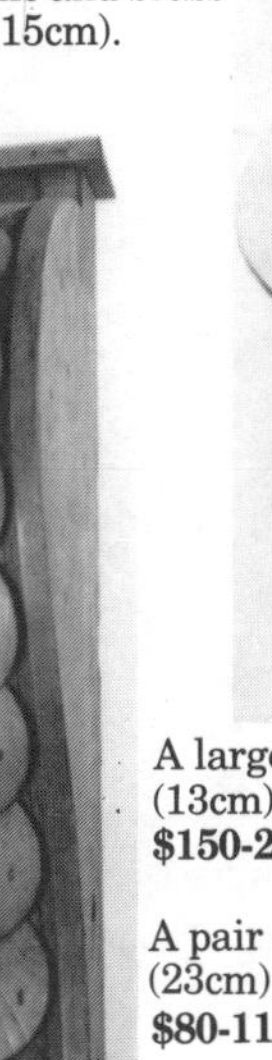

A large brass door handle, 5in (13cm).
$150-250

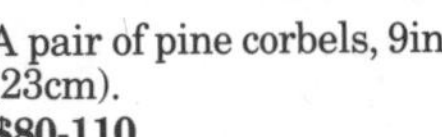

A pair of pine corbels, 9in (23cm).
$80-110

'rench stained glass church windows, St Corentin and St Edouard, 120in (304.5cm) high.
3,000-4,000 each

'rench stained glass windows by G P Dagrant of Bordeaux, c1900, Joan of Arc, St Michel, St Louis, 43in (109cm) high.
$3,000-4,000 each

A set of 11 mahogany corbels, 10in (25cm).
$550-650

A set of 4 pine corbels, 9in (23cm).
$150-200

An iron window frame, 34in (86cm) wide.
$250-400

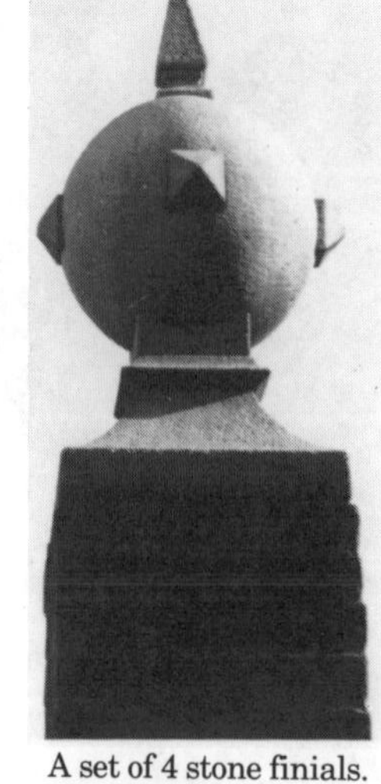

A set of 4 stone finials.
$5,000-5,500

A French bottle trolley, 39in (99cm) long.
$150-205

A Japanese stone lantern.
$550-700

A cast iron drain, c1910, 26in (66cm) high.
$120-140

A wrought iron house sign with copper letters, 53in (134.5cm) wide
$400-480

A dance hall ceiling from the German liner HV Columbus, c190
each panel 74in (188cm) wide.
$20,000-22,000 complete

A Victorian wrought iron arbour.
$3,000-3,500

An English cast iron boot scraper
c1870.
$100-110

A pair of Victorian ormolu and brass curtain tie backs.
$80-110

A miniature cannon, c1800, 15in (38cm) long.
$300-310

A pair of cast iron door stops, c1880, 10in (25cm).
$300-400

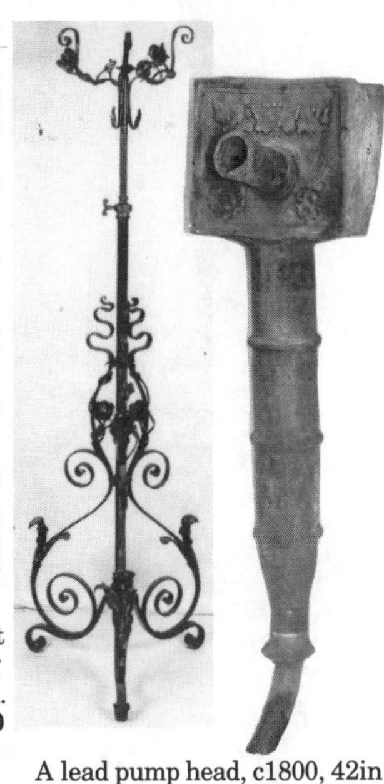

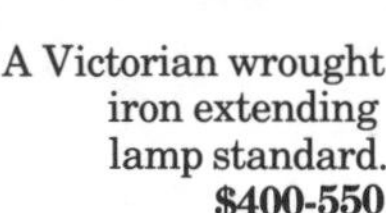

A Victorian wrought iron extending lamp standard.
$400-550

A lead pump head, c1800, 42in (106.5cm).
$250-260

A pair of Continental ormolu rococo design chenets, c1775.
$1,000-1,200

A lead pump head, c1800, 34in (86cm) high.
$200-210

A spirit percolator, 13½in (35cm).
$140-200

A mahogany stick stand, c1890.
$240-280

An iron boot scraper, 17½in (44cm) wide.
$140-145

A decorative cast iron finial, 19thC, 63in (160cm).
$500-650

A large wooden cog, 25in (64cm).
$100-120

A Victorian cog or casting mould, 16in (41cm).
$75-90

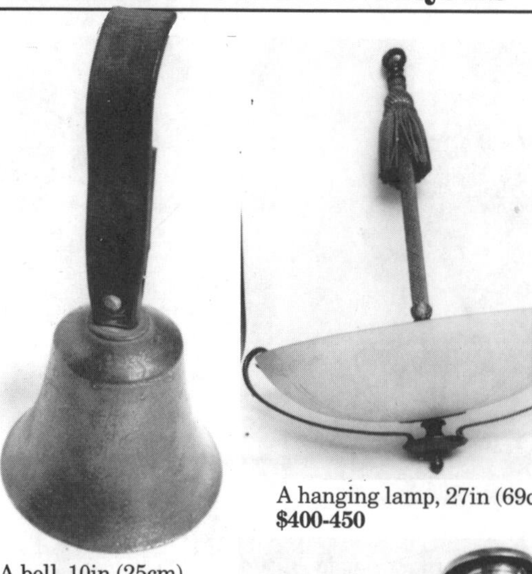

A bell, 10in (25cm).
$50-80

A hanging lamp, 27in (69cm).
$400-450

Four York stone balls, 10in (25cm).
$150-210

A wooden thermometer, 12in (31cm). **$10-15**

A wrought iron lantern with vaseline glass shade, c1885, 34in (87cm) high.
$650-700

A set of 4 brass casters, 4in (10cm).
$130-150

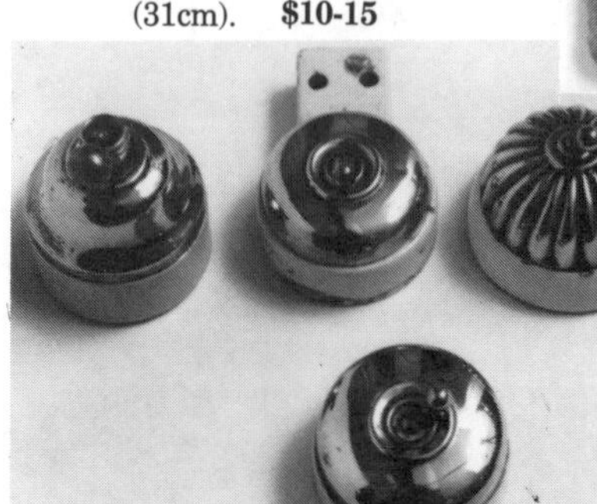

Four brass and ceramic light switches.
$30-50 each

A pair of iron troughs and feeder, c1800, 46in (116.5cm) wide.
$1,000-1,200

A brass boiler thermometer, 7in (18cm).
$17-25

A brass letter box cover, 7in (18cm).
$40-55

An elm country doo
18thC.
$140-150

A pair of oak woodcarvings from a Renaissance fireplace, 25in (64cm) wide.
$500-550

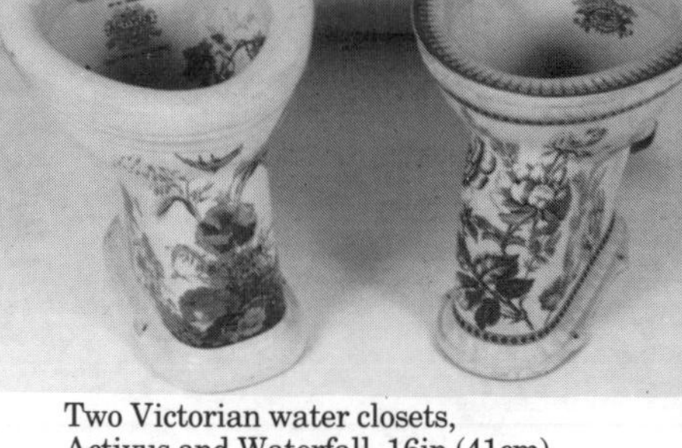

Two Victorian water closets, Activus and Waterfall, 16in (41cm) high.
$525-650 each

A gas flare brass dragon, 5in (13cm).
$80-100

A set of 2 Edwardian red terracotta chimney pots.
$145-200

A Victorian cast iron stove.
$350-400

A Victorian terracotta Tudor Rose design wall decoration.
$25-30

A pestle and mortar, 6in (15cm) high.
$120-150

A set of 2 stone plaques, 17thC.
$300-320

A decorated clay ridge tile.
$8-15

A clay ridge tile.
$6-8

A chimney pot, 16in (41cm) high.
$100-120

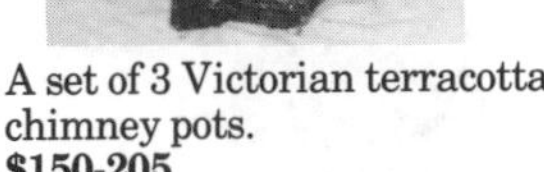

A set of 3 Victorian terracotta chimney pots.
$150-205

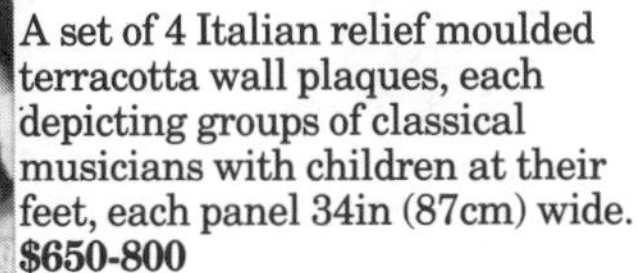

A set of 4 Italian relief moulded terracotta wall plaques, each depicting groups of classical musicians with children at their feet, each panel 34in (87cm) wide.
$650-800

A Bath stone carving with a Gothic cross.
$55-75

CLOCKS

Longcase Clocks

A George II scarlet lacquered chinoiserie longcase clock, with arched brass dial by Moses Abraham, Frome, 87in (221cm) high.
$4,000-5,000

A mahogany longcase clock, Wm. Aitken, Haddington, early 19thC.
$6,500-8,000

A mahogany longcase clock, by John Duffett, Bristol, with 'High water at Bristol Key' (sic), c1770.
$12,000-13,000

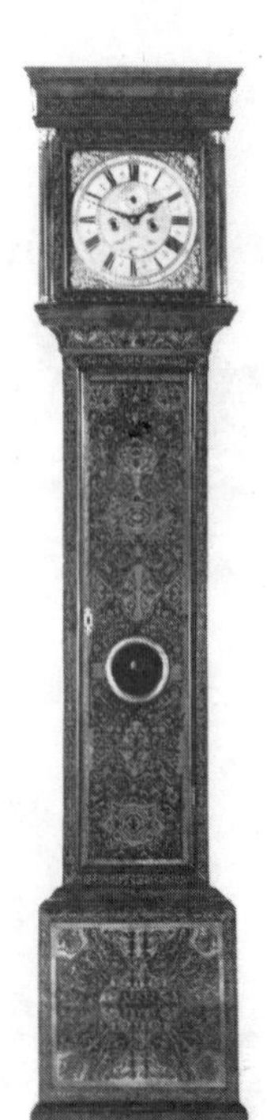

A longcase clock with arabesque marquetry, John Barron, London, early 18thC.
$14,000-16,000

A mahogany North Country 8-day longcase clock, with lunar painted dial, the case with swan-neck pediment, ropetwist columns and Gothic arched door, on plinth base, 90in (230cm).
$1,200-1,500

A lacquer longcase clock, by John Berry, London, the 8-day 5-pillar movement with brass dial showing seconds, date and with strike/silent, the case with chinoiseries of Oriental design on a tortoiseshell background, c1750, 86in (218.5cm) high.
$7,000-8,000

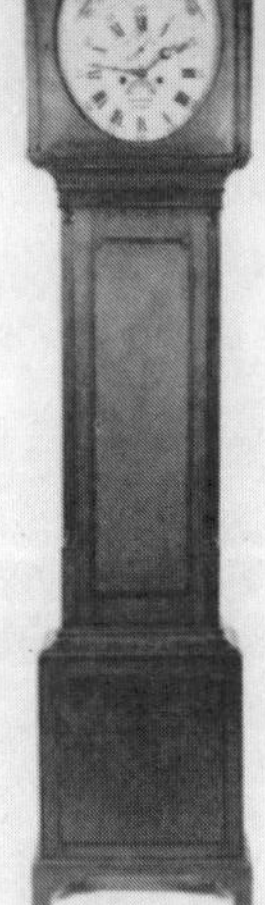

An oak and mahogany longcase clock, Thos. Bembow, Newport, late 18thC, 94in (238cm).
$2,000-3,000

A mahogany longcase clock, c1770.
$5,500-6,500

An oak longcase clock, Nat. Brown, Manchester, late 18thC.
$6,500-8,000

A Federal inlaid mahogany longcase clock, the hood with 3 brass ball-and-spire finials centering pierced fretwork above a arched, glazed door opening to a painted dial, signed Aaron Willar Boston, the waisted case with moulded rectangular door centerir an inlaid oval patera and edged wit chequered stringing, flanked by fluted quarter-columns with brass capitals and bases over a box base with pattern stringing, on French feet, repairs to case, works possibl not original, c1805, 91in (231cm) high.
$8,000-12,000

A George III oak and mahogany longcase clock, by John Warrone, Kirby Moorside, 96in (243.5cm).
$3,000-4,000

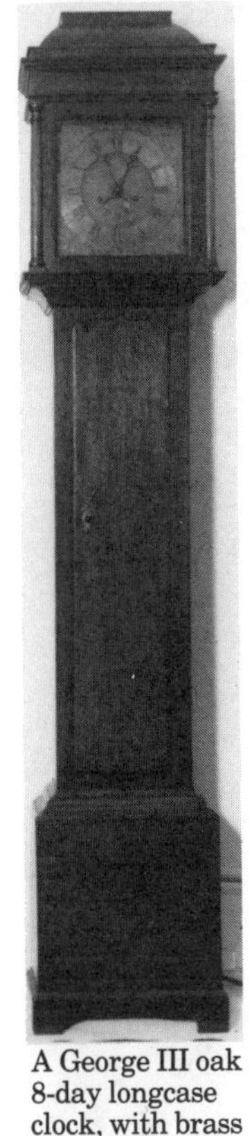

A George III oak 8-day longcase clock, with brass dial inscribed Jn. Agar & Son, York, 84in (213cm) high.
$1,000-1,100

A late Georgian Scottish longcase clock, with 8-day movement and brass dial, the mahogany case with shell motif inlay, satinwood stringing and fluted pilasters, inscribed J Ramage, Edinburgh, 84in (213cm).
$4,500-5,000

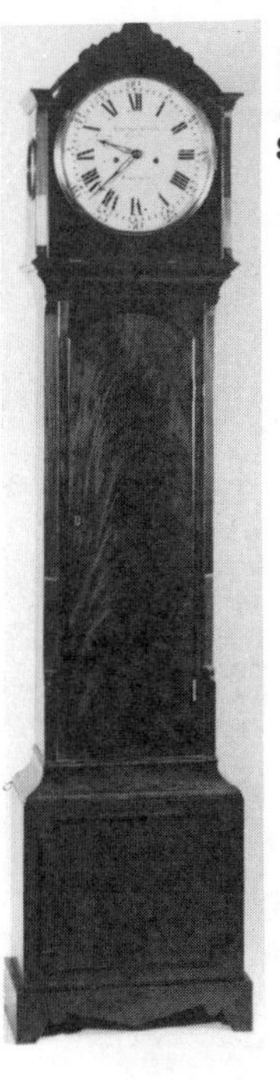

A mahogany longcase clock, c1815.
$5,000-6,500

An important walnut longcase clock, with hourly strike on a bell, 14in (35cm) arch brass dial, 5-pillar movement, 8-day duration, strike/silent in arch, by Joseph Bosley, London, c1720, 96in (243.5cm).
$20,800-21,500

A mahogany longcase clock, with 8-day duration, hourly strike on a bell, by Joseph Brown, Worcester, c1780, 79in (200.5cm).
$5,500-6,500

A mahogany 8-day longcase clock, with arched painted dial, boxwood strung case flanked with ropetwist columns, maker Neath, early 18thC, 86in (218cm).
$2,500-3,000

A mahogany longcase clock, by W B Cornforth, Macclesfield, early 19thC, 93in (236cm).
$2,500-3,000

A Victorian 30-hour longcase clock, with original case and movement, Vernis Martin oil painting on door.
$2,300-2,500

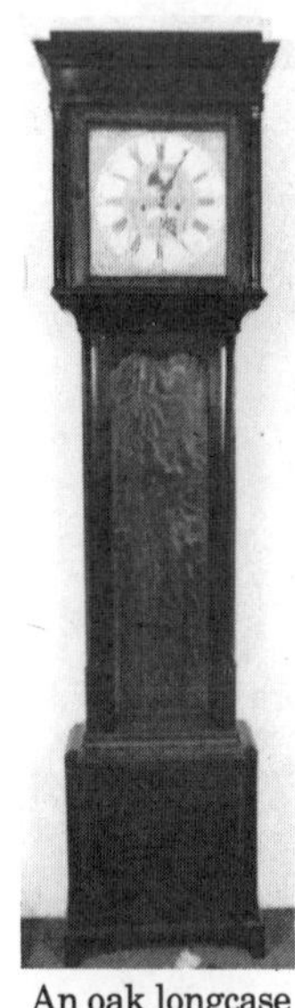

An oak longcase clock, 8-day duration, unusual bell aperture for the moon, by S Collier of Eccles, 80in (203cm).
$5,800-6,800

An early Georgian japanned 8-day longcase clock, with silvered ring dial and gilt vase spandrels with moving ship in the arch, inscribed The Duke of Cumberland, with seconds hand and date aperture inscribed Jno. Carter, London, the case with chinoiserie and scrolls on a dark ground, 96in (243.5cm).
$2,000-2,500

A Georgian mahogany and shell inlaid longcase clock, with arched brass dial, with pergoda style pediment, inscribed James Garvis, Darlington, 95in (241cm).
$5,000-6,500

A walnut and marquetry longcase clock, with 12in (30.5cm) brass dial and silvered chapter ring, date aperture and seconds dial, late 17thC, the movement perhaps early 18thC, and Victorian alterations, 100in (254cm).
$6,500-7,000

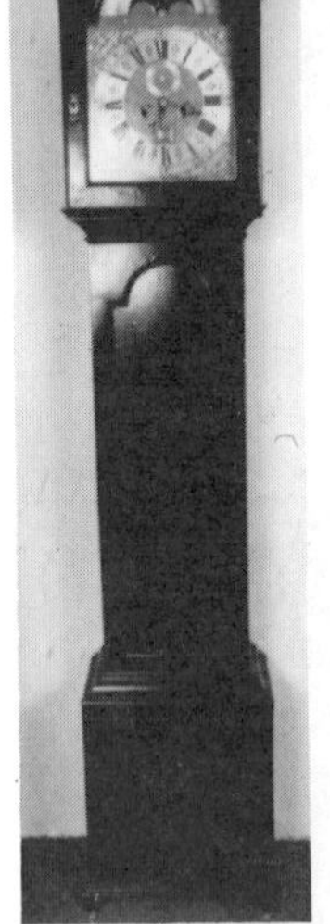

A Scottish red walnut longcase clock, with brass moon phase movement, sunburst inlay to the trunk, 8-day duration, 31-day calendar, subsidiary dial for seconds, hourly strike on a bell, by John Mearns, Aberdeen, c1760, 82in (208cm).
$10,000-12,000

A mahogany longcase clock with 8-day duration, by Rowden, Stapleford, c1820, 78in (198cm).
$4,000-5,000

An oak and mahogany crossbanded longcase clock, the 11½in (29cm) square brass dial with subsidiary seconds and date crescent, 4-pillar 8-day rack striking movement with anchor escapement, by Richardson, Weaverham, signed to the frieze J Andrews, Cabinet Maker, Weavering, late 18thC, 80in (203cm).
$1,400-2,000

An oak longcase clock, Rob Murray Lauder.
$5,000-5,500

A 30-hour verge longcase clock made by Humphrey Clarke of Hartford, c1680.
$9,000-9,500

A George III Scottish 8-day longcase clock, with brass and silvered dial, seconds dial and date aperture, in mahogany case with swan neck pediment, Corinthian columns and door with marquetry Brittania and lion and plumes in angles, inscribed Will Morvat, Aberdeen and motto 'Keep your end in view', 83½in (211cm).
$4,000-5,000

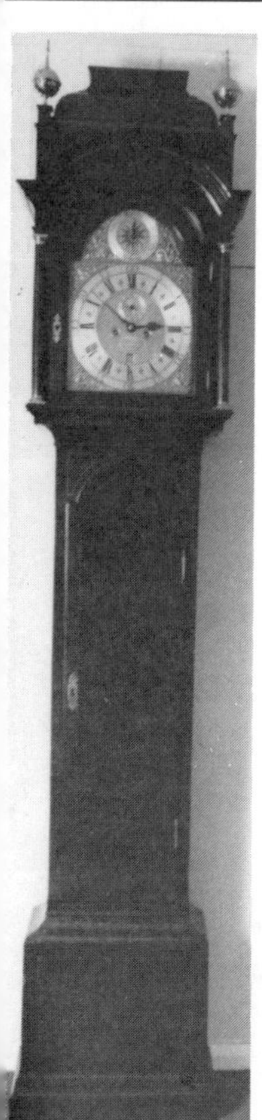

A walnut longcase clock, with 8-day duration, detachable caddy top, by Francis Dorrol, London, c1730, 94in (238cm).
$11,000-13,000

An oak longcase clock, with swan neck pediment and plain pillars to the hood, the case with mahogany crossbanding, the brass dial inscribed Thos, Hanxnell, Brampton, with pierced spandrels, seconds and date dials, 30-hour movement, late 18thC, 83in (210.5cm).
$900-1,000

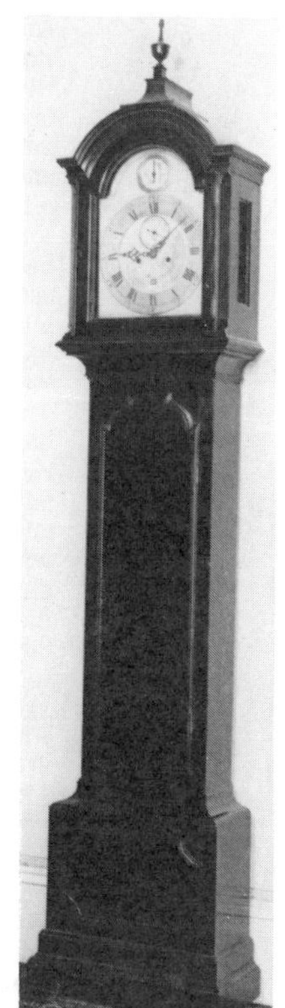

A George III longcase clock, in London mahogany style case, by Thomas Grignon, 95in (241cm).
$9,500-11,000

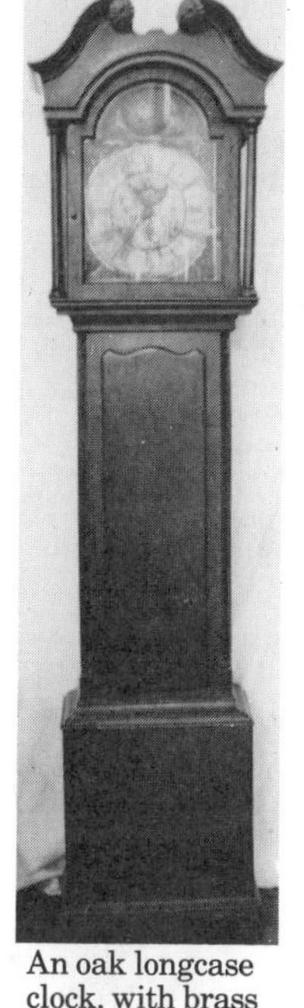

An oak longcase clock, with brass arched dial, with date and lunar ring and seconds dial, inscribed John Varley, mid-18thC, 82in (208cm).
$700-800

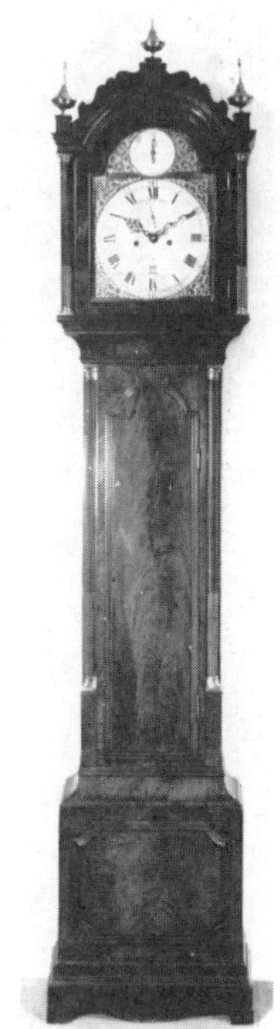

A mahogany longcase clock, Henry Daniel, London, late 18thC.
$12,000-13,000

A mahogany longcase clock, c1765.
$9,500-11,000

A mahogany longcase clock, with swan arch pediment and blind fretwork to trunk, 12in (30.5cm) arch silvered dial, 8-day duration, hourly strike on a bell, subsidiary dial for seconds, 31-day calendar, by John Durwood of Edinburgh, c1800, 89½in (227cm).
$9,000-9,500

A mahogany longcase clock, the painted movement of 8-day duration, 31-day calendar, subsidiary dial for seconds, hourly strike on a bell, by Colin Salmon, Dundee, c1811, 84in (213cm).
$8,000-9,500

A Scottish longcase clock, in original case, 8-day brass dial, by John Kirkwood, Melrose, c1770, 87in (221cm).
$8,000-9,500

A mahogany longcase clock, with swan arch pediment, the 12in (30.5cm) arched brass dial showing the phases of the moon, aperture for 31-day calendar and subsidiary dial for seconds, 8-day duration, hourly strike on a bell, by Richard Peyton, Gloucester, c1760, 94in (240cm).
$13,500-15,000

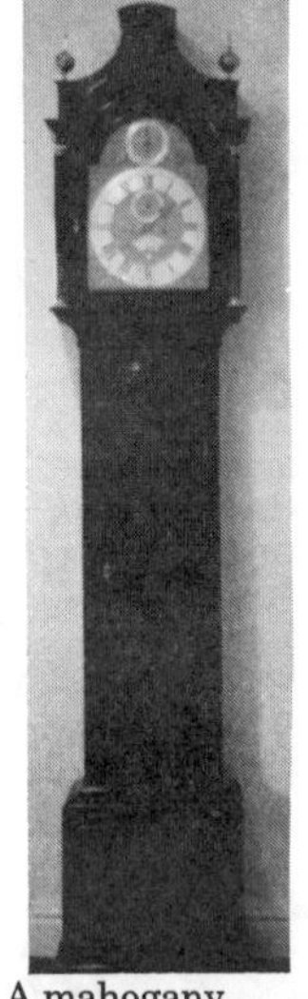

A mahogany longcase clock, by William Hughes, London, the 8-day movement striking the hours on a bell, the brass dial with seconds, date and strike/silent to the arch, c1765, 93in (236cm).
$9,000-9,500

An oak longcase clock, the hood with a shaped and broken pediment, gilt brass scale panels and turned pillars at the corners, the arched brass dial with an oscillating ship in an engraved harbour surrounded by a semi-circular band, gilt brass rococo spandrels, silvered chapter ring, the centre with date aperture, engraved seconds dial, bell striking 8-day movement, inscribed Richd. Lear Pinhey Plymouth Dock, 94in (238cm).
$2,500-3,000

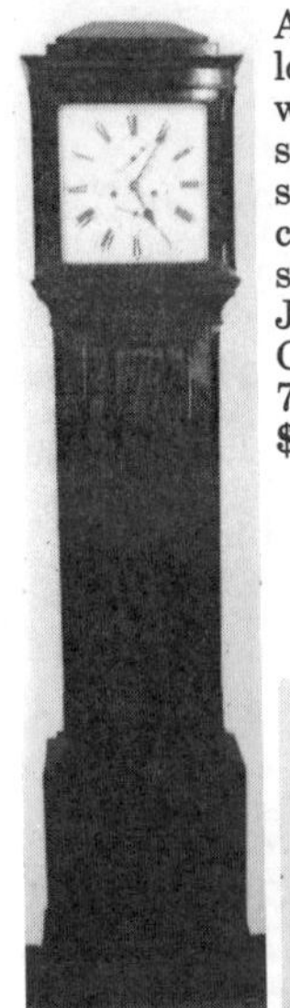

A mahogany longcase clock, with painted dial, subsidiary dial for seconds, 31-day calendar, hourly strike on a bell, by John Todd, Glasgow, c1825, 78in (198cm).
$5,500-6,500

A George III oak longcase clock, with 12in (30.5cm) brass dial, signed, with subsidiary seconds, date aperture and ringed winding holes, 8-day movement with inside count wheel, 4-finned pillars and anchor escapement, by Thomas Bridge, Wigan, 80in (203cm).
$1,500-2,500

An oak longcase clock, with 11in (28cm) brass dial, with subsidiary seconds, date aperture, 8-day bell striking movement and a pair of brass cased weights, inscribed Peter Horner, Ripon, 18thC, 81in (205.5cm).
$2,500-4,500

An oak longcase clock, with painted arched dial movement, 8-day duration, 31-day calendar, subsidiary dial for seconds, hourly strike on a bell, by P Miller-Alloa, c1800, 85in (216cm).
$3,000-4,000

An oak and mahogany longcase clock, with swan neck pediment, rosewood decorated trunk and shaped door, the white dial inscribed Count Sleaford, with second dial and 8-day movement, 19thC, 85in (216cm).
$1,200-1,300

A George III musical longcase clock, playing one tune of 7 bells every 4 hours, 8-day duration, hourly strike on a bell, subsidiary dial for seconds, in a mahogany case, inlaid with Sheraton shells, by James Pike, Newton Abbot, c1790, 83in (210.5cm).
$13,000-15,000

A marquetry longcase clock, with Transitional hood moulding and original frets, movement with internal count wheel and single latched pillar, by J Wiles, c1695, 88in (223.5cm).
$16,000-25,000

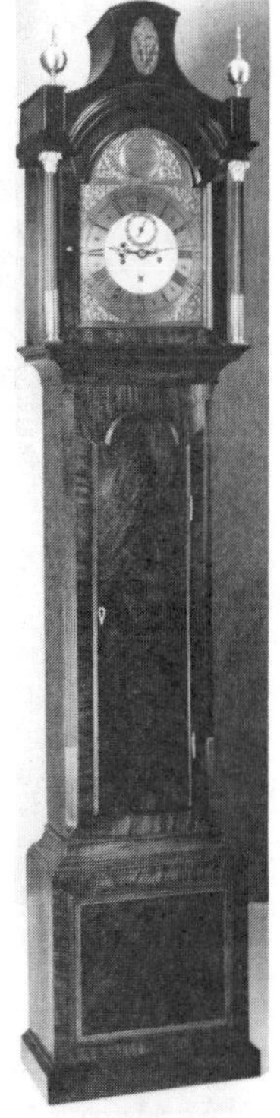

A mahogany longcase clock, c1790.
$7,000-9,000

A mahogany longcase clock with inlay, Wm. Bullock, Bath.
$6,500-8,000

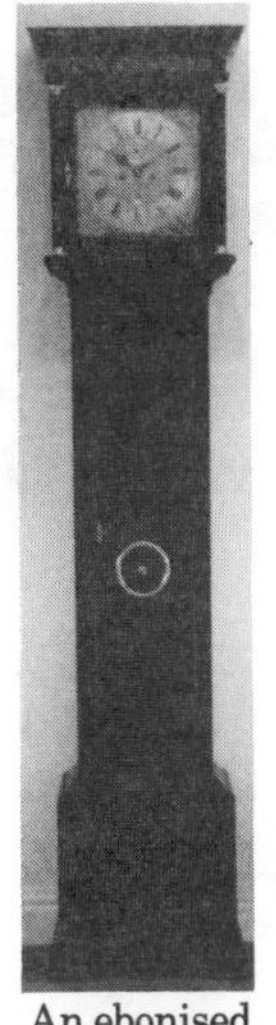

An ebonised longcase clock, by William Simes, London, the 8-day movement striking the hour on a bell, the movement with 5-plate pillars and rack striking, the brass dial with seconds and date, c1720.
$6,500-7,000

A Scottish oak longcase clock, by Walter Scott, the 8-day movement striking the hour on a bell and with seconds and date, with painted dial, c1780, 87in (221cm).
$3,000-5,000

A walnut marquetry longcase clock, by Joseph Windmills, London, the 8-day movement with inside count wheel striking on a bell and 6 latched pillars, c1690, 80in (203cm).
$45,000-50,000

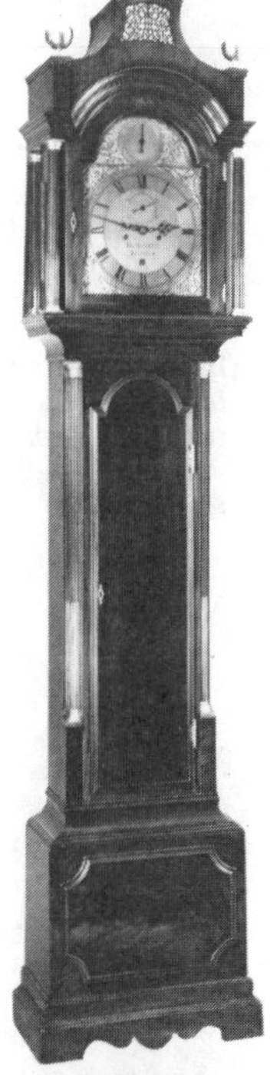

A mahogany longcase clock, c1770.
$9,000-10,000

An oak longcase clock, the 8-day movement with anchor escapement and Dutch striking on 2 bells, the 5-pillar movement with a verge alarm and strike/silent, with plaque to the centre inscribed Vincent Menil, Amsterdam, late 18thC, 92in (233.5cm).
$5,500-7,000

Regulators

Three Vienna regulators.
$2,000-2,500 each

A double weight Vienna regulator in walnut case, 44in (111.5cm).
$2,500-3,000

A single weight Vienna regulato in rosewood veneers edged with boxwood stringing, 8-day duration, maintaining pov dead beat escapement, G Becker, c1860 42in (106.5cm).
$4,500-5,300

Bracket Clocks

An ebonised bracket clock, repeating on 6 bells, by Benj. Cotton, c1760, 22½in (57cm).
$5,500-6,500

A George III scarlet japanned striking bracket clock, with pierced wood quarter frets and gilt patterned glazed side frets, the florally painted dial signed Dollif Rollison Halton 472 on disc to the arch, brass chapter ring, the 5-pillar, centre pillar latched, twin fusee, wire lines, movement with verge escapement, foliate engraved backplate, 23in (58.5cm).
$4,000-5,000

A George III bracket clock by Francis Dorrell, London, the 8-day movement striking and repeating the hour on a bell, with verge escapement and engraved backplate, the dial with date aperture and strike/silent in the arch, in ebonised case with brass carrying handle, c1765.
$5,500-6,500

A blue lacquered bracket clock, with original movement, finely engraved backplate and original verge, by Joshua Herring, c1750, 20in (51cm).
$8,000-9,500

A George III mahogany striking balloon bracket clock, with satinwood crossbanded case with gilt ball and eagle finial to bell top, white painted dial signed Evans Royal Exchange, London, with pierced gilt hands, 5-ringed pillar twin fusee movement, wire lines, with anchor escapement and pendulum holdfast, the similarly signed backplate with securing brackets to case, 33in (83.5cm).
$5,000-6,500

Regency mahogany bracket clock, ie white enamel dial inscribed ibbs, London, 8-day bell striking isee movement, 20in (51cm).
2,500-3,000

Georgian ebonised bracket clock vith 3½in (8.5cm) white enamel lial, with 2 subsidiary dials in the rch for strike/silent and regulation, rass fret work side panels, bracket eet and handles, and hole for repeat hord, missing, movement and dial nscribed Grant, Fleet Street, ondon No. 210, 10in (25cm).
16,000-20,000

A bracket clock, c1850.
6,500-8,000

A William IV mahogany bracket clock, with ring handles and brass mounts, the white dial with Roman numerals inscribed Henderson, Brigg, enclosing a brass 8-day single fusee non-striking movement, 19½in (49cm).
$800-1,200

An ebonised bracket clock, with silent escapement, by Wm. Hatton, 12in (31cm).
$4,000-5,000

A bracket clock, with web engraved back plate, by J Lawson of London, c1800. 16½in (42cm).
$4,000-5,000

A mahogany fusee bracket clock, by John Kemp, Yoxford, strikes the hour on a bell and repeats same at will, the original verge movement with engraved backplate and silvered brass dial incorporating strike/silent in the arch, c1790.
$7,000-8,000

A mahogany bracket clock, with painted dial, 8-day duration, by S Norris, London, c1820, 15in (38cm).
$5,500-6,500

A George III mahogany bracket clock, the arched brass dial signed on a silvered cartouche, John Newton, London, subsidiary strike/silent ring to the arch, applied gilt metal rococo spandrels, the movement with verge escapement and bob pendulum, with glazed rear door, together with an associated oak bracket, c1790, 16½in (42cm).
$6,500-8,000

A Regency mahogany bracket clock, the case with gilded metal ring handles and pineapple finial, fluted pediment, brass inlaid dial surround on platform base, the white painted dial with Roman numerals, signed Hyman Bass & Co Louth, enclosing a single fusee non-striking 8-day movement, together with a mahogany wall bracket, 18½in (47cm).
$1,000-1,300

A Gothic style double fusee bracket clock in bronze case, Peter Hay, Edinburgh, c1840, 16in (41cm).
$1,500-2,000

A Regency mahogany bracket cloc the chamfered top with gilt brass pineapple finial, brass beaded panels and canted corners, brass ball feet, the dial inscribed Thoma Reid, Edinburgh, bell striking fus movement, 17in (43cm).
$2,500-3,000

A late Regency rosewood striking bracket clock, with brass inlaid side angles, on wood bun feet, the engraved silvered dial signed in the arch G. Philcox Patentee London No 13, with blued Breguet hands, the 4-pillar twin fusee movement with shaped plates and anchor escapement, brackets to case, 11½in (30cm).
$2,500-4,000

A Georgian mahogany bracket clock, with repeating movement in lancet case, the silvered dial inscribed Recordon late Emery, London, with inlaid motifs and brass grilles and feet, on contemporary bracket with sliding front and secret key compartment, 17½in (45cm).
$2,500-3,000

A Georgian style mahogany bracke clock, with stepped pediment and base, the silvered dial enclosing a double fusee movement with strik on a single bell, 19in (49cm).
$650-800

An ebonised musical repeating bracket clock, made for the Turkish market, the silvered chapter ring with Turkish numerals, date aperture, the arch with subsidiary strike and chime, silent dial and tune selection dial flanking a shaped silvered panel signed Edward Pistor, London, the 3-train movement with verge escapement, striking the hours on a single bell and the quarters on 10 bells with 17 hammers operated from a pin barrel, together with an ebonised bracket with brass gallery and turned pendants, 18thC, 22½in (57cm).
$5,500-6,500

An Edwardian bracket fusee clock
$4,000-5,000

. bracket clock in a mahogany case, he brass and silvered dial signed Vm Smith, London, c1770.
15,000-20,000

A keyhole shaped mahogany bracket clock, by Simmons, London, the shaped 8-day movement striking the hour on a bell and with engraved border to the backplate, finely chased bezel to the dial, c1835, 15in (38cm) high.
$4,000-5,000

A mahogany bracket clock with applied gilded embellishment, 8-day duration, hourly strike on a bell/pull repeat strike, by Vulliamy of London, c1830, 15in (38cm).
$10,000-12,000

A George III fruitwood striking bracket clock, the dial signed Joseph Trattle Newport, on a shaped silvered chapter ring, pierced blue hands, scroll spandrels, strike/silent o the arch, the 4-pillar twin fusee, wire lines, movement with verge escapement, trip repeat, foliate engraved backplate, brackets to case, 16in (40.5cm).
$7,000-8,000

A mahogany bracket clock, by Edward Scales, London, the 8-day movement with verge escapement, engraved backplate, striking the hour on a bell, the brass dial with date and strike/silent, c1765.
$9,000-9,500

A Regency mahogany striking bracket clock, with brass lined quarter mouldings, the glazed painted dial signed James McCabe Royal Exchange London 1410, with pierced Breguet hands and strike/silent above XII, 19½in (50cm).
$2,500-3,000

A Regency mahogany bracket clock in Egyptian style, by John Wakefield, London, with sphinx caryatids to the front and engraved brass bezel to the face, the 8-day fusee movement with anchor escapement and striking the hours on a bell, c1820.
$5,500-6,500

A bracket clock, by Josephy Windmills, case restored, c1720.
$10,000-12,000

Clocks

All clock measurements refer to height unless otherwise stated

A George III mahogany striking bracket clock, with mock pendulum and calendar apertures, signed on a plaque W Turnbull, Darlington, with silvered chapter ring, twin chain fusee movement with scroll engraved backplate also signed, with vertical rack and pinion rise and fall, pull quarter repeat, brackets to case, 19½in (49cm).
$7,000-8,000

A Louis XV ormolu mounted polychrome boulle bracket clock, with glazed enamel dial, the bracket with a floral spray and pierced foliate boss, stamped A G Peridiez, 42½in (108cm).
$2,000-2,500

A rosewood and inlaid bracket or mantel clock, with a rounded arch pediment having four brass urn finials, brass mounted fluted columns at the corners, brass bracket feet and side grilles, inlai with a classical and foliate design, circular silvered dial, wire gong striking movement, late 19thC, 14½in (37cm).
$300-400

Carriage Clocks

A satinwood English 4 glass carriage clock, chain fusee movement, by Barwise London, c1830, 9in (23cm).
$3,000-4,000

A brass repeating carriage clock, in corniche case with white enamel dial and striking movement, 6½in (17cm), in morocco covered carrying case.
$550-650

Clocks
All clock measurements refer to height unless otherwise stated

A reproduction silver striking carriage clock, with uncut balance to lever platform, strike/repeat on bell on backplate signed Charles Frodsham London, similarly signed white dial with Roman numerals and blued spade hands within a florally engraved silver mask, anglaise case, base numbered 0012, 6½in (17cm).
$800-1,200

A gilt brass carriage clock, with strike repeat movement, with whi enamelled dial and filigree dial surround, early 20thC, 8½in (21cm with leather outer case.
$1,000-1,200

Did you know
MILLER'S Antiques Price Guide builds up year by year to form the most comprehensive photo-reference system available

A carriage clock, with repeating movement in engraved brass one-piece case, with lion's mask handle terminals, the white dial inscribed Martin Baskett & Cie, Paris, 5in (13cm).
$1,200-1,400

A brass carriage clock, striking a gong, c1880, 5in (13cm).
$1,000-1,200

A miniature carriage clock, 8-day duration, in serpentine case with cloisonné decoration, 3in (8cm).
$800-1,000

A brass case repeating alarm carriage clock, with white enamel dials on a silvered ground, 6in (15cm), in leather travelling case.
$700-800

A French striking carriage clock, signed Soldano, c1870, 5½in (15cm).
$1,200-1,400

A gilt brass striking carriage clock, with cut bimetallic balance to silvered lever platform strike/repeat/alarm on gong, white enamel dial signed Le Roy & Fils 57, New Bond Street, Made in France Palais-Royal Paris, with blued spade hands, subsidiary alarm ring below VI, corniche case, 5½in (15cm), leather travelling case.
$800-1,200

A gilt brass striking carriage clock, with uncut bimetallic balance to silvered lever platform, strike/repeat on gong, white enamel dial indistinctly signed, with blued Breguet hands, 5½in (15cm), leather travelling case.
$1,200-1,300

An early satinwood striking carriage clock, with plain 3 arm balance to gilt lever platform, strike on bell, backplate stamped Hy Marc Paris, similarly signed white enamel dial with blued Breguet hands within engraved gilt bevelled surround, one-piece satinwood case with carrying handle to top, 6in (15.5cm).
$800-1,000

A gilt brass one-piece striking carriage clock, with compensated 3 arm balance to lever platform strike/repeat on bell, backplate with stamp of Japy Frères, white enamel dial signed Brevet D'Invention S G D G, with blued Breguet hands, 5½in (15cm).
$1,400-2,000

A gilt brass grande sonnerie striking carriage clock, with later platform lever escapement, strike/repeat on 2 gongs, backplate with stamp of Richard & Cie, 3 position selection lever to base, the white enamel dial signed Smith & Sons, with Roman numerals and blued spade hands, corniche case, 6in (16cm).
$1,300-1,400

A French repeating alarm carriage clock, striking the hours and half hours, with enamel chapter ring and alarm dial within a floral fret work panel, all set in a gilt brass case with hobnail style decoration, 6½in (16cm).
$1,500-2,000

A miniature carriage clock, c1870 3in (8cm).
$700-800

A gilt brass striking carriage clock, with uncut bimetallic balance to silvered platform level escapement, strike/repeat on gong, white enamel dial with blued Breguet hands, 5½in (15cm).
$900-1,000

A gilt brass striking carriage clock, with uncut bimetallic balance to silvered lever platform, strike on gong, backplate with stamp of Jacot, white enamel dial, blued spade hands, corniche case, 5½in (15cm).
$1,000-1,200

A French cloisonné carriage clock, 4½in (11cm).
$900-1,000

A French carriage clock, the moulded case with fine decoration, lever escapement, 8-day duration, hourly and half-hourly strike on a bell, by Lucien, Paris, c1840, 5in (14cm).
$1,200-2,000

A German miniature carriage clock, with lever escapement, 8-day duration, c1890, 2½in (6cm).
$650-700

An Austrian carriage clock with date, month, days and full grande sonnerie strike alarm/strike/silent c1870, 7in (18cm).
$2,500-2,600

lantel Clocks

Regency satinwood mantel clock, ıse time piece with alarm by obert Ward, London, 13½in 34cm).
3,000-9,500

A mantel timepiece with silvered dial inscribed Jas Brown, London, with screw adjusting locking pendulum, in brass inlaid ebonized case, early 19thC, 9½in (24cm).
$550-700

A Gothic brass mantel clock, with enamel dial, 8-day duration, hourly strike on a gong, c1860, 9½in (24cm).
$1,400-1,500

ι mantel clock, with timepiece novement, c1820.
2,000-2,500

An ebonised mantel calendar timepiece, the engine turned gilt dial with Roman numerals and engraved arch below, numbered from the centre with mechanical day dial, with simple fusee movement, early 19thC, 7in (18cm).
$1,500-2,500

An early Victorian satinwood veneered case mantel timepiece, the 8-day fusee movement with an engraved silvered dial and backplate inscribed Birch Fenchurch St., London, bevelled glass panels, the ogee frieze to a plinth base, 8½in (21cm).
$2,000-2,500

ι late Regency rosewood mantel imepiece, the case with ball finial to tepped gadrooned top and on wood un feet, the arched engraved ilvered dial with Roman numerals nd signed Thos. Cox Savory 47 Cornhill London 762, blued steel Breguet hands, the 4-pillar single hain fusee movement with anchor scapement, 12in (30cm).
$2,000-2,500

A small gilt clock, 8-day duration, c1870, 4in (10cm).
$500-650

An Edwardian mantel clock, by J W Benson of Ludgate Hill, London, the 8-day movement with quarter strike, the brass dial and silvered chapter ring within an architectural rosewood case with classical inlay and stringing, with ogee pediment and faceted pilasters.
$1,000-1,200

A gilt spelter and alabaster cased mantel clock, the white dial enclosing a French brass movement with strike, late 19thC, 14½in (37cm).
$140-200

An English brass desk clock, c1870, 6in (15cm).
$500-650

A mahogany clock, 9in (23cm).
$1,000-1,200

A gilt metal and white marble mantel timepiece, surmounted by Cupid, 8in (20cm).
$650-700

A French balloon clock inlaid wit satinwood, c1900, 10in (25cm).
$300-500

A Federal mahogany eglomisé shelf clock, by Eli Terry and Sons, Plymouth, Connecticut, c1820, 30½in (77.5cm) high.
$3,500-4,000

A Federal inlaid mahogany shelf clock, the dial marked Aaron Willard, Boston, the pierced pediment above a slightly projectin cornice with contrasting banded inlay, the box base with stringing, on a shaped skirt with French feet, dial and surround restored, age cracks, small losses, acc. no. 1943.7.17, 31in (78.5cm) high.
$1,200-1,500

A Directoire ormolu and patinated bronze clock, depicting a porter carrying a basket, the later movement signed on the circular white enamel dial Barbot À Paris, with anchor escapement, thread suspension to pendulum, striking the hour and half-hour by means of a countwheel, 14in (35.5cm) high.
$10,000-12,000

A French 4-glass mantel clock, 11in (28cm).
$1,300-1,400

A Louis XVI ormolu and cream marble portico mantel clock, the enamel dial signed Piolaine A Paris.
$2,500-3,000

An English fusee clock, by Frodsham, with gilded and engraved dial, 19thC, 9½in (24cm). **$1,000-1,100**

A French rosewood and marquetry mantel clock, striking on a bell, 8-day duration, c1850, 13½in (34cm).
$1,600-2,000

A Victorian black marble clock, with female mask designs to the sides, striking French movement, Japy Frères.
$150-300

A French gilt clock, with Sèvres panels, c1860, 17in (43cm).
$2,500-3,000

A gilt brass 4-glass striking mantel clock, with perpetual calendar dial below the chapter ring with jewelled visible Brocot escapement in the recessed centre, signed Steward Glasgow, with blued Breguet hands, the movement with twin gong barrels striking on a bell on backplate, gorge type case, later plinth base, 17in (43cm).
$4,000-5,000

A small French boulle clock, 8-day duration, tortoiseshell case with brass inlay, c1860, 8in (20cm).
$1,400-2,000

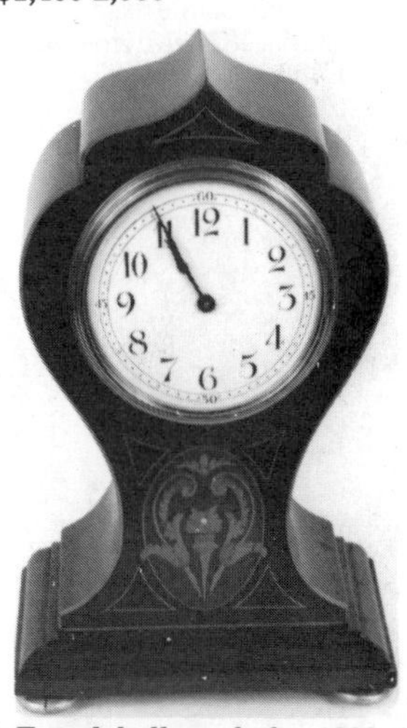
A French balloon clock, c1900, 10in (25cm).
$300-400

A French Empire mantel clock, by B P & F No. 4618, with 4½in (11.5cm) gilt dial to the 8-day striking movement, supported in bird's-eye maple veneered case with arched and moulded top, on 4 columns with gilt mounts, 19thC, 22½in (57cm).
$1,200-1,400

A French clock, by Morgan Paris, 8-day duration, boulle case with tortoiseshell, c1870, 13½in (34cm).
$1,300-1,400

A mahogany cased mantel clock, with fusee movement, the dial inscribed LNWR, 13in (33cm).
$300-400

An oak balloon clock, 8-day French movement, c1910, 10in (25cm).
$150-250

A French ormolu ebonised and boulle mantel clock, with French striking movement, 19thC.
$700-800

A French horseshoe mantel clock c1910, 5in (13cm).
$300-400

A French mantel clock, the movement stamped S Marti, with 4½in (11.5cm) white enamel dial, in ormolu mounted tortoiseshell veneered case, 13½in (34cm).
$900-1,000

A French gilt brass and porcelain mantel clock, the porcelain dial with Roman numerals, the movement striking the hours and half-hours on a gong, with giltwood stand, pendulum and winding key, late 19thC, 17½in (44cm).
$900-1,000

A Charles X French gilt bronze mantel clock, with engine turned gilt dial flanked by a dog and a classical figure playing a flute, surmounted by a 2-handled urn, with 2-train spring driven movement with count wheel mechanism striking on a bell, 17in (43cm).
$800-1,200

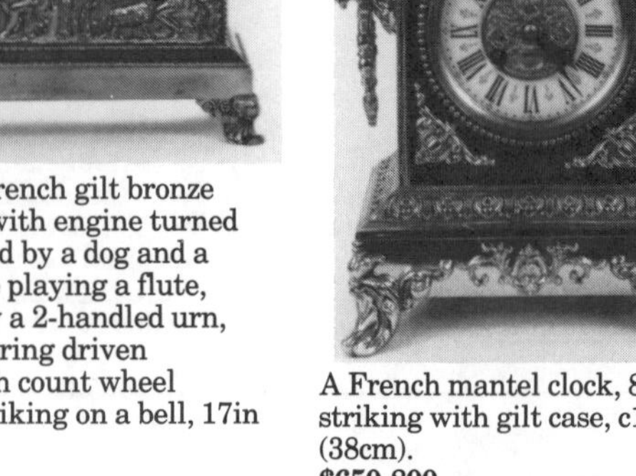

A French mantel clock, 8-day striking with gilt case, c1900, 15in (38cm).
$650-800

A French mantel clock, silk suspension, outside count strike on a bell, 8-day duration, by F C Paris, c1860.
$1,300-1,400

An ebony clock, with enamel decoration, Laine A Paris, 14in (36cm).
$600-680

A French ormolu and ebony clock, c1840, 26in (66cm).
$9,500-10,000

A similar clock is in the Royal apartments in Windsor Castle, and there is reason to believe that this piece has Royal connections.

Lantern Clocks

A lantern clock, half ting tang fusee movement, 19thC, 23in (59cm).
$4,500-5,000

A miniature winged brass lantern clock, with verge escapement and pendulum bob in the form of an anchor, the dial centre engraved with tulips, the front and wing frets also engraved, the arrow shaped steel hand indicating hours only, iron backplate fitted hoop and spikes, 9½in (24cm).
$2,500-3,000

A brass lantern clock, with anchor escapement, seconds pendulum and brass cased weight hoop and spikes to the rear, the chapter ring inscribed Danl. Hoskins, the single steel hand indicates hours only, lacking side and back doors, 15½in (39cm).
$900-1,000

A brass lantern clock, 10in (25cm).
$650-700

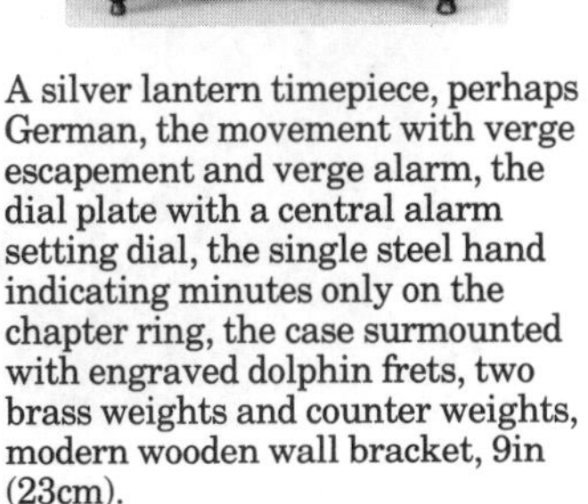

A silver lantern timepiece, perhaps German, the movement with verge escapement and verge alarm, the dial plate with a central alarm setting dial, the single steel hand indicating minutes only on the chapter ring, the case surmounted with engraved dolphin frets, two brass weights and counter weights, modern wooden wall bracket, 9in (23cm).
$4,500-5,000

A French lantern clock, 8-day duration, c1900, 9in (23cm).
$300-500

Wall Clocks

A lacquer wall clock with alarm, c1730, 18in (46cm).
$4,500-5,000

A Swedish wall clock by Carl Bergstein, striking 8-day duration, with silk work suspension, and giltwood case, c1790, 30in (76cm).
$3,000-4,000

An English single fusee dial clock, convex dial cast bezel 8-day duration, by H & E Gaydon of Brentford, London, c1830.
$900-1,000

An English 12-hour fusee dial clock, 8-day duration, mahogany case, by Dobell, Hastings, c1880, 15½in (39cm) diam.
$650-700

A mahogany clock with brass bezel, 8-day duration, c1830.
$650-800

A mahogany clock with brass bezel, 8-day duration, Fontana, High Wycombe, c1830.
$1,200-1,300

A mahogany and inlaid wall clock, c1840, 20in (51cm).
$700-800

An English mahogany wall clock, with dial spring movement, c1860
$400-500

An apprentice mahogany wall clock, with fusee movement, 8-day duration, c1840, 14in (36cm).
$3,000-3,500

A brass English ship's clock, ear 20thC, 9in (23cm).
$525-575

A single fusee clock in mahogany case, inlaid with brass stringing, c1830.
$1,400-1,500

A rosewood and brass inlaid wall clock, made in Germany, retailed in Exeter by S F Hettish, c1840, 27in (69cm).
$800-1,000

A mahogany cased trunk wall clock, with inlaid decoration, carved and fretwork design, the white dial enclosing a striking American movement, late 19thC, 28in (71cm).
$200-275

A Vienna wall clock, the case with rearing horse and ring turned pediment, turned pillar sides, enclosing a white dial with striking 8-day movement, 42in (106.5cm).
$250-300

A Georgian wall dial, the convex glazed engraved silvered 8in (20cm) dial, with mock pendulum aperture and pierced hands, the 4-pillar single gut fusee movement with knife-edge verge escapement and short bob pendulum, in later purpose made pegged mahogany case with side door, signed Thomas Harvey, London, 7½in (11cm).
$3,000-5,000

A Zaandam clock of typical form, the brass posted frame movement with Tuscan angle columns, Dutch strike on 2 bells above the velvet covered dial, signed Cornelis van Rossen on the chapter ring, 36in (91cm).
$3,000-6,500

Garnitures

A French garniture, c1870, 12½in (32cm).
$3,000-4,000

A French 3-piece clock set with 8-day striking movement, the clock surmounted by Nymphe de Torrent, by A Quintrand.
$300-400

A pink marble and ormolu clock garniture, the clock with enamel dial, inscribed Made in France for Jas Crighton & Co., Edinburgh, surmounted by an urn on a fluted column and canted plinth, the candlesticks with beaded festooned nozzles on fluted columns, the clock 8½in (22cm).
$1,000-1,300

A French 3-piece mantel clock set, with 8-day striking movement, surmounted by swan and girl, on marble base.
$150-250

Table clocks

An ormolu mounted ebony table clock, made for the Turkish market, the movement with verge escapement striking the hours on a bell and fitted with a six-bell repeater, the backplate engraved with scrolling foliate designs, the numerals changed from Turkish to Roman, engraved in the arch Geo. Prior London, 18thC, 20in (51cm).
$10,000-11,000

A French table clock, 8-day duration, c1890, 5½in (14cm).
$500-550

A Germanic brass table clock, with chain fusee for the going with spring balance, verge escapement, pierced square footed cock, resting barrels for hour strike and alarm on bell in hinged base, signed Wenzl Wachter in Gaya, No. 151, basically 18thC, 3½in (8cm) diam.
$3,000-4,000

A Germanic table clock, with steel frontplate and pillars, brass backplate, chain fusee for the going with spring balance verge escapement, resting barrels for the hour and quarter strike on 2 bells in the hinged base, going barrel alarm, copper gilt dial with brass chapter ring, on winged paw and alternating toupie feet, signed Charleson London, initially early 17thC, extensively reconstructed mid-18thC, 6in (15cm) diam.
$5,000-5,500

An English bird's-eye maple table clock, with fusee movement, 8-day duration, by William Hardy, c1830, 11in (28cm).
$2,500-2,700

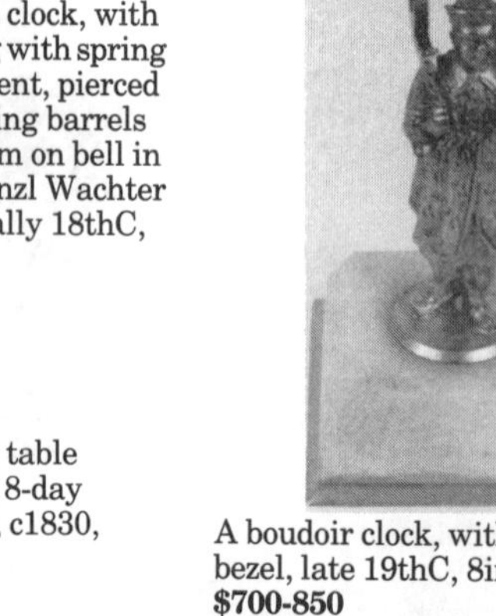

A boudoir clock, with engraved dia bezel, late 19thC, 8in (20cm).
$700-850

Miscellaneous

A Dutch walnut veneer longcase organ clock, numerous wood pipes, in need of restoration, early 19thC, 118in (300cm).
$1,400-1,450

A carriage or desk clock, by Howell & Jones, 7in (18cm).
$1,100-1,250

NB. This was given by Disraeli to his private secretary, Sir Charles Wilson, who later became the President of the Grand Trunk Railway of Canada and thereafter to his descendants.

A dark brass Gravity clock, made i USA, 10in (25cm).
$550-700

An English Organ clock, attributed to George Ryke, London, the engraved brass dial set in an elaborate cartouche flanked by Diana and Mercury, 2 subsidiary dials above for tune selection and lock/unlock for music, the timepiece fusee movement with verge escapement and a separate fusee organ movement driving a pinned wood barrel operating 15 valves and 44 pipes with 3 stops playing a choice of 9 tunes, c1750.
$32,000-40,000

A brass alarm clock, with stainless steel surround, 4in (10cm).
$400-500

A musical clock, playing any one of 8 tunes every four hours or at will, by Ellicot, c1770, 19thC, 27½in (70cm).
$11,000-12,000

A Gravity clock, with 30-hour duration, by Kee Less Clock Co, England, c1900, 10½in (26cm).
$300-500

A brass clock, 3in (8cm).
$300-500

A decorative silver front clock, with lizard skin sides and pine back, 4in (10cm).
$550-650

A travelling clock and case, c1920, 3in (8cm).
$250-300

A Marjaine miniature clock, 2½in (6cm).
$800-900

A small silver clock, top lifts to reveal a compass, by Mappin & Webb, c1904, 7in (18cm).
$1,000-1,200

A French automaton windmill clock, with timepiece, aneroid barometer and 2 thermometers in naturalistic gun metal case, with revolving sails worked from separate motor turned through front door, 17in (43cm).
$1,200-1,400

A ship's clock, by Seth Thomas, made in USA, 10½in (26cm).
$500-650

An American ship's clock, 8-day platform movement, by Waterbury, c1910, 8in (20cm).
$500-650

A mercury pendulum 400-day clock with glass dome, c1890, 11½in (29cm).
$1,000-1,150

Skeleton Clocks

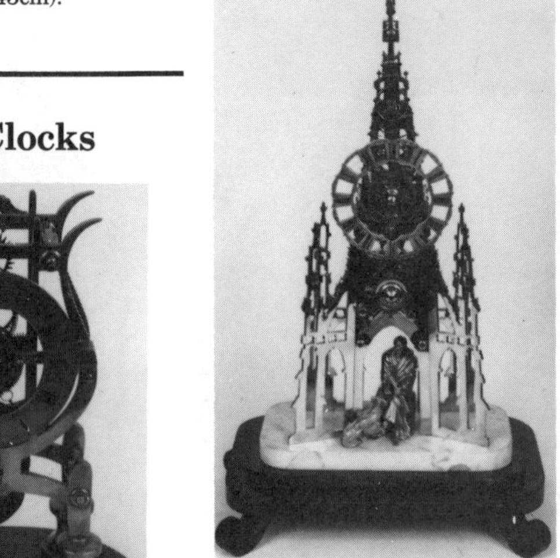

A skeleton clock by Read of Ipswich, 11½in (29cm).
$1,200-1,300

A Walter Scott memorial skeleton clock, with brass inlaid rosewood base, c1851, 20in (51cm).
$3,000-4,000

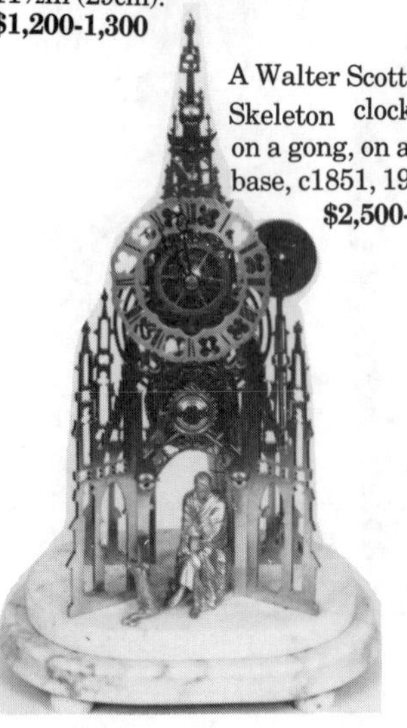

A Walter Scott Memorial Skeleton clock, striking on a gong, on a marble base, c1851, 19in (49cm).
$2,500-3,000

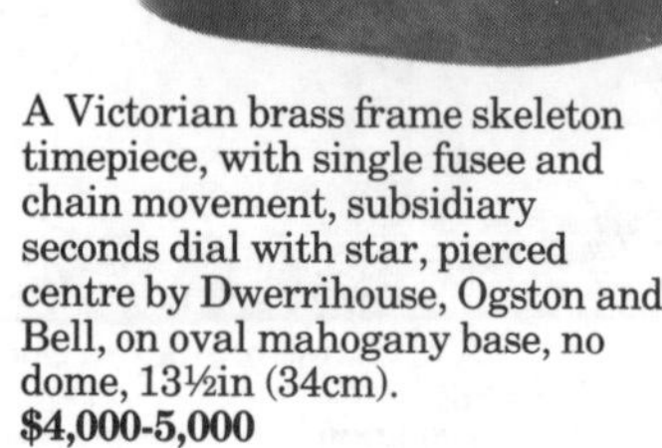

A Victorian brass frame skeleton timepiece, with single fusee and chain movement, subsidiary seconds dial with star, pierced centre by Dwerrihouse, Ogston and Bell, on oval mahogany base, no dome, 13½in (34cm).
$4,000-5,000

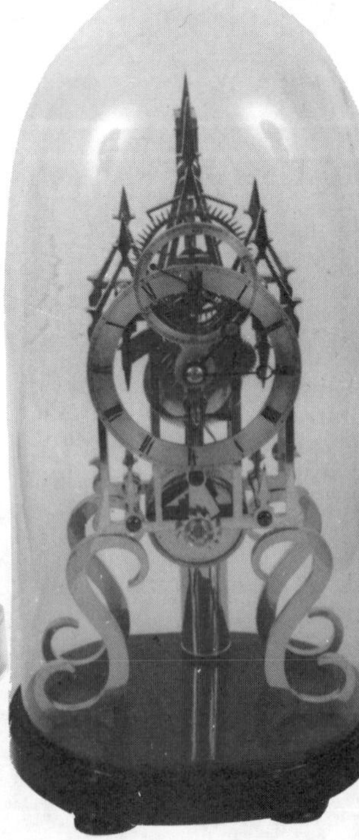

A rare English skeleton clock, Grant scope wheel and seconds dia semi dead beat.
$2,000-2,500

Watches

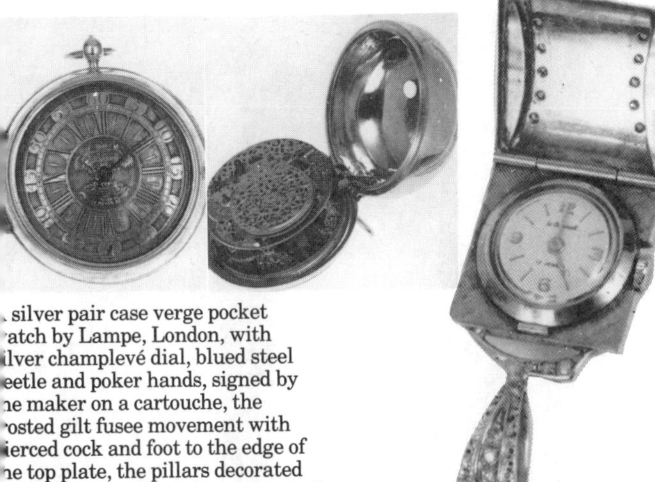

A silver pair case verge pocket watch by Lampe, London, with silver champlevé dial, blued steel beetle and poker hands, signed by the maker on a cartouche, the frosted gilt fusee movement with pierced cock and foot to the edge of the top plate, the pillars decorated with unusual pierced Royal Crest of King George I, the inner and outer cases bearing the mark TB surmounted by a crown, possibly Thomas Bamford, London, early 18thC, 5.5cm.
$3,000-4,000

A white gold and diamond pendant watch, 4cm.
$550-700

An English silver pocket watch, c1880, 3cm.
$130-150

A Victorian gold watch, with flower engraved dial, 4cm.
$400-500

A Victorian ladies gold fob watch, with cylinder movement, 3cm.
$150-200

An engraved silver pocket watch, with enamel flower decoration, 4cm.
$150-210

A Dine 18 carat gold hunter cased minute repeating centre seconds keyless chronograph, the white enamelled dial with black Roman numerals and Arabic minute ring, enclosing a subsidiary seconds dial, with centre seconds, the jewelled lever escapement striking on 2 gongs, with dust cap, in a plain case.
$1,300-2,000

A Victorian ladies Swiss silver fob watch, 3cm.
$50-80

A pink gold two-train independent seconds keyless hunter pocket watch, in rubbed engine turned case with engraved monogram to the front cover, with white enamel dial, decorative gold hands and sweep centre jumping seconds hand operated by a button in the band, 5.5cm.
$800-1,500

A keyless open face Mickey Mouse pocket watch, by Ingersoll, the subsidiary seconds indicated by revolving disc with 3 Mickeys, the time indicated by Mickey's arms, the signed three-quarter plate movement stamped P69, c1930, 5cm.
$500-800

Wristwatches

A Rolex Oyster gentleman's wristwatch, with subsidiary seconds dial, in stainless steel case, with later bracelet.
$500-550

A Rolex Oyster perpetual wristwatch, the dial inscribed Mappin and Chronometre, with luminous hands and numerals and subsidiary seconds dial, in stainless steel case.
$650-700

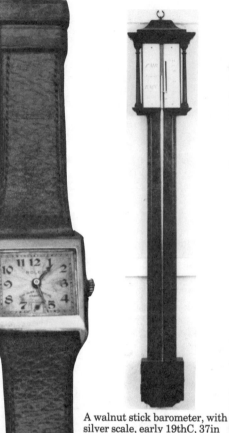

A Rolex Oyster gentleman's perpetual wristwatch, in stainless steel case.
$250-300

A Rolex gentleman's square faced wristwatch, in 9ct. gold case, inscribed 'The Alex Clarke Co., London', glass missing.
$650-700

Make the Most of Miller's

Every care has been taken to ensure the accuracy of descriptions and estimated valuations. Price ranges in this book reflect what one should expect to pay for a similar example. When selling one can obviously expect a figure below. This will fluctuate according to a dealer's stock, saleability at a particular time, etc. It is always advisable to approach a reputable specialist dealer or an auction house which has specialist sales

BAROMETERS
Stick

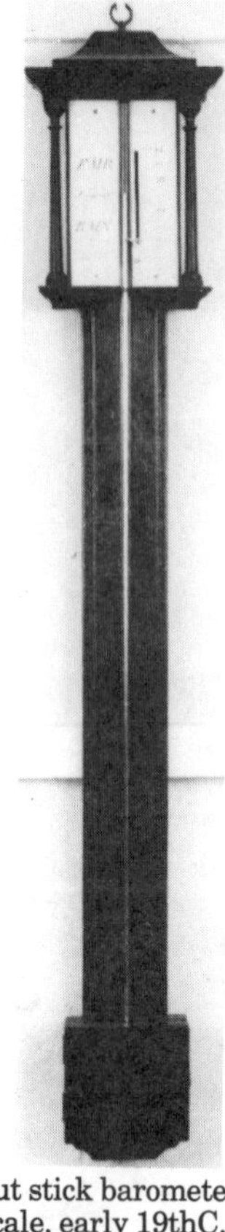

A walnut stick barometer, with silver scale, early 19thC, 37in (94cm).
$1,500-2,000

A mahogany stick barometer by Dolland of London, c1810.
$4,000-5,000

A mahogany stick barometer, by Edward Nairne, London, c1765.
$2,500-3,000

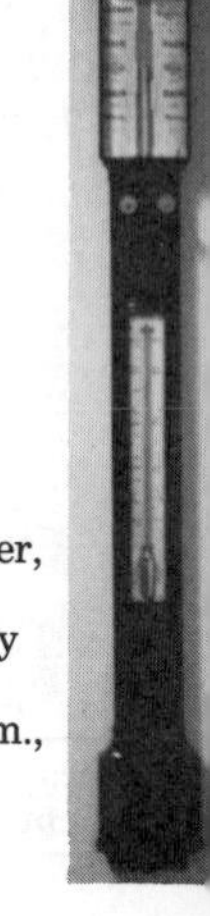

A bowfronted mercurial barometer, in an ebony veneered case, by Samuel Chare, Taunton, the ivory scales engraved and incorporate 2 setting verniers for a.m. and p.m., with a thermometer set into the front of the case, c1840.
$4,000-5,000

A walnut stick barometer, by Darcy of London, c1830. **$1,300-1,500**

A marine barometer by Adam Dundee, in mahogany case with brass gimballed vernier adjuster, c1830.
$4,000-5,000

A mahogany country/farmers barometer, c1860.
$550-700

A bowfronted mahogany barometer by Stebbing, Southampton, the brass silvered register plates with vernier and original mother-of-pearl setting key, c1840.
$5,500-6,500

A mahogany stick barometer, early 20thC, 37in (94cm).
$900-1,000

A mahogany stick barometer, in style of Adie, c1820.
$2,500-3,000

A George III mahogany stick barometer/thermometer, with silvered scale plate inscribed with maker's name Tagliabue Torre and Co, 294 Holborn, London, with broken apex pediment centred by a brass urn finial, the stick with chevron banded veneer, 38in (97cm).
$1,000-1,200

Wheel

A mahogany banjo barometer by Girletti of Glasgow.
$800-1,000

A mahogany banjo barometer inlaid with shell, 38in (97cm).
$1,000-1,200

A miniature ornamental brass aneroid barometer and thermometer, 7in (17.5cm).
$80-110

A rosewood mercury barometer and thermometer, with a picture of original owners set within, c1840.
$650-800

A barometer with thermometer in the dial, by Camble of Oswestry, c1840, 36in (90cm).
$1,400-1,500

A mahogany banjo barometer, c1860, 39in (99cm).
$900-1,000

A mahogany barometer with boxwood stringing, by Nicholson of Kircudbright, c1860.
$900-1,000

A Victorian rosewood wheel barometer with onion styled pediment, hygrometer, thermometer, 8in (20cm) registe and level, with mother of pearl banding to the case, 38in (97cm)
$550-700

Chronometers

A 2-day marine chronometer, the movement with Earnshaw spring, detent escapement compensation balance, blue steel helical spring maintaining power fusee, up-and-down winding dial dead beat, mahogany case, Barraud, No. 3422, 7in (17.5cm) square.
$3,000-4,000

A 'Hertfordshire' 8-day mantel chronometer, the dial signed Thomas Mercer Ltd, St Albans, England, No. 794, 11½in (29cm).
$4,000-5,000

A one-day marine chronometer, brass bezel to the white enamel dial, no up-and-down dial, all hands of gold, convex glass, top plate engraved Brockbank's, number 836, London, one-day Earnshaw escapement, Brockbank's steel three-armed balance, bimetallic three segment balance rim, the movement protected by outer drum cover, in brass bowl with gimbal, mounted in 3-tier mahogany brass bound box with drop handles, complete with outer guard box, 3in (8.3cm) dial diam.
$3,500-4,000

Use the Index!

Because certain items might fit easily into any of a number of categories, the quickest and surest method of locating any entry is by reference to the index at the back of the book. This has been fully cross-referenced for absolute simplicity

Miscellaneous

A mercury thermometer, 25in (64cm).
$80-100

Previously used outside a petrol station.

A Victorian rosewood stick cased ship's system barometer/thermometer, 39in (99cm).
$1,000-1,200

A pocket sundial with copper compass rose, with silvered scale and outer brass hour scale for latitudes 46° and 49°, with hinged adjustable small gnomon and bird indicator, contained in a mahogany case, 19thC, 3in (6.5cm).
$400-500

An Augsburg-type gilt and silvered brass universal equinoctial dial, signed Johan Schrettegger in Augsburg on the underside of the compass box, with silvered dial, blued needle on pivot with brass cap, 18thC, 2in (5.5cm).
$500-550

A German cube dial, inscribed HE1: FRANK, all faces with hand coloured engraved paper dials decorated with flowers, putti and geometric designs, string with plummet brass gnomons, on ball and socket joint over the base with compass and a table of latitudes for 38 Continental cities, on 4 bun feet, unsigned, 18thC, 7½in (19cm) high.
$1,300-1,500

A French silver dial, signed Butterfield A Paris, the upper surface engraved with hour scales for 43°, 46°, 49° and 52°, with inset compass and spring loaded bird gnomon, with a degree scale for latitudes 40°-60°, supplemented with scrolls and foliage, 18thC, 2in (5.5cm).
$1,000-1,200

SCIENTIFIC INSTRUMENTS Dials

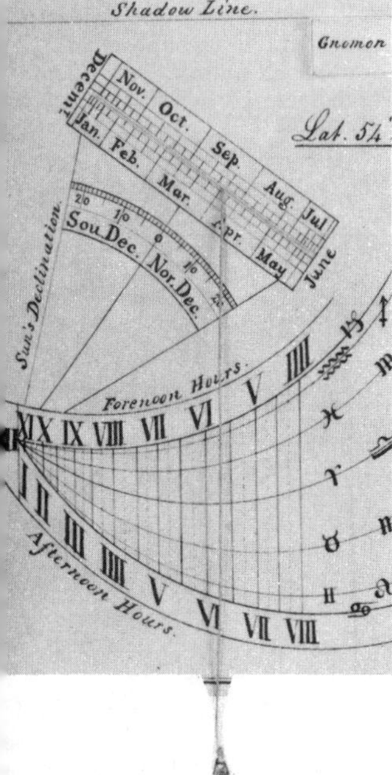

A paper rectilinear Capuchin dial, with sheet of written instructions forming the outer envelope, unsigned, 19thC, 4½in (11cm) high.
$250-400

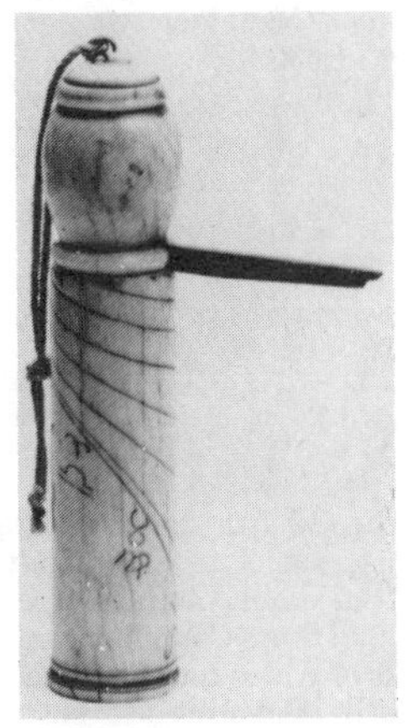

A bone-ivory pillar dial, incised for lines of hours, zodiac signs, with folding brass gnomon, bobbin turned cap with suspension loop and cord, unsigned, 18thC, 4½in (11.5cm).
$1,000-1,200

A brass universal equinoctial ring dial, engraved on one side, Robt. Fletcher, the other side Ex Dono Shan Divi Johann. Coll, Cantab. MDCCLV, the bridge with sliding pin hole sight and engraved with calendar and declination scales, unsigned, 18thC, 4½in (11.5cm) diam.
$800-900

A brass universal equinoctial compass dial, signed Newton & Co. 3 Fleet Street, London, with compass box, late 19thC, 4in (9.5cm) wide.
$550-700

Globes

A 6in (15cm) world time globe, the brass drum shaped base stamped Made in France No. 637, and containing the time clock mechanism, with equatorial hour ring, sun and hour pointer, the gores coloured and with the international cable route marked in red, 11½in (29.5cm) high.
$1,300-1,400

A 4in (10cm) instructional star globe, mounted on twin oxydised brass supports with scale 20° –0° –25° and vernier arm, on circular mahogany base stamped S & A.D., with 3 adjustable brass feet, late 19thC, 9½in (24cm) high.
$250-400

A German silver and gilt brass universal equinoctial dial, signed Johan Martin In Augsburg-48, the underside of the compass box with the names and latitudes of 23 European cities and towns, the plate engraved with scrolls and fitted with 3 bun feet, late 17thC, 2in (5cm) long.
$3,500-4,000

A mechanical orrery with 2½in (6cm) diam. globe, zodiac circle candle socket with reflector, on shaped iron steel, 19thC, the arm 19½in (49.5cm) long.
$1,400-1,500

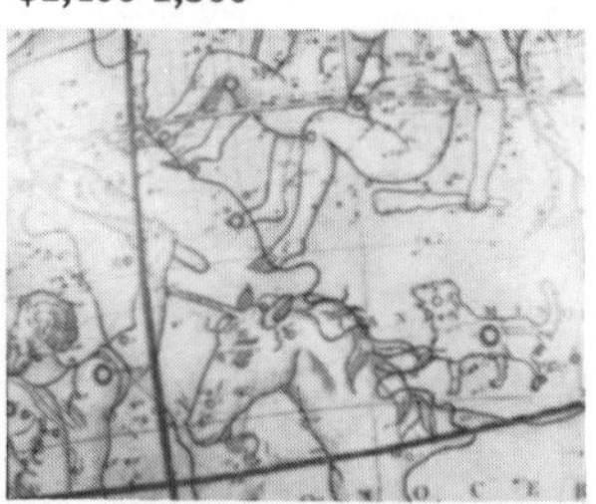

An 18in (45.5cm) diam celestial globe, the label inscribed Smith's Celestial Globe, Containing all the principal Stars Compiled from the Works of Wollaston, Flamsted, De La Caille, Havelius, Mayer, Bradley, Herschel, Maskelyne, the Transactions of the Astronomical Society of London & Co., Made in Great Britain, G. Phillip & Son Ltd, 32 Fleet Street, London E.C., 22in (56cm) high.
$2,500-4,000

A slate multiple sundial, the face carved with hour and calendar scales and the names of 70 world side cities and towns, with brass gnomon set for latitude 51° 30″ north, the apex of the corners wit subsidiary dials for New York (morning), Alexandria (afternoon Isle of Bornio (evening), New Zealand (night), mounted in a br frame with 2 suspension points, unsigned, 19thC, 14½in (36.5cm) square.
$2,000-2,500

A Philips 19in (48.5cm) terrestria globe, with brass support and turned oak stand, 28½in (72cm) high overall.
$400-550

An 8¼in (21cm) terrestrial globe, b Peter Bauer, Nürnberg, with brass meridian circle, mounted on horizc ring, printed with zodiac and calendar scales, on 4 quadrant supports, with inset compass on base, 19thC, 14½in (37cm) high.
$1,200-1,400

urveying

lacquered brass hydrograph with eel square, the quadrant engraved '-90°, unsigned, in mahogany case,)in (25cm) wide.
250-300

ʌn aluminium and brass miniature imple theodolite, signed Stanley ,ondon, with enclosed compass and ross bubble, the telescope with rack nd pinion focusing, level and half ircle engraved in 2 quadrants with taff mounting, 6in (15cm) long.
500-550

A lacquered brass miniature sextant, signed on the index arm Berge London, the frame with pin hole sight adjustable mirrors, index arm with vernier scale, the arc divided 0°-130° radius 2in (5cm), in plush lined leather covered case.
$5,000-5,500

An oxydised brass surveying level, the silvered compass dial signed Troughton & Simms, London, with rack and pinion focusing, bubble level, ray shade and dust slide, on 4 screw tripod mounting, in fitted mahogany case, 19thC, 19½in (49.5cm) long.
$300-400

An oxydised and lacquered brass surveying level, signed Troughton & Simms, London, with graduated level and cross bubble, rack and pinion focusing and fine vertical adjustment, on 4 screw tripod mounting in mahogany case, 20in (51cm) wide.
$200-300

A lacquered brass box sextant, signed Allan London, with silvered scale divided each 30 mins from 0°-150°, the index arm with vernier, tangent screw fine adjustment and magnifier, the drum shaped cover forming the base, early 19thC, 4½in (11cm) diam.
$650-800

A brass and aluminium transit theodolite, by Cooke, Troughton & Simms Ltd., No. Y2946, with silvered scales, levels, twin verniers and magnifiers on 3 screw tripod mounting, in mahogany case, 15½in (40cm) wide.
$650-800

ʌ brass sextant, by Troughton and ;imms Ltd., with white metal egree scale, the index arm with dog lip clamp, and with 2 sets of oloured filters, in stained wood box, ate 19thC.
500-550

ʌ pocket sextant, late 19thC.
250-300

A sextant compendium, comprising a sextant of small size, signed Bate, London, with vernier, magnifier, telescope and shades, the arc with silvered scale, 4in (10cm) radius, additional tube, folding artificial horizon trough and mercury jar, in brass bound mahogany case, early 19thC, 10in (25.5cm) wide.
$3,000-4,000

Telescopes

A 2½in (6cm) lacquered brass reflecting telescope, signed James Short London No. 211/1377 = 12, with screw rod focusing adjustment on tapering pillar support and tripod stand, in a fitted mahogany case, 18thC, 18½in (46.5cm) wide.
$2,500-3,000

James Short (1710-68) signed and engraved his reflecting telescopes with a coded numbering system where in this case 211 equals the serial number of the telescope for this size, 1377 indicates the number of telescopes constructed, and 12 equals the focal length of the large speculum mirror in inches.

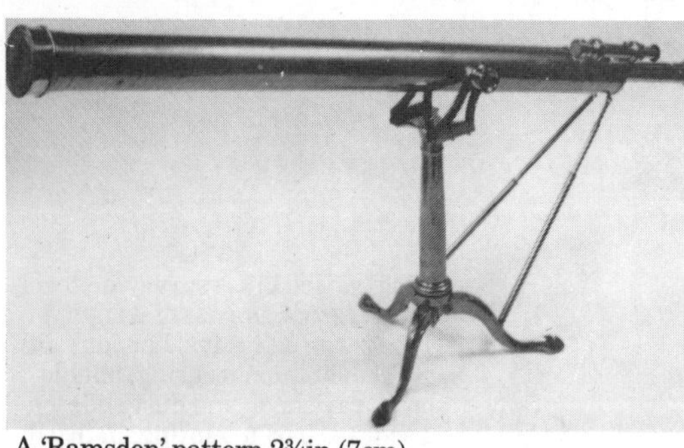

A 'Ramsden' pattern 2¾in (7cm) reflecting telescope, the 45in (115cm) long body tube with rack and pinion focusing, dust cap and located on the alt/azimuth trunnion by wedge and slot and 2 telescopic steadying bars, early 19thC.
$1,500-2,000

A vellum and horn 1in (2.5cm) 4-draw telescope, with brass caps and fishskin covered outer body tube, lens defective, unsigned, 18thC, 37½in (96cm) long extende
$800-1,000

A 6in (15cm) Newtonian reflector telescope, on an alt/azimuth stand, in teak case.
$9,500-11,000

A 2in (5cm) brass 4-draw refracting telescope, signed James Mann, Norwich, with dust cap and eye-piece slide, 3-eye pieces, mounted by a screw clamp on a tapering pillar support with folding tripod, the cabriole legs terminating in pad feet, in fitted mahogany case, 12½in (31.5cm) wide, with 2 clips and inset plaque to lid engraved John Harvey.
$1,300-1,400

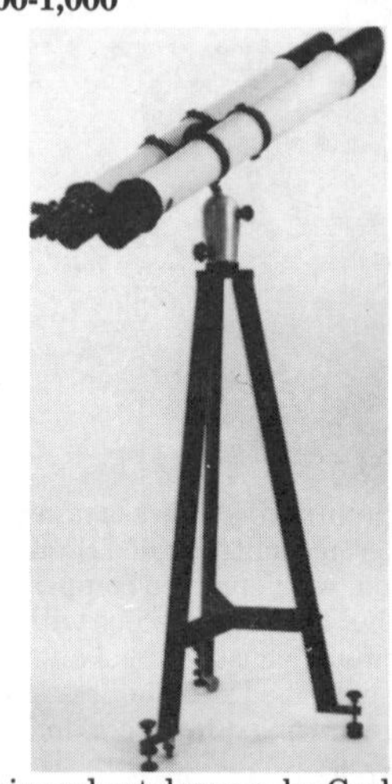

A binocular telescope, by Carl Zei Jena, the white painted body tube 41¼in (104.8cm) long, the objectiv 4½in (11cm) diam. clear aperture, with image erecting prism system with triple ×33, 53 and 72 magnifications, 5 screw adjustme and focusing, arranged for binocul observation for 1 person and monocular observation for 2 persons, in steel bound case, 62i (157.5cm) long, with a later steel tripod and mounting.
$5,000-5,500

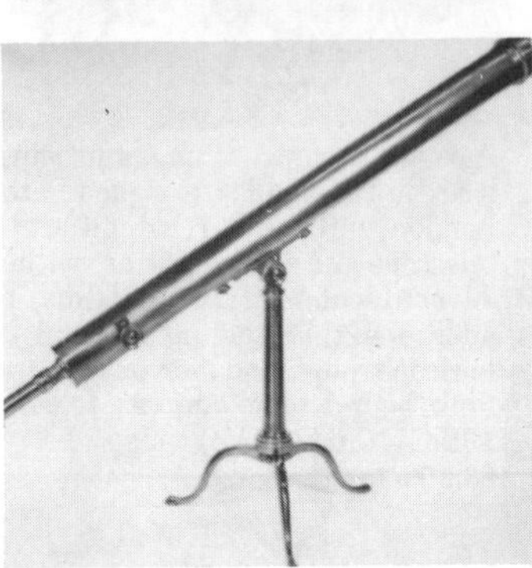

A lacquered brass 3in (7.5cm) refracting telescope, signed Watson & Son, 313 High Holborn, London, with rack and pinion focusing and dust cap, in a Broadhurst & Clarkson case with 2 eye-pieces, 45in (115cm) long.
$1,400-2,000

A brass 2¾in (7cm) refracting telescope, signed Wm. De Silva, 1 Duke St. & 25 Chapel St. Liverpo the 37¾in (96cm) long body tube with rack and pinion focusing, sta finder, object glass dust cap, on tapering pillar support with steadying bar and folding tripod stand, in pine carrying case, 19th 40½in (102cm) long.
$1,400-2,000

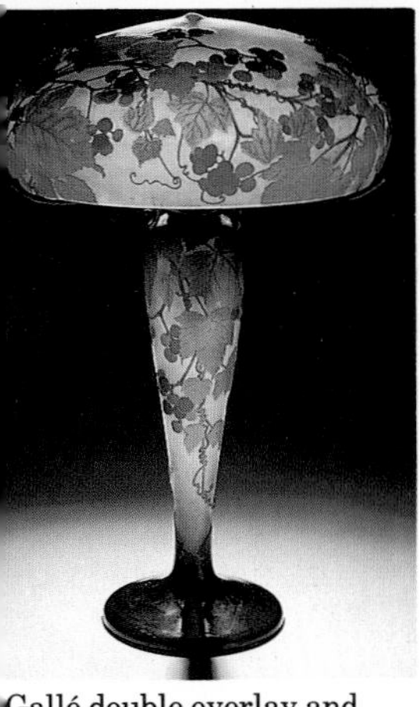

Gallé double overlay and
:hed table lamp, shade
ıd base signed, 21in (54cm).
0,000-50,000

A flowering dogwood leaded glass and bronze table lamp, stamped Tiffany Studios New York, 29½in (75cm) high.
$85,000-95,000

A Venetian leaded glass and gilt bronze table lamp, stamped Tiffany Studios New York 515, 20in (51cm).
$35,000-40,000

linenfold leaded glass and
onze table lamp, the 12-sided
ade stamped Tiffany Studios New
ork Pat. Appld. For 1927, the base
ffany Studios New York 370, 23in
9cm). **$16,000-20,000**

A peony leaded glass and bronze table lamp, the shade stamped Tiffany Studios New York 1475-66, the pineapple bronze base stamped Tiffany Studios New York 366, 26in (66cm).
$88,000-95,000

A Tyler leaded glass and bronze table lamp, stamped Tiffany Studios New York 1440-5, 22in (56cm) high.
$13,000-15,000

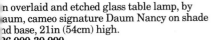

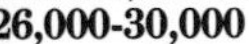

n overlaid and etched glass table lamp, by
aum, cameo signature Daum Nancy on shade
ıd base, 21in (54cm) high.
26,000-30,000
bove r. An internally decorated glass lamp,
Daum, etched signature Daum Nancy France,
3in (46cm) high.
22,000-25,000
A Gallé carved and acid etched double
rerlay table lamp, with carved signature
allé, 14½in (37cm) high.
20,000-22,000

A glass table lamp by Emile Gallé, the shade and base within a yellow and white frosted ground overlaid with purple-blue and etched to represent chrysanthemums, cameo signature Gallé on shade and base, 12½in (32cm) high.
$40,000-50,000

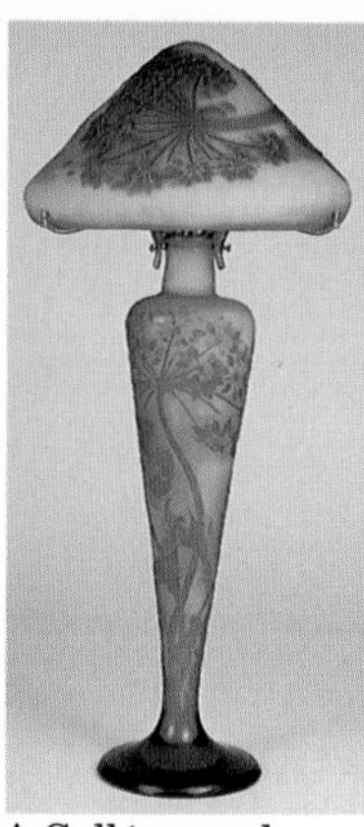

A Gallé carved and acid etched double overlay table lamp, carved signature Gallé, 25½in (65cm) high.
$25,000-32,000

A Gallé carved, acid etched and fire polished, double overlay table lamp, 23in (59cm) high.
$50,000-55,000

A double overlay and etched glass table lamp and shade, both parts signed Gallé in the overlay, 10½in (27cm) high.
$50,000-65,000

A double overlaid and etched glass table lamp, cameo signature Gallé, 22in (56cm) high.
$32,000-40,000

An overlaid and etched glass table lamp, cameo signature on shade and base Gallé, 20in (51cm) high.
$50,000-65,000

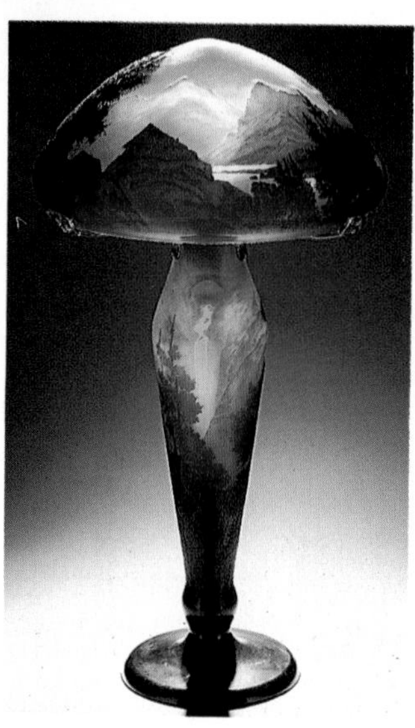

A double overlaid and etched glass table lamp, with original bronze mounts, cameo signature on shade and base Gallé, 30in (77cm) high.
$400,000+

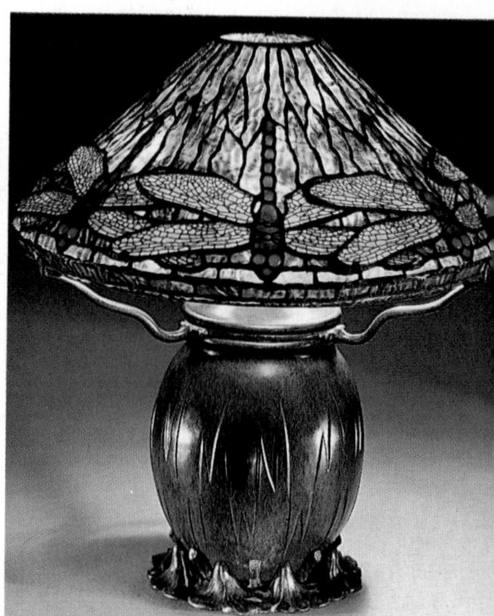

A 'dragonfly' leaded glass and bronze table lamp, both shade an base stamped Tiffany Studic 18in (46cm) high.
$50,000-80,00

A 'geranium' leaded glass and bronze table lamp, stamped Tiffany Studios New York, 16½in (42cm) high.
$50,000-80,000

A favrile glass and metal table lamp, stamped under fuel canister Tiffany Studios, 20½in (52cm) high.
$14,000-16,000

r. A leaded glass and bronze table lamp, by Tiffany Studios, 15½in (40cm) high.
$5,000-7,000

r. An 'autumn leaf' leaded glass and bronze table lamp, by Tiffany Studios, 31in (79cm) high.
$55,000-65,000

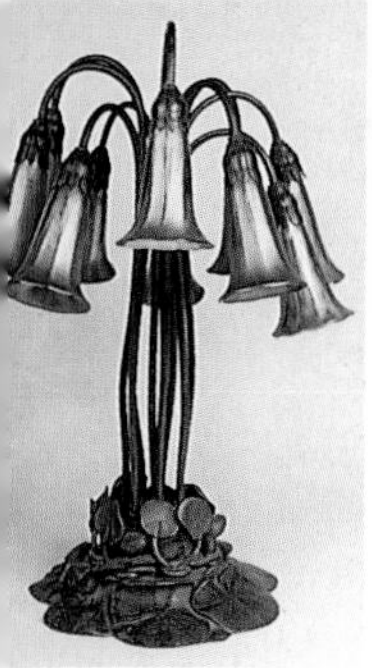

bronze base
ıter lily
np, with 10
descent
ades,
ned
ffany Studios.
2,000-14,000

A favrile lily 10-light glass and gilt bronze table lamp, by Tiffany Studios, 20½in (52cm) high. **$30,000-40,000**
r. 'L'Orchidée', a lamp, from a model by Louis Chalon, French, early 20thC, 29in (74cm) high. **$7,000-9,000**

A Cypriot glass hanging lantern, by Tiffany Studios, 18in (46cm) high. **$13,000-16,000**

geometric leaded glass and
onze lamp shade, by Tiffany
udios, 12½in (32cm) high.
,000-10,000

l. A geometric leaded glass and metal chandelier, by Tiffany Studios, the shade suspended from 6 link chains, 14in (36cm) high. **$16,000-18,000**

A 'Clematis' leaded glass shade, by Tiffany Studios, 18in (46cm) diam. **$40,000-50,000**

stained and leaded glass
me light shade, decorated
th grapes and leaves,
in (71cm) diam.
,000-1,200

An 'Iris' leaded glass and bronze chandelier, attributed to Tiffany Studios, 22½in (57cm) high. **$10,000-13,000**

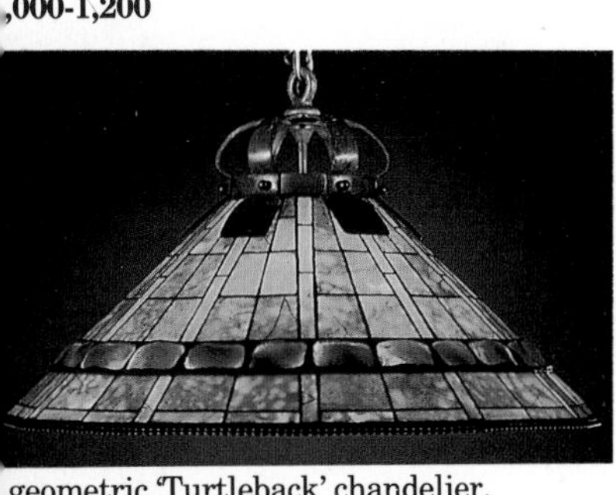

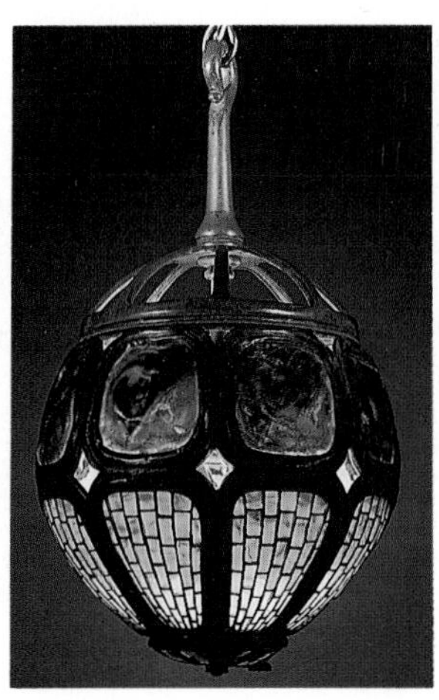

geometric 'Turtleback' chandelier,
 Tiffany Studios, 22in (56cm) high.
1,000-16,000
A geometric 'Turtleback' tile and
aded glass hanging lantern, by
ffany Studios. **$28,000-32,000**

An iridescent glass and brass chandelier, attributed to Kolo Moser, c1902, 25in (64cm) high. **$8,000-12,000**

A wrought iron and glass chandelier, stamped E. Brandt.
$8,000-10,000

A pair of wrought iron and glass sconces, by Edgar Brandt and Daum.
$6,500-8,000

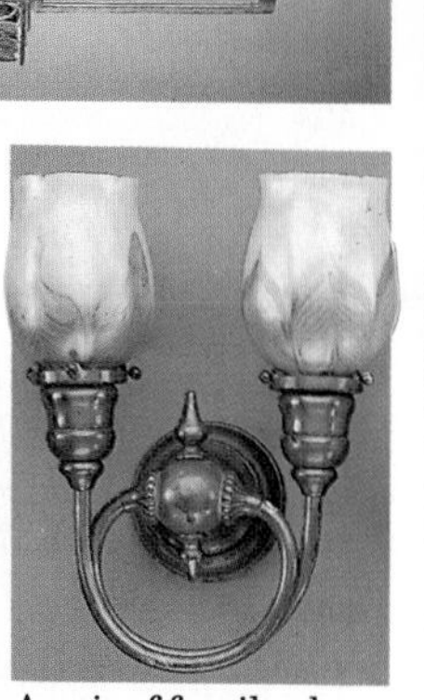

A pair of favrile glass and bronze wall sconces, by Tiffany Studios, inscribed L.C.T., 12in (31cm) high.
$6,500-8,000

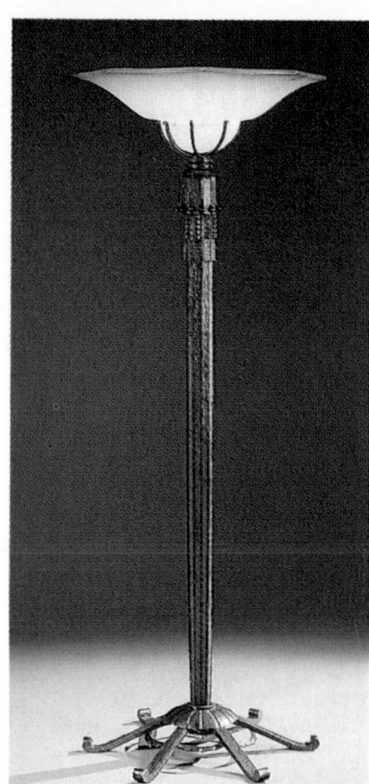

A pair of wrought iron and earthenware sconces, by the Roycrofters for Elbert Hubbard II.
$2,000-3,000

l. A wrought iron and alabaster floor lamp, by Raymond Subes, c1925 70½in (179cm) high.
$25,000-30,000

A bronze and favrile glass mirror, by Tiffany Studios, 18in (46cm) high.
$28,000-32,000

A favrile glass and gilt bronze candelabra, by Tiffany Studios, fitted for electricity.
$12,000-14,000

A cast and wrought iron door gate, by Louis Sullivan, c1895.
$25,000-30,000

r. A wrought iron fire screen, by Edgar Brandt, c1925.
$30,000-40,000

A bronze and favrile glass firescreen, by Tiffany Studios, 47in (119cm) wide. **$22,000-26,000**

Two cast iron frieze panels, by Louis Sullivan, c1895. **$2,500-3,000**

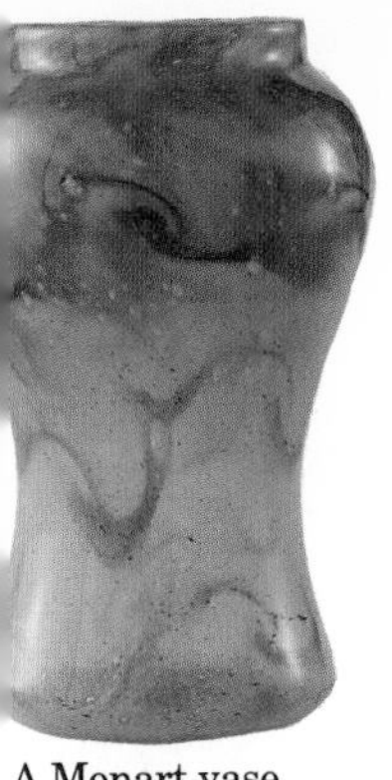

A Monart vase, blue and ochre, with whorls, 9in (23cm) high. **$300-350**

A Monart vase, the surface decorated in yellow and lustred white stripes, c1925, 8in (20cm) high. **$1,500-3,000**

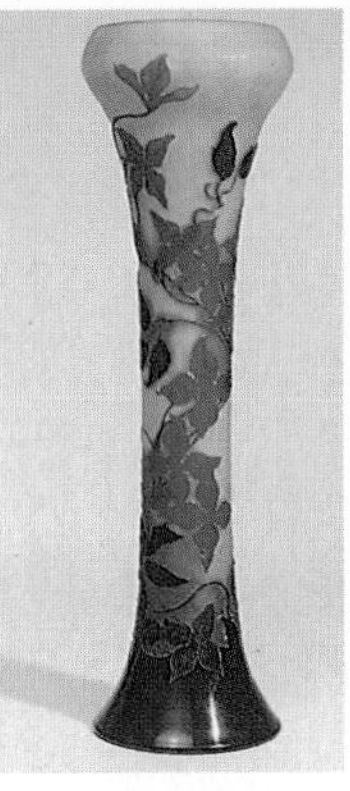

A Gallé carved, acid etched and partially fire polished vase. **$9,500-10,000**

A Gallé carved and acid etched, double overlay vase, with carved signature, 12½in (32cm) high. **$9,500-12,000**

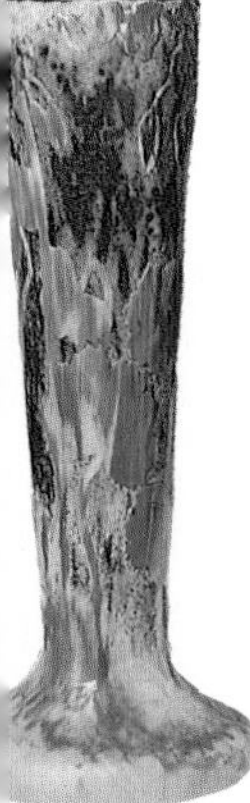

Daum martelé acid textured and
rved vase. **$8,000-9,500**
bove r. A Daum two-coloured
ass vase. **$26,000-28,000**

A frosted green glass vase, 'Perruches', by Rene Lalique et cie, with bronze stand, 10½in (26cm). **$16,000-18,000**

An amber glass vase by Rene Lalique et cie, 'Serpent', 10in (25cm) high. **$16,000-18,000**

l. A frosted amber glass vase, by Rene Lalique et cie, 'Languedoc'. **$14,000-16,000**

r. A paperweight favrile glass vase, by Tiffany Studios, 6in (15cm). **$14,000-16,000**

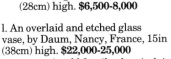

A Müller glass vase, c1900, 11in (28cm) high. **$6,500-8,000**

l. An overlaid and etched glass vase, by Daum, Nancy, France, 15in (38cm) high. **$22,000-25,000**

r. A gold favrile glass jack in the pulpit vase, by Tiffany Studios, 20in (51cm) high. **$15,000-18,000**

A double overlay and etched glass vase, signed Gallé, 22½in (57cm) high.
$32,000-40,000

A Gallé double overlay glass vase, 8in (20cm) high.
$25,000-30,000

A Tiffany favrile glass vase with engraved signature L.C. Tiffany Favrile, 12½in (32.5cm) high.
$3,000-4,000

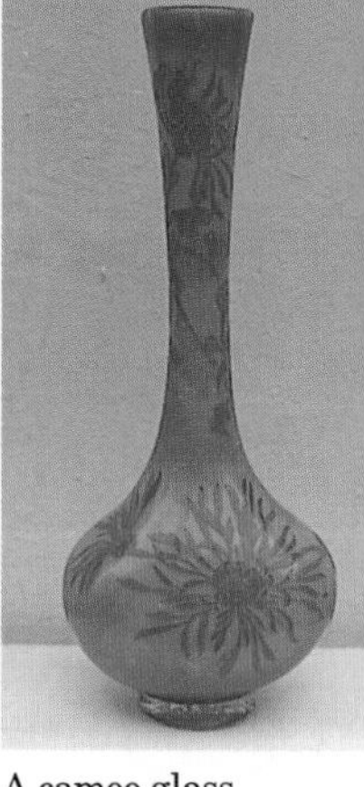

A cameo glass vase, engraved Gallé, 16in (41cm) high.
$8,000-9,500

A cameo glass vase, amethyst overlaid on amber, signed Gallé, 8in (20cm) high.
$5,500-6,500

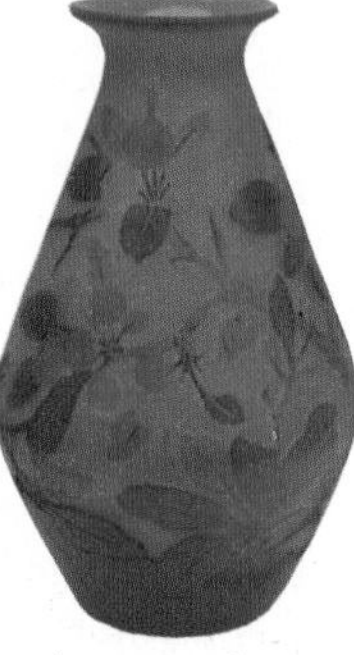

A cameo glass vase, signed Gallé, 6½in (16.5cm) high.
$2,500-3,000

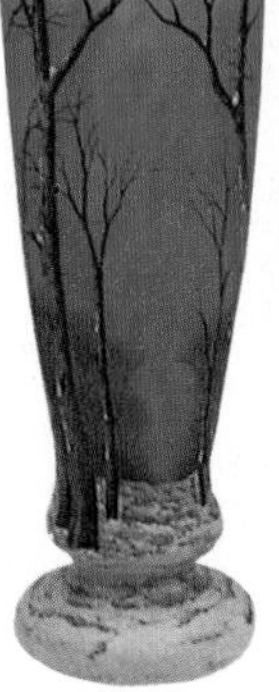

An etched and enamelled cameo glass vase, by Daum and with enamelled signature, 9in (22.5cm) high.
$4,300-5,000

A cameo glass landscape vase, etched and enamelled, by Daum with enamelled signature, 5in (12.5cm) high.
$3,000-4,000

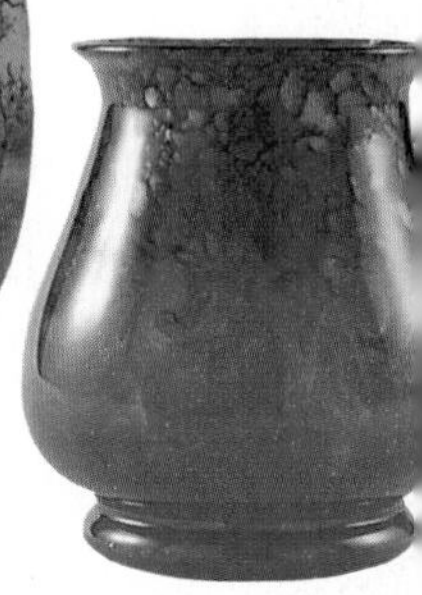

A Monart vase, in red, black and gold, rare colour, 5½in (14cm) high.
$650-700

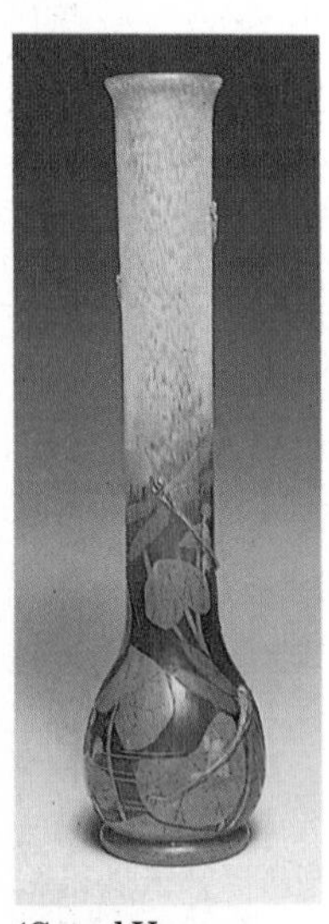

'Grand Vase Libellules', carved, acid-etched and applied, carved signature Daum Nancy, 23½in (60cm) high.
$95,000-103,000

A cameo glass vase, probably Thomas Webb, 6in (15cm) high.
$900-1,000

Two Lalique vases, 'Sophora' and 'Vases Davos', both signed, tallest 11½in (29cm).
l. **$9,000-9,500**
r. **$6,500-7,000**

r. A Daum étude vase 'Anemones', engraved Daum Nancy, 9½in (23.5cm) high.
$22,000-26,000

An acid-etched, carved, enamelled and gilt decorated landscape vase, signed Daum Nancy, 11in (28cm) high.
$11,000-13,000

A paperweight favrile glass bowl, by Tiffany Studios, inscribed 1333E L.C. Tiffany-Favrile, 8in (20cm) diam.
$7,000-8,000

A Le Verre Français cameo glass bowl, signed, 9in (22.5cm) high.
$1,400-1,500

A favrile glass plaque by Tiffany Studios, inscribed L.C.T., 19in (48cm). **$6,500-9,500**

An internally decorated and engraved glass coupe, 'La Vague', engraved Daum Nancy, 6½in (16cm) high.
$30,000-40,000

A mould blown, overlaid and etched glass bowl, signed Gallé, 12½in (32cm) diam. **$40,000-50,000**

A 'Grand vase de Tristesse', by Gallé for the Parish Exposition, 1889, base cracked, signed, 14in (36cm) high. **$9,000-12,000**

A glass vase, signed Daum.
$30,000-35,000

A triple overlaid and etched glass vase, cameo signature Gallé, 28½in (72cm).
$25,000-30,000

A double overlaid and etched glass vase, cameo signature Gallé, 26in (66cm) high.
$20,000-25,000

An overlaid and etched glass vase, cameo signature Gallé, 15½in (40cm) high.
$9,000-12,000

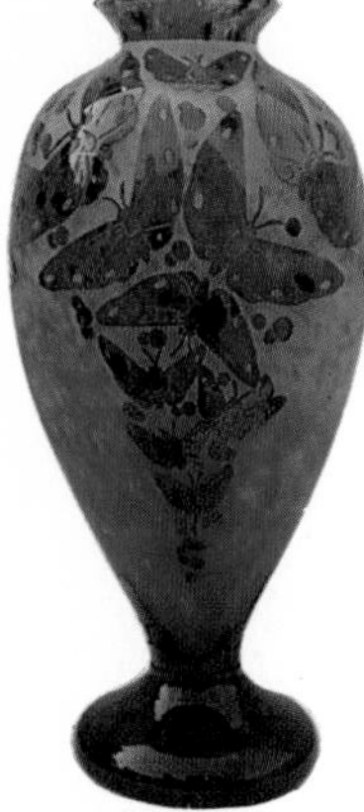
A cameo glass vase, signed Le Verre Français.
$1,300-1,500

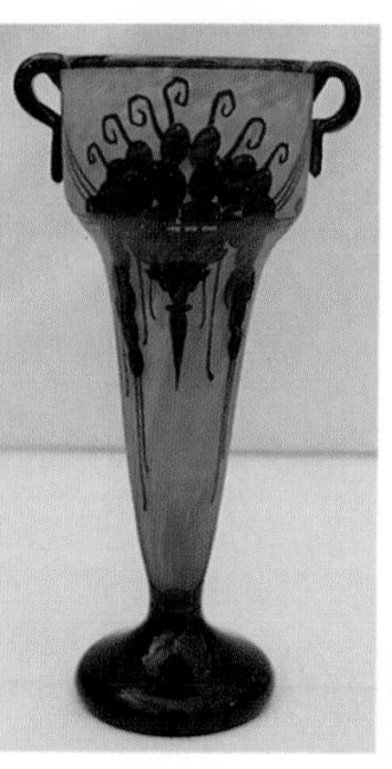

A cameo glass vase, signed Le Verre Français.
$1,300-1,500
r. An internally decorated glass vase, marked Gallé.
$80,000-100,000
l. A cameo glass vase, signed Le Verre Français, 19in (48cm). **$1,000-1,300**

'hree Powell guitar style vases, in tangerine, reen and blue, c1965, 7in (18cm) high. **30-65 each**

Three Powell 'log' vases, the coloured glass cased in clear, c1965, 6 to 9in (15 to 23cm) high. **$27-75 each**

. Concetta Mason blown lass bowl, entitled 3lue Fire, engraved narks, c1987, 12in 30.5cm). **900-2,000**

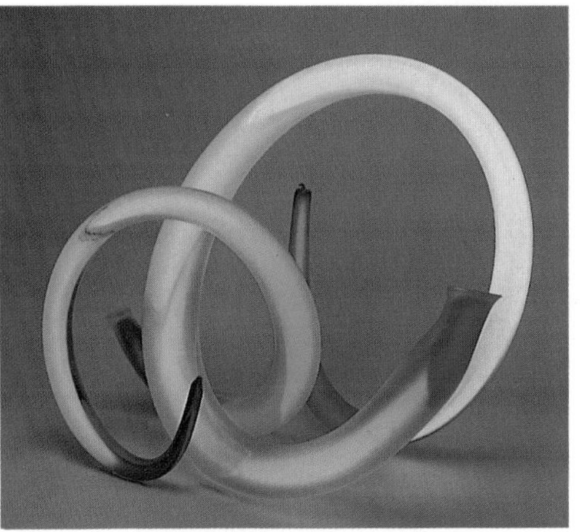

A Paul Seide frosted spiral radio light, complete with base and transmitter, 1 glass element engraved Seide, c1987. **$2,000-4,000**

A Paul Ysart crown weight, in pink, blue, green and white, original label, c1970. **$700-900**

A Paul Ysart paperweight, red and green salamander, very rare, c1970. **$1,500-3,000**

A Monart jug, in blue, black and gold, 10in 25cm) high. **550-700**

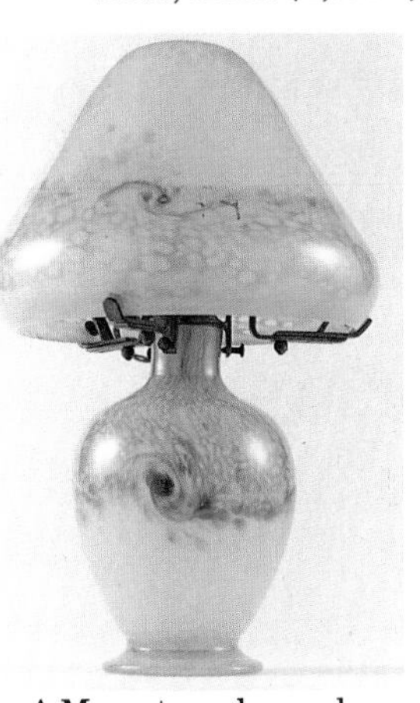

A Monart mushroom lamp, in yellow and white, probably post-war, with original label. **$2,500-4,000**

A Whitefriars lemonade set, comprising 6 glasses and jug, c1938, jug 6½in (17cm) high. **$120-130**

A clear glass vessel form, with surface application, by Joel Philip Myers, 1987. **$550-650**

An exotic bird series bowl form, by Toots Zynsky, 1987, 7½ by 16in (19 by 41cm). **$1,000-1,200**

l. An enamelled and metal vase, by Camille Faure, in abstract designs, 7in (18cm) high. **$1,500-2,500**

A Clarice Cliff plate with painted scene, Rock of Gibraltar, 9in (23cm).
$1,000-1,300

A Clarice Cliff painted plate, House and Tree, 9in (23cm).
$800-1,200

A Clarice Cliff painted plate, Crinoline Lady, 9in (23cm).
$500-800

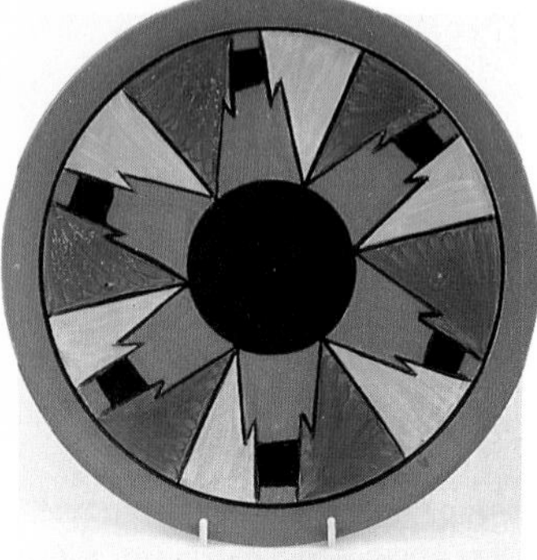

A Clarice Cliff plate, early geometric, by C. Cliff, c1925, 10½in (26cm). **$700-1,000**

A Clarice Cliff painted plate, 'Gardenia', 9½in (24cm).
$650-1,000

A Clarice Cliff blue and yellow un-named plate, 9in (23cm).
$650-1,000

A Clarice Cliff painted plate, Orange tree cottage, 9in (23cm). **$1,000-1,300**

A Clarice Cliff early geometric painted plate, 7in (18cm).
$300-500

A Clarice Cliff painted plate, Autumn, 9in (23cm).
$650-1,000

A Clarice Cliff painted plate, Solitude, 9in (23cm).
$650-1,000

A Maling ware charger, c1930, 16in (41cm).
$650-700

A Maling ware plate with an embossed design, Irises, 11in (28cm).
$250-300

A William de Morgan plate, 'Panthers', decorated on reverse, 9½in (24cm). **$1,500-2,000**

A Foley Intarsio tea caddy, c1900, 6in (15cm) high. **$500-650**

A 21-piece Shelley Deco tea service, in a blue, black and silver block pattern, c1931. **$1,300-1,400**

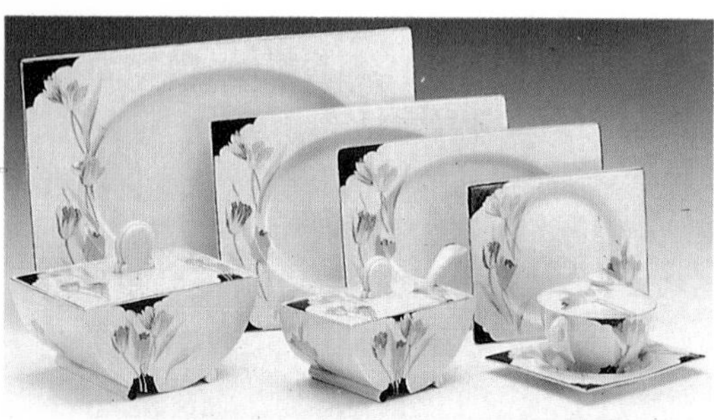

A Clarice Cliff 50-piece painted dinner service. **$3,000-4,000**

A Shelley Deco 21-piece Orange J pattern tea service, no teapot, c1931. **$1,300-1,400**

A Quimper cup and saucer, Deco period, signed, saucer 7½in (19cm), cup 4½in (11cm). **$40-50**

A Clarice Cliff Patina tea set, comprising: milk jug, sugar bowl, cup, saucer and plate, teapot 5in (13cm) high. **$1,400-1,500**

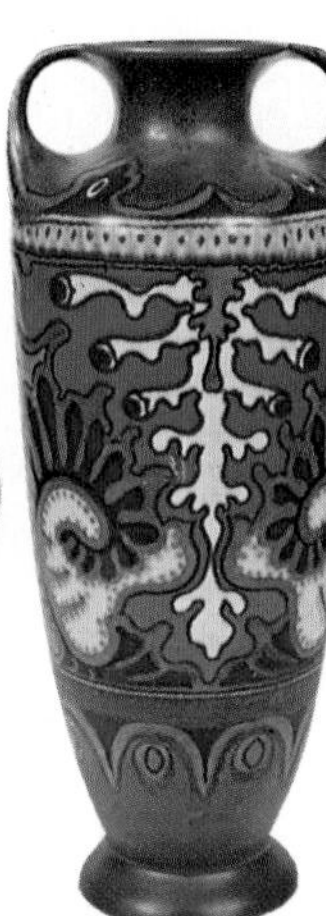

A pair of Villeroy and Boch vases, Dutch, c1900. **$550-700**

A pair of Villeroy and Boch jars, c1900, 7in (18cm) high. **$400-550**

A Minton vase, brown with gold decorations, Aesthetic influence, c1886, 12in (31cm) high. **$900-1,000**

r. A Moorcroft vase, 9½in (24cm) high. **$700-800**

A Foley Intarsio vase, Frederick Rhead design, chicken and hens, 9in (23cm) high. **$1,000-1,300**

r. A Frederick Rhead swan design vase, 12½in (32cm) high. **$1,400-1,500**

. Foley Intarsio bowl
'ith Shakespeare scene,
1900, 11½in (29cm).
800-1,000

A Clarice Cliff bowl with Kandina pattern, 8in (20cm). **$700-800**

A Shelley lustre bowl, signed by Walter Slater, c1920, 7in (18cm) high.
$250-300

A Bernard Moore bowl, initialled by Cicely Jackson, 9in (22.5cm).
$400-500

An Austrian amphora blue and white flower holder, 9in (22.5cm) high.
$300-350

An Ault Grotesque jug, 7in (17.5cm) high.
$500-550

A Clarice Cliff Lotus jug with the Inspiration Caprice pattern, rim cracked, 12in (30.5cm).
$1,500-2,000

A porcelain Limousine water jug, 8in (20cm) high.
$130-150

A Foley Intarsio jardinière in the Goose pattern, c1900, 4½in (11cm) high.
$500-650

l. A Foley Intarsio jardinière on stand by Frederick Rhead.
$3,000-4,000

A Clarice Cliff step jardinière, 3½in (8.5cm) high.
$300-400

. pair of Liberty & Co.
toneware jardinières,
lesigned by Archibald
Knox, 16in (41cm) high.
4,000-5,000

An earthenware charger by John Bennett, signed, 1878, 14½in (37cm).
$5,000-5,500

A Minton blank painted by an amateur painter, exhibited in 1883, 10in (25cm). **$150-250**

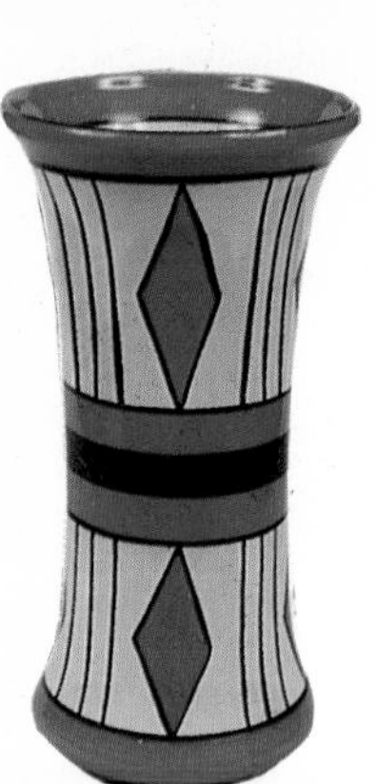

A Clarice Cliff early geometric vase, 8in (20cm) high. **$900-1,000**
Above r. A Clarice Cliff umbrellas and rain vase, 10in (25cm). **$1,300-1,500**

r. A Pilkington Lancastrian lustre vase and cover, decorated by Gordon Forsyth, 11½in (29cm). **$5,000-5,500**

Far r. A Pilkington Royal Lancastrian lustre vase, decorated by William S. Mycock, 11in (28cm). **$1,400-1,500**

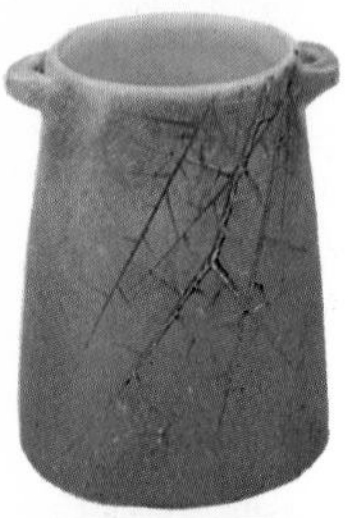

l. A Clément Massier vase, painted by Lucien Levy-Dhurmer, 4in (10cm) high. **$130-150**

A Goebels ceramic glass-eyed gnome, 8in (22cm). See below.

A Goldscheider figure, 15½in (39cm) high. **$1,300-1,500**

A Continental majolica vase, in yellow, blue and lime, 5in (13cm). **$100-130**

A Bernard Moore vase, initialled, 7½in (19cm). **$400-450**

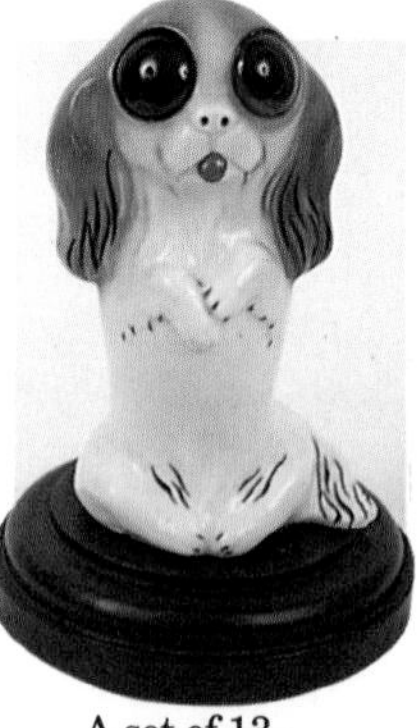

A set of 13 Goebels ceramic glass-eyed lamps. **$7,000-8,000**

r. A Goldscheider figure, 15in (38.5cm) high. **$1,400-1,500**

An Intarsio clock, by Frederick Rhead, 13½in (35cm) high. **$700-750**

A pair of bisque porcelain figures, c1910, 7½in (19cm) high. **$300-400**

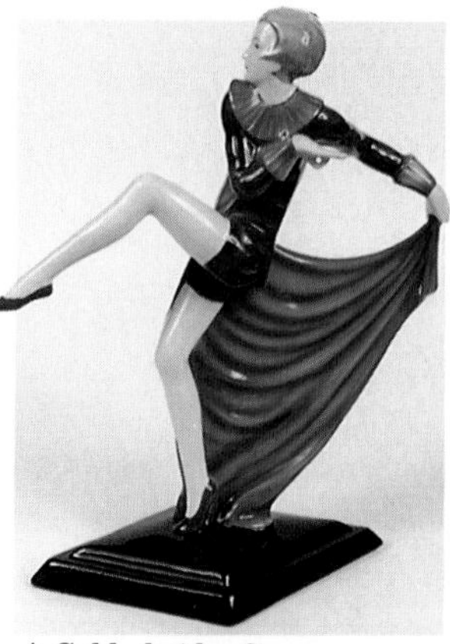

A Goldscheider figure, 12in (30.5cm) high. **$1,000-1,300**

r. A Goldscheider figure, 17in (43.5cm) high. **$2,000-2,500**

A Moorcroft brown chrysanthemum vase, signed W. Moorcroft, retailer's mark Spalding & Company, c1910, 12in (30.5cm). **$5,000-6,500**

A Pilkington Royal Lancastrian lustre vase, decorated by Gordon Forsyth, impressed, signed and dated 1911, 25in (63cm). **$6,500-7,000**

A porcelain centrepiece, by Adelaide Alsop Robineau, carved with artist's monogram and incised 1926, damaged in the firing, 13in (33cm) diam. **$35,000-40,000**

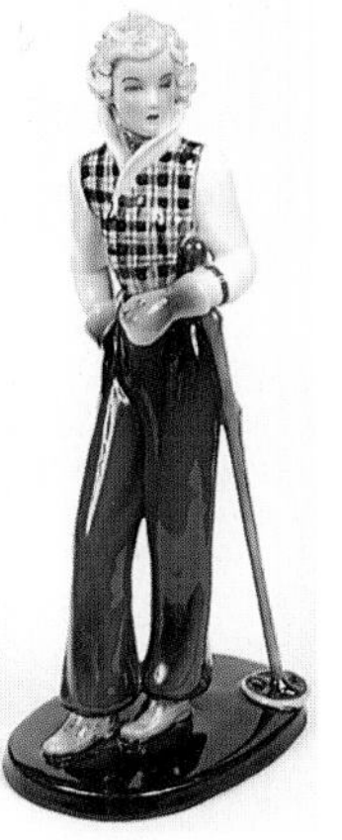

l. A Goldscheider figure of a skier, 11in (28cm). **$1,000-1,100**
r. A Goldscheider figure, 11in (28cm). **$650-700**

A Goldscheider figure based on the Ballet Russe, designed by Kestial, 17½in (44cm). **$4,000-5,000**

A Goldscheider golfing figure, 9in (23cm). **$550-650**

A Goldscheider figure by Clare Weiss, 13in (34cm). **$800-900**

A Daum etched and enamelled cameo glass bowl, etched signature, 6in (15cm) diam. **$1,500-2,000**

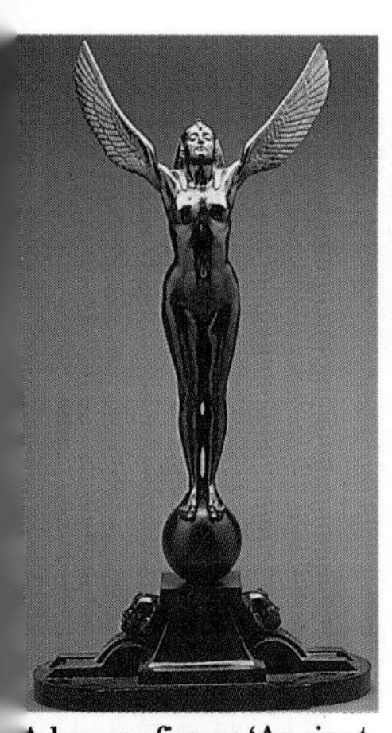

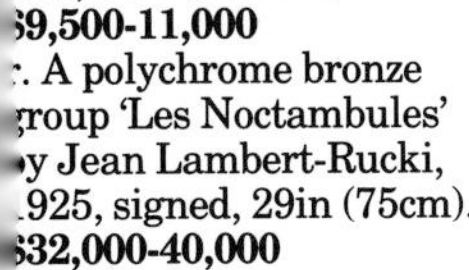

A bronze figure 'Ancient History' by Haig Patigian Paris, 1907, signed and impressed with foundry seal, 38in (96.5cm). **$9,500-11,000**
r. A polychrome bronze group 'Les Noctambules' by Jean Lambert-Rucki, 1925, signed, 29in (75cm). **$32,000-40,000**

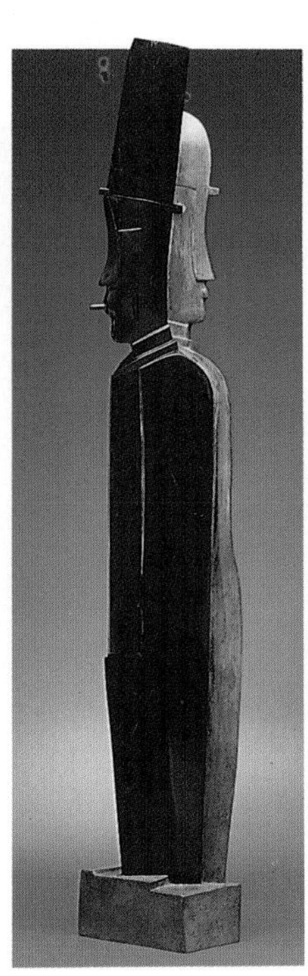

A monumental Lenci ceramic figure, with impressed signature Gnni Riva, 39in (99cm). **$10,000-13,500**

A Gallé cameo glass bowl, signed in cameo, 6in (15cm) diam. **$2,500-3,000**

A Daum etched and enamelled cameo glass bowl, signed in enamel, 6in (15cm) diam. **$2,500-3,000**

An oak inlaid double bed, by Gustav Stickley and used in his home at Morris Plains, New Jersey, c1909, 58in (147cm) wide.
$20,000-25,000

An oak double bed by Gustav Stickley, c1901, 58in (147cm) wide.
$13,000-14,000

A pair of oak beds by Gustav Stickley, c1909, 45in (114cm) wide.
$3,000-4,000

l. An Ebène de Macassar bed, by Emile Jacques Ruhlmann, 43in (109cm) wide.
$4,000-5,000
r. A walnut and ebonised bedroom suite, designed by Gio Ponti.
$5,000-5,500

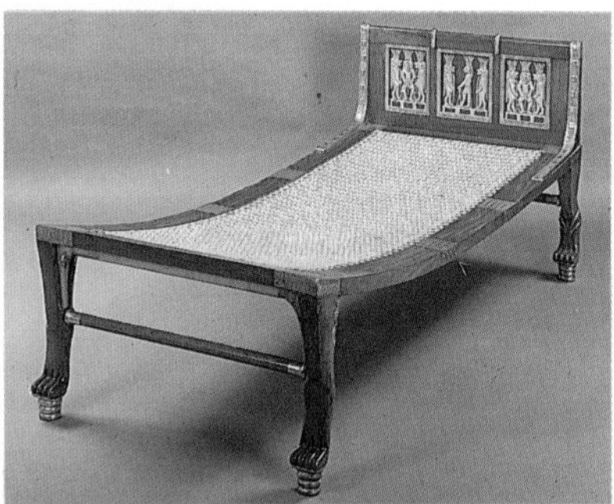

A 'Tutankhamun' gilt decorated mahogany daybed, in the style of J. Moyr-Smith, with cushion and bolsters, 69½in (176cm) long.
$5,000-5,500

An oak bookcase, by Gustav Stickley for the interior of his Craftsman Farms home, Morris Plains, New Jersey, c1909, 62in (157cm) wide.
$4,000-5,000

A chestnut bookcase in 2 sections, with adjustable shelves, by Gustav Stickley, c1909, 94½in (239cm) wide.
$5,000-6,500

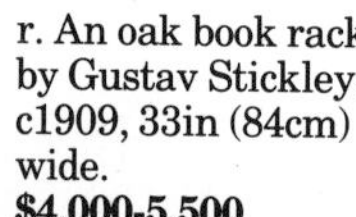

r. An oak book rack, by Gustav Stickley, c1909, 33in (84cm) wide.
$4,000-5,500

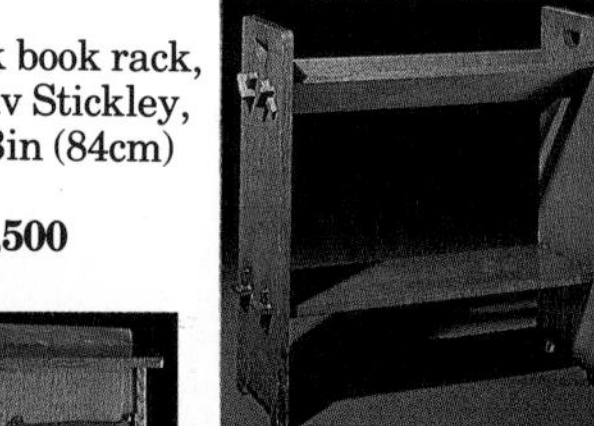

A rare oak book shelf and cabinet by Gustav Stickley, with 3 adjustable shelves, c1904, 38in (96.5cm) wide. **$6,000-7,500**

A Continental carved mahogany china cabinet, c1900, 81in (205.5cm) high.
$20,000-25,000
l. An oak armoire, by Gustav Stickley for the interior of his Craftsman Farms home, Morris Plains, New Jersey, c1909, 77in (195.5cm) high.
$9,000-10,000

An inlaid mahogany music cabinet, designed by Harvey Ellis, by Gustav Stickley, c1904, 48in (122cm) high.
$8,000-9,500

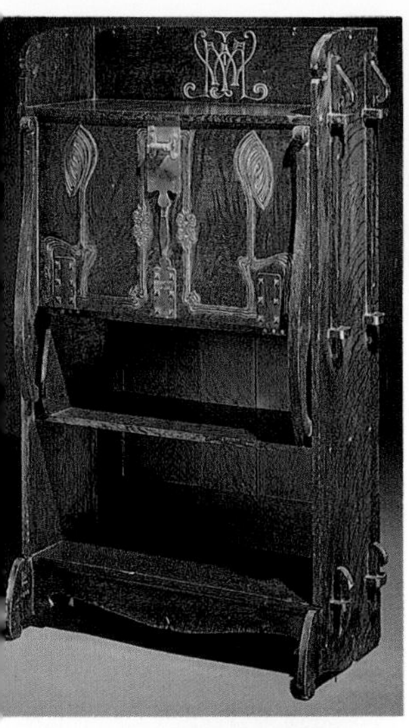

A burr walnut and marquetry, desk by Oscar Kaufmann, 1918, 102½in (260cm) wide. **$20,000-25,000**

l. An oak drop front desk by Charles Rohlfs, 1902, 54in (137cm) high. **$22,000-28,000**

r. An oak mirror, by Gustav Stickley, c1909. **$2,000-2,500**

l. A palissandre and ivory desk, by Jacques-Emile Ruhlmann, 1927, 47in (119cm) wide. **$160,000+**

r. An oak legged sideboard, by Gustav Stickley, c1902, 70in (178cm) wide. **$5,000-5,500**

A carved mahogany and marquetry sideboard, by Louis Majorelle, with inset marble top, 65in (165cm) wide. **$35,000-40,000**

l. A rare oak serving board, by Gustav Stickley, c1902, 60in (152cm) wide. **$13,000-14,000**

A carved and marquetry vitrine, by Louis Majorelle, 68½in (174cm) high. **$11,000-13,000**

l. A rosewood and walnut coffee table, by George Nakashima, 70½in (178cm) long. **$6,000-7,500**

r. A table by Jacques-Emile Ruhlmann, c1932, 134in (342cm). **$58,000-65,000**

l. An oak dining table by Gordon Russell, labelled and dated 1923, 66in (167.5cm). **$5,000-5,500**

r. A coffee table, by Jacques-Emile Ruhlmann, 31½in (80cm) diam. **$26,000-30,000**

A Majorelle walnut and marquetry etagère, 48½in (123cm) high.
$3,000-4,000

A marquetry two-tier table, inlaid with flowers and leaves, signed Gallé Nancy, 17in (43cm) wide.
$5,000-6,500

An oak director's table, by Gustav Stickley, with branded mark, c1912, 72in (182.5cm).
$10,000-12,000

A burr walnut and marquetry centre table, designed by Oskar Kaufmann, 41½in (105cm) diam.
$6,500-8,000

A pair of steel and marble consoles, 32in (81cm) high.
$14,000-16,000
r. A carved mahogany side table, by Louis Majorelle, 39in (99cm) high.
$6,500-8,000

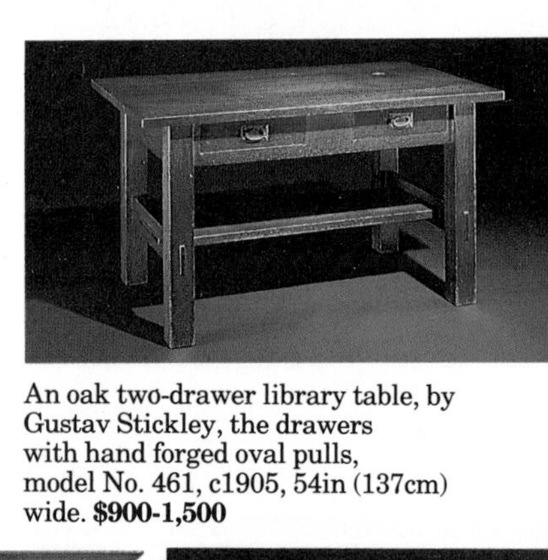

An oak two-drawer library table, by Gustav Stickley, the drawers with hand forged oval pulls, model No. 461, c1905, 54in (137cm) wide. **$900-1,500**

A rosewood desk, by Jacques-Emile Ruhlmann, the top inset with a leather panel, fitted with 2 drawers, branded, c1925, 60in (152cm) wide.
$200,000-250,000
l. An oak and brass dinner gong, by Gustav Stickley, c1909, 24in (61cm) wide.
$7,000-10,000

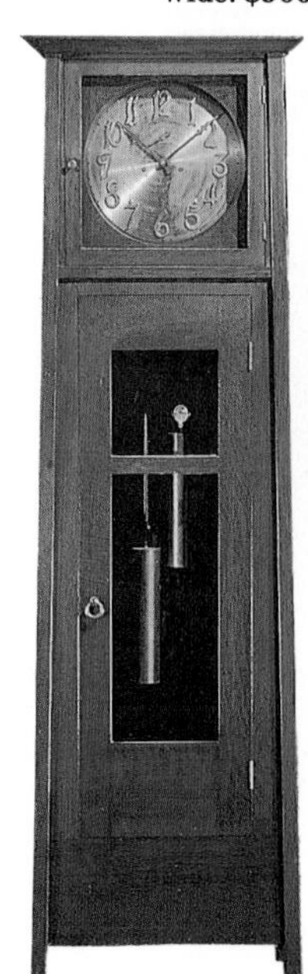

An oak tile top table, by Gustav Stickley, labelled, c1905, 24in (61cm) wide.
$14,000-18,000
l. A longcase clock, by Gustav Stickley, labelled, Model No. 3, 72in (183cm) high.
$50,000-65,000

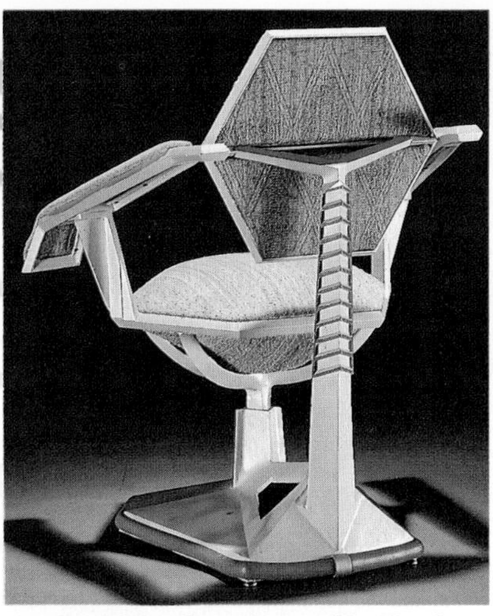

An aluminium chair, designed by Frank Lloyd Wright for the H. C. Price Co. Tower, Bartlesville, Oklahoma, c1954, 32½in (85cm) high.
$45,000-50,000

A Tidewater cypress end table, designed by Frank Lloyd Wright for the Misses Austin, Greenville, Carolina, c1951, 26in (66.5cm) high.
$28,000-32,000

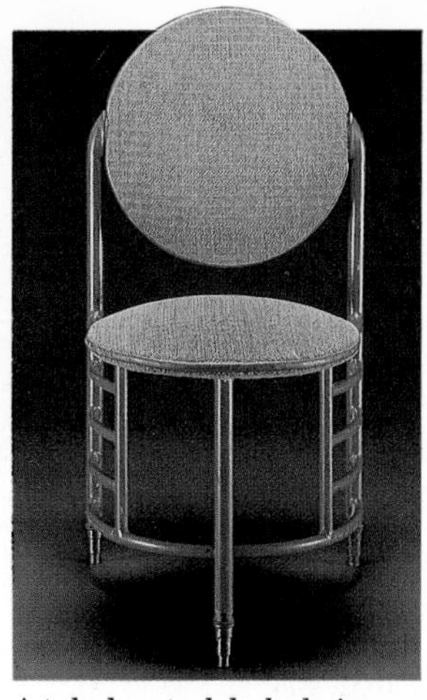

A tubular steel desk chair, designed by Frank Lloyd Wright for the S. C. Johnson Building, Racine, Wisconsin, c1936, 35in (89cm) high.
$73,000-80,000

Two Tidewater cypress dining tables and 6 chairs, by Frank Lloyd Wright for the Misses Austin, c1951.
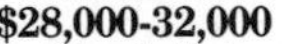
$28,000-32,000

r. A leaded glass window, by Frank Lloyd Wright for the J. J. Walser house, Chicago, Illinois, c1903, 65in (165cm) high. **$5,000-9,500**

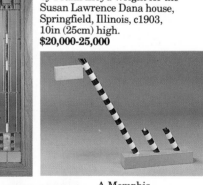

A gilt bronze and glass table lamp, by Frank Lloyd Wright for the Susan Lawrence Dana house, Springfield, Illinois, c1903, 10in (25cm) high.
$20,000-25,000

A pair of leaded glass doors, by Frank Lloyd Wright for the Francis W. Little house, Wayzata, Minnesota, c1913, each 79in (200.5cm) high.
$25,000-32,000

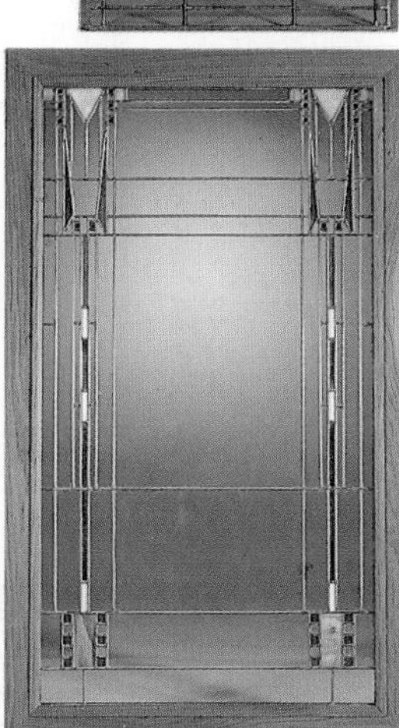

A leaded glass window, by Marion Mahony for the Gerald Mahony house, Elkhardt, Indiana, c1905, 47in (119cm) high framed.
$4,000-8,000

A Memphis lacquered metal table lamp, by Michele de Lucchi, 1981, 29in (74cm) high. **$1,000-1,300**

l. A table lamp by Ettore Sottsass, 1981, 27½in (69.5cm) high.
$1,500-2,500

An Art Deco maple 3-piece suite, the design attributed to Maurice Adams, the sofa with waved padded back, rounded upholstered seat and scroll end arms on platform base, comprising a sofa and 2 armchairs, sofa 71½in (181cm) wide. **$9,500-13,000**

r. A Carlo Bugatti ebonised, inlaid and painted vellum side chair. **$5,000-6,000** and table. **$11,000-13,000**

l. An Edwin Lutyens 'Napoleon' chair, 38½in (98cm) wide. **$9,500-13,000**

A carved mahogany dining table and a set of 12 dining chairs, by the firm of Louis Majorelle, the table with 3 additional leaves, 117in (297cm) extended. **$25,000-30,000**

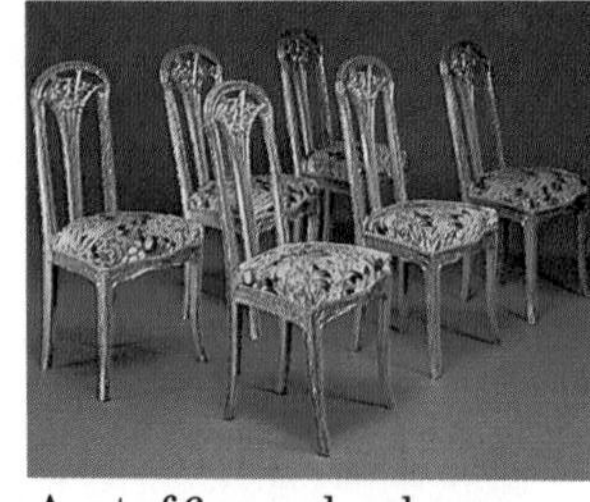

A set of 6 carved mahogany 'clematis' sidechairs, by the firm of Louis Majorelle, 37in (94cm) high. **$4,000-5,500**
l. A beechwood and mahogany 'Sitz Machine' chair, c1912, 39in (99cm) high. **$40,000-50,000**

A set of 4 mahogany dining chairs, from the oceanliner 'Normandie', 35in (89cm) high. **$20,000-25,000**

A chair, model No. MR 90, known as the 'Barcelona Chair', designed by Ludwig Mies Van Der Rohe, Director of the Bauhaus, c1931. **$130,000-150,000**
l. An inlaid oak armchair, designed by Harvey Ellis, c1904. **$12,000-18,000**

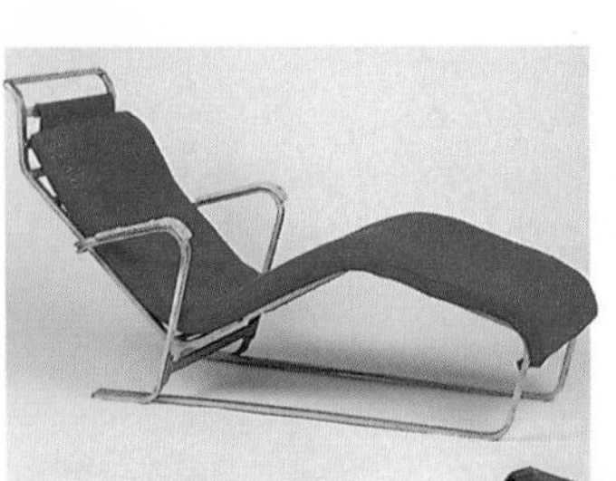

An aluminium chaise longue, designed by Marcel Breuer, Director of Bauhaus furniture workshop 1925-28, the arm supports set with wooden handles, c1935, 53in (134cm) long. **$16,000-20,000**

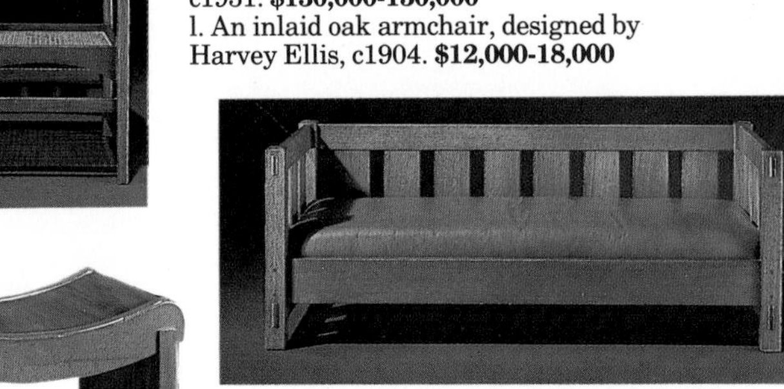

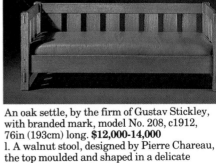

An oak settle, by the firm of Gustav Stickley, with branded mark, model No. 208, c1912, 76in (193cm) long. **$12,000-14,000**
l. A walnut stool, designed by Pierre Chareau, the top moulded and shaped in a delicate scroll, 18in (46cm) high. **$16,000-18,000**

An ashtray, executed at the Bauhaus metal workshop, stamped Bauhaus, c1924, 2½in (6cm) high.
$13,000-14,000

'Tee Extraktkannchen', a silver and ebony Bauhaus teapot, fitted with a tea strainer, by Marianne Brandt, c1924, 3in (7.5cm).
$200,000-208,000

A hand wrought hammered silver and ebony Bauhaus coffee pot, sterling and 925 silver mark, 8½in (21cm) high.
$14,000-18,000

A silver mounted iron cylindrical vase, by Tiffany & Co., New York, c1880, 9in (23cm) high.
$11,000-12,000

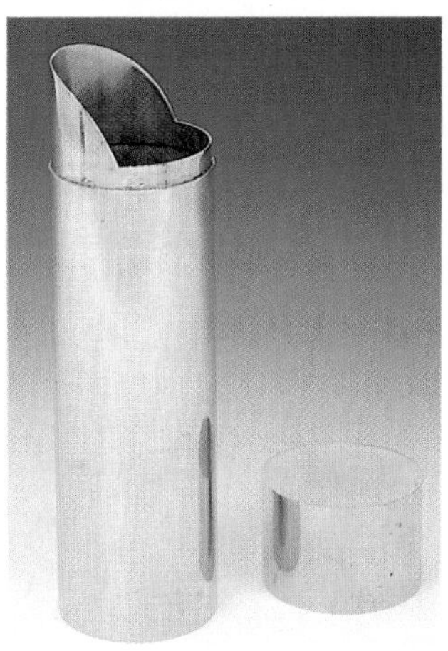

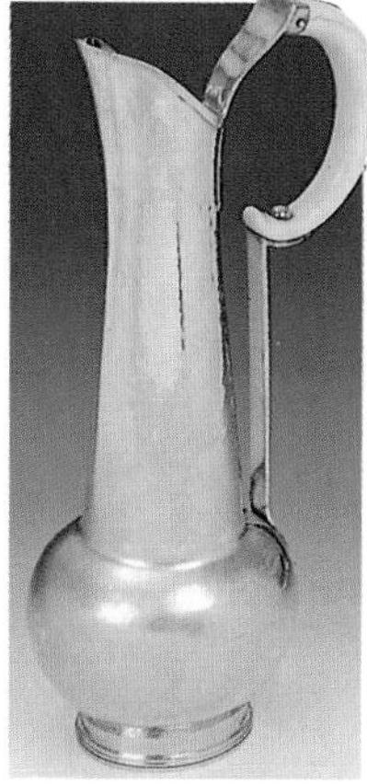

A metal plated brass tea caddy, stamped Bauhaus, c1925, 8½in (20cm) high. **$20,000-21,000**

Above r. A hand wrought hammered silver and ivory wine jug, with applied shaped strap handle, interrupted by a crescent shaped ivory grip, stamped with maker's monogram CD, with 800 silver mark, 11½in (30cm) high. **$35,000-40,000**

A hand wrought hammered silver and ebony, Bauhaus coffee pot, stamped CD and 900 silver mark, 9in (23cm) high. **$50,000-60,000**

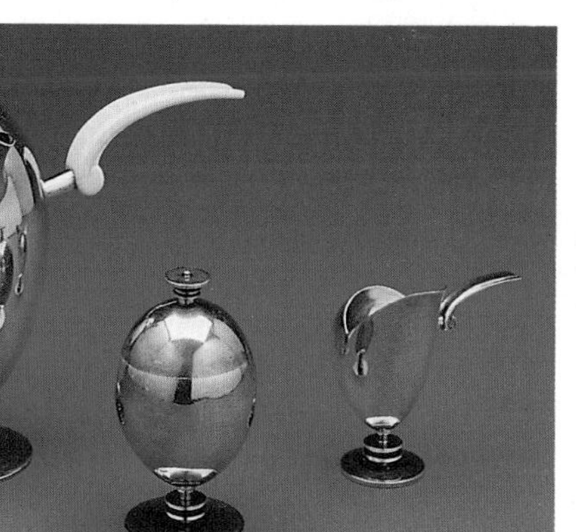

A silver and ivory espresso service, and 3 demi-tasse spoons, for Georg Jensen, c1935, 22oz gross.
$6,500-8,000

A silver espresso service, designed by Johan Rohde for Georg Jensen silversmithy, comprising: a coffee pot, cream pitcher, and sugar bowl, and a tray, maker's marks, coffee pot 7in (18cm) high.
$9,000-10,000

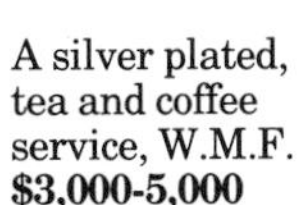

A silver plated, tea and coffee service, W.M.F.
$3,000-5,000

A Liberty gold, mother-of-pearl and pearl necklace, designed by Archibald Knox.
$5,000-5,500

An Art Nouveau 15ct gold turquoise and pearl brooch by Murlle Bennett & Co., c1910.
$650-700

A Liberty Art Nouveau opal pendant, possibly designed by Oliver Baker.
$2,000-2,500

A Liberty gold and opal ring designed by Archibald Knox, marked.
$1,400-2,000

A Liberty gold, opal and pearl pendant, designed by Archibald Knox.
$4,000-5,000

A gold, opal and pearl necklace, designed by Archibald Knox.
$4,000-5,000

A gold and turquoise pendant, designed by Archibald Knox.
$4,000-5,000

A Liberty gold and turquoise pendant, by Archibald Knox.
$9,000-9,500

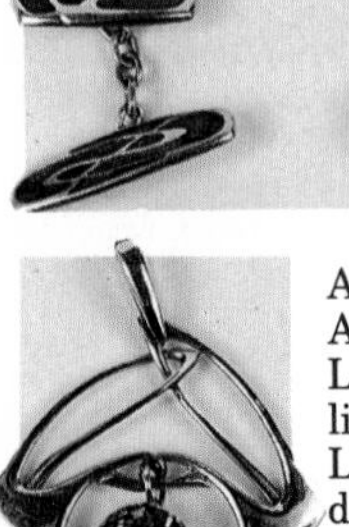

Above and l. A pair of Liberty cuff links and a Liberty pendant designed by Archibald Knox.
Cuff links,
$3,000-4,000
Pendant,
$1,500-2,500

A Liberty platinum pendant by Archibald Knox.
$6,500-7,000

A Liberty gold and mother-of-pearl bracelet by Archibald Knox.
$3,000-4,000

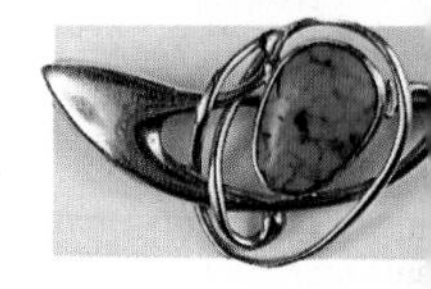

r. A Liberty gold and turquoise brooch, designed by Archibald Knox.
$2,000-2,500

A stoneware bowl by Lucie Rie, c1983. **$6,500-7,000**
l. A stoneware bowl by Lucie Rie, c1969.
$8,000-11,000

. stoneware bowl by Lucie Rie, white nd blue pitted glaze, impressed LR eal, c1982, 10½in (26cm) diam.
9,500-12,000

. deep pink porcelain bowl y Lucie Rie, impressed LR eal, c1979, 9in (23cm).
6,500-8,000

A shiny green porcelain bowl, with golden bronze 'running' rim, by Lucie Rie, impressed LR seal, c1980, 8in (20cm) diam. **$5,000-6,500**

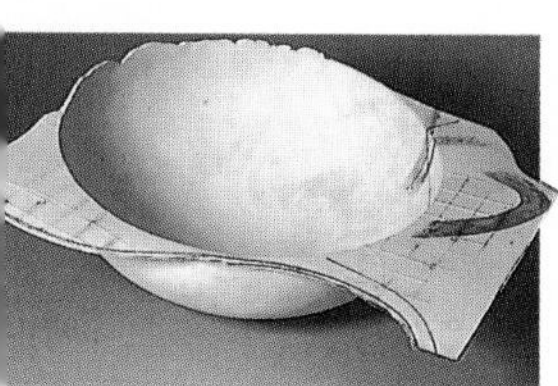

. white bowl form, by ordon Baldwin, signed B 80, 20in (50cm) diam.
1,300-1,500

A large stoneware bowl by Bernard Leach, c1960.
$1,300-1,500

A porcelain bowl by Bernard Leach, white with blue Chinese landscape, small repaired kiln crack, c1925. **$6,500-8,000**

. stoneware bowl y Lucie Rie, mpressed LR, 1984.
5,000-6,500

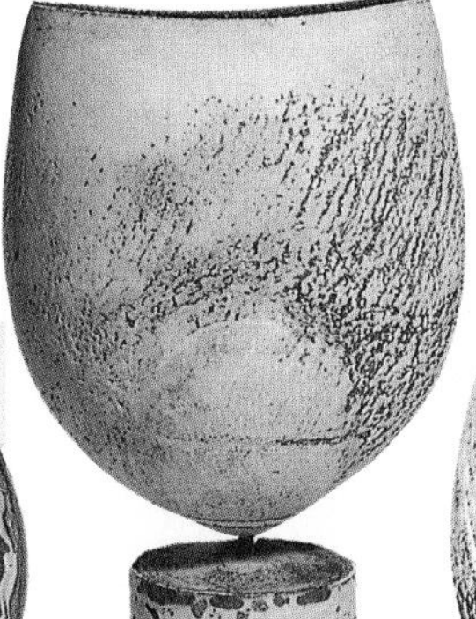

l. A stoneware cup form, by Hans Coper, on drum foot with ochre and matt manganese blistering, c1972, 6in (15cm) high.
$28,000-30,000

win candleholders, y Hans Coper, lack and bronze, npressed HC eals and 1966.
130,000-150,000

A large bowl by Katherine Pleydell-Bouverie, impressed KPB seal, c1955, 13½in (34cm) diam.
$800-1,500

r. A white stoneware cup form by Hans Coper, impressed HC seal, c1970, 7in (17cm) high.
$20,000-22,000

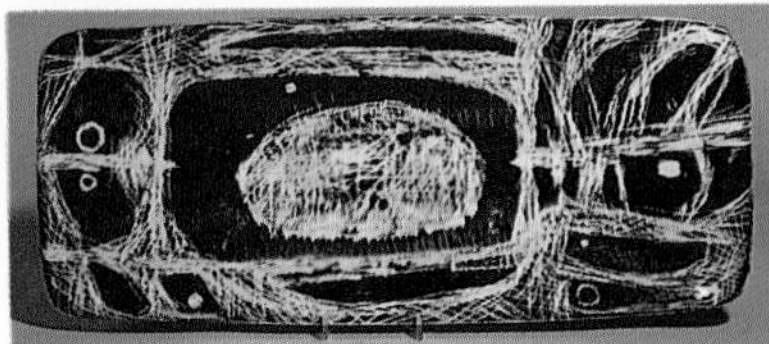

An earthenware shallow rectangular dish, by James Tower, inscribed J. Tower 1953, 22in (56cm) wide.
$2,500-3,000
r. A handbuilt stoneware irregular dish, by Ewen Henderson, 23½in (60cm) wide. **$1,000-1,300**

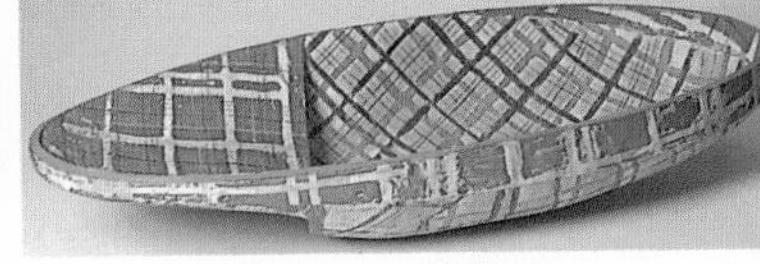

An eliptical boat vessel, by Jacqueline Poncelet, 23in (58cm) long.
$1,400-1,650

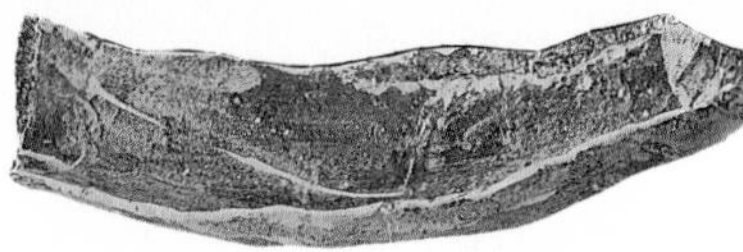

An earthenware dish by John Piper.
$1,000-1,300

A stoneware dish, by Hans Coper, impressed HC seal, c1952, 8in (20cm) wide.
$25,000-32,000

A shallow dish on 3 feet, by Rosanjin Kitaoji, incised RO signature, 8½in (21.5cm) wide.
$5,500-6,500

A stoneware charger, by Michael Cardew, marked MC.
$3,500-4,000

A stoneware spout pot, by Elizabeth Fritsch, 7in (17.5cm) high.
$5,000-5,500

A stoneware spout pot, by Elizabeth Fritsch, with undulating rim, c1974.
$6,500-7,000

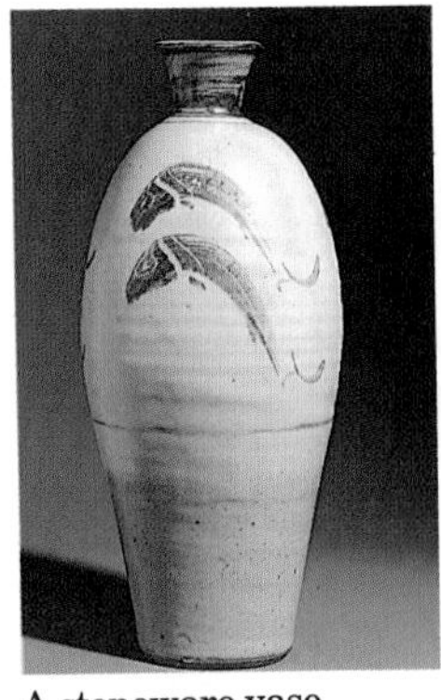

A stoneware vase, by Bernard Leach, impressed BL and St. Ives seals.
$7,000-8,000

A stoneware vase, by Lucie Rie, marked LR seal, c1960, 16in (41cm).
$11,000-16,000
l. A 'volcanic glazed' vase, by Hugh Cornwall Robertson for Dedham Pottery, marked by the artist and the Pottery, 8in (20cm) high.
$4,000-5,000

Above l. A porcelain vase by Lucie Rie, marked LR seal, c1980, 9½in (24cm). **$5,500-6,500**
Above r. A 'Cycladic' vessel form, by Hans Coper, 1976. **$40-50,000**

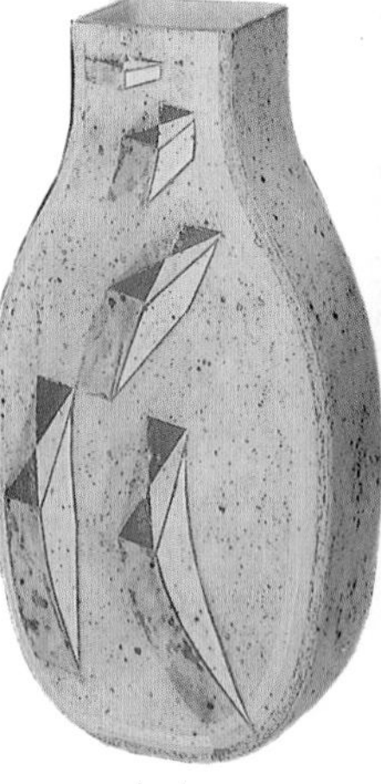

A stoneware vase by Elizabeth Fritsch, 13in (33cm).
$5,000-6,500
r. A vase by Shoji Hamada, c1950, 10in (25cm). **$9,500-11,000**

licroscopes

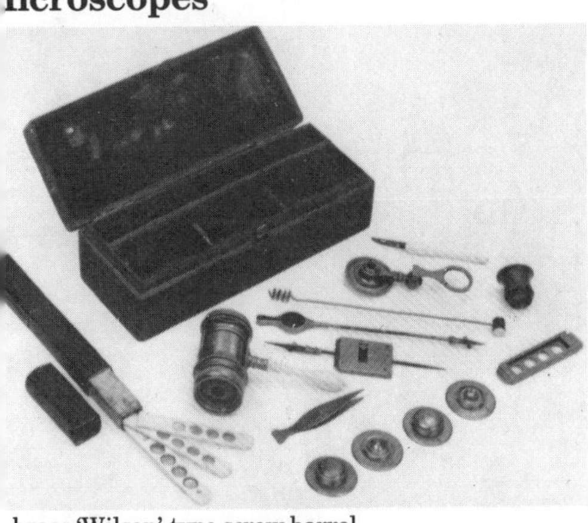

. brass 'Wilson'-type screw barrel nd simple microscope compendium, ith accessories, including objectives, ivory sliders, specimen, iewer, forceps and other items, nsigned, in fishskin covered case, 8thC, 7½in (18.5cm) wide.
1,500-2,500

A brass microscope lamp, the case with cast signature Swift & Son, London, W.C. with the glass reservoir, lamp and shade, height adjustment, in stained pine case with brass carrying handle, late 19thC, 12in (31cm) high.
$200-250

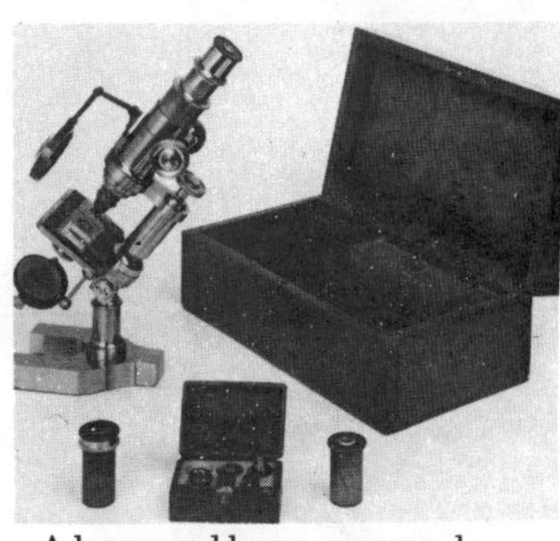

A lacquered brass compound monocular microscope, signed on the body tube E. Hartnack & A. Prazmowski, Rue Bonaparte, 7 Paris, complete with accessories and slides in the original fitted mahogany case, stamped 18140, 19thC, 11in (28cm) wide.
$650-700

A lacquered brass aquatic nicroscope, signed on the stage V&S Jones, 30 Holborn, London, he tubular pillar with rack and inion focusing, the arm with bjective adjustable both in the orizontal and vertical planes, the tage with forceps, the lower pillar vith concave swivel mirror, with ome accessories, in plush lined eather covered case, the lid with nounting ferrule, early 19thC, ½in (13.5cm) wide.
$500-550

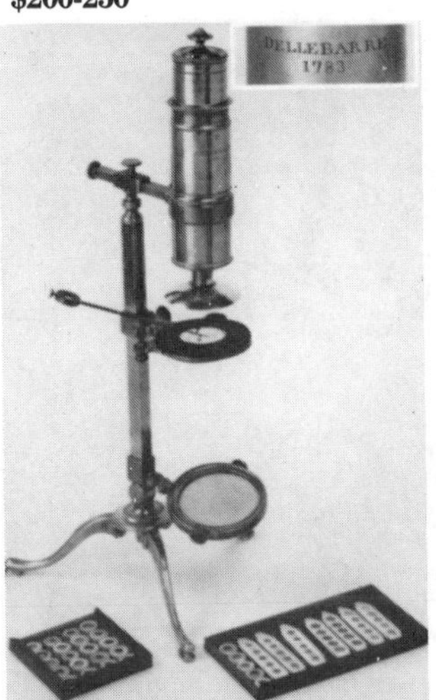

A brass compound monocular microscope, signed on the body tube Dellebarre 1783, located on an arm by friction leather band, now missing, on tripod stand, with a lieberkuhn, set of 5 objectives and other items including a case of ivory sliders and another with ivory specimen cups, in fitted walnut case, 12½in (32.5cm) wide.
$5,000-5,500

A black enamelled and lacquered brass monocular microscope, by Carl Zeiss Jena, No. 161198, with rack and pinion coarse focusing and micrometer fine adjustment, quadruple nose-piece, mechanical circuit stage, substage condenser and plane concave mirror, with a range of accessories including a binocular attachment, 2 cases, the largest 14½in (37.5cm) high.
$1,000-1,200

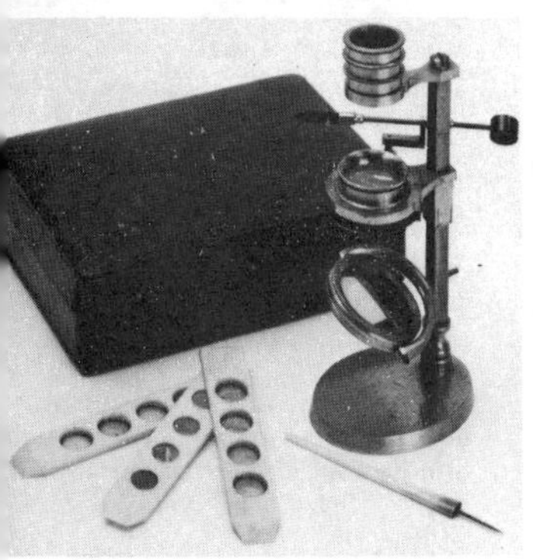

A lacquered brass aquatic pocket microscope, the pillar with arm for objectives, stage with forceps live box and swivel mirror, on oval base, unsigned, in fitted plush lined leather covered case with sliders and trade label inscribed Hawes, 95 Cheapside. From Dollands, 19thC, the case 4½in (11.5cm) wide.
$400-500

A lacquered brass solar microscope, signed on the rotating plate Cary, London, the mirror adjusted by worm drive screw and enclosed rack and pinion, with a bead glass objective carrier 1-6, spring loaded specimen clamp and other accessories, in mahogany case, lid missing, 19thC, 15½in (40cm) wide.
$1,300-1,400

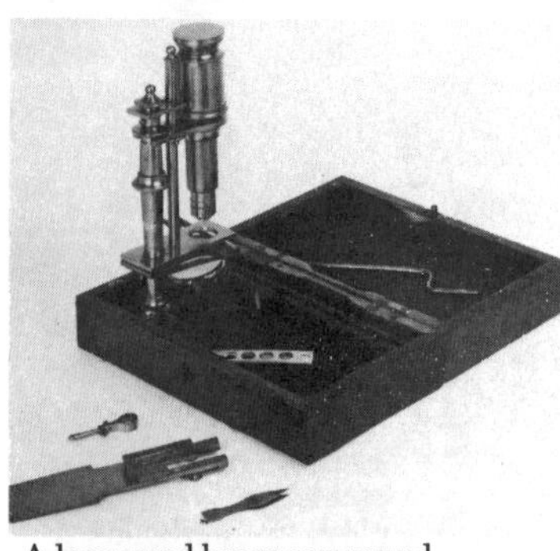

A lacquered brass compound monocular microscope, unsigned with 'quick thread' focusing, the stage with sprung slide holder, the pillar mounted on swivel attachment with mirror, forceps, frogplate and other accessories in fitted crossbanded mahogany case, early 19thC, 9in (22.5cm) wide.
$900-1,000

Medical Instruments

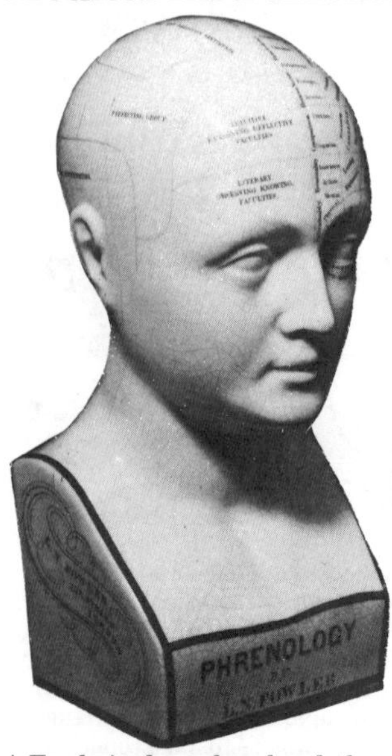

A Fowler's phrenology head, the cranium printed with the areas of the sentiments, the base with maker's label and title, crackle glaze finish, 11½in (29.5cm) high.
$1,000-1,200

A plaster model eye, signed on the base, 54 Anotomie Clostique Dr Auioux 1949, the stand 7½in (19.5cm) wide.
$400-500

A lacquered and oxidised brass microscope by W. Watson and Sons, with rack and pinion focusing, triple nose-piece, fully mechanical adjustable stage, sub-stage condenser and swivel mirror and various accessories, in mahogany case, late 19thC, 13in (33cm) high.
$300-400

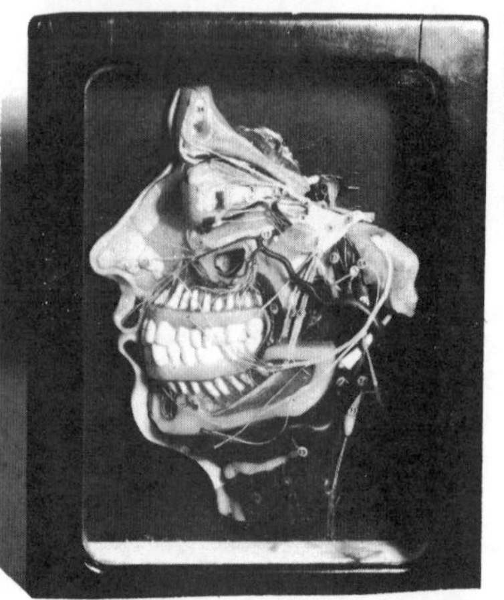

A wax model of the human head, the veins and arteries with numbered labels, in glazed ebonised case, 10in (25cm) high.
$400-500

A surgeon's instrument set, in a mahogany and brass banded folding case with inner tray, virtually complete with 75 items each stamped with the maker's mark and in original condition, by S. Mawson & Thompson, Aldersgate, London, 19thC.
$5,000-5,500

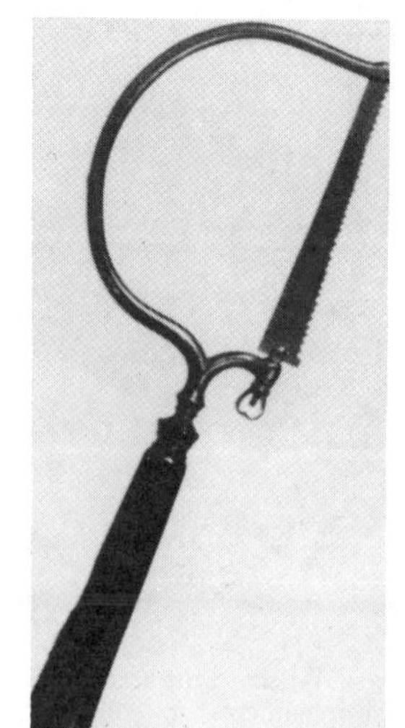

A medical saw, the blade secured rivet and wing nut, and with tapering octagonal section walnut handle, 18thC, 9½in (24.5cm) lon
$250-300

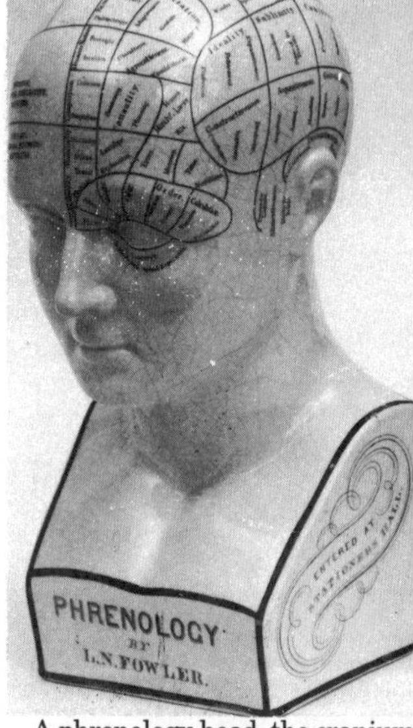

A phrenology head, the cranium printed with the areas of the sentiments, trade label, scroll an citation, by L. N. Fowler, 11½in (29.5cm) high.
$800-1,000

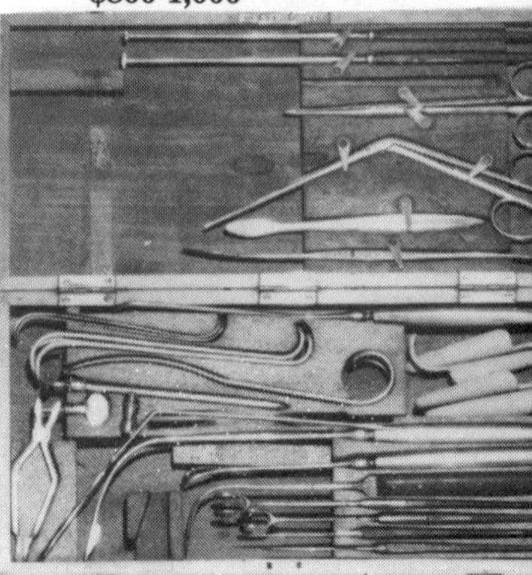

A mahogany cased set of surgical instruments, and a part set of ivor handled optician's instruments, by Weiss, 13in (33cm) wide.
$400-500

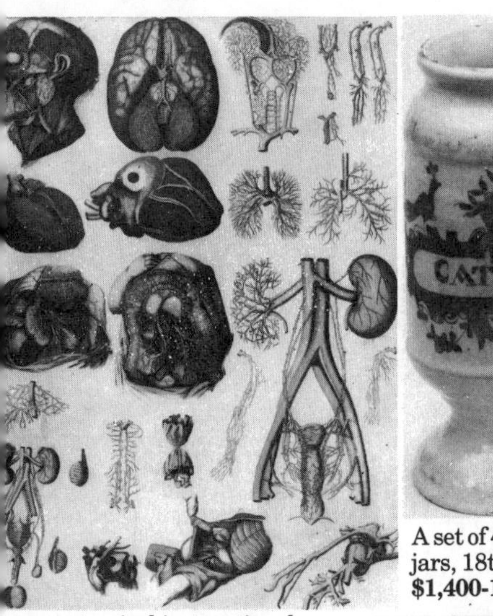

A set of 4 Dutch blue and white drug jars, 18thC, 7½in (19cm) high.
$1,400-1,500

our anatomical instructional ints, signed Impensis J. & P. napton Londini 1740, 1749 & 750, J.S Müller Sculp and G. rignion Sculp, 18thC, framed and azed, 22½in (57cm) by 16in 0.5cm).
,000-1,200

A brass binocular telescope, with range of lenses and fittings, in mahogany case with brass handle, by Broadhurst Clarkson & Co London, 19thC, 23in (59cm) high.
$1,300-1,500

A burnished steel tooth key, with single claw and ebony handle with chequered grip, 5½in (13.5cm) long, and another tooth key with 2 spare claws, early 19thC.
$300-400

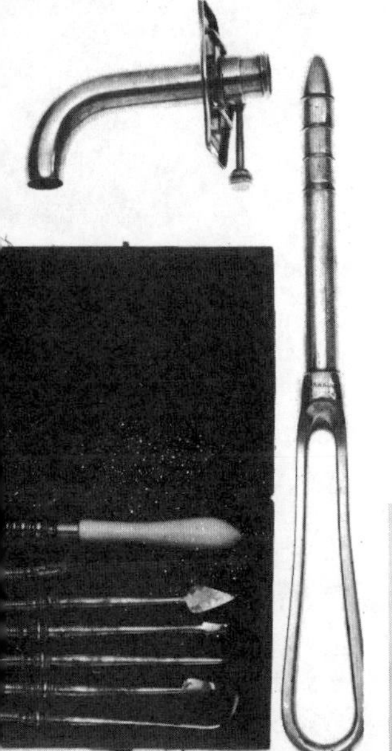

silver metal tracheotomy nnulae with lobster tail, 6½in 6cm) long, and a set of 6 dental struments with ivory combination andle, in plush lined case with irror, 19thC, 3in (7.5cm) wide.
300-400

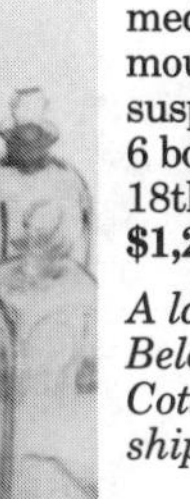

A leather covered domestic medicine casket, with chased silver mounts, the mansard lid with suspension loop rising to reveal 6 bottles, cup, funnel and scissors, 18thC, 7½in (19cm) wide.
$1,200-1,400

A label found with this casket says: Belonging to Adm. Sir Charles Cotton and taken by him on board ship when ever he went to sea.

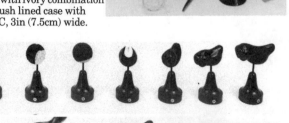

A collection of numbered coloured plaster demonstration and instructional models of the evolution of the common frog.
$250-300

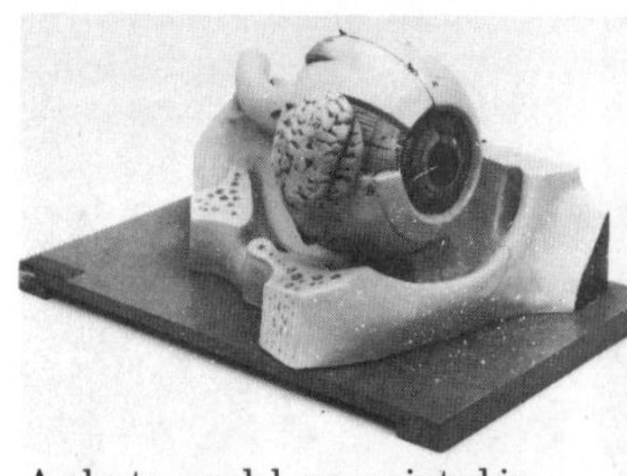

A plaster model eye, painted in colours with numbers corresponding to the nervous system, on wood base, by van de Knip, Utrecht, 15½in (40cm) wide.
$300-500

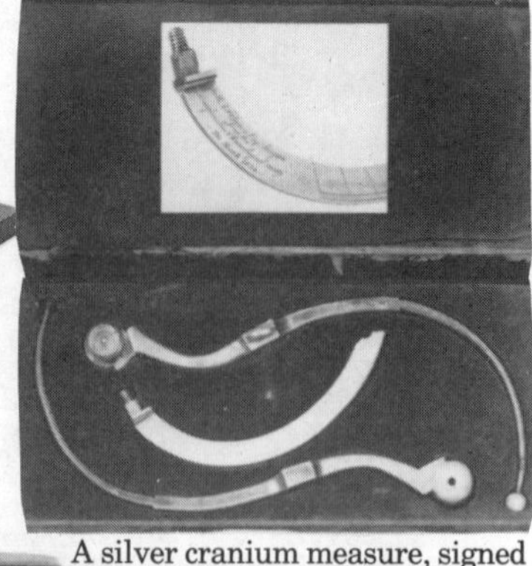

A silver cranium measure, signed and engraved in the quadrant arm to W.A.F. Brown Esqr. Surgeon, from the Dunfermline Phrenological Society 20 March 1834, in a plush lined leather case, 10½in (26.5cm) wide.
$2,500-3,000

A 35mm 'Ensign cinematograph camera, by Houghton-Butcher M Co. Ltd., England, with hand-cr and a brass bound Carl Zeiss, Je Tessar f.3.5 5cm lens No. 241252 in maker's leather case.
$650-700

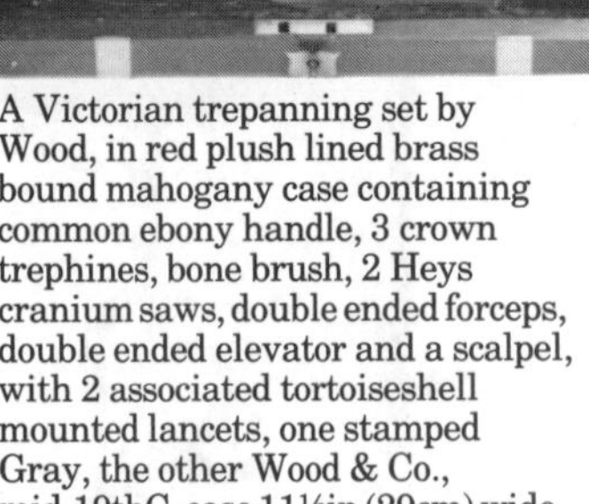

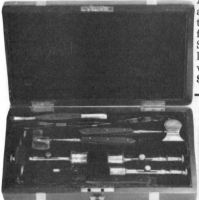

A Victorian trepanning set by Wood, in red plush lined brass bound mahogany case containing common ebony handle, 3 crown trephines, bone brush, 2 Heys cranium saws, double ended forceps, double ended elevator and a scalpel, with 2 associated tortoiseshell mounted lancets, one stamped Gray, the other Wood & Co., mid-19thC, case 11½in (29cm) wide.
$1,000-1,200

A half-plate brass and mahogany tailboard camera, by W. I. Chadwick, Manchester, with a brass bound R. and J. Beck 5 by 4in (12.5 by 10cm) rectalinear 7in (17.5cm) focus lens No. 3945.
$400-500

A quarter-plate mahogany bodi 'Rover' camera by J. Lancaster & Son, Birmingham, set into a 'Lancaster' patent See Saw shut in maker's original fitted leathe case.
$650-700

Cameras

A 5 by 4in (12.5 by 10cm) Transitional wet-plate/dry-plate mahogany bodied studio camera, by J. H. Dallmeyer, London, with brass fittings, rising and falling front, removable repeating back with 2 separate masks, mahogany single dark slide and a brass bound J. H. Dallmeyer Triple achromatic lens No. 5135 set into a non-original shutter mechanism.
$1,500-2,500

A postcard 'Xit' camera, by J. F. Shew and Co., London, with a C. Goerz Dogmar Series III 150mm f.6.8 lens No. 209149, in a leathe case.
$200-300

Two Eastman Kodak Co. Browni cameras, comprising a No. 2 Brownie camera in maker's origi box, featuring the Brownie characters, and a No. 2a Brownie camera in Art Deco styled blue b
$250-300

A 12cm diam. film 'Kinokam Style A' camera, with swinging taking and viewing lens, internal removable film holder and handle all contained in maker's original cardboard box, with paper label, by The Kinokam Co., London.
$2,500-3,000

The Kinokam camera was the subject of patent No. 17347 dated August 9, 1904, and taken out by S. H. Crocker. The specification described an apparatus for viewing or photographing moving pictures. The combined camera/viewer used a disc to hold the sensitised film or processed pictures and a revolving section mounted on the front of the camera carried a viewing lens, photographic lens and a view-finder. The apparatus could also be used for viewing transparencies.

The Kinokam produced 24 images on a circular disc of film. The subsequent paper print was viewed using the camera but with the lens section rotated 180 degrees bringing a magnifying lens into position.

metal enamelled advertising sign the form of a film spool, by Illingworth and Co. England, 20 7in (50 by 18cm).
275-300

brass bound portrait lens o. 14361, by Voigtlander & Son, raunschweig, Germany, with ass mounting flange and aterhouse stop, with engraved ns barrel.
00-900

A 6 by 9cm Ontoflex twin lens reflex camera, by Cornu, Paris, with a Berthiot Ontar f.3.5 viewing lens No. 316153 and a Berthiot Stellor f.3.5 90mm taking lens No. 257750 set into a Compur Rapid shutter and revolving roll film back, all in maker's case.
$300-400

A 5 by 4in (12.5 by 10cm) Micro-Technical Mk. VI camera with a Carl Zeiss, Jena Tessar f.4.5 13.5cm lens No. 2549254 set into a Compur shutter, a Kodak Ektar f.7.7 203mm lens set into a Prontor-SVS shutter, 3 double dark slides and a Polaroid 545 Land film holder, all in a fitted leather case, and a Gandolfi tripod.
$900-1,000

A Popular Photographic Co. Nodark camera, with polished wood body and nickel fittings and internal wooden holder for 26 plates, 3½ by 2½in (9 by 6.5cm).
$650-700

A 2¾ by 3¼in (7 by 8cm) mahogany bodied wet-plate camera, by A. Ross, London, with rising front, a brass bound A. Ross, London, lens No. 3892, with rack and pinion focusing and one wet-plate dark slide.
$7,000-9,500

A Votra stereo transparency viewer by E. Leitz, Wetzlar, with rear film holder for a 35mm mounted stereo transparency and with a very rare Votiv stand.
$1,300-1,500

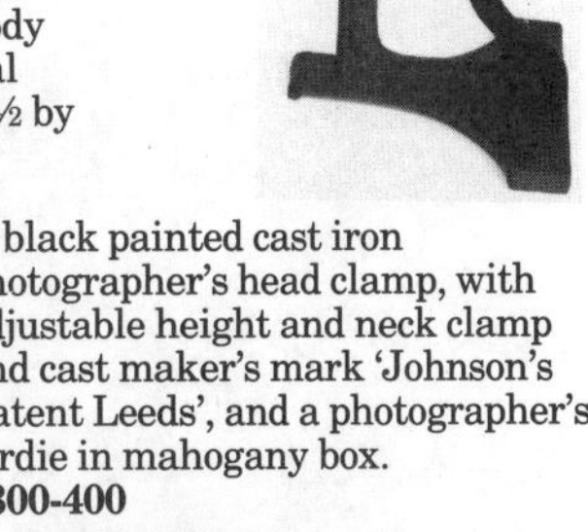

A black painted cast iron photographer's head clamp, with adjustable height and neck clamp and cast maker's mark 'Johnson's Patent Leeds', and a photographer's birdie in mahogany box.
$300-400

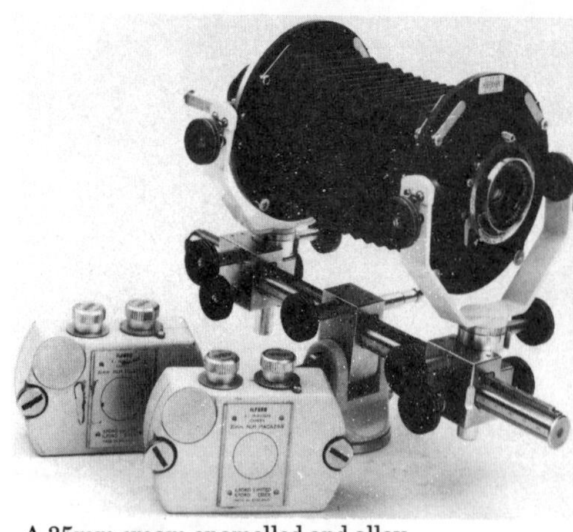

A 35mm cream enamelled and alloy K. I. Monobar technical camera, by Ilford/Kennedy Instruments Ltd., England, with a sliding viewfinder, a Schneider Angulon f.6.8 90mm lens No. 4805934 set into a Synchro-Compur-P shutter, two cream-enamelled K. I. Monobar film magazines and a shutter all in maker's original fitted box.
$1,200-1,400

A metal bodied 'Ticka' camera, by Houghtons Ltd., London, with lens cap and film spool in a cloth pouch with instruction booklets, all contained in maker's original box, and a wooden 'Ticka printing box' with 'Ticka pictures' instruction booklet, all in maker's original box.
$650-700

A 10 by 8in (25.5 by 20cm) mahogany and brass field camera No. 7148, by G. Hare, London, with inset brass binding strips, red square cut bellows and a brass bound J. H. Dallmeyer patent 3.D lens with rack and pinion focusing and aperture for Waterhouse stops, and a mahogany and brass fitted Morgan and Kidd patent roll film holder No. 144, in a fitted leather case.
$1,400-2,000

A rare 3 by 2in (8 by 5cm) 'Ensignette No. 2' camera, by Houghtons Ltd., London, Silver Plated model No. 2892 with a tim and instantaneous shutter, in maker's original box with paper label 'Silver Plated Ensignette P/A1235/1/2/12' standard box lab
$1,500-2,000

A quarter-plate brass and mahogany bodied 'The Sanderso camera, by Houghtons Ltd., London, No. 11.938, lacks focusi back, with a lens.
$250-300

An Elmarit-R f.2.8 35mm lens No. 1995370, with a 12564K lens hood, by E. Leitz, Wetzlar, all in maker's plastic case.
$250-300

A 35mm Contarex camera No. T92434, by Zeiss Ikon, Germany, with a Carl Zeiss Planar f.2.5mm lens No. 2368376, all in maker's leather ever ready case.
$300-400

A very rare left-hand shutter release device, by E. Leitz, Wetzla for use with the M-series Leica camera.
$1,000-1,200

rare 35mm Esco camera with a teinheil Cassar f.6.3 3.5cm lens o. 168632 set into a dial-set Pronto hutter, by Seischab, Germany.
5,000-5,500

he Esco camera was made by Otto eischab of Nuremburg from 1926. could take up to 400 exposures on andard 35mm cine film. The larged film chambers were copied y Leitz in their 250 exposure eporter camera of 1933.

A very rare hand held magnesium-ibbon flash unit with hand-crank magnesium-ribbon chamber and detachable reflector, all in original box.
$500-650

A 35mm mahogany cased, hand-cranked, cinematographic camera No. 50, by A. Darling and Son, Brighton, England, with brass binding strips, 2 internal mahogany W.K. Co. Ltd., film magazines, film transport mechanism and casing marked 'AD' and claw mechanism marked 'A 221. Pat. 21787-08', a Carl Zeiss, Jena Tessar f.3.5cm lens No. 236088 set into a brass focusing lens mount, hand crank, camera body stamped.
$1,400-2,000

An Eastman Kodak Co. rollfilm original Brownie camera with push-on back and simple meniscus lens set into a rotary shutter.
$550-600

A Kodak Ensemble outfit, comprising a beige coloured 127-film Kodak Petite camera with stylus, lacking cosmetics, contained in maker's presentation suede case, by Eastman Kodak Co., Rochester, N.Y., U.S.A.
$400-450

The Kodak Ensemble was available from October 1929 to 1933. Cosmetics with the set comprised a powder compact, lipstick and mirror supplied by the House of Tre Jur.

A 7½ by 5in (19 by 12.5cm) Transitional mahogany bodied tailboard camera, by W. W. Rouch, London, with brass fittings, rising and cross front, swinging back, screw-focusing back standard, red leather bellows, removable ground glass screen, a brass bound Wray, London 5 by 4in (12.5 by 10cm) lens No. 3792, a mahogany single wet-plate dark slide contained within the camera body and two mahogany dry-plate double dark slides with each plate holder numbered consecutively from 1 to 4 and 3 containing a mahogany quarter-plate reducing mask, camera with maker's plaque.
$550-700

Two Carl Zeiss Jena catalogues comprising 'Photo lenses. Reference P. 185' dated 1910 and 'Photo Objective. P. 185' dated 1910.
$150-250

An 8 by 8in (20 by 20cm) mahogany wet-plate camera with black bellows, brass locking clips, a sturdy brass handle, removable focusing screen, a brass bound Jamin a Paris lens with rack and pinion focusing and a mahogany wet-plate dark slide.
$650-1,000

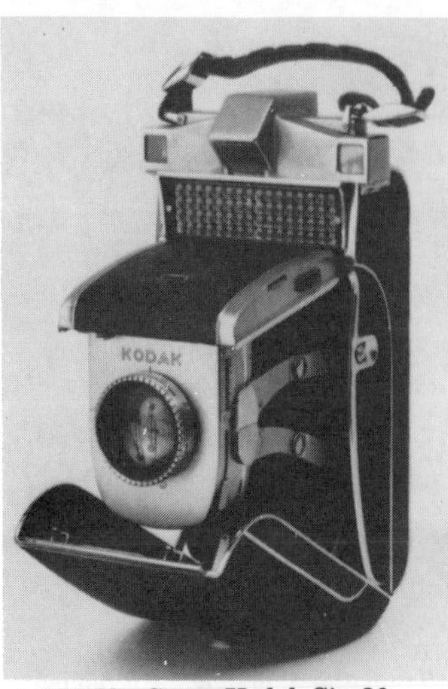

A 620-film Super Kodak Six-20 camera, No. 2125 with an Eastman Kodak Co. Kodak Anastigmat Special f.3.5 100mm lens, No. 1394.
$2,000-2,500

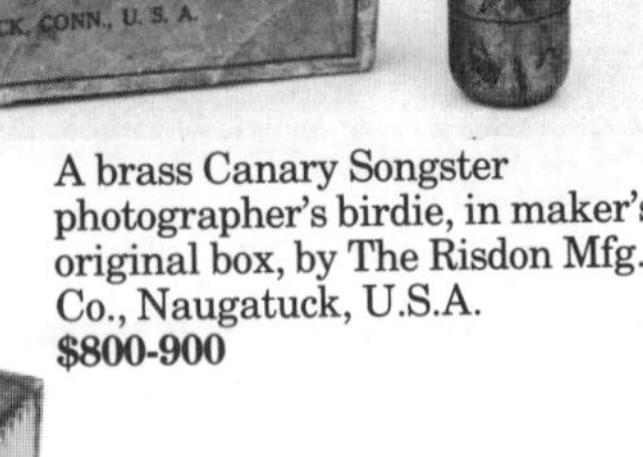

A brass Canary Songster photographer's birdie, in maker's original box, by The Risdon Mfg. Co., Naugatuck, U.S.A.
$800-900

An original Kodak camera No. 3784 with winding key, barrel shutter and film holder, camera stamped with serial number and 'Pat. May 1885, Other patents applied for in All Countries'.
$2,500-3,000

An Eastman Kodak Co. No. 3a U.S. Army Signal Corps K-3 camera No. 24, in gunmetal grey and brown leather finish with a Bausch and Lomb Kodak anastigmat f.6.3 lens No. 2946310 set into an Optimo la shutter.
$1,200-1,500

The Signal Corps Kodak camera was a specially finished version of the 3a Autographic Kodak Special camera. 100 of these cameras were made in 1916.

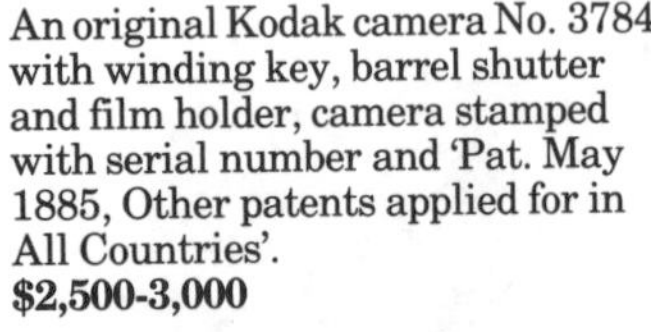

An American Stereoscopic Co. Brewster-pattern hand held stereoscope, with gilt tooled leather covered body, ivory feet and cover knob and wood moulding decoration.
$300-350

An Eastman Co. rollfilm C Daylight Kodak camera No. 2404, with a lens set into a sector shutter.
$500-550

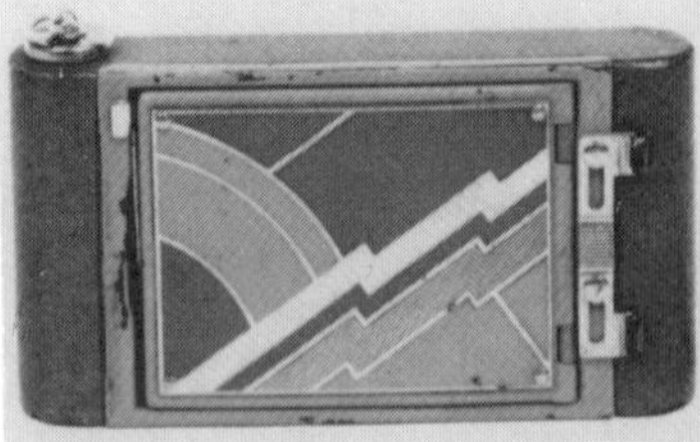

An Eastman Kodak Co. 127-film blue coloured Kodak Petite camera No. 41537 with blue and chrome Art Deco styled baseplate and blue cloth covered body.
$500-550

A Blair Camera Co., Boston, U.S.A., wooden bodied detective camera with lens and internally held double dark slides, 5 by 4in (12.5 by 10cm).
$400-450

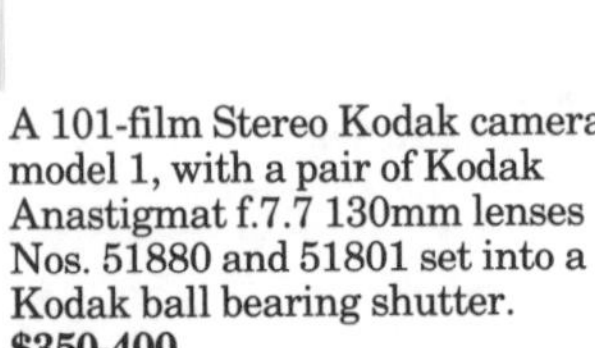

A 101-film Stereo Kodak camera model 1, with a pair of Kodak Anastigmat f.7.7 130mm lenses Nos. 51880 and 51801 set into a Kodak ball bearing shutter.
$350-400

RT NOUVEAU

'eramics

jug and basin set, with green and nk embossed design, jug 12½in 2cm) high.
200-230

A Continental green boat vase, 16in (41cm) wide.
$100-130

A Foley plate, produced for the American market, signed F Micklewright, c1893, 9in (23cm) diam.
$150-300

Two Foley Intarsio Toby jugs, John Bull and Scotsman, 7½in (19cm) high.
$400-550 each

n Eichwald tazza, c1920, 11in (28cm).
300-400

Two early E. Radford, Burslem, vases, tallest 6½in (16cm).
$65-100 each

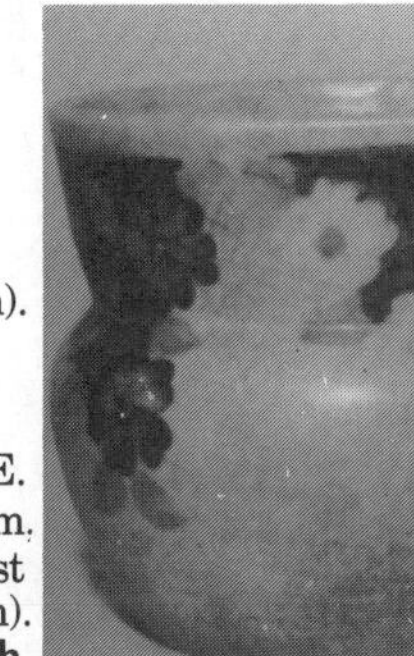

pair of Eichwald ases, 12in (31cm).
140-200

An E. Radford jug, Anemone pattern, 6½in (16cm).
$65-80

An E. Radford vase, Strawberry pattern, 9in (22cm).
$80-100

A large early E. Radford jug, Ranunculus pattern.
$140-200

An early E. Radford vase, Anemone pattern.
$120-140

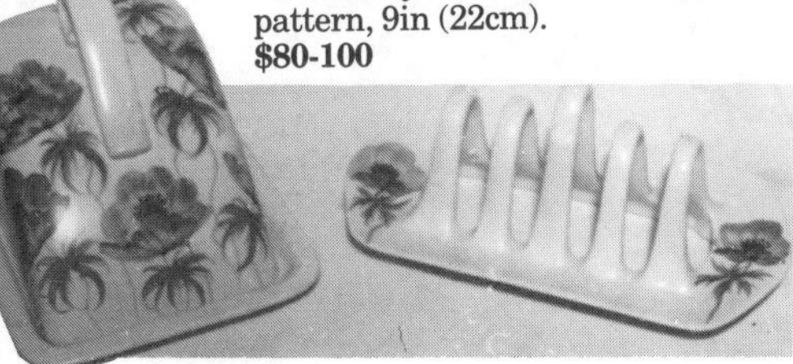

An E. Radford cheese dish and toast rack, Anemone pattern.
$90-120 each

An E. Radford 'coaching' jug, 10½in (27cm).
$150-200

Three pieces of Radford ware, Ranunculus pattern.
$40-150 each

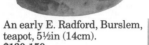

An early E. Radford, Burslem, teapot, 5½in (14cm).
$130-150

An E. Radford moulded vase, Ros pattern, 6in (15cm).
$80-110

A large E. Radford moulded jug, Indian Tree pattern, 8½in (21cm) high.
$100-130

Two E. Radford vases, Anemone pattern, 7½in (19cm) and 10in (25cm) high. **$65-100 each**

An early E. Radford, Burslem, jug 7in (17cm) high.
$110-140

Two E. Radford wall pockets, Anemone pattern, 4½in (11cm).
$65-100 each

An E. Radford plate and vase, vase 8in (20cm) high.
$65-100 each

An early E. Radford, Burslem, tal lamp base.
$110-130

Two early E. Radford, Burslem, vases. **$110-140 each**

Two early E. Radford, Burslem, jugs. **$65-100 each**

A collection of E. Radford Anemone ware.
$40-110 each

Two E. Radford pieces with the Anemone pattern, plate 10in (25cm) diameter. **$65-100 each**

Figures

A Royal Dux figure group, The Dolly Sisters, c1920, 16½in (42cm).
$2,500-3,000

A Royal Dux figure, The girl with the Golden Apple, c1920, 22in (56cm) wide.
$2,000-2,500

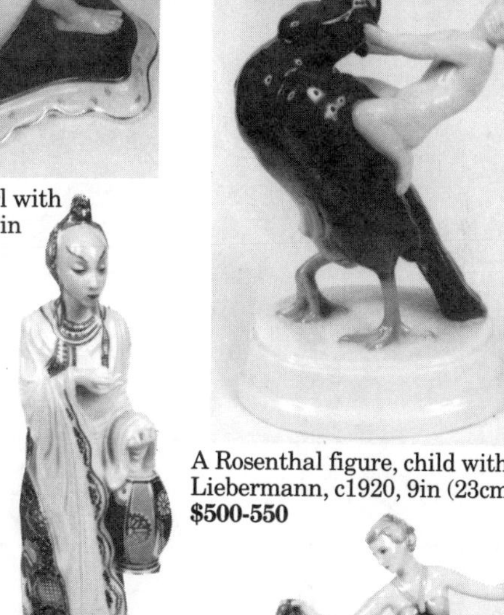

A Rosenthal figure, child with bird, Liebermann, c1920, 9in (23cm).
$500-550

A Royal Dux figure, Pierette, Schaff design, c1920, 14½in (37cm).
$650-1,000

A Rosenthal figure of an Eastern lady, Holzer de Fanti design, c1920, 18½in (47cm).
$1,200-1,300

A Goldscheider earthenware figure of a woman, wearing pink and grey skirt, the rose bodice with pink halter neck, restored, printed with factory mark, 'Made in Austria', signature and impressed number 6126 42 6, 15in (39cm) high.
$500-550

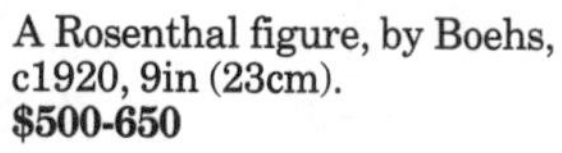

A Rosenthal figure, by Boehs, c1920, 9in (23cm).
$500-650

A Heals wardrobe, c1898, 41½in (105cm).
$1,200-1,400
Illustrated in A History of Heals.

A Thonet chair, No. 4 from their catalogue, 35in (89cm).
$100-140

A Georges De Feure carved cherrywood armchair, the carved apron and legs decorated with scrolling foliate motifs.
$3,000-4,000

An Art Nouveau desk, 20in (51cm). **$1,200-1,300**

An Art Nouveau hall stand, 22in (56cm).
$230-275

An Art Nouveau style oak and inlaid cabinet, 65in (165cm).
$1,400-1,500

An Art Nouveau sideboard, c1900, 54in (137cm).
$3,000-4,000

A bentwood nest of tables, by Thonet, 23½in (60cm).
$550-900

A bentwood table, with baize top, 27½in (70cm) high.
$500-650

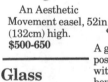

An Aesthetic Movement easel, 52in (132cm) high.
$500-650

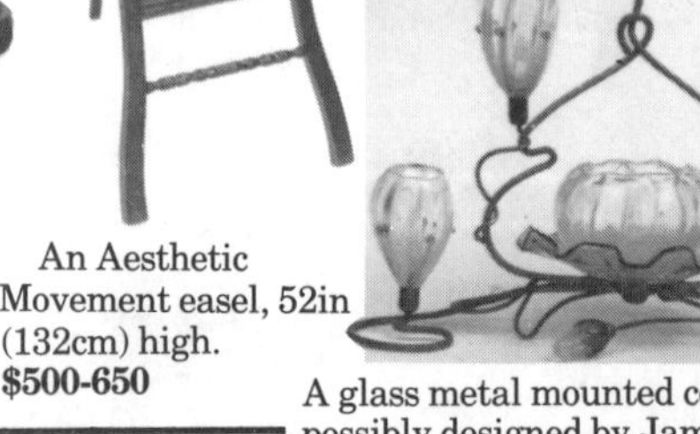

A glass metal mounted centrepiec possibly designed by James Powel with central glass water lily form bowl and 4 small water lily shape vases mounted on gilt metal stand 12in (31cm). **$550-800**

Glass

A Morris screen, 46in (116.5cm).
$650-800

A James Powell engraved glass decanter, on domed foot, the green tinted glass engraved with sprigs of flowers, with silver stopper stamped J & P and London hallmarks for 1912, 10½in (27cm).
$1,200-1,400

An Art Nouveau green iridescent glass inkwell, overlaid with a silv and gilt Art Nouveau design.
$140-200

A leaded glass triptych window, by Tiffany Studios for the Albert Mitchell House, Rose Hill, Ohio, in 3 sections, depicting purple wisteria vines and magnolia branches against a blue-green striated hammered glass sky, c1908, 75in (190.5cm) high.
$150,000-160,000

A Favrile glass vase, by Tiffany Studios, the iridescent blue bulbous form with everted rim and tripod feet decorated with a pewter swirled motif around the neck, engraved 02950, 5in (13cm) high.
$3,000-4,000

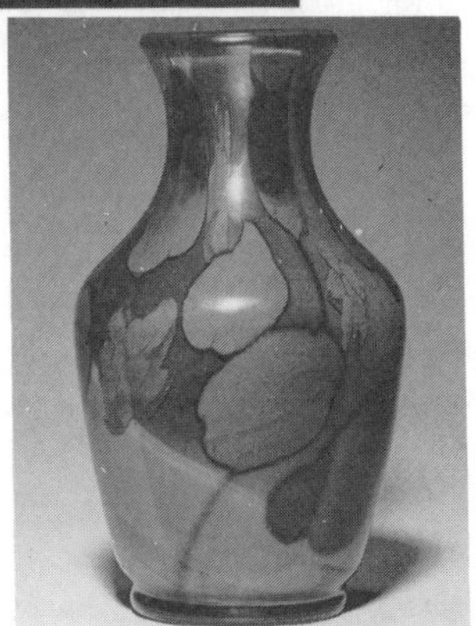

A 'paperweight' Favrile glass vase, by Tiffany Studios, with stylised aquatic plants in orange and green on a blue iridescent ground, cased in clear glass, inscribed 1735G L.C. Tiffany Favrile, 8½in (21cm) high.
$14,000-15,000

A Favrile glass vase, by Tiffany Studios, of gourd form in black iridescent glass with pulls and spatters of green, purple and blue, inscribed Louis C. Tiffany 05753, 6½in (17cm) high.
$5,000-6,000

Jewellery

An Art Nouveau pendant/brooch with gold, emerald and enamel decoration, made by John Hardman, Birmingham, design by Pugin, c1880.
$5,000-5,500

A German Art Nouveau pendant, in gold, with ruby, pearls and diamonds, signed F. Mahla Pforzheim.
$650-700

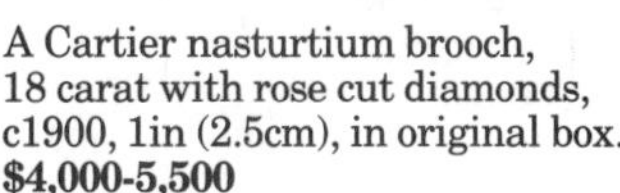

An Austrian golfer brooch in platinum, black onyx and diamonds, by Ernst Paltscho, c1925. **$4,000-5,500**

An Art Nouveau crystal and moonstone pendant, by Sybil Dunlop.
$700-800

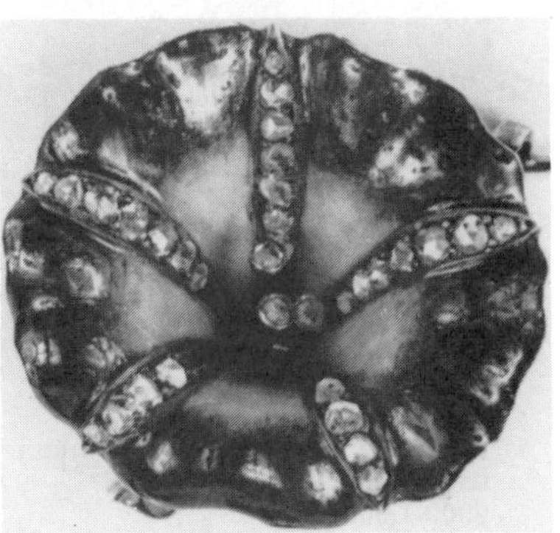

A Cartier nasturtium brooch, 18 carat with rose cut diamonds, c1900, 1in (2.5cm), in original box.
$4,000-5,500

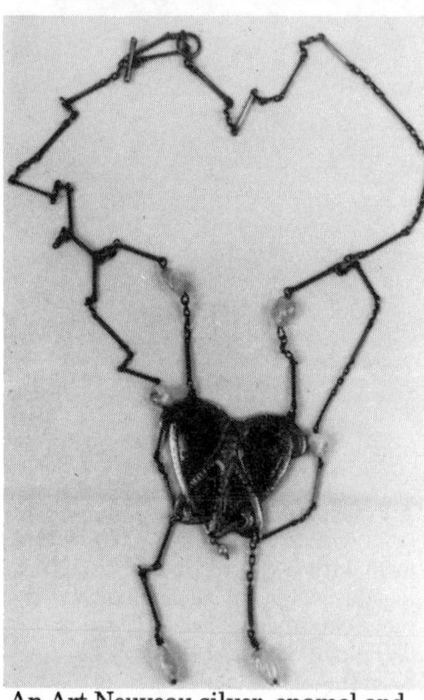

An Art Nouveau silver, enamel and pearl necklace by Mürlle Bennett & Co.
$510-350

An Art Nouveau carved horn pendant of a butterfly, on woven silk cord with 2 blue glass beads between wooden spacers, 3in (8cm) long.
$300-400

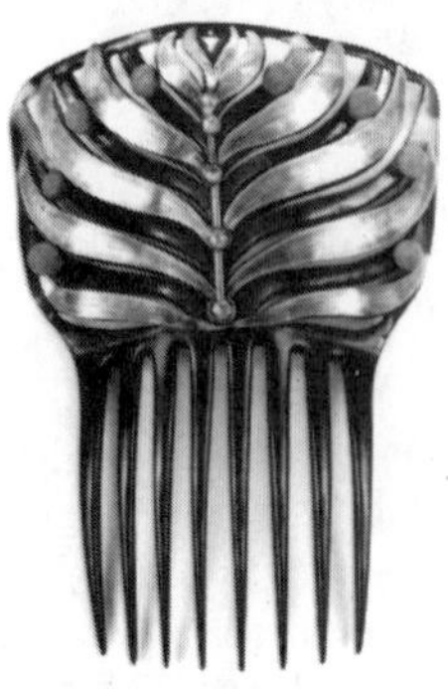

An Art Nouveau tortoiseshell comb, in silver and olivine, by Wm. Soper, 5½in (13cm).
$650-800

An Art Nouveau necklace made by Mürlle Bennett, in enamel and silver, c1900.
$800-1,000

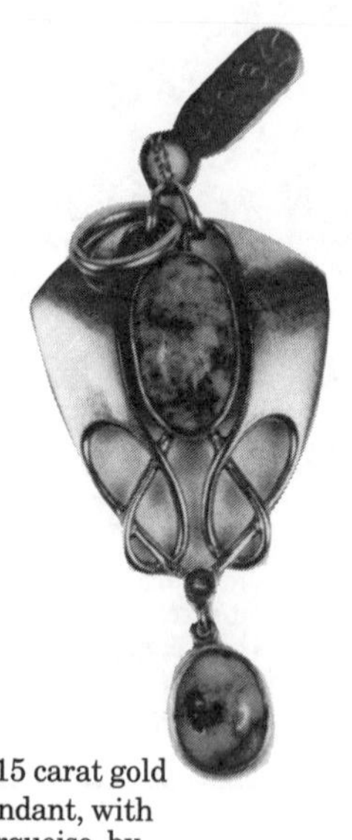

A 15 carat gold pendant, with turquoise, by Mürlle Bennett.
$550-650

Lamps

An American copper table lamp in the form of a Doric column, with two lamp holders, the shade in leaded green glass, the stepped base marked "Gorham Co., Q497" and trademark, 19in (48cm).
$900-1,000

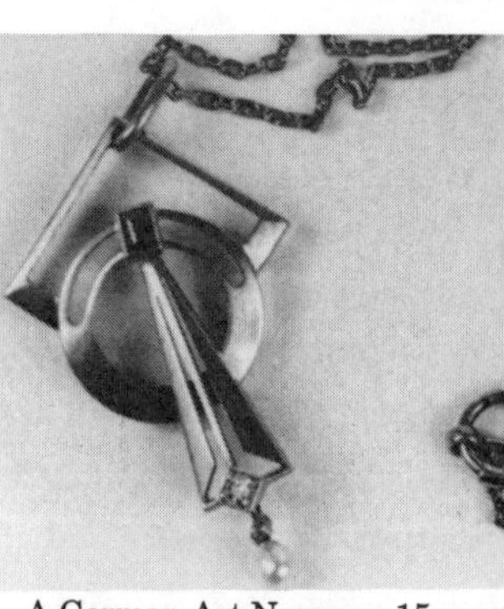

A German Art Nouveau 15 carat pendant, with ruby, diamond and pearl, Pforzheim in the style of Kleeman.
$800-1,000

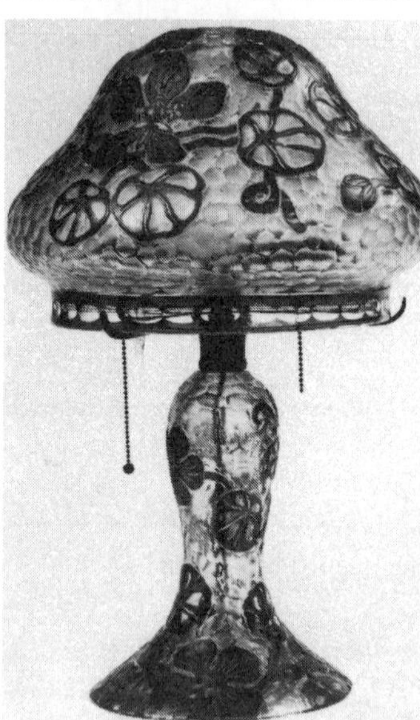

An acid etched and cut glass cameo table lamp, the clear glass overlaid in blue with flowers and foliage on a multi-faceted and textured surface, minor chips round the base 20½in (51cm).
$2,500-4,000

A 'Le Verre Français' cameo glass and wrought iron table lamp, designed by Schneider, the pale green ground overlaid and etched with thorny berry-laden branches, striped cane signature on base, 15½in (39.5cm).
$4,000-5,000

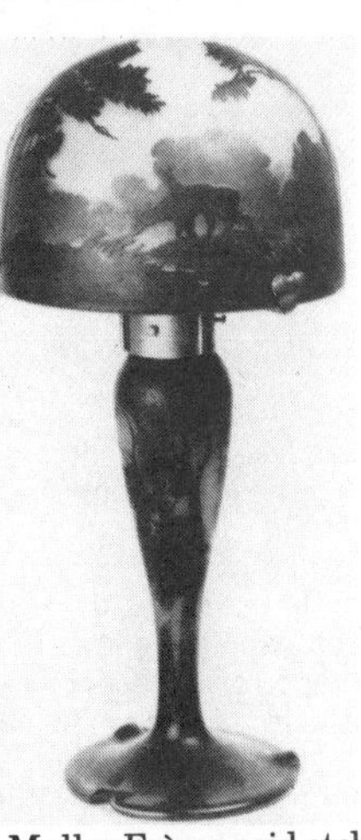
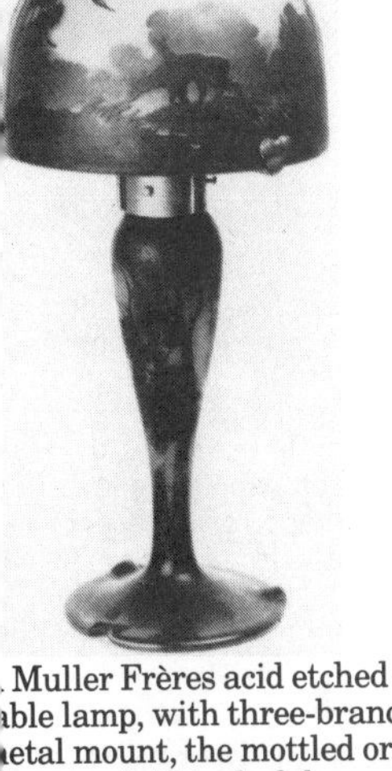

. Muller Frères acid etched cameo ıble lamp, with three-branch gilt ıetal mount, the mottled orange lass overlaid in dark brown with ›ntinuous river landscape and razing deer, cameo signature Iuller Frères, Luneville, in the ase, 19in (48.5cm).
·7,000-9,000

A 'Spider Web' leaded glass and bronze table lamp, the shade in a geometric pattern of blue and green Favrile glass amongst a canopy framework of bronze arms, the entire shade supported by a bronze base cast to depict the underside of a mushroom, the shade stamped Tiffany Studios New York 387-26, the base stamped Tiffany Studios New York 337, 18½in (47cm) high.
$15,000-18,000

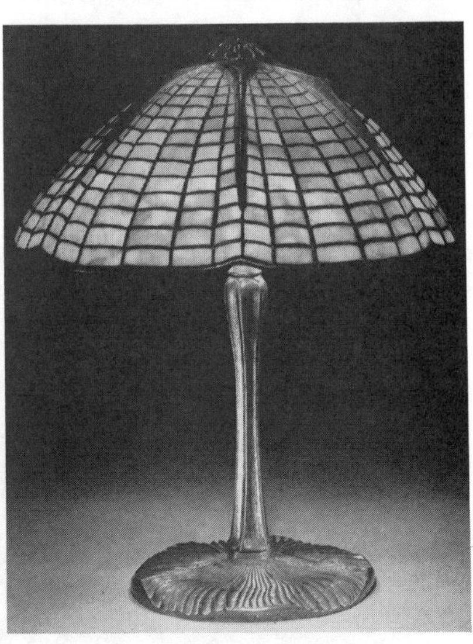

A Favrile glass and bronze desk lamp, the domed shade with green wave design and gold wave iridescence, the bronze base with 4 curving arms formed as a slender branch on a circular base, stamped Tiffany Studios New York 461, 19½in (49.5cm) high.
$5,500-6,000

A Favrile glass and bronze table lamp, the patinated brown/green telescoping cushion base with a ribbed motif and a beaded border with 2 arms supporting 2 rainbow iridescent mushroom-shaped shades, base stamped Tiffany Studios New York 28600 and with Tiffany Glass and Decorating Co. monogram, 26in (66.5cm) high.
$5,000-7,000

A set of 3 Art Nouveau gilt metal twin branch wall lights, with pineapple glass shades and one extra shade. **$500-550**

\ 'Pomegranate' leaded glass and ›ronze table lamp, the domed shade ›f square and rectangular green ;lass, with a circular frieze of yellow ;lass pomegranates, stamped Tiffany Studios New York 1457-37, he bronze base with brown patina ;tamped Tiffany Studios New York 333, 21½in (54.5cm) high.
$9,000-10,000

A reverse painted glass and bronze table lamp, the domed shade painted with brilliant red, yellow and blue parrots and butterflies amongst golden chrysanthemums and green foliage, on a deep green ground, supported on a faceted base cast with stylised foliage, the shade inscribed Handel 7025, 26in (66.5cm) high.
$20,000-22,000

Metal

An Art Nouveau W. M. F. bottle holder, 7in (17.5cm).
$400-500

A W. M. F. electroplated pewter three-piece coffee set, comprising: a coffee pot, a cream jug and sugar basin on trestle feet, each stamped with usual WMF marks, coffee pot 8in (19.5cm) high.
$700-1,000

A mixed metal sugar bowl and cream jug, applied with copper castings of foliage, birds and insect the sugar bowl with 2 bronze handles and the cream jug with on each cast in the form of a stylised elephant's head, with traces of gilding on the interiors, by Gorha Providence, both marked, 1882, sugar bowl 4in (10cm) diam, 11.5 gross.
$5,500-6,500

A Martele inkstand with removable glass liner, the stand repoussé and chased with serpentine ribs and flowers, on three ball feet, by Gorham, Providence, marked Martele.9584, c1905, 10in (25.5cm) wide, 9.5oz.
$2,000-2,500

A Liberty muffin dish, designed by Archibald Knox, 11½in (29cm) diam.
$650-800

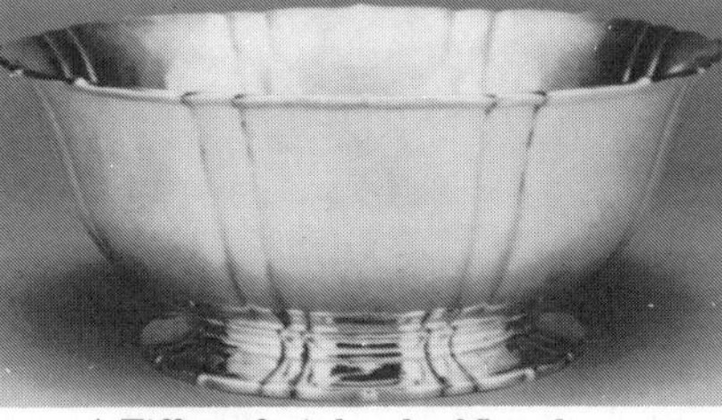

A Tiffany fruit bowl, of fluted circular form on spreading base with lightly hammered surface, mid-20thC, 10½in (27cm) diam.
$3,000-4,000

An Art Nouveau silver photo frame, Birmingham, 1902.
$440-500

A Mappin and Webb Art Nouveau silver and enamelled frame, on easel support, cast in relief with shamrocks, enamelled in green and pale turquoise, stamped M & W, Sheffield, 1904, 8in (20cm) high.
$1,200-1,300

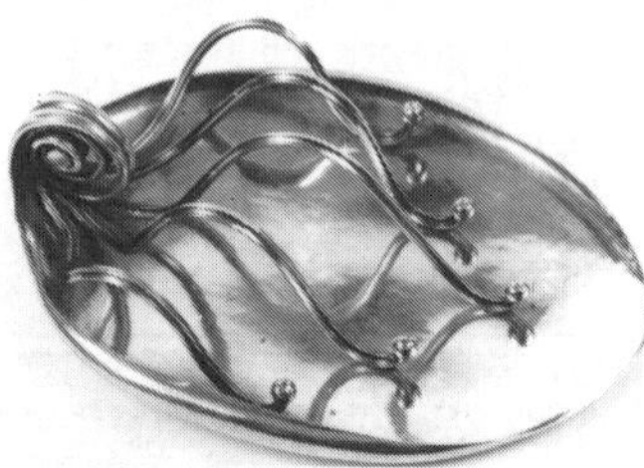

A silver toast rack, by Georg Jensen, c1930, 6in (15cm) wide.
$2,000-2,150

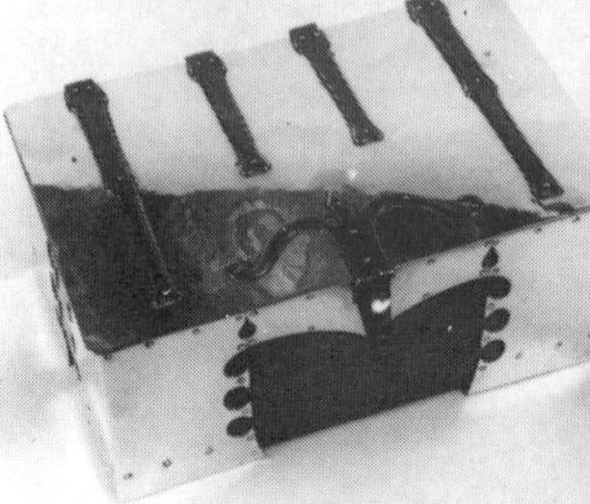

A silver and copper box, by Birmingham Guild of Handicraft signed B.G.H., c1900, 8½in (22cm wide.
$2,500-2,650

A W. M. F. candelabrum, with 2 urn shape sconces on brassed stems, the centre pewter figure of a young scantily clad girl wearing a long flowering dress, 10in (25cm) high.
$1,500-2,500

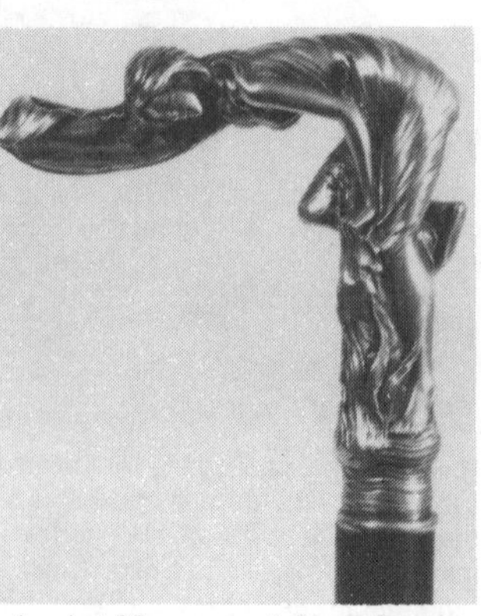

An Art Nouveau style malacca walking stick, the white metal handle modelled with a figure of a young woman kneeling amidst reeds.
$400-650

A hammered silver raised bowl, b A. E. Jones, the frieze cast with foxes chasing geese, on raised foot Birmingham, 1915, 4in (10.5cm) diam.
$500-550

A cake basket, marked Sterling and Tiffany & Co., c1895, 12in (30.5cm) long.
$2,500-3,000

A pear-shaped coffee pot on a rising circular foot, with a fluted rising curved spout, scroll handle and domed, hinged cover with foliate finial, by Tiffany & Co., 19thC, 11in (28cm) high, 21.5oz.
$550-650

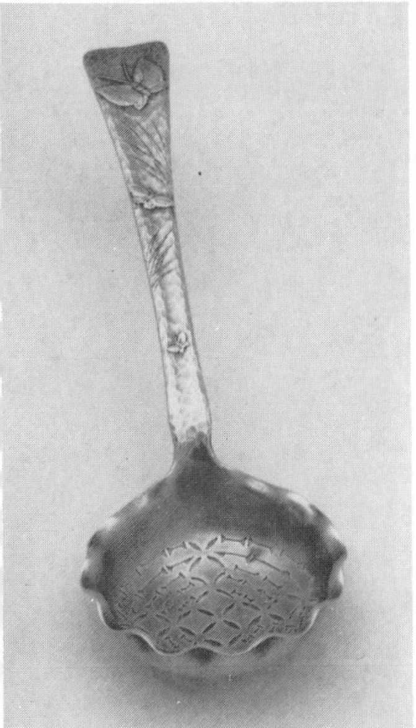

A two pint flask, with a threaded and hinged cap, the surface decorated with etched scenes of Brownies, the cap with 4 Brownie faces, the base with etched stylised monogram 'GWL', marked, by Tiffany & Co., New York, c1895, 8in (20cm) high, 15oz.
$8,000-10,000

A mixed metal pierced ladle, the hammered flaring handle applied with butterflies in copper and gold, the circular bowl with a ruffled edge and pierced with a geometric Japanese design, marked, by Tiffany & Co., New York, c1880, 8½in (21.5cm) long, 3oz.
$4,500-5,500

A silver gilt dish, in the form of an Indian basket, cast and chased to resemble coiled straw, marked Tiffany & Co. Makers Sterling Silver, New York, c1890, 6in (15cm) diam, 5.5oz.
$1,500-2,000

A silver coffee pot, Sheffield, 1899, 10in (25cm), 27oz.
$800-900

A neo-Classical style four-piece tea and coffee service, by Tiffany & Co., with ebony scroll handles to the tea and coffee pots, the milk jug with a laurel applique panelled handle, 67oz gross.
$2,500-3,000

A kettle on stand and a teapot, each globular, with an applied foliate mid-band and a circular cover with a bud finial, the shoulder engraved with a monogram and a crest, the handles with ivory insulating rings, the kettle stand squared, with 2 open supports, on 4 pierced bracket feet in the Oriental style, each marked, now without burner, surface wear, by Tiffany & Co., New York, c1880, kettle 13in (33cm) high, 85.5oz gross.
$2,000-2,500

An Adam style footed bowl, on pedestal foot with applied tongue-and-dart band above beading, the bowl with applied band of lozenges below beading and with stylised flowerheads at intervals with hanging husk festoons, by Tiffany & Co., 12in (30.5cm) diam, 63oz.
$3,000-4,000

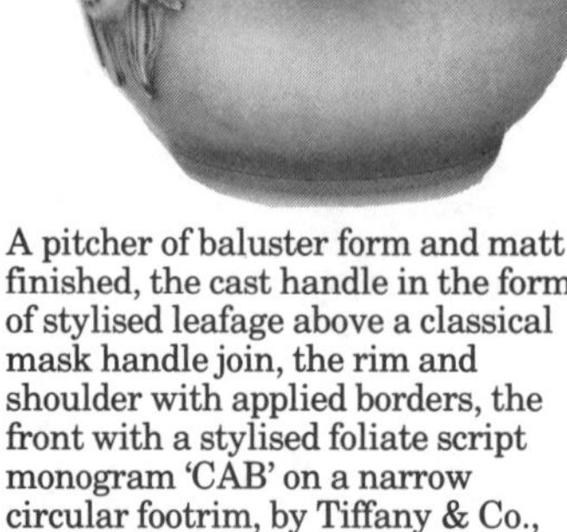

A pitcher of baluster form and matt finished, the cast handle in the form of stylised leafage above a classical mask handle join, the rim and shoulder with applied borders, the front with a stylised foliate script monogram 'CAB' on a narrow circular footrim, by Tiffany & Co., New York, c1880, 8½in (21.5cm) high, 36.5oz.
$3,500-4,000

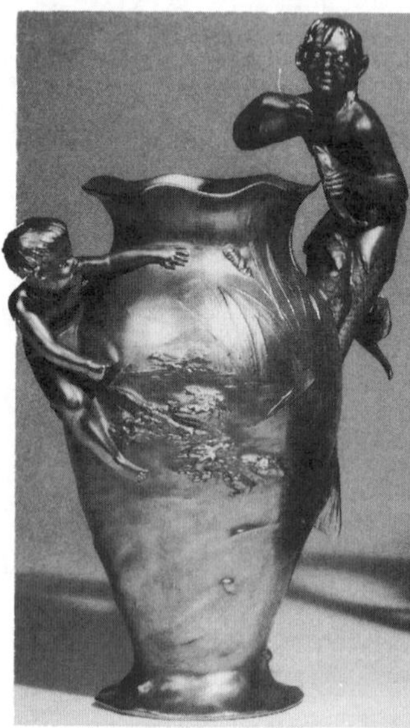

A pair of W. M. F. gilded pewter vases, moulded with rushes and rocks in a stream and adorned with water sprites and cherubim, stamped with WMF marks, 11½in (29.5cm) high.
$500-800

Price

Prices vary from auction to auction – from dealer to dealer. The price paid in a dealer's shop will depend on:

1) what he paid for the item
2) what he thinks he can get for it
3) the extent of his knowledge
4) awareness of market trends

It is a mistake to think that you will automatically pay more in a specialist dealer's shop. He is more likely to know the 'right' price for a piece. A general dealer may undercharge but he could also overcharge

An Arts and Crafts trophy pitcher, by Reed and Barton, the lower part of the body thinly applied with stylised Indians on horseback on grass ground, the side with partly applied and engraved inscription in rustic lettering dated 1914, 10½in (27cm) high, 62.5oz.
$9,000-10,000

A pair of Japanese style grape scissors, with overall hammered surface, the handles pierced with stylised clouds, by Tiffany & Co., New York, c1880, 8in (20cm) long.
$3,000-4,000

A two-handled covered bowl, by Tiffany & Co., on gadrooned foot, the sides chased, c1881, 8in (20cm) long, 17.5oz.
$1,500-2,000

four-piece tea and coffee service, ith two-handled plated tay, by rosjean & Woodward for Tiffany & o., comprising: teapot, coffee pot, ot water jug and two-handled overed sugar bowl, the bodies hased with flowerheads and atted scrolling foliage centering shaped oval cartouches, one ngraved with monogram, c1860, offee pot 12in (31cm) high, the tray y Reed & Barton, 1941, 25½in 55cm) long, 104.5oz.
3,000-4,000

A set of 4 open salts, each with a die-rolled Greek key border, on 3 cast ram's-head legs with hoof feet, each engraved with an original script monogram or name, the interior gilt, each marked, by Tiffany & Co., New York, c1860, 3in (7.5cm) diam, 8oz.
$1,200-1,800

A pair of covered entrée dishes, on square bracket feet with foliate joins and die-rolled borders, the domed covers engraved with strapwork and foliage surmounted by detachable leaf handles, by Moore for Tiffany & Co., c1860, 9in (22.5cm) diam, 54oz.
$5,000-6,000

Two bread baskets, by Tiffany & Co., with shaped borders pierced with trelliswork, the smaller c1896, the larger c1905, 11in (28cm) and 14½in (37cm) long, 48oz.
$3,000-3,500

Moorcroft

A Moorcroft pottery vase, the ovoid body boldly painted with a lily design on a cream and green ground, impressed marks, Walter Moorcroft initials and paper label, 13in (33.4cm).
$900-1,200

An Art pottery baluster vase, decorated with bulrushes in polychrome enamels, by Moorcroft.
$400-500

Miscellaneous

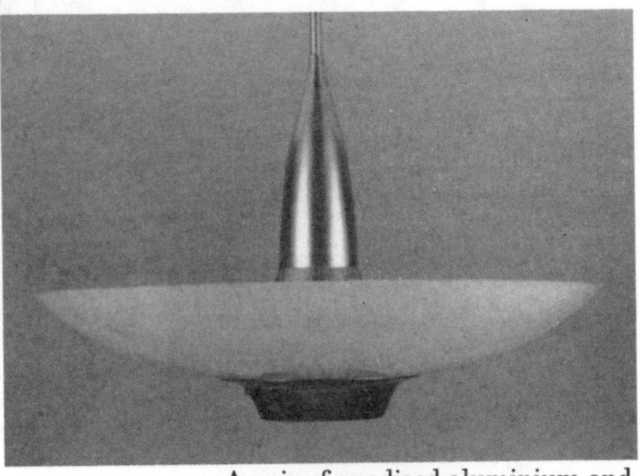

A pair of anodised aluminium and plastic hanging lamps.
$150-300

A set of 8 Richards tiles, 6in (15cm) square.
$120-230

A bronze 'Zodiac' desk set by Tiffany Studios, comprising: a picture frame, notepad, box, blotterends, clock, match holder message book, pen holders and letter tray, stamped Tiffany Studios New York 1090.
$2,500-3,500

A silver applied copper cigar lighter, by Gorham, Providence, formed as a globular spot hammered teapot, the sides applied with cast silver flower and frog, marked, c1882, 2½in (6cm) high, 5in (12cm) wide.
$700-1,000

A collection of 13 Goebels ceramic glass-eyed lights, comprising: monkey, cat, black mammy, orange gnome, spaniel, frog, googly-eyed girl, a pair of Dutch boys, fish, Turkish gentleman, owl, and elephant, 7 to 8in (17.5 to 20cm) high.
$7,000-8,000

Doulton

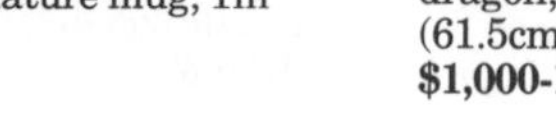

A Doulton miniature mug, 1in (2.5cm) high.
$65-80

A large Doulton Lambeth stoneware bulbous jug, by Mark V Marshall with incised and applied foliate decoration glazed in shades of brown, the undulated rim glazed in blue and brown, damage to dragon, impressed marks, 24in (61.5cm) high.
$1,000-1,500

A pair of Doulton vases, initialled E.B., c1910, 12in (30.5cm) high.
$275-350

A Doulton Burslem porcelain figure of a jester sitting on a pedestal, painted in pastel shades of salmon pink and mint green with gilt motifs, minor restorations, printed marks, 9½in (24cm) high.
$1,200-1,400

A Doulton Lambeth vase with incised band of cattle, by Hannah Barlow, dated 1888, 7½in (19cm) high.
$550-650

A Doulton Lambeth pottery lemonade jug, by Emily J Parrington, with silver plated hinged cover and thumbpiece, decorated in low relief within oval buff reserve panels, on flower decorated green and blue ground, impressed mark and initials, 9in (23cm) high.
$800-1,000

A pair of Doulton Burslem blue and white transferware soup plates, Madras pattern, 10in (25cm) diam.
$25-30

A Doulton Lambeth plaque, decorated by Hannah Barlow, dated 1874, 9in (23cm) square.
$650-800

Royal Doulton

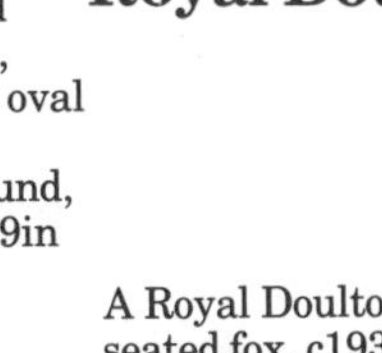

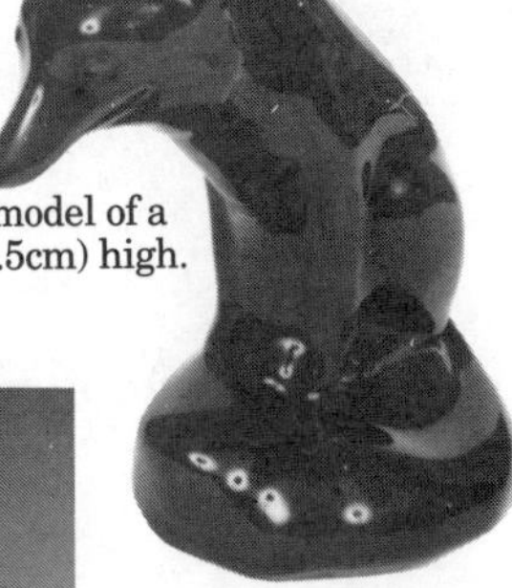

A Royal Doulton flambé model of a seated fox, c1930, 5in (12.5cm) high.
$500-550

A Royal Doulton tea service, D5104, entitled 'Fox-hunting', comprising: teapot and lid, 6 cups, saucers and plates, and a cake plate.
$275-300

The Henley Teddy, limited edition of 250, 1989, 9in (22.5cm) high.
$160-230

Shareholder, limited edition of 1,500, 1988, 9in (22.5cm) high.
$140-150

Churchill, a limited edition of 750, 1990, 9in (22.5cm) high.
$150-200

The Cavalier with goatee beard, c1939, 6in (15cm) high.
$2,500-3,000

Churchill, a limited edition of 5,000, 1989, 9in (22.5cm) high.
$150-210

Lord Nelson, No. D6336, 1952-69, 6in (15cm) high.
$300-350

Margaret Thatcher, limited edition of 1,000, 1989, 9in (22.5cm) high.
$160-210

The Gardener, No. D6630, 1973-81, 7in (17.5cm) high.
$150-230

White-haired Clown, No. D6322, 1951-55, 6in (15cm) high.
$700-1,000

The Vicar of Bray, No. D5615, 1936-60, 6in (15cm) high.
$150-210

Old King Cole, No. D6036, 1939-60, 6in (15cm) high.
$160-230

Miller's is a price Guide not a price List

The price ranges given reflect the average price a purchaser should pay for similar items. Condition, rarity of design or pattern, size, colour, provenance, restoration and many other factors must be taken into account when assessing values. When buying or selling, it must always be remembered that prices can be greatly affected by the condition of any piece. Unless otherwise stated, all goods shown in Miller's are of good merchantable quality, and the valuations given reflect this fact. Pieces offered for sale in exceptionally fine condition or in poor condition may reasonably be expected to be priced considerably higher or lower respectively than the estimates given herein

The Town Crier, No. D6530, 1960-73, 6in (15cm) high.
$230-275

The Collector, No. D6796, limited edition of 5,000, 1988, 6in (15cm) high.
$150-200

The Golfer, limited edition of 1,000, 1989, 9in (22.5cm) high.
$160-210

Mr. Pickwick, 1940-60, 6in (15cm) high.
$150-210

Farmer John, No. 5788, 1938-60, 6in (15cm) high.
$100-140

George Robey, with removable hat, c1925, 10½in (26cm) high.
$3,000-3,500

A Royal Doulton cabinet plate, painted and signed by W. E. J. Dean, dated 1916, 9in (23cm) diam.
$400-500

A Royal Doulton figure, 'The Curtsey', HN 334.
$650-700

A Royal Doulton boxed set of napkin rings, comprising the Dickens figures, Mr. Pickwick, Mr. Micawber, fat Boy, Tony Weller, Sam Weller and Sairey Gamp, printed marks.
$1,300-2,000

A Royal Doulton flambé model of a seated rabbit, restoration, c1925, 4in (10cm) high.
$200-300

A Royal Doulton porcelain figure, 'Matador and Bull', designed by M. Davies, HN 2011, printed and painted marks, 15½in (38cm) high.
$3,500-5,000

A Royal Doulton Lambeth stoneware figure of Samuel, by George Tinworth, on oval moulded base, with impressed initials, 6in (15cm) high.
$700-800

A Royal Doulton jug, 'The Pied Piper', number 252 of a limited edition of 600 by H. Fenton, 10in (25cm) high.
$275-400

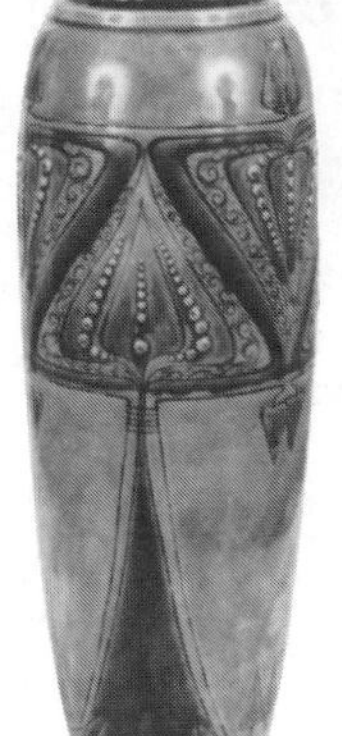
A Royal Doulton Art Nouveau vase, Artists' monogram Eliza Simmance and Bessie Newberry, incised date code for 1909, 15in (38.5cm) high.
$330-400

A Royal Doulton blue and white chamber pot, c1900.
$65-75

A Royal Doulton Holbein ware pottery vase, decorated by W. Nunn, in colours with 2 men seated drinking at a table, signed, impressed Doulton Ivory, 1920B and printed mark in green, 9½in (24cm) high.
$300-400

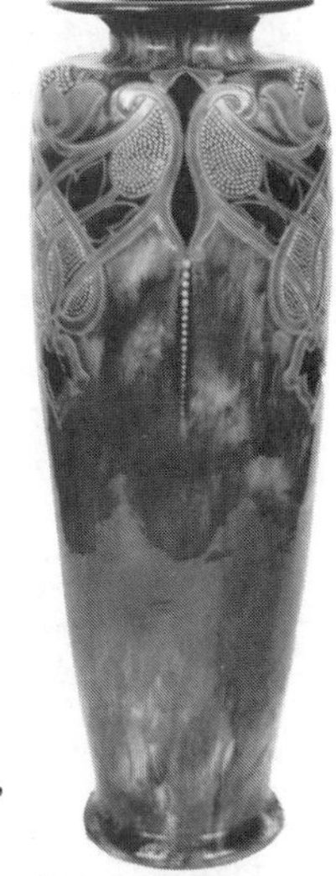
A Royal Doulton vase, restored, 14in (36cm) high.
$80-100

Arts & Crafts

A Royal Doulton figure, 'The Jester', HN 702, one ball on tunic stuck, one missing. **$500-550**

A Royal Doulton ovoid vase, by Eliza Simmance, with flared rim, the stylised flower decoration on brushed grey green ground with blue and brown banding, 15in (38.5cm) high.
$400-500

A Foley plaque, 10 by 8in (25 by 20cm), c1880.
$1,400-2,000

A very rare piece.

A Barum ware bottle vase, with blue bird and floral decoration on a cream ground, incised mark and dated 1890, 13½in (35cm) high.
$140-200

A Foley Intarsio tray, with typical Art Nouveau design, c1880, 10½ by 8in (25 by 20cm).
$500-650

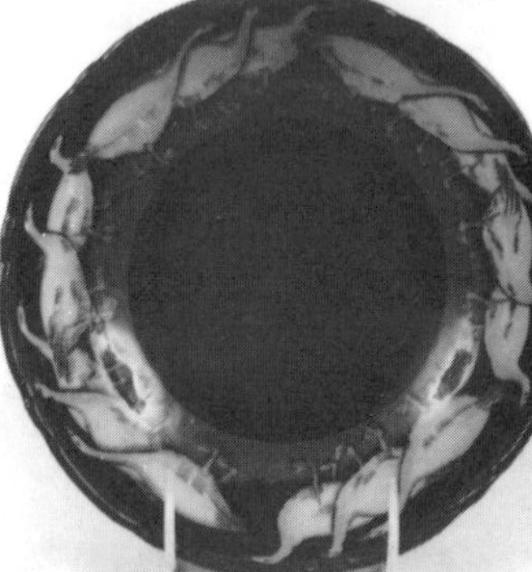

A Foley Intarsio bowl with geese, c1880, 8in (20.5cm) diam.
$500-650

A Foley Intarsio bowl with scenes from Hamlet, c1900, 11½in (29cm) diam.
$800-1,000

A French Longwy charger, c1900, 17in (43.5cm) diam.
$250-300

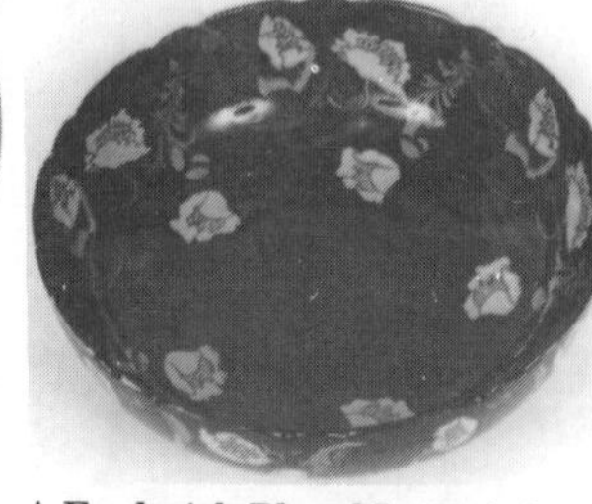

A Frederick Rhead Intarsio bowl c1900, 11½in (30cm) diam.
$400-500

A Ruskin amethyst shaded bowl, with applied embossed flowers, high fired, marked.
$800-1,000

A Ruskin grey and white mottled bowl, impressed mark, c1927, 8in (20cm) diam.
$650-800

A Ruskin dark green bowl, on three feet, 8in (20cm) diam.
$120-150

A Sèvres Art Pottery bowl, in blue tones sponged with yellow, c1930, 11in (28cm) diam.
$80-150

A Sèvres Art Pottery dish in red, green and brown, 7in (17.5cm) diam.
$65-100

A Brannam pink dog with toothache, 6½in (16.5cm) high.
$90-100

A Brannam green owl jar with lid, made for Liberty, 5in (12.5cm) high.
$80-130

A Brannam cat, green with black markings, 11in (28.5cm) high.
$300-330

An Upchurch pottery bowl with three handles, in blue and grey, 7in (17.5cm) diam.
$80-110

A Brannam flower holder, initialled 'B W', c1900, 10in (25cm) wide.
$275-300

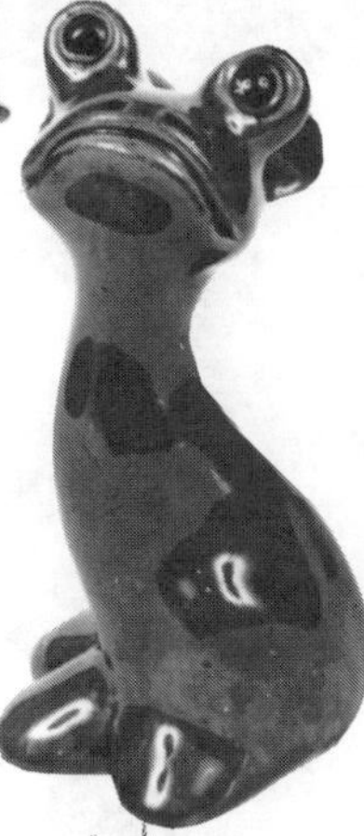

A Barum blue frog, 2½in (6cm) high.
$100-130

A Brannam chamber stick, initialled 'S W', 4in (10cm) high.
$200-250

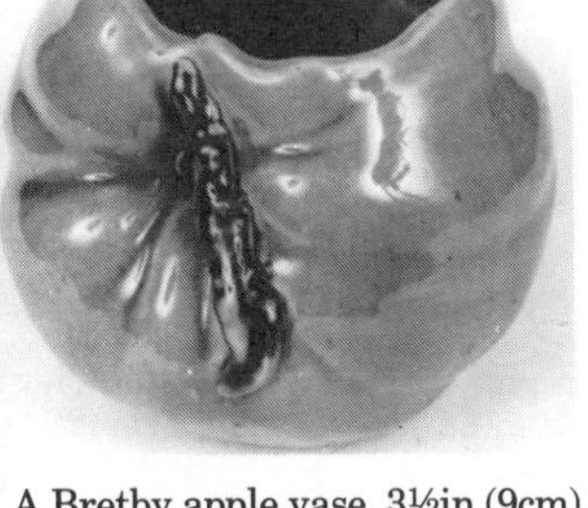

A Bretby apple vase, 3½in (9cm) high.
$50-75

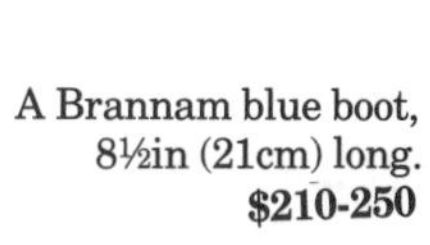

A Ruskin green cup and saucer, with decoration, 3½in (9cm) diam.
$100-130

A Brannam blue boot, 8½in (21cm) long.
$210-250

A Brannam beaker/mug, part of a lemonade set, with inscription.
$130-150

A Brannam blue Toby jug, 4in (10cm) high.
$50-80

A Barum jug, inscribed 'The Lundy Parrot', 5in (12.5cm) high.
$110-140

A Brannam jug, with inscription, initialled 'F B', 1901, 5½in (14cm) high.
$210-240

A Quimper cup and saucer, c1905, saucer 7in (18cm) diam.
$65-100

A Ruskin green cup and saucer, 5½in (14cm) diam.
$110-140

A Brannam puffin jug, c1900, 8in (20cm) high.
$130-150

An Elton ware loving cup, c1890, 8½in (21cm) high.
$500-590

A Barum blue puzzle jug, with inscription, 5in (12.5cm) high.
$55-65

A Ruskin dark green cup and saucer, from the Ferneyhough collection, saucer 6in (15cm) diam.
$140-165

A pair of Frederick Rhead Foley Intarsio ewers, c1880, 11in (28cm) high.
$1,300-1,400

Did you know

MILLER'S Antiques Price Guide builds up year by year to form the most comprehensive photo-reference system available

ARTS & CRAFTS

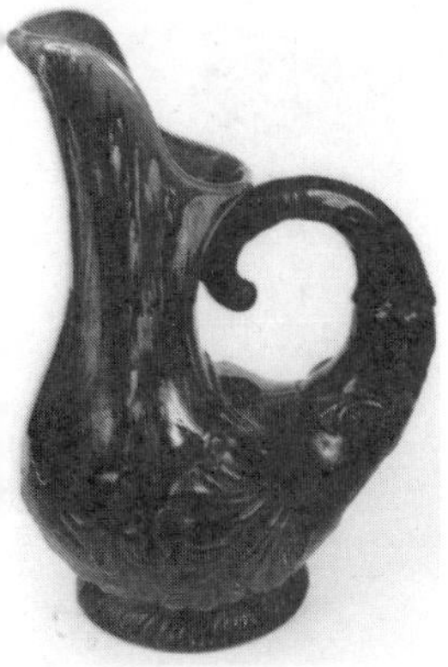

A Bretby jug, with flowing glaze spout, copperette handle and body, 12in (30.5cm) high.
$230-250

A Louis Desmant, Normandy, jug with scenes from the Bayeux Tapestry, 5½in (14cm) high.
$65-100

A Lauder green jug, 8in (20cm) high.
$150-215

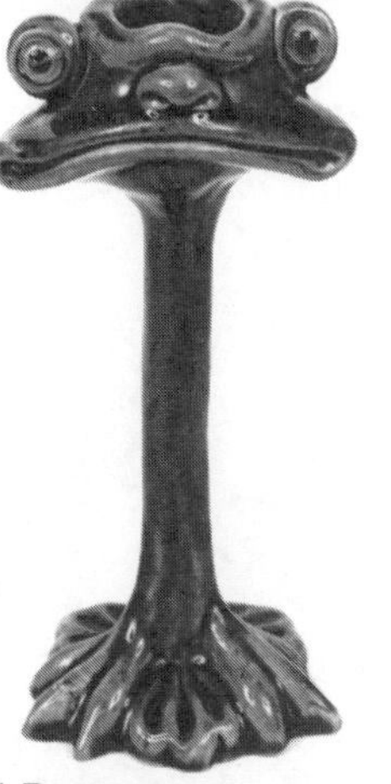

A Barum green frog candle holder, 6in (15cm) high.
$140-150

A Belgian pottery candle holder, 11½in (29cm) high.
$80-100

A Gouda ceramic candle holder, c1920, 8½in (21cm) high.
$110-130

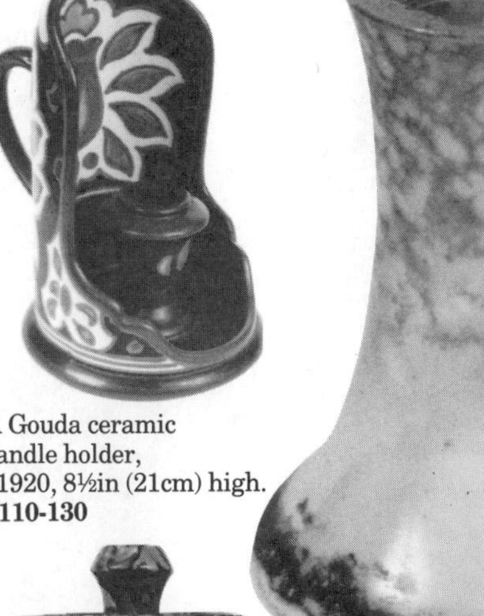

A Ruskin candlestick, marbled grey with burgundy trim, marked, 3in (7.5cm) high.
$250-300

A Wardle mauve candle holder, 9in (22.5cm) high.
$65-100

A Frederick Rhead candle holder, 15in (38cm) high.
$400-500

A Chameleon ware container with lid, 8½in (21cm) high.
$110-130

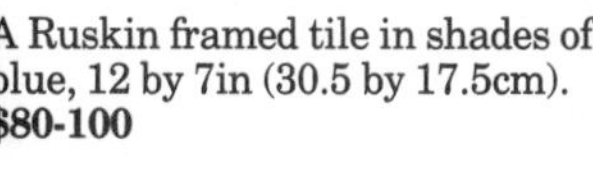

A Ruskin framed tile in shades of blue, 12 by 7in (30.5 by 17.5cm).
$80-100

A Minton Secessionist vase, with water lily design, 1903, 8in (20cm) diam.
$230-250

A Frederick Rhead Foley Intarsio vase, with fish decoration, 8½in (21cm) diam.
$550-700

A Ruskin blue and beige vase from the Ferneyhough Collection, ex W. Howson Taylor collection, impressed mark, dated 1927, 9in (22.5cm) high.
$1,200-1,400

A Charlotte Rhead vase, c1930, 12½in (32cm) high.
$550-700

A Charlotte Rhead vase, c1930, 10in (25cm) high.
$400-500

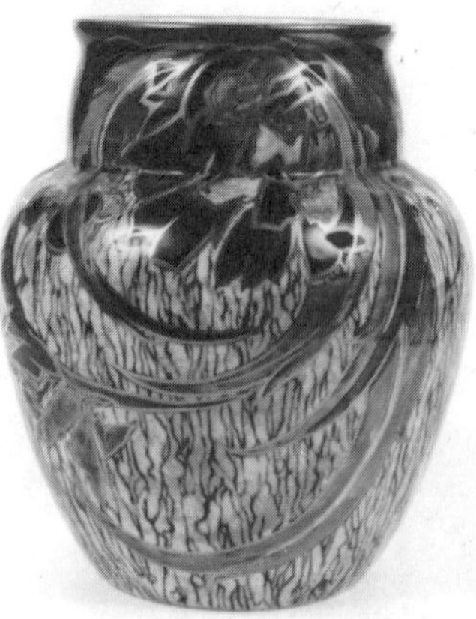

A Royal Winton ware vase, c1920, 8½in (21cm) high.
$300-400

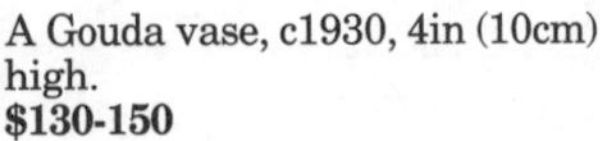

A Gouda vase, c1930, 4in (10cm) high.
$130-150

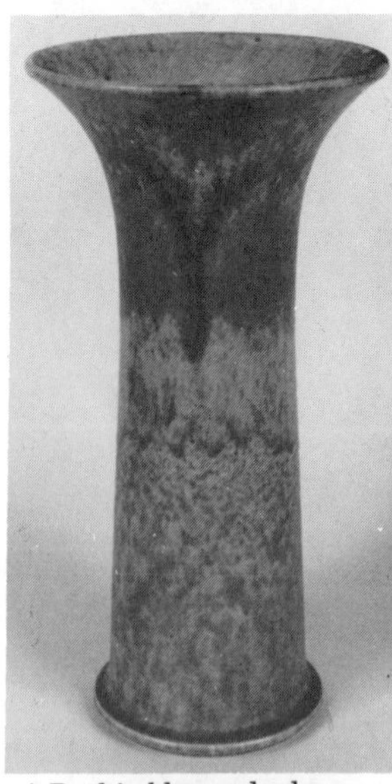

A Ruskin blue and ochre vase marked 12in (30.5cm) high.
$165-210

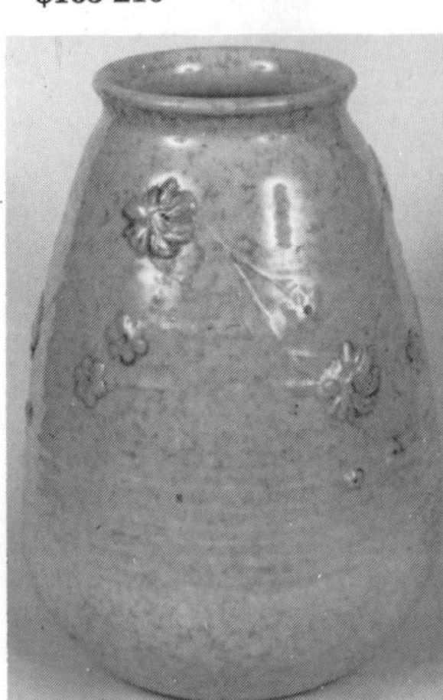

A Ruskin vase, with applied embossed decoration, impressed mark, dated 1927, 11in (28cm) hig
$120-150

A Royal Winton vase, c1920, 9½in (24cm) high.
$300-400

ARTS & CRAFTS

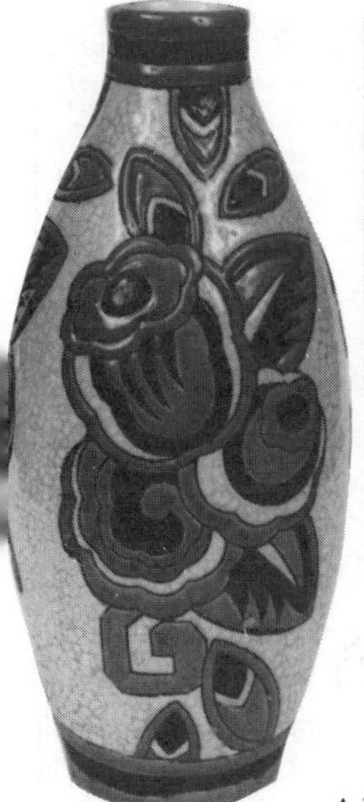

A pair of Villeroy and Boch vases, 10½in (26cm) high.
$500-550

A Boch blue and white vase, c1930, 12in (30.5cm) high.
$300-400

A Gouda vase, c1900, 14in (36cm) high.
$130-140

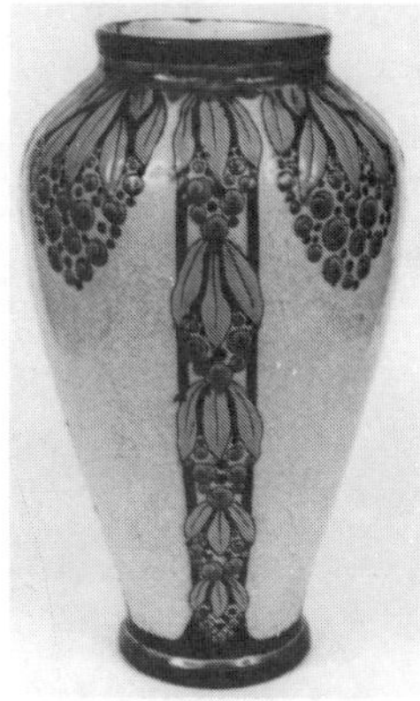

A Gouda vase, c1930, 4in (10cm) high.
$80-100

An early Frederick Rhead vase, 10in (25cm) high.
$500-550

A Maw's pink Art Nouveau vase, c1900, 12½in (32cm).
$200-230

A majolica vase, c1880, 6in (15cm).
$100-110

An E. B. Fisher vase, 8½in (21cm).
$400-500

An Upchurch pottery vase, in pink/grey, 10in (25cm).
$110-130

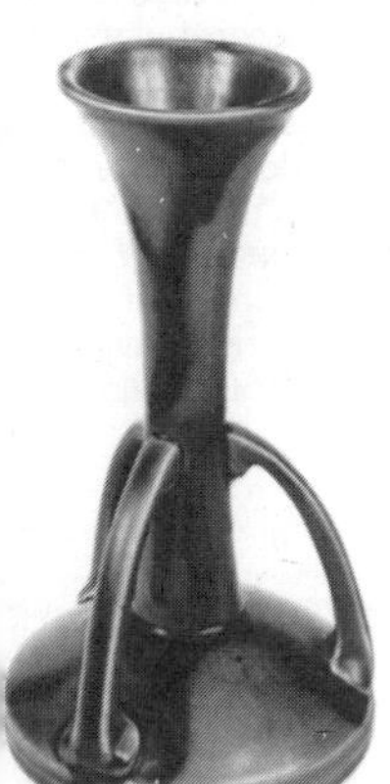

A Bretby deep blue vase.
$110-140

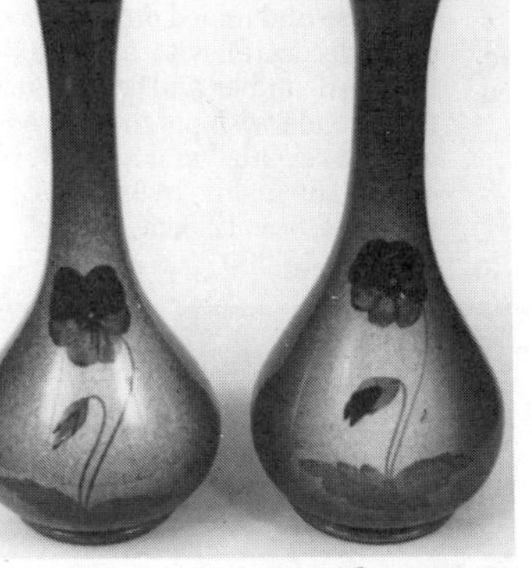

A pair of Ault vases with pansy decoration, one signed by William Ault, 9½in (24cm).
$130-150

A pair of Bretby vases, painted with ships on a chocolate coloured field, 13½in (34cm).
$150-200

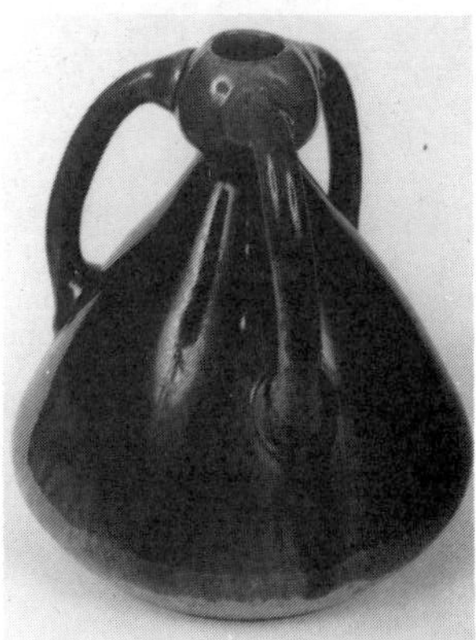

An Ashby Potters' Guild pink vase, 8in (20cm).
$150-200

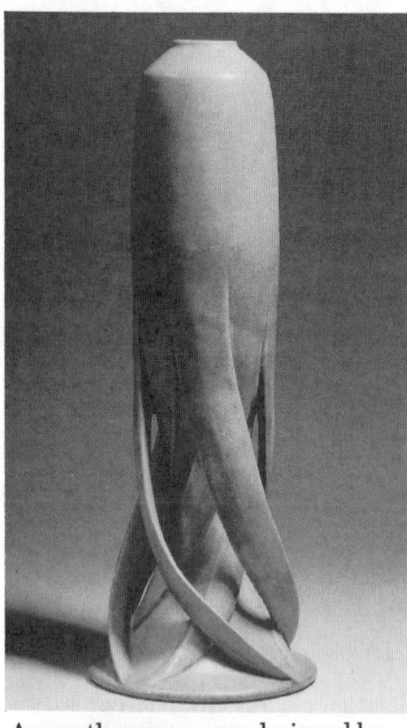

An earthenware vase designed by Fritz Albert, produced by Gates Potteries as Teco, stamped twice TECO and 310, c1910, 17in (43.5cm) high.
$25,000-30,000

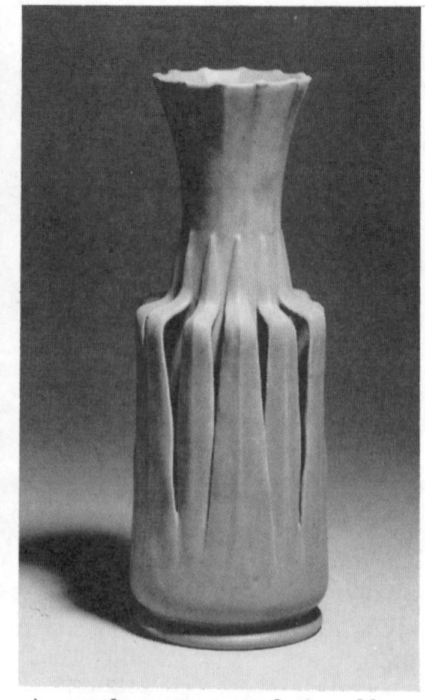

An earthenware vase designed by William J. Dodd, produced by Gates Potteries as Teco, stamped twice TECO, model 85, c1910, 11½in (29.5cm) high.
$16,000-18,000

An earthenware vase, the body finely carved with stylised leaves, in green glaze, impressed with the firm's mark, produced by the Grueby Faience Company, 22½in (57.5cm) high.
$18,000-24,000

An earthenware vase of double gourd form with 4 buttress arms, designed by W. B. Mundie, produced by Gates Potteries as Teco, stamped twice TECO and 287A, 13in (33.5cm) high.
$18,000-22,000

An earthenware vase, pinched at the base and folded on 4 sides of the body, decorated with a mottled mustard, amber and green glaze on the outside with patches of red clay ground revealed and a cobalt blue one on the inside, incised G.E. Ohr in script, 5in (12.5cm) high.
$15,000-18,000

An earthenware vase, a melon form vessel, the surface decorated with 3 groups of jonquils in bloom, the body in green impasto glaze, the blossoms in white glaze, impressed with the firm's mark and incised with the artist's monogram, designed by Wilhelmina Post, produced by the Grueby Faience Company, 11½in (29.5cm) high.
$30,000-35,000

An earthenware basket, the folded bowl with 2 applied handles and 4 applied lions heads as feet, one side decorated with a scene of alligators, palms and a pyramid along the Nile, the other decorated with a spider and fly on a spiderweb, overall with copper lustre highlights, impressed Rookwood, 1883, 45, 20in (50.5cm) long.
$5,000-6,000

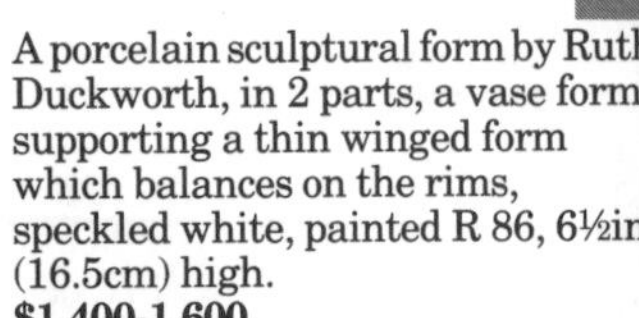

A porcelain sculptural form by Ruth Duckworth, in 2 parts, a vase form supporting a thin winged form which balances on the rims, speckled white, painted R 86, 6½in (16.5cm) high.
$1,400-1,600

n earthenware vase, the body ecorated with moulded irises about e body in green glaze, the ossoms, in yellow, impressed with e firm's mark and incised with the tist's initials and number 161, esigned and produced by the rueby Faience Company, 12½in 1.5cm) high.
12,000-15,000

An earthenware vase, with gunmetal glaze, impressed G.E. OHR, Biloxi, Miss, 12in (30.5cm) high.
$25,000-35,000

An earthenware pitcher, the waisted bulbous body with folded and cut-out handle, with mauve and green dappled glaze, the interior in lavender, with green G.E. Ohr in script, 5in (12.5cm) high.
$8,000-12,000

. 'Linenfold' leaded glass and ronze table lamp, stamped Tiffany tudios New York 561, 25in 3.5cm) high.
8,000-12,000

A 'Lotus' leaded glass and bronze table lamp, stamped Tiffany Studios New York, and with Tiffany Glass and Decorating Co. monogram, 20in (50.5cm) high.
$30,000-35,000

A Favrile glass and bronze table lamp, the domed shade of pale yellow glass with an elaborate bronze open work cover and beaded curtain border, the pumpkin-shaped base of deep and lime green striated glass with a patinated brown domed foot and an elaborate bronze shoulder plate supporting 6 upturned arms, the base stamped S1487, the fuel canister Tiffany Studios New York D967 and with Tiffany Glass and Decorating Co. monogram, fitted for electricity, 23½in (60cm) high.
$20,000-25,000

A 'Greek Key Pattern' leaded glass and gilt bronze table lamp, stamped Tiffany Studios New York, 26in (66.5cm) high.
$10,000-12,000

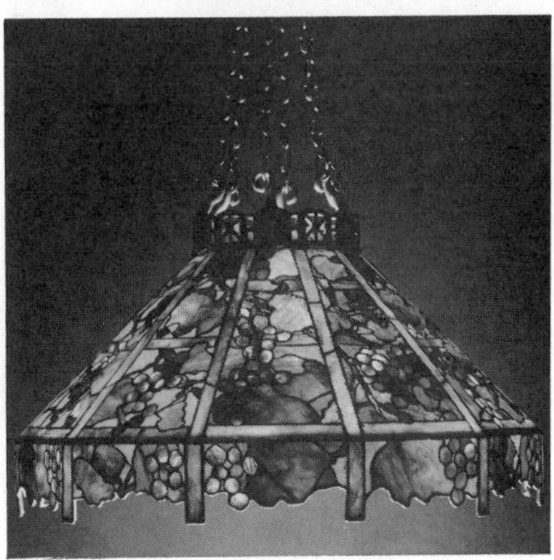

A 'Grape Trellis' leaded glass and bronze hanger, the conical shaped octagonal shade with purple, plum and blue grapes, amber, gold and green leaves on an amber and gold ground, by Tiffany Studios, shade 29½in (74.5cm) diam.
$45,000-50,000

ARTS & CRAFT

An oak drop front desk, designed by Harvey Ellis, by Gustav Stickley, the panelled front dropping to reveal an interior with partitions, drawer, and an original glass inkwell, with the firm's brown paper label and small red decal, model No. 706, c1907, 30in (76cm) wide.
$2,000-3,000

An oak umbrella stand, by Gustav Stickley, with square tapering posts and copper drip pan insert, with the firm's paper label, model No. 54, c1912, 33½in (85cm) high.
$5,000-6,000

An oak ladderback sidechair, by Gustav Stickley, used in the interior of his Craftsman Farms home, Morris Plains, New Jersey, with rush seat, with the firm's small red decal, model No. 306, c1909, 35in (89cm) high.
$350-400

An oak heavy ladderback sidechair, by Gustav Stickley, used in the interior of his Craftsman Farms home, Morris Plains, New Jersey, with rush seat, model No. 349, c1909, 37in (94cm) high.
$900-1,000

An oak sewing rocker, by Gustav Stickley, used in the interior of his Craftsman Farms home, Morris Plains, New Jersey, with rush seat, model No. 305, c1909, 30½in (77cm high.
$300-400

An oak double bed, by Gustav Stickley, with tapered posts and wide slats across the head and foot boards, with the firm's small red decal, model No. 923, 59in (149.5cm) wide.
$3,000-5,000

An oak and leather rocker, by Gustav Stickley, with the firm's small red decal and brown paper label, model No. 311, c1909, 34in (86cm) high.
$600-800

An oak costumer, by Gustav Stickley, on shoe feet, with the firm's small red decal, model No. 192, c1902, 60in (152cm) high.
$1,500-2,000

Two Arts and Crafts armchairs with matching side chairs.
1,500-2,000

An Arts and Crafts tub chair.
$400-500

An Arts and Crafts carver chair.
$250-300

A set of 8 Arts and Crafts rush seated chairs, including 2 carvers.
$1,300-1,400

A chestnut footstool, by Gustav Stickley, with tapering legs joined by arched cross stretchers, the arched apron frame covered in leather, model No. 725, c1901, 16½in (42cm) high.
$1,500-2,500

A set of 4 Arts and Crafts chairs.
$650-700

A set of 8 Arts and Crafts chairs, by William Birch.
$1,300-1,400

An oak mirror, by Gustav Stickley, with simple arched frame with hand wrought iron hooks and chain, with the firm's small red decal and brown paper label, model No. 910, c1909, 23½in (60cm) high.
$1,200-1,600

An oak trestle table, by Gustav Stickley, the top supported by 2 scrolling cut out legs, joined with 2 medial rails ending in keyed exposed tenons and surmounted by a shelf, with firm's red decal, model No. 403, c1903, 36in (92cm) wide.
$2,000-3,500

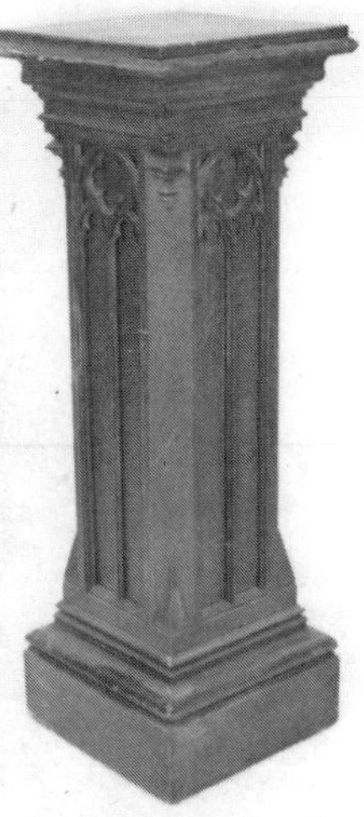

A pair of Gothic oak pillars, with painted decoration, 49in (124.5cm).
$1,000-1,200

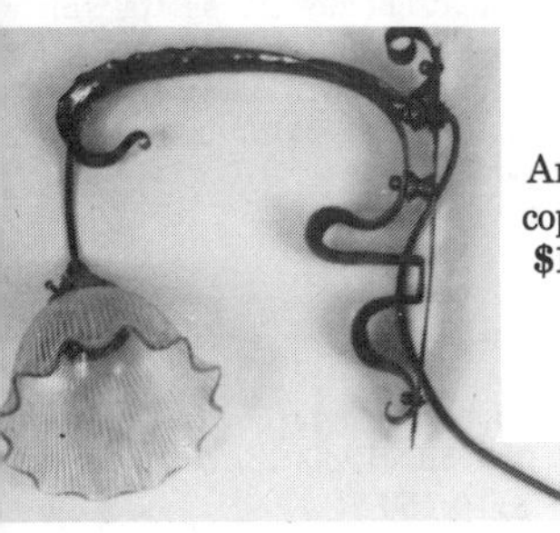

An Arts and Crafts copper wall light.
$100-110

A Newlyn copper repoussé tray, 17½in (44.5cm).
$250-300

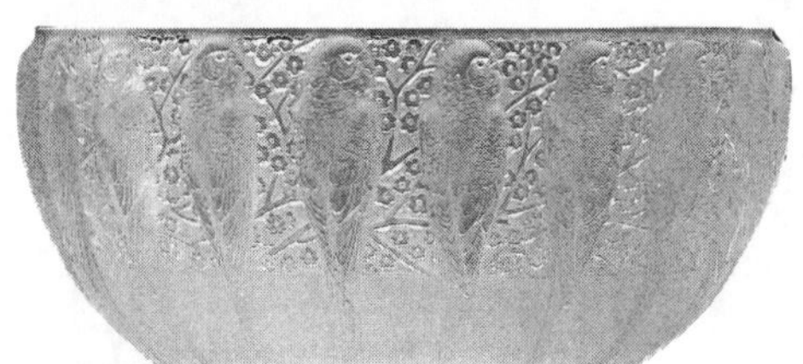

A Lalique opalescent glass bowl, moulded with an encircling band of budgerigars and blossom, etched 'R. Lalique, France', 9½in (24cm) diam.
$2,500-3,000

A Lalique black necklace, on silk cord, c1930.
$1,500-2,000

A Lalique opalescent table clock 'Inseparables', moulded R. Lalique 4½in (11cm) high.
$1,300-1,500

Ceramics

A Quimper basket, signed, 4in (10cm) wide.
$230-250

A Maling ware plate, with daffodils design, c1930, 11in (28cm) diam.
$250-300

A Maling ware plate, c1930.
$250-300

A set of 6 Fornasetti '12 Mesi, 12 Soli' ceramic plates, each with painted polychrome decoration of the sun against differing landscapes, with printed signature '12 Mesi 12 Soli, Fornasetti Milano Made in Italy', 10½in (25.5cm).
$700-1,000

A Shelley plate, Iris pattern, c1930, 10in (25cm) wide.
$40-50

A Goldscheider terracotta wall mask of a young woman, with gre curled hair, white face and yellow shoulder, slight damage, 10in (25cm) high.
$400-550

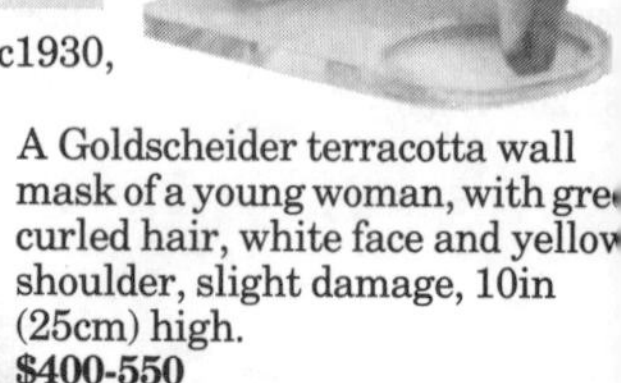

A Crown Devon bowl painted wit galleon, c1930, 13in (33.5cm) wi
$110-150

A Shelley lustre ware bowl, signed by Walter Slater, c1920, 12in (30.5cm) diameter.
$100-130

A Shelley Harmony ware strainer, c1930, 8in (20cm) diam.
$65-100

A Quimper cup, Pecheur pattern, signed, 2in (5cm).
$25-30

A Carlton ware Apple Blossom breakfast set, c1930.
$500-550

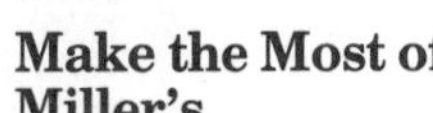

Make the Most of Miller's

CONDITION is absolutely vital when assessing the value of an antique. Damaged pieces on the whole appreciate much less than perfect examples. However a rare, desirable piece may command a high price even when damaged

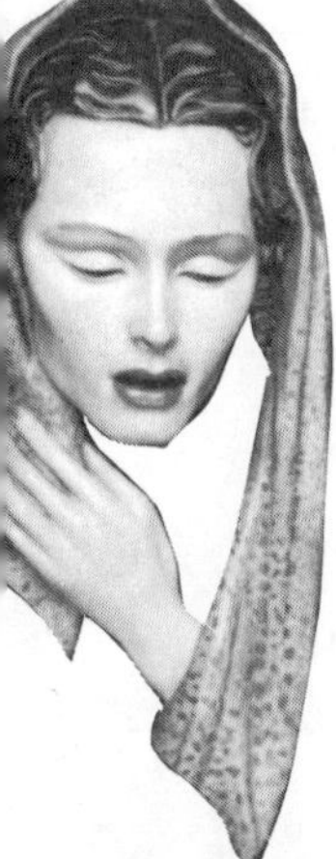

A wall mask by Leonardi, with mushroom coloured face and green scarf, Reg. No. 825795, c1930, 20½in (52cm) high.
$400-500

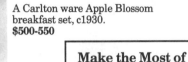

A Shelley ginger jar, in orange and yellow, c1930, 8½in (22cm) high.
$150-250

A Shelley Regent shape tea service, Mimosa pattern.
$550-700

A Robj earthenware bowl and cover, formed as a Red Indian's head, with dark red glazed feather headdress, with impressed mark Robj Paris Made in France, 8in (20cm) high.
$650-800

A Lenci bust, Essevi Samdo Vachetti, 8½in (21cm) high.
$330-400

A Lenci bust, Essevi Samdo Vachetti, c1938, 7in (17.5cm) high.
$350-400

A Shelley 22 piece tea service with teapot, English Cottage design, low Queen Anne shape.
$800-1,000

A Shelley 22 piece tea service, with green and silver pattern, c1933.
$700-900

A Wedgwood stoneware vase, designed by Keith Murray, of globular form with cylindrical n and ribbed body, covered in an emerald green glaze, inscribed w a facsimile signature Keith Mur and Wedgwood, Made in Englan 7½in (18.5cm) high.
$400-700

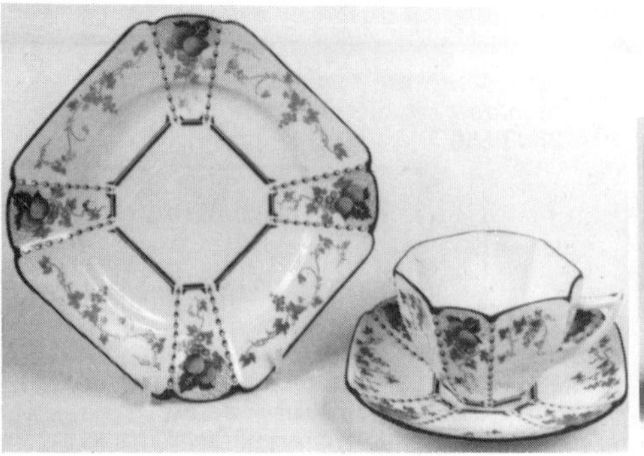

A Shelley 21 piece tea service, including teapot, low Queen Anne shape, with peaches and grapes design, c1920.
$550-650

A pair of Wedgwood bookends, designed by Keith Murray, each c right angle form, covered in a gre glaze, and with fluted decoration, stamped Wedgwood, 5½in (14.5cn high.
$650-1,000

A Shelley afternoon tea service, decorated with The Apple Blossom Pattern comprising: 12 teacups, 12 saucers, 12 square tea plates, a pair of bread plates, teapot, hot water jug, cream jug, sugar bowl and a circular teapot stand, pattern No. 12287, Reg. No. 756533.
$700-900

A Shelley 21 piece tea servic Sunburst pattern, c1931.
$1,400-1,500

A Wiener Keramik coffee service, decorated by Ida Schwetz, the cream ground decorated in grey and black with scalloped borders and handles, and flower patterns, with impressed Wiener Keramik marks and decorator's monogram IS, coffee pot 8in (19cm) high.
$700-1,000

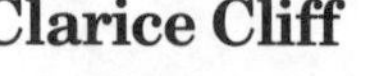

Clarice Cliff

A plate by John Armstrong for Clarice Cliff, 9in (22.5cm) diam.
$500-550

A Fantasque Bizarre flower bowl, modelled as a Viking longboat, decorated in the Trees and House pattern of orange cottage in a wooded landscape, painted in green, orange and black, lithograph marks, tiny chip to foot, 13in (33.5cm) long.
$2,000-2,500

A Clarice Cliff Fantasque Bizarre single handled Lotus jug, with reeded decoration painted with th Summerhouse pattern, 11in (28cn high.
$900-1,000

An Ernest Proctor, for Clarice Cliff, designer plate, with a bride and groom on horseback, in pale green with silver lustre, 9in (23cm) diam.
$400-550

A Clarice Cliff Fantasque charger, with coloured star-like motifs on a bubble ground within an orange border, 17in (43.5cm) diam.
$2,500-3,000

A Clarice Cliff single handled Isis jug, painted with the Forest Glenn pattern in bright, warm enamel colours, 10in (25cm) high.
$1,400-2,000

A Fantasque sandwich plate, decorated in the 7 colour version of the Trees and House pattern of cottage in a wooded landscape, painted in orange, yellow, blue, purple, green, rust and brown, minor wear, rubber stamp mark, 11½in (29cm) wide.
$700-800

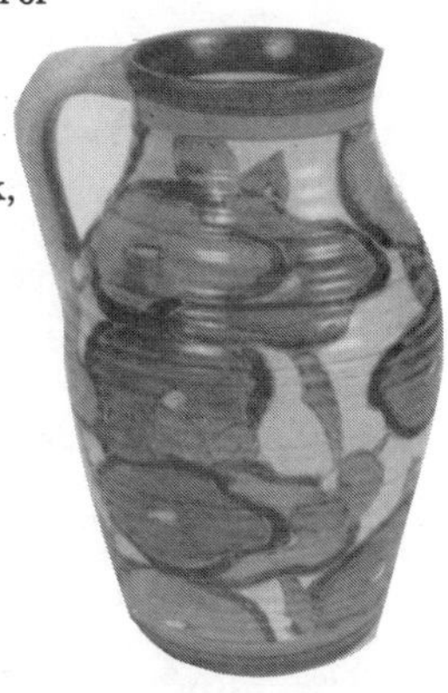
A Clarice Cliff Fantasque Bizarre pottery single handled Lotus jug, decorated in shades of blue, green and pink on a cream ground with the Blue Chintz pattern, cracked, printed mark, 11½in (29cm) high.
$80-110

A Clarice Cliff Fantasque Bizarre Football pattern, pottery two handled Lotus jug, decorated in shades of orange, yellow, blue, purple, green and black, printed mark, 11½in (29cm) high.
$2,500-3,000

A charger decorated to a design by Sir Frank Brangwyn, printed and painted in colours with a procession of figures of various nationalities in a tropical garden, hand painted inscription, 17in (43.5cm) diam.
$5,500-7,000

A pair of Clarice Cliff candlesticks, 3½in (9cm) high.
$250-275

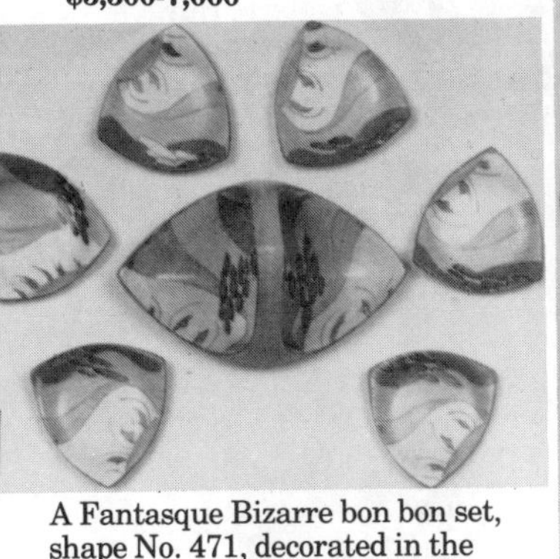
A Fantasque Bizarre bon bon set, shape No. 471, decorated in the Windbells pattern of blue foliate tree in stylised garden, painted in green, orange, yellow and blue, comprising: oval dish with overhead handle and 6 triangular dishes, minor wear, lithograph mark.
$1,400-1,500

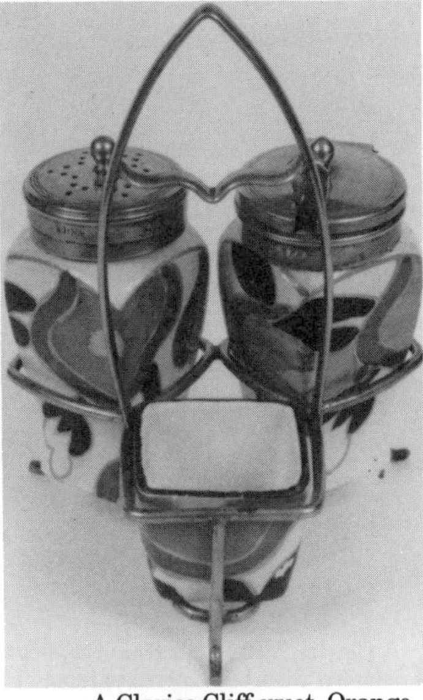
A Clarice Cliff cruet, Orange Chintz, 3½in (9cm) high.
$300-400

A pair of Clarice Cliff candlesticks, Football pattern, 8in (20cm) high.
$1,500-2,150

A Bizarre dinner service, decorate by Dod Proctor with a fish and seaweed, painted in shades of blue and green, comprising: 6 side plate 12 entrée plates, 6 dinner plates, 3 graduated oval platters, a fish platter, 2 tureens and 1 cover, and 2 sauceboats, some damage, printe marks.
$1,400-2,000

A Bizarre muffineer set, decorated to a design by Dame Laura Knight, of stylised head and scroll motifs, painted in pink, brown, orange, turquoise and black, comprising pepper and salt shakers, and mustard pot and cover, minute firing crack to salt, printed marks and facsimile signature.
$1,000-1,200

A Clarice Cliff Bizarre vase, Delicia pattern, painted with yellow, orange and green peaches, wi printed signature Delicia Ha Painted Bizarre by Clarice Cl and Newport Pottery Englan Provisional Patent No. 23385 retailer's mark China Glass Lawleys of Regent Street, London W1, 7in (18cm) high.
$700-1,000

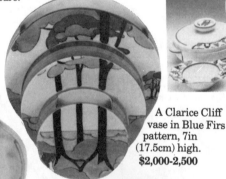

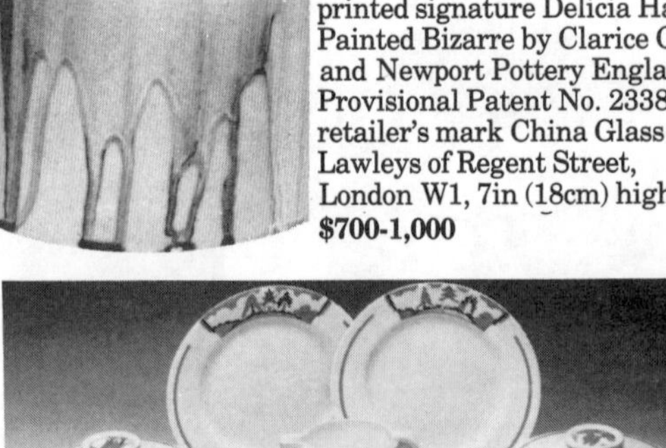

A Clarice Cliff Bizarre part dinner service, painted with Kew pattern o a red-roofed pagoda in parkland scenery, comprising: 3 tureens and 2 covers, 3 sauceboats and stands, 6 grapefruit dishes and 8 stands, 5 meat dishes, 12 dinner plates, 8 dessert plates, and 7 small plates, some damage.
$1,200-1,400

A Clarice Cliff vase in Blue Firs pattern, 7in (17.5cm) high.
$2,000-2,500

A Clarice Cliff Inspiration Caprice pattern vase, of inverted baluster form with pink and mauve trees on a turquoise ground, 9in (22.5cm) high.
$2,000-2,500

A Clarice Cliff Summer House pattern vase, Isis shape, 10in (25cm) high.
$3,000-3,500

Make the Most of Miller's

In Miller's we do NOT just reprint saleroom estimates. We work from realised prices either from an auction room or a dealer. Our consultants then work out a realistic price range for a similar piece. This is to try to avoid repeating freak results – either low or high

Figures – Ceramics

A Goldscheider group designed by Lorenzl, of Harlequin and Columbine embracing, wearing polychrome enamelled elaborate costume, on domed base, with printed facsimile signature Goldscheider Wien Made in Austria Hand decorated, and impressed Lorenzl, 16in (40cm) high.
$800-1,200

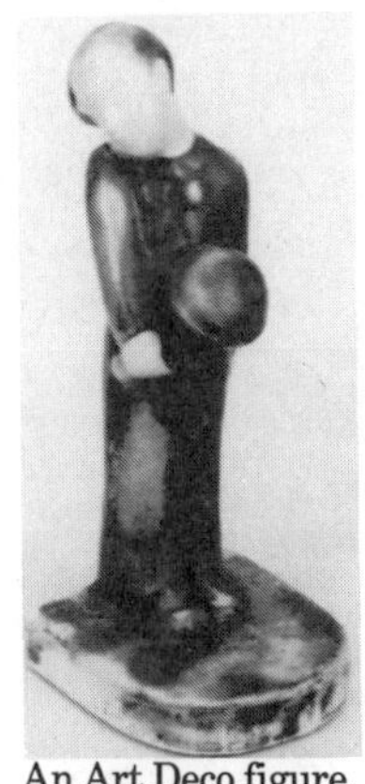

An Art Deco figure, 7½in (19cm) high.
$10-15

An Art Deco plaster figure of Diana the Huntress.
$250-400

A gold and silver patinated bronze and ivory figure 'Liseuse', cast and carved from a model by A. Carrier-Belleuse, on bronze plinth, signed in the bronze A. Carrier-Belleuse and with plaque inscribed Liseuse, par Carrier Belleuse, Grand-Prix du Salon, 23½in (60cm) high.
$5,000-5,500

An Art Deco spelter figure of a kneeling lady holding a bird of paradise, on marble plinth.
$300-350

Figures – Metal

A bronze figure 'Young Girl', cast from a model by Dêmetre Chiparus, on an amber-coloured onyx plinth, the base damaged, signed in the onyx Chiparus, 11½in (29.5cm) high.
$2,500-3,000

A bronze figure of a lady by Bruno Zack, in green swimsuit holding beachball, on oval green marble base, 14in (35.5cm) high.
$900-1,000

Bronze & Ivory Figures

A silvered bronze and ivory figure, cast and carved from a model by Lorenzl, on square stepped green onyx and marble base, bronze inscribed 'Lorenzl', 11in (28cm) high.
$800-1,200

A bronze figure, 'Dancer with Thyrsus', cast from a model by Pierre Le Faguays, on a stepped, black striated marble base, signed Le Faguays, 22½in (56cm) high.
$5,000-5,500

A gilt, bronze and ivory group of a little girl and a baby snuggled up in an armchair, signed A. Croisy, the reverse with studio stamp on mink onyx base, entitled 'Le Nid', early 20thC, 7in (17.5cm).
$2,500-3,000

A silver patinated bronze figure, 'Amazon', by Marcel Bouraine, the stylised nude female warrior kneeling on a dark patinated base, signed in the bronze Bouraine, 7in (16.5cm) high.
$1,500-2,500

An Art Deco gilt bronze and ivory figure, cast and carved from a model by E. Monier, wearing armbands and tight fitting feathered skirt, on rectangular base cast in relief with eagles, on yellow onyx base, bronze inscribed E. Monier, 14½in (37cm) high.
$2,500-3,000

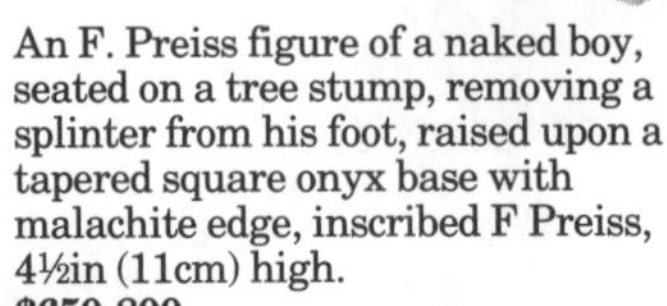

An F. Preiss figure of a naked boy, seated on a tree stump, removing a splinter from his foot, raised upon a tapered square onyx base with malachite edge, inscribed F Preiss, 4½in (11cm) high.
$650-800

A French bronze figure of the Pie
Piper playing a flute, with ivory fa
and hands, signed E. Barillot, on
slate socle, 10in (25cm).
$1,200-1,300

A bronze and ivory figure cast and carved from a model by A. Brandel, of a figure on tip-toe, dressed in a red and black cold-painted Oriental costume, on shaped repainted base indistinctly signed A. Brandel, 10½in (26.5cm) high.
$800-1,300

A Marquet gilt bronze and ivory figure, 'Draped Piper', in Egyptian costume, on veined black marble base, hand damaged, 17in (43.5cm) high.
$2,500-3,000

An F. Preiss carved ivory figure 'Girl with a skipping rope', signed.
$1,400-1,500

A French bronze and ivory figure of a jester holding a hand mirror, with an owl on his shoulder, signed E. Barillot, on a slate socle, 10½in (27cm).
$1,200-1,300

An Austrian bronze draped female by J. Benk, 1907, 11in (28cm) high.
$1,500-2,500

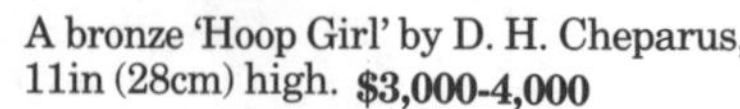

A bronze 'Hoop Girl' by D. H. Cheparus, 11in (28cm) high. **$3,000-4,000**

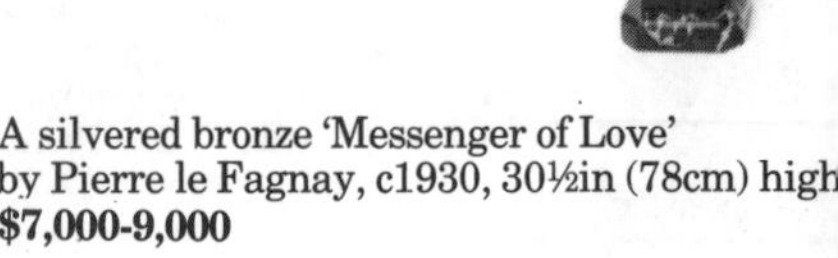

A silvered bronze 'Messenger of Love' by Pierre le Fagnay, c1930, 30½in (78cm) high
$7,000-9,000

A figure lamp by le Verrier, c1930, 19in (48.5cm) high. **$8,000-9,500**

A bronze and ivory figure of Mephistopheles, on onyx base, polished, c1925, 8½in (21.5cm) high.
$300-400

A bronze and ivory figure of a lady dancer in a tunic, on onyx base, by Lorenzl, signed Renz, patination polished, 7in (17.5cm) high.
$500-550

A bronze and ivory figure table lamp, 'The Stile', the young woman wearing a green shirt and bronze trousers, standing between 2 pillars supporting a lamp, on black base, signed F. Preiss, with shade, 22in (56cm) high.
$5,500-6,500

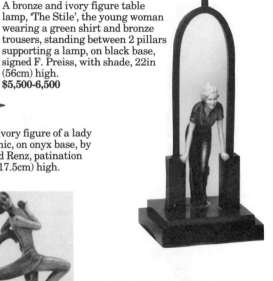

A gilt bronze figure of a female dancer, cast from a model by Lorenzl, standing on a green onyx base, base damaged, bronze inscribed Lorenzl, 8½in (21cm) high.
$500-650

Furniture

A pair of 'Barcelona' chairs, designed by Mies van der Rohe, with chromed steel 'X'-shaped frames strung with leather strap supports, with detachable black leather buttoned seat and cushions.
$800-900

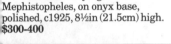

A cream leather three-piece suite, by Heal's.
$2,500-3,000

Illustrated in Heal's catalogue.

A pair of chrome chairs, 33in (84cm) high.
$300-500

A Heal's oak adjustable lounge chair, with solid back and seat flanked by arm forming two-tier shelf and drop-leaf table, with upholstered cushions.
$400-500

A pair of Heal's limed oak adjustable armchairs, the solid panelled backs and seats supported on rounded rectangular trestle ends with plank supports, with original fabric upholstered cushions.
$1,000-1,200

A set of 3 laminated beech side chairs, designed by Bruno Mathsson, the back and seat frames woven with brown hessian, each on moulded trestle ends joined by plain stretchers, paper label printed Designed by Bruno Mathsson, rubber stamped Made in Sweden.
$550-1,000

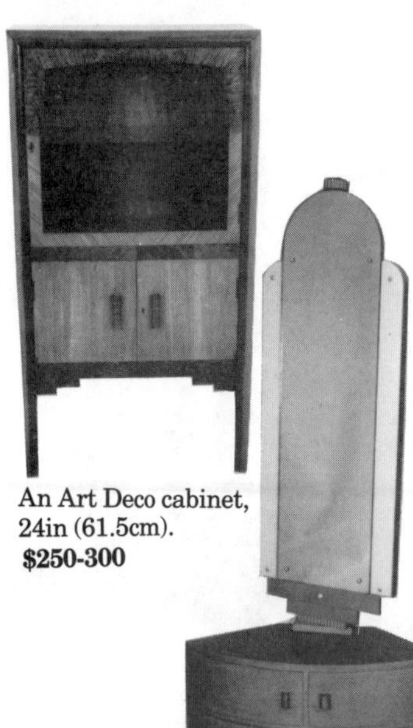
An Art Deco cabinet, 24in (61.5cm).
$250-300

A Rowley bedroom suite, comprising: dressing table, stool, chest and bedhead, with illuminated side panels, dressing table 34in (86cm).
$1,000-1,300

A dressing table from an Art Deco bedroom suite, comprising: dressing table, bedside cupboard and large cupboard in oyster maple, 48in (122cm) wide. **$1,300-1,500**

A Gordon Russell chestnut wardrobe, the top with chamfered finials above 2 panelled cupboard doors, on octagonal section legs wit printed paper label 'Design No 101/1283, Designer Gordon Russell, Foreman F. Shilton Cabinet Maker P. Wade, Timber used chestnut, Date 27.11.30', stamped 'E.A. Dorley', 76in (193.5cm) high.
$1,400-1,500

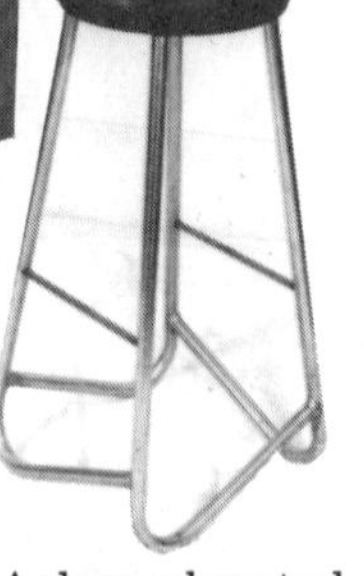
A chrome bar stool made by PEL, c1930, 30in (76cm) high.
$100-130

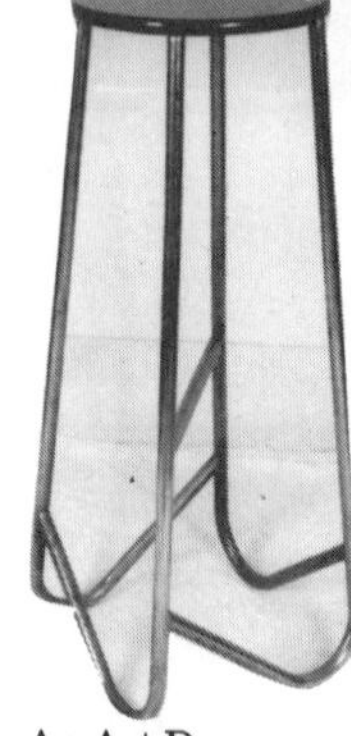
An Art Deco chrome stool, 37in (94cm) high.
$65-80

An Art Deco chrome and maroon glass cocktail trolley, 25½in (65cm) high.
$200-300

A Rowley Gallery corner unit, with inset picture of lion killing a deer, 44in (111.5cm) wide.
$300-500

A Robert Thompson 'Mouseman' oak wardrobe, with beaten iron fittings, on short square section legs with mouse signature carved in intaglio, 48in (122cm).
$4,000-5,000

An occasional table designed by Piero Fornasetti, with wooden top covered in black lacquer and decorated with a transfer printed sun and ray motif, on tripod steel legs modelled with nodules, with printed paper label, 29½in (75cm) high. **$1,400-2,000**

An Art Deco French table, c1930, 24in (61.5cm) high.
$250-300

An Art Deco rosewood and burr-maple walnut centre table, in the style of Emile Ruhlmann, inlaid with ivory lattice stringing above plain frieze and chamfered legs, 33in (84cm).
$1,500-2,500

An occasional table, designed and labelled by Waring and Gillow, 21in (53cm) high.
$300-400

An Art Deco table, 32in (81.5cm) diam.
$800-1,000

An Art Deco nest of tables, 30in (76cm) diam.
$400-650

An Art Deco circular table, 36in (91.5cm) diam.
$1,300-1,400

An Art Deco vitrolite occasional table by PEL, 29in (74cm) high.
$80-150

An Art Deco glass and walnut coffee table, 21in (53cm) high.
$250-300

Glass

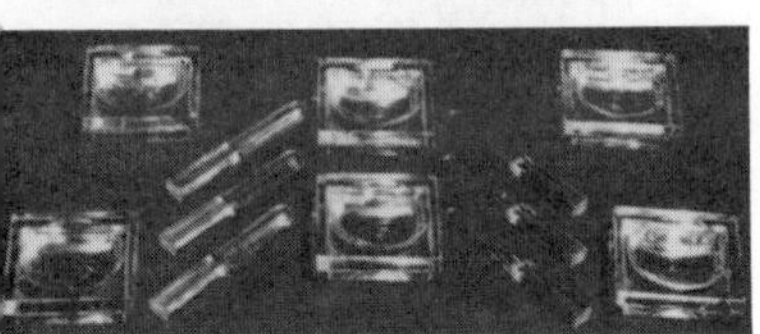

A set of 6 Asprey crystal butter dishes and knives, in original fitted box, marked Asprey 166 Bond Street London, butter knife 4in (10cm) long.
$800-1,000

An Orrefors 'Ariel' vase designed by Ingeborg Lundin, the thick clear glass decorated internally with a blue geometric pattern and air bubbles, with engraved signature Orrefors Ariel Nr 177-E7 Ingeborg London, 6½in (15.5cm) high.
$1,200-1,400

A Degué Art Deco acid-etched cameo vase, the acid-textured clear ground overlaid in high relief with mottled pink diamond pattern and chevron borders, with cameo signature Degué and acid-etched Made in France, 14in (35.5cm) high.
$1,500-2,500

A Venini bottle vase, the clear glass internally decorated with yellow diagonal lines, acid-stamped signature 'Venini Murano Italia', 14in (35.5cm) high.
$500-800

A pair of Art Deco glass hanging lamps, by Sabino, 12in (30.5cm) high.
$1,000-1,200

Jewellery

A lacquer, crystal and paste on silver bangle, c1920.
$500-1,000

An 18 carat gold ladies cocktail watch with synthetic rubies and diamonds, c1940.
$800-1,000

A Mexican silver and semi-precious stone bracelet, c1945, 7in (17.5cm) long.
$300-500

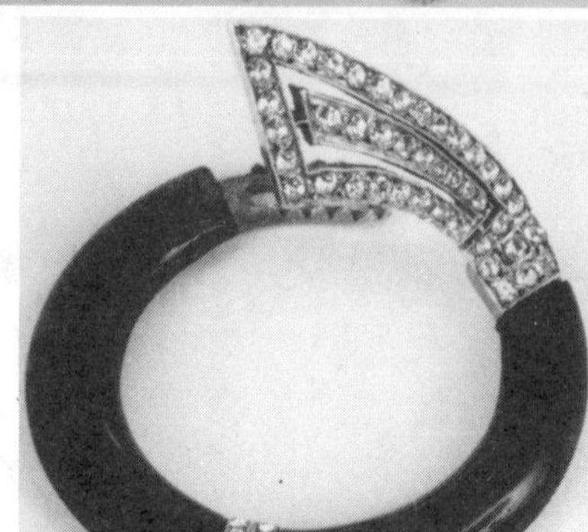

A Mexican silver and inlaid semi-precious stone necklace, designed by Ladesma, c1945.
$250-300

A silver, enamel and paste brooch/clip, c1920.
$250-300

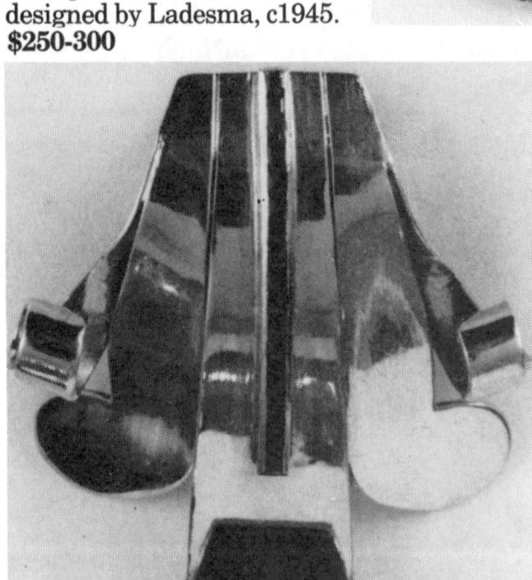

An 18 carat gold clip with rubies, c1940.
$650-800

An 18 carat gold watch ring, with cabochon sapphires, in original box, c1940.
$650-800

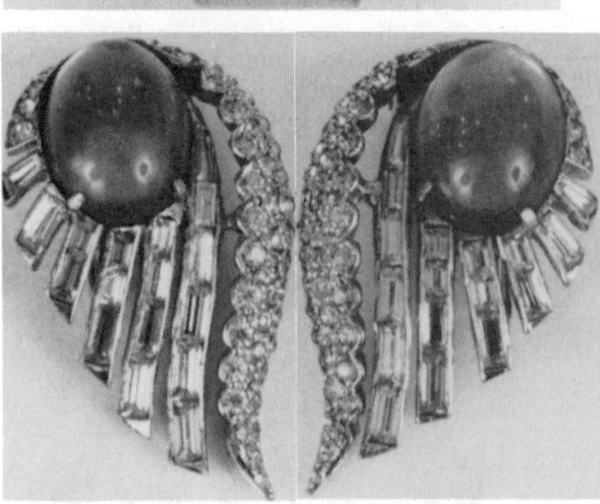

A pair of costume jewellery clips by Boucher, c1940.
$200-250

Metal

An Art Deco silver pepper and salt by Georg Jensen, design by Jorgen Jensen, c1930, 4½in (11cm) high.
$2,000-2,500

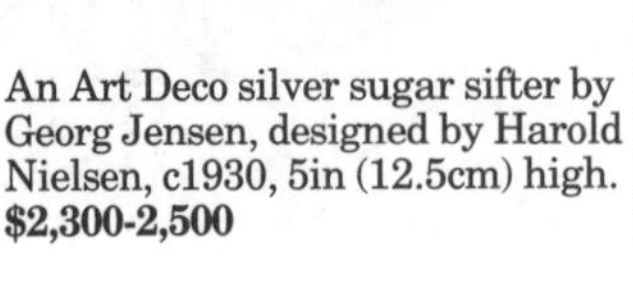

An Art Deco silver sugar sifter by Georg Jensen, designed by Harold Nielsen, c1930, 5in (12.5cm) high.
$2,300-2,500

An Art Deco lamp, with a silver and gold plaster figure of a lady.
$90-275

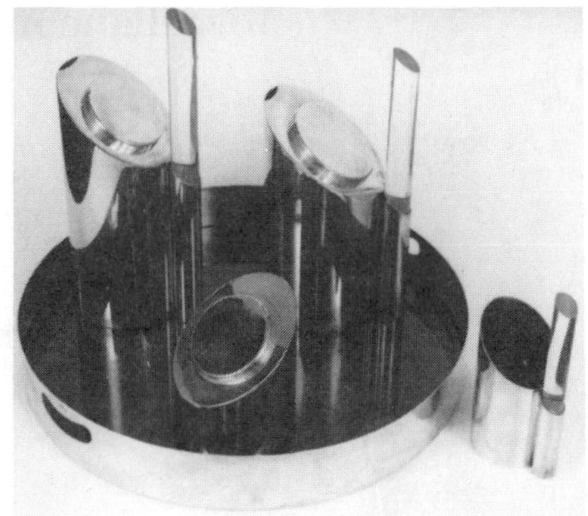

A silver plated teaset and tray, with French transparent Bakelite handles, c1960, 15in (38cm) diam.
$2,500-3,000

A hammered silver bowl and cover, with a stepped everted rim, gently domed cover and ring finial, stamped with German silver marks, c1930, 4in (10cm) high.
$2,500-3,000

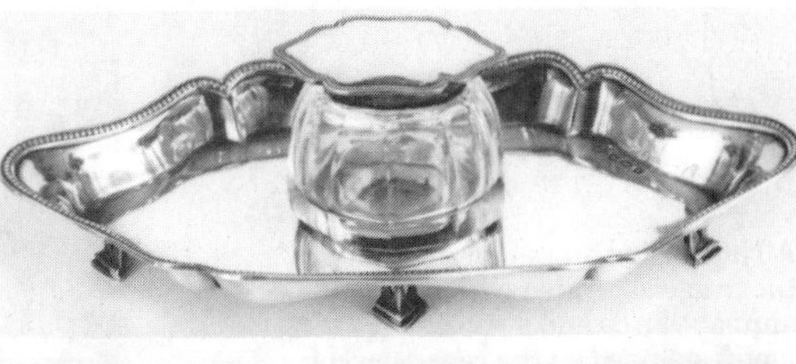

A silver inkstand, Birmingham, 1915, 7½in (19cm) wide.
$300-400

A Danish 3-piece demitasse service by Georg Jensen, comprising: coffee pot, sugar bowl and cream pitcher, with side bone handles and knop finials with beaded joins, c1945, 18.5oz gross.
$1,200-1,600

A chrome plated brass fruit bowl, with slightly domed centre and flaring well, stamped Bauhaus, 1929, 11½in (29cm) diam.
$5,000-5,500

A pair of Asprey chromium plated cocktail shakers, each dumb-bell shaped, with strainer, one end forming the lid, one dented, stamped mark A & Co. Asprey London 6333 Made in England, 10½in (25.5cm) high.
$800-1,200

A Hagenauer brass bowl, the shallow hammered bowl on a tapering foot with openwork decoration of horses, stamped mark wHw Hagenauer Wien Made in Austria, 12½in (32.5cm) diam.
$2,500-3,000

A three-piece Art Deco style silver tea service, Birmingham, 1935, 20oz gross.
$550-650

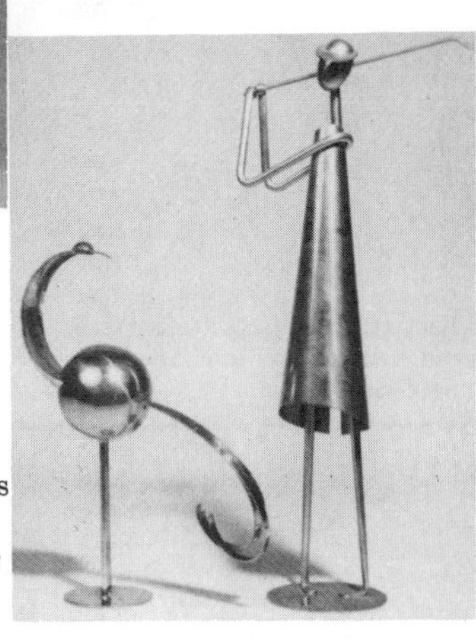

A Hagenauer brass sculpture of a bird and a golfer, the stylised forms on circular bases, stamped Hagenauer wHw Made in Austria, golfer 15in (38.5cm).
$1,200-1,400 each

A Hagenauer brass hanging mirror, the frame decorated with stylised animals, birds and a geometric motif, stamped on the reverse wHw Hagenauer Wien, Made in Austria, 16½in (42cm) high.
$3,500-9,500

An Art Deco four-piece fluted rounded oblong tea service, with polished wood handles, the domed hinged covers with carved wood finials, hot water jug 8in (20cm), 56.5oz gross.
$2,500-3,000

An Art Deco plated tea service, marked, teapot 5in (12.5cm) high.
$400-500

Miscellaneous

An Art Deco marble clock set, with a spelter panther figure and urns.
$400-500

An Art Deco marble clock set with spelter figure of a kneeling lady 'Time Flies'.
$500-550

An Art Deco marble clock set with brass decoration in the Epstein style.
$500-550

An Art Deco wall clock, 12in (30.5cm) square.
$150-250

A copper wall clock, c1930, with new quartz movement, 13½in (35cm) diam.
$150-200

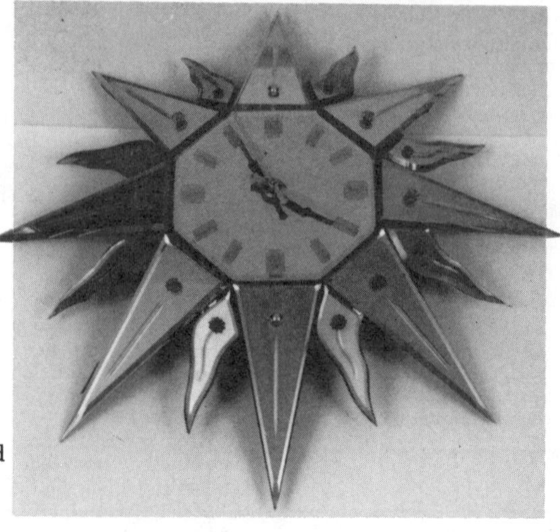

An Art Deco Sunburst mirrored clock, 26in (66cm) diam.
$400-500

An Art Deco chrome extractor fan.
$300-350

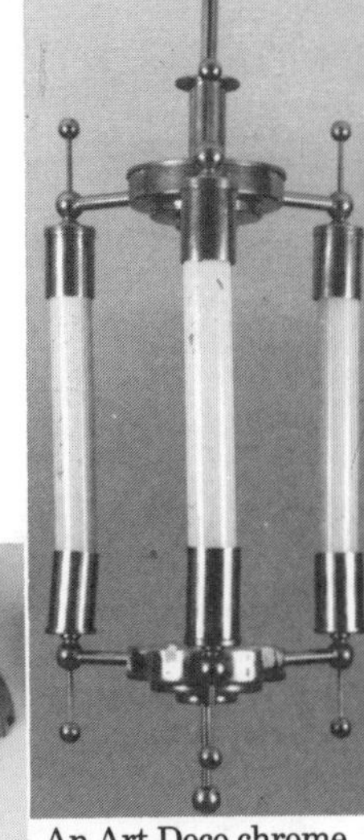

An Art Deco chrome hanging lamp.
$400-550

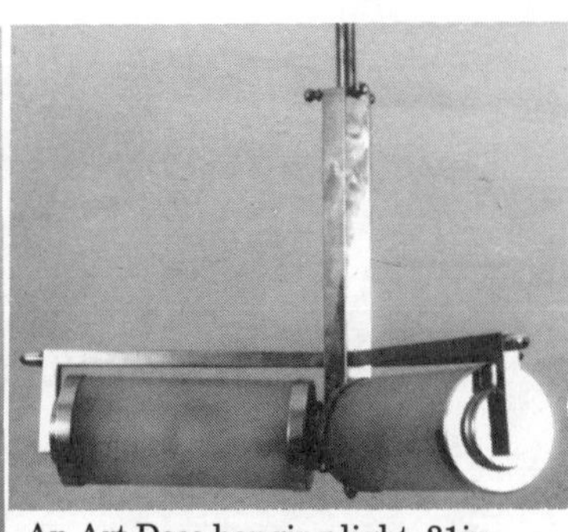

An Art Deco hanging light, 31in (79cm) high.
$150-300

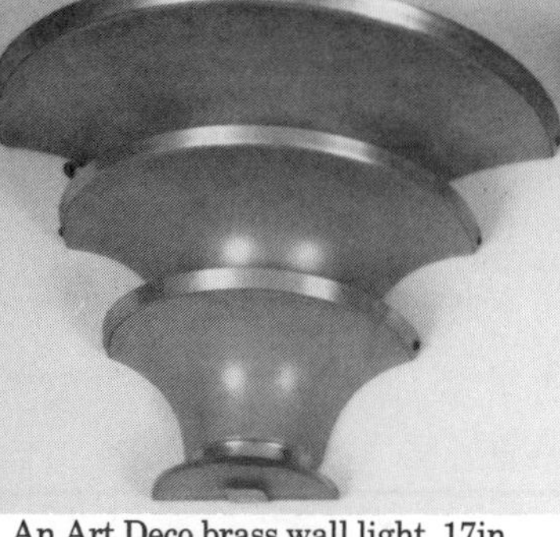

An Art Deco brass wall light, 17in (43.5cm) high.
$130-200

A Danish silver and enamel bracelet, c1960.
$250-300

Post-War Design

A James Powell ewer, with ovoid body on domed base, the tall neck with flaring trefoil rim, with applied elongated handle, milky vaseline glass, 14in (35.5cm) high.
$1,000-1,300

A Dino Martens vase, with pinched figure-of-eight shaped rim, the clear glass internally decorated with polychrome geometric fields and patterns, 7in (17.2cm) high.
$2,500-3,000

A chrome and vinyl settee and chair, c1945, 27in (68.5cm) high.
$1,000-1,300

Two pieces of Italian enamelled metal jewellery, design by Ettore Sotsass, c1980.
$40-80

A Hille plywood dining room suite, designed by Robin Day, comprising: rectangular table on tubular steel legs, sideboard with 2 smoked glass sliding doors enclosing shaped single shelves, on tubular steel legs, and 6 chairs with shaped plywood back and arm rests above upholstered seats, on tubular steel legs, with ivorine plaques Hille London, c1955.
$1,000-1,300

SILVER

Baskets

A George IV fruit basket, by John, Henry and Charles Lias, 1828, 13½in (34cm) diam, 53oz.
$2,650-3,500

A George III sugar basket, by Solomon Hougham, London, 1795, 3½in (9cm) high.
$1,000-1,200

A George III bread basket, engraved with a coat-of-arms within an oval cartouche, by Richard Morton & Co., Sheffield, 1784, 15in (38cm) long, 27oz.
$3,500-4,500

A George III cake basket, pierced and engraved with foliage, by Robert Breading, Dublin, 1794, 15½in (39.5cm) long, 38oz.
$5,000-6,500

A George IV cake basket, engraved with the Royal arms, by Paul Storr, 1829, stamped Storr & Mortimer, 16½in (42cm) wide, 38oz.
$13,000-14,000

Beakers

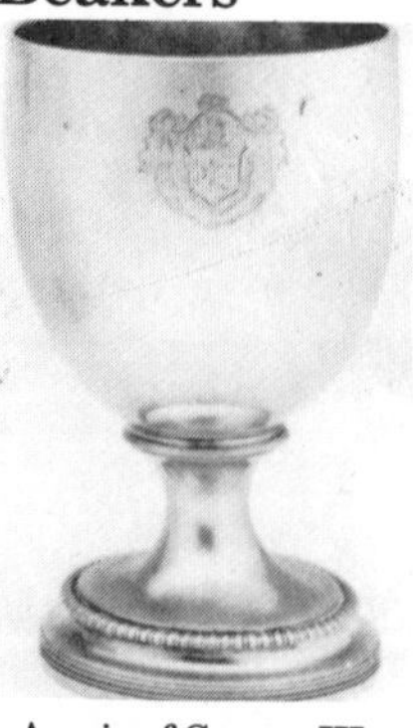

A pair of George III goblets, engraved with crest, maker C.H., London, 1808, 20oz.
$2,500-3,000

A beaker by William A. Williams, Alexandria, Virginia or Washington D.C., with reeded rim and footrim, engraved with monogram 'WAN' below armorials, marked, early 19thC, 3in (8cm) high, 4oz.
$1,500-2,500

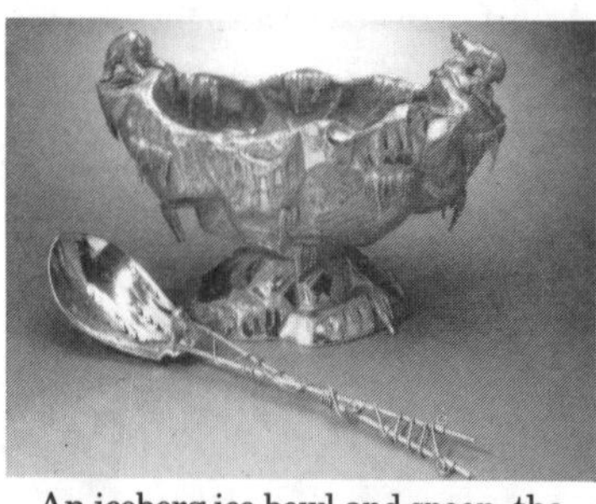

An iceberg ice bowl and spoon, the bowl partly matted and with applied pendant icicles surmounted by a roaring polar bear on each end, on similar base, by Gorham, 1872, 11in (28cm) long, the spoon with pierced bowl surmounted by a polar bear, the stem formed as 2 crossed harpoons applied with tied cable, 11½in (29cm) long, 27.5oz.
$15,000-20,000

Bowls

A George II Irish bowl, by Andrew Goodwin, Dublin, c1740, 6in (15.5cm) diam, 9oz.
$2,650-3,000

An Edwardian rose bowl with later presentation inscription, Birmingham, 1908, 11in (28.5cm), 32oz.
$1,500-2,000

A fruit bowl fitted with a glass liner, Birmingham, 1930, 9in (22.5cm), 29.75oz free.
$1,400-1,650

An Edwardian sugar bowl and tongs, London, 1905, 5in (12.5cm) diam.
$250-300

. Continental gilt lined toilet box, he lid inset with a circular ivory laque carved with bust portraits of ouis XVI and Marie Antoinette, by erthold Muller, bearing import narks for Chester, 1907, 6½in 17cm), 16.5oz. gross.
1,300-1,500

A late Victorian brazil nut shape ox, 2in (5cm) long.
$650-800

A Victorian vesta case, Birmingham, 1896, 1½in (4cm) high.
$50-65

An American vesta case, by Gorham Manufacturing Co., c1900, 2½ by in (6 by 5cm).
40-55

A hen on nest box, gilt to the interior, Chester import mark, 5½in (14cm), 10oz.
$1,000-1,200

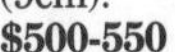

A George III Irish Freedom box, the detachable slightly domed cover engraved with the arms of Cork, the base with presentation inscription, dated 12 July 1780, the side with a crest and Earl's coronet, the maker's mark I.H., struck twice in the cover only, Cork, 3½in (9cm) diam, 5oz.
$5,500-6,500

The crest is that of Meade for the Right Hon. Sir John Meade, first Earl of Clanwilliam.

A Continental vesta case, the front enamelled with a bust portrait of a flaxen haired beauty on a blue ground, import marks for London 1907, 2in (5cm).
$500-550

A George III silver gilt mounted cowrie shell snuff box, the lid engraved with ornate initials within a beaded border, Phipps and Robinson, London 1789, 4in (10cm).
$800-900

A Continental gilt lined cigarette case, the front enamelled with a three-quarter length portrait of a lady holding a closed fan, 3½in (9cm).
$500-550

A Russian silver gilt box in the form of a book, the 'covers' and the 'spine' polychrome cloisonné enamelled with scroll work and flowers in shades of blue, red and white within blue beadwork borders, with fastening clip attached, 4in (11cm).
$900-1,000

A George III vinaigrette by Joseph Willmore, Birmingham, 1816, 4in (10cm) long.
$140-200

An Edwardian card case, Birmingham 1902, 3½in (9cm) long.
$200-300

A French embossed snuff box, possibly Rheims, import mark London, 1890, 2½in (7cm) long.
$330-400

Candelabra

A pair of George II style two-light candelabra, 1968, 8½in (21.5cm), 46oz.
$2,500-3,000

Candlesticks

A pair of George II cast silver candlesticks, with shaped bases decorated with angels, fluted, spiral fluted, and knopped stems and spool-like nozzles, by John Perry, c1752, 34oz.
$2,500-3,500

A pair of George III silver candlesticks, Sheffield 1813, 12in (31cm).
$2,500-3,000

A Dutch gilt lined jewel casket, on caryatid scroll feet, the sides and the hinged cover chased with carousing figures in the style of Tenniers, the underside with 2 presentation inscriptions, 19thC, 10in (26cm), 31oz.
$2,000-2,500

A pair of Victorian beaded four-light candelabra, by Frederick Elkington, Birmingham 1880, 23in (59cm), 180oz.
$6,500-7,000

A pair of early George III candlesticks with cast shaped and stepped square bases decorated with shell motifs, fluted stem and corded spool-shape sconces, by William Cafe, c1763, 36.5oz.
$3,000-4,000

An Edwardian miniature card cas London, 1901, 2in (5cm) high.
$75-90

A pair of candelabra, fitted for electricity, the knopped panelled baluster stems with spool shaped candleholders, on welled square bases with concave corners, the top with a central baluster ornamental candleholder, the detachable nozzle with a pineapple finial and with 3 scroll branches, the candleholder with drip pans, by Hawksworth Eyre & Co., 22½in (57cm).
$1,000-1,200

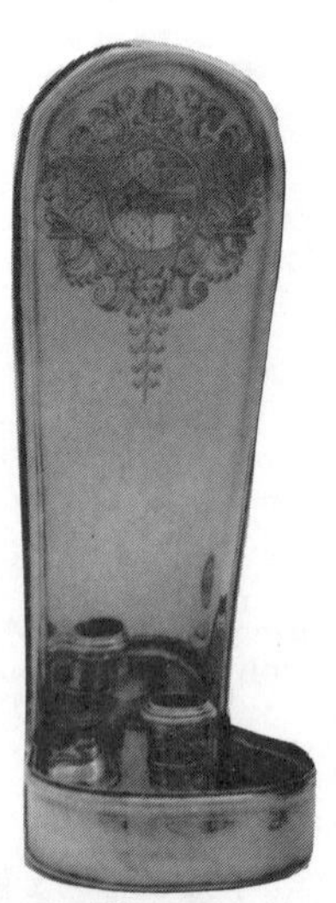
A pair of wall mounted candleholders, each with plain tapering backs and reeded urn shape candlesticks, engraved with an ornate armorial, Britannia Standard, London 1919, 11½in (30cm), 30oz.
$4,000-5,000

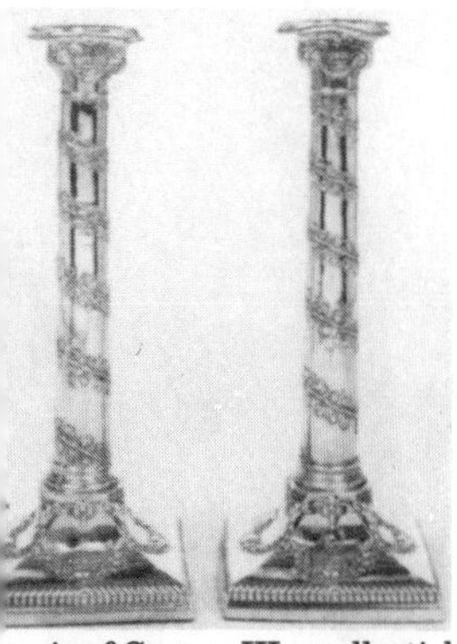

pair of George III candlesticks, ıased with a continuous band of ailing vines, the moulded sockets ith detachable shaped square ɔzzles, each engraved with crests, by Tudor and Leader, ıeffield, c1775, 12½in (32cm).
3,500-4,000

A pair of George III cast silver table candlesticks of baluster form, the knopped stems gadrooned and spiral fluted detachable sconces, gadrooned stepped square bases, by Ebenezer Coker, London 1766, 11in (28cm), 41½oz.
$3,000-4,000

A pair of William IV candlesticks, by Henry Wilkinson, Sheffield 1836, 9in (23cm) high.
$1,000-3,000

Four George III chamber candlesticks, with gadrooned borders and foliage capped scroll handles, with detachable nozzles and extinguishers, by Matthew Boulton and Co., Birmingham 1807, 35oz.
$6,500-7,000

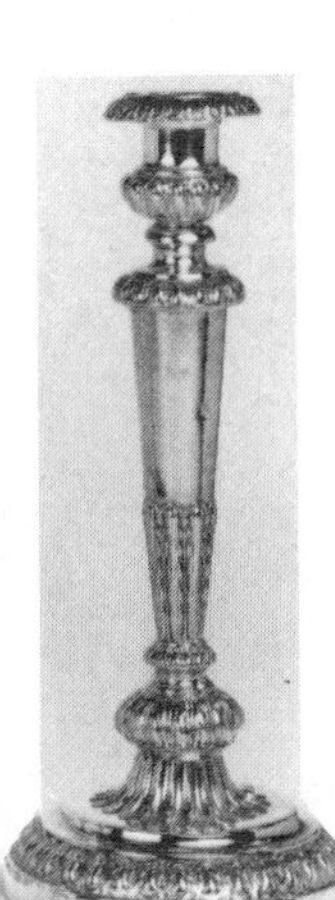

Four large table candlesticks, with ɔartly fluted vase shaped sockets ınd detachable nozzles, engraved with a crest, 2 by Matthew Boulton ınd Plate Co., Birmingham 1826, ınd 2 by R. E. Atkins, Birmingham 1844, 14in (36cm) high.
$6,500-7,000

A pair of silver pillar candlesticks, London 1904, 6in (16cm).
$140-200

A pair of George II cast silver candlesticks, the bases, knops and sconces with corner shell moulding, maker John Cafe, London 1756, 8½in (21cm), 30oz.
$3,000-4,000

Casters

A caster, the domed and pierced cover with bayonet mounts and a turned finial, the body with a moulded circular footrim, the base engraved 'IMP', marked 'HM', probably New York, c1700, 3½in (9cm) high, 3.5oz.
$4,000-6,000

A Queen Anne plain pear-shaped caster, or moulded foot, with a rib round the body and bayonet fitting cover pierced with stylised foliage and with baluster finial, by Charles Adam, probably 1708, marks worn, 8in (20cm), 9oz.
$1,000-1,400

A George II two-tier cruet stand, on 4 shell feet and with leaf capped scroll handle and applied rococo cartouche, fitted with 3 plain vase shaped casters in 2 sizes, each with pierced detachable domed cover with baluster finial and 3 silver mounted clear glass bottles, by Samuel Wood, the stand 1739, the casters 1740, 1742 and 1749, the bottle mounts unmarked, the larger bottle mounts engraved with a crest, largest caster 6in (15cm), 37oz.
$5,000-6,500

A mid-18thC style gadrooned and part spiral fluted vase shaped sugar caster, applied with rococo shell and scroll decoration and on a gadrooned rising circular foot, the spiral fluted cover with chased baluster finial, Goldsmiths and Silversmiths Co. Ltd., London 1915, 9in (22.5cm), 16oz.
$700-1,000

A Victorian coffee pot, in mid-18thC taste, with a leaf capped panelled rising curved spout, ebonised wood scroll handle, and panelled domed hinged cover with octagonal baluster finial, engraved with a crest, the interior fitted with a detachable filter, by W.H., London 1888, 9in (23cm), 18.25oz gross.
$1,000-1,200

Coffee & Chocolate Pots

A Victorian pear shaped coffee pot, chased with the signs of the zodiac in the Indian taste, and with several chased friezes of foliage, with a rising curved spout, double scroll handle and flat hinged cover with fluted finial, Houles & Co., London 1874, 9½in (24cm), 27oz.
$700-800

A George II coffee pot, on moulded foot with leaf capped curved spout, hinged domed cover and baluster finial, maker's mark indistinct, possibly John Lampfert, the cover unmarked, c1750, 9in (23cm), 21oz gross.
$2,500-3,000

A George II coffee pot, the domed hinged lid with turned finial, having a crested cartouche and wooden scroll handle, later engraved with scrolling acanthus and latticework, by Paul Crespin London 1736, 8in (21cm), 30.5oz gross.
$7,000-8,000

A George II coffee pot, on moulded foot, with curved spout and shaped domed cover with baluster finial, engraved with a crest, by R. Gurney and T. Cooke, 1742, 8½in (21cm), 19oz gross.
$3,000-4,000

A George II baluster coffee pot, on gadrooned foot and with leaf capped bird's head spout, and hinged domed cover with spirally fluted vase shaped finial, by Fuller White, 1757, 11in (28cm), 33oz gross.
$5,000-6,500

Cutlery

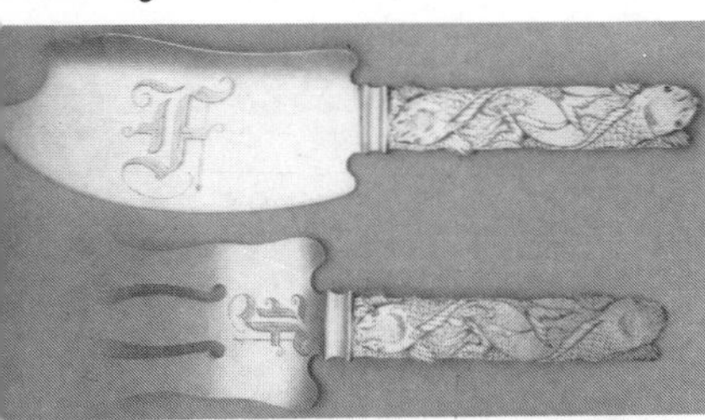

A parcel gilt fish slice and fork, each with a flat handle engraved with 2 intertwined carp, the gilt blade and tines engraved with initial 'F', marked Sterling pat. etching, c1885, slice 11½in (30cm) long, 8oz.
$600-800

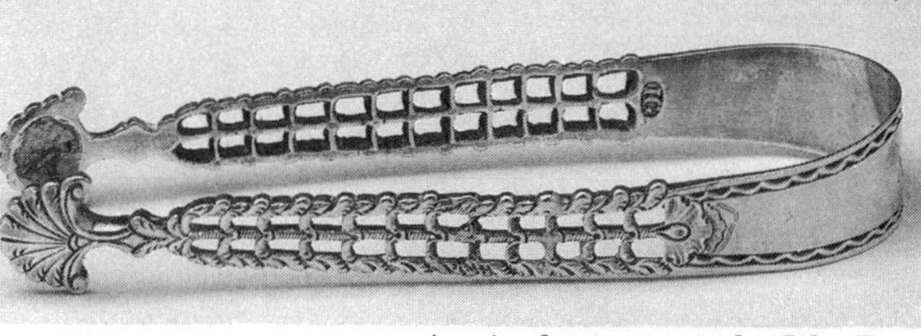

A pair of sugar tongs, by John D. Germon, Philadelphia, the arms pierced in the form of stylised leafage with shell shaped tips, the end with deeply bright cut borders and engraved 'TW' in block letters, marked inside each arm, c1805, 5½in (14cm) long, 1.5oz.
$800-1,500

A pair of tablespoons, by Adam Lynn, Alexandria, Virginia, each with a pointed oval handle and a pointed oval bowl, the handle engraved 'W' in script on front and 'DL' on back, marks partially struck, each marked, c1800, 7½in (19cm) long, 3oz.
$600-700

Three berry spoons, 7in (17.5cm) long. **$80-110**

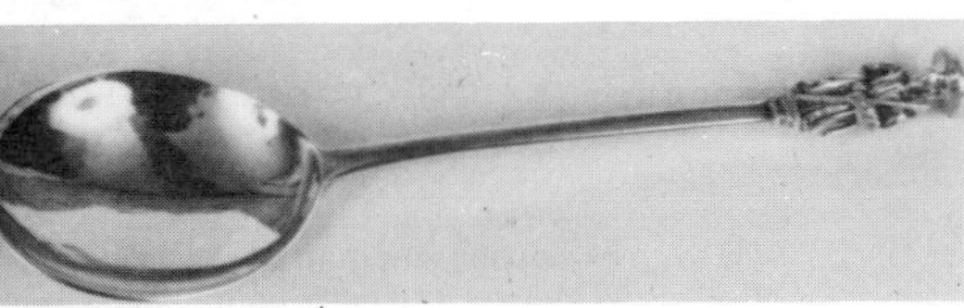

A George II silver Apostle spoon, London 1741, 7in (17.5cm).
$400-550

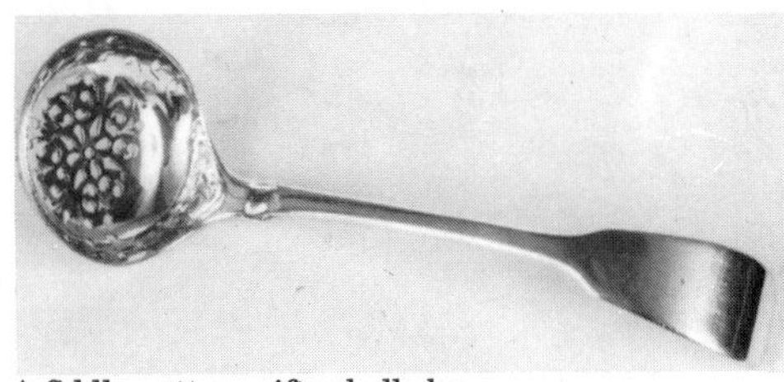

A fiddle pattern sifter ladle by George Adams, London 1844, 6in (15cm) long.
$110-150

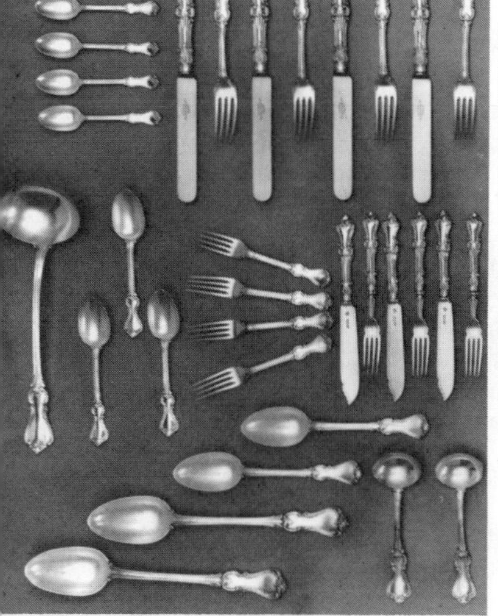

A canteen of Albert pattern cutlery comprising 205 pieces, with loaded tusk pattern handles, London 1859, all fitted with either stainless steel or silver blades, various makers, London and Sheffield 1904-5, in a fitted mahogany case.
$9,500-11,000

A flatware table service of 71 pieces, by Mappin and Webb, feather edge pattern, Sheffield assay, in stained oak canteen, 105oz excluding weighted items.
$2,500-3,000

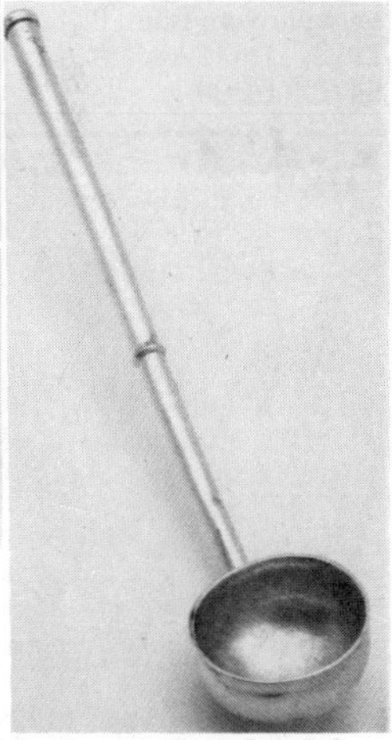

A punch ladle, attributed to John Hastier, New York, the hollow tapering cylindrical handle with a pierced and flower engraved cap at the end and applied with a mid moulding, the circular bowl with a heart shaped join and an everted rim, engraved on the back '3oz. 15dwt', marked, minor repair at handle join, c1735, 13½in (35cm) long, 3.5oz.
$2,000-2,500

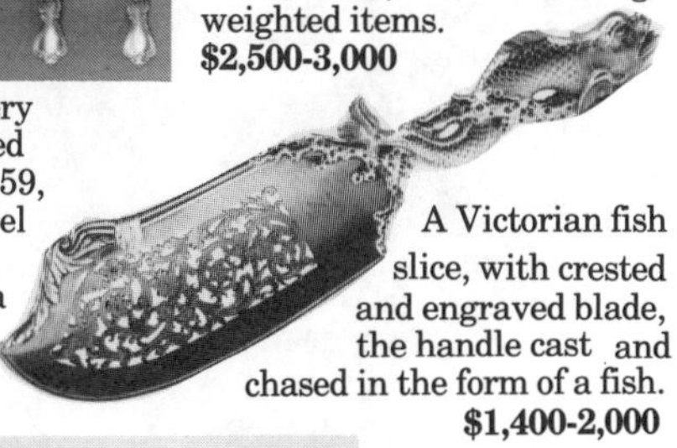

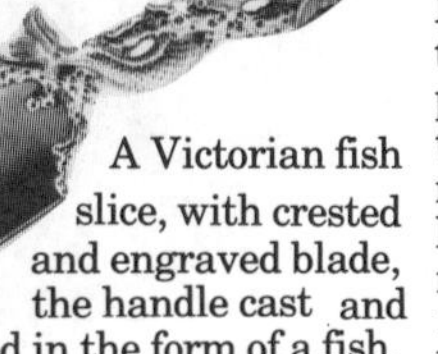

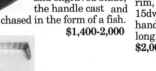

A Victorian fish slice, with crested and engraved blade, the handle cast and chased in the form of a fish.
$1,400-2,000

A pair of George III asparagus tongs, 10in (25cm) long.
$300-400

Dishes

A pair of George III entrée dishes and covers, with ovolo borders and detachable unmarked crest handles, engraved with a coat-of-arms and motto, by William Fountain, 1808, 11½in (29.5cm) long, 103oz.
$5,000-6,500

A pair of silver gilt bonbon dishes, c1862.
$1,400-1,500

Inkstands

A silver travelling inkstand, with central carrying handle, 2 hinged covers affording access to a glass lined interior, the whole supported on 4 claw-and-ball feet, London 1912, 11in (29cm), 92oz.
$4,000-5,000

A George III inkstand, on 4 lion's paw shell and foliage feet, fitted with 2 silver mounted glass inkwells and a wafer box, with detachable taperstick with shell capped ring handle, vase shaped socket and detachable nozzle and conical extinguisher, by Joseph Craddock and William K. Reid, 1819, 11in (28cm) wide, 29oz.
$6,500-7,000

Jugs

A George III foliate chased hot water jug, with chased spout, polished wood scroll handle and gadrooned foliate chased domed hinged cover with baluster finial, by Louis Hearn, London 1766, 10½in (27cm), 22oz gross.
$1,400-2,000

A late Victorian claret jug, in the form of a duck, with slice cut decoration to form the wings and breast feathers, loop handle and 2 front supports, with a silver mount to the neck and cover forming the head, richly chased with feathers, by Henry Wilkinson, Sheffield 1894, 8in (20cm) high.
$2,500-3,000

A lemonade jug, of oval baluster form with scroll handle, the rim moulded with scrolls and anthemia, marked Sterling, J E Caldwell & Co., 9in (23cm). **$650-700**

An Italian hot milk jug, on shell and hoof feet, with a polished wood scroll handle, domed hinged cover with scroll thumbpiece and stylised flower finial, the body and cover later chased with spiral fluting and arabesques, 18thC, 9½in (24cm), 21oz gross.
$4,000-5,000

Mugs & Tankards

A Queen Anne mug, chased with a band of spiral flutes and with applied moulded band above and scroll handle, engraved with a cypher, the base engraved with initials, by Benjamin Pyne, 1705, 4½in (11cm) high, 8oz.
$5,000-6,500

A George II silver tankard, with single girdle, domed form scroll handle and scroll thumbpiece, repair to hinge, by Francis Spilsbury I, London 1736, 23.25oz.
$4,000-5,000

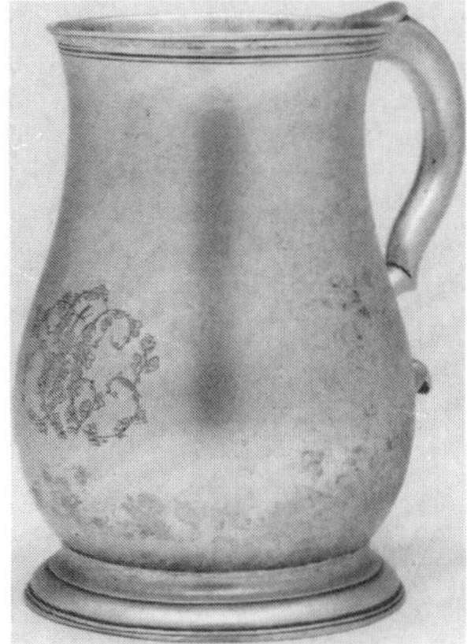

A can, by Joseph Richardson, Sr, Philadelphia, the double scroll handle with a spur terminal and a drop at the upper join, with a moulded rim and a moulded circular foot, the front with a foliate script monogram 'TCE', marked twice at rim near handle, c1764, 5½in (14cm) high, 11.5oz.
$3,000-5,000

A late George III gilt lined goblet, with presentation inscription, by Richard Gaze, London 1807, 8in (20cm) high, 18oz.
$2,000-2,500

A pair of George IV gilt lined goblets, on floral and foliate chased bases, on detachable turned wood plinths, by Edward Barton, London 1824, 7in (18cm) high, 28oz.
$1,400-2,000

Two Victorian silver gilt shell shaped salt cellars, after a design by Edward Hodges Baily, each on oval base cast and chased with simulated waves and shells, surmounted by a merman holding a shell, one by John S. Hunt, 1855, stamped Hunt & Roskell late Storr & Mortimer, 35oz.
$6,500-7,000

Salts

A George III mustard pot, of compressed melon form with leaf capped scroll handle, with blue glass liner, by William Elliott, London 1813, 7oz. **$650-700**

A George III mustard pot, by William Fountain, London 1801, 3in (8cm) high.
$400-500

A set of 6 Victorian salt cellars, with applied floral and foliate chased rims, each cast and chased with extensive rural scenes in the style of Tenniers and each also engraved with a crest, on mask and lion's paw feet, fitted with blue glass liners, maker's initials J.E., possibly James Edwards, London 1846, 3in (8cm) high, 49oz free.
$2,500-3,000

Salvers

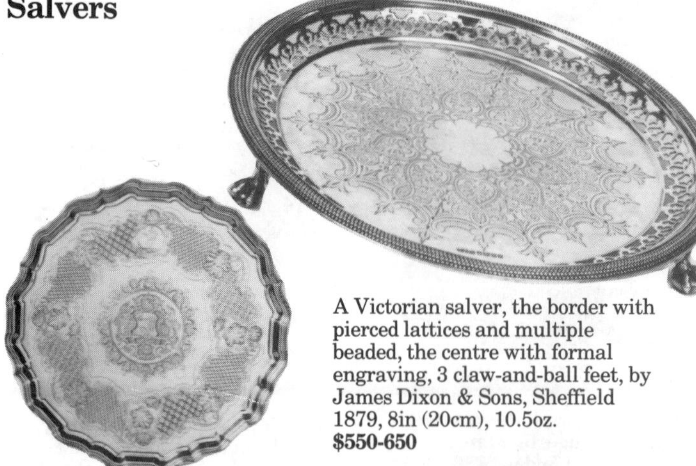

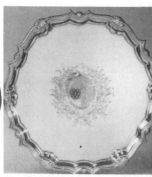

A Victorian salver, the border with pierced lattices and multiple beaded, the centre with formal engraving, 3 claw-and-ball feet, by James Dixon & Sons, Sheffield 1879, 8in (20cm), 10.5oz.
$550-650

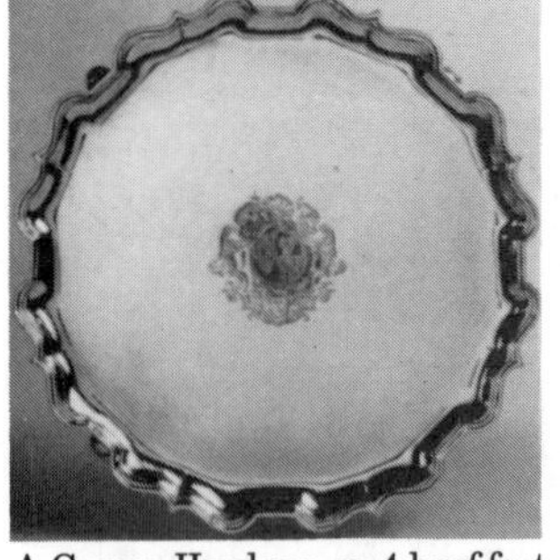

A George II salver, on 4 scroll feet, with moulded border, chased with a band of trellis-work, shells and scrolls enclosing a crest and engraved with a coat-of-arms within a baroque cartouche, by Augustine Courtauld, 1729, Britannia Standard, 13in (34cm) diam, 45oz.
$6,800-8,000

A George II salver, on 3 scroll hoof feet and with shell and scroll border engraved with a coat-of-arms within a floral cartouche, by Robert Abercrombie, 1739, 12in (30.5cm) diam, 27oz.
$3,000-4,000

A Victorian salver, engraved with scrolls and floral festoons, with raised hatched border with cast scroll and mask rim, by The Barnards, 1889, 16in (40.5cm) diam, 49oz.
$1,400-2,000

A George II salver, on 4 hoof feet, with waved moulded border, engraved with a coat-of-arms within a baroque cartouche, by Edward Cornock, 1734, 12½in (31.5cm) diam, 30oz.
$5,000-5,500

A mid-18thC style salver on hoof feet, with a moulded rim and plain ground, by Elkington & Co., 12in (30.5cm) diam, 26oz.
$650-700

A George III salver, with perforated rim, on 4 feet, maker E.R., London 1764, 42oz.
$2,000-2,500

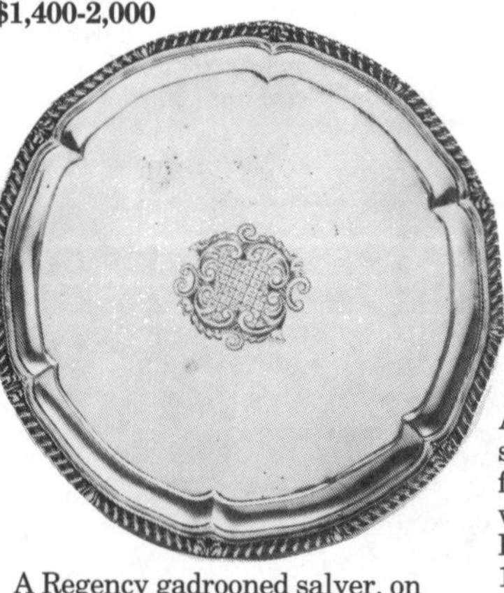

A Regency gadrooned salver, on foliate and floral capped pad feet, the ground engraved with a scrolling foliate cartouche containing an overall trellis design, by Paul Storr, London 1814, 12in (30.5cm), 26oz.
$1,200-1,300

A George III salver, on 4 foliage and scroll feet, with moulded flower, foliage and scroll border, engraved with a coat-of-arms, by William Bennett, 1816, 24in (61.5cm) diam, 178oz.
$6,500-8,000

A Victorian hand-made salver, London 1900, 10in (25cm) diam, 21oz.
$800-900

A George III Irish salver, on satyr's mask feet, applied with a broad border die-stamped with trailing vines with egg-and-dart rim, the ground with later presentation inscription and facsimile signatures, I.S., Dublin 1808, 11in (28cm), 32.75oz.
$1,400-2,000

Sauceboats

A George II plain brandy saucepan, with turned wood handle and moulded lip, engraved with a crest, by John Swift, 1757, 9in (22.5cm) long overall, 9oz gross.
$2,000-2,500

A pair of Victorian sauceboats, with ovolo borders, the lower part of the body chased with vertical fluting, applied above with rams' masks and laurel festoons and wreaths within beaded borders, with reeded scroll foliage handles, by John S. Hunt, 1865, stamped Hunt & Roskell Late Storr & Mortimer, 48oz.
$11,000-12,000

A pap boat, by William Thompson, New York, oval with an everted rim, a curving spout and a scroll handle, one side engraved 'TCD', rhw base engraved 'Sarah Wallace', marked, c1827, 6½in (16cm) long, 3oz.
$500-800

A pair of George III shell-shaped sauceboats, each on cast foot, the body and foot chased with alternate flutes and foliage ribs, with gadrooned and foliage borders and double scroll handles, engraved with a crest, by William Grundy and Edward Fernell, 1779, 34oz.
$6,800-7,300

A George III sauceboat by Samuel Meriton, London 1753, 8in (20cm) wide.
$1,200-1,280

A Victorian three-piece tea service, on open scroll feet, the milk jug and sugar basin gilt lined, each engraved with a crest and motto, by Reily and Storer, London 1850, teapot 8½in (21.5cm) high, 71oz.
$2,500-3,000

Services

A George III tea set, with everted gadrooned borders and leaf and florally engraved band to sides, the strap handles chased with flowers, shells and scrolls, on 4 lion mask bracket feet, the teapot with long shaped engraved handle, the domed hinged cover with oval finial, monograms engraved to sides, by Napthali Hart, London 1819, the sugar bowl and cream jug 1818, 36oz.
$1,400-2,000

A George III York tea service, comprising teapot, cream jug and two-handled sugar basin, with decorative reeded handles on plain circular bases, makers James Barber and William Whitewell, York 1815, 35oz gross.
$2,000-2,500

The base of the teapot is inscribed 'This plate purchased with money won at Doncaster Agricultural Meeting 1816 by a subscription of two guineas each (thirteen subscribers) for the best shearling wether sheep'.

A five-piece tea and coffee service, all of half fluted bulbous form topped with bright cut floral decoration and ebony handles, by Walker & Hall, 3 pieces Birmingham 1921, 2 pieces Sheffield 1902, 83oz gross.
$2,500-3,000

A four-piece tea and coffee service, each of bulbous form with gadrooned edges, angular handles, on ball supports, Sheffield, c1938, 64oz gross.
$1,200-1,300

A four-piece globular tea service, the teapot and hot water jug with foliage capped carved polished wood handles, slightly domed fluted hinged covers with mounted turned wood finials, and foliate capped spouts, the gilt lined milk jug and sugar basin with leaf capped scroll handles, by Rankin & Co., Birmingham 1938, hot water jug 7in (17.5cm) high, 61.75oz gross.
$1,500-2,500

A four-piece tea and coffee service comprising: teapot, coffee or hot water pot, with gauze filter, two-handled sugar bowl and helmet shaped cream jug, each of plain circular form with single ribbed decoration, scrolling handles and plain pedestal bases, Sheffield 1930-31, 57oz gross.
$700-900

A four-piece tea and coffee set, with applied bands to body, scroll handles and spreading bases, the coffee pot and teapot with wooden scroll handles, and scrolling spouts terminating in monsters' heads, the domed and hinged covers with ball finials, by Atkins Brothers, Birmingham 1948, coffee pot 1952, 94oz.
$2,500-3,000

A George III Scottish tea service, each engraved with monogram within a shield shaped cartouche, comprising a teapot and stand, a sugar basin with swing handle, a helmet shaped cream jug and a pair of sugar tongs, maker's mark G & M, Edinburgh 1795 and 1796, the tongs 1795, height of teapot and stand 7in (17.5cm), 40oz gross.
$5,000-5,500

A three-piece tea set, with embossed rococo cartouches, flowers, scrolling foliage and lattices on matted grounds, the teapot by Frederick W. Turton, Birmingham 1899, the sugar bowl and milk jug marked W * T., Birmingham 1902, 37.25oz gross.
$700-800

A Victorian composite tea and coffee service, comprising: 2 teapots, 2 coffee pots, 2 sugar basins and 2 cream jugs, each on circular rim foot, the lower part of the body chased with vertical fluting and with foliage shoulders and beaded rims, the covers with fluted baluster finials, the majority by Martin Hall & Co., London 1875 and Sheffield 1896, etc., 120oz gross.
$7,000-9,000

A five-piece tea and coffee service, by Ball, Black & Co., New York, comprising: a coffee pot, a teapot, a covered sugar bowl, a covered cream jug and a waste bowl, the cast handles with ivory insulating rings, each marked, c1865, coffee pot 10in (26cm) high, 102oz gross.
$3,000-5,000

An Edwardian four-piece coffee service, comprising: coffee pot, hot water jug, sugar basin with swing handle and cream jug, the coffee pot and hot water jug with leaf capped bracket handles, hinged domed covers and vase shaped finials, with reeded waved borders and bright cut with floral swags and vacant oval cartouches, by Walker and Hall, Sheffield 1905, hot water jug 12in (30.5cm) high, 73oz gross.
$4,000-5,000

An Indian Colonial tea and coffee service, of heavy gauge metal, comprising: coffee pot, teapot, two-handled sucrier, milk jug and pair of sugar bowls, by P. Orr & Sons, Madras, c1860, coffee pot 9½in (24cm) high, 119oz.
$2,000-2,500

A Victorian three-piece tea service, with plain loop handles and engine turned trellis decoration, by Elkington and Co., Birmingham 1863, 42oz, in fitted case.
$1,300-1,500

A three-piece tea set of oval lobed form, the teapot with composite handle and finial, maker's mark W A, Birmingham 1931, 38.5oz.
$650-800

A Victorian four-piece tea service of Japanese design, engraved with rosettes and having simulated bamboo spouts, makers R.M. and E.H., London 1881, 70oz.
$1,400-1,500

A six-piece tea and coffee service 2 handled plated tray, by Tiffany & Co., comprising: tea kettle, stand and lamp, teapot, coffee pot, two-handled covered sugar bowl, cream jug and waste bowl, engraved with initials 'RCW', the sugar bowl with upswept handles, the moulded raised cover surmounted by octagonal urn finial, the teapot and coffee pot with similar handle and hinged cover, with upcurved octagonal spout, the tea kettle with similar cover and overhead swing handle, the octagonal stand with 2 curved octagonal supports, the tray with moulded border and applied reeded rim, with 2 reeded scroll handles, 17in (69cm) long, 145oz gross.
$5,000-7,000

A Victorian compressed three-piece tea service, on rising bases and with scroll handles, engraved with monograms, the teapot with a panelled rising curved spout and baluster finial, the milk jug and sugar basin gilt lined, each bearing London hallmarks for 1853 as well as Aberdeen hallmarks, teapot 8in (20cm) high, 51oz.
$1,400-2,000

Tea Caddies

A George III tea caddy, the sides and curved top finely engraved with riband ornament, festoons of husks and foliage, with feather-edge borders and oblong cover with flower finial, maker's mark I.L., 1772, 4½in (11cm) high, 6oz.
$3,000-4,000

A George III tea caddy, with hinged cover and wood finial, bright cut with bands of foliage, floral swags and oval cartouches, each enclosing initials, fitted with lock plate and key, by William Skeen, 1788, 5in (12.5cm) high, 13oz gross.
$4,000-5,000

A pair of Victorian bombé shaped tea caddies in the 18thC taste, on rococo shell and scroll feet and with chased rococo floral and foliate decoration incorporating scroll cartouches engraved with armorials, crests and mottos, the chased and fluted detachable cover with pagoda finials, by Elkington & Co., Birmingham, 7in (17.5cm).
$1,000-1,080

A George III fluted tea caddy, with hinged cover and stained ivory finial, bright cut with bands of rosettes and foliage and engraved with a monogram, by Henry Chawner, 1790, 6in (15cm) high, 12oz gross.
$5,650-6,500

A Victorian tea caddy and cover, maker F.A.P., London 1896, 3½in (9cm) high.
$350-450

Tea Kettles

A George II inverted pear shaped tea kettle, stand and lamp, the stand on 3 leaf capped shell and scroll feet, the kettle with bird's head curved spout, hinged domed cover, flower finial and scroll handle, chased with scrolls and foliage on a matted ground and engraved with a coat-of-arms and crest, each within a scroll cartouche, by William Shaw and William Priest, 1752, 14½in (37cm) high overall, 69oz gross.
$4,000-5,500

A Dutch silver gilt kettle stand, on 3 shell feet with openwork flower and scroll aprons between, the stand engraved with flowers, with reeded border and circular partly fluted lamp, by Hendrik Swierink, Amsterdam, 1768, 317gr.
$1,200-1,400

Teapots

A George III teapot, with tapering angular spout, hinged domed cover, wood finial and beaded borders, engraved with a coat-of-arms and monogram, by Hester Bateman, 1783, 5in (12.5cm), 13oz.
$2,650-3,500

A George IV compressed melon fluted teapot, on a rising foot, with a leaf capped rising curved spout, leaf capped scroll handle and domed hinged cover with fluted button finial, with later presentation inscription, I.W., London 1828, 5½in (14cm), 24oz.
$1,000-1,200

A George III teapot with wood scroll handle and ivory finial, by John Emes, London 1804, 19.25oz gross.
$800-1,000

A George III teapot with scroll handle, allover embossed and engraved with rococo cartouches, flowers, mask, scrolls and foliage on a matted ground, maker's mark I pellet B, 24.75oz.
$800-1,000

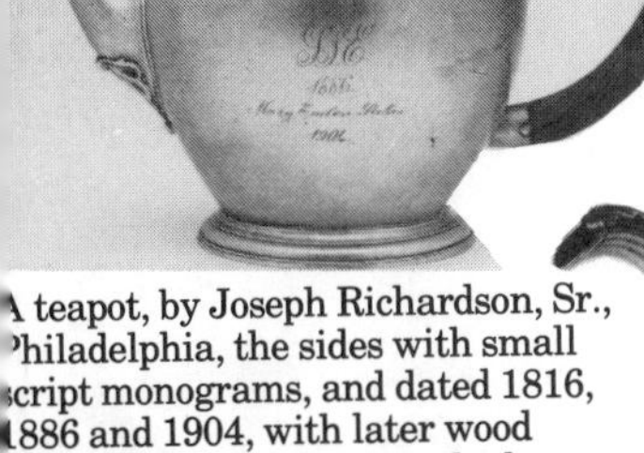

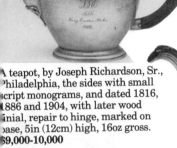

A teapot, by Joseph Richardson, Sr., Philadelphia, the sides with small script monograms, and dated 1816, 1886 and 1904, with later wood finial, repair to hinge, marked on base, 5in (12cm) high, 16oz gross.
$9,000-10,000

A George III reeded teapot, with rising curved spout, polished wood scroll handle and domed hinged cover with ivory pineapple finial, by Peter, Ann and William Bateman, London 1799, 6½in (16.5cm), 14.75oz gross.
$1,300-1,400

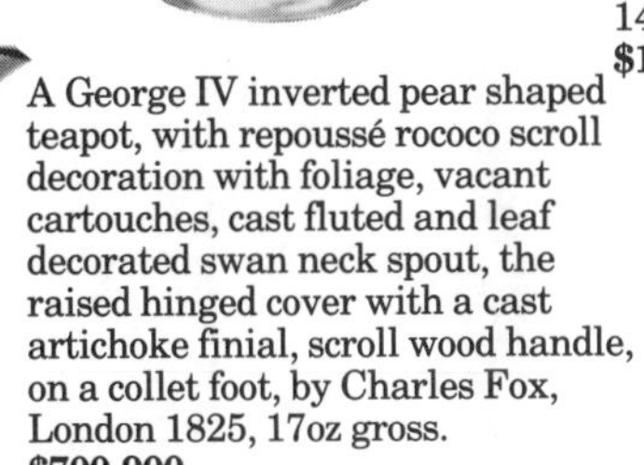

A George IV inverted pear shaped teapot, with repoussé rococo scroll decoration with foliage, vacant cartouches, cast fluted and leaf decorated swan neck spout, the raised hinged cover with a cast artichoke finial, scroll wood handle, on a collet foot, by Charles Fox, London 1825, 17oz gross.
$700-900

A George III teapot with domed, hinged cover, bone finial and curving handle, reeded edges and plain bulbous body, engraved with the Gilbert crest, maker's mark TH/JT, London 1798, 11in (28cm) overall, 15oz gross.
$500-650

A George III teapot, with fluted and chamfered corners, the body with engraved cartouches and bands of scrolls and foliage, ivory handle and finial, by Robert Hennell, London 1791, 15.75oz gross.
$1,000-1,200

A teapot with plain hinged cover, hardwood handle and finial, wrythen fluted body and a plain spout, engraved with the Gilbert crest, maker's mark GL(?), London 1883, 9in (22.5cm) overall, 14oz gross.
$700-900

A George III moulded teapot, with a raised acorn finial and engraved foliate band, by John Emes, London 1801, 8in (20cm), 16oz gross, with a matching stand and a milk jug, 3½in (8cm), 3.5oz.
$2,500-3,000

Tureens

Four George IV plain entrée dishes and covers, with gadrooned borders and detachable foliage, shell and scroll ring handles, engraved with a coat-of-arms, by John Edward Terrey, 1822, 11½in (29cm) wide, 244oz.
$13,500-14,500

Miscellaneous

A Victorian hip flask, London 1864, 5in (12.5cm) high.
$300-350

An Edwardian combined sovereign and half sovereign case, Birmingham 1906, 2in (5cm) high.
$140-150

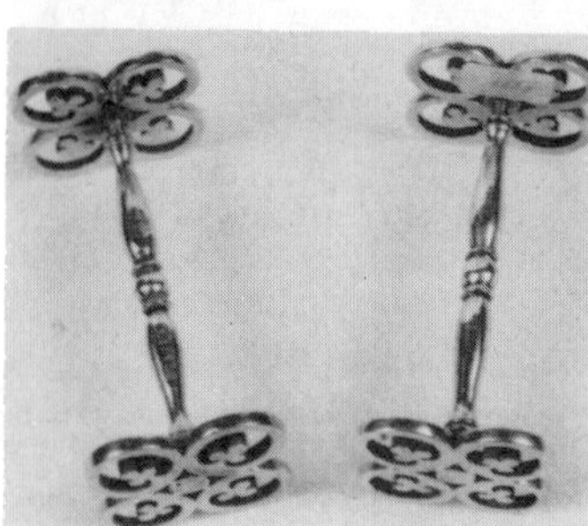

Two knife rests, London 1900, 2½in (6.5cm) long.
$100-130

Toys & Miniature Pieces

A pair of Victorian cast silver models of sheep, 2in (5cm), and a lamb, 1½in (4cm).
$300-400

A George III silver gilt embossed miniature tray, c1800, 3in (7.5cm) wide.
$150-250

An early George V baby's ratt with sliding action articulated monkey, Birmingham 1919 an 1904.
$150-250

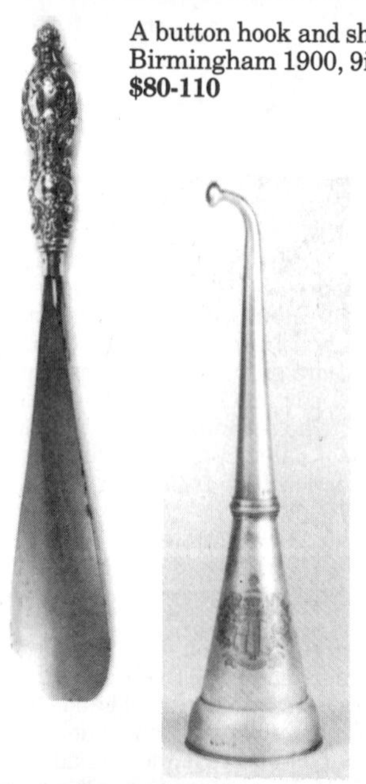

A button hook and shoe horn set, Birmingham 1900, 9in (22.5cm).
$80-110

A rare George IV ear trumpet, with ear piece and moulded borders, engraved with a coat-of-arms within foliate scroll mantling, by Mary Ann and Charles Reily, 1828, 13in (33.5cm) long, 5oz.
$5,000-5,500

The arms are those of Shirley, for Washington, 8th Earl Ferrers (d. 1842).

A George III anchovy collar, c1800, 1in (2.5cm) diam.
$65-80

A George III egg coddler, stand and lamp, on 3 reeded scroll and lion's paw feet and with detachable lamp, the boiler with wood scroll handle and 2 hinged covers each with fluted thumbpiece, containing a wirework frame with central handle and stained ivory finial, engraved with a crest, by Paul Storr, 1798, 9in (22.5cm) high, 27oz gross.
$6,500-7,000

A Victorian easel mirror, 11 by 13i (28 by 33.5cm).
$700-800

A pair of Victorian tapersticks, of slender fluted column form, on animal tripods and concave sided platform bases, by Henry Wilkinson & Co., Sheffield 1870, 6½in (16cm), 3.25oz.
$700-900

A Victorian cigar lighter formed as a lamp, the stem formed as entwined dolphins, the oval body similarly engraved to the foot, with bearded mask terminal and sphinx handle, the hinged cover with cone finial, by Charles and George Fox, 1842, 14oz.
$4,000-5,000

A tea urn of Classical proportions, on 4 reeded and tapered legs with claw feet on a gadrooned base on 4 ball feet, with lion masks carrying ring and a spherical finial on the domed lid, early 19thC.
$650-700

SILVER PLATE

Candlesticks

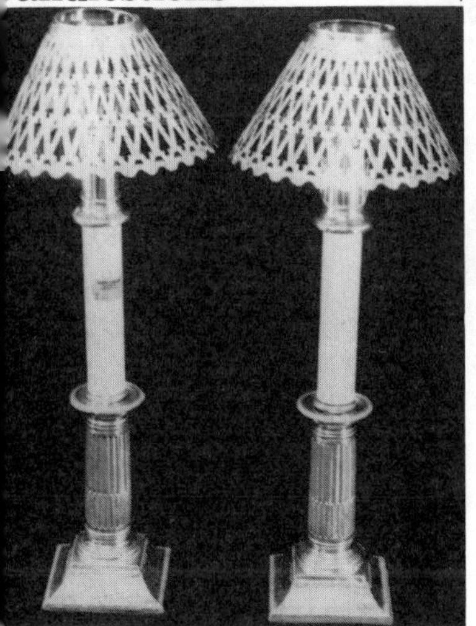

A pair of Georgian style candlesticks, with reeded column and square bases, having spring loaded candle feeds and with .1000 non-matching pierced shades.
$130-150

A candelabrum, c1820, 26in (66.5cm) high.
$1,400-1,500

A set of 8 Victorian table candlesticks, of lobed baluster form with domed bases and detachable sconces, bell marks, 11in (28cm) high.
$1,000-1,300

Services

A four-piece coffee set of demi-ribbed oval form comprising: coffee pot, hot water kettle, stand and burner, a sugar basin and creamer, by Mappin and Webb.
$550-650

Tureens

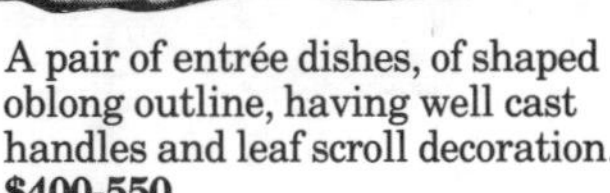

A pair of entrée dishes, of shaped oblong outline, having well cast handles and leaf scroll decoration.
$400-550

A Victorian/Edward VII four-piece tea service, comprising: spirit kettle-on-stand, teapot, sugar basin and cream jug, semi-fluted design embossed with ribbon swags, engraved initials L.B., London, 1898, 1907, 1909 and Sheffield 1898.
$2,000-2,500

Wine Antiques

A pair of English wine coasters, turned from single 'oysters' of laburnum wood, c1700.
$800-1,000

Four George III wine coasters, each on turned wood base, the sides pierced with slats and with beaded borders, by John Smith, Sheffield 1779.
$5,000-5,500

A pair of wirework wine coasters, c1790, 5in (12.5cm) diam.
$400-500

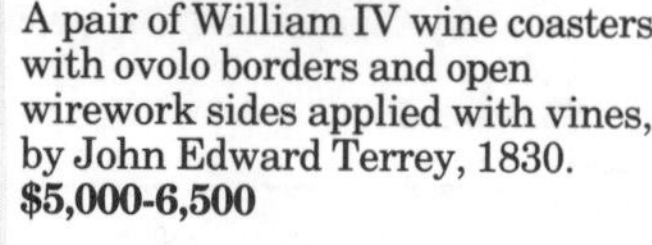

A pair of William IV wine coasters, with ovolo borders and open wirework sides applied with vines, by John Edward Terrey, 1830.
$5,000-6,500

Four George IV wine coasters, wi shaped sides and gadrooned rims, engraved with a coat-of-arms and motto, by Charles Marsh, Dublin 1821, also with the mark of Brow as retailer.
$5,500-6,500

The arms are those of Ruxton.

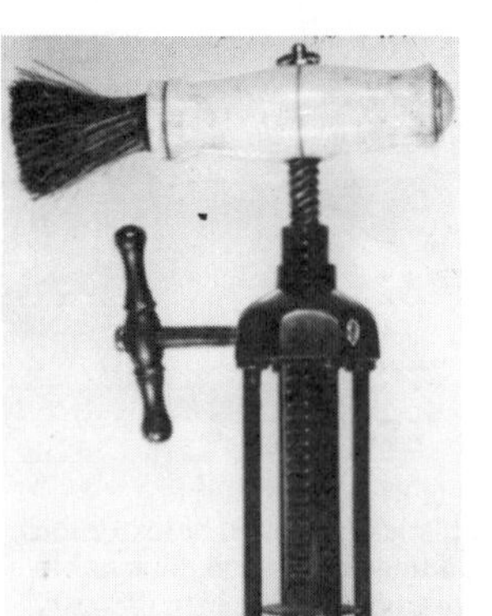

A King's Screw with 4 pillar open frame corkscrew, c1800.
$650-700

A pair of Sheffield plate wine coasters, c1835, 6½in (16.5cm) diam.
$500-550

A set of 4 William IV wine coaster the openwork sides cast with vine tendrils and grapes and with scroll borders, the turned wood bases inse with a silver print engraved with a crest, by Paul Storr, 1831.
$14,000-16,000

A Farrow and Jackson open barrel brass corkscrew, c1850.
$200-250

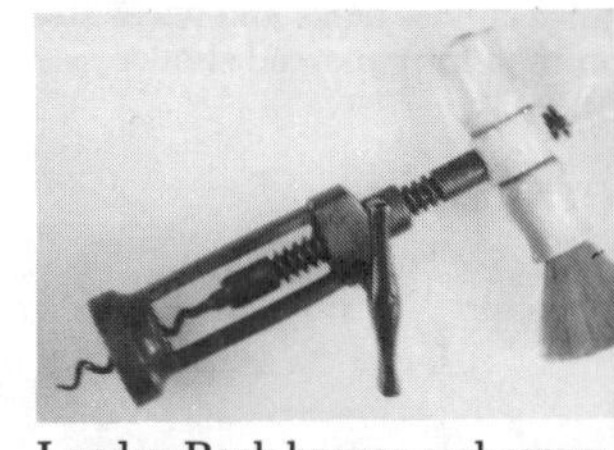

London Rack bronze corkscrew, with open frame and turned bon handle, c1855.
$400-500

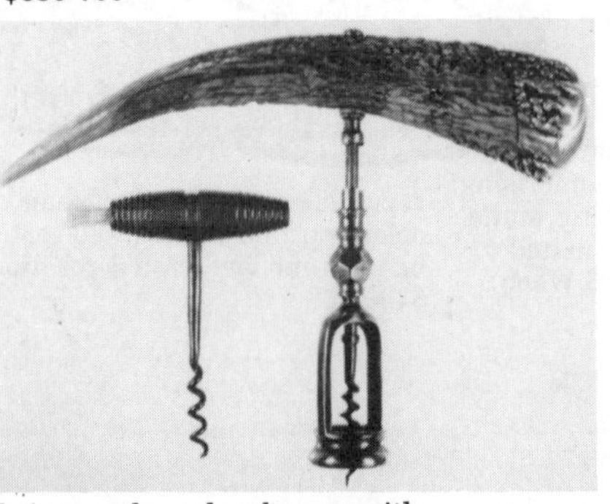

l. A turned wood corkscrew with brush, c1840.
$75-80

r. A gargantuan sized stag's horn handle corkscrew with 'diamant' mechanism.
$600-650

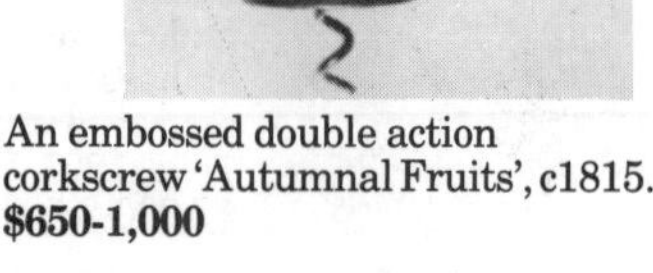

An embossed double action corkscrew 'Autumnal Fruits', c1815.
$650-1,000

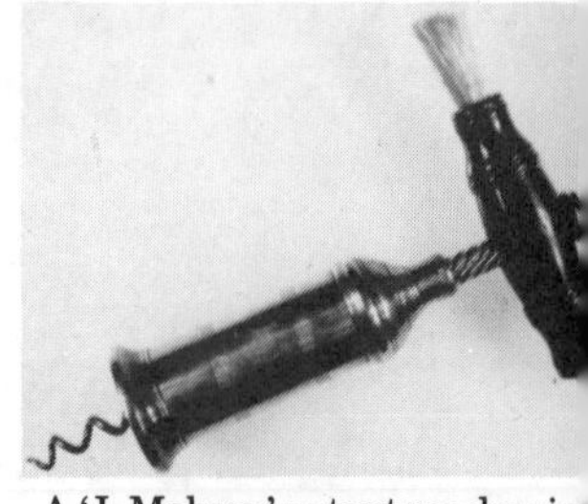

A 'J. Mabson' patent mechanic corkscrew, patented 1869.
$800-1,000

A Hans Eberl limousine, with clockwork motor, opening doors, adjustable brake and steering, near mint condition, c1907, 15in (38cm). **$6,500-8,000**

A very rare JEP Bugatti clockwork racer, near mint condition, c1930, 13in (33cm). **$32,000-40,000**

A Hans Eberl clockwork limousine, adjustable steering and opening doors, near mint condition, c1908, 11in (28cm). **$9,000-9,500**

A Mettoy Police Patrol motor cycle and rider, clockwork mechanism, mint condition, c1938, 8in (20cm). **$1,400-1,600**

A Karl Bub 4-seat tourer, clockwork mechanism and adjustable steering, near mint condition, 10½in (27cm). **$5,000-5,500**

A Bing hand painted lorry, trailer and load, near mint condition, c1908, 19in (48cm). **$26,000-27,000**

A German clockwork open tourer, very good condition, c1905, 8in (21cm). **$3,000-4,000**

A Märklin hand painted tramcar and suede horse, c1898, 11in (28cm). **$25,000-26,000**

A Gunthermann clockwork Town Sedan, mint condition, c1906, 6½in (16.5cm). **$5,000-5,500**

A Hess 4 seater, mint condition, c1925, 8½in (22cm). **$4,000-5,000**

A rare Bing clockwork limousine, minor paint damage, c1908, 11in (28cm). **$30,000-32,000**

A French clockwork runabout, with adjustable front wheels, c1898, 8½in (22cm). **$14,000-15,000**

A rare clockwork Moko open bullnosed Morris, c1930, 7in (18cm). **$5,000-5,500**

A Lehmann No. 555 'Uhu', clockwork amphibious car, c1907.
$5,000-6,500

A Louis Roussy Michelin railcar, powered by a 20 volt electric motor four gauge '0' in 1933.
$6,500-8,000

A Hess limousine, with working flywheel mechanism, opening door glass windows and chauffeur, c1908. **$5,000-6,500**

A Distler 'Standard' oil tanker, clockwork, with adjustable steering, c1935. **$9,000-10,000**

A Gunthermann fire engine, with clockwork motor, 2 firemen and bell, c1907, 6½in (16cm).
$5,000-6,500

A Bing open 4-seater car, with rubber-tyred wheels, clockwork motor, chauffeur and adjustable steering, c1922. **$9,500-11,000**

A Lehmann No. 595 clockwork 'Ihi' grocery van, with mechanically operated roller curtains.
$7,000-9,000

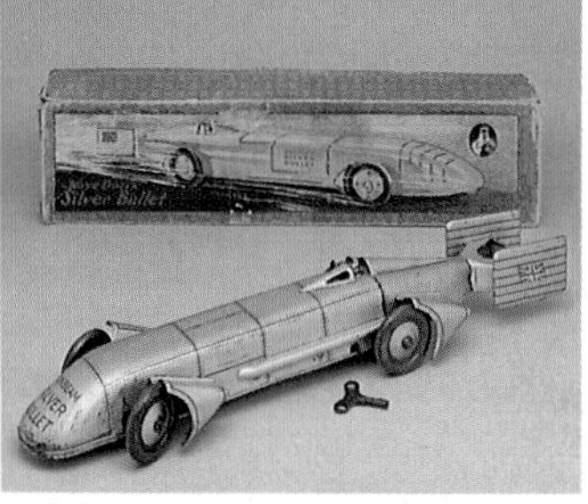

A Gunthermann 'Silver Bullet', Sunbeam record car, with powerful clockwork motor and adjustable steering, with box, 22in (56cm).
$1,500-2,000

A Lehmann No. 350 'Mikado Family', operated by a flywheel mechanism, c1897, 7in (18cm).
$6,500-8,000

A hand enamelled tinplate clockwork, De Dion car, No. 13654, by Bing, c1904. **$3,000-5,000**

A clockwork ship by Bing, c1912, 32½in (83cm) long.
$8,000-9,500

A Märklin, 'The Rheinuferbahn Set', electric, c1929.
$16,000-20,000

A clockwork ship by Bing, one lifeboat missing, c1908, 29in (74cm) long.
$5,000-6,500

A dining car by Bing, with detailed interior, c1904, 21½in (55cm) long
$2,500-5,000

A Jumeau closed mouth doll, all original, c1880, 15in (38.5cm).
$2,500-3,000

A Simon and Halbig lady doll, all original, c1900, 19in (48.5cm).
$2,000-2,500

A pedlar doll, all original, c1836, 13½in (34.5cm).
$800-1,300

A large Norah Wellings Dutch boy, 33in (84cm).
$400-550

An English golliwog, post-war, 27in (69cm).
$25-40

A pressed bisque headed bébé, by Emile Jumeau, marked, c1880, 16½in (42cm).
$8,000-9,500

A pair of poured wax headed character dolls, in original suits, some damage, c1880, 15in (38cm). **$2,500-3,000**

A bisque headed bébé, c1885, 19in (48cm).
$7,000-9,000

A wax over papier mâché headed doll, with spare clothes, in original box, c1785, with later letter, 17½in (45cm) high.
$1,300-2,000

A Steiff plush teddy bear, with some wear, c1910, 20½in (52cm).
$5,000-6,500

A bisque headed bébé, rubbed body, marked BRU Jne.15.
$11,000-16,000

Above. A carved and painted wooden doll with some damage, c1740, 18in (46cm).
$16,000-25,000

r. A clockwork musical automaton, by Phalibois, c1885.
$5,000-8,000

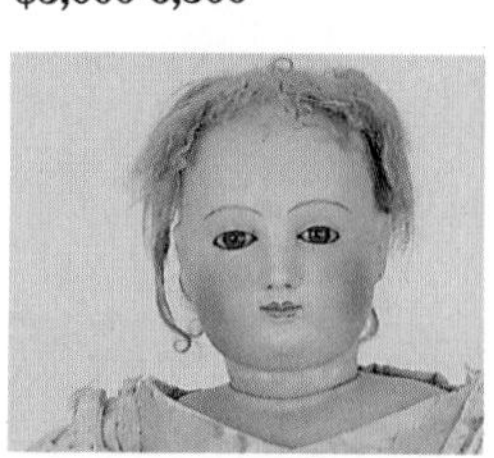

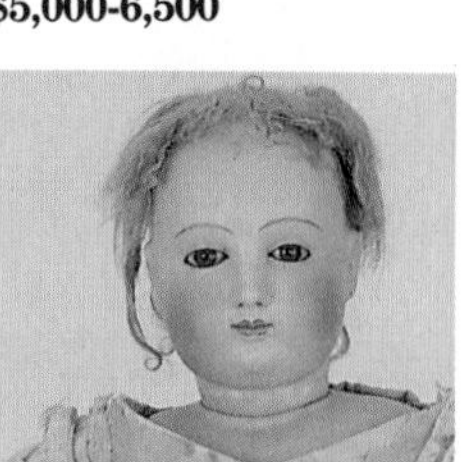

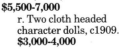

A bisque swivel headed Parisienne, probably Bru, 31½in (80cm).
$5,500-7,000

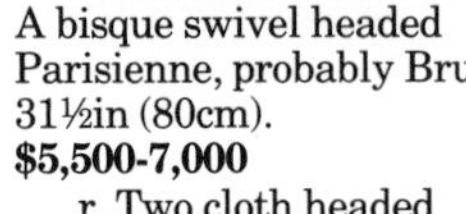

r. Two cloth headed character dolls, c1909.
$3,000-4,000

. fine Mycenaean chalice, painted
ith stylised lotus flowers around
owl with concentric bands below,
art of foot restored, 1400-1200 BC,
in (18cm) high. **$12,000-13,000**

An Attic black-figure exaleiptron or plemochoe, black-glazed inside and out, edge of foot reserved, a band of rays between lines with dots around the rim of the knop handled lid, late 6th Century BC, 8in (21cm) high. **$12,000-16,000**

An alabaster vase, with cuneiform inscription of Entemena, ruler of Lagash, 2404-2375 BC. **$13,000-20,000**

. Greek marble
ınerary stele,
ıscribed and
ıounted, 4th
'entury BC,
3in (83cm).
65,000-73,000

An Etruscan bronze helmet, 5th Century BC, 8in (20cm) high. **$220,000-250,000**

l. A Greek marble head of a female, Hellenistic 2nd-1st Century BC, 6½in (16.5cm). **$14,000-20,000**

A bronze handle, inlaid with gold and silver, c4th Century BC, 8½in (21.5cm). **$7,000-9,000**

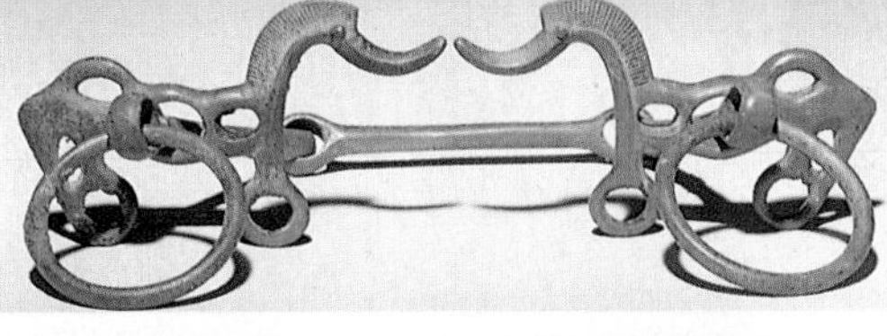

A Villanovan bronze horse bit, 8-7th Century BC, cheek-pieces, 4in (10cm). **$12,000-13,500**

. Celtic bronze terret,
st Century AD, 3½in (8.5cm)
ide. **$8,000-13,000**

Above l. A bronze wagon attachment, c2nd Century AD, 4in (11cm) high. **$4,000-5,500**

Above r. A Roman bronze figure of a gladiator, 1st Century AD, 3½in (9cm). **$5,500-7,000**

l. A Greek bronze mirror cover, 4th Century BC, 6in (15cm). **$13,500-16,000**

r. A bronze figure of Ptah, Late Period, 7½in (19cm). **$9,500-13,000**

A glazed composition syncretistic figure of Thoth, beak restored, Late Period, 4in (10cm). **$10,000-13,500**

A dragon dish, Daoguang seal mark and of the period, 6in (15cm) diam, fitted cloth box. **$1,000-1,500**

A small café-au-lait glazed bowl, Guangxu mark and of the period, 4½in (11cm) diam. **$1,000-1,500**

A Beijing glass carved bowl, Qianlong 4-character mark and of the period, 6in (15cm). **$15,000-20,000**

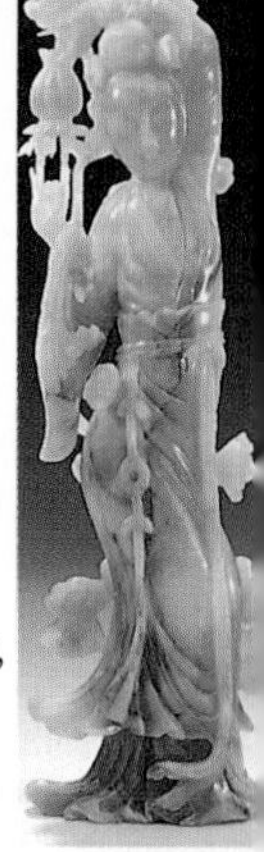

r. A mottled green jadeite figure of Lancaihe, some russet staining, 10in (25cm). **$32,000-40,000**

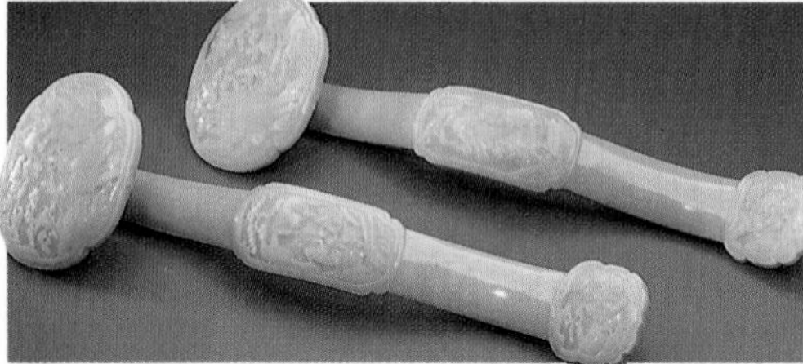

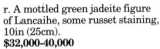

A pair of grey-green jade ruyi sceptres, 17½in (44.5cm) long. **$15,000-20,000**

r. A carved, mottled jadeite group in green and russet, some damage, 8in (20cm) high. **$10,000-15,000**

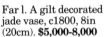

A pair of jade bowls, 19thC, 8in (20cm). **$5,000-7,000**

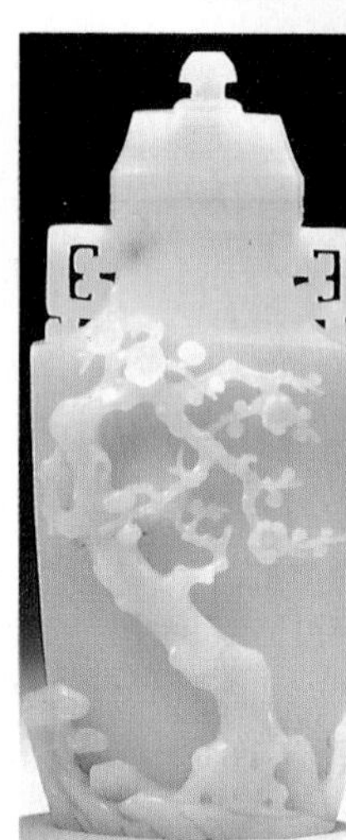

A jade vase and cover, c1800, 11in (28cm) high. **$15,000-20,000**

l. A jade beaker vase, c1700, 9in (23cm). **$15,000-18,000**

Far l. A gilt decorated jade vase, c1800, 8in (20cm). **$5,000-8,000**

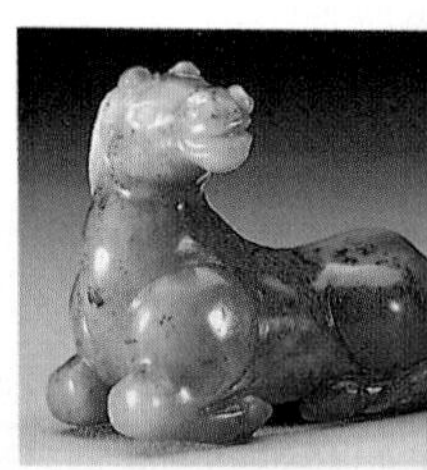

A jade figure of a horse, Tang Dynasty or later, 2in (5cm) long. **$7,000-10,000**

Above. A 2-colour jadeite goat group, 6½in (16cm) long. **$1,500-2,000**

A jade figure of a camel, Song Dynasty, 3in (7.5cm) long, wit wood stand and box. **$8,000-11,000**

Two jade figures, one male and one female, 19thC, 3in (7.5cm) high. **$2,500-3,000**

A jade horse shown in the process of rolling, 3½in (8.5cm) long. **$4,000-5,000**

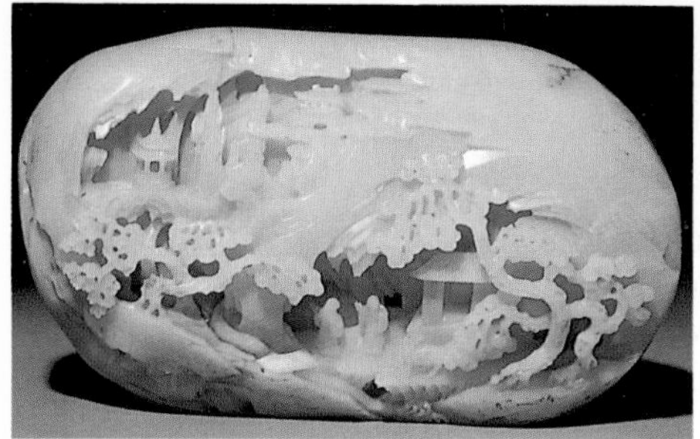

A jadeite flecked cylindrical box and cover, the base with shallow wide footring, 2½in (5.5cm) diam.
$1,500-2,500
r. A celadon jade mountain group, the stone flecked with russet inclusions, Kangxi, 11in (28cm) high. **$8,000-13,000**

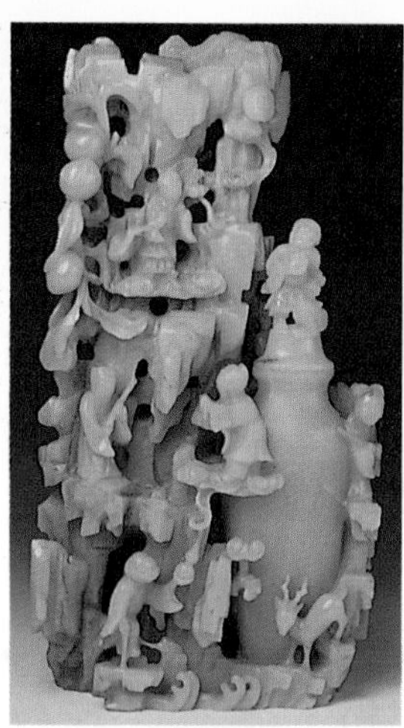

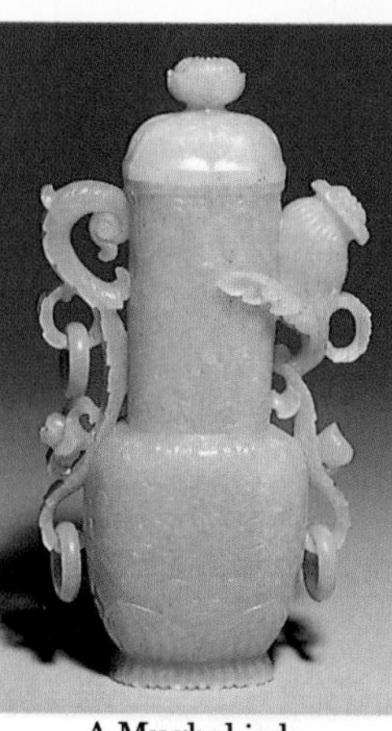

A Mughal jade ewer and cover, the stone of very even tones, 18thC, 8in (20cm) high.
$6,500-8,000

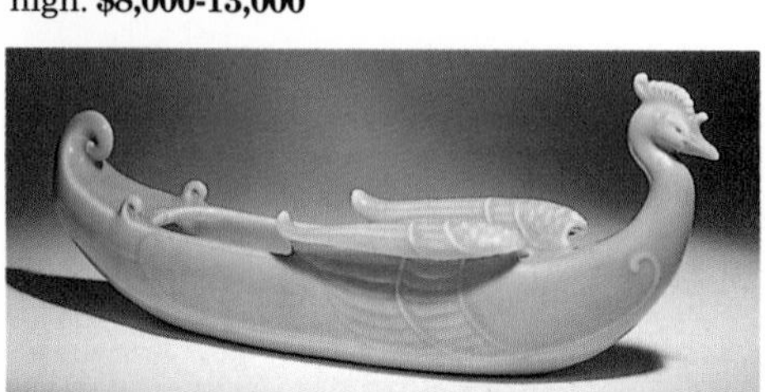

An ikebana vessel in the form of a celadon glazed boat, signed Makuzu Kozan, Meiji period, 17in (44cm) long. **$6,500-8,000**

A pair of black stone water buffalos, partially hollowed underside, late 17thC, 11½in (29cm) long.
$9,000-12,000

A silver and gilt inlaid bronze vase, minor dents, 17thC, 30in (76cm) high.
$6,000-8,000

A pair of bronze vases, 19thC, 23in (59cm) high.
$11,000-13,000

Two gilt splashed bronze censers and covers, mid Qing Dynasy, 10½in (27cm) and 12½in (32cm) high. **$4,000-5,500**
Above l. A Japanese bronze vase, marked, 9½in (24cm).
$5,500-6,500
Above r. An archaic bronze wine vessel, some malachite encrustation, Shang Dynasty, 8in (21cm) high. **$18,000-21,000**
l. An archaic bronze 2-handled vessel, some damage and malachite encrustations, Shang Dynasty, 10in (25.5cm) wide. **$5,000-6,500**
r. A large archaic bronze food vessel, worn in places, Shang Dynasty, 14in (36cm) diam.
$21,000-22,000

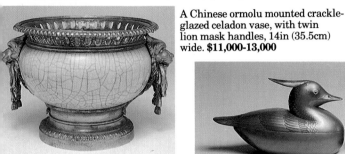

l. A roironuri cylindrical box and cover, Meiji period, 3½in (8.4cm). **$5,000-5,500**

Above. A roironuri suzuribako and bundai, minor chips to bundai, Meiji period, bundai 23in (58.5cm) wide. **$6,500-8,000**

A rare gold almond shaped openwork plaque, Five Dynasties, 3½in (9cm) high. **$21,000-25,000**

A Chinese ormolu mounted crackle-glazed celadon vase, with twin lion mask handles, 14in (35.5cm) wide. **$11,000-13,000**

A pair of gold fundame kobako, modelled as male and female mandarin ducks, both with some damage, late 19thC, 7½in (18.4cm) long. **$7,000-9,000**

An enamelled silver teapot and cover, the body worked in gold and silver wire, minor restoration, triangular mark with S.M., Meiji period, 7in (17cm) high. **$6,500-8,000**

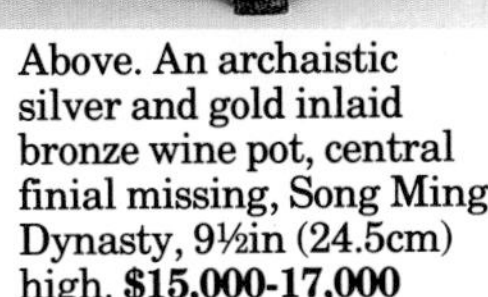

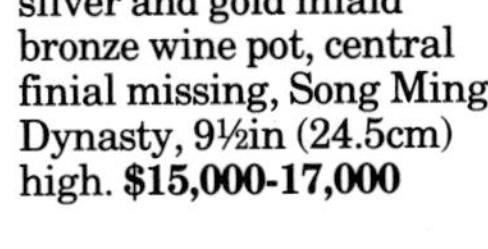

Above. An archaistic silver and gold inlaid bronze wine pot, central finial missing, Song Ming Dynasty, 9½in (24.5cm) high. **$15,000-17,000**

A pair of iron stirrups, 19thC, 11½in (29cm) long. **$5,000-6,500**

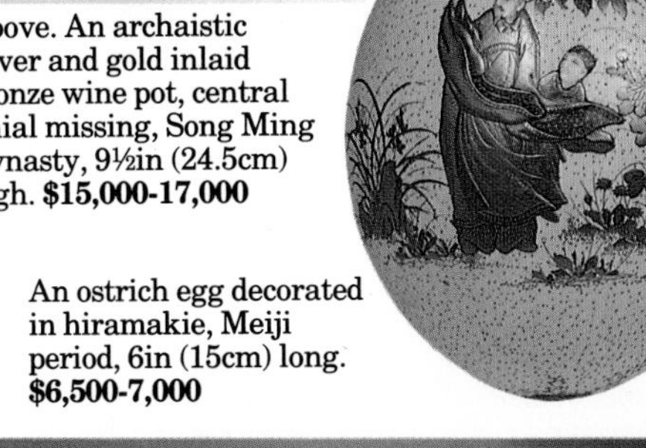

An ostrich egg decorated in hiramakie, Meiji period, 6in (15cm) long. **$6,500-7,000**

A lacquered tonkotsu, unsigned, with ivory netsuke and ojime signed Shogyoku, late 19thC. **$4,000-5,500**

A flat inkstone with bamboo box and lid, 17th/18thC, 4in (10cm). **$18,000-20,000**

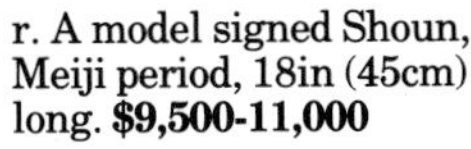

r. A model signed Shoun, Meiji period, 18in (45cm) long. **$9,500-11,000**

A late Ming gilt bronze seated figure of Guandi, his robe bordered with peony, 17thC, 14in (35.5cm) high, fitted box. **$24,000-26,000**

An enamelled and gilt bronze model of a Buddhistic lion, on layered rock with peony flowers, some restoration, 18thC, 10in (25.5cm) wide. **$16,000-20,000**

A pair of cloisonné enamel quail censers and covers, minor bruising, feet damage, Qianlong, 6in (14.5cm) high. **$14,000-16,000**

A Ming gilt bronze polychrome cloisonné enamel beaker vase, vajra on base, 15thC, 7in (18.5cm). **$150,000-160,000**

A pair of cloisonné enamel deer, each supporting a detachable double gourd vase, Qianlong, 9½in (24.6cm) high. **$13,000-15,000**

A pair of cloisonné enamel moon flasks, with gilt kui dragon handles, slight damage, 19thC, 26in (66cm) high. **$9,000-12,000**

A group of 4 cloisonné enamel tripod incense burners and covers and 2 vases, Qianlong, largest 11in (28cm) high. **$13,000-16,000**

r. A miniature lacquer kodansu, with fitted interior, 19thC, 5in (12.5cm) high. **$17,000-20,000**

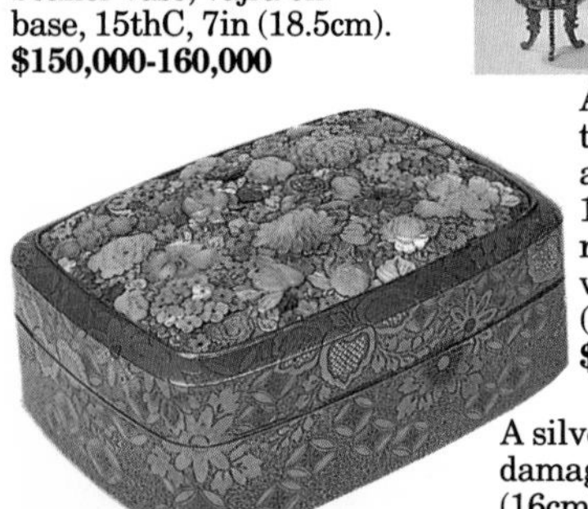

A silver rimmed shell box, damage, signed, 19thC, 6½in (16cm) wide. **$5,500-7,000**

l. A silver rimmed box and tray, presented by Prince Hirohito, slight damage to tray, 19thC, box 6in (14.5cm) wide. **$10,000-11,000**

r. A pewter rimmed bunko, brocade lined, worn, 18thC, 13in (33cm) wide. **$6,500-8,000**

l. A kobako with 3 hishigata on a nashiji tray, slight damage, 19thC, 4½in (12cm). **$16,000-20,000**

r. A lacquer box, minor damage, 19thC, 10in (25cm). **$4,000-5,000**

A jewelled, silver and nephrite ashtray, marked Fabergé, Moscow, c1910, 6½in (16cm) diam.
$9,000-10,000

A large shaded enamel silver-gilt kovsh, by Vasilii Agafanov, Moscow, c1910, enamelled overall in peonies and tulips, engraved with various donors' signatures under the handle, 13in (33cm) long.
$13,000-14,000

A Fabergé picture frame, c1890, 4½in (11.5cm).
$20,000-25,000

A Fabergé gold and guilloche enamel frame, c1900.
$25,000-32,000

A vodka service by the Imperial Glass Factory, Russian proverb on flask, 8 glasses and tray, dated 1875, flask 10in (25cm) high. **$5,000-6,500**

A five-piece shaded enamel desk set, some surface wear, with Imperial warrant of Pavel Ovchinnikov, Moscow, c1910, stand 8½in (21.5cm) wide.
$16,000-20,000

An enamel silver gilt beaker, by Khlebnikov, c1910.
$2,500-3,000

An ormolu mounted lapis lazuli and marble commemorative plaque, by Count Fedor Tolstoi, inscribed, 1824, 11in (28cm) square.
$7,000-10,000

A silver mounted hardstone lamp and matching glue pot, the mounts marked Fabergé, c1890, lamp 6in (15cm).
$20,000-25,000

A Russian neo-classical bone sewing box, with lidded compartments, probably Arkhangelsk, c1775, 8in (20cm) high.
$4,000-5,000

Mother of God Eleousa of Kykkos, 18thC, 17in (43cm).
$6,500-7,000

l. The Virgin Kazanskaya in silver-gilt cloisonné enamel, marked Borisov, c1890, 12½in (32cm) high.
$6,500-8,000

A pair of shaded enamel silver gilt tea caddies, marked Fabergé, c1910, 5in (13cm) high.
$22,000-26,000

A pair of panels of Archangels Michael and Gabriel for an Iconastas, repainted, 16thC, 30½in (77.5cm) high.
$9,000-9,500

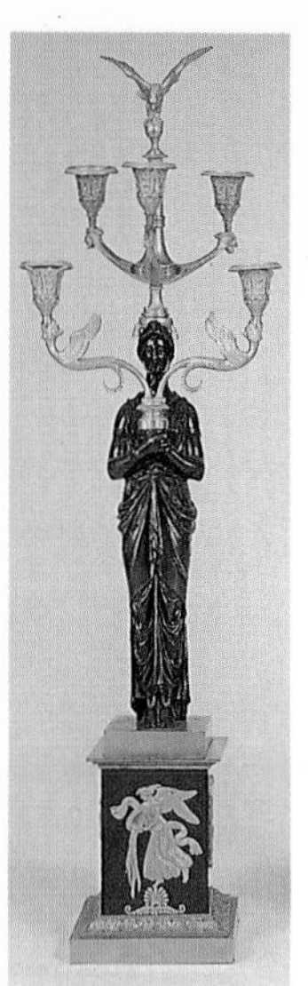

Above l. A pair of Empire bronze and ormolu candelabra, 34in (86cm) high. **$16,000-20,000**
Above r. A pair of Louis XVI bronze and ormolu candelabra, 31in (79cm) high. **$11,000-16,000**

Above. A set of 4 ormolu and bronze candlesticks, mid-19thC, 11in (28cm) high. **$9,500-13,000**

A gilt metal 10-branch chandelier, late 19thC, 33in (84cm) high. **$5,000-6,500**

l. A pair of Empire ormolu and patinated bronze candelabra, drilled for electricity, restorations, early 19thC, 34½in (87cm). **$25,000-30,000**

Above. A Continental gilt brass and copper hall lantern, fitted for electricity, late 19thC, 51in (129.5cm) high. **$6,500-9,500**

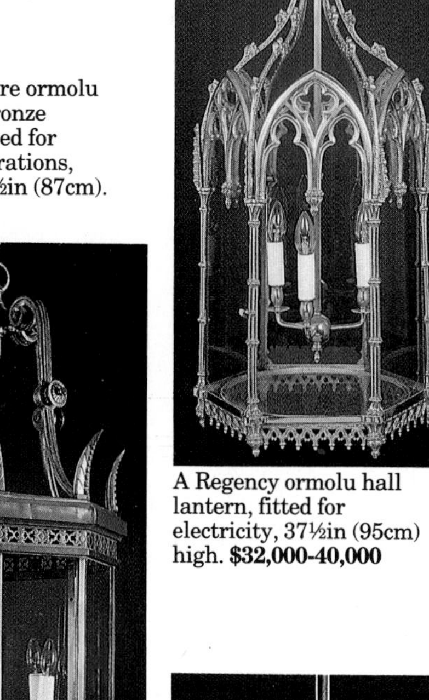

A Regency ormolu hall lantern, fitted for electricity, 37½in (95cm) high. **$32,000-40,000**

A pair of Louis Philippe ormolu and patinated bronze wall lights, drilled for electricity, mid-19thC, 36in. **$9,000-12,000**

l. A set of 6 ormolu wall lights, mid-19thC, 36½in (93cm) high. **$16,000-25,000**

A pair of ormolu wall lights, mid-19thC, 43½in (110cm). **$2,500-3,000**

l. A pair of Continental ormolu mounted rock crystal and malachite urns, fitted for electricity, 30in (76cm) high. **$8,000-11,000**

A pair of Regency ormolu, bronze and cut glass 3-light candelabra, 1 drip pan replaced, 21½in (54cm) high.
$13,000-16,000

A pair of Empire ormolu and patinated bronze 3-light candelabra, early 19thC.
$13,000-16,000

A matched pair of Empire ormolu and bronze 5-light candelabra, c1810, 33in (84cm).
$14,000-16,000

A pair of Empire ormolu 3-light candelabra, c1810, 17in (43cm).
$11,000-13,000

A pair of ormolu mounted Sèvres bleu nouveau 5-light candelabra, some cracks, 35in (89cm) high.
$11,000-14,000

A Louis XVI ormolu 6-light chandelier, drilled for electricity, c1780, 33½in (85cm) high.
$12,000-18,000

A Regency cut glass 21-light chandelier, restorations, 84in (213cm) high.
$50,000-65,000

A pair of ormolu and rock crystal 12-branch chandeliers, 19thC, 38in (97cm) high.
$25,000-30,000

A Regency ormolu hanging dish light, 25in (64cm) diam.
$14,000-16,000

An ormolu hall lantern, mid-19thC, 32in (82cm) high.
$13,000-16,000

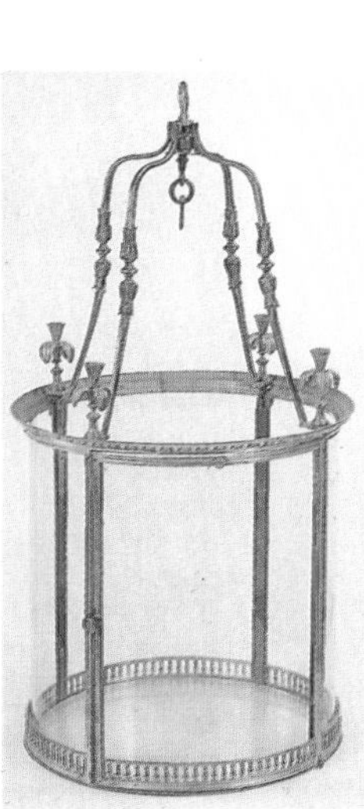

A pair of mahogany and painted copper wall lanterns, restorations, 29in (74cm) high.
$18,000-21,000

l. A Louis XVI ormolu hall lantern, 44in (112cm) high.
$50,000-65,000

A pair of early Victorian ormolu mounted ivory and ebonised candlesticks, inset with precious stones. **$2,000-3,000**

A pair of Regency ormolu, cut glass and Wedgwood porcelain candlesticks, 12in (31cm) high. **$2,500-3,000**

A pair of candlesticks. **$3,000-5,000**

A pair of ormolu and porcelain candelabra, late 19thC, 20½in (52cm) high. **$2,500-3,000**

A gilt brass and enamel 10-light chandelier, fitted for electricity. **$3,000-5,000**

A Victorian cut glass 10-light chandelier, restorations, 42in (107cm) diam. **$8,000-11,000**

A Danish ormolu and cut glass 6-light chandelier. **$6,500-8,000**

An Empire bronze and ormolu 6-branch hanging light, drilled for electricity, 40in (101.5cm) high. **$7,000-9,500**

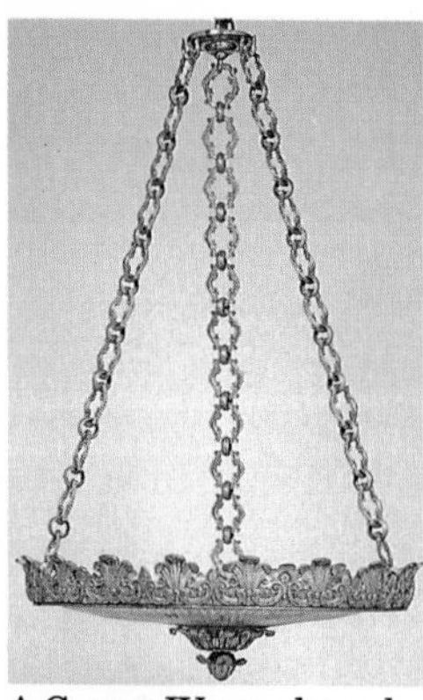
A George IV ormolu and cut glass dish light, 27in (69cm) diam. **$13,000-16,000**

A pair of Empire bronze and ormolu tripod brûle parfums. **$18,000-20,000**

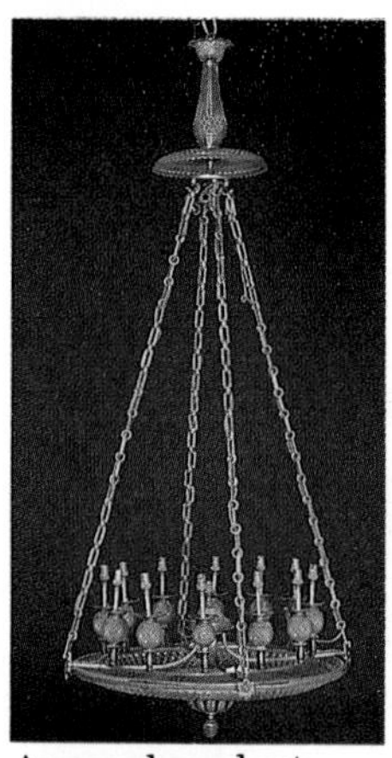
An ormolu and cut glass 12-light hanging light, part early 19thC. **$13,000-15,000**

l. An ormolu mounted, sang de boeuf vase, fitted for electricity. **$8,000-9,000**

A pair of parcel gilt mahogany, wall lanterns, 12in (31cm) wide. **$13,000-14,000**

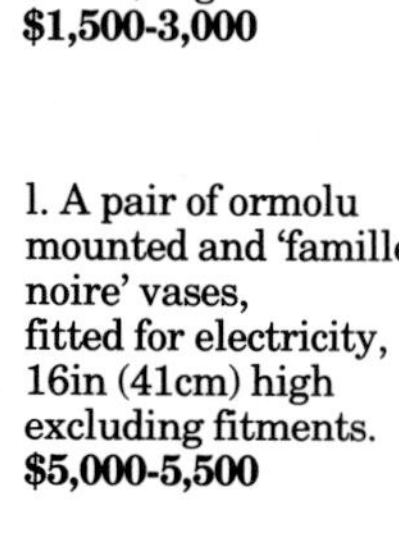
An ormolu and steel lampe bouillotte, 27in (69cm) high. **$1,500-3,000**

l. A pair of ormolu mounted and 'famille noire' vases, fitted for electricity, 16in (41cm) high excluding fitments. **$5,000-5,500**

An etched Italian Infantry half armour, probably Milanese, some damage and restoration.
$32,000-40,000

A relic Iberian dagger with scabbard.
$1,500-2,500

A British Life Guards helmet and cuirass, c1870.
$2,500-3,000

A French Caribinier trooper's brass faced cuirass, some cleaned rust, dated 1864.
Est. **$2,500-3,000**

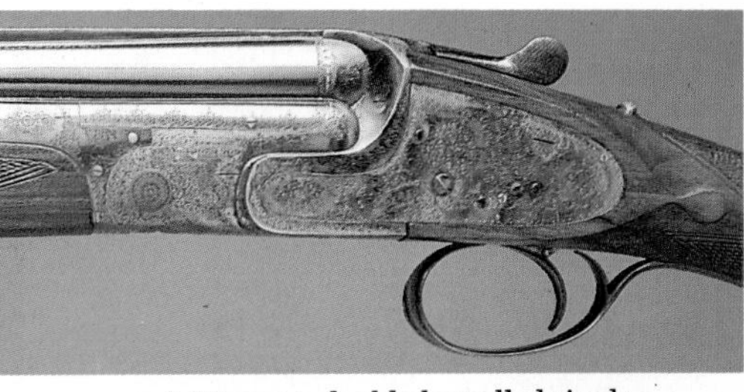

A 20-gauge double barrelled single trigger over-and-under hammerless sidelock ejector gun, by Boss, No. 9098, c1958. **$35,000-40,000**

A German seige weight helmet, c1600. **$3,000-3,500**
l. A lobster tail helmet, probably Polish, c1650. **$1,000-1,200**

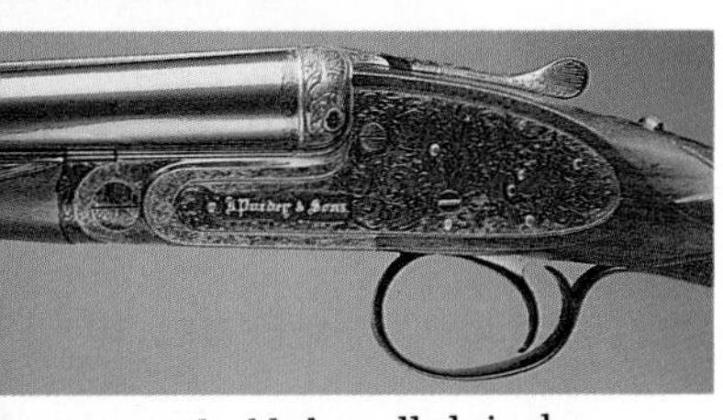

A 20-gauge double barrelled single trigger hammerless sidelock ejector gun by J. Purdey, No. 26166, c1959.
$25,000-30,000

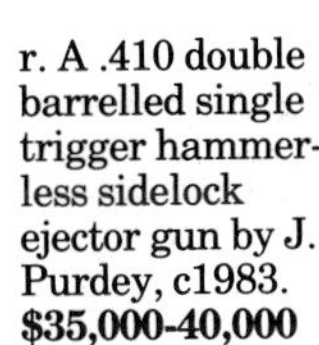

r. A .410 double barrelled single trigger hammerless sidelock ejector gun by J. Purdey, c1983.
$35,000-40,000

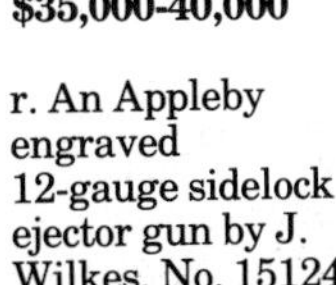

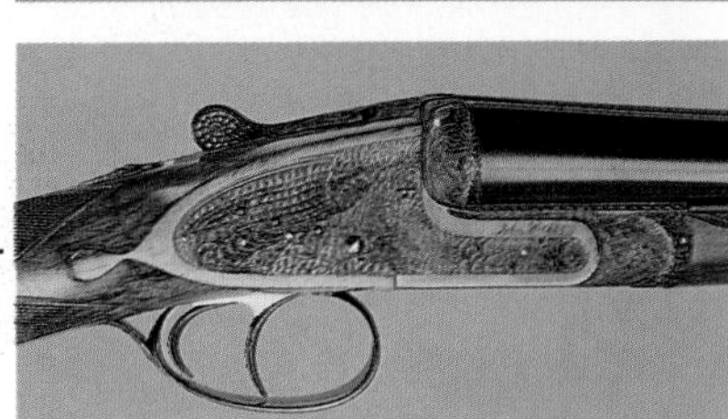

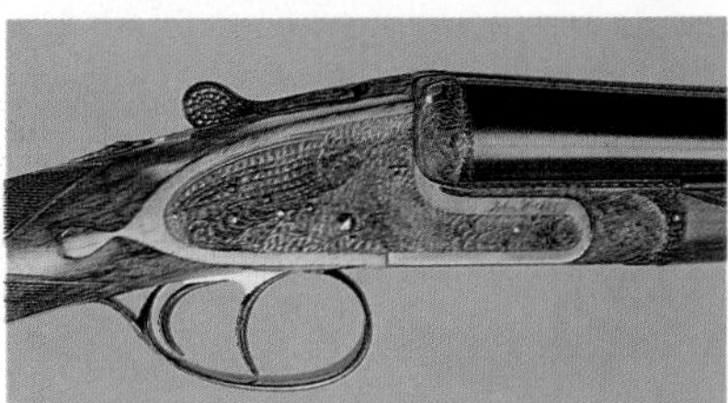

r. An Appleby engraved 12-gauge sidelock ejector gun by J. Wilkes, No. 15124.
$28,000-30,000

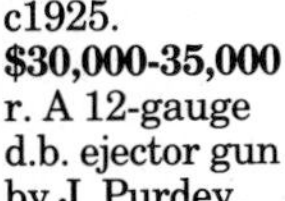

l. A pair of 12-gauge d.b. hammerless ejector guns by J. Purdey, c1925.
$30,000-35,000
r. A 12-gauge d.b. ejector gun by J. Purdey, c1965.
$16,000-25,000

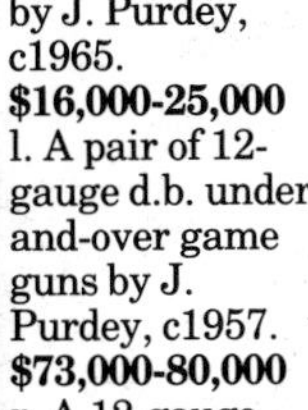

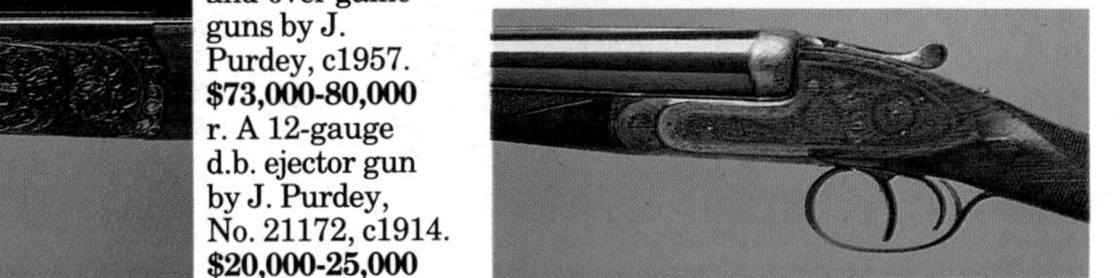

l. A pair of 12-gauge d.b. under-and-over game guns by J. Purdey, c1957.
$73,000-80,000
r. A 12-gauge d.b. ejector gun by J. Purdey, No. 21172, c1914.
$20,000-25,000

The Most Noble Order of the Garter, Lesser George sash badge, chips to cameo border, early 19thC, in fitted case.
$16,000-20,000

The Most Noble Order of the Garter, Lesser George sash badge, some chips to enamel.
$35,000-40,000

The Most Noble Order of the Garter, Lesser George sash badge, early 19thC, in case.
$18,000-20,000

The Most Noble Order of the Garter, Lesser George sash badge, some damage to enamel, early 19thC.
$30,000-32,000

The Most Noble Order of the Garter sash badge, c1800.
$35,000-40,000

The Most Noble Order of the Garter sash badge, mid-18thC.
$65,000-70,000

The Most Noble Order of the Garter badge.
$30,000-32,000

The Most Noble Order of the Garter badge, mid-17thC.
$50,000-55,000

A pre-1914 Imperial Austrian Artillery officer's shako, in its original case. **$1,500-2,500** and a Bavarian General officer's pickelhaube, with original lining. Est. **$1,500-2,080**

A pair of pre-1855 Light Company officer's dress wings. Est. **$400-500**

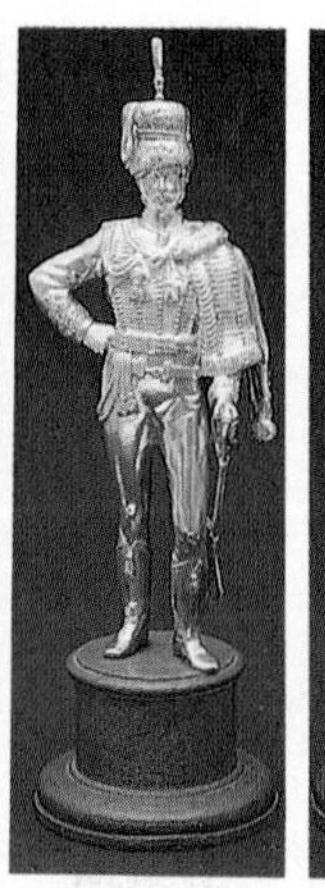

A set of 3 H.M. silver, London, military officer figures, 7in (18cm) high. **$1,500-3,000**

A bronze figure of Edward, Prince of Wales, 1936.
$1,500-3,000

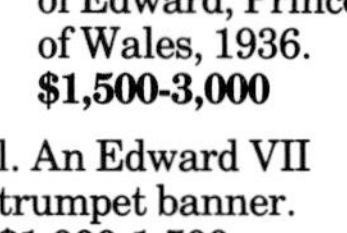

l. An Edward VII trumpet banner.
$1,000-1,500

A Spanish bronze cannon, barrel inscribed and dated 1639, on later carriage.
$7,000-8,000

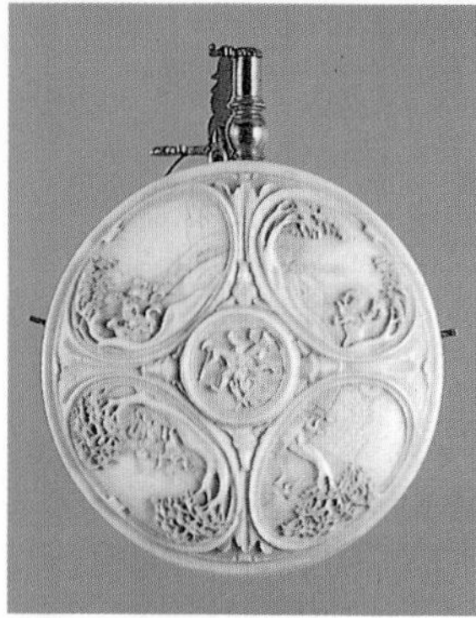

A German carved ivory powder flask, late 17thC, 5½in (14cm) high.
$16,000-20,000

A Partisan head of the Yeoman of the Guard with Edward VIII cypher, both sides etched, blued and gilt, with lined wooden case, c1936, 24½in (62cm) overall. **$2,000-3,000**

An Italian knightly sword, with double edged blade, c1400, 32in (81cm) blade.
$16,000-20,000

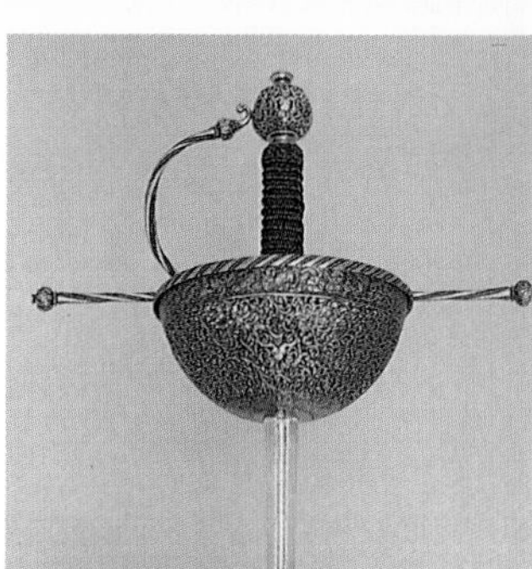

An Italian cup hilt rapier, with original wire bound wooden grip, c1660, 40½in (103cm) blade.
$13,000-20,000

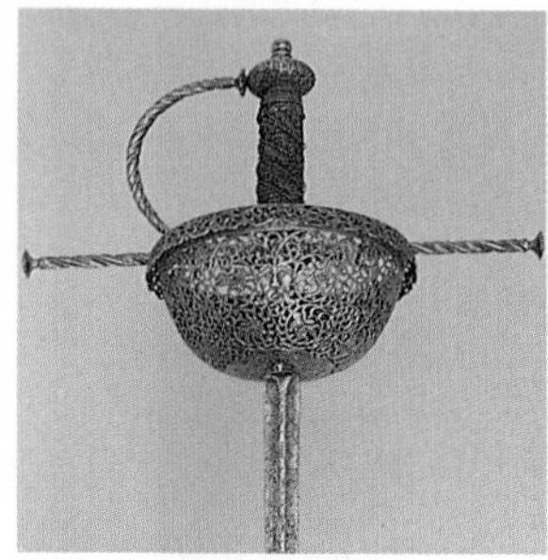

A Neapolitan cup hilt rapier, c1660, 44½in (113cm) blade.
$13,000-16,000

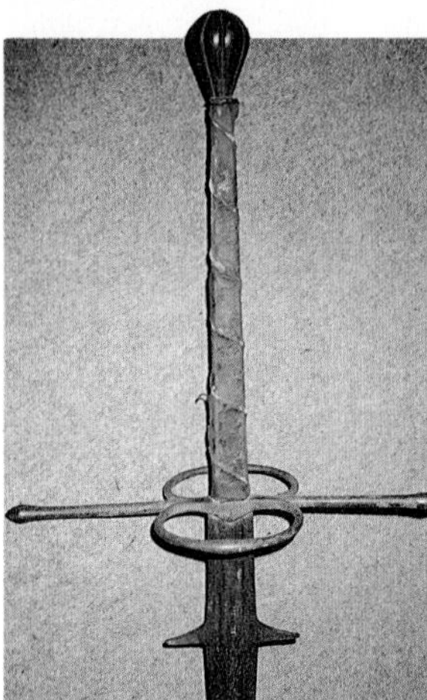

A German two-handed sword, c1500.
$2,500-3,000

An engraved gold medal, 1st Volunteer Movement, c1804.
$4,000-5,000

The Most Noble Order of the Garter Registrar's badge in gold and enamel, in original red leather case with riband, c1816.
$16,000-18,000

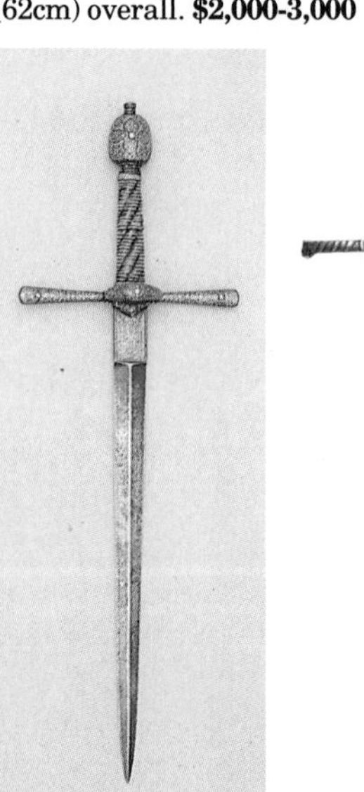

A left-hand dagger, with spirally fluted wooden grip, late 16thC, 18in (46cm). **$14,000-16,000**
Above r. A German main gauche dagger, c1620. **$2,000-2,500**

A German rapier, the hilt covered in silver, c1620.
$9,500-13,000
Above r. A basket hilt sword, c1740. **$550-650**

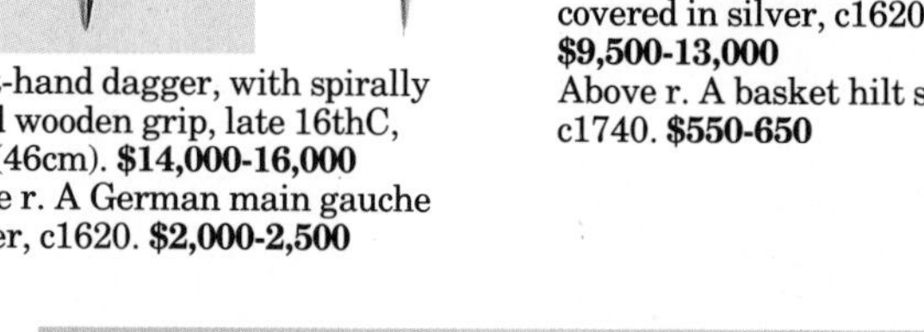

The Most Noble Order of the Garter breast stars, mid-19thC.
$5,000-6,500 each

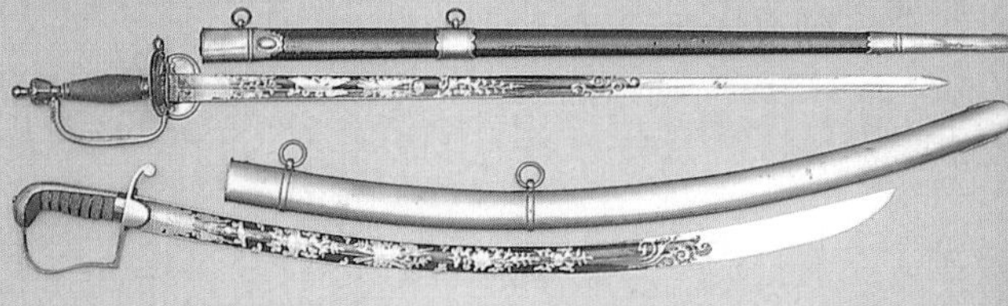

A Georgian 1796 pattern Light Cavalry officer's sabre with curved blade, 33in (84cm), steel scabbard.
$2,500-4,000
A Georgian 1796 pattern Infantry officer's sword, engraved 'Fras. Deakin Birmn', blade 32in (81cm). **$800-1,500**

A pair of French silver mounted double barrelled flintlock pistols by Chasteau à Paris, 1749 Paris silver marks, 14½in (37cm).
$14,000-16,000

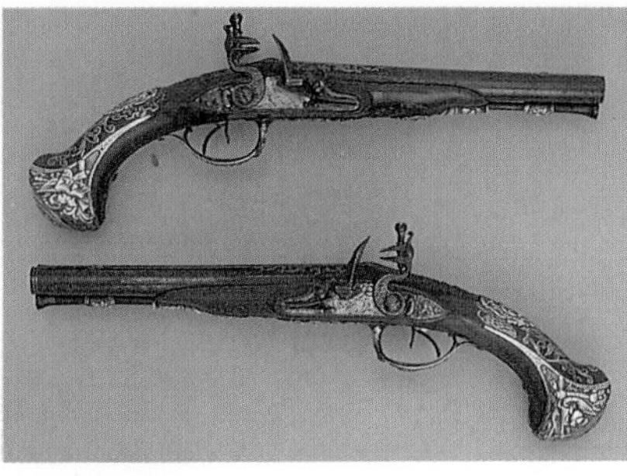

A pair of flintlock duelling pistols, by Joseph Manton, London, No. 4532 for 1805.
$9,500-16,000

A Spanish double barrelled miquelet pistol, the stock overlaid with brass, c1740.
$1,300-1,500

l. A 6-shot 120 bore revolver, by F. Barnes & Co. and engraved.
$1,300-1,500

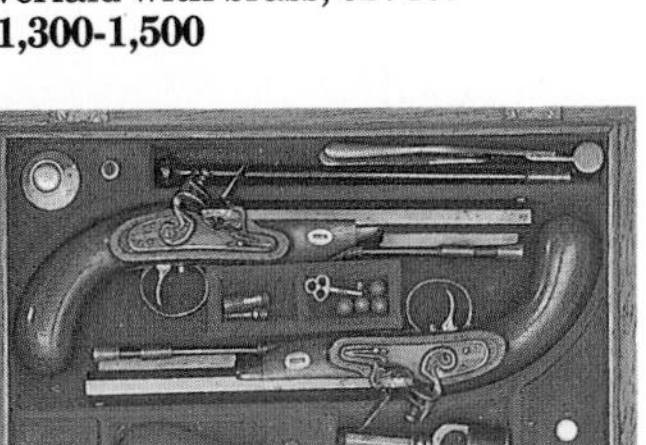

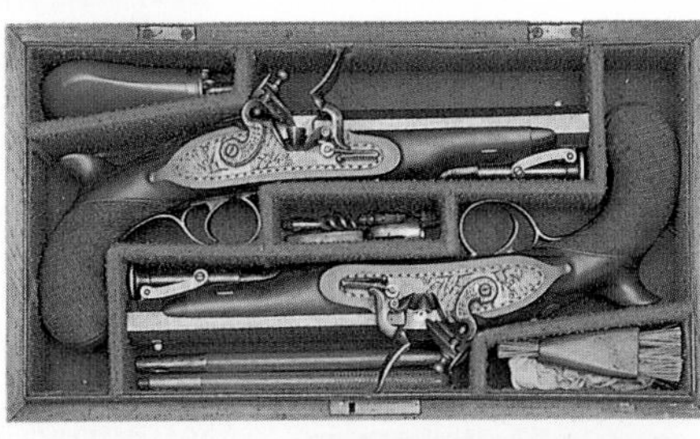

l. A pair of miniature flintlock duelling pistols, in the style of c1810.
$1,400-2,000
r. A pair of saw-handled flintlock officer's pistols, early 19thC.
$11,000-16,000

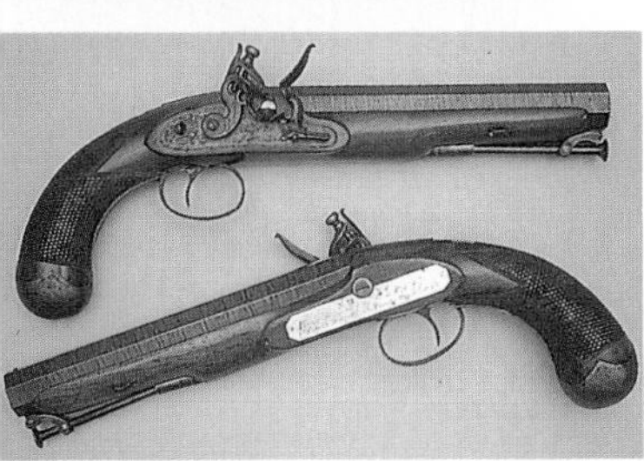

A pair of presentation 10 bore flintlock holster pistols by Westley Richards, 1832.
Est. **$5,000-6,500**

A pair of French double barrelled flintlock pistols, c1740.
$5,000-5,500

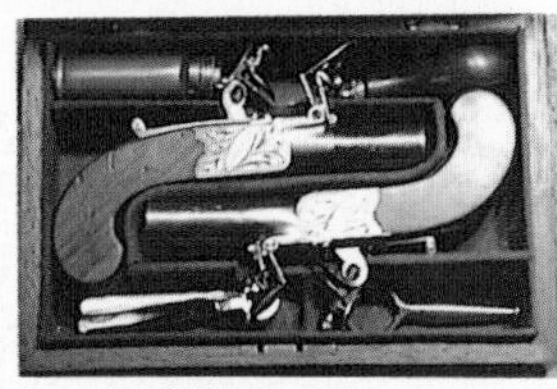

A pair of flintlock boxlock pocket pistols, complete in case, c1780.
$1,000-1,200

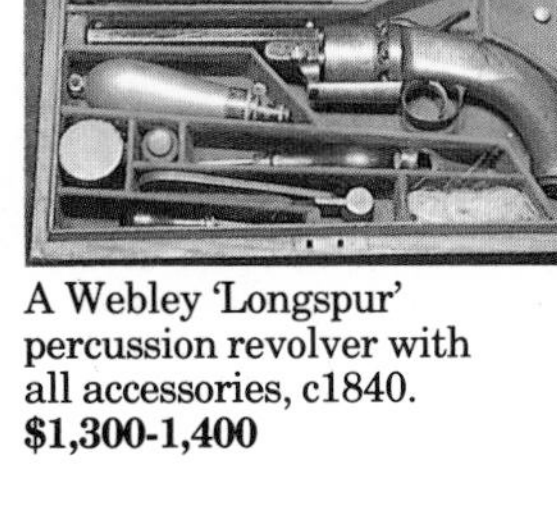

A Webley 'Longspur' percussion revolver with all accessories, c1840.
$1,300-1,400

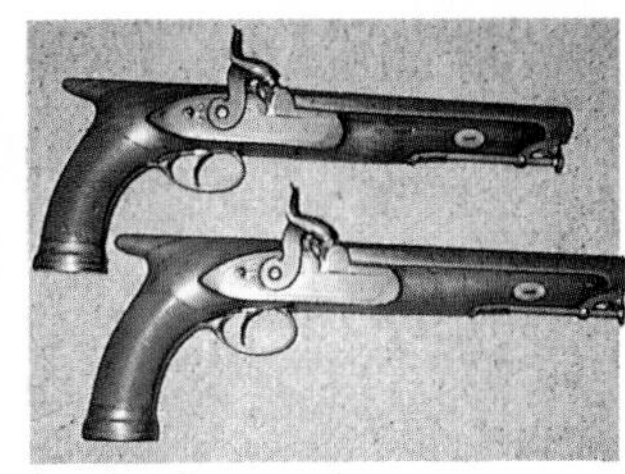

A pair of percussion saw handled pistols, c1840.
$2,500-3,000

A pair of flintlock duelling pistols by John Manton, 1831, 15in (38cm).
$14,000-20,000

A prototype-experimental Colt open top single action revolver, 'N.M. Navy 1871'.
$16,000-20,000

A Colt pocket percussion revolver, No. 102789, 1849, 9in (22.5cm).
$5,000-6,500

A 16-bore flintlock sporting rifle, with earlier Turkish browned etched twist octagonal barrel, by Bate, London proof marks, c1790, 32in (81cm) barrel. **$5,000-5,500**

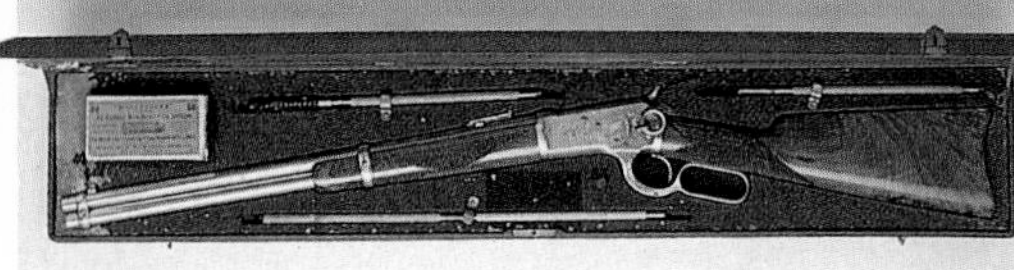

A factory engraved and cased Winchester model 1892 lever action carbine, No. 60909, .44-40 calibre, maker and calibre markings on the barrel, in excellent condition, case interior with some damage, 20in (51cm) barrel. **$32,000-40,000**

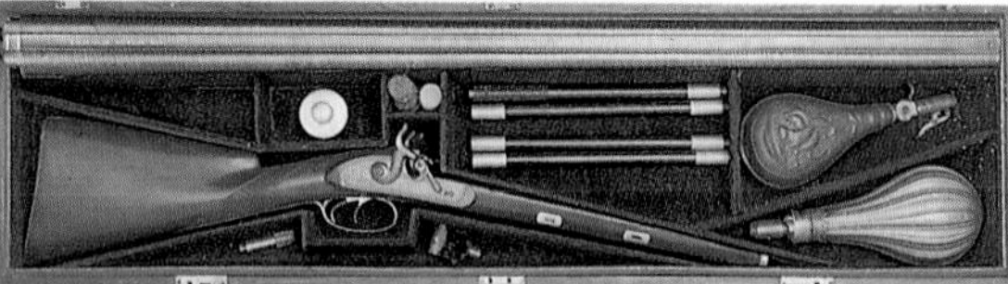

An 8-bore double barrel silver mounted tubelock fowling gun, original silver tipped ebony ramrod and much original finish, silver hallmarks for 1845, 42½in (108cm) barrels. **$8,000-9,000**

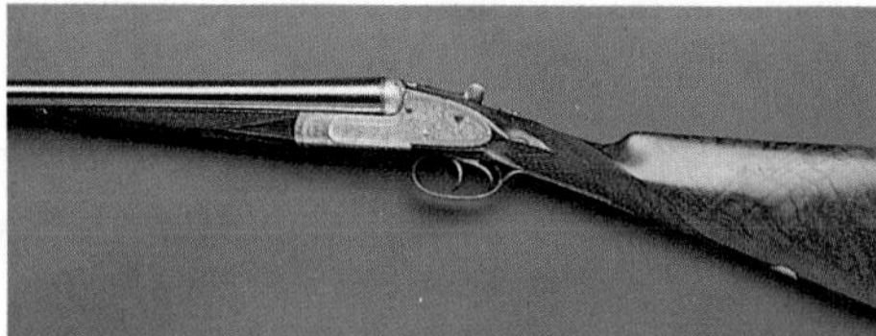

A light 12-gauge 'Royal' double barrel hammerless sidelock ejector gun, by Holland & Holland, No. 16567, the barrels possibly shortened, 28in (71cm) barrels. **$7,000-9,000**

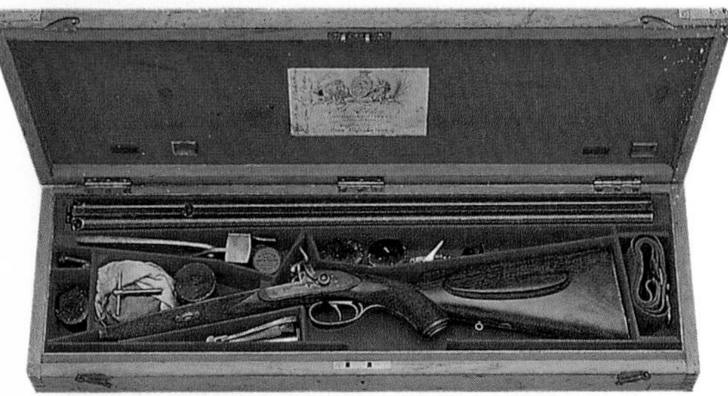

A 40-bore double barrel percussion sporting rifle, in its original oak case with London proof marks No. 6806 for 1864. **$8,000-9,500**

A 12-gauge double barrel hammerless sidelock ejector gun, by W. Evans, No. 15448, 30in (76cm) barrels. **$5,000-6,500**

A 12-gauge Winchester single trigger, over/under gun, 28in (71cm) barrels. **$3,000-3,500**

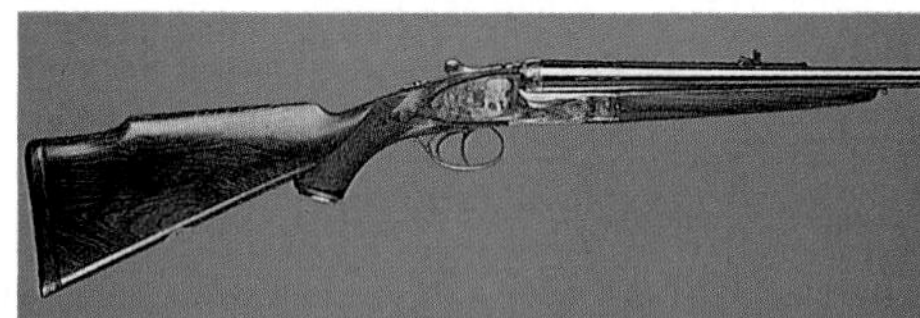

A Preater engraved .458 magnum 'modele de luxe' double barrel hammerless sidelock ejector rifle, by Holland & Holland, No. 35518, in oak and leather case, 24in (61cm) barrels. **$40,000-50,000**

A 12-bore self-opening sidelock ejector pigeon gun, by J Purdey, No. 24700, rebarrelled 1985. **$9,500-13,000**

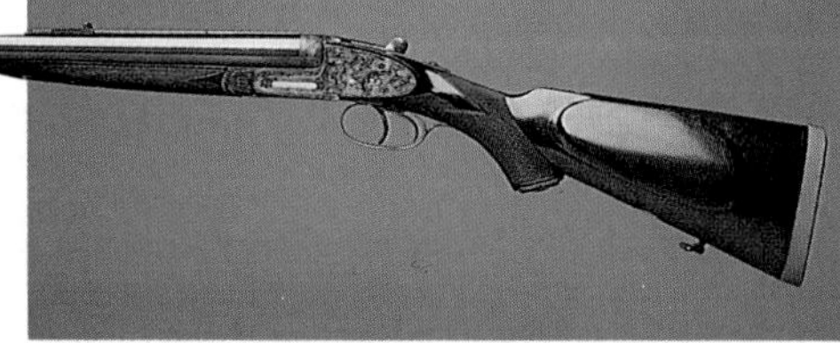

A .577 double barrel hammerless sidelock ejector rifle, by Holland & Holland, No. 19270, converted to ejector, with later goldwork by Philippe Grifnée, the rifle built c1900 and re-chambered and re-embellished in 1983, 26in (66cm) barrels. **$18,000-20,000**

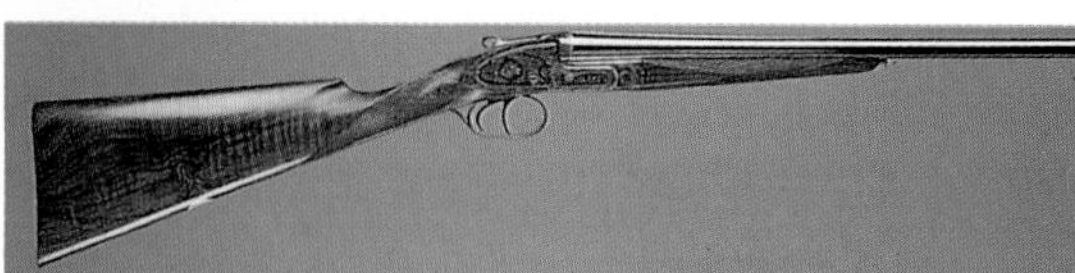

A Casbard engraved 28-gauge double barrel hammerless self-opening sidelock ejector gun, by Peter Chapman, No. 0029/28. **$18,000-20,000**

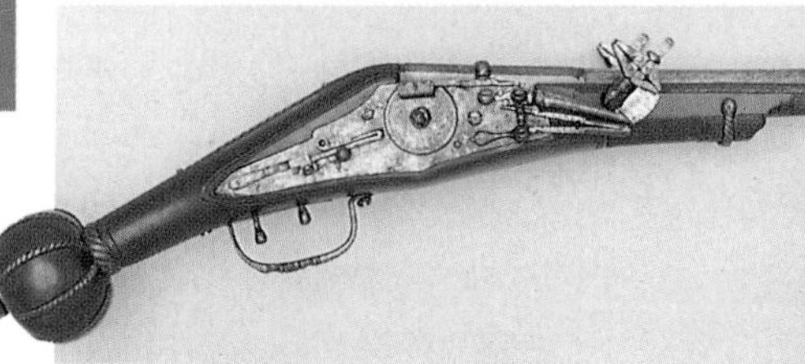

A Saxon double barrel wheel lock holster pistol, piece of stock and ramrods missing, late 16thC, 20in (51cm). **$25,000-26,000**

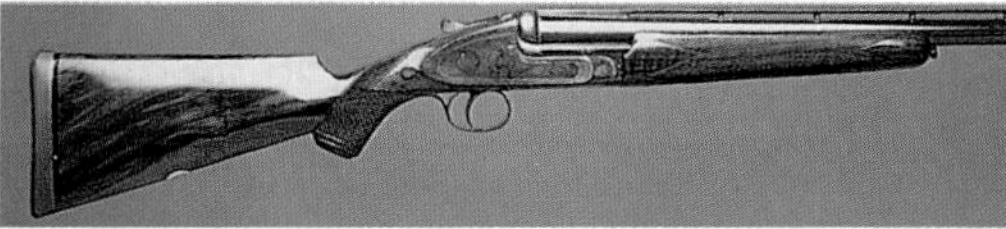

A 12-gauge single barrel hammerless self-opening sidelock ejector trap gun, by J. Purdey, No. 23870, c1930, 32in (81cm) barrel. **$8,000-9,500**

Lori Pambak rug, reas of wear and ear, 100 by 63in 254 by 160cm). **6,500-9,500**

A Ladik prayer rug, shows wear and repair, c1800, 72 by 47in (183 by 120cm). **$3,000-3,500**

A Lenkoran long rug, late 19thC, 92in (234cm). **$5,500-8,000**

An Ottoman embroidered cotton bokshe, late 18thC, 46 by 33in (117 by 84cm). **$2,500-3,500**

Mahal carpet, with an allover attern of meandering vines and almettes and a primary border f palmettes and rosettes, ome wear, c1900, 126 by 94in 320 by 239cm). **6,500-9,000**

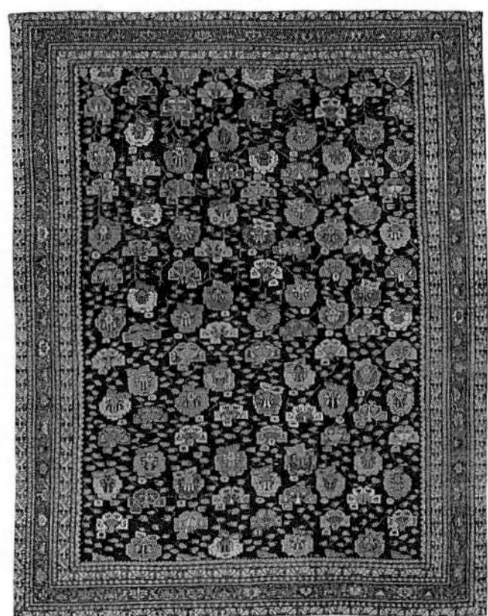

A Malayir carpet, the indigo field with a lattice of floral lozenges, surrounded by flowering vine, ends trimmed and rebound selvedges, 173 by 139in (439 by 354cm). **$8,000-9,500**

A Malayer prayer rug, the deep rust ground covered by a floral Tree of Life flanked by cypress trees leading to the prayer arch, 89 by 67in (226 by 170cm). **$4,000-6,500**

n antique Qashqai double bag, the ilim back with panels of multi-loured lappets, minor damage, 5in (114cm) long. **$6,500-8,000**
bove r. A Qashqai rug, very slight ear, 88 by 48in (224 by 122cm). **3,000-4,000**

A Serapi carpet, the rust ground covered by an allover pattern of floral vines with interconnecting spandrels, surrounded by a border, loss to ends and repaired, late 19thC, 134 by 110in (341 by 280cm). **$10,000-12,000**

A Marasali Shirvan rug, the midnight blue ground covered by flaming botehs, surrounded by an inner reciprocal trefoil border, 3 brown borders and 2 reciprocal latchhook borders with web ends, 51 by 47in (130 by 119cm). **$2,500-3,000**

A Heriz carpet, with pink field, areas of wear, repair and tinting, 148 by 116in (376 by 295cm).
$8,000-9,500

An Isfahan rug, 91 by 59in (231 by 150cm).
$3,000-5,000

A silk Kashan pictorial rug, depicting a cartoon by George McManus, entitled 'Bringing up Father', 71 by 61in (180 by 155cm).
$18,000-21,000

A silk Kashan prayer rug, a few areas of slight wear, 78 by 53in (198 by 135cm).
$13,000-16,000

A Kashan pictorial rug, with 2 registers of a seated Shah with womenfolk and courtiers, in a border, replaced fringes, 78 by 55in (198 by 140cm).
$5,000-6,500

A Chelaberd Karabagh rug, some repairs, mid-19thC, 78 by 50in (198 by 127cm). **$9,000-12,000**

Above r. A Kuba runner, corros browns, c1880, 138 by 36in (351 by 92cm).
$6,500-8,000

A Kazak rug, the brick field with 2 ivory and 2 mid blue medallions, with inner brick hooked motifs, 85 by 47in (216 by 120cm). **$1,000-1,500**

A Kuba rug, with indigo floral field in a red vine border, repairs, 127in (322cm) long.
$5,000-6,500

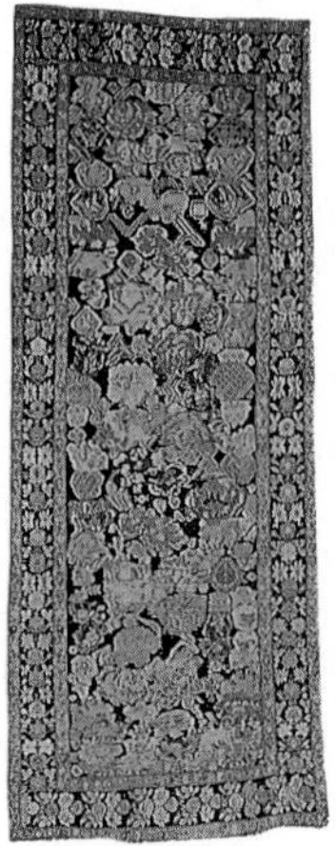
A Karabagh Kelleh rug, with indigo field and border, 180 by 61in (456 by 155cm).
$5,000-5,500

A Karatchoph Kazak rug, shows some wear, crease wear and slightly reduced end guard borders, late 19thC, 86 by 74in (219 by 188cm). **$4,000-6,500**

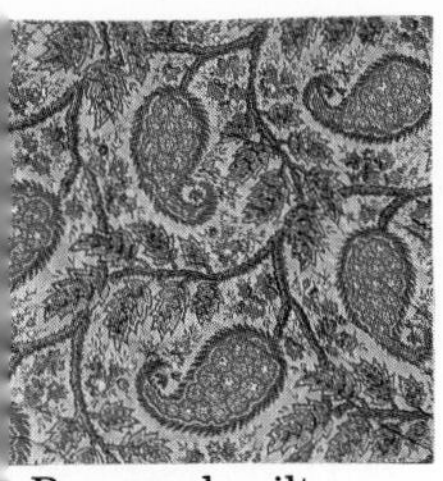

A Provençal quilt, early 19thC, new lining.
$550-700

A reversible Provençal quilt.
$530-550

A reversible Provençal quilt.
$400-500

Above l. A Provençal quilt, red reverse, c1800, 58in (147cm) square. **$550-700**
Above r. A Provençal quilt, c1915, 83in (210.5cm) long. **$350-450**

A pair of Beauvais tapestry pillows, late 18thC, 18in (45cm) square.
$6,500-8,000

r. A Brussels late baroque mythological tapestry, signed Behaegle, late 17thC, 86 by 182in (219 by 461cm).
$32,000-40,000

A European needlework panel, stained, 103in (261cm) long.
$5,500-6,500

A French embroidered silk panel, 19thC, 77 by 80in (196 by 203cm).
$3,500-4,000

A Brussels baroque mythological tapestry, lacking borders, early 18thC, 117 by 141in (297 by 356cm).
$20,000-30,000

A Brussels tapestry in silks and wools, with weavers' marks and Brussels town mark, early 18thC, 135 by 168in (342 by 427cm).
$50,000-60,000

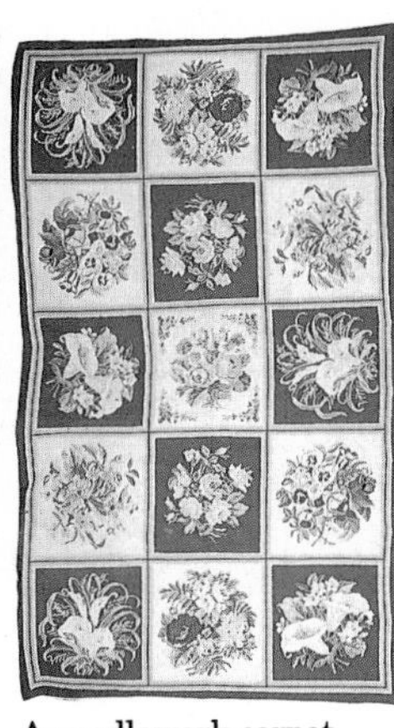

A needlework carpet, backed, 147 by 87in (373 by 221cm).
$6,500-7,000

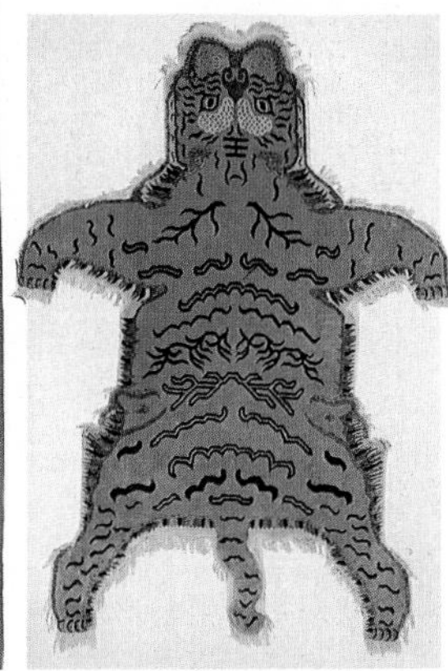

A Tibetan tiger shaped rug, 96in (243.5cm) long.
$25,000-32,000

A 4-colour wool and cotton Jacquard coverlet, by Andrew Corick, Maryland, with self fringe, mid-19thC, 68 by 56in (172 by 142cm). **$2,000-3,000**

A needlework sampler, by Alice Mather, Norwich, Connecticut, dated 1774, 14 by 11½in (36 by 30cm). **$50,000-80,000**

An appliquéd and pieced album quilt, slight staining, Maryland, mid-19thC, 85 by 95in (216 by 241cm). **$6,500-8,000**

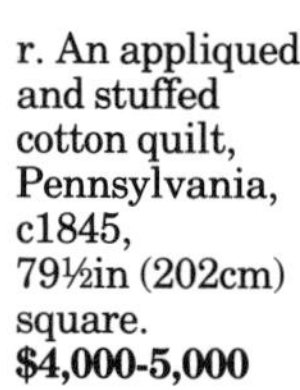

l. An appliquéd cotton and quilted coverlet, slightly stained, American, c1850, 88in (223cm) square. **$3,500-5,500**

r. An appliquéd and stuffed cotton quilt, Pennsylvania, c1845, 79½in (202cm) square. **$4,000-5,000**

A painted fireboard, Maine or New Hampshire, early 19thC. **$18,000-25,000**

r. A wool and cotton double woven Jacquard coverlet, attributed to James Alexander, c1830. **$2,000-5,000**

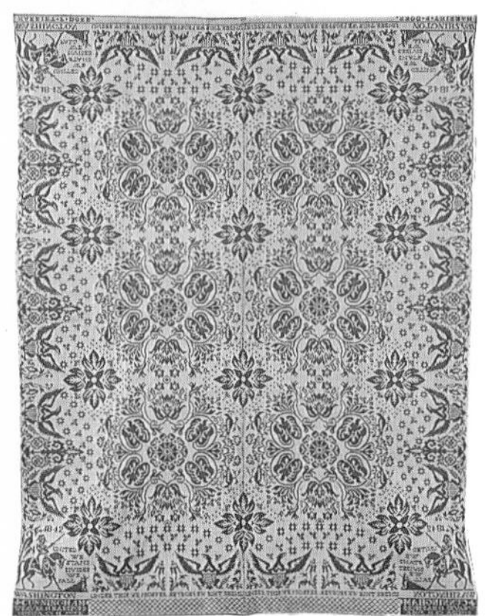

A needlework sampler, by Sarah Doubt, Massachusetts, 1765. **$6,500-9,000**

l. A wool and cotton double woven Jacquard coverlet, by James Cunningham, New York, 1842. **$3,000-5,000**

r. A wool and cotton double woven Jacquard coverlet, inscribed 'Delhi New York', 1845. **$2,000-3,000**

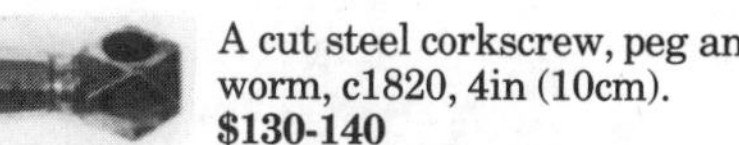

A cut steel corkscrew, peg and worm, c1820, 4in (10cm).
$130-140

Thomason type corkscrew, c1830.
300-350

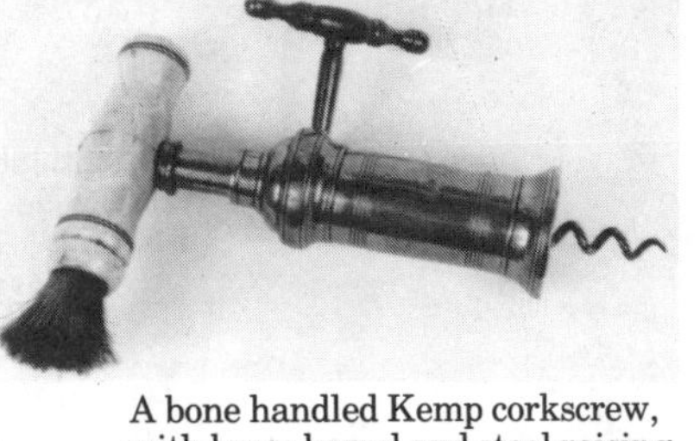

A bone handled Kemp corkscrew, with brass barrel and steel raising handle, c1830.
$550-650

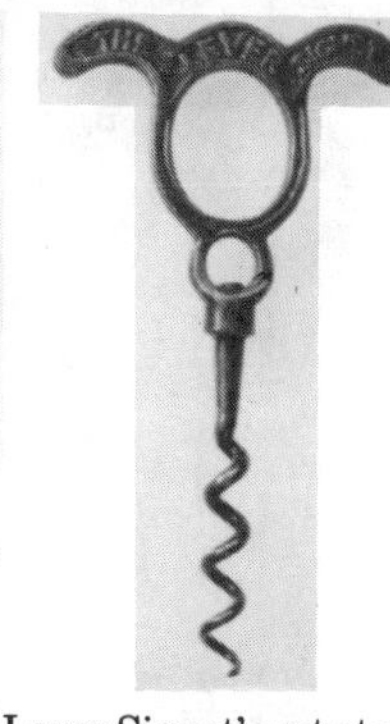

'The Lever Signet' cast steel corkscrew, c1880.
$55-80

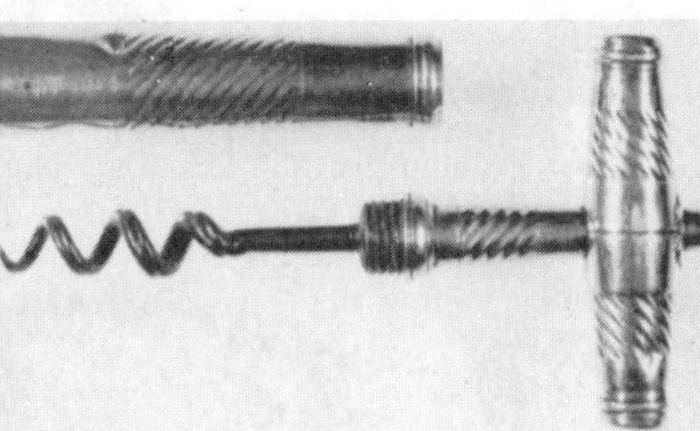

A silver pocket corkscrew, by Samuel Pemberton, 18thC.
$500-650

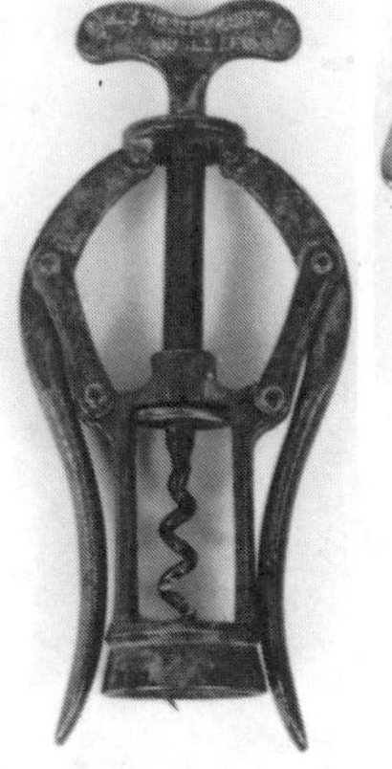

A Heeley A1 double lever corkscrew, patent 1888, 6½in (16cm) long.
$120-130

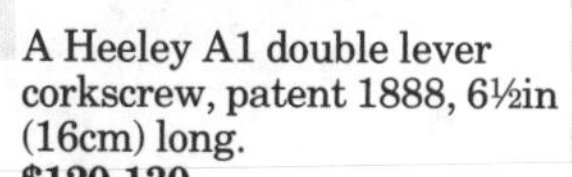

A Swiss corkscrew, with spring, c1920.
$150-200

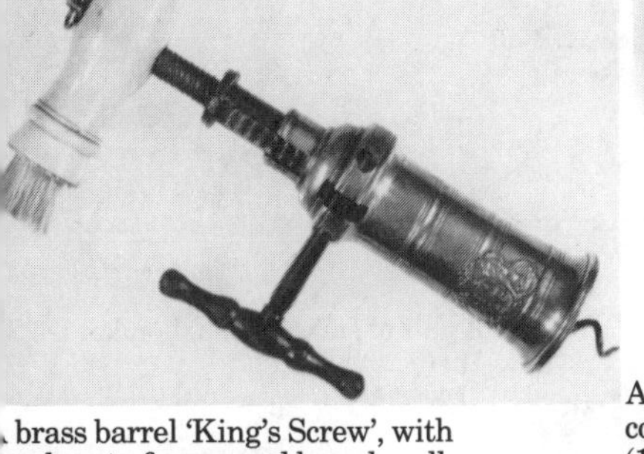

brass barrel 'King's Screw', with yal coat-of-arms and bone handle.
550-600

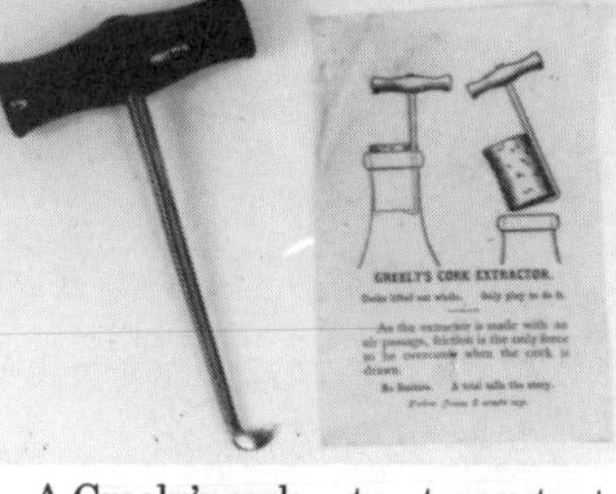

A Greely's cork extractor, patent March 6th, 1888.
$250-300

corkscrew, by J Hedley & Sons, narked Weirs patent 25th Sept 884, 13½in (34cm) long.
130-140

A brass barrel 'King's Screw', with royal coat-of-arms and bone handle.
$550-800

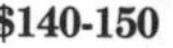

A peg and worm corkscrew, with baluster stems and reeded discs, 2½in (6cm) long.
$140-150

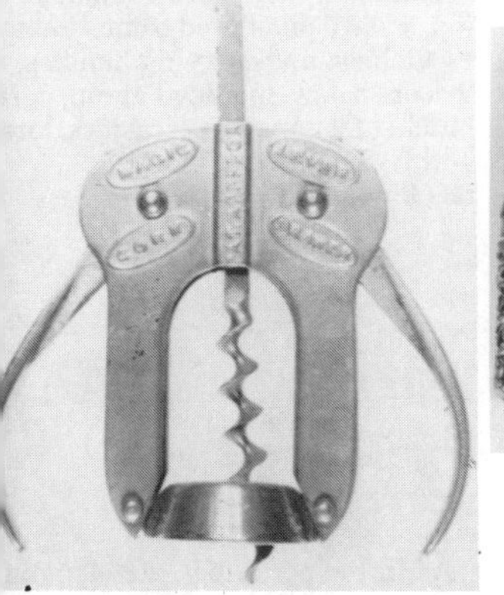

'Magic Lever' corkscrew.
80-100

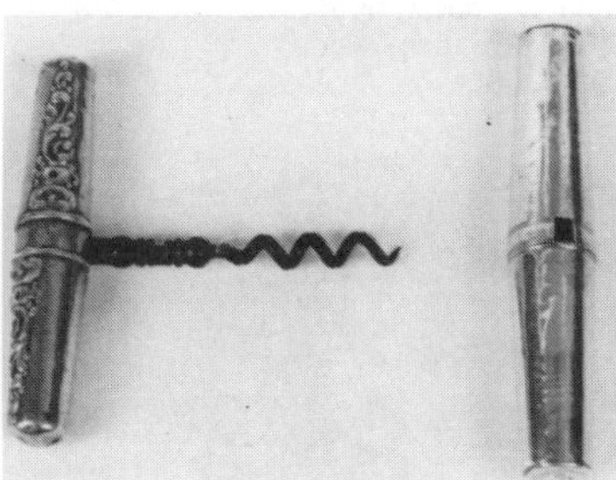

Two folding silver corkscrews.
l. Decorated handle.
$130-140

r. Unfolded corkscrew.
$200-210

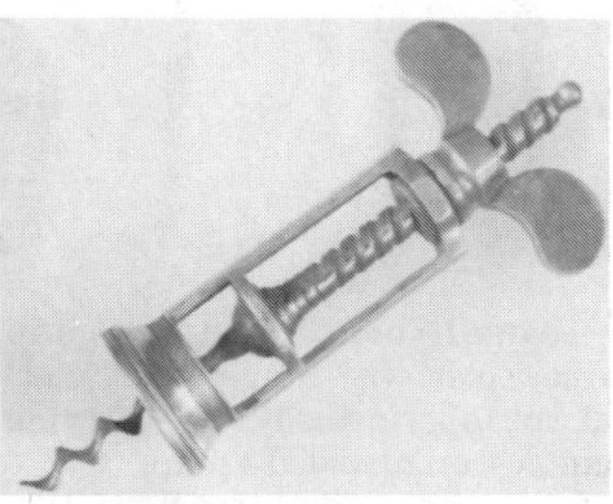

A brass Farrow and Jackson type wing nut corkscrew.
$275-400

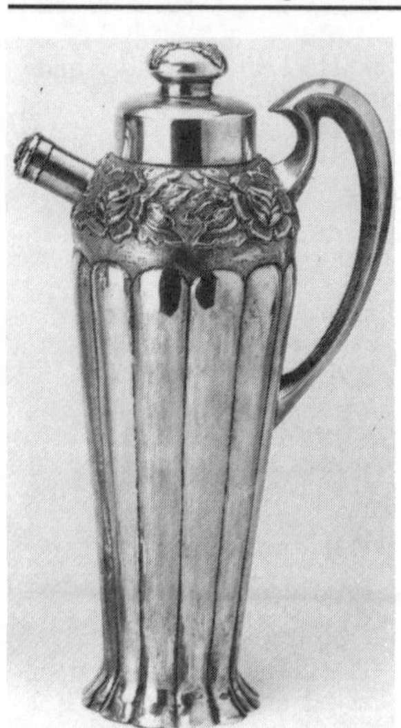

A Continental cocktail shaker, the fluted tapering cylindrical body with floral and leaf chased band to collar, scroll handle and angled spout, the pull off cover with floral finial and engraved monogram, 14in (36cm) high.
$550-650

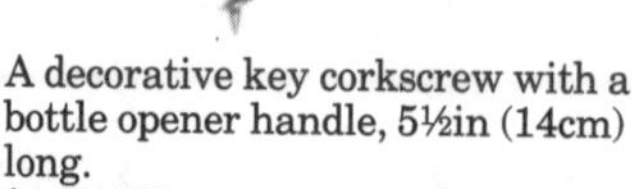

A decorative key corkscrew with a bottle opener handle, 5½in (14cm) long.
$140-150

A Bronti label, Sheffield 1981, 2½in (7cm) wide.
$40-65

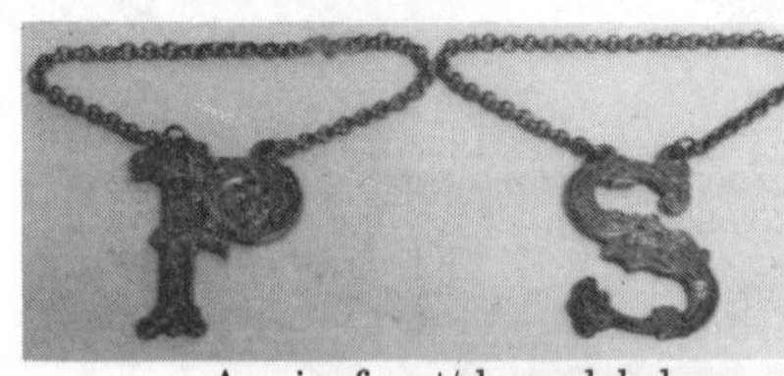

A pair of port/sherry labels, Edinburgh c1850, 2in (5cm) long.
$150-210

An early George III wine funnel, by Hester Bateman, London 1770, 5in (13cm) high.
$700-900

A pair of sauce labels, London 1822, 1in (3cm) wide.
$140-200

A gin bottle ticket, by Taylor & Perry, c1845, 2in (5cm) wide.
$80-90

A bottle ticket, by Hester Bateman, c1780, 2in (5cm) wide.
$275-300

A mahogany cellaret with domed top, square pilastered front, brass escutcheon and carrying handles, 2 doors below, moulded apron, ogee bracket feet and brass casters, late 18thC, 23in (59cm) wide.
$3,000-4,000

A George III brass bound mahogany wine cooler, with hinged octagonal lid, the tapering body with carrying handles, on moulded square tapering legs, later brass liner, 18in (46cm) wide.
$5,000-5,500

A George III open tub wine cooler, without a stand or liner.
$2,500-3,000

A Minton port label, c1874, 5½in (14cm) wide.
$90-100

. George IV mahogany wine cooler, ' sarcophagus shape inlaid with ɔony lines with stepped canted top, nclosing a lead lined divided nterior, the panelled tapering sides ıounted with lion mask ring andles, with reeded apron on paw et, 29½in (75cm) wide.
2,500-3,000

pair of Old Sheffield plate ımpana shaped wine coolers, each ı spreading base and with shell ıd foliate scroll handles, plain ıers and gadrooned, shell and liage collars, c1830, 9½in (24cm) gh.
,000-5,500

An early Victorian mahogany wine ooler, the hinged coffered top nclosing a fitted interior, the apered sides with chamfered angles arved with acanthus volutes, on tiff leaf scroll feet, 35in (90cm) vide.
$5,000-5,500

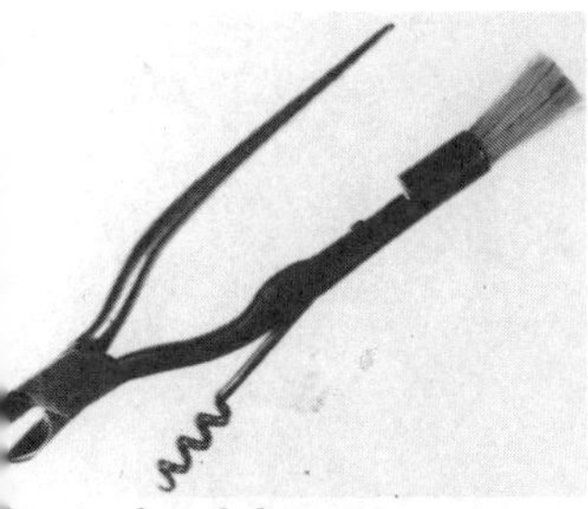

A pair of steel champagne wire ippers combined with a fluted vorm corkscrew, c1850.
$350-400

A George III brass bound mahogany wine cooler, with octagonal lid and carrying handles, the stand with fluted frieze and square tapering legs, 19½in (50cm) wide.
$5,000-5,500

Four Old Sheffield plate vase shaped wine coolers, the foot and lower part of the body chased with fluting, with foliage scroll handles and gadrooned borders, with detachable collars and liners, engraved with a crest, c1830, 10in (26cm) high.
$8,000-9,500

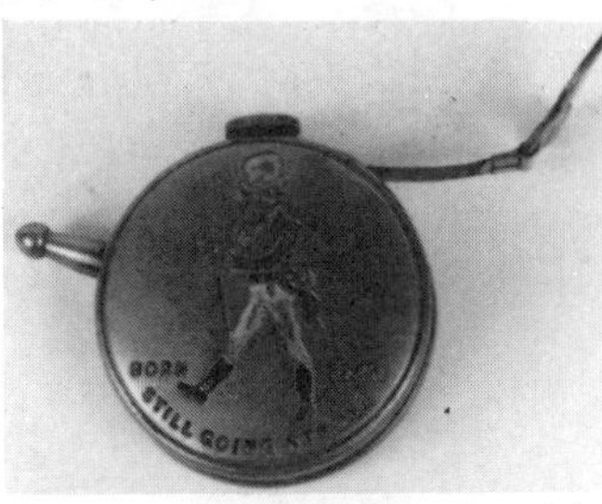

A brass bowls measure, advertising Johnny Walker, 1½in (4cm) diam.
$55-65

A cased champagne tap.
$80-100

A Wedgwood creamware sherry label, c1830, 5½in (14cm).
$90-100

A George III style mahogany brass bound wine cooler, with fanned top centred by a turned handle, on square tapered legs, 28in (71cm) wide.
$1,400-2,000

A Regency fiddle back mahogany cellaret, of sarcophagus form, with rectangular hinged top, the sides applied with lion's mask and ring handles, on hairy paw feet, 29in (74cm) wide.
$2,000-2,500

A George III brass bound mahogany wine cooler, with hinged top and lined interior, on a stand with 4 square tapered legs, 17½in (45cm) wide.
$1,500-2,500

A pair of William IV style Warwick vase wine coolers, each with a moulded rim decorated with classical masks, vines and acanthus leaves and with an egg-and-dart and bead rim, fitted with detachable liners and collars, 10½in (27cm), 231.5oz.
$7,000-8,000

A late Regency mahogany sarcophagus wine cooler, inlaid with boxwood with original interior and raised on carved hairy paw feet, 24in (62cm) wide.
$2,500-3,000

A mahogany cellaret, the top with ovolo moulded edge, hinged and opening to reveal a lift-out tray and fitted interior, with 4 dummy drawers to the fascia, brass baluster tied loop handles to the sides, raised upon gadroon carved ogee bracket feet, the whole strung with box and with fan shaped rosettes, early 19thC, 16½in (42cm) wide.
$4,000-5,000

A pair of Old Sheffield plate tapering wine coolers, moulded with ribbed hoops and engraved with simulated staves, each with 2 handles and with a detachable liner and collar, engraved with crests and mottos within garter cartouches, c1815, 9in (23cm).
$5,500-6,500

A George III mahogany and brass bound wine cooler, of octagonal form with partitioned lead lined interior, the stand with moulded square section legs, 18½in (47cm) wide.
$4,000-5,000

A Continental ewer and basin, with gadroon swirl band decoration, 18thC, the basin 12½in (32cm) diam.
$200-250

METALWARE

Pewter

A pedestal punch bowl, with pricked inscription 'The London Punch House, 1760', 10in (25cm) diam.
$700-800

An English wriggle-work plate, c1710, 8½in (21.5cm) diam.
$150-250

A Continental alms dish, c1700, 12in (30.5cm) diam.
$550-650

Three English pewter salts, c1780.
$80-150 each

A coffee pot, 19thC, 9½in (24cm) high.
$100-110

An inkstand with removable ink and pounce pots, centre taperstick and wax drawer, engraved 'For y use of y Great Vestry Room — Samuel Cooper (?) Vestry Clerk, 1743', 11in (28cm).
$1,300-1,500

Believed to be from Shoreham Old Church.

A pewter measure, Jersey, 18thC, 8in (20cm) high.
$250-300

A Scottish laver, the tapering banded body with scroll handle and twin lobed thumbpiece, late 18thC, 10½in (26.5cm) high.
$400-550

Brass

A pair of George II candlesticks, the cylindrical shafts with lobed knops on petal bases, 8in (20cm) high.
$650-1,000

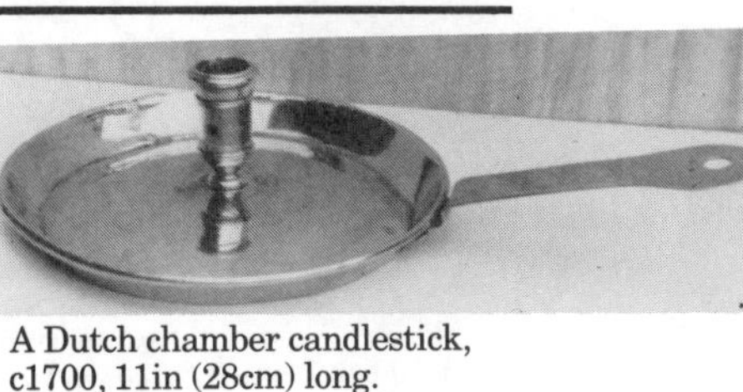

A Dutch chamber candlestick, c1700, 11in (28cm) long.
$150-250

A candlestick with heavy ribbed column, central reeded drip pan, on broad moulded circular foot, 17thC, 8in (20cm) high.
$6,500-7,000

A pair of candlesticks, with knopped baluster stems on shell cast petal bases, 18thC, 8½in (21.5cm) high.
$900-1,000

A pair of candle lamps, 8½in (21.5cm) high.
$550-650

A pair of chambersticks, 19thC.
$200-250

A Dutch jardinière, with repoussé scenes of drinking men, the sides with lion masks, previously with rings, 17in (43.5cm) wide.
$650-700

A mid-Victorian brass and ormolu miniature frame in the form of a five-bar double gate, inscribed 'Please shut these gates' centred by a miniature oval frame and flanked by trees, opening to reveal 4 miniature oval frames, the reverse engraved 'R. Betjeman & Sons' with registration mark for 1867 and 'Registration No. 34' and bracket engraved 'Toulmin & Gale, 7, New Bond Street, and 85 & 86 Cheapside'.
$1,000-1,200

A heavily patinated lantern bracket, 32in (81cm) high.
$1,400-1,600

A pair of candlesticks, with segmented cylindrical columns and narrow everted rims, wide drip pans and spreading bases, 17thC, 7in (17.5cm) high.
$4,000-6,500

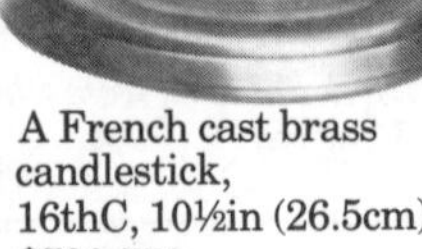

A French cast brass candlestick, 16thC, 10½in (26.5cm).
$500-550

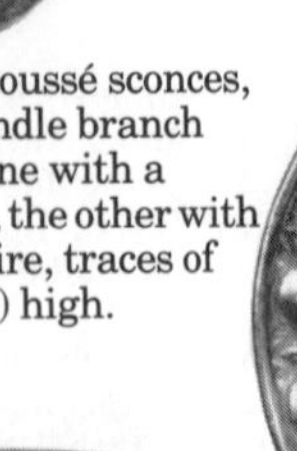

A Continental candlestick, repaired, c1600, 7in (17.5cm) high. **$650-1,000**

A cast brass oil lamp, the boat shaped reservoir applied with masks in the Renaissance style, supported upon a circular base with green tinted shade, 19thC, 22½in (57cm) high.
$800-900

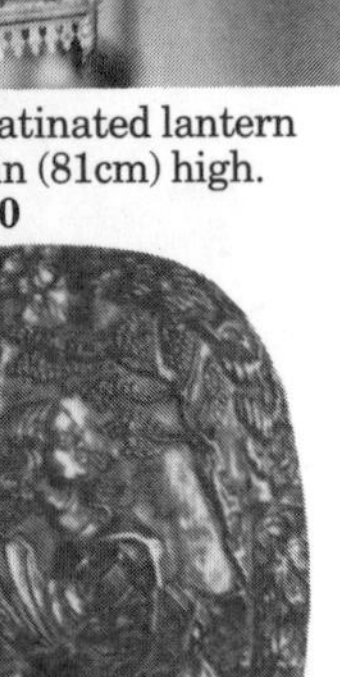

A pair of Flemish repoussé sconces, each with scrolled candle branch and oval backplate, one with a figure holding a tulip, the other with an old man before a fire, traces of silvering, 13in (33cm) high.
$2,600-3,000

A brass cat, the ring turned supports and legs around a central urn, early 19thC, 15½in (39.5cm) high.
$500-550

Cats were made of metal or wood and were used for keeping food or dishes warm beside a fire.

A pair of Adam and Eve chargers, 14in (35.5cm) diam.
$700-800

A gilt brass curfew of typical form, repoussé decorated with portraits, animals and figure subjects and pseudo coats-of-arms, surmounted by a carrying handle, 18thC, 17in (43.5cm) wide.
$1,200-1,300

A desk ink stand with glass liner, 19thC.
$150-230

A Nuremberg minnekästchen, in the manner of Michael Mann, the base engraved inside and out, the sides with pierced silver, enamel and gem set appliques, applique from lid missing, minor damage to lock, minor losses, associated key, early 17thC, 2 by 3in (5 by 7.5cm).
$2,600-3,000

A pair of five-light brass gilt candelabra, on a square marble base, mid-19thC, 20in (51cm) high.
$2,000-2,500

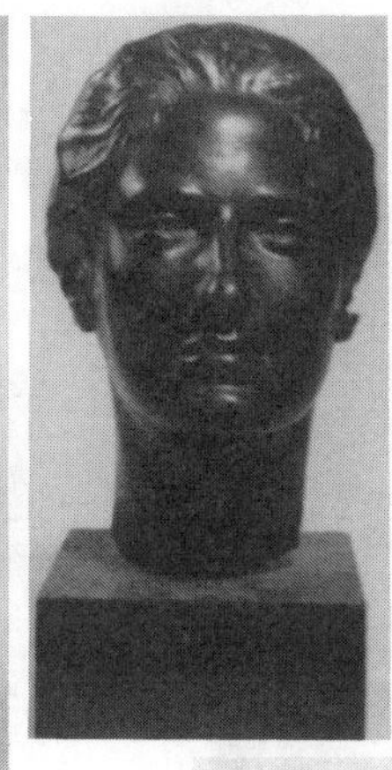

An English bronze mask of Mary Swainson, cast from a model by Alphonse Legros, pedestal chipped, late 19thC, 11½in (30cm) high.
$2,500-3,000

Mary Swainson was Legros' pupil at the Slade School from 1880 to 1883. Legros modelled the mask during one of his lessons and gave the original plaster mould to the sitter. A marble version was exhibited at the Grosvenor Gallery in 1884 and a bronze cast was made in Paris in 1890. The present mask is one of 3 bronzes cast.

A French bronze bust of the pensive Venus, signed J. Clessinger, Rome 1860, the integral socle stamped F. Barbedienne Fondeur, 19thC, 9½in (24cm) high.
$650-750

A French bronze bust of a lady, cast from a model by S. Salmson in Louis XVI costume, signed on one shoulder S. Salmson 1873 and inscribed on the other shoulder P. Baur, on turned marble socle, socle repaired, 19thC, 20½in (52cm) high.
$2,500-3,000

A French parcel gilt bronze figure of a recumbent bacchante, 19thC, 13 by 25½in (34 by 65cm).
$2,500-3,000

A French bronze figure, cast from a model by Eugene Aizelin, inscribed 'Conseils d'une mere a ses enfants', signed Aizelin, on marble base, 19thC, 14½in (36.5cm) high.
$1,400-2,000

A French bronze figure of a fisherboy, cast from a model by M. de Vasselot, the base inscribed 'Paris 1882, mon petit Charlot, M. de Vasselot', 19thC, 48½in (124cm) high.
$9,500-11,000

An Italian bronze bust of woman from Capri, cast from a model by Vincenzo Gemito, the base cast with twin dolphins, signed Gemito and with foundry stamp, early 20thC, 18½in (48cm) high.
$6,500-7,500

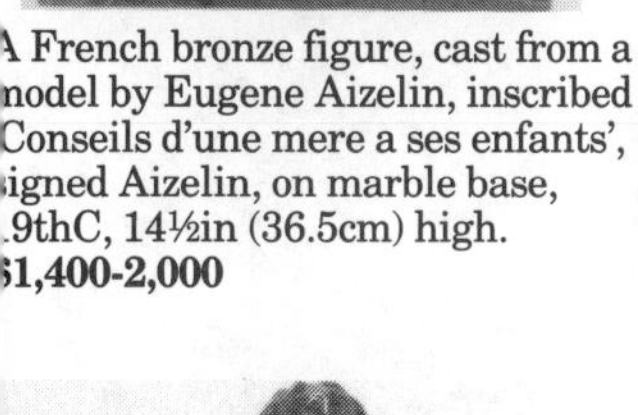

An Italian bronze heroic bust of Napoleon, cast from a model by A. Pandiani, the reverse signed A. Pandiani and dated Milano 1890, on rouge marble columnar base applied with bronze N, 19thC, 21in (54cm) high.
$4,000-5,000

A French bronzed metal group of 2 putti riding on the back of a giant tortoise, 10in (26cm) high.
$800-1,200

A French bronze figure of an animal trainer, cast from a model by Christopher Fratin, a self portrait caricature head of Fratin, the base stamped Fratin, mid-19thC, 8in (20cm) high.
$2,500-4,000

A pair of French statuettes of Painting and Sculpture, cast from models by Salmson, the bases signed Salmson, with ormolu pedestals with bronze reliefs of putti, with supports for candle holders behind, tops missing, mid-19thC, 15in (38.5cm) high.
$3,000-4,000

A Venetian bronze model of a small mechanical owl, opening to reveal a figure, c1900, 5½in (14cm) high.
$250-400

A Venetian bronze, The water seller, c1900, 7½in (19cm) high.
$700-900

A Venetian bronze model of a mechanical owl on tree trunk, opening to reveal a figure, 5½in (14cm) high.
$1,500-2,500

A Venetian bronze, Bacchus and a nymph, c1900, 4½in (12cm) wide.
$1,400-1,500

A Venetian bronze, an ashtray with camel, c1900, 7½in (19cm) diam.
$1,300-1,400

A Venetian bronze model of a large Egyptian dancer, c1900, 10½in (27cm) high.
$2,500-3,000

A bronze depicting a fat pig being ridden by the devil, 1½in (4cm).
$300-500

A Rheinhold bronze, The Philosophical Chimpanzee, the animal seated on a pile of books and contemplating a skull, on a square base, signed, 13in (34cm) high.
$1,000-1,200

A bronze bust of a Moroccan man cast from a model by Rachel Lucy Hautot, inscribed R. Hautot, and stamped France, rich greenish brown patina, 19thC, 20in (51cm) high.
$2,500-3,500

A Venetian bronze model of 2 small dogs, c1900, 3½in (9cm) wide.
$300-500

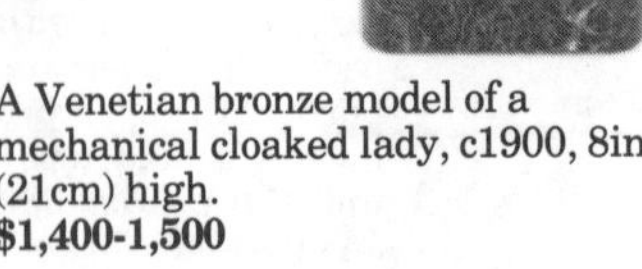

A Venetian bronze model of a mechanical cloaked lady, c1900, 8in (21cm) high.
$1,400-1,500

A Venetian bronze model of dogs frolicking, c1900, 3½in (9cm) wide.
$500-650

A Venetian bronze model of a large dog paper holder, c1900, 12½in (32cm) wide.
$1,200-1,300

A Venetian bronze, The arms seller, c1900, 4½in (12cm) wide.
$800-1,000

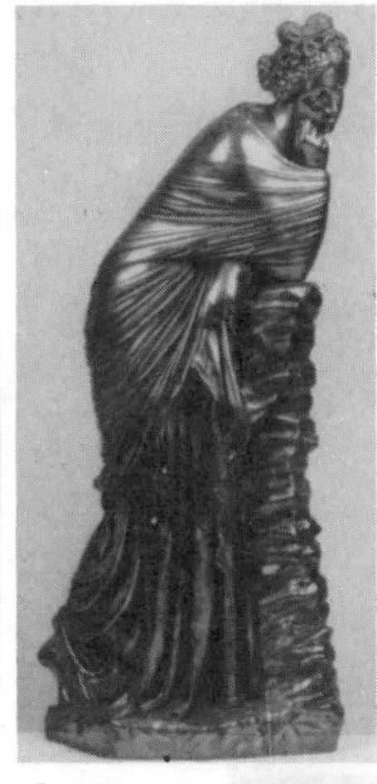

A French bronze statuette of Polyhymnia, after the antique, cast by Barbedienne, marked F. Barbedienne Fondeur, polished, 19thC, 29½in (75cm) high.
$2,500-3,000

A Venetian bronze, The elephant tusk seller, c1900, 8in (21cm) high.
$2,000-3,000

A Venetian bronze model of a fox pin holder, c1900, 7½in (19cm) wide.
$500-650

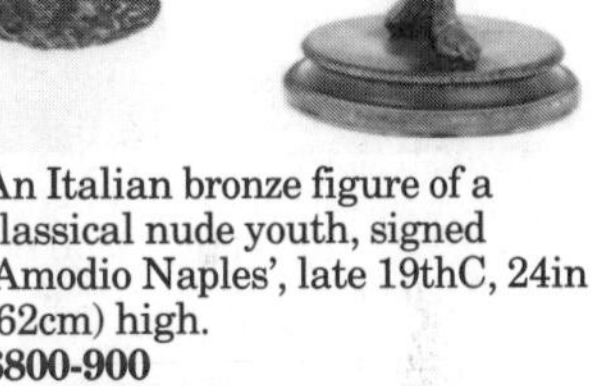

An Italian bronze figure of a classical nude youth, signed 'Amodio Naples', late 19thC, 24in (62cm) high.
$800-900

A Venetian bronze model of a pug dog, c1900, 3½in (9cm) wide.
$150-300

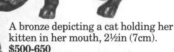

A bronze depicting a cat holding her kitten in her mouth, 2½in (7cm).
$500-650

A Venetian bronze model of a large tiger, c1900, 7in (18cm) wide.
$900-1,000

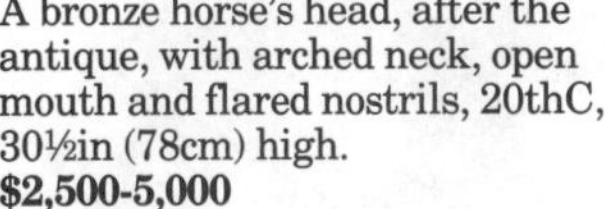

A bronze horse's head, after the antique, with arched neck, open mouth and flared nostrils, 20thC, 30½in (78cm) high.
$2,500-5,000

The bronze horse's head is a copy of the original excavated at Civitavechia near Rome, it was acquired by the Medici family, who almost certainly commissioned Giambologna or his studio to adapt it as a fountain in the courtyard of the Medici Palace.

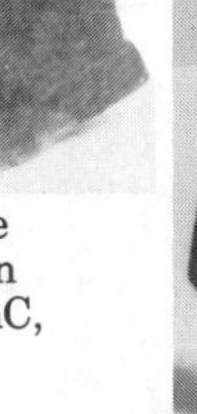

A French bronze model of a stag, cast from a model by Antoine-Louis Barye, on naturalistic base, signed Barye and stamped F. Barbedienne, Fondeur, the underside marked No. 640 and 43, 19thC, 7in (18cm) high.
$2,000-2,500

A French bronze model of a setter carrying a pheasant, cast from a model by Jules Moigniez, on naturalistic base signed J. Moigniez and stamped Exposition Paris 1900 M.D. Mlle d'or H.V., 19thC, 16in (40.5cm) high.
$5,000-6,500

A North Indian provincial bronze figure of Kali, standing with the principal hands holding patra and khadga handle, the secondary with staff and skull, slight corrosion, khadga blade and staff finial missing, 18thC, 19in (49cm) high.
$32,000-40,000

A Venetian bronze, a tent light fixture, c1900, 12½in (32cm) high.
$500-650

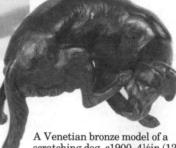

A bronze figure of the inventor Ambroise Pare, in 16thC costume, the base signed P.J. David, with Barbedienne foundry stamp, inscribed Ambroise Pare, 19thC, 19in (49cm) high.
$800-1,200

A Venetian bronze model of a scratching dog, c1900, 4½in (12cm) high.
$800-1,000

A French bronze group of a panther seizing a stag, cast from a model by Antoine-Louis Barye, on naturalistic base, signed Barye and inscribed Susse frères editeurs à Paris, late 20thC, 13in (33cm) high.
$3,000-5,000

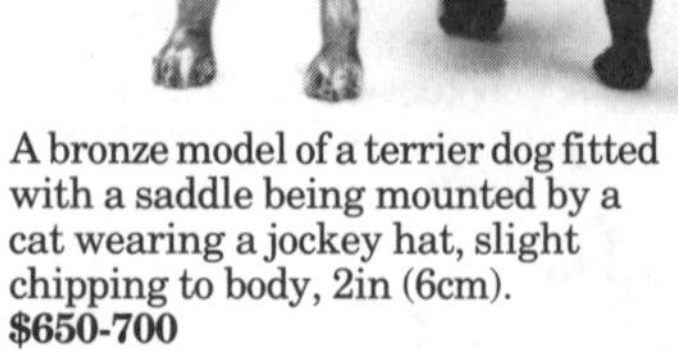

A bronze model of a terrier dog fitted with a saddle being mounted by a cat wearing a jockey hat, slight chipping to body, 2in (6cm).
$650-700

A bronze group of 2 dancing maidens, after Clodion, the infant Bacchus at their feet, on naturalistic base, incised Clodion and dated 1762, stamped 1937, 15½in (40cm) high.
$1,400-1,500

A French bronze group, by Louis Sauvageau, on plain base, dark patination, signed, mid-19thC, 31½in (80cm) high.
$2,500-3,000

A bronze figure of a lion, signed Kenworthy '65 and numbered 6/10, on marble plinth, 14½in (37cm) wide.
$900-1,000

An Austrian bronze model of a buffalo, with painted eyes, 19thC, 12in (31cm) long.
$2,000-2,500

A set of 6 bronze bell shaped standard weights, by Sewell & Young, Makers, London, each engraved Rygate 1795, 5616-216, each stamped with various George III proof marks, late 18thC.
$3,000-5,000

A Victorian gilt bronze and brass mounted four-piece desk set, with hardstone bosses, comprising an inkstand, blotter, pentray and holder, and a pen.
$1,000-1,200

A French bronze figure of the Cheval Turc, the base signed Barye, with gold F.B. stamp and F. Barbedienne Fondeur, the underside of the base stamped A.A. 45, 19thC, 7½in (19cm) high.
$5,000-8,000

A French table bronze and ormolu lamp, modelled with putti, 19thC.
$2,000-2,500

A gilt bronze inkstand, with central candle holder supported by a classical female figure, the 2 lotus cast ink pots on dolphin supports and shell base, 19thC, 12in (31cm) long.
$550-650

A large South Indian cast bronze ritual eating vessel, with rounded base and inturned mouth with small everted lip, the loop handle at each side with 3 ridges, an applied heart motif below, a brief Tamil inscription on the rim and shoulder below, Kerala, 18thC, 32½in (83cm) diam.
$1,500-2,500

The inscription on the rim states 'This belongs to the Panakel family', that on the shoulder gives the family house name 'Paramaswan' and another states that it has been disposed of by the family.

A pair of French bronze urns, after Clodion, the neck, handle and foot with foliate motifs, a musician putto seated on the handle, bearing the signature Clodion, on turned marble socles, 19thC, 19in (49cm) high.
$1,400-2,000

An Italo-Russian bronze model of a recumbent cow, cast from a model by Prince Paul Troubetskoy, on a naturalistic base, signed P. Troubetskoy 1914, and with the cire perdue stamp of the Valsuani foundry, and No. 10, early 20thC, 14½in (38cm) long.
$4,000-5,500

A pair of French bronze ornamental urns, from the Barbedienne foundry, with classical scenes on the bodies between anthemia with elegant handles and small heads each side of the tall necks, on black marble plinths, mid-19thC, 25in (64cm) high.
$2,500-3,000

A French bronze model of a roaring lion, cast from a model by Thomas Cartier, signed Th. Cartier and stamped Vrai bronze, early 20thC, 18in (46cm) high.
$1,300-2,000

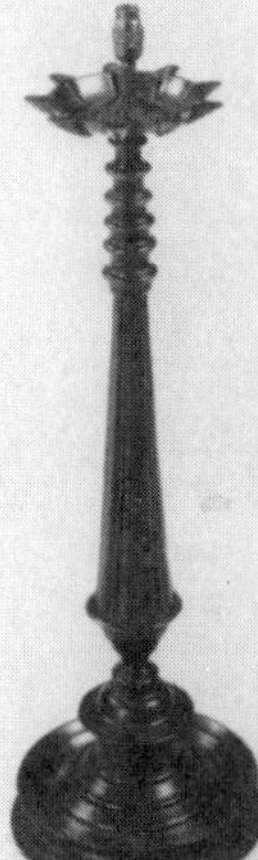
A bronze candlestick with spreading reeded stem, surmounted by a sun shaped dish, 17thC, fitted for electricity, 29in (73cm) high.
$4,000-5,000

A French bronze relief of Spring, cast from a model by Croisy, Spring shown as a seated naked nymph adorning herself with roses, with a putto holding a looking glass, signed Croisy and inscribed 'Printemps', within an ornate walnut frame with foliate brass inlay, late 19thC, with frame, 31½in (80cm) square.
$3,000-4,000

A copper preserving pan, with 2 carrying handles, c1820.
$150-210

Copper

A copper pan and lid, 19thC.
$150-250

A Tibetan gilt copper figure of a red hat lama, seated in dhyanasana, the left hand in dhyana, the right in abhaya, on double lotus base, sealed, 17thC, 7in (17.5cm) high.
$1,300-1,500

A copper jug, 15in (38cm) high.
$350-450

A English coffee pot, c1830, 7in (17.5cm) high.
$150-250

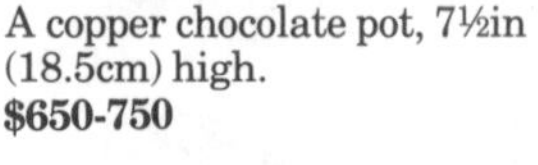

A copper chocolate pot, 7½in (18.5cm) high.
$650-750

A copper tea kettle, with flat arched swing handle, slightly domed lid with brass urn finial and curved spout, marked 'Hunneman' on handle, Boston, c1810, 11in (28cm) wide.
$2,500-3,000

A Nepalese gilt copper figure of a Dakini, the head with dharmapala crown and flaming nimbus behind, on 2 prostrate figures, on large double lotus base, scarf damaged, slight pitting, 17thC, 13½in (34.5cm) high.
$4,000-5,500

A Tibetan gilt copper figure of Vajrapani, the hair flaming behind, on double lotus base, vajra missing, 18thC, 8in (20cm) high.
$2,000-2,500

Firemarks

The London Assurance Co., c1890.
$40-55

The Yorkshire Fire and Life Insurance Co., copper, c1860, 9½in (24cm).
$80-130

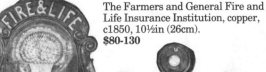

The Farmers and General Fire and Life Insurance Institution, copper, c1850, 10½in (26cm).
$80-130

The Royal Insurance Co., copper, c1850, 12in (30cm).
$65-80

The Royal Exchange Assurance, lead, c1830, 9in (22cm) high.
$100-110

Iron

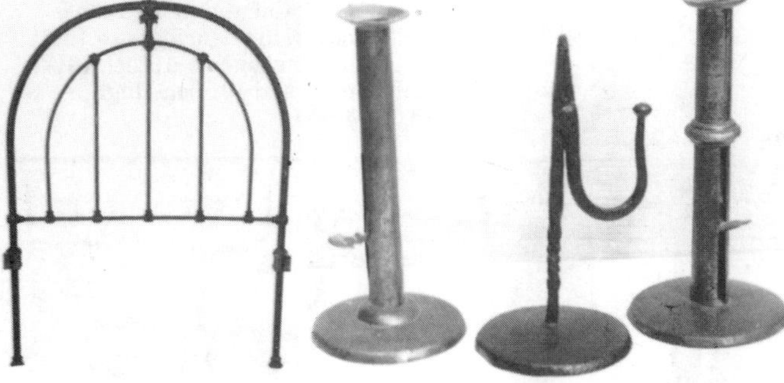

l. A plain hogscraper candlestick, c1800, r. a hogscraper rushnip, c1790, c. a wedding band hogscraper candlestick, c1800, 7½in (18.5cm) high. **$80-250 each**

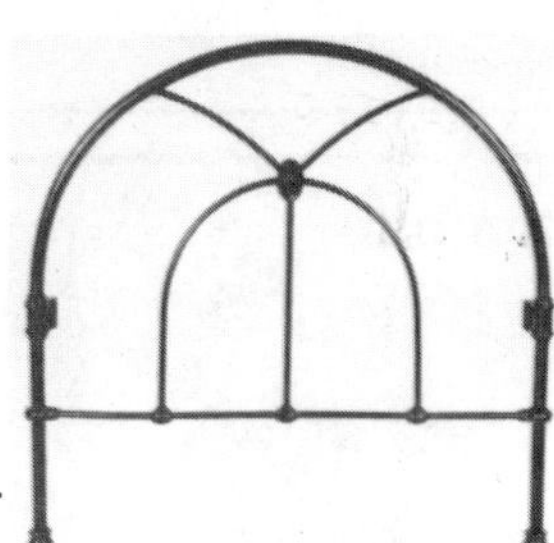

An iron bed head, 46in (116.5cm) high.
$200-210

An iron bed foot, 32½in (82cm) high.
$150-200

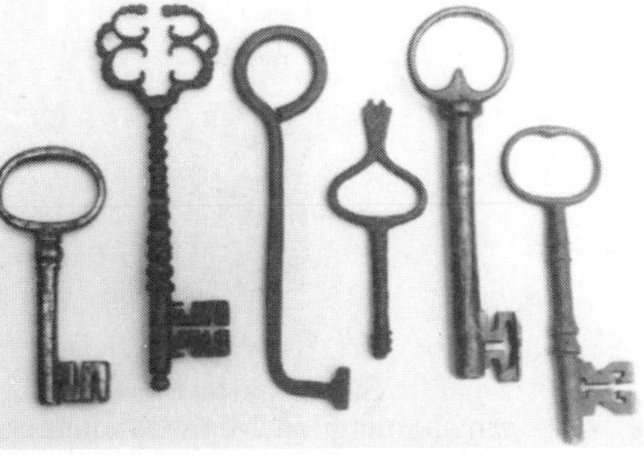

A group of keys dating from 1680 to 1860.
$6-200 each

A painted sheet iron weathervane in the form of an Indian, with feather headdress aiming a bow-and-arrow, traces of original paint, American, late 19th/early 20thC, 15½in (39.5cm) high.
$2,500-3,000

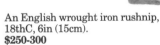

An English wrought iron rushnip, 18thC, 6in (15cm).
$250-300

A pair of gold painted cast iron figures of recumbent lions, their front paws crossed, 19thC, 31in (79cm) long.
$1,300-1,400

A painted cast iron trade sign, modelled in the form of a top hat, painted on 2 sides 'Hats' in white and red, American, 19thC, 7in (17.5cm). **$2,500-3,000**

A pair of wrought iron wafering irons, with blacksmith's tong handles, the 2 flat discs engraved with the Pascal Lamb and a coat-of-arms, both within foliate cartouche surrounds, inscribed 1750, 30in (76.5cm) long.
$700-800

Wafer irons, which are certainly known from the mid-14thC, were used in making wafer bread for the Mass and other religious ceremonies. Their use, however, was not entirely confined to the ecclesiastical.

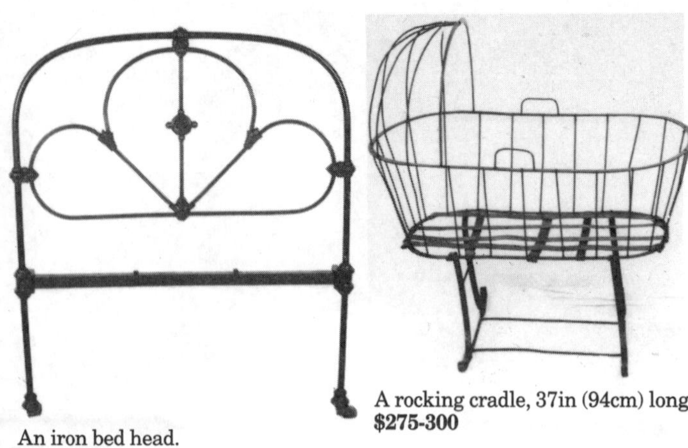

An iron bed head.
$150-230

A rocking cradle, 37in (94cm) long.
$275-300

Lead

A pair of Continental figures of a youth and girl in a dancing pose, the girl with a tambourine, 19thC, 38½ and 40in (97 and 101.5cm) high.
$3,000-4,000

Ormolu

A pair of ormolu and glass tazzas, each with fluted moulded shaped dish supported by foliate S-scrolls emerging from a column flanked by 3 putti, on concave sided triangular plinth, 16in (41cm) high.
$5,500-7,000

A pair of Sèvres pattern assembled ormolu mounted 3-light candelabra, with turquoise ground porcelain bodies painted within gilt floral and hatched cartouches and applied with ormolu goat's mask and foliage scroll handles, on spreading fluted ormolu feet above royal blue porcelain cylindrical plinths and square ormolu bases, late 19thC, 19in (48.5cm) high.
$2,500-3,000

An ormolu and enamel toilet mirror, with bevelled plate enclosed by a double door with amethyst enamel floral cartouches and mirrored back, the frame with cresting of ribbon tied trophies with garlands of roses and banded with laurel, on easel stand, late 19thC, 15 by 10in (38 by 25cm).
$2,500-3,500

A pair of Louis XVI design candlesticks, the fluted bodies hung with swags, on circular beadwork and foliate chased circular bases, 11½in (29cm) high.
$900-1,000

An ormolu-mounted opaline vase, the lid pierced with scrolls, the sides with winged caryatids on circular spreading base, 12½in (32cm) high.
$1,300-1,500

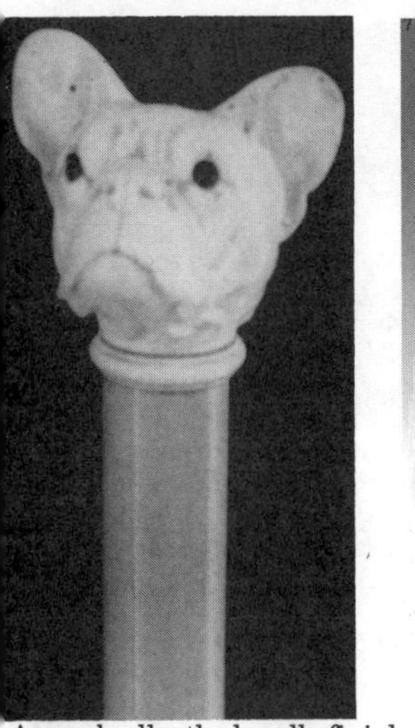

An umbrella, the handle finial of carved ivory in the form of a pug dog.
$300-400

A carved ivory figure of Mary Queen of Scots, opening to reveal a triptych with figures depicting a marriage ceremony, a Royal Pardon and a prison visitor, on a circular base, late 19thC, 9in (22.5cm) high.
$1,000-1,200

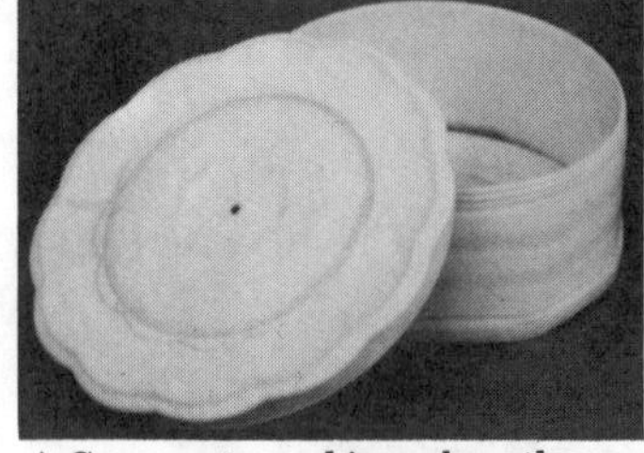

A German turned ivory box, the base and sides with wavy decoration, the screw-on lid with lobed border and flowerhead in centre, minor repair to lid, late 17thC, 4in (10cm) diam.
$2,000-2,500

An Anglo-Indian ivory inlaid wood cabinet, the doors opening to reveal 2 shelves with 2 small drawers below, surmounted by a cusped pediment, within chevron and floral lozenge borders, very slight damages to inlay, 19thC, 22in (55.5cm) high.
$1,000-1,400

Tortoiseshell

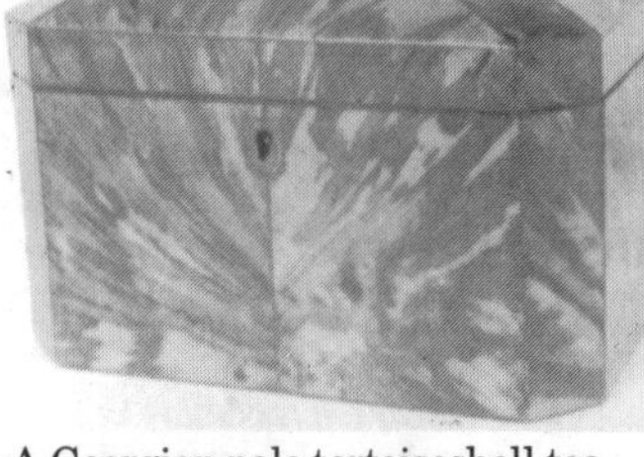

A Georgian pale tortoiseshell tea caddy, the domed top with segmented veneers, opening to reveal 2 caddies to the interior, 7in (18cm) wide.
$700-900

A Georgian tortoiseshell tea caddy, with sphere knop, the interior with 2 fitted compartments and supported upon sphere feet, 7in (18cm) wide.
$900-1,000

Marble

An English marble bust of Queen Victoria, signed L A Malempre 1887, on turned marble socle, 19thC, 19½in (50cm) high.
$1,000-1,200

A white marble relief of a youth, bust length and holding his hair in one hand, framed, probably English, 19thC, 22 by 17½in (56 by 45cm).
$1,500-2,500

A gilt mounted alabaster tazza, the shallow bowl with the monogram DL beneath a crown, the pierced handles mounted with confronting silver plate portrait medallions of Roman style, on spreading base, the base signed Mon. Alph. Giroux, Paris, late 19thC, 18in (46cm) diam.
$1,000-1,400

An Italian marble bust, 19thC, 25in (64cm) high.
$6,500-8,000

A white marble bust of Sir Joseph Hawley, 3rd Baronet, inscribed Joseph Henry Hawley, Bart, 26in (67cm) high.
$700-900

Sir Joseph Hawley (1813-75) was a patron of the Turf winning the Oaks in 1847, the 2,000 Guineas in 1858, the Derby in 1858, 1859 and 1868 and the St Leger in 1869. He also built a considerable library at his home at Leybourne Grange, Maidstone.

A pair of Italian marble busts of smiling and solemn children, wearing Roman togas, on turned socles, one repaired at neck with minor chips, 19thC, 10in (26cm) high.
$5,000-5,500

An English white marble figure of a recumbent bacchante, after Bartolini, lying on her discarded cloak, holding a tambourine and with a snake entwined around her right wrist, 19thC, 22in (56cm) long.
$3,000-4,000

A sculpted alabaster model of a snarling lion, with inset glass eyes, its head turned to dexter, on a naturalistic rocky base, 22in (56cm) long.
$1,000-1,200

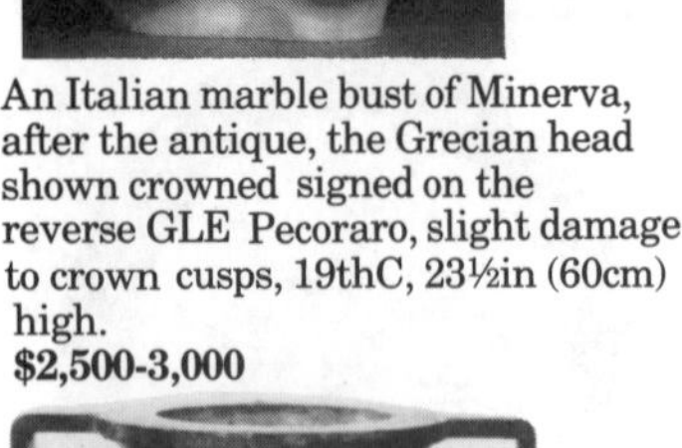

An Italian marble bust of Minerva, after the antique, the Grecian head shown crowned signed on the reverse GLE Pecoraro, slight damage to crown cusps, 19thC, 23½in (60cm) high.
$2,500-3,000

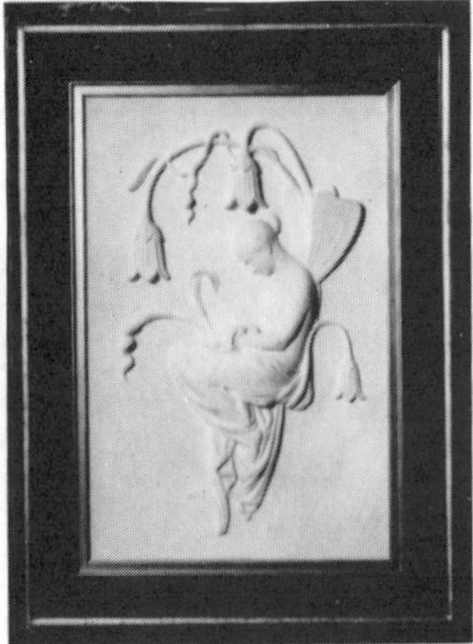

An English plaster relief of 'Bluebell', cast from a model by Sir Richard Westmacott Jr, a winged fairy seated amidst bluebell flowers and tendrils, signed Westmacott Jun Scp and dated Feby 1836, framed and glazed, 25½ by 19in (65 by 48cm).
$2,500-3,000

A variegated rouge marble twin-handled urn, 18thC, 16in (41cm) high.
$5,000-6,500

An Ashford-in-the-water black marble occasional table by Samuel Birley, inlaid with various coloured marbles, the underside bearing a label inscribed 'This table was made from black marble quarried at Ashford, Derbyshire, it was turned and inlaid by Samuel Birley at Ashford about 1899, this work is now a lost art and the black marble is no longer quarried', 18½in (47cm) wide.
$5,500-6,500

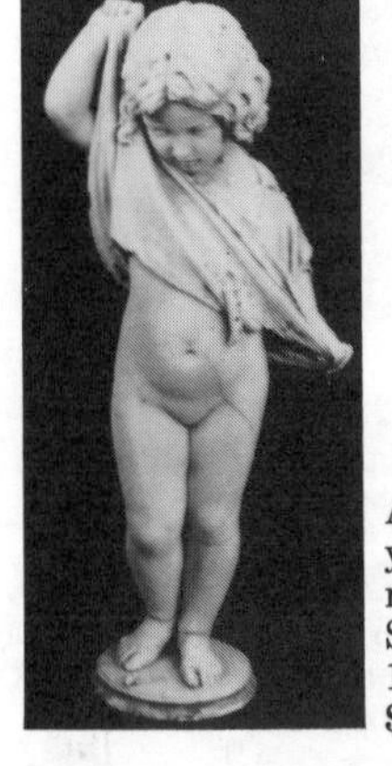

An Italian white marble figure of a young girl, the shy child raising her nightdress, signed P. Dal Nelro, Sculp, Milano, 1873, some damage, 19thC, 35in (90cm) high.
$3,000-4,000

An Italian white marble Medici vase, the urn carved with classical figures and handles, on a fluted socle, raised on an ebonised plinth the sides decorated with gilt wreaths, 19thC, 48in (121.5cm) high overall.
$11,000-14,000

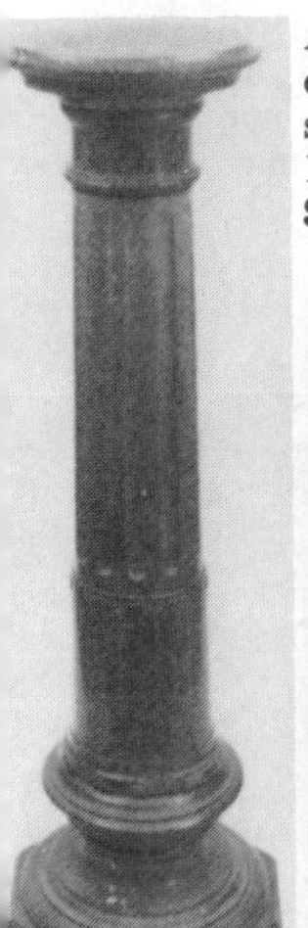

A verde antico marble column, the circular revolving top with fluted shaft and stepped hexagonal base, 19thC, 44in (111.5cm) high.
$550-700

A pair of French white marble urns, in the style of Clodion, carved with putti harvesting corn and fruit, with twin ram's head handles and fluted feet, one foot repaired in 2 places, 19thC, 16½in (41.5cm) high.
$5,500-8,000

A pair of Italian alabaster seated putti, one reading an alphabet book, the other writing Canova on a slate, both on naturalistic bases, minor damages to extremities, late 19thC, 16½in (42cm) high.
$3,000-4,000

A grey veined marble pedestal urn mounted in ormolu, the cover cast with fruiting vines, with ram's mask handles, garlands, swags and formal foliage, supported upon a square base, 24½in (63cm) high.
$1,000-1,200

A marble statue of a lady, 49in (124.5cm) high.
$5,000-5,500

An English marble portrait medallion of a young girl in profile, by S Terry, signed on the truncation S Terry, in walnut frame, late 19thC, 21in (54cm) high.
$1,500-2,500

Terracotta/Stone

A soapstone lotus bowl on stand, c1880, 9in (22.5cm) diam.
$100-130

A French terracotta bust of the 'Chanteuse Mauresque', by Charles-Henri-Joseph Cordier, the Moorish singer in folk costume, inscribed on the integral base and signed on the right side Cordier, 19thC, 18in (45cm) high.
$6,500-8,000

A South Indian granite figure of Nandi, kneeling with the right leg slightly raised, wearing jewellery and a backcloth, Vijayanagar, 15thC, 24in (61cm) high.
$8,000-9,500

An English terracotta relief of a nymph, after a model by Alexander Munro, shown bust length in a stream with rushes crowning her long hair, within an integral square frame, mid-19thC, 22½ by 20in (56.5 by 51.5cm).
$2,500-2,700

An Italian terracotta relief, with the introduction, on the battlefield, of a commander to a young boy, minor damages and repair, 16thC, 7in (17cm) diam.
$1,000-1,300

A French terracotta bust of a young boy, after Pajou, bearing the signature Pajou and the date 1780 under right shoulder, painted wooden socle, 15in (37.5cm) high.
$2,500-5,000

A Sicilian terracotta group of a peasant family, on oval base with giltwood stand and glass dome, signed with label by Giacomo & Giuseppe Bongiovannie Vaccaro, Caltagirone, 19thC, 17in (43cm) wide.
$1,300-1,400

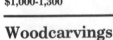

An Indian red sandstone bracket in the form of a peacock, a small bird at the breast, 3 pendant banded cones below, very slight damages, c17thC, 19in (48.5cm) high.
$1,000-1,300

An Austrian polychrome terracotta figure of a robed Arab, the base with the Goldscheide label, 19thC, 16½in (42cm) high.
$300-400

A red sandstone arched jali, the central panel pierced with a delicate octagonal lattice around a central rectangular opening, the spandrels carved with lilies and flowering vine, in a plain border, the reverse similar but simpler, slight weathering, reverse limed, 18th/19thC, 38 by 27½in (96.5 by 70cm).
$650-800

Woodcarvings

A carved and painted wooden figure modelled as Uncle Sam, standing on a box base, painted red, white and blue, some restoration and repair, marked Punching, American, early 20thC, figure 19½in (49.5cm) high.
$2,500-3,000

A South German polychrome wood group of Anna Selbdritt, St. Anne shown seated, holding the Virgin within her left arm and the Christ Child seated on her right knee, the integrally carved base dated 1519, all with damaged noses, the Virgin and the Child with arms lacking, other minor damages, early 16thC, 25½in (65cm) high.
$7,000-9,000

A pair of English oak carvings, c1660, 8in (20cm) high.
$400-500

A set of German carved wood and polychrome figures of itinerant musicians and peasants, on stepped bases, 18thC, tallest 12in (30.5cm) high.
$1,400-2,000

A German turned wood cup and cover, the ovoid cup gadrooned, with screw thread into the bulbous knop below, on a spreading foot, enriched allover with bone studs, screw to joint loose, c1700, 14in (36cm) high.
$2,500-4,000

A pair of wood appliqués, in the manner of Grinling Gibbons, carved and pierced with dead birds suspended amidst fruit and foliage, each attached to later backing, late 18thC, 75in (190.5cm) high.
$11,000-13,000

A set of 4 South German painted pinewood figures, the 2 women and 2 men in contemporary costume, emblematic of The Four Seasons, minor losses, 18thC, 12in (31cm) high.
$4,000-5,000

A Netherlandish boxwood relief of the Crucifixion, attributed to Albert Vinckenbrinck, carved in high relief on a naturalistic mound, signed with the monogram 'ALVB', 17thC, in contemporary but associated renaissance style ebonised wood frame, 10½in (26cm) high.
$9,500-12,000

Miscellaneous

A wax portrait relief bust of a gentleman, inscribed J.L. Elliot, early 19thC, 7in (18cm), in a glazed giltwood frame.
$300-500

An English bas relief medallion of a young girl, by C Pibworth, in a wreath with a stylised flower at the top and ribbons below, on voluted plinth, late 19th/early 20thC, 28½in (73cm) high.
$8,000-9,500

ANTIQUITIES

Marble

A marble relief panel, with head of a bearded male deity in relief, possibly Zeus Serapis, wearing crown with leaves around its base, and grape cluster earrings, mounted, 1st-2nd Century A.D., 18in (46cm) high.
$7,000-9,000

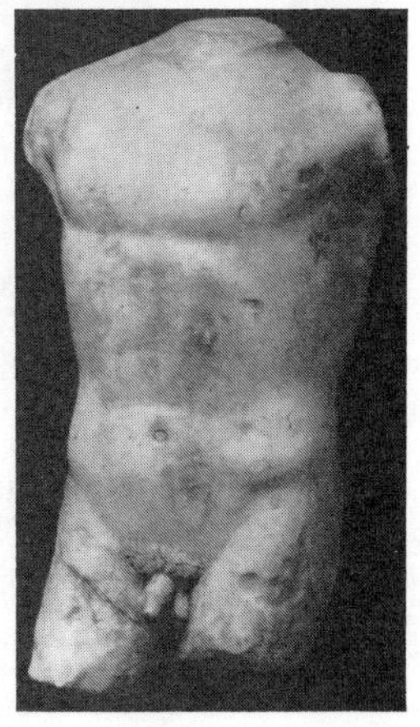

A marble torso of a youth, possibly copied from a 5th Century BC Greek original, lacking all extremities and surface marked and pitted, 1st-2nd Century A.D., 51in (129.5cm) high overall, on rectangular modern bronze base.
$20,000-22,000

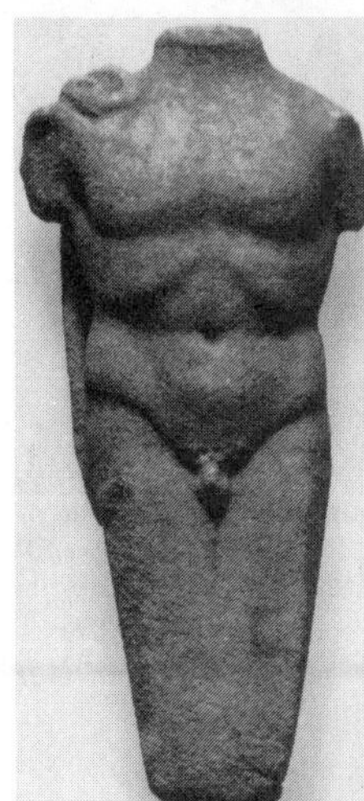

A Greek marble figure of a herm, showing strong muscular detail, incised pubes and cloak draped over right shoulder, head missing, Hellenistic, c3rd Century B.C.
$2,500-3,000

A Roman marble double head of a herm, on one side the head of a bearded satyr, on the other the head of a youth, both wearing ivy wreaths around their heads, mounted, 1st-2nd Century A.D., 5½in (14cm) high.
$8,000-9,500

Metalware

A bronze figure of Oriris, wearing atef crown and holding crook and flail, with detailed collar and wrist bands, mounted, c4th Century B.C., 10in (25cm) high.
$3,000-5,000

A bronze furniture attachment, in the form of the front part of a shrine, the cavetto cornice chased with a winged sun disc, each side bearing a dedication to Ptolemy II Philadelphus (?), the 4 tenons at the back pierced for attachment, Ptolemaic, 5in (13cm) high.
$2,500-3,000

A Greek bronze figure of a rabbit or hare, with head turned to the right, 2 tangs below feet, mounted on perspex stand, 5th Century B.C., 2in (5cm) high.
$5,500-7,000

A bronze appliqué of the bust of a child, with wavy locks, the top plaited and tied in a bunch at the front, mounted, 2nd-3rd Century A.D., 2in (5cm) high.
$1,000-1,200

A bronze seated figure of Harpocrates, the naked god wearing a double crown, figure-of-eight uraeus and broad collar, mounted, 4th-2nd Century B.C., 4in (10cm) high.
$1,500-2,500

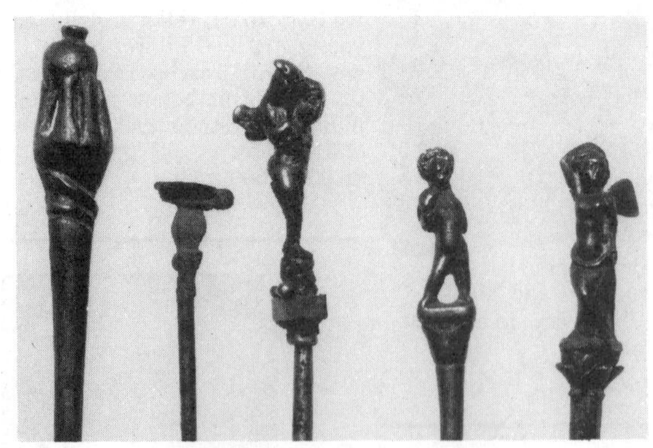

A set of 5 silver hairpins, each with plain shaft and elaborate finial, 1st-3rd Century A.D., 5½in (14cm) long.
$2,500-3,000

Many Roman hairstyles involved the use of elaborate tight curls made with hot tongs and arranged, rather than held, in place with the aid of such hairpins.

Pottery

A miniature Attic black figure hydria, the body with 3 naked komasts dancing between ivy border to each side, second half 6th Century B.C., 4½in (12cm) high.
$2,000-2,500

A complete bun shaped schoolboy's tablet, with 3 lines of text on each side, an extract from a lexical composition with river names including the Tigris, Old Babylonian, early 2nd Millennium B.C., 3½in (9cm) diam.
$2,500-3,000

The skills of reading and writing were not widespread in ancient Mesopotamia. Scribes had to train from an early age to master their craft, first learning how to shape the clay tablets on which they wrote, practising individual characters and gradually learning to write the script. On these round bun shaped tablets the teacher would typically write out 3 lines on one side, the schoolboy would carefully examine these then try to reproduce exactly the same text on the reverse of the tablet.

A Palmyran limestone portrait head of a man, with powerful features, mounted on variegated green base, 3rd-4th Century A.D., 9in (23cm) high.
$8,000-9,500

A terracotta figure of a woman and child, the woman wearing a long garment seated on a stool, holding naked child in both her hands, the child on her knees, traces of yellow white and red pigment, Boeotian, 5th Century B.C., 5in (13cm) high.
$21,000-25,000

Rugs & Carpets

A Heriz carpet, the red field with an allover design of brightly coloured stylised flowering vines within a dark blue floral border, 135 by 109in (342.5 by 276.5cm).
$1,500-2,500

A Chi Chi rug, the black field with multi-coloured patterns, a short kilim strip at each end, partly replaced selvedges, slight corrosion, 76 by 46in (193 by 116.5cm).
$6,500-8,000

A Chinese carpet, in ivory and royal blue stripes, areas of slight wear and staining, 138 by 110in (350.5 by 279cm).
$3,000-4,000

A Bidjar rug, the indigo field with fox brown, turtle palmette and flowering vine border between medium blue floral stripes, inner zig-zag stripe, slight overall wear, fringes replaced, 77 by 57in (196 by 145cm).
$4,000-5,000

An Iranian Sarouk rug, the shaded brick red field with a blue medallion and ivory spandrels, within an indigo palmette border, 56 by 39in (142 by 99cm).
$650-800

A Kazak carpet, the red field with 3 red, ivory and blue medallions, in turquoise, blue and red border stripes with stylised flowerheads and serrated leaves, 144 by 96in (365.5 by 243.5cm).
$1,300-1,500

An Armenian rug, with 5 indigo gabled and hooked medallions with pink floral panels surrounded by similar dart motifs, in a broad ivory floral border between shaded blue, yellow, rust red flowerhead floral and baton stripes, 133 by 56in (337 by 142cm).
$3,000-4,000

A Heriz carpet, with lozenge shaped brick field, large indigo centre jewel pendant medallion, inner medallions in rose, pale blue, ivory and indigo, 223 by 149in (566.5 by 378cm).
$22,000-26,000

A pair of part silk Isfahan rugs in ivory, tomato red, indigo, blue and sandy yellow, 91 by 58in (231 by 147cm).
$12,000-13,500

A Karadjar runner, the indigo field with stepped rows of alternately facing boteh in an ivory flowering vine border between brick red floral stripes, 196 by 42in (497.5 by 106.5cm).
$2,500-3,000

A Chinese silk rug, the apricot field with 5 imperial 5-clawed dragons surrounded by stylised clouds, within a stylised wave and mountain border, an inscribed panel above, areas of slight wear, 94 by 61in (238 by 155cm).
$1,400-2,000

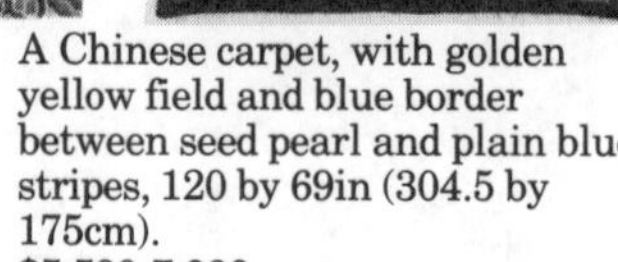

A Chinese carpet, with golden yellow field and blue border between seed pearl and plain blue stripes, 120 by 69in (304.5 by 175cm).
$5,500-7,000

A European carpet, with raspberry red, sandy yellow, ivory, brown and pistachio green stripes in an ivory border, slight staining and colour run, 111 by 86in (282 by 218.5cm).
$4,000-5,000

A Khotan carpet, the shaded lilac and blue field with stylised floral motifs around 3 blue shaded lilac floral roundels, plain outer lilac stripe, slight overall wear, 136 by 66in (345 by 167.5cm).
$4,000-5,500

A Chinese carpet, the ivory field with an indigo flowering vine border with light blue flowering vine and plain blue stripes, a few minor stains, 143 by 110in (363 by 279cm).
$5,000-6,500

A Kerman carpet with pink and blue Tree of Life pattern on a fawn field with a blue flowered border, 120 by 82in (304.5 by 208cm).
$2,600-3,000

A Kazak rug, the tomato red field with hooked lozenges, floral motifs and human figures in blue, indigo, mustard yellow and chocolate brown, slight overall wear, repaired, 110 by 75in (279 by 190.5cm).
$2,600-3,500

A Kirman carpet, the indigo field with a large flowering tree with perching birds, 127 by 89in (322 by 226cm).
$5,000-6,500

An Ushak carpet, the ivory field within a salmon pink border of alternate ivory and sea blue floral cartouches divided by floral bands, between sea blue floral and zig-zag stripes, slight overall wear, 214 by 210in (543.5 by 533cm).
$2,500-3,000

A Savonnerie carpet, on shaded olive green field with double narrow pink and white plain striped border, areas of wear and repair, backed, 151 by 48in (384 by 122cm).
$7,000-8,000

A Samarkand rug, with faded blue field with allover pomegranate design in soft brick with brown and brick fruiting branches, brick, faded blue, celadon green and pale gold narrow floral borders, 101 by 57in (256.5 by 144.5cm).
$1,500-2,500

A central Anatolian kilim, in indigo, ivory, brick and pale green, with an allover design of various hooked medallions, rosettes and 'S' motifs, ivory fret outer border, 19thC, 110 by 44in (279 by 111.5cm).
$400-550

A Tabriz carpet in blue, brick red and ivory, 267 by 174in (677 by 442cm).
$8,000-9,500

A Qashqai tribal rug, the blue field with an overall Herati-type design, with dark ivory spandrels, surrounded by brick red, ivory and dark mustard stripes, 90 by 57in (228.5 by 144.5cm).
$1,500-2,000

A Kazak rug, the tomato red field with 2 indigo floral medallions, in a light blue stylised flowering vine border between ivory boteh and brick red flowering vine stripes, slight overall wear, 83 by 59in (210.5 by 149.5cm).
$1,000-1,300

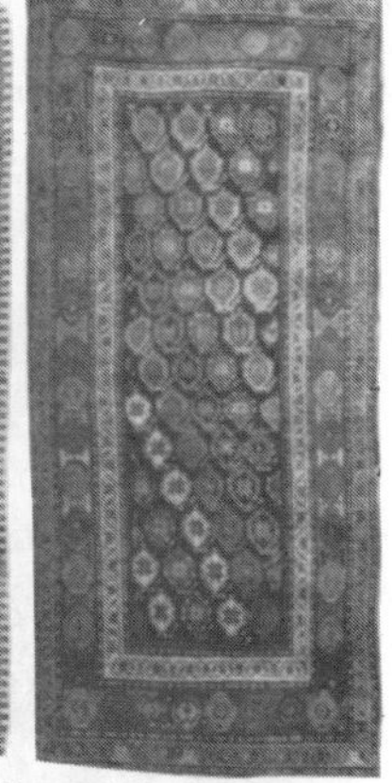

A Kazak-Gendje rug, the indigo field with columns of diagonal multi-coloured boteh, surrounded by ivory and mustard yellow inner and outer stripes with flowering vines and a brick red lozenge border, 106 by 50in (269 by 127cm).
$1,300-1,500

A Tabriz rug, in tan, ivory, indigo and brick red, very slight wear, 77 by 55in (195.5 by 139.5cm).
$2,500-3,500

TEXTILES
Costume

A Christening robe of Carrickmacross lace, the skirt threaded with ivory satin ribbons, the bodice worked with scrolling foliage, c1907.
$650-800

This robe was purchased in 1907 after it had won 1st prize in an exhibition in Chicago of Irish lace.

A young girl's dress of egg shell blue wool and silk, with a tiered skirt and short pleated cap sleeves, trimmed with lace, c1878.
$500-650

A complete highlander's outfit, comprising: green facecloth jacket and waistcoat, Gordon tartan kilt, shorts and sash, matching socks and sock tabs, tam-o'shanter, skhein dhu and sporran stamped R W Forsythe, Glasgow and Edinburgh.
$500-550

A child's matador fancy dress outfit, comprising black velvet breeches, trimmed with white satin and metal braid, a waistcoat and bolero similarly trimmed, a hat, cummerbund and pair of ivory silk stockings, early 20thC.
$140-200

A dress of red grosgrain silk, the bodice of rust coloured velvet trimmed with large bows and blue chiffon, with gigot sleeves, 1893.
$300-400

A wedding gown of ivory tamboured net, with a frilled lace yoke, leg of mutton sleeves, an ivory satin sash and orange blossom wreath, 1905.
$700-900

A densely embroidered jacke with Chinese scrolling embroidery with a sea wave border, the back worked with a phoenix, labelled Molyneux, 1937.
$400-500

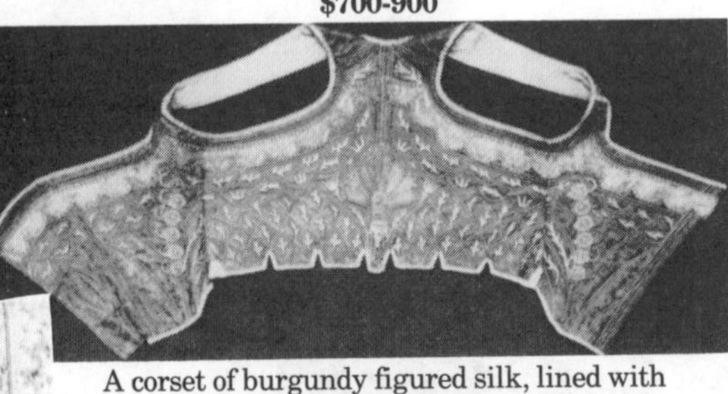

A corset of burgundy figured silk, lined with glazed printed cotton and embroidered with metal thread flowers and white metal hooks, regional, c1810. **$650-800**

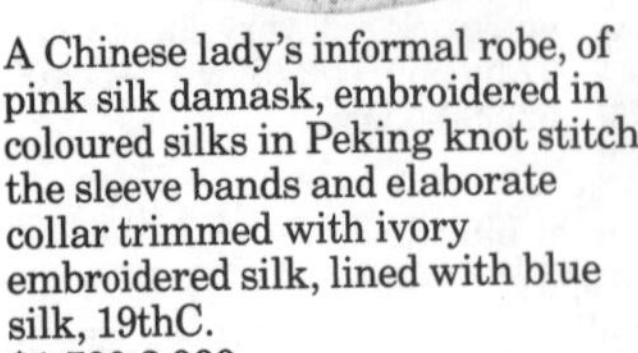

A Chinese lady's informal robe, of pink silk damask, embroidered in coloured silks in Peking knot stitch, the sleeve bands and elaborate collar trimmed with ivory embroidered silk, lined with blue silk, 19thC.
$1,500-2,000

A Chinese robe, of midnight blue silk embroidered with baskets of flowers and butterflies, the wide sleeve bands embroidered with large flowerheads, some in Peking knot on an ivory ground.
$250-400

A dress of red chiffon with a wrap-over bodice of red chiffon over cream net, trimmed with gilt bugle beads at the neck and sleeves, knotted at the hem a the back to show a Brussels lace appliqu underskirt, c1910.
$300-400

A Chinese robe of ivory silk, richly embroidered in various coloured silks, with a wave border worked in Peking knots.
$1,400-2,000

A Turkish robe of purple velvet, densely embroidered with beaten silver gilt wire arabesques, sprigged with ribboned sprays of flowers, 19thC.
$650-700

A cope of red velvet, the orphreys and hood finely embroidered in coloured silks and gilt threads, the hood with the Crucifixion, the orphreys with arched recesses framing scenes of the Passion, lined with crimson damask, the embroidery probably Flemish, late 15th/early 16thC.
$3,000-5,000

Cope: a long cloak worn in processions.

A Japanese furisode, of ivory silk, printed in black and rust to resemble tie-dyed patterns, embroidered in green, red and pink silk, and gilt threads, with padded hem, lined with red silk, early 19thC.
$1,400-2,000

A Chinese informal jacket, of red silk damask, with trimmings of ivory silk, embroidered in coloured silks, lined with fur, 19thC.
$500-650

A Chinese lady's informal coat of silver-green silk, embroidered in coloured silks, trimmed with black silk embroidered ribbon, lined with pink silk, late 19thC.
$700-800

A Chinese robe of red silk, embroidered mainly in shades of blue and white, with a pair of civil rank badges, worked with the seventh-rank mandarin duck, lined with blue silk, 19thC.
$650-800

A Chinese robe of yellow silk, trimmed with blue kossu silk, woven in many colours, the kossu from an earlier robe, late 18th/early 19thC.
$1,500-3,000

The robe made-up before 1860, when it was brought to England by Colonel John Desborough from the Summer Palace.

A Chinese dragon of blue kossu silk, woven in many colours, lined with pale blue silk, 19thC.
$1,000-1,500

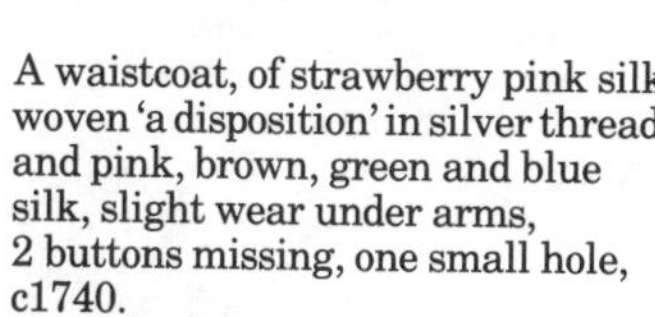

A waistcoat, of strawberry pink silk woven 'a disposition' in silver thread and pink, brown, green and blue silk, slight wear under arms, 2 buttons missing, one small hole, c1740.
$2,600-3,000

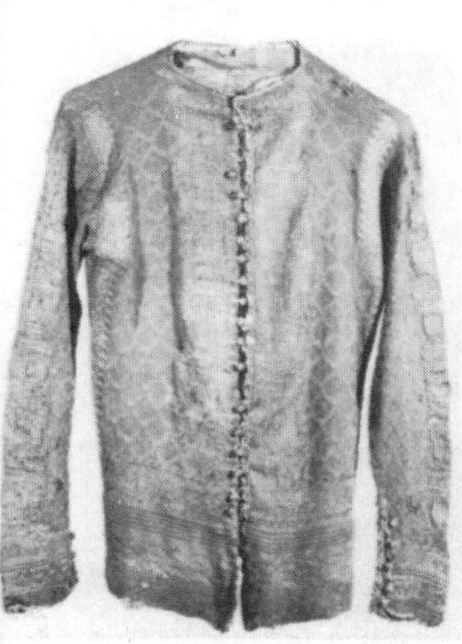

A knitted waistcoat, of burgundy coloured silk, knitted with gold lace patterns at the borders and seams, with ball-shaped buttons of gold thread, repairs, 17thC.
$1,500-2,500

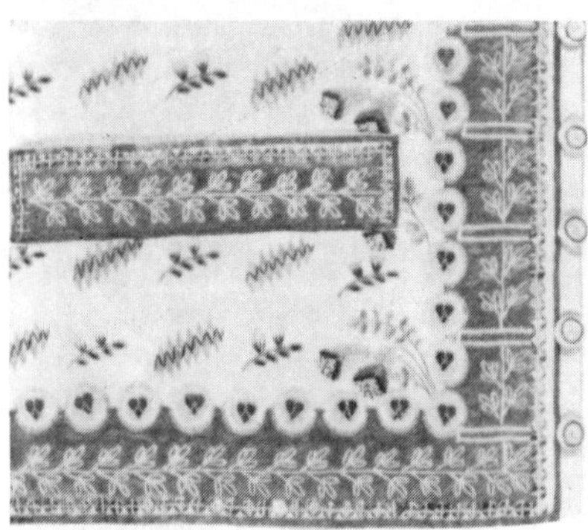

A waistcoat, of ivory satin embroidered with sprigs of flowers and zig-zag motifs, the borders applied with olive green satin and decorated with chenille work, paste and cut steel hearts, c1780.
$1,000-1,200

The lining stamped 'Sir. Tho: Cave'.

A pair of lady's beaded evening shoes, c1935.
$65-100

A pair of cherry red leather lace-up shoes, with circular heels labelled Ferrina, Created by Ferragamo, Made in England, and Harvey Nichols and Eros.
$65-100

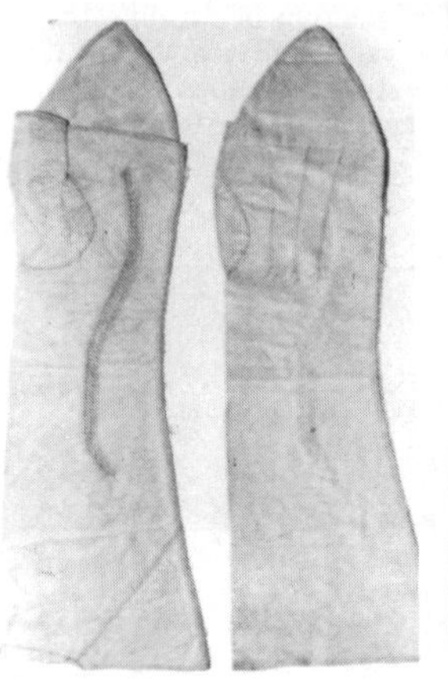

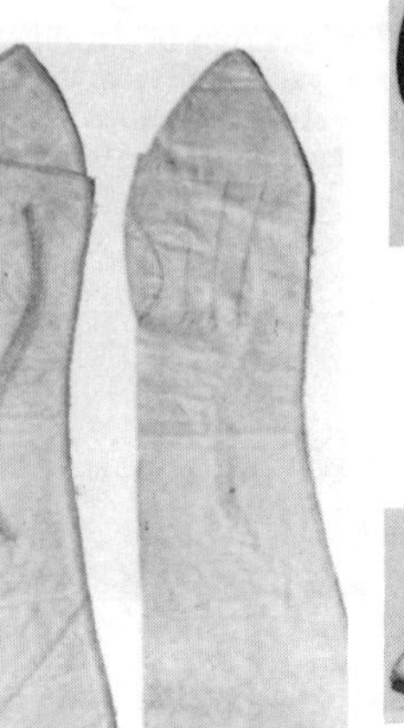

A pair of ivory silk mittens, with a long sinuous insertion at the inner wrists embroidered in pink silk, the borders also embroidered in pink silk, the tips lined in pink silk, c1770.
$800-1,300

A pair of mauve brocade slippers, woven with a thin green stripe with white scrolling flowers, trimmed with white silk ribbons and bows, with a low stepped heel, c1865.
$200-250

A Victorian Lord Chancellor's bourse, of honey coloured velvet, worked with metallic threads and sequins, with the Royal coat-of-arms and motto, surmounted by the royal coat-of-arms, with the initials VR, the border with putti, the corners with large tassels, 2 loose, with bag, 17in (43cm) square.
$1,400-2,000

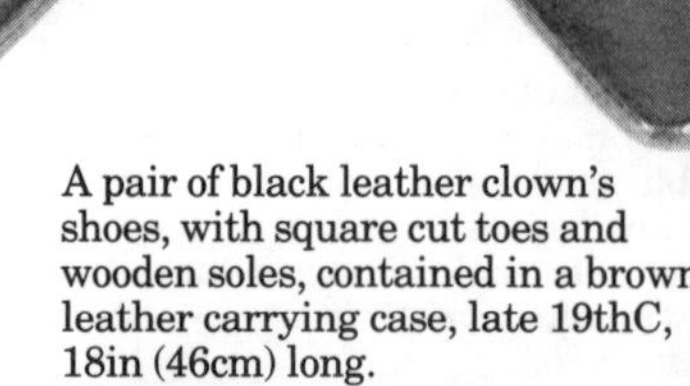

A pair of black leather clown's shoes, with square cut toes and wooden soles, contained in a brown leather carrying case, late 19thC, 18in (46cm) long.
$300-400

A Canton fawn silk shawl, embroidered with figures from Chinese life, with ivory painted faces, 60in (152cm) square.
$500-800

A Kashmir rumal shawl, with floral arches, with an indistinct description in pink silk, c1840, 72in (182.5cm) square.
$1,500-2,000

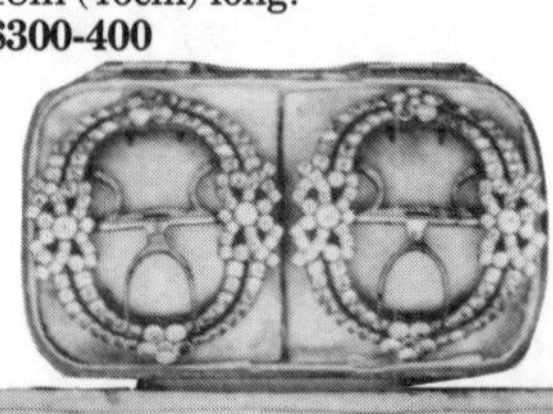

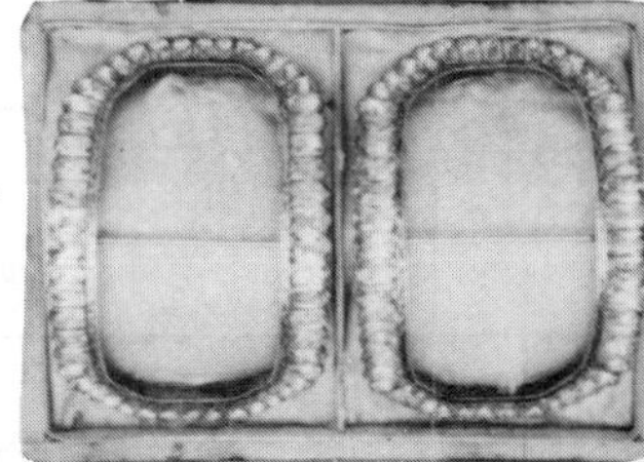

A pair of paste shoe buckles, with gold stamped trim, chapes missing, in fitted box, late 18thC; and another pair of oval shoe buckles, set with paste bows, with forked tongues, also late 18thC, in fitted box.
$800-1,000

A Kashmir shawl, with complex broad hashiya woven with S-motifs, the palla woven with 3 circular laurel wreaths and stylised sacred mountains, the boteh reserved in yellow, pink and blue, the dhor similar, with a black field, c1830, Sikh period, 130 by 56in (330 by 142cm).
$2,000-2,500

A double-sided Paisley shawl, woven with bright colours, the borders of palmette motifs, the field woven with swirling leafy cones arranged in informal columns, with fringes, c1860, 70 by 66in (177.5 by 167.5cm).
$700-900

A Paisley shawl, woven in fresh colours with curled tipped cones forming a central medallion, c1860, 64 by 128in (162.5 by 325cm).
$1,300-1,400

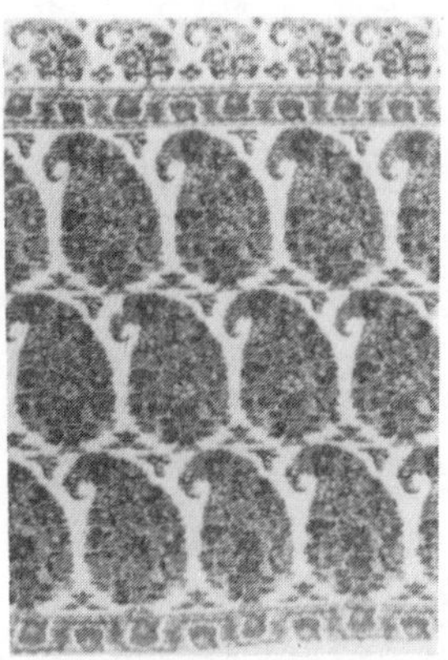

A shawl of ivory wool, the hashiya woven with an angular meandering vine with blue flowers, the palla woven with 3 rows of small mosaic boteh on ideogramme roots, woven in shades of red, blue and yellow, Afghan period, joined, c1820, 48 by 100in (122 by 254cm).
$1,200-1,300

An Indian ivory net stole, embroidered with brightly coloured floss silks, the ends worked with 3 cones against a floral background, the field sprigged with flowers, c1835, 20 by 100in (50.5 by 254cm).
$300-400

A turnover shawl, with red field and attached borders woven with flower filled cones amid angular trees, with a floral border, c1845.
$550-650

A double sided Paisley shawl, woven with an intricate design of palmettes and mihrabs in green, black, red and ivory, 69½ by 65in (176 by 165cm).
$650-700

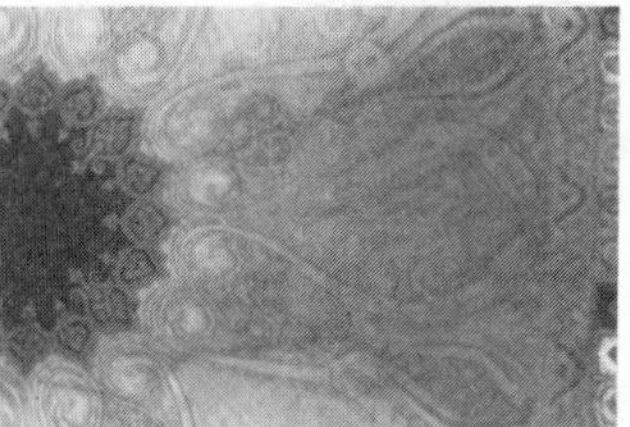

A rumal shawl, Doghra, c1850, 80in (203cm) square. **$1,000-1,200**

A Paisley shawl woven predominantly in burgundy and blue, with cones flanking 4 central cartouches, 2 ivory, 2 blue, c1858, 64 by 130in (162.5 by 330cm).
$650-700

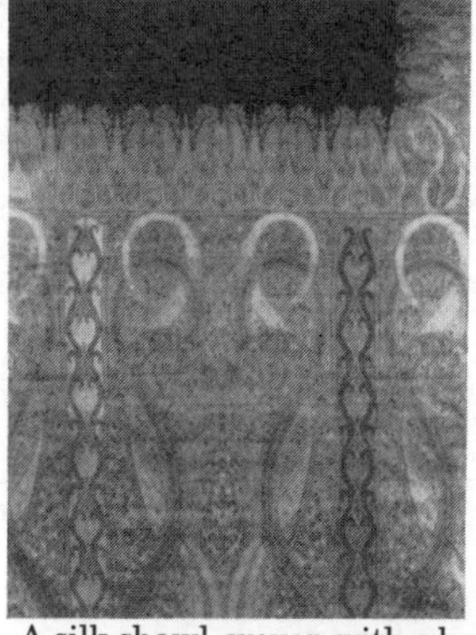

A silk shawl, woven with a border composed of serpentine cones separated by green and blue columns, with a twisted red silk fringe and black silk field, c1850, 70 by 140in (177.5 by 355cm).
$650-700

A Paisley shawl, woven with 2 spiral tipped opposing cones at either corner framing a red silk central medallion, c1855, 74in (188cm) square.
$650-800

A Paisley shawl, woven with a central palmette column flanked by cones and beneath a prayer arch, with a black silk residual field, c1860, 64 by 142in (162.5 by 360.5cm).
$2,000-2,500

A double sided shawl, woven with columns of bent tipped cones, c1865, 64 by 70in (162.5 by 177.5cm).
$650-800

A Paisley shawl, woven with elongated leafy columns, c1865, 12 by 64in (325 by 162.5cm).
$900-1,000

Embroidery

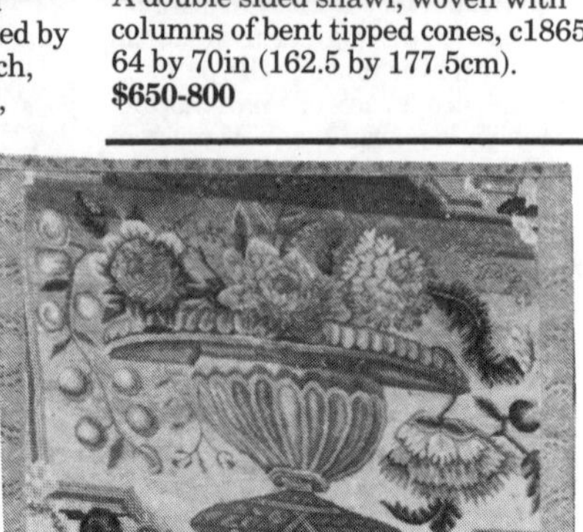

An embroidered panel from a chair back, worked in coloured wools against a sky blue ground, trimmed with later braid, made up into a cushion, French, late 17th/early 18thC, 15 by 20in (39 by 51cm).
$650-1,000

An embroidered picture, worked in coloured silks, 18thC, 18 by 16in (46 by 41cm), framed and glazed.
$1,200-1,300

A pair of 17thC style crewelwork curtains, embroidered in shades of green, blue, brown and red wool, 18thC, 82 by 34in (208 by 87cm), and a matching pelmet.
$2,000-2,500

An embroidered picture, worked in coloured silk, depicting an interior with children playing blind man's buff, late 18th/early 19thC, 13 by 18in (34 by 46cm), framed in black and gold glass.
$2,500-3,000

An embroidered silk chenille and gauze puffwork picture, of a spray of flowers on an ivory silk ground, early 19thC, 18 by 15½in (46 by 40cm).
$300-400

An embroidered scalloped pelmet, worked in coloured wools and whit beads, highlighted with silks, against a white beaded ground, c1840, 37 by 11in (94 by 29cm).
$550-650

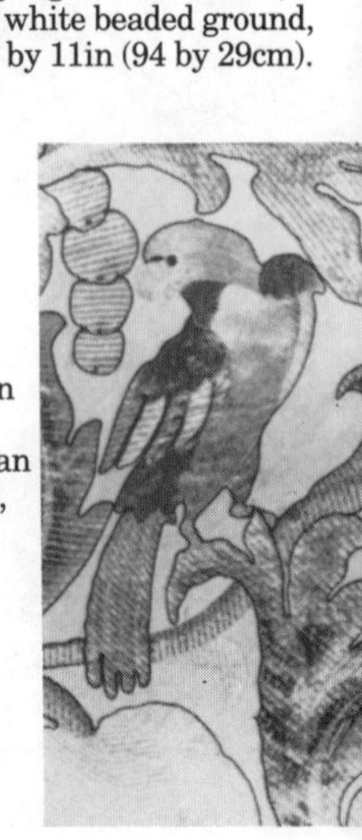

An embroidered panel, worked in coloured floss silks and couched black cord and gilt thread, with an early 18thC style pattern, c1880, 29 by 112in (74 by 284.5cm).
$700-900

An embroidered bag, worked in coloured silks with a swan and a lyre among flowers, the reverse with a spray of roses, the embroidery c1840, 8 by 6in (21 by 16cm).
$140-200

An embroidered picture, worked in coloured wools, highlighted with silks, with a spaniel sitting on a red cushion with large tassels at each corner, mid-19thC, 10 by 16in (26 by 41cm), framed and glazed.
$1,200-1,300

A pair of Japanese black silk hangings, embroidered in coloured silks, late 19thC, 120 by 45in (304.5 by 114cm).
$700-1,000

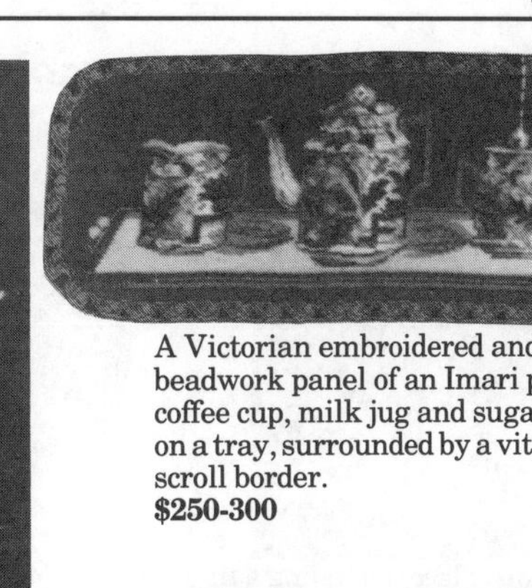

A Victorian embroidered and beadwork panel of an Imari pattern coffee cup, milk jug and sugar bowl on a tray, surrounded by a vitruvian scroll border.
$250-300

A Syrian silk and silver thread embroidered panel, the ivory field with a large baluster flowering vase within a golden yellow, ice blue and ivory scrolling frame with outer burgundy stripe, areas of repair and staining, 84 by 71in (213 by 180cm).
$2,500-3,000

Lace

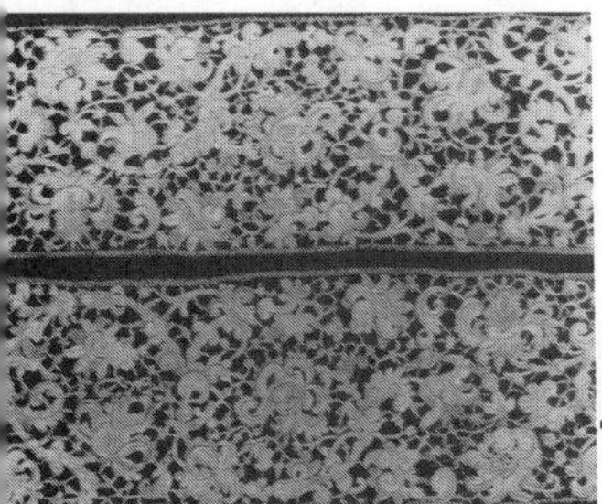

A flounce of gros point de Venise, 17thC, 112 by 7in (284.5 by 18cm).
$275-300

A collection of Italian lace, including 2 lengths of Punto in Aria, worked with bellflowers and flowers alternating with sunburst roundels, edged with bellflowers, 17thC.
$300-500

Two lengths of Venetian rose point lace, fragments of Venetian tape lace and another piece similar, late 17thC.
$80-150

A collection of lace, including 2 flounces of filet, worked with pomegranates, lilies and honeysuckle, probably 18thC, 8 by 92in (21 by 233.5cm) and 60in (152cm).
$300-400

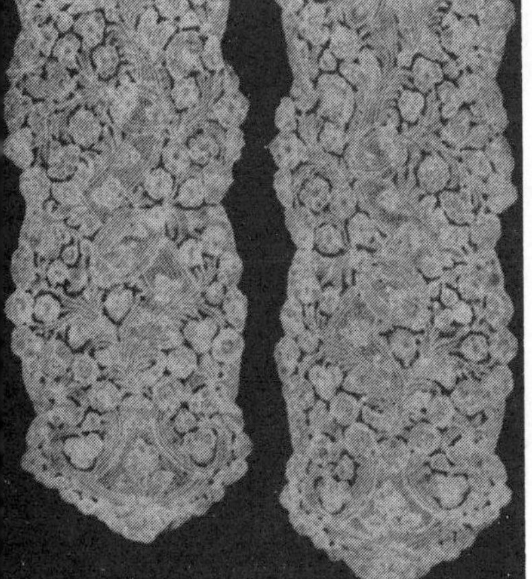

A pair of Brussels bobbin lace lappets, worked with a zig-zagging ribbon against a floral ground, mid-18thC, 4 by 23in (10 by 59cm).
$1,000-1,200

A flounce of fine Alençon needlelace, worked with flower filled cartouches above a scalloped border, late 19thC, 156 by 13in (396 by 33cm).
$1,400-1,500

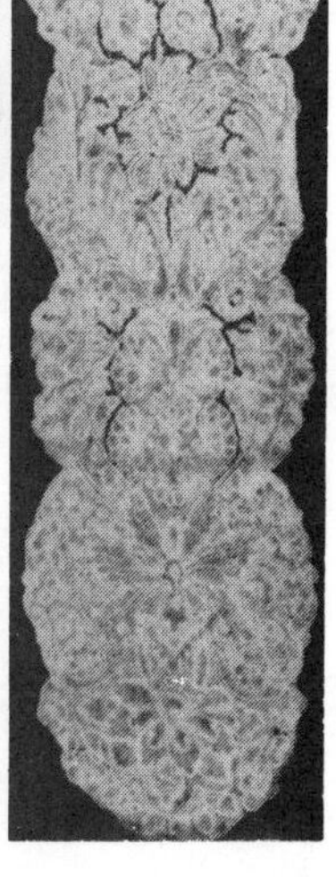

A pair of Brussels lace lappets, worked with a scalloped edge, with an orchid-like flower at either end, with various flowers above framed by informal garlands, c1730, 4 by 23in (10 by 59cm).
$550-800

A collection of lace, including a fine flounce of point de gaze, with shaped ends, worked with butterflies and birds, 18in (46cm) deep.
$2,000-2,500

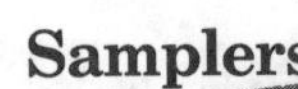

Samplers

A map sampler of England and Wales, worked in long and short stitch, and fine black cross stitch, with a border of entwining leaves and flowers, signed Mary Sutton, Cheadle School, Stoke 1797, Britannia is seated in the top right hand corner, late 18thC, 25 by 22in (64 by 56cm).
$500-650

A sampler by Ellen Greaves, 1846, worked in coloured wools, with a verse 'Jesus permit', 26 by 27in (67 by 69cm), mounted on a stretcher.
$300-500

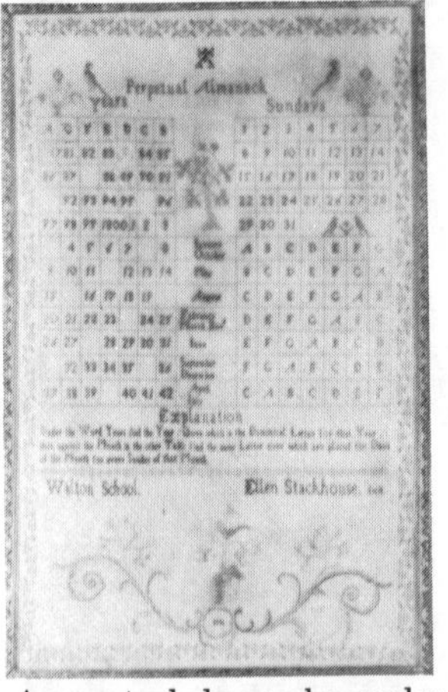

A perpetual almanack sampler, by Ellen Stackhouse, 1781, Walton School, the table and explanation in black silk, with a naturalistic pot of flowers and scrolling motifs worked beneath in coloured silks, with a trailing floral border, 16 by 11in (41 by 28cm), framed and glazed.
$500-650

A sampler, by E. B, embroidered in coloured silks, with a verse 'Let Gratitude', c1835, 14 by 12in (36 by 31cm), framed and glazed.
$800-1,000

A sampler by Matilda Andrews, 1837, worked in coloured silks with a verse 'Lord search, oh search', also with a picture of St Pauls Chapel New York, with a formalised floral border, 15 by 12in (39 by 31cm), framed and glazed.
$1,300-1,400

A sampler by Marthe Le Patuorel, 1827, worked in coloured silks with a French verse, Channel Islands, 19 by 22in (49 by 56cm), framed and glazed.
$900-1,000

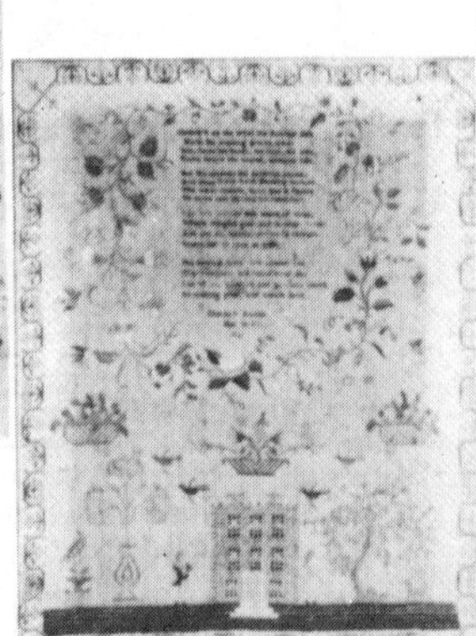

A sampler, by Elizabeth Rennie, 1811, worked in coloured silks with a verse 'stretched on the cross', the verse framed by a garland of naturalistic flowers, with a border of trailing flowers, 17 by 13in (43 by 33cm), framed and glazed.
$800-1,000

A needlework sampler by Sarah Hemsley, of Bexley Heath, Kent, dated April 21 1894, worked in fine coloured silks, unframed, late 19thC, 16½ by 13in (43 by 34cm).
$1,000-1,200

A needlework sampler, by Elizabeth Lloyd aged 11 years, dated 1800, of Adam and Eve flanking the Tree of Knowledge beneath rows of alphabets, small animals, winged putti, and a 3 lined text, 18 by 15in (46 by 39cm). **$500-650**

Tapestries

A tapestry panel woven in wools and silks, depicting 2 ladies hunting a fire breathing dragon within a landscape, flanked by centaurs, plain borders, restorations, 17thC, 30 by 22in (77 by 56cm).
$1,000-1,200

A French verdure tapestry panel, woven in shades of green, blue and brown, with leafy trees and foliage in the background and a small pavilion in the foreground, restored, Aubusson, late 17thC, 60 by 28in (152 by 72cm).
$800-1,000

A tapestry border, woven in many colours, with a central roundel depicting one of the Labours of Hercules, with a centurion and grotesque above, 16thC, 110 by 13in (279 by 34cm).
$2,000-2,500

A Louis XVI tapestry panel, woven in many colours depicting a scene after Oudry, against a cream ground, 22 by 18in (56 by 46cm).
$650-800

A French tapestry border, woven mainly in shades of cream, blue, brown and yellow, with a pale blue border woven with a yellow trailing pattern, restored, 17thC, 40 by 13in (101.5 by 34cm).
$300-400

A pair of Louis XVI Aubusson tapestry cushion covers, woven in many colours, backed with crimson damask, 14 by 16in (36 by 41cm).
$1,200-1,300

An Aubusson tapestry, woven in shades of brown, cream, green and yellow, 19thC, 80 by 22in (203 by 56cm). **$4,000-5,000**

A French tapestry, woven in muted colours, possibly the Aubusson Factory, 19thC, 49 by 67in (124.5 by 170cm).
$2,500-3,000

An Aubusson tapestry hanging, woven in many colours, within a frame entwined with roses, 19thC, 106 by 54in (269 by 137cm).
$4,000-5,000

Miscellaneous

A needlework mirror, with ivory satin frame, worked in coloured silks and gilt threads with raised work animals in each corner, the embroidery English, c1660, 22 by 20in (56 by 51cm), framed and glazed. **$5,500-6,500**

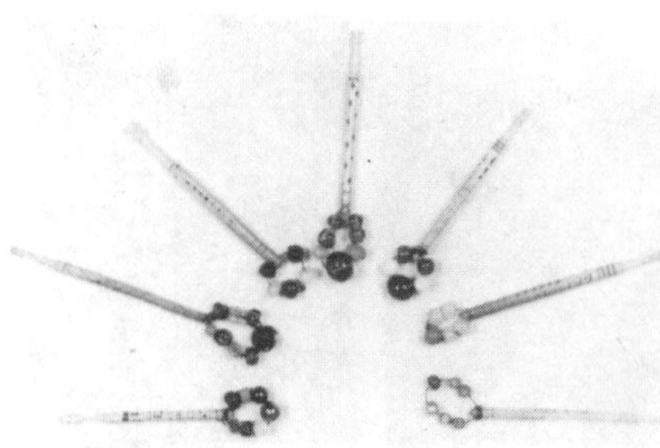

A collection of 7 named and initialled bone bobbins, including David Headland, Ann Gammons, David.
$110-150

A pair of George III needlework pictures by Ellen Foster, 1812, each with watercolour features on an ivory silk ground, 11 by 9in (29 by 23cm) with Victorian giltwood and gesso frames.
$1,500-2,500

A needlework panel, the ivory field with an acanthus oval enclosing a large bouquet, in a scrolled grey and green lattice with border bouquets in each corner, backed, 75 by 56in (190.5 by 142cm).
$1,500-2,500

A needlework picture, worked in coloured silks, late 18thC, 18 by 16in (46 by 41cm), framed and glazed.
$300-500

A pair of olive green velvet chair backs, woven to reveal a dark red silk ground, 19thC, 64 by 22in (162.5 by 56cm) each.
$1,000-1,200

A pair of cream cord tie backs, with elaborate tasselled heads trimmed with blue, red, green and cream silk, and a pair of tie backs of cream and peach coloured cord with matching tassells decorated with gilt threads, and 3 other tie backs.
$500-650

A needlework panel, the ivory ground divided into 4 groups of mustard yellow, green, raspberry red and blue open floral leafy palmettes, in a turquoise and mustard yellow plain striped border, backed, 91 by 60in (231 by 152cm).
$5,500-6,500

A needlework panel, the buff field divided by golden yellow floral strips into 6 panels, each with a floral wreath around a central golden flowerhead, backed, 62 by 42in (157 by 106.5cm).
$2,500-3,000

An early Georgian needlework panel, worked in tent stitch, of a lady and gentleman dressed as a shepherd and shepherdess tending their flock in a rural landscape, 23 by 17in (58.5 by 43cm).
$1,200-1,300

A Tulip and Rose hanging, woven in shades of blue, green, red and yellow wool, with a repeating pattern of flowerheads among curling leaves against a dark blue ground, designed by William Morris, late 19thC, 91 by 80in (231 by 203cm).
$2,600-3,500

This pattern was registered as a fabric on 20 January 1876.

A hanging, composed of 3 panels of natural embroidered linen framed with a border of blue arabesques, the field worked with 4 columns of bold palmettes in blue or red, with serpent motifs, Ottoman, 17th/18thC, 56 by 88in (142 by 223.5cm).
$7,000-9,000

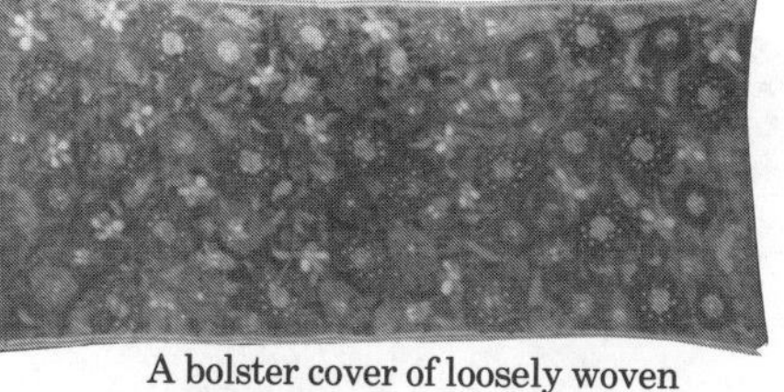

A bolster cover of loosely woven natural linen, embroidered with 2 arching flower sprays, worked with blue spikey florets, terracotta roses and pale green leaves and buds, 18thC, 21 by 47in (53.5 by 119cm).
$1,200-1,400

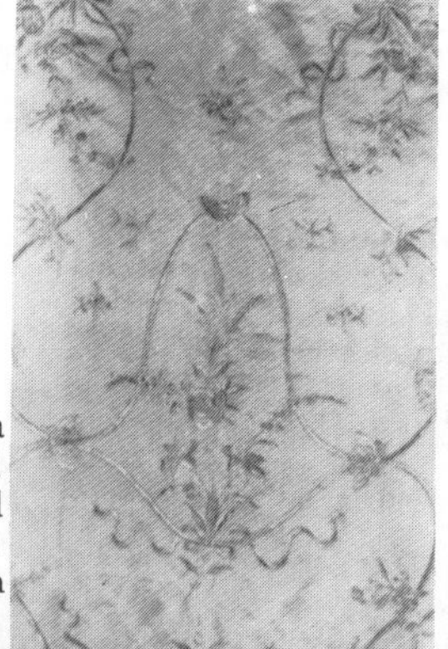

set of hangings for a ɔed, of lilac coloured silk, embroidered in pale blue silk, for European export, 19thC.
$500-650

A Turkish bolster cover, worked on ivory silk, embroidered with a border of alternating sky blue striped tents and trees, the field sprinkled with flowerbuds in silk and metal thread, 18thC, framed under polythene, 25 by 50in (64 by 127cm).
$550-800

A patchwork quilt, composed of various patterned chintzes, including some printed to commemorate Nelson's victories, against a cream coloured ground, backed with blue cotton, c1800, 114 by 126in (289.5 by 320cm).
$700-1,000

A pair of cushions, incorporating 17thC verdure tapestry panels, woven in wools and silks depicting figures among pillars and arches, 26 by 16in (66.5 by 40.5cm).
$1,400-2,000

A diamond patchwork coverlet, composed of 19thC cottons dating from c1810, 90in (228.5cm) square.
$650-800

A framed patchwork coverlet, composed of various plain and patterned silks, the central panel with 3 ovals woven with ladies in hats and the title 'Coventry Manufacturers', c1850, 96 by 82in (243.5 by 208cm).
$300-500

A Victorian taffeta patchwork quilt with geometric designs, 82in (208cm) square.
$500-650

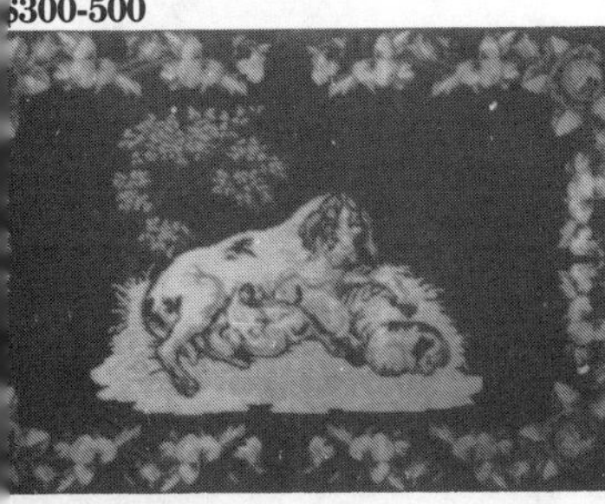

. large woolwork hanging, worked ı coloured wools, with a central lush stitch spaniel, with a tree in ıe background and framed by ailing plush stitch flowers, against n olive green ground, mid-19thC, 6 by 86in (142 by 218.5cm).
1,500-2,500

A pieced and appliqued quilted cotton coverlet, worked in red, green and maize on ivory ground with 4 spreadwing eagles centering a leaf-spoked star, framed by sawtooth band with a border stitched with a trailing vine, slight wear and discolouration, Pennsylvania, late 19thC, 78 by 70in (198 by 177.5cm).
$800-1,000

Fans

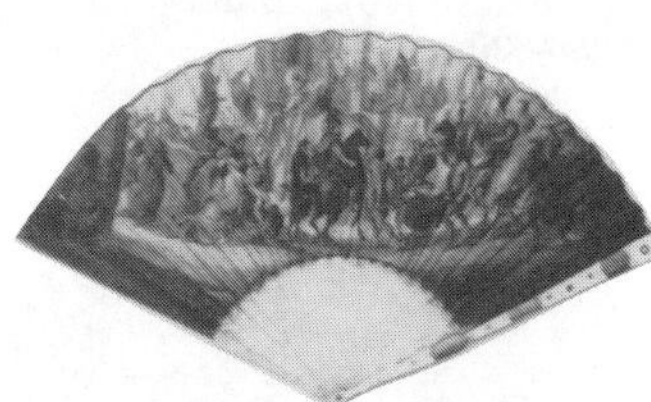

A fan, the leaf painted with the triumphal arrival of Alexander, with ivory sticks, the guardsticks clouté with mother-of-pearl and piqué with silver, c1700, 11in (29cm).
$2,500-3,000

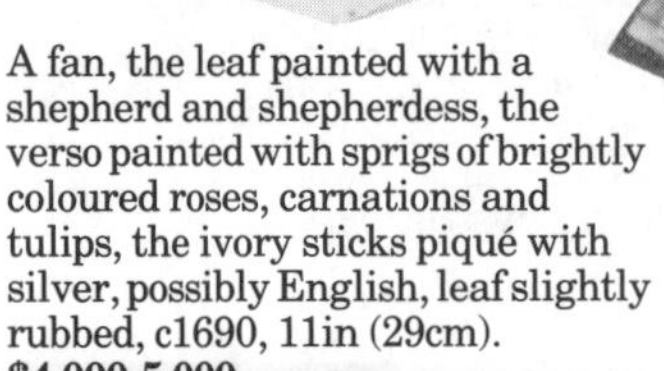

A fan, the leaf painted with a shepherd and shepherdess, the verso painted with sprigs of brightly coloured roses, carnations and tulips, the ivory sticks piqué with silver, possibly English, leaf slightly rubbed, c1690, 11in (29cm).
$4,000-5,000

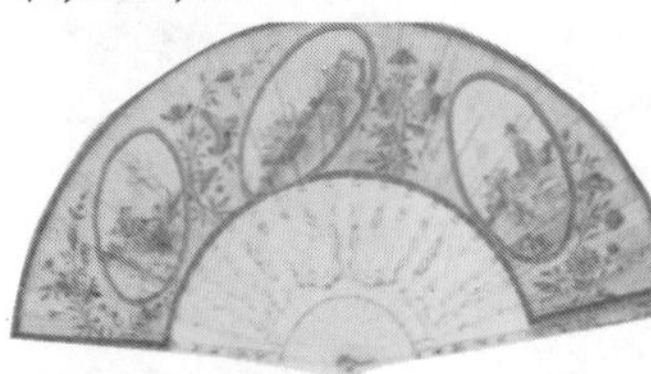

A fan, the leaf painted with a trompe l'oeil of 3 chinoiserie scenes against a pink and white striped ground strewn with flowers, the ivory sticks carved, pierced and painted, c1760, 10in (26cm).
$550-800

An ivory brisé fan, painted with Pan and Syrinx, the guardsticks carved with a portrait of a lady, early 18thC, 8½in (22cm).
$1,500-2,500

A fan, the leaf painted against a silver and green striped ground, the verso with a figure in a landscape, the ivory sticks gilt, worn and repaired, c1775, 10½in (27cm).
$650-800

A printed fan, with allegorical map of the Track of Youth to the Land of Knowledge, the leaf a hand coloured etching engraved by V. Woodthorpe, 27 Fetter Lane, and published by John Wallis June 25, 1796, 36 Ludgate Street, with wooden sticks, c1796.
$2,000-2,500

A fan, the leaf painted with Judith with the Head of Holofernes, the ivory sticks piqué with silver, the guardsticks clouté with tortoiseshell and mother-of-pearl, 2 pieces of mother-of-pearl missing, early 18thC, 10½in (28cm).
$2,500-3,000

A fan, the leaf painted in tones of green with figures, the ivory sticks carved and pierced with figures, guardsticks damaged, mid-18thC, 11in (29cm), in contemporary box.
$1,400-2,000

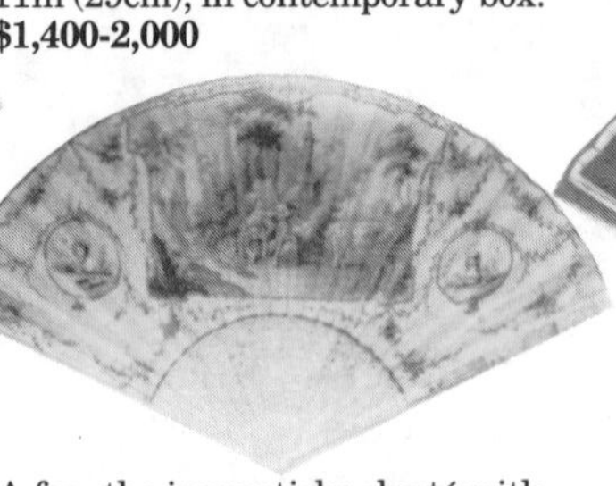

A fan, the ivory sticks clouté with mother-of-pearl, piqué with a trellis of silver and carved with a huntsman, c1770, the sticks c1730, 11½in (30cm).
$800-1,200

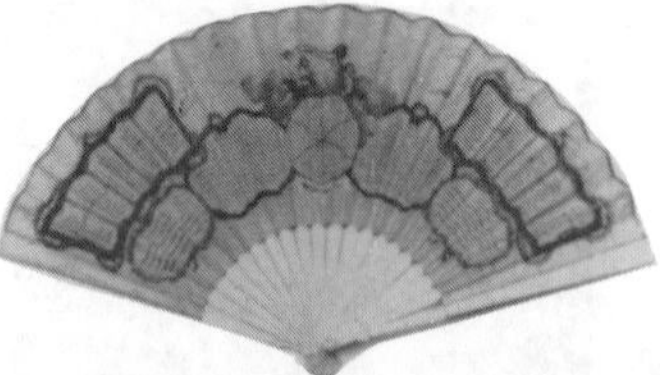

A printed fan, with bone sticks, the publication line overpainted but it is probably by John Cock, J. P. Crowder & Co., 21 Wood St., Cheapside, although in a contemporary fan box by Stunt, Fanmaker, 191 Strand, the old established shop late Sudlow, c1800, 9in (23cm).
$650-800

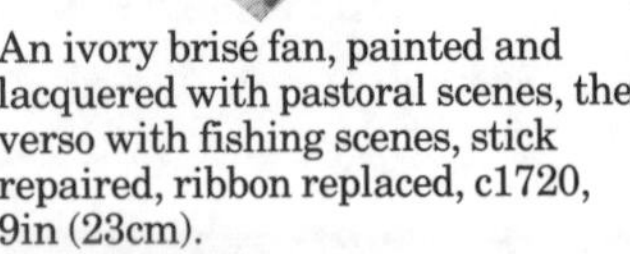

An ivory brisé fan, painted and lacquered with pastoral scenes, the verso with fishing scenes, stick repaired, ribbon replaced, c1720, 9in (23cm).
$2,000-2,500

A fan, the chickenskin leaf painte with a classical scene, the sticks lacquered in red, green and gold, th guardsticks clouté with mother-of-pearl, early 18thC, 11½in (30cm).
$1,200-1,400

A fan, the chickenskin leaf painte with 3 views of Vesuvius, includin the eruption of 1767, the ivory stick pierced, leaf torn, c1770, 10½in (27cm).
$1,400-2,000

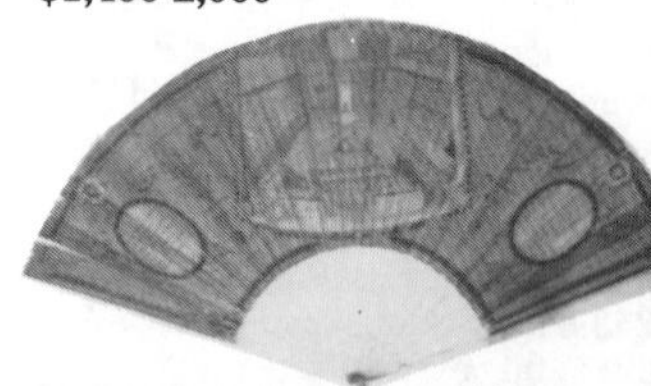

A fan, The trial of Warren Hasting the leaf a hand coloured line engraving of Westminster Hall printed in brown and edged with sequins, with bone sticks, English c1788.
$1,000-1,300

A pierced bone fan, early 19thC.
$300-400

A fan, the verso signed Alexandre, the mother-of-pearl sticks carved and pierced with putti and gilt with sunbursts, 3 sticks broken, the leaf c1860, the sticks 18thC, in glazed fan case.
$300-500

Rimmel's Cassolette fan, a hand coloured lithographic fan with bone sticks, 1 guardstick set with a gilt metal pomander, c1875, 11in (29cm).
$300-400

A card brisé fan, printed with views of London, c1870, 8in (21cm).
$200-250

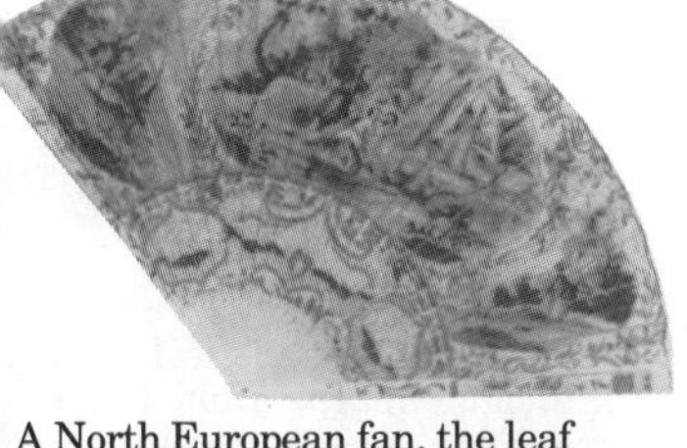

A North European fan, the leaf painted with a central vignette of Moses striking the rock and 2 smaller vignettes of Moses with the Tablets and staff, the verso with a Medieval castle and classical ruins from the sea, the ivory sticks carved and pierced, the guardsticks backed with red foil, c1740, 11½in (30cm).
$1,000-1,400

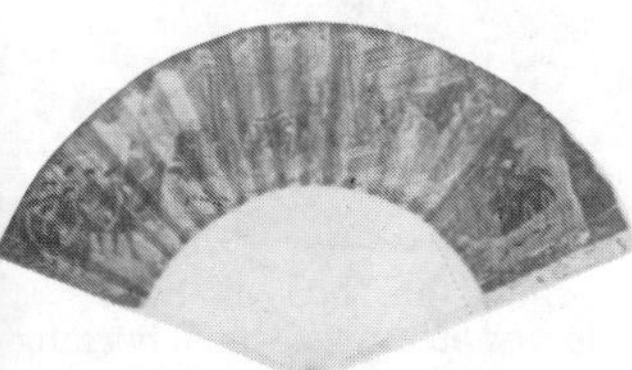

A Swedish fan, the leaf painted with a Court scene, the ivory sticks pierced, the guardsticks carved with a king, c1750, 10in (26cm).
$1,000-1,300

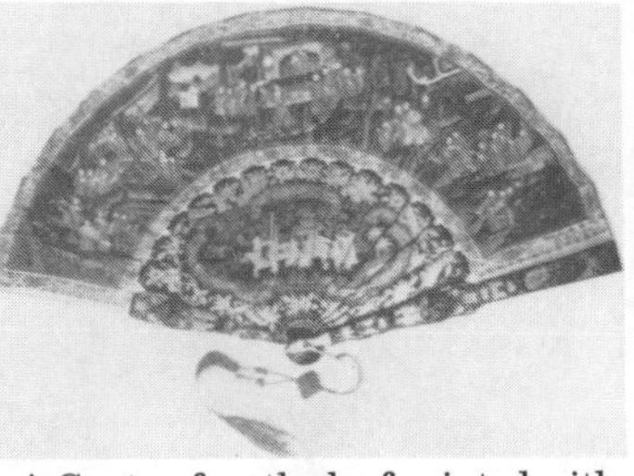

A Canton fan, the leaf painted with figures on a terrace, their faces of ivory, their clothes of silk, with lacquered sticks, c1860, 11in (29cm), in fitted lacquer box.
$800-1,000

An Austrian printed fan, the leaf an etching of a battle scene, with a key below, the verso with Joseph II and Turkish prisoners, published by Leonard Schielling, Vienna, with wooden sticks and bone fillet, slightly damaged, c1788, 11in (29cm).
$2,500-3,000

A Canton tortoiseshell parasol cockade fan, finely carved and pierced with roundels of buildings, figures and flowers, and slotted with blue and white ribbon, 2 sticks repaired, c1800, 9in (23cm).
$2,500-3,000

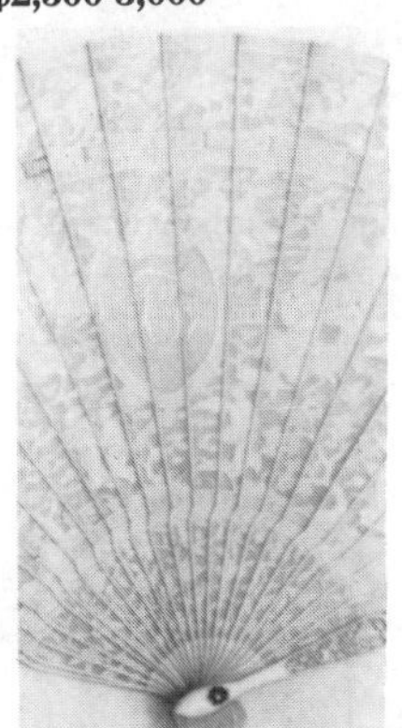

A Canton ivory brisé fan, carved and pierced with figures, animals and buildings and initials J.T., labelled J Threasher, c1820, 8in (21cm).
$800-1,000

A Japanese ivory brisé fan, lacquered in gold on each side with storks, the guardsticks decorated with shibayama work, late 19thC, 10in (26cm).
$3,000-4,000

A Flemish fan with painted leaf, the mother-of-pearl sticks carved, pierced and silvered gilt and backed, with German sticks, c1750, 11½in (30cm), in later glazed carved wood fan-shaped frame.
$700-900

A note on the back of the frame states: Marie Elizabeth A. Cartwright, née Sandigell. In the year 1833 this fan came into my possession at the death of Amelia, Duchess of Pflaz Zewybruken (sic) Duchess of Neubourg, Bavaria née Princess of Saxony with my group of old Saxon china . . . the Duchess Amelia died in 1833 aged 86 she was a dear friend of my family.

A fan, the leaf a pen and ink drawing of a Roman Triumph, the verso inscribed, the smokey grey mother-of-pearl sticks carved and pierced with figures and gilt, the leaf early 18thC, the verso and sticks mid-19thC.
$2,500-3,000

A fan, the chickenskin leaf painted with the Piazza del Popolo, Rome, the verso with a ruin, the ivory sticks pierced with a trellis, the guardsticks carved with figures and Chinese scenes, Italian with Chinese sticks, c1780, 10½in (27cm).
$2,500-3,000

A painted paper fan, on a gold sprinkled ground, the silk tassel with an ivory ojime, the ivory guards carved to simulate bamboo stalks with gold takamakie, shibayama and various flowering branches, signed Kunine, sealmark, Meiji period, 16in (41cm).
$1,000-1,300

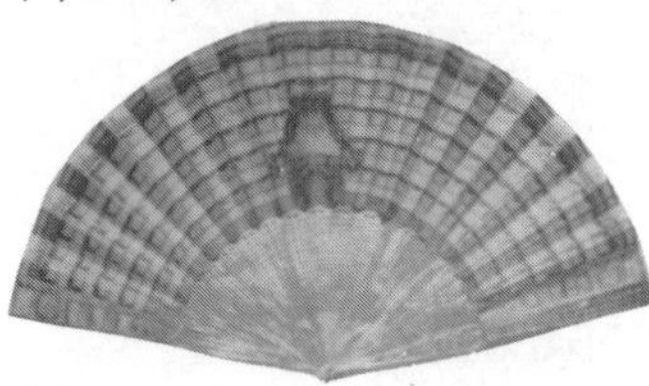

A fan commemorating the centenary of the Grand Theatre Royal de Turin, the leaves painted with the seating plan of the theatre in 1732 and 1782, decorated with garlands, with pierced and gilded mother-of-pearl sticks, 1832, 10in (26cm), in late 19thC box by A. Rodien, Eventailliste, 48 Rue Cambon Ancienne Rue de Luxembourg.
$2,500-3,000

A French fan, the leaf painted with a court scene, possibly Naples, the ivory sticks pierced and silvered, c1770, 11in (29cm), in glazed fan case.
$1,300-1,500

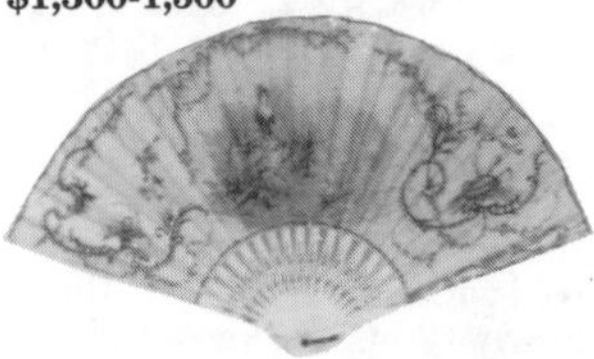

A French fan, the cream silk leaf hand painted in colours applied with gilt sequins, the ivory sticks decorated with stylised flowers and leaves, the guard stick carved and painted, 10in (24.5cm) long, in original box, upholstered in foliate fabric and inscribed in gilt J. Duvelleroy, Paris, By Appointment.
$200-275

An Italian fan, the chickenskin leaf painted with a view of Naples, the bone sticks pierced, c1780, 10½in (27cm), in 18thC fan case labelled Clarke, Fan Maker No 27, near Hungerford Street, Strand, London.
$1,500-2,500

A Canton white metal filigree brisé fan, worked with a deer, butterflies and plants and partly gilt, 19thC, 7½in (19cm), in box labelled Wang sin kee fan shop 727 Nanking Road, Shanghai, established 1875.
$1,400-2,000

An Italian fan, the chickenskin leaf painted with the Triumph of Aurora, the ivory sticks carved and pierced, in glazed case, repaired, late 18thC.
$2,000-2,500

A Souvenir de l'Exposition Universelle de 1867 fan, the leaf a hand coloured lithograph with a bird's eye plan of the exhibition, lithographed by Truillot, 21, rue Grange-aux-belles, with wooden sticks, 10in (26cm).
$1,000-1,200

A French fan, the leaf painted with an 18thC pastiche, the ivory sticks carved, pierced and painted with trophies of love, leaf slightly torn and splitting at folds, mid-19thC, 11in (28cm).
$550-700

A Dutch fan, the leaf painted with a Dutch fishing scene, and baskets of flowers, the verso with a bunch of flowers, the ivory sticks pierced and silvered, c1770, 11in (29cm).
$500-650

A fan, the canepin leaf painted with a trompe l'oeil of genre scenes and portraits against a wooden ground, signed A. Gomez, Madrid, with ivory sticks, c1880.
$500-650

A French fan, the leaves painted with figures and a windmill in a landscape, the ivory sticks carved with a cabriolet, painted and gilt with chinoiserie, 2 sticks damaged, leaf split at folds, c1750.
$2,500-3,000

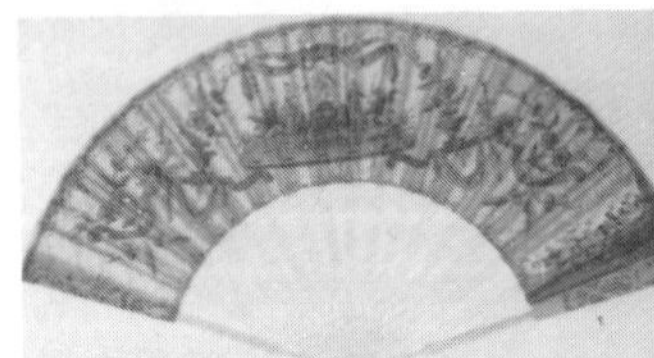

A French fan, the silk leaf painted with figures at the Altar of Love, and embroidered with gold braid and sequins, the ivory sticks carved and pierced with putti, c1760, 10in (26cm).
$550-700

A printed fan, the leaf a hand coloured etching of Cupid burning his wings inscribed, with gilt metal sticks, the guardsticks set with miniature vignettes of doves in red and white paste frames, repaired, c1820, 7in (18cm), in glazed case.
$250-300

An Indian fan, the ivory guards carved in low relief with trailing roses, the sticks pierced with keywork and roundels and with the name 'Elizabeth', with white feather and ostrich feather leaf, with gilt metal loop and white silk tassel, late 19thC, sticks 10in (26cm) high, boxed.
$110-150

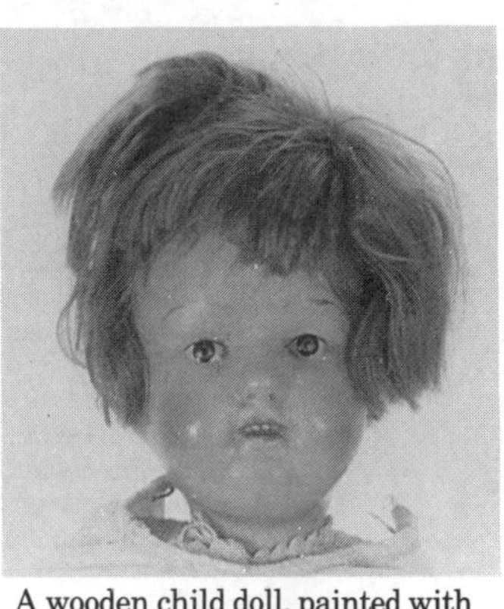

An Italian fan, the chickenskin leaf painted with the Birth of Jupiter, with ivory sticks, split at folds, c1730, 10½in (27cm).
$2,000-2,500

An Italian fan, the chickenskin leaf painted with a view of St Peter and the Vatican, the ivory sticks pierced and silvered, worn, c1780, 11in (29cm).
$2,500-3,000

DOLLS

Wooden Dolls

A George III wooden doll, with black and white enamelled eyes, pink mouth, jointed pine legs, sculptured shoes, fabric upper arms and wooden lower arms terminating in long fork like digits, wearing an early 19thC red and brown and white lace bonnet, hair missing and slight damage, c1780, 23in (59cm) high.
$1,200-1,300

A George III wooden doll, the carved ovoid head with the remains of a styled ginger wig, black and white enamelled eyes, dot painted eyebrows and eyelashes, pink mouth and cheeks, jointed pine legs and primitively carved feet, wearing a 19thC crimson silk bodice, cream skirt, pantaloons and woven stockings, some damage, c1800, 26in (67cm) high.
$2,500-3,000

A wooden child doll, painted with brown eyes, 4 teeth and with blonde wool wig, the spring jointed body wearing original combinations and contemporary underclothes, including a liberty bodice, with oval transfer mark reading Schoenhut Doll Pat. Jan. 17th 1911, U.S.A., 15in (39cm) high.
$500-550

A carved, turned and painted wooden doll, with rouged cheeks, dark enamel eyes, stitched brows and lashes and carved ears, the white painted wooden body with arms attached at shoulders with cloth, dressed as a child in contemporary 18thC silk frock with sack back, blue silk calash.
$11,000-13,000

Wax

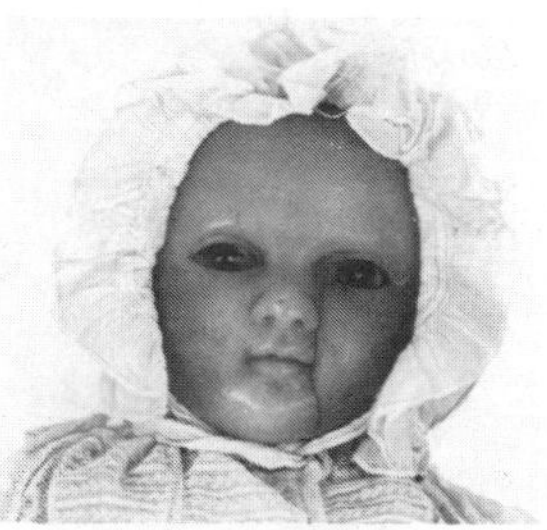

A poured wax baby doll, with blue sleeping eyes, blonde mohair wig, the stuffed body with wax limbs, dressed in original whitework gown, cracked face and damage to feet, eye mechanism lacks wire, c1820, 23in (59cm) high.
$650-800

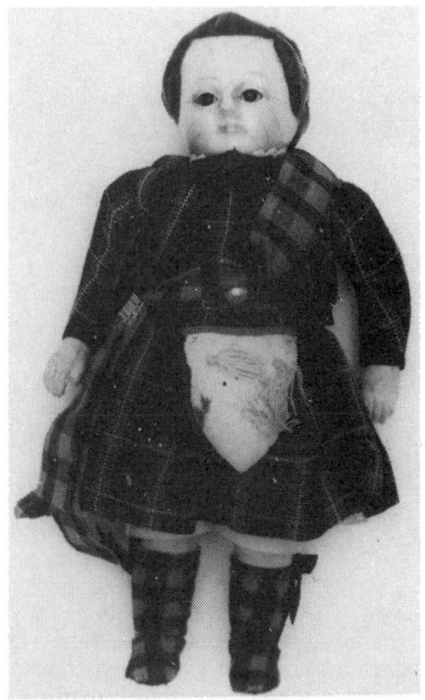

A wax over composition headed doll, with dark sleeping eyes, brown moulded hair, the composition body in original Highland outfit, c1850, 10½in (26.5cm) high.
$300-500

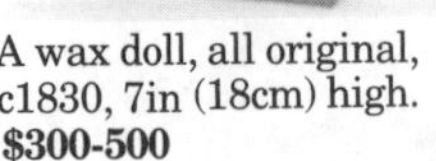

A wax doll, all original, c1830, 7in (18cm) high.
$300-500

A wax over composition doll, 'Eliza', with wired eye mechanism, brown mohair ringlets, the stuffed body with wax over composition limbs, in contemporary cotton print dress, white quilted cotton sun bonnet and underwear, wax cracked, c1845, 22in (56cm) high.
$800-1,000

A wax over papier mâché headed doll, with fixed bright blue eyes an hair wig, the stuffed body with waxed arms, wearing original cream gauze dress trimmed with lace, flowers and ribbons, standing on a red painted doll's house chair, c1840, 14in (35.5cm) high, in glaze case.
$300-500

A wax over papier mâché headed doll, with fixed eyes, the cloth body with pink kid arms, in contemporary black satin dress, with separate white collar, ribbon, lace bonnet and underclothes, extra clothes including a green silk dress, a white muslin flounced dress, 2 coloured printed wool dresses, a woven blue patterned wool dress and a green and white checked cotton frock, c1848, 14in (35.5cm) long. **$1,300-1,500**

A wax over papier mâché headed doll, the dark sleeping eyes wired from the waist, the brown ringlet set into a slit in the crown, the stuffed body with blue kid arms, wearing muslin frock with pink sash and straw hat decorated wit flowers, c1840, 28in (72cm) high.
$650-800

A wax over composition doll, with dark eyes, brown mohair ringlets and stuffed body with wax over composition limbs in contemporary cotton print dress and straw hat, wax cracked, c1840, 25in (64cm) high.
$400-550

A wax over composition headed doll, with fixed blue eyes and blonde ringlets, the stuffed body dressed as a child in original white silk and lace frock, with artificial flowers in her hair, hands and bosom, carrying a banner embroidered with the message 'Forget me not', mid-19thC, 12in (30.5cm) high, in glazed case.
$650-800

A wax headed doll, with bead eyes painted short hair, cloth body and wax arms, original blue wool skir white ribbed silk jacket, wired flower trimmed hat and underclothes, c1840, 7½in (19cm) high.
$800-1,000

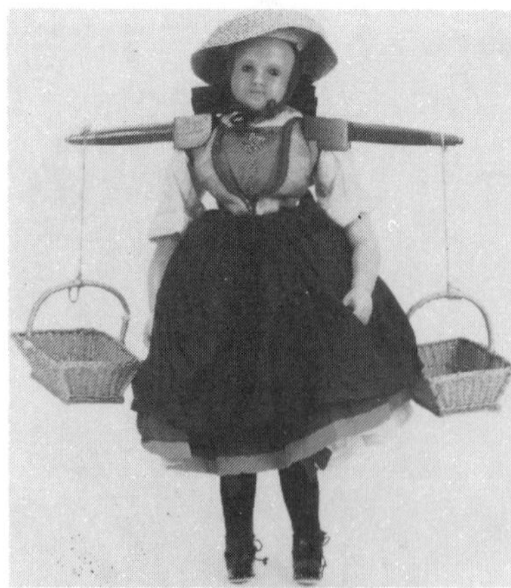

A poured wax headed doll, with dark eyes, the stuffed body with wax limbs, dressed in regional costume from Hamburg with wooden yoke and 2 baskets, broken at neck, c1850, 21in (53.5cm) high, with a letter written in German which accompanied the doll in 1850.
$1,000-1,200

A wax over papier mâché shoulder headed doll, with fixed pale blue eyes, fair hair ringlets, cloth body and waxed legs and arms with separate fingers, some cracking, old repair to eyelid, c1850, 34in (86.5cm) high.
$1,500-2,500

poured wax doll, all original, 1880, 21in (53.5cm) high.
500-700

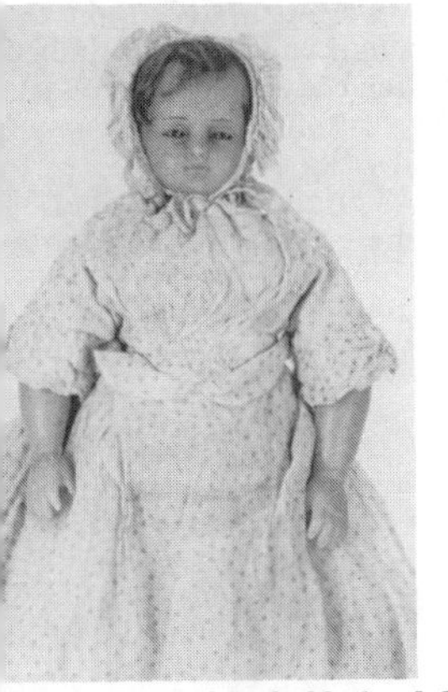
poured wax headed baby doll, with blue eyes, fair hair inset in lashes, the stuffed body with wax imbs in blue spotted muslin dress nd lace trimmed bonnet, probably y Pierotti, 16in (40.5cm) high.
1,000-1,200

A wax bride doll, c1925, 19in (48.5cm) high.
$130-150

A wax over composition headed doll, with dark eyes, moulded blonde hair with paper hair decoration, the stuffed body with composition limbs including blue boots with red tassels, original cotton print frock trimmed with purple braid and medallion marking the centenary of the founding of Sunday Schools in 1880, c1880, 15in (38.5cm) high, in glazed case.
$300-500

These medallions were given to children attending Sunday School in the centenary year.

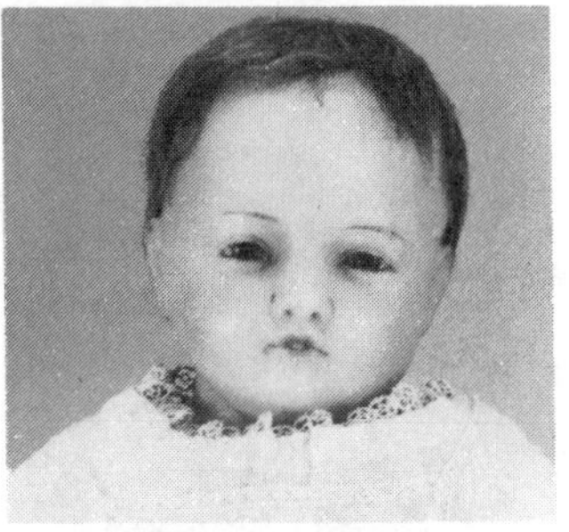
A poured wax headed doll modelled as a baby, with blue eyes, inset hair and eyelashes, the stuffed body with wax limbs dressed in white lace trimmed gown and underwear, probably by Pierotti, slight damage to forehead, 22in (55.5cm) high.
$1,200-1,300

A wax over composition headed doll, with black sleeping eyes operated with a wire, dark brown ringlets, the stuffed body with waxed limbs, dressed in original cream watered silk frock, mauve silk jacket, cream silk wired bonnet, underwear, shoes and socks, c1845, 30in (76.5cm) high.
$1,400-2,000

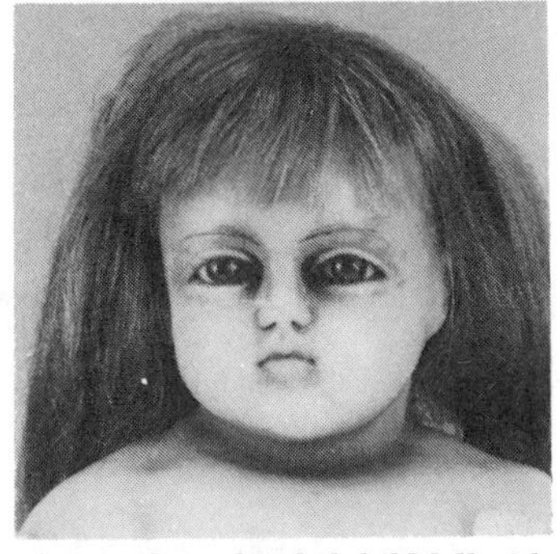
A poured wax headed child doll with pale grey eyes outlined in blue, with long blonde mohair inserted wig, the stuffed body with wax limbs, wearing original underclothes and knitted and beaded bootees, marked in ink on body 'B–/S', leg damaged, c1880, 17in (43.5cm) high.
$300-500

Bisque & Papier Mâché

A bisque headed character baby doll, with open closed mouth, blue sleeping eyes, short blonde wig and baby body dressed in cream silk robe and hat with tucks and lace insertions, marked 'D.I.P. 5' and stamped in green Geschutz, Germany S. & Co. for Swaine & Co.
$1,200-1,300

A bisque headed bébé, with fixed blue yeux fibres, pierced ears, blonde wig and jointed composition body, dressed in white, firing crack behind left ear, stamped in red 'Le Parisien' and on the body in purple Bebe 'Le Parisien' Medaille d'Or Paris, and impressed '11 Paris', 18in (45.5cm) high.
$1,400-2,000

A French Liane bébé bisque doll, by J. Verlingue.
$400-550

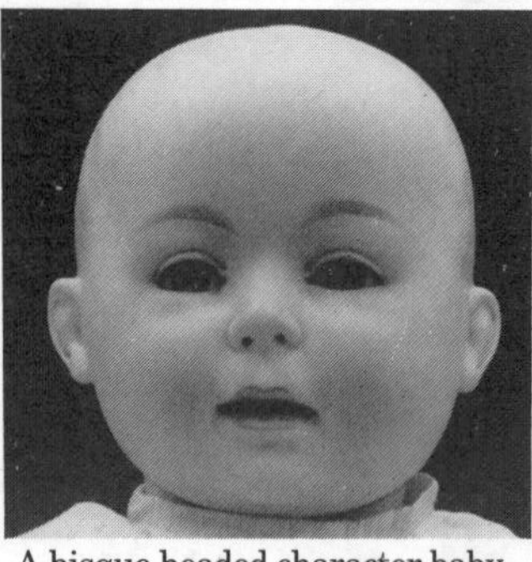

A bisque headed character baby doll, with blue sleeping eyes, moulded and painted hair, the bent limbed composition body dressed in white, marked D. Lori 1 and stamped S & Co., 23in (58.5cm) high.
$2,000-2,500

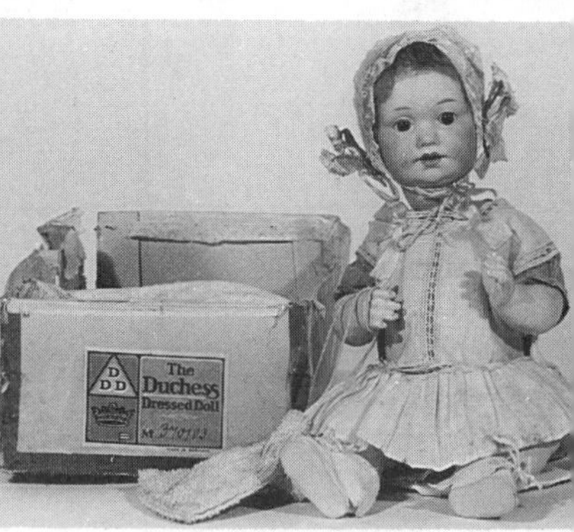

A bisque headed character baby doll with brown sleeping eyes, light brown mohair wig and bent limbed composition body in original blue and white cotton dress, lace bonnet, shoes and socks, marked 971 A.3/OM, in original box marked 'The Duchess Dressed Doll', 12in (30.5cm) high.
$1,200-1,300

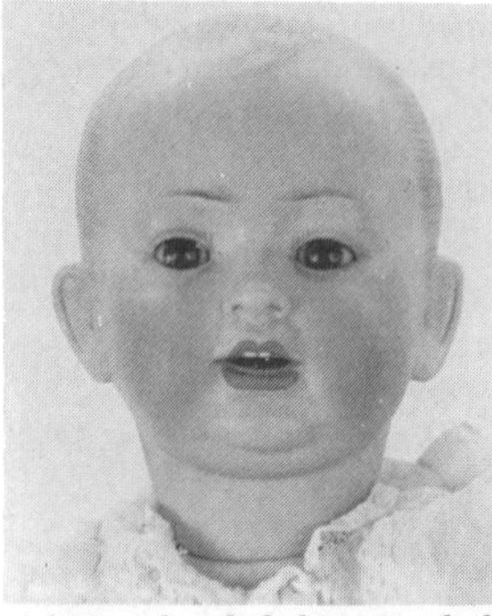

A bisque headed character baby doll, with brown sleeping eyes, painted brush strokes for hair and composition baby's body, dressed in cream, tiny chip to neck and eye, marked 151, 18in (45.5cm) high.
$500-550

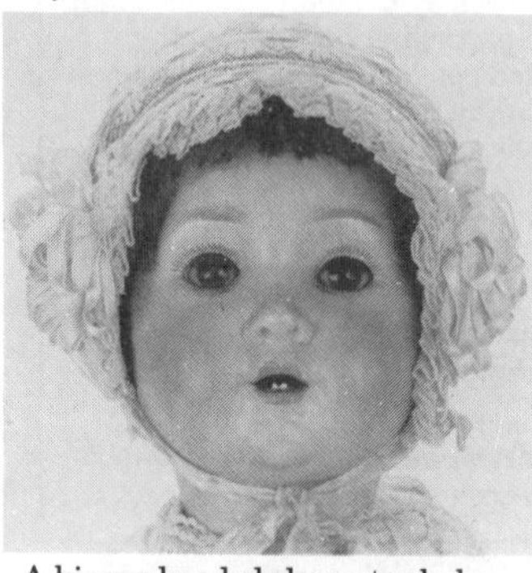

A bisque headed character baby doll, with brown lashed sleeping eyes, brown mohair wig, the bent limbed composition body in lace trimmed cream silk gown and bonnet, marked B & O B–3 3/4 by Bruckner & Och, 18in (45.5cm) high.
$300-500

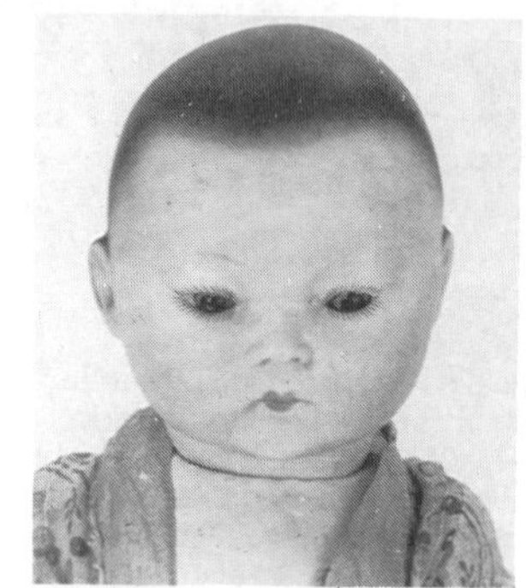

A bisque headed Oriental character baby doll, with closed sleeping eyes, the toddler body wearing a kimono, marked '2', 12in (30.5cm) high.
$1,000-1,300

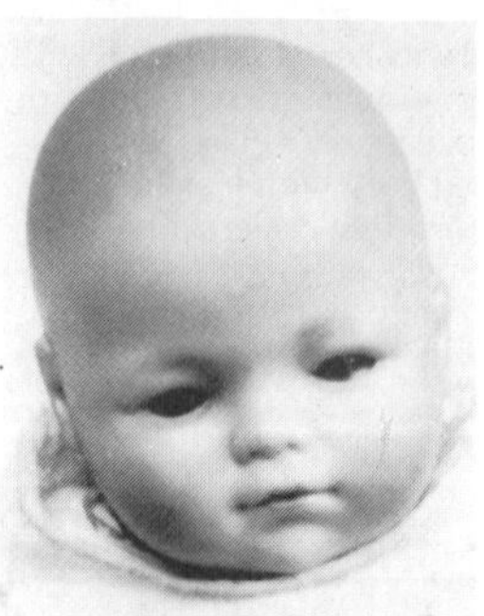

A bisque headed baby doll, with closed mouth, blue sleeping eyes, the stuffed body with composition arms and voice box, dressed in white, marked S PB in star H, N O B, 12in (30.5cm) high.
$650-800

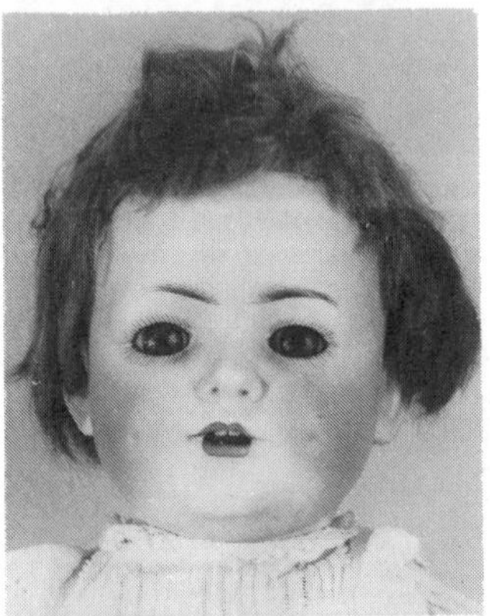

A bisque headed character doll, with blue sleeping eyes, feathered brows, dimples, light brown mohair wig, the jointed wood and composition toddler body in whitework dress and underwear, marked Harmus 660-10, 19in (48.5cm) high.
$650-800

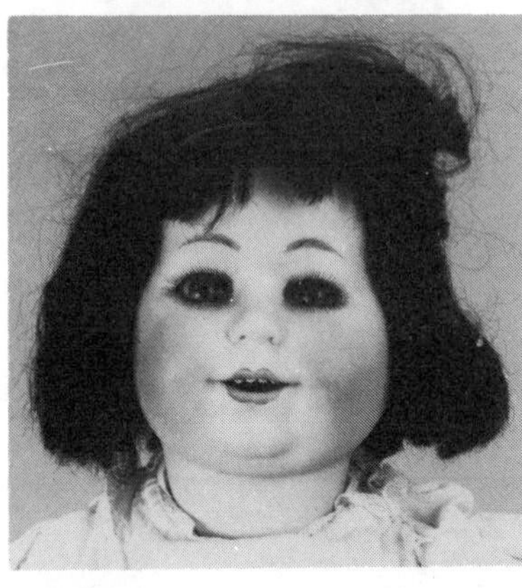

A bisque headed character baby doll, with smiling mouth, blue lashed sleeping eyes, feathered brows and bent limbed composition body in whitework dress and underwear, marked WG B1 – 8, 19in (48.5cm) high.
$800-1,000

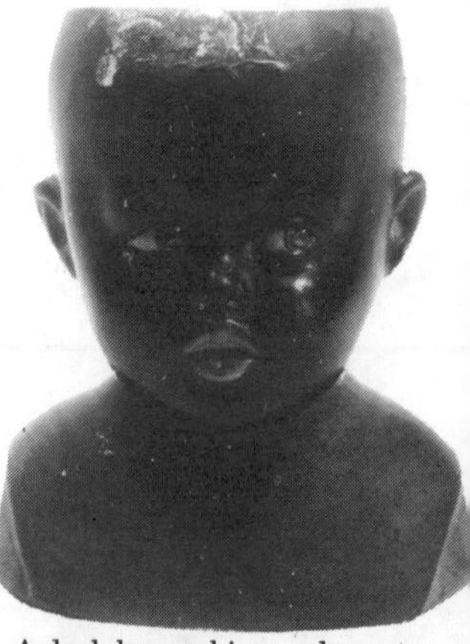

A dark brown bisque character shoulder-head, modelled as a frowning negro child, with open/closed mouth and brown intaglio eyes glancing to the left, impressed 93, Heubach Square 32, probably the shoulder head wigged version of mould 7671, 3½in (9cm) high.
$500-650

A bisque headed character doll, with sleeping googlie eyes, closed mouth and bent limbed composition body dressed in sailor suit and hat, marked 323 A.O.M, 12½in (32cm) high.
$1,400-2,000

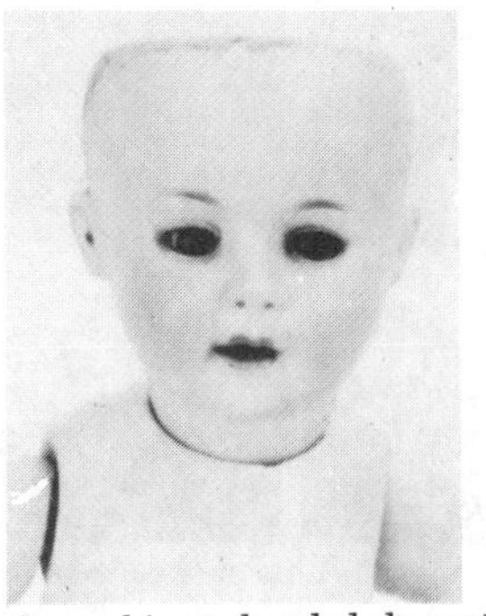

A rare bisque headed character baby doll, with blue lashed sleeping eyes and bent limbed composition body, probably the wigged version of Lori by Swaine & Co., tiny chip to neck, marked 233 7, 16in (40.5cm) high.
$1,200-1,300

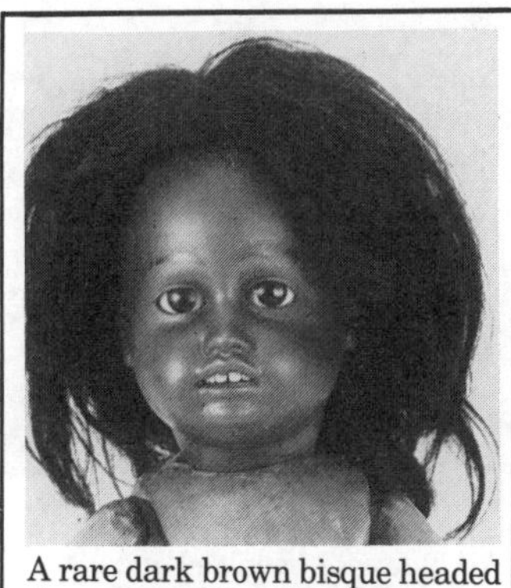

A rare dark brown bisque headed character doll, modelled as a negress with brown sleeping eyes black wool wig and brown jointed body, marked 34-27, possibly Gebruder Kühnlenz, restored hands, 16in (40.5cm) high.
$2,500-3,000

A bisque headed bébé, with fixed blue eyes, pierced ears and jointed body wearing a wedding dress, petticoat and underclothes, shoes and socks, marked 3, the shoes stamped 3 Paris Deposé with the Bee trademark, 12½in (32cm).
$1,500-2,500

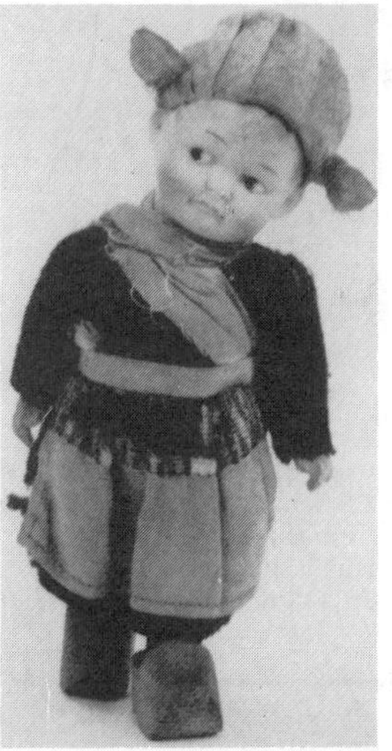

A bisque headed character doll, with googlie eyes, closed mouth with teeth over bottom lip, moulded and painted hair, the straight limbed composition body dressed in original Dutch regional costume, marked EH 262, 7½in (18.5cm) high.
$500-650

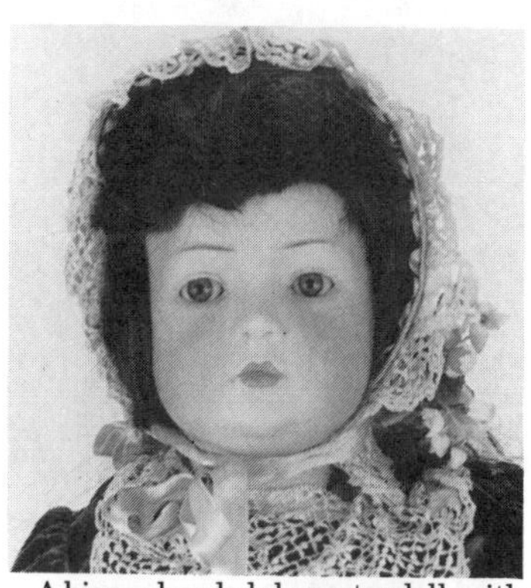

A bisque headed character doll, with closed mouth, blue fixed eyes, feathered brows and brown wig, the jointed wood and composition body dressed in blue velvet with leather shoes, wig pulls and overpainted body, marked BSW in Heart for Bruno Schmidt of Waltershausen, 27in (68.5cm) high.
$1,000-1,500

A bisque headed character doll, with blue lashed sleeping eyes and blonde mohair wig, the composition toddler body in original frilled dress and underwear and blue felt hat, marked Porzellanfabrik Burggrub Princess Elizabeth 3 1/2, 17in (43.5cm) high.
$1,200-1,300

A pair of bisque headed twin dolls, by Max Handwerck, 21in (53.5cm) high.
$800-1,200

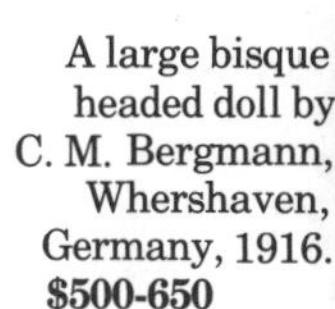

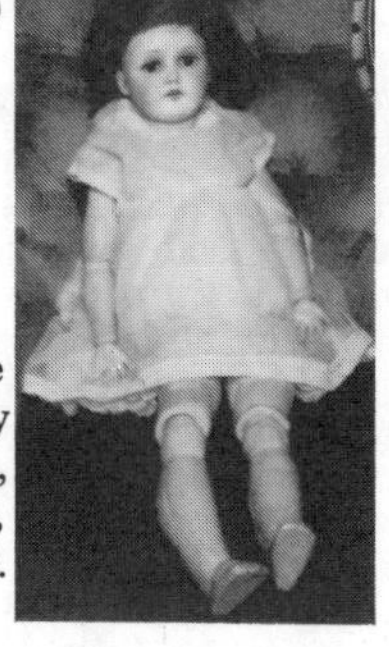

A large bisque headed doll by C. M. Bergmann, Whershaven, Germany, 1916.
$500-650

A bisque headed doll 'Queenie', with blue lashed sleeping eyes, moulded brows and brown wig, the jointed wood and composition body in sea green light woollen dress, underwear and blue leather shoes, hand overpainted, marked ABG 13641/214, 26in (66.5cm) high.
$1,200-1,300

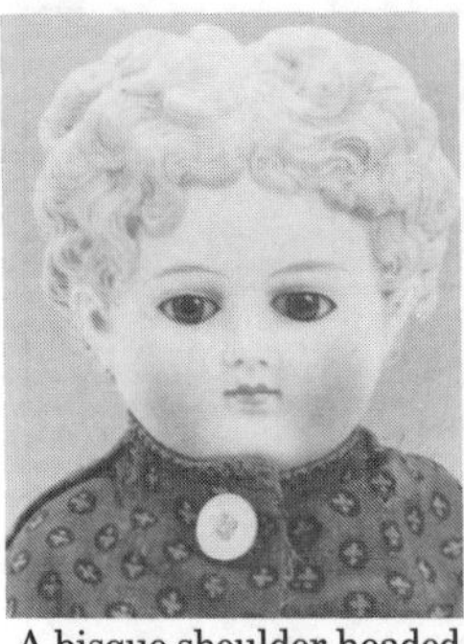

A bisque shoulder headed doll with fixed blue eyes, moulded and painted blonde hair, the stuffed body with kid arms in cotton print dress and underwear, 19½in (49.5cm) high.
$650-800

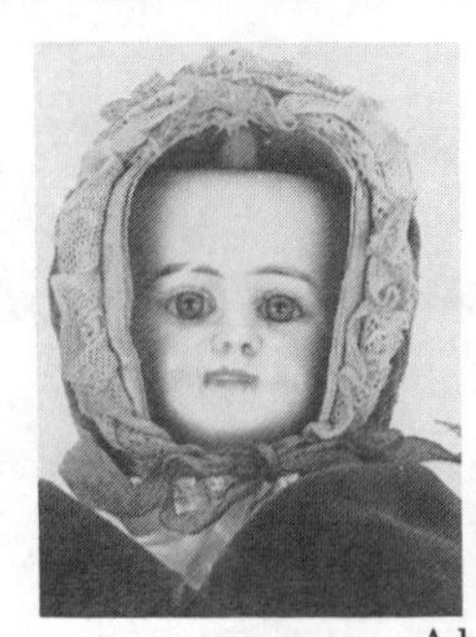

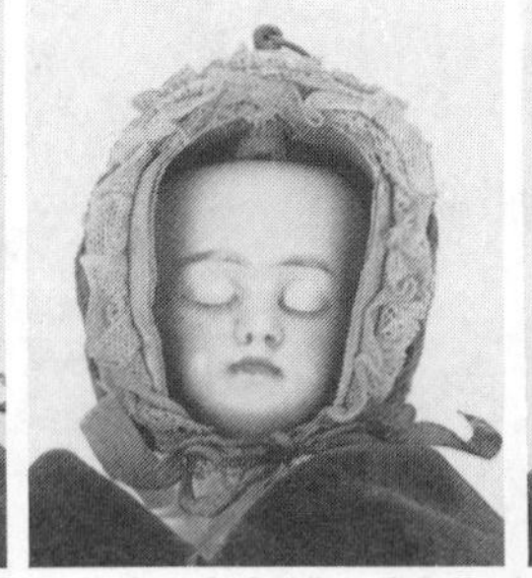

A bisque headed 3-faced doll, the faces smiling, crying and sleeping, under lace trimmed carton hood, the jointed wood and composition body dressed in corded silk coat, damaged hands, by Carl Bergner, c1900, 14in (35.5cm) high.
$1,300-1,500

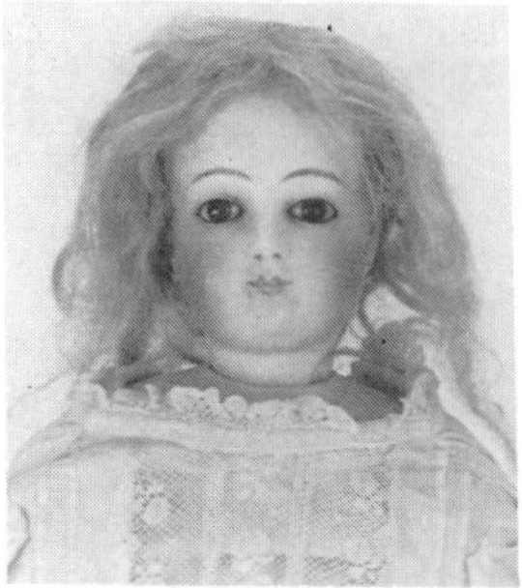

A bisque swivel headed Parisienne, with fixed deep blue eyes, pierced ears, blonde wig and gusseted kid body, filled firing crack above left ear, 16½in (42cm) high.
$1,200-1,400

An all bisque doll with closed mouth, blue fixed eyes and blonde mohair wig, the body with moulded and painted shoes and socks in elaborate original cream silk dress with train, tiny chip to neck, silk distressed, 7in (17.5cm) high.
$1,000-1,200

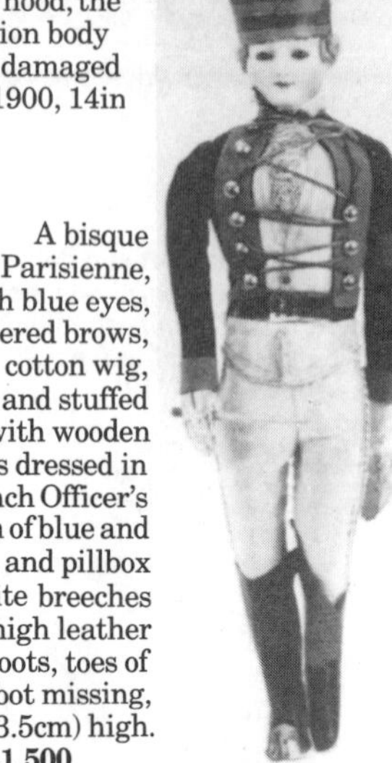

A bisque headed Parisienne, with blue eyes, feathered brows, white cotton wig, stock and stuffed body with wooden limbs dressed in French Officer's uniform of blue and red jacket and pillbox hat, white breeches and high leather boots, toes of one foot missing, 13in (33.5cm) high.
$1,300-1,500

A Victorian papier mâché doll, all original, 16in (40.5cm) high.
$250-400

Bru

A bisque swivel headed Parisienne with smiling mouth, pale blue paperweight eyes, feathered brows, pierced ears, fair mohair wig, and gusseted kid body with individually stitched fingers, dressed in blue woollen skirt and jacket, marked 'G', probably Bru, 18in (45.5cm) high. **$6,500-8,000**

A bisque swivel-headed Parisienne, with fixed blue eyes, pierced ears and gusseted kid body, wearing original peacock green silk dress with matching sleeveless jerkin, with spare flower printed wool dress trimmed with orange and yellow silk fringing, large flat chip to front shoulder plate, marked on head and shoulder D, by Bru, c1862, 15in (38cm) high. **$2,000-2,500**

A bisque headed Bébé Teteur, with brown eyes, feathered brows, pierced ears and blonde mohair wig with original cork pate, with kid body, bisque hands and composition legs, with drinking mechanism, dressed in original white muslin over pale blue, tucked and lace trimmed baby gown and bonnet, baby feeding bottle and dummy, in wicker moses basket with hood, draped in blue and white cotton, lace trimmed, one finger chipped, marked Bru Jne, 13in (33.5cm) high.
$6,500-9,500

J. D. Kestner

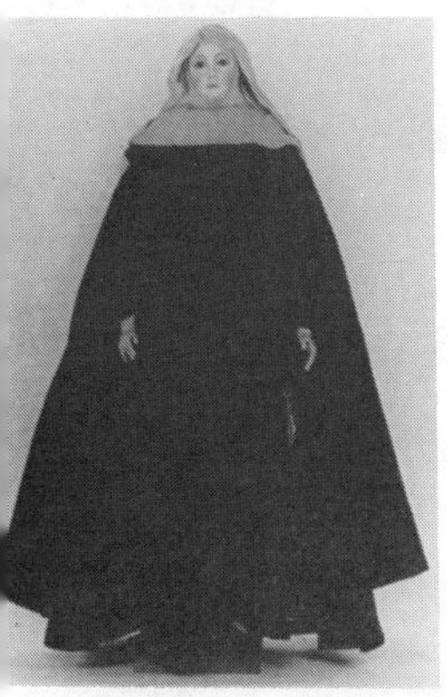

ι pressed bisque swivel headed lady loll, with fixed sky blue eyes with rey brows, pink nostrils, chin and heeks, pierced ears and cork pate, he shoulder plate with adult figure, he kid body wearing original ιovice's habit of the Augustinian rder, comprising voile fin, veil, andeau, wimple, serre-tête, choir loak, habit, fichu, black serge waist etticoat, linen petticoat, chemise, aced bodice, knitted cotton tockings, garters and black kid lippers, by Jumeau, c1875, 31in 78.5cm) high, with original stand.
$6,500-9,500

'his figure was kept in the roberie in he Convent des Oiseaux, a house of he Canonesses of Saint Augustine n Paris, as a model of how a Novice hould dress. It seems probable, as his was a well endowed Convent, hat the doll was ordered especially, s there are no gussets in the body; he hands, which would not be seen, re of poor quality, and there is no vig.

A Kestner 192 doll, in original clothes, c1915, 7½in (19cm) high.
$500-550

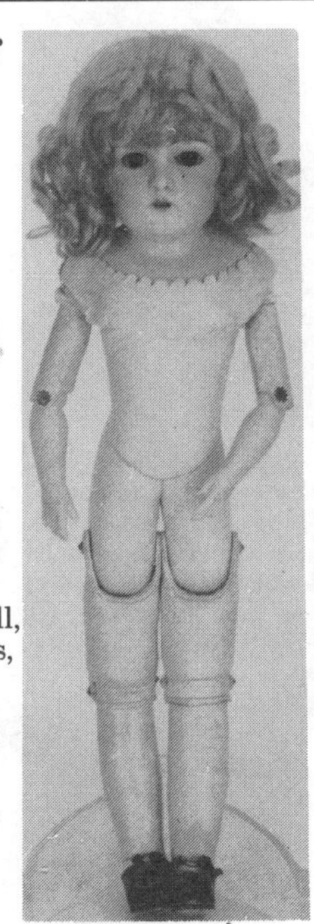

A bisque shoulder headed doll, with brown sleeping eyes, heavy feathered brows and blonde curly mohair wig, the pink jointed kid body with bisque arms, marked S 147, by Kestner, 16½in (42cm) high.
$1,500-2,500

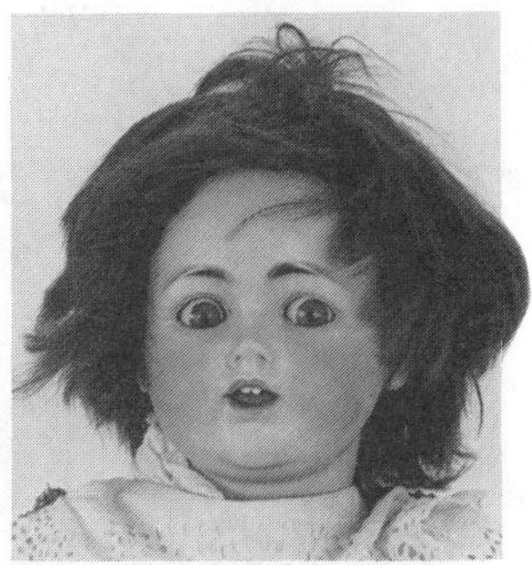

A bisque headed, flirty eyed, character baby doll, with blue eyes, trembling tongue, brown wig and bent limbed composition body dressed in white, hairline at neck, marked J.D.K. 257, 25½in (65cm) high.
$550-800

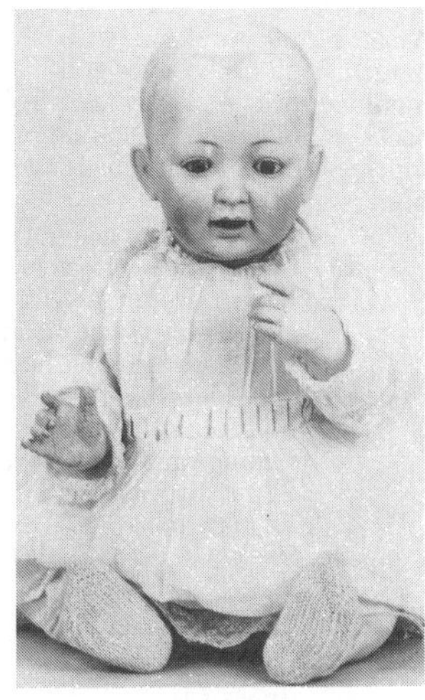

A bisque headed character baby doll, 'Peter', with blue sleeping eyes, feathered brows, painted hair with brushstrokes, the bent limbed composition body in white lace trimmed dress and underclothes, marked J.D.K., 25in (64cm) high.
$550-1,200

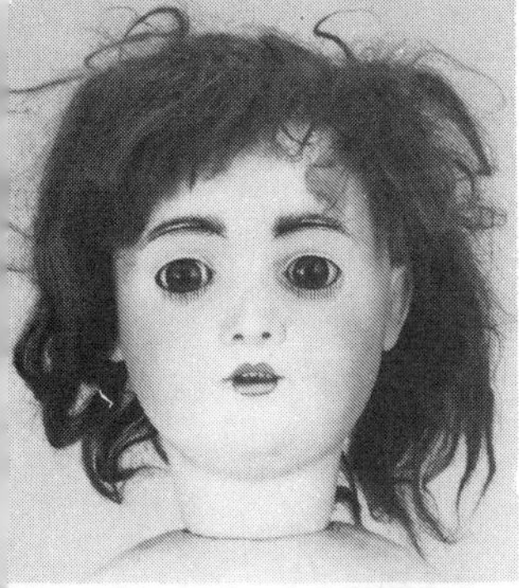

ι large bisque headed doll, with lue sleeping eyes, moulded and eathered brows, brown mohair wig nd jointed wood and composition ody, marked 136 15 by Kestner, 30in (77cm) high.
$800-900

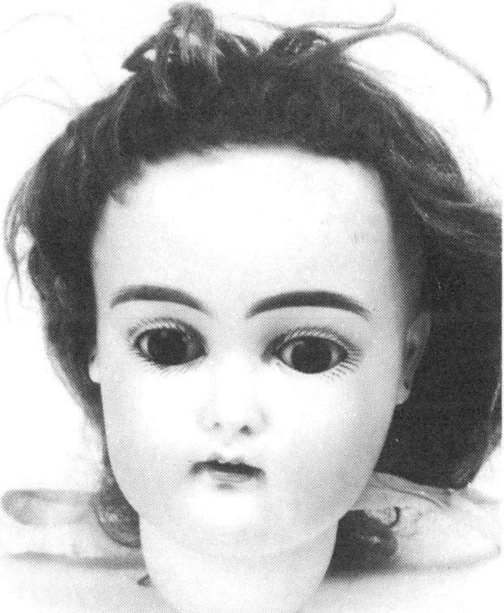

A bisque headed child doll, with brown sleeping eyes, pierced ears, light brown wig and jointed fixed wrist composition body, marked 192 10, Kestner, the head 5in (13cm) high.
$1,200-1,300

An all bisque googlie eyed doll, with blue painted eyes glancing to the left, closed watermelon mouth and moulded blue socks and black shoes, jointed at shoulder and hip, chips to legs at top, marked on the legs 310, by Kestner, 5½in (14cm) high.
$550-700

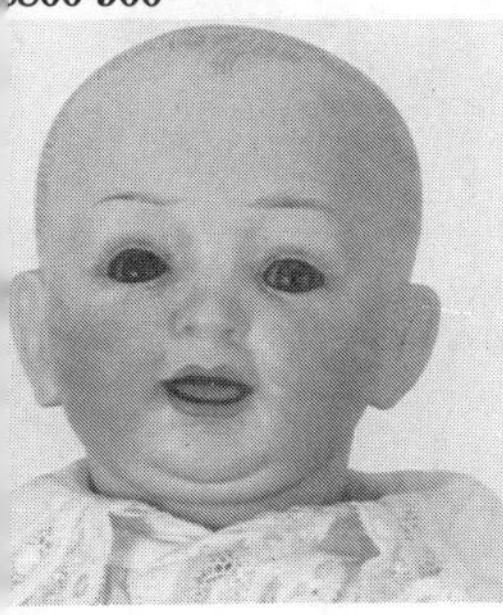

A bisque headed character baby doll, with blue sleeping eyes, moulded and painted hair, open/closed mouth and baby's body dressed in white, impressed 6 142, by Kestner, 14in (36cm) high.
$550-800

An all bisque child doll, with closed mouth, fixed brown eyes and moulded socks and grey tasselled boots, jointed at neck shoulder and hip, by J. D. Kestner, 6in (16cm) high. **$650-700**

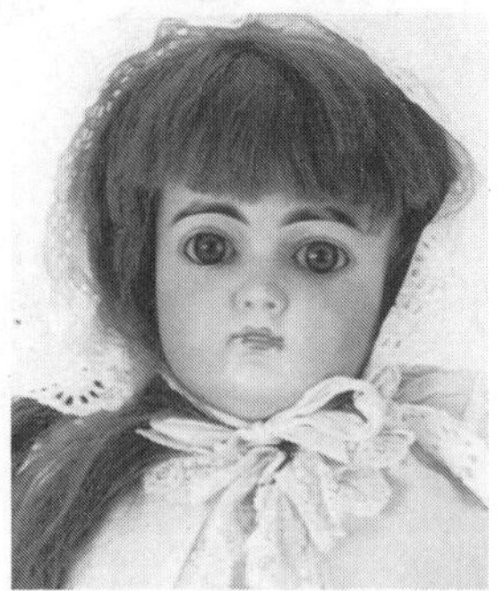

A bisque headed child doll, with fixed blue eyes, pierced ears, long fair hair wig and fixed wrist jointed composition body dressed in cream silk and wool, impressed 192 14, probably Kestner, 23in (59cm). **$3,000-4,000**

A pair of all bisque character dolls, modelled as Max and Moritz, with painted black and ginger hair, blue eyes glancing to the left and right, smiling watermelon mouths and moulded shoes, jointed at neck, shoulder, and hip, with bisque loop at shoulder and hip, by J. D. Kestner, 5in (13cm) high. **$2,500-3,000**

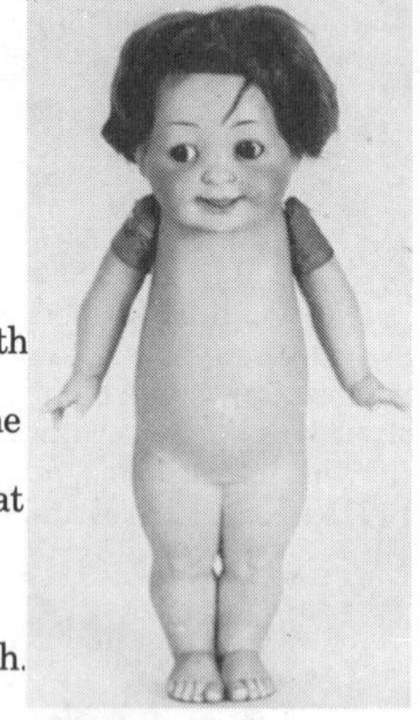

An all bisque googlie eyed doll, with open/closed watermelon mouth, brown sleeping eyes glancing to the side, light brown mohair wig, and all bisque body with arms jointed at shoulders and turned out hands, and a quantity of dolls clothes, damage at shoulders, marked 222 28 by Kestner, 11in (29cm) high. **$2,500-4,000**

Lenci

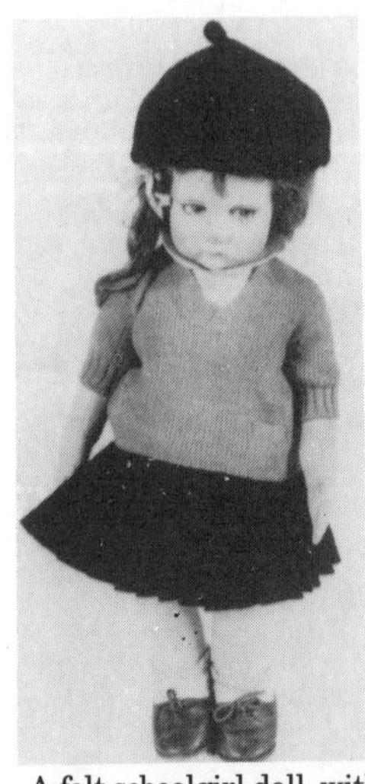

A felt schoolgirl doll, with long brown hair, painted moulded facial features, and moving limbs, with stitched fingers, wearing a blue felt beret, a white felt short sleeved blouse, pleated navy blue felt skirt, knitted orange wool short sleeved jumper, white ankle socks and brown kid shoes, stamped Lenci in black on both feet, c1930, 18in (45.5cm) high. **$700-900**

A painted brown felt character doll, with black mohair wig, modelled as an American Indian with swivel waist, original orange and tan felt skirt and bolero, some moth damage to neck, bolero and feet, No. 104 by Lenci, c1920, 16½in (42cm) high. **$1,000-1,200**

Armand Marseille

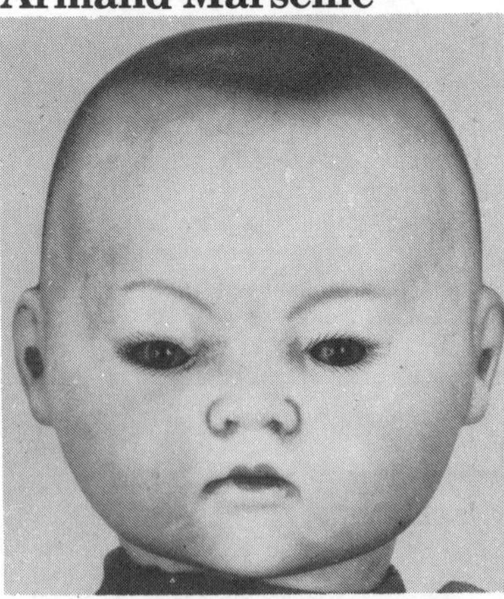

A bisque headed character baby doll modelled as an Oriental, with brown sleeping eyes and bent limbed composition body dressed in original shift, marked A.M. 353/3K, 13in (34cm) high. **$1,000-1,200**

A bisque headed child doll, with blue sleeping eyes, brown wig and jointed body, in contemporary Scottish outfit, impressed 390 A 7 M, 24in (62cm) high. **$800-1,000**

S.F.B.J.

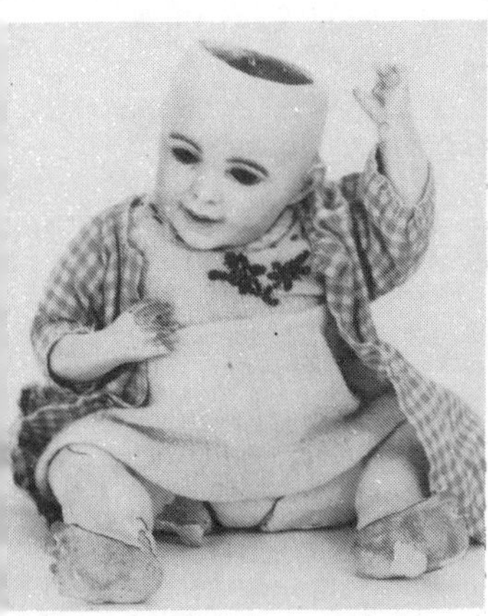

A bisque headed character baby doll, with sleeping eyes, open/closed mouth with 2 teeth, and bent limbed composition toddler body, marked SFBJ 236-2, 9½in (24cm) high.
$500-650

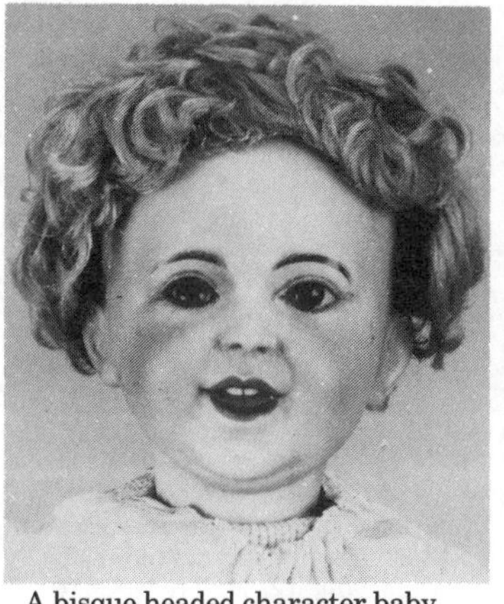

A bisque headed character baby doll, with brown sleeping eyes, open/closed mouth, curly blonde wig and bent limbed composition body dressed in cream baby gown, some damage to fingers, roughly moulded rim to head, marked SFBJ 236 10, 18in (46cm) high.
$800-1,000

Simon & Halbig/ Kammer & Reinhardt

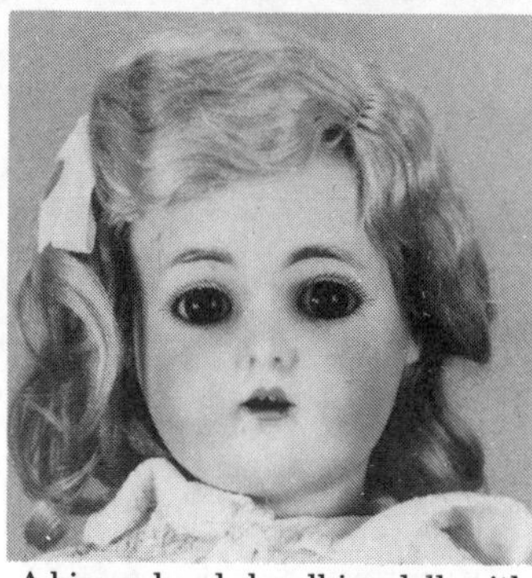

A bisque headed walking doll, with brown sleeping eyes, pierced ears, blonde mohair wig and rigid legs turning the head from side-to-side, marked Halbig K * R, 18in (46cm).
$1,000-1,200

A Simon and Halbig doll, all original, 15in (39cm) high.
$300-400

A Simon & Halbig doll, K * R 46, 18in (46cm) high.
$1,200-1,400

A bisque headed character doll, with blue sleeping eyes and baby's body dressed in white, marked K * R Simon & Halbig 122 28, 11in (29cm) high.
$800-1,000

A bisque headed character doll, with closed mouth, painted features and blonde mohair wig, the jointed wood and composition toddler body in cotton print dress and underwear, wig pulls, marked K * R 114 34, 13in (34cm) high.
$1,300-1,500

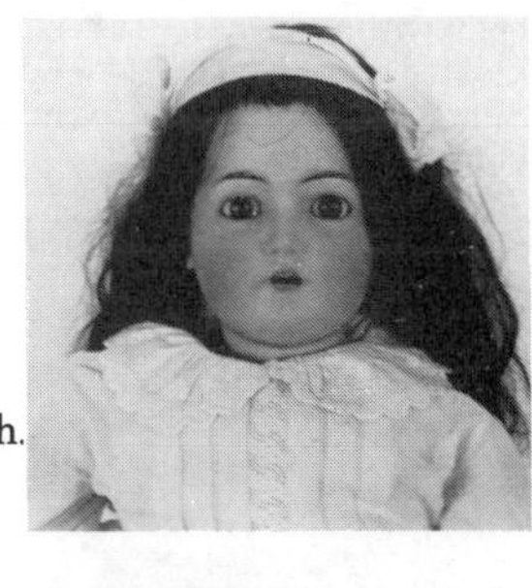

A bisque headed child doll, with brown sleeping eyes, jointed composition body dressed in pink cotton frock, impressed Simon & Halbig K * R 85, 34in (87cm) high.
$800-1,300

A bisque headed child doll, with blue sleeping eyes, pierced ears and jointed body dressed in white, marked Halbig K * R70, 27in (69cm) high.
$700-1,000

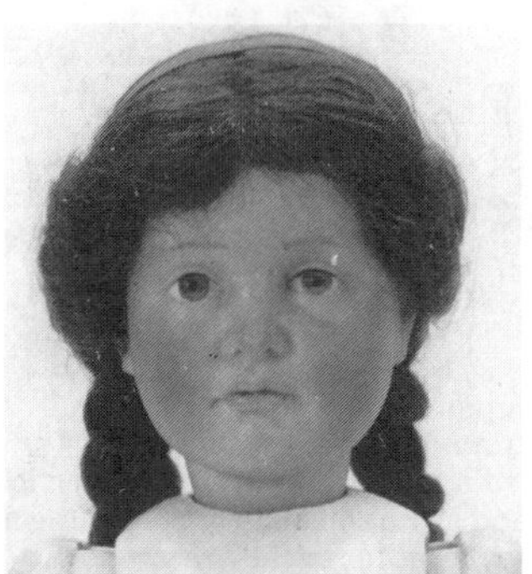

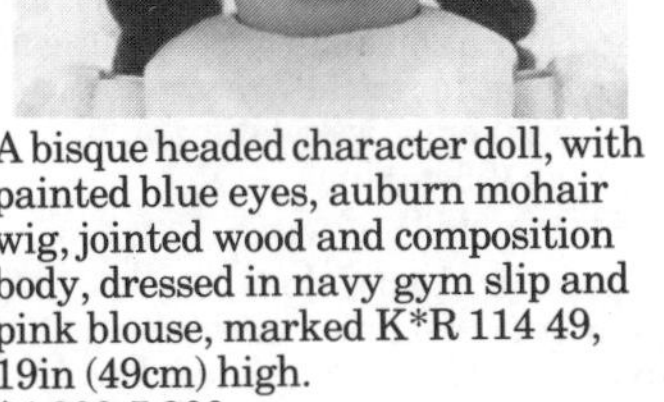

A bisque headed character doll, with painted blue eyes, auburn mohair wig, jointed wood and composition body, dressed in navy gym slip and pink blouse, marked K*R 114 49, 19in (49cm) high.
$4,000-5,000

A Simon and Halbig bisque head doll, with applied hair, sleeping eyes, open mouth and composition body with jointed limbs, stamped Simon and Halbig SH8, 19in (49cm) high.
$500-550

A bisque headed child doll, with blue sleeping eyes, pierced ears and blonde wig, the composition jointed body wearing robe with lace insertions and wool cape and bonnet, marked Simon & Halbig K*R50, 19in (49cm) high.
$1,000-1,200

A bisque headed child doll, with blue sleeping eyes, pierced ears and jointed body dressed in cream silk, marked Simon & Halbig K * R76, 30in (77cm) high.
$800-1,000

A bisque headed child doll, with blue sleeping eyes, pierced ears, blonde wig and jointed body wearing bronze kid boots with 3 ankle straps, marked S & H L.L. & S6½, 18in (46cm) high.
$550-700

A Simon & Halbig doll, early 20thC, 28in (72cm) high.
$700-900

A bisque headed character baby doll, with lidded flirting blue eyes, feathered brows and brown mohair wig, the bent limbed composition body with voice box, dressed in knitted suit, marked 1296 F.S.&Co. Simon & Halbig, 20in (51cm) high.
$650-1,000

Jules Steiner

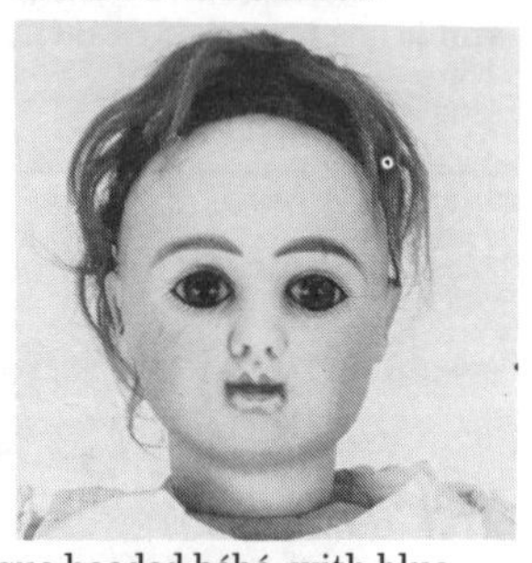

A bisque headed bébé, with blue yeux fibres, closed mouth, and pierced ears, the jointed composition body dressed in white shoes and socks, marked J. Steiner Paris A7, 14½in (37cm) high.
$5,000-5,500

A bisque headed Bébé Premier Pas, the solid pate with fixed blue eyes and blonde, curly wig, the composition body with walking mechanism, wearing earlier embroidered linen dress, by J. Steiner, 20in (51cm) high.
$2,500-3,000

A bisque headed bébé, with closed mouth, pierced ears, fixed bright blue eyes, skin wig and papier mâché fixed wrist body, wearing a petticoat, impressed Ste CO, and with grey Jules Nicholas Steiner trademark stamp on the body, 13½in (35cm) high.
$5,500-6,500

Dolls Houses

A mock Tudor style dolls house, possibly Triang, c1930.
$500-650

A painted wooden dolls house, simulating yellow stone with trompe l'oeil coining, dentil portico and imitation slate roof, opening at the front to reveal 7 rooms with original papers, on later stand, 37½in (95cm) high.
$2,500-3,000

A printed paper and wood dolls house, opening to reveal 4 rooms, each with fireplace, by G & J Lines Bros. DH/17, c1910, 25in (64cm) high. **$550-700**

A painted wooden dolls house, opening at the front to reveal 9 rooms, 55in (139.5cm) high.
$1,000-1,200

A box type wooden dolls house, the façade with brick paper ground floor and original cream paintwork with remains of gilt lines, opening to reveal 4 rooms, with varnished white wood pelmets, teak window sills and original papers on the inside of the façade, by G & J. Lines, c1910, 24in (62cm) high.
$800-1,000

A wooden dolls house, painted to simulate brickwork with grey roof and scalloped eaves, opening to reveal 4 fully furnished rooms, on shaped base, c1900, 50in (127cm) high.
$4,000-5,500

A printed paper on wood dolls house, with printed green slate roof, the door and windows with painted architectural details opening at the front and with roof removing to show 2 rooms with original floor, and wallpapers, the underside of the roof with paint and transfer decorations, stamped on the base Schutsmarke and C.H. in a monogram below a crown, for Christian Hacker, also inscribed in pencil R138/1, 20in (51cm) high.
$1,000-1,300

A group of dolls house furniture, including 2 soft metal chairs, a conversation seat and a cradle, and 3 printed paper on wood pieces, late 19thC.
$1,000-1,300

A Bing plated and tinplate child's live steam kitchen stove, with 5 burners, 3 ovens, adjustable rings, filling pipe and extra copper based utensils, not complete, some rusting, c1920, 19in (48cm) wide.
$800-1,000

A German painted wood toy grocer's shop, coloured cream with blue lines, the drawers with enamel content labels in English, 2 drawers missing, 21in (54cm) high.
$800-1,000

A Staffordshire child's china tea service for 6, painted with yellow and green tulips and gilt rims, c1840. **$550-650**

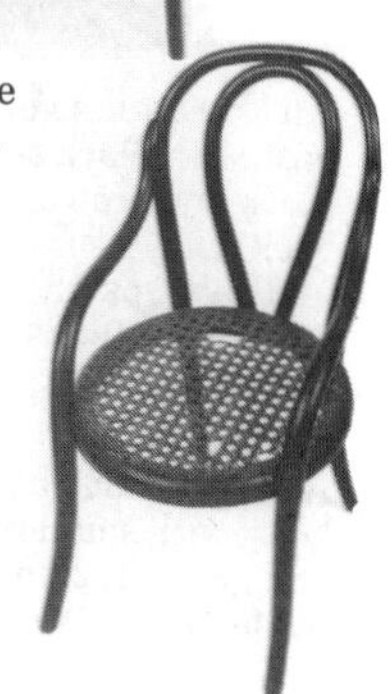

Dolls bentwood furniture, with cane seats, 4 chairs, a settee and a table, 19thC, settee 14in (36cm) wide.
$550-700

A Waltershausen gilt transfer decorated extending dining room table of serpentine shape, 6½in (17cm) long, a gilt transfer decorated writing desk, 4in (10cm) high, and a mantel clock with turned supports 3½in (9cm).
$500-650

TOYS

Automata

A hand operated musical automaton of a violin player, the bisque head with closed mouth and light brown wool wig, in original red and white suit, with wood hands, feet and violin, 7½in (19cm) high.
$650-800

A hand-operated musical automaton, of 3 bisque headed dolls seated at a table under an arbour, distressed, 11in (28cm) wide.
$1,500-2,500

A fur covered bear automaton with walking, turning head, and jaw mechanism, ivory teeth and wooden feet, inoperative, tail missing, probably number 77 in the Roullet and Decamps catalogue of 1878, 7in (17.5cm) high.
$400-500

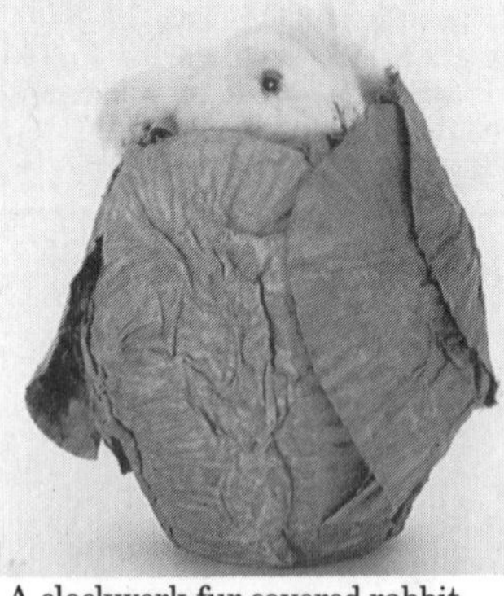

A clockwork fur covered rabbit automaton, with pink glass eyes, emerging from a carton and cloth cabbage, turning his head and raising his ears, by Roullet and Decamps, 7½in (19cm) high.
$1,400-2,000

Teddy Bears

An early golden plush covered teddy bear, with boot button eyes, hump, excelsior stuffing and elongated limbs, wearing tortoiseshell rimmed spectacles, hole on left paw, replaced pads, appendix scar squeaker inoperative, lacks stuffing, small blank Steiff button in ear, c1903, 20in (50.5cm) high
$650-1,000

A golden short plush covered teddy bear with boot button eyes, hump, low set ears, horizontally stitched nose, felt pads, firm stuffing and long straight legs, one pad recovered, some moth in paws, probably early American, 29in (73.5cm) high.
$1,300-1,400

An Edwardian gold plush teddy bear with black stitched snout, black and brown glass eyes, hump back, long arms, cloth pads to feet and paws, partly straw filled, with squeaker, 19in (48.5cm) high.
$500-550

A bear muff, c1920.
$300-400

Two Schuco perfume bottle bears, 5in (12.5cm) high. **$400-500 each**

A long blonde plush covered teddy bear, with small hump, large feet and growler, 20in (50.5cm) high.
$650-800

An English Chiltern teddy bear, c1950, 18in (45.5cm) high.
$100-130

Lead Soldiers

A set of 6 mounted Royal Life Guards by Britains, number 4284 from a limited edition of 7000, contained in original box together with a certificate of authenticity.
$80-110

A military marching band by Britains, comprising 12 figures, bass drum and mace missing, c1939.
$4,000-5,000

Money Banks

A cast iron mechanical moneybox, 'Stump Speaker', with movable right arm, opening bag and unusual counterbalanced 'talking' mouth, in original paintwork, Pat. June 8 1886, 10in (25cm) high.
$1,400-2,000

A cast iron mechanical moneybox, 'Jolly Nigger Bank', with movable right arm, cast iron base, in original paintwork, with patent details, by Shepard Hardware Co., Buffalo, N.Y., c1883, 7in (17.5cm) high.
$300-400

Tinplate

A clockwork motorcycle, c1935.
$120-130

A Camtoy clockwork 'Universal Transport' box wagon, 6½in (16.5cm) long, a Brimtoy clockwork 'Lyons Tea' articulated wagon, 6in (16cm) long, and a Mettoy clockwork caterpillar tractor and driver, in original box.
$130-150

A Gama fire engine with turntable, 9in (23cm) long, and a clockwork Red Cross van, slight damage, 8in (20cm) long.
$75-100

A Hessmobile, the clockwork automobile in crimson livery lined in black and white, the chauffeur in dark navy blue uniform with peaked cap, bearing the trade mark of John Leonard Hess, c1908, 9in (22.5cm) long.
$550-650

A Lehmann clockwork figure of a negro driving a 3-wheeled vehicle, with lithographed detail and concentric back wheels, c1925, 5in (12.5cm) long.
$550-600

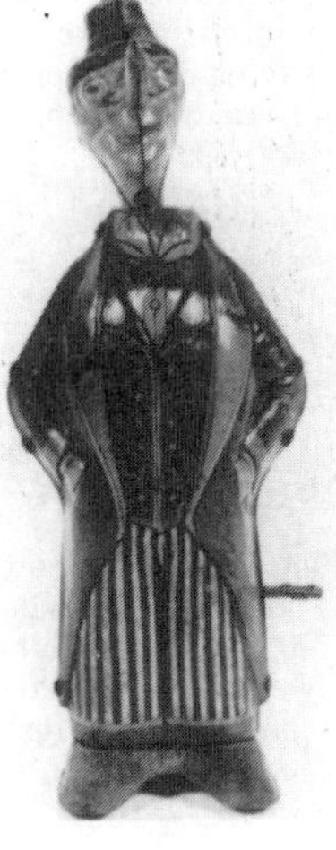

A German clockwork clown by H. Fischer, standing with upturned nose and moving head, early 20thC, 8in (20cm) high. **$250-300**

A Mettoy clockwork racing car, 12½in (32cm) long, and a Mettoy clockwork yellow plated express delivery van, 6in (15cm) long.
$150-200

A painted hansom cab, with clockwork mechanism, 'Li La Hansom Cab', spoked wheels, driver with steering wheel and brake, 2 lady passengers, a dog, in original paintwork, EPL No. 520, by Lehmann, c1910, 5in (12.5cm).
$1,400-2,000

A printed and painted teabox with 2 Chinese coolies, 'Kadi', clockwork mechanism concealed in box, one arm missing, box supports broken, EPL No. 723, by Lehmann, c1910, 7in (17.5cm) long.
$650-800

A clockwork camouflaged observation vehicle, with a driver and 3 figures to the flat back, operating a spot light, one figure missing, 14in (35.5cm) long.
$150-250

A felt covered and painted tinplate toy, 'Donald Duck', in sailor's uniform, with clockwork mechanism, slightly worn, by Schuco, c1936, 6in (15cm) high.
$400-550

An Alfa Romeo P2 Racing Car, C.I.J., painted tinplate, finished in blue, with cloverleaf insignia, operating steering and handbrake, dummy shock absorbers and drum brakes, and narrow tread tyres, early type, c1926. **$3,000-4,000**

A lithographed tinplate dancing negro, 'Oh My', EPL 690, with hand cranked clockwork mechanism concealed in base, in original paintwork, with stand, original lid with instructions, lid torn, by Lehmann, c1912, 10in (25cm) high.
$650-700

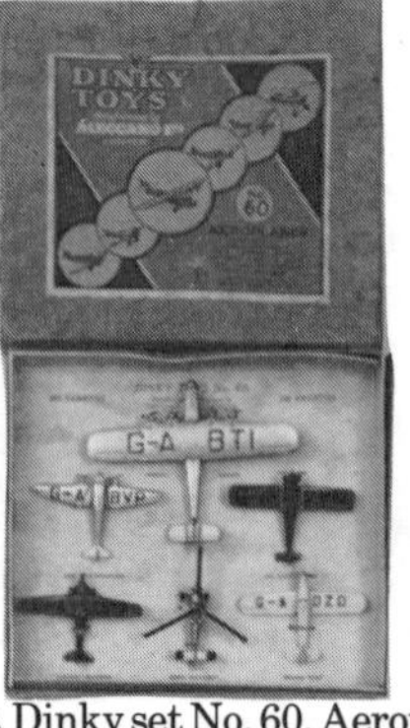

A Dinky set No. 60, Aeroplanes, 2nd Issue, with markings and instructions, in original box, some damage, pre-war, G, box F.
$800-1,000

A German painted tinplate steam riverboat, in red and white, blue and red lined, yellow funnel with red star, single cylinder engine with painted flywheel and brass boiler driving 3-screw propeller, c1905, 11½in (30cm) long.
$650-800

Three Dinky Supertoys, No. 901 Foden Diesel 8-Wheel Wagon, No. 903 Foden Flat Truck and No. 905 Foden Flat Truck with Chains, all in original boxes, E, boxes E.
$1,000-1,200

A German painted and lithographed tinplate clockwork pusher biplane, finished in cream, with front stabiliser, rear tailplane and 3-wheel under carriage, in the style of Gunthermann, propeller blades missing, c1910, 7in (18cm) long.
$1,200-1,300

A Carette painted pulley driven platen printing press, with operating mechanism, fly wheel, fount and tray of rubber type, finished in maroon, Cat. Ref. 634/1, c1911, 5in (12.5cm) wide.
$700-800

A Dinky original set 39 box containing green 39a Packard Super 8 Sedan, black 39b Oldsmobile, 6 Sedan and yellow 39f Studebaker State Commander Coupe, pre-war F-G, box G, no insert.
$1,000-1,200

A Dinky 977 Commercial Servicing vehicle, in original box, M, box E.
$300-400

Two Dinky 28 series delivery vans, one No. 28s Frys van, 1 No. 28f Mackintosh's van, and a No. 22c Motor Truck, 2nd types, damage, pre-war, F-G.
$250-300

Six Dinky Supertoys, No. 981 Horse Box, No. 982 Pullmore Transporter and 994 Loading Ramp, No. 932 Comet Wagon, No. 922 Big Bedford Lorry and No. 933 Leyland Comet Wagon, all in original boxes, E, boxes E.
$800-900

Miscellaneous

A child's wicker gig, with skin covered horse mounted over the front wheel, simulating a galloping motion as the pram is pushed, with whip and pram handle, restored, 63in (160cm) long.
$2,000-2,500

Advertised in Harrods Christmas Catalogue for 1911, priced 5gns.

Victorian dapple grey rocking horse.
$2,500-3,000

A Merrythought monkey, post war, 20in (51cm).
$65-80

A set of Britains painted diecast figures of Snow White and the Seven Dwarfs, c1938.
$110-140

A Meccano outfit No. 3X, red and green with electric motor, with manuals, in original wood box, good condition, c1928.
$400-500

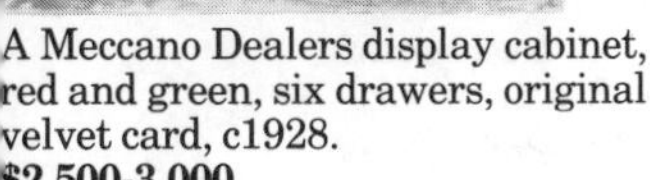

A Meccano Dealers display cabinet, red and green, six drawers, original velvet card, c1928.
$2,500-3,000

A coloured plastic one-armed bandit, 1962. **$120-130**

A German toy wooden grocer's shop, stencilled and lined in brown with printed paper labelled drawers, wooden canisters and cash and ledger books, c1930, 21in (54cm) wide.
$800-1,000

MODELS

Air

A detailed 1in:1ft scale static display model of the prototype Austin Whippet biplane, constructor's No. AUI registration letter G-EAGS, built by P. Veale, Barcombe, wingspan 21½in (54cm).
$1,500-2,500

G-EAGS was first given the temporary registration number K-158 in 1919 and the model represents the prototype in its final form when owned by C. P. B. Ogilvie at Hendon in 1920-21. In all five Austin Whippets were built.

A radio controlled flying model highwing monoplane 'Majestic Mayar', built by R. Golding, wingspan 90½in (227cm).
$300-500

A late Victorian gilt painted paper and cardboard scale model of a Ferris wheel, raised upon a canted square plinth with scroll brackets to the corners, in a glazed stained wood display cabinet, gilding worn in places, 22in (55cm) high.
$300-500

Land

A Richardson and Allwin painted wood and metal model Bullnose Morris pedal car, with folding hood, and painted metal Shell oil can, 45in (114cm) long.
$6,500-7,000

A 3in scale model Foden 'C' type twin cylinder steam lorry Patricia, having welded steel boiler, Ackerman steering, hand and foot brakes, wooden cab, opening doors, 29 by 72in (74 by 182.5cm).
$5,000-5,500

A Mamod steam driven lorry.
$65-110

A 3½in gauge model of the Shay 0–4–0 + 0–4–0 geared logging locomotive No. 2, with silver soldered copper boiler, hydraulic tested to 200 p.s.i., steam tested to 150 p.s.i., with fittings, finished in grey, red and polished brightwork, the tank sides lettered Renhold Timber Co, built by P. Higgins, Renhold, carrying box, 11 by 27½in (28 by 70cm).
$4,000-5,000

This model is new and has not been steamed.

An exhibition standard 5in gauge model of the L.M.S. 2–4–2 side tank locomotive No. 10637, built to the designs of Don Young by Major F. R. Pearce, West Byfleet, with brazed superheated copper boiler built by R. R. Chambers, Poole, finished in L.M.S. red livery and lining, with showtrack, 14 by 39½in (35.5 by 99.5cm).
$6,500-7,000

A Hornby Electric gauge 0 tinplate 0–4–0 Metropolitan locomotive and 4 Hornby tinplate gauge 0 accessories and track, in wooden box.
$250-300

A steam engine on a wood base.
$500-650

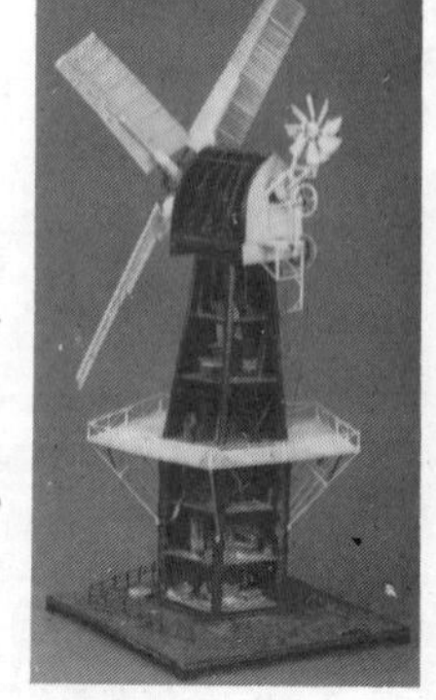

A well detailed wood and metal model of Orbel Mill, with sails and angle adjustment mechanism, wooden driving gears, internal rollers, chains, shoots, mill stones, ladders and much detailing, built by A. Williams, some old damage, c1805, 65in (165cm) high.
$1,000-1,500

Sea

A brass and wood one-twelfth scale model of a marine 32lb cannon of c1850, built by V. Pentecost, Falmouth, 8 by 19in (20 by 48cm).
$1,400-2,000

GAMES

Chess Sets

A set of boxwood chessmen.
$250-300

A Chinese red and white ivory chess set, each piece carved as a member of the court of a warrior, the knights mounted, with castellated elephant rooks, on waisted oval cases, 2 to 4in (5 to 10cm), displayed in a later mahogany box together with a wooden chess board and a volume of A History of Chess by Harry Golombek, 1976.
$550-650

MUSICAL

Musical Instruments

A mahogany 14-key table barrel organ with 10-air barrel, simulated pipes in 2-lancet Gothic front, list of tunes and trade label of J. Fentum, Music Printer & Publisher, early 19thC, 18½in (47cm) high.
$800-1,000

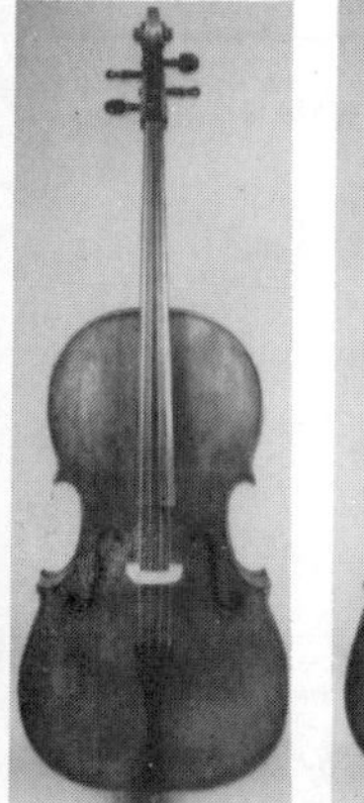

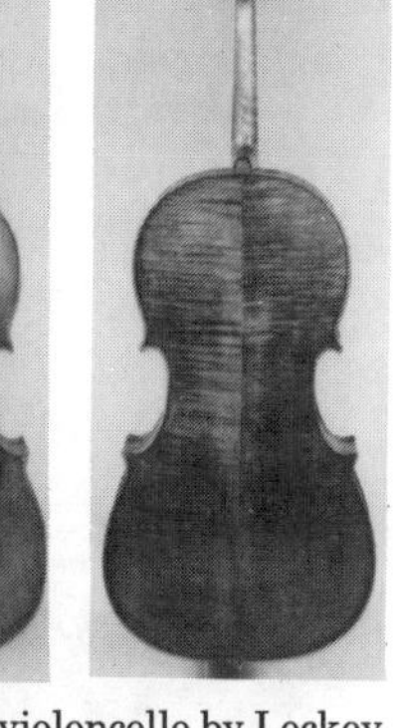

An English violoncello by Lockey Hill, labelled L. Hill/Violin & Violoncello/Maker/Boro'/London, with golden-brown varnish, length of back 29in (73.5cm).
$20,000-25,000

The fingerboard is numbered H 34.

A chamber barrel organ, by G. Astor & Co., 79 Cornhill, with 3 of 4 ten-air barrels, 4 ranks of pipes, drum, triangle, 6 stops, 18 keys and mahogany case with chequer stringing, oval simulated false-pipe panel, storage for 2 barrels in base and maker's label and later tune sheet in lid, 59in (149.5cm) high, the case stamped 588.
$3,000-4,000

An Italian violin attributed to Cesare Candi, labelled Enrico Rocca . . . 1906, with red-orange varnish over a golden ground, length of back 14in (35.5cm).
$13,000-16,000

A ten-air street barrel piano, in varnished wood case with incised decoration and glazed upper panel, with trade labels of A. O. Wintle, Lawshall, Bury St. Edmunds, on painted cart, 99in (251.5cm) long overall.
$3,000-4,000

A street barrel piano by Keith Prowse & Co. Ltd., with ten-air barrel pinned by Tomasso with popular tunes of c1900, the case with typical incised name and decoration, Tomasso transfer, modern colour prints and detached pediment with typed Tomasso tune sheet, in traditional handcart with leaf-sprung wheels, 83in (210.5cm) long overall.
$5,000-5,500

A Kessels 61-note automatic piano, in ebonised case with roll mechanism in cupboard below keyboard, driven by hand crank or electric motor, wood tracker bar, pneumatic action and electro-pneumatic controls, with 31 rolls, 59in (149.5cm) wide.
$650-1,000

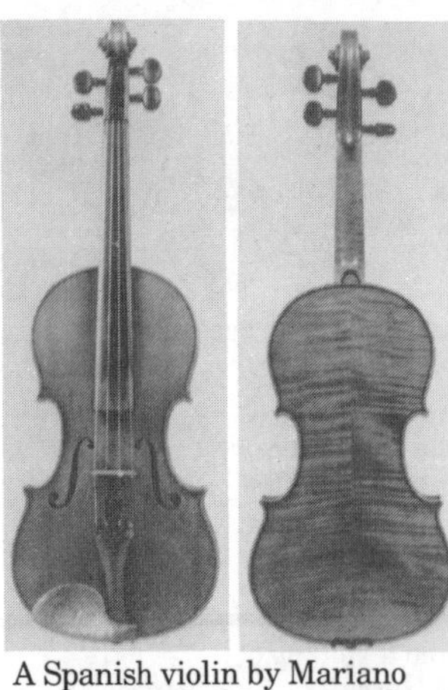

A Spanish violin by Mariano Ortega, labelled Marianus Ortega filius Silberi/fecit Matriti anno 1844, length of back 14in (35.5cm), in case.
$28,000-30,000

Sold with the certificate of W. E. Hill & Sons dated 11 September 1905.

A Classical stencilled and carved mahogany piano, by E. N. Scherr, Philadelphia, c1830, 68in (172.5cm) wide.
$3,500-5,500

A Bechstein boudoir grand piano, Model A, No. 108650, the mahogany case with 3 pairs of tapering square legs joined by stretchers and on brass casters, 72in (182.5cm).
$4,000-5,000

A Swiss gilt metal musical casket, the hinged lid containing singing bird mechanism with enamel cover, the base with timepiece and musical movement playing 4 airs listed underneath, early 20thC, 5in (12.5cm) wide.
$4,000-5,000

Musical Boxes

A 15⅝in (39.5cm) table Polyphon disc musical box, with double movement in panelled walnut case with carved mouldings, with 20 discs in storage case, with Nicole Freres index list, part lid missing.
$5,000-5,500

A Symphonion Eroica triple disc musical box, in walnut case with clock-backed fretwork door, small disc storage chute in base and balustraded top, with 16 sets of discs, 80in (203cm) high.
$20,000-21,000

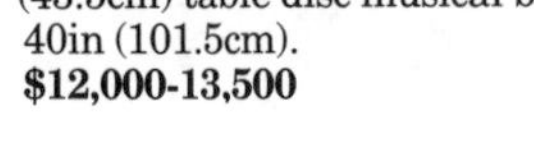

A Lochmann's original 17in (43.5cm) table disc musical box, 40in (101.5cm).
$12,000-13,500

Miscellaneous

A musical automaton tableau, with 3 pairs of bisque headed doll dancers on rotating turntable, in a rustic setting with waterfall, wooded background painted on glass dome, 2-train clock and ebonised wood base, 23½in (60cm) high.
$2,500-4,000

Gramophones

A Thorens No. 17 folding portable gramophone, in the form of a folding camera, in brown and yellow crackled enamel casing, 11in (28cm) wide.
$300-400

An early E.M.G. Mark X hand-made gramophone, with gooseneck tone-arm, later E.M.G. soundbox, oak case, electric motor and papier-mâché horn, 29in (73.5cm) diam, a Davey fibre cutter, a B.C.N. thorn sharpener, and a Davey dry-air jar for fibre needles, c1930.
$2,500-3,000

Leather & Luggage

An English stitched leather suitcase with old baggage labels, c1920, 23½in (60cm) wide.
$120-150

An English tin painted travel trunk with domed, faux grained top, c1875, 28in (71cm) wide.
$130-150

A Louis Vuitton travelling trunk, 44in (111.5cm) wide.
$550-700

A gentleman's travelling valise, probably Finnighans, Manchester, c1920.
$800-900

A tin hat box with original blue interior and wood grained paint exterior, c1890.
$110-150

A German green and gilt tooled leather stationery folder, the cover inset in brass, 19thC, 17 by 12½in (43.5 by 32cm).
$1,000-1,200

An English tin plated and painted faux oak hat box, c1880, 12½in (32cm) diam.
$50-100

An English tinware faux grained painted hat box, c1880, 11in (28cm) wide.
$130-150

An English painted tin hat box with original paint, c1890, 15in (38cm) wide.
$100-140

SPORTS

Fishing

A Fraser-Kilian Neo Caster reel, post war, elaborate for spin-casting but not working very well.
$30-50

A 4½in Farlow Patent Lever brass salmon fly reel, No. 2503, with rich bronze finish over brass, drag control on the back plate.
$50-65

A 5¼in Hardy Silex reel, for sea fishing, made of Ebona, Bickerdyke lineguard, 2 rim controls, rare.
$100-150

A 5in Horton of Glasgow brass and ebonite salmon reel, c1900.
$30-50

An unnamed pre-1939 sidecaster, wooden and metal, probably made in Australia, probably for sea fishing, 4in (10cm) diam.
$25-30

A 3⅜in Hardy multiplying Zenith fly reel, rare version, post war.
$30-50

A 2¾in Farlow brass crank-wind reel, with bone handle, c1870.
$50-80

A folding fishing stool, 15in (38cm) high.
$25-40

A table mat, with glass cover to hold one gut-eyed salmon fly, plus 4 smaller, 6in (15cm) square.
$6-10

A 123in Hardy Halford The Priceless rod, handle made with light and dark timber, the top joint pentagonal, made of 5 splices of cane rather than normal 6, extremely rare.
$130-150

Golfing

An electroplated pentray/inkstand, the centre with a golfer addressing the ball.
$250-300

A silver pint tankard inscribed for Lightcliffe Golf Club, Sheffield 1912, 5in (13cm), 10oz.
$110-150

A plated cruet set comprising salt, pepper and mustard pot, two with blue glass containers.
$300-350

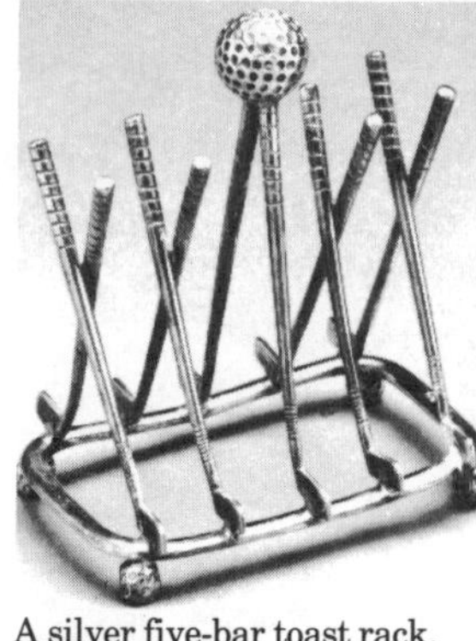

A silver five-bar toast rack, modelled from clubs and ball, London 1930, 4½in (11cm) tall
$550-650

An electroplated pentray/inkstand, the centre with a golfer playing a shot, club loose, on scrolled maskhead feet.
$300-400

A chrome and silver plate cocktail shaker, c1930, 7½in (19cm) high.
$130-150

Cricket

A model of a cricketer in early 19th dress, using a still earlier curved bat, on wood plinth, late 19thC, 13in (33cm).
$400-500

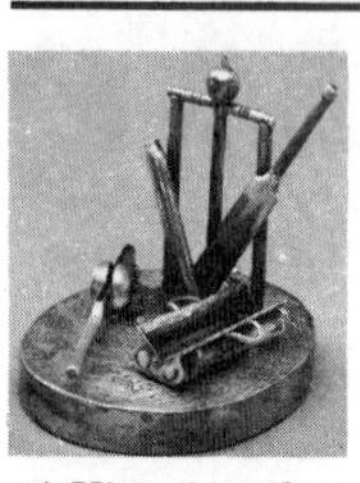

A Victorian silver smoker's condiment set, formed as a wicket with crossed bats, some damage, London, c1886, hallmark slightly rubbed, 5½in (14cm) long.
$500-550

A miniature model setting of a 19thC cricket match with glass wickets, 6 milk glass figures on flocked green pitch, in glazed case, 3 figures damaged, case 11in (28cm) wide.
$150-200

A black and white pot lid, with cartouche depicting bats, stumps and balls within leaf decoration, 2½in (6.5cm) wide.
$80-100

Boxes

A Regency tortoiseshell veneered two-division tea caddy with turned bone finial, 5½in (14cm) high.
$1,400-1,500

A tortoiseshell, ivory and mother-of-pearl inlaid tea caddy, with concave corners, on bun feet, early 19thC, 4in (10cm) wide.
$800-1,000

A pair of brass tea caddies, 6in (15cm) high.
$55-80 each

A Victorian coromandel games box, the cover with cruciform cut brass mount and agate bosses, the interior with bezique and whist markers, bearing the trade label of Carlisle & Watts, 49 Hanover Street, Edinburgh, 7in (17.5cm) square.
$550-700

A Louis XV tortoiseshell and gold snuff box piqué overall with vari-colour gold stripes, chased with a guilloche, by Jean-Louis Capette, Paris, c1772, with the charge and décharge of Julien Alaterre, 3in (7.5cm) diam.
$2,500-3,000

A Rosenthal porcelain cigarette case, 3in (7.5cm) high.
$130-200

A pair of fruitwood tea caddies modelled as apples, the hinged covers opening to reveal a zinc lined interior, with oval metal lock escutcheons, one damaged and repaired, traces of red staining, 4in (10cm) high.
$4,000-5,000

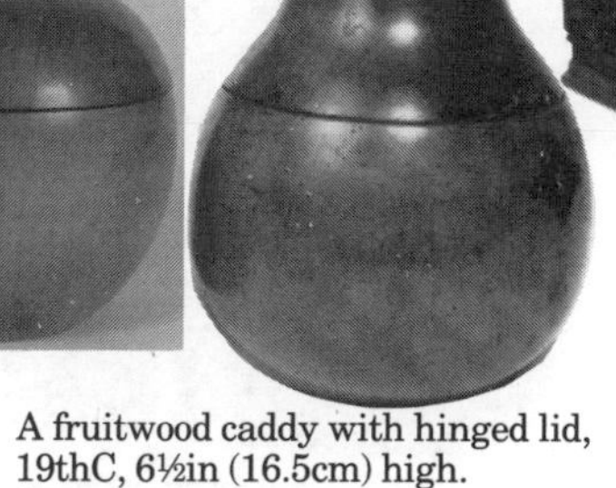

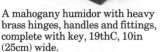

A fruitwood caddy with hinged lid, 19thC, 6½in (16.5cm) high.
$2,500-3,000

A mahogany humidor with heavy brass hinges, handles and fittings, complete with key, 19thC, 10in (25cm) wide.
$500-550

An Anglo-Indian micro-mosaic ebony and ivory stationery box, the lid enclosing a cedar divided interior, late 18th/early 19thC, 8in (20cm) wide.
$1,000-1,200

A Regency scarlet japanned 'coal box', the domed cover finely gilt with a band of wild roses and foliage outlined in black, with conforming painted cast iron loop handles and resting on bold paw feet, c1820, 19in (48.5cm) high.
$5,000-6,500

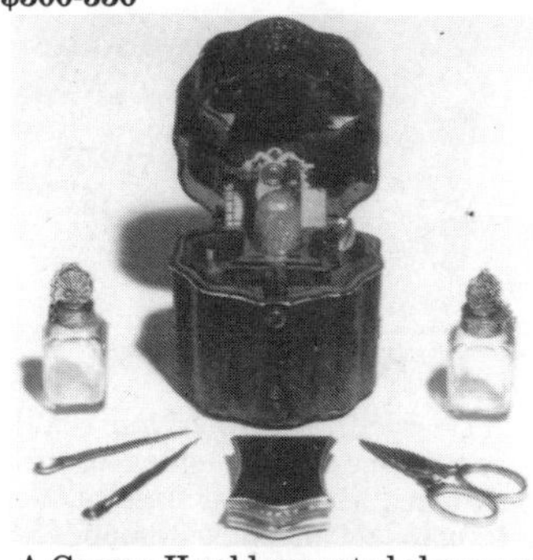

A George II gold mounted shagreen necessaire, containing a gold mounted agate patch box, a pair of glass scent bottles, tweezers, manicure stick, scissors and ivory tablets and a gold pencil holder, bodkin, spoon, ear pick and thimble and an ivory cotton reel, the base re-glued, c1755, 2½in (6.5cm) high.
$4,000-5,000

A Regency rosewood miniature lap desk, with brass inlaid decoration and fitted interior.
$450-500

A rosewood writing slope with burr wood banding, 19thC.
$275-300

A Swedish mahogany, rosewood and marquetry inlaid spice cabinet, with brass knob handles, early 19thC, 8in (20cm) wide.
$450-500

A George III mahogany knife box, later inlaid with a conch shell, with enclosed cutlery compartment, the front with later inlaid flutes, 9in (22.5cm) high.
$700-800

A walnut tantalus, with ivory and brass banding, 3 glass jars and stoppers, 7in (17cm) wide.
$450-550

An Anglo-Indian horn tea caddy, with ivory and ebony interior, fitted with 2 hinged zinc-lined caddies and a cut glass bowl, on ribbed bun feet, 15in (38cm) long.
$700-1,000

A finely carved Welsh love token snuff box, 18thC.
$550-650

An Edwardian silver and tortoiseshell dressing table box, on fluted tapering column legs with ball feet, inlaid with musical trophies, flowers and scrolling foliage and with stamped friezes of paterae, with 2 domed hinged covers, by William Comyns, London, 1905, 6in (15cm).
$2,500-3,000

A George III satinwood and scrolled paper tea caddy, the sides set with stamped white paper classical figures laid on a pine ground, decorated in original bright colours and gilt edged, opening to reveal an inner satinwood lid set with a walnut panel and chequered stringing, 6½in (16.5cm) wide, complete with its original protective wood carrying case of hexagonal form, the hinged cover with brass swan neck handle, 9in (22cm) wide.
$4,000-5,000

An Indian painted wooden box with hinged top, opening to reveal various compartments, inlaid with panels of ivory, and brass mounts, areas of slight damage and restoration, Rajasthan, 18thC, 21in (53cm) wide.
$650-800

A Birmingham enamel casket, with gilt metal mounts, c1758, 10½in (27cm) long.
$3,000-5,000

A casket with gilt brass ring and foliate handles, and with small drawers enclosed by a pair of panelled doors, the whole decorated with applied red wax seals, 19thC, 10½in (27cm) wide.
$550-650

A red damask covered casket, with domed hinged lid, enclosing a later marbled paper interior, 12in (31cm) wide.
$100-150

A brass snuff box with fleur-de-lys design, 2½in (6.5cm).
$65-100

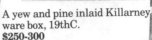

A yew and pine inlaid Killarney ware box, 19thC.
$250-300

A yew and pine Killarney box, 19thC.
$275-300

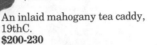

An inlaid mahogany tea caddy, 19thC.
$200-230

A Victorian mother-of-pearl card case, 4in (10cm) long.
$100-110

A mid-Victorian ormolu and porcelain mounted kingwood jewel box, crossbanded with rosewood and inlaid à quatre faces with cabochons and foliate border, the interior lined in green velvet, 27½in (70cm) high.
$2,500-3,000

A Victorian crossbanded coromandel and brass inlaid toilet case, the lined interior with silver mounted fittings, maker's mark W.N., London 1871, 12in (30.5cm) wide.
$700-900

A pair of George III mahogany knife boxes, carved with a shield containing Prince of Wales' Plumes, opening to reveal the original fitted interior.
$1,000-1,200

A French wood and cuir bouilli missal box, with iron bands, hasp and lock, key missing, 15thC, 1 by 3½in (6 by 9cm).
$2,500-3,000

A burr walnut humidor, lined with cedarwood, with lock and handles, c1850, 9in (22.5cm) high.
$700-900

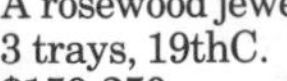

A rosewood jewellery box, with 3 trays, 19thC.
$150-250

A tortoiseshell and silver box, London 1918, 2in (5cm) diam.
$100-130

A tortoiseshell veneered and ivory line inlaid tea caddy, the interior with 2 lidded compartments, early 19thC, 7in (17.5cm) wide.
$650-800

A collage box, 12in (30.5cm) long.
$110-150

An unusual coromandel crab with central locking compartment.
$700-800

Transport

A Victorian child's horsedrawn carriage, the wicker seat lined with buttoned leatherette cushions, with brown leather restraining straps and green concertina action hood, 'pulled' by a pair of painted and carved wood figures of prancing horses, each with stitched leather harness and horse hair tail, 2 wheels replaced, 59in (150cm) long.
$3,000-4,000

An Edwardian governess cart, fitted with shaped bench seats and hinged access door to the rear, with 2 carriage lamp brackets, spoked wheels 36in (91.5cm) diam.
$800-1,000

An Austin 10/4 saloon car, 1141c.c., originally registered 1st March 1933, re-registered under new number, with maroon and black paintwork.
$3,000-5,000

An English child's tricycle, c1910, 25in (64cm) high.
$275-300

Car Mascots

A large green patinated bronze statue of a female archer on detachable marble base, one silver plated plaque inscribed 'Junior Car Club, International Trophy Race, 1938, presented by The Autocar', the other inscribed 'Group 2, won by H.W. Cook (E.R.A.), speed 84.34 M.P.H., driven by Raymond Mays', bow missing, slight damage to marble at foot of archer, 21½in (55cm) high overall.
$800-900

A chrome car mascot, c1930.
$120-140

Miscellaneous

A Fenton L.M.S. maroon enamelled totem.
$275-300

Fenton was the next station to Stoke-on-Trent on the N. Staffordshire Railway. Opened 7th August 1848, closed 6th February 1961, demolished shortly afterwards.

A London and North Eastern Railway cast brass nameplate, The Pytchley, being the left hand side plate removed from the D.49 Hunt Class 4–4–0 locomotive No. 62750, 33in (83cm) long.
$10,000-12,000

Two brass traction engine maker's plates, inscribed No. 2987 and No. 3665 Aveling & Porter Limited, Rochester, Kent, England, 10in (26cm) wide.
$300-500

A Western Australian Government Railways coats-of-arms transfer on wood panel.
$80-130

No. 657
WHITE STAR LINE.
R.M.S. "TITANIC."
This ticket entitles bearer to use of Turkish or Electric Bath on one occasion.
Paid 4/- or 1 Dollar.

A White Star Line, RMS Titanic, Turkish Bath ticket No. 657, 2 by 3in (5 by 8cm), together with letter of provenance.
$1,500-2,000

An Emile Monier bronze plaque, cast in relief with the figure of a motorist at the steering wheel of a car, c1920, 7½in (19cm) diam.
$200-250

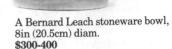

A stoneware cylindrical form by Hans Coper, incised with spiral, covered in a matt buff slip burnished towards the base to reveal areas of matt manganese, c1961, 17½in (45cm) high.
$5,000-6,500

A stoneware hot water flask, by Sven Bayer, incised with foliate decoration, covered in a lustrous iron glaze with olive green splashes, impressed SB and Wenford Bridge seals, 12in (30.5cm) high.
$200-250

A slab with thrown vase, by Adam Sutherland, with painted head of a youth, in blue, green, pink, beige, black, potter's painted signature, 9in (23cm) high.
$275-300

A large Raku plate by John Dunn, with cracked white glaze, impressed potter's seal, 23in (59cm) diam.
$110-150

A spherical porcellaneous Form, by Gabriele Koch, in tones of burnished grey, incised Gabriele Koch, 15in (38cm) high.
$800-1,000

An earthenware ovoid pot, by Elspeth Owen, with irregular inverted rim, smoked and burnished, 7in (17cm) high.
$400-500

A covered Raku pot, by Mike Saul, in mottled grey and pink with twin vertical grey lines, signed M. Saul, 81, 7in (17cm) high.
$400-500

A Raku bowl, by Mike Saul, covered with a pink glaze, with red line below rim, signed M. Saul, 81, 10½in (27cm) diam.
$550-650

Mike Saul studied with Lucie Rie and Hans Coper at Camberwell School of Art together with Ewen Henderson and John Ward. Over the last 10 years he has devoted himself to establishing a major teaching college in Sunderland.

A Bernard Leach stoneware bowl, 8in (20.5cm) diam.
$300-400

A 'Neptune' stoneware vase, by Abdo Nagi, with bands in tones of blue, impressed potter's seal, 12in (31cm).
$650-700

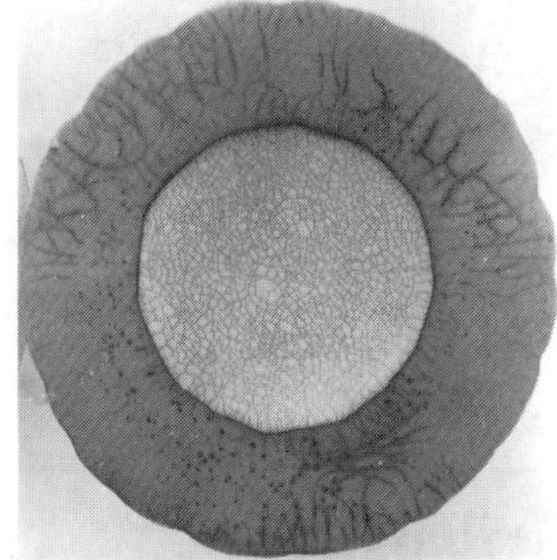

A large Raku bowl, by David Roberts, the interior well white with grey crackling, unglazed rim, impressed DR seal, 21½in (55cm) diam.
$400-550

A curved slab vase, by Adam Sutherland, with painted heads in blue, black and pink, potter's painted signature, 11½in (29cm).
$400-500

Adam Sutherland (b. 1958). After studying pottery with Colin Kellam and taking a B.A. in Fine Arts, Adam Sutherland studied at the Ecole des Arts Decoratifs, Paris. Since 1985 he has been teaching ceramics and printmaking at the Almond Road Workshops in North London, together with Ken Eastman.

A stoneware bowl, by William Staite Murray, with prominent potting rings, on shallow foot, covered in a mottled olive brown and green glaze, the interior with a pale mushroom glaze thinning to reveal glaze beneath, impressed M seal, 7½in (20cm) diam.
$500-650

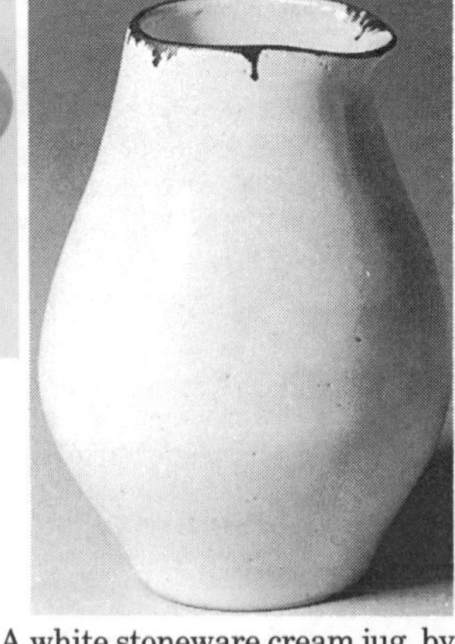

A white stoneware cream jug, by Lucie Rie, impressed LR seal, c1956, some restoration to rim, 4in (10cm).
$550-650

A stoneware goblet shaped vase by James Tower, the interior covered in a translucent black glaze, the exterior in a mottled brown and green glaze over white, inscribed Tower, 8in (20cm) high.
$500-800

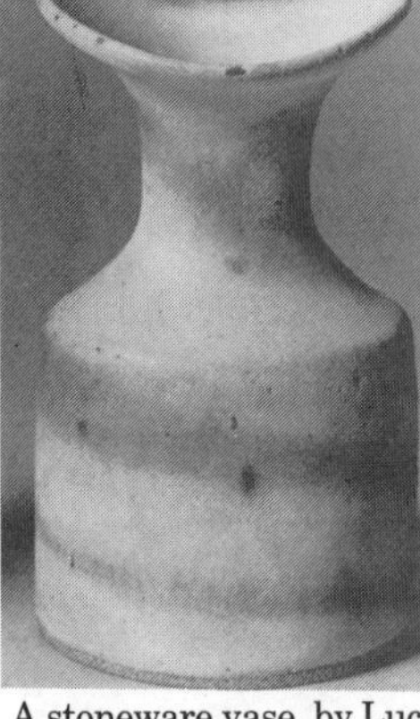

A stoneware vase, by Lucie Rie, white with brown spiral, impressed LR seal, c1970, 5in (13cm) high.
$2,000-2,500

A Raku vase, by Lorraine Robinson, black with splashed white glaze, incised potter's signature, 10in (25cm) high.
$150-200

An Abuja stoneware candlestick by Bawa Ushafa, covered in a mottled lavender blue glaze thinning to reveal areas of lustrous iron brown, impressed B.U.A. seal, 14½in (37.5cm) high.
$300-400

Tribal Art

A Nootka whalebone club, of spatulate form, the butt carved as a bird's head, the eyes as grooved circlets, the back of the head pierced 4 times, dark patina, 19thC, 22½in (57cm).
$5,500-6,500

A Maori greywacke hand club, the butt with 4 carved ridges and pierced for wrist thong, chipped, 15in (37.5cm) long.
$1,000-1,300

An Inca vessel, painted in colours with 2 panels each containing a pair of figures, minor damages, 8½in (21.5cm) high.
$1,500-2,500

A small kero, painted with a central band of 2 monkeys and a parrot within foliage, old repairs, 6½in (15.5cm) high.
$800-900

A Solomon Islands ornament, of twisted fibre sewn with 10 rows of porpoise teeth between bands of white trade beads, white bead border, nassa shells to each end, plaited fibre ties, one with tooth tassels, 8½in (22cm) long.
$2,500-3,000

A Benin bronze bell, cast in high relief, white painted collector's mark BC3, 19thC, 7in (18cm) high.
$300-500

A Baule bush cow mask, 24in (61cm) long.
$650-1,000

A rare Northwest coast bone figure, the spine and ribs carved in high relief, vestiges of applied skin remaining on the head with iron nails, Coastal Salish or Nootka, late 19thC, 9in (23cm) high.
$2,500-3,000

A Luba/Songye mask, with projecting square mouth and pierced eyes, the eyelids, nose and central band blackened, the remainder of the surface grooved and whitened, 18in (45cm) high.
$4,500-5,000

An unusual pipe, the stem bound with dark and pale copper strips, curved plump base to mouthpiece, on Inagaki stand, 12in (30cm) high
$800-1,000

A fine Senufo wood mask, the concave cheeks carved in relief, triple incisions on forehead, the cresting with 3 rows of raised knobs, dark brown partially crusty patina, 11½in (29.5cm) high.
$6,500-9,500

A Guro female figure, the coiffure dressed as 5 lobes, white beaded waistband with small gold nugget, the crack at the back with some native filler, reddish brown patina, 13in (33cm) high.
$5,000-8,000

A Seneca moccasin, of tanned and smoked skin, decorated in coloured quillwork ornament in blue, red and white, the dark brown silk borders edged with white seed beads, minor damages, 8in (20cm) long.
$1,400-1,500

A Baga female figure, with red glass beads about neck, loins and ankles, circular base, Inagaki wood stand, 18½in (47cm) high.
$6,500-8,000

Three Ibeji, 2 males and a female, with pierced and pointed blued coiffure, smoothly worn faces, necklaces of fine dark blue beads and larger beads about the wrists and ankles, one with repaired base, from the Shaki area, 9½in (23.5cm) high.
$700-1,000

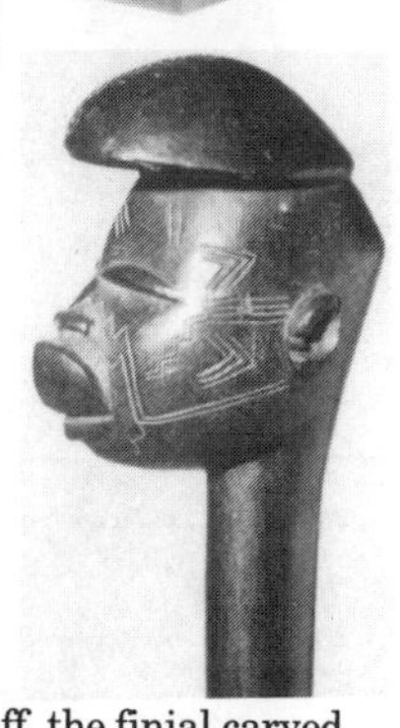

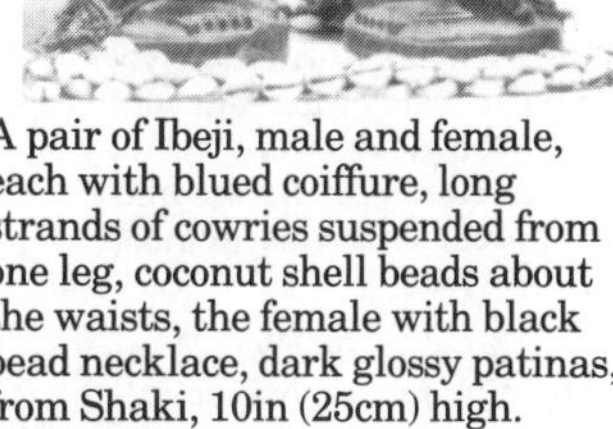

A rare Hungana male figure, encrusted red patina, termite erosion to left side, on Inagaki wood stand, 20½in (52cm) high.
$3,000-5,000

A Makonde staff, the finial carved as a head wearing rounded cap with incised band of circles, the face with large upper lip and incised scarification, the shaft with panels of incised geometrics, dark glossy patina, 58½in (148cm) long.
$800-1,000

A pair of Ibeji, male and female, each with blued coiffure, long strands of cowries suspended from one leg, coconut shell beads about the waists, the female with black bead necklace, dark glossy patinas, from Shaki, 10in (25cm) high.
$300-400

A pair of Yoruba female twin figures, with necklace of large black beads, one with red and blue beads about the wrists, dark glossy patinas, from Baba Magba, 10½in (26cm) high.
$300-500

A Northern Northwest coast bowl, each end incised with the mask of a beaver, the rim with upholstery nails, 3 missing, dark glossy patina, 19thC, 14in (35cm) long.
$2,500-3,000

A Benin bronze head, for the altars of the Queen Mother, dark brown and black patina, mid-19thC, 19½in (49.5cm) high.
$20,000-25,000

A Baule mask, the eyes pierced with slits beneath narrow brows, the small mouth pierced at the centre, lower lip chipped, glossy brown patina, 8in (20cm) high.
$2,500-3,500

EPHEMERA

Pop Ephemera

A three quarter length signed photograph of Tina Turner, 8 by 10in (20 by 26cm).
$50-65

Three Beatles twin track mono tapes.
$15-25 each

A Canadian presentation gold disc to The Boomtown Rats, inscribed 'Presented to Johnny Fingers to commemorate the sale of over 50,000 units of the Mercury album "The Fine Art of Surfacing" December 10th, 1979', 20 by 16in (51.5 by 41cm), framed.
$300-500

A pair of black leather gloves, and a certificate of authenticity from the Elvis Presley Museum confirming that the gloves were worn by Elvis when riding his horses and motorcycles at Graceland.
$900-1,000

Exhibited at the Elvis Presley Museum for several years.

A souvenir concert programme for The Beatles/Mary Wells tour, signed on the cover by each member of the group and inscribed 'love Paul McCartney xxx', 1964.
$2,500-3,000

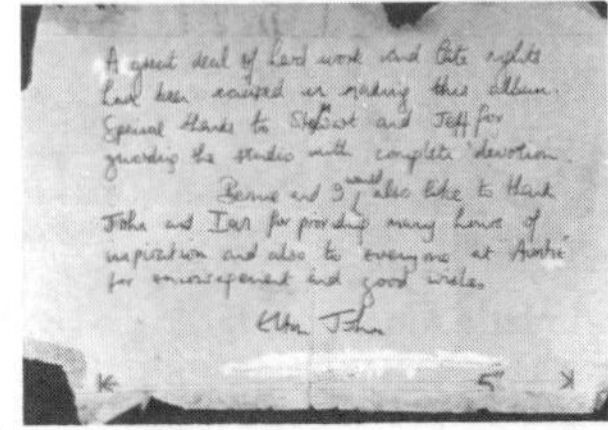

An autograph note signed by Elton John, the note reproduced on the reverse of the album cover 'Empty Sky', 1969.
$1,000-1,200

A black and white portrait photograph of Eric Clapton, signed and inscribed Eric Clapton 89, 10 by 8in (25 by 20cm).
$300-350

An album cover Slow Train Coming and a programme for European Concert Tour 1981, both signed by Bob Dylan in black felt pen.
$650-800

An A.M.I. JBJ 120 jukebox, Serial No. 461081, 45 r.p.m., finished in silver and black, 59½in (151cm) high.
$1,500-2,500

It is believed that the machine belonged to Malcolm MacLaren and was used by The Sex Pistols when miming for auditions.

A pair of tan leather zip-up boots, made by Verde, accompanied by an affidavit confirming that the boots were owned and worn regularly by Elvis, c1970.
$2,500-3,000

An embroidered banner for the winning band, 24 by 12in (61 by 30.5cm).
$55-65

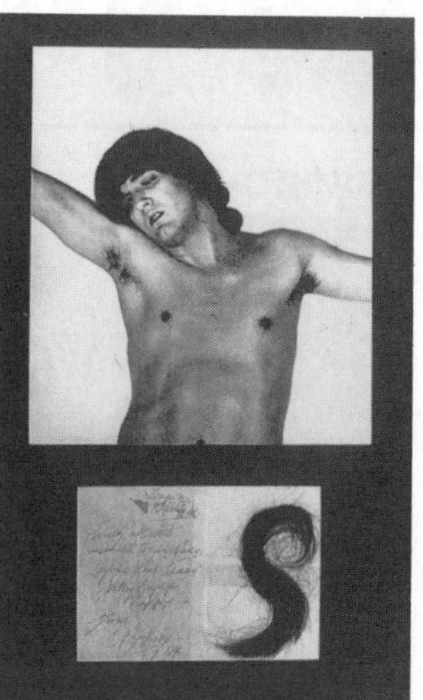

An autographed letter signed from P. J. Proby to a fan, inscribed 'With all best wishes to you Mary, hope this small token keeps you happy — from P. J. Proby xxx', in common mount with a lock of hair 9in (22.5cm) long, and a David Bailey portrait photograph of P. J. Proby, taken from 'David Bailey's Box of Pin-Ups', 1965, 28½ by 18½in (72.5 by 47cm) overall.
$150-300

A Fender Stratocaster guitar, Serial No. S 981810 on 'ivory', bleached rosewood neck, signed by Mark Knopfler, 38½in (97cm) long.
$2,500-3,000

A custom-made ring, the mouth and eyes set with navette cut rubies, accompanied by a certificate of authenticity from the Elvis Presley Museum stating that Elvis bought the ring from Schwartz and Ableser fine jewellery store.
$7,000-8,000

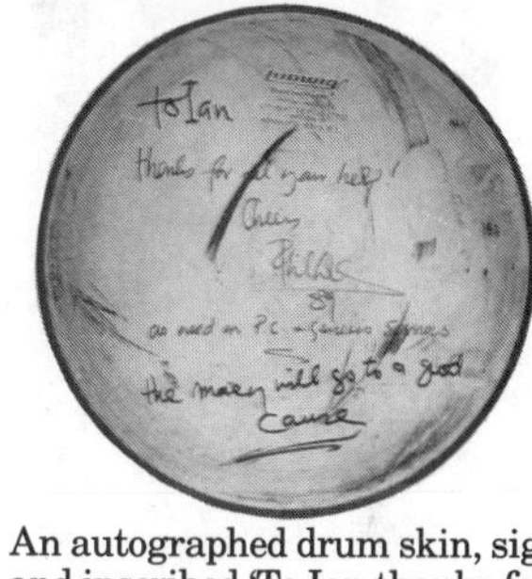

An autographed drum skin, signed and inscribed 'To Ian thanks for all your help, Cheers Phil Collins 89, as used on P.C. and Genesis sessions, the money will go to a good cause', in black felt pen, 13½in (34.5cm) diam.
$1,000-1,200

A rare single-sided acetate 'Good Rockin Tonight', Memphis Recording Service label stamped 'W.H.B.Q. Memphis', accompanied by a certificate of authenticity from The Elvis Presley Museum stating that 'this Elvis Presley's 2nd recording for the Sun label is the original first copy made on the night it was recorded . . .'.
$5,000-5,500

A polychrome film poster The Fall Of The House of Usher, featuring Vincent Price, 30 by 40in (76 by 101.5cm).
$80-150

Eighteen English polychrome horror posters, various titles, 1960s and 1970s, 30 by 40in (76 by 101.5cm).
$150-300

A Laurel and Hardy polychrome half sheet film poster The Dancing Masters, printed by Stafford & Co. Nottingham, 22 by 28in (56 by 72cm).
$80-110

A colour postcard Campbell's Soup Cans, signed Andy Warhol, 6 by 4in (15 by 10cm), mounted and framed.
$1,200-1,300

An August Leymarie Everest Film présente Charlot lithograph, in colours printed by L'Affiche d'Art, Paris, c1920, 62½ by 46½in (158 by 118cm), framed.
$700-1,000

Eleven English polychrome horror posters, largest 30 by 40in (76 by 101.5cm), and a collection of press, campaign books and related material.
$150-250

A French advertisement for Anic cigarettes, by Dransy, slight corner crease.
$65-130

Five polychrome English and American horror posters, c1960, largest 30 by 40in (76 by 101.5cm).
$110-150

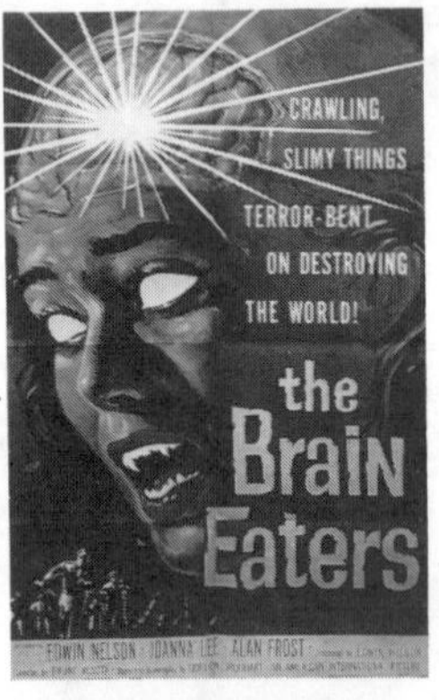

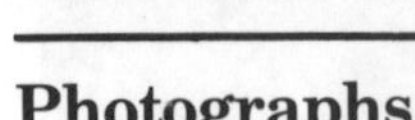

A Raphael Tuck, Celebrated Posters, Colman's Mustard, Returned from Klondyke poster, 1500, by Hassall, UB, album corner marks.
$50-80

A Raphael Tuck Hoe's Sauce poster, 1505.
$30-50

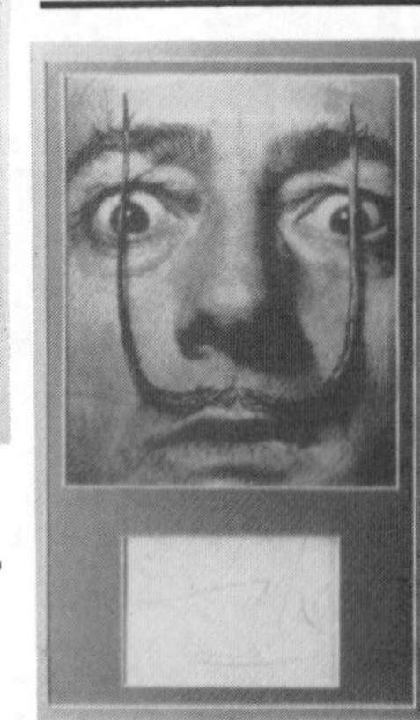

A signed reproduction portrait photo of Salvador Dali, overmounted in gold, silver and ivory, framed and glazed.
$200-300

Photographs

Eight publicity stills by Clarence Sinclair Bull of subject in the title role of the 1933 M.G.M. film Queen Christina, each with photographer's ink credit on reverse, 10 by 8in (25 by 20cm).
$550-700

Six 35mm colour transparencies of Marilyn Monroe, 5 with corresponding colour prints, largest 14 by 11in (36 by 28cm), sold with copyright.
$3,000-4,000

One of the above was used by William Carroll for his counter display card in 1945.

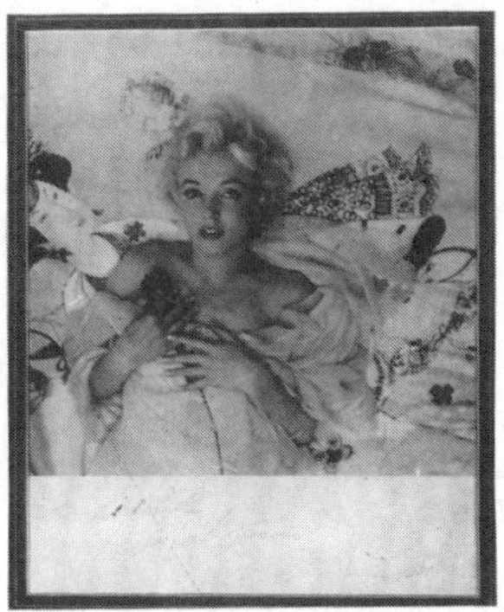
A half-length portrait photograph by Cecil Beaton, signed and inscribed on margin 'To Bridette (sic) Love & Kisses, Marilyn Monroe', 9 by 7½in (23 by 19cm), window mounted, framed, and a letter of authenticity on reverse.
$2,500-3,000

A colour publicity still of the Dynamic Duo, signed and inscribed, 10 by 8in (25 by 20cm).
$300-500

Disneyalia

A Mickey and Minnie Mouse Christmas card, signed Walt Disney, 4 by 5in (10 by 13cm), and a biro sketch of Mickey Mouse.
$700-900

Walt Disney Studios, Snow White And The Seven Dwarfs, 1937, Dopey And Woodland Animals, gouache on celluloid with airbrush background, 5½in (14cm) square, window mounted and framed.
$2,000-2,500

Walt Disney Studios, Alice in Wonderland, 1951, 4 celluloids, Red Rose, Red Rose and Rocking HorseFly, White Sleeping Rose and White Rose Awakes, each flower characterised with facial features, gouache on celluloid, largest 10 by 12in (25 by 31cm).
$1,000-1,300

Walt Disney Productions, Foul Hunting, a T.V. Production, Goofy and a Friend Duck Hunting, gouache on celluloid on watercolour background, 8 by 10in (20 by 25cm), window mounted.
$700-900

A piece of 'Cunard White Star R.M.S., Queen Elizabeth' headed paper, illustrated with a pencil drawing of Mickey Mouse, signed and inscribed 'Best Wishes, Walt Disney', 7 by 5½in (18 by 14cm).
$5,000-6,500

Walt Disney Studios, Snow White And The Seven Dwarfs, 1937, 'Doc With A Lantern In His Hand Tells Bashful And Sneezy To Keep Quiet', gouache on multi-cel set up applied to a Courvoisier airbrush background, 9 by 9in (23 by 23cm), window mounted and framed.
$5,000-5,500

A piece of paper illustrated with a crayon drawing of Mickey Mouse, signed Walt Disney, 8 by 6½in (20 by 17cm).
$3,000-5,000

Walt Disney Studios, Snow White And The Seven Dwarfs, 1937, 'The Seven Dwarfs' gouache on celluloid with wood veneer background, 10½ by 14in (27 by 36cm), window mounted.
$1,500-3,000

Film & Theatre

An ornate Elizabethan style dress of figured silver lame trimmed with silver gilt braid, and lace, with petticoat and slashed sleeves of oyster satin, and 'Warner Bros.Pic.Inc.', embroidered label stitched inside, accompanied by a film still of Olivia de Havilland wearing the dress as Lady Penelope Gray in the 1939 Warner Bros. film 'The Private Lives of Elizabeth And Essex', 8 by 10in (20 by 26cm).
$700-900

Roger Furse, 'Ulyses', Mr Torin Thatcher, armed costume, tunic BCC 71' signed, watercolour and pencil costume design for the Warner film 'Helen Of Troy', 1955, 18½in by 13in (47 by 35cm), window mounted and framed.
$300-400

A brass key ring, one side inscribed with the M.G.M. lion trade mark, the other inscribed 'Dressing Room 24 CLARK GABLE', 2½in (6cm) diam.
$500-550

An autographed photograph of Judy Garland, inscribed lower right 'David — Thank you for a perfect evening, love Judy, June 25, 1956', 13 by 10in (33.5 by 25cm).
$1,000-1,200

A half length colour photograph, signed by Adam West and Burt Ward, as Batman and Robin.
$110-130

ORIENTAL

Cloisonné & Enamel

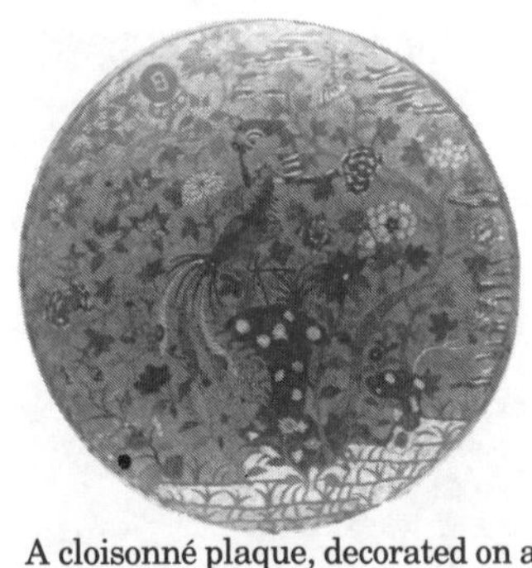

A cloisonné plaque, decorated on a turquoise ground, early 19thC, 23in (59cm).
$550-700

A Chinese cloisonné jardinière, decorated on a yellow ground of formal scrolling lotus flowers, 10in (26cm).
$400-550

A Chinese cloisonné teapot, with 8 Buddhistic emblems, c1800, 6in (16cm) high.
$400-650

A pair of Chinese cloisonné moon flasks, with gilt decoration on a flowerhead cell pattern ground, the necks with butterflies and stiff leaves, 14½in (37cm) high.
$1,200-1,300

Furniture

A Chinese ebonised wood desk and chair, on dragon carved cabriole legs, 52in (132cm) wide.
$700-1,000

A Japanese red lacquer cabinet and stand, some chipping, 18in (46cm) high.
$500-650

A Chinese redwood table cabinet with 2 sliding doors, decorated with applied hard stones, ivory and mother-of-pearl, the corners with silver mounts, hallmarked London 1894, 12½in (32cm) wide.
$2,500-3,000

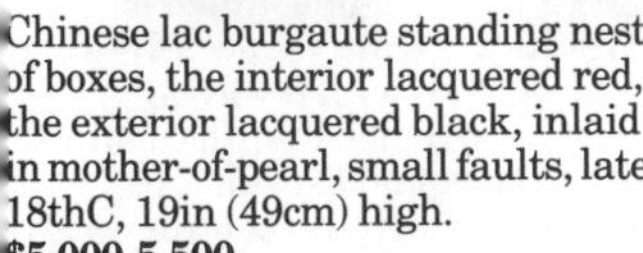

Chinese lac burgaute standing nest of boxes, the interior lacquered red, the exterior lacquered black, inlaid in mother-of-pearl, small faults, late 18thC, 19in (49cm) high.
$5,000-5,500

A Japanese painted paper two-panel screen, decorated on a gold ground, with a brocade border, the reverse with grey paper with silver flowers, 19thC, Rimpa School, 67in (170cm) high. **$1,500-2,000**

Glass

A deep red Peking glass box and cover, incised with the yinyang symbols, Qianlong 4-character mark and of the period, 5in (13cm) diam.
$3,000-4,000

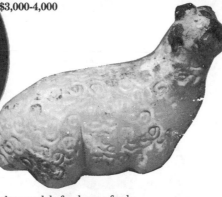

A glass model of a sheep, of pale celadon tone with amethyst coloured head, a whitish slightly degraded patination to most parts incised underneath with small curls imitating wool, chips, probably Han Dynasty, 2½in (7cm) wide.
$3,000-5,000

A pair of Chinese overlay glass vases, decorated in relief with birds in flight and perched on flowering prunus issuing from pierced rockwork, 9½in (24cm) high.
$400-650

Inros

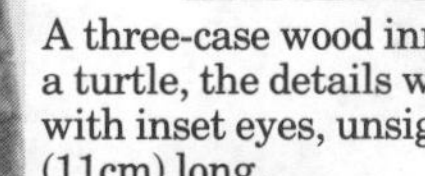

A three-case wood inro modelled as a turtle, the details well delineated, with inset eyes, unsigned, 4in (11cm) long.
$1,200-1,300

A four-case jidai inro, worked in gold and coloured takamakie with the legend of the 4 sleepers, the interior of nashiji, 18thC, 4in (11cm) long.
$800-1,300

A four-case wood inro, decorated with peony flowers issuing from pierced rockwork, the reverse with a butterfly, in gold takamakie, the interior black lacquered, signed Gyokushunsai, 3½in (9cm).
$650-800

A four-case gold lacquer inro, with a fundame ground decorated within shaped panels with the front and reverse of a hawk tethered to a tasselled perch, in grey, black and gold takamakie, the interior of nashiji, chips, signed Nikkosai, 3½in (9cm).
$2,000-2,500

A one-case wood inro modelled as a butterfly, the wings inlaid in wood, light wood, mother-of-pearl and tortoiseshell with ivory and cord holes, 3in (8cm).
$1,000-1,200

Ivory

A Japanese ivory group of musicians, 3½in (9cm) high.
$500-650

A Cantonese ivory box and hinged cover on paw feet, deeply carved with figures on bridges and terraces before buildings, trees and rockwork, 12in (31cm) wide.
$2,500-3,000

A set of 4 ivory counter boxes, by Mariaual le Jeune, tinted for the 4 suits in green, yellow, white and red, the lids with revolving markers, complete with counters and in original fishskin case accompanied by notes of 'Rewards Preference' in Quadrille, some counters replaced, 18thC, 7½in (18.5cm) wide.
$2,500-3,000

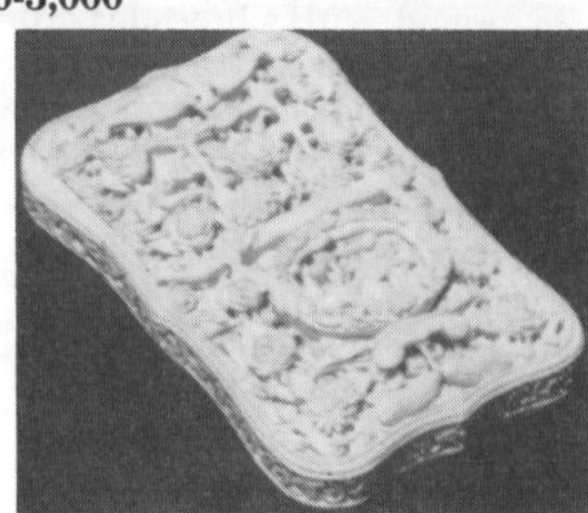

A Cantonese ivory card case, minor damage, 4in (10cm) long.
$500-650

An ivory figure of a Buddha, seated on a lotus throne, cracks, signed, Meiji period, 8½in (22cm), wood stand.
$1,500-2,000

A fine ivory tusk carving, on a pierced hardwood stand, 19thC, 18½in (47cm) long.
$1,000-1,200

Jade & Amber

A spinach green jade bowl, flecked with black inclusions and streaked with white areas, rim polished, small chips, Jiaqing, 7in (17.5cm) diam.
$2,500-3,000

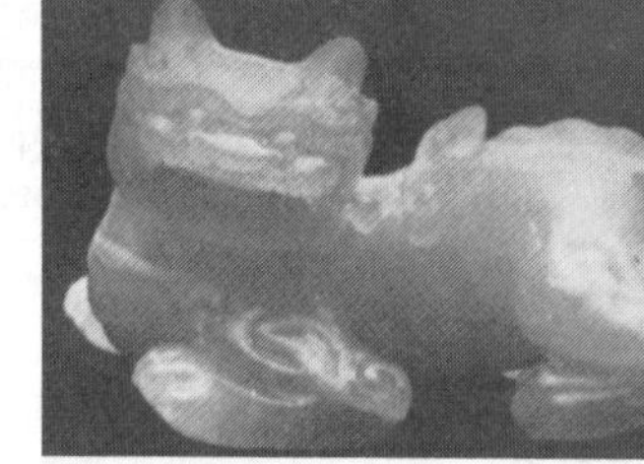

A Chinese jade carving of a crouching Buddhistic lion, grasping a lingzhi fungus in its mouth, its head turned to the left, 18thC, 3in (8cm) long.
$1,000-1,200

Amber group of the Virgin and Child, her cloak engraved with foliate decoration, Child's face restored, minor restorations, later base, late 17th/early 18thC, 5in (12.5cm) high.
$1,300-2,000

A Chinese dark green and mottled jade vase, modelled as a tree section and carved with pine and lingzhi, 4½in (11.5cm) high.
$550-700

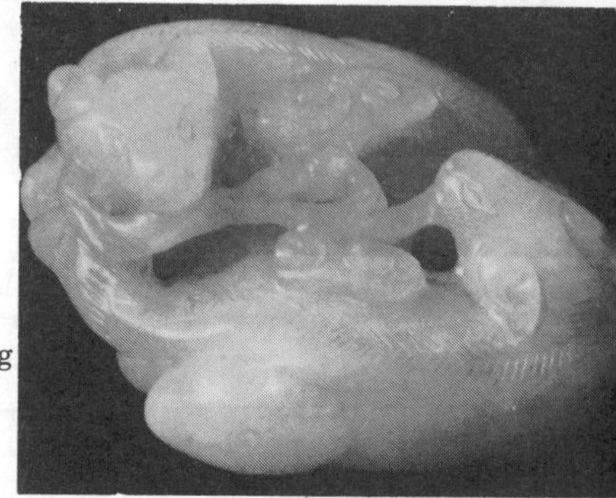

A Chinese pale celadon jade carving of 2 recumbent animals grasping a lingzhi fungus, 18thC, 2in (5cm) wide.
$300-500

Lacquer

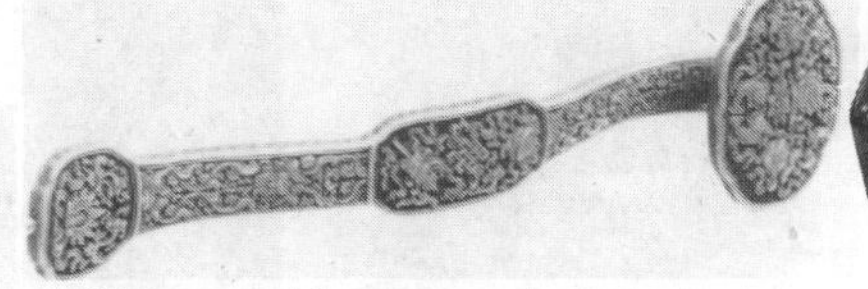

A Chinese red lacquer ruyi sceptre, carved in relief with the 8 Buddhist emblems amongst lotus and floral designs, the reverse with a T-pattern ground, 18th/19thC, 15½in (39.5cm) long.
$700-800

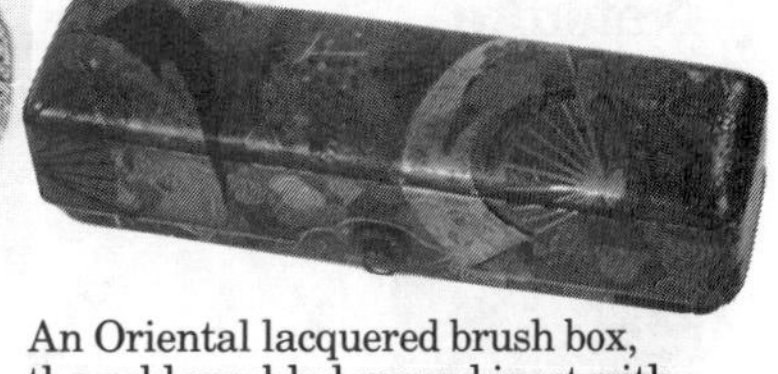

An Oriental lacquered brush box, the gold speckled ground inset with gold leaf, with a pair of metal ring handles with flowerhead backplates, 9½in (24cm) long.
$100-130

A Chinese export lacquer games box and domed cover, on paw feet, decorated and heavily gilt, with approx. 100 monogrammed mother-of-pearl counters, 14½in (37cm) wide.
$4,000-5,000

A Japanese red lacquer box and cover with black interior, carved in relief with flowerheads and foaming wave design, 2in (5cm) diam.
$100-140

Metal

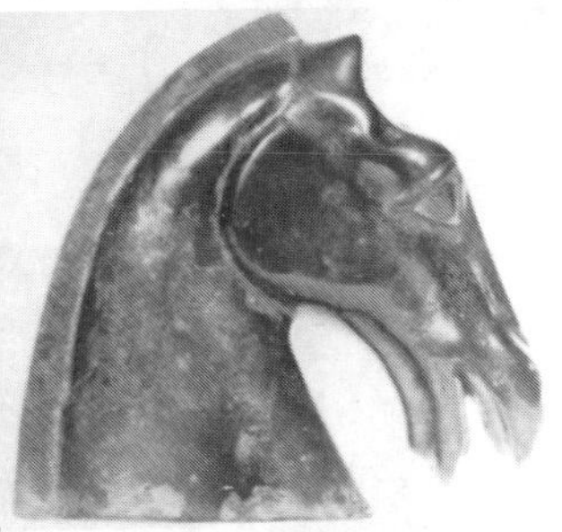

A Chinese Han-style bronze head of a horse, 8in (20cm) high.
$1,200-1,300

A Japanese white metal bowl, decorated with irises on a stippled ground, the interior plain, 7in (17.5cm) diam.
$1,000-1,100

A Chinese bronze ewer with a shallow domed cover, the spout with a dragon head, 16th/17thC, 9in (22.5cm) high.
$1,000-1,200

A bronze figure of a sage, holding a pearl in one hand, his robes cast with dragon, cloud and floral designs, 19thC, 10in (25cm) high.
$400-550

A Chinese silver tripod lobed teapot and domed cover, decorated in relief with butterflies among flowerheads, the handle with ivory insets, signed, 7in (17.5cm) long.
$1,000-1,200

A Japanese bronze dish inlaid in brass with a writhing dragon, the details in black and red, signed Inove and Ariake, 11in (28cm) diam.
$650-700

A Chinese white metal inlaid bronze tripod flattened censer, signed Shisou and with a Xuande 6-character mark, probably 18thC, 5in (12.5cm) diam.
$800-1,000

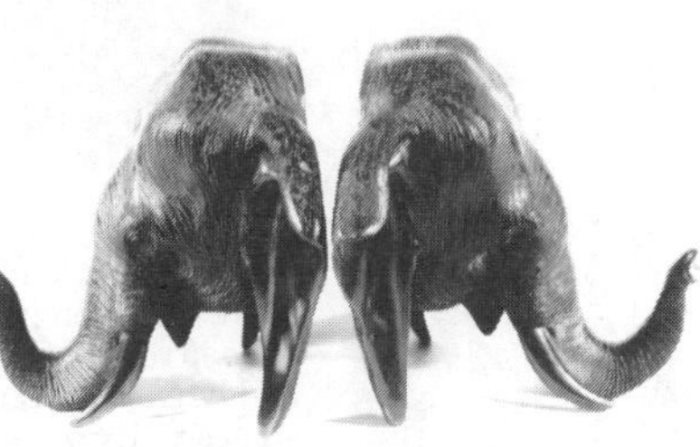

A pair of Japanese bronze elephant-head bookends, with deep red patinated decorated ears, undersides of trunks, and tusks, signed, late 19thC, 6in (15cm) high.
$700-800

Netsuke

A Japanese wood tobacco pouch, ojime and netsuke, the eyes inlaid in dark horn, the pouch signed and the netsuke signed, the pouch 4in (10cm) long.
$1,500-2,500

A bone netsuke of a bearded Chinese sage, wearing robes and leaning on a stick, age cracks, late 18thC, 4in (10cm) long.
$200-300

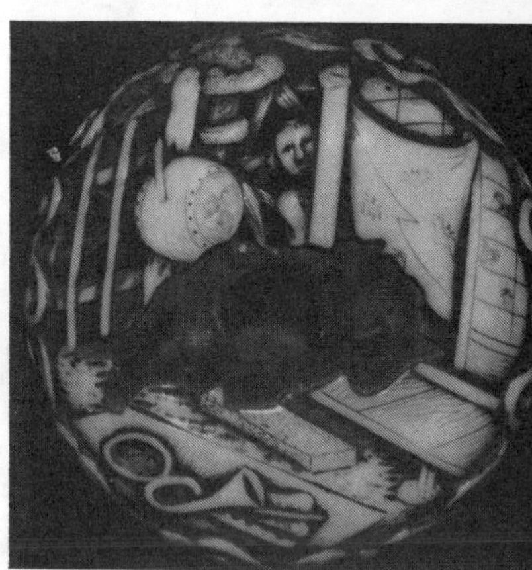

A marine ivory manju netsuke, signed Mitsu, 2in (5cm) diam.
$300-400

A set of 3 ivory netsuke, carved as the Three Mystic Apes, Iwazaru, Kikazaru and Mizaru, 2 signed in oval reserves 'Masatami' (Shomin), late 19thC, 1½in (3.5cm).
$2,500-3,000

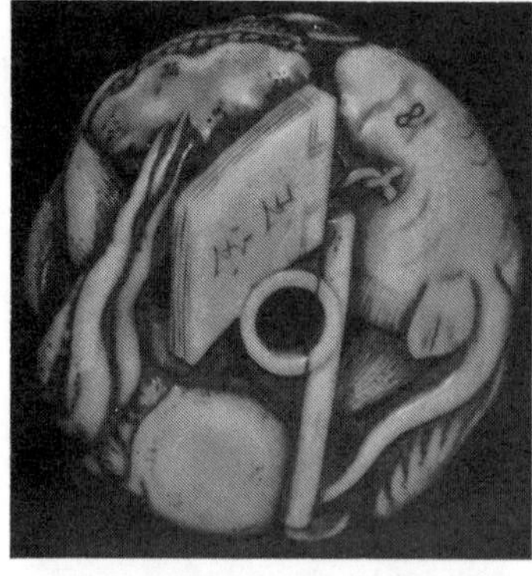

An ivory manju netsuke modelled with a variety of fish, shells and squid around a boat hook, signed Gyokuko, 2in (5cm) wide.
$700-800

An ivory netsuke of a man and boy completing a model of a karashishi and brocade ball with hammer and chisel, signed Gyokoku, 2in (5cm) long.
$450-500

Snuff Bottles

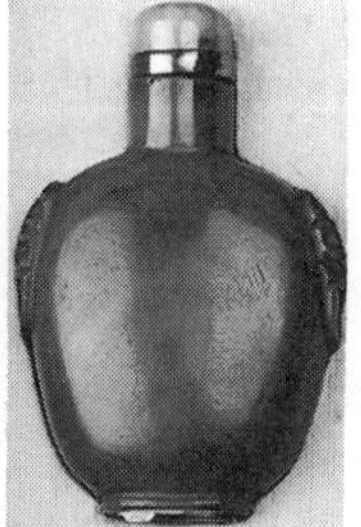

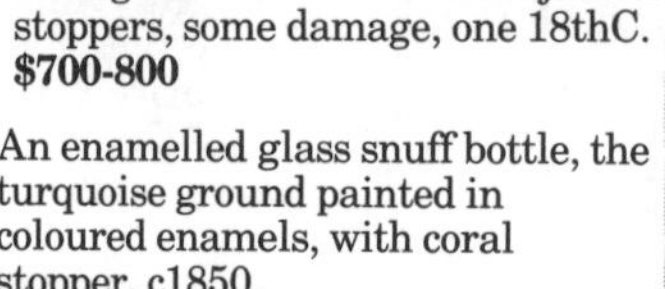

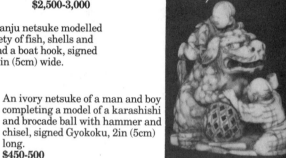

Four glass snuff bottles with jadeite stoppers, some damage, one 18thC.
$700-800

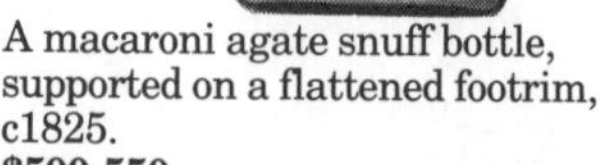

A macaroni agate snuff bottle, supported on a flattened footrim, c1825.
$500-550

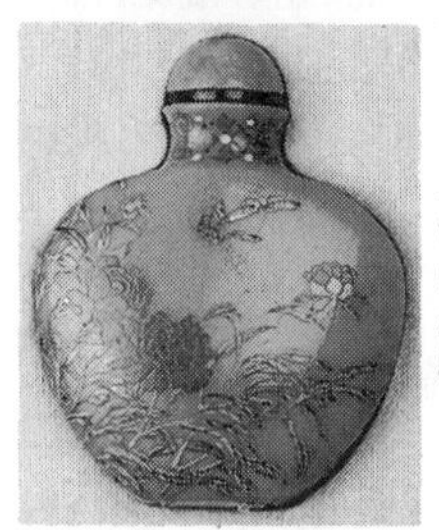

An enamelled glass snuff bottle, the turquoise ground painted in coloured enamels, with coral stopper, c1850.
$275-300

An amber snuff bottle, 18thC.
$700-800

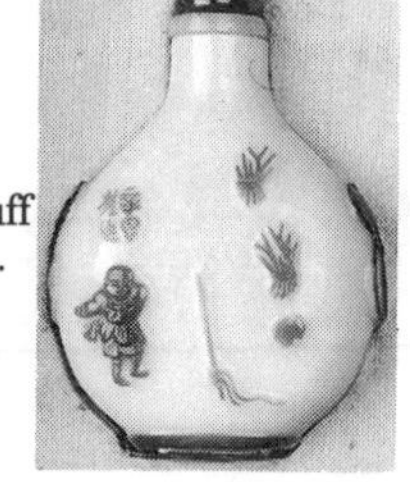

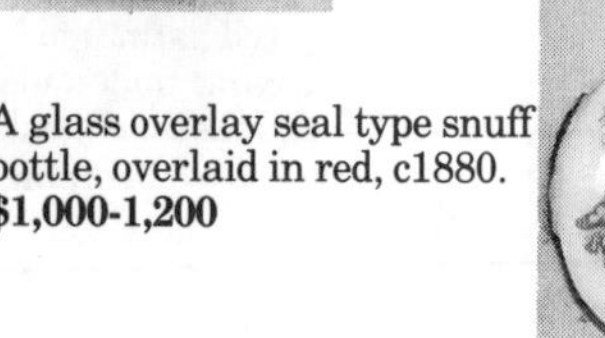

A glass overlay seal type snuff bottle, overlaid in red, c1880.
$1,000-1,200

A chalcedony snuff bottle, with an ochre inclusion in the front, carved in deep relief with a camel, monkey and lynx, yellow metal and jadeite stopper, c1830.
$1,150-1,200

An agate snuff bottle, the smoky stone with brown inclusions, c1800.
$150-200

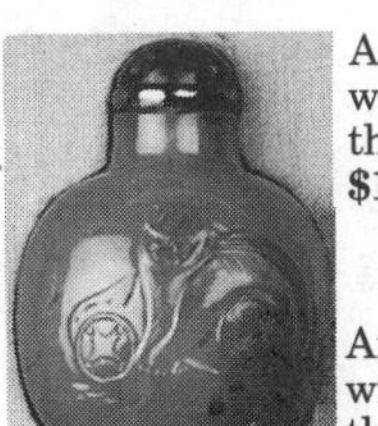

An agate snuff bottle, the reverse with pomegranates picked out using the ochre colours in the stone, c1830.
$110-150

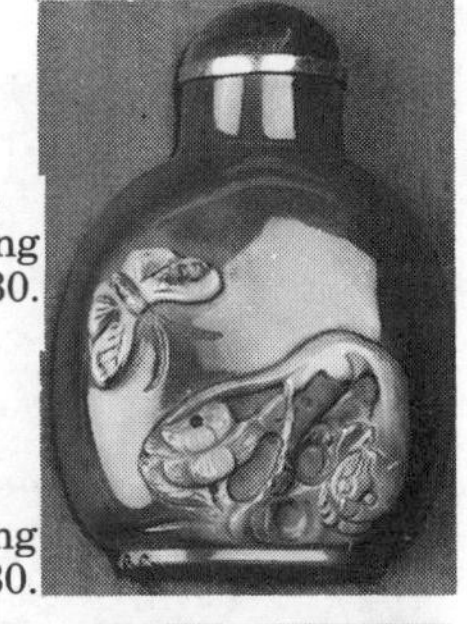

An agate snuff bottle, the reverse with pomegranates picked out using the ochre colours in the stone, c1830.
$110-140

A rock crystal snuff bottle, highlighted by brown inclusions in the stone, the reverse incised with bamboo stems, c1840.
$150-200

A porcelain snuff bottle, covered in a white glaze, foot and rim chipped, c1840.
$110-150

A porcelain snuff bottle, painted in underglaze blue with a 5-clawed dragon chasing the flaming pearl, silver jadeite stopper, 19thC.
$1,000-1,200

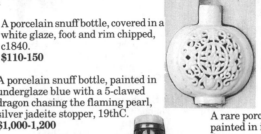

A rare porcelain snuff bottle, painted in iron red and gilt with dragons on each side, jadeite stopper, Daoguang 2-character mark, and period.
$1,000-1,200

An agate snuff bottle, with russet thumb print patterns, c1830.
$400-500

An amethyst snuff bottle, of ovoid form incised with Buddhist emblems, 19thC.
$250-300

A glass overlay and inside painted snuff bottle, overlaid in black with bands at the foot and neck and with mask ring handles at the shoulders, 19thC.
$80-150

A porcelain snuff bottle, painted in 'famille verte' enamels, Daoguang mark, and period.
$200-250

An agate snuff bottle, supported on a neatly finished footrim, 19thC.
$300-400

An agate snuff bottle carved with dragons, the reverse with an inscription, 19thC.
$200-250

An agate snuff bottle, the white, honey and grey striated stone carved with figures on rocks, 19thC.
$130-200

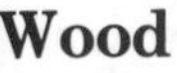

Wood

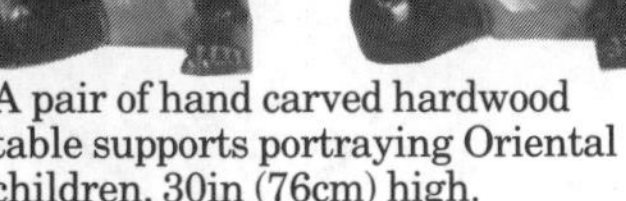

A pair of hand carved hardwood table supports portraying Oriental children, 30in (76cm) high.
$650-700

A polychromed wood Bodhisattva's head in the Song style, Qing Dynasty, 31in (79cm) high, mounted on metal base.
$3,000-4,000

A lacquered wood and ivory figure of a female immortal, seated in an aubergine coloured spoon shaped vessel, the robes painted with floral pattern, the mounted head and hands of ivory, mid-Qing Dynasty, 7in (17cm) wide, on wood stand.
$2,000-2,500

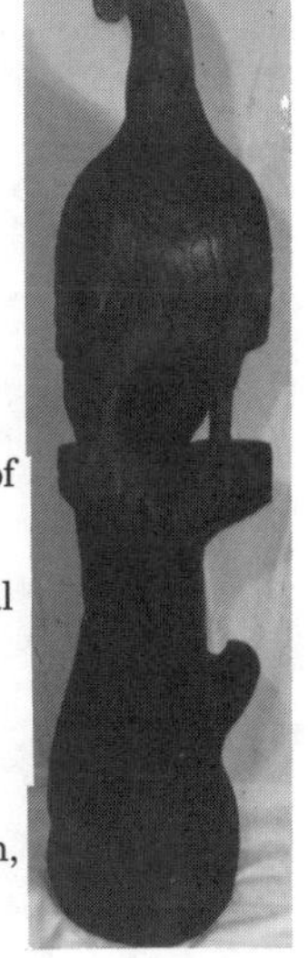

A hand carved hardwood peahen, 48in (122cm) high.
$450-550

LIGHTING

Four Regency mirror-backed double branch wall lights, with Wedgwood green and chinoiserie painted frames, with gilt shell and acanthus cresting.
$2,000-2,500

A pair of Victorian lacquered brass oil lamp brackets, with cranberry reservoirs and cranberry tinted and etched glass shades.
$700-800

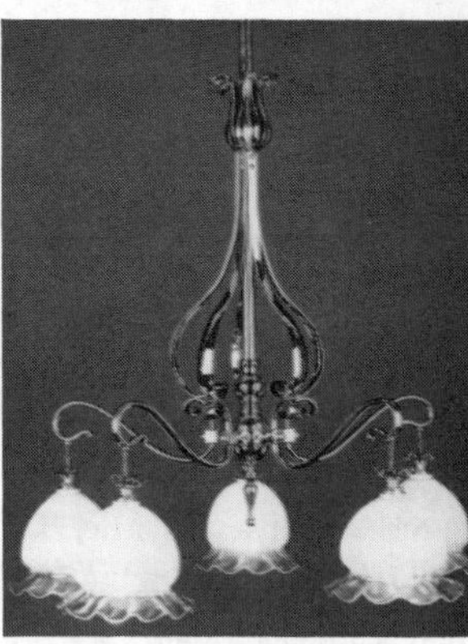

An Art Nouveau five-light electrolier with vaseline glass shades, c1905.
$1,200-1,400

A Dutch style brass twelve-light chandelier, the scrolling branches fitted with twin tiered nozzles and drip pans, 23½in (60cm) high.
$1,000-1,500

An Edwardian fringed ceiling electric light, c1906.
$350-450

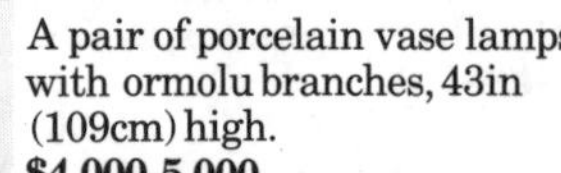

A pair of porcelain vase lamps with ormolu branches, 43in (109cm) high.
$4,000-5,000

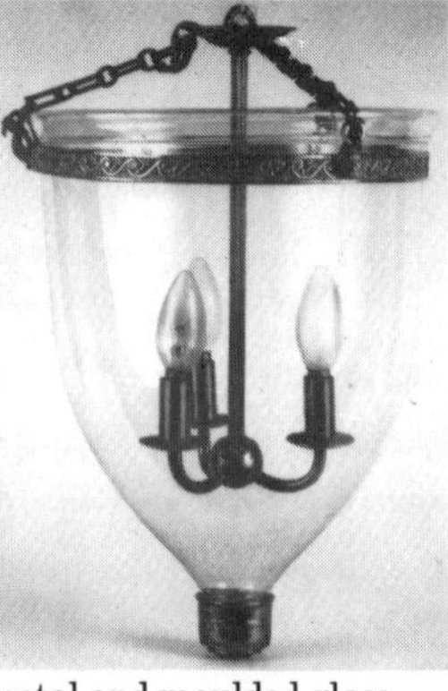

A gilt metal and moulded glass basket shaped hanging lantern, with vitruvian scroll banding and flowerhead boss, with later three-light fitment, 17in (43.5cm) high.
$1,000-1,300

A pair of wall lights, of wrought metal and white porcelain flowers with electric candle lights, some flowers missing, late 19thC, 20in (50.5cm) high.
$900-1,000

A brass ornamental table lamp supported on 4 paw feet, 17in (43.5cm) high.
$275-300

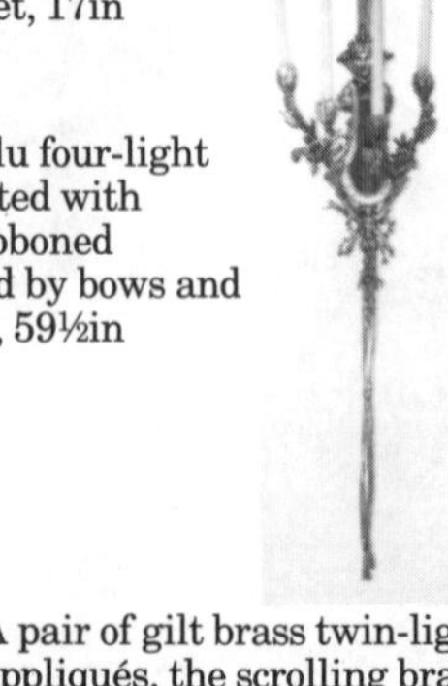

A pair of French ormolu four-light wall appliqués, decorated with female masks, with ribboned extensions surmounted by bows and terminating in tassels, 59½in (151cm) high.
$2,500-3,000

A pair of gilt brass twin-light wall appliqués, the scrolling branches emanating from oval backplates boldly chased with acanthus leaves, 14in (35.5cm) high.
$800-900

A brass three-light pendant, with white satin bell shades, early 20th
$200-250

PAPIER MÂCHÉ

Miscellaneous

A papier mâché tray, painted with chinoiserie figures and rococo gilt scrolls in an Oriental landscape, early 19thC, 31in (78.5cm) wide.
$1,200-1,300

A papier mâché comport in excellent condition, c1920, 14in (35.5cm) diam.
$130-200

A pair of papier mâché lacquer bulbous flared neck vases, 33in (83.5cm) high.
$2,500-3,000

A papier mâché collar box, c1900, 5½in (14cm) high.
$110-150

A set of 3 graduated papier mâché tea trays, painted in shades of blue, green, red and purple with flowering saxifrage with large gilt leaves and hairy stems, slight damage, 19thC, largest 31½in (80cm) wide.
$2,600-3,500

A Regency papier mâché tray, painted and heightened in gilt with peonies and clematis with stylised leaves, 22 by 30in (55.5 by 76.5cm).
$1,200-1,300

A papier mâché butler's tray, 19thC.
$400-500

A papier mâché blotter, 19thC.
$110-150

SEWING

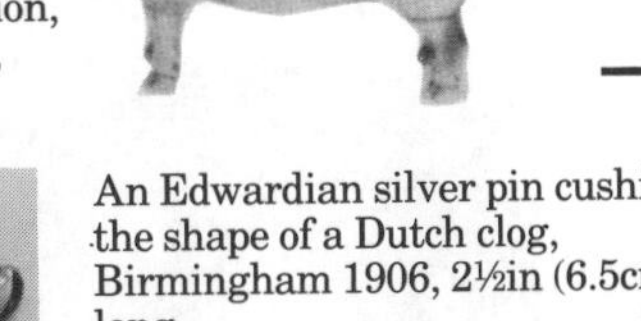

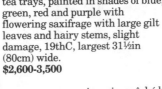

A novelty silver pig pin cushion, makers Adie & Lovekin Ltd., Birmingham, c1905.
$275-300

A bloodstone and gilt metal etui, the mount bright cut engraved, the hinged cover opening to reveal a penknife, a cylindrical needle holder, folding scissors and folding ivory rule, 2 panels damaged, early 19thC, 4in (9.5cm) high.
$650-800

An Edwardian silver pin cushion in the shape of a Dutch clog, Birmingham 1906, 2½in (6.5cm) long.
$150-210

An elephant novelty silver pin cushion, makers Adie & Lovekin Ltd., Birmingham 1905, 3in (7.5cm).
$300-400

A lacquered work box, with fitted interior and some original ivory fittings and bobbins.
$150-250

An Edwardian silver elephant pin cushion, by A. L. Davenport Ltd., Birmingham, c1907, marks rubbed, 3in (7.5cm) long.
$300-400

MINIATURES

A gentleman, in plum coloured coat with pearl buttons, white cravat, powdered hair en queue, gilt metal frame with blue enamel rim and simulated split-pearl border, slight damage, by Richard Cosway, R.A. 1742-1821, 2in (5cm) high.
$2,300-2,600

A lady, in lace bordered white dress with matching bonnet, trimmed with a large blue ribbon, gilt mounted rectangular black papier mâché frame, by John Barry, 1784-1827, 2in (5cm) high.
$1,500-2,000

A lady, in décolleté yellow dress with white underslip, wearing a red cloak on vellum, gold frame with pierced spiral cresting, School of Christian Friedrich Zincke 1683-1767, 2½in (6.5cm) high.
$650-1,000

A lady, in lace trimmed décolleté red dress with brooch at corsage and gold pendant earrings, chased gold brooch clasp frame, attributed to Simon Jacques Rochard, 1788-1872, 1½in (4cm) high.
$1,000-1,200

A young lady, wearing a décolleté white dress with blue sash, gilt metal mount in square giltwood frame, by Louis Lié Périn-Salbreux, 1753-1817, 2½in (6.5cm) diam.
$3,000-4,000

A lady, in gold trimmed white dress and shawl, matching turban headgear, drop pearl earrings, unframed, by Charles Shirreff, c1750, 3in (7.5cm) high.
$550-650

Mrs. Robinson, in white dress trimmed with blue ribbon, white bandeau in her powdered hair, in gold frame, the reverse with plaited hair, by Frederick Buck, 1771-1840, 2½in (6.5cm) high.
$550-650

Three portrait miniatures of gentlemen, American, c1800, 2 to 4in (5 to 10cm) high.
$500-800

A gentleman, believed to be Col. William Wasey, 1733-1817, of the Lifeguards, in white lined scarlet coat and grey cravat, powdered hair en queue, in gold frame, by Richard Cosway, R.A., 1742-1821, 1in (2.5cm) high.
$1,400-2,000

A lady, in décolleté white dress and a blue and yellow cloak gathered with a brooch on her right shoulder, enamel on gold, unframed, by the Huaud Brothers, c1700, 1in (2.5cm) high.
$1,400-1,500

A lady, in white dress with pearl brooch at her corsage, green bordered red shawl draped over her shoulders, fitted red leather case, lid missing, attributed to Andrew Robertson 1777-1845, 3in (7.5cm) high.
$700-1,000

A lady, in surcoat with frilled border, a dress with ribbon at corsage, lace stole, pearl studded choker and lace bonnet trimmed with ribbon, by James Fergusson 1710-1776, plumbago turned black wood frame, 2½in (6.5cm) high.
$700-1,000

A staff officer, in scarlet uniform with blue collar, gold embroidered loops, epaulette and black stock, in gilt metal frame, the reverse with plaited hair, by Thomas Richmond, 1771-1837, 2½in (6.5cm) high.
$1,200-1,300

Three Russian miniatures, of Elizabeth I, Paul I, her son, and Catherine I, his wife, in ormolu frames with Russian eagle emblem, 5in (12.5cm) high.
$5,000-5,500

A gentleman, in black habit with lace bordered lawn collar, embroidered cross sash, black bow on shoulder, oil on copper contemporary tortoiseshell case, Dutch School, c1660, 2in (5cm) high.
$2,000-2,500

A miniature of a lady's right eye, with blue iris and brown lashes, in gold frame formed as a serpent, brooch clasp reverse, English School, late 18thC, ½in (1.5cm) diam.
$1,500-2,500

A miniature of a lady's left eye, with blue iris and blonde lock of hair, in chased gold frame with black enamel inscribed 'In Memory Of', the reverse inscribed GCI/WY/1839, English School, 1839, ½in (1.5cm) high.
$700-800

A gentleman, in maroon coloured coat, white waistcoat and cravat, powdered hair, in gold frame, the reverse with plaited hair within blue glass border, by James Green, 1771-1834, 2in (5cm) high.
$4,000-5,000

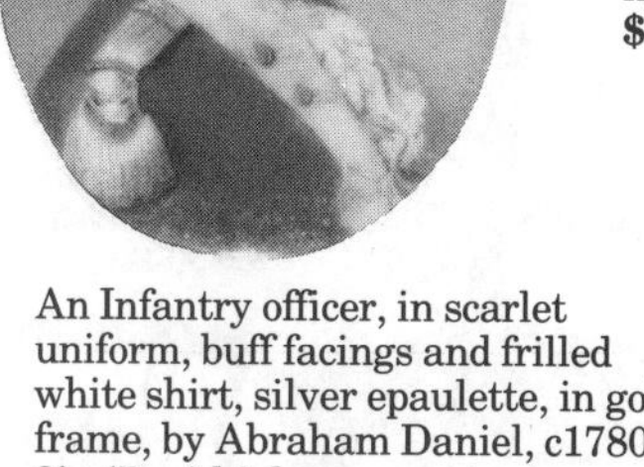

An Infantry officer, in scarlet uniform, buff facings and frilled white shirt, silver epaulette, in gold frame, by Abraham Daniel, c1780, 2in (5cm) high.
$2,500-3,000

A father and son, the father in blue coat, white waistcoat and cravat, the son in white and yellow gown, in gilt metal frame, ribbon cresting mounted with rubies and seed pearls, by James Nixon, A.R.A., c1741-1812, 2½in (6.5cm) high.
$2,000-2,500

PINE FURNITURE

Beds

Early pine rocking cradle, c1830, 39in (99cm) long.
$400-500

A pine dolls cradle, c1850, 18½in (47cm) long.
$100-110

Bookcases

An Irish pine glazed dresser/ bookcase, c1840, 80in (203cm) high.
$1,000-1,200

A Victorian pine bookcase, c1860, 82in (208cm) high.
$700-800

A Victorian original painte pine bookcase, Cumbrian, c1850, 83in (210.5cm) high
$1,000-1,200

A pine bookcase with adjustable shelves, original handles, c1860, 76½in (194cm) high.
$1,200-1,300

A pine bookcase, c1860, 77in (195.5cm) high.
$800-1,000

A red painted pine bookcase in 4 parts, each graduated and rectangular on base moulding, overall wear, New England, late 18th/early 19thC, 52in (132cm) wide.
$4,000-5,000

Chairs

A pine child's chair, 19in (49cm) high.
$50-80

A Victorian elm child's chair, fr the village school at Preston, Ke 24in (62cm) high.
$65-80

A pine child's chair, 30½in (78cm) high.
$50-80

A set of 4 pine chairs, pegged, 34½in (88cm) high. **$80-130 each**

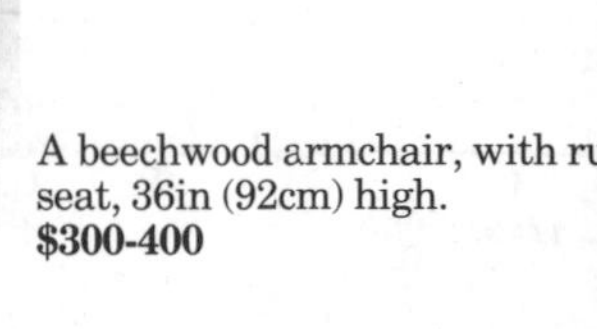

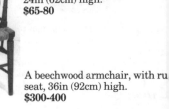

A beechwood armchair, with ru seat, 36in (92cm) high.
$300-400

A pine child's school chair, 24in (62cm) high.
$50-80

A painted pine child's folding chair, 22in (56cm) high.
$50-80

A beech corner chair, with rush seat, 27in (69cm).
$250-300

Chests

A pine chest of drawers with replacement handles, c1850, 46in (116.5cm) wide.
$650-800

A William and Mary painted pine blanket chest, the hinged top above an open compartment, with 2 false drawers, above 2 long drawers on base moulding with compressed ball feet on platforms, overall wear, New England, 18thC, 37in (94cm) wide.
$3,000-3,500

An English Regency pine and sycamore chest of drawers, with original feet and brasses, Suffolk, c1810, 37in (94cm) wide.
$1,400-2,000

An English pine five-drawer narrow chest, the top drawer containing 3 secret drawers, Lincolnshire, c1850, 41½in (105cm) high.
$1,200-1,300

A Scottish pine chest of drawers, original cock beading and handles, c1830, 42½in (108cm) wide.
$800-1,000

A Danish pine four-drawer chest, with replaced brassware, c1870, 36½in (92cm).
$900-1,000

An English two part chest-on-chest, with original ebonised handles, Yorkshire, c1860, 40in (101.5cm) wide.
$1,500-3,000

A Spanish pine coffer, with original ironwork, c1840, 43in (109cm).
$400-550

Cupboards

A pine hanging corner cupboard, c1840, 36in (92cm) high.
$275-300

A George III Cumbrian corner cupboard, 76in (193cm) high.
$1,200-1,300

A Scottish pine corner cupboard, 16in (41cm) wide.
$110-150

A pine glazed corner cupboard, c1860, on a new base, 84in (213cm) high.
$1,200-1,300

A Scottish pine linen press, late 18thC, 77½in (196cm) high.
$1,200-1,300

A Scottish pine linen press, with 2 interior drawers and a secret drawer, c1780, 72in (182.5cm) high.
$1,200-1,300

A bowfronted pine corner cupboard, with original handles, 12½in (32cm) high.
$200-250

A Queen Anne style pine corner cupboard, with cove moulded cornice above an open cupboard with 2 shelves and scalloped surround over double recess panelled cupboard door, on a moulded base, 34½in (87.5cm) wide.
$800-1,000

A pine linen press, with new feet, c1860, 78½in (199cm) high. **$1,000-1,200**

A Danish panelled pine two-part double armoire, on 2 drawer base, c1870, 73½in (186cm) high.
$1,500-2,000

A pine cupboard with shelves and drawer in base, c1800, 74in (188cm) high.
$900-1,000

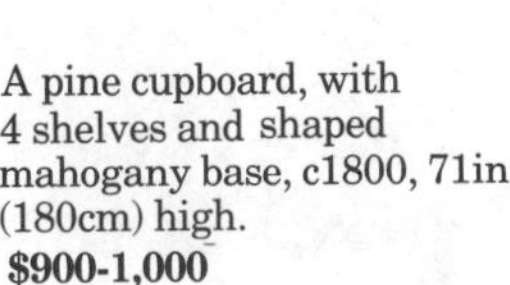

A pine cupboard, with 4 shelves and shaped mahogany base, c1800, 71in (180cm) high.
$900-1,000

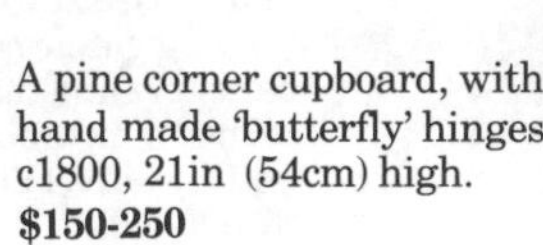

A pine corner cupboard, with hand made 'butterfly' hinges, c1800, 21in (54cm) high.
$150-250

Dressing Tables

A pine dressing table, with original paint, 36in (92cm) wide.
$400-500

A pine dressing table, with new handles, 36in (92cm) wide.
$550-650

A pine dressing table, with new handles, 36in (92cm) wide.
$400-500

A pine dressing table with elm top, 34in (87cm) wide.
$300-400

Mirrors

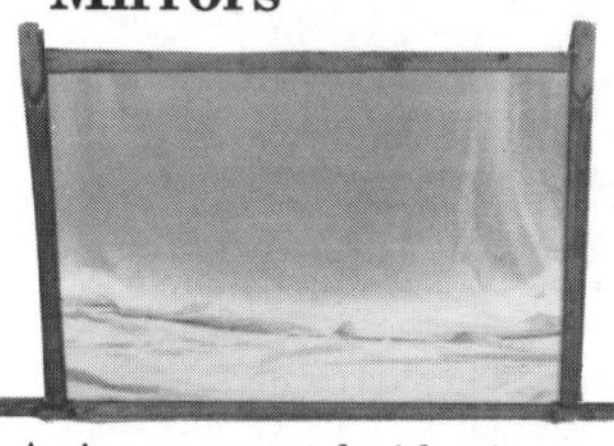
A pine overmantel with mirror and white china feet, c1860, 28in (71cm) high.
$130-150

A pine mirror, 44 by 30in (111.5 by 77cm).
$200-250

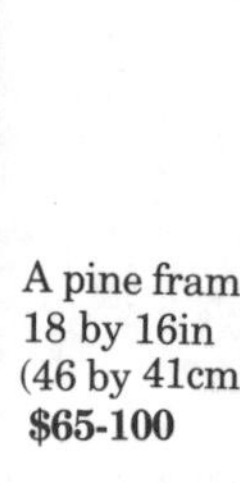
A pine frame, 18 by 16in (46 by 41cm).
$65-100

Stools

A pine bench with pegged back, c1840, 72in (182.5cm) long. **$500-550**

Tables

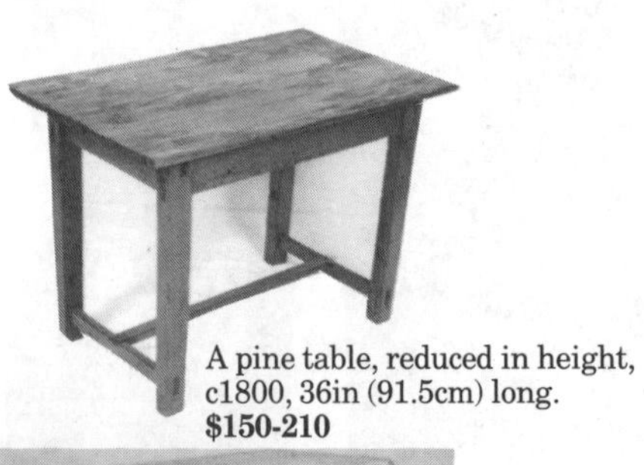
A pine table, reduced in height, c1800, 36in (91.5cm) long.
$150-210

A pine gateleg table, with 2 drop leaves above a moulded apron with a long drawer, on 4 baluster turned and incised stationary legs with 2 swing gatelegs with matching balusters and turned stretchers, on turned feet, probably Southern, 18thC, 44in (111.5cm) wide.
$2,500-3,000

Settles

A Georgian barrel-back settle, with cupboard, c1830, 81in (205.5cm) wide.
$1,000-1,200

A Welsh pine box settle, c1840, 66in (167.5cm) wide.
$700-900

A pine settle, c1850, 39in (99cm) wide.
$900-1,000

A pine table with drawer, c1840, 48in (122cm) wide.
$250-300

A pine writing table, c1860, 42½in (107cm) wide.
$200-250

An Irish pine bobbin leg 3-tier cake table, c1860, 27in (69cm) high.
$300-400

A pine writing table, c1860, 36in (91.5cm) wide.
$275-400

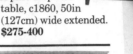

A pine drop-leaf table, c1860, 50in (127cm) wide extended.
$275-400

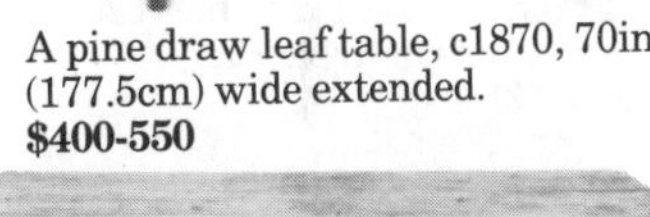

A pine draw leaf table, c1870, 70in (177.5cm) wide extended.
$400-550

Wardrobes

A pine wardrobe, with drawers under, 76in (193cm) high.
$900-1,000

A pine wardrobe, c1860, 81in (205.5cm) high.
$900-1,000

A pine wardrobe, 77in (195.5cm) high.
$400-550

A pine work table, c1860, 60in (152cm) long.
$400-500

A pine table, with single drop leaf, c1860, 35in (89cm) wide.
$200-250

Washstands

A pine washstand, panelled all round, with towel rail, c1840, 33in (84cm) high.
$300-400

A pine washstand in original condition, c1860, 22in (56cm) wide.
$150-250

A pine double washstand, 40½in (102cm) wide.
$275-400

A pine washstand, with original paintwork, 32in (82cm) wide.
$250-400

KITCHENALIA

An Austrian poplarwood dough trough, c1860, 31½in (80cm) long.
$110-150

A Dutch original painted metal milk churn, 25½in (65cm) high.
$150-300

An Austrian wicker linen basket and lid, Linz, c1920.
$200-250

A Scandinavian beechwood and lathe band flour barrel, with locking cover, c1900, 13½in (34cm) high.
$150-250

A lignum vitae treen pestle and mortar, 18thC, 9in (23cm).
$800-1,000

A French wicker grape harvester's basket, Burgundy, c1920.
$200-250

A pair of scales, minus weights, 26in (66cm) wide.
$65-100

A pair of brass letter scales, by Stevens & Son, London, 14in (45.5cm) wide.
$50-80

A set of scales and weights for butter or cheese, porcelain and brass pans, with mirror both sides, 28in (71cm) high.
$300-400

A treen nutcracker, shaped as a squirrel, c1840, 7in (18cm) long
$210-300

A pair of brass and iron parcel scales, 18in (45.5cm) wide.
$80-110

An English beechwood bath rack, c1910, 30 by 10in (77 by 26cm).
$30-100

An English ash and elm dolly stick, c1900, 35in (89cm) high.
$65-100

A pair of iron scales with weights, 20in (51cm) high.
$130-150

Walking Sticks & Canes

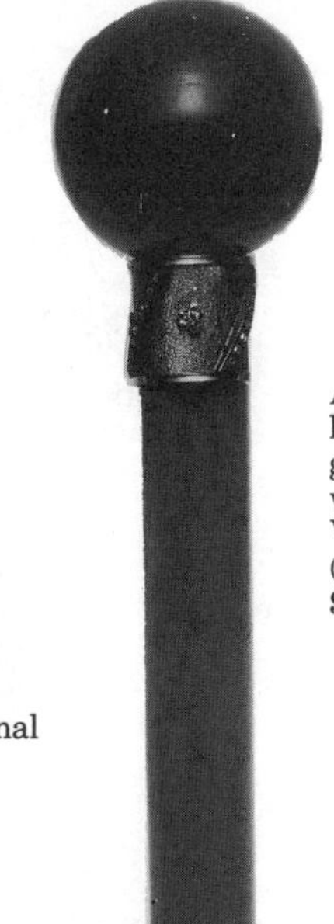

A French translucent blue guilloche enamel parasol handle, by Cartier, Paris, in original fitted case, 2½in (6cm) long.
$3,000-4,000

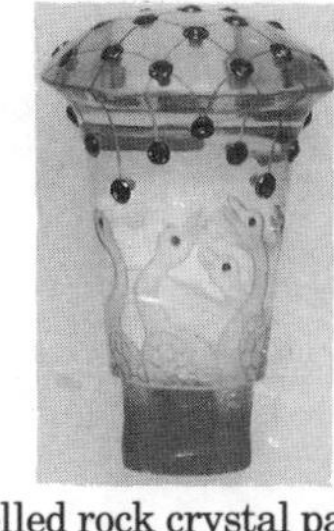

A jewelled rock crystal parasol handle, set with trellis of rubies in gold collets, in fitted case stamped with the retailer's name J.C. Vickery, Regent St., late 19thC, 2in (5cm) high.
$1,300-2,000

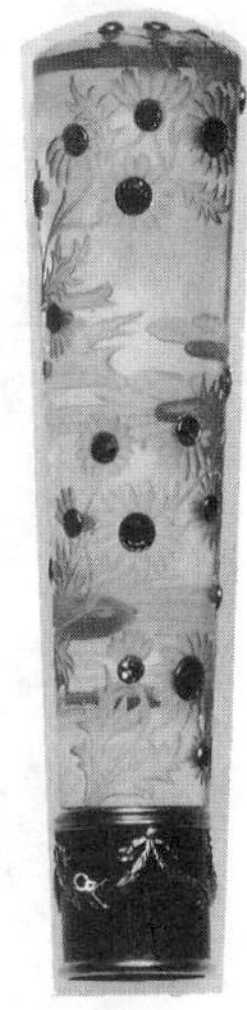

A gold mounted silver and rock crystal parasol handle, set with sapphires in gold collets, the silver collar enamelled in translucent blue and set with gold swags within reeded borders, by Tiffany and Co., in fitted case, late 19thC, 4½in (11cm).
$2,500-3,000

An Edward VII jewelled gold mounted tortoiseshell parasol handle, with a collar of matted gold set with diamonds and demantoid garnets, with spherical pommel, by Charles Cooke, 1906, in original fitted case stamped Brigg & Son, of London and Paris, 11in (28cm) long.
$1,300-2,000

An Edward VII jewelled gold mounted tortoiseshell parasol handle, with collar of matt gold set with turquoise, with writhen spherical pommel, by Charles Cooke, 1906, also stamped with retailer's name Brigg, in original fitted case, 6½in (16cm) long.
$1,200-1,300

Smoking & Snufftaking

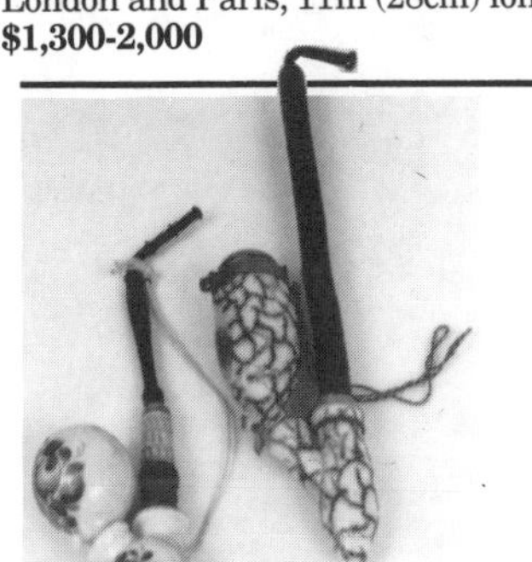

A small pipe, with two-piece porcelain bowl, the stem constructed of sections of ivory and ebony, a two-piece porcelain pipe depicting a dog, textured glaze, blue and gold pattern, natural fruitwood stem.
$200-250

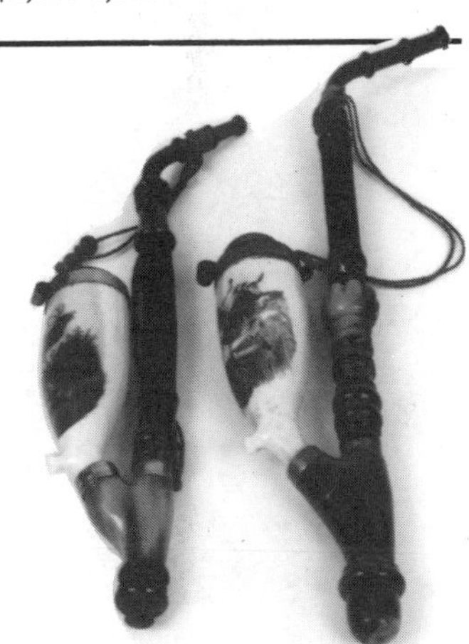

Two German two-piece porcelain pipes with rural scenes turned horn to stems, another similar of a stag.
$130-200

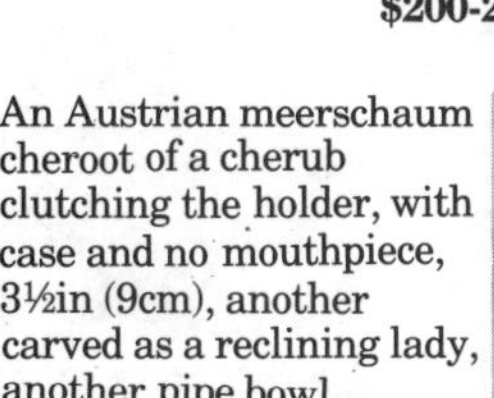

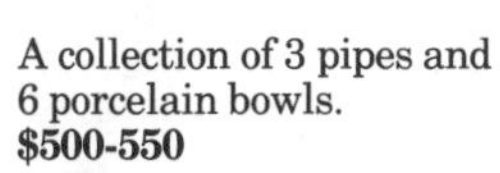

A collection of 3 pipes and 6 porcelain bowls.
$500-550

A comic clay pipe entitled 'The Whole Dam Family', 2 entitled 'The Arrest' and 'Victory', 3 RAOB's, a fish, an eagle claw, and a small black clay, contained in a pine box.
$200-250

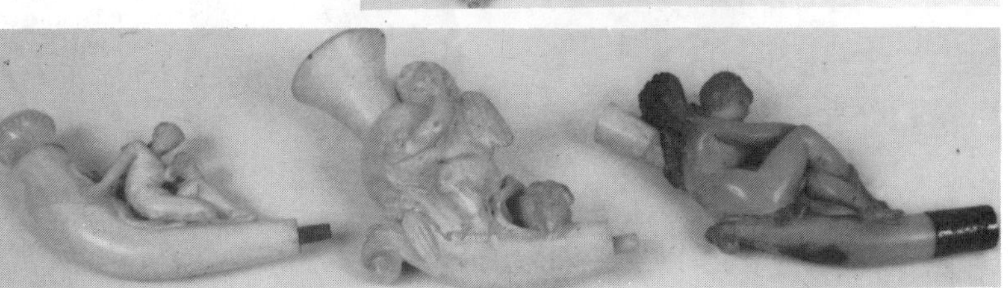

An Austrian meerschaum cheroot of a cherub clutching the holder, with case and no mouthpiece, 3½in (9cm), another carved as a reclining lady, another pipe bowl.
$150-200

JEWELLERY

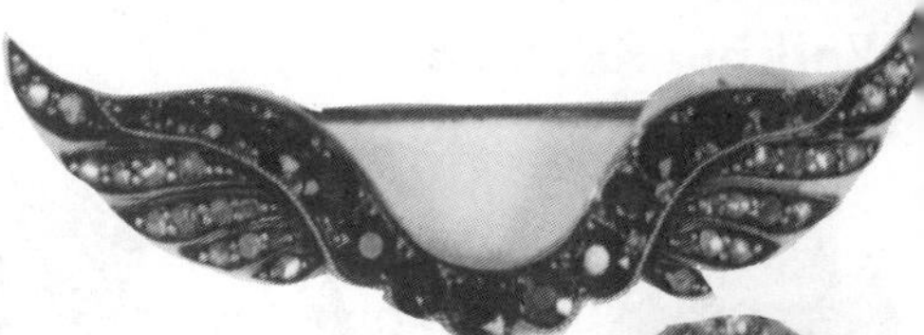

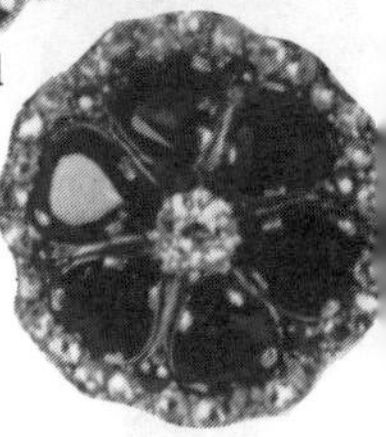

Top. An 18ct ruby and diamond wing brooch.
$1,500-1,600

Bottom. An 18ct garnet and diamond brooch.
$1,300-1,400

Four garnet brooches.
$250-500 each

An 18ct gold pendant, inset with garnets and emeralds, 1½in (4cm) long.
$800-1,000

Four pearl surrounded brooches:
Top l. A small 18ct gold pearl pendant, for photograph.
$250-300

Top r. An 18ct gold pearl rectangular shaped brooch, for photograph or hair, c1820.
$800-1,000

Bottom l. An 18ct gold pearl locket, with picture of Victorian girl.
$500-650

Bottom r. An 18ct gold graduated pearl locket.
$500-650

Make the Most of Miller's

In Miller's we do NOT just reprint saleroom estimates. We work from realised prices either from an auction room or a dealer. Our consultants then work out a realistic price range for a similar piece. This is to try to avoid repeating freak results – either low or high

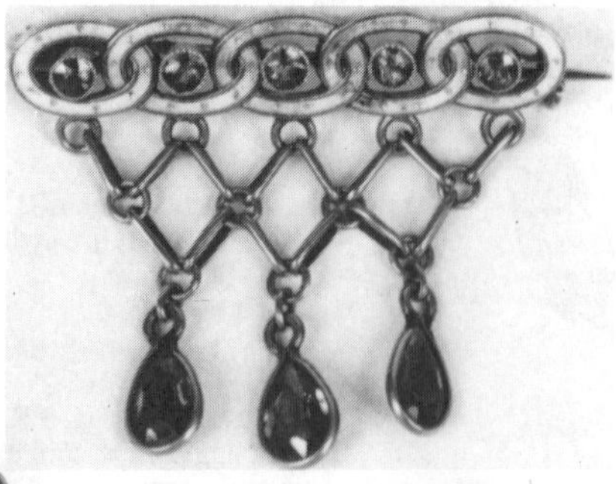

A garnet, enamel and gold brooch, 1½in (4cm) wide.
$400-550

A mother-of-pearl shell brooch, inset with pearl and gold flowers.
$650-800

An 18ct gold deeply carved agate cameo, in green, brown and white, 1½in (4cm) long.
$2,000-2,500

A demantoid garnet and sapphire openwork quatrefoil brooch.
$500-650

A 15ct gold butterfly brooch, 1½in (4cm) high.
$400-500

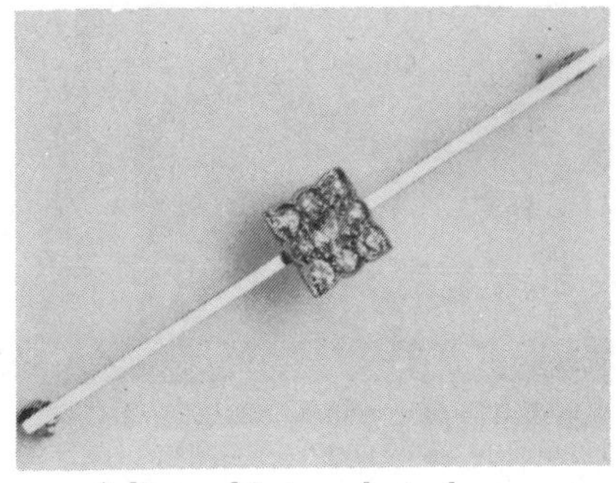

A diamond 9 stone cluster bar brooch.
$400-500

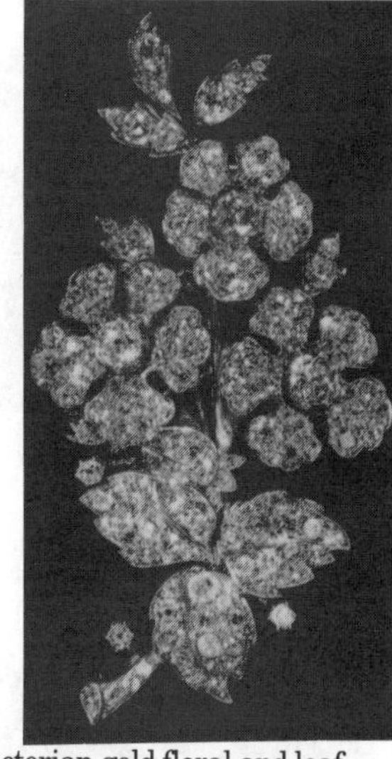

A Victorian gold floral and leaf trembler spray brooch, with approximately 168 diamonds set in silver.
$5,000-5,500

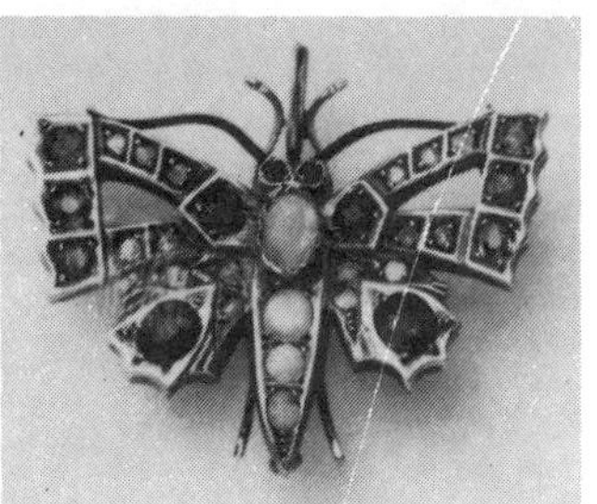

A rose diamond, opal, sapphire and garnet winged insect brooch.
$1,000-1,200

A cabochon sapphire and diamond turtle brooch with articulated limbs and diamond set eyes.
$550-650

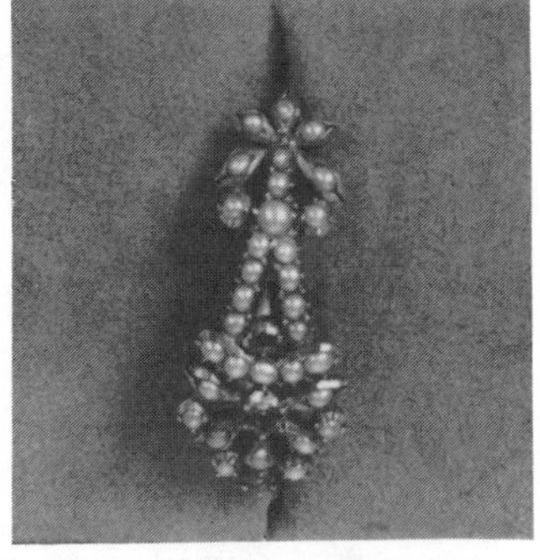

An 18ct gold Haley's comet style brooch, inset with pearls, rubies and emeralds.
$550-650

A 15ct gold bar brooch with pendant and monkey on a swing.
$650-800

A diamond, rose diamond and green guilloche enamel clover leaf brooch, with diamond centre.
$900-1,000

An opal and diamond openwork cluster bar brooch.
$500-650

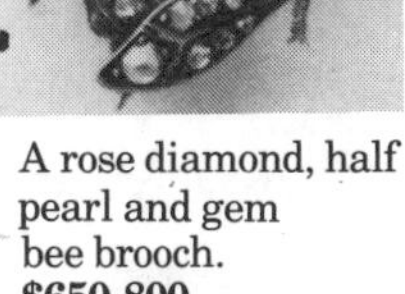

A rose diamond, half pearl and gem bee brooch.
$650-800

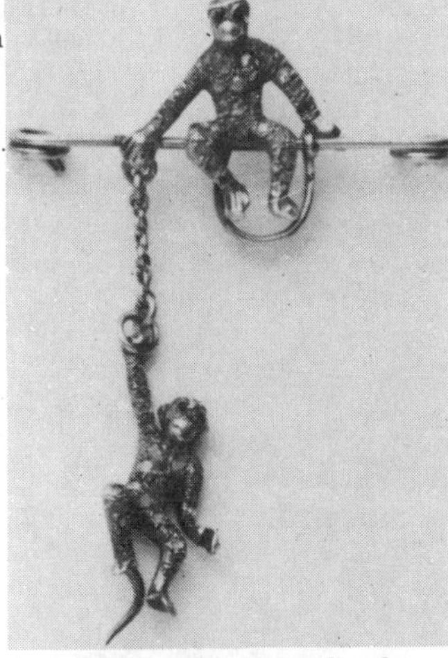

A rose diamond twin monkey bar brooch, 1 seated upon a bar, the other suspended beneath.
$800-1,000

A 22ct gold brooch inset with garnets, c1840, 2in (6cm) wide.
$1,000-1,200

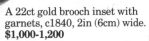

A diamond openwork double clip brooch, 4 stones damaged.
$1,000-1,200

An 18ct gold Georgian necklace, inset with pink topaz and turquoise.
$4,000-5,000

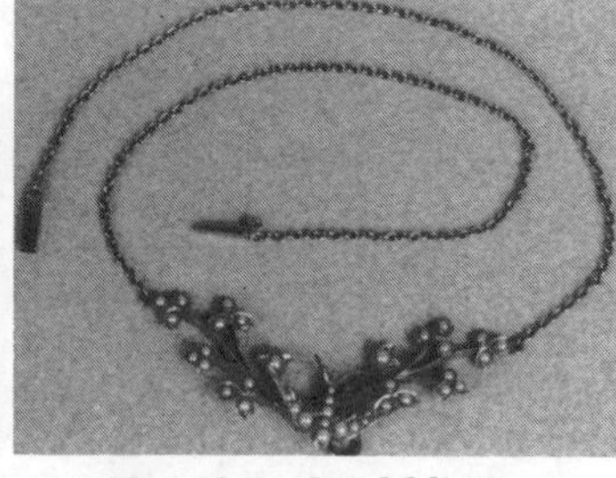

A gold, seed pearl and foliate pendant on a gold chain necklace.
$500-550

A drop cut ruby solitaire pendant with diamond border and suspension to an S-link integral necklet.
$2,500-3,000

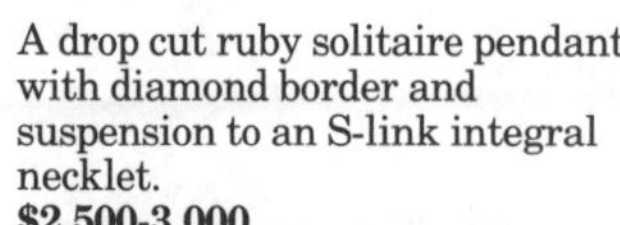

A French quatrefoil coral link necklace by Van Cleef and Arpels, Paris, with chain link connections, in maker's case.
$2,000-2,500

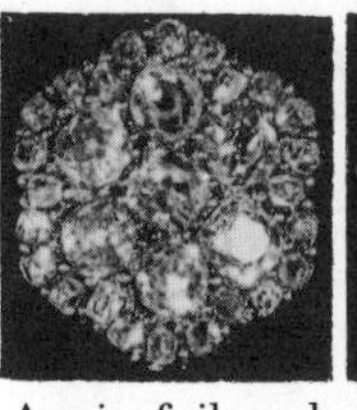

A pair of diamond set 1940s style bow design ear clips, with twin Brazilian link drops to diamond set terminals.
$1,000-1,200

A pair of silver cluster ear studs, each set with 31 diamonds in closed settings.
$5,000-5,500

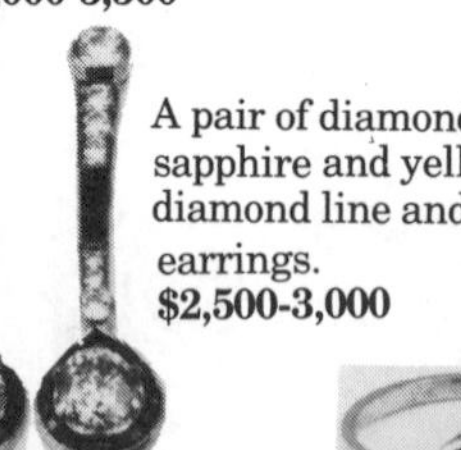

A pair of diamond, calibre sapphire and yellow diamond line and drop earrings.
$2,500-3,000

A rose diamond pendant seal, modelled as a sphinx, set with a blister pearl forming the body, engraved with the legend 'Remember the Tangible Now'.
$550-650

An emerald single stone ring with baguette diamond single stone shoulders.
$1,300-2,000

A scroll and foliate design paste set pendant with centre oval blistered pearl, 19thC.
$30-80

A diamond circular cluster ring.
$550-650

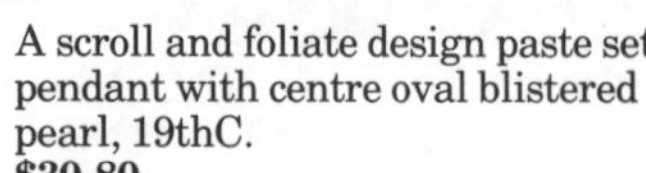

A diamond triple flower cluster half hoop ring.
$1,000-1,200

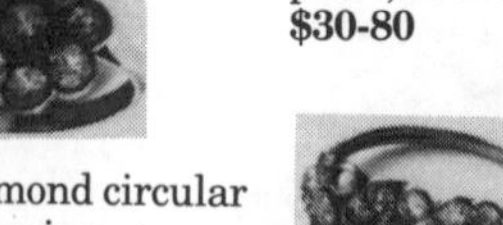

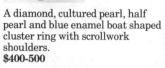

A diamond, cultured pearl, half pearl and blue enamel boat shaped cluster ring with scrollwork shoulders.
$400-500

A gold oval turquoise intaglio ring, depicting the profile head of an Egyptian Pharaoh, 19thC.
$900-1,000

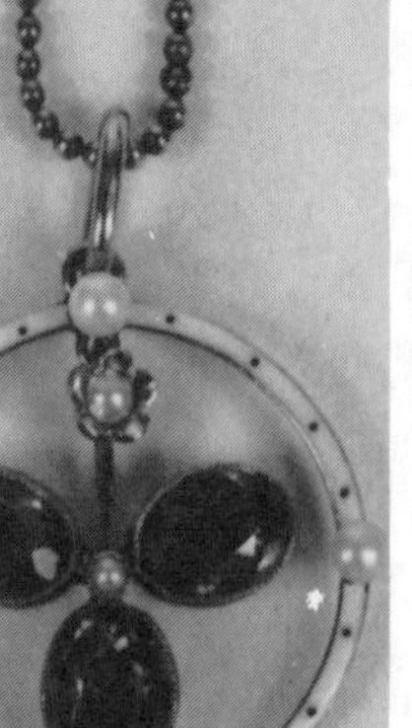

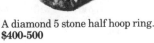

A diamond 5 stone half hoop ring.
$400-500

An 18ct white gold diamond cluster ring.
$800-1,300

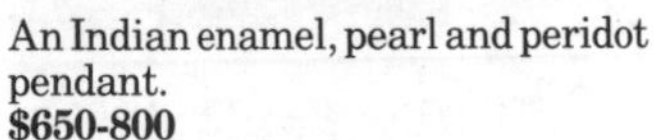

An Indian enamel, pearl and peridot pendant.
$650-800

ARMS & ARMOUR
Armour

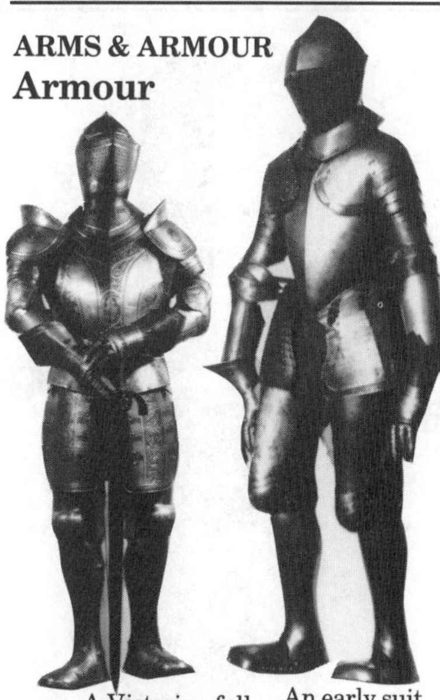

A Victorian full suit of armour. **$5,000-6,500**

An early suit of armour. **$15,000-18,000**

A pair of German gauntlets, of bright steel, with overlapping finger-plates with cusped edges bordered by incised lines, riveted to the original leathers, one damaged, separate hinged thumb guards, and original leather lining gloves (damaged), one retaining its original iron buckle for a wrist-strap, late 16thC, 11in (28cm). **$5,000-6,500**

Cannon

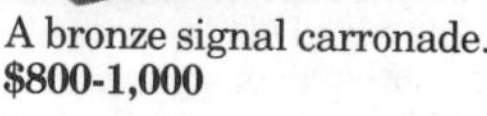

A bronze signal carronade. **$800-1,000**

Daggers

A Third Reich Luftwaffe 1934 pattern presentation dagger. **$3,000-4,000**

r. A Balkan dagger, jambiya. **$1,300-1,500**

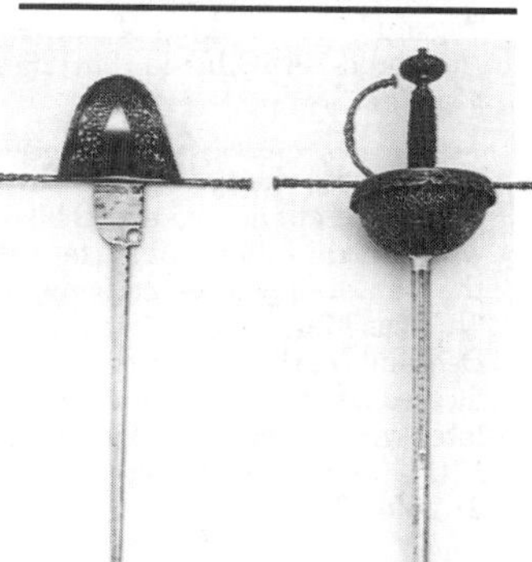

A Spanish cup hilt rapier and left-hand dagger, stamped respectively 'Antonio Picinio' and 'En Toledo', knuckle guard, cast and partly pierced, 41in (104cm) and 19in (48.5cm). **$3,000-4,000**

A Scottish silver mounted dirk with tapering hollow-ground single-edged blade back-edged towards the point and with incised device on each face, silver-mounted rootwood handle, and silver pommel-cap engraved with later owner's crest and motto, in original leather scabbard with silver locket and chape, the blade of the by-knife stamped 'Paton' on one side, some damage, c1745, 19in (48.5cm). **$1,500-2,500**

The crest and motto are of Macadam.

A Singhalese gold and silver mounted kastana, the hilt comprising knuckle guard and downturned quillons each terminating in a dragon's head, large pommel with gold tongue and eyes set with red stones, in original decorated silver scabbard, and 4 rings for suspension, together with its original gold brocade sash, 24in (61.5cm). **$2,000-2,500**

A rare Swiss 'Holbein' dagger, with double-edged blade of flattened diamond section struck on both sides with a mark, a dagger, the hilt of characteristic form with hardwood grip of slightly swollen diamond section, and brass lined iron mounts, in gilt bronze mounted scabbard covered in leather, repairs, iron parts pitted throughout, the dagger late 16thC, 15½in (39.5cm). **$4,500-5,500**

A Scottish Highland dirk, with straight fullered single-edged blade, the pommel-plate engraved with initials 'IC', in brass-mounted leather scabbard with side-pockets for the by-knife and fork each with flat pewter mounted cow horn handle, some damage, early 18thC, 15½in (39.5cm). **$1,400-2,000**

A Tibetan miniature gilt brass mounted ritual dagger, the terminal in the form of the head of a hawk with open beak, 17thC, 4½in (11.5cm). **$1,500-2,500**

Knives

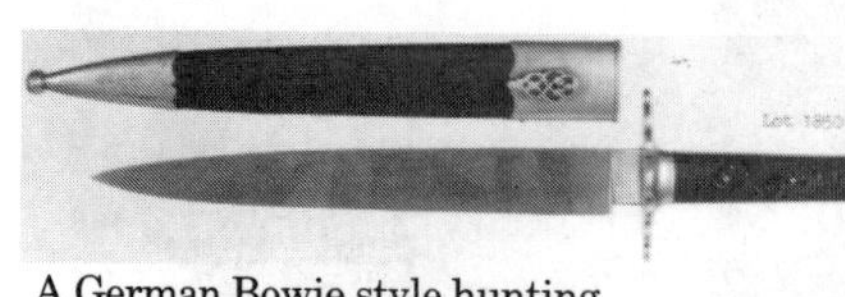

A German Bowie style hunting knife, probably made in Solingen for the American market, the grips of vulcanised rubber, decorated with a winged mythical beast and scrolling foliage, the nickel silver guard with scalloped edges, straight, unfullered single edged blade, in its black leather bayonet style scabbard with nickel silver mounts, the locket with frog stud, some flaking of leather glaze, mid-19thC, blade 10in (25cm).
$550-700

Swords

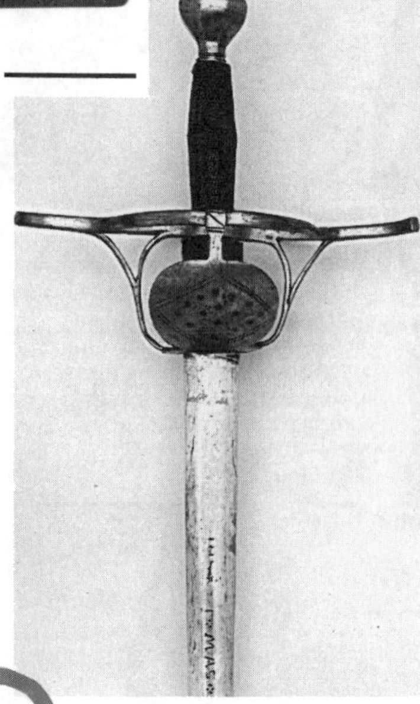

A composite riding sword, with broad straight double-edged blade with central fuller on each face at the forte stamped respectively 'Th(e)sus Maria' and '(To)mas Deaiala', leather-covered ricasso, faceted fig-shaped pommel, and later wire-bound wooden grip, early 17thC, blade 34in (86cm).
$1,200-1,300

A Polish sabre with leather covered wooden hilt, flattened iron quillons with button finials, one pierced for the knuckle-chain, and long slender langets, in original leather-covered wooden scabbard with embossed and pierced brass mounts, some damage, the hilt and scabbard painted black, early 17thC, blade 29in (73.5cm).
$1,000-1,300

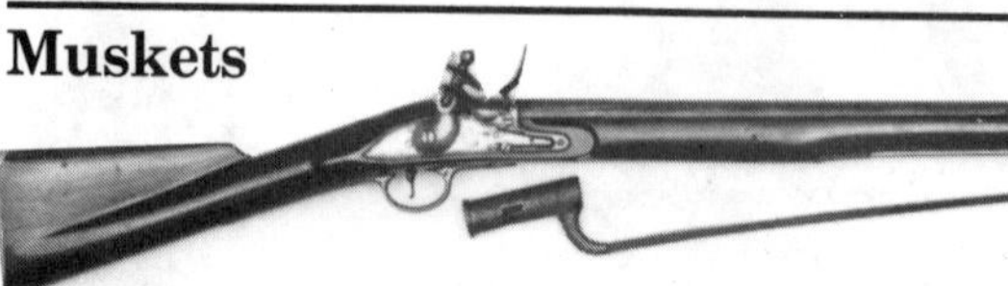

An English rapier, c1630.
$550-650

Muskets

An India pattern Brown Bess flintlock musket of the Royal Fusiliers.
$2,500-3,000

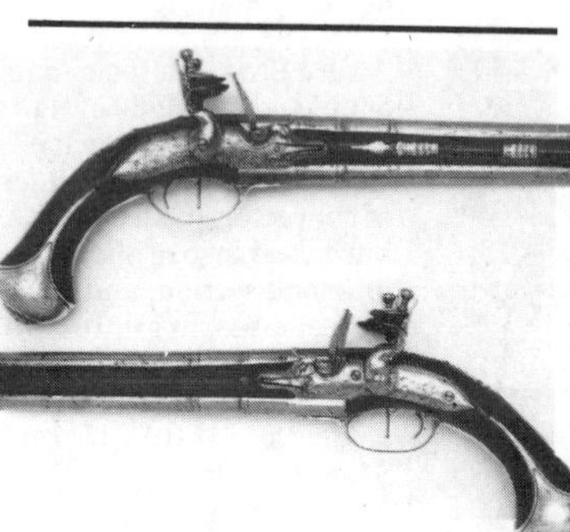

An Austrian military repeating air rifle, with carved figured walnut full stock, leather-covered butt reservoir, brass mounts engraved behind the breech, owner's crest and initials, and stamped with a small maker's mark, solid side-plate engraved with a trophy of arms and foliage, trigger-guard matching and brass fore-end cap, ramrod missing, in original lined and fitted wooden case with trade label and accessories including pump, spanner, bullet mould and spare reservoirs, one with leather covering missing, finished by Mortimer, 21 St. James's Strt., London, c1820, 33in (83.5cm) barrel.
$4,000-5,500

Sporting

A 20-bore double barrelled flintlock sporting gun, with rebrowned twist sighted barrels, with gold-lined maker's stamp, gold lines and vents, engraved case-hardened tang, signed border engraved flat locks with rollers, one cock and mainspring replaced, one steel damaged, figured walnut half-stock, chequered grip, repaired, in lined and fitted brass mounted mahogany case, lock replaced, with trade label and some accessories including Sykes patent leather shot-belt, by Joseph Manton, London, No. 615 for 1794, 32in (81.5cm) barrels. **$5,500-7,000**

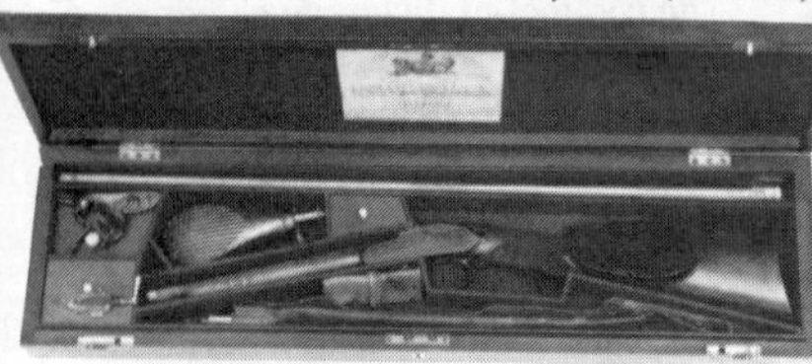

A flintlock sporting gun by Patrick, c1820.
$2,500-3,000

Pistols

A rare pair of over-and-under flintlock holster pistols, with cast and chased silver mounts, trigger-guards, vacant grotesque escutcheons pierced with foliage, and later wooden ramrods, iron parts pitted throughout, some replacements, by I. Steward, late 17thC, 17in (43.5cm).
$3,000-4,000

An unusual pair of flintlock over-and-under turn-over pistols, with rebrowned twist barrels octagonal changing to polygonal at the breeches, figured walnut butts, minor damage, engraved steel mounts, spurred pommels, one pitted, vacant silver escutcheons, and later brass-tipped wooden ramrods, by Samuel Brummit, Worksop, London proof marks, c1790, 19in (48.5cm).
$5,000-5,500

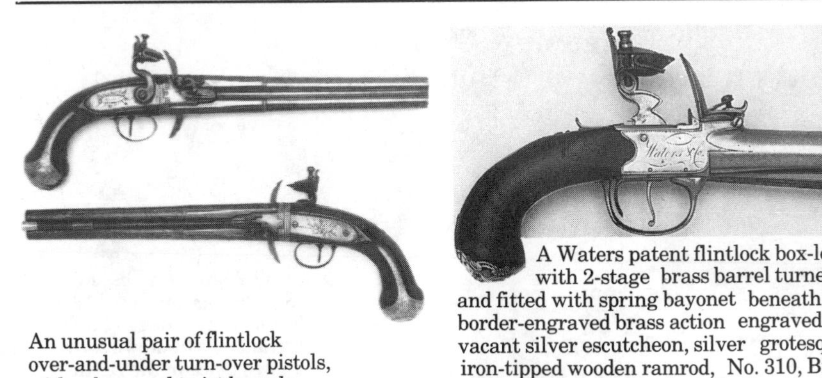

A Waters patent flintlock box-lock blunderbuss pistol, with 2-stage brass barrel turned at the muzzle and fitted with spring bayonet beneath stamped 'Tho. Gill', border-engraved brass action engraved 'Waters & Co., Patent', vacant silver escutcheon, silver grotesque mask butt-cap, and iron-tipped wooden ramrod, No. 310, Birmingham private proof marks, Birmingham silver hallmarks for 1781, maker's mark of Charles Freeth, 13in (33.5cm).
$2,000-2,500

This pistol embodies Waters' Patent No. 1284 of March 9, 1781.

A pair of flintlock duelling pistols, with gold lines and vents, barrel tangs engraved with rococo foliage, signed flat locks with rollers, engraved trigger-guards retaining traces of original blueing, and horn-tipped wooden ramrods, in later lined and fitted wooden case with some accessories including copper 3-way flask, by John Twigg, London, c1785, 15in (38.5cm).
$8,000-9,000

A pair of flintlock holster pistols, with 2-stage barrels with maker's mark at the breech, with later horn-tipped wooden ramrods, both pistols worn and lightly pitted throughout, by S. Blankle (sic), London proof marks, c1705, 19½in (49.5cm).
$3,000-4,000

A Balkan flintlock pistol with 3-stage barrel, engraved breech struck with maker's mark and 10 fleur-de-lys marks, signed Italian bevelled lock entirely covered in parcel gilt, silver gilt pierced trigger, and white metal tipped brass ramrod, the lock signed 'D. Lanoni', 18th/19thC, 16½in (42cm).
$1,200-1,400

A Balkan flintlock pistol, with lightly engraved flat lock with roller, covered in gilt brass decorated in relief against a granular ground with strapwork and foliage inhabited by birds, with sleeve around the muzzle and trigger-guard, and false ramrod, 19thC, 21in (53.5cm).
$1,300-1,400

A very rare breech-loading flintlock pistol with folding back-sight, signed border-engraved rounded lock engraved with stylised foliage, top of cock replaced, moulded figured walnut full stock, brass mounts cast and chased with foliage including pierced side-plate, repaired, with later brass-capped wooden ramrod, by Robert Rowland, London proof marks, c1715, 18in (45.5cm).
$3,000-4,000

A Colt Model 1861 Navy percussion revolver, No. 23786, .36 calibre, 7½in (18.5cm) barrel marked 'Address Col. Saml. Colt New York U.S. America', naval engagement roll scene on cylinder.
$3,000-4,000

A flintlock pistol with 4-stage barrel engraved with foliage, fluted breech and flared muzzle, signed, engraved lock, action defective, lobe butt engraved with later owner's crest and motto, turned iron trigger, 3 engraved silver panels on the underside of the stock, and engraved steel belt hook, ramrod missing, by Thomas Murdoch, late 18thC, 12½in (32.5cm).
$2,600-3,500

A Colt Model 1860 Army percussion revolver, No. 186376, .44 calibre, the 8in (20cm) round barrel marked 'Address Col. Saml. Colt New York U.S. America', naval engagement roll scene on cylinder.
$4,000-5,000

Revolvers

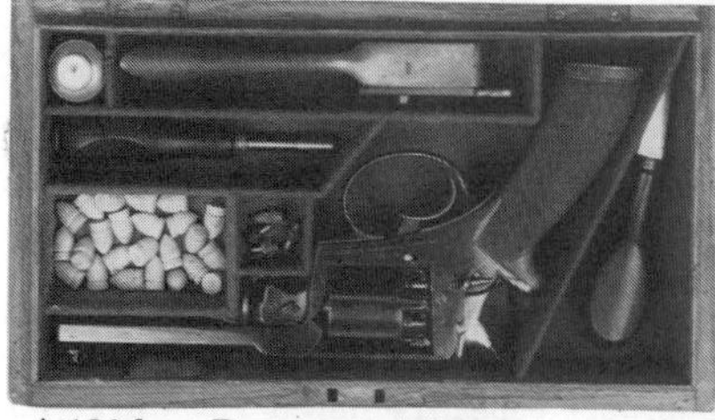

A 120-bore Beaumont-Adams double-action percussion revolver, with blued sighted rifled barrel stamped 'L.A.C.', blued cylinder, blued border engraved frame with safety-stop, blued rammer, chequered figured walnut butt, blued trigger-guard and butt-plate, No. 32239.R, in original lined and fitted oak case with accessories including bullet mould, London proof marks, 10in (25cm).
$1,500-2,500

Companion of the Order of St. Michael and St. George neck badge.
$300-350

Medals & Orders

A second World War Distinguished Flying Cross group, dated 1945, with ribbon, awarded to Flight Lieutenant Gretkiercwicz, who was shot down twice in the Battle of Britain.
$1,200-1,300

Union of South Africa medal 1910, un-named as issued.
$210-250

Distinguished Conduct Medal group, Edward VII, Q.M.Sgt. W. Dobbs, G. Coy., Royal Engineers.
$500-650

Order of The British Empire, for Meritorious Service, George V.
$90-100

1914-15 Star, British War medal, Victory medal, Pte. C. H. Bourne, C. of London Yeomanry.
$40-55

Badges & Plates

A shoulder belt plate of The 57th (West Middlesex) Regiment, pre-1855.
$650-700

A Boer War badge of the Commander in Chief's Yeomanry Escort.
$300-400

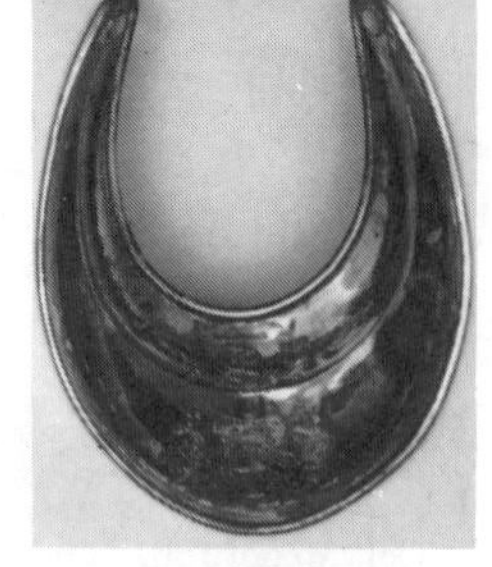

A Georgian gorget of the Royal Marines, c1795.
$900-1,000

A Victorian officer's special pattern waist belt plate, The Essex Regiment.
$300-400

DIRECTORY OF INTERNATIONAL AUCTIONEERS

This directory is by no means complete. Any auctioneer who holds frequent sales should contact us for inclusion in the 1992 Edition. Entries must be received by April 1991. There is, of course, no charge for this listing. Entries will be repeated in subsequent editions unless we are requested otherwise.

America

Acorn Farm Antiques,
15466 Oak Road, Carmel,
IN 46032
Tel: (317) 846-2383

ALA Moanastampt Cain (David H Martin),
1236 Ala Moana Boulevard,
Honolulu, HI 96814

Alabama Auction Room Inc,
2112 Fifth Avenue North,
Birmingham, AL 35203
Tel: (205) 252-4073

B Altman & Co,
34th & Fifth Avenue, New York,
NY 10016
Tel: (212) OR 9 7800 ext 550 & 322

Ames Art Galleries,
8729 Wilshire Boulevard, Beverly Hills, CA 9021
Tel: (213) 655-5611/652-3820

Arnette's Auction Galleries Inc,
310 West Castle Street,
Murfreesboro, TN 37130
Tel: (615) 893-3725

Associated Appraisers Inc,
915 Industrial Bank Building,
Providence, RI 02906
Tel: (401) 331-9391

Atlanta's ABCD Auction Gallery (Clark, Bate and Depew),
1 North Clarendon Avenue,
Antioch, IL 30002
Tel: (312) 294-8264

Bakers Auction,
14100 Paramount Boulevard,
Paramount, CA 90723
Tel: (213) 531-1524

Barridoff Galleries,
242 Middle Street, Portland,
ME 04 101
Tel: (207) 772-5011

C T Bevensee Auction Service,
PO Box 492, Botsford, CT 06404
Tel: (203) 426-6698

Frank H. Boos Gallery, Inc.,
420 Enterprise Ct., Bloomfield Hills, MI 48013

Richard A Bourne Co Inc,
Corporation Street, PO Box 141/A,
Hyannis Port, MA 02647
Tel: (617) 775-0797

Bridges Antiques and Auctions,
Highway 46, PO Box 52A,
Sanford, FL 32771
Tel: (305) 323-2801/322-0095

George C Brilant & Co,
191 King Street, Charleston,
SC 29401

R W Bronstein Corp,
3666 Main Street, Buffalo,
NY 14226
Tel: (716) 835-7666/7408

Brookline Auction Gallery,
Proctor Hill Road, Route 130,
Brookline, NH 03033
Tel: (603) 673-4474/4153

Brzostek's Auction Service,
2052 Lamson Road, Phoenix,
NY 13135
Tel: (315) 678-2542

Buckingham Galleries Ltd,
4350 Dawson Street, San Diego,
CA 92115
Tel: (714) 283-7286

Bushell's Auction,
2006 2nd Avenue, Seattle,
WA 98121
Tel: (206) 622-5833

L Butterfield,
605 W Midland, Bay City,
MI 48706
Tel: (517) 684-3229

Butterfield,
808 N La, Cienega Boulevard, Los Angeles, CA 90069

Butterfield & Butterfield,
1244 Sutter Street, San Francisco,
CA 94109
Tel: (415) 673-1362

California Book Auction Galleries,
358 Golden Gate Avenue, San Francisco, CA 94102
Tel: (415) 775-0424

C B Charles Galleries Inc,
825 Woodward Avenue, Pontiac,
MI 48053
Tel: (313) 338-9023

Chatsworth Auction Rooms,
151 Mamaroneck Avenue,
Mamaroneck, NY 10543

Christie, Manson & Wood International Inc,
502 Park Avenue, New York
Tel: (212) 826-2388 Telex: 620721

Christie's East,
219 East 67th Street, New York,
NY 10021
Tel: (212) 570-4141

Representative Offices:
California:
9350 Wilshire Boulevard, Beverly Hills, CA 902 12
Tel: (213) 275-5534

Florida:
225 Fern Street, West Palm Beach,
FL 33401
Tel: (305) 833-6592

Mid-Atlantic:
638 Morris Avenue, Bryn Mawr,
PA 19010
Tel: (215) 525-5493

Washington:
1422 27th Street NW, Washington,
DC 20007
Tel: (202) 965-2066

Midwest:
46 East Elm Street, Chicago,
IL 60611
Tel: (312) 787-2765

Fred Clark Auctioneer Inc,
PO Box 124, Route 14, Scotland,
CT 06264
Tel: (203) 423-3939/0594

Cockrum Auctions,
2701 North Highway 94,
St Charles, MO 63301
Tel: (314) 723-9511

George Cole, Auctioneers and Appraisers,
14 Green Street, Kingston,
NY 12401
Tel: (914) 338-2367

Coleman Auction Galleries,
525 East 72nd Street, New York,
NY 10021
Tel: (212) 879-1415

Conestoga Auction Company Inc,
PO Box 1, Manheim, PA 17545
Tel: (717) 898-7284

Cook's Auction Gallery,
Route 58, Halifax, MA 02338
Tel: (617) 293-3445/866-3243

Coquina Auction Barn
40 S Atlantic Avenue, Ormond Beach, FL 32074

Danny's Antique Auction Service (Pat Lusardi),
Route 46, Belvidere, NH 07823
Tel: (201) 757-7278

Douglas Galleries,
Route 5, South Deerfield,
MA 01373
Tel: (413) 665-2877

William Doyle,
175 East 87th Street, New York,
NY 10128
Tel: (212) 427-2730

DuMochelle Art Galleries,
409 East Jefferson, Detroit,
MI 48226
Tel: (313) 963-6255

John C Edelmann Galleries Inc,
123 East 77th Street, New York,
NY 10021
Tel: (212) 628-1700/1735

Robert C Eldred Co Inc,
Box 796, East Dennis, MA 02641
Tel: (617) 385-3116/3377

The Fine Arts Company of Philadelphia Inc,
2317 Chestnut Street,
Philadelphia, PA 19103
Tel: (215) 564-3644

Fordem Galleries Inc,
3829 Lorain Avenue, Cleveland,
OH 44113
Tel: (216) 281-3563

George S Foster III,
Route 28, Epsom, NH 03234
Tel: (603) 736-9240

Jack Francis Auctions,
200 Market Street, Suite 107,
Lowell, MA 01852
Tel: (508) 441-9708

S T Freeman & Co,
1808 Chestnut Street,
Philadelphia, PA 19103
Tel: (215) 563-9275

Col K R French and Co Inc,
166 Bedford Road, Armonk,
NY 10504
Tel: (914) 273-3674

Garth's Auctions Inc,
2690 Stratford Road, Delaware,
OH 43015
Tel: (614) 362-4771/369-5085

Gilbert Auctions,
River Road, Garrison, NY 10524
Tel: (914) 424-3657

Morten M Goldberg,
215 N Rampart Street, New Orleans, LA 70112
Tel: (504) 522-8364

Gramercy Auction Galleries,
52 East 13th Street, New York,
NY 10003
Tel: (212) 477-5656

Grandma's House,
4712 Dudley, Wheatridge,
CO 80033
Tel: (303) 423-3640/534-2847

The William Haber Art Collection Inc,
139-11 Queens Boulevard,
Jamaica, NY 11435
Tel: (212) 739-1000

Charlton Hall Galleries Inc,
930 Gervais Street, Columbia,
SC 29201
Tel: (803) 252-7927/779-5678

Hampton Auction Gallery,
201 Harwick Street, Belvidere,
NH 07823
Tel: (201) 475-2928

Hanzel,
1120 S Michigan Avenue, Chicago,
IL 60605
Tel: (312) 922-6234

Harbor Auction Gallery,
238 Bank Street, New London,
CT 06355
Tel: (203) 443-0868

Harmer's of San Francisco Inc,
49 Geary Street, San Francisco,
CA 94102
Tel: (415) 391-8244

Harris Auction Galleries,
873-875 North Howard Street,
Baltimore, MD 21201
Tel: (301) 728-7040

Hart,
2311 Westheimer, Houston,
TX 77098
Tel: (713) 524-2979/523-7389

Hauswedeil & Nolte,
225 West Central Park, New York,
NY 10024
Tel: (212) 787-7245

G Ray Hawkins,
7224 Melrose Avenue, Los Angeles, CA 90046
Tel: (213) 550-1504

Elwood Heller & Son Auctioneer,
151 Main Street, Lebanon,
NJ 08833
Tel: (201) 23 62 195

William F Hill Auction Sales,
Route 16, East Hardwick,
VT 05834
Tel: (802) 472-6308

Leslie Hindman,
215 West Ohio Street, Chicago,
IL 60610
Tel: (312) 670-0010

The House Clinic,
PO Box 13013A, Orlando, Fl 32859
Tel: (305) 859-1770/851-2979

Co Raymond W Huber,
211 North Monroe, Montpelier,
OH 43543

F B Hubley Et Co,
364 Broadway, Cambridge,
MA 02100
Tel: (617) 876-2030

Iroquois Auctions,
Box 66, Broad Street, Port Henry,
NY 12974
Tel: (518) 942-3355

It's About Time,
375 Park Avenue, Glencoe,
IL 60022
Tel: (312) 835-2012

Louis Joseph Auction Gallery (Richard L Ryan),
575 Washington Street, Brookline,
MA 02146
Tel: (617) 277-0740

Julia's Auction Service,
Route 201, Skowhegan Road,
Fairfield, ME 04937
Tel: (207) 453-9725

Sibylle Kaldewey,
225 West Central Park, New York,
NY 10024
Tel: (212) 787-7245

Kelley's Auction Service,
PO Box 125, Woburn, MA 01801
Tel: (617) 272-9167

Kennedy Antique Auction Galleries Inc,
1088 Huff Road, Atlanta,
GA 30318
Tel: (404) 351-4464

Kinzie Galleries Auction Service,
1002 3rd Avenue, Duncansville,
PA 16835
Tel: (814) 695-3479

La Salle,
2083 Union Street, San Francisco,
CA 94123
Tel: (415) 931-9200

L A Landry (Robert Landry),
94 Main Street, Essex, MA 01929
Tel: (603) 744-5811

Jo Anna Larson,
POB 0, Antioch, IL 60002
Tel: (312) 395-0963

Levins Auction Exchange,
414 Camp Street, New Orleans,
LA 70130

Lipton,
1108 Fort Street, Honolulu,
HI 96813
Tel: (808) 533-4320

F S Long & Sons,
3126 East 3rd Street, Dayton,
OH 45403

R L Loveless Associates Inc,
4223 Clover Street, Honeoye Falls,
NY 14472
Tel: (716) 624-1648/1556

Lubin Galleries,
30 West 26th Street, New York,
NY 10010
Tel: (212) 924-3777

Main Auction Galleries,
137 West 4th Street, Cincinnati,
OH 45202
Tel: (513) 621-1280

Maison Auction Co Inc,
128 East Street, Wallingford,
CT 06492
Tel: (203) 269-8007

Joel L Malter & Co Inc,
Suite 518, 16661 Ventura
Boulevard, Encino, CA 91316
Tel: (213) 784-7772/2181

Manhattan Galleries,
1415 Third Avenue, New York,
NY 10028
Tel: (212) 744-2844

Mapes,
1600 West Vestal Parkway,
Vestal, NY 13850
Tel: (607) 754-9193

David W Mapes Inc,
82 Front Street, Binghamton,
NY 13905
Tel: (607) 724-6741/862-9365

Marvin H Newman,
426 South Robertson Boulevard,
Los Angeles, CA 90048
Tel: (213) 273-4840/378-2095

Mechanical Music Center Inc,
25 Kings Highway North, Darien,
CT 06820
Tel: (203) 655-9510

Milwaukee Auction Galleries,
4747 West Bradley Road,
Milwaukee, Wl 53223
Tel: (414) 355-5054

Wayne Mock Inc,
Box 37, Tamworth, NH 03886
Tel: (603) 323-8057

William F Moon & Co,
12 Lewis Road, RFD 1, North
Attleboro, MA 02760
Tel: (617) 761-8003

New England Rare Coin Auctions,
89 Devonshire Street, Boston,
MA 02109
Tel: (617) 227-8800

Kurt Niven,
1444 Oak Lawn, Suite 525, Dallas,
TX 75207
Tel: (214) 741-4252

Northgate Gallery,
5520 Highway 153, Chattanooga,
TN 37443
Tel: (615) 842-4177

O'Gallerie Inc,
537 SE Ash Street, Portland,
OR 97214
Tel: (503) 238-0202

Th J Owen & Sons,
1111 East Street NW, Washington,
DC 20004

Palmer Auction Service,
Lucas, KS 67648

Park City Auction Service,
925 Wood Street, Bridgeport,
CT 06604
Tel: (203) 333-5251

Pennypacker Auction Centre,
1540 New Holland Road,
Kenhorst, Reading, PA 19607
Tel: (215) 777-5890/6121

Peyton Place Antiques,
819 Lovett Boulevard, Houston,
TX 77006
Tel: (713) 523-4841

Phillips,
867 Madison Avenue, New York,
NY 10021
Tel: (212) 570-4830

525 East 72nd Street, New York,
NY10021
Tel: (212) 570-4852

Representative Office:
6 Faneuil Hall, Marketplace,
Boston, MA 02109
Tel: (617) 227-6145

Pollack,
2780 NE 183 Street, Miami,
FL 33160
Tel: (305) 931-4476

Quickie Auction House,
Route 3, Osseo, MN 55369
Tel: (612) 428-4378

R & S Estate Liquidations,
Box 205, Newton Center,
MA 02159
Tel: (617) 244-6616

C Gilbert Richards,
Garrison, NY 10524
Tel: (914) 424-3657

Bill Rinaldi Auctions,
Bedell Road, Poughkeepsie,
NY 12601
Tel: (914) 454-9613

Roan Inc,
Box 118, RD 3, Logan Station,
PA 17728
Tel: (717) 494-0170

Rockland Auction Services Inc,
72 Pomona Road, Suffern,
NY 10901
Tel: (914) 354-3914/2723

Rome Auction Gallery (Sandra A
Louis Caropreso),
Route 2, Highway 53, Rome,
GA 30161

Rose Galleries Inc,
1123 West County Road B,
Roseville, MN 55113
Tel: (612) 484-1415

Rosvall Auction Company,
1238 & 1248 South Broadway,
Denver, CO 80210
Tel: (303) 777-2032/722-4028

Sigmund Rothschild,
27 West 67th Street, New York,
NY 10023
Tel: (212) 873-5522

Vince Runowich Auctions,
2312 4th Street North, St
Petersburg, FL 33704
Tel: (813) 895-3548

Safran's Antique Galleries Ltd,
930 Gervais Street, Columbia,
SC 29201
Tel: (803) 252-7927

Sage Auction Gallery,
Route 9A, Chester, CT 06412
Tel: (203) 526-3036

San Antonio Auction Gallery,
5096 Bianco, San Antonio,
TX 78216
Tel: (512) 342-3800

Emory Sanders,
New London, NH 03257
Tel: (603) 526-6326

Sandwich Auction House,
15 Tupper Road, Sandwich,
MA 02563
Tel: (617) 888-1926/5675

San Francisco Auction Gallery,
1217 Sutter Street, San Francisco,
CA 94109
Tel: (415) 441-3800

Schafer Auction Gallery,
82 Bradley Road, Madison,
CT 06443
Tel: (203) 245-4173

Schmidt's Antiques,
5138 West Michigan Avenue,
Ypsilanti, MI 48 197
Tel: (313) 434-2660

K C Self,
53 Victory Lane, Los Angeles,
CA 95030
Tel: (213) 354-4238

B J Selkirk & Sons,
4166 Olive Street, St Louis,
MO 63108
Tel: (314) 533-1700

Shore Galleries Inc,
3318 West Devon, Lincolnwood,
IL 60659
Tel: (312) 676-2900

Shute's Auction Gallery,
70 Accord Park Drive, Norwell,
MA 02061
Tel: (617) 871-3414/238-0586

Ronald Siefert,
RFD, Buskirk, NY 12028
Tel: (518) 686-9375

Robert A Siegel Auction Galleries
Inc,
120 East 56th Street, New York,
NY 10022
Tel: (212) 753-6421/2/3

Robert W Skinner Inc,
Main Street, Bolton, MA 01740
Tel: (617) 779-5528

585 Boylston Street,
Boston, MA 02116
Tel: (617) 236-1700

C G Sloan & Co,
715 13th Street NW, Washington,
DC 20005
Tel: (202) 628-1468

Branch Office:
403 North Charles Street,
Baltimore, MD 21201
Tel: (301) 547-1177

Sotheby,
101 Newbury Street, Boston,
MA 02116
Tel: (617) 247-2851

Sotheby Park Bernet Inc,
980 Madison Avenue, New York,
NY 10021
Tel: (212) 472-3400

1334 York Avenue, New York,
NY 10021

171 East 84th Street, New York,
NY 10028

Mid-Atlantic:
1630 Locust Street, Philadelphia,
PA 19103
Tel: (215) 735-7886

Washington:
2903 M Street NW, Washington,
DC 20007
Tel: (202) 298-8400

Southeast:
155 Worth Avenue, Palm Beach,
FL 33480
Tel: (305) 658-3555

Midwest:
700 North Michigan Avenue,
Chicago, IL 60611
Tel: (312) 280-0185

Southwest:
Galleria Post Oak,
5015 Westheimer Road, Houston,
TX 77056
Tel: (713) 623-0010

Northwest:
210 Post Street, San Francisco,
CA 94108
Tel: (415) 986-4982

Pacific Area:
Suite 117, 850 West Hind Drive,
Honolulu, Hawaii 96821
Tel: (808) 373-9166

Stack's Rare Coin Auctions,
123 West 57th Street, New York,
NY 10019
Tel: (212) 583-2580

Classic Auction Gallery
(formerly Sterling Auctions),
62 No. 2nd Avenue, Raritan,
NJ 08869
Tel: (201) 526-6024

Stremmel Auctions Inc,
2152 Prater Way, Sparks,
NV 89431
Tel: (702) 331-1035

Summit Auction Rooms,
47-49 Summit Avenue, Summit,
NJ 07901

Superior Stamp & Coin Co Inc,
9301 Wiltshire Boulevard,
Beverly Hills, CA 90210
Tel: (213) 272-0851/278-9740

Swann Galleries Inc,
104 East 26th Street, New York,
NY 10021
Tel: (212) 254-4710

Philip Swedler & Son,
850 Grand Avenue, New Haven,
CT 06511
Tel: (203) 624-2202/562-5065

Tait Auction Studio,
1209 Howard Avenue,
Burlingame, CA 94010
Tel: (415) 343-4793

Tepper Galleries,
110 East 25th Street, New York,
NY 10010
Tel: (212) 677-5300/1/2

Louis Trailman Auction Co,
1519 Spruce Street, Philadelphia,
PA 19102
Tel: (215) K1 5 4500

Trend Galleries Inc,
2784 Merrick Road, Bellmore,
NY 11710
Tel: (516) 221-5588

Trosby Auction Galleries,
81 Peachtree Park Drive, Atlanta,
GA 30326
Tel: (404) 351-4400

Valle-McLeod Gallery,
3303 Kirby Drive, Houston,
TX 77098
Tel: (713) 523-8309/8310

The Watnot Auction,
Box 78, Mellenville, NY 12544
Tel: (518) 672-7576

Adam A Wechsler & Son,
905-9 East Street NW,
Washington, DC 20004
Tel: (202) 628-1281

White Plains Auction Rooms,
572 North Broadway, White
Plains, NY 10603
Tel: (914) 428-2255

Henry Willis,
22 Main Street, Marshfield,
MA 02050
Tel: (617) 834 7774

The Wilson Galleries,
PO Box 102, Ford Defiance,
VA 24437
Tel: (703) 885-4292

Helen Winter Associates,
355 Farmington Avenue,
Plainville, CT 06062
Tel: (203) 747-0714/677-0848

Richard Withington Inc,
Hillsboro, NH 03244
Tel: (603) 464-3232

Wolf,
13015 Larchmere Boulevard,
Shaker Heights, OH 44120
Tel: (216) 231-3888

Richard Wolffers Inc,
127 Kearney Street, San
Francisco, CA 94 108
Tel: (415) 781-5127

Young,
56 Market Street, Portsmouth,
NH 03801
Tel: (603) 436-8773

Samuel Yudkin & Associates,
1125 King Street, Alexandria,
VA 22314
Tel: (703) 549-9330

Australia

ASA Stamps Co Pty Ltd,
138-140 Rundle Mall, National
Bank Building, Adelaide, South
Australia 5001
Tel: 223-2951

Associated Auctioneers Pty Ltd,
800-810 Parramatta Road,
Lewisham, New South Wales 2049
Tel: 560-5899

G J Brain Auctioneers Pty Ltd,
122 Harrington Street, Sydney,
New South Wales 2000
Tel: 271701

Bright Slater Pty Ltd,
Box 205 GPO, Lower Ground
Floor, Brisbane Club Building,
Isles Lane, Brisbane, Queensland
4000
Tel: 312415

Christie, Manson & Woods
(Australia) Ltd,
298 New South Head Road, Double
Bay, Sydney, New South Wales
2028
Tel: 326-1422

William S Ellenden Pty Ltd,
67-73 Wentworth Avenue,
Sydney, New South Wales 2000
Tel: 211-4035/211-4477

Bruce Granger Auctions,
10 Hopetoun Street, Huristone
Park, New South Wales 2193
Tel: 559-4767

Johnson Bros Auctioneers & Real
Estate Agents,
328 Main Road, Glenorchy,
Tasmania 7011
Tel: 725166 492909

James A Johnson & Co,
92 Boronia Road, Vermont,
Victoria 3133
Tel: 877-2754/874-3632

Jolly Barry Pty Ltd,
212 Glenmore Road, Paddington,
New South Wales 2021
Tel: 357-4494

James R Lawson Pty Ltd,
236 Castlereagh Street, Sydney,
New South Wales
Tel: 266408

Mason Greene & Associates,
91-101 Leveson Street, North
Melbourne, Victoria 3051
Tel: 329-9911

Mercantile Art Auctions,
317 Pacific Highway, North Sydey,
New South Wales 2060
Tel: 922-3610/922-3608

James R Newall Auctions Pty Ltd,
164 Military Road, Neutral Bay,
New South Wales 2089
Tel: 903023/902587 (Sydney ex)

P L Pickles & Co Pty Ltd
655 Pacific Highway, Killara, New
South Wales 2071
Tel: 498-8069/498-2775

Sotheby Parke Bernet Group Ltd,
115 Collins Street, Melbourne,
Victoria 3000
Tel: (03) 63 39 00

H E Wells & Sons,
326 Rokeby Road, Subiaco, West
Australia
Tel: 3819448/3819040

Young Family Estates Pty Ltd,
229 Camberwell Road, East
Hawthorn, Melbourne 2123
Tel: 821433

New Zealand

Devereaux & Culley Ltd,
200 Dominion Road, Mt Eden,
Auckland
Tel: 687429/687112

Alex Harris Ltd,
PO Box 510, 377 Princes Street,
Dunedin
Tel: 773955/740703

Roger Moat Ltd,
College Hill and Beaumont Street,
Auckland
Tel: 37 1588/37 1686/37 1595

New Zealand Stamp Auctions,
PO Box 3496, Queen and
Wyndham Streets, Auckland
Tel: 375490/375498

Alistair Robb Coin Auctions,
La Aitken Street, Box 3705,
Wellington
Tel: 727-141

Dunbar Sloane Ltd,
32 Waring Taylor Street,
Wellington
Tel: 721-367

Thornton Auctions Ltd,
89 Albert Street, Auckland 1
Tel: 30888 (3 lines)

Daniel J Visser,
109 and 90 Worchester Street,
Christchurch
Tel: 68853/67297

Austria

Christie's,
Ziehrerplatz 4/22, A-1030 Vienna
Tel: (0222) 73 26 44

Belgium

Christie, Manson & Woods
(Belgium) Ltd,
33 Boulevard de Waterloo, B-1000
Brussels
Tel: (02) 512-8765/512-8830

Sotheby Parke Bernet Belgium,
Rue de l'Abbaye 32, 1050 Brussels
Tel: 343 50 07

Canada

A-1 Auctioneer Evaluation
Services Ltd,
PO Box 926, Saint John,
NB E2L 4C3
Tel: (508) 762-0559

Appleton Auctioneers Ltd,
1238 Seymour Street, Vancouver,
BC V6B 3N9
Tel: (604) 685-1715

Ashton Auction Service,
PO Box 500, Ashton, Ontario,
KOA 180
Tel: (613) 257-1575

Canada Book Auctions,
35 Front Street East, Toronto,
Ontario M5E 1B3
Tel: (416) 368-4326

Christie's International Ltd,
Suite 2002, 1055 West Georgia
Street, Vancouver, BC V6E 3P3
Tel: (604) 685-2126

Miller & Johnson Auctioneers Ltd,
2882 Gottingen Street, Halifax,
Nova Scotia B3K 3E2
Tel: (902) 425-3366/425-3606

Phillips Ward-Price Ltd,
76 Davenport Road, Toronto,
Ontario M5R 1H3
Tel: (416) 923-9876

Sotheby Parke Bernet (Canada)
Inc,
156 Front Street, Toronto, Ontario
M5J 2L6
Tel: (416) 596-0300

Representative:
David Brown,
2321 Granville Street, Vancouver,
BC V6H 3G4
Tel: (604) 736-6363

Denmark

Kunsthallens,
Kunstauktioner A/S,
Købmagergade 11 DK 1150
Copenhagen
Tel: (01) 13 85 69

Nellemann & Thomsen,
Neilgade 45, DK-8000 Aarhus
Tel: (06) 12 06 66/12 00 02

France

Ader, Picard, Tajan,
12 rue Favart, 75002 Paris
Tel: 261.80.07

Artus,
15 rue de la Grange-Batelière,
75009 Paris
Tel: 523.12.03

Audap,
32 rue Drouot, 75009 Paris
Tel: 742.78.01

Bondu,
17 rue Drouot, 75009 Paris
Tel: 770.36.16

Boscher, Gossart,
3 rue d'Amboise, 75009 Paris
Tel: 260.87.87

Briest,
15 rue Drouot, 75009 Paris
Tel: 770.66.29

de Cagny,
4 rue Drouot, 75009 Paris
Tel: 246.00.07

Charbonneaux,
134 rue du Faubourg Saint-
Honoré, 75008 Paris
Tel: 359.66.57

Chayette,
10 rue Rossini, 75009 Paris
Tel: 770.38.89

Delaporte, Rieunier,
159 rue Montmartre, 75002 Paris
Tel: 508.41.83

Delorme,
3 rue Penthièvre, 75008 Paris
Tel: 265.57.63

Godeau,
32 rue Drouot, 75009 Paris
Tel: 770.67.68

Gros,
22 rue Drouot, 75009 Paris
Tel: 770.83.04

Langlade,
12 rue Descombes, 75017 Paris
Tel: 227.00.91

Loudmer, Poulain,
73 rue de Faubourg Saint-Honoré,
75008 Paris
Tel: 266.90.01

Maignan,
6 rue de la Michodière, 75002 Paris
Tel: 742.71.52

Maringe,
16 rue de Provence, 75009 Paris
Tel: 770.61.15

Marlio,
7 rue Ernest-Renan, 75015 Paris
Tel: 734.81.13

Paul Martin & Jacques Martin,
3 impasse des Chevau-Legers,
78000 Versailles
Tel: 950.58.08

Bonhams, Baron Foran,
Duc de Saint-Bar, 2 rue Bellanger,
92200 Neuilly sur Seine
Tel: (1) 637-1329

Christie's, Princess Jeanne-Marie
de Broglie,
17 rue de Lille, 75007 Paris
Tel: (331) 261-1247

Sotheby's, Rear Admiral J A
Templeton-Cotill, CB,
3 rue de Miromesnil, 75008 Paris
Tel: (1) 266-4060

Monaco

Sotheby Parke Bernet Group,
PO Box 45, Sporting d'Hiver, Place
du Casino, Monte Carlo
Tel: (93) 30 88 80

Hong Kong

Sotheby Parke Bernet (Hong
Kong) Ltd,
PO Box 83, 705 Lane Crawford
House, 64-70 Queen's Road
Central, Hong Kong
Tel: 22-5454

Italy

Christie's (International) SA,
Palazzo Massimo Lancellotti,
Piazza Navona 114, 00186 Rome
Tel: 6541217

Christie's (Italy) SR1,
9 Via Borgogna, 20144 Milan
Tel: 794712

Finarte SPA,
Piazzetta Bossi 4, 20121 Milan
Tel: 877041

Finarte SPA,
Via delle Quattro, Fontane 20,
Rome
Tel: 463564

Palazzo International delle Aste ed
Esposizioni SPA,
Palazzo Corsini, Il Prato 56,
Florence
Tel: 293000

Sotheby Parke Bernet Italia,
26 Via Gino Capponi, 50121
Florence
Tel: 571410

Sotheby Parke Bernet Italia,
Via Montenapoleone 3, 20121
Milan
Tel: 783907

Sotheby Parke Bernet Italia,
Palazzo Taverna, Via di Monte
Giordano 36, 00186 Rome
Tel: 656 1670/6547400

The Netherlands

Christie, Manson & Woods Ltd,
Rokin 91, 1012 KL Amsterdam
Tel: (020) 23 15 05

Sotheby Mak Van Waay BV,
102 Rokin 1012, KZ Amsterdam
Tel: 24 62 15

Van Dieten Stamp Auctions BV,
2 Tournooiveld, 2511 CX The
Hague
Tel: 70-464312/70-648658

Singapore & Malaysia

Victor & Morris Pte Ltd,
39 Talok Ayer Street, Republic of Singapore
Tel: 94844

South Africa

Ashbey's Galleries,
43-47 Church Street, Cape Town 8001
Tel: 22-7527

Claremart Auction Centre,
47 Main Road, Claremont, Cape Town 7700
Tel: 66-8826/66-8804

Ford & Van Niekerk Pty Ltd
156 Main Road, PO Box 8, Plumstead, Cape Town
Tel: 71-3384

Sotheby Parke Bernet South Africa Pty Ltd,
Total House, Smit and Rissik Streets, PO Box 310010, Braamfontein 2017
Tel: 39-3726

Spain

Juan R Cayon,
41 Fuencarral, Madrid 14
Tel: 221 08 32/221 43 72/222 95 98

Christie's International Ltd,
Casado del Alisal 5, Madrid
Tel: (01) 228-9300

Sotheby Parke Bernet & Co,
Scursal de Espana, Calle del Prado 18, Madrid 14
Tel: 232-6488/232-6572

Switzerland

Daniel Beney,
Avenue des Mousquines 2, CH-1005 Lausanne
Tel: (021) 22 28 64

Blanc,
Arcade Hotel Beau-Rivage, Box 84, CH-1001 Lausanne
Tel: (021) 27 32 55/26 86 20

Christie's (International) SA,
8 Place de la Taconnerie, CH-1204 Geneva
Tel: (022) 28 25 44

Steinwiesplatz,
CH-8032 Zurich
Tel: (01) 69 05 05

Auktionshaus Doblaschofsky AG,
Monbijoustrasse 28/30, CH-3001 Berne
Tel: (031) 25 23 72/73/74

Galerie Fischer,
Haldenstrasse 19, CH-6006 Lucerne
Tel: (041) 22 57 72/73

Germann Auktionshaus,
Zeitweg 67, CH-8032 Zurich
Tel: (01) 32 83 58/32 01 12

Haus der Bücher AG,
Baumleingasse 18, CH-4051 Basel
Tel: (061) 23 30 88

Adolph Hess AG,
Haldenstrasse 5, CH-6006 Lucerne
Tel: (041) 22 43 92/22 45 35

Auktionshaus Peter Ineichen,
CF Meyerstrasse 14, CH-8002 Zurich
Tel: (01) 201-3017

Galerie Koller AG,
Ramistrasse 8, CH-8001 Zurich
Tel: (01) 47 50 40

Koller St Gallen,
St Gallen
Tel: (071) 23 42 40

Kornfeld & Co,
Laupenstrasse 49, CH-3008 Berne
Tel: (031) 25 46 73

Phillips Son & Neale SA,
6 Rue de la Cité, CH-1204 Geneva
Tel: (022) 28 68 28

Christian Rosset,
Salle des Ventes, 29 Rue du Rhone, CH-1204 Geneva
Tel: (022) 28 96 33/34

Schweizerische Gesellschaft der Freunde von Kunstauktionen,
11 Werdmühlestrasse, CH-8001 Zurich
Tel: (01) 211-4789

Sotheby Parke Bernet AG,
20 Bleicherweg, CH-8022 Zurich
Tel: (01) 202-0011

24 Rue de la Cité, CH-1024 Geneva
Tel: (022) 21 33 77

Dr Erich Steinfels, Auktionen,
Rämistrasse 6, CH-8001 Zurich
Tel: (01) 252-1233 (wine) & (01) 34 1233 (fine art)

Frank Sternberg,
Bahnhofstrasse 84, CH-8001 Zurich
Tel: (01) 211-7980

Jürg Stucker Gallery Ltd,
Alter Aargauerstalden 30, CH-3006 Berne
Tel: (031) 44 00 44

Uto Auktions AG,
Lavaterstrasse 11, CH-8027 Zurich
Tel: (01) 202-9444

West Germany

Galerie Gerda Bassenge,
Erdener Strasses 5a, D-1000 West Berlin 33
Tel: (030) 892 19 32/891 29 09

Kunstauktionen Waltraud Boltz,
Bahnhof Strasse 25-27, D-8580 Bayreuth
Tel: (0921) 206 16

Brandes,
Wolfenbütteler Strasse 12, D-3300 Braunschweig 1
Tel: (0531) 737 32

Gernot Dorau,
Johann-Georg Strasse 2, D-1000 Berlin 31
Tel: (030) 892 61 98

F Dörling,
Neuer Wall 40-41, D-2000 Hamburg 36
Tel: (040) 36 46 70/36 52 82

Roland A Exner,
Kunsthandel-Auktionen, Am Ihmeufer, D-3000 Hannover 91
Tel: (0511) 44 44 84

Hartung & Karl,
Karolinenplatz 5a, D-8000 Munich 2
Tel: (089) 28 40 34

Hauswedell & Nolte,
Pöseldorfer Weg 1, D-2000 Hamburg 13
Tel: (040) 44 83 66

Karl & Faber,
Amiraplatz 3 (Luitpoldblock), D-8000 Munich 2
Tel: (089) 22 18 65/66

Graf Klenau Ohg Nachf,
Maximilian Strasse 32, D-8000 Munich 1
Tel: (089) 22 22 81/82

Numismatik Lanz München,
Promenadeplatz 9, D-8000 Munich 2
Tel: (089) 29 90 70

Kunsthaus Lempertz,
Neumarkt 3, D-5000 Cologne 1
Tel: (0221) 21 02 51/52

Stuttgarter Kunstauktionshaus, Dr Fritz Nagel,
Mörikestrasse 17-19, D-7000 Stuttgart 1
Tel: (0711) 61 33 87/77

Neumeister Münchener Kunstauktionshaus KG,
Barer Strasse 37, D-8000 Munich 40
Tel: (089) 28 30 11

Petzold KG- Photographica,
Maximilian Strasse 36, D-8900 Augsburg 11
Tel: (0821) 3 37 25

Reiss & Auvermann,
Zum Talblick 2, D-6246 Glashütten im Taunus 1
Tel: (06174) 69 47/48

Gus Schiele Auktions-Galerie,
Ottostrasse 7 (Neuer Kunstblock), D-8000 Munich 2
Tel: (089) 59 41 92

Galerie,
Paulinen Strasse 47, D-7000 Stuttgart 1
Tel: (0711) 61 63 77

J A Stargardt,
Universitäts Strasse 27, D-3550 Marburg
Tel: (06421) 234 52

Auktionshaus Tietjen & Co,
Spitaler Strasse 30, D-2000 Hamburg 1
Tel: (040) 33 03 68/69

Aachener Auktionshaus, Crott & Schmelzer,
Pont Strasse 21, Aachen
Tel: (0241) 369 00

Kunstauktionen Rainer Baumann,
Obere Woerthstrasse 7-11, Nuremburg
Tel: (0911) 20 48 47

August Bödiger oHG,
Oxford Strasse 4, Bonn
Tel: (0228) 63 69 40

Bolland & Marotz,
Feldören 19, Bremen
Tel: (0421) 32 18 11

Bongartz Gelgen Auktionen,
Münsterplatz 27, Aachen
Tel: (0241) 206 19

Christie's International Ltd,
Düsseldorf:
Alt Pempelfort 11a, D-4000 Düsseldorf
Tel: (0211) 35 05 77

Hamburg:
Wenzelstrasse 21, D-2000 Hamburg 60
Tel: (4940) 279-0866

Munich:
Maximilianstrasse 20, D-8000 Munich 22
Tel: (089) 22 95 39

Württenberg:
Schloss Langenburg, D-7183 Langenburg

Sotheby Parke Bernet GmbH,
Munich:
Odeonsplatz 16, D-8000 Munich 22
Tel: (089) 22 23 75/6

Kunstauktion Jürgen Fischer,
Alexander Strasse 11, Heilbronn
Tel: (07 131) 785 23

Galerie Göbig,
Ritterhaus Strasse 5 (am Thermalbad ad Nauheim)
Tel: (Frankfurt) (611) 77 40 80

Knut Günther,
Auf der Kömerwiese 19-21, Frankfurt
Tel: (611) 55 32 92/55 70 22

Antiquitaeten Lothar Heubel,
Odenthaler Strasse 371, Cologne
Tel: (0221) 60 18 25

Hildener Auktionshaus und Kunstgalerie,
Klusenhof 12, Hilden
Tel: (02103) 602 00

INDEX

C

D

Q

R

S